lonely planet

East Coast Australia

Cristian Bonetto, Lindsay Brown, Jayne D'Arcy, Peter
Dragicevich, Anthony Ham, Trent Holden, Anna Kaminski, Ali Lemer, Monique
Perrin, Tim Richards, Tamara Sheward, Tom Spurling, Andy Symington,
Benedict Walker

Contents

KOALA (P504) EATING
EUCALYPTUS LEAF

CENTRE PLACE,
MELBOURNE P223

BONDI BEACH (P69),
SYDNEY

Contents

FIRELIA/ACQUA ©

COVID-19

We have re-checked every business in this book before publication to ensure that it is still open after 2020's COVID-19 outbreak. However, the economic and social impacts of COVID-19 will continue to be felt long after the outbreak has been contained, and many businesses, services and events referenced in this guide may experience ongoing restrictions. Some businesses may be temporarily closed, have changed their opening hours and services, or require bookings; some unfortunately could have closed permanently. We suggest you check with venues before visiting for the latest information.

Left: Red bottlebrush tree

Welcome to East Coast Australia

The ultimate Aussie road trip, East Coast Australia connects Melbourne with the Great Barrier Reef, with picture-perfect beaches, hip cities and rainforests en route.

Into the Wild

Strung out for nearly 10,000km, Australia's east coast is a stirring succession of beaches and the country's best surf breaks. Offshore, the astonishing Great Barrier Reef is a 2000km-long hypercoloured haven for tropical marine life. Also here are hundreds of islands, from craggy nature reserves to palm-studded paradises. Inland are national parks with lush rainforests, jagged peaks and native critters that rate from cuddleworthy (koalas) to photogenic (cassowaries and Ulysses butterflies) and fearsome (saltwater crocs).

Action Stations

East Coast Australia is not just about seeing, and the doing is half the fun – jogging, swimming, surfing, cycling, kayaking, snorkelling, hiking... Why not join in? Get underwater on the Great Barrier Reef, the most photogenic submarine landscape on earth. Raft your way down white-water rapids, sea-kayak along the coast or set sail through a tropical archipelago. Hike up a mountain, through the rainforest of a national park or alongside a rushing river. Or just head for the beach, where the locals let it all hang out.

City Scenes

Home to Indigenous Australians for millennia, the east coast is also where modern Australia kicked off around Sydney. Sassy and ambitious yet unpretentious, Sydneysiders eat, drink, shop and party with hedonistic abandon. To the south, Melbourne is Australia's arts and coffee capital – a cafe-rich, European-style city with a bohemian soul. Wrapped around river bends, boom-town Brisbane is a glam patchwork of inner-city neighbourhoods. And don't forget Australia's capital, Canberra – so much more than a political filing cabinet!

Eat, Drink & Celebrate

Australia's big east-coast cities provide a rich culinary experience, with fantastic cafes, sprawling food markets and world-class restaurants. After dark, moody wine bars, student-filled speakeasies and boisterous Aussie pubs provide plenty of excuses to bend an elbow, chew the fat and maybe join in the local passion for watching sports. Beyond the cities, enjoy fish (straight off the fishing boats) and chips, the produce of cheesemakers and small-town bakeries, and fine-dining meals, all paired perfectly with high-quality wines from the Mornington Peninsula or Hunter and Yarra Valleys.

Why I Love East Coast Australia

By Anthony Ham, Writer

In the course of a travelling lifetime, I've ranged all along this gorgeous coast. Melbourne will always be home, and it's a city that just keeps getting better. Growing up in Sydney, I spent most of my summer holidays exploring the New South Wales coast, and still adore its wild coastline and rugged national parks. But Far North Queensland is a far more recent passion, and its combination of reef and rainforest, of wildlife and soulful Indigenous stories and encounters, go to the very heart of why I love this country.

For more about our writers, see p544

Above: The Rocks (p60) and the Sydney Habour Bridge (p60)

East Coast Australia

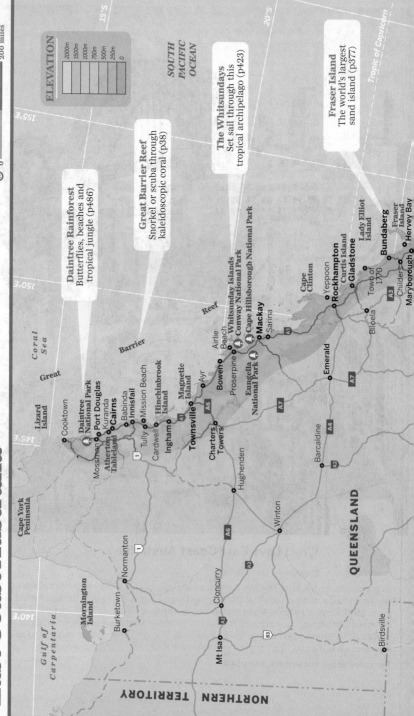

ELEVATION

2000m
1500m
1000m
750m
500m
250m
0

Daintree Rainforest
Butterflies, beaches and tropical jungle (p486)

Great Barrier Reef
Snorkel or scuba through kaleidoscopic coral (p38)

The Whitsundays
Set sail through this tropical archipelago (p423)

Fraser Island
The world's largest sand island (p377)

Gulf of Carpentaria

Cape York Peninsula

Coral Sea

Great Barrier Reef

SOUTH PACIFIC OCEAN

Tropic of Capricorn

NORTHERN TERRITORY

QUEENSLAND

Mornington Island

Burketown
Normanton
Cloncurry
Mt Isa
Birdsville
Winton
Hughenden
Barcaldine
Emerald
Bliela

Cooktown
Lizard Island
Mossman
Daintree National Park
Port Douglas
Kuranda
Atherton Tableland
Cairns
Babinda
Innisfail
Mission Beach
Tully
Cardwell
Ingham
Hinchinbrook Island
Magnetic Island
Townsville
Ayr
Charters Towers
Bowen
Airlie Beach
Proserpine
Whitsunday Islands
Conway National Park
Cape Hillsborough National Park
Mackay
Sarina
Eungella National Park
Cape Clinton
Yeppoon
Rockhampton
Curtis Island
Gladstone
Town of 1770
Lady Elliot Island
Bundaberg
Childers
Fraser Island
Maryborough
Hervey Bay

400 km
200 miles

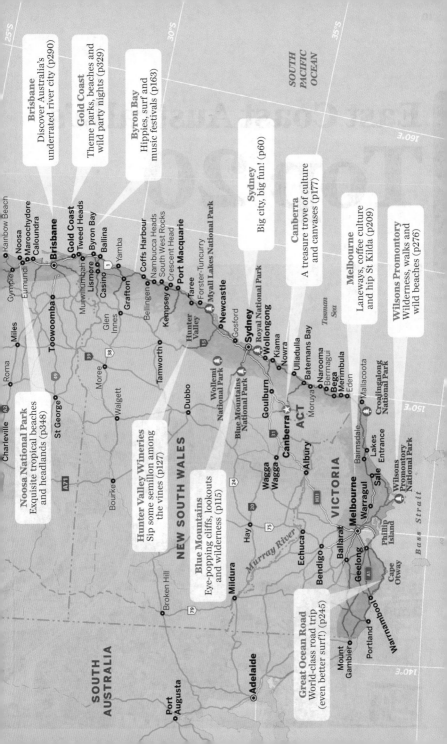

Brisbane
Discover Australia's underrated river city (p290)

Gold Coast
Theme parks, beaches and wild party nights (p329)

Byron Bay
Hippies, surf and music festivals (p163)

Sydney
Big city, big fun! (p60)

Canberra
A treasure trove of culture and canvases (p177)

Melbourne
Laneways, coffee culture and hip St Kilda (p209)

Wilsons Promontory
Wilderness, walks and wild beaches (p276)

Noosa National Park
Exquisite tropical beaches and headlands (p348)

Hunter Valley Wineries
Sip some semillon among the vines (p127)

Blue Mountains
Eye-popping cliffs, lookouts and wilderness (p115)

Great Ocean Road
World-class road trip (even better surf!) (p245)

SOUTH PACIFIC OCEAN

25°S
30°S
35°S
160°E
150°E
140°E

SOUTH AUSTRALIA

NEW SOUTH WALES

VICTORIA

ACT

Tasman Sea

Bass Strait

Murray River

Port Augusta
Adelaide
Broken Hill
Bourke
Charleville
Roma
Miles
Toowoomba
St George
Walgett
Moree
Mildura
Hay
Bendigo
Echuca
Wagga Wagga
Albury
Ballarat
Geelong
Warrnambool
Portland
Mount Gambier
Cape Otway
Melbourne
Warragul
Sale
Bairnsdale
Lakes Entrance
Phillip Island
Wilsons Promontory National Park
Mallacoota
Croajingolong National Park
Eden
Merimbula
Bega
Bermagui
Narooma
Moruya
Batemans Bay
Ulladulla
Nowra
Kiama
Wollongong
Goulburn
Canberra
Dubbo
Tamworth
Glen Innes
Bourke
Walgett
Tweed Heads
Byron Bay
Ballina
Casino
Lismore
Murwillumbah
Yamba
Grafton
Coffs Harbour
Bellingen
Nambucca Heads
South West Rocks
Crescent Head
Kempsey
Port Macquarie
Forster-Tuncurry
Taree
Myall Lakes National Park
Newcastle
Hunter Valley
Gosford
Sydney
Royal National Park
Wollemi National Park
Blue Mountains National Park
Gympie
Eumundi
Noosa
Maroochydore
Caloundra
Rainbow Beach
Brisbane
Gold Coast

East Coast Australia's
Top 20

Sydney

1 The big-ticket sights are all in Sydney (p58) – the Sydney Opera House, the Rocks and Sydney Harbour Bridge top most people's lists – but to really catch the city's vibe, spend a day at the beach. Stake out a patch of sand at Bondi Beach (or any of Sydney's stellar beaches), lather yourself in sunscreen and plunge into the surf; or hop on a harbour ferry from Circular Quay to Manly for a swim, a surf or a walk along the sea-sprayed promenade to Shelly Beach.

Great Barrier Reef

2 The Great Barrier Reef (p412) lives up to its reputation. Stretching more than 2000km along the Queensland coastline, it's a complex ecosystem populated with dazzling coral, languid sea turtles, gliding rays, timid reef sharks and 1500 species of colourful tropical fish. Whether you dive on it, snorkel over it, explore it via a scenic flight or glass-bottom boat, linger in an island resort or camp on a remote atoll, this vivid undersea kingdom and its 900 coral-fringed islands is an unforgettable world waiting to be discovered.

ZETTER / GETTY IMAGES ©

2

JEFF HUNTER / GETTY IMAGES ©

Daintree Rainforest

3 Lush green rainforest tumbles towards brilliant white-sand coastline in the ancient, World Heritage–listed Daintree Rainforest (p486). Upon crossing the Daintree River and entering this extraordinary wonderland – home to some 3000 plant species – you'll be enveloped by birdsong, the buzz of insects and the constant commentary of frogs. There are crocs, tree kangaroos and cassowaries. Continue exploring on wildlife-spotting tours, mountain treks, interpretive boardwalks, tropical-fruit orchard tours, canopy walks, 4WD trips, horse rides, kayak trips and cruises.

Indigenous Far North Queensland

4 The human history of Far North Queensland is as dramatic as its natural surrounds. Indigenous people have called the region's rainforests and beaches home for more than 40,000 years, and a boom in Aboriginal-led tours (p487) and experiences makes it easier than ever to see it all through Aboriginal eyes. Throw a spear, make a boomerang, sample bush tucker, interpret rock art, go on a rainforest walk, or learn the didgeridoo: a world of new – yet incredibly old – adventures awaits.

Wildlife Watching

5 Head to Phillip Island (p273) for a parade of adorable little penguins and fur seals cavorting along the rocky shore, or into tropical Far North Queensland for other-worldly cassowaries, tree kangaroos and dinosaur-like crocodiles. In between, you'll find a panoply of extraordinary animals found nowhere else on earth: koalas, kangaroos, wombats and platypuses. There's also great whale watching along the coast in season (May to November), plus the omnipresent laughter of kookaburras, to say nothing of the extraordinary marine life all along the Great Barrier Reef.

Sailing the Whitsunday Islands

6 You can hop around an entire archipelago of tropical islands for a seafaring lifetime and never find anywhere with the sheer tropical beauty of the Whitsundays (p408). Travellers of all stripes launch yachts from party town Airlie Beach and elsewhere to drift between these lush green isles in a slow search for paradise (you'll probably find it in more than one place). Sheltered, palm-fringed coves; some of the world's most beautiful beaches; and turquoise seas – what more could you wish for?

ANDRII SLONCHAK / SHUTTERSTOCK ©

Byron Bay

7 Australia's most easterly point, Byron Bay (p163) – Byron to its mates – is one of the enduring icons of Australian culture. Families on school holidays, surfers and sunseekers from around the globe and those seeking to escape the rat race gather here, drawn by fabulous restaurants, a laid-back ethos, surf beaches and an astonishing range of activities. This is one of the most beautiful stretches of coast in the country and, although it's markedly upmarket these days, the town's infectious hippie vibe will still put a smile on your dial.

Melbourne

8 Why the queue? Oh, that's just the line to get into the latest 'no bookings' restaurant in Melbourne (p209). The next best restaurant, cafe, barista or bar may be the talk of the town, but there are things locals would never change: the galleries and dynamic cultural life, the leafy parks and gardens in, the trams that whisk creative 'northerners' to sea-breezy southern beaches and the allegiances that living in such a sports-mad place brings. And the city's world-renowned street-art scene expresses Melbourne's fears, frustrations and joys. Above: Flinders St Station (p210)

Great Ocean Road

9 Jutting out of turbulent waters, the Twelve Apostles on the Great Ocean Road (p244) are one of Victoria's defining sights, but it's the getting-there road trip that doubles their impact. Take it slow along roads that curl beside Bass Strait beaches, then whip inland through wildlife-rich rainforest and quaint little towns. The Great Ocean Road doesn't stop at the Twelve Apostles – further along is maritime treasure Port Fairy and hidden Cape Bridgewater. And for the ultimate in slow travel, hike the Great Ocean Walk from Apollo Bay to the Apostles.

Blue Mountains

10 Just a few hours from Sydney, the views from Katoomba's Echo Point and Blackheath's Govetts Leap in the Blue Mountains (p114) are so good that you'll find yourself pushing to the front of the crowd then pushing your camera's memory card to the limit. After the photo shoot, hike a trail into the magnificent Jamison Valley or Grose Valley, accompanied by the scent of eucalyptus oil, a fine mist of which issues from the dense tree canopy and gives these World Heritage–listed mountains their name. Right: Echo Point (p117), Blue Mountains

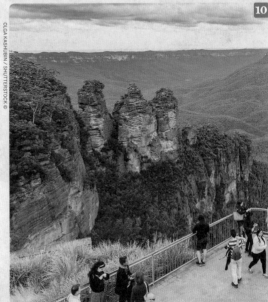

OLGA KASHUBIN / SHUTTERSTOCK ©

Fraser Island

11 Fraser Island (p377) is an ecological wonderland created by drifting sand, where dingoes roam free and lush rainforest grows on sand. It's an elemental place, a primal island utopia, home to a profusion of wildlife, including the purest strain of dingo in Australia. The best way to explore the island is in a 4WD – cruising up the seemingly endless Seventy-Five Mile Beach and bouncing along sandy inland tracks. Tropical rainforest, pristine freshwater pools and beach camping under the stars will bring you back to nature.

Wilsons Promontory

12 Victoria's southernmost point and finest coastal national park, Wilsons Promontory (p278) – aka 'Wilson's Prom', or just 'the Prom' – is heaven for bushwalkers, wildlife watchers, surfers and photographers. A short detour from the park base at Tidal River (pictured below) will access swathes of white-sand beaches and bays. But with more than 80km of marked walking trails, the best of the Prom requires some leg work. Serious hikers should tackle the three-day Great Prom Walk, staying a night in gloriously isolated lighthouse keepers' cottages.

FLIPHOTO / SHUTTERSTOCK ©

MARCO CASAVECCHIA / SHUTTERSTOCK ©

Noosa National Park

13 Cloaking the headland beside the stylish resort town of Noosa, Noosa National Park (p507) features a string of perfect bays fringed with sand and pandanus trees. Surfers come here for the long, rolling waves; walkers make the trip for the unspoiled natural vibes. Lovely hiking trails crisscross the park: our pick is the scenic coastal trail to Hell's Gates, on which you might spy sleepy koalas in the trees around Tea Tree Bay, and dolphins swimming off the rocky headland.

Brisbane

14 Forget the nasty gossip. Once considered little more than a provincial sidekick to Sydney and Melbourne, Brisbane (p288) has reinvented itself as one of Asia Pacific's hippest hubs. No longer happy to settle for 261 days of sunshine a year, Queensland's new and improved capital is smashing it on the cultural front, with an ever-expanding variety of ambitious street art and galleries, boutique bookshops, secret cocktail bars and award-winning microbreweries. The result: big-city Australian cool with a laid-back, subtropical twist.

Hunter Valley Wineries

15 Picture this: a glass-fronted pavilion overlooking gently rolling hills covered with row after row of grape-heavy vines. Inside, you're sipping a glass of golden-hued semillon and pondering a lunch menu of top-quality local produce. Make your choice, lean back, nurse a glass or two of earthy shiraz and settle in to enjoy your meal. Such experiences (and culinary riches) are just another day in New South Wales' premier wine district, the Hunter Valley (p124).

ARTIE PHOTOGRAPHY (ARTIE NG) / GETTY IMAGES ©

Canberra

16 Though Canberra (p177) is only a century old, Australia's purpose-built capital has always been preoccupied with history. So it's not surprising the major drawcards here are lavishly endowed museums and galleries that focus on recounting and interpreting the national narrative. Institutions such as the National Gallery of Australia, National Museum of Australia, National Portrait Gallery and Australian War Memorial offer visitors a fascinating insight into the country's history and culture. An emerging culinary scene, a small-town feel and beautiful natural surrounds top it all off. Above: Australian War Memorial (p179)

Montague Island

17 Montague Island (p197) is one of wild Australia's most underrated destinations. Offshore from Narooma, bald, boulder-strewn Montague is a haven for nesting seabirds, including 10,000 little penguins. Indigenous sacred sites, an unusual granite lighthouse, refurbished cottage accommodation and guided eco-tours set Montague apart from the mainland by more than the 9km boat ride it takes to get there. Diving (spot some grey nurse sharks!), seal watching and occasional pods of passing whales all add to the island's appeal.

Gold Coast

18 Brash, trashy, hedonistic, overhyped...Queensland's Gold Coast (p329) is all of these things. But if you're looking for a party, bring it on! Beyond the clubs you'll find rapidly growing food and craft-brew scenes, and an improbably gorgeous coastline of clean sand, warm water and peeling surf breaks. Here, Australia's bronzed surf lifesavers patrol the sand and pit their skills against one another in surf carnivals – gruelling events involving ocean swimming, beach sprints and surf-boat racing. Australia's biggest theme parks are also here, making this place a roller-coaster nirvana.

Lady Elliot Island

19 This ecofriendly resort island (p397) is one of the loveliest and most peaceful places to experience the Great Barrier Reef. Snorkel straight off Lady Elliot's white sands – the living reef that surrounds the tiny coral cay is teeming with tropical fish, turtles and the island's resident manta rays. At hatching time (January to April) you can see baby turtles scamper across the sand, and from June to October humpback whales pass by. Getting to the island, with a scenic flight over the turquoise reef-filled waters, is equally memorable.

Bridge Climbing

20 Vertigo not an issue? Make a bee-line for Sydney's iconic Harbour Bridge or Brisbane's Story Bridge and scale their steely heights. Once only the domain of bridge painters and trespassing daredevils, Sydney's big arch can now be tackled by anyone on a BridgeClimb (p80). Story Bridge Adventure Climb is a newer experience, but no less mesmerising. And it's not just about the sublime city views – the bridges themselves are amazing structures!

19

20

Need to Know

For more information, see Survival Guide (p515)

Currency
Australian dollar ($)

Language
English

Visas
All visitors to Australia need visas; only New Zealanders are granted a visa on arrival. Apply online through the Department of Immigration & Border Protection (p521)

Money
ATMs widely available. Credit cards accepted at most hotels, restaurants and shops.

Mobile Phones
Many service providers offer free roaming in Australia. If yours doesn't, buy a SIM card and prepaid charge card at airport mobile-phone outlets.

Time
Australia's east coast is on Australian Eastern Standard Time (AEST) – GMT/UTC plus 10 hours. Australia (except Queensland) observes daylight-saving time (October to early April).

When to Go

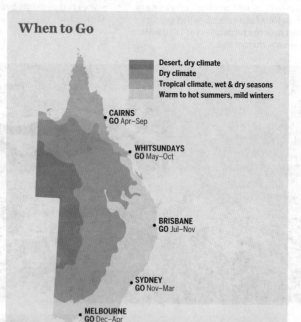

- Desert, dry climate
- Dry climate
- Tropical climate, wet & dry seasons
- Warm to hot summers, mild winters

CAIRNS GO Apr–Sep

WHITSUNDAYS GO May–Oct

BRISBANE GO Jul–Nov

SYDNEY GO Nov–Mar

MELBOURNE GO Dec–Apr

High Season
(Dec–Feb)

➡ Summertime: hot and humid up north, warm and dry down south.

➡ Prices rise 25% for big-city accommodation.

➡ Low season, unsafe swimming from November to May (jellyfish, aka 'stingers') in the tropical north.

Shoulder
(Sep–Nov & Mar–May)

➡ Warm sun, clear skies, shorter queues.

➡ Spring flowers (October); autumn colours in Victoria (April).

➡ Locals not yet stressed by summer crowds.

Low Season
(Jun–Aug)

➡ Cool, rainy days and lower prices down south.

➡ Tropical high season: mild days, low humidity, pricey beds.

➡ Good visibility on the Great Barrier Reef.

Useful Websites

Lonely Planet (lonelyplanet.com/australia) Destination information, hotel bookings, traveller forum and more.

Tourism Australia (www.australia.com) Government tourism site with loads of visitor info.

Queensland Tourism (www.queenslandholidays.com.au) Queensland coverage.

Visit NSW (www.visitnsw.com) New South Wales information.

Visit Victoria (www.visitvictoria.com) Victoria's official site.

Coastalwatch (www.coastalwatch.com) Surf reports and cams.

Important Numbers

Country code	☏61
International access code	☏0011
Emergency (ambulance, fire, police)	☏000
Directory assistance	☏1800 810 211
Area codes	Vic ☏03, NSW & ACT ☏02, Qld ☏07

Exchange Rates

Canada	C$1	$1.12
Eurozone	€1	$1.62
Japan	¥100	$1.33
New Zealand	NZ$1	$0.96
UK	UK£1	$1.90
USA	US$1	$1.46

For current exchange rates, see www.xe.com.

Daily Costs

Budget: Less than $150

➡ Hostel dorm bed: $25–35

➡ Double room in a hostel: $80–100

➡ Budget pizza or pasta meal: $15–20

➡ Short bus or tram ride: $4

Midrange: $150–300

➡ Double room in a motel or B&B: $130–250

➡ Breakfast or lunch in a cafe: $20–30

➡ Car hire per day: from $35

➡ Short taxi ride: $25

Top end: More than $300

➡ Double room in a top-end hotel: from $250

➡ Three-course meal in a classy restaurant: from $80

➡ Adventure activities: sailing the Whitsundays from $300 per night, diving course $650

➡ Domestic flight Sydney to Melbourne: from $100

Opening Hours

Business hours vary from state to state, but use the following as a guide:

Banks 9.30am–4pm Monday to Thursday, to 5pm Friday

Bars 4pm–late

Cafes 7am–5pm

Nightclubs 10pm–4am Thursday to Saturday

Post Offices 9am–5pm Monday to Friday; some also 9am–noon Saturday

Pubs 11am–midnight

Restaurants noon–2.30pm and 6–9pm

Shops 9am–4pm

Supermarkets 7am–9pm

Arriving in Australia

Sydney Airport (p524) Airport Link trains to central Sydney every 10 minutes, 4.22am to 12.57am. Prebooked shuttle buses service city hotels. A taxi into the city costs $45 to $55 (30 minutes).

Melbourne Airport (p524) SkyBus services (24 hours) to central Melbourne every 10 to 30 minutes. A taxi into the city costs around $50 to $55 (25 minutes).

Brisbane Airport (p524) Air-train trains to central Brisbane every 15 to 30 minutes, 5am to 10pm ($19.50). Prebooked shuttle buses service city hotels. A taxi into the city costs $45 to $55 (25 minutes).

Etiquette

There are several rules of etiquette in Australia.

Greetings A simple 'G'day', smile or nod suffices when passing people. Shake hands with men or women when meeting for the first time.

Aboriginal Communities Direct eye contact can be considered overbearing. Be respectful, wait to be acknowledged and respond in a like manner.

Dry Communities Check whether alcohol restrictions apply when visiting remote communities. You may be breaking the law by having booze in your vehicle.

BBQs Bring your own drinks and some sausages (aka 'snags') if invited to a barbecue.

Photography For Aboriginal Australians, photography can be highly intrusive, and photographing people, cultural places, practices, images, sites of significance and ceremonies may not be welcomed.

For much more on **getting around**, see p524

What's New

Here's what's happening in Australia right now. From a must-visit remote island and a surge in plant-based dining to boutique distilleries and mineral swimming pools, there's plenty to entice both new visitors and old-timers. As the country recovers from wildfires, these visits will be more appreciated than ever.

Best in Travel

Tiny, remote Lord Howe Island was awarded fifth place in Lonely Planet's list of top 10 regions internationally in 2020. Rising from the Pacific some 600km from the New South Wales (NSW) mainland, the visually breathtaking World Heritage–listed island is a refuge for endemic species and an excellent example of sustainably managed tourism. Only 400 visitors are allowed at any time, and they are encouraged to participate in a series of ecological projects.

Cutting-Edge Art Gallery

A bastion of culture in Surfers Paradise, HOTA (p334) is due to add an art gallery consisting of six floors of angular, colourful glass, inspired by William Robinson's *Rainforest* painting, in 2021.

Plant-Based Dining

Foodie-mad Melbourne and Sydney continue along the path of a vegan revolution, with new all-vegan restaurants, and vegan options conspicuously being added to meat-laden menus, too. Places to try include Eden (p98), Lentil as Anything (p214), Smith & Daughters (p227) and Yellow (p96).

Ganyamalbaa Camping Trial

At the Aboriginal-owned Worimi Conservation Lands, the Ganyamalbaa Campground (p142) in Port Stephens offers a unique camping experience on the largest moving sand dune system in the southern hemisphere.

Must-Try Restaurants

Tiny, graffiti-pimped and hidden down a laneway, the 10-seat, omakase-inspired, Brisbane-based Joy (p310) is creating

---

LOCAL KNOWLEDGE

WHAT'S HAPPENING IN EAST COAST AUSTRALIA

Anna Kaminski, Lonely Planet writer

Australia is facing some of its biggest challenges yet, both in the political arena and on a purely existential level. The surprise defeat of the Labour Party and election of Scott Morrison of the Liberal Party in 2019 has left the country divided, not least because Morrison's government refused to move away from Australia's reliance on fossil fuels and opted to open the world's largest coal mine in the face of the environmental changes that the country has been facing for some time. The bushfires of 2019–20 have been the worst on record, and the prime minister's inadequate response saw his ratings plummet, but not sufficiently to cause his government to pivot on policies that don't take climate change into account. Immigration also continues to be a divisive issue, though Australia remains a relatively outward-looking, welcoming country.

culinary waves across the country. Other don't-miss Mod Oz places are Ester (p99), Cutler & Co (p232) and Quay (p91).

Boutique Distilleries

Boutique distilleries continue to blossom in Australia. Noosa's first brewery, Land & Sea Brewery (p353), has a new venture called Fortune Distillery. It will launch its first whisky in 2021, but there are already gins, vodka and a white malt to sample, and a rum on its way.

Fresh Sydney Museums

Sydney University's impressive new Chau Chak Wing Museum (p73) shows off treasures from its 450,000-piece collection, while the Australian Museum (p69) has a new Pacific Spirit Gallery, among other exciting additions. Both were due to open in mid-2020.

Light Rail in Sydney

South East Light Rail has new tram lines up and running in Sydney, allowing you to cruise from Circular Quay through the city and out to Randwick in the Eastern Suburbs, and giving you easy tram access to the beach at Newcastle.

Budj Bim Cultural Landscape

While this ancient aquaculture system developed by the Gunditjmara people is anything but new (dating back 6600 years!), what has changed is that it's been recognised by Unesco as a World Heritage Site. It's the only place in Australia listed exclusively for its Aboriginal culture. It's near Portland in Victoria.

From Bushfires to Solutions

South coast NSW faced a harrowing spate of bushfires over the summer of 2019–20. For towns like Mogo, almost everything will have to be rebuilt. Yet the renewed sense of community spirit is palpable as those who choose to stay and work in tourism-related industries seek practical solutions for dealing with climate change.

Mineral Pools

Swimming pools are no longer just pools, with a growing number of smaller hotels,

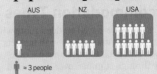
such as Byron Bay's Bower (p167), opting for magnesium/mineral swimming pools. With no chlorine, guests smell better after a soak, and the magnesium reputedly has healing qualities.

Aboriginal-led Wildlife Excursions

Aboriginal-led excursions in search of wildlife in rainforest and rivers, such as Kuku-Yalanji Dreamtime Gorge Walk (p487) and diving and snorkelling operations like Dreamtime Dive & Snorkel (p462), are increasingly a part of the traveller experience in north Queensland.

Accommodation

Find more accommodation reviews throughout the On the Road chapters (from p57)

PRICE RANGES

The following price ranges refer to a double room with bathroom in high season (December to February down south, June to September up north).

$ less than $130

$$ $130–$250

$$$ more than $250

Expect to pay $20 to $50 more in expensive areas – notably Sydney – and during school and public holidays.

Accommodation Types

The east coast is a well-trodden route with plenty of accommodation for all budgets, but you still need to book ahead – especially through summer, over Easter and during school holidays.

Camping & Caravan Parks East coast camping grounds and caravan parks are often close to the beach.

Hostels Backpacker joints along the east coast are certainly characterful.

Boutique Hotels From ritzy city boltholes to remote eco-retreats.

Resorts Tropical island luxury – need we elaborate?

Self-Contained Apartments & Cottages Beach houses, city apartments and hinterland cottages.

Motels Drive-up motels line the east coast highways – unremarkable, perhaps, but clean, convenient, reliable and affordable.

Best Places to Stay

Best on a Budget

Backpacker hostels are a wonderfully affordable and sociable way of seeing the east coast. There are dense clusters of them in cities and popular destinations (Sydney, Melbourne, Airlie Beach, Cairns) and they range from modest, family-run places to huge, custom-built party resorts. Dorm bed prices start at around $30 and increase to $55 in flash city hostels.

➡ Nomads Arts Factory Lodge, Byron Bay (p167)

➡ Nunnery, Melbourne (p224)

➡ No 14, Katoomba (p119)

➡ On the Wallaby, Yungaburra (p467)

➡ Brisbane Quarters, Brisbane (p300)

➡ Keiraleagh, Wollongong (p187)

Best Tropical Resorts

Plenty of islands in Queensland have resorts. Here's your chance to sleep for a week (with the odd cocktail and dip in the pool), or bring the family along for a fun-filled tropical holiday full of activities (snorkelling, kayaking, bushwalking, windsurfing, swimming, sailing…). Most resorts are at the pricey end of the scale – at least $260 a night, often a *lot* more – but some offer good family rates, particularly out of peak season.

➡ Elysian Retreat, Long Island (p426)

➡ Lizard Island Resort, Lizard Island (p492)

➡ InterContinental Hayman Island Resort, Hayman Island (p429)

➡ Orpheus Island Lodge, Orpheus Island (p443)

➡ Armana Resort, Port Stephens (p143)

➡ Kingfisher Bay Resort, Fraser Island (p381)

Best for Nature Lovers

Those wanting to get up close and personal with nature have almost unlimited options when it comes to roughing it. The majority of national parks have campgrounds, ranging from very basic (pit toilets and little else) to swish (hot showers, restaurant, wi-fi access). On the Great Barrier Reef, you can camp for a pittance ($6.55) on several uninhabited islands. At the high end of the spectrum are wilderness lodges, with safari tents, cabins and wildlife guides.

➡ Cedar Park Rainforest Resort, Kuranda (p476)

➡ Platypus Bushcamp, Eungella National Park (p416)

➡ Takarakka Bush Resort, Carnarvon National Park (p405)

➡ Bombah Point Eco Cottages, Myall Lakes National Park (p145)

➡ Great Ocean Ecolodge, Cape Otway (p261)

➡ Paperbark Camp, Jervis Bay (p192)

Best Boutique Hotels

A rarer beast than the ubiquitous, cookie-cutter motels, boutique accommodation ranges from lovingly restored historic houses in remote locations turned into intimate luxury retreats, to characterful small hotels in the big cities, distinguished by their contemporary design. They may have fewer amenities than larger luxury hotels, but tend to be distinguished by personalised service.

➡ Bailey, Cairns (p464)

➡ Spicers Vineyards Estate, Hunter Valley (p128)

➡ Emporium Hotel, Brisbane (p303)

➡ Cullen, Melbourne (p224)

➡ Songbirds, Tamborine Mountain (p344)

➡ Drift House, Port Fairy (p268)

Best for Families

Caravan parks are among the best options for those travelling with children. They usually have self-catering facilities and are often located near a beach and/or playground; the swisher ones come with swimming pools. In towns and cities, apartment hotels are a good bet, while in the countryside, some farmstays offer fun activities for kids.

➡ Stoney Creek Farmstay, Mackay (p416)

➡ Tyrian Serviced Apartments, Melbourne (p224)

ELLINNUR BAKARUDIN / SHUTTERSTOCK ©

PLAN YOUR TRIP ACCOMMODATION

➡ Bower, Byron Bay (p167)

➡ Great Keppel Island Holiday Village, Great Keppel Island (p403)

Booking

Book all accommodation well ahead, particularly in national parks and in popular beach destinations. During peak season, minimum stays may apply at some hotels and resorts. Some camping grounds and wilderness resorts are seasonal and close outside certain months.

Useful websites:

Lonely Planet (lonelyplanet.com/australia/hotels) Find independent reviews, as well as recommendations on the best places to stay – and then book them online.

Couchsurfing (www.couchsurfing.com) Find a free bed on the fly.

Flatmate Finders (www.flatmatefinders.com.au) For longer-term share-house stays.

Find a Camp (www.findacamp.com.au) Camping and caravan park bookings all over Australia.

Getting Around

For more information, see Transport (p524)

Travelling by Car

Urban exploration aside, having your own wheels is the quintessential way to get around this vast nation, allowing you to set your own schedule and reach remote corners. Whether you're focusing your visit on one state or several, road trips are a popular Australian experience.

Car Hire

Major car-rental companies have desks at all major airports, including Sydney, Melbourne, Brisbane, Cairns and Townsville. To rent a car, most companies require drivers to have a credit card and be over the age of 21, though in some cases it's 18 and in others it's 25. Know precisely what is included in the price: given the vast distances, having unlimited kilometres is essential, and check whether you're covered on unavoidable unsealed roads. Renting a campervan saves on lodging.

Driving Conditions

East coast Australia has an excellent network of roads, ranging from motorways to bucolic roads through the scenic countryside. Most are in excellent condition, but it's a bad idea to drive after dark due to a good chance of hitting wildlife. To drive some unsealed roads (and anywhere on sand), you'll need a 4WD.

No Car?

Bus

Australia's extensive bus network is a reliable and reasonably inexpensive way to get around, but distances are often vast. Most Australian buses are equipped with air-con, comfortable seats and decent toilets; all are smoke-free and some have wi-fi and USB chargers. The main companies include Greyhound Australia (www.greyhound.com.au), Firefly Express (www.fireflyexpress.com.au) and Premier Motor Service (www.premierms.com.au).

Another way to get around is by bus tour. Some include accommodation and meals; others are a means of getting from A to B and seeing the sights on the way.

AAT Kings (☎02-9028 5180; www.aatkings.com)

Adventure Tours Australia (☎1300 654 604; www.adventuretours.com.au)

Autopia Tours (☎1300 944 334; www.autopiatours.com.au)

Oz Experience (☎1300 473 946; www.ozexperience.com)

Train

Long-distance train travel falls into one of two categories. The expensive, scenic, once-in-a-lifetime category includes journeys between Sydney and Perth, Brisbane and Adelaide. Whereas the relatively inexpensive category includes somewhat slow services from Brisbane to Cairns, and Sydney to Brisbane, Melbourne and Canberra. The most notable long-distance rail journeys in East Coast Australia are run by the following:

Queensland Rail (p529)

NSW TrainLink (p529)

V/Line (p529)

Bicycle

Cycling around Australia is possible, but will take considerable fitness and excellent planning, given the distances involved.

If you're bringing your own bike, bus companies within Australia require you to dismantle your bicycle. Trains sometimes have separate bike-storage facilities on board.

Bike helmets are compulsory in all states and territories, as are white front lights and red rear lights for riding at night.

Carry plenty of water at all times. Distances between towns can be gruellingly far. Avoid cycling in the middle of the day in hot weather. Wear high-vis outerwear.

DRIVING FAST FACTS

→ Right or left? Left
→ Manual or automatic? Automatic
→ Top speed limit: 110km/h
→ Blood alcohol limit: 0.05%
→ Legal driving age: 16
→ Signature car: Hyundai i30
→ Alternative vehicle: Honda CB125E motorbike

ROAD DISTANCES (KMS)

	Brisbane	Cairns	Mackay	Melbourne
Cairns	1647			
Mackay	923	724		
Melbourne	1923	3570	2846	
Sydney	904	2551	1827	1019

Sydney to Melbourne distance is via the coastal road (A1).
All others are the shortest distances on the road; other routes may be considerably longer.

If You Like...

Beaches

Bondi Beach Essential Sydney: carve up the surf or laze around and people-watch. (p69)

Wilsons Promontory Victoria's premier coastal wilderness, with deserted beaches. (p278)

Fraser Island The world's largest sand island is basically one big beach. (p377)

Whitehaven Beach The jewel of the Whitsundays, with 5km of powdery white sand and gin-clear waters for snorkelling. (p430)

Cape Tribulation The rainforest sweeps down to smooch the reef at empty stretches of sand loved by crocs. (p489)

The Spit A long, wild stretch of pristine Gold Coast sand and dunes, beyond the high-rises and the crowds. (p334)

Four Mile Beach Take a stinger-safe swim at Port Douglas, or go for a 4-mile beachcomb. (p481)

Clarkes Beach Iconic strip of Byron Bay sand – at low tide you can walk to the lighthouse. (p168)

Greenfield Beach White squeaky sand at Jervis Bay, ringed by gum trees and lapped at by gentle teal waters. (p191)

Long Beach Long, pristine stretch of white sand on Great Keppel Island, with a naturist section for sunning your buns. (p401)

Indigenous Culture

Big Bend Walk Peruse centuries-old Aboriginal cave paintings and rock carvings in the Carnarvon National Park gorge. (p2405)

Dreamtime Southern X Fascinating walking and coach tours of Aboriginal sites in Sydney. (p80)

Koorie Heritage Trust A great place to discover southeastern Aboriginal culture, in Melbourne. (p211)

Kuku-Yalanji Dreamtime Walks Walks through Queensland's Mossman Gorge with knowledgeable Indigenous guides. (p487)

Tjapukai Aboriginal Cultural Park Interactive tours and vibrant performances in Cairns by local Tjapukai people. (p462)

Dreamtime Dive & Snorkel Indigenous sea rangers present the Great Barrier Reef in a new – read ancient – way. (p462)

Mandingalbay Ancient Indigenous Tours Sample the bush tucker and rainforest remedies of Far North Queensland's Mandingalbay Yidinji people. (p462)

Bingi Dreaming Track This accessible coastal walk passes through ancient Yuin country in south coast NSW. (p195)

Queensland Art Gallery This must-see Brisbane gallery includes a significant collection of art from modern and contemporary Aboriginal artists. (p291)

Bataluk Cultural Trail Visit sites sacred to the Gunai and Kurnai people in east Gippsland. (p281)

Wildlife Encounters

Phillip Island Penguins The world's largest little penguin colony; catch them at sunset marching up from the sea. (p274)

Whale watching in Eden In season (July to November) you can spy whales offshore from Eden right up to the Great Barrier Reef. (p204)

Ben Boyd National Park Muddle-headed wombats aplenty at this rambling national park near Eden. (p205)

Montague Island (Barranguba) Spy some seals, seabirds and penguins offshore from Narooma. (p197)

Solar Whisper Croc-seeking tours along the Daintree River and rainforest (p488)

Eungella National Park Sit in silence by the creek and watch for the elusive platypus at dusk and dawn. (p415)

Port Macquarie Koala Hospital Learn how you can help the native koala population devastated by the 2019 bushfires. (p147)

Top: Whitehaven Beach (p423), Hamilton Island.

Bottom: :Members of the Tjapukai Dance Theatre (p462)

Noosa National Park Koalas, dolphins and seasonal whales are easy to spot at this highly accessible pocket of green. (p348)

Fraser Island The dingoes here are the purest breed in Australia. (p377)

Port Douglas Go snorkelling out on the reef among an astonishing proliferation of marine life. (p479)

Islands

Montague Island (Barranguba) Seabirds, little penguins, fur seals...plus revamped lighthouse accommodation. What's not to like? (p197)

Cockatoo Island Amazing Sydney Harbour isle with a dazzling history. (p71)

Lady Musgrave Island Camp on this tiny cay and swim and snorkel in a turquoise lagoon. (p389)

Fraser Island Rev up your 4WD: the largest sand island in the world has giant sand dunes, freshwater lakes and rampant wildlife. (p377)

The Whitsundays Jump aboard a yacht or speedboat, and explore as many of these amazing islands as you can. (p423)

Lady Elliot Island Ringed by the Great Barrier Reef and reachable by light aircraft – the perfect place to play castaway. (p397)

Fitzroy Island One of a handful of lovely islands off Cairns, with enticing beaches, rich coral and a hilly interior. (p471)

Great Keppel Island Combine bushwalking with daydreaming on 17 white-sand beaches and turtle watching below the waves. (p401)

Lizard Island Pitch a tent or check into the plush resort on this far-north island. (p492)

Frankland Islands These five uninhabited, coral-fringed isles are custom-made for adventurers and beach bums alike. (p471)

Month by Month

January

January yawns into action as Australia recovers from its Christmas hangover, but then everyone realises, 'Hey, it's summer!'. Heat and humidity along the coast; monsoonal rains up north.

✲ Sydney Festival

'It's big' says the promo material. Indeed, sprawling over three summer weeks, the Sydney Festival, a fab mixture of music, dance, talks, theatre and visual arts – much of it free and family-focused – is an artistic behemoth. (p79)

☆ Australian Open

Held at Melbourne Park in late January, the Australian Open draws tennis fanatics from around the planet as the world's best duke it out on the courts. Invariably it's baking hot. (p221)

✲ Australia Day

Australia Day (www.australiaday.com.au) is the nation's 'birthday' – when the First Fleet landed on 26 January 1788. Expect picnics, barbecues, fireworks and, increasingly, nationalistic chest beating. In less of a mood to celebrate are Indigenous Australians and others sympathetic to the date's relevance to their history, who refer to it as 'Invasion Day'.

February

February is usually Australia's warmest month: hot and sticky up north as the wet season continues, but divine in Victoria.

✲ Sydney Gay & Lesbian Mardi Gras

Mardi Gras is a two-week-long arts festival running into March and culminating in a flamboyant parade along Sydney's Oxford St that attracts 300,000 spectators. After-party tickets are gold. (p518)

March

Heat and humidity ease down south – crowds dissipate and resort prices drop. Meanwhile, high temperatures and general irritability prevail in the north.

☆ Australian Formula One Grand Prix

Melbourne's normally tranquil Albert Park explodes with four days of Formula One (www.grandprix.com.au) rev-head action in late March. The 5.3km street circuit around the lake is known for its smooth, fast surface.

April

Autumn brings golden colours to Victoria and cooler, mild temperatures to New South Wales (NSW). Up north it's the end of the wet season: smiling faces and warm, pleasant weather.

★ Byron Bay Bluesfest

Music erupts over the Easter weekend when 20,000 festivalgoers swamp Byron Bay to hear blues-and-roots bands from all over the world (Ben Harper, Neil Young, Bonnie Raitt). Held on Tyagarah Tea Tree Farm, 11km north of Byron. Some folks camp. (p167)

May

Days grow noticeably cooler down south; beach days are unlikely anywhere south of the Gold Coast.

★ Biennale of Sydney

Held in even-numbered years between March and June, Sydney's Biennale showcases the work of hundreds of contemporary artists and is the country's largest visual-arts event. Expect tours, talks, screenings and cutting-edge exhibitions. Most events are free. (p80)

★ Noosa Eat & Drink

One of Australia's best regional culinary fests, with cooking demonstrations, wine tastings, cheese exhibits, feasting on gourmet fare and live concerts at night. Over three days in mid-May. (p351)

★ Sydney Writers' Festival

Books, words, books full of words... For one week in May, the Sydney Writers' Festival hosts 300-plus novelists, essayists, poets, historians and philosophers – from Australia and beyond – who read their work, run workshops and host edifying panel discussions. (p79)

★ Whale Watching

Between May and November along the southeastern Australian coast, migrating southern right and humpback whales come close to shore to feed, breed and calve. See them at Eden (NSW), Warrnambool (Victoria), and Hervey Bay and North Stradbroke Island (Queensland).

June

The south shivers into winter, while tourist season kicks into high gear in the warm, clear tropical north with stinger-free beaches. Migrating whales cavort off the coast (until November).

★ Vivid Sydney

Immersive light installations and projections in the city, plus performances from local and international musicians, and public talks and debates with leading global creative thinkers. Held over 18 days in August 2021. (p79)

★ Sydney Film Festival

Held in venues across town, this excellent, highly regarded film festival screens art-house gems from Australia and around the world. (p80)

★ State of Origin Series

Rugby league fanatics consider this series of three matches (www.nrl.com) between Queensland and New South Wales the pinnacle of the game. One of the three is held in Sydney. The final match is held in July.

July

Pubs with open fires, cosy coffee shops and empty beaches down south; packed markets, tours and accommodation up north. Bring warm clothes for anywhere south of Brisbane.

★ Cairns Indigenous Arts Fair

Thousands of collectors, curators and curious folk head to CIAF each year to experience a whirlwind of Aboriginal and Torres Strait Islander art and culture. (p462)

★ Splendour in the Grass

A splendid alt-rock music festival in Byron Bay, Splendour draws the big names from around Australia and overseas for three days in late July (winter, so the grass can get a tad muddy). (p167)

August

August is when southerners, sick of winter's grey-sky drear, head to Queensland for some sun.

★ Melbourne International Film Festival

As wildly popular as Toronto and Cannes, the Melbourne International Film Festival has been running since 1952. Myriad short films, feature-length spectaculars and documentaries flicker across inner-city screens. (p222)

🏃 Airlie Beach Race Week

Taking place over the second week in August, this is one of Australia's largest yacht-racing regattas. Sailing aside, there's live music and other festivities. (p418)

🎆 Melbourne Winter Festival

Scheduled to start from 2020, Melbourne will combine the long-running Melbourne International Arts Festival and White Night into a single monolith major event that will run annually from 20 August to 6 September.

🎆 Cairns Festival

Running for two weeks from late August into September, the massive art-and-culture Cairns Festival delivers a stellar program of music, theatre, dance, comedy, film, Indigenous art and public exhibitions. Lots of outdoor events. (p461)

September

Winter ends and spring returns, bringing wildflowers and brighter spirits in the south.

🎆 Bigsound Festival

Brisbane's new music festival, held over four nights in September, showcases dozens of up-and-coming artists in 18 venues across Fortitude Valley, attracting those on the lookout for fresh Aussie music. (p299)

🏃 Australian Football League Grand Final

The pinnacle of the AFL season is this high-flying spectacle in Melbourne, watched (on TV) by millions. At half-time everyone's neighbourhood BBQ moves into the local park for a little amateur kick-to-kick. (p222)

☆ Brisbane Festival

One of Australia's largest, most diverse arts fiestas, the Brisbane Festival runs for 22 days in September. An impressive schedule includes concerts, plays, dance and fringe events. It finishes off with 'Riverfire', an elaborate fireworks show over the Brisbane River. (p299)

October

The weather avoids extremes everywhere: a good time to go camping or hit some vineyards.

☆ Caloundra Music Festival

Held at Kings Beach, this family-friendly music festival spans four days and attracts crowds of up to 40,000 with its diverse line-up of musicians spanning all genres. Acts range from current and veteran Australian rock and indie pop to blues and soul acts and international guests. (p357)

November

Northern beaches may close due to 'stingers' – jellyfish in the shallows north of Agnes Water.

☆ Airlie Beach Festival of Music

The Airlie Beach Festival of Music entails three days of letting it all hang out in the famous party town, with loads of live tunes to rock out to. (p418)

December

Holidays begin a week or two before Christmas. Up north, monsoon season is underway: afternoon thunderstorms bring pelting rain.

☆ Sydney to Hobart Yacht Race

Pack a picnic and join the Boxing Day (26 December) crowds along Sydney's waterfront to watch the start of the Sydney to Hobart, the world's most arduous open-ocean yacht race (628 nautical miles!). (p80)

☆ Sydney Harbour New Year's Eve Fireworks

A fantastic way to ring in the new year: join the crowds overlooking the harbour as the Sydney Harbour Fireworks light up the night sky on 31 December. There's a family display at 9pm; the main event erupts at midnight. (p80)

Itineraries

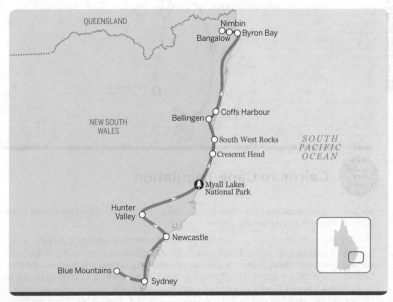

QUEENSLAND

Nimbin
Bangalow ○○ ○○ Byron Bay

NEW SOUTH WALES

Bellingen ○ ○ Coffs Harbour

○ South West Rocks

SOUTH PACIFIC OCEAN

○ Crescent Head

Myall Lakes National Park

Hunter Valley ○

○ Newcastle

Blue Mountains ○

○ Sydney

10 DAYS Sydney to Byron Bay

Mountains, cities, wine, beaches and quirky towns: this road trip is an Australian classic.

Kick-start your tour in **Sydney**, checking out the big-ticket sights, seeing and being seen on Bondi Beach, bar hopping and shopping. Don't miss the seaside Bondi to Coogee Clifftop Walk. Dart inland to explore the **Blue Mountains**, with misty Katoomba's cache of art-deco architecture and the amazing Three Sisters lookout. Alternatively, a couple of days drifting on the Hawkesbury River in a houseboat is serenity itself.

Next stop is the the arts- and surf-loving city of **Newcastle**. Thirsty? Detour inland to the hedonistic vineyards of the **Hunter Valley**. Back on the coast, explore the pristine beaches of **Myall Lakes National Park**.

Northern New South Wales basks in subtropical glory. Surf the excellent breaks at **Crescent Head** and splash around in the sea at **South West Rocks**. Hit **Bellingen** for a mix of bushwalking, canoeing and culture, then proceed to **Coffs Harbour**, where the kitsch Big Banana awaits your appreciation. Further north, **Byron Bay** is inescapable – a chilled-out beach town where surfers, hipsters and hippies share the sands. Meditating in Byron's hinterland is the alt-stoner haven of **Nimbin** and laid-back **Bangalow** – both worthy day trips.

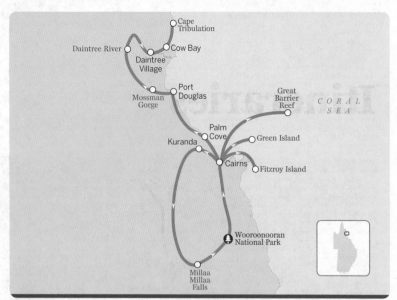

Cairns to Cape Tribulation

2 WEEKS

Far North Queensland is like nowhere else on earth – a dizzying array of coral reefs, tropical atolls, rainforests and interesting towns.

Australia's reef-diving capital and gateway to the Daintree Rainforest, **Cairns** is an obligatory east-coast destination. Spend a few days visiting botanic gardens, hip restaurants and buzzy watering holes. A short hop offshore, reef-trimmed **Green Island** and **Fitzroy Island** have verdant vegetation and lovely beaches. Further afield, a snorkelling or dive trip to the **Great Barrier Reef** is an essential east-coast experience, or plan a few days on a live-aboard expedition to Cod Hole (Lizard Island), one of Australia's best dive spots.

Next up, head inland on a gondola cableway or scenic railway to **Kuranda** for rainforest walks and a wander around the town's famous markets. If you have your own wheels you can explore further: swing by the picturesque **Millaa Millaa Falls** and take a rainforest hike in spectacular **Wooroonooran National Park**.

Back at sea level, treat yourself to a night in a plush resort at **Palm Cove**, just north of Cairns. An hour further north is **Port Douglas**, an up-tempo holiday hub with fab eateries, bars and a beaut beach. It's also a popular base for boat trips to the outer reef. Next stop is **Mossman Gorge**, where lush lowland rainforest surrounds the photogenic Mossman River. Take a guided walk and cool off in a waterhole.

Further north is the **Daintree River**, where you can go on a crocodile-spotting cruise then stop for lunch at the low-key **Daintree Village**. Afterwards, cross by vehicle ferry to the northern side of the river. From here continue driving north (easy does it – this is cassowary country!) to the Daintree Discovery Centre – a great place to learn about this magnificent jungle wilderness. The beach at nearby (and rather agriculturally named) **Cow Bay** is perfect for a few hours of beachcombing among the seashells and driftwood.

Last stop on your tropical tour is **Cape Tribulation**, a magnificent natural partnership between rainforest and reef. Spend a few nights taking in the splendour at one of the camping or backpacker places nooked into the rainforest.

Top: City Hall,
Bundaberg (p388),
Queensland

Bottom: Noosa Heads
(p348), Queensland

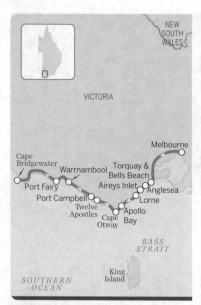

5 DAYS Melbourne & the Great Ocean Road

Dip into east-coast Australia's deep south, exploring hip Melbourne and the gorgeous Great Ocean Road.

Melbourne can keep visitors engaged for months – bars, galleries, live music, shopping, AFL football...but the Great Ocean Road, a classic Aussie road trip, beckons.

Start in the surfing mecca of **Torquay** and check the swell at **Bells Beach**, then head to family-focused **Anglesea** for a surf lesson and a riverside picnic. **Aireys Inlet** is next: tour the lighthouse, then spend the night in the resort town of **Lorne**.

West of here, the Great Ocean Road gets seriously scenic, winding between the sea and the rainforest-clad Otway Ranges. Wind down in the artsy fishing town of **Apollo Bay**, then swing by **Cape Otway** to see some koalas and the lighthouse.

Next up is Port Campbell National Park and its famed **Twelve Apostles**. Count them from the cliff tops, then spend a night in **Port Campbell** to get a real feel for the area. Scan for whales along the **Warrnambool** coast, then continue west to quaint, rather Irish-feeling **Port Fairy**. If there's time, **Cape Bridgewater** is worth a visit.

10 DAYS Melbourne to Sydney

This 10-day coastal run offers lots of wilderness, bookended by Australia's biggest cities. And don't overlook Canberra!

Kick off in savvy, coffee-scented **Melbourne** before exploring **Phillip Island**. Next stop is **Wilsons Promontory** with its fab bushwalks and beaches. Truck northeast through the Gippsland Lakes district to **Mallacoota**, a Victorian seaside town.

Entering warmer south-coast NSW, sleepy **Eden** is famed for whale watching. Don't miss picture-perfect **Central Tilba**. Continue to **Narooma**, with its pretty beaches and solid surf. From here, ferry out to **Montague Island**, an important Aboriginal site and nature reserve. Tracking north, detour inland to Australian capital **Canberra** to see the country's best museums.

Jervis Bay offers beaches, dolphins and national parks. Heading north, zip through pretty **Kiama** then **Wollongong** to the Grand Pacific Drive. South of Sydney are the dramatic cliffs of **Royal National Park**.

Welcome to **Sydney**. Tour the Opera House, catch a harbour ferry and dunk yourself in the Bondi Beach waves. Leave time for the awe-inspiring **Blue Mountains**.

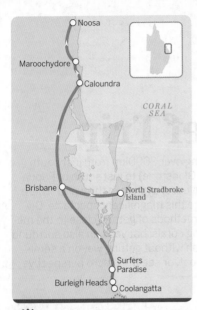

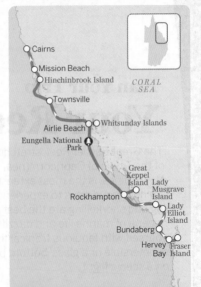

5 DAYS South Queensland Coast

Check out Queensland's big smoke, and the sun-baked Gold and Sunshine Coasts.

Semitropical **Brisbane** is dappled with brilliant bars, cafes and bookshops. Don't miss the Gallery of Modern Art and neighbouring Queensland Art Gallery on the South Bank riverfront. The neighbourhoods here are a characterful patchwork: check out raffish West End, ever-changing Fortitude Valley, and side-by-side Teneriffe and Newstead with their emerging crop of hip eateries, breweries and live-music venues.

An hour south, the Gold Coast exhibits the flip side of Queensland's soul: beachy, brassy and boozy. The hub is **Surfers Paradise**, with its after-dark sexiness and theme parks. More relaxed and surf-centric are **Burleigh Heads** just to the south, and **Coolangatta** on the NSW border.

Tack on a few days roaming the beaches on **North Stradbroke Island** in Moreton Bay. Otherwise, truck north to the Sunshine Coast towns of up-and-coming **Caloundra** and vibrant **Maroochydore**. Another half-hour north is **Noosa**, a classy resort town with sublime beaches, a lush national park and a string of top-flight restaurants.

12 DAYS Hervey Bay to Cairns

Track north along the central section of Queensland's eastern seaboard, with islands to visit en route.

Two hours north of Noosa is amiable **Hervey Bay**, from where you can explore the huge dunes and crystalline lakes on **Fraser Island**. Not far north, sip Australia's favourite rum in **Bundaberg**.

Sample Queensland's coral wonders at **Lady Musgrave Island** or **Lady Elliot Island**, then devour a steak at 'beef city' **Rockhampton**. Offshore, unwind for a few days on the trails and beaches on **Great Keppel Island**.

Spot a platypus in peaceful **Eungella National Park** then wheel into buzzy **Airlie Beach**, gateway to the azure waters and powdery white-sand beaches of the **Whitsunday Islands** – sail, dive, snorkel, relax at a resort or camp on an uninhabited atoll.

Townsville is next with a hip eating and drinking scene. Don't miss hiking the Thorsborne Trail on magnificent **Hinchinbrook Island**. Recover at **Mission Beach**, where the rainforest meets the sea. End your epic road trip in touristy **Cairns** with a trip to the Great Barrier Reef and a seafood feast.

Plan Your Trip

Your Reef Trip

The Great Barrier Reef, stretching over 2000km from just south of the Tropic of Capricorn (near Gladstone) to just south of Papua New Guinea, is the most extensive reef system in the world. There are numerous ways to experience this magnificent spectacle. Diving and snorkelling are the best methods of getting close to the menagerie of marine life and dazzling corals, but you can also surround yourself with fabulous tropical fish without getting wet on a semi-submersible or a glass-bottom boat, or see the macro perspective on a scenic flight.

Best for...

Wildlife

Viewing sea turtles around Lady Elliot Island or Heron Island.

Looking for reef sharks and rays while kayaking off Green Island.

Spotting wild koalas on Magnetic Island.

Snorkelling

Getting underwater at Knuckle, Hardy and Fitzroy Reefs.

Enjoying the offshore delights at Magnetic Island or the Whitsunday Islands.

Views from Above

Taking scenic chopper or plane rides from Cairns or the Whitsunday Islands.

Skydiving over Airlie Beach.

Sailing

Sailing from Airlie Beach through the Whitsunday Islands.

Exploring Agincourt Reef from Port Douglas.

When to Go

High season on the reef is from June to December. The best overall underwater visibility is from August to January.

From December to March, northern Queensland (north of Townsville) has its wet season, bringing oppressive heat and abundant rainfall (it's cooler from July to September). Stinger (jellyfish) season is between November and May; most reef operators offer Lycra stinger suits to snorkellers and divers, or bring your own.

Anytime is generally good to visit the Whitsundays. Winter (June to August) can be pleasantly warm, but you will occasionally need a jumper. South of the Whitsundays, summer (December to March) is hot and humid. Southern and central Queensland experience mild winters – pleasant enough for diving or snorkelling in a wetsuit.

Picking Your Spot

There are many popular and remarkable spots from which to access the 'GBR', but bear in mind that individual areas change over time, depending on the weather or recent damage.

Mainland Gateways

There are several mainland gateways to the reef, all offering slightly different experiences and activities. Here's a brief overview, south to north.

Agnes Water & Town of 1770 Small towns and good choices if you want to escape the crowds. Tours head to Fitzroy Reef Lagoon, one of the most pristine sections of the reef with great snorkelling, where visitor numbers are still limited.

Gladstone The closest access point to the southern or Capricorn reef islands and innumerable cays, including Lady Elliot Island.

Airlie Beach A small town with a full range of sailing outfits. The big attraction here is spending two or more days aboard a boat and seeing some of the Whitsunday Islands' fringing coral reefs, with tours to match all budgets.

Townsville Whether you're learning or experienced, a four- or five-night diving safari around the numerous islands and pockets of the reef is a great choice. Kelso Reef and the wreck of the SS *Yongala* are teeming with marine life. There are also a couple of day-trip options on glass-bottom boats, but for more choice you're better off heading to Cairns. The gigantic Reef HQ Aquarium (p433) is also here.

Mission Beach Closer to the reef than any other gateway destination, this small, quiet town offers a few boat and diving tours to sections of the outer reef.

Cairns The main launching pad for reef tours, with a staggering number of operators offering everything from relatively inexpensive day trips on large boats to intimate five-day luxury charters. Tours cover a wide section of the reef, with pricier operators going as far north as Lizard Island.

Port Douglas A swanky resort town and a gateway to the Low Isles and Agincourt Reef, an outer-ribbon reef featuring crystal-clear water and stunning corals. Diving, snorkelling and cruising trips tend to be classier, pricier and less crowded than in Cairns.

Cooktown Close to Lizard Island, but most tour operators here shut down between November and May for the wet season.

Islands

Speckled throughout the reef is a profusion of islands and cays that offer some of the most stunning access. Here is a list of some of the best islands, travelling from south to north.

Lady Elliot Island The coral cay here is twitcher heaven, with 57 resident bird species. Sea turtles also nest here and it's possibly the best spot on the reef to see manta rays. It's also a famed diving location. There's a resort here, but you can also visit Lady Elliot on a day trip from Bundaberg.

Heron Island A tiny, tranquil coral cay sitting amid a huge spread of reef. It's a diving mecca, but the snorkelling is also good and it's possible to do a reef walk from here. Heron is a nesting ground for green and loggerhead turtles and home to 30 bird species. The sole resort on the island charges accordingly.

Great Keppel Island Arguably the best island for bushwalking, Great Keppel is surrounded by fringing reefs. There's excellent swimming and snorkelling here, with a good chance of spotting turtles. There's accommodation to suit all budgets and it's easily accessed from Yeppoon on a day trip.

Hamilton Island The big daddy of the Whitsundays, Hamilton is a sprawling, family-friendly resort laden with infrastructure. While the atmosphere isn't exactly intimate, there's a wealth of tours going to the outer reef. It's also a good place to see patches of the reef that can't be explored from the mainland.

Orpheus Island A national park and one of the reef's most exclusive, tranquil and romantic hideaways. Orpheus is particularly good for snorkelling – you can step right off the beach and be surrounded by colourful marine life. Clusters of fringing reefs also provide plenty of diving opportunities.

Green Island Another of the reef's true coral cays. The fringing reefs here are considered to be among the most beautiful surrounding any island, and the diving and snorkelling are spectacular. Covered in dense rainforest, the entire island is a national park. Bird life is abundant. Accessible as a day trip from Cairns.

Lizard Island Remote, rugged and the perfect place to escape civilisation, Lizard has a ring of talcum-white beaches, remarkably blue water and few visitors. It's home to the Cod Hole, arguably Australia's best-known dive site, where you can swim in the same waters as docile potato cod weighing as much as 60kg. Accommodation here has no grey areas: it's either five-star luxury or bush camping.

TOP SNORKELLING SITES

Some nondivers may wonder if it's really worth going to the Great Barrier Reef 'just to snorkel'. The answer is a resounding yes! Much of the rich, colourful coral lies just underneath the surface (coral needs bright sunlight to flourish) and is easily viewed by snorkellers. Here's a round-up of some top snorkelling sites.

➡ Fitzroy Reef Lagoon (Town of 1770)

➡ Heron Island (Capricorn Coast)

➡ Great Keppel Island (Capricorn Coast)

➡ Lady Elliot Island (Capricorn Coast)

➡ Lady Musgrave Island (Capricorn Coast)

➡ Hook Island (Whitsundays)

➡ Hayman Island (Whitsundays)

➡ Border Island (Whitsundays)

➡ Hardy Reef (Whitsundays)

➡ Knuckle Reef (Whitsundays)

➡ Lizard Island (Cairns)

➡ Michaelmas Reef (Cairns)

➡ Hastings Reef (Cairns)

➡ Norman Reef (Cairns)

➡ Saxon Reef (Cairns)

➡ Opal Reef (Port Douglas)

➡ Agincourt Reef (Port Douglas)

➡ Mackay Reef (Port Douglas)

Diving & Snorkelling the Reef

Much of the diving and snorkelling on the reef is boat-based, although there are some excellent reefs accessible by walking straight off the beach of some islands. Free use of snorkelling gear is usually part of any day cruise to the reef. Overnight or liveaboard trips obviously provide a more in-depth experience and greater coverage of the reefs. If you don't have a diving certificate, many operators offer the option of an introductory dive, where an experienced diver conducts an underwater tour. A lesson in safety and procedure is given beforehand and you don't require a five-day Professional Association of Diving Instructors (PADI) course or a 'buddy'.

Key Diving Details

Your last dive should be completed 24 hours before flying – even in a balloon or for a parachute jump – in order to minimise the risk of residual nitrogen in the blood that can cause decompression injury. It's fine to dive soon after arriving by air.

Find out whether your insurance policy classifies diving as a dangerous-sport exclusion. For a nominal annual fee, the Divers Alert Network (www.diversalert network.org) provides insurance for medical or evacuation services required in the event of a diving accident. DAN's hotline for emergencies is +1 919 684 9111.

Visibility for coastal areas is 1m to 3m, whereas several kilometres offshore visibility is 8m to 15m. The outer edge of the reef has visibility of 20m to 35m and the Coral Sea has visibility of 50m and beyond.

In the north, the water is warm all year round, from around 24°C to 30°C. Going south it gradually gets cooler, dropping to a low of 20°C in winter.

Top Reef Dive Spots

The Great Barrier Reef is home to some of the world's best diving sites. Here are a few of our favourite spots to get you started:

SS Yongala A sunken shipwreck that has been home to a vivid marine community for more than 90 years.

Cod Hole See potato cod as you dive.

Heron Island Join a crowd of colourful fish straight off the beach.

Lady Elliot Island With 19 highly regarded dive sites.

Wheeler Reef Massive variety of marine life, plus a great spot for night dives.

Boat Excursions

Unless you're staying on a coral-fringed island, you'll need to join a boat excursion to experience the reef's real beauty. Day trips leave from many places along the coast, as well as from island resorts, and typically include the use of snorkelling gear, snacks and a buffet lunch, with scuba diving an optional extra. On some boats, naturalists

Reef Highlights

N 0   200 km
    0   100 miles

Lizard Island

○ Cooktown

CORAL
SEA

PORT DOUGLAS

Book yourself onto an upmarket catamaran day-trip out to Agincourt Reef. (p479)

● **PORT DOUGLAS**
Green Island
○
Fitzroy Island
CAIRNS

GREAT

○ Innisfail

CAIRNS

Hop over from Cairns for a luxurious sojourn on Green Island, with its rainforest and fringing coral. On a budget? Take a day trip to Fitzroy Island and/or Green Island. (p456)

Tully ○ **MISSION BEACH**
Dunk Island

BARRIER

Hinchinbrook Island

Ingham ○

MISSION BEACH

Unwind on Mission Beach with rainforest walks, and overnight on nearby Dunk Island, which has good swimming, kayaking and hiking. (p447)

Magnetic Island

TOWNSVILLE ○

REEF

○ Charters
Towers

Bowen ○

Airlie ○
Beach

Hamilton Islnd
Lindeman Island

Whitsunday Islands

TOWNSVILLE

In Townsville, visit the excellent Reef HQ Aquarium for a dry-land reef encounter. If you're an experienced diver, book a trip on a liveaboard boat to dive the SS *Yongala* wreck. And don't miss the koalas on Magnetic Island. (p433)

○ Mackay

THE WHITSUNDAYS

From party-prone Airlie Beach, explore some white-sand Whitsundays beaches and encircling coral reefs via a tour or sailing cruise. (p423)

Tropic of Capricorn

Emerald ○

Rockhampton ○

Great Keppel Island

○ Gladstone
Lady
Musgrave
Island
○ **TOWN OF 1770**

TOWN OF 1770

Head to the Town of 1770 and day-trip out to Lady Musgrave Island for semisubmersible coral-viewing, plus snorkelling or diving in the definitive blue lagoon. (p393)

Bundaberg ○

*Fraser
Island*
Hervey Bay ○
Maryborough ○

○ Miles

Noosa ○

or marine biologists present talks on the reef's ecology.

Boat trips vary dramatically in passenger numbers, type of vessel and quality – which is reflected in the price – so get all the details before committing. When selecting a tour, consider the vessel (motorised catamaran or sailing ship), the number of passengers (from six to 400), what extras are offered and the destination. The outer reefs are usually more pristine. Inner reefs often show signs of damage from humans and coral-eating crown-of-thorns starfish. Coral bleaching is a major issue in far northern sections of the reef. Some operators offer the option of a trip in a glass-bottom boat or semi-submersible.

Many boats have underwater cameras for hire, although you'll save money by hiring these on land (or using your own). Some boats also have professional photographers on board who will dive and take high-quality shots of you in action.

Liveaboards

If you're eager to do as much diving as possible, a liveaboard is an excellent option as you'll do three dives per day, plus some night dives, all in more remote parts of the Great Barrier Reef. Trip lengths vary from one to 12 nights. The three-day/three-night voyages, which allow up to 11 dives (nine day and two night dives), are among the most common.

Some boats offer specialist itineraries, following marine life and events such as minke whales or coral spawning, or offer trips to less-visited spots like the far-northern reefs, Pompey Complex, Coral Sea Reefs or Swain Reefs.

Go with operators who are Dive Queensland (www.dive-queensland.com.au) members: this ensures they follow a minimum set of guidelines. Ideally, they'll also be accredited by Ecotourism Australia (www.ecotourism.org.au).

Popular departure points for liveaboard dive vessels, along with the locales they visit are:

Bundaberg The Bunker Island group, including Lady Musgrave and Lady Elliot Islands, possibly Fitzroy, Llewellyn and the rarely visited Boult Reefs or Hoskyn and Fairfax Islands.

Town of 1770 Bunker Island group.

Gladstone Swains and Bunker Island group.

Mackay Lihou Reef and the Coral Sea.

Airlie Beach The Whitsundays, Knuckle Reef and Hardy Reef.

Townsville SS *Yongala* wreck, plus canyons of Wheeler Reef and Keeper Reef.

MAKING A POSITIVE CONTRIBUTION TO THE REEF

The Great Barrier Reef is incredibly fragile and it's worth taking some time to educate yourself on responsible practices while you're there.

➡ No matter where you visit, take all litter with you – even biodegradable material such as apple cores – and dispose of it back on the mainland.

➡ It is an offence to damage or remove coral in the marine park.

➡ If you touch or walk on coral you'll damage it and get some nasty cuts.

➡ Don't touch or harass marine animals.

➡ If you have a boat, be aware of the rules in relation to anchoring around the reef, including 'no anchoring areas' to avoid coral damage.

➡ If you're diving, check that you are weighted correctly before entering the water and keep your buoyancy control well away from the reef. Ensure that equipment such as secondary regulators and gauges aren't dragging over the reef.

➡ If you're snorkelling (especially if you're a beginner), practise your technique away from coral until you've mastered control in the water.

➡ Hire a wetsuit rather than slathering on sunscreen, which can damage the reef.

➡ Watch where your fins are – try not to stir up sediment or disturb coral.

➡ Do not enter the water near a dugong, whether you're swimming or diving.

➡ Note that there are limits on the amount and types of shells that you can collect.

Cairns Cod Hole, Ribbon Reefs, the Coral Sea and possibly far northern reefs.

Port Douglas Osprey Reef, Cod Hole, Ribbon Reefs, Coral Sea and possibly the far northern reefs.

Dive Courses

In Queensland, there are numerous places where you can learn to dive, take a refresher course or improve your skills. Dive courses here are generally of a high standard, and all schools teach either PADI or Scuba Schools International (SSI) qualifications. Which certification you choose isn't as important as choosing a good instructor, so meet with the instructor before committing to a programme.

A popular place to learn is Cairns, where you can choose between courses for the budget-minded (four-day courses cost between $540 and $785) that combine pool training and reef dives, and longer, more intensive courses that include reef diving on a liveaboard (five-day courses, including three-day/two-night liveaboard, cost between $850 and $1100).

Other places where you can learn to dive, and then head out on the reef, include Bundaberg, Mission Beach, Townsville, Airlie Beach, Hamilton Island, Magnetic Island and Port Douglas.

Camping on the Great Barrier Reef

Pitching a tent on an island is a hugely fun and affordable way to experience the Great Barrier Reef. Campsite facilities range from extremely basic (read: nothing) to fairly flash, with showers, flush toilets, interpretive signage and picnic tables. Most islands are remote, so ensure you're adequately prepared for medical and general emergencies.

Wherever you stay, you'll need to be self-sufficient, bringing your own food and drinking water (5L per day per person is recommended). Weather can often prevent

---

REEF RESOURCES

Dive Queensland www.dive-queensland.com.au

Tourism Queensland www.queenslandholidays.com.au

Great Barrier Reef Marine Park Authority www.gbrmpa.gov.au

Department of National Parks, Sport & Racing www.nprsr.qld.gov.au

Australian Bureau of Meteorology www.bom.gov.au

PLAN YOUR TRIP YOUR REEF TRIP

---

planned pick-ups, so have enough supplies to last an extra three or four days in case you get stranded.

Camp only in designated areas, keep to marked trails and take out all that you brought in. Fires are banned, so you'll need a gas stove. National park camping permits need to be booked in advance online through the Queensland government's **Department of National Parks, Sport & Racing** (📞13 74 68; www.nprsr.qld.gov.au). Here are our top camping picks:

Whitsunday Islands Nearly a dozen beautifully sited camping areas, scattered on Hook, Whitsunday, South Molle and Lindeman islands.

Capricornia Cays Camping available on three separate coral cays – Masthead Island, North West Island and Lady Musgrave Island.

Dunk Island Easy to get to, with good swimming, kayaking and hiking.

Fitzroy Island Resort and national park with short walking trails through bush, and coral just off the beaches.

Frankland Islands Coral-fringed islands with white-sand beaches off Cairns.

Lizard Island Eye-popping beaches, magnificent coral and abundant wildlife; visitors mostly arrive by plane.

Orpheus Island Secluded island (accessible by air) with pretty tropical forest and superb fringing reef.

Great Barrier Reef (p412)

Plan Your Trip
East Coast Australia Outdoors

With ancient rainforests, magnificent islands and craggy ranges as the venues, plus the amazing Great Barrier Reef, the east coast is tailor-made for outdoor action. Scuba diving and snorkelling are daily indulgences, while the surfing here is world-class. There's also sailing and kayaking, and loads of other watery pursuits. Back on dry land, head off on a hike, go mountain biking or try rock climbing. For an adrenaline rush, try abseiling, bungee jumping or skydiving.

BERNARD RADVANER / GETTY IMAGES ©

Best For...

Wildlife Watching

➡ Penguins on Phillip and Montague Island

➡ Whales off Eden and Hervey Bay

➡ Koalas at Cape Otway and Magnetic Island

➡ Cassowaries in the Daintree Rainforest and Mission Beach

➡ Crocodiles in the Daintree River

Aquatic Activities

➡ Diving and snorkelling on the Great Barrier Reef.

➡ Surfing at Bondi, Byron Bay and Noosa.

➡ Sailing the Whitsundays.

➡ Kayaking at North Stradbroke Island, Noosa Everglades and Airlie Beach.

Daredevils

➡ Canyoning in the Blue Mountains.

➡ Skydiving over Mission Beach.

➡ Bungee jumping in Cairns.

➡ White-water rafting on the Tully River.

Bushwalking

➡ Blue Mountains

➡ Dorrigo National Park

➡ Wilsons Promontory National Park

➡ Croajingolong National Park

➡ Wooroonooran National Park

➡ Springbrook National Park

On Land

Hiking

The east coast is laced with brilliant bushwalks (hikes) of every length, standard and difficulty. Coastal and hinterland national parks and state forests, many easily accessible from the cities, provide some of the best opportunities.

New South Wales

Prime hiking terrain includes the Blue Mountains, Ku-ring-gai Chase National Park and Royal National Park. If you'd rather mix a surf and a soy latte in with your hike, the brilliant semi-urban Bondi to Coogee Coastal Walk and Manly Scenic Walkway are within Sydney itself.

Victoria

For coastal treks, head down to Wilsons Promontory National Park in Gippsland, with marked trails from Tidal River and Telegraph Saddle that can take anywhere from a few hours to a couple of days. Expect squeaky white sands and clean aquamarine waters, untouched bushland and beautiful coastal vistas. The Great Ocean Road coast also offers sublime bushwalking.

Queensland

Prime spots in Queensland include Hinchinbrook Island, Springbrook National Park and D'Aguilar Range National Park. For peak baggers, Wooroonooran National Park, south of Cairns, contains Queensland's highest peak, the eccentrically named Mt Bartle Frere (1622m). Mt Sorrow, in the far north at Cape Tribulation, is a fine rainforest walk.

Resources

Bushwalking clubs and information:

Brisbane Bushwalkers www.brisbanebush walkers.org.au

Bushwalking NSW www.bushwalkingnsw.org.au

Bushwalking Queensland www.bushwalking queensland.org.au

Bushwalking Victoria www.bushwalking victoria.org.au

Cairns Bushwalkers Club www.cairnsbush walkers.org.au

Tablelands Bushwalking Club www.tablelands bushwalking.org

Cycling & Mountain Biking

Cyclists along the east coast have access to plenty of routes and can go touring for days or weekends, or even tackle multiweek trips. The landscape is, for the most part, not seriously mountainous, and the sun is often shining. Or you can just rent a bike for a few hours and wheel around a city.

Rates charged by rental outfits for road or mountain bikes range from $15 to $20 per hour and $30 to $50 per day. Security deposits range from $50 to $200, depending on the rental period. See www.bicycles. net.au for links to state and territory cycling organisations.

PLAN YOUR TRIP EAST COAST AUSTRALIA OUTDOORS

GREAT WALKS OF QUEENSLAND
....
The Great Walks of Queensland is a $16.5-million project that has created a world-class set of 10 walking tracks. For complete track descriptions, maps and camp-site bookings, visit www.nprsr.qld.gov.au/experiences/great-walks.

Wildlife Watching

Native wildlife animates the Australian bush and tracking down iconic species can be the highlight of any trip. National parks along the east coast are the best places to meet the residents, although many species are nocturnal (bring a torch). Australia is also a birdwatching nirvana, with a wide variety of habitats and more than 700 species. For more about birds visit https://birdlife.org.au.

Where to See...

Kangaroos Canberra (p180); Anglesea (p254); Wilsons Promontory National Park (p278); Cape Hillsborough National Park (p417)

Koalas Kennett River (p259); Cape Otway (p261); Raymond Island (p282); Noosa National Park (p348); Magnetic Island (p439)

Wombats Kangaroo Valley (p189); Ben Boyd National Park (p205)

Platypuses Carnarvon National Park (p404); Eungella National Park (p416); Paluma Range National Park (p441); Yungaburra (p477)

Wallabies Wilsons Promontory National Park (p278); Point Nepean National Park (p273); Cape Hillsborough National Park (p417); Long Island (p426); Magnetic Island (p439); Tyto Wetlands, Ingham (p444)

Whales Port Macquarie (p147); Hat Head National Park (p151); Muttonbird Island (p157); Jervis Bay (p191); Eden (p204); Warrnambool (p264); Great Sandy National Park (p365)

Echidnas Point Nepean National Park (p273); Raymond Island (p282); Magnetic Island (p439)

Dingoes Fraser Island (p377)

Crocodiles Daintree (p488); Innisfail (p452)

Tree Kangaroos Mt Hypipamee (p479); Daintree (p486)

Wilsons Promontory National Park (p278)

On the Water

Going to an east coast beach isn't just about sun, sand and wading ankle deep in the water – there are plenty of more active pursuits for those eager for thrills. You can try jet skiing in Cairns, Southport on the Gold Coast, Caloundra, Airlie Beach and in Batemans Bay; and parasailing on Sydney Harbour, Victoria's Mornington Peninsula, and in Queensland at Cairns, Rainbow Beach and the Gold Coast beaches. Try stand-up paddleboarding in NSW at Manly and Cronulla in Sydney, Jervis Bay and Newcastle; in Queensland at Noosa and on the Gold Coast; and in Victoria on the Mornington Peninsula and at Melbourne's St Kilda.

Surfing

The southern half of the east coast is jam-packed with sandy surf beaches and point breaks. North of Agnes Water in Queensland, the Great Barrier Reef shields the coast from the ocean swells. If you're keen to learn, you'll find plenty of good waves, board hire and lessons

Humpback whale off Phillip Island (p273)

available – notably in Sydney and Byron Bay in NSW, the Gold Coast and Noosa in Queensland and along the Great Ocean Road in Victoria. Two-hour lessons cost around $60.

In Queensland and much of NSW you can get away with wearing board shorts and a 'rashie', but Victoria's chilly water will have even the hardiest of surfers reaching for their wetsuit. A full-length, up-to-7mm-thick wetsuit is the norm.

The Best Breaks

There are endless surf breaks from which to choose. Our picks:

New South Wales
➡ Bondi Beach
➡ Byron Bay
➡ Crescent Head

Queensland
➡ The Superbank
➡ Burleigh Heads
➡ North Stradbroke Island

Victoria
➡ Torquay (Bells Beach, Jan Juc and Winki Pop) and numerous spots along the Great Ocean Road
➡ Point Leo, Flinders, Rye and Portsea back beaches
➡ Phillip Island (Woolamai Beach)

WILDLIFE FIELD GUIDES

➡ *The Complete Guide to Finding the Mammals of Australia* (David Andrew; 2015)

➡ *A Field Guide to the Mammals of Australia* (Peter Menkhorst & Frank Knight; 3rd ed, 2011)

➡ *The Complete Guide to Finding the Birds of Australia* (Richard Thomas et al; 2nd ed, 2011)

➡ *The Australian Bird Guide* (Peter Menkhorst et al; 2017)

➡ App: The Michael Morcombe eGuide to Australian Birds

Left: Yarra River, Melbourne (p207)

Diving & Snorkelling

Even if the Great Barrier Reef wasn't just off the east coast, the diving and snorkelling here would still be world-class. Coral reefs, rich marine life (temperate, subtropical and tropical species) and hundreds of shipwrecks paint an enticing underwater picture.

Diving is generally possible year-round, although in Queensland avoid the wet season (December to March), when floods can impair visibility and stingers (jellyfish) are present (November to May, north of Agnes Water).

Diving Courses

Every major town along the east coast has a dive school, but standards vary – do some research before signing up. Budget outfits tend to focus on shore dives; pricier outfits sometimes run multiday liveaboard boat tours. Multiday Professional Association of Diving Instructors (PADI) Open-Water courses cost anywhere from $550 to $825; one-off introductory dives start at $120.

For certified divers, renting gear and going on a two-tank day dive generally costs between $180 and $250. You can also hire a mask, snorkel and fins from a dive shop for around $30 to $50.

Where to Dive

With the Great Barrier Reef a day trip offshore, Queensland is paradise for divers: most diving and snorkelling trips set sail from Cairns and Port Douglas. You can also organise dive trips at North Stradbroke Island, Moreton Island, Mooloolaba, Rainbow Beach and Bundaberg. In NSW you can dive all along the coast, including Sydney, Byron Bay, Jervis Bay, Coffs Harbour and Narooma. In Victoria try Port Campbell on the Great Ocean Road and Bunurong Marine Park in Gippsland.

Kayaking & Canoeing

Kayaks and canoes let you paddle into otherwise inaccessible areas, poking your nose into mangroves and estuaries, river gorges, island beaches and remote wilderness inlets. In NSW you can kayak on Sydney Harbour and at Byron Bay, Coffs Harbour, Port Stephens and Jervis Bay.

In Queensland head for Mission Beach, Magnetic Island, Noosa and the Whitsundays. In Victoria you can kayak around Melbourne itself (on the Yarra River), plus there are operators running trips around Apollo Bay, Phillip Island, Wilsons Promontory and Gippsland. Two-hour paddles cost around $70.

White-Water Rafting

In Queensland, the mighty Tully, North Johnstone and Russell Rivers between Townsville and Cairns are renowned white-water-rafting locations. The Tully (p447) is the most popular of the three, with 44 rapids graded III to IV.

Sailing

Sailing is the second-most-popular ocean activity (after surfing) on Australia's east coast. It has its own affluent marina culture and its own migratory patterns: during the winter, the yachties sail north, following the warmer weather.

Where to Sail

In NSW, Sydney Harbour and boats are inextricably and historically intertwined – this is one of the world's great nautical cities. The easiest way to get out there is on a ferry: hop a ride to Manly or Balmain and see the sea. There are also harbour cruises and yacht charters available. Beyond Sydney, Port Stephens, Jervis Bay and Ballina are busy sailing centres. Yachties shouldn't miss the annual spectacle that is the Sydney to Hobart Yacht Race on 26 December.

In Queensland, the postcard-perfect Whitsunday Islands are magical for a sail. You can join a full- or multiday cruise, or charter your own craft in Airlie Beach. You can also explore the Great Barrier Reef and some of the islands off the Far North Queensland coast on board a chartered boat or cruise from Cairns or Port Douglas. Joining a yacht crew is also possible in Port Douglas.

In Victoria, city-based yachties gravitate to the sailing clubs around Port Phillip Bay. Other popular boating areas include the sprawling Gippsland Lakes and Mallacoota Inlet near the NSW border.

Plan Your Trip
Family Travel

Travelling Australia's east coast as a family can create so many highlights of a lifetime. Yes, distances are long, but there's much to see and do, from family-friendly beaches, boat excursions, theme parks and national parks to museums and wildlife parks where you can get a stellar view of the native fauna..

Keeping Costs Down

Accommodation
Many motels, hotels and the better-equipped holiday parks have playgrounds, swimming pools and children-focused activities to keep kids entertained without spending extra.

Car safety seats
Ideally bring your own child safety seats rather than pay hire fees. You can pick up a secondhand one in Australia from reselling websites like eBay, but there are safety concerns (age or damage) to consider. Do your research.

Concessions
Child concessions (and family rates) often apply to accommodation, tours, admission fees and transport, with some discounts as high as 50% off the adult rate. However, the definition of 'child' varies from under five years, 12 years or 18 years so always check. Museums and art galleries are often free.

Eating out
Most cafes, pubs and restaurants offer children's menus, or will provide a child-sized (entrée) portion for a smaller price on request. The best news for travelling families is the free or coin-operated barbecues in many public parks. Often outdoors dining is the best way forward with little ones.

Children Will Love...
Zoos & Wildlife Parks

Taronga Zoo (p70), **Sydney** World-famous zoo with respected programmes focusing on native animals.

Melbourne Zoo (p215), **Melbourne** Outstanding city zoo with a good mix of local and international wildlife.

Australia Zoo (p355), **Beerwah** Zoo made famous by Steve Irwin, with plenty of chances to get close to wildlife.

Hartley's Crocodile Adventures (p474), **Ellis Beach** Crocodiles in all their glory between Cairns and Port Douglas.

Wildlife Habitat (p481), **Port Douglas** Wildlife from Far North Queensland in its natural habitats.

Free-Range Wildlife Watching

Phillip Island (p274) Watch the penguins arrive at sunset in one of nature's great spectacles.

Eden (p204) Watch for whales from July to November in Australia's whale-watching capital.

Magnetic Island (p439) Koalas and wallabies, not to mention birds, in a stunning island setting.

Fraser Island (p377) The best place in Australia to see dingoes.

Daintree (p486) Cruise the river looking for crocs then look for cassowaries and tree kangaroos.

Theme Parks

Dreamworld (p344), **Gold Coast** The biggest amusement park in Australia, with incredible rides.

Warner Bros Movie World (p344), **Gold Coast** Hollywood transplanted onto Aussie soil with rides and movie-themed attractions.

Wet'n'Wild (p344), **Gold Coast** Part of the Gold Coast's big three, including epic water slides.

Luna Park (p71), **Sydney** World-famous amusement park with big rides, and big views for parents while they wait.

Luna Park (p219), **Melbourne** The city's premier amusement park with a nostalgic look at theme parks of old.

Beaches & Snorkelling

Bondi Beach (p69), **Sydney** Your kids haven't been to Sydney if they haven't swum at Bondi.

Wilsons Promontory (p278) Some of Victoria's best beaches, with wildlife never far away.

Fraser Island (p377) Endless beaches for the perfect family holiday.

Main Beach (p168), **Byron Bay** Byron in all its glory with the family-friendly town alongside.

Port Douglas (p479) Four Mile Beach and world-class (and family-friendly) snorkelling on the reef.

Region by Region

Melbourne & Coastal Victoria

Melbourne is a family-friendly city with excellent beaches, interactive museums and fantastic food. Beyond the city, the Great Ocean Road, Phillip Island and Wilsons Prom are all stellar wildlife-watching destinations.

Canberra & South Coast New South Wales

Canberra's museums are among the best in the country and most have interactive exhibits. South coast NSW has some of Australia's best beaches and towns well set up for the summer influx of families.

Sydney & Around

In Sydney and the surrounding coast you'll find dozens of brilliant beaches, while downtown Sydney has a fine zoo (p70), famous theme park (p71) and fun ferries to zip between everything.

Byron Bay & North Coast New South Wales

Generations of Aussie families have spent time by this stretch of sea and with good reason – mile after mile of fabulous beaches with friendly towns as a backdrop.

The Gold Coast

Theme parks, endless sands and a tourist industry experienced in catering for families – the Gold Coast may be tacky, but the kids won't care at all.

Brisbane & Around

Brisbane's transformation into one cool city includes museums kids will love, all manner of activities and a sport obsession that will appeal to many children.

Noosa & the Sunshine Coast

Noosa is a seaside resort that's as good for families as for the high-rollers. A national park (p348) on the doorstep, fine beaches and one of eastern Australia's best zoos (p51) should be enough to fill a summer.

Fraser Island & the Fraser Coast

Sand dunes and sandy beaches, dingoes and days spent exploring this most unusual rainforest – few regions of Australia can provide so many attractions in one small space quite like Fraser Island.

Capricorn Coast & the Southern Reef Islands

Beaches and snorkelling off reef islands are the main drawcards here, but wild national parks, numerous opportunities to get active, fun towns and plenty of wildlife all help make this a major draw for families.

Whitsunday Coast

The beaches here are near perfect, and most are protected from rough seas by the reef. Go sailing, snorkel alongside marine life and do everything from bushwalking to kayaking.

Townsville to Mission Beach

Magnetic Island, off Townsville, is one of Australia's best places to see wildlife, while Mission Beach has plenty of activities. Up in the hills near Paluma, there are platypuses.

Cairns & the Daintree Rainforest

Take a boat trip looking for crocs (p488), learn Indigenous bush knowledge at Mossman Gorge (p487), take the train-and-cable-car excursion at Kuranda, go snorkelling on the outer reef – there's not much you can't do.

Good to Know

Look out for the 🛈 icon for family-friendly suggestions throughout this guide.

Change Rooms & Breastfeeding All cities and major towns have public rooms where parents can breastfeed or change nappies (diapers).

Car Safety Seats Safety restraints are compulsory for all children up to seven years of age. If you don't bring your own, major hire-car companies will sup-

ply and fit child safety seats, charging a one-off fee of around $25.

Restaurants Kids' menus are common, but selections are usually uninspiring. Find something on the regular menu and ask the kitchen to adapt it.

High Chairs Many places can supply high chairs, but numbers may be limited.

Health Care Australia has high-standard medical services and facilities. Travel with insurance.

Useful Resources

Lonely Planet Kids (lonelyplanetkids.com) Loads of activities and great family travel blog content.

Book: Travel with Children (shop.lonelyplanet.com) Lonely Planet's print guide to travelling with your kids contains plenty of useful information.

Book: City Trails Sydney (shop.lonelyplanet.com) Sydney's best-kept secrets, amazing stories and loads of other cool stuff. Ages eight to 12.

My Family Travel Map: Australia (shop.lonelyplanet.com) Unfolds into a colourful and detailed poster for kids to personalise with stickers to mark their family's travels. Ages five to eight.

Kids' Corner

Say What?

Hello.	Hi, g'day.
You're welcome.	Too easy.
Everything will be ok.	She'll be right.
Really?	Fair dinkum?

Did You Know? 🛈

- Kangaroos and emus cannot walk backwards.
- Wombat poo is cube shaped.

Have You Tried?

Lamington A small sponge, chocolate and coconut cake

ROBYNMAC / GETTY IMAGES ©

Regions at a Glance

Byron Bay & North Coast NSW

Nightlife
Surfing
Small Towns

Drinking in Byron

Byron Bay has bars and pubs for every day of the week, be it beer barns serving local craft beer, live-music pubs or classy wine bars. Just name your poison!

North-Coast Surf

The water's warm, and perfect point breaks are rolling in at legendary north-coast surf spots such as the Pass in Byron Bay and Lennox Head.

Nimbin & Bangalow

A short detour into the Byron Bay hinterland unveils some fine small towns. Wander through the smoke haze in hippie Nimbin, or have a pub lunch in upmarket (but unpretentious) Bangalow.

p138

Canberra & South Coast NSW

History & Culture
Beaches
Politics

Canberra Museum Scene

Spend some culture-filled days exploring Canberra's National Gallery, with its magnificent Indigenous art, the imaginative National Museum, the moving War Memorial and the impressive National Portrait Gallery.

South-Coast Beaches

Track into southern NSW, where you'll find impressive, wide stretches of white sand, with reliable surf and, in places, barely a footprint to be seen.

Parliament House

Attend Question Time at Australia's grass-topped Parliament House, pay a visit to Old Parliament House and check out the Museum of Australian Democracy.

p175

Sydney & Around

Beaches
Food
Wilderness

Perfect Surf

Sydney's surf beaches are outstanding. Bondi is the name on everyone's lips, but the waves here get crowded. Head south to Maroubra or Cronulla, or to the Northern Beaches for a bit more elbow room.

Modern Australian

The term 'Modern Australian' is starting to sound a little dated, but this pan-Pacific fusion of styles and ingredients is still the name of Sydney's culinary game. Serve it up with a harbour view and you've got a winning combo.

National Parks

This region has some of the best national parks in Australia. Around Sydney there's Royal National Park, with fab walks and beaches; waterways and wildlife in Ku-ring-gai Chase National Park; and vast tracts of native forest in Wollemi National Park in the Blue Mountains.

p58

Melbourne & Coastal Victoria

Food
Bushwalking
Beaches

Eating in Melbourne

Melbourne is a foodie's paradise with produce markets, eat streets, arty cafes and sassy restaurants, all infused with the ebullient multiculturalism that defines this city.

Hiking Wilsons Prom

Wilsons Promontory National Park – mainland Australia's southernmost point – offers everything from short jaunts along the beach to multiday circuits covering most of the peninsula.

Great Ocean Road

This stretch of coast hosts some of Australia's prettiest beaches, from the big breaks at Bells Beach to Lorne's gentle bay and the dramatic rock formations near Port Campbell.

p207

Brisbane & Around

Cafes
Neighbourhoods
Nightlife

Coffee Culture

Brisbane is hot and humid, but that doesn't mean the locals can't enjoy a steaming cup of coffee. Cool cafes abound, well supplied by a clutch of quality local bean roasters.

Inner-City Hip

Brisbane is a tight-knit web of distinct neighbourhoods. Check out the bohemian West End and postindustrial Newstead and Teneriffe, with their ever-growing number of on-point cafes, brew-bars and music rooms.

Small-Bar Scene

It's taken a while, but Brisbane has joined in on the Australia-wide boom in small speakeasies, down laneways and behind compact shopfronts across town.

p288

The Gold Coast

Surfing
Nightlife
National Parks

Surfers Paradise

They don't call it Surfers Paradise for nothing! The beach here is one of the best places in Australia to learn to surf, or head for the more challenging breaks around Burleigh Heads and Kirra.

Clubs, Pubs & Bars

All along the Gold Coast, from Surfers Paradise's throbbing clubs to the pubs and surf-lifesaving clubs in Coolangatta, you'll never be far from a cold après-surf beer (or tequila).

Hinterland Greenery

Ascend into the Gold Coast hinterland to discover some brilliant national parks: Springbrook, Lamington and Tamborine feature waterfalls, hikes and native birdsong.

p329

Noosa & the Sunshine Coast

Surfing
Food
Nature

Sunshine Coast Surf

The relaxed surfer ethos of the Sunshine CoasNoosat permeates the backstreets and the beaches, with surf shops aplenty and reliable breaks and warm waves right along the coast.

Noosa Dining Scene

You know you're *really* on holiday when you wake up and the choice of where to have breakfast, lunch and dinner is the most important item on the day's agenda. Welcome to Noosa!

Noosa National Park

Bathed by the South Pacific, with photogenic beaches reaching up to hillsides awash with subtropical bush, accessible Noosa National Park is perfect for bushwalking, swimming or just chilling out.

p346

Fraser Island & the Fraser Coast

Islands
Marine Life
Small Towns

Fraser Island

Sandy Fraser Island hosts a unique subtropical ecosystem that's pretty darn close to paradise. A day tour merely whets the appetite; camp overnight and wish upon countless shooting stars.

Whale Watching

Off Hervey Bay, migrating humpback whales breach, blow and tail slap. Controversy shrouds the whale-watching business worldwide, but eco-accredited tours give these amazing creatures the space they need.

Rainbow Beach & Childers

One on the coast and one inland, these two little towns are absolute beauties: Rainbow Beach for its magnificent cliffs, and Childers for its country vibe and historic architecture.

p370

Capricorn Coast & the Southern Reef Islands

Diving & Snorkelling
Islands
Accessible Outback

Southern Reef Encounters

From the Town of 1770, book a snorkelling cruise out to the reef or a bunk on a liveaboard dive vessel. Or base yourself on an island in this technicolour underwater world.

Lady Elliot Island

Tiny, coral-ringed Lady Elliot is superb for snorkelling, with reefs directly off the beach. The resort is eco-attuned, and the flight here is a scenic tour in itself.

Rockhampton

Australia's 'beef capital', 40km from the coast, gives visitors a true taste of the bush, with bucking broncos and big hats. Further west, cattle-station stays offer full immersion into outback living.

p391

Whitsunday Coast

Islands
Sailing
Nightlife

The Whitsundays

With 74 tropical beauties to choose from, the Whitsunday Islands archipelago is truly remarkable. There are numerous ways to experience the islands: bushwalking, kayaking or just lounging around on a yacht.

Island Hopping

The translucent seas around the Whitsundays would seem incomplete without billowing sails in the picture. Climb aboard a yacht and find your perfect island.

Airlie Beach

The main jumping-off point for trips around the Whitsundays, Airlie Beach is a party town full of party people. Join those up for a good time in the bars after dark.

p408

Townsville to Mission Beach

Coastline
Nature
Architecture

Beaut Beaches

Between Townsville's palm-shaded Strand and Flying Fish Point near Innisfail is a stretch of coastline that shelters sandy expanses such as the namesake shore at Mission Beach, through to intimate coves like Etty Bay.

National Parks

Hiking, camping, swimming and picnicking abound in the region's national parks, with prehistoric-looking cassowaries roaming the rainforest. Top picks include bushwalking paradise Hinchinbrook Island and Paluma Range National Park.

Historic Buildings

See the gold-rush-era streetscapes of Charters Towers, 19th-century buildings in Townsville and art-deco edifices in Innisfail.

p431

Great Barrier Reef

Marine Life
Diving & Snorkelling
Islands

Coral & Fish

Believe the hype: the World Heritage–listed Great Barrier Reef is home to a mind-blowing spectrum of colourful coral and fish of all shapes, sizes and hues.

Reef Day Trips

Don't delay – book yourself onto a diving or snorkelling trip to explore the reef. Cairns and Port Douglas offer multiple operators that can take you there for the day (or longer).

Castaway Cays

Play castaway for a day: studded along the 2000km spine of the reef are myriad sandy cays, islands and atolls, most with no one else on them.

p412

Cairns & the Daintree Rainforest

Nightlife
Food
Indigenous Culture

Cairns After Dark

There are so many tourists in Cairns, it's sometimes hard to spot a local. You can usually find one or two in the city's boisterous pubs and bars.

Regional Produce

Many of the Atherton Tableland's farms, orchards and plantations can be visited on tours. Or simply taste the good stuff at regional restaurants.

Daintree

Several Aboriginal-led tour companies take you on a cultural journey through the timeless Daintree Rainforest, offering insights into its rich Indigenous heritage. Deserted beaches and wildlife encounters add further depth to the experience.

p453

On the Road

Sydney & Around

Best Places to Eat

➡ Quay (p91)

➡ Ester (p99)

➡ Subo (p135)

➡ Mr Wong (p93)

➡ EXP. (p130)

➡ Dead Ringer (p96)

Best Places to Sleep

➡ ADGE Boutique Apartment Hotel (p89)

➡ Sydney Harbour YHA (p84)

➡ Ovolo 1888 (p85)

➡ Tonic (p127)

➡ Carrington Hotel (p119)

➡ Cockatoo Island (p89)

Why Go?

Chances are Sydney will be your introduction to Australia's east coast and there simply isn't a better place to start. The city's spectacular harbour setting, sun-kissed beaches and sophisticated sheen make it unique in Australia, and its out-doorsy population endows it with a confident charm that every city yearns for but few achieve.

It would be reasonable to assume that the areas surrounding Sydney would be content to bask in the reflected and undeniably golden glow of the metropolis, but that's not the case. Each has its own delights. The Blue Mountains offer magnificent bush-clad vistas and opportunities to snuggle in front of log fires; Newcastle has surf beaches in profusion; the Royal National Park offers spectacular coastal walking and top beaches; and the Hunter Valley has leafy country roads scattered with producers of fine wine, chocolate and cheese. The broader region is home to world-class restaurants that rival even those in the big smoke.

When to Go

Sydney

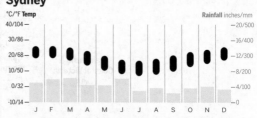

Jan The year kicks off with a spectacular fireworks display over Sydney Harbour.

Feb–Mar Sydney's summer party season culminates with the Gay & Lesbian Mardi Gras.

Jul Enjoy wood fires, wine and winter menus in the Blue Mountains and Hunter Valley.

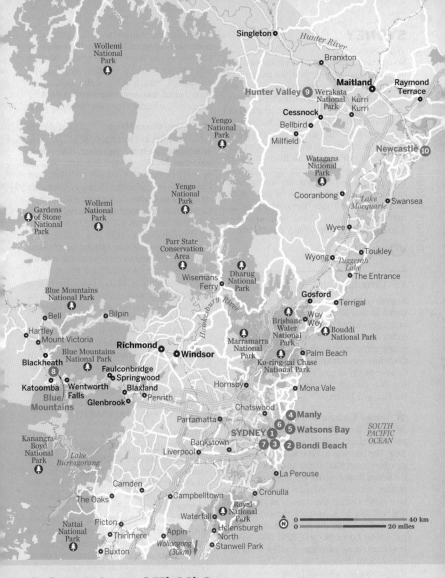

Sydney & Around Highlights

1 Sydney Opera House
(p60) Coming face to face with the symbol of the city.

2 Bondi Beach (p69)
Relaxing on the golden sands.

3 Surry Hills (p96) Eating in the gastronomic heartland.

4 Manly Scenic Walkway
(p79) Hopping between headlands and beaches.

5 Watsons Bay (p70)
Exploring South Head and claiming a spot for sunset.

6 Taronga Zoo (p70)
Meeting Australia's weird and wonderful native fauna.

7 White Rabbit (p71)
Challenging your stereotypes at Sydney's best art gallery.

8 Blue Mountains (p115)
Exploring the eucalyptus-scented valleys on a bushwalk.

9 Hunter Valley (p124)
Indulging yourself with boutique hotels, fine food and excellent wines.

10 Newcastle (p131) Enjoying a post-surf breakfast at one of the city's cafes.

SYDNEY

📍 02 / POP 5.2 MILLION

No one can deny that Sydney is blessed with incredible good looks, from its magnificent harbour to its stunning coastline, and this big show-off of a city flaunts them at every turn. You'll find Sydneysiders stretched out on gleaming beaches, sipping harbourside cocktails and taking to the water by yacht, kayak or ferry on any day of the week. And come sundown they're still living it up, enjoying a boundary-pushing arts scene, sizzling nightlife and top-notch international cuisine. Sydney's also home to three of the country's major icons – the Harbour Bridge, the Opera House and Bondi Beach – making it an unmissable stop on any coastal trip.

◉ Sights

◉ Circular Quay & the Rocks

Several of Sydney's key sights are concentrated in this area. Museums and venerable buildings dotted about the Rocks give insights into Australia's colonial history, while major attractions such as the Museum of Contemporary Art and Royal Botanic Garden deserve plenty of your time. The indisputable Big Two, though, are the Opera House and the Harbour Bridge.

★ **Sydney Harbour Bridge**   BRIDGE

(🚇 Circular Quay, Milsons Point) Sydneysiders love their giant 'coathanger', which opened in 1932. The best way to experience this majestic structure is on foot. Stairs and lifts climb up the bridge from both shores, leading to a footpath on the eastern side (the western side is a bike path). Getting the train to Milsons Point and walking back towards the city is most spectacular. Climb the southeastern pylon to the **Pylon Lookout** (📞 02-9240 1100; www.pylonlookout.com.au; adult/teen/child $19/12.50/9.50; ⊙ 10am-5pm) or ascend the arc on the popular if expensive BridgeClimb (p79).

The harbour bridge is a spookily big object – moving around town you'll catch sight of it in the corner of your eye, sometimes in the most surprising places. Its enormous dimensions (the arch is 134m high, the span measures 503m and it has 53,000 tonnes of steel) make it the biggest (if not the longest) steel arch bridge in the world.

The two halves of chief engineer JJC Bradfield's mighty arch were built outwards from each shore in what was a huge source of Depression-era employment. In 1930, after seven years of merciless toil by 1400 workers, the two arches were only centimetres apart when 100km/h winds set them swaying. The coathanger hung tough and the arch was finally bolted together. Extensive load-testing preceded the bridge's opening two years later.

★ **Sydney Opera House**   NOTABLE BUILDING

(📞 02-9250 7111, tour bookings 02-9250 7777; www.sydneyoperahouse.com; Bennelong Point; tours adult/child $42/22; ⊙ tours 9am-5pm; 🚇 Circular Quay) Designed by Danish architect Jørn Utzon, this magnificent building is Australia's most famous landmark. Visually referencing a yacht's sails, it's a soaring, commanding presence that comprises five performance spaces for dance, concerts, opera and theatre. Wander around the outside to your heart's content. The best way to experience the interior is to attend a performance, but you can also take a one-hour guided tour (available in several languages), with optional food. Ongoing renovation work, scheduled to be completed in 2022, may disrupt visits.

There's also a two-hour 'access all areas' backstage tour ($175), which departs at 7am and includes breakfast in the Green Room restaurant. Another way to experience the Opera House includes a seven-minute narration of Aboriginal stories, *Badu Gili*, that is spectacularly projected onto the sails nightly at sunset, at 9pm, 9.30pm and 10pm.

★ **Royal Botanic Garden**   GARDENS

(📞 02-9231 8111; www.rbgsyd.nsw.gov.au; Mrs Macquarie's Rd; ⊙ 7am-dusk; 🚇 Circular Quay) 🆓 Southeast of the Opera House, this garden was established in 1816 and features plant life from around the world. Within the gardens are hothouses with palms and ferns, as well as the **Calyx** (www.rbgsyd.nsw.gov.au; ⊙ 10am-4pm; 🚇 Martin Place) 🍃, a striking exhibition space featuring a curving glasshouse gallery with a wall of greenery and temporary plant-themed exhibitions. Grab a park map at any main entrance.

The gardens include the site of the colony's first paltry vegetable patch, but their history goes back much further than that: long before the convicts arrived, this was an initiation ground for the Gadigal (Cadigal) people. Free 1½-hour guided walks depart from the visitor centre (open 10am to 3pm) at 10.30am daily, plus 1pm on weekdays from March to November. Book ahead for an **Aboriginal Heritage Tour** (📞 02-9231 8134; www.rbgsyd.nsw.gov.au;

SYDNEY IN...

Two Days

Start your first day by getting a train to Milsons Point and walking back to the Rocks across the Harbour Bridge. Then explore the Rocks area, delving into all the narrow lanes. Next, follow the harbour past the Opera House to the Royal Botanic Garden and on to the Art Gallery of NSW (p65). That night, enjoy a performance at the Opera House (p107) or check out the action in Chinatown or Darlinghurst. The next day, it's time to soak up the sun and scene at Bondi – be sure to take the clifftop walk to Coogee and then make your way back to Bondi for a sunset dinner at Icebergs Dining Room (p97).

Four Days

On day three, board a ferry and sail through the harbour to Manly, where you can swim at the beach or follow the Manly Scenic Walkway (p77). That night, head to Surry Hills for drinks and dinner. On day four, learn about Sydney's convict heritage at the Hyde Park Barracks Museum (p65) and then spend the afternoon shopping in Paddington or Newtown.

One Week

With a week, you can spare a couple of days to visit the majestic Blue Mountains, fitting in a full day of bushwalking before rewarding yourself with a gourmet dinner. Back in Sydney, explore Watsons Bay (p70), Darling Harbour (p66) and Taronga Zoo (p70).

---

adult $41; ⊙10am Wed, Fri & Sat) with an Indigenous guide.

A hop-on, hop-off **tourist train** (www.choochoo.com.au; adult/child $10/5; ⊙11am-4pm May-Sep, 10am-4.30pm Oct-Apr) runs a route around the main points of interest in the garden.

★**Rocks Discovery Museum** MUSEUM (☑02-9240 8680; Kendall Lane; ⊙10am-5pm; ♿; ⊠Circular Quay) FREE Divided into four displays – Warrane (pre-1788), Colony (1788–1820), Port (1820–1900) and Transformations (1900 to the present) – this small, excellent museum, tucked away down a Rocks laneway, digs deep into the area's history on an artefact-rich tour. Sensitive attention is given to the Rocks' original inhabitants, the Gadigal (Cadigal) people, and there are interesting tales of early colonial characters. The 3rd floor holds temporary exhibitions.

Sydney Observatory OBSERVATORY (☑02-9217 0111; www.maas.museum/sydney-observatory; 1003 Upper Fort St; ⊙10am-5pm; ⊠Circular Quay) FREE Built in the 1850s, Sydney's copper-domed, Italianate sandstone observatory squats atop **Observatory Hill** (Upper Fort St), overlooking the harbour. Inside is an intriguing collection of vintage apparatus as well as background on Australian astronomy and transits of Venus. Fun family-focused tours (adult/child $26/22), including telescope viewing and a planetarium show, are on offer at twilight daily and during the day

at weekends and on school holidays. More serious stargazing is available during daily night-time sessions (adult/child $40/34). Book tours a week ahead at busy times.

Walsh Bay WATERFRONT (www.walshbaysydney.com.au; Hickson Rd; ⊠324, 325, ⊠Wynyard) This section of Dawes Point waterfront was Sydney's busiest before the advent of container shipping and the construction of port facilities at Botany Bay. This century has seen the Federation-era wharves morphing into luxury hotels, apartments, a renovated arts precinct, power-boat marinas, and restaurants. It's a picturesque place to stroll, combining the wharves and harbour views with the Barangaroo Reserve waterfront park.

Museum of Contemporary Art GALLERY (MCA; ☑02-9245 2400; www.mca.com.au; 140 George St; ⊙10am-5pm Thu-Tue, to 9pm Wed; ⊠Circular Quay) FREE The MCA is a showcase for Australian and international contemporary art, with a rotating permanent collection and temporary exhibitions. Indigenous art features prominently. The original art deco building has had a modern space grafted onto it, the highlight of which is the rooftop cafe with stunning views. There are free guided tours daily, in several languages.

Susannah Place Museum MUSEUM (☑bookings 02-8239 2211; www.sydneylivingmuseums.com.au; 58-64 Gloucester St; adult/child

Sydney Harbour

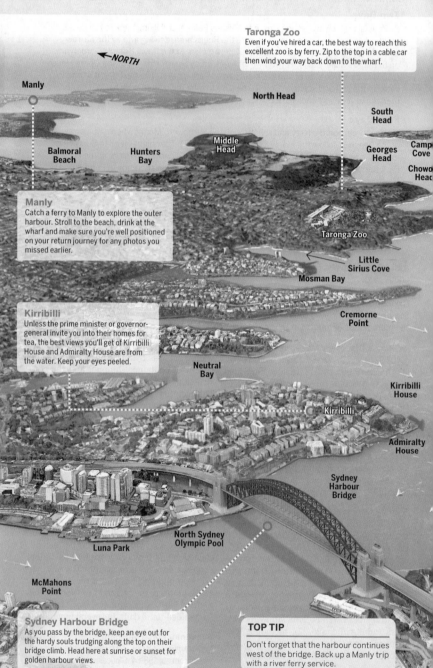

←NORTH

Taronga Zoo
Even if you've hired a car, the best way to reach this excellent zoo is by ferry. Zip to the top in a cable car then wind your way back down to the wharf.

Manly

North Head

South Head

Balmoral Beach

Hunters Bay

Middle Head

Georges Head

Camp Cove

Chowo Head

Manly
Catch a ferry to Manly to explore the outer harbour. Stroll to the beach, drink at the wharf and make sure you're well positioned on your return journey for any photos you missed earlier.

Taronga Zoo

Little Sirius Cove

Mosman Bay

Kirribilli
Unless the prime minister or governor-general invite you into their homes for tea, the best views you'll get of Kirribilli House and Admiralty House are from the water. Keep your eyes peeled.

Cremorne Point

Neutral Bay

Kirribilli House

Kirribilli

Admiralty House

Sydney Harbour Bridge

North Sydney Olympic Pool

Luna Park

McMahons Point

Sydney Harbour Bridge
As you pass by the bridge, keep an eye out for the hardy souls trudging along the top on their bridge climb. Head here at sunrise or sunset for golden harbour views.

TOP TIP

Don't forget that the harbour continues west of the bridge. Back up a Manly trip with a river ferry service.

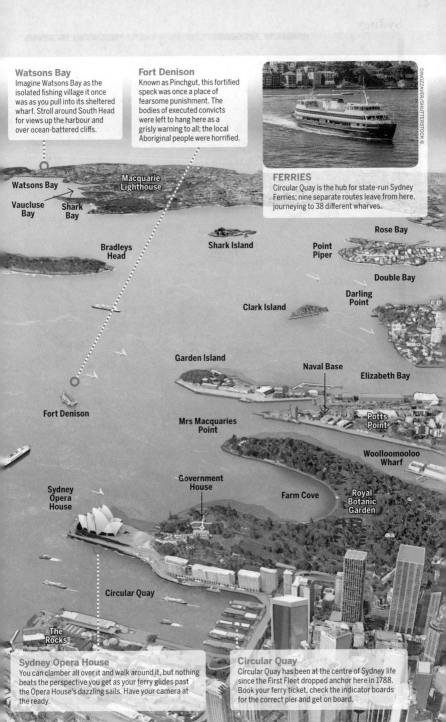

Watsons Bay
Imagine Watsons Bay as the isolated fishing village it once was as you pull into its sheltered wharf. Stroll around South Head for views up the harbour and over ocean-battered cliffs.

Fort Denison
Known as Pinchgut, this fortified speck was once a place of fearsome punishment. The bodies of executed convicts were left to hang here as a grisly warning to all; the local Aboriginal people were horrified.

DINOZZAVER/SHUTTERSTOCK ©

FERRIES
Circular Quay is the hub for state-run Sydney Ferries; nine separate routes leave from here, journeying to 38 different wharves.

Watsons Bay

Macquarie Lighthouse

Vaucluse Bay

Shark Bay

Bradleys Head

Shark Island

Rose Bay

Point Piper

Double Bay

Darling Point

Clark Island

Garden Island

Naval Base

Elizabeth Bay

Mrs Macquaries Point

Potts Point

Fort Denison

Woolloomooloo Wharf

Government House

Sydney Opera House

Farm Cove

Royal Botanic Garden

Circular Quay

The Rocks

Sydney Opera House
You can clamber all over it and walk around it, but nothing beats the perspective you get as your ferry glides past the Opera House's dazzling sails. Have your camera at the ready.

Circular Quay
Circular Quay has been at the centre of Sydney life since the First Fleet dropped anchor here in 1788. Book your ferry ticket, check the indicator boards for the correct pier and get on board.

Sydney

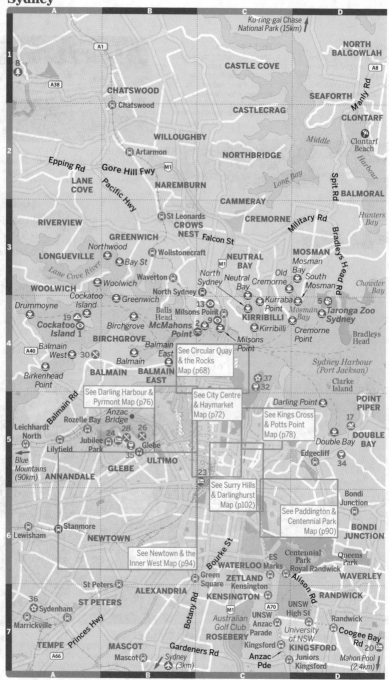

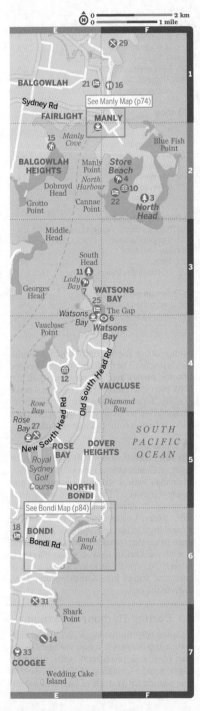

$15/12; ⊙ tours 2pm, 3pm & 4pm; ℝ Circular Quay) Dating from 1844, this diminutive terrace of four houses and a shop is a fascinating time capsule of life in the Rocks. A personable guide takes you through the claustrophobic homes, decorated to reflect different eras and brought to life by the real stories of the people that inhabited them. The visit lasts an hour. Groups are limited to eight, so book ahead online or by phone.

⊙ City Centre & Haymarket

★ Art Gallery of NSW   GALLERY
(☏ 1800 679 278; www.artgallery.nsw.gov.au; Art Gallery Rd; ⊙ 10am-5pm Thu-Tue, to 10pm Wed; 🚌 441, ℝ St James) **FREE** With its neoclassical Greek frontage and modern rear, this much-loved institution plays a prominent and gregarious role in Sydney society. Blockbuster international touring exhibitions arrive regularly and there's an outstanding permanent collection of Australian art, including a substantial Indigenous section. The gallery also plays host to lectures, concerts, screenings, celebrity talks and children's activities. A range of free guided tours is offered on different themes and in various languages. Construction of a second building, Sydney Modern, is due to be completed in 2022.

★ Hyde Park Barracks Museum   MUSEUM
(☏ 02-8239 2311; www.sydneylivingmuseums.com. au; Queens Sq, Macquarie St; adult/child $24/16; ⊙ 10am-5pm; ℝ St James) This noble brick building was designed by the convict architect Francis Greenway to house prisoners arriving in the colony. Now a flagship museum, the barracks house an entertaining modern display. Beautifully constructed dioramas tell the story of expanding colonial settlement and its devastating impact on the lives and culture of Indigenous Australians. All information is given via an automatic audioguide, which can be clunky but gives charismatic narration from the point of view of participants in the building's history.

Museum of Sydney   MUSEUM
(MoS; ☏ 02-9251 5988; www.sydneylivingmuse ums.com.au; cnr Phillip & Bridge Sts; adult/child $15/12; ⊙ 10am-5pm; ℝ Circular Quay) Built on the site of Sydney's first Government House, the MoS is a fragmented storytelling museum, which uses installations to explore the city's history. The area's long Indigenous past is highlighted throughout, plus there's interesting coverage of the early days of contact

Sydney

between the Gadigal (Cadigal) people and the colonists. Key figures in Sydney's planning and architecture are brought to life, while there's a good section on the First Fleet itself, with scale models.

Sydney Tower Eye   TOWER
(www.sydneytowereye.com.au; Level 5, Westfield Sydney, 188 Pitt St; adult/child $29/20; ⊙9am-9pm, last entry 8pm; ⬜St James) The 309m-tall Sydney Tower (still known as Centrepoint by many Sydneysiders) offers unbeatable 360-degree views from the observation level 250m up. The visit starts with the 4D Experience, a short film giving you a bird's-eye view of city, surf, harbour and what lies beneath the water, accompanied by mist sprays and bubbles. Then it's up the lift to the viewing area. The guided **Skywalk** (adult/child $80/50) takes you outside to circumnavigate the tower along a ledge.

Anzac Memorial   MEMORIAL
(☑02-8262 2900; www.anzacmemorial.nsw.gov.au; Hyde Park; ⊙9am-5pm; ⬜Museum) **FREE** This dignified memorial commemorates WWI soldiers of the Australia and New Zealand Army Corps (Anzac). The interior dome is studded with 120,000 stars: one for each New South Wales (NSW) soldier who served. These

twinkle above Rayner Hoff's poignant sculpture *Sacrifice*. The downstairs Hall of Service features names and soil samples of all the NSW places of origin of WWI soldiers. There's a daily 11am remembrance service here; alongside is a poignant exhibition with stories and artefacts of some of those who fought.

★ **Chinatown**   AREA
(⬜Paddy's Markets, ⬜Town Hall) Dixon St is the heart of Chinatown: a narrow, shady pedestrian mall with a string of restaurants and insistent hawkers. The ornate dragon gates (*paifang*) at either end have fake bamboo tiles, golden Chinese calligraphy and ornamental lions to keep evil spirits at bay. Chinatown in general (outside of the dragon gates) is a fabulous eating district, which effectively extends for several blocks north and south of here, and segues into Koreatown and Thaitown to the east.

◉ **Darling Harbour & Pyrmont**

Unashamedly tourist-focused, Darling Harbour will do its best to tempt you to its shoreline bars and restaurants with fireworks displays and a sprinkling of glitz. The eastern side unfurls three strips of bars and restaurants at Cockle Bay, King Street Wharf and

Barangaroo South. On its western flank, Pyrmont still has a historic feel, and strolling its harbourside wharves is a real pleasure.

⭐ **Australian National Maritime Museum** MUSEUM
(MU-SEA-UM; 📞02-9298 3777; www.sea.museum; 2 Murray St, Pyrmont; permanent collection free, temporary exhibitions adult/child $20/12; ⏰9.30am-5pm, to 6pm Jan; 🚻; 🚌389, 🚤Pyrmont Bay) Beneath a soaring roof, the Maritime Museum sails through Australia's inextricable relationship with the sea. Exhibitions range from Indigenous canoes to surf culture, and from immigration to the navy. The worthwhile 'big ticket' (adult/child $35/20) includes entry to some of the vessels moored outside, including the atmospheric submarine HMAS *Onslow* and the destroyer HMAS *Vampire*. The high-production-value short film *Action Stations* sets the mood with a re-creation of a mission event from each vessel. Excellent free guided tours explain the features of each vessel.

⭐ **Chinese Garden of Friendship** GARDENS
(📞02-9240 8888; www.darlingharbour.com; Harbour St; adult/child $6/3; ⏰9.30am-5pm Apr-Sep, to 5.30pm Oct-Mar; 🚇Town Hall) Built according to Taoist principles, the Chinese Garden of Friendship is usually an oasis of tranquillity – although one increasingly dwarfed by assertive modern buildings nearby. Designed by architects from Guangzhou (Sydney's sister city) for Australia's bicentenary in 1988, the garden interweaves pavilions, waterfalls, lakes, paths and lush plant life. There's also a tea house. Various tours are available.

Sydney Sea Life Aquarium AQUARIUM
(📞1800 614 069; www.sydneyaquarium.com.au; Aquarium Pier; adult/child $46/33; ⏰10am-6pm, last entry 5pm; 🚇Town Hall) 🦈 As well as regular tanks, this impressive complex has large pools that you can walk through – safely enclosed in Perspex tunnels – as an intimidating array of sharks and rays pass overhead. Other highlights include a two-minute boat ride through a king and gentoo penguin enclosure, a dugong, disco-lit jellyfish, evolutionary throwbacks and the brilliant finale: the enormous Great Barrier Reef tank, which cycles you through different times of day in the life of coral, turtles, rare sharks and numerous fish.

Sydney Fish Market MARKET
(📞02-9004 1108; www.sydneyfishmarket.com.au; Bank St, Pyrmont; ⏰7am-4pm; 🚤Fish Market)

This piscatorial precinct on Blackwattle Bay shifts around 15 million kilograms of seafood annually, and has retail outlets, restaurants, sushi and oyster bars, delis and a highly regarded **cooking school** (📞02-9004 1111; 2/4hr courses $95/170; 🚤Fish Market). Chefs, locals and overfed seagulls haggle over mud crabs, Balmain bugs, lobsters and salmon at the daily fish auction, which kicks off at 5.30am on weekdays. Check it out on a behind-the-scenes tour (adult/child $45/20). A flash new market is being built a little further west, due to open in 2023.

Wild Life Sydney Zoo ZOO
(www.wildlifesydney.com.au; Aquarium Pier; adult/child $44/31; ⏰10am-5pm, last entry 4pm; 🚇Town Hall) Complementing its sister and neighbour, the Sea Life Aquarium this surprisingly spacious complex houses an impressive collection of Australian native reptiles, butterflies, spiders, snakes and mammals (including koalas and a walk-through kangaroo area). The nocturnal section is particularly good, bringing out the extrovert in the quolls, potoroos, echidnas and possums. The up-close look at a sizeable saltwater croc is also memorable, while upstairs visitors queue for cute koala selfies (from $25). Talks throughout the day fill you in on key species.

👁 Kings Cross & Potts Point

Traditionally Sydney's seedy red-light zone, the Cross has changed markedly in recent years. Controversial lockout laws killed the late-night bar life, and major building programmes have accelerated gentrification in this so-close-to-the-city district. The area's blend of backpackers and quirky locals is still enticing though, and its leafy streets and good eateries make for surprisingly pleasant daytime meanders.

Adjoining the Cross, gracious, tree-lined Potts Point and Elizabeth Bay seem worlds away. By the water below the old sailors' district of Woolloomooloo has glitzy wharf restaurants and a handful of characterful pubs.

Elizabeth Bay House HISTORIC BUILDING
(📞02-9356 3022; www.sydneylivingmuseums.com.au; 7 Onslow Ave, Elizabeth Bay; adult/child $15/12; ⏰10am-4pm Fri-Sun; 🚌311, 🚇Kings Cross) Now dwarfed by 20th-century apartments, Colonial Secretary Alexander Macleay's elegant Greek Revival mansion was one of the finest houses in the colony when it was completed in 1839. The architectural highlight is an

Circular Quay & the Rocks

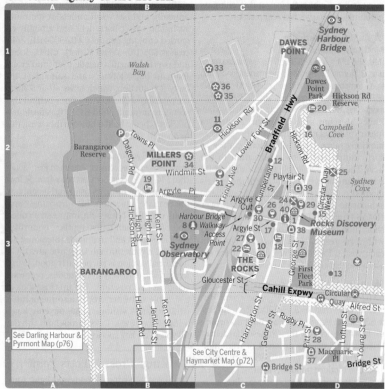

See Darling Harbour & Pyrmont Map (p76)

See City Centre & Haymarket Map (p72)

exquisite oval saloon with a curved and cantilevered staircase. There are lovely views over the harbour from the upstairs rooms. Drop down to the twin cellars for an introductory audiovisual with a weird beginning.

◉ Surry Hills & Darlinghurst

Sydney's hippest neighbourhood with a clutch of great LGBTIQ+ establishments is also home to its most interesting dining and bar scene. The plane trees and steep inclines of increasingly chic Surry Hills merge into the pretty terraces of Darlinghurst. They are pleasant, leafy districts appealingly close to the centre.

★ **Brett Whiteley Studio**   GALLERY
(☑02-9225 1881; www.artgallery.nsw.gov.au/ brett-whiteley-studio; 2 Raper St, Surry Hills; ⊙10am-4pm Thu-Sun; ☒Surry Hills, ☒Central) **FREE**
Acclaimed local artist Brett Whiteley (1939–1992) lived fast and without restraint. Many

of his multimillion-dollar paintings were created in this studio (look for the signs on Devonshire and Bourke Sts), which has been preserved as a gallery. Pride of place goes to his astonishing *Alchemy*, a giant multi-panel extravaganza that could absorb you for hours with its broad themes, intricate details and humorous asides. The studio room upstairs gives insight into the character of this master draughtsman and off-the-wall genius.

★ **Sydney Jewish Museum**   MUSEUM
(☑02-9360 7999; www.sydneyjewishmuseum. com.au; 148 Darlinghurst Rd, Darlinghurst; adult/ teen/child $15/9/free; ⊙10am-4.30pm Mon-Thu, to 3.30pm Fri, to 4pm Sun; ☒Kings Cross) One of Sydney's best museums revolves around a detailed and expertly curated exhibition on the Holocaust, with sobering testimonies and moving personal belongings as well as a memorial section for the 1.5 million child victims. Other sections cover the history and practice of Judaism and Australian Jewish history,

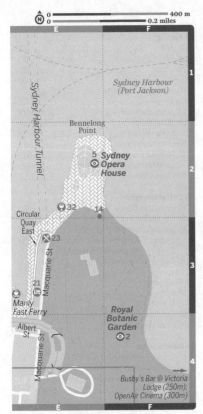

Paddington & Centennial Park

A byword for eastern suburban elegance, these areas are distinctly well heeled – and in Paddington's case, they're probably Manolo Blahniks. This is Sydney's upscale fashion and art heartland, full of pretty corners, quality commercial galleries and eye-catching boutiques. Curiously, Paddington's gorgeous Victorian terraces, so desirable nowadays, once formed a desperately poor slum.

★**Centennial Park** PARK
(☑ 02-9339 6699; www.centennialparklands.com.au; Oxford St, Centennial Park; ☺ gates sunrise-sunset; ☒; ☐ Moore Park, ☐ Bondi Junction) Scratched out of the sand in 1888 in grand Victorian style, Sydney's biggest park is a rambling 189-hectare expanse full of horse riders, joggers, cyclists and in-line skaters. Grab a park map at any of the entrances or the information centre in the middle. During summer the Moonlight Cinema (p107) attracts crowds.

Bondi, Coogee & the Eastern Beaches

Sydney sheds its suit and tie, ditches the strappy heels and chills out in the eastern suburbs. Beach after golden-sand beach, alternating with sheer sandstone cliffs, are the classic vistas of this beautiful, laid-back and egalitarian stretch of the city.

★**Bondi Beach** BEACH
(Campbell Pde; ☐ 333) Definitively Sydney, Bondi is one of the world's great beaches. It's the closest ocean beach to the city centre (8km away), has consistently good (though crowded) waves, and is great for a rough-and-tumble swim (the average water temperature is a considerate 21°C). If the sea's angry, try the child-friendly saltwater sea baths at either end of the beach, both of which received an upgrade in 2019. Free beach-friendly wheelchairs (adult or child) can be booked through the **Bondi Pavilion** (☑ 02-9083 8400; www.waverley.nsw.gov.au; Queen Elizabeth Dr; ☺ 9am-5pm) FREE.

Sydney Harbourside

Stretching inland for 20km until it morphs into the Parramatta River, the harbour has shaped the local psyche for millennia, and today it's the city's sparkling playground. Its inlets, beaches, islands and shorefront parks

culture and tradition. A section on the top floor examines contemporary human rights challenges, while temporary exhibitions are always excellent. Free tours run at 2pm.

★**Australian Museum** MUSEUM
(☑ 02-9320 6000; www.australianmuseum.net.au; 1 William St, Darlinghurst; ☐ Museum) Australia's first museum was established just 40 years after the First Fleet dropped anchor and behind its sandstone facade are modernised halls showcasing a 21-million-piece collection. Standouts include exhibits on Aboriginal history and spirituality, a new Pacific Spirit Gallery to rehouse the colourful Pacific Island collection and a showcase of Australian dinosaurs such as the *Muttaburrasaurus*.

Closed for renovation at the time of research, the redevelopment will expand the touring exhibitions halls for global blockbuster exhibits. Check the website before you plan to visit.

Circular Quay & the Rocks

provide endless swimming, sailing, picnicking and walking opportunities. A fantastic way to explore the harbour is to hop aboard a ferry at Circular Quay – the beloved green-and-cream vessels are certainly not speedsters, but they're usually faster, and always more relaxed, than Sydney's congested roads.

★**Watsons Bay** AREA
(🚌324, 325, 380, 🛥Watsons Bay) Lovely Watsons Bay, east of the city centre and north of Bondi, was once a small fishing village, as evidenced by the heritage cottages that pepper the suburb's narrow streets (and now cost a fortune). It's a lovely day trip by ferry for an exploration of South Head and a leisurely lunch. While you're here, tradition demands that you sit in the Beach Club (p106) beer garden at sunset and watch the sun dissolve behind the Harbour Bridge.

★**Taronga Zoo Sydney** ZOO
(🖉02-9969 2777; www.taronga.org.au; Bradleys Head Rd, Mosman; adult/child $49/29, under 4 free;

🕑9.30am-4.30pm Jun-Aug, to 5pm Sep-May; 👪; 🚌M30, 🛥Taronga Zoo) 🖉 A 12-minute ferry ride from Circular Quay, this bushy harbour hillside is full of kangaroos, koalas and similarly hirsute Australians, plus imported guests. The zoo's critters have million-dollar harbour views, but are blissfully unaware of the privilege. Encouragingly, Taronga sets benchmarks in animal care and welfare. Highlights include the nocturnal platypus habitat, the Great Southern Oceans section and the Asian elephant display. Feedings and encounters happen throughout the day, while in summer, twilight concerts jazz things up (see www.twi lightattaronga.org.au).

★**McMahons Point** VIEWPOINT
(Henry Lawson Ave; 🛥McMahons Point) Is there a better view of the bridge and the Opera House than from the wharf at this point, a short hop by ferry northwest of the centre? It's all unfolded before you and this is a stunning spot to be when the sun is setting. Between Luna Park and McMahons

Point, at the head of Lavender Bay, **Wendy Whiteley's Secret Garden** (www.wendys secretgarden.org.au; Lavender St; ⊙24hr; ⛴Milsons Point, 🚇Milsons Point) **FREE** is a guerrilla garden created by the widow of artist Brett Whiteley (an artist herself) on an old railway siding.

★**Cockatoo Island**   ISLAND
(☑02-8969 2100; www.cockatooisland.gov.au; ⛴Cockatoo Island) Studded with photogenic industrial relics, convict architecture and art installations, fascinating Cockatoo Island (Wareamah) opened to the public in 2007 and has regular ferry services, a camping ground (p89), rental accommodation, and two cafe-bars. Information boards and audioguides ($5) explain the island's time as a brutal convict prison, a shipyard and a naval base. A range of tours run from the **Visitor Centre** (⊙10am-4pm), from straight-up heritage tours to Ghostyard Paranormal and Convict Escape Attempts (from $16). The island is a major venue for the Biennale (p80).

Vaucluse House   HISTORIC BUILDING
(☑02-9388 7922; www.sydneylivingmuseums. com.au/vaucluse-house; Wentworth Rd, Vaucluse; adult/child $15/12; ⊙10am-4pm Wed-Sun; 🚌324, 325, 386) Construction of this imposing, turreted specimen of Gothic Australiana, set amid 10 hectares of lush gardens, commenced in 1805, but the house was tinkered with into the 1860s. Atmospheric and decorated with beautiful European period pieces, the house offers visitors a rare glimpse into early Sydney colonial life, as lived by the well-to-do. The history of the Wentworths, who occupied it, is fascinating, and helpful guides give great background on them. In the grounds is a popular tearoom.

South Head   NATIONAL PARK
(www.nationalparks.nsw.gov.au; Cliff St, Watsons Bay; ⊙5am-10pm; 🚌324, 325, 380, ⛴Watsons Bay) At the northern end of Camp Cove, the **South Head Heritage Trail** kicks off, leading into a section of Sydney Harbour National Park distinguished by harbour views and crashing surf. It passes old fortifications and a path heading down to **Lady Bay** (Cliff St, Watsons Bay; 🚌324, 325, 380, ⛴Watsons Bay) nude beach, before continuing on to the candy-striped **Hornby Lighthouse** and the sandstone **Lightkeepers' Cottages** (1858). Between April and November, look out to sea where whale-watching boats have congregated and you'll often see cetaceans.

Luna Park   AMUSEMENT PARK
(☑02-9922 6644; www.lunaparksydney.com; 1 Olympic Dr, Milsons Point; ⊙10am-10pm Fri & Sat, 10am-6pm Sun, 11am-4pm Mon; ⛴Milsons Point, 🚇Milsons Point) **FREE** A sinister, gigantic chip-toothed clown face forms the entrance to this old-fashioned amusement park overlooking Sydney Harbour. It's one of several 1930s features, including the Coney Island funhouse, a pretty carousel and the nausea-inducing Rotor. There are two-ride passes ($22), or height-based unlimited-ride passes (adults $57, kids $25 to $47; cheaper online) but you can also wander through without buying a ticket. Hours are extended during school and public holidays. There's a bar-restaurant on-site with a great harbour view.

⊙ Newtown & the Inner West

The bohemian sweep of the Inner West is an array of suburbs crowded with great places to eat and drink. The quiet streets of Glebe and the louder Newtown, grouped around the University of Sydney, are the best known of these tightly packed suburbs, but Enmore, Marrickville, Redfern and more are all worth investigating. All the essential hang-outs for students – bookshops, cafes, pubs and live-music venues – are present in abundance, but the Inner West is a lifestyle choice for a whole swathe of Sydney society.

★**White Rabbit**   GALLERY
(☑02-8399 2867; www.whiterabbitcollection.org; 30 Balfour St, Chippendale; ⊙10am-5pm Wed-Sun, often closed Dec, Feb & Aug; 🚇Central) **FREE** In many ways Sydney's best contemporary-art gallery, White Rabbit is tucked behind the Central Park development in Chippendale. It's the project of billionaire philanthropist Judith Neilson, who has amassed one of the world's largest collections of cutting-edge, contemporary Chinese art (works produced since 2000) and has so many pieces that only a fraction can be displayed at one time. You'll find art here that is edgy, funny, sexy and idiosyncratic. An on-site cafe does speciality teas and dumplings.

★**Carriageworks**   ARTS CENTRE
(☑02-8571 9099; www.carriageworks.com.au; 245 Wilson St, Eveleigh; ⊙10am-6pm; 🚇Redfern) **FREE** Built between 1880 and 1889, this intriguing group of huge Victorian-era workshops was part of the Eveleigh Railyards. The rail workers chugged out in 1988, and

City Centre & Haymarket

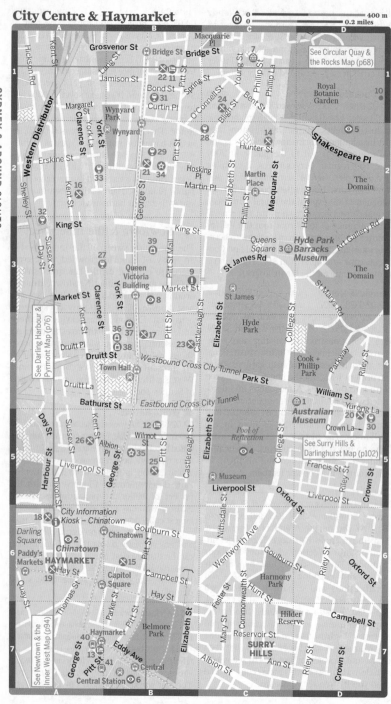

N

0   400 m
0   0.2 miles

Macquarie Pl

Grosvenor St

Bridge St   Bridge St

7

See Circular Quay & the Rocks Map (p68)

Jamison St

Lang St

Spring St

Young St

Phillip La

Bond St

Pitt St

O'Connell St

Bent St

Phillip St

Royal Botanic Garden

10

Margaret St

Curtin Pl

31

24

Blight St

Wynyard Park

Clarence St

York St

Wynyard

28

Hunter St

14

5

Shakespeare Pl

Erskine St

Kent St

29

Pitt St

Hosking Pl

Elizabeth St

Martin Place

Macquarie St

The Domain

33

34

21

Martin Pl

16

King St

King St

Queens Square

Hyde Park Barracks Museum

3

Art Gallery Rd

The Domain

32

Sussex St

Day St

27

Queen Victoria Building

39

Pitt St Mall

9

St James Rd

Market St

Market St

St James

Hospital Rd

St Marys Rd

Market St

Clarence St

York St

Kent St

8

Pitt St

Castlereagh St

Elizabeth St

Hyde Park

College St

Cook + Phillip Park

36

37

17

23

Druitt Pl

38

Druitt St

Town Hall

Westbound Cross City Tunnel

Park St

William St

1

Australian Museum

Yurong La

20

30

Druitt La

Bathurst St

Eastbound Cross City Tunnel

Crown La

See Darling Harbour & Pyrmont Map (p76)

Day St

Harbour St

12

Wilmot St

26

Albion Pl

35

25

Elizabeth St

Pool of Reflection

College St

See Surry Hills & Darlinghurst Map (p102)

Francis St

Riley St

Crown St

Liverpool St

Sussex St

Kent St

George St

Liverpool St

4

Oxford St

Liverpool St

Museum

Castlereagh St

Oxford St

18

City Information Kiosk – Chinatown

Darling Square

Chinatown

2

Chinatown

Goulburn St

Nithsdale St

Wentworth Ave

Goulburn St

Riley St

Oxford St

Paddy's Markets

HAYMARKET

Hay St

19

15

Pitt St

Campbell St

Foster St

Commonwealth St

Hunt St

Harmony Park

Campbell St

Capitol Square

Hay St

Belmore Park

Elizabeth St

Mary St

Hilder Reserve

Reservoir St

SURRY HILLS

Crown St

See Newtown & the Inner West Map (p94)

40

Haymarket

13

41

Eddy Ave

Central

6

Quay St

Thomas St

Parker St

Pitt St

George St

Central Station

Albion St

Ann St

Riley St

Campbell St

City Centre & Haymarket

in 2007 the artists moved in. It's now home to an impressive artist-led programme of inventive visual arts and performance, often on a monumental scale. Expect anything from Indigenous dance retrospectives to aura photography or giant incense sculptures; have a look on the website to see what's on.

Chau Chak Wing Museum   MUSEUM
(☏ 02-9351 2222; www.sydney.edu.au/museum; University Pl, University of Sydney; 🚌 412, 413, 436, 438-40, 461, 480, 483, M10) FREE This excellent new museum at the University of Sydney was scheduled to open in 2020. It combines the three former university museums and greatly expand the space to exhibit the university's collections and host temporary exhibitions. Highlights include Indigenous cultural objects and the important collections of 19th- and 20th-century Australian, European and Asian art and Australian natural history. It will also house an impressive Mediterranean archaeological ensemble, including a Mummy Room with a 2500-year-old Egyptian mummified cat.

◉ Manly

With both a harbour side and a glorious ocean beach, Manly is Sydney's only ferry destination with surf. Capping off the harbour with scrappy charm, it's a place worth visiting for the ferry ride alone. The surf is good, there are appealing contemporary bars and eating spots and, as the gateway to the northern beaches, it makes a popular base for the board-riding brigade. There's also some great walking to be done.

★**Manly Beach**   BEACH
(🚢 Manly) Sydney's second most famous beach is a magnificent strand that stretches for nearly two golden kilometres, lined by Norfolk Island pines and midrise apartment blocks. The southern end of the beach, nearest the Corso, is known as South Steyne, with North Steyne in the centre and Queenscliff at the northern end; each has its own surf lifesaving club.

★**North Head**   NATIONAL PARK
(☏ 1300 072 757; www.nationalparks.nsw.gov.au; North Head Scenic Dr; ☉ sunrise-sunset; 🚌 135) FREE About 3km south of central Manly, spectacular North Head offers dramatic cliffs,

Manly

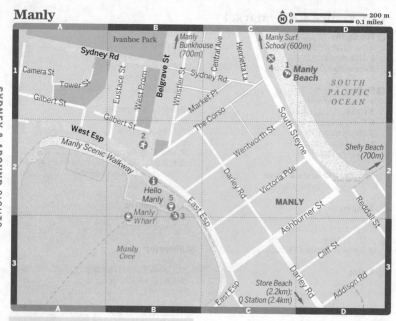

Manly

◎ Top Sights
1 Manly Beach C1

✛ Activities, Courses & Tours
2 Manly Bike Tours................................B2
3 Manly Kayak Centre...........................B2

✖ Eating
4 The Pantry...C1

◉ Drinking & Nightlife
5 Manly Wharf Hotel B2

lookouts, secluded beaches, pretty paths through the native scrub, and sweeping views of the ocean, harbour and city. It's great to explore, by bike or on foot, along the Manly Scenic Walkway (p77). Grab a map and plot your own path through the headland, which takes in former military barracks, WWII gun emplacements, a quarantine cemetery and a memorial walk commemorating Australia's military. At the tip, **Fairfax Lookouts** offer dramatic clifftop perspectives.

★ **Store Beach** BEACH
(⊙ dawn-dusk; 🚢 Manly) A hidden jewel on North Head, magical Store Beach can only be reached by kayak – you can hire them from **Manly Kayak Centre** (📞 02-9976 5057; www. manlykayakcentre.com.au; Manly Wharf; hire per

1/2/4/8hr from $25/45/55/75; ⊙ 9am-6pm, last booking 5pm; 🚢 Manly) – or you can go by boat. It's a breeding ground for **fairy penguins**, so access is prohibited from dusk, when the birds waddle in to settle down for the night.

Q Station HISTORIC BUILDING
(Quarantine Station; 📞 02-9466 1551; www.qstation. com.au; 1 North Head Scenic Dr; ⊙ visitor centre 10am-4pm Sun-Thu, 10am-8pm Fri & Sat; 🚌 135) **FREE** From 1837 to 1984 this sprawling historic complex in beautiful North Head bushland was used to isolate new arrivals suspected of carrying disease. These days it has been reborn as a tourist destination, offering appealing accommodation (p90) and various tours. Shuttle buses whisk you from reception down to the wharf, where there's a lovely beach, a museum in the old luggage shop telling the site's story, an information desk and a cafe. Nearby is a bar and restaurant.

◎ Northern Beaches

Wilder and more distant than Sydney's eastern strands, the northern beaches are a must-see, especially for surfers. Although you'll most likely approach them as a day trip, they're very much a part of the city, with a string of seaside suburbs vying for the title of best beach. Some neighbourhoods are ritzier than others, but what they all have in common is a devotion to the sand and surf.

★ Palm Beach
BEACH

(Ocean Rd; 🚌199, L90) Long, lovely Palm Beach is a crescent of bliss that's famous as the setting for the cheesy TV soap *Home and Away*. The 1881 **Barrenjoey Lighthouse** (☑02-9451 3479; www.nationalparks. nsw.gov.au; 🚌199, L90) **FREE** punctuates the northern tip of the headland in an annexe of Ku-ring-gai Chase National Park (p80). Palm Beach has two sides: the magnificent ocean beach and a pleasant strip on Pittwater, where the calmer strands are good for young kids. From here you can get **ferries** (☑02-9974 2411; www.fantasea.com.au/ palmbeachferries; Barrenjoey Rd; each way adult/ child Pittwater ferries $8.60/4.30, Broken Bay ferries $12.20/6.10; ⊙office 9am-5pm Mon-Fri, from 10am Sat & Sun; 🚌199, L90) to other picturesque Pittwater destinations, including other park sections.

Avalon
BEACH

(Barrenjoey Rd, Avalon; 🚌188, 199, L90) Caught in a sandy '70s time warp, Avalon is the mythical Australian beach you always dreamed of but could never find. Challenging surf and sloping, tangerine-gold sand have a boutique headland for a backdrop. There's a sea pool at the southern end. Good, cheap eating options abound in the streets behind.

👁 Parramatta

Parramatta, 23km west of central Sydney, was founded in 1788 by Governor Phillip, who needed a place to grow grain to supply the colony. The Indigenous Darug people called the area Burramatta for the area's plentiful eels, which are still the symbol and nickname of Parramatta's famous rugby league team. Most of Parramatta's historic sights are a short detour off the lovely river walk (p77).

Big things are afoot in Parramatta, which is undergoing a massive and ambitious development programme to establish it as a real alternative to central Sydney.

Experiment Farm Cottage
HISTORIC BUILDING

(☑02-9635 5655; www.nationaltrust.org.au; 9 Ruse St, Harris Park; adult/child $10/8; ⊙guided tours 10.30am-3.30pm Wed-Sun; 🚃Harris Park) This colonial bungalow stands on the site of Australia's first official land grant. In 1789 Governor Phillip allocated 12 hectares to emancipated convict James Ruse as an experiment to see

how long it would take Ruse to wean himself off government supplies. The experiment was a success, and Ruse became Australia's first private European farmer. He sold the land to surgeon John Harris, who built this house around 1835. It's decked out in period style with lovely early colonial furniture.

Elizabeth Farm
HISTORIC BUILDING

(☑02-9635 9488; www.sydneylivingmuseums.com. au; 70 Alice St, Rosehill; adult/child $15/12; ⊙10am-4pm Wed-Sun; 🚌909 from Parramatta Station, 🚃Harris Park) Elizabeth Farm contains part of Australia's oldest surviving colonial building (1793), built by renegade pastoralist and rum trader John Macarthur. Heralded as the founder of Australia's wool industry, Macarthur was a ruthless capitalist whose politicking made him immensely wealthy and a thorn in the side of successive governors. The pretty homestead is now a hands-on museum where you can recline on the reproduction furniture and thumb voyeuristically through two of Elizabeth Macarthur's letters.

Old Government House
HISTORIC BUILDING

(☑02-9635 8149; www.nationaltrust.org.au; Parramatta Park, Parramatta; adult/child $15/10; ⊙10am-4pm Tue-Sun; 🚃Parramatta) The country residence of the early governors, this elegant Georgian Palladian building in **Parramatta Park** (www.parrapark.com.au; cnr Pitt & Macquarie Sts) is now a preciously maintained museum furnished with original colonial furniture. It was built by convicts and dates from 1799, making it the oldest remaining public building in Australia.

ℹ DISCOUNT PASSES

Sydney Museums Pass (www.sydney livingmuseums.com.au; adult/child $35/28) Allows a single visit to each of 12 museums in and around Sydney, including the Museum of Sydney, Hyde Park Barracks, Elizabeth Bay House and Susannah Place. It's valid for a month and available at each of the participating museums. It's a good deal.

Four Attraction Pass (adult/child $75/53) Provides access to the high-profile, costly attractions operated by British-based Merlin Entertainment: Sydney Tower Eye, Sydney Sea Life Aquarium, Wild Life Sydney Zoo and Madame Tussauds. It's often cheaper online; various combinations are available.

Darling Harbour & Pyrmont

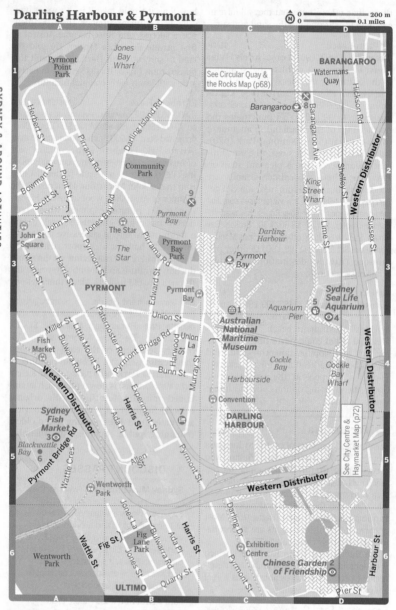

Temporary exhibitions add to the building's interest and there are volunteers stationed around the building to answer your questions. A vine-draped restaurant is in the courtyard.

🏃 Activities

Cycling

Manly Bike Tours   CYCLING
(☎ 02-8005 7368; www.manlybiketours.com.au; Belgrave St, Manly; hire per hour/day from $18/35, extra days from $15; ⏰ 9am-6pm Oct-Mar, to 5pm Apr-Sep;

Darling Harbour & Pyrmont

Manly) Hires out bikes and provides maps and suggested routes for self-guided tours. There's a big variety of bikes available and it's right across from the ferry wharf. Lockers are available for you to store gear while you ride.

Diving

Dive Centre Bondi
DIVING
(02-9369 3855; www.divebondi.com.au; 198 Bondi Rd, Bondi; 2 guided dives incl equipment from shore/boat $175/230, PADI Open Water courses $495; 9am-6pm Mon-Fri, from 8am Sat & Sun; 333, 380, 381) Friendly and professional, this centre offers guided dives from shore or boat as well as equipment hire. It runs PADI Open Water courses as well as other certifications.

Gordons Bay
Underwater Nature Trail
DIVING
(www.gordonsbayscubadivingclub.com; Victory St, Clovelly; 338, 339) Accessed from beyond the car park just south of Clovelly Beach, this is a 620m underwater chain that guides divers around reefs, sand flats and kelp forests. On clear days you can snorkel the trail.

Kayaking

Sydney By Kayak
KAYAKING
(1300 503 889; www.sydneybykayak.com.au; 1 Railway Ave, Lavender Bay; tours from $125; Milsons Point, North Sydney) Small-group tours on Sydney Harbour, including sunrise kayak-and-coffee tours, private couples tours and clean-up paddles to pull rubbish out of Lavender Bay (two hours, $45). No experience necessary.

Surfing

Sydney is a surf city, with a string of brilliant beaches running both north and south of the harbour. For updates on what's breaking where, see www.coastalwatch.com, www.surf-forecast.com, www.magicseaweed.com or www.swellnet.com.

Most beaches have surfboard hire available and several have companies offering surfing lessons.

★ Let's Go Surfing
SURFING
(02-9365 1800; www.letsgosurfing.com.au; 128 Ramsgate Ave, North Bondi; board & wetsuit hire 1hr/2hr/day/week $25/30/50/200; 9am-5pm; 333) North Bondi is a great place to learn to surf, and this well-established surf school offers lessons catering to practically everyone. There are classes for 'grommets' (young surfers) aged seven to 15 (1½ hours, $49) and adults (two hours, $119; women-only classes are also available), or you can book a private tutor (1½ hours, $230/350 for one/two people). Prices drop outside summer.

Manly Surf School
SURFING
(02-9932 7000; www.manlysurfschool.com; North Steyne Surf Club, Manly; surf lessons adult/child $80/70, private classes $125 per hr; 136, 139, Manly) Reliable and well established, this outfit right on the sand offers good two-hour surf lessons year-round, as well as private tuition. It's a fair bit cheaper if you book a multi-class package. Let them know your level in advance so they can match you with the ideal tidal conditions. You can also book classes at Palm Beach in summer.

Swimming

Fancy a dip? Sydney has sheltered harbour coves, saltwater rock pools, more than 100 public pools and brilliant ocean beaches. Always swim between the flags on life-saver-patrolled beaches, and avoid swimming in the ocean for a day and in the harbour for three days after heavy rains.

Bondi Icebergs Pool
SWIMMING
(02-9130 4804; www.icebergs.com.au; 1 Notts Ave, Bondi Beach; adult/child $9/6; 6am-6.30pm Mon-Wed & Fri, from 6.30am Sat & Sun; 333) Sydney's most famous pool commands the best view in Bondi, and is one of its more community-oriented spaces. There's a sauna and a cute little cafe (0450 272 223; www.facebook.com/thecrabbehole; Lower Level, 1 Notts Ave; breakfasts $5-15; 7am-3pm Mon-Fri, to 5pm Sat & Sun; 333). The saltwater lapping pool

Kings Cross & Potts Point

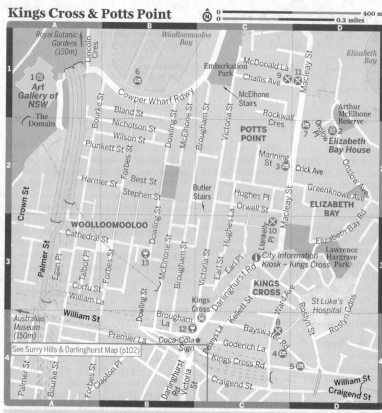

N 0 ————————— 400 m
   0 ————————— 0.2 miles

Kings Cross & Potts Point

◎ Top Sights
1	Art Gallery of NSW	A1
2	Elizabeth Bay House	D2

◎ Sleeping
3	Blue Parrot Backpackers	C2
4	Hotel 59	C4
5	Mad Monkey Bayswater	D4
6	Ovolo Hotel Woolloomooloo	B1
7	The Macleay	D2

◎ Eating
8	Farmhouse	C4
9	Fratelli Paradiso	C1
10	Room 10	C3
11	Yellow	D1

◎ Drinking & Nightlife
12	Kings Cross Hotel	B4
13	Old Fitzroy Hotel	B3

◎ Entertainment
	Old Fitz Theatre	(see 13)

is doused by the bigger breakers, but there's a more sheltered pool for kids. It closes on Thursdays so they can clean the seaweed out, though it sometimes opens once the job's done.

Murray Rose Pool   SWIMMING
(Redleaf Pool; 536 New South Head Rd, Double Bay; ⊙ 24hr; ☐ 323-326, ☐ Double Bay) Not a pool as such, family-friendly Murray Rose (named

after a champion Olympic swimmer) is a large, shark-netted enclosure that is one of the harbour's best swimming spots. As one of the closest harbour beaches to the city, it attracts an urbane cross-section of inner-eastern locals. A boardwalk runs around it, and there are two sought-after floating pontoons.

Walking

As well as standard urban strolling, there are two main types of walks in Sydney: coastal or harbour walks, and bushwalks in the city's national parks.

The most famous coastal walk is Bondi to Coogee (p92), but there are numerous trails, with some of the most rewarding ones around the harbour. The Harbour Bridge to Spit Bridge walk is recommended, and the Spit Bridge to Manly is another excellent stretch. Or do the 80km Bondi to Manly stretch over a few days (www.bonditomanly. com). Get inspired at www.walkingcoastal sydney.com.au.

There are great bush trails in Ku-Ring-Gai Chase National Park (p80), **Lane Cove National Park** (🕙 weekdays 02-8448 0400, weekends 02-9472 8949; www.nationalparks.nsw.gov.au; Lady Game Dr, Chatswood West; per car $8; 🕙 9am-6pm Apr-Sep, to 7pm Oct-Mar; 🚌 545, 550, 🚇 North Ryde) and the Royal National Park (p121), as well as other protected areas of bush.

A nice way to explore some of these areas is to hike sections of the **Great North Walk** (www.thegreatnorthwalk.com). Starting at Sydney Harbour, this runs 250km up to Newcastle. The Sydney section passes reasonably close to lots of train stations, meaning you can easily walk a section as a half- or full-day walk. The 10km stretch from Thornleigh to Hornsby in Sydney's northern suburbs is one of several lovely ones; Berowra to Cowan is another.

★ **Manly Scenic Walkway**   WALKING
(www.manly.nsw.gov.au; 🚢 Manly) This marvellous coastal walk has two major components: the 10km western stretch between Manly and Spit Bridge, and the 9.5km eastern loop around North Head (p73). Either download a map or pick one up from the information centre near the wharf.

Parramatta River Walk   WALKING
(🚢 Parramatta) There's no better way to explore this part of Sydney than by walking along the Parramatta River. There's a path on both the north and south sides of the river in Parramatta itself, and plenty of birdlife in places. You can head towards Sydney, or go upstream and discover **Lake Parramatta**. Download the *Parramatta River Walk* brochure for a map.

 Tours

Boat Tours

There's a wide range of harbour cruises available, from paddle steamers to maxi yachts and jet boats. If you're pinching pennies, take the return ferry trip to Manly and consider yourself very clever.

Whale-watching boats run from May to November. As well as spotting cetaceans, these give you a pretty good look at the harbour as well as the heads and a perspective from the ocean.

Kayaking or stand-up paddleboarding (SUP) tours are a fun way to explore the harbour.

★ **Whale Watching Sydney**   WILDLIFE
(WWS; 🕙 02-9583 1199; www.whalewatchingsyd ney.com.au; adult/child $87/56; 🕙 mid-May-early Dec) Humpback and southern right whales habitually shunt up and down the Sydney coastline, sometimes venturing into the harbour. Between mid-May and December, WWS runs three-hour tours beyond the heads. For a faster ride that also offers a more intimate whale experience, there are two-hour jet-boat expeditions ($77). Sunset cruises are also available.

Sydney Harbour Tallships   BOATING
(🕙 02-8015 5571; www.sydneytallships.com.au; tours from $59) These elegant, high-masted, replica 19th-century vessels offer a variety of cruises around the harbour, leaving from one of two docks in the Rocks. You can book online.

Captain Cook Cruises   CRUISE
(🕙 02-9206 1111; www.captaincook.com.au; Wharf 6, Circular Quay; from $35; 🚇 Circular Quay) As well as sightseeing ($39 to $55), lunch and dinner cruises, and whale watching, this crew offers an aquatic version of a hop-on, hop-off bus tour, with two main routes that include Watsons Bay, Taronga Zoo, Shark Island and Manly. It costs $50/29 per adult/child for two days and includes some commentary. Departures from Circular Quay, Darling Harbour and Barangaroo.

Bike Tours

Bonza Bike Tours   CYCLING
(🕙 02-9247 8800; www.bonzabiketours.com; 30 Harrington St; tours from $99; 🕙 office 9am-5pm; 🚇 Circular Quay) These bike boffins run a 2½-hour Sydney Highlights tour (adult/child $99/79) and a four-hour Sydney Classic tour ($129/99). Other tours include a Manly option. They also hire out bikes ($15/30/40/130 per hour/half-day/day/week).

SYDNEY & AROUND FESTIVALS & EVENTS

KU-RING-GAI CHASE

The spectacular 14,928-hectare **Ku-ring-gai Chase National Park** (☑02-9472 8949; www.nationalparks.nsw.gov.au; per car per day $12, landing fee by boat adult/child $3/2; ☺sunrise-sunset), 20km to 30km from the city centre, forms Sydney's northern boundary. It's a classic mix of sandstone, bushland and water vistas, taking in over 100km of coastline along the southern edge of Broken Bay, where it heads into the Hawkesbury River. There are two unconnected principal sections, **Bobbin Head** (Bobbin Head Rd, North Turramurra; vehicles $12; ☺6am-8pm Oct-Mar, to 5.30pm Apr-Sep; ☑577 from Turramurra station, ☑Mt Colah) and the **West Head** (West Head Rd, Terrey Hills; per car $12; ☺6am-6pm Apr-Sep, to 8.30pm Oct-Mar) area. The Barrenjoey headland (p74) at Palm Beach is also part of the park.

Declared in 1894, Ku-ring-gai takes its name from its original inhabitants, the Guringai people, who were all but wiped out just after colonisation through violence at the hands of settlers and the devastating introduction of smallpox. It's well worth reading Kate Grenville's *The Secret River* for an engrossing but harrowing telling of this story.

Remnants of pre-colonial Aboriginal life are visible today thanks to the preservation of more than 800 sites, including rock paintings, middens and cave art.

Elevated park sections offer glorious views over Cowan Creek, Broken Bay and Pittwater.

For information about the park, stop at the Bobbin Head Information Centre, operated by the NSW National Parks & Wildlife Service, where there are also picnic areas, a marina, a cafe and a boardwalk leading through mangroves

Access to the park is by the Palm Beach Ferry (p74), by **water taxi** (☑0415 408 831) or by car via McCarrs Creek Rd (off Mona Vale Rd, Terrey Hills) for West Head; or via Bobbin Head Rd (North Turramurra) or Ku-ring-gai Chase Rd (Mount Colah) for Bobbin Head.

Walking Tours

Sydney Architecture Walks WALKING
(☑0403 888 390; www.sydneyarchitecture.org; adult walks $49-59, cycle not incl bike $90) These bright young archi-buffs run two 3½-hour cycling tours and six themed two- to three-hour walking tours. There's a focus on explaining modern architectural principles and urban design. It's cheaper if you book in advance.

Dreamtime Southern X WALKING
(☑02-9517 4390; www.dreamtimesouthernx.com.au; adult/child $44/33) Indigenous-owned and operated, this friendly set-up takes you on a leisurely 90-minute stroll around the Rocks area, evoking something of what it used to be before the First Fleet arrived, and providing insights into traditional and contemporary Aboriginal culture. Meet at **Cadman's Cottage** (☑02-9337 5511; www.nationalparks.nsw.gov.au; 110 George St; ☑Circular Quay) FREE; tours must be prebooked. They also run twice-weekly coach tours visiting important Indigenous heritage sites around the city (adult/child $175/131).

The Rocks Walking Tours WALKING
(☑02-9247 6678; www.rockswalkingtours.com.au; Shop 4a, cnr Argyle & Harrington Sts; adult/child/family $32/15/79; ☺10.30am & 1.30pm; ☑Circular Quay) Two daily 90-minute tours through the historic Rocks, with plenty of tales and interesting minutiae. The office is in a shopping arcade; you can book online too.

Other Tours

★BridgeClimb WALKING
(☑02-8274 7777; www.bridgeclimb.com; 3 Cumberland St; adult $268-388, child $188-278; ☑Circular Quay) Don a headset, a safety cord and a dandy grey jumpsuit and you'll be ready to embark on an exhilarating 3½-hour climb to the top of Sydney's famous bridge. The priciest climbs are at dawn and sunset. A cheaper, 90-minute 'sampler' climb (to a lower point) is also available, as are 'express climbs', ascending to the top via a faster route (2½ hours).

★ Festivals & Events

★Sydney Festival CULTURAL
(www.sydneyfestival.org.au; ☺Jan) Sydney's premier arts and culture festival is a three-week showcase of music, theatre and visual art.

★Sydney Gay & Lesbian Mardi Gras LGBT
(www.mardigras.org.au; ☺Feb-Mar) This two-week cultural and entertainment festival celebrating all things LGBTIQ+ culminates in the world-famous massive parade and party. Lots of international visitors means the city is buzzing.

★ **Sydney Writers' Festival**   LITERATURE
(www.swf.org.au; ⊘ Apr/May) The country's pre-eminent literary shindig is held over a week in various prime locations around the central city. It pulls some big names and the programme is always extremely interesting.

Vivid Sydney   LIGHT SHOW
(www.vividsydney.com; ⊘ late May-mid Jun) This impressive and popular festival features spectacular immersive light installations and projections onto the sails of the Opera House and other locations right across the city. There are also performances and public talks, and debates with leading global creative thinkers. As a result of the covid pandemic, it will be held in August in 2021.

★ **New Year's Eve**   FIREWORKS
(www.sydneynewyearseve.com; ⊘ 31 Dec) The biggest party of the year, with flamboyant firework displays shooting off the Harbour Bridge. A family-friendly show starts at 9pm, with the main event at midnight. There's a variety of regulated zones where you can watch the fireworks – some ticketed, some alcohol-free.

Sydney Film Festival   FILM
(www.sff.org.au; ⊘ Jun) Held in venues across town, this excellent, highly regarded film festival screens art-house gems from Australia and around the world. Flexipasses offer the best ticketing deals and can be shared between friends.

Sculpture by the Sea   ART
(www.sculpturebythesea.com; ⊘ Oct) For 17 days from late October, the clifftop trail (p92) from Bondi Beach to Tamarama transforms into the world's largest free sculpture exhibition. Serious prize money is on offer for the most creative, curious or quizzical offerings from international and local sculptors. Try to visit midweek as it is crammed at weekends.

Chinese New Year   CULTURAL
(www.sydneychinesenewyear.com; ⊘ Jan/Feb) Based in Chinatown, but with around 100 elements and events across Sydney, this two-week celebration features food, fireworks, dragon dancers and dragon-boat races to see in the lunar new year. Actual dates vary slightly; the new year day can be from late January to mid-February.

Biennale of Sydney   ART
(www.biennaleofsydney.com.au; ⊘ Mar-Jun even years) This high-profile festival of contemporary art and ideas is held between March and June in even-numbered years. It originated as an opening celebration for the Opera House.

Sydney to Hobart Yacht Race   SPORTS
(www.rolexsydneyhobart.com) On 26 December Sydney Harbour is a sight to behold as hundreds of boats crowd its waters to farewell the yachts competing in this gruelling ocean race.

🛏 Sleeping

Sydney offers a vast quantity and variety of accommodation, especially concentrated in the city centre, Rocks and Darling Harbour

---

SYDNEY FOR CHILDREN

With boundless natural attractions and relaxed, outdoor living, Sydney is great for kids.

The calm waters of the harbour beaches are tops for youngsters, and most of Sydney's surf beaches have saltwater ocean pools, some with kids' sections, such as the spectacular Bondi Icebergs (p77). Most surf schools, like Let's Go Surfing (p75), cater for kids and have special holiday packages.

At Darling Harbour there's Wild Life Sydney Zoo (p67) and the Sydney Sea Life Aquarium (p67), plus the fascinating Australian National Maritime Museum (p67) and its excellent collection of boats and ships. There's also a great playground at Darling Harbour, **Tumbalong Park**, which boasts squirting jets, a stepping-stone pool, spiderweb climbers, giant slides and an Archimedes water screw.

Another harbourside attraction is the excellent Museum of Contemporary Art (p61) which has a great hands-on kids programme. Across town, the Australian Museum (p69) is a real hit with the younger crowd, especially its excellent dinosaur exhibition. A certain winner is the ferry ride to the wonderful Taronga Zoo (p70). Luna Park (p73), also a ferry ride from the centre, has been thrilling kids for over 80 years. Little astronomers might want to do some stargazing or see the Time Ball drop at the free and very kid-focused Sydney Observatory (p61).

Where to Stay in Sydney

0 —————— 2 km
0 —————— 1 mile

**Circular Quay
& the Rocks**
Big-ticket sights, vibrant
nightlife, top hotels and
restaurants but full of
tourists and expensive.

Best For Honeymoons,
convenience

Transport Short walk to
city centre

Price Mostly top end

*Sydney
Harbour
Bridge*

Parramatta
Intriguing multicultural
hub on the rise with his-
toric sights, but far from
Sydney's central areas.

Best For Budget trav-
ellers

Transport Two trains to
city centre

Price Budget

**Darling Harbour &
Pyrmont**
Plenty to see and do;
lively nightlife but can be
a little soulless.

Best For Waterfront
strollers

Transport Light rail or a
short walk to the centre

Price Midrage to top end

**Circular Quay
& The Rocks**

**City Centre
& Haymarket**

Parramatta
← *(13km)*

**Darling
Harbour
& Pyrmont**

**Surry Hills &
Darlinghurst**

**Newtown &
the Inner West**
Bohemian zone with
great cafes, cheap res-
taurants and interesting
shops. Priced for locals.

Best For Vintage
shopping, cutting-edge
culture

Transport Train to city
centre

Price Midrange

**Newtown &
the Inner West**

**Surry Hills &
Darlinghurst**
Sydney's hippest eating
and drinking precinct;
heart of the LGBT+ scene.

Best For LGBT+ travel,
foodies

Transport Short walk or
bus to city centre

Price Midrange

Northern Beaches

A string of marvellous beaches with a buzzy summer scene, but it's a long way from the city.

Best For Camping

Transport One bus to the city

Price Budget and midrange

Northern Beaches (5km)

Manly

Manly

Beautiful beaches and a community feel, wiht both harbour and ocean on hand.

Best For Families, surfers, backpackers

Transport Ferry to the centre

Price Budget and midrange

City Centre & Haymarket

Good transport links, lots of sights, numerous bars and fantastic Asian restaurants.

Best For Business travellers, shoppers

Transport Great connections to the rest of Sydney

Price Midrange to top end, some budget

Sydney Harbourside

Waterfront choices in a range of picturesque suburbs around the harbour.

Best For Romantic weekends

Transport Ferries to centre

Price Mostly top end

Sydney Harbourside

Kings Cross & Potts Point

Interesting and idiosyncratic; numberous hostels, bars and clubs; good transport links. Still some sleaze.

Best For Backpackers

Transport Short train ride to centre

Price Budget

Kings Cross & Potts Point

Bondi, Coogee & the Eastern Beaches

Sand, surf and good times at this string of brilliant beaches.

Best For Surfers, people-watchers, families

Transport Slow bus to city centre

Price Budget to top end

Paddington & Centennial Park

Leafy and genteel with boutique shopping and gourmet food. Not many accommodation options.

Best For Glitz and glamour

Transport Bus to city centre

Price Midrange

Paddington & Centennial Park

Bondi, Coogee & the Eastern Beaches

Bondi

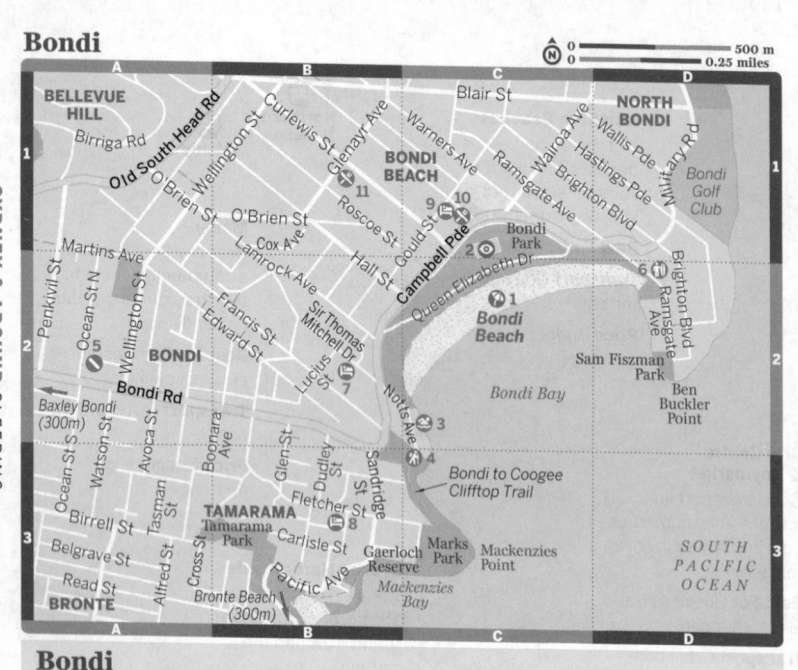

Bondi

areas. Even so, the supply shrivels up under the summer sun, particularly around weekends and big events, so be sure to book ahead. Prices, even in the budget class, are high; city-centre hotels charge stratospheric rates.

🛏 Circular Quay & the Rocks

★ **Sydney Harbour YHA**　　　HOSTEL **$**
(☑ 02-8272 0900; www.yha.com.au; 110 Cumberland St; dm $41-69, d $165-250; ⊜ ❄ @ ☎; ☒ Wynyard)
🖊 Any qualms about the prices will be shelved the moment you head up to the ample rooftop space of this sprawling, modern hostel and see the superb views of Circular Quay. Very well run, the hostel has spacious en-suite four-

and six-berth dorms and a selection of decent-value-for-Sydney private rooms.

Harbour Rocks Hotel　　　BOUTIQUE HOTEL **$$**
(☑ 02-8220 9999; www.harbourrocks.com.au; 34 Harrington St; r $269-449; ⊜ ❄ @ ☎; ☒ Circular Quay) This deluxe boutique hotel on the site of Sydney's first hospital has undergone a chic and sympathetic transformation from a colonial warehouse and workers' cottages to a series of New York loft–style rooms, with high ceilings, distressed brick and elegant furnishings. It maintains a historic feel and has a great little garden balcony terrace. Superior rooms are worth the upgrade.

Pullman Quay Grand Sydney Harbour APARTMENT $$$
(☑ 02-9256 4000; www.pullmanquaygrandsyd neyharbour.com; 61 Macquarie St; apt $550-800; ⓟ☒⏣◉ 🛈⏥; ◨Circular Quay) With the Opera House as its neighbour, the building complex known locally as 'The Toaster' has a scorching-hot location. These large, well-equipped and well-designed contemporary apartments set you in Sydney's glitzy heart, encircled by top restaurants, cocktail bars and that attention-seeking harbour. The small number of rooms and blend of residents and visitors gives it a quiet ambience.

Lord Nelson Brewery Hotel PUB $$
(☑ 02-9251 4044; www.lordnelsonbrewery.com; 19 Kent St; r incl breakfast $210-250; ⏥☒🛈; ◨Circular Quay) Built in 1836, this atmospheric sandstone pub has a tidy set of seven upstairs rooms, with exposed stone walls and dormer windows with harbour glimpses. Rooms are all en suite; one is smaller and cheaper than the others. The downstairs microbrewery is a welcoming place for a pint and a meal. Rates include a continental breakfast.

Park Hyatt HOTEL $$$
(☑ 02-9256 1234; www.hyatt.com; 7 Hickson Rd; r $1200-1800; ⓟ⏥☒◉🛈⏥; ◨Circular Quay) At Sydney's most expensive hotel the impeccable service and facilities are second to none, as is the location on the waterfront promenade. With full-frontal views across Circular Quay, you can catch all the action from your bed, balcony or bathtub. From the rooftop pool it feels as if you could almost touch the Harbour Bridge. A most luxurious urban experience.

🛏 City Centre & Haymarket

★**Railway Square YHA** HOSTEL $
(☑ 02-9281 9666; www.yha.com.au; 8-10 Lee St; dm $33-44, d $112-144; ⏥☒@🛈; ◨Central) 🏄 A lovely piece of industrial renovation has converted Central Station's former parcel shed into a really appealing and relaxing hostel, in a great location but away from the bustle. Dorms with corrugated roofs and underfloor-heated bathrooms are spotless; some are actually in converted train carriages. There's a cafe with cheap lunch and dinner deals, as well as daily activities and laundry facilities.

★**Sydney Central YHA** HOSTEL $
(☑ 02-9218 9000; www.yha.com.au; 11 Rawson Pl; dm $36-54, d $100-140; ⓟ⏥☒@🛈⏥; ◨Haymarket, ◨Central) 🏄 By Central Station, this

565-bed mega-hostel has brilliant facilities, including a travel agent, help with organising working holidays, workspaces for digital nomads and a rooftop pool. Dorms and private rooms are spacious, with colourful murals and thoughtful features like charging points in lockers. Kitchens are fab; there's also an on-site cafe with cheap meal deals, a bar, and loads of activities on offer.

Primus Hotel Sydney HOTEL $$
(☑ 02-8027 8000; www.primushotelsydney.com; 339 Pitt St; r $220-380; ⓟ⏥☒🛈⏥; ◨Town Hall) In the former Water Board building, this slick conversion has a magnificent lobby with red pillars and glorious art deco details. There's space to spare here, with wide corridors and ample, commodious rooms; excellent service is a noteworthy feature. Though the pool itself is tiny, the deck surrounding it is a fabulous spot; the bar here is open to the public.

★**QT Sydney** BOUTIQUE HOTEL $$$
(☑ 02-8262 0000; www.qthotelsandresorts.com/ sydney-cbd; 49 Market St; r $360-540; ⓟ⏥ ☒@🛈; ◨Queen Victoria Building, ◨Town Hall) Fun, sexy and relaxed, this ultra-theatrical, effortlessly cool hotel is located in the historic **State Theatre** (☑ box office 13 61 00; www. statetheatre.com.au; 49 Market St; tours adult/ child $25/17; ☉ tours 10am and/or 1pm, usually on Mon, Tue or Wed; ◨Town Hall) complex. Art deco eccentricity is complemented by quirky extras in the rooms, which are distinct and decorated with real style and flair – there's a definite wow factor. Service is personable and upbeat; there's also a luxurious spa plus a fashionable bar and restaurant.

Establishment Hotel BOUTIQUE HOTEL $$$
(☑ 02-9240 3100; www.merivale.com.au; 5 Bridge Lane; r $380-600; ⏥☒🛈; ◨Wynyard) In a discreet laneway, this designer boutique hotel in a refurbished 19th-century warehouse evokes Asia with its incense aromas and dark-wood fittings. There are two principal room styles: 'light' (all white-and-tan contemporary colouring) and sexier 'dark' (with wooden floorboards and a nocturnal feel). Decadent nights out are assured with the hotel owners' numerous acclaimed bars and restaurants.

🛏 Darling Harbour & Pyrmont

★**Ovolo 1888**
Darling Harbour BOUTIQUE HOTEL $$
(☑ 02-8586 1888; www.ovolohotels.com.au; 139 Murray St, Pyrmont; r $239-539; ⏥☒@🛈⏥; ◨Convention) In a heritage-listed wool store, this

Sydney's Beaches

Whether you join the procession of the bronzed and the beautiful at Bondi, or surreptitiously slink into a deserted nook hidden within Sydney Harbour National Park, the beach is an essential part of the Sydney experience. Even in winter, watching the rollers break while you're strolling along the sand is exhilarating.

Where to Go

Sydney's ocean beaches divide into the eastern beaches, south of the harbour, running from Bondi southwards as far as Botany Bay; and the northern beaches, north of the harbour, starting at Manly and ending at Palm Beach. The numerous harbour beaches are mostly east of the bridge on both the north and south sides.

Beach Culture

For Australians, going to the beach is all about rolling out a towel on the sand with a minimum of fuss. And they're certainly not prepared to pay for the privilege; you won't find loungers or parasols for rent here, let alone bars.

Surf life-savers have a hallowed place in the culture and you'd do well to heed their instructions, not least of all because they're likely to be in your best interests. Surf Life Saving Clubs are an Australian institution; swim between the flags and they'll be watching over your safety.

Ocean Pools

If you have children, shark paranoia, or surf just isn't your thing, you'll be pleased to hear that Sydney's blessed with a string of 40 artificial ocean pools up and down the coast, most of them free. Some,

1. Manly Beach (p73)
2. Bondi Icebergs pool (p77)
3. Palm Beach (p74)

like **Mahon Pool** (www.randwick.nsw.gov.au; Marine Pde, Maroubra; ☐353, 376-77) FREE, are what are known as bogey holes – natural-looking rock pools where you can safely splash about and snorkel, even while the surf surges in. Others are more like swimming pools; **Bondi Icebergs** (☏02-9130 4804; www.icebergs.com.au; 1 Notts Ave, Bondi Beach; adult/child $9/6; ⊗6am-6.30pm Mon-Wed & Fri, from 6.30am Sat & Sun; ⊞; ☐333) is a good example of this type. It normalls closes one day a week so the seaweed can be cleaned out.

Harbour Beaches & Pools

The pick of Sydney's harbour beaches includes Camp Cove and Lady Bay near South Head (the latter is mainly a gay nude beach), Shark Beach at Nielsen Park in Vaucluse, and Balmoral Beach on the North Shore. Also popular are the netted swimming enclosures at Cremorne Point on the North Shore and Murray Rose Pool near Double Bay. There are plenty of little sandy gems scattered about that even Sydneysiders would be hard-pressed to find, including Parsley Bay and Milk Beach right in the heart of residential Vaucluse.

Beaches by Neighbourhood

Sydney Harbour Lots of hidden coves and secret sandy spots; the best sites are out near the heads and around Mosman.

Eastern Beaches High cliffs frame a string of surf beaches, with excellent coffee and cold beer just a short stumble away.

Northern Beaches A steady succession of magical surf beaches stretching 30km north from Manly to Palm Beach.

SYDNEY & AROUND SLEEPING

stylish gem combines industrial minimalism with the warmth of ironbark-wood beams, luxury appointments and engaged staff. Rooms range from the aptly named Shoebox to airy lofts and attic suites with harbour views. Booking direct earns you a free minibar, breakfast buffet and a daily happy hour in the jazzy downstairs wine bar, **Mister Percy**.

Kings Cross & Potts Point

Blue Parrot Backpackers HOSTEL **$**
(☑02-9356 4888; www.blueparrot.com.au; 87 Macleay St, Potts Point; dm $35-46; ☺@� ; ☒Kings Cross) This colourful hostel is the antithesis of some of the backpacker barns around the Cross, offering a warm, personal experience that feels more like a share-house (but much cleaner!). There's a great back courtyard and high-ceilinged dorms with good bunks and mattresses. Netflix, PlayStation, free SIM cards and a BBQ add points. For 18- to 35-year-olds only.

Mad Monkey Bayswater HOSTEL **$**
(☑02-9331 0520; www.madmonkey.com.au; 79 Bayswater Rd, Kings Cross; dm $31-42; ☺✻@☞; ☒Kings Cross) Nicely set in a quieter part of the Cross, this is a well-run, fun-oriented place with fan-cooled dorms that sleep four to 12 and come with lockers and under-bed storage. The kitchen-lounge and sweet roof terrace are the places to hang out. Security is good and the price fair. Breakfast is included and there are regular activities from yoga to BBQs.

Hotel 59 GUESTHOUSE **$**
(☑02-9360 5900; www.hotel59.com.au; 59 Bayswater Rd, Kings Cross; s $110, d $140-150; ☺✻☞; ☒Kings Cross) With just nine simple, spot-less, comfortable rooms, family-run Hotel 59 offers great value on a quiet but still very convenient part of Bayswater Rd. A good breakfast is available in their downstairs cafe for $8.50.

The Macleay APARTMENT **$$**
(☑02-9357 7755; www.themacleay.com; 28 Macleay St, Elizabeth Bay; apt $180-280; P☺✻@☞☒; ☒Kings Cross) This understated place is at the posh end of Kings Cross, surrounded by fabulous restaurants. The studios are a little faded, but all have small kitchenettes and there's a laundry on each floor. An added plus is the rooftop pool and gym. Staff are welcoming and helpful; it's worth upgrading to the city- and harbour-view rooms on higher floors.

★**Ovolo Hotel Woolloomooloo** HOTEL **$$$**
(☑02-9331 9000; www.ovolohotels.com.au; 6 Cowper Wharf Rdwy, Woolloomooloo; r $400-700; P☺✻@☞☒; ☐311, ☒Kings Cross) Superbly set in Woolloomooloo Wharf, this excellent smart-casual hotel has extremely friendly staff and very likeable features. 'Superoo' rooms are mostly either road-facing or skylit, so for water views upgrade to a 'deluxe' (facing east) or 'city' (facing west) room. It's ultra characterful with long corridors, industrial machinery and unusually shaped, artfully designed rooms, some split-level. A Sydney standout.

If you book direct, there are nice touches such as a complimentary minibar, breakfast thrown in, and a free happy hour in the bar.

Surry Hills & Darlinghurst

Big Hostel HOSTEL **$**
(☑02-9281 6030; www.bighostel.com; 212 Elizabeth St, Surry Hills; dm $35-40, s/tw/d $109/120/130; ☺✻@☞; ☒Central) A bright and breezy, no-frills hostel with a rooftop terrace and a crowded but decent communal area and 24-hour kitchen. Dorms do the job, with lockers, high ceilings and enough space. The four-bed ones cost a little more but have a bathroom and small TV. The price is good for central Sydney; continental breakfast is included.

57 Hotel HOTEL **$**
(☑02-9011 5757; www.57hotel.com.au; 57 Foveaux St, Surry Hills; s $100-150, d $115-190; ☺✻☞; ☒Central) Converted from a technical college, this business hotel goes to town on modish grey, black and chocolate colouring. Rooms vary widely, from the extremely compact 'shoebox' twins (from $115) to large, light king-bedded rooms on the corners of the building. Free coffee

and morning pastries are great for a quick breakfast on the hoof.

★ **Little Albion**   BOUTIQUE HOTEL **$$**
(📞02-8029 7900; www.littlealbion.com.au; 21 Little Albion St, Surry Hills; r incl breakfast $270-800; ❂❄🅿🛜🅿; 🚆Central) This boutique hotel combines an attractive heritage building with a more modern development to great design success. Rooms range from compact 'crash pads' to generous suites; characterful art in the public spaces leans more towards Albion St's gangster and brothel heritage than this former convent's history. A great honesty-bar area encourages socialising and there's a gorgeous rooftop garden.

★ **ADGE Boutique Apartment Hotel**   APARTMENT **$$$**
(📞02-8093 9888; www.adgehotel.com.au; 222 Riley St, Surry Hills; apt $350-700; 🅿❂❄🛜; 🚆301, 302, 352, 🚆Central) Modern, catchy and bold, ADGE puts a clever, upbeat twist on the ubiquitous serviced apartment experience. The idiosyncratic but extremely comfortable two-bedroom apartments have gloriously striped liquorice-all-sorts carpets, floor-to-ceiling windows, quality kitchens with Smeg fridges and appealing balconies. Little extras, including a welcome drink, add a wonderful touch. It's an ideal urban experience and great value for two couples.

🛏 Bondi, Coogee & the Eastern Beaches

★ **Baxley Bondi**   BOUTIQUE HOTEL **$**
(📞02-9388 0895; www.thebaxleybondi.com; 44 Flood St, Bondi; d from $170, s/d without bathroom from $104/126; ❂❄🛜; 🚆333, 380, 381, 🚆Bondi Junction) Halfway between the beach and Bondi Junction train station (10 to 15 minutes' walk to either) this pleasantly scented guesthouse is great value. Rooms are small (the building used to be a hostel) but the recent refit is stylish and contemporary, with quality linen and an airy blue-and-white theme. All rooms have sinks, kettles and fridges. Prices drop in low season.

Bondi Beachouse YHA   HOSTEL **$**
(📞02-9365 2088; www.yha.com.au; 63 Fletcher St, Tamarama; dm $30-36, tw & d without bathroom $90, d/f $110/162; ❂🛜; 🚆333, 380, 381) Perched on a hillside between Bondi and Tamarama Beaches, this 95-bed hostel has fan-cooled dorms that sleep four to eight and come with bright colours, wooden

floors and spacious lockers. Some of the private rooms have ocean views – all are clean and well maintained. Facilities include surfboard hire, cinema room, courtyard barbecue and a beanbag-strewn rooftop with million-dollar views.

★ **Bondi Beach House**   GUESTHOUSE **$$**
(📞02-9300 0369; www.bondibeachhouse.com.au; 28 Sir Thomas Mitchell Rd, Bondi Beach; s from $130, d $160-340; 🅿❂❄🛜; 🚆333) In a tranquil pocket behind Campbell Pde, this charming place offers a homey atmosphere decorated in beachy-botanical style with rustic-chic furnishings. Though only a two-minute walk from the beach, you may well be tempted to stay in all day – the courtyard and terrace are great spots for relaxing, and the breezily arty rooms are conducive to long sleep-ins.

Dive Hotel   BOUTIQUE HOTEL **$$**
(📞02-9665 5538; www.divehotel.com.au; 234 Arden St, Coogee; standard r from $230, ocean-view r from $355; 🅿❂❄@🛜; 🚆313, 314, 353, 372, 373) In a cracking location right across the road from the beach, this relaxed, family-run affair is, thankfully, very inaccurately named. Simple, likeable contemporary rooms come with fridges, microwaves and small stylish bathrooms. A sociable continental buffet breakfast (included) in an appealing indoor-outdoor area is a highlight, as are the personable owners.

★ **QT Bondi**   APARTMENT **$$$**
(📞02-8362 3900; www.qtbondi.com.au; 6 Beach Rd, Bondi Beach; apt $459-900; 🅿❂❄🛜🛋; 🚆333) Colourful, chic and appropriately beachy, this apartment hotel is steps from the sand and offers an appealing combination of facilities, location and chatty staff. All the rooms and suites are spacious, with light-coloured furniture and an airy feel. King Deluxe rooms and above have balconies, but there are no ocean views. Price can halve in low season.

🛏 Sydney Harbourside

★ **Cockatoo Island**   CAMPGROUND **$**
(📞02-8969 2111; www.cockatooisland.gov.au; campsites $45-50, simple tents $89-99, 2-bed tents $130-175, apt/house from $265/625; 🛜; 🚢Cockatoo Island) Waking up on an island (p71) in the middle of the harbour is an extraordinary Sydney experience. Bring a tent (or just sleeping bags) or 'glamp' in a two-person tent (with stretcher beds) on the water's edge.

Paddington & Centennial Park

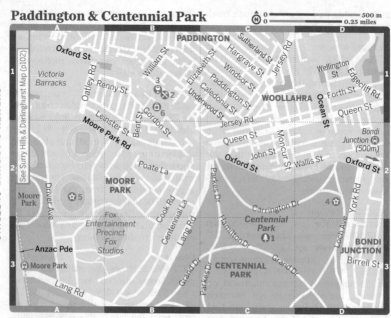

Paddington & Centennial Park

Non-campers will enjoy the elegant houses and apartments. For self-caterers, there's a well-equipped camp kitchen; for everyone else, there are two cafe-bars.

★**Watsons Bay**
Boutique Hotel   BOUTIQUE HOTEL **$$$**
(☑02-9337 5444; www.watsonsbayhotel.com.au; 1 Military Rd, Watsons Bay; d from $299, with harbour view from $329, ste from $489; P❄✳☎; ☒324, 325, 380, ⛴Watsons Bay) Often filled with wedding parties, or Watsons Bay locals who are renovating, this personable hotel is a great place to slip into the barefoot-millionaire vibe of this secluded Sydney neighbourhood. The ferry pulls up right outside and rooms are light and super-spacious with a lounge area and slick, glassed-in en suites; many have balconies. Rates include breakfast, bikes and beach towels.

🛏 Newtown & the Inner West

Village   HOSTEL **$**
(☑02-9660 8133; www.thevillagehostels.com.au; 256 Glebe Pt Rd, Glebe; dm/r from $18/74; ✳☎; ☒431, 433, ☒Jubilee Park) Located in a quiet, but still central, part of town, this pleasant hostel has simple, clean, four- to 12-bed dorms (including one for women only) and basic en-suite rooms. There's also a TV room, big communal kitchen, pool table and free barbecues on Fridays. A lovely tree-shaded courtyard offers relaxing space and period details like stained-glass windows add charm.

St Paul's Serviced Apartments APARTMENT **$$**
(☑02-9550 7440; www.stpaulseventsandstays. com.au; 9 City Rd, Camperdown; s without bathroom from $110, d $220-280, 2-bed apt $160-260; P❄✳☎; ☒423, 426, 428) Get your Harry Potter on at Sydney University's first college

(dating from 1857), featuring gracious sandstone buildings and well-tended gardens. Single rooms in the ivy-clad heritage buildings are popular with nostalgic alumni returning for a lecturing gig, while the modern wing (built in 2018) has contemporary rooms with kitchenettes and a rooftop common area with an open fire and great views.

Old Clare Hotel BOUTIQUE HOTEL **$$$**
(☑02-8277 8277; www.theoldclarehotel.com.au; 1 Kensington St, Chippendale; r $250-500, ste from $650; P❄☀🐾🛜; ☒Central) A sensitive brewery-office conversion is now a 69-room hotel in a primo Chippendale location. Rooms are well back from noisy Broadway, high-ceilinged and easy on the eye, with artful bespoke details such as lamps made of salvaged toolshed paraphernalia. Superior room categories are much larger, but the cheapest rooms still have king beds, attractive amenities and a good sense of space.

Manly

Manly Bunkhouse HOSTEL **$**
(☑02-9976 0472; www.bunkhouse.com.au; 35 Pine St; dm/d $45/118; P❄@🛜; ☒151, 158, 159, 🚲Manly) An easy walk from the beach, this laid-back hostel has a distinct surf vibe. High-ceilinged en-suite dorms have modern furnishings, plenty of room to move and lots of storage space, making them popular with long-termers. Private rooms (also en-suite) are a great deal. There's a surfboard rack and bodyboards and snorkels are available, and there's a top backyard with a BBQ.

Q Station LODGE **$$**
(☑02-9466 1500; www.qstation.com.au; 1 North Head Scenic Dr; r $250-450; P❄☀🛜; ☒135, 🚲Manly) Hidden away in shrubland rolling down to a beautiful harbour beach, the former quarantine station (p74) offers a wide variety of accommodation. Minibuses shuttle you around this sizeable complex of historic buildings; rooms have their own balconies and many have harbour views. Kayaks, bikes and snorkels are available, and there's an on-site cafe and restaurant. It's an out-of-the-way, utterly relaxing spot.

Eating

Sydney's cuisine is exceptional and rivals that of any great world city. The city truly celebrates Australia's place on the Pacific Rim, marrying the freshest local ingredients – excellent seafood is a particular highlight – with

the flavours of Asia, the Mediterranean, the Americas and, of course, its colonial past. Sydneysiders are real foodies, always seeking out the latest hot restaurant.

Sydney's top restaurants are pricey, but eating out needn't be expensive. There are plenty of budget places where you can grab a cheap, zingy pizza or a bowl of noodles. Cafes are a good bet for a solid, often adventurous and usually reasonably priced meal. Pubs either do reliable standard fare, often with excellent prices, or casual but high-quality Modern Australian dining. The numerous BYO (bring your own alcohol) restaurants offer a substantially cheaper eating experience; Inner West Sydney is brimful of them.

Circular Quay & the Rocks

There are several upmarket places in this area, many with winning water views. There are also quite a few mediocre spots feeding off visitors. This most touristy of precincts is also one of the priciest.

★Fine Food Store CAFE **$**
(☑02-9252 1196; www.finefoodstore.com; cnr Mill & Kendall Lanes; light meals $10-19; ⏰7am-4pm Mon-Sat, from 7.30am Sun; 🛜🍴; ☒Circular Quay) The Rocks sometimes seems like it's all pubs, so it's a delight to find this contemporary cafe that serves a better, cheaper breakfast than your hotel. Staff are genuinely welcoming, make very respectable coffee and offer delicious panini, sandwiches, brunches and generously proportioned cocktails. The outside tables on this narrow lane are the spot to be.

★Quay MODERN AUSTRALIAN **$$$**
(☑02-9251 5600; www.quay.com.au; Level 3, Overseas Passenger Terminal, Circular Quay West; 6-/10-course degustation $240/295; ⏰6-9pm Mon-Thu, noon-1.30pm & 6-9pm Fri-Sun; ☒Circular Quay) What many consider to be Sydney's best restaurant matches a peerless bridge view with brilliant food. Chef Peter Gilmore never rests on his laurels, consistently delivering exquisitely crafted, adventurous cuisine, coaxing unlikely bedfellows such as abalone and pig cheek into perfect matches. It's polished but never prissy. Book online in advance.

★Aria MODERN AUSTRALIAN **$$$**
(☑02-9240 2255; www.ariasydney.com.au; 1 Macquarie St; 3-/4-course dinner $150/175, degustation $210; ⏰noon-2.15pm & 5.30-10.30pm Mon-Fri, noon-1.30pm & 5-11pm Sat, noon-2.15pm & 5.30-10pm Sun; ☒Circular Quay) Aria is a star in Sydney's

🏃 City Walk
Bondi to Coogee Clifftop Trail

START BONDI BEACH
END COOGEE BEACH
LENGTH 6KM; TWO TO THREE HOURS

Sydney's most famous and most popular walk, this coastal path really shouldn't be missed. Both ends are well connected to bus routes, as are most points in between should you feel too hot and bothered to continue – although a cooling dip at any of the beaches en route should cure that (pack your swimmers). There's little shade on this track, so make sure you dive into a tub of sunscreen before setting out. A hat's also a good idea.

Starting at iconic **1 Bondi Beach** (p69), take the stairs up the south end to Notts Ave, passing above the glistening **2 Icebergs** (p77) pool complex. Step onto the clifftop trail at the end of Notts Ave.

Walking south, the windswept sandstone cliffs and boisterous Pacific Ocean couldn't be more spectacular (watch for dolphins, whales and surfers). Small but perfectly formed **3 Tamarama** has a deep reach of sand that is totally disproportionate to its width.

Descend from the clifftops onto **4 Bronte Beach**. Take a dip, lay out a picnic under the Norfolk Island pines or head to a cafe for a caffeine hit. After your break, pick up the path on the southern side of the beach.

Some famous Australians are among the subterranean denizens of the amazing cliffedge **5 Waverley Cemetery**. On a clear winter's day this is a prime vantage point for whale-watchers.

Pass the locals enjoying a beer or a game of lawn bowls at the **6 Clovelly Bowling Club**, then breeze past the cockatoos and canoodling lovers at **7 Burrows Park** to sheltered **8 Clovelly Beach**.

Follow the footpath up around the car park then down the steps to the upturned dinghies lining **9 Gordons Bay** (p75), one of Sydney's best shore-dive spots.

The trail continues past **10 Dolphins Point**, which offers great ocean views, then lands you smack-bang on glorious **11 Coogee Beach**. Swagger into the Coogee Pavilion (p105) and toast your efforts with a cold beverage.

fine-dining firmament, an award-winning combination of chef Joel Bickford's stellar dishes, floor-to-ceiling windows staring straight at the Opera House, a stylishly renovated interior and faultless service. A good-value pre- and post-theatre menu is perfect for a special meal before or after a night at the Opera House (two/three courses $90/120).

City Centre & Haymarket

Chinatown is your best bet for a cheap, satisfying meal – especially late at night. Chinese food dominates, but you'll also find superb Vietnamese, Malaysian, Japanese, Korean and Thai. There's also a Koreatown along Pitt St near Liverpool St, and a Thaitown on Campbell St.

★ Gumshara
RAMEN $

(☑ 0410 253 180; Shop 211, 25-29 Dixon St; ramen $12-19; ⊙ 11.30am-9pm Tue-Sat, to 8.30pm Sun & Mon; 🚇 Paddy's Markets, 🚉 Central) Prepare to queue for some of Sydney's best broth at this cordial ramen house in a popular but unglamorous Chinatown budget-price food court. They boil down over 100kg of pork bones a week to make the gloriously thick and sticky liquid. There are lots of options, including some that pack quite a punch. Ask for extra back fat for a real indulgence.

Pablo & Rusty's
CAFE $

(☑ 02-9283 9543; www.pabloandrustys.com.au; 161 Castlereagh St; lunches $9-25; ⊙ 6.30am-5pm Mon-Fri, 8am-3pm Sat, 9am-3pm Sun; 🖥 🍴 ; 🚉 Town Hall) Mega-busy and loud, with close-packed tables, this excellent cafe is high energy. The inviting wood-and-brick decor and seriously good coffee (several single-origins available daily) are complemented by a range of appealing, generously proportioned breakfast and lunch specials, ranging from large sourdough sandwiches to wholesome, globally influenced combos featuring on-trend ingredients. Try to visit off-peak. No cash accepted.

Cross Eatery
CAFE $

(☑ 02-9279 4280; www.facebook.com/crosseatery; 155 Clarence St; light meals $10-16, mains $20-25; ⊙ 7am-4pm Mon-Fri; 🖥 🍴 ; 🚉 Wynyard) Given so many tiny, jam-packed cafes around, it's very pleasant to cruise in here and enjoy a bit of elbow room. Set in the lobby of an office building, there's space to spare and a bright, luminous ambience. Come for coffee and good-value, healthy breakfasts and lunches. Add daily salad specials to creative mains or munch tasty ciabatta rolls and sandwiches.

★ Mr Wong
CHINESE $$

(☑ 02-9114 7317; www.merivale.com.au/mrwong; 3 Bridge Lane; mains $26-56; ⊙ lunch noon-3pm Mon-Fri, 10.30am-3pm Sat & Sun, dinner 5.30-11pm Mon-Wed, to midnight Thu-Sat, to 10pm Sun; 🖥 🍴 ; 🚉 Wynyard) Classy but comfortable in an attractive, low-lit space on a central business district (CBD) laneway, this place has exposed-brick colonial warehouse chic, a huge team of staff and hanging ducks in the open kitchen. Lunchtime dim sum offerings bristle with flavour and the salads are mouth-freshening sensations. Mains such as crispy pork hock are sinfully sticky, while the Peking duck pancake rolls are legendary.

Restaurant Hubert
FRENCH $$

(☑ 02-9232 0881; www.restauranthubert.com; 15 Bligh St; mains $20-50; ⊙ 4pm-1am Mon-Sat, plus noon-3pm Thu & Fri; 🚉 Martin Place) The memorable descent into the sexy old-time ambience plunges you straight from suity Sydney into a 1930s movie. Delicious French fare comes in old-fashioned portions – think terrine, black pudding or escargots, plus a few more avant-garde creations. Candlelit tables and a long whisky-backed counter provide seating. There's no bookings for small groups, so wait it out in the bar area.

Ho Jiak
MALAYSIAN $$

(☑ 02-8040 0252; www.hojiak.com.au; 92 Hay St; mains $25-48; ⊙ 11am-midnight Mon-Sat, 11am-10pm Sun; 🚇 Paddy's Markets) Drawing on Penang home-cooking and street-food traditions, this is a wonderful den of aromas and flavours. Satisfying bowls of noodles come with rich seafood broth, while Wagyu rendang or crispy fish skin with runny duck egg are deliciously comforting dishes. Decadent milky concoctions and decent wines back up the food. There are so much here that you're bound to want to return.

Mercado
MODERN AUSTRALIAN $$

(☑ 02-9221 6444; www.mercadorestaurant.com.au; 4 Ash St; share plates $27-48; ⊙ lunch noon-2.30pm Mon-Fri, dinner 5.30-9.30pm Mon, to 10pm Tue-Thu, to 10.30pm Fri & Sat; 🚉 Wynyard) Set in a busy, buzzy basement, Mercado riffs on Spanish themes to produce an excellent menu of tapas-style dishes backed up by succulent spit-roasted meats. The chef produces cheeses and smoked meats on-site, and the generous depth of flavour in their inventive creations is truly impressive. An interesting selection of Spanish wine is a bonus.

Newtown & the Inner West

Grounds of the City
CAFE $$

(☑02-9699 2235; www.thegrounds.com.au; 500 George St; mains $25-35; ☺7am-5pm Mon, 7am-9pm Tue-Thu, 7am-10pm Fri, 8am-10pm Sat, 8am-9pm Sun; ☎; ☒Town Hall) Peddling everything from takeaway snacks and scientifically roast-ed coffee to fuller meals and cocktails in a striking curiosity-shop interior, this place rep-resents a significant, modern bohemian style conquest of the somewhat staid CBD fortress. There's an amazing range of quality eating and drinking, from freshly baked breakfast rolls to flower-strewn gin concoctions, gen-erous mains like bouillabaisse, and delights wheeled around on the dessert trolley.

Chat Thai
THAI $$

(☑02-9211 1808; www.chatthai.com.au; 20 Camp-bell St; mains $14-34; ☺10am-2am; ☑; ☒Capitol Square, ☒Central) Cooler than your average Thai joint, this Thaitown linchpin is so pop-ular that a list is posted outside for you to affix your name to should you want a table. Expat Thais flock here for the dishes that don't make it on to your average suburban Thai restaurant menu – particularly the more unusual sweets.

Sydney Madang
KOREAN $$

(☑02-9264 7010; www.facebook.com/madang 2006; 371a Pitt St; mains $17-26; ☺11.30am-2am;

extraordinary restaurant is for those seeking a culinary journey rather than a simple stuffed belly. Settle in for 10-plus courses of French- and Japanese-inflected food from the genius of legendary Sydney chef Tetsuya Wakuda. It's all great, but the seafood is sublime. Excellent wine list. Book well ahead.

★**Azuma**   JAPANESE $$$
(📞02-9222 9960; www.azuma.com.au; Level 1, Chifley Plaza, Hunter St; mains $33-57, tasting menus $88-115; ⊗noon-2.30pm & 6-10pm Mon-Fri, 6-10pm Sat; ℝMartin Place) Tucked away upstairs in Chifley Plaza, this is one of Sydney's finest Japanese restaurants. Sushi and sashimi are of stellar quality and too pretty to eat – almost. Other options include sukiyaki and hot-pot DIY dishes and excellent tasting menus. It's a great place to get acquainted with high-class modern Japanese fare. It also has moreish sake by the carafe.

🍴 Darling Harbour & Pyrmont

Rows of restaurants line Darling Harbour, many of them pairing their sea views with seafood. Most are pricey, tourist-driven affairs that are OK but not outstanding, but Barangaroo South has upped the ante, serving quality meals to local businessfolk. Over in Pyrmont, the Star has sought to assert itself as a fine-dining destination, luring many a gifted restaurateur. There are some truly excellent restaurants here, but the shopping-mall atmosphere won't be for everyone.

★**LuMi**   ITALIAN $$$
(📞02-9571 1999; www.lumidining.com; 56 Pirrama Rd, Pyrmont; tasting menus $155-185; ⊗6.30-10.30pm Wed & Thu, noon-2.30pm & 6-10.30pm Fri & Sat, noon-2.30pm & 6.30-10.30pm Sun; 🔊; 🚢Pyrmont Bay, 🚟The Star) This wharf spot sits alongside bobbing boats, though views aren't quite knock-me-down. Just steps from the Star Casino, it offers strikingly innovative Italian-Japanese cuisine in an atmosphere of casual competence. Degustations are a tour de force; memorable creations include extraordinary pasta dishes. The open kitchen is always entertaining, service is smart, and both the wine and sake lists are great.

Cirrus   SEAFOOD $$$
(📞02-9220 0111; www.cirrusdining.com.au; 10/23 Barangaroo Ave; mains $40-52; ⊗noon-3pm & 6-10.30pm; 🚢Barangaroo, 🚟Wynyard) 🌿 The curved glass windows of this excellent Barangaroo seafood restaurant offer a water

ℝMuseum) Down a teensy Koreatown lane is this alleyway gem – an authentic, good-value BBQ joint that's low on interior charisma but high on quality and quantity. Noisy, cramped and chaotic, yes, but the chilli seafood soup will have you coming back. Try the delicious cold noodles too. Prepare to queue at weekends.

★**Tetsuya's**   FRENCH, JAPANESE $$$
(📞02-9267 2900; www.tetsuyas.com; 529 Kent St; degustation menu $240, matching wines from $125; ⊗5.30-10pm Tue-Fri, noon-3pm & 6.30-10pm Sat; ℝTown Hall) Concealed in a villa behind a historic cottage amid the high-rises, this

Newtown & the Inner West

view more ambient than spectacular, but the tinny (a simple fishing boat) suspended from the ceiling hints at another focus. Sustainably sourced fish and extremely tasty molluscs and crustaceans form the backbone of the menu, which features dishes with exquisite flavour pairings and presentation, designed to share. Outdoor seating is available.

Kings Cross & Potts Point

Room 10   CAFE $
(☑ 0432 445 342; www.facebook.com/room10e spresso; 10 Llankelly Pl, Kings Cross; mains $8-15; ☺ 7am-4pm Mon-Fri, from 8am Sat & Sun; ☑; ☷ Kings Cross) With a real neighbourhood feel, this tiny cafe is the sort of place where staff know all the locals by name. The coffee is delicious and the menu is limited to sandwiches, salads and such – tasty and uncomplicated. Watch them make it in front of you as you sit at impossibly tiny tables, or do some people-watching on the lovable laneway.

Farmhouse   MODERN AUSTRALIAN $$
(☑ 0448 413 791; www.farmhousekingscross. com.au; 4/40 Bayswater Rd, Kings Cross; set menu $65; ☺ sittings 6.30pm & 8.30pm Wed-Sat, 2pm & 6.30pm Sun; ☷ Kings Cross) Occupying a space between restaurant and supper club, this narrow sliver of a place has a tiny kitchen and charming hospitality. Diners sit at one long table and eat a set menu that features uncomplicated, delicious dishes made from high-quality produce. There are good wines and a buzzy, fun atmosphere. Prebooking is essential.

Fratelli Paradiso   ITALIAN $$
(☑ 02-9357 1744; www.fratelliparadiso.com; 12-16 Challis Ave, Potts Point; breakfast $12-17, mains $25-35; ☺ 7am-11pm Mon-Sat, to 10pm Sun; ☑ 311, ☷ Kings Cross) Striking a lovely balance between cosy neighbourhood trattoria and stylish upmarket restaurant, Paradiso offers very fairly priced, super-flavoursome dishes from a short, market-driven menu and a welcoming vibe despite the prowling fashionistas. The street-side tables are the place to be, whether for morning espresso or night-time feasting; the annexe is a bit less comfy than the main dining room. No bookings.

★ **Yellow**   VEGETARIAN $$$
(☑ 02-9332 2344; www.yellowsydney.com.au; 57 Macleay St, Potts Point; 5-/7-course degustation menu $85/105; ☺ 5-11pm Mon-Fri, 11am-2.30pm & 5-11pm Sat & Sun; ☑; ☑ 311, ☷ Kings Cross) This sunflower-yellow former artists' residence is now a top-notch contemporary vegetarian restaurant. Dishes are prepared with real panache; the tasting menus, which can be vegan, take the Sydney meat-free scene to new levels and the service is happily not too formal. A flight of delicious juice combinations is a fine accompaniment. Weekend brunch is also a highlight, as is the wine list.

Surry Hills & Darlinghurst

Scruffy Surry Hills' transformation into Sydney's foodie nirvana was sudden, roughly commencing with the 1999 opening of the Eastern Distributor motorway, which made peaceful tree-lined backstreets out of Crown and Bourke Sts (once the main routes to the airport). Some of the city's top-rated restaurants now inhabit surprising nooks amid terrace houses and former warehouses, with new places opening all the time. Cafes are another highlight, from hole-in-the-wall coffee innovators to decadent brunching spots.

⭐ **Bourke Street Bakery** BAKERY $
(☑ 02-9699 1011; www.bourkestreetbakery.com.au; 633 Bourke St, Surry Hills; items $5-12; ☉ 7am-6pm Mon-Fri, to 5pm Sat & Sun; ☑; ☐ 301, ☐ Surry Hills, ☐ Central) Queuing outside this teensy bakery, which has sprouted branches across the city, is an essential Surry Hills experience. It sells a tempting selection of pastries, cakes, bread and sandwiches, along with near-legendary sausage rolls. There are a couple of spots to sit inside, but on a fine day you're better off on the street. Check online for sourdough-bread-making classes.

Reuben Hills CAFE $
(☑ 02-9211 5556; www.reubenhills.com.au; 61 Albion St, Surry Hills; mains $9-22; ☉ 7am-4pm Mon-Fri, from 7.30am Sat & Sun; ☎ ☑; ☐ Central) An industrial design and creative Latin American menu await at Reuben Hills, set in a terraced house and its former garage. The star is the fantastic single-origin coffee, roasted on the premises, but the refreshing homemade *horchata* (rice milk), stellar fried chicken, tacos and *baleadas* (Honduran tortillas) are no slouches either.

Messina ICE CREAM $
(☑ 02-9331 1588; www.gelatomessina.com; 241 Victoria St, Darlinghurst; 1/2/3 scoops $5.30/6.80/8.80; ☉ noon-11pm Sun-Thu, to 11.30pm Fri & Sat; ☑; ☐ Kings Cross) Join the queues of people who look like they never eat ice cream at the counter of the original store of Sydney's most popular gelato shop – clearly even they can't resist quirky flavours such as vegan pandan and coconut sorbet, or panna cotta with fig jam and amaretti biscuit.

⭐ **Spice I Am** THAI $$
(☑ 02-9280 0928; www.spiceiam.com; 90 Wentworth Ave, Surry Hills; mains $12-30; ☉ 11.30am-3.30pm & 5-10pm Tue-Sun; ☑; ☐ Central) Once the preserve of expat Thais, this little red-hot chilli pepper now has queues out the door – no mean feat in a town awash with Thai restaurants. But it's no wonder: everything from the 70-plus dishes on the menu is super-fragrant and super-spicy. The sign is very unobtrusive so it's easy to walk past: don't. BYO alcohol. No reservations.

⭐ **Porteño** ARGENTINE $$
(☑ 02-8399 1440; www.porteno.com.au; 50 Holt St, Surry Hills; sharing plates $22-36, mains $42-85; ☉ 6-10pm Tue-Sat, plus noon-3pm Fri; ☐ Central) This upbeat and deservedly acclaimed Argentine restaurant is a great place to eat. The 'animal of the day' is slow-roasted for eight hours before the doors even open and is always delicious. Other highlights include homemade chorizo and morcilla, but lighter touches are also in evidence, so it's not just a meat feast. There's a decent Argentine wine list too.

⭐ **Dead Ringer** MODERN AUSTRALIAN $$
(☑ 02-9046 8460; www.deadringer.wtf; 413 Bourke St, Surry Hills; small share plates $8-20, large plates $29-39; ☉ 5-11pm Mon-Wed, to midnight Thu & Fri, 10am-midnight Sat, 11am-11pm Sun; ☎ ☑; ☐ 333, 440) This charcoal-fronted terrace is a laid-back haven of quality eating and drinking. Graze on the short, brilliant menu that changes daily and runs from bar snacks and tapas to mains. Though well presented, the food's all about flavour combinations rather than airy artistry. The 'feed-me' menu ($59) is great value and there's always something interesting to accompany by the glass.

Lankan Filling Station SRI LANKAN $$
(☑ 02-8542 9936; www.lankanfillingstation. com.au; 58 Riley St, East Sydney; curries $16-22; ☉ noon-10pm Tue-Sat, from 10am Sun, 10am-4pm Sun; ❋ ☑; ☐ Museum) Come here for traditional favourites like *pol sambol* (coconut-chilli salad), short eats (snacks) and the house speciality, *hoppers*. These bowl-shaped rice-flour pancakes are spongy in the middle and crispy on the outside when they're done right – and they're done right here. No dinner reservations for tables under six people, so put your name on the list and grab a drink nearby.

Malabar SOUTH INDIAN $$
(☑ 02-9332 1755; www.malabarcuisine.com.au; 274 Victoria St, Darlinghurst; mains $16-29, meat or veg banquet $49; ☉ 5.30-10.15pm Mon & Tue, noon-2.15pm & 5.30-10.15pm Wed-Sun, to 11.15pm Fri & Sat; ☑; ☐ Kings Cross) Delicious dosas, piquant Goan curries and the soft seductive tastes of India's south make this sizeable, well-established Darlinghurst restaurant a standout. The open kitchen and decor, with large black-and-white photos adorning the walls, add atmosphere. The owner and staff are very genial and will guide you through the substantial menu. You can bring your own wine. It's wise to book ahead.

Paddington & Centennial Park

Fred's ITALIAN $$$

(02-9114 7331; www.merivale.com/venues/freds; 380 Oxford St, Paddington; entrees $25-58, mains $38-110; ◷noon-midnight Tue-Fri & Sun, 8-11am & noon-midnight Sat; 🛜; 🚌333, 352, 440, 340) Fresh, local ingredients are given an Italian spin and roasted over an open hearth in this airy and convivial space. But the real treat here is peeking behind the curtain as award-winning chef Danielle Alvarez weaves her magic in the kitchen. The cooking is done right in the middle of the dining room, with four seats actually at the food-preparation benches.

Bondi, Coogee & the Eastern Beaches

★Lox Stock & Barrel CAFE $$

(02-9300 0368; www.loxstockandbarrel.com.au; 140 Glenayr Ave, Bondi Beach; breakfast & lunch dishes $15-22, dinner mains $30-34; ◷7am-3.30pm daily plus 6-10pm Wed & Thu, 6-11pm Fri & Sat; 🛜🅿🗘; 🚌379, 333, 380) Stare down the barrel of a smoking hot bagel and ask yourself one question: Wagyu corned-beef Reuben, or chicken liver with extra pickle? And be sure to add a side of hash. In the evening the menu sets its sights on the likes of steak, lamb and slow-roasted eggplant dishes. It's always busy, even on a wet Monday.

Three Blue Ducks CAFE $$

(02-9389 0010; www.threeblueducks.com; 141-143 Macpherson St, Bronte; breakfasts $15-19, lunches $22-34, dinner $28-48; ◷7am-2.30pm Mon & Tue, to 9pm Wed-Sat, to 3pm Sun; 🅿; 🚌379) 🍃 These ducks are a fair waddle from the water at Bronte Beach, but that doesn't stop queues forming outside the art-covered walls for weekend breakfasts. The adventurous chefs have a strong commitment to using local, organic and fair-trade food whenever possible – including from the bees, chooks and herb garden in the backyard.

Eden VEGAN $$

(0406 630 660; www.edenbondi.com; 180 Campbell Pde, Bondi Beach; mains $24-26; ◷5-10pm Wed-Sun, plus 11.30am-3pm Sat & Sun; 🅿; 🚌333, 380) Colourful comfort foods from pizzas and cheeseburgers to 'fysh' tacos and watermelon 'sashymi' are served sans animal products at this leafy courtyard space, which aims to replicate the protein quota of meat in its dishes. Gluten-free, nut-free, garlic-and-onion-free and and sugar-free options ensure everyone is catered for.

★Icebergs Dining Room ITALIAN $$$

(02-9365 9000; www.idrb.com; 1 Notts Ave, Bondi Beach; mains $48-52; ◷noon-3pm & 6.30-11pm daily, from 10am Sun; 🚌333) Poised above the famous swimming pool (p77), Icebergs has sweeping views across the Bondi Beach arc to the sea. Inside, bow-tied waiters deliver fresh, sustainably sourced seafood and steaks cooked with elan. There's also an elegant cocktail bar. In the same building, the Icebergs club has a bistro and bar with simpler, cheaper fare.

Sydney Harbourside

★Riverview Hotel GASTROPUB $$

(02-9810 1151; www.theriverviewhotel.com.au; 29 Birchgrove Rd, Balmain; bar mains $18-30, restaurant mains $29-39; ◷restaurant 6pm-midnight Mon-Fri, from noon Sat & Sun; 🛜; 🚌433, 444, 445, 🚢Balmain) Foodies flock here to try the excellent seafood dishes (such as Balmain bug) and nose-to-tail meat creations in the elegant upstairs dining room, while locals are equally keen on the pizzas, tasty fish and chips, and Sunday roasts served in the downstairs bar. It's a lovely pub in itself, with hanging baskets and a characterful interior.

Catalina MODERN AUSTRALIAN $$$

(02-9371 0555; www.catalinarosebay.com.au; Lyne Park, Rose Bay; mains $54-56; ◷noon-3pm & 6-10pm Mon-Sat, noon-4pm Sun; 🚌323-5, 🚢Rose Bay) Named after the flying boats once based here, this excellent Rose Bay restaurant has marvellous views, a lively eastern suburbs vibe and an impressive wine list. With this location, on stilts over the water, you'll expect seafood, and it doesn't disappoint. Sit in the elegant dining room, or stop in just for a drink; the balcony does all-day bar food.

Doyles on the Beach SEAFOOD $$$

(02-9337 2007; www.doyles.com.au; 11 Marine Pde, Watsons Bay; mains $45-52; ◷noon-3pm & 5.30-9pm Mon-Fri, noon-4pm & 5.30-9pm Sat & Sun; 🚌324, 325, 380, 🚢Watsons Bay) Perhaps not Sydney's absolute best seafood, but few can compete with Doyles' location or history – it first opened in 1885. Catching the harbour ferry to Watsons Bay for a fishy lunch is a quintessential Sydney experience. If the prices make you think twice, grab fish and chips (from $15.90) from its outlet (open 10am to 5pm, longer in summer) at the ferry wharf.

✗ Newtown & the Inner West

Newtown's King St and Enmore Rd are among the city's most diverse eat streets, with Thai restaurants sitting alongside Vietnamese, Greek, Lebanese and Mexican. A stretch on south King St, opposite the Newtown High School of Performing Arts, features half a dozen vegan restaurants. And when it comes to coffee culture, all roads point this way too.

★ Cow & the Moon   GELATO $
(🗐 02-9557 4255; www.cowandthemoon.com.au; 181 Enmore Rd, Enmore; small gelati $6.50; ⊙ 8.30am-10.30pm Sun-Thu, to 11.30pm Fri & Sat; 🛜 🖉 ♿; 🚇 Newtown) Forget the diet and slink into this cool corner cafe, where an array of sinful truffles and tasty tarts beckons seductively. Ignore them and head straight for the world's best gelato – the title this humble little place won in 2014 at the Gelato World Tour competition in Rimini, Italy. There's decent coffee too – expect to queue.

Lentil as Anything   VEGAN $
(🗐 02-8283 5580; www.lentilasanything.com; 391 King St, Newtown; suggested donation $15; ⊙ noon-3pm & 6-9pm Mon-Fri, from 10am Sat & Sun; 🛜 🖉; 🚇 Newtown) 🍃 This Melbourne import stands out by offering tasty fare (usually South Asian–influenced) on a voluntary-contribution basis. You can give money for your meal, or volunteer time, creativity or other skills. The heartening project is deservedly popular with everyone, from latte-sipping laptoppers to backpackers, students and some people who really need the feed.

Black Star Pastry   BAKERY $
(🗐 02-9557 8656; www.blackstarpastry.com.au; 277 Australia St, Newtown; snacks $6-12; ⊙ 7am-5.30pm; 🖉; 🚇 Newtown) Wise folks follow the black star to pay homage to excellent coffee, brilliant cakes and a few very good savoury things (gourmet pies and the like). Queues form for the famous strawberry-watermelon cake (dubbed 'the world's most Instagrammed cake' by the *New York Times*), but some say the raspberry-lychee is better. Other outposts have cropped up around town.

Faheem Fast Food   PAKISTANI $
(🗐 02-9550 4850; 194 Enmore Rd, Enmore; dishes $12-13; ⊙ 5pm-midnight Mon-Fri, from noon Sat & Sun; 🖉; 🚍 423, 426, 428) This Enmore Rd stalwart offers a totally no-frills dining atmosphere but very tasty and authentic curry and

tandoori options served until late. Its Haleem lentil-and-beef curry is memorably tasty, while the brain *nihari* is another standout, and not as challenging as it sounds.

Thai Pothong   THAI $$
(🗐 02-9550 6277; www.thaipothong.com.au; 294 King St, Newtown; mains $17-32, banquets from $30; ⊙ noon-3pm daily, plus 6-10.30pm Mon-Thu, 6-11pm Fri & Sat, 5.30-10pm Sun; 🖉; 🚇 Newtown) This crowd-pleasing restaurant is a favourite for birthdays and family dinners. The army of staff are efficient and friendly, and the food is reliably excellent. Top choice is a window seat to watch Newtowners pass by. If you pay cash, you get a 'discount', paid in a local currency only redeemable in the gift shop. Vegan and gluten-free menus are available.

Stinking Bishops   CHEESE $$
(🗐 02-9550 6116; www.thestinkingbishops.com; 63 Enmore Rd, Newtown; 2-/3-/4-cheese boards $22/30/38; ⊙ 5-10pm Tue-Thu, from noon Fri & Sat; 🖉; 🚇 Newtown) A pungent array of artisanal cheeses is the raison d'être of this popular shop and place to eat. Choose the varieties you want, pick a wine or local craft beer to accompany them, and off you go. There are also very tasty charcuterie boards. All its wares are sourced from small producers and available to take home too.

★ Ester   MODERN AUSTRALIAN $$$
(🗐 02-8068 8279; www.ester-restaurant.com.au; 46-52 Meagher St, Chippendale; share plates $10-60; ⊙ 6pm-midnight Mon-Fri, from noon Sat, noon-4.30pm Sun; 🖉; 🚇 Central) Ester exemplifies Sydney's contemporary dining scene: informal but not sloppy; innovative without being overly gimmicky; hip, but never try-hard. The menu specialises in well-sourced Australian fish, molluscs and crustaceans prepared with a variety of global influences, but don't miss the blood-sausage sandwich, or the excellent vegetarian creations. Leave room for dessert.

★ Boathouse on
Blackwattle Bay   SEAFOOD $$$
(🗐 02-9518 9011; www.boathouse.net.au; 123 Ferry Rd, Glebe; mains $40-48; ⊙ 6-10pm Tue-Thu, noon-2.45pm & 6-11pm Fri-Sun; 🚍 Glebe) The best restaurant in Glebe, and one of the best seafood restaurants in Sydney. Oysters are sourced from mid-north NSW to southeast Tasmania, but so fresh you'd think you'd shucked them yourself, and the snapper pie will go straight to the top of your favourite-dish list. The views over the Anzac Bridge are stunning.

Arrive by water taxi for maximum effect.

FOOD COURTS

Sydney's CBD is absolutely riddled with food courts, though they aren't necessarily visible from the street. They can be great places for a budget meal, especially at lunchtime. Look for them in shopping centres and major office towers. Some worthwhile ones are in Westfield Sydney, in Australia Square, underground at the north end in the Queen Victoria Building,, between George and Pitt Sts north of Liverpool St, in World Square and in the Sussex Centre.

Sushi places in particular tend to start discounting that day's fare in the mid-afternoon; Friday afternoons see a big sell-off at CBD food courts, which are mostly closed at weekends.

Glebe Point Diner MODERN AUSTRALIAN **$$$**
(☑ 02-9660 2646; www.glebepointdiner.com.au; 407 Glebe Point Rd, Glebe; mains $30-36; ☺ noon-2.30pm Wed-Sun, plus 6-10pm Mon-Thu, 5.30-11pm Fri & Sat; ☐ 431, ☐ Jubilee Park) A sensational neighbourhood bistro, where only the best local produce is used and where almost everything is made from scratch. The compact menu is creative and comforting at the same time: a rare combination that aims to keep loyal locals happy. On the wine list you'll find 150 carefully chosen drops. The $49 lunch deal is top value.

✗ Manly

The Pantry MODERN AUSTRALIAN **$$**
(☑ 02-9977 0566; www.thepantrymanly.com; Ocean Promenade, North Steyne; mains $28-41; ☺ 7.30am-9pm; ☎; ☒ Manly) Right on the beach, this Manly favourite is perfect for watching the goings-on in the water and on the sand while kicking back with anything from a hearty breakfast to a cocktail or something off the appealing lunch and dinner menu. The food revolves around quality Australian meats and plenty of seafood, served with style. Ther are some nice wines too.

✗ Northern Beaches

Pilu Baretto CAFE **$**
(☑ 02-9938 3331; www.pilu.com.au; Moore Rd, Freshwater; dishes $12-22; ☺ 6.30am-3pm Sun-Thu, to 9pm Fri & Sat; ☐ 139, E65) It may be attached to the upmarket **Pilu restaurant** (2-/3-course à la carte $78/98, 7-course tasting menu $160;

☺ noon-2.30pm & 6-10pm Tue-Sat, noon-2.30pm Sun), but this casual deck cafe is an altogether more relaxed, beachy affair. It's a top spot for Italian-influenced pre-surf breakfasts, delicious post-surf lunches or evening grazing. The coffee is great, but so is the Sardinian wine by the glass.

Boathouse Palm Beach SEAFOOD **$$**
(☑ 02-9974 5440; www.theboathousepb.com.au; Governor Phillip Park, Palm Beach; lunch mains $19-28; ☺ 7am-4pm; ☎ ☑; ☐ 199, L90) Sit on the large timber deck right by the sand at Pittwater or grab a garden table – either option is alluring at this casual seafood cafe. The food (try the legendary fish and chips or the vibrant salads) is nearly as impressive as the views. No bookings or table service; expect queues to order.

★ **Jonah's** MODERN AUSTRALIAN **$$$**
(☑ 02-9974 5599; www.jonahs.com.au; 69 Bynya Rd, Whale Beach; 2/3 courses $89/110; ☺ 7.30-9am, noon-2.30pm & 6.30-11pm; ☎; ☐ 199, L90) Perched above Whale Beach, luxurious Jonah's has fabulous perspectives over the ocean. The food is easy on the eye too, with immaculate presentation and excellent fish dishes. For the ultimate Sydney indulgence, take a seaplane from Rose Bay, order the seafood platter for two and stay overnight in one of the ocean-view rooms (dinner, bed and breakfast $522 per person).

♟ Drinking & Nightlife

In a city where rum was once the main currency, it's little wonder that drinking plays a big part in the Sydney social scene – whether it's knocking back some tinnies at the beach, schmoozing after work or warming up for a night on the town. Sydney offers plenty of choice in drinking establishments, from the flashy to the trashy.

☕ Circular Quay & the Rocks

★ **Opera Bar** BAR
(☑ 02-8587 5900; www.operabar.com.au; lower concourse, Sydney Opera House; ☺ 10am-midnight Mon-Thu, 10am-1am Fri, 9am-1am Sat, 9am-midnight Sun; ☎; ☒ Circular Quay) Right on the harbour with the Opera House on one side and the bridge on the other, this perfectly positioned terrace manages a very Sydney marriage of the laid-back and the sophisticated. It's an iconic spot for visitors and locals alike. There's live music or DJs most

nights and excellent food, running from oysters to fabulous steaks and cold fish dishes.

★ Glenmore Hotel   PUB
(📋02-9247 4794; www.theglenmore.com.au; 96 Cumberland St; ⏰10am-midnight Sun-Thu, to 1am Fri & Sat; 🚻; 🚆Circular Quay) Downstairs it's a predictably nice old Rocks pub with great outdoor seating, but head to the rooftop and the views are beyond fabulous: the Opera House, harbour and city skyline are all present and accounted for. It gets rammed up here on the weekends, with DJs and plenty of wine by the glass. The food's decent too.

★ Hero of Waterloo   PUB
(📋02-9252 4553; www.heroofwaterloo.com.au; 81 Lower Fort St; ⏰10am-11.30pm Mon-Wed, to midnight Thu-Sat, to 10pm Sun; 🚌311, 🚆Circular Quay) Enter this rough-hewn 1843 sandstone pub to meet some locals, chat to the Irish bar staff and grab an earful of the swing, folk and Celtic bands (Friday to Sunday). Downstairs is a dungeon where, in days gone by, drinkers would sleep off a heavy night before being shanghaied to the high seas via a tunnel leading to the harbour.

Bulletin Place   COCKTAIL BAR
(www.bulletinplace.com; 10 Bulletin Pl; ⏰4pm-midnight Mon-Wed, to 1am Thu-Sat; 🚆Circular Quay) A discreet entrance on this little street conceals the staircase up to one of Sydney's most talked-about cocktail bars. Personable, down-to-earth staff shake up five great daily creations that are high on zinginess and freshness and low on frippery. It's a small space, so get here early. Cocktails are about $22 each.

Doss House   BAR
(📋0457 880 180; www.thedosshouse.com.au; 77 George St; ⏰4pm-1am Tue-Thu, to 2am Fri & Sat, to midnight Sun; 🚆Circular Quay) With a curious origin story involving two Irish pals, a lottery win and a hostel in Peru, this hidden-away jewel is an atmospheric Rocks basement space. Historic sandstone melds seamlessly with a romantic, cosy interior studded with venerable furniture and lined with whisky bottles. There's a serious malt menu as well as delicious cocktails and attractively tiled seating in the narrow courtyard.

Lord Nelson Brewery Hotel   BREWERY
(📋02-9251 4044; www.lordnelsonbrewery.com; 19 Kent St; ⏰11am-11pm Mon-Sat, noon-10pm Sun; 🚻; 🚌311, 🚆Circular Quay) This atmospheric boozer is one of three claiming to be Sydney's old-

est (all using slightly different criteria). The on-site brewery cooks up its own natural ales; a pint of dark, stouty Nelson's Blood is a fine way to partake. Pub food downstairs is tasty and solid; the upstairs brasserie is an attractive space doing fancier food, including good seafood.

Argyle   BAR
(📋02-9247 5500; www.theargylerocks.com; 18 Argyle St; ⏰11am-1am Sun-Wed, to 3am Thu-Sat; 🚻; 🚆Circular Quay) This stylish and wildly popular conglomeration of bars is spread throughout the historic Argyle Stores buildings, including a cobblestone courtyard and an atmospheric wooden-floored downstairs bar. The decor ranges from rococo couches to white extruded plastic tables, all offset with kooky chandeliers and moody lighting. During the day the courtyard is a pleasant place for a drink or spot of lunch.

Busby's Bar @ Victoria Lodge   BAR
(📋02-9241 2419; www.rbgsyd.nsw.gov.au; Royal Botanic Garden; ⏰10am-5.30pm Sep & Apr, 10am-7pm Oct-Mar; 🚆Circular Quay) This casual summer pop-up cabin will infuse you with the picnic spirit as you lounge on deckchairs or on the lawns of the Botanic Garden. There's a stunning view across Farm Cove to the Opera House, backed by the bridge. Offerings range from gin cocktails to antipasto platters, but they mix things up yearly.

Australian Hotel   PUB
(📋02-9247 2229; www.australianheritagehotel.com; 100 Cumberland St; ⏰11am-midnight; 🚻; 🚆Circular Quay) With its wide awning shading lots of outdoor seating, this handsome early-20th-century pub is a favoured pit stop for a cooling ale; it was doing microbrewed beer long before it became trendy and has a great selection. The kitchen also does a nice line in gourmet pizzas ($17 to $28), including toppings of kangaroo, emu and crocodile.

🍴 City Centre & Haymarket

The city centre has long been known for upmarket, after-work booze rooms, none of which you would describe as cosy locals. Much more interesting is the wide network of 'small bars', which are speakeasy-style places lurking in the most unlikely back alleys and basements.

★ Frankie's Pizza   BAR
(www.frankiespizzabytheslice.com; 50 Hunter St; ⏰4pm-3am Sat-Thu, from noon Fri; 🚻; 🚆Martin

SYDNEY & AROUND DRINKING & NIGHTLIFE

Surry Hills & Darlinghurst

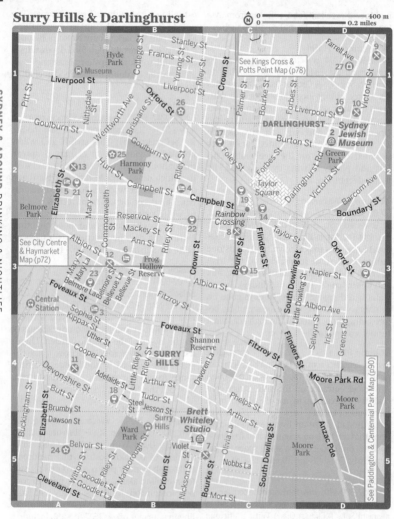

N 0   400 m
0   0.2 miles

Place) Descend the stairs and you'll think you're in a 1970s pizzeria, complete with plastic grapevines, snapshots covering the walls and tasty pizza slices ($6). But open the nondescript door in the corner and an indie wonderland reveals itself. Bands play here at least four nights a week (join them on Tuesdays for live karaoke) and there's another bar hidden below.

★ **Uncle Ming's**   COCKTAIL BAR
(www.unclemings.com.au; 55 York St; ☉ noon-midnight Mon-Thu, to 1am Fri, 4pm-1am Sat; ☒ Wynyard) We love the dark, romantic opium-den atmosphere of this small bar secreted away

in a basement by a shirt shop. It's an atmospheric spot for anything from a quick beer to a leisurely exploration of the cocktail menu. It also does excellent dumplings and usually has very welcoming bar staff.

Baxter Inn   BAR
(www.thebaxterinn.com; 152-156 Clarence St; ☉ 4pm-1am Mon-Sat; ☒ Town Hall) Yes, it really is down that dark lane and through that unmarked door (there are two easily spotted bars on this courtyard, but this place is through a door to your right). Whisky's the main poison and the friendly bar staff really know their stuff. There's an elegant speakeasy atmosphere and

Surry Hills & Darlinghurst

some mighty impressive bottles – over 900 whiskies at last count.

Ivy CLUB
(☑ 02-9240 3000; www.merivale.com/ivy; Level 1, 330 George St; ☺ noon-late Mon-Sat, plus pool party 1pm-midnight Sun Oct-Mar; ☎; ☒ Wynyard) Down a lane off George St, Ivy is the HQ of the all-pervading Merivale Group. It's a fashionable complex of bars, restaurants and even a swimming pool. It's also Sydney's most hyped venue; expect lengthy queues for the club nights, which at the time of research included a backpacker special on Thursdays and an LGBT club, Poof Doof, on Saturdays.

Slip Inn & Chinese Laundry CLUB
(☑ 02-9114 7327; www.chineselaundry.club; 111 Sussex St; ☺ 11am-1am Mon-Thu, to 3am Fri, 2pm-3am Sat, Chinese Laundry 9pm-3.30am Fri, 9pm-4am Sat; ☎; ☒ Wynyard) Slip in to this cheerfully colourful and atmospheric warren on the edge of Darling Harbour and bump hips with the kids. There are bars, pool tables, a pleasantly packed beer garden and Mexican food courtesy of El Loco. On Friday and Saturday nights the bass cranks up at the long-running attached Chinese Laundry nightclub ($28 to $43), accessed via Slip St.

O Bar COCKTAIL BAR
(☑ 02-9247 9777; www.obardining.com.au; Level 47, Australia Square, 264 George St; ☺ 5pm-midnight Sat-Thu, noon-midnight Fri; ☎; ☒ Wynyard) The cocktails at this 47th-floor revolving bar aren't cheap, but they're still substantially cheaper than admission to Sydney Tower (p66) – and it's considerably more glamorous.

The views are truly wonderful; get up there shortly after opening time, and kick back to enjoy the sunset and transition into night. There's also smart food on offer.

Kings Cross & Potts Point

★**Old Fitzroy Hotel** PUB
(☑ 02-9356 3848; www.oldfitzroy.com.au; 129 Dowling St, Woolloomooloo; ☺ 11am-midnight Mon-Fri, noon-midnight Sat, noon-10pm Sun; ☎; ☒ Kings Cross) Hidden in the backstreets, this totally unpretentious **theatre pub** (☑ 0416 044 413; www.redlineproductions.com.au; 129 Dowling St, Woolloomooloo; tickets $25-48; ☒ Kings Cross) is also a decent old-fashioned boozer in its own right, with a great variety of beers on tap and a convivial welcome. Prop up the bar, grab a seat at a street-side table or head upstairs to the bistro, serving smart English-inspired pub grub, with a pool table and couches.

Kings Cross Hotel PUB
(☑ 02-9331 9900; www.kingscrosshotel.com.au; 244-248 William St, Kings Cross; ☺ 10am-1am Sun-Thu, to 3.30am Fri & Sat; ☎; ☒ Kings Cross) This grand old brick building guards the entrance to the Cross and is one of the area's best pubs, with several levels of boozy entertainment. The balcony bar is a very pleasant spot for lunch, while the rooftop that opens weekend evenings has the drawcard vistas. Saturdays are good, with DJs on all levels.

Surry Hills & Darlinghurst

Once upon a time, this neighbourhood was known for its grungy live-music pubs and high-octane gay scene. Many of the music venues have subsequently been converted into chic bar-restaurants and the gay bars have dwindled, but this area still contains some of Sydney's best nightspots – you just have to look harder to find them. The 'small bar' phenomenon has taken off here, with many of the city's best lurking down the most unlikely lanes.

★ Love, Tilly Devine
WINE BAR

(☑02-9326 9297; www.lovetillydevine.com; 91 Crown Lane, Darlinghurst; ⊘5pm-midnight Mon-Sat; ☒Museum) Tilly Devine was a notorious Sydney madam and crime boss in the '30s, and her namesake bar is hidden down a back alley, in true furtive style. The dark, good-looking, split-level bar is compact, but the wine list certainly isn't. It's an extraordinary document, with some exceptionally well-chosen wines and a mission to get people away from their tried-and-tested favourites.

★ Wild Rover
BAR

(☑02-9280 2235; www.thewildrover.com.au; 75 Campbell St, Surry Hills; ⊘4pm-midnight Mon-Sat; ☒Central) Look for the wide, unsigned door and enter this supremely cool brick-lined speakeasy. Ask the bar staff to recommend a whisky from the huge range on offer, or pick a craft beer from the menu written on a vintage train-station spinner sign. The upstairs bar opens for trivia on Tuesday and occasional live bands.

★ Shakespeare Hotel
PUB

(☑02-9319 6883; www.shakespearehotel.com.au; 200 Devonshire St, Surry Hills; ⊘10am-midnight Mon-Sat, to 10pm Sun; ☒Surry Hills, ☒Central) The 'Shakey' is a classic Sydney pub (1879) with art nouveau tiled walls, scuzzy carpet, the horses on the TV and cheap bar meals. There are plenty of cosy hidey holes upstairs and a cast of local characters. It's a proper convivial all-welcome place that's the antithesis of the more gentrified Surry Hills drinking establishments.

Shady Pines Saloon
BAR

(www.shadypinessaloon.com; 4/256 Crown St, Darlinghurst; ⊘4pm-midnight; ☒333, ☒Museum) With no sign or street number on the door and entry via a shady back lane (look for the white door before Bikram Yoga on Foley St), this subterranean honky-tonk bar caters to the urban boho. Sip whisky and rye with the good ole boys amid Western memorabilia and enormous North American taxidermy.

WyNo X Bodega
WINE BAR

(☑02-9212 7766; www.bodegatapas.com; 50 Holt St, Surry Hills; share plates $16-36; ⊘noon-10pm Tue-Fri, from 5pm Sat; ☒Central) Sydney tapas legend Bodega moved in with wine bar WyNo in 2019. The petite space seats 28 at one long table and retains some of the Bodega favourites, including its famous fish fingers. But the focus has shifted somewhat from the tapas to the carefully curated 400-bottle wine list, all available by the glass.

Winery
WINE BAR

(☑02-8322 2007; www.thewinerysurryhills.com.au; 285a Crown St, Surry Hills; ⊘noon-midnight; ☒Central) Beautifully situated in the leafy grounds of a historic water reservoir, behind the Pieno restaurant, this oasis serves dozens of wines by the glass to the swanky Surry Hills set. Sit for a while and you'll notice all kinds of kitsch touches lurking in the greenery: headless statues, upside-down parrots, iron koalas. It's a fun, boisterous scene on weekend afternoons.

Stonewall Hotel
GAY

(☑02-9360 1963; www.stonewallhotel.com; 175 Oxford St, Darlinghurst; ⊘noon-3am; ☒333) A stalwart of the Oxford St LGBTIQ+ strip, Stonewall has three levels of bars and dance floors. Cabaret, karaoke and quiz nights spice things up; there's something on every night of the week. Wednesday's notorious Malebox, which has been running for over two decades, is an official Mardi Gras (p79) event and an inventive way to meet people.

Darlo Bar
PUB

(Royal Sovereign Hotel; ☑02-9331 3672; www.darlobar.com.au; 306 Liverpool St, Darlinghurst; ⊘10am-midnight Mon-Sat, noon-midnight Sun; ☒Kings Cross) Something of a locals' lounge room, the Darlo's triangular retro space is a magnet for urban bohemians, fluoro-clad ditch diggers and architects with a hankering for pinball or pool. It's quiet during the day, but DJs fire things up on Saturday nights. The partly open-air rooftop bar is a pleasant spot.

🍷 Paddington & Centennial Park

The Paddington
BAR

(☑02-9114 7329; www.merivale.com.au/thepaddington; 384 Oxford St, Paddington; ⊘noon-midnight Tue-Sat, to 10pm Sun; ☎; ☒333, 352, 440, 340) There's a kick to Paddington's weekend nightlife, and this bar-restaurant is a key player. Drinks and service are excellent, while chickens spinning on the rotisserie provide a simple but classy eating choice. The design, all white tiles, distressed brick and black-and-white photos of ancestors brandishing haunches of meat, deliberately recalls a butcher's shop – a little cynically, as it wasn't one.

Unicorn PUB
(www.theunicornhotel.com.au; 106 Oxford St, Paddington; ☺4pm-midnight Mon, to 1am Tue, to 3am Wed, 11am-3am Thu-Sat, 11am-midnight Sun; 🔊; 🚌333, 352, 440, 340) This spacious pub is casual and unpretentious, and a fine place to sink a few craft beers, sip some Australian wines or join in nightly events like dragqueen-hosted Cards Against Humanity (Wednesday). Burgers are the highlight of the OK eating offerings. There's a cosy downstairs bistro and small beer garden.

Bondi, Coogee & the Eastern Beaches

Coogee Pavilion BAR
(☎02-9114 7321; www.merivale.com.au/coogeepavilion; 169 Dolphin St, Coogee; ☺7.30am-midnight Sun-Thu, to 3am Fri & Sat; 🔊🚼; 🚌313, 314, 353, 370-4) With numerous indoor and outdoor bars and restaurants, and a large kids' play area, this cavernous complex packs them in, especially at weekends. The ground floor feels a bit like a food court, but the middle level has three more intimate venues, and the adults-only rooftop has sweeping views. Built in 1887, the building originally housed an aquarium and swimming pools.

Speakeasy WINE BAR
(☎02-9130 2020; www.speakeasybarbondi.com.au; 83 Curlewis St, Bondi Beach; ☺5-11pm Mon-Sat, from 1pm Sun; 🚌333, 379, 380) Skip Bondi's beachside boozers and head a few blocks inland to this tiny red-and-black den with Persian rugs, mismatched furniture and a few footpath seats. Share plates take a Mediterranean slant, or come for the Sunday roast (with a glass of Tempranillo) for $25.

Sydney Harbourside

⭐**Golden Sheaf** PUB
(☎02-9327 5877; www.thegoldensheaf.com.au; 429 New South Head Rd, Double Bay; ☺10am-1am Mon-Wed, to 2am Thu-Sat, to midnight Sun; 🔊🚼; 🚌323-327, 🚢Double Bay, 🚆Edgecliff) A cracking pub, especially at weekends when it thrums with life all day, this is a real eastern suburbs favourite. The beer garden is among Sydney's best: large, with good wines by the glass, heaters, fairy lights, evening entertainment and

SYDNEY & AROUND DRINKING & NIGHTLIFE

LGBTIQ+ SYDNEY

Sydney's LGBTIQ+ community is visible, vibrant and an integral part of the city's social fabric. Partly because of that integration, partly because of phone apps facilitating contact, and partly because of licensing law changes, the gay nightlife scene has died off substantially. But the action's still going on and Sydney is indisputably one of the world's great LGBTIQ+ cities.

The famous Sydney Gay & Lesbian Mardi Gras (p79) is now the biggest annual tourist-attracting date on the Australian calendar. The gay and lesbian community throws itself wholeheartedly into the entire festival, including the blitzkrieg of partying that surrounds it. There's no better time for LGBTIQ+ travellers to visit Sydney than the two-week lead-up to the parade and party, held in February or March.

Darlinghurst and Newtown have traditionally been the the most LGBTIQ+-friendly neighbourhoods, although all of the inner suburbs have a higher-than-average proportion of LGBT IQ+ residents. Most of the venues are on the Darlinghurst section of Oxford St, with classic spots like casual Stonewall Hotel, or, around the corner, Arq (☎02-9380 8700; www.arqsydney.com.au; 16 Flinders St, Darlinghurst; ☺9pm-late Thu-Sun; 🚌333). However, some of the best events are held at mixed pubs, such as the legendary Sunday afternoon session at the **Beresford Hotel** (☎02-9114 7328; www.merivale.com.au/theberesfordhotel; 354 Bourke St, Surry Hills; ☺noon-midnight Mon-Wed, to 1am Thu-Sun; 🔊; 🚌374, 397, 399).

Beach scenes include the north end of Bondi; Lady Bay (p71), a pretty nudist beach tucked under South Head; **Obelisk**, a secluded nude beach with a bush hinterland; and Murray Rose Pool (p77), another harbour beach. Women-only **McIvers Baths** at Coogee is extremely popular with lesbians.

Free LGBTIQ+ media includes *LOTL* (www.lotl.com) and the *Star Observer* (www.starobserver.com.au).

AT THE DOOR

Sydney's bouncers are often strict, arbitrary and immune to logic. They are usually contracted by outside security firms so have no problem with turning away business. Being questioned and searched every time you want a drink after 8pm on a weekend can definitely take the shine off a Sydney night out.

It is against the law to serve people who are intoxicated and you won't be admitted to a venue if you appear drunk. Expect to be questioned about how much you've had to drink that night: it's more to see if you're slurring your words than actual interest in the answer. Plenty of places won't admit you if you are wearing tank tops, thongs (flip-flops) or sandals.

If security staff suspect that you're under the legal drinking age (18 years), you'll be asked to present photo ID with proof of your age. Many places have a policy of checking the ID of anyone who looks under 25, and some bars scan ID for everyone entering.

Some pubs have smoking areas, but you aren't allowed to take food into those areas – even if you're happy to do so.

brilliant pub food. Check the website for fun events like poker night or Dating with Dogs.

★ **Watsons Bay Beach Club** PUB
(②02-9337 5444; www.watsonsbayhotel.com.au; 1 Military Rd, Watsons Bay; ⊙7am-11pm; 🚌324, 325, 380, 🛳Watsons Bay) One of the great pleasures in life is languoring in the pumping beer garden of the Watsons Bay Hotel, mere metres from the ferry wharf, after a day at the beach. It goes off here at weekends, with a rowdy good time had by all. Stay to watch the sun go down over the city. The food is OK, if pricey.

🍷 Newtown & the Inner West

Courthouse Hotel PUB
(②02-9519 8273; www.facebook.com/TheCourty; 202 Australia St, Newtown; ⊙10am-midnight Mon-Sat, to 10pm Sun; 🚆Newtown) A block back from the King St fray, the 150-year-old Courthouse is one of Newtown's best pubs, the kind of place where everyone from goth lesbians to magistrates can have a beer and feel at home. It packs out for Sydney Swans games. The beer garden is one of Sydney's best: spacious, sheltered and cheerful, with decent pub food available.

Young Henry's BREWERY
(②02-9519 0048; www.younghenrys.com; 76 Wilford St, Newtown; ⊙noon-7pm; 🚆Newtown) Conviviality is assured in this craft brewery bar, where the beer, found on taps all over Sydney, is as fresh as you'll get. Basically, they've filled a bit of street-art-splattered warehouse with high tables, a loud stereo system and a counter to serve their delicious beer, then opened the roller door and filled it with happy locals.

★ **Earl's Juke Joint** BAR
(www.facebook.com/earlsjukejoint; 407 King St, Newtown; ⊙5pm-midnight; 🚆Newtown) Swinging Earl's serves craft beers and killer cocktails to the Newtown hip-erati. It's hidden behind the down-at-heel facade of the Betta Meats butcher shop it used to be, but once in, you're in downtown New Orleans, with a bar as long as the Mississippi.

Bearded Tit BAR
(②02-8399 0067; www.thebeardedtit.com; 183 Regent St, Redfern; ⊙4pm-midnight Tue-Fri, 2pm-midnight Sat, 2-10pm Sun; 🚆Redfern) Redfern is home to a cluster of offbeat hangouts for misfits, creatives and subcultural scallywags, and the Tit is one of the best. A sexy, super-inclusive crowd sips cocktails amongst the eclectic decor inside, or around the retro caravan out back. There are occasional (free) live shows and art exhibitions.

★ **Timbah** WINE BAR
(②02-9571 7005; www.facebook.com/Timbah WineBar; 375 Glebe Point Rd, entrance on Forsyth St, Glebe; ⊙4-10pm Tue-Sat; 🚌431, 🛳Glebe) 🌿 Quite a way down Glebe Point Rd is an excellent independent wine shop; turn right to find the convivial wine bar it runs downstairs. Staff will happily talk you through the select wine list, and help you pick your wine by the glass. Tapas-style food features Australian native flavours and homegrown herbs.

Imperial Hotel GAY & LESBIAN
(②02-9516 1766; www.imperialerskineville.com.au; 35 Erskineville Rd, Erskineville; ⊙4pm-midnight Mon-Thu, noon-4am Fri & Sat, noon-midnight

Sun; ⊠ Erskineville) The Imperial is legendary as the starting point for *The Adventures of Priscilla, Queen of the Desert*. This old, late-opening LGBTIQ+ favourite put on a new frock in 2018, reopening with a mainly vegetarian restaurant offering Drag N' Dine shows, a dungeon-like basement theatre and a completely contrasting gelati-coloured rooftop cocktail bar.

🍴 Manly & the Northern Beaches

⭐ Manly Wharf Hotel PUB
(☑ 02-9977 1266; www.manlywharfhotel.com.au; East Esplanade, Manly; ⊙ 11.30am-midnight Mon-Fri, 11am-1am Sat, 11am-midnight Sun; 🛜 🚹; ⛴ Manly) Just along the wharf from the ferry, this remodelled pub is all glass and water vistas, with loads of seating so you'll have a good chance of grabbing a share of the views. It's a perfect spot for sunny afternoon beers. There's good pub food too (mains $22 to $30), with pizzas, fried fish and succulent rotisserie chicken all worthwhile.

⭐ The Newport PUB
(Newport Arms Hotel; ☑ 02-9114 7337; www.merivale.com; cnr Beaconsfield & Kalinya Sts, Newport; ⊙ 9am-midnight Mon-Sat, 9am-11pm Sun; 🛜 🚹; 🚌 188, 199, L90) This legendary northern beaches pub actually overlooks not the ocean but the Pittwater side, with its bobbing boats and quiet strands. It's an absolutely enormous complex, with acres of appealing outdoor seating, several bars, good food from various kitchens, table tennis and all sorts of stuff going on. It's a great, family-friendly place to while away a sunny afternoon.

⭐ Entertainment

Take Sydney at face value and it's tempting to unfairly stereotype its good citizens as shallow and a little narcissistic. But take a closer look: the arts scene is thriving, sophisticated and progressive.

Spectator sports, led by rugby league, are huge and attending a match is highly recommended.

Cinema

⭐ Golden Age Cinema & Bar CINEMA
(☑ 02-9211 1556; www.ourgoldenage.com.au; 80 Commonwealth St, Surry Hills; adult/concession tickets from $22.50/18; ⊙ 4pm-midnight Tue-Fri, from 2.30pm Sat & Sun; 🚇 Museum) In what was once the Sydney HQ of Paramount Pictures, a heart-warming small cinema occupies the

former screening room downstairs. It shows old favourites, art-house classics and a few recherché gems. There's a great small bar here too, with free gigs on Saturdays. All up, it's a fabulous place for a night out.

Moonlight Cinema CINEMA
(www.moonlight.com.au; Belvedere Amphitheatre, cnr Loch & Broome Aves, Centennial Park; adult/family $20/65; ⊙ sunset Dec-Mar; 🚌 333, 352, 440, 340, 🚇 Bondi Junction) Take a picnic and join the bats under the stars in magnificent Centennial Park; enter via the Woollahra Gate on Oxford St. A mix of blockbuster, kid-friendly, art-house and classic films is screened.

OpenAir Cinema CINEMA
(☑ 1300 366 649; www.westpacopenair.com.au; Mrs Macquaries Rd; tickets $40; ⊙ early Jan–mid-Feb; 🚇 Circular Quay) Right on the harbour, the outdoor three-storey screen here comes with surround sound, sunsets, skyline views and swanky food and wine. Most tickets are purchased in advance – look out for the dates in early December as they go fast – but a limited number go on sale at the door each night at 6.30pm; check the website for details.

Classical Music

⭐ Sydney Opera House PERFORMING ARTS
(☑ 02-9250 7777; www.sydneyoperahouse.com; Bennelong Point; 🚇 Circular Quay) The glamorous jewel of Australian performance, Sydney's famous Opera House has five main stages. Opera may have star billing, but it's also an important venue for theatre, dance and classical concerts, while big-name bands sometimes rock the forecourt. Ongoing renovation works have closed the concert hall until 2022, but in other theatres the show goes on.

Sydney Symphony Orchestra CLASSICAL MUSIC
(SSO; ☑ 02-8215 4600; www.sydneysymphony.com; cnr Harrington & Argyle Sts) The excellent SSO plays around 150 concerts annually with famous local and international musicians. Catch them at the Sydney Opera House (not until 2022), the Town Hall or the City Recital Hall (☑ 02-8256 2222; www.cityrecitalhall.com; 2 Angel Pl; ⊙ box office 9am-5pm Mon-Fri; 🚇 Wynyard).

Dance

Bangarra Dance Theatre DANCE
(☑ 02-9251 5333; www.bangarra.com.au; Pier 4, 15 Hickson Rd; 🚌 324, 325, 🚇 Circular Quay) Bangarra is hailed as Australia's finest Aboriginal performance company. Artistic director

🛈 ENTERTAINMENT BOOKING WEBSITES

Moshtix (☑1300 438 849; www.moshtix. com.au)

Ticketek (☑13 28 49; www.ticketek. com.au)

Ticketmaster (☑13 61 00; www.ticket master.com.au)

Stephen Page conjures a fusion of contemporary themes, Indigenous traditions and Western technique. When not touring internationally, the company performs at the Opera House or at Walsh Bay.

Sydney Dance Company DANCE
(SDC; ☑02-9221 4811; www.sydneydancecompany. com; Pier 4, 15 Hickson Rd; ☐324, 325, ☒Circular Quay) Australia's number-one contemporary-dance company has been staging wildly modern, sexy and sometimes shocking works since 1979. Performances are usually held at the Roslyn Packer Theatre (☑02-9250 1999; www.roslynpackertheatre.com.au; 22 Hickson Rd) or Carriageworks (p71).

Live Music

★Metro Theatre LIVE MUSIC
(☑02-9550 3666; www.metrotheatre.com.au; 624 George St; ☒Town Hall) The Metro is Sydney's best midsized venue for catching alternative local and international rock acts in intimate, well-ventilated comfort. Other offerings include comedy, cabaret and dance parties.

Oxford Art Factory LIVE MUSIC
(☑02-9332 3711; www.oxfordartfactory.com; 38-46 Oxford St, Darlinghurst; tickets from $11; ☒Museum) Indie kids party against an arty backdrop at this two-room multipurpose venue modelled on Andy Warhol's NYC creative base. There's a gallery, a bar and a performance space that often hosts international acts and DJs. Check the website for what's on.

★Lazybones Lounge LIVE MUSIC
(☑0450 008 563; www.lazyboneslounge.com. au; 294 Marrickville Rd, Marrickville; ☉7pm-midnight Mon-Wed, 5pm-3am Thu-Sat, 5-10pm Sun; 🛜; ☒Marrickville) Roomy and decadently decorated with erotic ceiling paintings, Lazybones has live music nightly and decent cocktails and food. At weekends it gets likeably louche, with a fun crowd dancing until late over two floors. Even the bouncers are friendly. There's

a cover charge for the bands ($10 to $20); it's free later on. Enter from Illawarra Rd.

Spectator Sport

★Sydney Cricket Ground SPECTATOR SPORT
(SCG; ☑02-9360 6601; www.scgt.nsw.gov.au; Driver Ave, Moore Park; ☐372, 374, 376, ☒Moore Park) During the cricket season (October to March), the stately SCG is the venue for interstate cricket matches (featuring the NSW Blues), family-friendly Big Bash (www.bigbash. com.au; ☉Dec-Feb) extravaganzas and sell-out international five-day test, one-day and T20 limited-over cricket matches. As the cricket season ends, the Australian Rules Football (AFL) season starts, and the stadium becomes a blur of red-and-white-clad Sydney Swans (www.sydneyswans.com.au) fans.

Theatre

★Belvoir St Theatre THEATRE
(☑02-9699 3444; www.belvoir.com.au; 25 Belvoir St, Surry Hills; ☐372, ☒Surry Hills, ☒Central) In a quiet corner of Surry Hills, this intimate venue, with two small stages, is the home of an often experimental and consistently excellent theatre company that specialises in quality Australian drama. It often commissions new works and is a vital cog in the Sydney theatre scene.

Sydney Theatre Company THEATRE
(STC; ☑02-9250 1777; www.sydneytheatre.com.au; Pier 4, 15 Hickson Rd; ☉box office 9am-7.30pm Mon, to 8.30pm Tue-Fri, 11am-8.30pm Sat, 2hr before show Sun; ☐324, 325, ☒Circular Quay) Established in 1978, the STC is Sydney theatre's most prominent company and has played an important part in the careers of many famous Australian actors (especially Cate Blanchett, co-artistic director from 2008 to 2013). Performances are staged here in the renovated Wharf Theatre, opposite at the Roslyn Packer Theatre and also at the Opera House.

🔒 Shopping

Sydney's city centre is brimming with department, chain and international fashion stores and arcades – shopping here is about as fast and furious as Australia gets. Paddington is the place for art and fashion, while new and secondhand boutiques around Newtown and Surry Hills cater to a hmore alternative crowd.

Newtown and Glebe have the lion's share of book and record shops, though the city centre has good options too. For surf gear, head to Bondi or Manly. Woollahra, Newtown (around St Peters Station) and Surry Hills are good for antiques. For souvenirs – from exquisite opals to tacky T-shirts – try the Rocks, Circular Quay and Darling Harbour.

★ Gannon House Gallery   ART
(☑ 02-9251 4474; www.gannonhousegallery.com; 45 Argyle St; ⊙10am-6pm; ⍟Circular Quay) Specialising in contemporary Australian and Aboriginal art, Gannon House purchases works directly from artists and Aboriginal communities. You'll find the work of prominent artists such as Gloria Petyarre here, alongside lesser-known names. There are always some striking and wonderful pieces.

★ Craft NSW   ARTS & CRAFTS
(☑ 02-9241 5825; www.artsandcraftsnsw.com.au; 12 Argyle Pl; ⊙10am-5pm; ⍟Circular Quay) This craft association gallery at the quiet end of the Rocks is full of beautiful and original creations. It's the perfect spot to pick up a unique gift for someone special. They also offer regular craft workshops.

★ Artery   ART
(☑ 02-9380 8234; www.artery.com.au; 221 Darlinghurst Rd, Darlinghurst; ⊙10am-5pm; ⍟Kings Cross) ∅ Step into a world of mesmerising dots and swirls at this small gallery devoted to Aboriginal art, particularly from the central and western deserts. Artery's motto is 'ethical, contemporary, affordable', and while large canvases by more established artists cost in the thousands, small, unstretched canvases start at around $50. There's also an offbeat sideline in preserved insects.

★ Abbey's   BOOKS
(☑ 02-9264 3111; www.abbeys.com.au; 131 York St; ⊙8.30am-6pm Mon-Wed & Fri, to 8pm Thu, 9am-5pm Sat, 10am-5pm Sun; ⍟Town Hall) Easily central Sydney's best bookshop, Abbey's has many strengths. It's good on social sciences and has excellent resources for language learning, including a great selection of foreign films on DVD. There's also a big sci-fi and fantasy section. Staff are great and generally very experienced.

Strand Arcade   SHOPPING CENTRE
(☑ 02-9265 6800; www.strandarcade.com.au; 412 George St; ⊙9am-5.30pm Mon-Wed & Fri, to 9pm Thu, to 4pm Sat, 11am-4pm Sun; ⍟Town Hall) Constructed in 1891, the beautiful Strand rivals the Queen Victoria Building in the ornateness stakes. The three floors of designer fashions, Australiana and old-world coffee shops will make your shortcut through here considerably longer. Some of the top Aus-

ℹ WHAT'S ON LISTINGS

Sydney Morning Herald (www.smh.com.au) Online and in Friday's 'Shortlist' section.

What's On Sydney (www.whatsonsydney.com)

What's On City of Sydney (http://whatson.cityofsydney.nsw.gov.au)

Time Out Sydney (www.timeout.com/sydney)

Eventbrite (www.eventbrite.com.au)

The Music (www.themusic.com.au) Online and printed guide to the live-music scene.

tralian designers and other iconic brands have shops here – chocolatiers included!

Carriageworks
Farmers Market   MARKET
(www.carriageworks.com.au; Carriageworks, 245 Wilson St, Eveleigh; ⊙8am-1pm Sat; ⍟Redfern) ∅ Over 70 regular stallholders sell their goodies at Sydney's best farmers market, established to connect small NSW producers with consumers in the big city. It's held in the heritage-listed Carriageworks gallery (p71). Food and coffee stands do a brisk business and vegetables, fruit, meat and seafood are sold in a convivial atmosphere of kids, dogs and people juggling big bunches of sunflowers.

Queen Victoria Building   SHOPPING CENTRE
(QVB; ☑ 02-9265 6800; www.qvb.com.au; 455 George St; ⊙9am-6pm Mon-Wed, Fri & Sat, to 9pm Thu, 11am-5pm Sun; 🛗; ⍟Town Hall) The magnificent QVB takes up a whole block and boasts nearly 200 shops on five levels. It's a High Victorian neo-Gothic masterpiece and Sydney's most beautiful shopping centre.

Australian Wine Centre   WINE
(☑ 02-9247 2755; www.australianwinecentre.com; 42 Pitt St; ⊙9.30am-8pm Mon-Thu & Sat, to 9pm Fri, 10am-7pm Sun; ⍟Circular Quay) This shop, with multilingual staff, is packed with quality Australian wine, beer and spirits. Smaller producers are well represented, along with a range of prestigious Penfolds Grange wines and other bottle-aged gems. The service is excellent and international shipping can be arranged.

Gleebooks   BOOKS
(☑ 02-9660 2333; www.gleebooks.com.au; 49 Glebe Point Rd, Glebe; ⊙9am-7pm Mon-Sat,

SYDNEY SPECTATOR SPORTS

Sydneysiders are sports crazy. Going to a match is a great way to absorb some local culture and atmosphere.

Rugby League

For many Sydney sports fans, rugby league is an all-consuming passion. The superfast, supermacho National Rugby League competition runs from March to October. The season climaxes in the sell-out Grand Final, which will be played at the Sydney Cricket Ground (p108) in 2020 and 2021 while Sydney's other two big stadiums, the ANZ Stadium and Sydney Football Stadium, are both being rebuilt; it's expected to return to the Sydney Football Stadium in 2022. You can catch games every weekend during the season, played at the home grounds of Sydney's various tribes; women play in the NRLW competition. Tickets start around $10/26 for the women's/men's competitions via www.tickets.nrl.com.

Rugby Union

Union (www.rugby.com.au), despite its punishing physical component, has a more upper-class rep than rugby league and a less fanatical following in Sydney. The men's annual southern hemisphere Rugby Championship (formerly the Tri-Nations) between Australia's Wallabies, New Zealand's All Blacks, South Africa's Springboks and Argentina's Pumas provokes plenty of passion. In the Super Rugby, the Waratahs bang heads with other teams from Australia, New Zealand, Argentina and South Africa. The Waratahs field a women's team in the local Super W competition.

Netball

Netball, the most popular women's team sport in Australia, is an exciting, fast-paced and high-scoring sport; the premier league Super Netball season runs from April to September. Sydney has two teams in the competitio, the Giants and the Swifts, who share home grounds at Sydney Olympic Park's Ken Rosewall Arena. Buy tickets via www.supernetball.com.au.

AFL

See the Sydney Swans in their red-and-white splendour from March to September at the Sydney Cricket Ground (p108). Sydney's other club, the Greater Western Sydney Giants (with men's and women's teams), play home games at Giants Stadium in the Olympic Park complex. Tickets start at around $25, available via www.afl.com.au.

Soccer

The A-League bucks convention, playing games from late August to February rather than through the depths of winter. Sydney FC (www.sydneyfc.com) won the men's championship in 2017 and 2019. The newer Western Sydney Wanderers haven't won a grand final yet but the men landed an even bigger prize in 2014: the Asian Champions League. Both clubs have W-League teams garnering rapidly increasing support.

Cricket

Sydney Thunder and the Sydney Sixers field men's and women's teams in the all-action Big Bash (p108) competits, which draw big crowds over the summer (tickets from $20/5 for adults/kids). Major international test, one-day and T20 matches take place at the SCG (p108) in summer. Women's cricket is attracting an increasing following in Australia, thanks in part to the world-dominating national team.

10am-6pm Sun; 🚌 431, 433, 🚊 Glebe) Gleebooks is one of Sydney's best bookshops, with its aisles full of politics, arts and general fiction titles, and the staff really know their stuff. Check its calendar for author talks and book launches.

Paddington Markets   MARKET
(📞 02-9331 2923; www.paddingtonmarkets.com.au; 395 Oxford St, Paddington; ⊙ 10am-4pm Sat; 🚌 333, 352, 440, 340) Originating in the 1970s, when they were drenched in the scent of patchouli oil, these markets are considerably more mainstream these days.

They're still worth exploring for their new and vintage clothing, crafts and jewellery. Expect a crush.

Glebe Markets   MARKET
(www.glebemarkets.com.au; Glebe Public School, cnr Glebe Point Rd & Derby Pl; ⊙10am-4pm Sat; ☐431, 433, ☐Glebe) The best of the west: Sydney's bohemian inner-city contingent beats a course to this crowded retro-chic market. There are some great handicrafts and designer pieces on sale, as well as an inclusive community atmosphere and live music.

Opal Minded   JEWELLERY
(☑02-9247 9885; www.opalminded.com; 55 George St; ⊙9am-6:30pm; ☐Circular Quay) This shop in the Rocks is one of several spots around here where you can stock up on opal, that quintessential piece of Aussie bling. The quality and service are both excellent.

Red Eye Records   MUSIC
(☑02-9267 7440; www.redeye.com.au; 143 York St; ⊙9am-6pm Mon-Wed, Fri & Sat, to 9pm Thu, 10am-5pm Sun; ☐Town Hall) Partners of music freaks beware: don't let them descend the stairs into this shop unless you are prepared for a lengthy delay. The shelves are stocked with an irresistible collection of new, classic, rare and collectable LPs, CDs, crass rock T-shirts, books, posters and music DVDs.

ⓘ Information

MEDICAL SERVICES

Royal Prince Alfred Hospital (RPA; ☑02-9515 6111; www.slhd.nsw.gov.au/rpa; Missenden Rd, Camperdown; ☎; ☐412)

St Vincent's Hospital (☑02-8382 1111; www.svhs.org.au; 390 Victoria St, Darlinghurst; ☐Kings Cross)

Kings Cross Clinic (☑02-9358 3066; www.kingscrossclinic.com.au; 13 Springfield Ave, Kings Cross; ⊙9am-1pm & 2.30-6pm Mon & Fri, 9am-1pm & 2-6pm Tue-Thu, 10am-1pm Sat; ☐Kings Cross) General and travel-related medical services.

POST

Australia Post (☑13 76 78; www.auspost.com.au) Has branches throughout the city.

TOURIST INFORMATION

Parramatta Heritage & Visitor Information Centre (☑02-8839 3311; www.discoverparramatta.com; 346a Church St; ⊙9am-5pm; ☐Parramatta) Knowledgeable staff here are genuinely passionate about Parramatta and will point you in the right direction with loads of brochures and leaflets, info on local events, access

for visitors with impaired mobility, and details on local Aboriginal cultural sites. They run free **walking tours** on certain days, including Aboriginal cultural tours led by elders; phone to book.

Customs House Tourist Information (www.cityofsydney.nsw.gov.au; Alfred St, Circular Quay; ⊙9am-8pm Mon-Sat, to 5pm Sun; ☐Circular Quay) This information desk is in the lobby of the **Customs House** (☑02-9242 8551; www.sydneycustomshouse.com.au; 31 Alfred St; ⊙8am-midnight Mon-Fri, from 9am Sat, 9am-5pm Sun; ☐Circular Quay).

City Information Kiosk – Chinatown (www.cityofsydney.nsw.gov.au; Dixon St; ⊙11am-7pm; ☐Town Hall) Under a pagoda-style roof in the heart of Chinatown.

City Information Kiosk – Kings Cross (☑0477 344 125; www.cityofsydney.nsw.gov.au; cnr Darlinghurst Rd & Springfield Ave; ⊙9am-5pm; ☐Kings Cross)

Hello Manly (☑02-9976 1430; www.hellomanly.com.au; East Esplanade, Manly; ⊙9am-5pm Mon-Fri, 10am-4pm Sat & Sun; ☐Manly) This helpful visitor centre, just outside the ferry wharf and alongside the bus interchange, has free pamphlets covering the Manly Scenic Walkway (p77) and other Manly attractions, plus local bus information. Staff can book a variety of tours, including short **walking tours** of Manly (most weekdays depending on volunteer availability, $15).

Sydney Visitor Centre (☑02-8273 0000; www.sydney.com; cnr Argyle & Playfair Sts; ⊙9.30am-5.30pm; ☐Circular Quay) In the heart of the Rocks, this Harbour Authority–run branch has a wide range of brochures, and staff can book accommodation, tours and attractions.

ⓘ Getting There & Away

AIR

Also known as Kingsford Smith Airport, Sydney Airport (p524), just 10km south of the centre, has separate international (T1) and domestic (T2 and T3) terminals, 4km apart on either side of the runways. A free shuttle bus runs between the two terminals, taking around 10 minutes. They are also connected by train ($6.70). Each has **left-luggage services** (☑02-9667 0926; www.baggagestorage.com.au; 24hr suitcase/carry-on $17/14; ⊙6am-9.30pm), ATMs, currency-exchange bureaux and rental-car counters; trains, buses and shuttles depart from both.

Airlines

Virgin Australia (☑13 67 89; www.virginaustralia.com), **Qantas** (☑13 13 13; www.qantas.com), and their budget division **Jetstar** (☑13 15 38; www.jetstar.com), run frequent flights to and from other Australian capitals. **Regional Express** (REX; ☑13 17 13;

www.rex.com.au) and **FlyPelican** (☏ 02-4965 0111; www.flypelican.com.au) connect smaller centres.

Numerous international airlines fly to Sydney from Asia, the Pacific and the Americas as well as from Europe with a refuelling stop. See info. flightmapper.net/airport/SYD for a list of airlines and destinations.

BUS

Long-distance coaches arrive outside Central Station. From here you can access the suburban train network, buses and light rail.

Firefly (☏ 1300 730 740; www.fireflyexpress. com.au) Runs from Sydney to Melbourne and on to Adelaide.

Greyhound (☏ 1300 473 946; www.greyhound. com.au) Greyhound has the most extensive nationwide network.

Murrays (☏ 13 22 51; www.murrays.com.au) Links Sydney with Melbourne and Canberra, with connections to the south coast.

Port Stephens Coaches (☏ 02-4982 2940; www.pscoaches.com.au) Coaches to Newcastle and Nelson Bay.

Premier Motor Service (☏ 13 34 10; www. premierms.com.au) Runs Cairns to Eden, via Brisbane, the Gold Coast and Sydney. Also books services for Firefly.

TRAIN

Intercity trains pull into the old (Country Trains) section of Sydney's historic **Central Station** (☏ 02-9379 1777; Eddy Ave; ☒ Central), in the Haymarket area of the south inner city. From here you can connect to the suburban train network, catch the light rail, or follow the signs to Railway Sq or Eddy Ave for suburban buses.

NSW TrainLink (☏ 02-4907 7501, 13 22 32; www.transportnsw.info/regional) The government-owned train network, connecting Sydney to Canberra, Melbourne, Griffith, Orange, Broken Hill, Dubbo, Moree, Armidale, Coffs Harbour, Casino and Brisbane.

Sydney Trains (☏ 13 15 00; www.trans-portnsw.info) Services Sydney and connects the city with the Blue Mountains, the south coast and the central coast.

ⓘ Getting Around

TO/FROM THE AIRPORT

Bus

Service from the airport is limited. The slow 400 route runs to Bondi Junction (one hour; from $4.80 from the international terminal), which departs roughly every 20 minutes and stops at both the domestic and international terminals.

Shuttle

Airport shuttles head to hotels and hostels in the city centre, and some reach surrounding suburbs and beach destinations. There are numerous airport-to-downtown operators, some with desks in the arrivals hall. For Manly and the northern beaches, try **Airport Shuttle North** (☏ 02-9997 7767; www.asntransfers.com; to Manly 1/2/3 people $44/56/68) or **Manly Express** (☏ 02-8068 8473; www.manlyexpress.com.au; airport to Manly 1/2/3 people $37/52/62).

Taxi

Fares from the airport are approximately $45 to $55 to the city centre, $55 to $65 to North Sydney and $90 to $100 to Manly. There are pick-up areas for Uber and other ride-shares.

Train

Trains from both the domestic and international terminals, connecting into the main train network, are frequent (at least every 10 minutes), quick (15 minutes to Central Station) and easy to use, but airport tickets are charged at a hefty premium ($17 to $19 to Central Station). If there are a few of you, it can be cheaper to catch a taxi or Uber. The cheapest way into town is to take bus 420 to Banksia train station ($2.24, eight minutes from the international terminal) and then catch the regular train to Central (from $2.52, 17 minutes).

CAR & MOTORCYCLE

Avoid driving in central Sydney if you can: there's a confusing one-way-street system, parking's elusive and expensive, and parking inspectors, tolls and tow-away zones proliferate. Conversely, a car is handy for accessing Sydney's outer reaches (particularly the beaches) and for day trips.

Car Hire

Car-rental prices vary depending on season and demand. Read the small print to check age restrictions, exactly what your insurance covers and where you can take the car; for example many rental agreements prohibit driving on unsealed roads.

If you take a small car for a few days, you can hope to find deals for around $30 a day.

The big players have airport desks and city offices (mostly around William St, Darlinghurst). Local companies also compete on rates and quality.

For motorbike hire, try **Bikescape** (☏ 02-8123 0917; www.bikescape.com.au; cnr Parramatta Rd & Young St, Annandale; ☺ 8.30am-5.30pm Mon-Fri, 9-11.30am Sat; ☒ Stanmore).

Car-rental companies:

Ace Rentals (☏ 02-9222 2595; www.acerentalcars.com.au; 50 Ross Smith Ave, Mascot; ☺ 6am-10.30pm)

Avis (☏ 02-9246 4600; www.avis.com.au; 200 William St, Woolloomooloo; ⊙7.30am-5.30pm Mon-Fri, to 2pm Sat & Sun; ☒ Kings Cross)

Bayswater Car Rental (☏ 02-9360 3622; www.bayswatercarrental.com.au; 180 William St, Woolloomooloo; ⊙7am-6.30pm Mon-Fri, 8am-3.30pm Sat, 9am-3.30pm Sun; ☒ Kings Cross)

Budget (☏ 02-8255 9600; www.budget.com.au; 93 William St, Darlinghurst; ⊙7.30am-5.30pm Mon-Fri, to 2pm Sat & Sun; ☒ Kings Cross)

Europcar (☏ 02-8255 9050; www.europcar. com.au; Pullman Hotel, 26-36 College St, Sydney; ⊙7.30am-6pm Tue-Fri, 8am-5pm Sat & Sun, 8am-4pm Mon; ☒ Museum)

Hertz (☏ 02-9360 6621; www.hertz.com.au; 65 William St, Darlinghurst; ⊙7.30am-5.30pm Mon-Fri, 8am-4pm Sat & Sun; ☒ St James)

Jucy (☏1800 150 850; www.jucy.com.au; 96 Princes Hwy, Arncliffe; ⊙8am-5pm Mon-Fri, 8am-2pm Sat, 9am-2pm Sun; ☒ Arncliffe)

Sixt (☏ 0413 639 068, 07-5555 8908; www.sixt. com.au; 191 William St, Darlinghurst; ⊙8.30am-3.45pm Mon-Fri, 8-11.45am Sat & Sun; ☒ Kings Cross)

Thrifty (☏ 02-8374 6177; www.thrifty.com.au; 191 William St, Darlinghurst; ⊙7.30am-4.15pm Mon-Fri, to 11.45am Sat & Sun; ☒ Kings Cross)

Toll Roads

There are hefty tolls on most of Sydney's motorways and major links (including the Harbour Bridge, Harbour Tunnel, Cross City Tunnel, WestConnex and Eastern Distributor). The tolling system is electronic, meaning that it's up to you to organise an electronic tag or visitors' pass through any of the following websites: www.linkt.com.au, www.tollpay. com.au or www.myetoll.com.au. Note that most car-hire companies supply e-tags, but they may well try to sell you an expensive all-inclusive rate. You may be better off or- ganising your own pass after hiring.

Buying & Selling

Sydney is a popular spot for travellers to buy and sell cheap vehicles to tour the country in. Check out www.sydneytravellerscarmarket. com.au for advice and vehicle listings, or check the used-car outlets lining Parramatta Rd.

To drive in NSW, a vehicle must be reg- istered. Registration involves a technical inspection (pink slip), compulsory third-party insurance (green slip) and payment of a fee through Service NSW (www.service.nsw.gov. au). Expect the whole process to cost around $1000, so buying a vehicle with plenty of reg- istration ('rego') is a good idea. Beware: cars may be sold cheaply if the owner knows they aren't likely to pass the upcoming technical inspection. There's also a small fee to transfer registration.

PUBLIC TRANSPORT

Transport NSW (☏13 15 00; www.trans portnsw.info) coordinates all of the state-run bus, ferry, train, metro and light-rail services. You'll find a useful door-to-door journey planner on its website. The system-wide Opal ticketing system is used for travel – pay with a contact- less credit or debit card or linked device, or purchase an Opal card. The TripView app is very useful for real-time public transport info and journey planning.

Bus

➤ Transport NSW has an extensive bus network, operating from around 4.30am to midnight, when less frequent NightRide services commence.

➤ Bus routes starting with an M or E indicate express routes; those with an L have similarly limited stops; all are somewhat quicker than the regular bus lines.

➤ There are several bus hubs in the city centre: Wynyard Park by Wynyard train station; Railway Sq by Central Station; the QVB close to Town Hall Station; and Circular Quay by the ferry, train and light-rail stops of the same name.

➤ Use your contactless credit or debit card, linked device or Opal card to ride buses (adult fares start at $2.24); tap on when you board, and remember to tap off when you alight, or you'll be charged the maximum fare.

Ferry

➤ Most Transport NSW ferriesoperate between 6am and midnight. The standard adult one-way fare for most harbour destinations is $6.12; ferries to Manly, Sydney Olympic Park and Parramatta cost $7.65. Ferries use the Opal ticketing system.

➤ Private company **Manly Fast Ferry** (☏02-9583 1199; www.manlyfastferry.com.au; Wharf 2, Circular Quay; adult one way $9.90) offers boats that blast from Circular Quay to Manly in 18 minutes. Other routes link Manly with Darling Harbour, Barangaroo and Watsons Bay.

➤ Captain Cook Cruises (p79) offers services with several stops around the harbour and all the way to Lane Cove.

Light Rail

➤ Trams run on two connecting routes. One runs between Central Station and Dulwich Hill, stopping at Chinatown, Darling Harbour, the Star casino, Sydney Fish Market, Glebe and Leichhardt en route. The second runs from Circular Quay through the city centre to Cen- tral Station, then shoots east through Surry Hills, heads past the Sydney Cricket Ground and on to Kingsford, with a branch veering to Randwick.

➤ Tickets use the Opal ticketing system and cost $2.24 to $4.80.

OPAL TICKETING SYSTEM

Sydney's public transport network runs on a ticketing system called Opal (www.opal.com.au).

The easiest way to use the system is to tap on and off with a contactless credit or debit card (Visa, MasterCard or Amex), or linked device; you'll be charged an adult fare. Most contactless cards issued overseas can be used, though you may be charged an overseas transaction fee by your card issuer.

You tap on when you start your trip at an electronic reader, and then tap off when you complete your trip, and the system calculates and deducts the correct fare. Readers are located at train and metro station gates, inside the doors of buses, on light-rail platforms and at ferry wharves.

You can also obtain dedicated Opal cards (for free) online or at numerous newsagencies and convenience stores across Sydney. They must be loaded with credit (minimum $10/5 for adult/child; $35 at airport stations). Child/youth Opal cards offer discounted travel for kids aged four to 15 years; kids three and under travel free. For student and pensioner discount Opal cards (available only to Australians or those studying in Australia), you have to apply online. You can still buy single adult or child tickets (Opal single-trip tickets) from machines at many train stations, ferry wharves and light-rail stops, or from bus drivers. These are more expensive than using a card or device.

You get a discount when transferring between services, and after a certain number of journeys in the week, and daily charges are capped at $16.10 ($2.80 on Sundays). Weekly charges are capped at $50. You can use the Opal system at the airport train stations, but none of these bonuses apply.

Train

→ Sydney Trains (p112) has a large suburban railway network with relatively frequent services, although there are no lines to the northern or eastern beaches.

→ Trains run from around 5am to midnight – check timetables for your line. They run a little later at weekends. Trains are replaced by NightRide buses in the small hours. These mostly leave from around Town Hall Station and pass through Railway Sq at Central Station.

→ Trains are significantly more expensive at peak hours, which are from 7am to 9am and 4pm to 6.30pm, Monday to Friday.

→ Trains use the Opal ticketing system; a short one-way trip costs $3.61, or $2.52 off-peak.

TAXIS & RIDE-SHARING SERVICES

Metered taxis are easy to flag down in the central city and inner suburbs, except at changeover times (3pm and 3am). Fares are regulated, so all companies charge the same. Flagfall is $3.60, with a $2.50 'night owl surcharge' after 10pm on Friday and Saturday until 6am the following morning. After that the fare is $2.19 per kilometre, with an additional surcharge of $2.63 per kilometre between 10pm and 6am.

Ride-sharing apps like Uber (www.uber.com) and Ola (https://ola.com.au) operate in Sydney and are very popular. Shebah (www.shebah.com.au) is an all-women (and children) ride-share service. Other apps such as GoCatch and Rydo offer taxi bookings, which can be very handy on busy evenings.

Zero200 (☑ 02-8332 0200; www.zero200.com.au) is a wheelchair-accessible taxi service.

Major taxi companies:
13CABS (☑ 13 22 27; www.13cabs.com.au)
Legion Cabs (☑ 13 14 51; www.legioncabs.com.au)
Premier Cabs (☑ 13 10 17; www.premiercabs.com.au)
RSL Cabs (☑ 02-9581 1111; www.rslcabs.com.au)
Silver Service (☑ 13 31 00; www.silverservice.com.au)

WATER TAXI

Water taxis are a fast way to shunt around the harbour (Circular Quay to Watsons Bay in as little as 15 minutes, for example). Companies will quote on any pick-up point within the harbour and the river, including private jetties, islands and other boats. All have a quote generator on their websites; you can add in extra cruise time for a bit of sightseeing. It's much better value for groups than singles or couples.

Water-taxi companies:
Fantasea Yellow Water Taxis (☑ 1800 326 822; www.yellowwatertaxis.com.au; ☺ 8am-9pm, prebooking required for services outside these hours)
H2O Maxi Taxis (☑ 1300 420 829; www.h2owatertaxis.com.au)
Water Taxis Combined (☑ 02-9555 8888; www.watertaxis.com.au)

AROUND SYDNEY

Blue Mountains

With stunning natural beauty, the World Heritage region of the Blue Mountains is an Australian highlight. The slate-coloured haze that gives the mountains their name comes from a fine mist of oil exuded by the huge eucalypts, forming a dense canopy across the landscape of deep, often inaccessible valleys and chiselled sandstone outcrops.

The foothills begin 65km inland from Sydney, rising to a 1100m-high sandstone plateau riddled with valleys eroded into the stone. There are eight connected conservation areas in the region offering truly fantastic scenery, excellent bushwalks (hikes) and Aboriginal heritage: this is the country of the Darug and Gundungurra peoples.

Although it's possible to day trip from Sydney, consider staying a night (or longer) so you can explore the towns, do at least one bushwalk and eat at some of the excellent restaurants. The hills can be surprisingly cool throughout the year, so bring warm clothes.

♞ Activities

The mountains are a popular cycling destination, with many people taking their bikes on the train to Woodford and then cycling downhill to Glenbrook Station on the **Woodford–Oaks trail** (www.nationalparks.nsw.gov.au/things-to-do/cycling-trails/woodford-oaks-trail), a ride of two to three hours. Cycling maps are available from the visitor centres.

Blue Mountains Adventure Company   ADVENTURE
(☑ 02-4782 1271; www.bmac.com.au; 84a Bathurst Rd, Katoomba; half-/full-day abseiling $195/225, canyoning $245-325; ☺ 8am-6pm Oct-Mar, 9am-5pm Apr-Sep) Opposite Katoomba Station (upstairs), this welcoming set-up offers year-round abseiling, canyoning, bushwalking and rock climbing. They'll leave any day of the week with bookings of three or more people. Lunches are included on full-day trips.

☞ Tours

★ Emu Trekkers   HIKING
(www.emutrekkers.org; 1-/2-day hikes from $79/249) ✐ Award-winning, not-for-profit tours by volunteer guides, with profits going to children's charities like the Indigenous Literacy Foundation and Unicef. Two-day treks include camping out in the bush (food and equipment are included). Meet at Central Station in Sydney and take the train to the mountains. It also runs tours in Sydney Harbour National Park and Royal National Park.

Blue Mountains Explorer Bus   BUS
(☑ 1300 300 915; www.explorerbus.com.au; 283 Bathurst Rd, Katoomba; adult/child $55/27.50; ☺ departures 9.15am-4.15pm) Significantly better than its city equivalents, this is a useful way to get around the most popular Blue Mountains attractions. It offers a hop-on, hop-off service on a Katoomba–Leura loop. Buses leave from Katoomba Station every 30 minutes and feature entertaining live commentary. Tickets are valid for one to three days.

✮✮ Festivals & Events

Winter Magic Festival   FAIR
(www.wintermagic.com.au; Katoomba; ☺ late Jun) This one-day festival, held at the winter solstice in June, sees Katoomba's main street taken over by a parade, market stalls, costumed locals and performances.

⌦ Sleeping

There's a good range of accommodation, but book ahead during winter and for Friday and Saturday nights. Leafy Leura is your best bet for romance, while Blackheath is a good base for hikers; larger Katoomba has excellent hostels and some good B&Bs. Two-night minimum stays are standard at weekends, when prices are higher.

There are bush campgrounds in the parks, some free, but check the contract conditions of your rental vehicle before taking it on dirt roads. Tourist offices have a comprehensive list of campsites.

❶ Information

For more information on the national parks (including walking and camping), contact the NPWS Blue Mountains Heritage Centre at Blackheath (p121), about 2.5km off the Great Western Hwy and 10km north of Katoomba.

There are information centres at the gateway to the mountains in **Glenbrook** (☑ 1300 653 408; www.bluemountainscitytourism.com.au; Hamment Pl; ☺ 8.30am-4pm Mon-Sat, to 3pm Sun; ☜), opposite the station in **Katoomba** (☑ 02-4760 8990; www.visitbluemountains.com.au; 76 Bathurst Rd; ☺ 8.30am-3pm Sat-Tue, to 2pm Wed-Fri) and at Echo Point (p120) (also in Katoomba). All can provide plenty of information on the region.

❶ Getting There & Away

Trains (☑13 15 00; www.transportnsw.info) run hourly from Sydney's Central Station to Katoomba and beyond via a string of Blue Mountains towns. The journey takes two hours to Katoomba and costs from $6.20 on the Opal ticketing system.

To reach the Blue Mountains by road, leave Sydney via Parramatta Rd. Parramatta Rd feeds into the WestConnex tollway (p113) between Haberfield and Parramatta ($8.20), though there are free (slower) alternative routes. After Parramatta the motorway continues (toll-free) to become the Great Western Hwy west of Penrith and takes you to all of the Blue Mountains towns. It takes approximately 1½ hours to drive from central Sydney to Katoomba. A scenic alternative is the Bells Line of Road (p120).

❶ Getting Around

There are limited local bus services run by **Blue Mountains Transit** (☑02-4751 1077; www.cdcbus.com.au) between the main mountains towns; you can also take the train. **Botanica Touring** (☑02-4760 8862; www.botanicatouring.com) runs services along the Bells Line of Road. In Katoomba and Leura, the hop-on, hop-off bus service is a good way to get around the main sights with little fuss, though walking between most of them isn't too burdensome either.

Wentworth Falls

As you head into the town of Wentworth Falls, you'll get your first real taste of Blue Mountains scenery: views to the south open out across the majestic Jamison Valley. The village itself is pleasant for a short potter along the main street.

Wentworth Falls Reserve　NATURE RESERVE
(Falls Rd; ᰡ Wentworth Falls) The falls that lend the town its name launch a plume of spray over a 300m drop. This is the starting point of several walking tracks that delve into the sublime Valley of the Waters, with waterfalls, gorges, woodlands and rainforests. Be sure to stretch your legs along the 1km return walk to **Princes Rock**, which offers excellent views of Wentworth Falls and the Jamison Valley. The reserve is 2.5km from Wentworth Falls Station on the other side of the highway.

Fed　CAFE **$$**
(☑02-4757 1429; 6 Station St; light meals $10-16; ☺6.30am-4pm Mon-Fri, 7.30am-3pm Sat & Sun; ☏☝) A top spot for a pre-walk breakfast or post-falls lunch, this handsome place strikes you on entry with its display cabinets bulging with good-looking food. Homemade pies, delicious daily salads, good-value sandwiches, salmon cakes, vegan rice balls, plus hot breakfasts and decent coffee mean there's something for everyone. Sit in the cosy, ferny interior or out on the street.

Leura

Leura is the Blue Mountains' prettiest town, fashioned around undulating streets, well-tended gardens and sweeping Victorian verandahs. Leura Mall, the tree-lined main street, offers rows of shops selling upmarket homewares and handicrafts, and cafes for the daily tourist influx. Leura adjoins Katoomba, which is slightly higher into the range.

◉ Sights

★**Sublime Point**　VIEWPOINT
(Sublime Point Rd) Southeast of Leura, this sharp, triangular outcrop narrows to a dramatic lookout with sheer cliffs on each side. It's much, much quieter than Katoomba's more famous Echo Point, and on sunny days cloud shadows dance across the vast blue valley below. You can spot the backside of the Three Sisters from here too.

**Leuralla NSW
Toy & Railway Museum**　MUSEUM
(☑02-4784 1169; www.toyandrailwaymuseum.com.au; 36 Olympian Pde; adult/child $15/5, gardens only $10/5; ☺10am-5pm) The striking art deco mansion is the home of the Evatt family, the most famous member of which was HV 'Doc' Evatt, the third president of the UN General Assembly, who helped draft the Universal Declaration of Human Rights. The building is packed with an incredible array of collectables – from grumpy Edwardian baby dolls and *Dr Who* figurines to a rare set of Nazi propaganda toys. Model trains are a highlight and railway memorabilia is scattered throughout the handsome heritage gardens.

🛌 Sleeping

★**Greens of Leura**　B&B **$$$**
(☑02-4784 3241; www.thegreensleura.com.au; 24-26 Grose St; r $215-225; 🅿☝☏) On a quiet street parallel to the Mall, this pretty centenarian house set in a fountain-filled garden offers genuine hospitality and five rooms named after British literary figures. All are individually decorated; some have four-poster beds and spas. Rates include

BLUE MOUNTAINS BUSH FIRES

In the terrible summer of 2019–20, the Gospers Mountain 'megafire', the largest bush fire in Australian history, destroyed an area seven times the size of Singapore. It impacted on the Blue Mountains, including the Blackheath region and especially the Bells Line of Road, wiping out almost 100 homes. But thanks to extraordinary work by emergency services and volunteer firefighters, no human lives were lost in this fire and around 1500 homes were saved. Other fires flared in the area, including one that burned around the Ruined Castle rock formation, visible from Echo Point, and another that claimed four buildings at Jenolan Caves. Some parts of the bush in the affected area were severely impacted, but many parts, including most major walking trails and lookouts, were not. Wilderness areas were expected to regenerate quickly in most places, with green shoots emerging from blackened stumps just weeks after the fires. There's no reason to put off a visit to the mountains.

breakfast as well as afternoon tea with sparkling wine and other goodies.

✕ Eating & Drinking

Leura Garage   MEDITERRANEAN $$
(☑ 02-4784 3391; www.leuragarage.com.au; 84 Railway Pde; lunches $19-25, mains $22-38; ⊙ noon-9pm or later; 🛜 ✐) In case you were in any doubt that this hip cafe-bar was once a garage, the suspended mufflers, stacks of old tyres and staff in overalls emphasise the point. The menu shifts gears from burgers to rustic shared plates served on wooden slabs, deli-treat-laden pizzas and substantial mains.

Silk's Brasserie   MODERN AUSTRALIAN $$$
(☑ 02-4784 2534; www.silksleura.com; 128 Leura Mall; lunch mains $26-43, 2-course dinner $59-75; ⊙ noon-3pm & 6-10pm) A warm welcome awaits at Leura's long-standing fine diner. Despite its contemporary approach, it's a brasserie at heart, so the food is generous and flavoursome. It's a comfortable space, its chessboard tiles and parchment-coloured walls creating an inviting, semiformal atmosphere. There's a two-course minimum at dinner. Make sure you save room for the decadent desserts.

Alexandra Hotel   PUB
(☑ 02-4782 4422; www.alexandrahotel.com.au; 62 Great Western Hwy; ⊙ 10am-10pm Sun-Thu, to midnight Fri & Sat; 🛜) On the highway, the Alex is a gem of an old pub, with lots of character, including cosy fireside nooks, a breezy dining area and a convivial outdoor space. Join the locals playing pool or listening to live bands on Sunday afternoons in summer. There's also a more-than-decent line in pub food, including wood-fired pizza.

Katoomba

There's something a little *Twin Peaks* about this town, with swirling, otherworldly mists, steep streets lined with art deco buildings, astonishing valley views, and a quirky miscellany of buskers, artists, bawdy pubs, retro restaurants and classy hotels. Katoomba is the biggest town in the mountains and manages to be bohemian and bourgeois all at once. It's got a great selection of accommodation and is a logical base, particularly if you're on a budget or travelling by public transport.

◎ Sights & Activities

★ Echo Point   VIEWPOINT
(Echo Point Rd) FREE Echo Point's clifftop viewing platform offers a magical prospect of the area's most essential sight, a rocky trio called the **Three Sisters** (Echo Point Rd), sacred to the Gundungurra people. Warning: the point draws vast, serenity-spoiling tourist gaggles, their idling buses farting fumes into the mountain air. Arrive early or late to avoid them, or skip the scene by heading along the escarpment-hugging **Prince Henry Cliff walk**; you'll soon leave the crowds behind. Parking is pricey in nearby streets. There's a tourist office (p120) here.

Scenic World   CABLE CAR
(☑ 02-4780 0200; www.scenicworld.com.au; Violet St; adult/child $49/27; ⊙ 9am-5pm) This long-time favourite, the Blue Mountains' most touristy attraction, offers spectacular views. Ride the glass-floored **Skyway** gondola across the gorge and then take the vertiginously steep **Scenic Railway**, billed as the steepest railway in the world, down the 52-degree incline to the Jamison Valley floor. From here

Blue Mountains

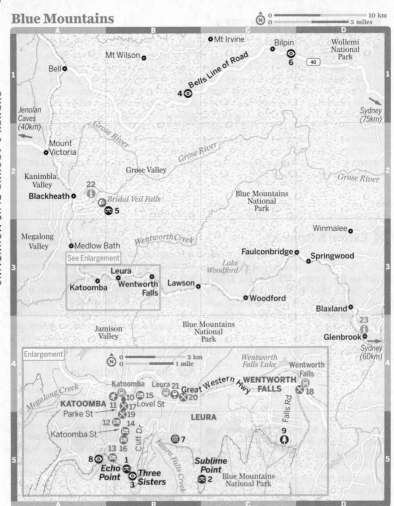

you can wander a 2.4km **forest boardwalk** before catching a **cable car** back up the slope.

Giant Stairway HIKING
(www.nationalparks.nsw.gov.au) This stunning but steep 4.7km walk (two to three hours) links Echo Point and Scenic World via the Giant Stairway, 900 or so steel and stone steps clinging to the edge of the cliff, some of which date from 1909. Views are incredible, and if you can't bear the climb out, you can take the Scenic Railway (the last train leaves at 4.50pm). Those keen for a challenge can take the Furber Steps at Scenic World to the top.

Blue Mountains Bike Hire CYCLING
(📞 0432 052 899; www.bmbikehire.com.au; 144 Bathurst Rd; mountain bike for 3-7hr $88, urban/mountain e-bike $88/140; ⏰ 8.30am-4.30pm Tue-Sun) A few minutes' walk from the train station, this outfit hires electric or mountain bikes, runs cycling tours and offers information on trails and conditions. There's also a drop-to-trail service. No day hires after 1pm.

🛏 Sleeping

⭐ **Blue Mountains YHA** HOSTEL $
(📞 02-4782 1416; www.yha.com.au; 207 Katoomba St; dm $26-34, d $84-120; 🅿 ❄ 🛜) Behind the

Blue Mountains

brick exterior of this popular 200-bed hostel are dorms and family rooms that are simple, but light filled and spotlessly clean. Facilities include a lounge (with an open fire), a pool table, an excellent communal kitchen and an outdoor space with barbecue. Staff can book activities and tours and there's an on-site canyoning and abseiling operator.

No 14　　　　　　　　　　HOSTEL $
(☑ 02-4782 7104; www.14lovelst.com; 14 Lovel St; dm $32, d without bathroom $83, tr with bathroom $120; ☺@☎) 🖉 In a rather lovely century-old house, this hostel has a friendly vibe, colourful interiors, polished floorboards and helpful managers. There's a no-music policy and no TV, so guests tend to actually talk to each other. A basic breakfast is included, or purchase a $6, two-person bacon-and-egg bundle to cook up. The verandah is a top spot to chill out.

★ Carrington Hotel　　　BOUTIQUE HOTEL $$
(☑ 02-4782 1111; www.thecarrington.com.au; 15-47 Katoomba St; d with/without bathroom from $210/135; ❋☎) Like stepping into a game of Cluedo, this 1883 gem has a billiard room and a ballroom, a wood-panelled library, and a bar with a stained-glass dome. But far from being a posh retreat for the elite, the Carrington is a much-loved community treasure, sheltering crochet circles and ukulele jams under its

elderly but genteel wings. Upstairs, there are rooms for different budgets.

Shelton-Lea　　　　　　　　B&B $$
(☑ 02-4782 9883; www.sheltonlea.com; 159 Lurline St; r $170-240; P☺☎) 🖉 This sweet bungalow has four spacious suites, each with its own entrance and sitting area, some with spa bathtub and three with kitchenette. There's a hint of art deco in the decor and lots of plush furnishings. There's a two-night minimum stay at weekends, when you get a cooked breakfast (midweek it's continental). No kids allowed.

Lurline House　　　　　　　B&B $$
(☑ 02-4782 4609; www.lurlinehouse.com.au; 122 Lurline St; r $125-170, with spa $145-190; P☺❋☎) Handsome, spacious rooms with four-poster beds and dark-wood furniture are true to the Federation features of this sizeable, excellently run guesthouse. Some rooms come with spa baths or fireplaces, and there's a lounge where guests can help themselves to fruit or drinks. Rooms are immaculately presented, and it's a cheerful, laid-back place. Breakfast is an impressive event, with an open kitchen.

Lilianfels　　　　　　　　　HOTEL $$$
(☑ 02-4780 1200; www.lilianfels.com.au; 5-19 Lilianfels Ave; r $320-619; P☺❋@☎≋≋) Very close to Echo Point and enjoying spectacular views, this luxury resort set in a lush garden

WORTH A TRIP

BELLS LINE OF ROAD

Hard hit by the devastating bushfires of 2019–20, the stretch of road between North Richmond and Lithgow is an alternative route across the Blue Mountains, which can make a nice loop if you're visiting from Sydney. It's far quieter than the highway.

Bilpin, at the base of the mountains, is known for its apple orchards; check out the **Hillbilly Cider Shed** (☑ 02-4567 2662; www.hillbillycider.com.au; 2230b Bells Line of Road; ⊙ noon-5pm Thu-Mon; 🚻) FREE and try their brews. The Bilpin Markets are held at the district hall every Saturday from 10am to noon.

Midway between Bilpin and Bell, the **Blue Mountains Botanic Garden Mount Tomah** (☑ 02-4567 3000; www.bluemountainsbotanicgarden.com.au; Bells Line of Road, Mount Tomah; ⊙ 9am-5.30pm Mon-Fri, from 9.30am Sat & Sun) 🅿 FREE is a cool-climate annexe of Sydney's Royal Botanic Garden. It was (mostly) saved from destruction in the fires, and provided a much-needed haven for devastated wildlife in the aftermath. Here native plants cuddle up to exotic species, including some magnificent rhododendrons.

To access Bells Line from central Sydney, head over the Harbour Bridge and take the M2 and then the M7 (both have tolls; total $12.71). Exit at Richmond Rd, which becomes Blacktown Rd, then Lennox St, then (after a short dog-leg) Kurrajong Rd and finally Bells Line of Road.

sports an array of facilities including a spa, heated indoor and outdoor pools, a tennis court, a billiards/games room, a library and a gym. Rooms come in a variety of categories; some have excellent vistas. Decor is classical with floral fabrics and tasteful wallpaper.

🍴 Eating

Hominy Bakery　　　　　　　BAKERY $
(☑ 02-4782 9816; 185 Katoomba St; pies from $5, loaves $7-8; ⊙ 6am-5.30pm; 🚻) Brilliant pies and sandwiches, delicious sourdough loaves and tempting sweet treats make this organic bakery an excellent stop.

Station Bar & Woodfired Pizza　　PIZZA $$
(☑ 02-4782 4782; www.stationbar.com.au; 287 Bathurst Rd; pizzas $11-25; ⊙ noon-midnight; 🛜🚻) Bringing visitors and locals together, this is an upbeat spot that combines three happy things: craft beer, pizza and live music (on Friday and Saturday nights). It's in a very likeable space next to the train station. It only does pizzas (plus a couple of salads), but they're delicious, with unusual gourmet toppings.

Aunty Ed's　　　　　　　　DINER $$
(☑ 02-4760 8837; www.auntyeds.com.au; 122 Katoomba St; mains $16-27; ⊙ 5-10pm Wed & Thu, noon-10pm Fri, 9am-10pm Sat & Sun; 🛜🚻) Descend the stairs to travel back 40 years, with Australian classics like milkshakes, spiders (fizzy drinks with a scoop of ice cream) and artfully retro food evoking nostalgia. One thing the nation certainly lacked in the 1970s was decent beer, but happily the 40 tinnies available here are filled with excellent modern craft brews.

Pins on Lurline　　　MODERN AUSTRALIAN $$$
(☑ 02-4782 2281; www.pinsonlurline.com.au; 132 Lurline St; 2-/3-course dinner $55/75; ⊙ 6-9pm, plus noon-2pm Sat & Sun; 🅿🚻) Push through the unpromising entrance to this charming dining room inside a heritage home. It's a local favourite for its seasonal dishes drizzled in carefully composed sauces, and impressive tasting menus (including one for vegetarians). Each dish offers a suggested wine pairing, or ask the staff for a recommendation.

ℹ Information

Echo Point Visitors Centre (☑ 1300 653 408; www.bluemountainscitytourism.com.au; Echo Point Rd; ⊙ 9am-5pm) A sizeable centre with can-do staff and a gift shop.

Blackheath

The crowds and commercial frenzy fizzle considerably 11km north of Katoomba in neat, petite Blackheath. It's a great base for visiting the Grose and Megalong Valleys. Though its fringes were charred in the 2019–20 fires, there are several memorable lookouts around town, and trailheads for some top hikes.

◉ Sights & Activities

★ **Grand Canyon Walk**　　　　HIKING
(Evans Lookout Rd) This spectacular 6km circuit plunges you from Evans Lookout into the valley for a memorable walk along the 'Grand Canyon' before looping back up to the Neates Glen car park, 1.5km from the lookout along the road. Though strenuous on the descent

and ascent, it's one of the area's shadier walks and takes most people around three hours.

Evans Lookout
VIEWPOINT

(Evans Lookout Rd) Signposted 4km from the highway in Blackheath, this lookout presents a magnificent perspective of sandstone cliffs dropping to the valley and canyon below. It's one of the most scenic of the Blue Mountains lookouts, and is also a trailhead for the majestic Grand Canyon Walk, perhaps the area's best half-day excursion.

🛏 Sleeping & Eating

Glenella Guesthouse
GUESTHOUSE $$

(☑02-4787 8352; www.glenella.com.au; 56 Govetts Leap Rd; d or tw $125-150, without bathroom $88-105; ☸❋🛜) Gorgeous, welcoming Glenella has been a guesthouse since 1909. There are several attractive lounge spaces, a stunning dining room and an ex-commercial kitchen where you can cook. Marvellous period features include ceiling mouldings and lead lighting. Rooms range from en-suite heritage rooms (the ones with verandah access are best) to more modern, basic ones with shared bathroom. No children under 16.

Anonymous
CAFE $$

(www.anonymouscafeblackheath.com.au; 237 Great Western Hwy; meals $10-25; ⊘7am-3pm Mon, Wed & Thu, to 4pm Fri & Sat, 7.30am-3pm Sun; 🛜) It's hard to stay anonymous when you do the best coffee in town, so you might only just squeeze into this bijou two-roomed cafe. There's an appetising array of breakfast fare on offer, along with a few lunch mains (go for the daily specials). Upbeat service keeps things buzzy.

Cinnabar
FUSION $$$

(☑02-4787 7269; www.cinnabar.kitchen; 246 Great Western Hwy; share plates $28-38; ⊘5.30-11pm Wed-Sat; 🍴) With a mission to take you around the world in a single sitting, this elegant place on the highway offers very tasty fusion share plates. They play fast and loose with international influences – Tunisian pork balls? – but the enthusiasm and culinary competence makes it easy to relax and enjoy the experience and flavours. Takeaway is also available.

ℹ Information

Blue Mountains Heritage Centre (☑02-4787 8877; www.nationalparks.nsw.gov.au; Govetts Leap Rd; ⊘9am-4.30pm; 🛜) The helpful, official NPWS visitor centre has information about local walks and national parks. It's at the end of Govetts Leap Rd, near the Govetts

Leap Viewpoint, and has a free exhibition on the local wildlife, geology and Indigenous culture. There's also a virtual reality exploration of the Claustral Canyon ($10 for 15 minutes).

Beyond Blackheath

★ Jenolan Caves
CAVE

(☑02-6359 3911; www.jenolancaves.org.au; 4655 Jenolan Caves Rd, Jenolan; adult/child/family from $42/28/95; ⊘tours 9am-6pm) Far from other Blue Mountains attractions, the limestone Jenolan Caves is one of the most extensive, accessible and complex systems in the world – a vast network that's still being explored. The numerous caverns are a spectacular sight with vast subterranean spaces, otherworldly limestone formations and an underground river. Cave visits run throughout the day but book up fast, so it's worth reserving in advance online. If you don't, you may face a substantial wait at busy periods.

Royal National Park

This prime stretch of wilderness is at Sydney's doorstep, and encompasses secluded wilderness beaches, vertiginous cliffs, scrub, heath, rainforest, swamp wallabies, lyrebirds and raucous flocks of yellow-tailed black cockatoos. The **park** (☑02-9542 0648; www.nationalparks.nsw.gov.au; cars $12, pedestrians & cyclists free; ⊘gates 7am-8.30pm) protects 15,091 hectares along 32km of beautiful coast and is the world's second-oldest national park (1879).

◎ Sights & Activities

Wattamolla Beach
BEACH

(www.nationalparks.nsw.gov.au; Wattamolla Rd) About halfway along the coast, Wattamolla Beach is one of the favourite picnic spots in the park and gets pretty busy in summer. It has the great advantage of having both a surf beach and a lagoon, allowing for safe swimming (though it's not patrolled). There's also a waterfall; jumping is strictly prohibited as shifting water levels make it deadly dangerous. The beach is 3.3km from the main road, accessed from very near the Bundeena turn-off.

Garie Beach
BEACH

(www.nationalparks.nsw.gov.au; Garie Beach Rd) Three kilometres down a turn-off from the main road, this excellent surf beach is a picturesque spot. Like all of the Royal National Park surf beaches, swimming can be

DON'T MISS

BLUE MOUNTAINS BUSHWALKING

For tips on walks to suit your level of experience and fitness, call the National Parks' Blue Mountains Heritage Centre (p121) in Blackheath, or the information centres in Glenbrook (p115) or Katoomba (p120). All three sell a variety of walk pamphlets, maps and books.

The three most popular bushwalking areas are the Jamison Valley, south of Katoomba, the Grose Valley, north of Blackheath, and the Wentworth Falls area. Some top choices include the Giant Stairway (p117) and the Grand Canyon Walk (p120). One of the most rewarding long-distance walks is the 46km, three-day **Six Foot Track** from Katoomba along the Megalong Valley to Cox's River and on to the Jenolan Caves. It has campgrounds along the way, but remember to prebook a return shuttle from the caves.

Note that the bush in the Blue Mountains is dense and it can be easy to get lost – there have been deaths – and fires can flare up unexpectedly. Always check conditions before you embark, and leave your name and walk plan with your accommodation, the Katoomba police or at the National Parks centre. You can do this online via the National Parks website (www.nationalparks.nsw.gov.au). The police and the national parks lend personal locator beacons for longer hikes. You can also download the Emergency+ app (https://emergencyapp.triplezero.gov.au) to help locate you in an emergency.

Take plenty of food and, whatever you do, take lots of water; it can get powerfully hot in summer (the gum particles that lend the mountains their blue hue also create a hothouse effect that concentrates the heat), and the steep gradients can dehydrate you fast at any time of year.

treacherous. There's a toilet block but no other facilities despite the large building complex, though the beach is patrolled on summer weekends and daily from late December to late January. A food kiosk opens on weekends and school holidays.

Figure Eight Pools NATURAL POOL
(www.nationalparks.nsw.gov.au/figure8pools) Shaped like the number eight, this pool on a rock shelf near Burning Palms Beach is an Instagram favourite. However it is imperative to pay attention to conditions: tides and weather mean that the shelf is frequently far too dangerous to visit, if not wholly submerged. Read the website forecast in detail before planning a trip here. It's a tough 6km return walk from Garrawarra Farm car park, off Garie Rd. National Parks recommends you visit with a Barefoot Downunder tour.

Coast Track HIKING
(www.nationalparks.nsw.gov.au) This spectacular walk traces the coastline of the Royal National Park between Bundeena and Otford, both of which are accessible by public transport. It is a tough 26km and usually tackled in two days with an overnight at North Era campground (prebook via the website). Doing it north to south offers the best perspectives and keeps the sun at your back.

Barefoot Downunder WALKING
(0476 951 741; www.barefootdownunder.com.au; half-/full-day trips $118/138, student $108/128; 8am-7pm) This husband-and-wife team run friendly and recommended half- and full-day coastal hiking trips from Sydney to the Royal National Park. Theirs is the only operator licensed to take trips to the Figure Eight Pools, which is the safest way to visit that spot. Pick-up is from George St, near Central Station.

🛏 Sleeping & Eating

⭐**Beachhaven** B&B $$$
(02-9544 1333; www.beachhavenbnb.com.au; 13 Bundeena Dr, Bundeena; r $325-475; P❄❀🛜) Right on gorgeous Hordens Beach, this classy B&B is run by a welcoming couple who offer two fabulous rooms. Both have kitchenettes, king beds with plush fabrics, and some fine antique furnishings, as well as a generously stocked fridge and lovely patio area. Beach House is right by the sand, while Tudor Suite is tucked away in a little subtropical garden.

Vinegar & Brown Paper FISH & CHIPS $
(02-9527 6655; www.vinegarandbrownpaper.com.au; 46 Brighton St, Bundeena; fish & chips $18, burgers $12; 11am-7pm Thu-Sun) Classic fish and chips and burgers, well made with fresh ingredients: that's about it, and that's about all you need. Grab some and head to the sand.

ℹ Information

Royal National Park Visitor Centre (✆02-9542 0600; www.nationalparks.nsw.gov.au; 2 Lady Carrington Dr, Audley; ⏰8.30am-4.30pm) This helpful office can sort out entrance fees, maps and bushwalking information. The centre is at Audley, 2km inside the park's northeastern entrance, off the Princes Hwy. There's also a cafe with very pleasant verandah seating.

ℹ Getting There & Away

Cronulla Ferries (✆02-9523 2990; www.cronullaferries.com.au; adult/child $7.10/3.55) travels to **Bundeena** from Cronulla, which is accessible by train from Sydney. **Park Connections** (✆0415 720 100; www.parkconnections.com.au; single trip/day pass $9/15) operates three interconnecting bus routes in the park; stops include Sutherland and Otford train stations, Bundeena Wharf, Garie Beach, Wattamolla, and the trailheads for the Coast Track and Figure Eight Pools.

You can also get a train to Waterfall or Otford and hike into the park from there.

THE CENTRAL COAST

The Central Coast runs between Sydney and Newcastle and includes some gorgeous beaches, swathes of national park and a series of inlets and saltwater lagoons that makes the geography here fascinating. There's demographic diversity too, with working-class coastal communities combined with weekending Sydney socialites and a solid corpus of lifestyle retirees and property-price refugee commuters.

The area's largest town is the transport and services hub of **Gosford**, but visitors tend to head to the iconic nearby beaches of **Avoca** or **Terrigal**. Further south towards the mouth of the Hawkesbury are national-park enclaves such as **Killcare** or **Pearl Beach**.

Further north, a series of salt 'lakes' spreads up the coast; good stopping points include the pelican-infested town of The Entrance and deep, placid **Lake Macquarie**.

◎ Sights & Activities

Bouddi National Park   NATIONAL PARK
(✆02-4320 4200; www.nationalparks.nsw.gov.au; vehicle access to Putty Beach area $8 per day) At this spectacular park, short walking trails lead to isolated beaches and dramatic lookouts from where you can experience the annual whale migration between June and November. There are campgrounds ($24 to $34 for two people) at Little Beach, Putty Beach and Tallow Beach; book ahead. Only the Putty Beach site has drinkable water. From Putty Beach, the **Bouddi Coastal Walk** runs eight easy and picturesque kilometres to Macmasters Beach. There are also good mountain-biking options in the park.

Brisbane Water National Park NATIONAL PARK
(✆02-4320 4200; www.nationalparks.nsw.gov.au; Woy Woy Rd, Kariong; vehicle access at Girrakool & Somersby Falls picnic areas $8) Bordering the Hawkesbury River, 9km southwest of Gosford, this park, despite its name, is mostly sandstone outcrops and forest, with only a small amount of water frontage. It's famed for its explosions of spring wildflowers and Guringai stone engravings, the most impressive gallery of which is the **Bulgandry Aboriginal Engraving Site**, 3km south of the Pacific Hwy on Woy Woy Rd. A favourite retreat for Sydneysiders is the pretty village of Pearl Beach, on the southeastern edge of the park.

Australian Reptile Park   ZOO
(✆02-4340 1022; www.reptilepark.com.au; Pacific Hwy, Somersby; adult/child $39/21; ⏰9am-5pm; ♿) Get up close to koalas and pythons, gaze in awe at big crocs, and watch funnel-web spiders being milked (for the production of antivenom) and a Galapagos tortoise being fed. There are wonderful tours for kids. It's signposted off the M1 Pacific Motorway, or you could get a cab from Gosford Station.

The Entrance   AREA
The Entrance has sprawled beyond its origins at the mouth of Tuggerah Lake to become one of the Central Coast's main centres. With excellent beaches, including landside family-friendly paddling, it's a popular destination. The daily pelican feeding in the town centre draws crowds at 3.30pm.

Central Coast Mountain Bike Tours   MOUNTAIN BIKING
(✆0410 523 612; www.ccmtbtours.com.au; 2hr/half-day ride $100/150) There's some great mountain biking to be done in the Central Coast's national parks and state forests, and these guys will take you out there. From two-hour leisure rides to more challenging half-days, there are options for all abilities. They also do other rentals and pick-ups.

🛏 Sleeping

There are numerous holiday lets right up and down the coast, as well as a wide selection of hotel and motel accommodation. National parks offer rustic camping, while better-equipped sites are dotted around the population centres.

Tiarri on Terrigal HOTEL $$

(📞 02-4384 1423; www.tiarriterrigal.com.au; 16 Tiarri Cres, Terrigal; r $160-200; P 🅿 ❄ 🛜) This small, eight-room hotel in a leafy gully just above Terrigal has clean, modern and comfortable rooms; we prefer the lighter upstairs ones. All have fridges; a couple come with a spa bath and one has a full-sized kitchen. It's very well managed and small enough to feel like a personal experience. On a quiet street five minutes from the beach. Adults only.

Kims Beachside Retreat BUNGALOW $$$

(📞 02-4332 1566; www.kims.com.au; Charlton St, Toowoon Bay; bungalow incl breakfast & dinner from $560; P 🅿 ❄ 🛜 🏊) Boardwalks through a beachside forest of bamboo, palms and pines connect luxurious wooden bungalows at Kims, which has been in business for over 130 years. The beach here, a short drive south of the Entrance, is beautiful, and the accommodation, which includes buffet dinner and breakfast, is ultra-relaxing. The most upmarket villas have their own pool and spa.

✖ Eating

Bon Pavilion PUB FOOD $$

(📞 02-4302 1593; www.thebonpavilion.com.au; 159 Mann St, Gosford; mains $28-43, cafe lunches $12-18; ⊙ food noon-3pm & 5-9.30pm Mon-Fri, 8am-9.30pm Sat & Sun; 🚹 ♿) Bringing a bit of glam to central Gosford, this bar-restaurant complex on the main drag is very OTT, with a vast interior, dark-wood fittings and a sweeping spiral staircase fit for a palace. There's an upmarket restaurant upstairs and more casual bar/cafe eating choices at ground level, including good-value light lunches. It's family-friendly and the bar does tasty wines by the glass.

Pearls on the Beach MODERN AUSTRALIAN $$$

(📞 02-4342 4400; www.pearlsonthebeach.com.au; 1 Tourmaline Ave, Pearl Beach; small plates $23-25, large plates $45; ⊙ noon-2.30pm & 6-10pm Thu-Sun) Share tasty, unpretentious, flavourful Modern Australian creations at this very cute wooden beach house right on the sand at idyllic Pearl Beach. Dishes have a Japanese inflection and are generously proportioned. The atmosphere is likeably casual. There's a good range of wines available by the glass and carafe. Opening hours are reduced in winter.

Reef MODERN AUSTRALIAN $$$

(📞 02-4385 3222; www.reefrestaurant.com.au; The Haven, Terrigal; restaurant mains $36-46, degustation $120, cafe mains $18-32; ⊙ noon-3pm & 6-9pm, cafe 7am-4pm; 🛜) The short, seafood-heavy menu does a fine job of stealing attention from the spectacular views at this white-linen place at Terrigal beach's southern end. The food is beautifully prepared and staff are cheery. Downstairs, the Cove Cafe offers unluxurious balcony seating with sea breezes and a relaxed atmosphere. It opens some evenings in high summer. Check the website for good-value specials.

ℹ Information

The Entrance Visitor Centre (📞 02-4334 4213; www.visitcentralcoast.com.au; 46 Marine Pde, The Entrance; ⊙ 9am-5pm) This tourist office covers the entire Central Coast region.

ℹ Getting There & Away

Driving from Sydney, you can choose to head straight up the M1 Pacific Motorway towards Newcastle (via various Central Coast exits) or take the Gosford exit then meander along the coast.

Gosford is a stop on the Newcastle & Central Coast line, with frequent trains from Sydney and Newcastle (both adult/child peak $8.86/4.43, 1½ hours). There are several other Central Coast stops, including Woy Woy. Trains also stop at Wondabyne within Brisbane Water National Park upon request (rear carriage only).

Local buses connecting the various towns and beaches are operated by **Busways** (📞 02-4368 2277; www.busways.com.au) and **Redbus** (📞 02-4332 8655; www.redbus.com.au).

Southern destinations such as Patonga and Ettalong can be reached by ferry from Sydney's Palm Beach.

THE HUNTER VALLEY

A filigree of picturesque roads criss-crosses this verdant valley, but a pleasant country drive isn't the main motivator for visitors – sheer decadence is. The Hunter Valley is one big gorge fest: fine wine, gourmet restaurants, boutique beer, chocolate, cheese, olives, you name it. Bacchus would surely approve.

The Hunter wineries – over 150 at last count – are refreshingly laid-back and welcoming to novices. They nearly all have a cellar door with cheap or free tastings.

While some deride the Disneyland aspect of the Hunter Valley, the region also offers everything from hot-air balloon rides and

LORD HOWE ISLAND

Rising dramatically from the Pacific 780km from Sydney, little Lord Howe's tropical, World Heritage–listed beauty and its forward-thinking approach to sustainable tourism have thrust this island into the international spotlight. From above it could be mistaken for a Bond villain's lair, with two lofty mountains overlooking an idyllic lagoon, gorgeous white-sand beaches and a lush sub-tropical jungle interior criss-crossed with walking trails.

Lord Howe's isolation and comparatively recent appearance – it was formed by hot-spot volcanic activity around seven million years ago – lends it a unique ecology, with approximately 50% of the flora and fauna endemic to the island. Birdwatchers rejoice as birds rule the roost here, with nesting terns noisily ever-present and the eerie cries of muttonbirds in their burrows punctuating the night. Ongoing ecological projects are seeking to remove introduced species with the aim of making the island rodent-free.

If you crave a slower pace and less crowds, the island's restricted accommodation and flight capacity ensure that visitor numbers are capped. This does mean it's not cheap here, but relaxation is guaranteed: there's limited internet and no mobile-phone signal.

Activities

There's great scope for outdoors fun on Lord Howe Island. On land, walking is the main attraction, with the guided hike up Mt Gower the highlight. A network of well-marked trails covers the rest of the island, offering super viewpoints and secluded beaches. The island's Instagram 'money shot', encompassing the full length of the island, can be snapped from Kim's Lookout via the Malabar Hill walk on the island's northern end. On water, grab a kayak or paddleboard to explore the lagoon, or go snorkelling, surfing or take a turtle-spotting boat trip. Other boat excursions include fishing trips, circumnavigations of the island or journeys to magnificent Ball's Pyramid. Lord Howe Island Marine Park is home to the world's southernmost coral reef, containing a unique mix of temperate and tropical species and over 85 species of hard coral. There's an aquatic adventure available for all ages and abilities.

Sleeping & Eating

Seriously, you'll need to book accommodation before finalising your flight, as the island fills fast, especially during Australian school holidays. There's no camping ground on the island nor is wild camping allowed. The island website www.lordhoweisland.info lists all the accommodation choices. Low-season prices are significantly cheaper, but during summer prices will double.

For a touch of luxury there's no going past the world-class Arajilla Retreat (☑1800 063 928, 02-6563 2002; www.arajilla.com.au; Old Settlement Beach; r from $890), while Pinetrees Lodge (☑02-6563 2177, reservations 02-9262 6585; www.pinetrees.com.au; Lagoon Rd; tw per person all-inclusive 5 nights from $2750; ☺Sep-May; Ⓟ) is a Lord Howe institution. Leanda Lei Apartments (☑02-6563 2195; www.leandalei.com.au; Middle Beach Rd; d from $350; Ⓟ🛜) ⚐ offers 19 fully self-contained units and is the most value-for-money option. Anchorage Restaurant (☑02-6563 2029; www.earlsanchorage.com; Ned's Beach Rd; dinner mains $34-45; ☺8am-9.30pm; 🛜) is the island's best place to eat.

Information

There's a tourist desk in the Lord Howe Island Museum, which also happens to be the hub for the island's limited wi-fi. Excellent details can also be found on www.lordhoweisland.info.

There's no mobile coverage on the island and many locals are keen to keep it that way, as it's an appealing feature for most visitors. Pay phones dot the island, and there are a few free phones around for making local calls.

Getting There & Away

Qantaslink (www.qantas.com) flies direct to Lord Howe from Sydney, which has connections to Brisbane, Melbourne, Port Macquarie and beyond. Flights are expensive for the distance, typically costing well over $1000 return, a little less in low season. One way around this is to fly using frequent flier miles/points: there aren't many dates available, but you don't need many points to get here as it's a domestic flight.

horse riding to open-air concerts. Accordingly, it is a hugely popular weekender for Sydney couples, wedding parties and groups of friends wanting to drink hard while someone else drives. Every Friday they descend and prices leap accordingly.

◉ Sights

Most attractions lie in an area bordered to the north by the New England Hwy and to the south by Wollombi/Maitland Rd, with the main cluster of wineries and restaurants in Pokolbin. The main gateway town is Cessnock, a sprawling agricultural centre that grew on the back of coal mining.

Tulloch Wines
WINERY

(☑ 02-4998 7580; www.tullochwines.com; cnr De Beyers & McDonalds Rds, Pokolbin; ☻ 10am-5pm) The flexibility offered is a particularly appealing aspect of the tastings at this upmarket winery. Choose six bottles from a selection of around 30 to try as part of its free tasting; or kick back with charcuterie or chocolate matches. Better still is the option to pay for fabulous cellar-aged 'museum' drops – it's great to contrast these awesome wines with their younger siblings.

Brokenwood
WINERY

(☑ 02-4998 7559; www.brokenwood.com.au; 401-427 McDonalds Rd, Pokolbin; tasting $10-25; ☻ 9.30am-5pm Mon-Sat, from 10am Sun) Known for semillon and shiraz, plus the popular 'Cricket Pitch' range, this acclaimed winery has a slick, modern visitor centre appropriately decked out in wood. Gather round a sociable circular tasting pod and try the range. It's well worth investing in the $25 tasting, which covers lots of high-quality single-vineyard wines. There's also a viewpoint over the barrel room, a cafe – Cru – doing deli plates, and a restaurant, The Wood.

Wine House
WINERY

(☑ 02-4998 7668; www.winehousehuntervalley.com.au; 426 McDonalds Rd, Pokolbin; redeemable tasting fee $10; ☻ 11am-5pm) With a sweet location by a little dam, this winery has a good attitude and showcases numerous varieties of wine from five great small estates, some of which don't have cellar doors. The upbeat tasting sessions include up to eight wines. There's also a casual eatery here.

Keith Tulloch Winery
WINERY

(☑ 02-4998 7500; www.keithtullochwine.com.au; cnr Hermitage & Deasys Rds, Pokolbin; redeemable tasting fee $5; ☻ 10am-5pm) Keith Tulloch is a fourth-generation winemaker who creates small-batch premium drops. His estate has one of the most inviting tasting settings in the region, upstairs overlooking the vineyard. They invite you to take your time over the nine or so wines in the basic tasting and to linger to enjoy the atmosphere. You can taste premium wines for $25. There's also a chocolate shop and the excellent restaurant Muse Kitchen (☑ 02-4998 7899; www.musedining.com.au; 2/3 courses $70/85; ☻ noon-3pm Wed-Sun, plus 6-9pm Sat; ☜☑).

Petersons
WINERY

(☑ 02-4990 1704; www.petersonswines.com.au; 552 Mt View Rd, Mount View; ☻ 9am-5pm Mon-Sat, from 10am Sun) Though this winery has a cellar door on the main road in Pokolbin, it's worth heading up to this location, where the ultra-friendly staff have more time for a chat and to guide you through the tasty, classically styled wines. It's a very welcoming experience. The Back Block shiraz is particularly delicious, though it's not often available for tasting.

Moorebank Vineyard
WINERY

(☑ 02-4998 7610; www.moorebankvineyard.com; 150 Palmers Lane, Pokolbin; redeemable tasting fee $5; ☻ 10am-5pm) ✎ This off-the-beaten-track, family-run winery makes a great visit; it's a picturesque spot and the owners are warmly welcoming. As well as the tasty wine, there's a great range of homemade condiments including spicy grape sauce, perfect for a bit of pre-barbecue glazing.

First Creek Wines
WINERY

(☑ 02-4998 2992; www.firstcreekwines.com.au; 600 McDonalds Rd, Pokolbin; ☻ 9am-6pm Mon-Wed, to 7pm Thu-Sat, 10am-5pm Sun) Very centrally located, this winery produces a range of elegant, well-balanced styles from local chardonnay, semillon and shiraz as well as from varietals sourced from other parts of the state. The expertly crafted wines offer great value. Tastings are free and it opens later than most.

Tamburlaine
WINERY

(☑ 02-4998 4200; www.tamburlaine.com.au; 358 McDonalds Rd, Pokolbin; free tasting; ☻ 9am-5pm) ✎ Australia's largest producer of certified organic wines, Tamburlaine has a busy, attractively rustic cellar door. It does a full range of white varietals, some tasty cabernet and shiraz, and a couple of dessert wines. Vegan options are available, and the winery also produces preservative-free drops (not usually available for tasting).

Glandore Estate   WINERY
(🕿 02-4998 7140; www.glandorewines.com; 1595
Broke Rd, Pokolbin; redeemable tasting fee $10;
⊙ 10am-5pm) This sweet spot has a smartly kitted-out tasting area and some under-the-radar
but rather tasty whites and reds, including a
couple with the unusual white grape savag-
nin. Staff members are knowledgeable and
make it fun. Try to book one of the wine and
chocolate matchings in the afternoon.

Gundog Estate   WINERY
(🕿 02-4998 6873; www.gundogestate.com.au; 101
McDonalds Rd, Pokolbin; redeemable tasting fee $5-
10; ⊙ 10am-5pm) In a little bungalow, Gundog
offers a plush tasting area that looks like a
posh living room except with wine on the
shelves instead of encyclopedias. It's a very
personable experience, with staff that give as
good as they get. The $10 tasting can include
some striking single-vineyard reds.

🏃 Activities

Balloon Aloft   BALLOONING
(🕿 02-4990 9242; www.balloonaloft.com; Peterson
House, Broke Rd, Pokolbin; adult/child $339/235)
Take to the skies for a sunrise hot-air-
balloon ride over the vineyards. The jaunt
lasts for about an hour and is followed up
with bubbles and breakfast at Peterson
House Winery.

Grapemobile   CYCLING
(🕿 02-4998 7660; www.grapemobile.com.au; 307
Palmers Lane, Pokolbin; day route $45-50; ⊙ 10am-
6pm Wed-Sun) Located at laid-back Pokolbin
Brothers vineyard, Grapemobile offers bikes
(for adults and kids) for a self-guided tour
on a series of safe off-road tracks, which let
you take in nine wineries. Add an extra $20
for transport to and from the starting point.
Want to buy wine on your way around? No
problem; the wineries will deliver it back for
you.

👉 Tours

If no one's volunteering to stay sober enough
to drive, don't worry: there are plenty of
winery tours available, ranging from minibuses providing basic transport between
wineries to full-on gourmet extravaganzas.
Some operators will collect you in Sydney or
Newcastle for a lengthy day trip. See www.
winecountry.com.au.

⭐ Two Fat Blokes   FOOD & DRINK
(🕿 deli 02-4998 6699, tours 0414 316 859; www.
twofatblokes.com.au; 691 Hermitage Rd, Pokolbin;

half-day $79-95, full day $189-259; ⊙ deli 8.30am-
5pm daily, cafe 8.30am-3pm Wed-Sun) These
standout, immersive gourmet experiences
are a great way to discover the region. Upbeat guided tours take you to some excellent
vineyards, but there's plenty more besides
the wine, with cheese, beer, delicious lunches and plenty of entertaining background.
Even if you're not doing a tour, their deli
and cafe is well worth a breakfast or lunch
stop.

🎉 Festivals & Events

Big international names (think Elton John
and Bruce Springsteen) drop by for weekend
concerts at the larger vineyards. If there's
something special on, accommodation
books up well in advance. Check for info at
www.winecountry.com.au.

🛏 Sleeping

Numerous wineries offer accommodation,
and there are lots of boutique self-catering
places. There are literally hundreds of places to stay. Prices shoot up savagely on Friday and Saturday nights, when two-night
minimum stays are common and weddings
also put a strain on available accommodation. Many places don't accept children.

⭐ Hunter Valley YHA   HOSTEL $
(🕿 02-4991 3278; www.yha.com.au; 100 Wine Country Dr, Nulkaba; dm $37-44, r with/without bathroom
$126/105; 🅿 ❄ 🛜 🏊) After a long day's wine
tasting or grape picking, there's plenty of
bonhomie around the barbecue and pool at
this attractive hostel at the northern outskirts
of Cessnock. Set in a characterful wooden
building on spacious grounds, the dorms are
four-berth and spotless, and there's a sweet
verandah, as well as bike hire and a nearby
brewery pub. Rooms can get hot.

⭐ Tonic   BOUTIQUE HOTEL $$$
(🕿 02-4930 9999; www.tonichotel.com.au; 251
Talga Rd, Lovedale; d incl breakfast $290-350, apt
$580-700; 🅿 ❄ ✳ 🛜 🏊) The polished con-
crete floors and urban minimalist style of
this handsome complex work a treat in the
vivid Hunter light. There's a lovely outlook
over a dam into the sunset from the impres-
sive rooms and two-bedroom apartment.
Bathrooms and beds are great, breakfast
supplies are placed in your room, and an ex-
cellent common area and genial host make
for an exceptional experience.
No children under 15 years.

Hunter Valley

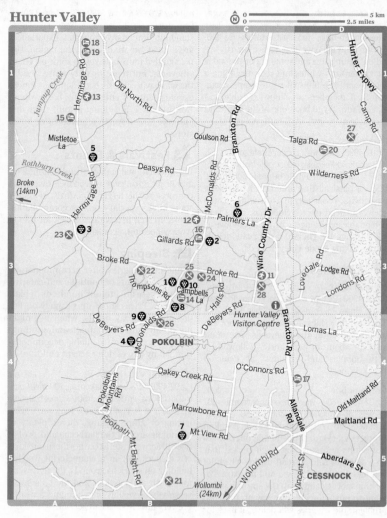

Grange on Hermitage
B&B $$$

(📞 02-4998 7388; www.thegrangeonhermitage.com.
au; 820 Hermitage Rd, Pokolbin; r $220-285, cottages
$450-980; 🅿 ➗ ❄ 🛜) Spacious grounds, euca-
lypts and vines make this a most appealing
place to relax. Rooms are enormous, with
modern amenities, kitchenette and spa bath,
and there are lots of lovely touches, like fresh
flowers and just-baked muffins delivered to
your door as part of breakfast. There are also
two cottages sleeping four to six.

Thistle Hill
B&B $$$

(📞 02-6574 7217; www.thill.com.au; 591 Hermitage
Rd, Pokolbin; r $240-295; 🅿 ➗ ❄ 🛜 🖾) This
idyllic 8-hectare property features rose gardens, a lime orchard, a vineyard, a self-contained cottage sleeping five and a luxurious
guesthouse with eight double rooms. Rooms
and common areas have an elegant French
provincial style and are strikingly attractive.
There's a great lounge and deck by the pool. A
full breakfast is included, even for the cottage.

Spicers Vineyards Estate
RESORT $$$

(📞 02-6574 7229; www.spicersretreats.com; 555 Her-
mitage Rd, Pokolbin; ste $599-699; 🅿 ❄ 🛜 🖾) 🎋
Surrounded by bushland, these 12 modern,
high-end spa suites have king-sized beds and
cosy lounge areas with open fireplaces: per-

Hunter Valley

fect for sipping shiraz in winter. The luxury suites are worth the extra $100 a night, with balconies or private courtyards, and particularly stunning bathrooms. Unwind at the day spa or in the pool before a meal at the top-notch **Restaurant Botanica** (www.spicersvineyards.com; 2-/3-course lunch $69/79, degustation $110; ☺ 6-8.30pm Wed-Fri, noon-2.30pm & 6-8.30pm Sat & Sun, plus 8-10.30am daily; ☎ ☒) ☞.

Cam Way Estate CABIN $$$
(☎ 02-4998 7655; www.camwayestate.com.au; Campbells Lane, Pokolbin; r $225-295; ☒ ☺ ☀ ☎ ☒) Though very central and within walking distance of several wineries, this is a peaceful spot, with well-spaced cabins surrounding a typically Australian rural scene with grazing kangaroos and laughing kookaburras. Studios and apartments are spacious and comfortable; there are flexible interlinking options, making it good for any size family. There's a swimming pool and tennis court. Wi-fi doesn't reach most rooms.

Hermitage Lodge CABIN $$$
(☎ 02-4998 7639; www.hermitagelodge.com.au; 609 McDonalds Rd, Pokolbin; r $225-475; ☒ ☺ ☀ ☎ ☒) Located within walking distance of a variety of cellar doors, this well-run spot has rooms ranging from fairly basic motel-style doubles to bright, modern, spacious studios and suites, with sunny decks overlooking a shiraz vineyard; two have a secluded upstairs deck with spa bath. There's a good northern Italian restaurant on-site, as well as a guest laundry.

✕ Eating

There's some excellent eating to be done in the Hunter Valley, which has a reputation as a gourmet destination. Many restaurants don't open midweek. Bookings are essential. Many of the wineries have restaurants or some form of eating option.

Hunter Valley Smelly Cheese Shop DELI $
(☎ 02-4998 6713; www.smellycheese.net.au; Roche Estate, 2144 Broke Rd, Pokolbin; light meals $10-18; ☺ 10am-5pm Mon-Thu, to 5.30pm Fri & Sat, 10am-5pm Sun) Along with the great range of stinky desirables filling the cheese counter and gloriously whiffy fromagerie fridge, there are deli platters, pizzas, burgers and baguettes to take away or eat on the deck, as well as superb gelato. Good daily specials and a cheery attitude prevail despite the besieging hordes. There's another branch in Pokolbin Village.

Enzo CAFE $$
(☎ 02-4998 7233; www.enzohuntervalley.com.au; cnr Broke & Ekerts Rds, Pokolbin; breakfast mains $16-28, lunch $23-38; ☺ 8am-4pm Sun-Thu, to 5pm Fri & Sat; ☎ ☒) Claim a table by the fireside in winter or in the garden in summer to enjoy the rustic dishes served at this deservedly popular Italian-inflected cafe in a picturebook setting. The food is reliably excellent (succulent lamb, splendid salads), service is casually friendly and a David Hook cellar door is here, so you can add a tasting to your visit.

Fawk Foods CAFE $$
(☎ 02-4998 6585; www.fawkfoods.com; 2188 Broke Rd, Pokolbin; breakfasts $18-24; ☺ 7am-3pm; ☎ ☒) Pokolbin needed an open-daily

WORTH A TRIP

HAWKESBURY RIVER

Less than an hour from Sydney, the tranquil Hawkesbury River flows past honeycomb-coloured cliffs, historic townships and riverside hamlets into bays and inlets and between a series of national parks, including Ku-ring-gai Chase (p80) and Brisbane Water (p123).

Accessible by train, the riverside township of **Brooklyn** is a good place to hire a houseboat and explore the river. Further upstream, a narrow forested waterway diverts from the Hawkesbury and peters down to the chilled-out river town of **Berowra Waters**, where a handful of businesses, boat sheds and residences cluster around the free, 24-hour ferry across Berowra Creek.

breakfast option and this stellar bakery and cafe lays down perfect foundations for a day of tasting. Dishes like beetroot hummus or smoked ocean trout are absolutely beautifully presented, and sandwiches (also takeaway) are delicious in their home-baked breads. They have the best bacon-and-egg roll in a substantial radius. Outdoor deck seating is a pleasure too.

Lillino's   ITALIAN $$
(✒02-4930 7799; www.lillinos.com.au; St Clements Estate, 136 Talga Rd, Rothbury; pizza/pasta $22-28, mains $34-43; ☻noon-3pm & 6-10pm Thu-Mon) It's a romantic, dreamy outlook over vines and hills from the outdoor tables here at sunset. Pleasantly removed from the busy heart of things, this Sardinian-leaning restaurant is an enticing spot for delicious homemade pasta, delicate fish dishes and hearty roast pork. Aged semillon and shiraz from the winery here provide great accompaniments.

★**EXP.**   MODERN AUSTRALIAN $$$
(✒02-4998 7264; www.exprestaurant.com.au; 1596 Broke Rd, Pokolbin; 2/3 courses $68/86; ☻noon-10pm Wed-Sat, noon-3pm Sun; ✐) Frank Fawkner's compact space in a corner of Oakvale winery makes you feel you are all – chefs, waiters, diners – on a convivial shared mission. There are some impressive bravura touches but the entrees and mains are all about deep flavours and texture contrasts; go for the more unusual offerings like quail or take on the degustation ($110).

★**Bistro Molines**   FRENCH $$$
(✒02-4990 9553; www.bistromolines.com.au; Tallavera Grove, 749 Mt View Rd, Mount View; mains $45-47; ☻noon-3pm Thu-Mon, plus 7-9pm Fri & Sat) Set in Carillion's Tallavera Grove winery, this French restaurant run by the Hunter Valley's most storied chef (Robert Molines) has a carefully crafted, seasonally driven menu that is nearly as impressive as the vineyard views. It's a wonderfully romantic location with lovely seating in the paved courtyard. Daily specials supplement the menu.

★**Muse Restaurant**   MODERN AUSTRALIAN $$$
(✒02-4998 6777; www.musedining.com.au; 1 Broke Rd, Pokolbin; 2-course lunch $80, 4-course dinner $115; ☻6-9pm Wed-Sat, noon-3pm Sat & Sun; ✐) Inside the Hungerford Hill winery complex is the area's highest-rated restaurant, offering contemporary fare and stellar service in an a glass-walled, high-ceilinged space. Presentation is exquisite; this is reliably impressive fine dining without pushing boundaries. Their trademark coconut dessert is sensational. Vegetarians get their own menu (with the same prices) and children are also decently catered for. Book well ahead at weekends.

Margan   MODERN AUSTRALIAN $$$
(✒02-6579 1317; www.margan.com.au; Margan Wines, 1238 Milbrodale Rd, Broke; 2/3/5 courses $65/85/115; ☻noon-2.30pm & 6.30-10pm Fri & Sat, noon-2.30pm Sun) ✐ There's a tempting array of dishes at this Broke restaurant, where much of the produce is sourced from the kitchen garden and farm. The luscious food is beautifully accompanied by the excellent estate-made wines. Views stretch across the vines to the Brokenback Range.

Hunters Quarter   MODERN AUSTRALIAN $$$
(✒02-4998 7776; www.huntersquarter.com.au; Cockfighter's Ghost, 576 De Beyers Rd, Pokolbin; mains $36-44; ☻6-10pm Mon, noon-3.30pm & 6-10pm Thu-Sat, noon-3.30pm Sun; ☎) With a lovely outlook over the vines, this place is bustling but intimate. Flavoursome dishes are produced from high-quality ingredients; a good range of wines by the glass lets you taste your way around this and nearby vineyards. Monday is 'locals' night', when two/three courses are $65/85 and it's BYO.

ⓘ Information

Hunter Valley Visitor Centre (✒02-4993 6700; www.huntervalleyvisitorcentre.com.au; 455 Wine Country Dr, Pokolbin; ☻9am-5pm Mon-Sat, to 4pm Sun; ☎) Has a huge stock of leaflets and info on valley accommodation, attractions and dining.

ℹ Getting There & Away

BUS

Rover Coaches (☏ 02-4990 1699; www.rovercoaches.com.au) Has four buses heading between Newcastle and Cessnock ($4.80 Opal card, 1¼ hours) on weekdays and two on Saturday; no Sunday service. Other buses head to Cessnock from the train stations at Maitland (50 minutes, hourly or more frequently Monday to Saturday, six Sunday).

CAR

From Sydney, you can head straight up the M1 motorway, then head to the valley via the exit near Gosford (which allows you to take the scenic route up through Wollombi), the Cessnock turn-off, or the Hunter Expressway (which begins near Newcastle).

TRAIN

A Transport NSW train line heads through the Hunter Valley from Newcastle. Branxton ($6.89, 50 minutes) is the closest station to the vineyards, although only Maitland has bus services to Cessnock.

ℹ Getting Around

There are several options for exploring without a car. The Hunter Valley YHA (p127) hires out bikes and **Sutton Estate** (☏ 0448 600 288; www.suttonestateelectricbikehire.com; 381 Deasys Rd, Pokolbin; half-/full day $75/85) rents out electric bikes. Other choices are to take a tour (p127) or a **taxi** (☏ 02-6572 1133; www.taxico.com.au).

iHop Hunter Valley (☏ 0455 535 035; www.ihophuntervalley.com.au; half-/full day $39/59; ☉ Thu-Mon) This friendly hop-on, hop-off minibus service has 16 stops around the Hunter Valley, allowing you to plan your own flexible winery exploration. A second loop around Lovedale operates only on Saturdays.

Vineyard Shuttle (☏ 02-4991 3655; www.vineyardshuttle.com.au; ☉ 6pm-midnight Tue-Sat) Offers a door-to-door service between Pokolbin accommodation and restaurants, and offers winery tours during the day.

NEWCASTLE

POP 322,300

The port city of Newcastle may be a fraction of the size of Sydney, but Australia's second-oldest city punches well above its weight. Superb surf beaches, historical architecture and a sun-drenched climate are only part of its charm. Fine dining, hip bars, quirky boutiques, a diverse arts scene and a laid-back attitude combine to make 'Newy' well worth a couple of days of your time.

Newcastle, located on traditional Awabakal and Worimi lands, had a rough trot at the end of the 20th century, with a major earthquake and the closure of its steel and shipbuilding industries. Its other important industry, shipping coal, has a decidedly sketchy future too, but Novocastrians always seem to get by with creative entrepreneurship and a positive attitude.

◎ Sights

Newcastle Art Gallery   GALLERY
(☏ 02-4974 5100; www.nag.org.au; 1 Laman St; ☉ 10am-5pm Tue-Sun, plus Mon school holidays; ♿) **FREE** Ignore the brutalist exterior, as inside this remarkable regional gallery are some wonderful works. There's no permanent exhibition; displays rotate the gallery's excellent collection, whose highlights include art by Newcastle-born William Dobell and John Olsen as well as Brett Whiteley and modernist Grace Cossington Smith. There are often child-friendly activities at weekends and school holidays.

Newcastle Museum   MUSEUM
(☏ 02-4974 1400; www.newcastlemuseum.com.au; 6 Workshop Way; ☉ 10am-5pm Tue-Sun, plus Mon school holidays; ♿) **FREE** This attractive museum in the restored Honeysuckle rail workshops tells a tale of the city from its Indigenous Awabakal origins to its rough-and-tumble social history, shaped by a cast of convicts, coal miners and steelworkers. Exhibitions are interactive and engaging, ranging from geology to local icons like Silverchair and the Newcastle Knights rugby league club. If you're travelling with kids, check out hands-on science centre Supernova and the hourly sound-and-light show on the steelmaking process. There's also a cafe.

Fort Scratchley   FORT
(☏ 02-4929 3066; www.newcastle.nsw.gov.au/Fort-Scratchley; Nobbys Rd; tunnel tour adult/child $12.50/6.50; ☉ 10am-4pm Wed-Mon, last tour 2.30pm) Perched above Newcastle Harbour, this intriguing military site was constructed during the Crimean War to protect the city against a feared Russian invasion. During WWII the fort returned fire on a Japanese submarine, making it the only Australian fort to have engaged in a maritime attack. It's free to enter, but the guided tours are worth taking, as you venture into the fort's labyrinth of

Newcastle

SOUTH
PACIFIC
OCEAN

Nobby's Head
(1.2km)

Nobbys Rd

Parnell Pl

Stevenson Pl

Wharf Rd

Newcastle Scott St

Bond St

Pacific St

Ocean St

Shortland Esp

1 Newcastle
Beach

Newcastle
Beach

Hunter St

Watt St

Bolton St

Newcomen St

King St

Church St

Tyrrell St

Reserve Rd

King Edward
Park Obelisk

King
Edward
Park

Bathurst's Way

Stockton
(500m)

Stockton
Ferry

Queens
Wharf

Wharf Rd

Port Hunter

Hunter St Mall

Wolfe St

Perkins St

Brown St

Crown
Street

Crown St

High St

Bar Beach (900m);
Merewether Beach (3km)

Kitchener Pde

Nesca Pde

Brooks St

Darby St

Newcastle
Harbour

Lee Wharf

Lee Wharf Rd

Honeysuckle Dr

HONEYSUCKLE
PRECINCT

Merewether St

Newcastle Visitor
Information Centre

Civic

Hunter St

Civic
Park

King St

Darby St

Council St

Bull St

Bruce St

Laman St

Dawson St

COOKS
HILL

Centennial
Park

Cambridge Hotel (800m);
Newcastle Interchange (850m);
Lass O'Gowrie Hotel (1.2km);
Hamilton Heritage B&B (2.5km)

The Edwards
(800m)

Junction
Hotel (850m)

400 m
0.2 miles

Newcastle

underground tunnels. Head to the shop for tickets or for a self-guided-tour brochure.

Nobby's Head   VIEWPOINT
Originally an island, this headland at the entrance to Newcastle Harbour was joined to the mainland by a stone breakwater built by convicts between 1818 and 1846, many of whom were lost to the wild seas during construction. The walk along the spit towards the lighthouse and meteorological station (open on Sundays) and along the long breakwater is exhilarating, but don't do it in high seas.

Christ Church Cathedral   CATHEDRAL
(☑ 02-4929 2052; www.newcastlecathedral.org.au; 52 Church St; ☺ 7am-6pm, tower 10.15am-3.15pm Mon-Sat, 11.15am-4.15pm Sun) FREE Dominating the city skyline, Newcastle's Anglican cathedral is filled with treasures like a gold chalice and a remembrance book made from jewellery donated by locals who lost loved ones in WWI. The self-guided tour offers an insight into features such as the fine pre-Raphaelite stained-glass window by Edward Burne-Jones and William Morris. Climb the claustrophobic spiral stairs to the tower ($10 donation) for splendid views across the mouth of the Hunter and the long dunes beyond.

Lock-Up   ARTS CENTRE
(☑ 02-4925 2265; www.thelockup.org.au; 90 Hunter St; ☺ 10am-4pm Wed-Sat, 11am-3pm Sun) FREE These days artists in residence, rather than prisoners, occupy this former police station (1861). There's a dynamic contemporary-art programme, artists studios and such creepy jailhouse relics as the padded cell, whose leather walls are stuffed with horsehair.

Hunter Wetlands Centre   NATURE RESERVE
(☑ 02-4951 6466, Segway tours 02-4943 7223; www.wetlands.org.au; 1 Wetlands Pl, Shortland; entry $5; ☺ 9am-4pm) 🚲 Transformed from a dump and abandoned sporting fields into a magnificent conservation sanctuary, this swampy centre is home to over 200 species of bird, including magpie geese, freckled ducks and egrets, and a huge diversity of animal residents. Extensive walking and bike trails criss-cross the site, or you can hire a canoe ($10/3 per adult/non-paddling child for two hours, times tide-dependent) and paddle along picturesque Ironbark Creek.

🏃 Activities

★ Bathers Way   WALKING
(www.visitnewcastle.com.au) This scenic coastal path from Nobby's Beach to Merewether Beach winds along spectacular cliffscapes and the city's finest stretches of sand. Interpretative signs describing Indigenous, convict and natural history dot the 6km trail. The most spectacular section is the board-walked Memorial Walk between Bar Beach and Strzelecki Lookout, with magical sea views.

At the far end of Merewether Beach, look out for the **Merewether Aquarium** (Henderson Pde, Merewether), a charming pedestrian tunnel transformed into a pop-art underwater world by local artist Trevor Dickinson.

DON'T MISS

HUNTER WINE TRAILS

Home to some of the oldest vines (dating from the 1860s) and biggest names in Australian wine, the Hunter Valley is known for its semillon, shiraz and chardonnay, which are of exceptional quality. The valley's 150-plus wineries range from small-scale, family-run affairs to massive commercial operations. Most offer tastings either free or for a small fee, which is usually redeemable against a purchase.

Grab a copy of the free touring map from the visitor centre at Pokolbin and use it to plot your course, or just follow your nose, hunting out the tucked-away small producers.

Most wineries offer significant discounts if you join their wine club, which means you have to buy another case or two in the next year.

🛏 Sleeping

Newcastle has a good choice of midrange accommodation, from remodelled pub rooms to B&Bs and business hotels. Hostels and camping are also available.

Newcastle Beach YHA HOSTEL $
(☑02-4925 3544; www.yha.com.au; 30 Pacific St; dm $30-39, s/d $70/93; ☻@🛜) It may have the look of a grand English mansion, but this sprawling, brick, heritage-listed YHA has the ambience of a laid-back beach bungalow, with great common spaces and airy, comfortable dorms in varying sizes. Just a minute away from the surf, it offers complimentary bodyboards, surfboards, barbecue nights and weekly pub meals.

★ Junction Hotel BOUTIQUE HOTEL $$
(☑02-4962 8888; www.junctionhotel.com.au; 204 Corlette St, The Junction; r $149-189; ☻❄🛜) The upstairs of this pub has been transformed with nine flamboyantly appointed rooms featuring moody lighting, lush fabrics and offbeat colours. All have generous-sized beds, coffee machines and flashy bathrooms with disco lights and (in some) little privacy. Well located among the Junction's boutiques and cafes, it's just a 10-minute walk to the beach.

★ Lucky Hotel BOUTIQUE HOTEL $$
(☑02-4925 8888; www.theluckyhotel.com.au; 237 Hunter St; r $149-229; ☻❄🛜) A slick but

sympathetic revamp of this grand old 1880s dame means it's an upbeat, modern place to stay above a great pub. The 28 light-filled rooms are tastefully decorated, with pleasing touches like luxe bedding and toiletries, not to mention a hand-painted quote about luck in case you need the inspiration. Corridors showcase black-and-white photos of old Newcastle.

Crown on Darby APARTMENT $$
(☑02-4941 6777; www.crownondarby.com.au; 101 Darby St; apt midweek $176-286; P☻❄🛜) Close to cafes and restaurants, this excellent modern complex of 38 apartments is right on Newcastle's coolest street. Studios are reasonably sized and have kitchenettes. One-bedroom apartments are a worthwhile upgrade, with interconnecting options, full kitchens and huge living rooms; some have spa baths. Both open and closed balconies are available, so request your preference.

Hamilton Heritage B&B B&B $$
(☑02-4961 1242; www.accommodationinnewcastle.com.au; 178 Denison St, Hamilton; r $140-155; P☻❄🛜) Offering genuine courtesy and a cosy atmosphere, this Federation-era home near the Beaumont St cafe strip makes for a characterful stay. The house has some beautiful original features, and the two old-style rooms have en suites, fridges and tea- and coffee-making facilities. Guests can use the kitchen and back deck overlooking a lovely subtropical garden.

Grand Hotel PUB $$
(☑02-4929 3489; www.thegrandhotel.net.au; 32 Church St; r $135-169; ☻❄🛜) A short stroll from the beach, this old pub has some lovely details and is a romantic place to stay. Rooms vary widely in size but are modernised; some have access to partitioned private sections of the beautiful wraparound verandah balcony, though top-floor rooms are quieter. Prices are fair. The pub is decent, with two bars and a cellar with Tuesday jazz.

Novotel Newcastle Beach HOTEL $$$
(☑02-4037 0000; www.novotelnewcastlebeach.com.au; 5 King St; r $199-329; P☻❄@🛜) Ideally situated for Newcastle Beach, this breezy hotel seamlessly checks out the business guests on Friday morning and welcomes families that afternoon. Rooms are moderately sized but stylishly furnished. It's worth the upgrade to the superior rooms, which offer bigger windows and better views. There are

good perks and facilities for under-16s. Wi-fi is free if you join the loyalty programme.

Eating

Newcastle has a thriving eating scene. Darby St is a local icon for cafes, Thai and Vietnamese restaurants, and pizza, while the harbourfront has lots of options, particularly in the Honeysuckle Precinct near the tourist office and at Queens Wharf near the Stockton ferry. In Hamilton, places to eat cluster along Beaumont St, while the Junction is well stocked and the beaches have plenty of options too.

Estabar
CAFE $

(☑ 02-4927 1222; www.estabar.com; 61 Shortland Esplanade; breakfasts & lunches $13-18; ⏱ 6.30am-3pm Feb-Dec, 6am-4pm Jan; 🛜 ⓹) 🍴 The punchy single-origin coffee, refreshing frappés and delicious gelato are great at this hugely welcoming spot, and the location right opposite Newcastle Beach is unbeatable. The owner makes an effort to source ethically and locally; the quality of the breakfasts (served until 2.30pm) and light lunch options is very high.

One Penny Black
CAFE $

(☑ 02-4929 3169; www.onepennyblack.com.au; 196 Hunter St; mains $14-20; ⏱ 7am-4.30pm; 🛜 ⓹) Nicely located on the mall, this place is perpetually popular for a reason – excellent coffee, served by staff who know their stuff. Toasties and healthy, well-presented breakfasts and light lunches are another plus.

Momo
CAFE, VEGAN $$

(☑ 02-4926 3310; www.facebook.com/momone wcastle; 227 Hunter St; dishes $12-22; ⏱ 7.30am-3pm; 🛜 ⓹) In a striking, high-ceilinged former bank building that at first seems too big for it, this friendly cafe specialises in wholefoods. Textures, colours and flavours make the vegetarian and vegan dishes very appealing, and influences range from Himalayan – the eponymous *momos* – to local.

The Edwards
MODERN AUSTRALIAN $$

(☑ 02-4940 0112; www.theedwards.com.au; 148 Parry St; medium dishes $16-28; ⏱ 7am-midnight Tue-Sat, 7am-10pm Sun; 🛜) Stylishly flaunting its warehouse chic on this light industrial street in the West End, the Edwards is back from the ashes after a disastrous 2018 fire. It's an out-of-the-way but special place to visit for delicious breakfasts, hefty share plates for lunch and dinner and great wines by the glass. Light, cool and relaxed.

Coal River & Co
ITALIAN $$

(☑ 02-4929 4265; www.coalriverandco.com.au; 120 Darby St; pasta $26-32; ⏱ 6-9.30pm Tue-Thu, noon-2.30pm & 6-9.30pm or later Fri-Sun; ⓹) The focus here is on delicious homemade pasta dishes, which are the only main courses available, though there are some good starters and salads designed to share. The pasta is super-fresh and tasty, and there are some interesting wines available to accompany it.

Signal Box
MODERN AUSTRALIAN $$

(☑ 0423 444 844; www.signalbox.com.au; 155 Wharf Rd; breakfast $16-23, mains $21-37; ⏱ 7am-4pm Sun-Tue, 7am-10pm Wed-Sat; ⓹) This happy indoor-outdoor venue had just opened at the time of research and brings new life to the former railway signal box near the waterfront. Eggs, avocados or garlic mushrooms are among the breakfast dishes that are superseded by Josper-grilled steaks, vegetarian bowls and grilled fish as lunchtime approaches. Fairly priced local wines are also on offer.

Bocados
SPANISH $$

(☑ 02-4925 2801; www.bocados.com.au; 25 King St; share plates $18-35; ⏱ 5-9.30pm daily, plus noon-2.30pm Fri & Sat) A block away from Newcastle Beach, Bocados (the name means 'mouthfuls') has a menu featuring an intriguing range of small and large tapas plates that trawl the Iberian peninsula for their inspiration. There are some pretty authentic ingredients as well as plenty of Spanish wines on the menu. It's BYO from Monday to Wednesday (corkage $10 per bottle).

★ Subo
MODERN AUSTRALIAN, VEGAN $$$

(☑ 02-4023 4048; www.subo.com.au; 551d Hunter St; 5 courses $95; ⏱ 6-10pm Tue-Sat; ⓹) Sweet little Subo gets everything right, from the generous attitude of its enthusiastic young team to its interesting wine selection and romantic atmosphere, particularly in the rear conservatory. The five-course dinner is beautifully presented, with dietary requirements superbly catered for. Optional oyster and cheese courses, plus moreish sourdough, add ballast to a feast of innovative, flavoursome dishes that are creative but without frippery.

Mason
MODERN AUSTRALIAN $$$

(☑ 02-4926 1014; www.restaurantmason.com; 3/35 Hunter St; 2-/3-/5-/7-course meals $75/92/105/130; ⏱ 6-9pm Wed-Sat, plus noon-3pm Fri; ⓹) This elegant dining room near the beach opens pleasantly to the street, where extra tables sit under the plane trees. The cuisine is refined

DON'T MISS

NEWCASTLE'S BEACHES

At the eastern end of town, easily reached on the light rail, surfers and swimmers adore **Newcastle Beach**; the **ocean baths** (www.newcastle.nsw. gov.au; Shortland Esplanade) FREE are a mellow alternative, encased in wonderful multicoloured art deco architecture. There's a shallow pool for toddlers and a backdrop of heaving ocean and chugging cargo ships. Surfers should goofy-foot it to **Nobby's Beach**, just north of the baths – the fast left-hander known as the Wedge at its northern end.

South of Newcastle Beach, below King Edward Park, is Australia's oldest ocean bath, the convict-carved **Bogey Hole**. It's an atmospheric place to splash about when the surf's crashing over its edge. The most popular surfing breaks are at **Bar Beach** and **Merewether Beach**, two ends of the same beach a bit further south. Merewether has huge **ocean baths** (www.newcastle.nsw.gov.au; Frederick St) of its own.

The city's famous surfing festival, **Surfest** (www.surfest.com; Merewether Beach; ⊙Feb-Mar), is the largest of its kind in the country.

and stylishly presented, focusing on subtle flavour and texture combinations, with a Japanese inflection to several of the dishes. Service is notably pleasant and helpful and there are separate tasting menus for vegetarians.

Paymasters FUSION $$$
(☑02-4925 2600; www.paymasters.com.au; 18 Bond St; breakfast dishes $20-26, lunch & dinner mains $37-45; ⊙noon-2pm & 6-9pm Wed-Fri, from 9.30am Sat, 9.30am-2pm Sun; 🖉) In a heritage weatherboard cottage overlooking a park and the river, this is a charming spot indeed. It packs out for weekend breakfasts and offers classy, creative à la carte dishes with a sizeable Asian influence in other meals. It feels a mite overpriced, but the setting is divine. There are good vegan choices.

🍷 Drinking & Nightlife

★**Coal & Cedar** COCKTAIL BAR
(☑0499 345 663; www.coalandcedar.com; 380 Hunter St; ⊙5pm-midnight Mon-Sat) Pull up a stool at the long wooden bar in this Prohibition-style speakeasy where you'll find

Newcastle's finest drinking Old Fashioneds to the sounds of the blues. The cocktails are great; let the expert bartenders guide you. Normal procedure is to text them to open the door: instructions are at the entrance.

The Koutetsu COCKTAIL BAR
(☑0431 760 025; www.facebook.com/thekoutetsu; 555 Hunter St; ⊙4pm-midnight Wed-Sat) Wire mesh and upside-down lampshades give an offbeat industrial vibe to this dark and atmospheric West End bar. A sizeable number of carefully selected spirits, including some fine Japanese whiskies, backs the helpful bartenders, who shake some brilliant house cocktails off the CD-box menu.

Grain Store CRAFT BEER
(☑02-4023 2707; www.grainstorenewcastle.com; 64 Scott St; ⊙11am-10.30pm Tue-Thu, to 11.30pm Fri & Sat, to 10pm Sun; 🖘) Once the grain and keg store for the old Tooheys beer factory, this rustic bar-cafe is an atmospheric with one of the great rotating selections of no fewer than 21 eclectic Australian-brewed craft beers on tap. There's all-day food, with pizzas, burgers and American-style dishes featuring prominently.

Honeysuckle Hotel PUB
(☑02-4929 1499; www.honeysucklehotel.com.au; Lee Wharf, Honeysuckle Dr, Honeysuckle Precinct; ⊙10am-11pm Mon-Thu, to midnight Fri & Sat, to 10pm Sun; 🖘) The deck at this waterfront place, located in a cavernous but cool converted warehouse looking across at the port, is a perfect spot for a sundowner. The food is less impressive.

☆ Entertainment

Newcastle Knights SPECTATOR SPORT
(☑02-4028 9100; www.newcastleknights.com.au; McDonald Jones Stadium, Turton Rd, New Lambton) The pride of Newcastle, the Knights are the local rugby league side. They've had a rough trot of late, but there's plenty of passion around them, and going to a game is a great experience. In summer the stadium is used by the Newcastle Jets A-League soccer team.

Cambridge Hotel LIVE MUSIC
(☑02-4962 2459; www.thecambridgehotel.com.au; 789 Hunter St; ⊙5-9pm Wed, 7-11.30pm Thu, 11.30am-3am Fri & Sat, 8pm-midnight Sun) A backpacker favourite that launched Silverchair, Newcastle's most famous cultural export, this pub continues to showcase touring and local bands. Check the website for upcoming gigs.

Lass O'Gowrie Hotel LIVE MUSIC
(☑ 02-4962 1248; www.lassogowriehotel.com.au;
14 Railway St, Wickham; ⏰ 2pm-midnight Wed-Sat,
2-10pm Sun; 🛜) Built in 1877, this tiled beauty is
the oldest pub in Newcastle and has been the
heart of the local music scene for the last two
decades. It's near the Newcastle Interchange
train station.

ℹ️ Information

Newcastle Visitor Information Centre (☑ 02-
4974 2109; www.visitnewcastle.com.au; Civic
Railway Station, Hunter St; ⏰ 9am-4.30pm
Mon-Fri, 10am-3pm Sat & Sun; 🛜) Set in the
former Civic Railway Station in the heart of
town, this friendly and helpful office has lots of
information on what to see and do in Newcastle.

ℹ️ Getting There & Away

AIR

Port Stephens Coaches has frequent buses
stopping at the **airport** (☑ 02-4928 9800;
www.newcastleairport.com.au; 1 Williamtown
Dr, Williamtown), located around 25km north
of the city in Williamtown, en route between
Newcastle ($4.80 Opal, $6 cash, 40 minutes)
and Nelson Bay. A taxi from the airport to Newcastle city centre costs about $60 and Uber
and shuttle services are also available.

Jetstar (☑ 13 15 38; www.jetstar.com) flies to/
from Melbourne, the Gold Coast and Brisbane;
Qantas (☑ 13 13 13; www.qantas.com) flies to/
from Brisbane; **Regional Express** (Rex; ☑ 13
17 13; www.rex.com.au) flies to/from Sydney;
Fly Pelican (☑ 02-4965 0111; www.flypelican.
com.au) services Sydney, Canberra, Dubbo and
Ballina; and **Virgin Australia** (☑ 13 67 89; www.
virginaustralia.com) flies to/from Brisbane,
Melbourne and Auckland.

BUS

While the new bus station next to the Newcastle
Interchange is under construction, check with
your coach operator where their Newcastle services are leaving from. Buses in the broader Hunter
area accept Opal cards.

Busways (☑ 02-4983 1560; www.busways.com.
au) At least two buses daily to Tea Gardens ($22,
1¾ hours), Hawks Nest ($22, 1¾ hours), Bluey's
Beach ($29, three hours), Forster ($33, 3½
hours) and Taree ($36, four hours).

Greyhound (☑ 1300 473 946; www.grey
hound.com.au) Two to three daily coaches to/
from Sydney ($36, 2¾ hours), Port Macquarie
($60 to $72, 3½ hours), Coffs Harbour ($84 to
$101, six to seven hours), Byron Bay ($132 to
$144, 10½ hours) and Brisbane ($172 to $219,
14 hours).

Port Stephens Coaches (☑ 02-4982 2940;
www.pscoaches.com.au) Regular buses to Anna
Bay (1¼ hours), Nelson Bay (1¾ hours), Shoal
Bay and Fingal Bay (two hours). All these fares
are $4.80 on Opal card or $6 cash.

Premier Motor Service (☑ 13 34 10; www.
premierms.com.au) Daily coaches to/from
Sydney ($35, three hours), Port Macquarie ($48,
3¾ hours), Coffs Harbour ($60, six hours), Byron
Bay ($73, 11 hours) and Brisbane ($78, 14½
hours).

Rover Coaches (☑ 02-4990 1699; www.rover-
coaches.com.au) Four buses to/from Cessnock
($4.80 Opal, 1¼ hours) on weekdays and two on
Saturday.

TRAIN

Sydney Trains (p112) runs regular services
to **Newcastle Interchange**, 2km west of the
centre and easily accessed on the light rail,
from Gosford ($8.86, 1½ hours) and Sydney
($8.86, three hours). A line also heads to the
Hunter Valley; Branxton ($6.89, 50 minutes) is
the closest stop to wine country.

ℹ️ Getting Around

BICYCLE

Bykko (☑ 1300 129 556; www.bykko.com.au)
This electric-bike-share scheme has a lot of
docks around Newcastle. Download the app and
away you go. Pay-as-you-go rates are $2 for 10
minutes or $10 for an hour; monthly rates are
$40 but that still only includes 60-minute rides
so it's designed for cross-town trips rather than
exploration.

Lynch's Hub (☑ 02-4925 2926; www.lynchs
hub.com.au; 292 Wharf Rd; bike 1hr/2hr/day
$9/15/25; ⏰ 7am-3pm Mon-Fri, to 5pm Sat &
Sun) This friendly waterfront cafe rents decent
bikes, with family-friendly options like tandems
and trailers available, as well as handcycles.

BUS

Newcastle has an extensive network of **local buses** (☑ 13 15 00; www.newcastletransport.info);
use an Opal card or pay-and-go credit or debit
card. The main hub is next to the former Newcastle train station in the east of the city.

FERRY

Stockton Ferry (www.transportnsw.info; adult/
child Opal card $2.24/1.12) Leaves every
half-hour from Queens Wharf to the suburb of
Stockton.

TRAIN

The new light rail service runs from the **Newcastle
Interchange** through the centre of town and on to
the beach. Tickets cost $2.24 with an Opal card,
or just 20¢ if you're transferring from the train or
ferry.

Byron Bay & North Coast New South Wales

Includes ➜

Best Places to Eat

➜ Little Beach Boathouse (p143)

➜ Qudo Cafe & Sake (p155)

➜ Bill's Fishhouse (p150)

➜ Fleet (p170)

➜ Paper Daisy (p171)

➜ Shelter (p163)

Best Places to Sleep

➜ Armana Resort (p143)

➜ Promised Land Retreat (p154)

➜ Bombah Point Eco Cottages (p145)

➜ 28° Byron Bay (p167)

➜ Halcyon House (p171)

➜ Sails Motel (p170)

Why Go?

Providing a buffer between New South Wales' capital-city sprawl to the south and Queensland's Gold Coast strip up over the border, northern NSW offers an altogether simpler way of life. Lovely, lazy beach towns and pristine national parks leapfrog each other all the way up this stupendous stretch of scenic coast.

Inland, lush farmland and ancient tracts of World Heritage–listed rainforest do the same, punctuated by hinterland towns with a character and charm all to themselves – seemingly more bohemian the further you venture towards the Queensland border. Farmers rub shoulders with folk who've abandoned the city for the sea and post-hippie alternative lifestylers here: if you're looking for stellar local produce, a single-origin coffee or a psychic reading, you won't be disappointed. And if you're searching for a surf break, rest assured there will be an awesome one, right around the next corner.

When to Go
Byron Bay

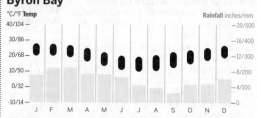

Jun & Jul
Migrating whales visit the coast and big-name musos visit Byron Bay.

Sep–Nov
Swimming weather and blooming jacarandas, though school-leavers hit mid-November.

Dec–Apr
Life's a beach; book ahead for January and Easter.

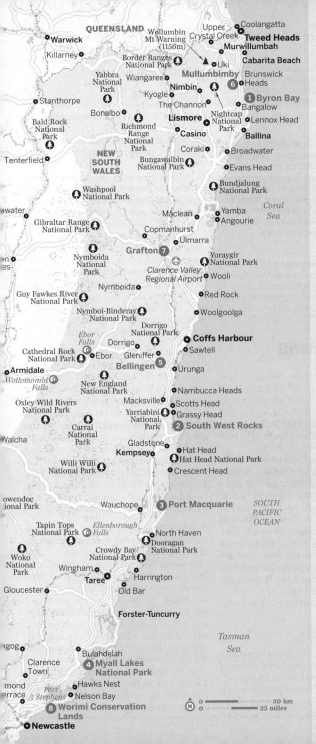

QUEENSLAND

Warwick

Killarney

Wollumbin Mt Warning (1156m)

Upper Crystal Creek

Coolangatta

Tweed Heads

Murwillumbah

Border Ranges National Park

Uki

Cabarita Beach

Yabbra National Park

Wiangaree

Mullumbimby

Brunswick Heads

6

Stanthorpe

Kyogle

Nimbin

❶ Byron Bay

The Channon

Bonalbo

Lismore

Nightcap National Park

Bangalow

Lennox Head

Bald Rock National Park

Richmond Range National Park

Casino

Ballina

Tenterfield

NEW SOUTH WALES

Coraki

Broadwater

Bungawalbin National Park

Evans Head

water

Washpool National Park

Bundjalung National Park

Coral Sea

Gibraltar Range National Park

Maclean

Yamba

Angourie

Copmanhurst

Grafton ❼

Ulmarra

Nymboida National Park

Yuraygir National Park

es

Clarence Valley Regional Airport

Wooli

Nymboida

Guy Fawkes River National Park

Red Rock

Nymboi-Binderay National Park

Woolgoolga

Ebor Falls

Dorrigo National Park

Cathedral Rock National Park

Dorrigo

Ebor

Gleniffer

Coffs Harbour

Sawtell

Armidale

Bellingen

❺

Urunga

Wollomombi Falls

New England National Park

Nambucca Heads

Oxley Wild Rivers National Park

Macksville

Scotts Head

Yarriabini National Park

Grassy Head

Walcha

Carrai National Park

Gladstone

❷ South West Rocks

Kempsey

Hat Head

Hat Head National Park

Willi Willi National Park

Crescent Head

owendoc ional Park

Wauchope

❸ Port Macquarie

SOUTH PACIFIC OCEAN

Tapin Tops National Park

Ellenborough Falls

North Haven

Dooragan National Park

Woko National Park

Crowdy Bay National Park

Wingham

Harrington

Taree

Gloucester

Old Bar

Forster-Tuncurry

Tasman Sea

ngog

Bulahdelah

Clarence Town

❹ Myall Lakes National Park

Hawks Nest

mond errace

Port Stephens

Nelson Bay

❽ Worimi Conservation Lands

Newcastle

0   50 km
0   25 miles

ℹ️ Getting There & Around

BUS
Greyhound (www.greyhound.com.au) and Premier (www.premierms.com.au) both have coach services linking Sydney and Brisbane via the Pacific Hwy. Other companies cover smaller stretches along the way.

CAR
The Pacific Hwy (Hwy 1) is an adventure in itself. It's been greatly improved (which, some might say, makes it easier for Sydneysiders to drive their luxury SUVs to Byron Bay) with eased curves and dual carriageways, but some parts remain a minefield of narrow curves, stoplights, traffic (eg Coffs Harbour) and speed cameras. Take the detours east to the coast or west up into the hills when you get the chance.

TRAIN
NSW TrainLink (www.nswtrainlink.info) services between Sydney and Brisbane stop at Wingham, Taree, Nambucca Heads, Coffs Harbour, Grafton and Casino. At Casino, coach connections to Tweed Heads stop at Lismore, Ballina and Byron Bay.

PORT STEPHENS

POP 72,695

Fringed by national parks and the largest moving sand dunes in the southern hemisphere, Port Stephens has something for every beach bum. It boasts sheltered bays perfect for lazy beach days and ideal for families, as well as rugged ocean shores favoured by surfers, fishers and even rock climbers.

Nelson Bay, the area's main town, self-bills as the 'dolphin capital of Australia'. It has a compact shopping and dining precinct and a bustling marina from where you can embark on all manner of aquatic adventures and activities. Just east of town, Tomaree National Park arcs southwest along the coast, skirting the sleepy villages of Boat Harbour and Anna Bay, just over the rise from wide and wild Birubi Beach, gateway to the expansive and incredible dune-filled landscape of the Worimi Conservation Lands.

All this, under an hour's drive from downtown Newcastle!

👁️ Sights

East of Nelson Bay, the pretty community of Shoal Bay has a wonderful sheltered swimming beach as well as ocean beaches. To its south, adjacent Fingal Bay has a pretty harbour beach and coastal beaches within Tomaree National Park. The park follows a southwest arc and encompasses clothing-optional Samurai Beach and magnificent One Mile Beach. Anna Bay is the gateway to the Worimi Conservation Lands.

⭐ Worimi Conservation Lands
NATURE RESERVE

(📞02-4984 8200; www.worimiconservationlands.com; 3-day driving permit $33) Located at Stockton Bight, these are the longest moving sand dunes in the southern hemisphere, stretching more than 35km. Thanks to the generosity of the Worimi people, the traditional owners who now manage the area, you're able to roam around and drive along the beach (4WD only). Be sure to check driving conditions and where to get your driving permit online.

It's possible to become so surrounded by shimmering sand that you'll lose sight of the ocean or any sign of life. As spectacular as this might be, it's the rich cultural heritage of the Worimi that makes this a truly special place to visit. The area includes numerous shell middens, some dating back tens of thousands of years. At the far western end of the beach, the wreck of the *Sygna* founders in the water.

⭐ Oakvale Wildlife Park
ANIMAL SANCTUARY

(📞02-4982 6222; www.oakvalewildlife.com.au; 3 Oakvale Dr, Salt Ash; adult/child $29.50/17.50; ⏰10am-5pm) What began its life as a humble petting zoo with a handful of farm animals in 1979 has grown into one of Australia's finest family-owned-and-operated wildlife sanctuaries, where visitors are free to 'roam with the animals'. Native Australian wildlife, including some endangered species, are represented, as well as furry, scaly and winged friends from around the world. Don't miss the fantastic koala breeding and education centre. Check the website for educational show times.

Tomaree National Park
NATIONAL PARK

(📞02-4984 8200; www.nationalparks.nsw.gov.au/visit-a-park/parks/tomaree-national-park; ⏰24hr) This wonderfully wild expanse offers beautiful hiking in an area that can feel far more remote than it actually is. The park harbours angophora forests and several threatened species, including the spotted-tailed quoll and powerful owl, and you can spot outcrops of the rare volcanic rock rhyodacite. In spring, the Morna Point trail (5.5km return, 2½ hours) is strewn with wildflowers.

At the eastern end of Shoal Bay there's a short walk to the surf at unpatrolled Zenith Beach (2km return, 30 minutes), or you can tackle the Tomaree Head Summit Walk

---

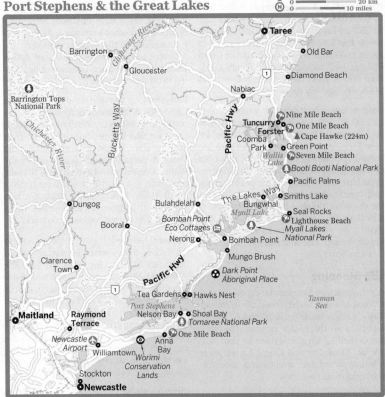

(2.2km, 1½ hours return) and be rewarded with stunning ocean views. For picnics and rock pool snorkelling try Fishermans Bay.

Nelson Head Lighthouse Cottage
HISTORIC BUILDING

(☑ 02-4981 3585; Lighthouse Rd, Nelson Bay; ⏰ 10am-4pm Mon-Fri, from 9am Sat & Sun) **FREE** Built in 1875, this restored lighthouse now hosts a small maritime museum with displays on the history of the building and the area's coast guard patrol. You can also visit the working Coastal Patrol radio base, staffed by volunteers; be sure to plan to visit in time for a light lunch or cuppa at the wonderful cafe (p143) with sweeping views.

🏃 Activities & Tours

There are dozens of operators offering various action-packed ways to spend your days in the area. As a general rule, cruises and aquatic adventures depart from **d'Albora Marinas** in Nelson Bay, while tour camel rides, sandboarding and 4WD adventures

in the Worimi Conservation Lands depart from **Birubi Beach** in Anna Bay – you'll find various trailers in the Birubi Point car park. Book ahead, or just show up.

Port Stephens 4WD Tours
TOURS

(☑ 02-4984 4760; www.portstephens4wd.com. au; James Patterson St, Anna Bay; tours from adult/ child $28/20) Offers a 1½-hour Beach & Dune tour (adult/child $52/31) and a sandboarding experience ($28/20) out on the magnificent dunes of the Worimi Conservation Lands. You can stay as long as you like if sandboarding; just jump on the shuttle when you want to go home. Check the website for operating times.

Port Stephens Surf School
SURFING

(☑ 0411 419 576; www.portstephenssurfschool. com.au; 1½hr group surf lessons $65) Operating for over 20 years, the region's first surf school offers both group and private surf lessons for adults and kids at One Mile and Fingal Bay Beaches. Board hire is also available (one/two hours $30/40).

Port Stephens Paddlesports   KAYAKING
(☑0405 033 518; www.paddleportstephens.com.
au; 35 Shoal Bay Rd, Shoal Bay; kayak/paddleboard
hire per hour $30; ☉Sep-May) Offers a range of
kayak and stand-up-paddleboard hire (from
$30) as well as excursions, including 1½-
hour sunset tours (adult/child $50/40) and
2½-hour discovery tours ($60/50).

Dolphin Swim Australia   WILDLIFE WATCHING
(☑1300 721 358; www.dolphinswimaustralia.com.
au; 6 Teramby Rd, Nelson Bay, d'Albora Marinas; 4hr
swim $329; ☉tours 5-10am Thu-Sun) There are
several operators in Port Stephens that offer
swimming with dolphins. Animal-welfare experts have concerns about the health effects
such human-animal interactions can have on
the dolphins. Dolphin Swim Australia operates the only state-sanctioned wild-dolphin
swim tour where six guests at a time are
towed through the water as the inquisitive
dolphins approach.

🛏 Sleeping

Accommodation here can be expensive and
tending towards bland, especially in Nelson
Bay – though some bargains can be found,
especially in the cooler months. It's often
worth shelling out a little more for your stay.
We like Shoal Bay and Fingal Bay for their
selection of relaxed options and access to
the region's best beaches.

Halifax Holiday Park   CAMPGROUND $
(☑02-4988 0990; www.beachsideholidays.com.
au; Beach Rd, Little Beach; powered sites from $48,
cabins from $180; P� ☎ ☎) This holiday park
boasts one of Port Stephen's best locations
and features powered camp sites and a variety of comfortable cabins ranging from two
bedroom to four bedroom, most with direct
beach access. Some include spa baths and
have water views. An amenities block including showers, bathrooms, camp kitchen
and guest laundry opened in 2019. Highly
recommended.

There's no pool, but the park has direct access to both Shoal Bay Beach and Little Beach.

Melaleuca Surfside Backpackers   HOSTEL $
(☑02-4981 9422; www.melaleucabackpackers.
com.au; 2 Koala Pl, One Mile Beach; sites/dm/
cabins from $20/32/70; @☎) Pitch your tent
among bushland, dosh out in a dorm, or
kick back in cosy architect-designed cabins
set amid peaceful scrub inhabited by koalas, kookaburras and sugar gliders at this
friendly, well-run and bilssfully car-free

place. There's a welcoming lounge area and
a kitchen, along with surfboard hire, sandboarding and other excursions. Make booking enquiries on the website; rates vary.

A nice touch is the $10 'day-stay' option
for travellers seeking a hot shower or wanting to do some washing.

Ganyamalbaa Campground   CAMPGROUND $
(☑02-4984 8200; www.worimiconservationlands.
com/camping; Worimi Conservation Lands, enter via
Lavis Lane; sites $33; P) Stay under the stars
on Australia's largest moving coastal sand
dunes, as part of a camping trial run by the
Worimi Conservation Lands (p140). To make
a booking, you must first watch an instruc-
tional video. Park permits ($33) are also
required in addition to the site fee. Bring
everything you need, and leave no trace.

★Hotel Nelson   BOUTIQUE HOTEL $$
(☑02-4916 4600; www.hotelnelson.com.au; 3
Government Rd, Nelson Bay; d/apt from $175/220;
P✳☎☎) Fresh from renovation and re-
branding, the Nelson boasts an excellent
location a stones' throw from the Marina,
Foreshore Reserve and the downtown shop-
ping and dining precinct. Styling is crisp and
clean with woody accents and splashes of col-
our. Many rooms and apartments have balco-
nies with pleasant views across the Marina to
the Bay. The on-site cafe is a local fave.

Dutchies Motel   MOTEL $$
(☑02-4984 9299; https://dutchies-motel.busi
ness.site; 16 Christmas Bush Ave, Nelson Bay; d
from $130; P☎) The best thing about this lit-
tle motel, with its handful of pleasantly renovated (though not air-conditioned) rooms
with teeny kitchenette, painted brickwork
and real-deal 70's soft-pink bathroom tiles
is its almost-beachfront location. It's set in
the utterly delightful, sleepy cove known as
Dutchman's Beach ('Dutchies', to locals); just
over the hill and yet half-a-world away from
Nelson Bay's main drag.

Marty's at Little Beach   HOTEL $$
(☑02-4984 9100; www.martys.net.au; cnr Gow-
rie Ave & Intrepid Close, Nelson Bay; r/apt from
$140/210; ✳☎☎☎) This uberpopular, pri-
vately run motel is an easy stroll to Little
Beach and Shoal Bay. Simple beach-house-
inspired rooms and modern, self-contained
apartments feel fresh and quietly stylish.
Families with kids older than babes in cots
are only accommodated in the two-bedroom
executive suites.

★ Armana Resort
BOUTIQUE HOTEL $$$
(✆02-4981 1644; www.amarnaluxurybeachresort.com.au; 16 Christmas Bush Ave, Nelson Bay; apt from $460; P❋☎☀) Not for those on a budget, this boutique collection of fully self-contained, one-, two- and three-bedroom apartments and penthouses in a waterfront, resort-style setting on delightful Dutchman's Beach, is unrivalled in Port Stephens for its location, style and luxury. For that special occasion, why not splurge on Apartment 201, with its own private pool and spa.

All apartments have full ocean views and there is generally a two-night minimum stay.

✖ Eating

With a particular emphasis on fresh seafood, Port Stephens has some excellent restaurants, not all of which are located in downtown Nelson Bay. You may have to travel a little further afield to some outlying villages to sample some of the better establishments.

★ Inner Light Tearooms
CAFE $
(✆02-4984 2505; www.innerlighttearooms.com.au; 5a Lighthouse Rd, Nelson Bay; light meals $6-21; ☉9am-3pm; P) Enjoy stunning vistas over the Port Stephens' headlands to the great blue yonder of the Pacific Ocean from this breezy breakfast and lunch spot in the historic Lighthouse Cottage (p141) atop Nelson Head. If you're only in the Bay for a day and don't have time for lunch, you must stop by for famous, freshly baked scones and incredible views.

Note: the walk up from the beach isn't ideal for those with mobility challenges, and parking spaces at the top are limited.

Peter's Chinese
CHINESE $
(✆02-4981 2685; 3/47 Donald St, Nelson Bay; lunches $10, mains $12-22; ☉11am-9.30pm) If you're looking for a cheap alternative to the Bay's oversaturation of seafood, pop upstairs to Peter's Chinese for $10 lunches and no-fuss dinners and takeaways. The backyard veggie garden and the wonderfully kitsch signage and decor let you know that this is a tried and true ma-and-pa kitchen from way back.

★ Shoal Bay Country Club
PUB FOOD $$
(✆02-4981 1555; www.shoalbaycountryclub.com.au; 35-45 Shoal Bay Rd, Shoal Bay; pizza $19-26, mains $23-40; ☉7am-2am Mon-Sat, to midnight Sun) Fresh from a fabulous, multi-million-dollar refurbishment, the iconic 1930s Shoal Bay Country Club, opposite gorgeous Shoal Bay beach, isn't a country club at all by American standards. But it is the place to be and be seen in Port Stephens. Drop in for brekky in its 1950s Mermaids diner for a wood-fired pizza or fresh seafood, or simply for a sunset cocktail.

Crest Birubi Beach
CAFE $$
(✆02-4919 0446; www.crestbirubibeach.com.au; 73 James Paterson St, Anna Bay; mains $10-24; ☉8am-3pm; P) This stylish, smart-casual cafe within the Birubi Point surf club boasts an absolute beachfront location with stunning views over Stockton Bight and the Worimi Conservation Lands (p140), perfect for a post-camel-ride Avocado Smash or bucket of prawns. Crest's full bar licence means you can trade Tea Gardens kombucha for Hunter Valley verdelho, or simply sip beers in the sun.

Holbert's Oyster Farm
SEAFOOD $$
(✆02-4982 7234; www.holbertsoysterfarm.com; Lot 52 Diemars Rd, Salamander Bay; oysters by-the-dozen from $15; ☉7am-5pm Mon-Fri, from 9am Sat-Sun; P) If one was to draw a line in the sand, you could fairly safely put shucker-lovers on the left, and haters on the right, without the need for other distinctions such as 'sometimes like'. If you'd put yourself left of that line, you'd best get here quick for some of the best briny bivalves in the oyster capital of the nation.

Sienna's
ITALIAN $$
(✆02-4984 4900; www.siennas.com.au; 85 Magnus St, Nelson Bay; pizza $16-26, mains $21-33; ☉8am-2.30pm & 6-9pm) Sienna's offers a budget-conscious alternative to the myriad of Port Stephens' tourist-priced seafood restaurants. Now in its second decade of operation, this family-run Italian joint has found its niche. Service is fast and friendly, starting with mouthwatering brunches, a tempting menu of pizzas and pastas from lunchtime onwards, your favourite *secondi piatti* for dinner and decadent continental cakes for dessert.

★ Little Beach Boathouse
SEAFOOD $$$
(✆02-4984 9420; www.littlebeachboathouse.com.au; Little Beach Marina, 4 Victoria Pde, Nelson Bay; mains $33-40; ☉noon-2pm & 5-9pm Tue-Sat, 11.30am-2.30pm Sun) In an airy but intimate dining room, right on the water, you can order fabulous seafood dishes such as Hervey Bay scallops, Port Stephens oysters and lightly battered squid, all with a side of truffle and Parmesan fries. If you're not a seafood lover, go for the crispy pork belly or ravioli of the day. Book well ahead for dinner.

The Little Beach Bar decking on the marina is perfect for a sundowner and also does great bar food (noon to late, closed Monday).

BYRON BAY & NORTH COAST NEW SOUTH WALES PORT STEPHENS

The Point
SEAFOOD $$$
(☑02-4984 7111; www.thepointrestaurant.com.au; 1 Sunset Blvd, Soldiers Point; 2-course lunch from $28, dinner mains $28-52; ⊘11.30am-2.30pm & 5.30-9.30pm Tue-Sun) A local favourite for special occasion dining, patrons enjoy lovely views from the balcony and glassed-in dining room of this flagship restaurant at the Soldier's Point Marina. As you'd expect, there's plenty of seafood on offer, including oysters from Holbert's Oyster Farm (p143) and extravagant seafood platters (for two, $160); but many come for the excellent steaks and salads, plus duck and vegetarian options too. Book ahead.

🍷 Drinking & Nightlife

Many cafes are licensed, and you'll find a few upmarket spots to savour a glass of Hunter wine. There are plenty of pubs and clubs (of the sporting and ex-services variety) for post-beach beer consumption, but not a lot by way of nightlife.

Hope Taphouse
BREWERY
(☑02-4984 2076; www.hopebrewhouse.com.au; 3 Stockton St, Nelson Bay; ⊘4-9pm Thu, from noon Fri-Sun) Head upstairs and grab a seat under the striped umbrellas on the balcony overlooking the main street at this relaxed brewhouse. Sample some of the Hunter Valley–based brewery's core beers and seasonals on eight taps and pair them with tasty bar snacks, pizzas or burgers ($14 to $30).

Murray's Craft Brewing Co
BREWERY
(☑02-4982 6411; www.murraysbrewingco.com.au; 3443 Nelson Bay Rd, Bob's Farm; ⊘10am-6pm, tours 2.15pm) This brewery, 20km south of Nelson Bay, is the creator of cult recipes such as the award-winning Murray's Grand Cru, a hybrid of Belgian trippel and golden strong-ale styles, along with inventive seasonal flavours. The brewery has a family-friendly feel with plenty of open space, bocce and live music on Sunday afternoons. Beer is a key ingredient in the restaurant meals, too.

Also on-site is the Port Stephens Winery, with an expansive cellar door. A shuttle bus runs to/from Nelson Bay on weekends, and the $5 fee includes a brewery tour.

ℹ Information

Visitor Information Centre
(☑1800 808 900; www.portstephens.org.au; 60 Victoria Pde, Nelson Bay; ⊘9am-5pm) Has interesting displays about the marine park and can help book tours and excursions.

National Parks & Wildlife Service Office
(NPWS; ☑02-4984 8200; www.nationalparks.nsw.gov.au; 12b Teramby Rd, Nelson Bay; ⊘8.30am-4.30pm Mon-Fri) Also houses the representative offices for Worimi Conservation Lands (p140).

ℹ Getting There & Away

Port Stephens Coaches
(☑02-4982 2940; www.pscoaches.com.au) Zips around Port Stephens' townships heading to Newcastle and Newcastle Airport ($4.80, one hour). A daily service runs to/from Sydney (one-way/return $43/63, four hours) stopping at Nelson Bay and Shoal Bay, and on weekdays at Anna Bay.

Port Stephens Ferry Service
(☑0412 682 117; www.portstephensferryservice.com.au; return adult/child $26/13) Runs two services a day on a historic timber ferry between Nelson Bay and Tea Gardens (stopping at Hawks Nest en route), with more services running from November to January and over Easter. The journey takes one hour and there's a good chance of seeing dolphins. Bookings are necessary.

MID-NORTH COAST

The NSW Mid-North Coast runs for approximately 400km from Seal Rocks, in the Myall Lakes National Park (www.nationalparks.nsw.gov.au/visit-a-park/parks/myall-lakes-national-park), to Woolgoolga, just north of Coffs Harbour. The landscape here is textured by swaths of dense bushland and subtropical rainforest and is sprinkled with lakes and estuaries that glisten under sunny days.

The Pacific Hwy is the region's main arterial, snaking its route for the most part, somewhat inland from the coast. Branching off it at regular intervals, bumpy byways traverse dense bushland and meander through bucolic horse and cattle country, towards the Pacific Ocean. The Mid-North Coast is home to some of the country's most expensive beachfront real estate, but despite the often visible presence of significant wealth, there remains a delightfully unpretentious vibe to many communities here. Explorations off the beaten track reveal rustic bush camp sites, old-school fishing shacks, and sleepy seaside hamlets where surfing and fishing are a way of life.

Coffs Harbour is the largest and northernmost city. Intersected by a busy section of the highway which detracts from the quiet stretches of coast beyond, and ringed by resorts and shopping plazas built when timeshare was all the rage and domestic air travel wasn't yet affordable for many, parts of Coffs can feel a bit lost.

Port Macquarie is the region's second largest city, and despite its reputation as a giant retirement community it's a historic and pretty city with plenty going on and lots of appeal.

The Lakes Way

A scenic alternative to the Pacific Hwy, The Lakes Way is a 77km tourist route which begins outside the riverside town of Buladelah. A heavily potholed gem of a drive, the Lakes Way makes two winding mountain passes, darts in and out of Myall Lakes National Park, is bounded by several State Forests (one is home of 'the Grandis', the tallest tree in NSW). It then skirts along the shores of Myall, Smiths and Wallis Lakes, past the turnoff to pretty Seal Rocks and the picture-perfect paradise of Pacific Palms and onwards to tourist-fave Forster-Tuncurry before rejoining the Pacific Hwy, south of Taree.

Seal Rocks

One of the prettiest spots on this stretch of the coast, sleepy Seal Rocks is protected from further development by its inclusion within the 448-sq-km Myall Lakes National Park. This remarkably unpretentious hamlet hugging Sugarloaf Bay has a trio of beaches whose secluded breaks rank as legendary among the surfing community at home and abroad. The steep 660m walk to the historic **Sugarloaf Point Lighthouse** for epic ocean views is a must. On your way back down, take a detour to lonely **Lighthouse Beach**, a popular surfing spot. In contrast, **Number One Beach** has beautiful rock pools, a usually mellow and sometimes beautifully nonexistent swell, and soft white sand. If you don't surf, beach fish, snorkel or dive, there's not much to do here but to deepen your sense of bliss in the beautiful environment.

Accommodation at 'Seal' is limited to private holiday cabins and a handful of campgrounds. **Reflections** (☑02-4997 6164; www.reflectionsholidayparks.com.au; Kinka Rd; sites/cabins from $55/122; 🐾) is the most luxe option, with a range from grassed tent sites to basic cabins and luxury villas. **Treachery Camp** (☑02-4997 6138; www.treacherycamp.com.au; 166 Thomas Rd; sites adult $17-22, child $10-13, cabins $80-260) is set behind the dunes and coastal scrub of Treachery Beach, offering basic camping and amenities and uberpopular

BOMBAH POINT ECO COTTAGES

In the heart of the Myall Lakes National Park, these architect-designed glass-fronted **luxury eco cottages** (☑02-4997 4401; www.bombah.com.au; 969 Bombah Point Rd, Bombah Point; cottages from $260; 🏊) 🐾 sleep up to six guests. The 'eco' in the name is well deserved: sewage is treated on-site using a bio-reactor system; electricity comes courtesy of solar panels; and filtered rainwater tanks provide water. Cottages are quietly luxurious with huge rainwater spa baths and stylish cast-iron fireplaces. You can collect eggs from the local chickens or pick fresh herbs from the garden to supplement your catering supplies, and there is a communal coffee machine stocked with fresh beans.

From the town of Hawks Nest, scenic Mungo Brush Rd heads through the park to Bombah Broadwater, where the **Bombah Point ferry** makes the five-minute crossing every half-hour from 8am to 6pm ($6 per car). Note that, continuing north, a 10km section of Bombah Point Rd heading to the Pacific Hwy at Bulahdelah is unsealed.

cabins. There's an on-site cafe open weekends and school holidays.

Seal Rocks Rd branches off the Lakes Way at Bungwahl. It's a further 10km on a partially unsealed road from the turnoff to the village.

If you don't have your own wheels, Busways route 150 from Newcastle stops on demand at Bungwahl, near the turnoff.

Pacific Palms

A delightfully languid tiny coastal town, bounded by pristine **Booti Booti National Park** (☑02-6591 0300; www.nationalparks.nsw.gov.au/booti-booti-national-park; vehicle entry $8), Pacific Palms is a popular spot for surfers who are drawn to its swells at **Blueys** and **Boomerang** beaches. Patrolled during holiday periods, **Elizabeth Beach** is a tranquil choice for families. The 'Palms' also lures its fair share of multimillionaires who are drawn to its cache of beachfront holiday homes – weekenders for Sydney's nouveau riche. Many of the properties in the village, whose year-round residents number less than 300, are holiday rentals. If you can visit outside summer and the busy school holidays, there are beach-pad bargains to be had along with blissfully empty beaches.

If you're passing through, pop in to the friendly **Pacific Palms Visitor Centre** (☑ 02-6554 0123; www.greatlakes.org.au; Boomerang Dr; ⊙ 10am-4pm) for the local lowdown.

Forster-Tuncurry

POP 19,918

At the northern end of the Lakes Way, the twin towns of Forster and Tuncurry (known as Forster-Tuncurry) are joined by a 631m-long vehicular and pedestrian bridge. Opened in 1959, yet still officially unnamed, the bridge spans Cape Hawke Harbour as it feeds into Wallis Lake. The views from it, of the vibrant azure and aquamarine waters, and the harbour's innumerable white sandy spits and islands, are spectacular. Forster, to the south, is the larger of the twinned towns and has the mainstay of shopping, dining and tourist draws, while Tuncurry, to the north, has a markedly slower pace.

◉ Sights & Activities

Amaroo Cruises CRUISE
(☑ 0419 333 445; www.amaroocruise.com.au; Memorial Dr, Forster; 3hr tours from $49) Departing 10am on most days, this popular operator runs dolphin and whale-watching (June to November only) cruises. Boats depart from Forster Wharfs and head out into open ocean (not for the easily seasick) before returning for a scenic meander around the beautiful sandy islands of Wallis Lake.

Bennett's Head Lookout VIEWPOINT
(Bennett's Head Rd, Forster) **FREE** Follow Bennett's Head Rd to the top for dramatic views of the east coast as it arcs its way northward in spectacular fashion. There's also a small coastal walk here which takes you down to **One Mile Beach** for more ooh-and-aah vistas.

🛌 Sleeping

Lani's Holiday Island CARAVAN PARK $
(☑ 02-6554 6273; www.lanis.com.au; 33 The Lakes Way; sites/cabins from $22/80; **P 🛜 🏊**) The bushland camping section of Forster's largest camping and caravan park stretches back almost for almost 2km beyond the park entrance, giving campers that real in-the-bush feeling, despite being in the heart of town. In the main section of the park are

a wide selection of on-site vans and cabins, and all the usual amenities.

Simple Pleasures Camping Co ACCOMMODATION SERVICES $$
(☑ 0405 171 444; www.simplepleasurescamping.co; camping packages from $180) Got an urge to merge with Mother Nature, but lack outdoors expertise? These happy campers can score you a spot in the regions' best camping grounds and set you up with a safari tent with a full-sized bed, soft furnishings, cooking gear, lights and an outdoor dining setting.

Sevan Apartments HOTEL $$$
(☑ 02-6555 0300; www.sevan.com.au; 14-18 Head St, Forster; 1-/2-/3-bed apt from $225/275/310; **P 🛜 ❄ 🛜**) These modern apartments are located close to the town centre and Forster's main beach. Higher floors offer sea views.

🍴 Eating & Drinking

Gold Medal Chinese Restaurant CHINESE $$
(☑ 02-6555 9391; 4-6 Wallis St, Forster; mains $12-24; ⊙ 11.30am-2pm & 5-9pm Wed-Mon, 5-9pm Tue) This no-frills restaurant, popular with locals, has friendly staff, is invariably spotlessly clean, and serves a wide range of Chinese and Malaysian dishes, including excellent *san choy bao* and sizzling platters.

Deck @ Tuncurry AUSTRALIAN $$
(☑ 02-6555 6060; 2 Ray St, Tuncurry; breakfasts $10-21, dinner mains $23-35; ⊙ 7.30am-2.30pm & 5-9.30pm) This cheery spot by the water in Tuncurry has an airy, open atmosphere and serves great breakfasts (try the Eggs Benny!) and burgers, salads and seafood for lunch. In the evenings it's turned up a notch with a regularly changing menu often influenced by the head chef's love of Spanish cuisine.

★ Plunge Forster CAFE
(www.plungeforster.org; 5/21 Boundary St, Forster; ⊙ 7am-2.30pm) Serving organic fair-trade coffee, all-day breakfasts, and using sustainable and locally sourced produce wherever possible, Plunge has that Melbourne cafe feel. In the sleepy backstreets of town, next to an 18-hole golf course, it's a short walk to beautiful One Mile beach. Hip, friendly, tasty and strong.

ℹ Information

Forster Visitor Information Centre (☑ 1800 802 692; www.greatlakes.org.au; Little St, Forster; ⊙ 9am-5pm Mon-Fri, to 4pm Sat-Sun)

ℹ Getting There & Away

Forster-Tuncurry is 165km north of Newcastle via the Pacific Hwy.

If your final destination is Forster, it is sometimes quicker and always more scenic to take The Lakes Way. If you're heading to Tuncurry, turn off the highway at Failford Rd, from where it's a further 13km into town.

Busways (☑ 02-4997 4788; www.busways. com.au) operates one to two coach services per day from Newcastle's Broadmeadow railway station, into Forster, then Tuncurry (three hours, from $22).

Port Macquarie

POP 47,973

Making the most of its position at the entrance to the subtropical coast, Port, as it's commonly known, might be a minimetropolis but it remains overwhelmingly holiday focused. A string of beautiful beaches fans out either side of town, all a short driving distance from the centre. Most are great for swimming and surfing, and they seldom get crowded. There are enough interesting museums and attractions, plus a decent culinary scene, to warrant a stay of at least a couple of nights.

The local Birpai people are the traditional custodians of this land.

◉ Sights

★ **Tacking Point Lighthouse**   VIEWPOINT
(☑ 02-6581 8111; Lighthouse Rd) This little lighthouse (1879) commands a headland offering immense views along the coast. It's a great spot from which to watch the waves roll in to long, beautiful Lighthouse Beach; it's particularly lovely at sunset. The viewpoint looks out to the **Three Brothers Mountains**, a place of spiritual importance to the local Birpai Aboriginal people.

Koala Hospital   WILDLIFE RESERVE
(☑ 02-6584 1522; www.koalahospital.org.au; cnr Roto Pl & Lord St; by donation; ⊘ 8am-4.30pm) Chlamydia, traffic accidents and dog attacks are the biggest causes of illness and injury for koalas living near urban areas; about 250 end up in this shelter each year. You can walk around the open-air enclosures any time of the day, but you'll learn more on a free 40-minute tour and have the chance to see them being fed (3pm).

Signs detail the stories of some of the longer-term patients. Check the website for volunteer opportunities.

Sea Acres Rainforest Centre   NATIONAL PARK
(☑ 02-6582 3355; www.nationalparks.nsw.gov.au/ sea-acres-national-park; 159 Pacific Dr; boardwalk adult/child $9/5; ⊘ 9am-4.30pm) The 72-hectare pocket of Sea Acres National Park protects the state's largest and most diverse stand of coastal rainforest. At the Rainforest Centre you can take a self-guided tour on the wheelchair-accessible 1.3km-long elevated boardwalk through the forest, keeping an eye out for water dragons, brush turkeys, diamond pythons and birdlife, or join a free one-hour guided tour run by knowledgeable volunteers. The centre also has audiovisual displays about the local Birpai people ($2 entry).

Glasshouse Regional Gallery   GALLERY
(☑ 02-6581 8888; www.glasshouse.org.au/region al-gallery; cnr Clarence & Hay Sts; ⊘ 10am-5pm Tue-Fri, to 4pm Sat & Sun) FREE This dynamic multilevel space provides an interesting overview of local creativity, and hosts regular touring exhibitions from Australia's top museums and galleries. Exhibitions change approximately every four to six weeks.

Port Macquarie Historical Museum MUSEUM
(☑ 02-6583 1108; www.portmuseum.org.au; 22 Clarence St; adult/child $7/5; ⊘ 9.30am-4.30pm Mon-

---

LEWIS THE KOALA

In November 2019, footage of a woman, Toni Doherty, taking off her shirt and darting into a raging bushfire to rescue a fully grown male koala (around 12kg) from the flames, went viral around the world. The injured marsupial was taken to the Koala Hospital in Port Macquarie, where he was named Ellenborough Lewis and treated for severe burns to his hands, feet, arms and legs. Lewis was euthanised on 27 November due to the severity of his condition. Melting the hearts of millions around the world, Toni and Lewis brought the plight of Australia's most unique and best-loved marsupial onto the world stage. At time of writing, the Mid-North Coast was home to an estimated 15,000 to 28,000 koalas, though it is thought that 30% of those were killed during the 2019 bushfire season. If you'd like to learn more about our furry friends, and find out what you can do to help save this fast-becoming-endangered species, visit the Koala Hospital in Port Macquarie.

Port Macquarie

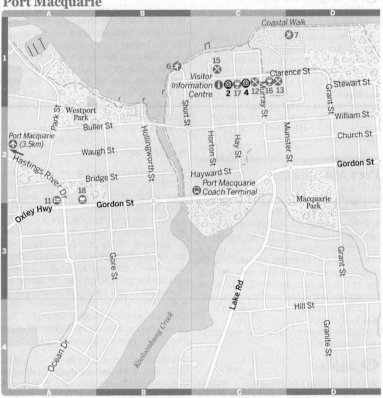

Port Macquarie

Sat) An 1830s house has been transformed into this surprisingly interesting and detailed museum. Aboriginal and convict history are given due regard before moving on to everything from archaeological artefacts to a 'street of shops' and a display of beautiful old clothes in the costume gallery.

🏃 Activities

Surfing is particularly good at **Town**, **Flynn's** and **Lighthouse** beaches – all patrolled in

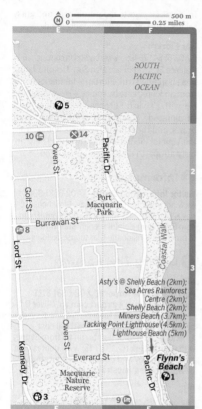

summer. The rainforest runs to the sand at **Shelly** and **Miners** beaches, the latter of which is an unofficial nudist beach.

Whale season is from May to November; there are vantage points around town, or go on a whale-watching cruise **with Port Cruise Adventures** (✆02-6583 8811; www.portjet.com.au; 1 Short St; tours from adult/child $55/45).

★**Port Macquarie Coastal Walk** WALKING
This coastal walk begins at Westport Park near the Town Green foreshore and winds for about 9km along the coast to Tracking Point Lighthouse in Sea Acres National Park. There are plenty of opportunities for swimming (it takes in eight beaches) and between May and November you can often view the whale migration. The walk can be divided into shorter 2km to 3km sections.

Soul Surfing SURFING
(✆02-6582 0114; www.soulsurfing.com.au; 2hr class $50, 1-day workshop $245) A family-run school,

it also runs school-holiday intensives, as well as women's workshops that include yoga, relaxation and food along with the surf lessons. Private lessons start at $85 for 90 minutes.

🛏 Sleeping

Port Macquarie Backpackers HOSTEL $
(✆02-6583 1791; www.portbackpackers.com.au; 2 Hastings River Dr; dm/s/d from $36/72/82; @🛜⛶) This heritage-listed house has pressed-tin walls and a leafy backyard with a small pool. Traffic can be noisy, but the freebies (including bikes and bodyboards) and a relaxed attitude more than compensate.

Eastport Motor Inn MOTEL $$
(✆02-6583 5850; www.eastportmotorinn.com.au; cnr Lord & Burrawan Sts; d from $120; P❄🛜⛶) This fully renovated three-storey motel offers friendly service and good-value rooms with comfortable beds and smart furniture.

Flynns on Surf VILLA $$
(✆02-6584 2244; www.flynns.com.au; 25 Surf St; 1-/2-/3-bedroom villas from $180/240/280; P❄🛜⛶) These smart one-, two- and three-bedroom villas are set on their own private estate. Each has a gorgeous bush outlook and is fully self-contained, with extra comforts such as Nespresso machines. The surf is 200m away.

Mantra the Observatory HOTEL $$
(✆02-6586 8000; www.mantratheobservatory.com.au; 40 William St; d from $170, 1-bedroom apt from $200; P❄🛜⛶) Rooms and apartments are more attractive than most and well equipped at this upmarket hotel; many have balconies overlooking the water. There's an indoor heated lap pool but you probably won't need it being opposite Town Beach.

🍴 Eating

Asty's @ Shelly Beach FAST FOOD $
(✆02-6582 5472; 2/141 Pacific Dr; breakfasts $9-14, burgers $6-13; ⏰8am-7pm) This takeaway joint at the top of the hill leading down to Shelly Beach does great greasy breakfasts and burgers, killer milkshakes and awesome loaded fries, topped with cheese, gravy and your choice of bacon, beef brisket, chicken schnitty-bits, or lamb. Naughty...but oh so nice!

Suzu Japanese Dining Bar JAPANESE $$
(✆02-6584 4559; www.facebook.com/suzu.japanese.dining.bar; Shop 3, 2 Horton St; dishes $13-29; ⏰11.30am-2pm & 5.30-9pm Wed-Mon) Vintage Japanese posters, *noren* (hanging curtains) and large sake bottles set the scene at this

authentic and intimate Japanese restaurant. Choose from fresh sushi and sashimi, udon soups, teriyaki mains and tempura dishes and finish with delicious black-sesame ice cream.

Burger Rebellion
BURGERS $$

(☑02-6584 1403; www.theburgerrebellion.com.au; 14/6 Clarence St; burgers $12-18; ⊙11.30am-3pm & 5-9pm) A smart space with wooden communal counters, booths and street-side tables, it delivers tasty gourmet burgers, craft beer and friendly service. Vegetarians are not overlooked here – any burger can be substituted by a mushroom, a veggie pattie or halloumi – and there are gluten-free options too.

★ Bill's Fishhouse
AUSTRALIAN $$$

(☑02-6584 7228; www.billsfishhouse.com.au; 2/18-20 Clarence St; mains $28-38; ⊙5.30pm-late Mon-Sat) A light and pretty space to escape the heat and eat the freshest of seafood. The menu changes regularly and might include local snapper fillet in a shiitake broth or blue-swimmer-crab risotto. It's augmented daily with the chef's pick from the fish market. Bookings are advised for dinner.

★ Stunned Mullet
INTERNATIONAL $$$

(☑02-6584 7757; www.thestunnedmullet.com.au; 24 William St; mains $32-52; ⊙noon-2.30pm & 6-10pm) This fresh, seaside spot is one serious dining experience. The inspired contemporary menu features dishes like award-winning Tajima Wagyu beef, alongside exotic listings such as Patagonian toothfish. Note, all fish is wild caught. The extensive international wine list befits Port's best restaurant and there's a small but impressive wine-by-the-glass and half-bottle selection.

◉ Drinking & Nightlife

★ Botanic Wine Garden
WINE BAR

(☑02-6584 3685; www.botanicwinegarden.com.au; Shop 3, 26 Clarence St; ⊙4-10pm Tue-Thu & Sun, to 11pm Fri & Sat) Sit under the fairy lights debating whether the food or the wine is better here at Botanic. Short answer: too close to call. The alfresco setting invites relaxed balmy evenings pairing cheese and cured-meat platters, or mains of 16-hour pork belly and fish of the day, with a bottle of wine from the impressive list highlighting small Australian producers.

Social Grounds Cafe
CAFE

(☑0423 240 635; 151 Gordon St; mains $9-20; ⊙6am-2pm Mon-Fri, to 11.30am Sat, from 7am Sun; ☏) Pull up a chair at the shared tables of this hip local hang-out. The wall menu wanders from spiced eggs to flaky croissants and gutsy salads. The coffee is dependably good.

Bar Florian
BAR

(☑02-6584 7649; www.barflorian.com.au; 6-14 Clarence St; ⊙4pm-late Mon-Sat) Despite being in a shopping strip, Florian – taking its name from an iconic cafe in Venice – is a welcoming bar with a stylish European feel. Italian beers sit alongside a selection of Australian craft brews, and the wine list features bottles from the Veneto, Piedmont and Tuscany. There are tasty antipasto platters and pizzas, too.

ⓘ Information

Visitor Information Centre (☑02-6581 8000; www.portmacquarieinfo.com.au; Glasshouse, cnr Hay & Clarence Sts; ⊙9am-5.30pm Mon-Fri, to 4pm Sat & Sun) Helpful friendly staff with plenty of brochures; inside the Glasshouse building.

ⓘ Getting There & Away

AIR

Port Macquarie Airport (☑02-6581 8111; www.portmacquarieairport.com.au; Oliver Dr) is 5km west from the town centre; it's served by regular local buses and a taxi will cost around $25. Regular flights run to/from Sydney with **QantasLink** (☑13 13 13; www.qantas.com.au), and Sydney and Brisbane with **Virgin** (☑13 67 89; www.virginaustralia.com).

BUS

Regional buses depart from **Port Macquarie Coach Terminal** (Gordon St).

Busways (☑02-6583 2499; www.busways.com.au) Runs local bus services from outside the Glasshouse to Port Macquarie Airport ($4, 30 minutes) and Kempsey ($10, one hour).

Greyhound (☑1300 473 946; www.greyhound.com.au) Buses head to/from Sydney (from $58, six hours, twice daily), Newcastle (from $61, 3¾ hours, twice daily), Coffs Harbour (from $40, 2½ hours, three daily), Byron Bay (from $84, 6½ hours, three daily), Surfers Paradise (from $116, 8½ hours, three daily) and Brisbane (from $128, 9½ hours, three daily).

Premier Motor Service (☑13 34 10; www.premierms.com.au) Daily coaches to/from Sydney ($62, 6½ hours), Newcastle ($48, 3¾ hours), Coffs Harbour ($48, 2¼ hours), Byron Bay ($68, 7½ hours), Surfers Paradise ($69, 8½ hours) and Brisbane ($69, 11 hours).

TRAIN

The closest train station is at Wauchope, 18km west of Port Macquarie. Buses connect with trains.

HAT HEAD NATIONAL PARK

Covering almost the entire coast from Crescent Head to South West Rocks, this 74-sq-km national park (vehicle entry $8) protects scrubland, swamps and some amazing beaches, backed by one of the largest dune systems in NSW.

The isolated beachside village of **Hat Head** (population 307) sits at its centre. At the far end of town, behind the holiday park, a picturesque wooden footbridge crosses the Korogoro Creek estuary. The water is so clear you can see fish darting around.

The best views can be had from **Smoky Cape Lighthouse** (02-6566 6168; www.nationalparks.nsw.gov.au/things-to-do/historic-buildings-places/smoky-cape-lighthouse; Lighthouse Rd; 1-3pm Mon, Wed, Fri), at the northern end of the park. During the annual whale migration (May to September) it's a prime place from which to spot them.

Camp at **Hungry Gate** (02-6651 6700; www.nationalparks.nsw.gov.au/hat-head-national-park; sites per adult/child $6/3.50), 5km south of Hat Head, for a beautifully back-to-basics holiday among native figs and paperbarks. The site operates on a first come, first served basis and does not take bookings; a ranger will come around and collect fees. There are nonflush toilets and a BBQ area, but you'll need to bring your own drinking water. Kangaroos provide entertainment.

Crescent Head

POP 1531

This beachside, palm-tree-filled hideaway has a quiet relaxed coastal village feel and one of the best right-hand surf breaks in the country. Many come simply to watch the longboard riders surf the epic waves of **Little Nobby's Junction**. There's also good shortboard riding off Plomer Rd. Picturesque **Killick Beach** stretches 14km north.

🛏 Sleeping & Eating

Surfari HOSTEL $
(02-6566 0009; www.surfaris.com; 353 Loftus Rd; sites/dm/d $20/40/140; @🕸🛜🏊) Surfari started the original Sydney–Byron surf tours and now base themselves in Crescent Head because 'the surf is guaranteed every day'. Surf-and-stay packages are a speciality. The rooms are clean and comfortable, and there's a large pool. It's 3.5km along the road to Gladstone and offers pickup ($10) from the train station in Kempsey, 25km from Crescent Head.

The Med MOTEL $$
(0409 968 076; www.themedch.com.au; 35 Pacific St; from $205; P🕸🛜🏊) The Med is going for a Spanish hacienda vibe with rounded arches, Acapulco chairs and swaying palms, but while the end result feels fun, it's more kitsch than cool. Clean, simple rooms feature whitewashed walls, tiled floors and coffee-pod machines, but it's more likely you'll want to hang out on a deck chair by the pool or in the bar.

Crescent Head Tavern PUB FOOD $$
(02-6566 0166; www.crescentheadtavern.com; 2 Main St; mains $14-32; noon-2pm & 6-8pm) The local pub has cold beer, a sun-soaked deck and a massive menu of Vietnamese dishes and pub classics, as well as takeaway pizza ($14 to $28), which in off-season is sometimes the only food you'll be able to get at 7.50pm.

ⓘ Getting There & Away

Busways (02-6562 4724; www.busways.com.au) runs between Crescent Head and Kempsey ($5, 30 minutes), with three services per day on weekdays, one on Saturdays and no services on Sundays.

South West Rocks

POP 4603

One of many pretty seaside towns on this stretch of coast, South West Rocks has great beaches and enough interesting diversions for at least a night.

The lovely curve of **Trial Bay**, stretching east from the township, takes its name from the *Trial,* a boat that sank here during a storm in 1816 after being stolen by convicts fleeing Sydney. The eastern half of the bay is now protected by **Arakoon National Park**, centred on a headland that's popular with kangaroos, kookaburras and campers. On its eastern flank, **Little Bay Beach** is a small grin of sand sheltered from the surf by a rocky barricade. It's both a great place for a swim and also the starting point for some lovely walks.

◎ Sights

★ Trial Bay Gaol   MUSEUM
(☑ 02-6566 6168; www.nationalparks.nsw.gov.
au/things-to-do; Cardwell St; adult/child $11/8;
☺ 9am-4.30pm) Occupying Trial Bay's eastern
headland, this sandstone prison was built
between 1877 and 1886 to house convicts
brought in to build a breakwater. When nature intervened and the breakwater washed
away, the imposing structure fell into disuse,
aside from a brief, rather tragic, interlude in
WWI when men of German and Austrian
heritage were interned here. Today it contains a museum devoted to its unusual history; even if you don't go inside, it's worth a
detour for the views and the resident roos.

🛏 Sleeping & Eating

Trial Bay Gaol Campground   CAMPGROUND $
(☑ 02-6566 6168; www.nationalparks.nsw.gov.au/
arakon-national-park; Cardwell St, Arakon National
Park; sites per 2 people from $32) Behind the Trial
Bay Gaol, this stunning NPWS campground
affords generous beach views from most
campsites and hosts ever-present kangaroos.
Amenities include drinking water, a coin-operated laundry, flush toilets, hot showers, a
camp kitchen and gas BBQs. There's a cafe
(☑ 02-6566 7100; www.trialbaykiosk.com.au;
mains breakfast $10-22, lunch $20-35, dinner $26-
35; ☺ 8am-2pm Tue-Sun & 5.30-8.30pm Fri & Sat)
nearby too.

Rockpool Motor Inn   MOTEL $$
(☑ 02-6566 7755; www.rockpoolmotorinn.com.au;
45 McIntyre St; d from $150; P ❄ 🛜 ⛶) Just a
few streets from the beach, this motel has
smartly furnished rooms and superhelpful
staff. There's an on-site restaurant, too.

★ Malt & Honey   CAFE $
(☑ 02-6566 5200; 5-7 Livingstone St; mains $12-
26; ☺ 7.30am-4pm Wed-Sun) An urban sensibility combines with beach-town charm at this
busy cafe. Pick up an early-morning latte or
grab a seat for crumpets with macadamia
crumble, house-made muesli or French toast
with maple-glazed bacon and banana. Big
salads and other healthy but satisfying options appear on the lunch menu. The cakes
are the best: moist and moreish.

❶ Information

Visitor Information Centre (☑ 02-6566 7099;
www.macleayvalleycoast.com.au; 1 Ocean Ave;
☺ 9am-4pm)

❶ Getting There & Away

Busways (☑ 02-6562 4724; www.busways.com.
au) Runs to/from Kempsey ($7.50, 50 minutes).
There are three services daily Monday to Friday,
two services Saturdays and none on Sundays.

Nambucca Heads
POP 6327

Nambucca Heads is languidly strewn over
a dramatically curling headland interlaced
with the estuaries of the glorious Nambucca
River. It's a quiet place, evoking sun-soaked
holidays of the 1970s and '80s.

Nambucca (nam-*buk*-a) means 'many
bends', and the river valley was ruled by the
Gumbaynggirr people until European timber
cutters arrived in the 1840s. Strong Aboriginal communities remain in Nambucca Heads
and up the valley in Bowraville; the activist
and historian Gary Foley hails from here.

◎ Sights

Yarriabini National Park   NATIONAL PARK
(www.nationalparks.nsw.gov.au/yarriabini-nation-
al-park; ☺ 7am-7pm) The highlight of this rain-
forest-filled park is the dramatic coastal view
from the lookout on the summit of Mt Yarriabini, accessible via a detour from scenic Way
Way Creek Rd. Pack a picnic and stop off at
the tranquil Pines picnic area where there is
a sculptural mosaic artwork by local Aboriginal artists conveying the importance of the
mountain to the Dunghutti, Ngambaa and
Gumbaynggirr Aboriginal people.

Captain Cook Lookout   VIEWPOINT
(Parkes St) Of the area's numerous viewpoints, Captain Cook Lookout, set on a
high bluff, is the best to ponder the array of
beaches, and to look for whales during the
migration season. A road here leads down to
the tide pools of **Shelly Beach**.

V-Wall   LANDMARK
(1 Wellington Dr) FREE For decades residents
and holidaymakers have decorated the rocks
of Nambucca's breakwater with vivacious
multicoloured artwork, and with notes to lovers, families and new-found friends. Visitors
are encouraged to paint their own messages.

🛏 Sleeping & Eating

Riverview Boutique Hotel   GUESTHOUSE $$
(☑ 02-6568 6386; www.riverviewlodgenambucca.
com.au; 4 Wellington Dr; d from $169; P ❄ 🛜)
This former pub, built in 1887, is a wooden,

Nambucca Heads

Nambucca Heads

⊙ Sights
1 Captain Cook Lookout D3
2 V-Wall C3

🛏 Sleeping
3 Riverview Boutique Hotel....................B2

⊗ Eating
4 Matilda's...B3
5 Wharf St Cafe.......................................B3

two-storey charmer with nine neat, smart
rooms; all have a private balcony and some
rooms have views. Your choice of a cooked
or continental breakfast is included.

Wharf St Cafe   CAFE **$$**
(☑ 02-6568 9440; 9/1 Wellington Dr; mains $14-26;
⊙ 7am-3.30pm Tue-Fri, from 8am Sat & Sun; 🛜)
Choose river views from inside or on the re-
laxed front deck for a lazy breakfast and Cam-
pos coffee, or drop by to lunch on a crumbed
fish burger or salt and pepper squid.

Matilda's   SEAFOOD **$$$**
(☑ 02-6568 6024; 6 Wellington Dr; mains $26-42;
⊙ 6-9pm Mon-Sat) This stylish seafood shack
has an old-fashioned beach-town character,
excellent service and a menu of mostly seafood, including local oysters.

ℹ Information

Nambucca Heads Visitor Information Centre
(☑ 02-6568 6954; www.nambuccatourism.
com.au; cnr Riverside Dr & Pacific Hwy;
⊙ 9.45am-4pm)

ℹ Getting There & Away

Long-distance buses stop at the Nambucca
Heads Visitor Information Centre.

The train station is 4km northwest from the
town centre.

NSW TrainLink (☑ 13 22 32; www.nswtrainlink.
info) Trains to/from Sydney ($94, eight hours),
Kempsey ($12, one hour) and Coffs Harbour
($7, 40 minutes).

Bellingen
POP 3074

Buried in deep foliage on a hillside above the
Bellinger River, this gorgeous town dances
to the beat of its own bongo drum. 'Bello' is
flush with organic produce, and the creative
community has an urban sensibility. Located
inland between the spectacular rainforest of
Dorrigo National Park and a spoilt-for-choice
selection of beaches, it is easily accessible from
Coffs Harbour and a definite jewel on the
East Coast route. Bellingen is also a natural
starting point for a number of scenic drives,
including the spectacular Waterfall Way.

WATERFALL WAY

Considered the most scenic drive in NSW, the 200km Waterfall Way links a number of beautiful national parks between Coffs Harbour and Armidale, taking you through pristine subtropical rainforest, Edenic valleys and, naturally, spectacular waterfalls. As you emerge into the tablelands, there is green countryside and wide plains.

Guy Fawkes River National Park (☑ 02-6739 0700; www.nationalparks.nsw. gov.au/guy-fawkes-river-national-park) and the stunning Ebor Falls are 50km past Dorrigo.

Make your way into the **Cathedral Rock National Park** (☑ 02-6739 0700; www. nationalparks.nsw.gov.au/cathedral-rock-national-park) or take a detour down Point Lookout Rd to **New England National Park** (☑ 02-6652 0900; www.nationalparks. nsw.gov.au/new-england-national-park), a section of the Gondwana Rainforests World Heritage Area.

Further west **Oxley Wild Rivers National Park** (☑ 02-6738 9100; www. nationalparks.nsw.gov.au/oxley-wild-rivers-national-park) is home to the towering plunge waterfall beauty of Wollomombi Falls.

◉ Sights

Bellingen Museum MUSEUM
(☑ 02-6655 0382; www.bellingenmuseum.org.au; 33-39 Hyde St; adult/child $3/free; ⊙ 10am-2pm Mon & Wed-Fri, or by appointment) Enthusiastic volunteers run this odd collection of local ephemera: old photos, clothes, tools etc.

Bellingen Island WILDLIFE RESERVE
This little semi-attached island on the Bellinger River (it's only completely cut off when the river is in flood) is home to a colony of grey-headed flying foxes. Take the ramp down from the Old Caravan Park on Dowle St at the northern end. The best months to visit are October to January, when the babies are being born and nursed. Wear long trousers and use insect repellent to ward off stinging nettles, leeches, ticks and mosquitoes.

At dusk the flying foxes fly out in their thousands to feed, though this impressive sight is best viewed from the bridge in the centre of town.

✿ Festivals & Events

Bellingen Readers & Writers Festival LITERATURE
(www.bellingenwritersfestival.com.au; ⊙ Jun) Established and emerging writers appear at talks, panels, readings, poetry slams and workshops over the Queen's Birthday long weekend.

Bello Winter Music MUSIC
(www.bellowintermusic.com; ⊙ mid-Jul) A nicely chilled music festival with local and international folk, roots, blues, world, hip-hop and pop acts, along with great food. Returning in summer 2022.

▭ Sleeping

Much of the region's accommodation is in small B&Bs and cottages scattered across the hillsides, and riverside cabins and cottages just outside Bellingen. In town, options include the YHA, pub accommodation and a couple of guesthouses.

Bellingen YHA HOSTEL $
(Belfry Guesthouse; ☑ 02-6655 1116; www.yha.com. au; 2 Short St; dm $38, r with/without bathroom from $150/90; @ 🛜) A tranquil, homey atmosphere pervades this lovely renovated weatherboard house, with impressive hinterland views from the swinging hammocks hanging on the broad verandah. Pickups from the bus stop and train station in Urunga are sometimes possible if you call ahead ($20).

Federal Hotel HOTEL $
(☑ 02-6655 1003; www.federalhotel.com.au; 77 Hyde St; d without bathroom from $90; 🛜) This beautiful old country pub has renovated weatherboard rooms, some of which open onto a balcony facing the main street, and modern clean bathrooms. It's a popular pub with live music on weekends so, of course, expect noise until closing.

Bellingen Riverside Cottages CABIN $$
(☑ 0413 317 635; www.bellingenriversidecottages. com.au; 224 North Bank Rd; cottages from $195; P ❄🛜🐾) These four polished cabins have cosy interiors with country furnishings and big windows. Timber balconies overlook the river, which you can tackle on a complimentary kayak. Your first night includes a DIY breakfast hamper.

★Promised Land Retreat CABIN $$$
(☑ 02-6655 9578; www.promisedlandretreat.com. au; 934 Promised Land Rd, Gleniffer; cabins from $325; P ❄🛜) A 10-minute drive from town over the evocatively named Never Never Riv-

er, these three stylish and private cottages feature spa baths and open-plan living areas attached to decks with dramatic views to the Dorrigo escarpment. Two of the chalets are suitable for families. Facilities include a tennis court, a games room and mountain bikes.

✗ Eating

Eating in Bellingen is a pleasure: it has a large and ever-growing number of cafes and casual restaurants, most of which make use of local and organic produce. There's a well-stocked IGA on Hyde St in the heart of town for self-caterers.

Hearthfire Bakery   BAKERY $
(☑02-6655 0767; www.hearthfire.com.au; 73 Hyde St; light meals $9-18; ⊙7am-5pm Mon-Fri, to 2pm Sat & Sun) Follow the smell of hot-from-the-woodfire organic sourdough and you'll find this outstanding country bakery and cafe. Try the famous macadamia fruit loaf or settle in with a coffee and a beautiful savoury pie. There is a full breakfast menu daily, and lunch dishes – including meze plates, soups and salads – are served during the week.

★ Qudo Cafe & Sake   JAPANESE $$
(☑02-6655 9757; www.domaandqudocafe.com; 121 Hyde St; mains $19-30; ⊙11.30am-2.30pm & 6-8.30pm Wed-Sat) Japanese chefs work their magic in this imposing and beautifully rustic two-storey former Freemason building. It's run by the same owners as Federal's **Doma Cafe** (☑02-6688 4711; 3-6 Albert St, Federal; mains $16-28; ⊙7.30am-2.30pm Mon-Fri, to 3pm Sat & Sun) ⌀, and the menu offers delicious delights such as sushi and sashimi, miso-glazed lamb cooked on a grill over bincho charcoal, tempura halloumi and kingfish carpaccio.

Purple Carrot   CAFE $$
(☑02-6655 1847; 105 Hyde St; mains $14-28; ⊙8am-3pm Mon-Sat, to noon Sun & 5pm-late Thu-Sat in summer) The breakfast-based menu offers eggs galore alongside dishes such as brioche French toast, smoked trout on a potato rösti, and a creamy pesto mushroom and haloumi burger. Get in early for Sunday brunch.

☮ Drinking & Nightlife

Bellingen Brewery & Co   MICROBREWERY
(☑02-6655 2210; www.bellingenbrewery.com.au; 3/5 Church St; ⊙5-11pm Wed-Fri, from noon Sat & Sun) Tucked away in a car park with a plant-strewn facade, the Bellingen Brewery packs punters in for its range of brews – from English-style bitters to a popular summer ale – along

with organic wine, excellent wood-fired pizzas ($18) and a soundtrack of live music.

People of Coffee   CAFE
(☑1300 720 799; www.peopleofcoffee.org; 84-90 Hyde St; ⊙6am-3pm Mon-Fri, to 1pm Sat; ☎) ⌀ While there's no shortage of good coffee in Bellingen, People of Coffee roasts on-site with beans that are not only organic, but also bird-friendly, rainforest-alliance and fair- and direct-trade certified. Toasties and delicious cakes are also on offer.

No 5 Church St   BAR
(☑02-6655 0155; www.5churchstreet.com; 5 Church St; ⊙9am-4pm Sun, Tue & Wed, to late Thu-Sat; ☎) Morphing effortlessly from cafe to bar, this vibrant venue stages an eclectic roster of live music, movie nights and community gatherings. The menu (mains $16 to $20), be it breakfast, lunch or dinner, comes with a directory of local growers who have produced the ingredients for the egg dishes, pizzas, salads and burgers.

🛍 Shopping

Tree-O Gallery   ART STUDIO
(☑0427 462 585; www.bimmortonfurniture.com; 16 Alex Pike Dr, Raleigh) It's free to browse the creations of local furniture maker Bim Morton in this workshop and gallery, which also showcases the creations of fellow homegrown artisans working wonders with wood. If you're a fan of fine bespoke furniture, be sure to have a chat with Bim before you go.

The gallery is located in an industrial complex in Raleigh, 10km southeast of Bellingen.

ℹ Information

Waterfall Way Information Centre (☑02-6655 1522; www.visitnsw.com/visitor-information-centres/waterfall-way-visitor-centre-bellingen; 29-31 Hyde St; ⊙9am-4.30pm Mon-Sat, 9.30am- 2.30pm Sun) Stocks brochures on scenic drives, walks and an arts trail.

ℹ Getting There & Away

Bellingen is a short drive inland from the coast along the spectacular Waterfall Way. Local buses service the town from Coffs, via Sawtell.
Busways (☑02-6655 7410; www.busways. com.au) Bus 361 runs to/from Coffs Harbour on weekdays ($7.50, 1¼ hours).
New England Coaches (☑02-6732 1051; www.newenglandcoaches.com.au) Three coaches per week to Urunga ($40) and Coffs Harbour ($35).

Coffs Harbour

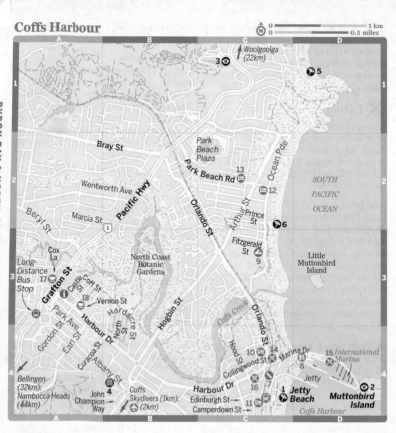

Coffs Harbour

◎ Top Sights
1 Jetty Beach	C4
2 Muttonbird Island	D4

◎ Sights
3 Big Banana	C1
4 Bunker Cartoon Gallery	B4
5 Diggers Beach	D1
6 Park Beach	C2

⊕ Activities, Courses & Tours
7 Jetty Dive	C4
8 Lee Winkler's Surf School	D4

🛏 Sleeping
9 BIG4 Park Beach Holiday Park	C3

10 Coffs Harbour YHA	C4
11 Observatory Apartments	C4
12 Ocean Paradise Motel	C2
13 Pacific Property Management	C2

✕ Eating
14 Fiasco	C4
15 Fishermen's Coop	D4
Lime Mexican	(see 16)
16 Old John's	C4

🍷 Drinking & Nightlife
17 Dark Arts Brew & Bar	A3
18 Palate & Ply	A3

Coffs Harbour

POP 71,822

The largest city on the Mid-North Coast, Coffs Harbour's iconic jetty was built in 1892 to load cedar and other logs. Bananas were first grown here in the 1880s and the industry reached its peak in the 1960s. A tourist boom town in the 1980s and '90s, Coffs remains popular. There's plenty to do here in terms of activities and wildlife encounters. Coffs is also home to the famous Big Banana.

Coffs has three main areas: the touristy jetty area, the downtown/commercial area and a string of attractive though far-flung beaches. A busy section of the Pacific Hwy snakes through the middle. Most visitors will check out the jetty area and a beach or two, but, many newcomers find that although tourism is the city's key draw, Coffs lacks a sense of cohesiveness and charm...and feels more like a good place to live than a great place to visit.

The city occupies the land of Gumbaynggirr country and there are important sites here you can visit to learn about the cultures and traditions of the Gumbaynggirr people.

⊙ Sights

Park Beach is a long, lovely stretch of sand backed by dense shrubbery and sand dunes, which conceal the buildings beyond. **Jetty Beach** is more sheltered and protected by a breakwater, creating calm swimming conditions. **Diggers Beach**, reached by turning off the highway near the Big Banana, is popular with surfers. Naturists let it all hang out at **Little Diggers Beach**, just inside the northern headland.

★Muttonbird Island   ISLAND

(☑1300 072 757; www.nationalparks.nsw.gov.au/ muttonbird-island-nature-reserve; tour adult/child/ family $20/10/50; ☺7am-7pm) The Gumbaynggirr people knew this island as Giidany Miirlarl (Place of the Moon). It was joined to Coffs Harbour by the northern breakwater in 1935. From late August to early April it's occupied by thousands of wedge-tailed shearwaters (muttonbirds). Muttonbirds by Moonlight tours – led by respected Gumbaynggirr Elder Uncle Mark Flanders – are a great way to see them and to learn about the Aboriginal significance of the island.

The island is also a great spot to see the humpback-whale migration between May and November.

Solitary Islands Aquarium   AQUARIUM

(☑02-6659 8131; www.solitaryislandsaquarium. com; Bay Dr, Charlesworth Bay; adult/child $12/8; ☺10am-4pm Sat & Sun, daily during school holidays) On weekends this small aquarium belonging to Southern Cross University's Marine Science Centre is open to the public. Touch tanks and enthusiastic, well-qualified guides provide close encounters with an octopus and the fish and coral that inhabit the waters of the Solitary Islands Marine Park.

Bunker Cartoon Gallery   GALLERY

(☑02-6651 7343; www.bunkercartoongallery. com.au; John Champion Way; adult/child $5/3; ☺10am-4pm) Displays rotating selections from its permanent collection of 23,000 cartoons from the 1920s to current day in a WWII bunker.

Big Banana   AMUSEMENT PARK

(☑02-6652 4355; www.bigbanana.com; 351 Pacific Hwy; ☺9am-5pm) **FREE** Built in 1964, the Big Banana started the craze for 'Big Things' in Australia. Admission is free, with charges for associated attractions, such as ice skating, toboggan rides, minigolf, the waterpark, plantation tours and the 'World of Bananas Experience'. Beyond the kitsch appeal there's little to see, but kids might get a kick out of it.

⅍ Activities

Coffs offers an abundance of action-packed adventure. The nearby Solitary Islands Marine Park provides an excellent environment for diving, and a number of surf schools offer lessons for all levels.

★Wajaana Yaam Adventure Tours   WATER SPORTS

(☑0409 926 747; www.wajaanayaam.com.au; 2hr tour $80) 🌿 This Aboriginal-owned business runs highly enjoyable and informative scenic stand-up paddleboard tours of Coffs Creek, Moonee Beach and Red Rock, depending on the tides. Along the way guides tell stories and teach about local Indigenous culture from the Gumbaynggirr language to bush tucker. It directly supports a not-for-profit organisation that runs after-school learning centres for Aboriginal children. Tours depart 7am to 9.30am daily.

Lee Winkler's Surf School   SURFING

(☑0438 535 560; www.surfschoolcoffsharbour.com. au; Coffs Harbour Yacht Club, 30 Marina Dr; 2hr lessons from $50) One of the oldest surf schools in Coffs. Group and private lessons available.

Coffs Skydivers   SKYDIVING

(☑02-6651 1167; www.coffsskydivers.com.au; Coffs Harbour Airport; tandem jumps from $180) Throw yourself out of a plane from 4572m on a tandem beach skydive, with a freefall of 70 seconds!

Jetty Dive   DIVING

(☑02-6651 1611; www.jettydive.com.au; 398 Harbour Dr; ☺8am-5pm) The Solitary Islands Marine Park is a meeting place of tropical waters and southern currents, making for a wonderful combination of corals, reef fish and seaweed. This dive shop offers spectacular diving and snorkelling trips (double boat dives from $195) and PADI certification (from $495). From June to October it runs whale-watching trips (adult/child $65/55).

Sleeping

There's plenty of choice for budget travellers and those looking for a midrange option, but little in the upmarket category. Contact Pacific Property Management (02-6652 9888; www.coffsholidayrentals.com.au; 3/29-33 Orlando St; 9am-5pm Mon-Fri) for private holiday apartment rentals.

Coffs Harbour YHA   HOSTEL $
(02-6652 6462; www.yha.com.au; 51 Collingwood St; dm/d from $30/90; @) A superfriendly and nicely positioned hostel with spacious dorms. Private rooms have bathrooms and wi-fi in the rooms, and the TV lounge (with Netflix) and kitchen are clean and colourful. You can use the free surfboards and hire bikes ($10 per day).

BIG4 Park Beach Holiday Park   CAMPGROUND $
(02-6648 4888; www.coffscoastholidayparks.com.au; 1 Ocean Pde; sites/cabins from $38/100;) This holiday park is massive but has an ideal location at the beach. Kids are well catered for with a shaded jumping pillow and a pool featuring slides and fountains.

Observatory Apartments   APARTMENT $$
(02-6650 0462; www.theobservatory.com.au; 30-36 Camperdown St; apt from $165;) The studio, two- and three-bedroom apartments in this attractive modern complex are bright and airy, with cook-up-friendly kitchens. All have a balcony, with views to the ocean across the road and parkland, and some have a spa bath.

Ocean Paradise Motel   MOTEL $$
(02-6652 5133; www.oceanparadisecoffs.com; 85 Ocean Pde; d from $100;) Towering palms and a lush garden give this cheerful motel a leg-up. Rooms are eye-poppingly bright and come with kitchenette. The central lawn and saltwater pool are family-friendly with a kids' playground area.

Eating

The strip of dining spots on Harbour Dr in the town's Jetty neighbourhood is great for dinner and there are a few decent options on the harbour itself that come with views. Downtown is good for lunch and all-day coffee; however, most places close early. You'll also find budget Vietnamese, Thai and Indian here.

★**Old John's**   CAFE $
(02-6699 2909; www.facebook.com/oldjohns; 360 Harbour Dr; mains $10-19; 7am-3.30pm) Join Coffs' cool kids propped up at the open window or on a street-side table sipping on the town's best coffee and digging into delights from a menu of chia 'pud', eggy breakfasts, and superfood bowls or lunch salads and toasted sandwiches.

Fishermen's Coop   FISH & CHIPS $
(02-6652 2811; www.coffsfishcoop.com.au; 69 Marina Dr; mains $12-20; 10am-7pm) Grab some excellent fish and chips and devour them right beside the fishing trawlers of Coffs' sizeable fleet. Call ahead for take-away.

Lime Mexican   MEXICAN $$
(0421 573 570; www.limemexican.com.au; 366 Harbour Dr; dishes $13-32; 5-9pm Tue-Sat;) Lime does modern Mexican tapas-style, designed to share. The taco line-up includes tempura fish, braised lamb and halloumi, and there are share plates of pork belly on spicy rice, cheese-stuffed jalapeño peppers and smoky paprika corn. Choose between the dark, moody interior or a street-side table. Daily happy hour is 5pm to 6pm for $10 cocktails and $5 beers.

★**Fiasco**   ITALIAN $$$
(02-6651 2006; www.fiascorestaurant.com.au; 22 Orlando St; pizzas $20-28, mains $29-45; 5-9pm Tue-Sat) Upmarket Italian fare is prepared in an open kitchen using local produce and herbs from the restaurant's own garden. Expect authentic delights such as wood-grilled octopus, gnocchi with beef and pork ragu, and well-done pizzas.

You can also choose to sit at the bar for antipasti and a glass of Italian vermentino or barbera. It's next to the Pacific Marina Apartments.

Drinking & Nightlife

Dark Arts Brew & Bar   COFFEE, BAR
(02-6600 1505; www.facebook.com/darkarts brewandbar; Cox Lane; 6am-3pm Mon-Thu & Sun, to 9.30pm Fri & Sat) Dark Arts is set in a nondescript central business district lane with a moody Goth interior and splashes of '80s-style graffiti on the walls. It operates as a cafe doing well-made coffee by day then transitions into an intimate cocktail bar come the weekend, with, of course, espresso martinis on the menu.

Palate & Ply COFFEE
(📱0434 700 910; www.palateandply.com.au; 37
Vernon St; ⊙6.30am-4pm Mon-Fri, to 2pm Sat)
The aroma of coffee hits you as you enter this
vast cafe with high ceilings and hessian sacks
of coffee beans lying around. The barista on
hand will deliver your brew however you
take it, from V60 and Aeropress to siphon,
espresso or nitro on tap, using beans roasted
locally by Artisti. There's also great cafe fare.

ⓘ Information

Visitor Information Centre (📱02-5622 8900;
www.coffscoast.com.au; Coffs Central, 35-61
Harbour Dr; ⊙9am-5pm)

ⓘ Getting There & Away

AIR

QantasLink (📱13 13 13; www.qantas.com.au),
and **Virgin** (📱13 67 89; www.virginaustralia.
com) fly to **Coffs Harbour Airport** (📱02-6648
4767; www.coffsharbourairport.com.au; Airport
Dr), 4km southwest of town. Qantas and Virgin
fly to/from Sydney. There are **Fly Corporate**
(📱1300 851 269; www.flycorporate.com.au)
services to Brisbane.

BUS

Long-distance and regional buses operated by
Greyhound, Premier and New England Coaches
link Coffs with Sydney, Byron Bay, Surfers Paradise and Brisbane. Services arrive and depart
from the **bus stop** on the corner of McLean St
and the Pacific Hwy.

TRAIN

NSW TrainLink (📱13 22 32; www.trans
portnsw.info/regional) Trains head to/from
Sydney ($96, nine hours), Kempsey ($20, 1¾
hours), Nambucca Heads ($8, 40 minutes) and
Grafton ($16.50, 1¼ hours) daily. There is one
service to Brisbane ($85, 5½ hours), per day.

FAR NORTH COAST

Where back-to-nature and surf-or-die lifestyles meet, this stretch of coast offers family-friendly destinations and some of the
world's most stunning beaches. Towns such
as Brunswick Heads and Yamba are being
touted as the new Byron; though both can
only be pretenders to the crown, they do have
enormous appeal all of their own – some of
that appeal is actually owing to the fact that
they are not Byron but a more relaxed, traf-
fic-free version.

Much of this coastline is situated on Bundjalung country, which stretches inland from

Grafton to Tweed Heads and over the border
into Queensland.

Grafton
POP 19,078

North of Woolgoolga, the Pacific Hwy leaves
the coast and skirts Yuraygir National Park
on its way to the small city of Grafton on the
Clarence River. This is the start of the Northern Rivers region, which stretches all the way
to the Queensland border. It's an area defined
as much by its beaches and clement weather
as it is by its three major waterways (the Clarence, Richmond and Tweed Rivers).

Don't be fooled by the franchises along the
highway – Grafton's grid of gracious streets
has grand pubs and some splendid old houses. In late October the town is awash with the
soft lilac rain of jacaranda flowers. Susan Island, in the middle of the river, is home to a
large colony of fruit bats.

⊙ Sights

Clarence River Historical Society MUSEUM
(📱02-6642 5212; www.clarencehistory.org.au; 190
Fitzroy St; by donation; ⊙1-4pm Tue-Thu & Sun)
Based in pretty Schaeffer House (1903), this
little museum displays treasures liberated
from attics across town.

⚝ Festivals & Events

★**Jacaranda Festival** CULTURAL
(www.jacarandafestival.org.au; ⊙late Oct) For
two weeks from late October, Australia's
longest-running floral festival paints the
town mauve, and there are fireworks, float
parades and markets.

🛏 Sleeping & Eating

Annie's B&B B&B $$
(📱0421 914 295; www.anniesbnbgrafton.com; 13
Mary St; s/d $145/160; ❄❀🛜🏊) This beauti-
ful Victorian heritage house on a leafy corner
has private rooms with an old-fashioned am-
bience, set apart from the rest of the family
home. A breakfast is provided, and you can
dine on your verandah or by the pool.

Heart & Soul Wholefood Cafe CAFE $
(📱02-6642 2166; www.cafeheartandsoul.com.au;
124a Prince St; mains $10-20; ⊙7.30am-5pm Mon-
Fri, to 3pm Sat, to noon Sun; 🍃) This beautiful
cafe is the work of two couples who love plant-
based eating. Expect warming Asian soups
and stir-fries, bright nourishing salads, and
delicious raw, sugar-free and dairy-free sweet

treats. Drop by the bar on Friday evenings (5pm to 10pm) for craft beer and cocktails.

Roches Family Hotel   PUB FOOD $$
(☑02-6642 2866; www.roches.com.au; 85 Victoria St; mains $16-34; ⊙10am-10pm Mon-Thu, to midnight Fri & Sat, 11am-10pm Sun) Breaking the rule that states regional pubs must be cavernous and starkly lit, this historic corner hotel is a cosy spot for a drink or a bite to eat in its contemporary bistro. It's worth calling in just for a peek at the beer-can collection and the croc in the public bar.

❶ Information

Clarence Valley Visitor Information Centre (☑02-6643 0800; www.myclarencevalley. com; Grafton Regional Gallery, 158 Fitzroy St; ⊙10am-4pm; 🛜) has helpful staff.

❶ Getting There & Away

AIR
Regional Express (Rex; ☑13 17 13; www.rex. com.au) flies to Sydney on weekdays from the **Clarence Valley Regional Airport** (GFN; ☑02-6643 0200; www.clarence.nsw.gov.au), 12km southeast of town.

BUS
Grafton is a popular hub for coach travel and is serviced by **Busways** (☑02-6642 2954; www. busways.com.au) (Maclean and Yamba), **Forest Coach Lines** (☑02-9450 2277; www.forestcoachlines.com.au) (Woolgoolga and Coffs Harbour), **Greyhound** (☑1300 473 946; www.greyhound. com.au) (Sydney, Coffs Harbour, Byron Bay, Surfers Paradise and Brisbane), **Northern Rivers Buslines** (☑02-6626 1499; www.nrbuslines. com.au) (Maclean and Lismore) and **Premier** (☑13 34 10; www.premierms.com.au) (Sydney, Coffs Harbour, Byron Bay and Brisbane).

Check websites for pricing and stop locations.

TRAIN
NSW TrainLink (☑13 22 32; www.nswtrainlink. info) Trains head to/from Sydney ($103, 10½ hours), Kempsey ($36, three hours), Nambucca Heads ($27, two hours) and Coffs Harbour ($18, 1¼ hours). There is one service per day to Brisbane ($68, four hours).

There are also road coach services to Maclean ($9, 30 minutes), Yamba ($14, 45 minutes), Ballina ($30, three hours), Lennox Head ($33, 3¼ hours) and Byron Bay ($36, 3¾ hours).

Yamba & Angourie

At the mouth of the Clarence River, the fishing town of Yamba is rapidly growing in popularity thanks to its gently bohemian lifestyle, splendid beaches, and excellent cafes and restaurants. Oft-heard descriptions such as 'Byron Bay 20 years ago' are not unfounded. Neighbour Angourie, 5km to the south, is a tiny, chilled-out place that has long been a draw for experienced surfers and was proudly one of Australia's first surf reserves.

◉ Sights & Activities

Bundjalung National Park   NATIONAL PARK
(☑02-6627 0200; www.nationalparks.nsw.gov.au/visit-a-park/parks/bundjalung-national-park; vehicle entry $8) Stretching for 25km along the coast north of the Clarence River to South Evans Head, this national park is largely untouched. Most of it is best explored with a 4WD. However, the southern reaches can be easily reached from Yamba via the passenger-only **Clarence River Ferries** (☑0408 664 556; www.clarenceriverferries.com.au; return adult/child $8.30/4.20; ⊙11am-3pm) to Iluka (at least four daily). This section of the park includes **Iluka Nature Reserve**, a stand of rainforest facing Iluka Beach, part of the Gondwana Rainforests World Heritage Area.

On the other side of Iluka Bluff the literally named **Ten Mile Beach** unfurls.

Angourie Blue & Green Pools   SPRING
(The Crescent) These springwater-fed waterholes south of Spooky Beach are the remains of the quarry used for the breakwater. Daring folk climb the cliff faces and plunge to the depths. Those with a little more restraint can slip silently into the water, surrounded by bush, only metres from the surf.

Yamba Kayak   KAYAKING
(☑02-6646 0065; www.yambakayak.com; 2hr tour adult/child from $60/40) Explore the Clarence River on one of these recommended kayaking tours. The popular three-hour River Islands tour includes a morning-tea stop (adult/child $75/50), or you can head out on the two-hour sunset oyster tour to the nearby oyster farm (adult/child $75/40).

🛏 Sleeping & Eating

Pacific Hotel   PUB $
(☑02-6646 2466; www.pacifichotelyamba.com. au/accommodation; 18 Pilot St, Yamba; dm/d from $30/130, without bathroom $80; ℗🛜) 'Motel-style' rooms in this lovely old pub have lots of charm. If you don't mind sharing a bathroom and you snare a corner cheapie, you've hit the view jackpot of a lighthouse out one window and the sea out the other. Rooms

with bathroom have a balcony as well as fridge and TV, and there are backpacker bunk rooms.

Seascape Ocean
Front Apartments   APARTMENT $$
(☑0429 664 311; www.seascapeunits.com.au; 4 Ocean St, Yamba; apt from $170; P⟨wifi⟩) Four ocean-view apartments and a riverside cottage are all furnished in bright, contemporary nautical style. Apartment views are spectacular and each space has retained its '50s Australian coastal bones. Prices are cheaper for multiple-night stays.

★ Beachwood Cafe   TURKISH $$
(☑02-6646 9781; www.beachwoodcafe.com.au; 22 High St, Yamba; mains $12-28; ⊙7am-2pm Tue-Sun) Cookbook author Sevtap Yüce steps out of the pages to deliver her bold *Turkish Flavours* to the plate at this wonderful little cafe. Most of the tables are outside, where the grass verge has been commandeered for a kitchen garden. The seasonal menu might include treats from organic mandarin juice and passion-fruit polenta cake to braised octopus for lunch.

French Pan Tree   FRENCH $$$
(☑02-6646 2335; www.thefrenchpantree.com.au; 15 Clarence St, Yamba; 2-/3-course menu $50/60; ⊙6-10pm Wed-Mon) 🌱 Dusky pink walls and candlelight set the scene at this atmospheric restaurant on the hill. Traditional French cuisine is tweaked with a modern approach by the Parisian chef, using the best of the Clarence Valley's local produce. The short and regularly changing menu features beautifully presented dishes. Book ahead.

ℹ Getting There & Away

Yamba is 15km east of the Pacific Hwy; turn off at the Yamba Rd intersection just south of the Clarence River.

Busways (☑02-6645 8941; www.busways.com. au) There are four to eight buses from Yamba to Angourie ($3.80, 15 minutes), Maclean ($5.20, 25 minutes) and Grafton ($10, 1¼ hours) daily.

Greyhound (☑1300 473 946; www.greyhound. com.au) Has a daily coach to/from Sydney (11 hours), Coffs Harbour (two hours), Byron Bay (2¼ hours), Surfers Paradise (four hours) and Brisbane (five hours). Greyhound uses dynamic pricing across its routes – check the website for current fares and specials.

NSW TrainLink (☑13 22 32; www.nswtrainlink. info) Has a daily coach to Maclean ($5, 25 minutes), Grafton ($10, one hour), Lennox Head ($14, 2½ hours), Ballina ($14, 2¼ hours) and Byron Bay ($14, 2¾ hours).

Ballina
POP 16,506
At the mouth of the Richmond River, Ballina made it as a timber town, but today it's better known for its recreational allure, with white-sand beaches, swimming spots at Shaws Bay, and the wide river itself. The Big Prawn's location (in a hardware-store car park) points to this town's commercial heart, and its 'find anything' main street heads away from the water. Ease into the Byron lifestyle by sampling Ballina's destination eating spots, and exploring its small but excellent art gallery. Ballina is home to the region's airport.

⊙ Sights

Northern Rivers
Community Gallery   GALLERY
(NRCG; ☑02-6681 0530; www.nrcgballina.com; 44 Cherry St; ⊙10am-4pm Wed-Fri, 9.30am-2.30pm Sat & Sun) **FREE** An excellent regional gallery representing the strong creative community that is an essential part of this region. Housed in the historic former Ballina Municipal Council Chambers, built in 1927, it showcases local artists and craftspeople, and also includes edgy, contemporary works and interesting events. There's a terrific cafe too.

Big Prawn   LANDMARK
(Ballina Bunnings, 507 River St) Ballina's big prawn was nearly thrown on the BBQ in 2009, but no one had the stomach to dispatch it. After a $400,000 restoration in 2013 by hardware giant Bunnings to add a much-needed tail, the 9m, 35-tonne crustacean is looking good enough to eat.

☞ Tours

Aboriginal Cultural Concepts   CULTURAL
(☑0405 654 280; www.aboriginalculturalconcepts. com; half-/full-day tours per person $95/190; ⊙Wed-Sat) Gain an Indigenous Australian perspective on the local area with heritage tours exploring mythological sites and sampling bush tucker around Ballina. Self-drive options mean meeting up with your guide at middens, former campgrounds, contact sites, fertility sites, fish traps and hunting areas.

🛏 Sleeping

Ballina Travellers Lodge   MOTEL $
(☑02-6686 6737; www.ballinatravellerslodge.com. au; 36-38 Tamar St; d $125-135, without bathroom $89; ⊛❄⟨wifi⟩) The motel rooms here are plush, with feature walls, pretty bedside

lamps and nice linen. Budget rooms (that is, the ones that share a bathroom) are a rung down in the decor stakes but represent good value. There's a kitchen with cooking facilities next to the games room, and a guest laundry.

**Reflections Holiday
Parks Shaws Bay** CARAVAN PARK **$$**
(📞02-6686 2326; www.reflectionsholidayparks.com.au; 1 Brighton St, East Ballina; sites/cabins from $45/123; 🅿️@🛜) Manicured and well positioned, this park is on the lagoon with cafes and a pub next door. Self-contained units include six deluxe and five premium villas. It has a basic camp kitchen and SUP hire.

Ballina Palms Boutique Motel MOTEL **$$**
(📞02-6686 4477; www.ballinapalms.com.au; cnr Bentinck & Owen Sts; d from $135, 2-bed studio from $275; 🅿️🛜) With its lush garden setting and Bali-style decor, this is a great-value motel. The rooms aren't overly large, but they all have a kitchenette, floorboards, marble in the bathrooms and high comfort levels. Watch traffic noise in front rooms, though.

✕ Eating

★**Belle General** CAFE **$**
(📞0411 361 453; www.bellegeneral.com; 12 Shelly Beach Rd, East Ballina; dishes $12-28; ⊙8am-3pm) Out of town opposite Shelly Beach, this destination cafe attracts local and travelling bohemians and their respective entourages. Bliss out over eggs on kale, paleo bowls or the Belle Granola — its house-made grain-, gluten-, dairy- and cane-sugar-free granola. Gluten free? Sub in quinoa loaf for sourdough.

★**Ballina Gallery Cafe** CAFE **$**
(📞02-6681 3888; www.linktr.ee/ballinagallerycafe; 46 Cherry St; mains breakfast $11-20, lunch $14-30; ⊙6.30am-3pm Tue-Sun; 🅿️) Sit out underneath the mango tree, or admire the art inside Ballina's 1920s-era former council chambers while enjoying some of Ballina's best produce. The owners pickle their own veg, smoke their own fish, and offer it up in gluten-free dishes like house-cured ocean-trout gravlax. The menu changes every six weeks.

★**Che Bon** FRENCH **$$**
(📞02-6687 8221; www.chebonrestaurant.com; 37-41 Cherry St; 2-course lunch $23, 3-course dinner $51; ⊙5.30-10.30pm Tue-Sat, 11.30am-2.30pm Thu-Fri; 🅿️) Relocating from the country town of Tintenbar to the rather suburban centre of Ballina, Che Bon, headed by chef

Rodolphe from Lyon, is a firm favourite for its well-executed French cuisine.

🍷 Drinking & Nightlife

Seven Mile Brewing BREWERY
(📞0421 841 373; www.sevenmilebrewing.com.au; 202 Southern Cross Dr; ⊙noon-6pm Thu-Sun) Flight delayed? Lucky you. Located next to Ballina airport, this family-run warehouse brewery has six to eight beers on tap, including seasonal varieties and the popular West Coast IPA made with four different hops. Tasting flights get you four beers for $14.

Old Quarter Coffee COFFEE
(📞0423 415 980; www.oldquartercoffee.com.au; 2/6 Endeavour Close; ⊙6am-1.30pm Mon-Fri) Old Quarter Coffee sits in an industrial estate, but it's a great place to grab a well-made single-origin filter coffee or stock up on beans (ethically sourced direct from farmers and roasted on-site). Pastries, toasties and fresh wraps tempt from the glass display.

ℹ️ Information

Ballina Visitor Information Centre (📞1800 777 666; www.discoverballina.com.au; 6 River St; ⊙9am-5pm Mon-Sat, 10am-2pm Sun) Grab your Ballina prawn T-shirt or apron here (as well as tourist information).

ℹ️ Getting There & Away

AIR
Ballina Byron Gateway Airport (📞02-6681 0555; www.ballinabyronairport.com.au; 210 Southern Cross Dr) is 5km north of the town centre. **Jetstar** (📞13 15 38; www.jetstar.com.au), **Virgin** (📞13 67 89; www.virginaustralia.com) and **Regional Express** (Rex; 📞13 17 13; www.regionalexpress.com.au) run services to/from Sydney; Jetstar also has services to Melbourne. **Fly Pelican** (📞02-4965 0111; www.flypelican.com.au) runs services to/from Newcastle.

Transport Options
A **taxi** (📞02-6686 9999; www.ballinataxis.com) to central Ballina costs around $20. There are regular buses and shuttle services and rental-car options for Ballina and beyond.

Byron Easy (📞02-6685 7447; www.byronbayshuttle.com.au) Scheduled door-to-door bus service from the Ballina Byron Gateway Airport to Byron Bay ($25, 40 minutes) and Bangalow ($27, 20 minutes).

Steve's Airport Transfers (📞0414 660 031; www.stevestransport.com.au) Ballina Byron Gateway Airport to Byron Bay costs $20 one-way.

Go Byron (☑ 02-6620 9200; www.gobyron. com.au) From Ballina Byron Gateway Airport to Byron Bay costs $25 one-way.

BUS

A number of bus lines service local towns and beyond, to Sydney and Brisbane, including NSW TrainLink buses that connect to rail services in Casino, 33km west from Lismore.

Blanch's (☑ 02-6686 2144; www.blanchs.com. au) Local buses, including services to Lennox Head ($5.10, 25 minutes), Bangalow ($7.60, 30 minutes), Byron Bay ($7.60, 50 minutes) and Mullumbimby ($10.10, 1½ hours).

Greyhound (☑ 1300 473 946; www.greyhound. com.au) Has coaches to/from Sydney ($168, 11½ hours, twice daily), Coffs Harbour ($45, three hours, twice daily), Byron Bay ($7, 30 minutes, twice daily), Surfers Paradise ($38, three hours, twice daily) and Brisbane ($46, 4½ hours, twice daily).

NSW TrainLink (☑ 13 22 32; www.trans-portsnw.info/regional) Coaches to Byron Bay ($5, 35 minutes, twice daily).

Premier (☑ 13 34 10; www.premierms.com.au) Daily coaches to/from Sydney ($95, 13¼ hours), Port Macquarie ($68, 6½ hours), Coffs Harbour ($48, four hours), Surfers Paradise ($40, four hours) and Brisbane ($40, 4½ hours).

Northern Rivers Buslines (☑ 02-6626 1499; www.nrbuslines.com.au) Buses to Lismore ($7.60, one hour).

Lennox Head

POP 7741

A protected National Surfing Reserve, Lennox Head's picturesque coastline has some of the best surf on the coast, with a world-class point break at Lennox Point. It's a bustling spot in summer, popular with campers who can choose from swimming in tannin-stained Lake Ainsworth, or the adjacent beach.

◉ Sights

Seven Mile Beach   BEACH
Long Seven Mile Beach starts at the township and stretches north. It's accessible to 4WDs, but you need a permit from the automated kiosk on Camp Drewe Rd (one day $15). The best place for a dip is the beach near the surf club at the northern end of town.

⌂ Sleeping

**Reflections Holiday
Park Lennox Head**   CAMPGROUND $
(☑ 02-6687 7249; www.reflectionsholidayparks.com. au; Pacific Pde; sites/cabins from $44/119; 🐕) By Lake Ainsworth and the patrolled section of

Seven Mile Beach, this family-friendly holiday park has a wide range of units, from economy cabins without bathrooms to a superior cabin sleeping seven. It offers more amenity blocks than the usual campsite, and has an excellent kitchen/TV room for chilling out.

Lennox Holiday Apartments   APARTMENT $$
(☑ 0429 328 556; www.lennoxholidayapartments. com; 20-21 Pacific Pde; apt $195-250; ❄🐕🏊) Gaze at the surf from your airy apartment in this stylish complex (all units face the ocean), then take a splash with a borrowed board from reception. The one-bedroom apartments are the same size as the two-bedroom, so feel more spacious. All apartments have a different style, and some have fold-up beds, leaving more play space during the day.

✕ Eating

Willams St Kitchen & Bar   CAFE $
(☑ 02-6687 4333; www.williamsstlennox.com; 50 Pacific Pde; mains $13.50-26; ⊘6.30am-2.30pm Mon-Wed, 6.30am-2.30pm & 4-10.30pm Thu-Sun; 🚸) This airy cafe is part beachside kiosk, part easy-going cafe with a large wooden deck for taking in the sea breeze. The all-day menu ranges from burgers to smoothie bowls while the latter half of the week and weekend you can drop by for music with your dinner and cocktails.

★**Shelter**   AUSTRALIAN $$
(☑ 02-6687 7757; www.shelterlennox.com.au; 41 Pacific Pde; mains $20-44; ⊘6.30am-3pm Mon-Wed & Sun, 6.30am-3pm & 5-9pm Thu-Sat) 🌿 One of the region's tastiest offerings, head here for generous lashings of entrées (like 'eat 'em whole' Clarence River school prawns) and sides like Brussels sprouts with cultured cream and mustard. Sit out front for beach glimpses during the day. Book ahead for dinner.

ⓘ Getting There & Away

Ballina Byron Gateway Airport is 15km away and is serviced by local bus company **Blanch's** (☑ 02-6686 2144; www.blanchs.com.au), with coaches to Lismore ($7.60, one hour), Mullumbimby ($7.60, one hour), Byron Bay ($5.10, 30 minutes) and Ballina ($5.10, 30 minutes), as well as local taxis.

Byron Bay

POP 9246

When some of Byron Bay's properties hit the $20 million mark, alarm bells rang

Byron Bay

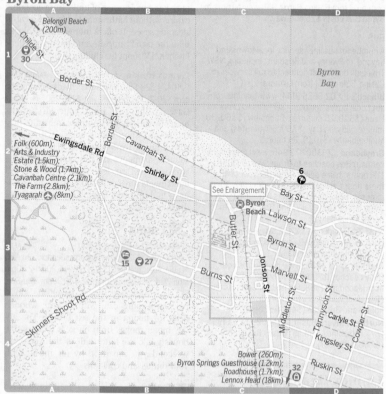

among those who loved it the best: 'Paradise lost!' And yes, Byron is suffering under the weight of its popularity – traffic-choked streets, expensive parking and lengthy cafe queues – but there's also a community passionate to fight for it, and save it from further development (coal seam gas exploration, for instance). While it's changing, Byron is still essentially a beachside town with a beautiful hill-filled backdrop.

The local Arakwal people know it as Cavanbah, which translates to 'meeting place', a fitting name when you consider its wonderful mishmash of young international backpackers, boho-parents with gold-skinned children, actors and musicians. Come here to surf epic breaks at dawn and sigh at the enchanting sunsets, refine your yoga moves and watch the street buskers, enjoy good food, then kick on at the pub. Wake up, hit repeat.

◉ Sights

★ The Farm
FARM

(www.thefarmbyronbay.com.au; 11 Ewingsdale Rd, Ewingsdale; tours adult/child $20/10; ⊗7am-4pm) FREE This photogenic, 32-hectare green oasis outside Byron is shared by Three Blue Ducks restaurant (p168), a produce store, the Bread Social bakery, an ice-cream shop and a nursery. Pick up a self-guided-tour map and roam the veggie plots and cattle-and-pig-dotted fields. Book in advance for guided tours (9am Friday to Sunday); Zephyr Horses offers tours from 7am Saturdays ($89).

Cape Byron State Conservation Park
STATE PARK

(www.nationalparks.nsw.gov.au/cape-byron-state-conservation-area; ⊗8am-sunset; 🅿) The Cape Byron State Conservation Park is home to the Cape Byron lighthouse, stunning lookouts (including from the most eastern point of the Australian mainland) and the excellent 3.7km Cape Byron Walking Track.

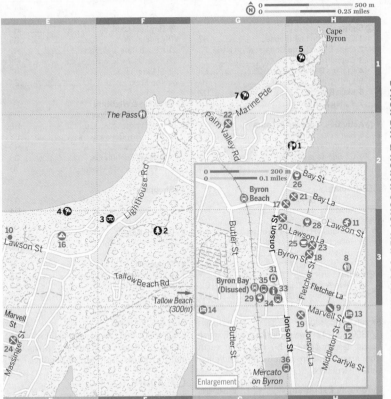

Cape Byron Lighthouse LIGHTHOUSE
(www.nationalparks.nsw.gov.au/things-to-do/his
toric-buildings-places/cape-byron-lighthouse;
Lighthouse Rd; ⊙ museum 10am-4pm) FREE This
1901 lighthouse is Australia's most easterly
and also its most powerful shipping beacon.
Inside there are maritime and nature displays. Take one of the volunteer-run tours
in the morning or afternoon to venture to
the top ($10). The cafe has great views and
serves up cones of local ice cream. Gate
opens at 8am and parking is $8 per hour.

🏃 **Activities**

From champagne-sipping hot-air ballooning, to hang gliding and kayaking, adventure sports are big in Byron, though surfing
and diving are the biggest draws. Most operators offer a free pickup service.

★ **Gaia Retreat & Spa** SPA
(☑ 02-6687 1670; www.gaiaretreat.com.au; 933
Fernleigh Rd, Brooklet; massage & treatments

$150-599) 🖉 This luxury retreat, tucked
away in the verdant hinterland in Bundjalung country, is famously co-owned by
Olivia Newton-John. If you want to save
the minimum $1500 it costs to stay, spend
a day in the spa, and book in for lunch: it's
$35, red-meat-free, and all produce is grown
on-site.

★ **Cape Byron Walking Track** WALKING
(www.nationalparks.nsw.gov.au/things-to-do/walk
ing-tracks/cape-byron-walking-track) Spectacular views reward those who climb up from
the **Captain Cook Lookout** (Lighthouse Rd)
on the Cape Byron Walking Track. Ribbon-
ing around the headland and through rainforest, the track dips and soars its way to
the lighthouse. Look out for dolphins and
migrating whales (June to November). Allow about two hours for the entire 3.7km
loop.

Byron Bay

Skydive Australia SKYDIVING
(☑ 1300 815 241; www.skydive.com.au; Tyagarah Airfield; tandem jumps $319) Hurtle to earth from around 4500m with friendly and energetic instructors.

Byron Bay Ballooning BALLOONING
(☑ 1300 889 660; www.byronbayballooning.com. au; Tyagarah Airfield; adult/child $269/175) Byron and its green surrounds are wonderful to balloon over; one-hour sunrise flights with this outfit include a champagne breakfast.

Byron Bay Dive Centre DIVING
(☑ 02-6685 8333; www.byronbaydivecentre.com. au; 9 Marvell St; dives without/with gear $80/100, snorkelling tours $80; ⊙ 9am-5pm) Offers guided dives and snorkelling trips as well as introductory ($195), freediving ($590) and open-water ($650) courses.

Black Dog Surfing SURFING
(☑ 02-6680 9828; www.blackdogsurfing.com; 11 Byron St; 3½hr group lesson $65, 3hr private lesson $140) One of four Byron Bay–based surf schools that can hold lessons at a Byron Bay beach, rather than further afield. There's a max of 10 people in group lessons, with one instructor per seven.

Surf & Bike Hire CYCLING
(☑ 02-6680 7066; www.byronbaysurfandbikehire. com.au; 31 Lawson St; ⊙ 9am-5pm) Rents bikes and surfboards (from $15/18 per day).

🌱 Tours

Rise Up Byron Conscious Tours ECOTOUR
(☑ 0450 913 145; www.riseupbyrontours.com; tours $89) Feeling smashed by the busyness of Byron? Take one of Cris' 'hinterland magic' tours to experience the best of the area, from secret waterfalls to glow worms and (optional) sound healing and meditation. A vegan meal is included.

Go Sea Kayaks KAYAKING
(☑ 0416 222 344; www.goseakayakbyronbay.com. au; adult/child $75/50) 🍃 Reputable three-hour sea-kayak tours in Cape Byron Marine Park led by a team of local surf lifesavers, who go out daily at 9.30am and 2pm. Sunrise tours run on fine days. If you don't see a whale, dolphin or turtle on the tour, book again for free.

Aboriginal Cultural Concepts CULTURAL
(☑ 0405 654 280; www.aboriginalculturalconcepts. com; half-/full-day tours $95/190; ⊙ Wed-Sat) Heritage tours led by Lois Cook – a traditional custodian of Nyangbul country in the region – explore cultural and mythological

sights, and visitors can sample bush tucker along the Bundjalung coast.

✦ Festivals & Events

Byron Bay Bluesfest
MUSIC

(www.bluesfest.com.au; Tyagarah Tea Tree Farm; ⊙Apr) Held over the Easter long weekend at the Tyagarah Tea Tree Farm in between Byron Bay and Brunswick Heads, this popular festival attracts high-calibre international performers (Iggy Pop, Brian Wilson and Patti Smith in recent years) and local heavyweights.

Splendour in the Grass
MUSIC

(www.splendourinthegrass.com; North Byron Parklands, 126 Tweed Valley Way, Yelgun; ⊙late Jul) This huge three-day festival featuring big-name artists celebrated 20 years in 2020. Recent past acts include Lorde, The Cure, Chvrches and LCD Soundsystem.

Byron Bay Writers' Festival
LITERATURE

(www.byronwritersfestival.com; ⊙early Aug) Gathers together big-name, predominantly Australian writers and their readers.

🛏 Sleeping

By any standards, Byron accommodation is expensive. If you're in the market for 'barefoot luxury' – relaxed but stylish – you're in luck. Backpackers are also catered for but it's the middle bracket that can be hard to find. Book well in advance for January, during festival times and school holidays, and avoid mid-to-late November when school-leavers hit the town to party.

★ Nomads Arts Factory Lodge
HOSTEL $

(☑02-6685 7709; www.nomadsworld.com/arts-factory; Skinners Shoot Rd; sites $17-22, dm/tepee $35-43, d $85-115; 🛜🏊) 🅿 For an archetypal Byron experience, try this rambling minivillage next to a picturesque swamp set on 2 hectares, 15 minutes' walk from town. Choose from colourful four- to 10-bed dorms, gritty festival-like campsites, a female-only lakeside cottage or shared tepee.

Reflections Holiday Park Clarkes Beach
CAMPGROUND $

(☑02-6685 6496; www.reflectionsholidayparks.com.au; 1 Lighthouse Rd; sites/cabins from $60/165; ❄🛜) The cabins sit within attractive bush high up above the beach and overlooked by the Cape Byron lighthouse. Architecturally designed premium villas and superior cabins have a 'boutique hotel' feel.

Barbara's Guesthouse
GUESTHOUSE $$

(☑0401 580 899; www.byronbayvacancy.com; 5 Burns St; d $170-330; 🅿➡❄🛜) This pretty 1920s weatherboard house in a quiet residential street has five elegant but beachy guest rooms with private bathroom, as well as a self-contained loft. The communal kitchen has breakfast supplies and a coffee machine, and the back deck's perfect for relaxing.

★ Byron Springs Guesthouse
GUESTHOUSE $$

(☑0457 808 101; www.byronsprings.com.au; 2 Oodgeroo Garden; r $150-350; 🅿🛜🏊) With a mineral pool set beside a Palm Springs–esque open-plan shared kitchen and chill-out-worthy verandah, a lot of thought has gone into keeping this space Insta-inspirational. Six unique rooms have been created from the area's original farmhouse.

★ 28° Byron Bay
BOUTIQUE HOTEL $$$

(☑02-6685 7775; www.28byronbay.com.au; 12 Marvell St; d from $450-650; 🅿❄🛜🏊) There's not a TV in sight at this stunning homestyle hotel. From the paleo granola in the in-room breakfast provisions, to the filtered water system that even feeds the pools, everything has been considered. Three rooms have plunge pools and one has lighthouse views, while rooms in the main house share a lounge, lap pool and gourmet kitchen.

Elements
RESORT $$$

(☑02-6639 1500; www.elementsofbyron.com.au; 144 Bayshore Dr; 1-bedroom villa from $380; 🅿❄🛜🏊) 🅿 Behind 2km of Belongil dunes, with its own section of sand, Byron's biggest resort is home to over 200 private villas. While none have ocean views, some do sit beside a lagoon. There's an adults-only pool, and some villas have almost Japanese-style bathhouses.

★ Bower
BOUTIQUE HOTEL $$$

(☑02-6680 9577; www.thebowerbyronbay.com.au; 28 Bangalow Rd; d from $250; 🅿❄🛜🏊) The NYC-inspired Bower is a former motel that's undergone a luxury makeover straight from the pages of an interior-design magazine (and now features in them). Expect luxury linen and excellent features and finishes. Take a dip in the circular heated mineral pool or jump on a Lekker bike to the beach.

Atlantic
BOUTIQUE HOTEL $$$

(☑02-6685 5118; www.atlanticbyronbay.com.au; 13 Marvell St; r from $295-550; ❄🛜🏊) Converting Byron's older homes into boutique accommodation is a thing, and here, four different

BYRON BEACHES

One of the toughest choices you'll need to make in Byron is deciding which beach it is for the day. Northwest of the town centre, wild **Belongil Beach** with its high dunes avoids the worst of the crowds and is clothing-optional in parts. At its eastern end lies the **Wreck**, a powerful right-hand surf break.

Immediately in front of town, lifesaver-patrolled **Main Beach** is busy from sunrise to sunset with yoga classes and buskers. As it stretches east it merges into **Clarkes Beach**. The most popular surf break is at the **Pass** near the eastern headland.

Around the rocks is gorgeous **Watego's Beach**, a crescent of white sand surrounded by rainforest that fringes Byron's most affluent enclave. A further 400m walk brings you to secluded **Little Watego's** (inaccessible by car; accessible by steps leading down from the lighthouse), another lovely patch of sand directly under rocky Cape Byron. Head here at sunset for an impressive moonrise. Tucked under the south side of the Cape (entry via Tallow Beach Rd) is **Cosy Corner**, which offers a decent-sized wave and a sheltered beach when the northerlies are blowing elsewhere.

Tallow Beach is an incredible, deserted sandy stretch that extends for 7km south from Cape Byron. This is the place to flee the crowds. Much of the beach is backed by **Arakwal National Park**, but the suburb of **Suffolk Park** sprawls along the sand near its southern end. **Kings Beach** is a popular gay-friendly beach, just off Seven Mile Beach Rd past the Broken Head Holiday Park.

houses make up 28 rooms. Check online to see what grabs you: go for the private verandah with outdoor shower, or get yourself a room close to the shared pool. Guests hang out by the firepit and cook dinner in open-air kitchens.

✖ Eating

Byron could well be the clean-eating capital of the country: golden lattes are ubiquitous and açaí bowls are more common than bacon and eggs. Upmarket restaurants serve Modern Australian dishes, and casual cafes travel the globe with tacos, tapas, pad thai and sushi. Ingredients are usually sourced from local organic producers.

★ Chihuahua   MEXICAN $
(☑02-6685 6777; Feros Arcade, 25 Jonson St; tacos $8-9; ☺11am-8.30pm) Ignore the rather un-Byron arcade location of Chihuahua to delight fully in the fresh and tasty Mexican on offer. The nachos with slow-cooked brisket feed two, and the battered halloumi with cumin aioli and sweet-potato chips is a winner, too.

Top Shop   CAFE $
(65 Carlyle St; mains $10-17; ☺6.30am-4pm) High up on the hill east of town, Top Shop has long been the choice of local surfers. Today it's a casually upmarket version of the old-school takeaway, with diners ripping into chilli chicken and chorizo rolls, as well as açaí bowls, while lazing on the lawn.

★ Bay Leaf Café   CAFE $$
(www.facebook.com/bayleafcoffee; 2 Marvell St; mains $17-24; ☺7am-2pm) Squeeze into this busy cafe and relax: everything is made with attention to detail and a passion for produce and the environment. Breakfasts, from the granola and Bircher muesli to the poached eggs with house-made dukkah, are fantastic.

★ Three Blue Ducks at the Farm   CAFE $$
(☑02-6684 7888; www.thefarmbyronbay.com.au; 11 Ewingsdale Rd, Ewingsdale; breakfast $18-25, lunch & dinner $27-43; ☺7am-3pm Mon-Thu, to 10pm Fri-Sun) The legendary Sydney team behind Three Blue Ducks moved up north to showcase its paddock-to-plate food philosophy. The heaving barn cafe and restaurant forms the beating heart of The Farm (p164) and features typical Byron healthy options, as well as surprises like spanner-crab scramble and roasted farm eggplant.

★ Balcony Bar   INTERNATIONAL $$
(☑02-6680 9666; www.balcony.com.au; cnr Lawson & Jonson Sts; mains $18-34; ☺noon-11pm Mon-Thu, to late Fri, from 9am Sat & Sun; ☺) The eponymous architectural feature here wraps around the building and gives you tremendous views of the passing Byron parade (and the ever-busy traffic circle). Decor is an appealing postcolonial pastiche, while the food is a great mix of tasty tapas-style dishes, Med-inflected warm-weather-appropriate salads and

sophisticated main meals from chilli crab linguine to a dry-aged beef burger.

Il Buco Cafe & Pizzeria
PIZZA $$

(☑02-6680 9186; www.ilbucobyronbay.com; 4/4 Bay Lane; pizza $18-28; ☺5.30pm-late) The best pizza in town, with authentic thin-crust wood-fired pizzas sparingly topped with outstanding flavours using as much local produce as possible – Bangalow sweet pork, for instance. BYO (no corkage!).

Folk
CAFE $$

(www.folkbyronbay.com; 399 Ewingsdale Rd; mains $15-18; ☺7.30am-2.30pm) 🍃 This delightful wooden-cottage cafe sits beside a busy caravan park but is a world unto itself, with a pretty garden setting and even prettier plating up. Find your menu of vegetarian and gluten-free treats in an old record sleeve.

Bang Bang
ASIAN $$

(☑0412 530 695; www.bangbangbyronbay.com; 4/1 Byron St; mains $29-47; ☺5pm-midnight) Byron's gone bonkers for Bang Bang and it's obvious why: outdoor eating on high benches, hot and tasty Asian food served up plate after sizzling plate and a cocktail list almost as long as the wine one. Keep an eye on the kitchen, and the beautifully presented dishes (listed as 'big bangs' or 'little bangs') coming out of it.

★St Elmo
SPANISH $$

(☑02-6680 7426; www.stelmodining.com; cnr Fletcher St & Lawson Lane; dishes $16-30, chef's tasting menu $60; ☺5-11pm Mon-Sat, to 10pm Sun) Perch on a stool at this moody modern tapas restaurant, where bar staff can whip up inventive cocktails or pour you a glass of wine from the largely Australian and Spanish list (including natural and minimal intervention drops). The solidly Iberian menu is bold and broad.

Raes Dining Room
SEAFOOD $$$

(☑02-6685 5366; www.raes.com.au; 6-8 Marine Pde, Watego's Beach; mains $34-41, tasting menu $105; ☺noon-3pm & 6-11pm) The sound of the surf perfectly sets off the excellent Mediterranean-influenced dishes at this exclusive little retreat overlooking Watego's Beach. Seafood features heavily with a strong focus on sourcing local produce from the Northern Rivers region. Beachgoers head to the Cellar Bar for a less formal taste from midday.

🍷 Drinking & Nightlife

★Locura
CLUB

(☑02-6675 9140; www.locura.com.au; 6 Lawson St; ☺9pm-late Fri-Sun) The folk from Three Blue Ducks opened Locura ('madness' in Spanish), a sleek and sophisticated alternative to Byron's backpacker nightspots. Get your late night techno/DJ fix with a host of guests curated by DJ/producer Jono Ma.

Stone & Wood
BREWERY

(☑02-6685 5173; www.stoneandwood.com.au; 100 Centennial Circuit; ☺10am-5pm Mon-Fri, noon-6pm Sat & Sun, meals noon-3pm) This independent and proudly local brewery, with a core family of ales, experimental pilot batches and seasonal beers, upgraded to this warehouse space in late 2018. Drop by for a paddle and to pick up a few beers or a carton; or book online for a tour (except Tuesdays; $35 per person).

Treehouse on Belongil
BAR

(☑02-6680 9452; www.treehouseonbelongil.com; 25 Childe St; mains $24-34; ☺7am-11pm) A homespun beach bar where wooden decks spill out among the trees, afternoons are for drinking, and live, original music is played Thursday to Sunday, with DJs playing over summer. Soak up the drinks with a menu of well-made woodfired pizzas, burgers, steaks and seafood.

Byron Bay Brewery
BREWERY

(☑02-6639 6100; www.byronbaybrewery.com.au; 1 Skinners Shoot Rd; ☺noon-late Wed-Sun) This old piggery-turned-booze-barn comes to life for events. Drink frosty glasses of house pale ale or lager in a light, louvred space by the brewing vats or outside in the tropical courtyard shaded by a giant fig tree. Entertainment includes live music, DJs and open-mic nights.

Railway Friendly Bar
PUB

(The Rails; ☑02-6685 7662; www.therailsbyronbay.com; 86 Jonson St; ☺10am-midnight) The Rails sure smells like a beer-stained pub, and its indoor-outdoor beer mayhem draws everyone from lobster-red British tourists to high-on-life earth mothers. The front beer garden – conducive to long, beery afternoons – has free live music.

Beach Hotel
PUB

(☑02-6685 6402; www.beachhotel.com.au; cnr Jonson & Bay Sts; ☺8am-late, Green Room from 4pm) Soak up the atmosphere and catch a gig in the iconic beachfront beer garden, or get your night started with $12 happy-hour cocktails and $2 freshly shucked oysters with finger lime in the sleeker Green Room.

WORTH A TRIP

BRUNSWICK HEADS

About 15km north of Byron Bay, Brunswick Heads is home to a top restaurant. With a teeny-tiny and simple (if effortlessly stylish) shopfront (entered from Fingal St) and most bookings snapped up on release, **Fleet** (☑ 02-6685 1363; www.fleet-restaurant.com.au; Shop 2/16 The Terrace; dishes $16-28, kitchen pick $118; ⊙ 3-11pm Thu-Sat, noon lunch only Sun) is one of Australia's most cultish dining destinations. Josh Lewis (chef) and Astrid McCormack (front of house) pursue a purist but joyful passion for produce. Dishes use local, sometimes foraged ingredients, cuts and animals that other restaurants leave behind, and produce that farmers give the restaurant on the day, say a bunch of wild amaranth. The series of small dishes that appear from the open kitchen, from cream of smoked mullet served with crisps of fish skin and potato or a 'schnitzel sandwich' of crumbed veal sweetbreads on a soft roll with anchovy mayo are punchy with flavour and pretty on the plate.

If you're staying overnight, try the **Sails Motel** (☑ 02-6685 1353; www.thesailsmotel.com. au; 26-28 Tweed St; d from $125-245, 2-bed apt $195-325; P ⊜ ❄ 🛜 🐾), a genteel 1960s motel that has been transformed. Its 22 rooms are light and simple with the occasional design piece, great eco toiletries, comfortable beds and pretty dishes and cups for balcony picnics. Owners Amanda and Simon can help you decide where to eat, swim or hike.

Barefoot Brew Room COFFEE
(www.barefootroasters.com.au; 1a Lanteen Lane; ⊙ 6am-4pm Mon-Fri, 7am-12.30pm Sat & Sun) Sneak away from the crowds down a laneway to this hole-in-the-wall coffee spot, frequented by locals, for expertly made brews by the team at Barefoot Coffee Roasters.

🛍 Shopping

Byron Farmers Market MARKET
(www.byronfarmersmarket.com.au; Cavanbah Centre; ⊙ 8-11am Thu) Local producers gather to sell their organic goods here, with hot coffee and hot-food stalls providing breakfast and brunch as you listen to live music. The Byron Magic Bus departs from the Byron Visitor Centre ($2/free adult/child) every half hour from 7:30am to 10:30am.

Spell & the Gypsy Collective FASHION & ACCESSORIES
(www.spelldesigns.com.au; 15 Browning St; ⊙ 10am-5pm) A locally grown business that's hit the big time (with 1 million Instagram followers), this fashion empire's floaty patterned dresses are seen all over Byron and the hinterland and shipped around the world. The flagship store is a calm oasis of luxe boho threads.

Arts & Industry Estate ARTS & CRAFTS
(www.byronartstrail.com) A minicity around 3km inland from Byron proper, the Arts & Industry Estate is home to Byron's community of creative businesses including Circus Arts, which runs circus programs. Check the website or grab the *Industry Trail* map available from the Visitor Centre.

Byron Twilight Market MARKET
(Railway Park, Jonson St; ⊙ 4-9pm Sat Nov-Apr) Local artists and designers show their wares at this popular night market. Expect leather, jewellery and clothing.

ℹ Information

Byron Central Hospital (☑ 02-6639 9400; https://nnswlhd.health.nsw.gov.au/about/hospitals/byron-central-hospital; 54 Ewingsdale Rd; ⊙ 24hr)

Byron Visitor Centre (☑ 02-6680 8558; www.visitbyronbay.com; Old Stationmaster's Cottage, 80 Jonson St; ⊙ 9am-5pm Mon-Sat, 10am-4pm Sun; 🛜) Helpful staff with accurate tourist information, and last-minute accommodation and bus bookings. Luggage storage (two hours $5, all day $10).

ℹ Getting There & Away

AIR

The closest airport is in Ballina (p162). Jetstar, Virgin and Rex run services to/from Sydney, and Jetstar also has services to Melbourne. Shuttle services and rental cars are available at the airport for Byron travellers. **Byron Easy Bus** (☑ 02-6685 7447; www.byronbayshuttle.com. au), **Steve's Airport Transfers** (☑ 0414 660 031; www.stevestransport.com.au; one-way/return $20/35) and **Go Byron** (☑ 02-6685 5008; www.gobyron.com.au) all serve Ballina Byron Gateway Airport (20 minutes).

Gold Coast Airport (p524) at Coolangatta has a greater range of services. **Skybus** (☑ 1300 655 655; www.skybus.com.au/byron-bay-express; one-way adult/child $15/2; 🛜) runs daily services between Byron Bay and Gold Coast Airport ($15, 55 minutes), as does Byron Easy Bus ($32),

Go Byron ($32) and **Byron Bay Express** (www.byronbayexpress.com.au) ($30).

Brisbane Airport (p524) is served by all domestic airlines and most international carriers. The **Brisbane 2 Byron Express bus** (☑1800 626 222; www.brisbane2byron.com) ($58), Byron Easy Bus ($62) and Go Byron ($70) travel from Brisbane Airport to Byron in around three hours.

BUS

Coaches stop on **Jonson St** near the Byron Visitor Centre. Operators include **Premier** (☑13 34 10; www.premierms.com.au), **Greyhound** (☑1300 473 946; www.greyhound.com.au) and **NSW TrainLink** (☑13 22 32; www.nswtrainlink.info).

Blanch's (☑02-6686 2144; www.blanchs.com.au) Regular buses to/from Ballina Byron Gateway Airport ($7.60, one hour), Ballina ($10.10, 55 minutes), Lennox Head ($5.10, 25 minutes), Bangalow ($5.10, 25 minutes) and Mullumbimby ($5.10, 25 minutes).

Brisbane 2 Byron Express Bus Three daily buses to/from Brisbane (adult/child $42/36, two hours).

Byron Bay Express Four buses daily to/from Surfers Paradise (1½ hours) for $30 one way.

Byron Easy Bus Minibus service to Brisbane ($46, three hours).

Northern Rivers Buslines (☑02-6626 1499; www.nrbuslines.com.au) Buses to/from Lismore (1½ hours), Bangalow (30 minutes) and Mullumbimby (20 minutes), all $7.60.

TRAIN

People still mourn the loss of the popular CountryLink train service that ran from Sydney. NSW Trainlink now has buses connecting to trains at the Casino train station (70 minutes), which is 33km west of Lismore.

Cabarita Beach

POP 103

Cabarita is a deliciously undeveloped beach town, though a recent win as Australia's best beach may change that. The beach is renowned for its surf breaks and also has a unique frontage, with a pandanus-fringed walking path behind the dunes. Come here for an old-school beach holiday, but let yourself get swept up in its glam side.

🛏 Sleeping

Hideaway TENTED CAMP **$$**
(☑1300 611 392; www.hideawaycabaritabeach.com.au; 2-6 Tweed Coast Rd; d from $189-239; P ☻ ❄ ☎) This purpose-designed Bell Tent village popped up on a former caravan-park site, and makes the most of its 'steps to the beach' location. 'Deluxe' and 'Bigger' tents

have air-con, but they all include quality bed linen, towels, lighting, and local teas and goodies. Even the communal area and stylish shared bathrooms are Instagrammable.

⭐**Halcyon House** BOUTIQUE HOTEL **$$$**
(☑02-6676 1444; www.halcyonhouse.com.au; 21 Cypress Cr; d $650-2000; P ❄ ❄ ☎ ☎) This former surfers' motel has kept its vintage curves to become one of East Coast Australia's most lauded boutique hotel and spas. The location is idyllic, nestled just back from the beach in a sea of pandanus, while the decor and blue and white colour palette is whimsical-meets-Hamptons luxury.

🍽 Eating

Stunned Mullet FISH & CHIPS **$**
(☑02-6676 0318; 1/16 Tweed Coast Rd; mains $9-12; ⊙10am-8pm) Everything seems to look photogenic in this town, including this fish and chip shop. It's really not often you can get a 'good green stuff' smoothie to go with your 'lonely mullet' combo meal or calamari burger, but it does suit the local vibe.

⭐**Paper Daisy** AUSTRALIAN **$$**
(☑02-6676 1444; www.halcyonhouse.com.au; 21 Cyprus Cr; mains $18-44, 5-course dinner $95; ⊙7-11am & noon-10pm) The award-winning poolside restaurant of Halcyon House is one of the area's best, with chef Jason Barrett, formerly at Raes (p169), at the helm. The sprawling space is rather (deliberately) cluttered, and the menu features locationally apt meals like kelp-baked fish with sea grapes and agnolotti with wild sea spinach.

ⓘ Getting There & Away

Cabarita is a 15-minute drive south from Gold Coast Airport in Coolangatta and its transport links, and a 40-minute drive north from Byron Bay.

NORTH COAST HINTERLAND

As Byron Bay gets busier, locals have headed to the hinterland. You'll find exciting little cafes and restaurants, great pubs and boutique accommodation set high in the hills, and more social-media-friendly vistas that you can poke a selfie stick at. With plenty of fresh-produce markets, and purportedly magic hills surrounding the area, wandering around in the incense-scented air is not a bad way to while away the days. During the busy times (school holidays and schoolies), many remain in the hinterland, emerging only for day trips to the coast, or to hit the hiking trails of one of the region's extraordinary national parks.

Mullumbimby

POP 3596

A pyramid-shaped mountain is the backdrop for Mullumbimby (aka Mullum), an attractive inland country town lined with lazy palms, tropical architecture and a spread of cafes, boutiques and pubs. Visit during its weekly farmers market to people-watch its bumper crop of locals.

Sleeping & Eating

★Blackbird Byron BOUTIQUE HOTEL $$$
(☑0467 904 123; 210 Frasers Rd, Mullumbimby Creek; d $485-545; P❋❋) Gaze at Cape Byron and the Pacific Ocean over the hinterland from one of three individual and specifically designed boltholes set high up above Mullumbimby. The magnesium mineral swimming pool and communal area share the same awe-inspiring vista.

★Punch & Daisy CAFE $
(☑02-6684 6564; www.punchanddaisy.com; 105 Stuart St; breakfast $10-18, lunch $14-20; ⊙7am-2pm) The coffee is the best in town at this delightful cafe with a relaxed rear garden. Dishes range from coconut chia porridge and avocado on sourdough with preserved lemon and pine nuts for breakfast, to wild-caught swimmer-crab cakes or filling seasonal salads at lunch.

Shopping

★Mullumbimby Farmers Market MARKET
(www.mullumfarmersmarket.org.au; Mullumbimby Showground, 51 Main Arm Rd; ⊙7-11am Fri) This vibrant food market is set under shady fig trees. Tuck into excellent organic produce while catching some live, local tunes.

Getting There & Away

Blanch's (☑02-6686 2144; www.blanchs.com. au) Runs regular buses to/from Byron Bay ($5.10, 25 minutes), Lennox Head ($7.60, 40 minutes) and Ballina ($10.10, 1½ hours).

NSW TrainLink (☑13 22 32; www.nswtrainlink. info) Services to Lismore ($9, 1½ hours).

Northern Rivers Buslines (☑02-6626 1499; www.nrbuslines.com.au) Weekday services to Bangalow ($7.60, 30 minutes) and Byron Bay ($7.60, 20 minutes).

Bangalow

POP 2021

Surrounded by subtropical forest and rolling green farmland 14km from Byron, Bangalow is home to a creative community, a dynamic, sustainable food scene and a range of urbane boutiques. The little town heaves during the monthly Bangalow Market. Stop at nearby tiny country towns of Federal and Newrybar for surprisingly good restaurants.

Sleeping & Eating

Bangalow Guesthouse GUESTHOUSE $$
(☑02-6687 1317; www.bangalowguesthouse.com. au; 99 Byron St; r $165-205, cottages $225-305; P❋❋) This timber villa houses four guest rooms on the river's edge, so guests can spot platypuses and large lizards from the expansive verandah. Private rooms have elegant, soulful decor. Three cottages have their own wooden verandah overlooking the river.

Woods Bangalow CAFE $$
(www.woodsbangalow.com.au; 5/10 Station St; mains $16-22; ⊙7.30am-2pm Tue-Sun, to 2.30pm Sat; ☑) This plant-based cafe is a lovely place of polished concrete and wood that serves Sydney's Single O coffee, the healthiest of sweets, drinks (complete with elixir powders) and beautiful brunches, such as Japanese-inspired soba noodles or quinoa with kale, pickles and hemp-seed dressing.

★Town Restaurant & Cafe AUSTRALIAN $$
(☑02-6687 1010; www.facebook.com/townbanga low; 33 Byron St; cafe mains $18-24, restaurant degustation $95; ⊙cafe 7.30am-3pm Mon-Sat, from 9am Sun, restaurant 7-9.30pm Thu-Sat; ☑) Upstairs (uptown, if you will) is one of northern NSW's perennially excellent restaurants, serving a seven-course degustation menu carefully and imaginatively constructed from seasonal local produce. There are vegetarian and vegan options too. Downstairs offers beautiful cafe breakfasts, light lunches and a counter heaving with sweet baked things.

★Harvest CAFE $$
(☑02-6687 2644; www.harvestnewrybar.com.au; 18-22 Old Pacific Hwy, Newrybar; breakfast $14-23, mains $21-94; ⊙noon-11pm Mon-Fri, from 8am Sat & Sun) ☞ Putting the tiny hinterland town of Newrybar on the map is Harvest: a restaurant in a rustic open-air Queenslander with a 'wild harvest' menu inspired by what the chef can get from the land, local farms and sea when you are there.

WORTH A TRIP

HINTERLAND NATIONAL PARKS

Nightcap National Park (www.nationalparks.nsw.gov.au/nightcap-national-park; vehicles $8) The spectacular waterfalls, the sheer cliff of solidified lava and the dense rainforest of 80-sq-km Nightcap National Park, the traditional land of the Widjabul people, are perhaps to be expected in an area with the highest annual rainfall in NSW. It's part of the Gondwana Rainforests World Heritage Area and home to many native birds and protected creatures.

The **Historic Nightcap Track** (18km, 1½ days), which was stomped out by postal workers in the late 19th century, runs from Mt Nardi to Rummery Park, a picnic spot and campground. The **Minyon Loop** (7.5km, 4½ hours) is a terrific half-day hike around the spectacular Minyon Falls, which are usually good for an icy splash. The lookout over the top of the falls is an easy 50m walk from the car park. A largely unsealed but very scenic road leads from the Channon to the Terania Creek Picnic Area, where an easy track (1.4km return, 1½ hours) heads to the base of **Protestor Falls**; swimming not permitted. It was closed at the time of research due to fires.

The park is around 30km west of Mullumbimby and 25km north of Lismore. From Nimbin, it's a 12km drive via Tuntable Falls Rd, from where Newton Dr leads to the edge of the park and then on to Mt Nardi (800m).

Border Ranges National Park (www.nationalparks.nsw.gov.au/visit-a-park/parks/border-ranges-national-park; vehicles $8) The vast Border Ranges National Park covers 317 sq km on the NSW side of the McPherson Range, which runs along the NSW–Queensland border. It's part of the Gondwana Rainforests World Heritage Area and it's estimated that representatives of a quarter of all bird species in Australia can be found here.

The eastern section of the park can be explored on the 64km **Tweed Range Scenic Drive** (gravel, and usable in dry weather), which loops through the park from Lillian Rock (midway between Uki and Kyogle) to Wiangaree (north of Kyogle on Summerland Way). The signposting on access roads isn't good (when in doubt take roads signposted to the national park), but it's well worth the effort.

The road runs through mountain rainforest, with steep hills and lookouts over the Tweed Valley to Wollumbin/Mt Warning and the coast. The five-minute walk out to the **Pinnacle Lookout** is a good alternative to climbing Wollumbin/Mt Warning to see the sunrise. A one-way drive takes you to lush rainforest, swimming holes and a picnic area at **Brindle Creek**. If you take a dip, be sure you're not wearing sunscreen or insect repellent as the chemicals are dangerous for the local rare frogs. You can walk the 5km-long walking path to **Antarctic Beech** picnic area, near a forest of 2000-year-old beech trees, or continue via the road.

Wollumbin National Park (www.nationalparks.nsw.gov.au/wollumbin-national-park) This park surrounds Wollumbin/Mt Warning (1156m), the most dramatic feature of the hinterland, towering over the valley. Its Aboriginal name, Wollumbin, means 'cloud catcher', 'fighting chief of the mountain' or 'weather maker'. Its English name was given to it by James Cook in 1770 to warn seafarers of offshore reefs.

The summit is the first part of mainland Australia to see sunlight each day, which encourages some to make the rather risky trek to the top. Under the law of the local Bundjalung people, only certain people are allowed to climb the sacred mountain; they ask you not to climb it, out of respect. Alternatively, see the sunrise from Pinnacle Lookout. More information is available from the **Murwillumbah Visitor Information Centre** (☏ 02-6672 1340; www.visitthetweed.com.au; Tweed Valley Way; ⊙ 9am-4.30pm Mon-Sat, 9.30am-4pm Sun).

Wollumbin is part of the Gondwana Rainforests World Heritage Area. Keep an eye out for the elusive Albert's lyrebird on the Lyrebird Track (300m return).

🛍 Shopping

Bangalow Farmers Market　　　MARKET
(Bangalow Hotel Car Park, 1 Byron St; ⊙8-11am Sat) One of the most favoured of the farmers markets, because of its pretty setting.

❶ Getting There & Away

Blanch's (☏ 02-6686 2144; www.blanchs.com.au) Weekday buses to/from Ballina ($7.60, 25 minutes), Lismore ($7.60, 40 minutes) and Byron Bay ($5.10, 20 minutes).

Northern Rivers Buslines (☑ 02-6626 1499; www.nrbuslines.com.au) Weekday buses to/from Lismore ($7.60, 40 minutes).

NSW TrainLink (☑ 13 22 32; www.nswtrainlink. info) Byron Bay ($5, 15 minutes), Murwillumbah ($10, 1¼ hours), Tweed Heads ($12, 1¾ hours), Burleigh Heads ($20, 1½ hours) and Surfers Paradise ($16, two hours).

Nimbin

POP 1477

Welcome to Australia's original alternative-lifestyle capital, a little town famous for its hemp culture. Nimbin was once an un-remarkable dairy village, but was changed forever in May 1973 when thousands of counter-culture kids and back-to-earth-movement types descended on the town for the Aquarius Festival. Many stayed on and created new communities in the beautiful countryside, hoping to continue the ideals expressed during the 10-day celebration. Genuine remnants of the peace-and-love generation remain, like the psychedelic rainbow-serpent murals on the main street. Depending on the day, those enjoying the local scents vary from the original hippies to the dodgier vibe of dealers, so the bus-loads of backpackers descending on the town from Byron can't be too sure what they'll find. But dig deep and you'll discover a strong community spirit and a focus on sustainability.

◉ Sights

Djanbung Gardens   GARDENS
(☑ 02-6689 1755; www.permaculture.com.au; 74 Cecil St; $5 donation for self-guided tours; ⊙10am-4pm Wed-Sat) Nimbin was an inno-vator of the organic gardening movement and this world-renowned permaculture ed-ucation centre, created out of a degraded cow pasture just a wander out of town, is home to food forests, vegetable gardens, a drought-proof system of dams, ponds and furry farm animals. Pick up a map for a self-guided wander, or sign up for a short course.

Hemp Embassy   CULTURAL CENTRE
(☑ 02-6689 1842; www.hempembassy.net; 51 Cul-len St; ⊙10am-5pm) Part shop, part strong-hold for minor political group the Hemp Party, this colourful place raises conscious-ness about impending marijuana legalisa-tion, and sells all the paraphernalia you'll need to attract police attention as well as

now legal edible hemp products. It organ-ises the **MardiGrass festival** (www.nimbin mardigrass.com) in May. An attached cafe-bar sells teas, smoothies and snacks.

✗ Sleeping & Eating

Nimbin Rox YHA   HOSTEL $
(☑ 02-6689 0022; www.nimbinrox.com.au; 74 Thorburn St; sites/dm/d/bell tents from $15/28/80/100; ☏ ▣) Escape the coastal crowds at this hostel perched on a lush hill at the edge of town offering dorms, pri-vate rooms and lovely bell tents. There are plenty of spots to unwind, with hammocks strung among the trees, an inviting pool and a nearby swimming creek. There's a communal kitchen for cooking hemp burg-ers and a regular shuttle into town.

★Grey Gum Lodge   GUESTHOUSE $
(☑ 02-6689 1713; www.greygumlodge.com; 2 High St; d $89-135; ▣ ☏) Enjoy serene valley views from the front verandah of this palm-draped wooden Queenslander-style house with six rooms with their own bathroom.

★Nimbin Hotel   PUB FOOD $$
(☑ 02-6689 1246; www.nimbinhotel.com.au; 53 Cul-len St; mains $15-25; ⊙11.30am-9.30pm) This clas-sic boozer has a vast back porch overlooking a verdant valley with seats taken up by a slice of all Nimbin life. The Mended Drum Bistro serves large plates of pub grub from classics such as chicken parma or fish and chips to fresh specials on the 'transient and specials' board. There's live music most weekends.

ℹ Information

Nimbin Visitor Information Centre (☑ 02-6689 1388; www.visitnimbin.com.au; 3/46 Cullen St; ⊙10am-4pm) Good info and local products on sale. Closes for lunch.

ℹ Getting There & Away

Various operators offer day tours or shuttles to Nimbin from Byron Bay, sometimes with stops at surrounding sights.

Gosel's (☑ 02-6677 9394) Two buses on week-days to Murwillumbah ($10.10, 1¼ hours) via Uki.

Grasshoppers (☑ 0438 269 076; www.grass-hoppers.com.au) Tours to Nimbin ($79, including BBQ lunch).

Happy Coach (☑ 02-6685 3996; www.happy-coachbyron.com) Runs tours to Nimbin ($55); lunch is included in the price.

Northern Rivers Buslines (☑ 02-6626 1499; www.nrbuslines.com.au) Weekday services to Lismore ($7.60, 45 minutes).

Canberra & South Coast New South Wales

Best Places to Eat

➡ Wheelers (p203)

➡ Quarterdeck Marina (p199)

➡ Cupitt's Estate (p194)

➡ Hayden's Pies (p194)

➡ Caveau (p187)

➡ Akiba (p182)

Best Places to Sleep

➡ Paperbark Camp (p192)

➡ Laurels B&B (p190)

➡ Keiraleagh (p187)

➡ East Hotel (p181)

➡ Little National Hotel (p181)

Why Go?

If the glamour of Sydney feels oh-too-much, or the drive up from Melbourne seems oh-so-drab, then seek out South Coast New South Wales, a gorgeous stretch of sandy coves, sea pools and sparsely visited national parks bristling with wildlife and laid-back local communities galvanised by recent bush fires.

The land has deep significance for Aboriginal communities: Montague Island (Barranguba), with its multitude of seals and birdlife; pert Pigeon House Mountain (Didthul); and ancient sites across Murramarang and Booderee National Parks.

Meanwhile, a couple of hours inland sits Canberra, the architecturally bold national capital that materialised in the scrub. Forget what you thought you knew about Canberra, the city is awash with intellectual, political, artistic and culinary exploits of the highest calibre.

When to Go
Canberra

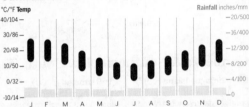

Feb & Mar Surf and swim in your boardies and bikinis, free from the holiday crowds.

Sep Meander through Canberra's galleries and museums amid the scent of Floriade Festival.

Apr & May Tackle the Light to Light Walk in Ben Boyd National Park.

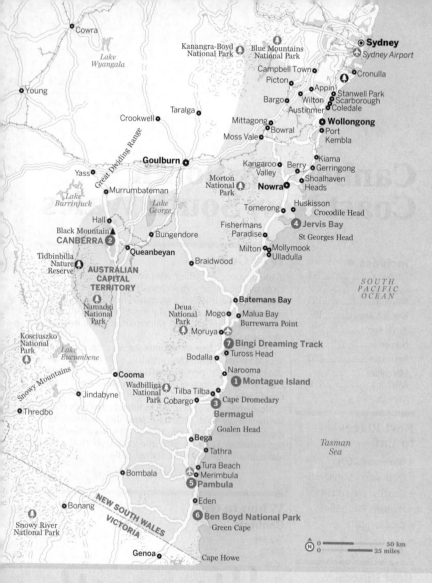

Canberra & Southern New South Wales Highlights

1 Montague Island (p197)
Circling the lighthouse on this pristine island sanctuary and snorkelling with curious seals.

2 Canberra (p177)
Surveying fine art and architecture in our new favourite national capital.

3 Bermagui (p200)
Swimming in the famous Blue Pool at this coastal town blessed with a deep harbour and a tinge of the alternative.

4 Jervis Bay (p191)
Kayaking crystal-clear waters before retiring to a dazzling white beach.

5 Pambula (p202) Slurping cheap, fresh oysters straight from roadside stalls.

6 Ben Boyd National Park (p205) Hiking other-worldly coastal reserves.

7 Bingi Dreaming Track (p195) Learning about sacred country and foraging with an Indigenous guide.

ℹ️ Getting There & Away

Trains from Sydney (📞 13 15 00, 02-4907 7501; www.sydneytrains.info) get as far as Nowra (Bomaderry) via Wollongong, Kiama and Berry, but beyond here it's buses. **Premier** (📞 02-4423 5233, 13 34 10; www.premierms. com.au) is the major operator, linking Eden with Sydney via all coastal towns twice daily. **Murrays** (📞 13 22 51; www.murrays.com.au) links South Coast towns with Canberra (the closest railway station to many of them), while V/Line (p196) offers a bus and train connection to Melbourne.

ℹ️ Getting Around

As everywhere in Australia, a car or motorcycle offers the best flexibility. Buses and trains supplemented by bike hire reduce costs significantly, though trips take longer. Forward planning is everything: in smaller places, you may have to rely on local buses timetabled for schoolchildren (that is, one or two services in the morning, and again in the afternoon).

CANBERRA

POP 410,199

Long the brunt of jokes from sneering bigger city folk, Canberra has been reimagined in recent years as Australia's unsung, sophisticated capital embedded in a bona fide bush landscape. Built in 1927 to solve a squabble between the political elite in Sydney and Melbourne, Canberra has long been recognised for its superb art galleries and avant garde architecture, and a sprawling, world-class university. But its resurgence as a travel destination is largely due to the impressive food and bar scene, and a number of hip new hotels catering to families and couples and the usual political entourage. There's plenty of history too, both past and in the making – visitors can see Australian democracy in action at Parliament House before exploring its bygone days at some of the city's many museums.

Canberra is also a great biking destination, with easy trails around Lake Burley Griffin and some world-class trails around Black Mountain and Majura Pines.

History

Canberra is built on Ngunnawal country. The Ngunnawal people are the Indigenous Australian nation that lived on the land around Canberra at the time of European settlement, along with the Gundungurra to the north,

the Ngarigo to the south, the Yuin to the west and the Wiradjuri to the east. Rock paintings found in nearby Tharwa indicate that Indigenous Australians have lived in this region for at least 20,000 years, though evidence from nearby regions suggests an even longer duration.

The Ngunnawal people called this place Kanberra, believed to mean 'Meeting Place'. The name was probably derived from huge intertribal gatherings that happened annually when large numbers of bogong moths – a popular food source – appeared in the region.

The Ngunnawal way of life was violently disrupted following the arrival of Europeans in 1820, when settlers began to move into the Canberra basin, bringing sheep and other introduced species. Indigenous Australians resisted the intrusion of the graziers, most notably in 1826 when over a thousand people gathered at Lake George to protest their displacement. Despite their efforts, the Aboriginal inhabitants of the area were gradually forced further north as their hunting grounds were diminished by the actions of the settlers, and by the 1860s very few remained here.

During the first stage of European settlement, the Canberra area was part of the colony of New South Wales. In 1901, when Australia's separate colonies federated, the rivalry between Sydney and Melbourne meant neither could become the new nation's capital, so a location between the two cities was carved out of southern NSW as a compromise. This new city was officially named Canberra in 1913, and became the national capital in 1927.

⊙ Sights

★**National Gallery of Australia** GALLERY (📞 02-6240 6502; www.nga.gov.au; Parkes Pl, Parkes; temporary exhibition prices vary; ⊙ 10am-5pm) **FREE** This Australian national art collection is showcased in an impressive purpose-built gallery within the parliamentary precinct. You can justifiably bypass the ticketed exhibitions as almost every big name you could think of from Australian and international art, past and present, is represented in the permanent collection. Famous works include *Blue Poles* by Jackson Pollock, one of Monet's *Waterlilies,* a Hockney *Diver,* several of Sidney Nolan's *Ned Kelly* paintings, Salvador Dalí's *Lobster Telephone,* an Andy Warhol *Elvis* print and a triptych by Francis Bacon.

Highlights include the extraordinary *Aboriginal Memorial* from Central Arnhem

Central Canberra

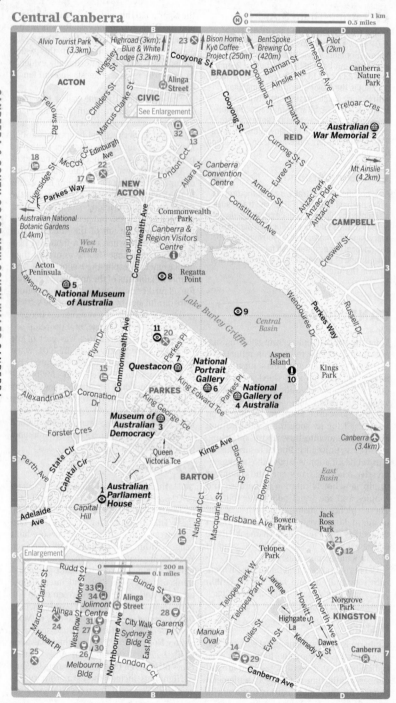

N
0 ——————— 1 km
0 ——————— 0.5 miles

Alvio Tourist Park
(3.3km)

Highroad (3km);
Blue & White
Lodge (3.2km)

23
Cooyong St

Bison Home;
Kyō Coffee
Project (250m)

BentSpoke
Brewing Co
(420m)

Pilot
(2km)

ACTON

Kingsley St
Childers St
Marcus Clarke St
Fellows Rd

CIVIC

Alinga
Street

See Enlargement

BRADDON

Doonkuna St
Cooyong St
Batman St
Ainslie Ave
Limestone Ave

Canberra
Nature Park

Treloar Cres

32
13

REID

Currong St

Elimatta St

Australian
War Memorial 2

18

McCoy Cct
Edinburgh
Ave

22

17
Parkes Way

Liversidge St

NEW
ACTON

London Cct

Allara St

Canberra Convention
Centre

Euree St
Amaroo St

Constitution Ave

Mt Ainslie
(4.2km)

Anzac Park
Anzac Pde
Anzac Park

CAMPBELL

Australian National
Botanic Gardens
(1.4km)

West
Basin

Commonwealth
Park

Canberra &
Region Visitors
Centre

Creswell St

Acton
Peninsula

Lawson Cres

5
National Museum
of Australia

Barrine Dr

Commonwealth Ave

8
Regatta
Point

Lake Burley Griffin

9

Central
Basin

Wendouree Dr

Parkes Way

Russell Dr

Flynn Dr

11
20
Parkes Pl

7
Questacon

National
Portrait
Gallery

6

Parkes Pl

Aspen
Island

10

Kings
Park

15

Alexandrina Dr
Coronation
Dr

Forster Cres

King Edward Tce

PARKES

King George Tce

Museum of
Australian
Democracy

3

4
National
Gallery of
Australia

Perth Ave
State Cir
Capital Cir

Queen
Victoria Tce

Kings Ave

BARTON

Blackall St

Bowen Dr

Canberra
(3.4km)

East
Basin

Adelaide
Ave

1
Australian
Parliament
House

Capital
Hill

National Cct

Macquarie St

Brisbane Ave

Bowen
Park

Jack
Ross
Park

21
12

Telopea
Park

Enlargement
0 ——————— 200 m
0 ——————— 0.1 miles

Telopea Park W
Telopea Park E
Jardine St

Highgate
La

Howitt St
Wentworth Ave

Norgrove
Park

KINGSTON

Rudd St

Bunda St

Marcus Clarke St

Moore St

33
34

Alinga
Street

Jolimont
Centre

19

Alinga St
City Walk
Sydney
Bldg

28
Garema
Pl

Giles St

Manuka
Oval

Eyre St

Kennedy St

Dawes St

Canberra

7

24
31
27
26
30

West Row
Northbourne Ave
East Row
London Cct

Hobart Pl

25

Melbourne
Bldg

14
29

Canberra Ave

Central Canberra

Land in the lobby, created for Australia's 1988 bicentenary. The work of 43 artists, this 'forest of souls' presents 200 hollow log coffins (one for every year of European settlement) and is part of an excellent collection of Aboriginal and Torres Strait Islander art. Most of the Australian art is on the 1st floor, alongside a fine collection of Asian and Pacific art. The outdoor sculpture garden offers a dramatic site for repose. A children's programme runs on weekends and school holidays.

Free guided tours are offered hourly from 10.30am to 2.30pm.

★ **National Portrait Gallery**   GALLERY
(☑ 02-6102 7000; www.portrait.gov.au; King Edward Tce, Parkes; ⊙ 10am-5pm) FREE Occupying a flash, purpose-built building, this wonderful gallery is a striking representation of Australia's shifting self-image and a must-see for art- and history-lovers. From wax cameos of Indigenous Australians to colonial portraits of the nation's founding families, to Howard Arkley's DayGlo portrait of musician Nick Cave and a host of modern Australian icons portrayed in various mediums, the gallery is an inspiring account of a nation's many faces. Only around 10% of the collection of more than 3500 works is on display at any one

time, so there's always something different to see. New portraits of contemporary Australian figures are also commissioned every year.

There is a good **cafe** (☑ 02-6102 7162; www.portrait.gov.au; National Portrait Gallery, King Edward Tce, Parkes; mains from $12.50; ⊙ 9am-4.30pm; ✸ 🛜) for post-exhibition coffee and reflection.

★ **Australian War Memorial**   MUSEUM
(☑ 02-6243 4211; www.awm.gov.au; Treloar Cres, Campbell; ⊙ 10am-5pm) FREE Canberra's glorious art-deco war memorial is a highlight in a city filled with interesting architecture. Built to commemorate 'the war to end all wars', it opened its doors in 1941 when the next world war was already well underway. Each section depicts Australia's involvement in significant conflicts, including displays on recent battles in Afghanistan and Iraq. Attached to the memorial is a large, exceptionally well-designed museum devoted to the nation's military history. Try to time your visit for the Last Post and accompanying ceremony each day just before closing.

★ **Australian Parliament House**   NOTABLE BUILDING
(☑ 02-6277 5399; www.aph.gov.au; ⊙ 9am-5pm) FREE Built in 1988, Australia's national parliament building is a graceful and deeply

symbolic piece of architecture. Sitting atop Capital Hill, the building is crossed by two axes, north–south and east–west, representing the historical and legislative progression of Australian democracy. There's plenty to see inside, whether the politicians are haranguing each other in the chambers or not.

Visitors are free to explore large sections of the building and watch parliamentary proceedings from the public galleries. The only time that tickets are required is for **Question Time** in the House of Representatives (2pm on sitting days); tickets are free but must be booked through the Serjeant-at-Arms. See the website for a calendar of sitting days.

Free guided tours (40 minutes) depart from the desk in the foyer at 9.30am, 11am, 1pm, 2pm and 3.30pm. We highly recommend the one-hour 'Behind the Scenes' tour ($15, 10am, noon and 3pm, outside parliamentary sitting weeks), which gives a more intimate look into the machinations of Australian democracy.

Australian National Botanic Gardens
GARDENS

(☑ 02-6250 9588; www.nationalbotanicgardens. gov.au; Clunies Ross St; ☺ 8.30am-5pm) FREE On the lower slopes of Black Mountain, these sprawling gardens showcase Australian floral diversity over 35 hectares and a further 50 hectares of remnant bushland. Various themed routes are marked out, with the best introduction being the main path (45 minutes return), which takes in the eucalypt lawn, rock garden, rainforest gully and Sydney Region garden. A 3.2km bushland nature trail leads to the garden's higher reaches. On weekends and summer school holidays, you

---

WILDLIFE ON THE HOP

Canberra is one of the best cities in Australia for spotting wild kangaroos. Some of the most likely spots include Weston Park on the shores of Lake Burley Griffin northwest of Parliament House, Government House, **Mt Ainslie** (www.environment.act.gov.au/parks-conservation/parks-and-reserves; Ainslie Dr) and **Namadgi National Park** (☑ 02-6207 2900; www.environment.act.gov.au; Naas Rd, Tharwa; ☺ visitor centre 9am-4pm) FREE . You're also practically guaranteed to see kangaroos if you visit **Tidbinbilla** (☑ 02-6205 1233; www.tidbinbilla.act.gov.au; 141 Paddys River Rd, Paddys River; entry per car $13; ☺ 7.30am-6pm Apr-Sept, to 8pm Oct-Mar, visitor centre 9am-5pm).

---

can take the Flora Explorer (adult/child $8/5, 45 minutes) at 10.30am or 1.30pm.

Questacon
MUSEUM

(☑ 02-6270 2800; www.questacon.edu.au; King Edward Tce, Parkes; adult/child/family $23/17.50/70; ☺ 9am-5pm; ▣) Most families visiting Canberra head straight for Questacon, Australia's premier science museum, where they can play around with fun interactive exhibits and tinker in supervised workshops. Permanent features include earthquake simulators, a ginormous model of the moon, and a terrifying vertical slide. If you're travelling to other states, it can be good value to purchase a national membership online. Regular science shows take place at the on-site theatre – usually at 11am, noon, 1.30pm and 2.30pm, but check online for updated times.

National Museum of Australia
MUSEUM

(☑ 02-6208 5000; www.nma.gov.au; Lawson Cres, Acton Peninsula; ☺ 9am-5pm) FREE As well as telling Australia's national story, this museum hosts blockbuster touring exhibitions (admission prices vary), which often outpoint the permanent collection by some margin. Highlights include the Gallery of First Australians, which explains the history and traditions of Aboriginal and Torres Strait Islander peoples, and the Garden of Australian Dreams, an interactive outdoor exhibition. One way to get the best out of the museum is to take a one-hour guided tour (adult/child $15/10, 10am, 1pm and 3pm daily). The views from the cafe and the grassy banks are very pleasant.

Lake Burley Griffin
LAKE

Every morning you'll see politicians running off the night before around this majestic lake, with perhaps a few journos hot on their trail. This lake was constructed in 1963 when the 33m-high Scrivener Dam was erected on the Molonglo River. It's lined with important institutions and monuments, including the **National Carillon** (www.nca.gov.au; Aspen Island) and **Captain Cook Memorial Water Jet** (Captain Cook's Fountain). You can cycle the entire 28km perimeter in two hours or walk it in seven. Alternatively, you can make a smaller 'loop' by making use of the two bridges – the popular central loop is 5km and can be walked in one to 1½ hours.

🏃 Activities & Tours

GoBoat
BOATING

(☑ 02-6100 7776; www.goboatcanberra.com.au; Wharf 2, Trevillian Quay, Kingston Foreshore; 1/2/3hr

$99/189/249; ⊙10am-8pm) Fancy pottering around Lake Burley Griffin on your own private boat? These little electric-powered dinghies can fit up to eight people and have a table in the centre just made for picnicking. You don't need a boat licence to captain your own cruise, just a sense of adventure. Bookings (via the website) are recommended.

Balloon Aloft   BALLOONING
(☑02-6249 8660; www.balloonaloftcanberra.com.au; 120 Commonwealth Ave, Yarralumla; adult/child from $330/240) Meet in the foyer of the Hyatt for an early-morning flight over Canberra – the ideal way to view the city's unique design.

★ Festivals & Events

Enlighten   CULTURAL
(www.enlightencanberra.com; ⊙Mar) For two weeks in early March, various Canberra institutions are bathed in light projections and keep their doors open late, while musical performances and other outdoor events culminate in an explosive fireworks display.

★ Floriade   FAIR
(www.floriadeaustralia.com; Commonwealth Park; ⊙mid-Sep–mid-Oct) This renowned spring flower festival is one of the city's biggest events, drawing the crowds to Commonwealth Park from mid-September to mid-October to delight in elaborate floral displays.

The festival includes evening events such as concerts and Night Fest, promising music, comedy and more.

🛏 Sleeping

Canberra's high-end hotel scene has blossomed. Accommodation is most expensive on parliamentary sitting days, but there is a buzz in town at these times so it can be worth the extra expense. Hotels charge peak rates midweek, but often have reduced rates at weekends. Peak rates also apply during the spring Floriade festival

Blue & White Lodge   MOTEL $
(☑02-6248 0498; www.blueandwhitelodge.com.au; 524 Northbourne Ave, Downer; s/d $95/100; P🌸🛜) On the main approach into Canberra from the north, this long-standing motel-style place and its indistinguishable sister, the Canberran Lodge, are reliable budget options in what can be a pricey city. It's a long walk into town, but there's a light-rail stop right out the front. Owners Maria and Michael are adept at meeting the needs of weary travellers.

KIDS IN THE CAPITAL

Canberra is a family-friendly city, with plenty of space to roam and no huge crowds. Kids like Canberra because there's stacks of cool stuff for them to do. Most of the museums and galleries have kids' programmes, and many offer dedicated tours and events for little people – check websites for details.

Canberra City YHA   HOSTEL $
(☑02-6248 9155; www.yha.com.au; 7 Akuna St; dm $35-41, d with/without bathroom $135/115; 🌸@🛜🏊) The Canberra City YHA is a bit of a winner: friendly staff, lots of amenities for a hostel, excellent pedestrian access. The basement pool and sauna are nice features year-round, while the large kitchen and on-site cafe ensure easy intermingling.

★ East Hotel   HOTEL $$
(☑02-6295 6925; www.easthotel.com.au; 69 Canberra Ave, Kingston; apt from $180; P🌸@🛜) The East's stylish mini-apartments make the perfect destination for a weekender or a family getaway, located near delightful Manuka Pool (guests swim free), Manuka Oval, which hosts major cricket and AFL matches, and the hip Kingston shopping strip. East offers stylish spaces and smile-inducing extras like free lollies and design magazines for loan. Even the studios have a work desk, an espresso machine and kitchenette, and there are one- and two-bedroom suites if you need to spread out. Plus downstairs there are two superb restaurants, **Agostini's** (☑02-6178 0048; pizzas $21-25, mains from $25; ⊙noon-3pm & 5.30pm-late) and Muse (p185).

★ University House   HOTEL $$
(☑02-6125 5211; www.unihouse.anu.edu.au; 1 Balmain Cres, Acton; tw/d/apt from $174/180/224; P🌸🛜) This 1950s-era building, with original custom-built furniture, resides in the tree-lined grounds of the Australian National University (ANU) and is favoured by research students, visiting academics and the occasional politician. The spacious rooms and two-bedroom apartments are unadorned but comfortable. There's also a peaceful central courtyard and a friendly cafe downstairs. Discounts are available for longer stays and for solo travellers.

Little National Hotel   HOTEL $$
(☑02-6188 3200; www.littlenationalhotel.com.au; 21 National Circuit, Barton; r from $116; P🌸@🛜)

Part of the respected Doma Group, which boasts five boutique hotels in the same precinct, Little National is the pick of the bunch. Housed within a stark black cube, this brilliant boutique hotel delivers affordable style by way of small but well-designed rooms with exceptionally comfortable beds. Compensating for the lack of cat-swinging space is an appealing 'library' and bar offering panoramic views of the city.

Ovolo Nishi
HOTEL $$$

(☑ 02-6287 6287; www.ovolohotels.com.au/ovolonishi; 25 Edinburgh Ave, New Acton; d $238-373; P❄🖥) ⚟ The Ovolo group are making waves globally for their cutting-edge art hotels, and Canberra's very own is a fine example of the brand. A spectacular exterior and an equally hip interior, rooms are quirkily decorated and have all the mod cons, from rain showers to high-tech electronics. Not a lot of functionality in the space and layout for a typical business stay, but the service and quality are exceptional and the spaces encourage an informal interaction between guests. Go for the Sung room.

Reception is filled with nooks, crannies and minilibraries, and the **Monster Kitchen & Bar** (www.monsterkitchen.com.au; breakfast $11-20, shared plates $20-34; ⊙6.30am-late; P🖥) is just as interesting.

★ Hyatt Hotel Canberra
HOTEL $$$

(☑ 02-6270 1234; www.hyatt.com; 120 Commonwealth Ave, Yarralumla; r/ste from $295/690; P❄@🖥💢) The Hyatt is almost a destination in Canberra, even if you don't need a bed for the night. Diplomats and dignitaries rub shoulders with journalists and dealmakers in the many communal spaces, including a fine tea lounge and a hopping bar. It may be the city's oldest luxury hotel, but the large rooms are distinctly modern and well-equipped, and facilities include an indoor pool, spa, sauna and gym.

🍴 Eating

Canberrans have always enjoyed access to some fine restaurants thanks to the politicians' and powerbrokers' love of the long lunch, but the city now impresses on every level. Established dining hubs include Kingston and Manuka, while the Kingston foreshore development, Civic (the central business district, or CBD) and Lonsdale St in Braddon have some strong players.

Two Before Ten
CAFE $

(www.twobeforeten.com.au; 1 Hobart Pl, Acton; mains $11-18; ⊙7am-4pm Mon-Fri, 8am-2pm Sat & Sun) Two Before Ten is our pick of Canberra's vibrant coffee scene. Bringing a touch of Cape Cod to the centre of a city block, the excellent coffee comes from its own roastery in Aranda, where there is also another outpost of the cafe. Meals are good, especially breakfast. There's a new branch in the airport too, so you can hit the ground running.

★ Akiba
ASIAN $$

(☑ 02-6162 0602; www.akiba.com.au; 40 Bunda St; noodle & rice dishes $10-21, share plates $16-33; ⊙11.30am-midnight Sun-Wed, to 2am Thu-Sat) Here's a place to kickstart a night out or savour 'New Asian' food with attitude. Canberra's coolest bar-restaurant is cocktails first, questions later. Slick staff can recommend dishes like octopus with duck-fat potatoes, king-prawn fried rice and crab dumplings, but the eight-plate dinner ($49) will ensure you don't miss out. A raw bar serves delectable sashimi, freshly shucked oysters and zingy ceviche.

★ Rye
CAFE $$

(☑ 02-6156 9694; www.ryecafe.com.au; 9 Lonsdale St, Braddon; breakfast $14-20, lunch $9-20; ⊙6.30am-4pm) Scandi-inspired Rye is all blonde wood, bright lights and modish furniture, with a menu to match. Danish *smørrebrød* (open sandwiches on dark rye bread) are a popular choice at lunch, while breakfast options are headed by the Rye Breakfast Board ($20) featuring soft eggs and hard cheese. Great coffee and smoothies.

★ Terra
AUSTRALIAN $$

(☑ 02-6230 4414; www.terracanberra.com.au; Shop G2, No Name Lane, 40 Marcus Clarke St; mains breakfast & lunch $10-16, dinner $18-38, set menu per person $65; ⊙7.30am-4pm Mon-Wed, to late Thu & Fri, from 10.30am Sat) By day this atmospheric, contemporary space creates delectable seasonal brunch dishes and fabulous coffee. At night the rotisserie takes centre stage, with six-hour roasted meats alongside innovative sides like charred lettuce, or crumbed egg salad. The best option, though, is the 'Feed Me' set menu (minimum two people) – you won't go home hungry.

Bookplate
CAFE $$

(☑ 02-6262 1154; www.bookplate.com.au; National Library of Australia, Parkes Pl W, Parkes; dishes $16-25; ⊙7.30am-5pm Mon-Thu, to 4pm Fri, from 9am Sat & Sun; ☑) In the foyer of

the **National Library** (☑ 02-6262 1111; www.
nla.gov.au; ☉ 10am-8pm Mon-Thu, to 5pm Fri &
Sat, from 1.30pm Sun, galleries 10am-5pm daily)
FREE you'll find Bookplate, an award-winning cafe with a technicolour stained-glass
backdrop. It's equally good as a lunch stop
– with daily specials including pulled-pork
tacos or poke bowls – or just for coffee and
cake. The wine list is also excellent.

Lazy Su   ASIAN $$
(☑ 02-5105 3812; www.lazy-su.com.au; 9 Lonsdale St, Braddon; dishes $12-29; ☉ 5-11pm Mon,
from noon Tue-Thu & Sun, to 1am Fri & Sat) Lazy
Su's playful Asian vibe is obvious as you enter past the wall of lucky cats. You can't go
far wrong with the menu, but if you can't
decide between Grandma's Tofu and the
fried-chicken ramen, opt for the seven-dish
'Mi-So Hungry' ($49 per person).

Highroad   CAFE $$
(www.highrd.com.au; cnr Cape & Woolley Sts, Dickson;
brunch $11-24, dinner $16-30; ☉ 7am-4pm Mon-Wed,
to late Fri, from 8am Sat, to 3pm Sun) Locals fill the
tables in the spacious corner building from
lunch to dinner, supping on speciality-blend
coffee in the mornings and local wines as the
sun sets. The menu spans the gamut of Mod
Oz cafe fare, from French toast to burgers.

Morning Glory   CAFE $$
(☑ 02-6257 6464; www.morning-glory.com.au;
2/15 Edinburgh Ave, New Acton; dishes $12-27;
☉ 6am-3pm; ✸ ♥) Nestled in the heart of
the New Acton complex, this sprawling
cafe has a sleek, contemporary vibe and is
a popular coffee stop for local office workers. The menu offers modern cafe dishes
with an Asian twist, like matcha hotcakes
at breakfast, or a sublime eggplant burger
at lunch.

Morks   THAI $$$
(☑ 02-6295 0112; www.morks.com.au; 19 Eastlake Pde, Kingston; mains $18-44; ☉ noon-2pm
& 6-10pm Wed-Fri & Sun, 6-10pm Tue & Sat) Not
exactly cheap, but nonetheless one of the
best restaurants on the Kingston foreshore,
Morks offers a contemporary spin on Thai
cuisine, with Chinese and Malay elements
added to the mix. Ask for a table outside
to watch the passing promenade, and tuck
into multiple starters; the crispy eggplant is
highly recommended.

★ **Pilot**   MODERN AUSTRALIAN $$$
(☑ 02-6257 4334; www.pilotrestaurant.com; 5/6
Wakefield Gardens, Ainslie; mains $25-45, set menu

per person $90, with paired drinks nonalcoholic/
alcoholic $120/150; ☉ 6pm-late Wed-Sat, noon-
3.30pm Sun) Elegant, seasonal dishes are
the highlight at this classy fine-dining restaurant in suburban Ainslie. The menu
changes daily but features local produce
and interesting flavour combinations. À la
carte options are available, but for the full
experience try the 'prix fixe' tasting menu,
available paired with either alcoholic or
nonalcoholic beverages. There's also a Sunday 'long lunch' ($60 per person).

🍷 Drinking & Nightlife

Canberra's village-like suburban centres are
great for cafes. In the evenings, though, nightlife tends to be concentrated in Civic and
around Lonsdale and Mort Sts in Braddon.

★ **Bar Rochford**   WINE BAR
(☑ 02-6230 6222; www.barrochford.com; 1st fl, 65
London Circuit; ☉ 5pm-late Tue-Thu, 3pm-1am Fri,
from 5pm Sat) Bartenders concentrate earnestly on their cocktail constructions and
wine recommendations at this sophisticated
but unstuffy bar in the Melbourne Building.
Dress up and hope for a table by one of the
big arched windows.

★ **Molly**   BAR
(www.molly.bar; Odgers Lane; ☉ 4pm-midnight
Mon-Wed, to 2am Thu-Sat, 5pm-late Sun) The
doorway to this little gem, hidden away
down quiet Odgers Lane, is illuminated only
by a light bulb. It may take some courage
to push through the unmarked wooden
door, but have faith: inside you'll find an atmospheric 1920s-style speakeasy, with dim
lighting, cosy booths and a very impressive
whisky selection. Try the cocktails.

Hippo Co   BAR
(☑ 02-6247 7555; www.hippoco.com.au; Level 1,
17 Garema Pl; ☉ 5pm-late Mon-Thu & Sat, from
4pm Fri) This cosy upstairs lounge-bar is
popular with young whisky and cocktail
slurpers who file in for Wednesday-night
jazz – the turntable rules other evenings.
The gin and whisky lists are more than
impressive; ask the friendly bartenders for
recommendations.

Highball Express   COCKTAIL BAR
(www.highballexpress.com.au; Level 1, 82 Alinga St;
☉ 4pm-late Tue-Sat) You'll need all your travel nous to find this louche tropical take on
a 1920s Cuban rum bar. Among the barrels
and the palms are Canberra's smoothest

cats, sipping on rum-soaked cocktails and bopping their heads.

Kingston Hotel
PUB

(☑ 02-6295 0123; www.kingstonhotel.com.au; 73 Canberra Ave, Griffin; ⊙ 11.30am-10.30pm) The 'Kingo' is an old Labor Party stalwart and an easy place near leafy Manuka to have a few frothies either in its neat, busy beer garden or inside the homely wooden interior. Decent pub food too. A popular starting point for a crawl through Kingston.

BentSpoke Brewing Co
MICROBREWERY

(☑ 02-6257 5220; www.bentspokebrewing.com.au; 38 Mort St, Braddon; ⊙ 11am-midnight) Bike-themed BentSpoke is one of Australia's best craft brewers, with 18 excellent beers and ciders on tap. For a crisp taste, go for the Mort's Gold. For the yeast lovers, the raspberry wheat beer is very popular. There's good pub food, too.

Smith's Alternative
BAR

(☑ 02-6257 1225; www.smithsalternative.com; 76 Alinga St, Civic; ⊙ 8am-midnight Mon-Thu, to late Fri, from 9am Sat, noon-midnight Sun) Smith's is an arty cafe-bar and performance space, with a makeshift stage in one corner and cakes in the cabinet. In the evenings, expect to be bemused by anything from live music to slam poetry to theatre.

★ Kyō Coffee Project
COFFEE

(www.kyocoffeeproject.com; 5/27 Lonsdale St, Braddon; ⊙ 7am-4pm Tue-Sat, 7.30am-3.30pm Sun) In a little courtyard just off Lonsdale St, achingly hip Kyō serves coffee just as good as its slick, minimalist fit-out promises. Options are limited to black, white or a batch brew. There's a petite, mildly Japanese-inspired menu if you're peckish.

🛍 Shopping

★ Bison Home
CERAMICS

(☑ 02-6128 0788; www.bisonhome.com; 14/27 Lonsdale St, Braddon; ⊙ 10am-5pm Mon-Fri, to 4pm Sat & Sun) A Braddon outpost of Pialligo-based ceramics label Bison, this aesthetically pleasing shop will have you rethinking every object in your kitchen, from mugs to mixing bowls. Smaller items – like tiny ceramic milk bottles in a rainbow of colours – make lovely souvenirs or gifts.

Craft ACT
HOMEWARES

(☑ 02-6262 9993; www.craftact.org.au; 1st fl, North Bldg, 180 London Circuit; ⊙ 10am-5pm Tue-Fri,

noon-4pm Sat Feb-Dec) Part design shop, part museum, this beautiful space showcases local art and stages temporary exhibitions.

ℹ Information

The CBRfree public wi-fi network covers most of central Canberra and provides users with 250MB of data per day.

Canberra & Region Visitors Centre (☑ 02-6205 0044; www.visitcanberra.com.au; Regatta Point, Barrine Dr, Commonwealth Park; ⊙ 9am-5pm Mon-Fri, to 4pm Sat & Sun) Staff at this exceptionally helpful centre can dispense masses of information and brochures, including the free quarterly *Canberra Events* brochure. Detailed maps for cycling and short drives are available too.

ℹ Getting There & Away

AIR

Canberra Airport (☑ 02-6275 2222; www.canberraairport.com.au; Terminal Ave, Pialligo) is located within the city itself, only 7km southeast of Civic.

Daily domestic flights service most Australian capital cities and some regional destinations. Qantas (www.qantas.com) flies to/from Adelaide, Brisbane, Melbourne, Perth and Sydney. Virgin Australia (www.virginaustralia.com.au) flies to/from Adelaide, Brisbane, Gold Coast, Melbourne and Sydney. FlyPelican (www.flypelican.com.au) heads to Newcastle.

Most international travellers transit through Sydney. Singapore Airlines (www.singaporeair.com) flies daily to/from Singapore (with a brief stop in Sydney inbound), while Qatar Airways (www.qatarairways.com) flies daily to/from Doha also with a brief stop in Sydney. Direct flights to/from China are in the pipeline.

BUS

Greyhound (☑ 02-6211 8545; www.greyhound.com.au; 65 Northbourne Ave) runs regular bus services between Canberra and Sydney ($43, 3½ hours). **Murrays** (☑ 13 22 51; www.murrays.com.au; 65 Northbourne Ave; ⊙ 3.30am-6pm) links South Coast towns with Canberra the closest railway station to many of them), while V/Line (p529) offers a bus and train connection to Melbourne.

CAR & MOTORCYCLE

Most visitors to Canberra arrive in their own car, along the Hume Hwy from Sydney or Melbourne. Coastal convoys approach from the west along Kings Hwy from Batemans Bay. The Monaro Hwy to/from Cooma offers glorious views of the Great Dividing Range, its mountainous terrain ideal for skiing in winter.

TRAIN

Three trains run daily in each direction between Sydney Central Station and Canberra's Kingston station. The four-hour journey via the Southern Highlands, Goulburn and Bungendore costs $38. Passengers for Melbourne must change trains in Albury.

ⓘ Getting Around

TO/FROM THE AIRPORT

A taxi to the city centre costs from $25 to $35.

Bus routes 11 and 11A run between city platform 9 and the airport at least hourly between 6am and 6pm (adult/child $5/2.50, 20 to 40 minutes).

BICYCLE

Canberra has an extensive network of on-road bicycle lanes and off-road cycling routes, making two wheels an excellent option for getting around the city. Many hotels and accommodation providers offer bicycle hire for guests. Other options include **Share a Bike** (☑ 1300 588 533; www.shareabike.com.au; 1/4/24hr rental $12/24/36), which has seven stations scattered across the city outside various hotels. Hotel reception provides locks and helmets in the price ($12/24/36 per one/four/24 hours).

BUS

The bus network, operated by **Transport Canberra** (☑ 13 17 10; www.transport.act. gov.au; single adult/child $5/2.50, day pass $9.60/4.80), will get you to most places of interest in the city. A useful journey planner is available on the website.

Travellers can use the MyWay smart-card system, but if you're only here for a week or so you're better off paying the driver in cash, as a card costs a nonrefundable fee of adult/child $5/2.50. A day pass costs less than two single tickets, so purchase one on your first journey of the day.

What is referred to as the City Bus Interchange is actually a set of 11 bus stops scattered along Northbourne Ave, Alinga St, East Row and Mort St.

TAXI

Cabxpress (☑ 02-6181 2700; www.cabxpress.com.au) is a taxi service.

LIGHT RAIL

Canberra's light-rail line from Civic to Gungahlin via Dickson began taking passengers in 2019. The 12km route stops along Northbourne Ave. At this stage it's only really useful for travellers staying around Braddon. Check the Transport Canberra website (www.transport.act.gov.au) for updates.

WOLLONGONG & AROUND

POP 295.669

Nestled on a pretty harbour some 80km south of Sydney, on the edge of the Illawarra Valley, Wollongong is a laid-back, lovable coastal city with an easy Aussie surf charm. The third largest city in NSW has an enviable stretch of coastline peopled by cheerful retirees and heart-in-the-sand locals who proudly call the 'Gong' home. A vibrant food and bar scene and good transport network make for a pleasant weekender or stopover on southern road trips.

Countless generations of the Wodi Wodi, a subgroup of the Dharawal people, have inhabited the Illawarra region for some 40,000 years, leaving tangible traces such as shell middens. The town's 19th-century history as a seaside resort, and today's surf-centred culture, dominate. But visitors can glimpse Wollongong's Aboriginal past and present at the botanic garden, the art gallery and windswept Bellambi Point.

◉ Sights

⭐ **Wollongong Botanic Garden** GARDENS
(☑ 02-4227 7667; www.wollongong.nsw.gov.au/botanicgarden; 61 Northfields Ave, Keiraville; ⊙ 7am-5pm Apr-Sep, to 6pm Mon-Fri, to 6.45pm Sat & Sun Oct-Mar; 🅿; 🚌 55A/55C) **FREE** Wollongong's botanic gardens delight with their attractive lily ponds, manicured lawns and contrastingly gnarled gum trees, all against the rugged green backdrop of the Illawarra Escarpment. Don't miss the **rose garden** with its dedication to the Stolen Generations, Aboriginal Australians who, as children, were forcibly institutionalised away from their families.

Also worth exploring is the **Towri Bush Garden**, featuring native edible plants. In summer there's an outdoor cinema (www.sunsetcinema.com.au).

It's easily accessed by the free Gong Shuttle bus (p188).

North Beach BEACH
(🅿) Stretching north from the harbour, North Beach is an excellent all-rounder: shallows for kids to splash in, breaks suitable for various levels and conveniently close to the city centre. North Beach has lifesavers year-round at its southern end; pay close attention to the ocean conditions.

For more challenging waves, head to the Acids Reef break near the rocks opposite Stuart Park.

Wollongong

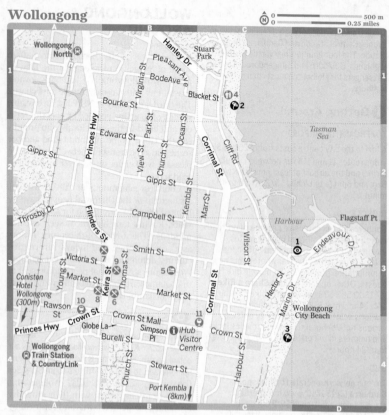

Wollongong

Illawarra Escarpment State Conservation Area PARK
(www.nationalparks.nsw.gov.au) **FREE** Spectacular rainforest hugs the edge of the ever-eroding sandstone cliffs of the Illawarra Escarpment, a 30-million-year-old feature that rises to 534m at Mt Kembla's pointed summit. A winding, 15-minute drive from Wollongong, through knotted tunnels of trees, leads to the dramatic **Mt Keira Lookout** (464m) across Wollongong and the coast.

Signs point to the 5.5km **Mt Keira Ring Track**; it's steep with many stairs, so allow up to 4½ hours for the full loop.

Wollongong City Beach BEACH
The southern of Wollongong's two city beaches is a popular stretch of golden sand with good swimming (especially at the northern end) and, depending on the wind, surfing.

Belmore Basin   HARBOUR
The basin, cut from solid rock in 1868, is a good place to orient yourself in Wollongong. The harbour beach is great for young children, with sand and gentle waves.

🏃 Activities

HanggglideOz   ADVENTURE SPORTS
(☑0417 939 200; www.hangglideoz.com.au; tandem flights midweek/weekend $260/285) 🏄 A reliable hang-gliding operator, established in 1987 by one of the first daredevils to glide from Stanwell Park, HanggglideOz offers tandem flights and courses from Bald Hill, which overlooks dazzling beaches. Prebooking is essential.

Pines Surfing Academy   SURFING
(☑0410 645 981; www.pinessurfingacademy.com. au; 1a Cliff Rd, North Wollongong; 2hr group lesson $50, 6hr set $130) This seasoned operator (established in 1989) offers surf lessons at either North Beach or the Farm Beach. There are lessons year-round, but book at least 48 hours ahead. Wetsuits included.

🛏 Sleeping & Eating

Keiraleagh   HOSTEL $
(☑02-4228 6765; www.backpack.net.au; 60 Kembla St; 6/4-bed dm from $25/30, s/d with shared bathroom from $65/85, d/f from $110/140; @ 🗍) 🐾 Keiraleagh is one of the picks of the South Coast backpacker scene. This historic mansion just a short walk from the city centre and the beach has a huge garden with Balinese-style benches and a barbecue area. The dorm rooms are clean, and spacious private doubles have new bathrooms; the family room ($150) is a fun option too for families who like to be part of the action. Friendly managers (and dogs!). Latest check-in is 10pm. Cash only.

Coniston Hotel Wollongong   BOUTIQUE HOTEL $$
(☑02-4229 1666; www.conistonhotel.com.au; 28 Bridge St, Coniston; r/ste from $143/225; P ❄ 🗍) Conveniently located near Coniston train station, but a few blocks back from the beach, this refurbished pub lodging is actually rather smart. Modern, stylish rooms with a minimalist aesthetic sit above a cracking bistro and popular bar.

His Boy Elroy   BURGERS $
(☑02-4244 8221; www.hisboyelroy.com.au; 176 Keira St; burgers $13-17; ⊙11am-9pm Sun-Wed, to midnight Thu-Sat) With a menu equally balanced between burgers and booze, His Boy Elroy is one of Wollongong's trendier picks

for a bite. Burgers range from Wagyu beef heavy with toppings (like the bacon, egg and barbecue-sauce 'Duke') to smoky pulled pork, veggie burgers and fish patties.

The cocktail list makes use of interesting spirits (how about chai vodka or hibiscus gin), though the burgers taste best with an IPA.

Miss Lee   CANTONESE $
(☑02-4226 1132; www.misslee.com.au; 155 Keira St; mains $12-18; ⊙10.30am-9.30pm Sun-Wed, from 11am Thu-Sat) The daughter of a local Cantonese matriarch oversees this big, buzzing restaurant which recreates the fast, cheap, authentic diners of Southeast Asia for an Aussie crowd. Sizzling stir-fries and spicy curries are distributed to packed tables. Plus you can BYO (Bring Your Own) booze.

★**Caveau**   AUSTRALIAN $$$
(☑02-4226 4855; www.caveau.com.au; 122-124 Keira St; 7-course degustation menu $110, with wine from $165; ⊙6-11pm Tue-Sat; 🖉) Award-winning Caveau is at the forefront of native Australian cooking. This lauded restaurant serves gourmet fare such as barramundi broth and fat, wallaby-tail pie and bunya-nut quail. There's a separate degustation for vegetarians and vegans, which is easily as inventive as the meat-eater menu.

★**Babyface**   JAPANESE, AUSTRALIAN $$$
(☑02-4295 0903; www.babyfacekitchen.com.au; 179 Keira St; mains $24-49, tasting menus $80-92; ⊙noon-3pm & 6-10pm or 11pm Thu-Sat, 6-10pm or 11pm Tue, Wed & Sun) The risk of fusion food pays off at Babyface, where Aussie meets the rest of the world. You can try smaller dishes like crumbed pig's head on a saltbush stick, or larger plates like a sublime Moreton Bay schnitzel. Tasting menus allow diners to sample a smorgasbord: king prawns, wattle-seed tarts, wasabi-spiked salmon and other morsels. There are some interesting wines by the glass and upbeat, friendly staff.

🍷 Drinking & Nightlife

★**Humber**   BAR
(☑02-4263 0355; www.humber.bar; 226 Crown St; ⊙4-11pm Tue & Wed, to midnight Thu & Fri, from 8am Sat, to 10pm Sun; 🗍) Rising above the Gong CBD, this multistorey bar culminates in an attractive roof terrace with retro parasols, overseen by very competent mixologists ('Flaming Peach Sour' or 'Ruby Red Hemmingway'?). The ground level does coffee and food before morphing into a stylish cocktail bar.

Scarborough Hotel
BEER GARDEN

(☑02-4267 5444; www.thescarboroughhotel. com.au; 383 Lawrence Hargrave Dr, Scarborough; ⊙8.30am-4pm Mon-Fri, to 5pm Sat & Sun; 🅿🐕) Built in 1886 and heritage listed, the Scarborough Hotel boasts one of Australia's finest beer gardens. The ocean view is truly spectacular and the main reason to come: there are long queues for decent but fairly standard pub seafood ($24 to $32).

Moominn
BAR

(☑0412 871 884; www.moominn.com.au; 68 Crown St; ⊙5-10pm Tue & Wed, to midnight Thu & Sat, from 4pm Fri) With tulips, checked tablecloths and greenery dangling from the ceiling, there's no more darling setting than Moominn. Along with a bluesy soundtrack, the wide-ranging wines and cocktails can be accompanied by globe-spanning tapas, which rotate monthly. Look out for the odd two-hour all-you-can-sip gatherings peddling various concoctions.

ℹ️ Information

IHub Visitor Centre (☑02-4267 5910; www. visitwollongong.com.au; 93 Crown St; ⊙9am-5pm Mon-Fri, 10am-3pm Sat & Sun; 🕾) Local information and bookings.

Southern Gateway Centre (☑02-4267 5910; www.visitwollongong.com.au; Princes Motorway, Bulli Tops; ⊙9am-5pm; 🕾) On the clifftops north of Wollongong, this helpful centre is a worthwhile information stop if you're approaching the city by car from Sydney (and the viewing platform outside is glorious).

ℹ️ Getting There & Away

Trains (p177) on the **South Coast Line** (Station St) undertake the scenic journey to/from Sydney's Central Station ($6.10, 90 minutes), and continue south as far as Nowra (Bomaderry; $6.10 to $8.70, 1¼ hours), via Kiama ($4.70, 45 minutes) and Berry ($4.70, 1¼ hours).

All long-distance buses leave from the eastern side of the railway station. Premier (p177) has two daily buses to Sydney ($18, two hours) and Eden ($69, 8½ hours). Murrays (p177) has buses to Canberra ($48.40, 3¼ hours).

ℹ️ Getting Around

Bringing a bike on the train from Sydney is a great way to get around. A cycle path runs north to Bulli and south to Port Kembla (download maps from the council website: www.wollongong.nsw.gov.au).

The free Gong Shuttle (buses 55A and 55C) runs every 10 to 20 minutes from 7am to 10pm (8am to 6pm at weekends) on a loop from the station to the university, and North Wollongong, useful for reaching North Beach, the botanic garden and Science Space.

KIAMA & AROUND
POP 23,006

Ancient volcanic vents have given touristy Kiama a distinctively ragged coastline. Most famous for its blowhole, which launches sea spray high into the air, Kiama is also close to coastal and forest walking trails, many of them easy and family-friendly. It's a likeable place, if a little touristy, but in summer the scent of lemon myrtle floats on the sea breeze and an easy-going ambience suffuses the town.

For millennia the land was tended by Aboriginal Australians from the Dharawal language group, the Wodi Wodi. Most of them perished or became displaced when European settlers arrived in the late 19th century to till the land for wheat production and, when that failed, dairy and mining.

⊙ Sights

★ Seven Mile Beach
BEACH

(www.nationalparks.nsw.gov.au; 🅿) This superlative crescent of sand, stretching south from Gerroa to Shoalhaven Heads, is one of the South Coast's most memorable beaches thanks to its pale-golden sand and sheer size. Gazetted as a national park, Seven Mile Beach has picnic areas, shaded walking tracks and kilometres of bright foam lashing the shore, making it almost impossible not to kick off your shoes and jump in.

Minnamurra Rainforest Centre
NATURE RESERVE

(☑02-4236 0469; www.nationalparks.nsw.gov.au; Minnamurra Falls Rd; car $12; ⊙9am-5pm, last entry 4pm; 🅿) At the eastern edge of **Budderoo National Park**, 15km inland from Kiama via Jamberoo, this is a surprisingly lush subtropical rainforest. A 1.6km loop walk weaves through the rainforest following a cascading stream (an early section is wheelchair accessible). Look out for water dragons and lyrebirds scurrying among more than a dozen types of fern. A secondary 2.6km walk on a steepish track leads to the **Minnamurra Falls**; allow two hours to combine the walks. The helpful visitor centre has a worthwhile cafe.

A weekday bus from Kiama Station gets up here, but it's six hours between arrivals.

Kiama Blowhole
NATURAL FEATURE

A tourist draw for well over a century, Kiama's blowhole sits on the point by the centre of town. Girded by basalt columns and wave-thrashed rocks, the blowhole has a setting that's arguably more impressive than its occasional spurt of seawater. It's floodlit at night.

The **Little Blowhole** (Marsden Head) along the coast to the south is less impressive but much more regular.

🛏 Sleeping & Eating

Bellevue Accommodation APARTMENT **$$$**
(📞 02-4232 4000; https://bellevueaccommoda-tion.com.au; 21 Minnamurra St; apt from $220; P ❄ 🛜) This 1890s manor, one of the oldest buildings in Kiama, is the grand dame of the seaside town and run by a generous organic farmer (produce available!). Bay windows and palm-shaded decks with wicker chairs lend plantation-style elegance, while glossy kitchens, coral-tiled bathrooms and amenities such as washer-dryers bring apartments into the 21st century.

Kiama Harbour Cabins CABIN **$$$**
(📞 02-4232 2707; www.kiamacoast.com.au; Blowhole Point; 1-/2-/3-bed cabins from $220/255/325; P ❄ 🛜) Overlooking the beach and the nearby ocean pool, these one- to three-bedroom cabins are decorated in pleasing earth tones, with airy lounge rooms and barbecues on front verandahs.

Little Blowhole Art Bar TAPAS **$**
(📞 02-4232 4990; www.littleblowholeartbar.com; 4 Tingira Cres, Kiama; small dishes $8-16) The Little Blowhole is a fun concept. Delicious tapas – go for the $35 'Feed Me' option if peckish – accompanied by fine wines, cocktails, local art for purchase and local music to set the social mood. It's perched away from the main drag.

Silica SEAFOOD **$$**
(📞 02-4223 0572; 72 Manning St; mains $24-32; ⊙ 11am-3pm & 5-9pm Wed-Fri, 8.30am-3pm & 5-9pm Sat, 8.30am-8pm Sun) Directly opposite the northern pocket of the main beach, Silica is Kiama's finest seafood restaurant, emphasising subtle flavour and elegant presentation, but it's the more casual 'Silica To Go' which caught our attention. Grab a box of fish and chips ($16) and a garden salad ($2.50) and trot to the sand.

ℹ Information

Visitor Centre (📞 02-4232 3322; www.kiama.com.au; Blowhole Point Rd; ⊙ 9am-5pm) Helpful with finding accommodation and full of tips on places to ramble, eat and drink.

ℹ Getting There & Away

Kiama is most easily reached by train, with frequent **Sydney Trains** (📞 13 15 00; www.sydneytrains.info; Railway Pde) departures to Wollongong ($6.80, 40 minutes), Sydney ($8.70, 2¼ hours) and Bomaderry (for Nowra; $5, 30 minutes).

Premier (p177) buses run twice daily to Eden ($69, 6¼ hours) and Sydney ($25, 2½ hours). **Kiama Coaches** (📞 02-4232 3466; www.kiamacoaches.com.au) runs to Gerroa, Gerringong and Seven Mile Beach on weekdays ($5, twice in the morning and twice in the afternoon).

KANGAROO VALLEY

POP 328

The roads wind and bend into idyllic Kangaroo Valley, a small, creative township which feels a long way from Sydney. Cradled by mountains, the region is a pastoral paradise, home to rural manors and warm hospitality. Kayaking, canoeing, wildlife and waterfalls round out the experience.

⊙ Sights & Activities

Cambewarra Lookout VIEWPOINT
(⊙ 7.30am-9pm) Signposted off the Cambewarra Lookout Rd between Kangaroo Valley and Nowra, this vantage point (678m) offers a stupendous perspective over the winding Shoalhaven River and the alluvial agricultural lands far below and along the coast.

There's a cafe here whose deck takes full advantage of the vista.

Fitzroy Falls WATERFALL
(www.nationalparks.nsw.gov.au; Morton National Park; per vehicle $4) Tumbling 81m from near-vertical sandstone cliffs, Fitzroy Falls can be a dramatic torrent or, in the heat of summer, a mere trickle. Regardless, you can rely on mesmerising views across the Yarrunga Valley (640m) from various lookouts along the easy trails in **Morton National Park** (per vehicle at Bundanoon/Fitzroy Falls $8/4; 🅿).

The falls are about 17km northwest of the bridge in Kangaroo Valley, up a steep mountain road.

The **visitor centre** (📞 02-4887 7270; 1301 Nowra Rd; ⊙ 9am-5pm) at the trailhead is the best resource for wildlife and walking information in the area, and has a cafe.

Kangaroo Valley Canoes KAYAKING, CANOEING
(Kangaroo Valley Safaris; 📞 02-4465 1502; www.kangaroovalleycanoes.com.au; 2031 Moss Vale Rd;

canoe & kayak hire from $45; 🚗) 🚶 North of Hampden Bridge, this well-established operator offers a range of guided or self-guided canoeing and kayaking trips into Shoalhaven Gorge and the national parks.

🛏 Sleeping & Eating

Boutique B&Bs and farmstays cluster in and around town, and along the road to Berry. There are a couple of camping grounds in the centre of the village; for a bush-camping experience, head west of town to Bendeela picnic spot (it's signposted), though check for bush-fire damage.

Kangaroo Valley Golf
& Country Resort   CABIN $$$
(☑02-4465 0200; www.kangaroovalleygolf.com.au; 390 Mount Scanzi Rd; cabins from $235; P✳🛜😣) This welcoming, gorgeous country property, about a five-minute drive out of town, has 30-odd neat, self-contained two-bedroom cabins tucked between the trees. Wombats, wallabies and goannas abound. There's also a nice pool, tennis court and giant chess board for the kids.

★Laurels B&B   B&B $$$
(☑02-4465 1693; www.thelaurelsbnb.com.au; 2501 Moss Vale Rd; d incl breakfast $285; P✳🛜) Situated within a former dairy farmer's residence 4km north of Hampden Bridge, Laurel's is arguably the finest B&B on the South Coast. Walls lined with bookshelves, and late-afternoon wine and cheese urge relaxation in the lounge. Four individually decorated rooms are similarly refined, with antiques and king-size beds. Breakfasts are cooked to order and served on fine china in a dining room that overflows with richly carved furniture.

Mango Tree   INDIAN $$
(☑02-4465 2618; www.mangotreerestaurant.com.au; 146 Moss Vale Rd; lunch mains from $15, dinner mains $15-25; ⏱11am-2.30pm & 5.30-9pm; 🛜🚗) The third instalment of this delicious Indian restaurant business (the flagship is on the beach in North Wollongong) opened in late 2019. Authentic Punjabi and South Indian dishes are complemented by astute service and a bright, breezy space overlooking the main street. It's hard to see this restaurant not fast becoming a favourite in the valley.

❶ Getting There & Away

Nowra-based Kennedy's (p195) runs a few buses a week from Kangaroo Valley to central Nowra via Bomaderry train station, which has regular links to Berry and Sydney (via Kiama).

SHOALHAVEN COAST

White sands, turquoise waters and small-town ambience lure Sydney weekenders to the Shoalhaven Coast. Jervis Bay's sensuous beaches, upmarket Ulladulla and fun-loving Wollongong each have their own appeal. But the most magical encounters are found deep in the national parks, where you can pitch a tent in the company of kangaroos and awaken to the roar of the sea. After roughing it in rustic campgrounds, the Shoalhaven's river cruises, wineries and good old-fashioned bakeries and pie shops are restorative pleasures.

Indigenous Australians belonging to the Dharawal and Yuin language groups have lived here for a colossal 20,000 years (and, by some estimates, many more). Travellers can access Aboriginal culture and history along national-park walking trails and on Indigenous-led tours, particularly in Murramarang National Park and around Ulladulla.

Berry
POP 2667

Berry is a sophisticated country town popular with artists, landed gentry and Sydney weekenders. The food and shopping scene, scattered across heritage buildings constructed during an era of agricultural prominence, is some of the best per capita on the South Coast. Most visitors pass through for immersion in the old-timey surroundings, complete with wholesome B&Bs and design stores. Eight kilometres inland of stunning Seven Mile Beach, it's a pleasant way station between Kiama and Nowra on Rte 1.

European settlement began in the early 19th century, displacing the Indigenous Wodi Wodi of the Dharawal group, the land's traditional owners. The modern town built its wealth on cedar trees and dairy farming, but these days Berry is best known for tourism and fine food.

◉ Sights

The town's short main street features National Trust–classified buildings and there are good-quality vineyards in the rolling countryside around Berry.

🛏 Sleeping & Eating

Berry is a popular weekender in winter as well as summer; upmarket B&Bs with verdant gardens and heritage features meet demand.

★ Berry B&B   B&B $$$
(📞0414 433 046; www.berrybandb.com.au; 146 Kangaroo Valley Rd; r incl breakfast & with shared bathroom $200-235; P🗺❄) Fringed by flower gardens, this three-room charmer is tucked away in a former dairy. Genial hosts usher guests into a big, elegantly furnished lounge. The fan-cooled rooms vary in size, but all have artful features, like book-shaped nightstands and the occasional ukulele, and there's a pool in the lush back garden. The breakfast is a sumptuous repast.

Bellawongarah at Berry   B&B $$$
(📞02-4464 1999; www.accommodation-berry. com.au; 869 Kangaroo Valley Rd, Bellawongarah; r $250-270; P❄🗺) Rainforest surrounds this wonderful place, 8km from Berry on the mountain road to Kangaroo Valley. There are two rooms. One is a sumptuous loft space in the main house, which features a large spa bath overlooking the greenery, and a cosy lounge and sleeping area under the eaves. The other is a cute 1868 church with an airy, French-provincial feel.

Famous Berry Donut Van   CAFE $
(📞02-4464 2753; 73 Queen St; 1/12 doughnuts $2.20/18; ⊘8am-6pm; 🖐) Parents driving the family down the South Coast for the holidays have long bribed the kids by promising a stop at this food truck if they were good along the way. The doughnuts are made fresh and rolled in cinnamon sugar. Up the ante with the 'donut & cream': split in half with a blob of vanilla ice cream ($7). Get in line with the Instagrammers!

Figbird Cafe   CAFE $$
(📞02-4464 2283; 4/58 Albert St; sandwiches from $10, breakfast $11-25, lunch $12-22; ⊘8am-4pm Mon-Sun) It can be difficult to choose between the many cafes dotting Berry's streets, but Figbird, with its lovely sunny locale on the town fringe, won us over with its homely decor, stunning breakfast, and yummy sandwiches and pies.

★ Bussola   PIZZA, ITALIAN $$
(📞02-4464 1188; www.bussolarestaurant.com.au; cnr Queen & Alexandra Sts; pizzas $16-26, mains $24-28; ⊘11am-9pm Wed-Sat, to 8pm Sun; 🍴) Unusual flavour combos like pineapple, ricotta and barbecue sauce, or Gorgonzola, ham and pickled pear, give pizzas at Bussola an edge. Moreish sweet-potato gnocchi and some truly unique *cichetti* (Venetian tapas) take taste buds on even more of an adventure. Just ask if you want your pizza vegan and/or gluten free.

Deftly prepared desserts and accommodating service complete the package.

🛍 Shopping

Treat Factory   FOOD
(📞02-4464 1112; www.treatfactory.com.au; 6 Old Creamery Lane; ⊘9.30am-4.30pm Mon-Fri, from 10am Sat & Sun; 🖐) One of the commercial success stories of the region, the Treat Factory is as much a feast for the eyes as for sweet-inclined appetites. This old-fashioned factory shop is chock-full of marshmallows, salted caramel, chocolate-covered macadamias and freckles (chocolate discs dotted with sugar sprinkles) bigger than your head.

❶ Getting There & Away

Trains run every hour or two to Nowra (Bomaderry; $3.10, 10 minutes) and to Kiama ($3.50, 30 minutes), where you can change to trains heading north to Wollongong ($4.70, 1¼ hours) and Sydney ($6.10, 2¾ hours).

Premier (p177) has buses to Sydney ($25, three hours, twice daily) via Kiama, and south to Eden via all coastal towns.

Local buses run two to three times Monday to Saturday to Nowra, Gerringong and Gerroa.

Jervis Bay

Wide, sheltered Jervis Bay is the darling of the South Coast, its blissfully protected coastline heaven for low-key family holidays, aquatic sports and beach camping.

A historical quirk means that Jervis Bay is actually under the jurisdiction of the Australian Capital Territory. But a few days lolling about on the pearl-white sand of this sea-meets-bush paradise makes you feel a long way from the political intrigue of Canberra.

◎ Sights & Activities

Jervis Bay National Park   NATIONAL PARK
(www.nationalparks.nsw.gov.au; 🖐) **FREE** North of Huskisson, Jervis Bay National Park spreads outwards from the graceful arc of Callala Bay. More than 4850 hectares of low scrub and woodland clasp the bay, itself a marine park. There are also pockets of protected land further south, around Huskisson and white-sand Hyams Beach, which

are replete with easy walking paths and family-friendly beaches. There are picnic areas (and toilets) at Red Point, Hammerhead Point and Greenfield Beach, which also has barbecue facilities and drinking water.

Huskisson is the centre for most activities on the water in Jervis Bay, including whale and dolphin watching, kayaking and kitesurfing.

Jervis Bay Maritime Museum MUSEUM
(☑02-4441 5675; www.jervisbaymaritimemuseum.asn.au; 11 Dent St, Huskisson; adult/child $10/free; ⊙10am-4pm; ⛟) This engaging museum tells of Jervis Bay's shipbuilding past and Aboriginal history. Interesting displays explain the Wreck Bay Aboriginal community's struggle for land rights. Back rooms are filled with imagination-firing maritime miscellany like brine-splashed wooden chests and ship figureheads. The gardens, laid out like an old ship-building yard, are fun to ramble.

Jervis Bay Kayaks & Paddlesports KAYAKING
(☑02-4441 7157; www.jervisbaykayaks.com.au; 13 Hawke St, Huskisson; kayak hire 2hr/day from $50/70, bike hire 2hr/day $29/50, snorkel hire from $25, 2hr kayak tours $59-79; ⊙9.30am-4.30pm Mon & Wed-Fri, to 3pm Sat & Sun Dec-Feb, hours vary Mar-Nov; ⛟) This friendly, family-owned place offers rentals of simple sit-on-top kayaks, stand-up paddleboards and single and double sea kayaks on St Georges Basin or Jervis Bay (for those with experience). Oar-enthusiast staff can also organise various guided trips, including two-hour, kid-friendly paddles, or arrange self-guided camping and kayaking expeditions. Also hires out bikes.

Private lessons to finesse your SUP or kayak technique start at around $60 for 1½ hours.

☞ Tours

Dolphin Watch Cruises WILDLIFE, BOATING
(☑02-4441 6311; www.dolphinwatch.com.au; 50 Owen St, Huskisson; ⊙dolphin-/whale-watching tour $35/65; ⛟) 🌱 This well-established setup on the main street in Huskisson offers cruises in a small, fast jetboat and a larger, more sedate double-decker. Sightings depend on the luck of the day, but it's common to see pods of dolphins frolicking around Callala Bay, and whale watching is great in season (September to November). Kids' tickets are a little over half-price.

🛏 Sleeping

There are options in various settlements around the bay, but Huskisson is the principal accommodation hub. Booderee National Park offers camp sites, as does the Beecroft Peninsula.

Huskisson B&B B&B $$$
(☑02-4441 7551; www.huskissonbnb.com.au; 12 Tomerong St, Huskisson; d incl breakfast $225-275; ℗❄️🛜📺) A beachy theme and kindly service make this boutique operation one of Huskisson's most characterful places to stay. There's luxury in all the right places, like excellent mattresses, claw-foot tubs and big bath towels, while antique-effect tiles and vintage glass add charisma. The continental breakfast, complete with homemade produce, a great cappuccino and lime marmalade, sweetens the package.

Hyams Beach Seaside Cottages COTTAGE $$$
(☑02-4443 0242; www.hyamsbeachseasidecottages.com.au; 53-55 Cyrus St, Hyams Beach; cottages from $290, 2-night minimum) Targeted at couples, these quaint, pastel-coloured cottages sit directly across the road from a long section of beautiful beaches. Each cottage, though small, is eclectically decorated, and the beds and bathrooms are excellent. There's a good cafe down the street, which is very busy in summer, but other times it's mostly you and the deep blue sea.

Be sure to walk from Hyams Beach to Greenfield Beach. Shoes optional.

★ Paperbark Camp LODGE $$$
(☑02-4441 6066; www.paperbarkcamp.com.au; 571 Woollamia Rd, Woollamia; d incl breakfast $525-750; ℗🛜) 🌱 Glamp in ecofriendly style in these 12 safari tents with en suites, wraparound decks and billowing mosquito nets. It's set in dense bush 4km from Huskisson, with only the chorus of cicadas to distract you from back-to-nature bliss. Borrow kayaks to paddle up the creek to the bay, or grab a bike to ride into town.

There's an excellent restaurant here open to the public (call ahead for reservations), and an impressive breakfast is included in rates.

🍴 Eating & Drinking

Huskisson is a trendy weekend spot for Sydneysiders and has a couple of excellent cafes. There are also options in Vincentia, Hyams Beach, Callala Bay and elsewhere.

5 Little Pigs
CAFE $$

(📞 02-4441 7056; www.5littlepigs.com.au; 64 Owen St, Huskisson; mains $11-25; ⏰ 7am-4pm; 📶 🍴) Everything hits the spot here, from the fun 5 Little Piggy Breakfast (boiled egg, baguette, jam, granola, yoghurt, juice, coffee) to the broccolini-based Breaky Salad. Fresh diner-style burgers constitute lunch. It's a bit of a social hub too.

Pilgrims
BURGERS, VEGETARIAN $

(📞 02-4441 6118; www.pilgrims.cafe; 57 Owen St, Huskisson; breakfasts $10-22, burgers $10-15, pies from $6; ⏰ 7am-3pm daily & 5.30-8pm Fri & Sat; 🍴) Aussie post-surf comfort food like pies and sourdough-based brunches come 100% meat-free at Pilgrims, which also has a popular branch at nearby Milton. Honey-drowned pancakes and generous cooked breakfasts dispel any fears of abstemious health food, while the lentil-based burger varieties are exemplary. Some vegan options are available.

Wild Ginger
ASIAN $$

(📞 02-4441 5577; www.wild-ginger.com.au; 42 Owen St, Huskisson; entrees/mains $22/32; ⏰ 3-11pm Tue-Sun; 📶 🍴) The most urbane restaurant in the Jervis Bay area, appealing to a Southeast Asian palate, Wild Ginger is a showcase of flavours complemented by trendy decor and outdoor seating. Find coconut-crusted squid, perch in Penang curry and light-soy blackfish.

★ Huskisson Hotel
PUB

(Husky Pub; 📞 02-4441 5001; www.thehuskisson.com.au; 73 Owen St, Huskisson; ⏰ 11am-midnight Mon-Sat, to 10pm Sun; 📶 🍴) The social centre of Huskisson is this light and airy pub that offers fabulous bay views from its deck, which packs out in summer. There's live music most weekends, tending towards rock, country and local DJs.

ℹ Information

Jervis Bay Visitor Information Centre (📞 02-4441 5999; www.jervisbaytourism.com.au; 11 Dent St, Huskisson; ⏰ 10am-4pm) Helpful tourist information centre set up within the Jervis Bay Maritime Museum building.

ℹ Getting There & Away

Nowra Coaches (p195) runs buses around the Jervis Bay area, with connections to Nowra and the train station at Bomaderry (1½ hours, four daily, fewer at weekends), which has connections north to Sydney and south to Eden.

Booderee National Park

Occupying Jervis Bay's southeastern spit, the sublime **Booderee National Park** (📞 02-4443 0977; www.booderee.gov.au; 2-day car or motorcycle entry $13), jointly managed by the government and the local Indigenous community, offers good swimming, surfing and diving on both bay and ocean beaches. Walking-trail maps and camping information are available at the **visitor centre** (⏰ 9.30am-3pm Sun-Thu, 9am-4pm Fri & Sat Feb-Dec, 9am-4pm daily Jan).

Surfing is good at Cave Beach and **Bherwherre Beach**, though beware the nasty rips. There's back-to-nature camping at **Green Patch** (camp sites $25, plus per adult/child $13/6; P), **Bristol Point** (camp sites $25, plus per adult/child $13/6; P) and secluded **Cave Beach** (camp sites $14, plus per adult/child $13/6; P) (tents only). Book online through the visitor centre, and do it a month in advance if you're coming at the height of summer.

Ulladulla & Mollymook

POP 15,278

The South Coast's coolest twin towns offer similarly unpretentious beach experiences, though harbour-side Ulladulla is perhaps the service centre 'big' brother and Mollymook the laid-back kid who surfs. Just close enough to Sydney to attract some of its high-heeled clientele, the towns boast better than expected gastronomic experiences, plus amazing, semiremote waves in Murramarang National Park and a fabulous hike up Pigeon House Mountain.

Beyond sand and surf, Aboriginal-led guided tours, a cultural trail and a small gallery create numerous possibilities for exploring the area's Yuin heritage.

◎ Sights & Activities

★ Pigeon House Mountain (Didthul)
HIKING

(Morton National Park) One of the best South Coast walks is to the top of this iconic mountain. The steep hike involves two climbs through bush, separated by a flat phase through heathland, then an ascent up ladders to a summit with magnificent views. It's just over 5km return from the car park; allow three to four hours and look out for lyrebirds and kangaroos.

The mountain (roughly 720m) has long been significant for the Indigenous Yuin people, who named it Didthul after its distinctive shape, like a woman's breast. Less poetic European settlers thought it resembled a dovecote and named it Pigeon House Mountain in the 1770s.

Didthul is in the Morton National Park (p189) section of the Budawang range, 33km west of Ulladulla by road.

Murramarang National Park   NATIONAL PARK
(www.nationalparks.nsw.gov.au; per car per day $8) Stretching along a secluded section of coast, this scenic park offers excellent beaches, opportunities to learn about Indigenous culture, and plentiful animal and birdlife. Surfing is good at several beaches, and marked walking trails access views of rainforest and shore; a standout is the tough **Mt Durras** walk (which takes up to five hours).

Wasp Head is a rewarding place to explore the area's Aboriginal past and present.

Bring $2 coins to feed the machines that issue entry tickets for the national park (it's pay and display).

Milton   VILLAGE
The town of Milton, 6km northwest of Ulladulla on the Princes Hwy, is a cheerful caricature of its 19th-century history. European settlers flocked to the area in the 1820s, lured by logging, and a township was founded some 40 years later. A courthouse, a theatre and dozens of other heritage buildings preserve Milton's lost-in-time feel. Nowadays craft shops, boutiques and cafes have earned the town a spot on tourist itineraries.

🛏 Sleeping

Mollymook Shores   HOTEL $$
(☑02-4455 5888; www.mollymookshores.com. au; 11 Golf Ave, Mollymook; studio/d/ste from $170/180/200; P🅿❄🛜🏊) Uplifted by friendly service and its location opposite a dreamy sand beach, Mollymook Shores has brightly decorated rooms arranged around a small pool. There are several room types, from doubles with dining tables and balconies right up to spa suites with large living areas.

Ulladulla Guest House   B&B $$$
(☑02-4455 1796; www.guesthouse.com.au; cnr Burrill & South Sts, Ulladulla; incl breakfast d $190-298, apt $350; P🅿❄🛜🏊) 🌿 New owners have maintained the subtropical vibes at this cosy, resort-style B&B. Highlights include neat rooms laden with local art, and an exceptional wine bar. Homegrown bananas, papayas and herbs find their way to the

breakfast table, and there's a barrel-shaped solar-heated sauna and a rainforest garden.

★**Bannisters Pavilion**   HOTEL $$$
(☑02-4455 3044; www.bannisters.com.au; 87 Tallwood Ave, Mollymook; r $275-445; P🅿❄🛜🏊) Set back from Mollymook Beach, this visually striking hotel operates with breezy style. There's space to spare, with wide hallways, plush, light rooms with pleasant woody outlooks and a private patio or balcony space. The two penthouses are worthy of a design magazine.

🍴 Eating & Drinking

★**Hayden's Pies**   BAKERY $
(☑02-4455 7798; www.haydenspies.com.au; 166 Princes Hwy, Ulladulla; pies from $5.90, sausage rolls $4.10; ⊙6am-5pm Mon-Sat, from 7am Sun; 🍴) With traditional pies – the likes of Sunday roast or chicken and bacon – and a range of gourmet fillings (such as Atlantic salmon, or mushroom and goat's cheese), this excellent bakery is awash with crusty goodness and delicious aromas.

Tallwood   AUSTRALIAN, CAFE $$$
(☑02-4455 5192; www.tallwoodeat.com.au; 85 Tallwood Ave, Mollymook; breakfast $12-22, dinner mains $24-52; ⊙6.30am-noon & 5.30-9.30pm, coffee served all day; 🍴) 🌿 From its stylish, open-plan kitchen, Tallwood kicks off the day with excellent coffee and out-of-the-ordinary breakfasts, such as crème-fraiche hash browns, or fried eggs with chilli and anchovy. Dinner is at the very high end of seasonal fish, meat and vegetable creations. Desserts have unexpected flavour pairings. Book in summer.

★**Cupitt's Estate**   AUSTRALIAN $$$
(☑02-4455 7888; www.cupitt.com.au; 58 Washburton Rd, Ulladulla; 2-/3-course menu $65/80; ⊙restaurant noon-2.30pm daily & 6-8.30pm Fri & Sat, bar food 10am-3pm, winery 10am-5pm; P🛜) 🌿 All gourmet tastes are satisfied at this restored 1851 creamery, 3km west of town. The cellar door showcases exceptional wine, accompanied by cheeseboards. The busy restaurant serves choice cuts of Wagyu and locally sourced seafood. Plenty of space for kids to run about.

Rick Stein at Bannisters   SEAFOOD $$$
(☑02-4455 3044; www.bannisters.com.au/rick-stein; 191 Mitchell Pde, Mollymook; mains $36-48; ⊙12.30-2pm Fri-Sun, 6-10pm Tue-Sun; P🛜) Served in an elegant setting on Bannister's

Point, the British celebrity chef Rick Stein's excellently selected and presented seafood matches the fine views. The menu is informed by local produce but has touches of French and Asian influences. In summer, hang around the poolside bar before or after your meal.

Mollymook Golf Club
Beachside Bistro   PUB FOOD
(📞02-4455 1911; 72 Golf Ave; mains $17-29) Enjoy stupendous views over the northern end of Mollymook Beach at this popular sporting club and bistro. Bypass the food for the tap beer and sunset.

ℹ Information

Shoalhaven Visitor Centre (📞02-4444 8819; www.shoalhaven.com; Princes Hwy, Ulladulla; ⊙9am-5pm Mon-Fri, to 2pm Sat & Sun) Bookings and information are offered in the civic centre and library, just off the highway.

ℹ Getting There & Away

Premier (p177) runs twice daily between Sydney ($35, five hours) and Eden ($50, 3½ to 4½ hours), via Batemans Bay ($14, 45 minutes) and Nowra ($18, one hour).

EUROBODALLA COAST

Known as 'the Land of Many Waters', this southern coastline luxuriates in long, sandy beaches and jewel-like coves, an irresistible draw for surfers and swimmers. Lakes and forest-backed inlets have ensured a lively market in kayak and SUP rentals, particularly around Batemans Bay. Wildlife entices visitors to Narooma, especially the playful seals of Montague Island and the promise of seasonal encounters with little penguins and whales. Meanwhile, Australia's gold rush and old quarrying days are feted in Moruya and the Tilba towns, all of them frozen in time.

Bush fires devastated this area in 2019/20, affecting many people's lives and livelihoods. Scenes of residents evacuated to local beaches amid darkened daytime skies shocked and scared the world.

The area is part of the homelands of the Yuin people and includes their sacred mountain, Gulaga (806m). Routes like the Bingi Dreaming Track (www.nationalparks. nsw.gov.au) thread their way through sites linked to the land's traditional owners.

Batemans Bay
POP 11,294

A popular family holiday destination since the 1950s, and more recently a retiree haven, Batemans Bay epitomises the South Coast adage of life in the slow lane. Outside a busy service centre, replete with car dealerships and fast-food joints, the town is blessed with a watery calm. Sandy, wave-kissed beaches extending south provide countless options for surfers and windsurfers, while the nearby Tomaga River estuary draws SUPs and kayaks to its calm waters.

The area's longest residents are the Yuin people, in particular the Walbunja group, whose gifts of food are thought to have been instrumental in saving early settlers from starvation.

⊙ Sights & Activities

The closest beach, 3km south of town, is Corrigans Beach. North of the bridge, beaches lead into Murramarang National Park. Surfers flock to Pink Rocks, gentle, regular Surf Beach, Malua Bay, McKenzies Beach and long Bengello Beach. Broulee has a wide crescent of sand and no rocky surprises, but there's a strong rip at the northern end.

Total Eco Adventures   WATER SPORTS
(📞02-4471 6969; www.totalecoadventures.com. au; 77 Coronation Dr, Broulee) This set-up offers various excursions on the river, including snorkelling safaris, kayaking, SUP lessons and water-sports-gear hire (from $35). Enquire ahead; departures are from Tomakin boat ramp.

Surf the Bay Surf School   SURFING
(📞0432 144 220; www.surfthebay.com.au; group/ private lesson $50/100) This surfing and paddleboarding school has personable instructors and operates at Batemans Bay, Broulee and Narooma. It also has equipment for hire (from $30 for a surfboard or $40 for an SUP) and runs special courses for kids during school holidays.

🛏 Sleeping & Eating

Zorba Waterfront Motel   MOTEL $$
(📞02-4472 4804; www.zorbamotel.com.au; Orient St; r $130-300; P❋🐾) With blue-dappled fittings to match the bay setting, Zorba's has 17 attractive, contemporary-style motel rooms with walk-in showers. Handily located right by the string of bayside restaurants, this is

an accommodating, family-run place that's been a reliable option for years.

Bay Breeze   MOTEL $$

(☑ 02-4472 7222; www.baybreezemotel.com.au; 21 Beach Rd; d $175-350; P ❋ 🖘) Balinese-style headboards and other stylish flourishes give rooms at the Bay Breeze a distinctive, luxurious air. Facilities at this boutique motel are pleasingly broad, from in-room standards like fridges and coffee makers to table tennis, laundry and massage on demand. It's discreetly shaded from the main promenade by a hedge, but the bay views from waterfront rooms (from $195) are excellent.

★ Mossy Cafe   CAFE $

(☑ 02-4471 8599; www.themossy.com.au; 31 Pacific St, Mossy Point; breakfasts from $11, lunch mains $14-20; ⊙ 7.30am-3pm; ☑ 🖈) Post-surf recovery is made much easier at this charming cafe in a converted 1930s general store. Brunch classics like smashed avocado, poached eggs on sourdough and chia bowls are joined on the menu by pulled-pork tacos and Korean-spiced veg bowls, plus enticing cakes and great coffee. It's a short walk from Mossy Point's boat ramp, 1.5km north of Broulee's surf beach.

Innes' Boatshed   FISH & CHIPS $

(☑ 02-4472 4052; 1 Clyde St; fish from $10, 6 oysters $10, prawns $7; ⊙ 8am-7pm; 🖈) Since the 1950s this has been one of the South Coast's best-loved fish-and-chip and oyster joints. Innes' has undergone some major renovations – for better or worse – but you can still find a decent seafood feed here. Head out to the spacious deck, which hangs pleasantly over the water. Mind the pelicans.

❶ Information

Batemans Bay Visitor Centre (☑ 02-4472 6900; www.eurobodalla.com.au; cnr Princes Hwy & Beach Rd; ⊙ 9am-5pm Oct-Apr, to 4pm May-Sep) Offers above-and-beyond advice and assistance for travellers in town and the wider Eurobodalla area.

❶ Getting There & Away

Just north of Batemans Bay, the scenic Kings Hwy climbs the escarpment and heads to Canberra.

Premier (p177) runs buses to Sydney ($45, six hours) and Eden ($46, three to 3½ hours) via Ulladulla ($14, 45 minutes) and Moruya ($11, 30 minutes).

Murrays (p177) runs buses to Canberra ($37.60, 2½ hours), Moruya ($13.60, 40 minutes) and Narooma ($20.90, 1¾ hours).

V/Line (☑ 1800 800 007; www.vline.com.au) runs a bus-train combination to Melbourne ($67.20, 11¾ hours), via Bairnsdale, Victoria, on Tuesday, Friday and Sunday.

Priors (☑ 02-4472 4040; www.priorsbus.com.au) runs regional services, including a bus to Broulee and Moruya via various surf beaches (bus 760; $7.40, nine times daily, less frequently at weekends).

Moruya

POP 2525

Moruya is a genteel regional town which serves primarily as an agricultural centre and a springboard for spectacular beaches. But its meandering river setting and well-maintained Victorian architecture offer reason enough to use it as a base.

When you gaze on Sydney Harbour Bridge, spare a thought for this little place: the town's quarries supplied the granite for this Australian icon. Other than this claim to fame, Moruya is locally known for its popular Saturday market. Before an agricultural land grab by European settlers in the 19th century, the area was populated by various Yuin groups, such as the Bugelli-Manji tribe, for whom the estuary and shoreline were abundant sources of shellfish.

Inland, the little-visited Deua National Park is a rugged bush landscape, popular with locals and clued-up travellers for its hiking, camping and freshwater swimming.

The area around Moruya was severely affected by the 2019 bush fires.

🛏 Sleeping & Eating

★ Post & Telegraph B&B   B&B $$

(☑ 02-4474 5745; cnr Page & Campbell Sts; s/d incl breakfast $130/160; P ❋ 🖘) This 19th-century post and telegraph office is now an enchanting four-room B&B with great historical character. High ceilings, marble fireplaces and the occasional claw-foot tub combine with friendly, genuine hospitality and numerous thoughtful details (including a gourmet breakfast). There's a shared verandah, decanters of port and an attractive common lounge. You couldn't ask for a lovelier spot.

The family room has one queen and one single bed.

Moruya Health Cafe   HEALTH FOOD $

(☑ 02-4474 3192; 11 Church St; mains $12-18; ⊙ 8am-5pm Mon-Fri, to 2pm Sat) Moruya's version of the socially conscious community cafe doubles as a healthy grocer, but hang around for amazing salads, slices and a plate of baked eggplant ricotta. Local coffee roasters Guerilla spill the beans to a return crowd.

The River
AUSTRALIAN $$

(02-4474 5505; www.therivermoruya.com.au; 16 Church St; mains $26-37, 5-course degustation $100, with matching wines $130; ⊙ noon-2pm & 6-8pm Wed-Sat, noon-2pm Sun) Perched right over the river and attired in nautical blue and white, this understated restaurant offers flavourful presentations, with a French influence. Smoked chicken and duck terrine, saffron gnocchi and pork belly with squid impress as much as the hilly views across the water. It's just west of the bridge.

Moruya Country Markets
MARKET

(www.facebook.com/moruyacountrymarket; Shore St; ⊙ 7.30am-12.30pm Sat) This riverside market is a popular Saturday event in Moruya, whether you're looking for cupcakes and ice cream, farm-fresh fruit and veg or honeys and olive oils.

ⓘ Getting There & Away

Moruya Airport (MYA; 0409 037 520; www.esc.nsw.gov.au; George Bass Dr) is 7km east of town, near North Head. Rex (www.rex.com.au) flies to/from Merimbula and Sydney daily.

Murrays (p177) buses head to Canberra ($40.80, 3½ hours), Batemans Bay ($13.60, 40 minutes) and Narooma ($14.80, one hour), stopping in Mogo by request.

Premier (p177) runs buses to Sydney ($49, six to seven hours) via Batemans Bay ($11, 30 minutes) and in the other direction to Eden ($46, 2½ to three hours) via all coastal towns.

V/Line runs a bus-train combination to Melbourne ($60.60, 11½ hours), via Bairnsdale, Victoria, on Tuesday, Friday and Sunday.

Narooma
POP 3342

Narooma is popular as the jumping-off point for Montague Island (Barranguba), an offshore excursion as rich in wildlife-spotting opportunities as in its history of the Yuin people, the land's traditional owners. But its stunningly clear (and cold!) waters are also home to rich sea life – including an incredible seal colony – while a tree-lined estuary wraps around a chilled-out town rich with surfer folklore and some surprisingly fine restaurants.

MAGICAL MYSTERY BAY TOUR

South of Narooma, 5km before the turn-off to the Tilbas, take the road to gorgeously undeveloped **Mystery Bay** and the southernmost pocket of **Eurobodalla National Park**. It's a special place, with fine sand and tar-black rocks framing a **natural swimming pool** at the southern end of the main surf beach. There's a council-run camping ground under the trees. It's so close to the beach that you could boil a kettle with your tootsies in the sand – well, almost.

Narooma is an excellent base for exploring the heritage towns inland along this magnificent stretch of the Eurobodalla Coast.

⊙ Sights & Activities

★ Montague Island (Barranguba)
NATURE RESERVE

(www.montagueisland.com.au) Wildlife thrives on this small, pest-free island, 9km offshore from Narooma, where fur seals frolic and 90 bird species wheel overhead. Little penguins nest here from September to February, while, offshore, whales are most numerous from September to November.

Book ahead for tours led by park rangers. Boat operators can combine the island visit with snorkelling and whale watching. Snorkelling and diving are made even more exciting by the presence of fur seals, whose underwater acrobatics are enchanting to watch.

Be warned: seals delight in speeding towards unsuspecting snorkellers before veering off course at the last moment (boats, meanwhile, keep a respectful distance from the animals).

All tours are number- and weather-dependent, and independent visits to the island aren't permitted. Once ashore, the island's whale, shark and turtle rocks, named by the Aboriginal community, are off limits to most visitors.

Underwater Safaris
DIVING

(0415 805 479; www.underwatersafaris.com.au; 2 dives $120) Unlike catch-all operators, this outfit focuses on underwater experiences amid Montague Island's marvellous wildlife. There are PADI courses, guided dives and snorkelling with seals ($89); the chances are good that you'll also spot grey

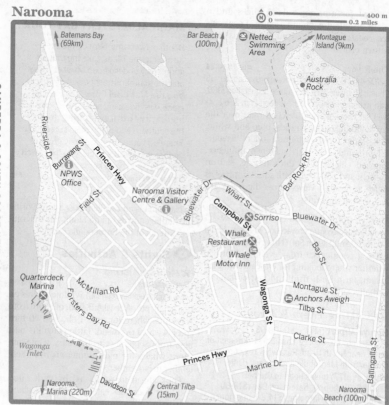

nurse sharks and bull rays gliding in the big blue. From September to November there are whale-watching excursions ($60).

Underwater Safaris is an eco-minded company that aims to tread lightly (no fishing tours are offered).

Snorkelling tasters for kids cost $35.

Narooma Marina BOATING
(☑02-4476 2126; www.naroomamarina.com.au; 30 Riverside Dr; boat per 1/3hr $60/155, surfboard half-/full day $20/40, kayak 1st/subsequent hour $25/20; ⊞) This chipper set-up on the river hires out canoes, kayaks, pedalos, fishing boats (with sunshades), surfboards and stand-up paddleboards. It's a one-stop shop for getting you out on the water.

⌖ Tours

Montague Island
Nature Reserve Tours WALKING, CULTURAL
(☑02-4476 2881; www.montagueisland.com.au; per person $90-120) A number of operators run

boat trips to Montague Island, where you link up with a national-park guide to lead you around. You'll dodge shearwater burrows on a walk across the pristine island, learn about its Aboriginal history and climb inside the lighthouse. Evening tours from September to November let you watch little penguins march ashore.

🛏 Sleeping

Whale Motor Inn MOTEL $$
(☑02-4476 2411; www.whalemotorinn.com; 102 Wagonga St; d from $135, ste $170-215; ᴾ❋⑀⊠⊠) From the balcony views to the comfy beds and tasteful splashes of colour, the Whale is a standout among Narooma's many motels. 'Premier' rooms are a real bargain, capacious and modern, while suites have a lounge and kitchenette. Zany decorative details increase the fun, as do the lounge bar and small pool.

There's also a refined restaurant, serving locally sourced food alongside sea views, and a popular cocktail bar.

★**Anchors Aweigh** B&B **$$**
(✆02-4476 4000; www.anchorsaweigh.com.au; 5 Tilba St; s/d incl breakfast from $115/155; P❀☎)
🏃 Rooms at this family-run B&B are furnished like a well-off aunt's bedroom, with heavy wooden dressers and floral decor; a couple of rooms (from $193) have spa baths. Authentic Aboriginal artwork hangs in common areas, competing for attention with garlands of teddy bears and old-fashioned toys. Breakfasts are cooked fresh from local and organic produce. No kids or pets.

★**Lighthouse Keepers' Cottages** COTTAGE **$$$**
(✆02-9585 683; www.nationalparks.nsw.gov.au; Montague Island; 3-/5-bedroom cottages $1200/1800) 🏃 For oneness with nature, elegantly renovated cottages on Montague Island offer a uniquely beautiful retreat. Cottages sleep up to eight or 12. Rooms are true to the buildings' 19th-century history, with fireplaces and polished wooden floors. Rates include boat transport; bring food supplies to make use of the barbecues and full kitchen (the tap water's drinkable). Book ahead. Two-night minimum. No wi-fi.

✖ **Eating**

Quarterdeck Marina CAFE, SEAFOOD **$$**
(✆02-4476 2723; www.quarterdecknarooma.com.au; 13 Riverside Dr; mains $24-35; ☺10am-4pm Thu, to 8pm Fri, 10am-3pm & 6-8pm Sat, 8am-3pm Sun; ☎) This 'little red house of tunes' overlooking Forsters Bay is a dreamy venue, ideal for farewelling the sun and welcoming a plate of lime-buttered scallops or blue-cheese oysters. The tiki-themed bar is busy on weekends, but the friendly owner is all over it, ensuring a great night out.

Sorriso ITALIAN **$$**
(✆02-4476 3362; 107 Campbell St; mains $24-30, pizzas from $18; ☺6-9pm Mon-Sat; 🚸) This much-loved place is a sociable spot doing hearty Italian home cooking, including very fine pizzas. Save space for the decadent dessert menu. The back deck has great views over the estuary. It's very family-friendly and there's a kids' menu. Reservations recommended.

Whale Restaurant AUSTRALIAN **$$**
(✆02-4476 2411; www.whalemotorinn.com; 102 Wagonga St; mains $31-39; ☺6-9pm Tue-Sat; ☎🏃) 🏃 Attached to a neat motor inn at the top of the hill is the surprisingly chic Whale Restaurant. Local knowledge gained by years of exploring the waves and tracks of the region

has been put to use by the chefs who showcase local oysters, homemade pasta, foraged herbs, Tilba cheeses, sustainable fish and aged beef. There's a pleasant lounge for a predinner drink.

ℹ **Information**

Narooma Visitor Centre & Gallery (✆02-4476 2881; www.narooma.org.au; Princes Hwy; ☺9.30am-4.30pm Mon-Fri, to 1.30pm Sat & Sun) This friendly, volunteer-run visitor centre is great for local information.

It also includes a gallery stocked by the local arts-and-crafts society and a free historical museum (with the original glass from Montague Island's lighthouse).

ℹ **Getting There & Away**

Premier (p177) runs two daily buses to Eden ($31, 2½ hours) and Sydney ($60, 6½ to eight hours) via Wollongong ($56, 4½ to six hours).

V/Line (p196) runs a daily bus-train combination from Narooma to Melbourne ($67.20, 11 hours) via Bairnsdale, Victoria.

Murrays (p177) has daily buses to Moruya ($14.80, one hour), Batemans Bay ($20.90, two hours) and Canberra ($48.40, 4½ hours).

Tilba Tilba & Central Tilba

Set in lovely hillside country, the twin heritage towns of Central Tilba and Tilba Tilba make for an idyllic detour from the Princes Hwy. The heritage buildings and cafes lining Bate St in the smaller, but busier, Tilba Tilba delight many visitors. Others may find it twee, and raise an eyebrow at the blurry line between historic buildings and antique-style homeware and souvenir shops. Either way, it's worth getting a sense of the locally made wine, cheese and art, or having a beer at the Dromedary Hotel.

The walk up to the water tower reveals magnificent views of Mt Gulaga (also referred to as Mt Dromedary).

🅞 **Sights**

Foxglove Gardens GARDENS
(✆02-4473 7375; www.thefoxglovegardens.com; 282 Corkhill Dr, Tilba Tilba; adult/child $9/2; ☺9am-5pm Oct-Mar, shorter hours Apr-Sep) Attractively landscaped with tree-shaded alcoves and neoclassical statues, this 1.4-hectare English-style private garden is an enchanting place to explore. It's worth sparing an hour to amble through the rose garden and duck

beneath tunnels draped in greenery. It's at the southern end of Tilba Tilba.

Sleeping & Eating

★ Bryn at Tilba
B&B $$$

(☑ 02-4473 7385; www.thebrynattilba.com.au; 91 Punkalla-Tilba Rd, Central Tilba; r $260-305; P 🔊) Follow Central Tilba's main street 1km out of town to this fabulous building that sits on a green-lawned hillside. It's a lovely, peaceful spot with expansive views from the rooms and a wide verandah. Three rooms with hardwood floors, a light, airy feel and characterful bathrooms share sumptuous common spaces; there's also a separate self-contained cottage.

Tilba Coastal Retreat
GUESTHOUSE $$

(☑ 0403 627 037; www.tilbacoastalretreat.com; 27 Victoria Creek Rd, Central Tilba; ste $150-220; P ➔ ❄ 🔊) It may be a few clicks from the coast, but this luxurious yet affordable property set in rolling farmland is an astute choice for families, groups or romantic weekenders. You can choose from the main 'Residence', with its spacious two-bedrooms, the adjoining 'Spa', or the 'Orchard', a self-contained separate abode. The styling in each is gorgeous and the friendly ex-Sydney owners will espouse the wisdom of the sea change.

Dromedary Hotel
PUB FOOD $$

(Bate St; mains $16-24; ⊙ noon-2pm & 6-8pm) If you're thirsty as a dromedary, stop at this weatherboard beauty sitting proudly above the main drag. New owners have revamped the menu to include some yummy Malaysian dishes, a couple of first-class burger choices and a huge Buddha Bowl for the vegetarians. The beer is ice cold and served with a smile.

ℹ Information

Bates Emporium (☑ 02-4473 7290; www.visittilba.com.au; 2 Bate St, Central Tilba; ⊙ 8am-5pm Mon-Fri, 8.30am-4.30pm Sat, from 9am Sun; 🔊) There's information, fuel, groceries and postal services at Bates Emporium, at the start of the main street of Central Tilba.

It also acts as the reception for **Tilba Two-Story** (☑ 02-4473 7290; www.tilbatwostory.com; r incl breakfast $180-195; 🔊).

ℹ Getting There & Away

Premier (p177) runs a daily bus to Sydney ($59, eight hours) via Narooma ($8, 25 minutes) and to Eden ($36, two hours). Daily services also reach Bermagui ($7, 20 minutes) and Merimbula ($28, 1½ hours).

SAPPHIRE COAST

Aside from NSW folk, many Australians have spent sadly little time along the glorious Sapphire Coast, due mostly to its relatively long distance (approximately six hours) from both Sydney and Melbourne. Yet a treasure trove of natural delights awaits those who venture off the Princes Hwy proper: empty, unblemished beaches wedged between saw-edged sea cliffs, dense forests and lonely lighthouses. The communities here are easy-going but intensely connected to the land they choose to live or play in. Whale watching from September to November is some of the country's best and many gastronomes visit purely for the local oysters.

The Sapphire Coast is a fulfilling place to trace the long history of the Yuin people, the traditional owners of the land. Former whaling town Eden has an especially fascinating history: Aboriginal fishers worked together with orcas to hunt and trap whales for thousands of years. Interpretative trails in Ben Boyd and Bournda National Parks are also enriching ways to learn about the land's ancient traditions.

Bermagui

POP 1481

'Bermie' is an iconic South Coast town, known for its rich Aboriginal history, wild surf beaches and laid-back state of mind. Tucked away off the highway, the pretty town hugs quiet lagoons and often empty shores, attracting youthful road-trippers who offer an alternative aesthetic to the typical fishing community.

The area's original inhabitants, the Djiringanj group of the Yuin people, have seen many changes since European settlers arrived in the 19th century. The land was turned to cattle farming and then hastily dug up during a three-year gold rush that began in 1880. North of town, bird-filled Wallaga Lake has been significant to Aboriginal people for millennia, as evidenced by numerous middens and cutting stones. Merriman Island in the middle of the lake is gazetted as an Aboriginal site of significance and is off limits to visitors.

Sleeping

Reflections Holiday Park Bermagui
CAMPGROUND $

(☑ 02-6493 4382; www.reflectionsholidayparks.com.au/park/bermagui; 1 Lamont St; unpowered/

powered/en-suite sites from $26/38/51, cabins $112-267; P 🛜 🐾) Very central but pretty crowded in summer, this all-purpose holiday park has accommodation at all budget levels, generous amenities (like laundry, barbecues and playgrounds), and a great location for access to the beach and pub.

Prices increase by at least a third in the summer high season when there is also a two-night minimum.

Harbourview Motel   MOTEL $$
(📞 02-6493 5213; www.harbourviewmotel.com.au; 56-58 Lamont St; s $150-185, d $160-230; P ❄ 🛜) A standout among Bermagui's motels for its spacious, high-standard rooms, the Harbourview is run in very shipshape fashion by the helpful owner, who is a top source of local information. Each room has a full kitchenette and its own gas barbecue, and there's boat parking to boot. It's well located for the beach or Fishermen's Wharf.

Laundry facilities on-site.

Captain's Quarters
Townhouses   BOUTIQUE HOTEL $$
(📞 02-6493 4946; www.captainsquarters.com.au; 6 George St; townhouses from $180) These bargain two-bedroom townhouses have elevated views back towards the beach and township. There are only three available so be sure to book ahead. The owners are tremendous and the shared saltwater pool is just lovely.

✕ Eating

Boneless Vegetarian Cafe   VEGETARIAN $$
(📞 02-6493 4057; 1/14 Lamont St; mains $13-24; ⊙ 8am-3pm Wed-Sun) A friendly skeleton adorns the logo of this inventive veggie hangout in the middle of pretty Lamont St. Aside from the fine coffee and sweets, you can feast on creative mains like nachos with jackfruit, 'cheeseburger' toasties and killer hemp-based smoothies. It's quickly becoming a local institution.

★ Il Passaggio   ITALIAN $$
(📞 02-6493 5753; www.ilpassaggio.com.au; Fishermen's Wharf, 73 Lamont St; pizzas $14-23, mains $28-35; ⊙ 6-9pm Wed & Thu, noon-2pm & 6-11pm Fri-Sun) Cheerfully located on the top deck of the wharf, Il Passaggio whips up authentic pizzas and a few out-of-the-ordinary Italian dishes, like saltimbocca with silver beet and spaghetti with purple broccolini. Well-chosen antipasti platters pair nicely with wines by the glass. There's a popular provedore on-site.

WORTH A TRIP

TATHRA ON THE COAST

Tathra is a beautiful coastal town which was rocked by bush fires back in 2018. The town is often bypassed by travellers, but its beach is a beauty, blessed with emerald waters and a long stretch of sand, and backed by Mimosa National Park.

Since 1905 live bands have rocked the rafters of the historic Tathra Hotel (www.tathrahotel.com.au; 8-12 Bega St), which was thankfully spared by the fires. Most of the live music is at weekends and it really draws a crowd. There are occasional midweek events; check the schedule on the website.

❶ Information

Visitor Centre (📞 02-6493 3054; www.visitbermagui.com.au; Bunga St; ⊙ 10am-4.30pm Mon-Sat, to 2pm Sun) The information centre near the town's main intersection has a great gift shop, along with the usual maps and pamphlets.

❶ Getting There & Away

Premier (p177) buses run daily between Sydney ($60, 8½ hours) and Eden ($31, 1¾ hours). V/Line (p196) runs four coaches a week to Bairnsdale, Victoria, connecting with a train to Melbourne (total $67.20, 10½ hours).

Merimbula & Pambula

POP 9102

Long a favourite destination of the retiree set and school holidaymakers, Merimbula is in fact a humble coastal town laid across a richly diverse natural environment. Beaches and inlets carve out the shared spaces, which always seem to turn towards the sea. A few kilometres south, smaller Pambula has wetlands to cycle, and a more urbane sensibility in its charming main street.

Aboriginal middens testify to the Yuin people's use of local oysters as a food source for tens of thousands of years. Today the area remains deservedly famous for its wonderful oysters – sample them in both towns and enter into the lively debate about whether Merimbula or Pambula oysters taste better...

Merimbula

```
0                    200 m
0                    0.1 miles
```

Tathra (24km)

Merimbula Aquarium (2km); Merimbula Wharf (2km)

NPWS Office

Main St

Merimbula Dr (Princes Hwy)

Beach St

Bega (36km)

Park St

Merimbula Visitor Information Centre

Monaro St

Market St

Short St

Merimbula Lake

Coastlife Adventures (230m)

Fishpen Rd

Marine Pde

Merimbula Beach (150m)

Top Lake

Elizabeth St

Merimbula (1.4km); Pambula Beach (7km); Eden (24km)

Merimbula

Sights

Panboola   NATURE RESERVE
(02-0414 864 873; www.panboola.com; Bullara St, Pambula) An admirable community project has protected 77 hectares of wetlands for native bird species. The well-managed realm of mangroves and salt marshes is threaded by walking and cycling trails, including an easy 3.4km loop trail along which you can spot black swans, royal spoonbills and other birdlife.

The river plain has been trodden by the Thaua group of the Yuin people for millennia. When European settlers arrived in 1835, the land was converted to dairy farming.

Activities

Cycle 'n' Surf   CYCLING, SURFING
(02-6495 2171; www.cyclensurf.com.au; 1b Marine Pde, Merimbula; bicycle hire per hour/half-day/full day $12/25/35, surfboard hire per half-/full day $40/60;) This reliable and friendly operator near the beach specialises in bikes but also hires out bodyboards and surfboards.

Coastlife Adventures   SURFING, KAYAKING
(02-6494 1122; www.coastlife.com.au; group/private surfing lessons $70/160, kayaking tours from $70, kayak & stand-up paddleboard rental per hour $25) Offers surfing and stand-up paddleboarding lessons and hire, plus sea-kayaking tours and kayak hire, in Merimbula and at Pambula Beach and Tathra.

Merimbula Marina   WILDLIFE WATCHING
(02-6495 1686; www.merimbulamarina.com; Merimbula jetty, Market St, Merimbula;) This operator runs popular whale-watching tours (adult/child $69/50) from mid-August to late November, as well as two-hour dolphin-watching cruises (adult/child $50/30) and fishing trips ($100 for four hours, December to May).

Merimbula Divers Lodge   DIVING
(02-6495 3611; www.merimbuladiverslodge.com. au; 15 Park St, Merimbula; 1/2 boat dives $69/120, equipment for 1/2 dives $55/99) Offers basic instruction, PADI courses and snorkelling trips – good for beginners. It runs guided dives to nearby wrecks, which include the *Empire Gladstone*, a now-collapsed 135m vessel that sank in 1950. Guided snorkelling including gear costs from $33.

Tours

★ Captain Sponge's Magical Oyster Tours   BOATING
(0429 453 545; www.magicaloystertours.com.au; Pambula; 2hr tour adult/child $70/30;) An experienced oyster farmer and master shucker, the charismatic Captain Sponge zips his boat around Pambula Lake, explaining mollusc mysteries along the way. The best part is the fresh oysters, which taste all the better on the water. Tours leave at 9am on Monday, Wednesday and Friday whenever there's demand; enquire ahead.

Sleeping

Wandarrah Lodge   HOSTEL $
(02-6495 3503; www.wandarrahlodge.com.au; 8 Marine Pde, Merimbula; 6-/4-person dm $34/36, s/d/f with shared bathroom from $59/76/142;

P 🛜) All the basics are done well at Wandarrah Lodge: clean, if institutional, dorm and private rooms, a lounge and TV room, and backpacker must-haves like laundry and lockers. It's a place for a peaceful night rather than a party, though the barbecue area and dining room are pleasant places to mingle ('Wandarrah' is an Aboriginal word meaning 'meeting place').

Note the late check-in (4pm) and early check-out (8am).

Sapphire Waters Motor Inn   MOTEL $$
(📞 02-6495 1999; www.merimbulamotel.com.au; 32-24 Merimbula Dr, Merimbula; d from $145; P ❄ 🛜 ≋) The pick of the town's more affordable digs, and resembling a row of terraced houses in England more than a motel, Sapphire Waters has ample rooms (more like suites, with separate living areas) featuring fresh decor, balconies and good shower pressure.

A small pool gives this motor inn almost the feel of a resort. Staff are warm and full of local tips, and there's a barbecue area and a self-service laundry ($3).

Pelican Motor Inn   MOTEL $$
(📞 02-6495 1933; www.pelicanmotorinn.com.au; 18 Merimbula Dr, Merimbula; d/f from $150/230; P ❄ 🛜) This classic coastal Aussie Motor Inn has good-value spotless rooms, tricked up in a mildly nautical theme. Rooms are thoughtfully attired (with hairdryers, kettles and toasters) and open onto shared balcony terraces, the best with soothing lake views. The pool area is pleasant to linger in. Easy-going service, too.

Prices jump in late December and January.

🍴 Eating & Drinking

Dulcie's Cottage   BURGERS $
(www.dulcies.com.au; 60 Main St, Merimbula; burgers $14-17; ⏱ 4pm-midnight Wed-Thu, from noon Fri & Sat, to 10pm Sun; 🛜) A renovated 1920s cottage is the scene for the Sapphire Coast's coolest, and surely tastiest, burger bar. Food truck outside, bartenders inside, lots of tables in between. Expect live music on most weekends.

Wild Rye's Baking Co   BAKERY $
(📞 02-6495 6649; www.wildryes.com.au; 26 Quondola St, Pambula; snacks from $3; ⏱ 6.30am-4pm Mon-Fri, to 2.30pm Sat; P) The best bread in these parts, from pillowy rolls to the signature light-rye sourdough, comes second only to the freshly baked pies and cakes at this appealing bakery.

This counter-service place is ideal for picnic supplies before a ramble in Panboola.

Ritzy   TAPAS $$
(📞 02-6495 1085; www.facebook.com/ritzywinebar.com.au; 56 Market St, Merimbula; tapas $10-24; ⏱ 4pm-midnight Mon-Sat; 🛜) Ritzy does a clever take on Aussie tapas in its cocktail-infused, playful restaurant just above the town centre. Dishes like kingfish sashimi on crispy wontons or grilled chorizo and scallops are juicy fresh. Prawns come by the bucketful and there's a killer dessert menu.

Merimbula Wharf   AUSTRALIAN, SEAFOOD $$
(📞 02-6495 4446; www.merimbulawharf.com.au; Lake St, Merimbula; mains $24-37; ⏱ 10am-5pm year-round, plus 6-9pm Wed-Sun Dec-Apr; 🛜) As much a destination venue as a restaurant, the views over bay and beach are stunning from the windows of the Wharf southeast of central Merimbula. Pop in for a glass of wine and a few oysters. Larger dishes are uncomplicated and tasty but presented with flair. Seafood platters, scallops and other fish dishes dominate the menu, though the desserts look as good as they taste. Book ahead for dinner.

There's an **aquarium** (adult/child $22/15; ⏱ 10am-5pm daily Oct-May, closed Tue Jun-Sep; ♿) underneath the restaurant.

★**Wheelers**   SEAFOOD $$
(📞 02-6495 6330; www.wheelersoysters.com.au; 162 Arthur Kaine Dr, Pambula; 12 oysters from shop $15-18, restaurant mains $26-42; ⏱ shop 10am-5pm Sun-Thu, to 6pm Fri & Sat, restaurant noon-2.30pm daily & 6pm-late Mon-Sat; 🍴♿) The lake-to-plate experience is offered in style at the region's premier oyster farm and restaurant. Set back from the highway between Merimbula and Pambula, the cherished molluscs can be slurped casually from the takeaway counter or enjoyed with inventive garnishes (avruga caviar, wasabi aioli) in the restaurant. Beyond house-smoked fish linguini and seafood laksa, nonpescatarians can feast on tremendous steaks and slick vegetarian dishes. Tours of the oyster farm depart 11am Tuesday to Saturday ($22, 45 minutes).

Longstocking Brewery   MICROBREWERY
(📞 02-6495 7373; www.longstocking.com.au; 3546 Princes Hwy, Pambula; ⏱ 11am-5pm Mon-Thu, to 10pm Sat-Sun) Sharing lovely grounds with the wholesome Oaklands Cafe, the Sapphire Coast's hottest microbrewery sets a cracking pace on Friday and Saturday when group bookings descend for growlers and paddles

of sweet ale and hoppy lagers. Oysters are available, plus strong coffee.

ℹ️ Information

Merimbula Visitor Information Centre (☑ 02-6495 1129; www.sapphirecoast.com.au; 4 Beach St; ⊙ 9am-5pm Mon-Fri, to 4pm Sat, from 10am Sun) In the centre of town by the lake.

ℹ️ Getting There & Away

Merimbula Airport (MIM; ☑ 02-6495 4211; www.merimbulaairport.com.au; Arthur Kaine Dr) is 1.5km south of town on the road to Pambula. Rex (www.rex.com.au) flies daily to Melbourne, Sydney, Cooma and Moruya.

Premier (p177) has two daily buses to Sydney ($69, 8½ hours) and Eden ($11, 30 minutes). **NSW TrainLink** (☑ 13 15 00; www.nswtrainlink.info) runs a daily bus to Canberra (from $30, 4½ hours). V/Line (p196) runs buses to Bairnsdale in Victoria (five hours), from where you can connect to Melbourne (four hours) by train; full-fare tickets are around $61.

Local **buses** (Market St) run Monday to Friday to Eden, Bega and Tathra at schoolkid-friendly hours.

Eden

POP 3151

For thousands of years, whales have breached the waters of Eden's Twofold Bay. An extraordinary relationship evolved between the Yuin Thaua people and their cetaceous neighbours: dolphins and killer whales helped the locals to corral their catch and bring it ashore, in return for a share of the spoils. Aboriginal Australians shared these skills with European settlers, who began whaling here in 1791.

The town of Eden is still famous for whales. Cries of 'Rusho!' – the whalers' call to action after a sighting – have fortunately fallen silent and now the annual Whale Festival welcomes the return of whales during their southern migration from Antarctic waters during September, October and November.

Eden's wide, elevated main street is a pleasant place to stroll, while the harbour bustle below offers a reminder of the town's past and present. Eden is also wedged between two sections of Ben Boyd National Park, home to one of East Coast Australia's finest walks.

The bushfires did considerable damage to local communities in and around Eden; your visit here will make a difference.

👁 Sights

Killer Whale Museum   MUSEUM
(☑ 02-6496 2094; www.killerwhalemuseum.com.au; 184 Imlay St; adult/child $12/3; ⊙ 9.15am-3.45pm Mon-Sat, from 11.15am Sun) This long-running museum satisfies appetites for tales of seabound adventures, local Aboriginal history and blubber-based medical cures. As its centrepiece, it displays the monster skeleton of Old Tom, a killer whale and local legend.

Whale Lookout   VIEWPOINT
(Rotary Park) Between late September and late November, a good spot to look for whales is at the scenic lookout south of the wharf. This can also save you the time and money of an organised cruise.

👉 Tours

Cat Balou Cruises   WILDLIFE
(☑ 0427 962 027; www.catbalou.com.au; Main Wharf, 253 Imlay St; adult/child $95/75; 🚢) This crew operates scenic and wildlife-spotting cruises aboard a 16m catamaran. Most popular are the 3½-hour whale-spotting voyages (late September to late November); there are also shorter trips aimed at families (adult/child $79/55). At other times of the year, dolphins and seals can usually be seen during the whistle-stop bay cruise (adult/child $45/25).

Kiah Wilderness Tours   KAYAKING
(☑ 0429 961 047; www.kiahwildernesstours.com.au; 1167 Princes Hwy, Kiah; 🚢) On the Towamba River 12km south of Eden, these guided kayaking tours explore the coastal estuary, with plenty of breaks to check out seabirds, take a dip and snack on complimentary refreshments. For wildlife and tranquil waters, the pick is the leisurely morning tour ($99).

There are also two-hour tasters aimed at families ($340 per group) and more challenging full-day excursions ($175 per person).

🎊 Festivals & Events

Whale Festival   STREET CARNIVAL
(www.edenwhalefestival.com.au; ⊙ late Oct or early Nov) During the old whaling days, hunters would herald the seasonal return of their prey towards the end of the year. Fortunately these days it's all about the excitement of the start of whale-*watching* season, marked by a carnival, a street parade and stalls, plus guided whale watching and documentary screenings.

🛏 Sleeping

Cocora Cottage B&B $$

(☑ 02-6496 1241; www.cocoracottage.com; 2 Cocora St; s/d incl breakfast $130/160; ⓟ 🤶) At this heritage-listed B&B adjoining the courthouse, original features amplify the sense of intrigue, like exposed, convict-picked rock by the kitchen and the lounge's old fireplace. Two rooms are available: an attractive, antique-style room at the front, and contemporary lodgings at the back with bay windows overlooking the back garden.

Twofold Bay Motor Inn MOTEL $$

(☑ 02-6496 3111; www.twofoldbaymotorinn.com. au; 164-166 Imlay St; r $170-240; ⓟ 🌂🤶🏊) Splashes of turquoise and chirpy management each do their part to enliven the ambience at Twofold Bay. The 24 rooms vary in size and bed configuration, but all are tidy and modern and have a kitchenette.

The best rooms have views of the sea. There's also a small heated indoor pool.

🍴 Eating & Drinking

Sprout CAFE, VEGAN $

(☑ 02-6496 1511; www.sprouteden.com.au; 134 Imlay St; mains $11-22; ⊙ 7.30am-4pm Mon-Fri, 8am-2pm Sat & Sun; 🤶🍴) 🍃 Sprout is a health-conscious street cafe which taps right into the local community spirit. Coffee, sandwiches and 'nourish bowls' are the main attractions, but the sweet treats in the counter are popular with the morning-tea set. There's a small organic grocery store and a sunny courtyard out back.

★ Drift SEAFOOD, AUSTRALIAN $$

(☑ 02-6496 3392; www.drifteden.com.au; Main Wharf, 253 Imlay St; snacks & share plates $9-36, mains $18-30; ⊙ 5-11pm Mon-Thu, 4pm-midnight Sat & Sun; 🤶) Eden mussels, Tilba cheeses and Gippsland wines find their perfect setting in this shack-chic, upper-floor restaurant overlooking the wharf. The sunset views and attention to detail in the food preparation belie the town's sleepy feel. We recommend the Bloody Mary oysters and a charcuterie board assembled from the best of the **smokehouse** (☑ 02-6496 2331; www.edensmokehouse.com.au; 18-20 Weecoon St; ⊙ 7.30am-4pm Mon, Tue, Thu & Fri) across the road.

Great Southern Inn PUB

(☑ 02-6496 1515; www.greatsoutherninn.com.au; 121 Imlay St; mains $14-24; 🤶) The pub in the heart of town offers good-value meals, views and beer-first service. There are cheap beds

---

BOURNDA LAGOON

Part of Bournda National Park, Bournda Lagoon is hidden at the end of an easy 2km walk along North Tura Beach, accessible from the well-signed car park. The watering hole is popular with huge goannas and skittish wallabies; expect to see plenty of pied oyster catchers bobbing about too. It's a prehistorically gorgeous spot, offering both tranquil and more adventurous open ocean swimming. Bring a picnic lunch, skirt through the regrowth forest past the odd friendly surfer with a board under their arm, and spend a few hours in this untouched paradise.

---

upstairs if you need one ($40 to $100), but it's best enjoyed as an unofficial information centre.

ℹ Information

Eden Visitor Centre (☑ 02-6496 1953; www. visiteden.com.au; cnr Mitchell St & Princes Hwy; ⊙ 9am-5pm) offers bookings and information by the main-road roundabout in the centre.

ℹ Getting There & Away

Premier (p177) runs services north to Sydney ($71, nine to 10 hours) twice daily via all major coastal towns. NSW TrainLink (p203) runs a daily bus service to Canberra (from $32, 4½ hours, 7am). For Melbourne ($57, 8½ hours), V/ Line (p196) runs a bus and train combination via Bairnsdale.

Local buses have limited services to Merimbula and Bega on weekdays; contact **Sapphire Coast Buslines** (☑ 02-6495 6452; www. scbuslines.com.au).

Ben Boyd National Park

With two sections either side of Eden covering almost 105 sq km, **Ben Boyd National Park** (www.nationalparks.nsw.gov.au; vehicle in southern/northern section $8/free) has colourful views, distinctive histories and one of NSW's most photogenic multiday hikes, the Light to Light Walk (p206; closed at time of research due to fire damage).

Ironstone cliffs give sections of Ben Boyd's shoreline a deep orange hue. The colour scheme is especially vivid at the **Pinnacles** in the northern section of the park, where reddish clay contrasts against white sand. Nearby, the **Pambula River Walk** follows the footsteps of the land's traditional owners, the Yuin people, passing significant Aboriginal sites, such as a 3000-year-old midden.

The southern section is just as interesting, with heritage buildings standing monument to 19th-century Scottish wheeler-dealer Ben Boyd and offering a glimpse of the area's by-gone whaling industry. Walking trails here are very rewarding, running between euca-lyptus forests and sparkling blue coves, of-ten ideal for snorkelling and swimming.

At the time of research, the southern sec-tion of the park, including the Light to Light Walk, was closed due to bushfire damage.

Sights & Activities

Green Cape Lightstation   LIGHTHOUSE
(02-6495 5000; www.nationalparks.nsw.gov.au; Green Cape Rd; tours adult/child/family $12/6/30) At the southern tip of Ben Boyd's southern section, elegant Green Cape Lightstation (1883) offers awesome views. There are tours (by appointment only) and three elegantly restored keepers' cottages. This is a great spot to see whales in season (May to August) and multitudes of muttonbirds during their migration (October).

The heritage **lightstation keepers' cottages**, with gas-heated lounge and dining room and high-ceilinged bedrooms accented in nautical blue, are available for overnight stays ($295 to $350). It's a place for travellers who want to enjoy the silence: there's no wi-fi or TV.

Boyd's Tower   HISTORIC BUILDING
FREE At the end of Edrom Rd is the turn-off for Boyd's Tower, built in the late 1840s from Sydney sandstone. It was built as a lighthouse, but the government wouldn't give Boyd, a once-wealthy landowner, permission to operate it (he later fled to California in massive debt). Instead it served as a whaling

lookout and still stands, an enigmatic struc-ture surrounded by eucalypts. Step inside (it's empty) before taking in the views of **Red Point's** claret-coloured shoreline. It's reached via an easy 500m walk from the car park.

Boyd's Tower is also one of the trailheads for the Light to Light Walk.

★Light to Light Walk   HIKING
(www.nationalparks.nsw.gov.au) The South Coast's premier walking trail, this 30km coastal route links Boyd's wannabe light-house to the real one at Green Cape, along russet-coloured shores, forest-backed beach-es and in view of somersaulting seals. The trail is growing in popularity on the back of government upgrades and group tour book-ings, but it's still a superb and challenging hike. There are campgrounds along the route at Saltwater Creek (12km from Boyd's Tower) and Bittangabee Bay (22km); allow two to three days to complete it one way. This path was closed due to fire damage at time of research, so check ahead to make sure it's open.

Sleeping

Bittangabee Bay Campground   CAMPGROUND $
(10am-3pm Mon-Fri 02-6495 5000; www.national parks.nsw.gov.au; tent sites per 2 people $24, per additional adult/child $12/6, plus park entry fee per vehicle $8; P) One of two national-park camp-grounds along the 30km Light to Light Walk, basic Bittangabee Bay has 30 unpowered sites, pit toilets and barbecue facilities. Oh, and plenty of lyrebirds. Book ahead online or by phone.

Getting There & Away

The park is divided into two sections – north and south – both reached via turn-offs from the Princes Hwy either side of Eden. Take Haycock Rd, 9km south of Pambula, or Edrom Rd, 16km south of Eden.

Melbourne & Coastal Victoria

Best Places to Eat

➡ Attica (p237)
➡ Minamishima (p227)
➡ Brae (p261)
➡ IGNI (p246)
➡ Sardine (p283)
➡ Lune Croissanterie (p227)

Best Places to Sleep

➡ QT Melbourne (p222)
➡ Cullen (p224)
➡ Drift House (p268)
➡ Lon Retreat (p255)
➡ Bimbi Park (p261)
➡ Wilsons Promontory Lightstation (p278)

Why Go?

Victoria may be Australia's smallest mainland state but it punches well above its weight with the country's second-biggest city in cosmopolitan, food-obsessed and culture-packed Melbourne, and to either side some of the nation's most gorgeous coastline, filled with windswept beaches, charming seaside towns and legendary surf spots.

Head west to wind along the impossibly scenic Great Ocean Road, home of world-class surfing beaches, a string of popular seaside communities and iconic limestone stacks the Twelve Apostles.

Southeast of Melbourne, fairy penguins waddle across the beach at Phillip Island, hikers find their paradise on Wilsons Promontory and a long ribbon of uninterrupted golden beach leads to activity-filled Lakes Entrance, where you'll find Australia's largest inland waterway system. More stunning national parks await further on, as you approach the border with New South Wales.

When to Go
Melbourne

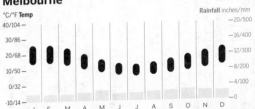

Dec & Jan Beaches are packed during school holidays; book hotels months ahead.

Feb & Mar Quieter but still plenty of activities, though late summer can get hot.

Apr–Nov Crisp mid-year winters lead into rainy and then glorious springtime weather.

Melbourne & Coastal Victoria Highlights

1 Great Ocean Road (p245)
Curling past spectacular beaches and through rainforests.

2 Dining & Drinking in Melbourne (p209) Exploring

cool cafes, hidden bars and the hottest restaurants.

3 Wilsons Prom Wilderness (p278) Strapping on your hiking boots to admire this national park's sheer natural beauty.

4 Penguin Parade, Phillip Island (p274) Cooing over the parade of cute little penguins waddling out of the sea.

5 Twelve Apostles (p262)

Being mesmerised by these iconic limestone pillars.

6 Mornington Peninsula (p270) Treating yourself to wine tasting, fine dining and natural hot springs.

7 Mallacoota (p285) Hiring a boat and exploring the inlet of this gorgeous place.

8 Ninety Mile Beach (p281) Camping in the dunes at this legendary stretch of sand.

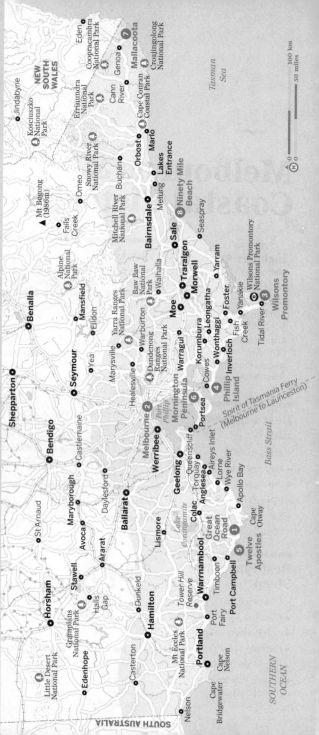

MELBOURNE

POP 4.96 MILLION

Dynamic, cosmopolitan Melbourne is stylish, arty and incredibly proud of its place as Australia's sporting and cultural capital. In the centre, you'll want to explore the dozens of laneways radiating through the grid to find the inner city's true nature: narrow lanes concealing internationally recognized restaurants, drinking dens and street art. But Melbourne is best experienced as a local would, through its diverse collection of inner-city neighbourhoods, each very much with their own quirky character. Despite a long-standing north–south divide – flashy South Yarra versus hipster Fitzroy – there's an effortless style to the city's bars, cafes, restaurants, festivals and people that transcends these borders. Sport is a crucial part of the social fabric here, too: Aussie Rules football ('footy') is practically a local religion, while cricket, Grand Slam tennis, horse racing and Formula One also draw fans in droves.

◉ Sights

◎ City Centre

★ Federation Square
SQUARE

(☑ 03-9655 1900; www.fedsquare.com; cnr Flinders & Swanston Sts, Melbourne; ℝ Flinders St) One of the city's newest public spaces and an urban focal point, Federation Sq is a place to meet, celebrate, protest, watch major sporting events or simply hang out on deckchairs. Occupying a prominent city block, 'Fed Square' is far from square: its undulating and patterned forecourt is paved with 460,000 hand-laid cobblestones from the Kimberley region in WA, with sight lines to important landmarks. Its buildings are clad in a fractal-patterned reptilian skin. Check the website to see what's on.

★ Ian Potter Centre: NGV Australia
GALLERY

(☑ 03-8620 2222; www.ngv.vic.gov.au; Federation Sq, Melbourne; ☉ 10am-5pm; ℝ Flinders St) FREE The National Gallery of Victoria's impressive Fed Sq offshoot was set up to showcase its extraordinary collection of Australian works. Set over three levels, it's a mix of permanent (free) and temporary (ticketed) exhibitions, comprising paintings, decorative arts, photography, prints, sculpture and fashion. Free 50-minute

tours are conducted daily at 11am, noon, 1pm and 2pm.

★ Queen Victoria Market
MARKET

(☑ 03-9320 5822; www.qvm.com.au; cnr Elizabeth & Victoria Sts, Melbourne; ☉ 6am-3pm Tue, Thu & Fri, to 4pm Sat, 9am-4pm Sun; ℙ; ℚ 58, ℝ Flagstaff) With more than 600 traders, 'Vic Market' is the largest open-air market in the southern hemisphere. Visit early morning to shop for fresh produce, accepting tasters and dodging the booming cries of spruiking stall holders. The wonderful deli hall with art deco features is lined with everything from soft cheeses and Polish sausages to Greek dips and kangaroo biltong. Check if the Wednesday Summer Night Market or Winter Night Market (5pm to 10pm) are on for hawker food, bars, entertainment and shopping.

Australian Centre for the Moving Image
MUSEUM

(ACMI; ☑ 03-8663 2200; www.acmi.net.au; Federation Sq; ☉ 10am-5pm, cinemas until late; ⊞; ℚ 1, 3, 5, 6, 16, 64, 67, 70, 72, 75, City Circle, ℝ Flinders St) FREE Managing to educate, enthral and entertain in equal parts, ACMI is a visual feast that pays homage to Australian cinema and TV, offering insight into the modern-day Aussie psyche. A $40 million renewal project in 2020 freshened things up, with newly designed exhibitions, a cafe, shop and sitting areas, making ACMI a perfect choice to while away a rainy day. Enquire about daily free exhibition tours, as well as cinema screenings, regular talks and great workshops (prices vary).

★ Hosier Lane
PUBLIC ART

(Hosier Lane, Melbourne; ☉ 24hr; ℝ Flinders St) Melbourne's most celebrated laneway for street art, Hosier Lane's cobbled length draws camera-wielding crowds and wannabe Instagram models posing in front of edgy graffiti, stencils and art installations (watch them from the comfort of the window seats at Bar Tini). Subject matter runs to the mostly political and countercultural, spiced with irreverent humour. Be sure to also see Rutledge Lane, which horseshoes around Hosier.

★ Birrarung Marr
PARK

(Batman Ave, Melbourne; ℝ Flinders St) Multi-terraced Birrarung Marr is one of Melbourne's most unique parks, featuring grassy knolls, river promenades, thoughtful planting of Indigenous flora and great

MELBOURNE IN...

Two Days

Head over to check out the Ian Potter Centre: NGV Australia (p209) art collection and have a look around Federation Square (p209) before joining a walking tour to see Melbourne's street art or learn about local Aboriginal history. Enjoy lunch at MoVida (p226) then find a rooftop bar to test the city's cocktails and take in the views before an evening kayak tour (p219) down the Yarra River. Finish the night off dining at one of Melbourne's best restaurants, Chin Chin (p225). Start day two with a stroll along Birrarung Marr (p209) and into the Royal Botanic Gardens (p218), then discover the gastronomic delights of the Queen Victoria Market (p209). Catch a tram to St Kilda (p219) to wander along the foreshore and pier before having a sundowner at beachside bar Pontoon (p237).

One Week

Spend a couple of hours at the Melbourne Museum (p215) then head into Fitzroy to boutique shop along Gertrude St and grab lunch and coffee at Proud Mary (p234) in Collingwood. Back in the city centre, wander through Chinatown and check out Ned Kelly's armour at the State Library before grabbing some dumplings at HuTong Dumpling Bar (p226) for dinner. Spend the rest of the week exploring the bars and live music of northern suburbs Fitzroy and Collingwood, shopping and cafe-hopping in hip Windsor and Prahran, hitting the South Melbourne Market (p215) and heading out to the Abbotsford Convent (p214). Make sure to fit in a meal at Supernormal (p226) and a drink at Bar Americano (p233).

viewpoints of the city and the river. There's also a scenic route to the MCG (p211) via the 'talking' William Barak Bridge – listen out for songs, words and sounds representing Melbourne's cultural diversity as you walk.

★ **Chinatown** AREA
(www.chinatownmelbourne.com.au; Little Bourke St, btwn Swanston & Exhibition Sts; ⊠ Melbourne Central, Parliament) For more than 150 years this section of central Melbourne, now flanked by five traditional arches, has been the focal point for the city's Chinese community. It remains a vibrant neighbourhood of historic buildings filled with Chinese and other restaurants. A must-visit for foodies, come here for yum cha (dim sum) or to explore the attendant laneways for late-night dumplings and cocktails. Some restaurants stay open until the wee hours. Chinatown also hosts the city's **Chinese New Year celebrations** (www.melbournechinesenewyear.com; Little Bourke St, Melbourne; ⊠ Jan/Feb; ⊡).

Chinese miners arrived in Victoria in search of the 'new gold mountain' in the 1850s and started to settle in this strip of Little Bourke St from the 1860s. To learn more about the Chinese-Australian story, visit the excellent **Chinese Museum** (☑03-9662 2888; www.chinesemuseum.com.au; 22 Cohen Pl; adult/child $11/9; ⊠ 10am-4pm; ⊠ Parliament).

Flinders St Station HISTORIC BUILDING
(cnr Flinders & Swanston Sts, Melbourne; ⊠ Flinders St) Melbourne's first railway station, which turned 100 years old in 2010, is also its most iconic building. You'd be hard-pressed to find a Melburnian who hasn't uttered the phrase 'Meet me under the clocks' – the popular rendezvous spot at the front entrance. Stretching along the Yarra, the neoclassical building is crowned with a striking octagonal dome that contains an abandoned ballroom (sadly closed to the public).

Parliament House HISTORIC BUILDING
(☑03-9651 8911; www.parliament.vic.gov.au; Spring St, Melbourne; ⊠ 8.30am-5.30pm Mon-Fri; ⊠ Parliament) FREE The grand steps of Victoria's parliament (1856) are often dotted with tulle-wearing brides smiling for the camera as well as placard-holding protesters. On sitting days the public is welcome to view proceedings from the galleries. On nonsitting days there are eight guided tours daily; times are posted online and on a sign by the door. Numbers are limited to 25 people, so arrive at least 15 minutes before time. Check online to book architecture or art tours.

State Library of Victoria LIBRARY
(☑03-8664 7000; www.slv.vic.gov.au; cnr Russell & La Trobe Sts; ⊠ 10am-9pm Mon-Thu, to 6pm Fri-Sun, galleries 10am-6pm; ⊡; ☑1, 3, 5, 6, 16, 30, 35, 64, 67, 72, ⊠ Melbourne Central) FREE This

grand neoclassical building has been at the forefront of Melbourne's literary scene since 1856. When its central **La Trobe Reading Room** was completed in 1913, the six-storey-high, reinforced-concrete octagonal dome was the world's largest; its natural light illuminates ornate plasterwork and studious Melburnians. The library's original reading room, the **Ian Potter Queen's Hall**, recently reopened after a glorious refurbishment. Galleries offer free exhibitions of Victorian artefacts (including outlaw Ned Kelly's armour). Free 45-minute tours depart daily (10.45am) from **Readings** (☑ 03-8664 7540; www.readings.com.au; State Library, 285-321 Russell St; ☉ 10am-8pm Tue-Thu, to 6pm Fri-Mon; ⓡ Melbourne Central).

Koorie Heritage Trust　　CULTURAL CENTRE
(☑ 03-8662 6300; www.koorieheritagetrust.com; Level 1 & 3, Yarra Building, Federation Sq, cnr Swanston & Flinders Sts, Melbourne; tours adult/child $30/15; ☉ 10am-5pm; ⓡ Flinders St) FREE Devoted to southeastern Aboriginal culture, this centre houses interesting artefacts and oral history. There's a shop and gallery downstairs; upstairs, carefully preserved significant objects can be viewed in display cases and drawers. It also runs hour-long tours along the Yarra (subject to weather conditions) led by Koorie guides that evoke the history and memories that lie beneath the modern city. You can book online or in person.

◉ Southbank

Prior to the 1980s Southbank was a gritty industrial zone supporting a major shipping port. Since then it has been built and rebranded as Melbourne's glitzy tourist precinct. This riverside promenade is peppered with big-name international restaurants, hotels and the distinct whiff of 'casino', but its Yarra River views and multiple top-draw arts institutions make it make it a worthwhile visit.

★**NGV International**　　GALLERY
(National Gallery of Victoria International; ☑ 03-8620 2222; www.ngv.vic.gov.au; 180 St Kilda Rd, Southbank; ☉ 10am-5pm; ⓡ Flinders St) FREE Housed in a vast, brutally beautiful, bunker-like building, the international branch of the NGV has an expansive collection, from ancient artefacts to the cutting edge. Regular blockbuster exhibitions (prices vary) draw crowds, and there are free 50-minute highlight tours on the hour from 11am to 2pm daily. It's a rite of passage to touch the water wall at the entrance.

Buxton Contemporary　　GALLERY
(☑ 03-9035 9339; www.buxtoncontemporary.com; cnr Southbank Blvd & Dodds St, Southbank; ☉ 11am-5pm Wed-Sun; ⓠ 1, 3, 5, 6, 16, 64, 67, 72) FREE Weird and wonderful Buxton Contemporary, located at the University of Melbourne's art school, opened in 2018 powered by the Michael Buxton Collection of contemporary Australian art. The four public galleries contain various exhibitions with works ranging from contemporary to creepy. Check online for talks and lectures, and to make sure it's not closed for installations.

Eureka Skydeck　　VIEWPOINT
(☑ 03-9693 8888; www.eurekaskydeck.com.au; 7 Riverside Quay, Southbank; adult/child $25/16.50, Edge extra $12/8; ☉ 10am-10pm; ⓡ Flinders St) Melbourne's tallest building, the 297m-high Eureka Tower was erected in 2006, and a wild elevator ride takes you to its 88th floor in less than 40 seconds (check out the photo on the elevator floor if there's time). The Edge – a slightly sadistic glass cube – cantilevers you out of the building; you have no choice but to look down. Book on the website for a slightly discounted admission.

If you want to experience a similar view in comfort, it's plusher and more affordable to head to the Rialto Tower – hit **Lui Bar** (☑ 03-9691 3888; www.luibar.com.au; 55th fl, Rialto, 525 Collins St, Melbourne; ☉ 5.30pm-midnight Mon-Wed, 11.30am-1am Thu, 11.30am-3am Fri & Sat, 11.30am-midnight Sun; ⓡ Southern Cross), on the same floor as fine-dining restaurant Vue de Monde (p226), for a world-class cocktail.

◉ Richmond & East Melbourne

Richmond and East Melbourne are the nexus for all things sporting, featuring the mighty Melbourne Cricket Ground. The genteel streets of East Melbourne centre on the gorgeous Fitzroy Gardens, while Richmond is a residential and commercial expanse. Bridge Rd, its declining shopping hub, has seen better days, but grittier Victoria St is a destination for Vietnamese food, and once-dowdy Swan St has developed into a hip strip.

★**Melbourne Cricket Ground**　　STADIUM
(MCG; ☑ 03-9657 8888; www.mcg.org.au; Brunton Ave, East Melbourne; tour adult/child/family $25/14/60, incl museum $35/18/76; ☉ tours 10am-3pm; ⓠ 48, 70, 75, ⓡ Jolimont) With a capacity of 100,000 people, the 'G' is one of the world's great sporting venues, hosting cricket in summer and AFL (Australian Football League, Aussie rules or 'footy') in winter – for

Melbourne

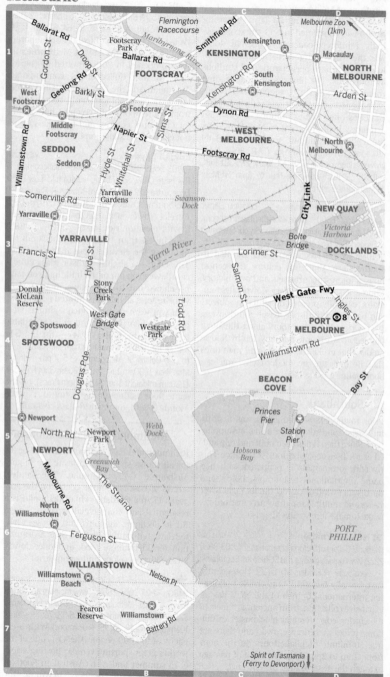

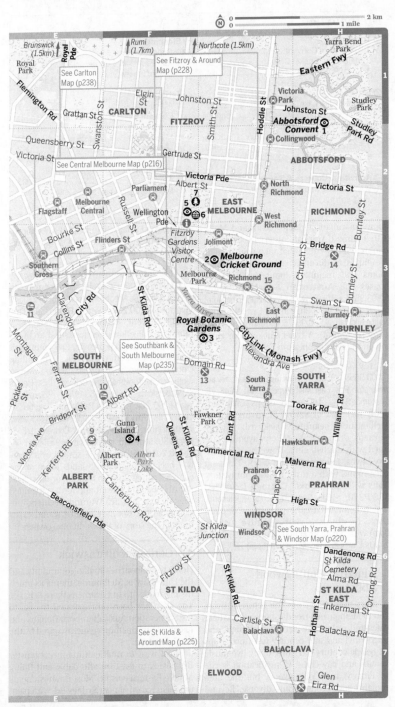

N
0 ⸺⸺⸺⸺⸺⸺⸺ 2 km
0 ⸺⸺⸺⸺⸺⸺⸺ 1 mile

Yarra Bend Park
Eastern Fwy

Brunswick (1.5km)
Royal Pde
Rumi (1.7km)
Northcote (1.5km)

Royal Park
Flemington Rd

See Carlton Map (p238)
Elgin St
CARLTON
Grattan St
Swanston St
Queensberry St

See Fitzroy & Around Map (p228)
Johnston St
FITZROY
Smith St
Hoddle St

Victoria Park
Johnston St
Abbotsford Convent 1
Studley Park
Studley Park Rd

Collingwood

Gertrude St

ABBOTSFORD

See Central Melbourne Map (p216)
Victoria St

Victoria Pde
Albert St
7
EAST MELBOURNE
North Richmond
Victoria St
RICHMOND
Burnley St

Parliament
Melbourne Central
Flagstaff
Russell St
5
6
Wellington Pde
West Richmond

Bourke St
Collins St
Flinders St
Fitzroy Gardens Visitor Centre
Jolimont

Bridge Rd
14
Church St

Southern Cross
Clarendon St
City Rd
St Kilda Rd
2
Melbourne Cricket Ground
Melbourne Park
Richmond
15
Swan St
Burnley
BURNLEY

11
Montague St
Ferrars St
Yarra River
Royal Botanic Gardens 3
East Richmond
CityLink (Monash Fwy)
Alexandra Ave

SOUTH MELBOURNE
See Southbank & South Melbourne Map (p235)
Domain Rd
13
South Yarra
SOUTH YARRA
Toorak Rd
Williams Rd

Pickles St
Bridport St
10
Albert Rd
Fawkner Park
Punt Rd
Hawksburn

Victoria Ave
Kerferd Rd
9
Gunn Island 4
Albert Park
Albert Park Lake
St Kilda Rd
Queens Rd
Commercial Rd
Prahran
Malvern Rd
Chapel St
PRAHRAN

ALBERT PARK
Canterbury Rd
Beaconsfield Pde
St Kilda Junction
High St
WINDSOR
Windsor

See South Yarra, Prahran & Windsor Map (p220)

Fitzroy St
St Kilda Rd
Dandenong Rd
St Kilda Cemetery
Alma Rd
Orrong Rd
ST KILDA EAST
Inkerman St

ST KILDA
See St Kilda & Around Map (p225)
Carlisle St
Balaclava
Hotham St
Balaclava Rd

BALACLAVA

ELWOOD
12
Glen Eira Rd

MELBOURNE & COASTAL VICTORIA

Melbourne

many Australians it's hallowed ground. Make it to a game if you can, otherwise there are non-match-day **tours** that take you through the stands, media and coaches' areas, change rooms and members' lounges. The MCG houses the **Australian Sports Museum** (✆03-9657 8879; www.australiansportsmuseum.org.au; Gate 3, MCG, Brunton Ave, East Melbourne; adult/child/family $30/15/75; ⊙10am-5pm; 🚃48, 70, 75, ☒Jolimont). A two-night outdoor cinema on the field happens in February.

Fitzroy Gardens   PARK
(✆03-9658 9658; www.melbourne.vic.gov.au; Wellington Pde, East Melbourne; 🚻👶; 🚃48, 75, ☒Jolimont) FREE The city drops away suddenly just east of Spring St, giving way to Melbourne's beautiful backyard, Fitzroy Gardens. The park's stately avenues are lined with English elms, flowerbeds, expansive lawns, fountains and a creek. There's a playground with a dragon slide, but history buffs will love **Cooks' Cottage** (adult/child $6.90/3.70; ⊙9am-5pm; 🚃48, 75, ☒Jolimont), which belonged to the parents of Captain Cook. Nearby is a **visitor centre** (⊙9am-5pm) with a cafe attached and the delightful 1930s **Conservatory** (⊙9am-5pm) FREE.

⊙ Fitzroy, Collingwood & Abbotsford

A short tram ride from the centre delivers you to Melbourne's trendiest enclaves, where cafes and restaurants are open all night and retro vinyl and mid-century furniture shops sit beside century-old pubs, divey live-music venues and gay clubs. Gentrification is rife in Fitzroy and Collingwood, but the area remains socioeconomically diverse. Beyond Collingwood is largely industrial Abbotsford, bordered by a scenic stretch of the Yarra River with ever more cafes.

★**Abbotsford Convent**   HISTORIC SITE
(✆03-9415 3600; www.abbotsfordconvent.com.au; 1 St Heliers St, Abbotsford; tours $15; ⊙7.30am-10pm; 🚻; 🚃200, 207, ☒Victoria Park) FREE This former convent, dating back to 1863, is a rambling collection of ecclesiastical architecture that's home to a thriving arts community of galleries, studios and cafes – including **Convent Bakery** (✆03-9419 9426; www.conventbakery.com; Abbotsford Convent, 1 St Heliers St, Abbotsford; mains $9.50-19.50; ⊙7am-5pm; 🚻; 🚃200, 207, ☒Victoria Park) and vegetarian **Lentil as Anything** (✆03-9419 6444; www.lentilasanything.com; Abbotsford Convent, 1/3 St Heliers St, Abbotsford; by donation; ⊙9am-9pm; 🚻; 🚃200, 207, ☒Victoria Park) – spread over nearly 7 hectares of riverside land. Tours of the complex run at 2pm on Sunday, or download the Abbotsford Convent app for a self-guided walking tour in which Wurundjeri elders, musicians and artists have created soundscapes that tell the story of the traditional owners.

⊙ Carlton & Brunswick

Home to Melbourne's Italian community and the University of Melbourne, there's as much history to absorb in Carlton as there is pasta. The strip has been reinvigorated thanks to next-generation Australian-born Italians and restaurateurs opening venues inspired by the area's heritage.

Head west to multicultural-meets-hipster Brunswick to feast on affordable and filling Middle Eastern cuisine. Most establishments are clustered on or near Sydney Rd, with plenty of cafes and secondhand shopping during the day and bar-hopping come nightfall.

★ **Melbourne Museum**   MUSEUM
(📞13 11 02; www.museumvictoria.com.au; 11 Nicholson St, Carlton; adult/child $15/free; ☺10am-5pm; 👶; 🚋City Circle, 86, 96, 🚆Parliament) This museum provides a grand sweep of Victoria's natural and cultural histories, incorporating dinosaur skeletons, a 600-species-strong taxidermy hall, a 3D volcano and an open-air forest atrium of Victorian flora. There's a children's gallery, and the excellent **Bunjilaka** on the ground floor presents Indigenous Australian history told through objects and Aboriginal voices with state-of-the-art technology. There's also an **IMAX cinema**.

★ **Royal Exhibition Building**   HISTORIC BUILDING
(📞13 11 02; www.museumvictoria.com.au/reb; 9 Nicholson St, Carlton; tours adult/child $10/7; 🚋City Circle, 86, 96, 🚆Parliament) Built for the 1880 International Exhibition, this Victorian edifice in Carlton Gardens symbolises the glory days of 19th-century Melbourne's economic supremacy. It was the first Australian building to fly the country's flag, house an aquarium, hold parliament (in 1901) and receive Unesco World Heritage status (in 2004). Tours of the building leave from the Melbourne Museum at 2pm; call to confirm.

The building and gardens host everything from craft fairs to car shows. While you're there, **Carlton Gardens** is a stunning place to picnic or rest by the grand fountain, and if visiting in March, you can attend the **Melbourne International Flower and Garden Show**, the largest in the southern hemisphere, attracting more than 100,000 people over five days.

👁 North Melbourne & Parkville

This strip of central Melbourne stretches from the shabby railway yards and gridlocked thoroughfares of West Melbourne, through the surprisingly quiet and awfully pretty Victorian neighbourhood of North Melbourne, and into the ample green spaces of Parkville. The big attraction here is the zoo, but if you're in the area, it's worth stopping by to sample a low-key neighbourhood cafe or restaurant in North Melbourne's Victoria, Errol or Queensberry Sts.

★ **Melbourne Zoo**   ZOO
(📞1300 966 784; www.zoo.org.au; Elliott Ave, Parkville; adult/child $38/19, child weekends &

WORTH A TRIP

HEIDE MUSEUM OF MODERN ART

The former home of John and Sunday Reed, **Heide** (📞03-9850 1500; www.heide.com.au; 7 Templestowe Rd, Bulleen; adult/child $20/free; ☺10am-5pm Tue-Sun; 👶; 🚌903, 🚆Heidelberg) is a prestigious not-for-profit art gallery with a stunning sculpture garden. It holds regularly changing exhibitions, many of which include works by the famous artists that called Heide home, including Sidney Nolan and Albert Tucker. The collection is spread over three buildings: a large purpose-built gallery, the Reeds' original farmhouse and the wonderful modernist house built in 1963 as 'a gallery to be lived in'. There's also a cafe, or you can pack a picnic to eat by the Yarra.

holidays free; ☺9am-5pm; 👶; 🚌58, 🚆Royal Park) 🍃 Established in 1862, this compact zoo remains one of the city's most popular attractions and continues to innovate, having become the world's first carbon-neutral zoo. Set in prettily landscaped gardens, the enclosures aim to simulate the animals' natural habitats and give them the option to hide if they want to (the gorillas and tigers are particularly good at playing hard to get).

👁 South Melbourne, Port Melbourne & Albert Park

Hugging Port Phillip Bay, this well-heeled trio of suburbs is leafy and sedate. South Melbourne has a namesake market surrounded by cafes and curated design shops. Albert Park offers culture in a former gasworks and the world-renowned Grand Prix in March, while near the end of shop-studded Bay St in Port Melbourne, ferries cruise south to Tasmania.

South Melbourne Market   MARKET
(📞03-9209 6295; www.southmelbournemarket.com.au; cnr Coventry & Cecil Sts, South Melbourne; ☺8am-4pm Wed, Sat & Sun, to 5pm Fri; 🅿👶; 🚋1, 12, 96, 109) Trading since 1867, this market is an institution, its labyrinthine guts packed with a brilliant collection of stalls selling everything from organic produce and arts and crafts to Indigenous Australian deli products. It's famed for dim sims (sold here since 1949), and there's no shortage of international food options. From early January to early February,

Central Melbourne

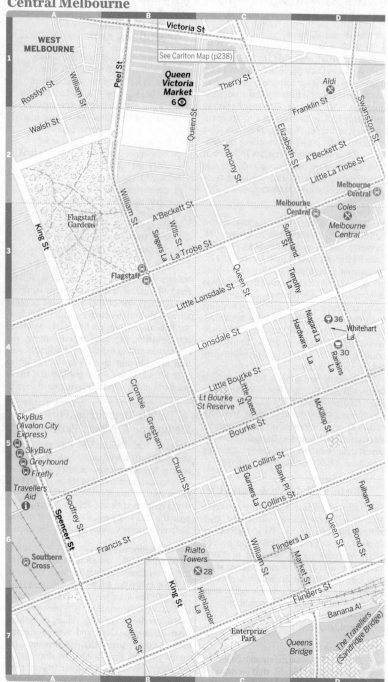

Victoria St

See Carlton Map (p238)

WEST MELBOURNE

Rosslyn St

William St

Peel St

Therry St

Queen Victoria Market
6

Aldi

Franklin St

Walsh St

Queen St

Swanston St

Anthony St

Elizabeth St

A'Beckett St

Little La Trobe St

Melbourne Central

King St

Flagstaff Gardens

William St

A'Beckett St

Wills St

Singers La

La Trobe St

Melbourne Central

Coles

Melbourne Central

Flagstaff

Little Lonsdale St

Queen St

Sutherland St

Timothy La

Lonsdale St

Hardware La

Niagara La

36
Whitehart La

Rankins La

30

Cromble St

Gresham St

Little Bourke St

Little Queen St

Lt Bourke St Reserve

Lt Bourke St

McKillop St

SkyBus (Avalon City Express)

SkyBus

Greyhound

Firefly

Church St

Bourke St

Little Collins St

Gurners La

Bank Pl

Collins St

Travellers Aid

Godfrey St

Spencer St

Francis St

Queen St

Fulham Pl

Southern Cross

William St

Flinders La

Market St

Bond St

Rialto Towers
28

King St

Highlander La

Flinders St

Banana Al

Downlie St

Enterprize Park

Queens Bridge

The Travellers (Sandridge Bridge)

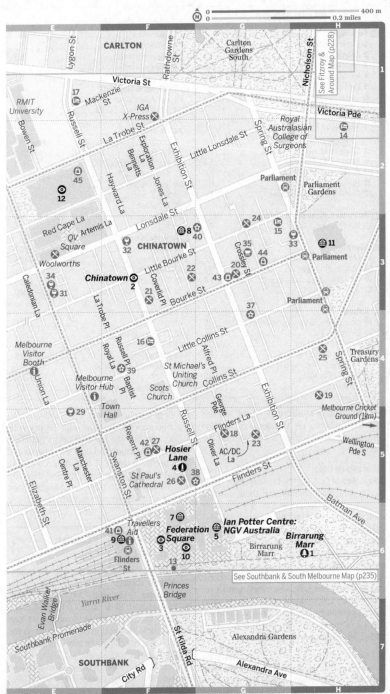

0   400 m
0   0.2 miles

N

MELBOURNE & COASTAL VICTORIA

CARLTON

Carlton
Gardens
South

See Fitzroy &
Around Map (p228)

Lygon St

Rathdowne St

Nicholson St

Victoria St

Victoria Pde

14

*RMIT
University*

17

Mackenzie
St

Russell St

IGA
X-Press

La Trobe St

Little Lonsdale St

Spring St

*Royal
Australasian
College of
Surgeons*

Bowen St

Exploration
La

Bennetts
La

Jones La

Exhibition St

Parliament

*Parliament
Gardens*

45

12

Red Cape La

*QV
Square*

Artemis La

Lonsdale St

8
40

24

15

33

11

32

CHINATOWN

35

44

Parliament

Woolworths

Little Bourke St

20

Crossley St

34

Chinatown
2

Coverlid Pl

21

22

43

31

La Trobe Pl

Bourke St

37

Parliament

16

Little Collins St

Alfred Pl

25

*Treasury
Gardens*

Royal La

39

Baptist
Pl

*St Michael's
Uniting
Church*

Collins St

Spring St

*Melbourne
Visitor
Booth*

Union La

Scots
Church

George
Pde

Exhibition St

19

*Melbourne Cricket
Ground (1km)*

*Melbourne
Visitor Hub*

*Town
Hall*

29

Flinders La

Wellington
Pde S

Regent Pl

42 27

**Hosier
Lane**

18

23

AC/DC
La

Batman Ave

Manchester
La

Centre Pl

Swanston St

4

St Paul's
Cathedral

26

38

Oliver La

Flinders St

Russell St

Elizabeth St

7

*Ian Potter Centre:
NGV Australia*

**Birrarung
Marr**

41

*Travellers
Aid*

**Federation
Square**

5

*Birrarung
Marr*

1

9

3

10

Flinders
St

13

See Southbank & South Melbourne Map (p235)

Yarra River

*Princes
Bridge*

Evan Walker
Bridge

Alexandra Gardens

Southbank Promenade

SOUTHBANK

City Rd

St Kilda Rd

Alexandra Ave

Central Melbourne

the lively **South Melbourne Night Market** runs until 9.30pm on Wednesdays. It's also home to a cooking school. See the website for details.

Albert Park Lake   LAKE
(btwn Lakeside Dr & Aughtie Dr, Albert Park; ⊟12, 96) Elegant black swans give their inimitable bottoms-up salute as you jog, cycle or walk the 5km perimeter of this artificial lake. Lakeside Dr was used as an international motor-racing circuit in the 1950s, and since 1996 the revamped track has been the venue for the **Australian Formula 1 Grand Prix** (☑1800 100 030, 03-9258 7100; www.grandprix. com.au; Albert Park Lake, Albert Park; general admission from $30; ⊘Mar) every March. Also on the periphery is the Melbourne Sports & Aquatic Centre, with an Olympic-size pool and child-delighting wave machine.

Starward Distillery   DISTILLERY
(www.starward.com.au; 50 Bertie St, Port Melbourne; tours $15; ⊘3-8pm Wed, to 9pm Thu, noon-10pm Fri & Sat, to 8pm Sun; ⊟235, ⊟109) This sleek distillery-warehouse-bar is massive, with a public area up the front and copper stills at the rear. Sample the Distillery's Selection flight ($15) or enjoy cocktails over cheese and charcuterie. Tours ($15 including two 15mL pours) run on Friday evenings and throughout the day on Saturday and Sunday. Book via the website, where you can also lock in masterclasses.

South Yarra, Prahran & Windsor

★**Royal Botanic Gardens**   GARDENS
(Melbourne Gardens; ☑03-9252 2300; www. rbg.vic.gov.au; Birdwood Ave, South Yarra; ⊘7.30am-sunset; ⓟⓠ; ⊟1, 3, 5, 6, 16, 64, 67, 72) **FREE** From the air, these stunning, 38-hectare gardens suggest a set of giant green lungs in the middle of the city. Drawing over two million visitors annually, it's considered one of the finest examples of Victorian-era landscaping in the world. Here you'll find global plantings and a range of Australian

flora. Mini ecosystems, a herb garden and an indigenous rainforest are set amid vast, picnic-friendly lawns and black-swan-spotted ponds. Be sure to book the Aboriginal Heritage Walk (p221).

⭐ **Shrine of Remembrance**   MONUMENT
(📞03-9661 8100; www.shrine.org.au; Birdwood Ave, South Yarra; ⊙10am-5pm, last entry 4.30pm; 🚊3, 5, 6, 16, 64, 67, 72) FREE One of Melbourne's icons, the Shrine of Remembrance is a commanding memorial to Victorians who have served in war and peacekeeping, especially those killed in WWI. Built between 1928 and 1934, much of it with Depression-relief, or 'susso' (sustenance) labour, its stoic, classical design is partly based on the Mausoleum of Halicarnassus, one of the seven ancient wonders of the world. The shrine's upper balcony affords epic panoramic views of Melbourne's skyline and all the way up tram-studded Swanston St.

⭐ **Justin Art House Museum**   GALLERY
(JAHM; 📞0411 158 967, 0403 052 641; www.jahm.com.au; 3 Lumley Ct, Prahran; $25; 🚊5, 6, 64) The geometric, zinc-clad home of Melbourne art collectors Charles and Leah Justin doubles as the Justin Art House Museum. Book ahead for a tour of the couple's dynamic collection of contemporary art, consisting of more than 300 pieces amassed over four decades. There's a strong emphasis on video and digital art, with the works rotated regularly. Guided tours take around two hours (check online for tour availability). The house was designed by the couple's daughter, Elisa.

👁 **St Kilda**

St Kilda is Melbourne's tattered bohemian heart, long featured in songs, plays, novels, film and TV. Originally a 19th-century seaside resort, it's also served as a post-war Jewish enclave, red-light district and punk-rocker hub. It's a complex jumble of boom-era Victorian mansions, raffish Spanish Moorish apartments, seedy side streets and a vintage roller coaster.

⭐ **St Kilda Foreshore**   BEACH
(Jacka Blvd, St Kilda; 🚻👶; 🚊3, 12, 16, 96) FREE Despite the palm-fringed promenades and golden stretch of sand, St Kilda's seaside appeal is more Brighton, England, than Venice Beach, California – with the exception of the regular rollerbladers. There's a kiosk at the

end of **St Kilda Pier** (🚻; 🚊3, 12, 16, 96) that offers a knockout panorama of Melbourne's skyline.

During summer, **Port Phillip EcoCentre** (📞03-9534 0670; www.ecocentre.com; 55a Blessington St, St Kilda; ⊙9am-5pm Mon-Fri; 🚊3, 16, 67, 78, 79, 96) 🌱 runs a range of tours including urban wildlife walks and coastal discovery walks, and offers information on a little-penguin colony that lives in the breakwater behind the pier's kiosk.

Luna Park   AMUSEMENT PARK
(📞03-9525 5033; www.lunapark.com.au; 18 Lower Esplanade, St Kilda; single ride adult/child $11/10, unlimited rides $50/40; ⊙hours vary; 🚻; 🚊3, 16, 96) Luna Park opened in 1912 and still has an old-style amusement-park feel, with creepy Mr Moon's gaping mouth swallowing you up as you enter. There's a heritage-listed wooden roller coaster, the oldest of its kind in the world, which stayed open during WWI when the rest of the park was closed; a beautiful baroque carousel with hand-painted horses, swans and chariots; and the full complement of gut-churning rides, with something for all ages and levels of adrenaline-seeker.

🏃 **Activities**

⭐ **Kayak Melbourne**   KAYAKING
(📞0418 106 427; www.kayakmelbourne.com.au; tours $82-110; 🚻; 🚊11, 48) City Sights tours (1¾ hours) paddle past Southbank to Docklands, while two-hour River to Sky tours include entry to the Eureka Skydeck (p211). Start your day sun-saluting on a two-hour Yoga Sunrise tour or end it with a 2½-hour Moonlight tour (which starts at 912 Collins St, Docklands). Most tours start here at Boathouse Dr, across the Yarra River from Federation Sq.

Fitzroy Swimming Pool   SWIMMING
(📞03-9205 5522; https://leisure.yarracity.vic.gov.au; 160 Alexandra Pde, Fitzroy; adult/child/under 5yr $7.10/3.60/free; ⊙6am-8pm Mon-Fri, 8am-6pm Sat & Sun; 🚻; 🚊11) Between laps in the heated, 50m outdoor pool, locals love catching a few rays up in the bleachers or on the lawn at this local favourite; there's also a toddler pool.

Melbourne Sports & Aquatic Centre   SWIMMING
(MSAC; 📞03-9926 1555; www.melbournesportscentres.com.au; 30 Aughtie Dr, Albert Park; adult/child from $8.50/5.80; ⊙5.30am-10pm Mon-Fri, 7am-8pm Sat & Sun; 🚻; 🚊96, 112) Flanking Albert Park Lake, Melbourne's premier

South Yarra, Prahran & Windsor

Ⓝ 0   500 m
0   0.25 miles

South Yarra, Prahran & Windsor

aquatic centre was a venue for the 2006 Commonwealth Games. Facilities include indoor and outdoor 50m pools, an indoor 25m pool, sauna and steam room, and spacious common areas. Kids will love SplashOUT, with inflatables, a wave pool, waterslide and more (adult/child $10.20/7.10). Childcare is available.

Kite Republic KITESURFING
(☑ 03-9537 0644; www.kiterepublic.com.au; St Kilda Sea Baths, 4/10-18 Jacka Blvd, St Kilda; 1hr lesson kitesurfing/SUP $95/85; ⊙ 10am-6pm Mon-Fri, 9.30am-5pm Sat & Sun; 📮 96) Offers kiteboarding lessons, tours and equipment, and is a good source of info. Most people opt for a two-hour kitesurfing lesson for $185. Also rents out stand-up paddleboards (SUPs) for $25 per hour.

🚶 Tours

Aboriginal Cultural Heritage Walk WALKING
(☑ 03-9252 2429; www.rbg.vic.gov.au; Royal Botanic Gardens, Birdwood Ave, South Yarra; adult/child $35/12; ⊙ tours from 11am Sun-Fri; 📮 3, 5, 6, 8, 16, 64, 67, 72) 🌿 The Royal Botanic Gardens (p218) is a significant cultural site for the Kulin people. This 90-minute walk starts with a smoking ceremony (don't take photos without asking) and continues with a leisurely, informative stroll led by an Aboriginal guide. Learn about traditional uses for plants and animals, before finishing with a lemon myrtle tea. Not suitable for wheelchairs.

Melbourne Street Art Tours TOURS
(☑ 03-9328 5556; www.melbournestreettours.com; tours adult/child $69/34.50; ⊙ city centre 1.30pm Tue, Thu & Sat, Fitzroy 11am Sat) Three-hour tours exploring the street art that makes Melbourne's laneways and buildings famous. Tours take place either in the city

centre or Fitzroy – meet out the front of ACMI (p209) or **Easey's** (☑ 03-9417 2250; www.easeys.com.au; 3/48 Easey St, Collingwood; burgers $13-20; ⊙ 11am-10pm Sun-Thu, to 11pm Fri & Sat; 🚻; 📮 86) respectively – and the guides are street artists themselves, so you'll leave with a much better insight into this art form.

Rentabike CYCLING
(☑ 0417 339 203, 03-9654 2762; www.rentabike.net.au; Vault 14, Federation Wharf, Federation Sq, Melbourne; rental per hour/day $15/35, 4hr tour incl lunch adult/child $120/89; ⊙ 10am-5pm; 🚻; 📮 Flinders St) 🚲 Renting out bikes for more than 40 years, this outfit also runs **Real Melbourne Bike Tours**, offering a local's insight into the city with a foodie focus. Tours max out at eight people. Electric bikes are also available.

🎉 Festivals & Events

Australian Open SPORTS
(www.ausopen.com; Melbourne Park, Olympic Blvd, Melbourne; ⊙ Jan; 🚻; 📮 70, 📮 Richmond) The world's top tennis players and huge, merry-making crowds descend on Melbourne Park for Australia's Grand Slam tennis championship. Along with the tennis, check out the AO Live Stage at Birrarung Marr (p209) for international music acts, the mini theme park for kids and dining options from local restaurants that improve each year.

★ **Melbourne Food & Wine Festival** FOOD & DRINK
(www.melbournefoodandwine.com.au; ⊙ Mar) Foodies travel to Melbourne especially for this festival, which celebrates the world-class food and wine scene with more than 200 events. From the sell-out 'World's Longest Lunch' – served on a 500m-long table that snakes through a different area each year – to international Michelin-starred chefs taking over

restaurants, masterclasses and free events, there's something for every gastronome.

Melbourne International Film Festival FILM
(MIFF; www.miff.com.au; ⏰ Aug) Midwinter movie love-in that brings out local cinephiles in droves, featuring dramas, comedies, documentaries, animation, shorts and more.

AFL Grand Final SPORTS
(www.afl.com.au; MCG, Brunton Ave, East Melbourne; ⏰ Sep) It's easier to kick a goal from the boundary line than to pick up sought-after tickets to the Aussie Rules Grand Final, usually held on the final Saturday in September – but it's not hard to get your share of finals fever anywhere in Melbourne.

Melbourne Cup SPORTS
(www.springracingcarnival.com.au; Flemington Racecourse; ⏰ Nov) Culminating in the prestigious Melbourne Cup, the Spring Racing Carnival is as much a social event as a sporting one. Melbourne Cup Day, held on the first Tuesday in November, is a Victorian public holiday. Expect to see Melburnians frocked up in their finest during the horse races – before getting frocked up at bars around town later on.

In recent years the Melbourne Cup has come under heated criticism for animal cruelty – in the 2018–19 season 122 horses were euthanised on Australian racetracks due to injury – as well as for contributing to the larger national issues of irresponsible alcohol consumption and gambling addiction, leading many Australians to protest the event via the 'Say Nup to the Cup' campaign.

🛏 Sleeping

◉ City Centre

Space Hotel HOSTEL $
(📞 03-9662 3888; www.spacehotel.com.au; 380 Russell St; dm from $37, r with/without bathroom from $130/89; ❄ 🛜; Ⓡ Melbourne Central) This sleek place walks the line between hostel and budget hotel. Private rooms have iPod docks and flat-screen TVs, while dorms have touches like large lockers with sensor lights and lockable adapters. Some doubles have en suites and balconies. The rooftop hot tub and free St Kilda shuttle (summer only) are big ticks. Book direct to avoid wi-fi fees.

Mansion Melbourne HOSTEL $
(📞 03-9663 4212; www.themansionmelbourne. com.au; 80 Victoria Pde, East Melbourne; dm/r from $30/110; ❄ 🛜; Ⓡ Parliament) Located within a castle-like former Salvation Army building with grand double staircases, this two-storey, 86-bed hostel has genuine character. A recent renovation has spruced things up – besides new paint and carpeting, there are privacy curtains, lights and powerpoints for every bed, plus two private rooms, two female dorms, laundry machines and a TV room. Some rooms have air-con. No lift.

★ **Ovolo Laneways** BOUTIQUE HOTEL $$$
(📞 03-8692 0777; www.ovolohotels.com.au; 19 Little Bourke St, Melbourne; r from $275; ❄ 🛜; Ⓡ Parliament) This 43-room boutique hotel has a cool city vibe. It's friendly, fun and loaded with goodies – on the free list are self-service laundry, minibar, a Nespresso machine and candy bar in the lobby and, for direct bookings, happy-hour booze and breakfast. Suites are more impressive than studios; all have Amazon's Alexa. We love the personalised welcome messages and treats.

★ **QT Melbourne** HOTEL $$$
(📞 03-8636 8800; www.qtmelbourne.com.au; 133 Russell St, Melbourne; r from $350; ❄ @ 🛜; 🚋 86, 96) Arty vibes, industrial surfaces, brass trim, lifts with tapestry light boxes that spurt random utterances in a Russian accent – this is one of Melbourne's quirkiest and best boutique hotels. The 188 rooms are beautifully kitted out – a contrast of concrete and soft, colourful fabrics – and there's a guide to the artwork in the building. Don't miss the gorgeous rooftop (⏰ noon-midnight Mon-Fri, from 2pm Sat & Sun; 🚋 86, 96) bar.

◉ Southbank

Pan Pacific Melbourne HOTEL $$$
(📞 03-9027 2000, 1800 049 610; www.panpacific.com; 2 Convention Centre Pl, South Wharf; r from $259; 🅿 ❄ @ 🛜; 🚋 35, 70, 75) Polished wood and natural fibres provide an earthy feel in this luxurious hotel. Suites are huge and some offer dazzling views across Melbourne. Red Desert Dreamings Gallery, an independent Aboriginal art gallery, is on the 4th floor, with art for sale. On the ground floor is a restaurant, cafe and an impressive artwork (made from scourers) depicting a coral reef.

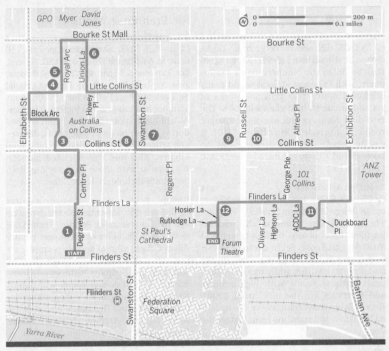

City Walk
Arcades & Laneways

START DEGRAVES ST
END RUTLEDGE LANE
LENGTH 3KM; 2½ HOURS

Central Melbourne is a warren of 19th-century arcades and gritty-turned-hip cobbled bluestone laneways featuring street art, basement restaurants, boutiques and bars.

Start on ① **Degraves St**, an archetypal Melbourne lane lined with shops and cafes. Grab a coffee at Cup of Truth, then continue north, crossing over Flinders Lane to cafe-filled ② **Centre Pl**, good for spotting street art.

Cross Collins St and enter ③ **Block Arcade**. Built in 1892 and featuring ornate plasterwork and mosaic floors, it's based on Milan's Galleria Vittorio Emanuele II arcade. Ogle the window display at the Hopetoun Tea Rooms, then continue through the arcade, turning left and exiting right onto Elizabeth St.

Walk to Little Collins St and turn right. Stop for an afternoon tipple at pocket-sized ④ **Chuckle Park** (or a coffee further down at Sensory Lab), before turning left into wonderfully ornate ⑤ **Royal Arcade**; look out for Gog and Magog, hammering away under the dome. Wander through to Bourke St Mall, then turn right and continue until you find street-art-covered ⑥ **Union Lane** on the right.

Follow Union Lane south to the end, turn left onto Little Collins St, then right on Swanston St. Walk past ⑦ **Melbourne Town Hall** (it's across the road) and pop into the 1932 ⑧ **Manchester Unity Building** to snoop around its impressive foyer, then cross Swanston St and head uphill to the 'Paris End' of Collins St. You'll pass the 1873 Gothic ⑨ **Scots Church** (the first Presbyterian church in Victoria) and the 1866 ⑩ **St Michael's Uniting Church**, built in an unusual Lombardic Romanesque style.

Turn right into Exhibition St, then right into Flinders Lane, and continue to ⑪ **Duckboard Pl**. Head down the laneway and admire the street art, horseshoeing around AC/DC Lane. Keep heading west on Flinders Lane to the street-art meccas of ⑫ **Hosier Lane** (p209) and Rutledge Lane before finishing with tapas and a hard-earned drink at MoVida or adjoining Bar Tini.

Fitzroy

Nunnery
HOSTEL $

(☑ 1800 032 635; www.nunnery.com.au; 116 Nicholson St; dm/s/d from $36/95/130; 🛜; 🚌96) Built in 1888, the Nunnery oozes atmosphere, with sweeping staircases and many original features plus religious works of art and ornate stained-glass windows. The next-door Nunnery Guesthouse has larger rooms in a private setting (from $140). It can be popular with long-term guests, so book ahead. All rates include breakfast. Free bike hire.

Brooklyn Arts Hotel
B&B $

(☑ 03-9419 9328; www.brooklynartshotel.com. au; 48 George St; s/d from $115/155; 🛜; 🚌86) There are seven rooms in this character-filled hotel owned by film-maker and artist Maggie Fooke. Set in a terrace house, rooms vary in size but all are clean, quirky and decorated with worldly treasures. Spacious upstairs rooms with high ceilings and balconies are the pick (from $200). Expect lively conversation over the included breakfast and attention from Badger the dog.

★Tyrian
Serviced Apartments
APARTMENT $$

(☑ 03-9415 1900; www.tyrian.com.au; 91 Johnston St; apt from $209; 🅿🛜; 🚌11) Big couches and balconies add to the appeal of these spacious, self-contained serviced apartments, while plenty of restaurants and bars are right at your door. It's rounded off with free wi-fi and parking. Rooms facing Johnston St can get noisy, but room 301 has an especially huge balcony with city views.

South Melbourne

★Coppersmith
BOUTIQUE HOTEL $$

(☑ 03-8696 7777; www.coppersmithhotel.com.au; 435 Clarendon St; r from $235; 🛜; 🚌12) Low-key, contemporary and elegant, 15-room Coppersmith has every right to call itself a boutique property. Designer furniture, heavenly beds and fine woollen rugs set a seductive tone in minimalist rooms, each with Nespresso machine, work desk, free wi-fi, recordable cable TV and a minibar customisable to your dietary requirements. There's also a smart bistro-bar and rooftop deck with skyline views.

Prahran & Windsor

Back of Chapel
HOSTEL $

(☑ 03-9521 5338; www.backofchapel.com; 50 Green St, Windsor; dm $26-36, d $60-80; ⊙ reception 9am-noon & 3-5pm; 🛜; 🚌6, 78, 🚆Windsor) Just 20 steps from the cool end of Chapel St, Back of Chapel offers budget-conscious slumber in a 150-year old Victorian terrace. A laid-back spot with four- and six-bed dorms, it also offers private twins, doubles and triples. Facilities include a communal kitchen, BBQ and coin-operated laundry. It's popular with those on a working holiday. Rates include basic breakfast.

Cullen
BOUTIQUE HOTEL $$

(☑ 03-9098 1555; www.artserieshotels.com.au/cullen; 164 Commercial Rd, Prahran; r from $239; ❄🛜; 🚌72, 78, 🚆Prahran) Grunge painter Adam Cullen's vibrant and often graphic art provides such visions as Ned Kelly shooting you from the bedroom-bathroom dividers. Rooms are stylish and comfy with handy kitchenettes, but you can order room service from HuTong and Gramercy Social downstairs. Standard studios are small. Rooms facing north and west from level four up offer the best views.

St Kilda

★Base Backpackers
HOSTEL $

(☑ 03-8598 6200; www.stayatbase.com; 17 Carlisle St, St Kilda; dm/d from $30/100; ❄🛜; 🚌3, 16, 96) This place has streamlined dorms with en suites and slick doubles, and one floor of women-only dorms, although cleanliness can be an issue. There's a free breakfast and a bar hosting nightly events (eg Boozy Bingo) and live music. Ask about free walking tours. Buy a pint on Friday to score a free steak. The party vibe may torment light sleepers.

Hotel Tolarno
HOTEL $

(☑ 03-9537 0200; www.tolarnohotel.com.au; 42 Fitzroy St, St Kilda; s/d/ste from $130/160/200; ❄@🛜; 🚌3, 12, 16, 96) Once home to the namesake gallery of a local bohemian couple – art dealer Georges Mora and his painter wife Mirka – the Tolarno features eclectically furnished rooms, with good beds, bold artwork, Nespresso machines and free wi-fi. (Note that the 'small' rooms are *quite* small.) Front-facing rooms have balconies but can get a bit noisy. The bar-bistro features occasional live music.

St Kilda & Around

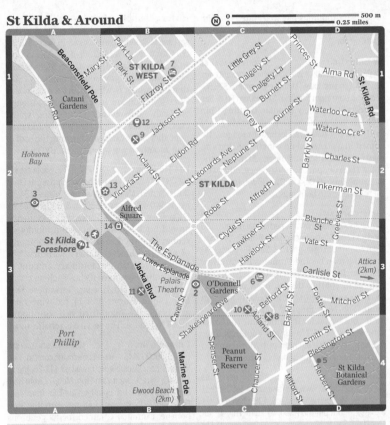

N 0 ————— 500 m
0 ————— 0.25 miles

MELBOURNE & COASTAL VICTORIA MELBOURNE

St Kilda & Around

 Eating

◉ City Centre

★ Hakata Gensuke — RAMEN $

(☑ 03-9663 6342; www.gensuke.com.au; 168 Russell St, Melbourne; ramen $15-16; ⊘ 11.30am-10pm Mon-Thu, to 1am Fri, noon-1am Sat, to 10pm Sun; ☒ Parliament) The original of four locations, Gensuke only does one thing and does it extraordinarily well: *tonkotsu* (pork broth) ramen. Choose from four types – 'signature', garlic and sesame-infused 'black' broth, spicy 'god fire' or the lighter *shio* – and then order extra toppings like marinated *cha shu* pork, egg, seaweed and black fungus. Worth queuing for.

★ Chin Chin   SOUTHEAST ASIAN $$

(✆ 03-8663 2000; www.chinchinrestaurant.com.au; 125 Flinders Lane, Melbourne; mains $25.50-37.50; ⊙ 11am-11pm Sun-Thu, to 11.30pm Fri & Sat; ☒ Flinders St) Insanely popular, bustling Chin Chin serves Southeast Asian hawker-style food with big flavours, designed to share. It's housed in a glammed-up warehouse that's all marble, white tiles and neon. Arrive on the dot at 11am or 5pm to avoid queues, otherwise kill some time at Go Go Bar downstairs until there's space. No bookings.

Supernormal   ASIAN $$

(✆ 03-9650 8688; www.supernormal.net.au; 180 Flinders Lane, Melbourne; dishes $16-43; ⊙ 11am-11pm Sun-Thu, to midnight Fri & Sat; ☒ Flinders St) From the man behind Cumulus Inc, Andrew McConnell, comes this creative selection of pan-Asian sharing dishes, from dumplings to raw seafood to slow-cooked Sichuan lamb. The New England lobster roll is famous, but we prefer the lunchtime *tonkatsu* sandwich special. No dinner bookings after 5.30pm, so arrive early to put your name on the list. Look for the neon cherries.

Mamasita   MEXICAN $$

(✆ 03-9650 3821; www.mamasita.com.au; 1st fl, 11 Collins St, Melbourne; 2 tacos $14-18, shared plates $25-39; ⊙ 5-10pm Mon-Wed, to 11pm Thu, 12.30-11pm Fri & Sat, to 10pm Sun; ✍; ☒ Parliament) Up a staircase above a 7-Eleven is the restaurant responsible for kicking off Melbourne's obsession with Mexican food. Mamasita remains one of the city's best. Chargrilled corn sprinkled with cheese and chipotle mayo is a legendary starter and there's a fantastic range of corn-tortilla tacos. Instead of a sommelier, there's a *mezcalier*. Vegan and gluten-free options are available. Bookings recommended.

MoVida   TAPAS $$

(✆ 03-9663 3038; www.movida.com.au; 1 Hosier Lane, Melbourne; tapas $4.80-9.50, raciones $13-38; ⊙ noon-10pm Sun-Wed, to 10.30pm Thu-Sat; ☒ Flinders St) MoVida's location in graffitied Hosier Lane is about as Melbourne as it gets. Line up by the bar, cluster around little window tables or, if you've booked, take a seat in the dining area for Spanish tapas and *raciones*. MoVida Next Door – yes, right next door – and newer Bar Tini are the perfect places for pre-show drinks and tapas.

HuTong Dumpling Bar   CHINESE $$

(✆ 03-9650 8128; www.hutong.com.au; 14-16 Market Lane, Melbourne; dumplings $8-15, mains $16-39; ⊙ 11.30am-3pm & 5.30-10.30pm Sun-Thu, to 11pm Fri & Sat; ☒ Parliament) Are these Melbourne's best *xiao long bao* (soup dumplings)? We think so, which is why getting a seat in this three-level building isn't always easy, though you can book ahead. Downstairs, watch chefs make the delicate dumplings, and then hope they don't catch you burning the roof of your mouth as you inhale them. BYO wine.

Lee Ho Fook   CHINESE $$$

(✆ 03-9077 6261; www.leehofook.com.au; 1st fl, 11 Duckboard Pl, Melbourne; sharing plates $24-30, mains $40-45; ⊙ noon-2.30pm & 6-10pm Tue-Fri, 6-10pm Sat & Sun; ☒ Parliament) Occupying an old brick warehouse down a fabulously scungy laneway, Lee Ho Fook is the epitome of modern Chinese culinary wizardry. The kitchen packs an extraordinary amount of flavour into signature dishes such as crispy eggplant with red vinegar, 'Taiwanese beer hall' clams, Wagyu beef in red-wine miso and crab-and-scallop fried rice with homemade XO sauce. The service is terrific, too.

Cumulus Inc   MODERN AUSTRALIAN $$$

(✆ 03-9650 1445; www.cumulusinc.com.au; 45 Flinders Lane, Melbourne; breakfast $12-26, mains $28-48; ⊙ restaurant 7am-11pm Mon-Fri, from 8am Sat & Sun, wine bar 5pm-late Tue-Thu, from 4pm Fri & Sat; ☒ Parliament) Quintessentially Melbourne, Cumulus is famed for its generous slow-roast lamb shoulder. It's all about beautiful produce and artful cooking here, served at the long marble bar and little round tables. Reservations are for groups only. The wine bar upstairs, Cumulus Up, is worth a visit as well – peruse the veritable tome of a wine list and order duck waffles.

Longrain   THAI $$$

(✆ 03-9653 1600; www.longrain.com; 40-44 Little Bourke St, Melbourne; share plates $25-38; ⊙ 6pm-late Mon-Thu, from 5.30pm Fri, from 5pm Sat & Sun; ☒ Parliament) Get in early or expect a long wait – upstairs, Longsong (✆ 03-9653 1611; www.longsong.com.au; 1st fl, 44 Little Bourke St, Melbourne; ⊙ 5pm-late Tue, from 4.30pm Wed-Sat; ☒ Parliament) is a beautiful holding space – before sampling this delicious Thai cuisine. Communal tables are great for checking out everyone else's meals. Dishes are designed to share; try the pork-belly-filled eggnet and whole fried fish, sweet and spicy with tamarind, chilli and lime.

Vue de Monde   MODERN AUSTRALIAN **$$$**
(📞 03-9691 3888; www.vuedemonde.com.au; 55th
fl, Rialto, 525 Collins St, Melbourne; set menu $275-
310; ⊘ reservations from noon-1pm & 6-8.45pm
Thu-Sun, 6-9pm Mon-Wed; 🚇 Southern Cross)
Surveying the world from the old observa-
tion deck of the Rialto tower, Melbourne's
favoured spot for occasion dining has views
to match its storied reputation. Wunder-
kind chef Hugh Allen recently took over the
reins from original visionary Shannon Ben-
nett, but rest assured you'll still be treated
to sophisticated and theatrical set menus
showcasing the very best Australian ingre-
dients. Book months ahead.

Grossi Florentino   ITALIAN **$$$**
(📞 03-9662 1811; www.grossiflorentino.com; 1st
fl, 80 Bourke St, Melbourne; 2-course lunch $65,
3-course dinner $150, degustation $180; ⊘ noon-
3pm & 6-10pm Mon-Fri, 6pm-late Sat; 🚇 Parliament) Celebrating its 90 years in 2018, Grossi
is an Italian institution. Gilded plasterwork,
chandeliers and 1930s Florentine Renaissance murals engender a heady sense of
occasion. Decadent set menus are accompanied by exquisite canapés and bread, and
the service is extremely slick. The **Grill** and
Cellar Bar below are more affordable and
rustic (but still fabulous), with street tables
perfect for people-watching.

◉ Southbank

Crown has done a solid job of luring people
into its casino complex by installing both
famous Australian and international restaurateurs in glamorous riverside venues (ever
heard of Nobu?). While prices are steep, quality is high – unlike many restaurants in this
touristy stretch. Newer additions, including
a locally famed pizzeria, Argentine grill and
spice-fuelled Thai restaurant, have somewhat
upped the ante. South Wharf has a couple of
good dining options at the river's edge that are
especially atmospheric when the sun is out.

Spice Temple   CHINESE **$$$**
(📞 03-8679 1888; www.spicetemple.com.au;
Crown, Yarra Promenade, Southbank; mains $45-
60, yum cha lunch banquet from $59; ⊘ 6-11pm
Mon-Wed, noon-3pm & 6-11pm Thu-Sun; 📶; 🚋 55)
When he's not at **Rockpool** (📞 03-8648
1900; www.rockpoolbarandgrill.com.au; Crown,
Yarra Promenade, Southbank; mains $39-58,
grill $54-150, bar mains $29-39; ⊘ noon-3pm &
6-11pm Sun-Fri, 6-11pm Sat; 🚋 55) or in one of
his Sydney restaurants, chef Neil Perry pays

homage to the spicy cuisines of China's cen-
tral provinces on the waterfront (hot dishes
are printed in red on the menu). By day you
can gaze at the river while tucking into a
yum cha banquet. By night, descend to the
atmospheric, darkened tabernacle beneath.

◉ Richmond

★**Minamishima**   JAPANESE **$$$**
(📞 03-9429 5180; www.minamishima.com.au; 4
Lord St, Richmond; per person $225; ⊘ 6-10pm
Tue-Sat; 🚋 48, 75) Arguably Australia's best
Japanese restaurant – if you care to empty
your pockets and book two months in advance. It's hidden down a side street; the
best seats are at the bar, where sushi master
Koichi Minamishima prepares seafood with
surgical precision and serves it one piece at
a time. Sake or wine pairings available for an
additional $125 per head.

◉ Fitzroy & Collingwood

★**Lune Croissanterie**   BAKERY **$**
(📞 03-9419 2320; www.lunecroissanterie.com; 119
Rose St, Fitzroy; pastries $5.90-13.50; ⊘ 7.30am-3pm
Mon-Fri, 8am-3pm Sat & Sun; 🚋 11) Good things
come to those who queue, and here they
come in the form of unrivalled pastries, from
innovative cruffins to plain croissants often
dubbed the world's best. In the centre of this
warehouse space is a glass, climate-controlled
cube where the magic happens. Book well in
advance for the Lune Lab experience, an innovative three-course pastry flight ($65).

Smith & Deli   DELI, VEGAN **$**
(📞 03-9042 4117; www.smithanddeli.com;
111 Moor St, Fitzroy; sandwiches $12-16; ⊘ 8am-
6pm Tue-Sat; 📶; 🚋 11) A stylish deli with a
full-vegan twist, this spin-off from the popular **Smith & Daughters** (📞 03-9939 3293;
www.smithanddaughters.com; 175 Brunswick St,
Fitzroy; brunch $16-22, dinner $22-27; ⊘ 6pm-late
Mon-Fri, 10am-late Sat,10am-3pm Sun; 📶; 🚋 11)
restaurant creates the closest thing vegetarians will get to meat – it's been known to
fool carnivores. Takeaway sandwiches are
filled with all the (mock) favourites; try the
deliciously filling 'Rubenstein' loaded with
'pastrami', sauerkraut and pickles, or choose
the memorable 'Club Sandwiches Not Seals'.

Gelato Messina   GELATO **$**
(www.gelatomessina.com; 237 Smith St, Fitzroy;
1 scoop $5.30; ⊘ noon-10.30pm Sun-Thu, noon-
11.30pm Fri & Sat; 🚋 86) Messina is hyped as

Fitzroy & Around

Northcote
(2km)

FITZROY NORTH

Alexandra Pde (Eastern Fwy)

Queens Pde

CLIFTON HILL

Princes St

Nicholson St

Station St

Kay St

CARLTON

Cecil St

Westgarth St

Leicester St

Rose St

Kerr St

Spring St

Argyle St

Johnston St

Elgin St

See Carlton Map (p238)

Fitzroy St

Brunswick St

Young St

Napier St

George St

Gore St

Smith St

Emma St

Cecil St

Westgarth St

Rose St

25

10

24

4

19

Victoria St

Mahoney St

Bell St

Nicholson St

John St

Fitzroy St

Brunswick St

11

Kent St

15

Kerr St

Argyle St

Johnston St

Chapel St

FITZROY

Greeves St

St David St

12

Keele St

Easey St

17

Sackville St

Perry St

Otter St

Young St

Moor St

King William St

13

3

Hanover St

Little Hanover St

Palmer St

Royal La

18

7

Gertrude St

14

George St

Gore St

Hodgson St

9

Moor St

Condell St

Atherton Reserve

Charles St

Little Charles St

Napier St

Webb St

Smith St

Stanley St

20

Little Oxford St

Oxford St

Bedford St

Peel St

See Central Melbourne Map (p216)

Fitzroy St

Brunswick St

Young St

Little Napier St

Napier St

Little George St

Little Gore St

Little Smith St

26

5

16

Gertrude St

23

Langridge St

Derby St

George St

2

Gore St

Little Smith St

Smith St

Victoria Pde

Victoria Pde

Little Victoria St

Mason St

Cambridge St

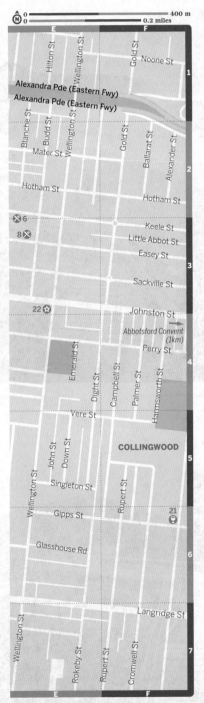

Fitzroy & Around

🏃 Activities, Courses & Tours
1 Fitzroy Swimming Pool C1

🛏 Sleeping
2 Brooklyn Arts Hotel C7
3 Nunnery A5
4 Tyrian Serviced Apartments B3

🍴 Eating
5 Charcoal Lane B6
6 CIBI E3
7 Cutler & Co A6
8 Easey's E3
9 Gelato Messina D5
10 Industry Beans B2
11 Lune Croissanterie C2
12 Red Sparrow D2
13 Smith & Daughters B5
14 Smith & Deli B4

🍸 Drinking & Nightlife
15 Black Pearl B3
16 Everleigh C6
17 Everyday Coffee D3
18 Marion A6
19 Naked for Satan B3
20 Proud Mary D5
21 Stomping Ground Brewery &
   Beer Hall F6

🎭 Entertainment
22 The Tote E3

🛍 Shopping
23 Crumpler D6
24 Hares & Hyenas B3
25 Rose St Artists' Market B2
26 Third Drawer Down C6

Melbourne's best ice creamery, and while purists might gawk at specials like peanut butter gelato with white-chocolate-covered potato chips, its popularity is evident in the queues of people, irrespective of the weather. You can watch the ice-cream makers at work through glass windows inside.

CIBI JAPANESE $
(☑ 03-9077 3941; www.cibi.com.au; 33 Keele St, Collingwood; dishes $14-21.50; ⏰ 7.30am-5pm Mon-Fri, 8am-5pm Sat & Sun; ☑; ☐ 86) It's ironic that 'Cibi' translates to 'little one' in Japanese given this incredibly aesthetically pleasing and zen cafe has expanded into a massive, airy warehouse. Along with having a traditional Japanese breakfasts you can browse the adjoining plant nursery and shop that stocks beautifully made products, from Japanese knives and sake sets to selected pantry items and vases.

MELBOURNE & COASTAL VICTORIA MELBOURNE

1. Smashed avocado and poached eggs
Melbourne has an abundance of cafes serving fresh, modern and healthy food (p225).

2. Surfing on Bells Beach, Victoria
Home of Australlalia's premier surfing (p254) event, the Bell's Classsic, since 1973.

3. State Library of Victoria, Melbourne
The Latrobe Reading Room is the centrepiece of this library, at the forefront of Melbourne's literary scene.(p210).

4. Cape Schanck (p273), Mornington Peninsula
A famous boardwalk leads to a majestic working lighthouse.

Red Sparrow
PIZZA, VEGAN $$

(☑03-9417 1454; www.redsparrowpizza.com; 406 Smith St, Collingwood; pizza $18-23; ⊙5-10pm Tue-Fri, noon-10pm Sat, 5-9pm Sun; ☑; ☐86) This cool all-vegan pizzeria with matte black walls breaking into bare brick serves a range of tasty vegan-cheese pizzas ranging from a spicy Puttanesca to 'sausage' with jalapeños. There are dessert pizzas too, interesting sides such as 'Buffalo Chicken' drumsticks, and a good drinks list including cocktails. A second branch is at 260 Chapel St, Prahran.

Charcoal Lane
MODERN AUSTRALIAN $$

(☑03-9418 3400; www.charcoallane.com.au; 136 Gertrude St, Fitzroy; mains $28-36; ⊙noon-3pm & 6-9pm Tue-Sat; ☐86, 11) 🍴 Housed in a former bluestone bank, this training restaurant for Indigenous and disadvantaged young people is one of the best places to try native flora and fauna; menu items may include chargrilled kangaroo sirloin or roasted emu crépinette. The chef's tasting plate for two ($30) is a great place to start. Weekend bookings advised, especially since Prince Harry and Meghan Markle dined here.

★Cutler & Co
MODERN AUSTRALIAN $$$

(☑03-9419 4888; www.cutlerandco.com.au; 55-57 Gertrude St, Fitzroy; mains $46-58; ⊙5-11pm Tue-Sat, noon-11pm Sun; ☐86) Hyped for all the right reasons, this is Andrew McConnell's flagship Melbourne restaurant and its attentive, informed staff and joy-inducing dishes make it one of Melbourne's top places for fine dining. The menu incorporates the best seasonal produce across the à la carte offering, degustation menu (from $170), and casual Sunday lunch designed for sharing ($85).

◉ Carlton & Brunswick

D.O.C. Espresso
ITALIAN $$

(☑03-9347 8482; www.docgroup.net; 326 Lygon St, Carlton; dishes $9-27; ⊙7am-9.30pm Mon-Sat, 8am-9.30pm Sun; ☐200, 207, ☐1, 3, 5, 6, 16, 64, 67, 72) Run by third-generation Italian Australians, D.O.C. is one of the best casual Italian options at the Carlton end of Lygon St. The espresso bar specialises in homemade pasta and sells microbrewery beers from Italy. During *aperitivo* (4pm to 7pm), you can enjoy a complimentary nibble board with your negroni.

Rumi
MIDDLE EASTERN $$

(☑03-9388 8255; www.rumirestaurant.com.au; 116 Lygon St, Brunswick East; mains $10.50-29; ⊙6-10pm; ☐1, 6) A well-considered place that mixes traditional Lebanese cooking

with contemporary interpretations of old Persian dishes. The *sigara boregi* (cheese and pinenut pastries) are a local institution, and generous mains from the charcoal BBQ are balanced by an interesting selection of vegetable dishes.

★King and Godfree
DELI, ITALIAN $$

(☑03-9347 1619; www.kingandgodfree.com.au; 293 Lygon St, Carlton; dishes $12-38; ⊙rooftop & restaurant noon-late, deli 9am-6pm, espresso bar 8am-late; ☐200, 207, ☐1, 6) It took three years to transform King and Godfree, an Italian grocer since 1884, into this multi-venue wonder. There's **Johnny's Green Room**, with 360-degree rooftop views and a glitterati cocktail vibe; a deli with cold cuts, cheese and food to take away; **Agostino** wine bar and restaurant; and the all-day espresso bar for coffee, panini, pasta or a negroni or two.

◉ South Melbourne

St Ali
CAFE $$

(☑03-9132 8960; www.stali.com.au; 12-18 Yarra Pl, South Melbourne; mains $18-25; ⊙7am-6pm; ☎; ☐12) The coffee is guaranteed to be good at this hideaway warehouse-conversion cafe. If you can't decide between house blend, speciality, black or white, there's a six-coffee tasting flight ($20). The food menu covers all bases with creativity, from secret-recipe corn fritters with poached eggs, halloumi and sweetcorn salsa to pancakes stuffed with banana jam, whipped cream and white caramel sauce.

Simply Spanish
SPANISH $$

(☑03-9682 6100; www.simplyspanish.com.au; South Melbourne Market, cnr Coventry & Cecil Sts, South Melbourne; tapas $9-18, paellas $17-25; ⊙8.30am-8.30pm Wed, 10am-8.30pm Thu, 8am-9pm Fri & Sat, 8am-4pm Sun; ☑; ☐12, 96) When a Melbourne restaurant repeatedly wins the title of 'Best Paella Outside of Spain' in Valencia, you know you're on to a good thing. This casual eatery is *the* place for paella, available here in classic and numerous other styles: smoked pork and mushroom, baked snapper, chicken and chorizo – there's even a vegan version. The tapas, however, can be hit-and-miss.

Bellota Wine Bar
ITALIAN $$

(☑03-9078 8381; www.bellota.com.au; 181 Bank St, South Melbourne; starters $15-24, mains $31-38; ⊙11am-11pm Tue-Sat; ☎; ☐1, 12) This handsome wine bar and bistro is an extension of adjoining **Prince Wine Store**, with an ever-changing wine list and seasonally driven dishes to match. Whether dining at the bar or at one of the intimate back tables (the latter require bookings), expect to swoon over dishes like green olive and mozzarella arancini and confit duck with *spaetzle* and mushrooms.

South Yarra & Prahran

⭐ Maker & Monger   CHEESE $
(📞0413 900 490; www.makerandmonger.com.au; Prahran Market; toasted sandwiches $14-16; ⏰7am-5pm Tue & Thu-Sat, 8am-3pm Sun; 🚋72, 78, 🚉Prahran) What was a small cart now has a shop complete with 40 seats, neon, pretty sage-colour tiling and Savignac-inspired posters. This cheap-eats favourite continues to sell *raclette* in winter and blow-torched reuben sandwiches oozing with cheese year-round, but now also makes cheese on-site. Try the luxurious *fontin bleu* for breakfast.

Matilda 159   AUSTRALIAN $$$
(📞03-9089 6668; www.matilda159.com; 159 Domain Rd, South Yarra; starters $24-36, mains $38-49; ⏰noon-3pm & 6-10pm; 🚋58) Across from the Royal Botanic Gardens (p218) and beneath United Places (📞03-9866 6467; www.unitedplaces.com.au), this classy restaurant focuses on cooking over flames, be it whole tiger flathead or Wagyu beef with smoked bone marrow. Starters steal the spotlight, especially spanner crab with prawn butter served in its shell. With glass cabinets containing seasonal botanic installations, plus smooth surfaces and slick service, this is what Australian fine dining looks like.

St Kilda

Monarch Cake Shop   DESSERTS $
(📞03-9534 2972; www.monarchcakes.com.au; 103 Acland St, St Kilda; slice of cake from $5; ⏰8am-9pm; 🚋96) Family-owned Monarch is a favourite among St Kilda's Eastern European cake shops and its *kugelhopf* (chocolate marble cake), plum cake and Polish baked cheesecake can't be beaten. In business since 1934, the shop hasn't changed much, with a soft, old-time atmosphere and wonderful, buttery aroma – not to mention framed snaps of local football players and film stars who've visited.

⭐ Stokehouse   SEAFOOD $$$
(📞03-9525 5555; www.stokehouse.com.au; upstairs, 30 Jacka Blvd, St Kilda; mains $38-54; ⏰dining room noon-3pm & 6-9.30pm, bar noon-midnight; 🚋3a, 16, 96) Striking contemporary architecture and floor-to-ceiling bay views set the tone at Stokehouse, a top draw for its waterside setting and modern, seafood-centric dishes (plus its devilishly good bombe: strawberry sorbet, white chocolate and toasted meringue). It's one of Melbourne's most-loved occasion restaurants, so book ahead. For a cheaper view, watch the sunset from adjoining Stokebar with a cocktail and snacks.

Lau's Family Kitchen   CHINESE $$$
(📞03-8598 9880; www.lauskitchen.com.au; 4 Acland St, St Kilda; mains $29-66; ⏰noon-3pm & 6-10pm Mon-Fri, 6-10pm Sat, 12.30-3.30pm & 6-10pm Sun; 🚋16, 96) This polished spot with service to match offers beautiful, home-style Cantonese with a few Sichuan surprises. Start with delicate dumplings and spanner crab and sweet corn soup, then order one of Melbourne's best *ma po* tofu dishes with minced pork and steamed rice. Reserve ahead and check out the elegant wall panels, made from 1930s kimonos.

Cicciolina   ITALIAN $$$
(📞03-9525 3333; www.cicciolinastkilda.com.au; 130 Acland St, St Kilda; mains lunch $18.50-29.50, dinner $27.50-48.50; ⏰restaurant noon-10pm Sun-Thu, to 11pm Fri & Sat, back bar from 5pm; 🚋3, 16, 96) This hideaway of dark wood, subdued lighting and pencil sketches is a St Kilda institution. The menu is Italian, with dishes that might see signature linguini twirled with Atlantic salmon, braised leek, capers, baby spinach, lemon and olive oil. Bookings for lunch only; for dinner eat early or start in the moody back bar, worth a visit on its own.

🍸 Drinking & Nightlife

Melbourne's drinking scene is easily the best in Australia and is a major player on the world stage. There's a huge diversity of venues, from basement dives hidden down laneways and award-winning cocktail lounges to rooftop wine bars and urban breweries and distilleries. Many pubs have pulled up beer-stained carpet and polished the concrete, but don't dismiss the character-filled oldies.

City Centre

⭐ Bar Americano   COCKTAIL BAR
(www.baramericano.com.au; 20 Presgrave Pl; ⏰4-10.30pm Mon, to 11pm Tue & Wed, to midnight Thu, to 1am Fri & Sat; 🚉Flinders St) A hidden laneway bar off Howey Pl, Bar Americano is a teensy standing-room-only affair with black-and-white chequered floors complemented by subway-tiled walls and a subtle speakeasy air.

Once the 14-person max is hit, the door grille gets pulled shut. The cocktails here don't come cheap, but they are classic and superb – try their Negroni. Credit cards only.

★ Siglo
ROOFTOP BAR

(☑ 03-9654 6631; 2nd fl, 161 Spring St, Melbourne; ☺ 5pm-3am; ꤪ Parliament) Siglo's sought-after terrace comes with Parisian flair, wafting cigar smoke and serious drinks. It fills with suits on Friday night, but any time is good to mull over a classic cocktail and admire the 19th-century vista of Parliament and St Patrick's Cathedral. Refined bar snacks are available. Enter via the unsigned door of **Melbourne Supper Club** (☑ 03-9654 6300; www.melbournesupperclub.com. au; 1st fl, 161 Spring St, Melbourne; ☺ 5pm-4am Sun-Thu, to 6am Fri & Sat; ꤪ Parliament).

★ Whitehart
BAR

(☑ 03-9602 2260; www.whitehartbar.com.au; 22 Whitehart Lane, Melbourne; ☺ noon-11pm Sun-Wed, to midnight Thu, to 1am Fri & Sat; ⛟ 19, ꤪ Melbourne Central) At the end of a laneway is this two-storey container bar festooned with giant staghead ferns and graceful palms. Grab a local beer on tap and head upstairs for alfresco drinking, or stay downstairs under cover in Melbourne's notoriously changeable weather. DJs spin most nights, and a rotating cast of food trucks feeds the crowds. Unsurprisingly, it's packed on weekend nights.

★ Heartbreaker
BAR

(☑ 03-9041 0856; www.heartbreakerbar.com.au; 234a Russell St; ☺ 3pm-3am Mon-Thu, from noon Fri & Sat, noon-1am Sun; ꤪ Melbourne Central) Black walls, ripped leather banquettes, skeleton beer-tap handles and a rockin' jukebox offer a nice change from too-slick CBD bars. The tough-looking sweethearts behind the bar offer craft beer and a big selection of bourbon, as well as pre-made artisanal cocktails in wee bottles. Order **Connie's Pizza** slices from the bar and pick up behind the pool table.

Cookie
BAR

(☑ 03-9663 7660; www.cookie.net.au; 1st fl, Curtin House, 252 Swanston St; ☺ noon-midnight Sun-Thu, to 1am Fri & Sat; ꤪ Melbourne Central) Part bar, part Thai restaurant, this kooky-cool venue with grand bones is one of the more enduring rites of passage of the Melbourne night. The bar is unbelievably well stocked with fine whiskies, wines and almost 200 craft beers, with over two dozen on tap. The staff also know how to make a serious cocktail.

Rooftop Bar
ROOFTOP BAR

(☑ 03-9654 5394; www.rooftopbar.co; 7th fl, Curtin House, 252 Swanston St, Melbourne; ☺ noon-1am Apr-Nov, from 11am Dec-Mar; ꤪ Melbourne Central) This alfresco bar sits atop happening Curtin House. From December to March there are daily DJs, and it transforms into an outdoor night-time cinema with striped deckchairs and a calendar of new and classic favourite flicks. Hit up the burger shack, order a cocktail jug and make some new friends.

⦿ Southbank

Ponyfish Island
BAR

(www.ponyfish.com.au; Southbank Pedestrian Bridge, Southbank; ☺ 11am-late; ꤪ Flinders St) Not content with hiding bars down laneways or on rooftops, Melburnians are finding ever more creative spots to do their drinking. Where better than mid-river, atop the pylon of a bridge arcing over the Yarra? It's a surprisingly good spot to knock back beers while snacking on beer-friendly Mexican food. It packs out in good weather.

⦿ Fitzroy & Collingwood

★ Black Pearl
COCKTAIL BAR

(☑ 03-9417 0455; www.blackpearlbar.com.au; 304 Brunswick St, Fitzroy; ☺ 5pm-3am, Attic Bar 7pm-1am Thu, 7pm-3am Fri & Sat; ⛟ 11) After more than 15 years in the game, Black Pearl goes from strength to strength, winning awards and receiving global accolades. Low lighting, leather banquettes and candles set the mood downstairs. Prop at the bar to study the extensive cocktail list or let the expert bartenders concoct something to your tastes. Upstairs is table-service **Attic Bar**; book ahead.

★ Naked for Satan
BAR

(☑ 03-9416 2238; www.nakedforsatan.com.au; 285 Brunswick St, Fitzroy; ☺ noon-late; ⛟ 11) Reviving an apparent Brunswick St legend (a man nicknamed Satan who would get naked because of the heat of his illegal vodka distillery), this place is packed with travellers vying for a seat on the roof terrace with wrap-around balcony, **Naked in the Sky**. The downstairs bar has a simple menu of inexpensive snacks such as oysters ($2.50 each) and sliders ($5 to $6).

★ Proud Mary
CAFE

(☑ 03-9417 5930; www.proudmarycoffee.com.au; 172 Oxford St, Collingwood; ☺ 7am-4pm Mon-Fri, 8am-4pm Sat & Sun; 🛜; ⛟ 86) A champion of direct-trade, single-origin coffee, this industrial

Southbank & South Melbourne

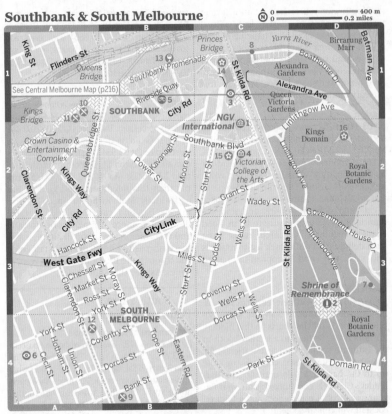

Southbank & South Melbourne

red-brick space takes its caffeine seriously. It's consistently packed, not only for its excellent brews but also for top-notch food, such as soft-shell-crab burger, and hotcakes with lemon curd and white chocolate.

**Stomping Ground
Brewery & Beer Hall** BREWERY
(☏ 03-9415 1944; www.stompingground.beer; 100 Gipps St, Collingwood; ⏲11.30am-11pm Sun-Thu, 11.30am-1am Fri & Sat; ☜; ℝ Collingwood) This

inviting brewery–beer hall set in a former textile factory is a relaxed, leafy retreat with exposed-brick walls, hanging plants, a kids' play area (featuring a cubby) and a large central bar. There's a 30-tap bar with rotating guest beers and a menu of wood-fired pizzas and share dishes. There are free brewery tours at noon on weekends.

Marion   WINE BAR
(☑ 03-9419 6262; www.marionwine.com.au; 53 Gertrude St, Fitzroy; dishes $12-39; ⊙ 5-11pm Mon-Thu, noon-11pm Fri, 11am-11pm Sat & Sun; ☐ 86) Melbourne's poster-boy chef, Andrew McConnell, knew what he was doing when he opened Marion. The wine list is one of the area's most impressive and the space – catering to both stop-ins and long romantic chats – is a pleasure to be in. Food changes regularly, but might range from such delights as confit duck leg to mussels and salsa roja, and European-influenced specials.

Everleigh   COCKTAIL BAR
(☑ 03-9416 2229; www.theeverleigh.com; upstairs, 150 Gertrude St, Fitzroy; ⊙ 5pm-1am; ☐ 86) Sophistication is off the charts at this hidden, upstairs nook. Settle into a leather booth in the intimate setting with a few friends for conversation and classic cocktails, or sidle up to the bar for a solo martini. The Bartender's Choice is encouraged: state your flavour and alcohol preferences and a tailored cocktail will appear soon after.

Everyday Coffee   COFFEE
(www.everyday-coffee.com; 36 Sackville St, Collingwood; ⊙ 7am-4pm Mon-Sat, 8am-4pm Sun; ☐ 86) You'll never guess how many days of the year Everyday is open... It's set in a brick warehouse with bench seating and stools out the front; come here for one of Collingwood's best cups of joe – the cold versions are divine during summer. Also has stores in the city, Carlton and Northcote.

◉ Carlton

Seven Seeds   CAFE
(☑ 03-9347 8664; www.sevenseeds.com.au; 114 Berkeley St, Carlton; dishes $12-22; ⊙ 7am-5pm Mon-Sat, 8am-5pm Sun; ☐ 19, 58, 59) This inconspicuous warehouse cafe a little north of Queen Victoria Market (p209) has plenty of room to store your bike and sip a splendid coffee with something from the all-day menu. On Wednesdays at 8am you can join a cupping session ($5). It also owns Traveller (www.

sevenseeds.com.au; 2/14 Crossley St; bagels from $7; ⊙ 7am-5pm Mon-Fri; ☐ 86, 96) and Brother Baba Budan (☑ 03-9347 8664; www.sevenseeds. com.au; 359 Little Bourke St, Melbourne; ⊙ 7am-5pm Mon-Thu, 7am-7pm Fri & Sat, 8am-5pm Sun; ☐ 19, 57, 59, ☐ Melbourne Central) in the CBD.

Carlton Wine Room   WINE BAR
(☑ 03-9347 2626; www.thecarltonwineroom. com.au; 172 Faraday St, Carlton; ⊙ 4-11pm Tue & Wed, noon-11pm Thu-Mon; ☐ 200, 207, ☐ 1, 6) There's no better place for a pre- or post-Nova (☑ 03-9347 5331; www.cinemanova. com.au; 380 Lygon St, Carlton; adult/student/ child $21/16/13; ☐; ☐ 200, 207, ☐ 1, 6) tipple than this neighbourhood gem. It has a distinctly Melbourne-European vibe: a marble bar and raised communal table downstairs, more dining space upstairs and food ranging from small share dishes to a daily pasta. Knowledgeable staff guide you through the 100-bottle list and reserve wines. Ask for the 'staff choice'.

◉ South Yarra, Prahran & Windsor

★ Leonard's House of Love   BAR
(☑ 0428 066 778; www.leonardshouseoflove.com. au; 3 Wilson St, South Yarra; ⊙ noon-1am Sun-Thu, noon-3am Fri & Sat; ☐; ☐ 58, 72, 78) Inside what appears to be someone's '70s love-shack party house you'll find this American bar touting 'free love and cold beer'. The menu is mostly burgers, fried chicken and loaded fries, which can be scoffed outside when warm or by the fire when chilly. Challenge a stranger to a game of pool and try the house Bathtub Lager.

Woods of Windsor   BAR
(☑ 03-9077 4407; www.thewoodsofwindsor.com; 108 Chapel St, Windsor; ⊙ 5pm-1am Mon-Thu, 4pm-1am Fri & Sat, 4-11.30pm Sun; ☐ 5, 6, 64, 78, ☐ Windsor) Dark timber, kooky taxidermy and a speakeasy vibe make the Woods a suitable place to hide on those brooding, rainy Melbourne nights. Bunker down for a standout selection of whiskies, or ditch them altogether for the whimsical cocktail menu, including an alcoholic pot of tea for two.

Market Lane Coffee   CAFE
(☑ 03-9804 7434; www.marketlane.com.au; Shop 13, Prahran Market, 163 Commercial Rd, South Yarra; ⊙ 7am-4pm Mon & Wed, 7am-5pm Tue & Thu-Sat, 8am-5pm Sun; ☐ 72, 78, ☐ Prahran) The first Market Lane speciality coffee shop and roastery hides at the back of Prahran Market. The beans here are strictly seasonal,

producing cups of coffee that are beautifully nuanced and best paired with a scrumptious pastry. There's only whole, organic milk or nothing here. On weekends the cafe serves locally famous mushroom burgers.

Revolver Upstairs CLUB
(☑ 03-9521 5985; www.revolverupstairs.com.au; 229 Chapel St, Prahran; ☉ 5pm-4am Tue & Wed, 5pm-6am Thu, 5pm Fri-noon Sat, 5pm Sat-9am Mon; ☐ 6, 78, ☑ Prahran) Rowdy Revolver – or 'Revs', if you're local – can feel like an enormous version of your lounge room. But with nonstop music come the weekend and the ability to party for 24 hours straight, you're probably glad it's not. Live music, art exhibitions and interesting local, national and international DJs and bands keep the mixed crowd wide awake.

◉ St Kilda

★ Bar Di Stasio WINE BAR
(☑ 03-9525 3999; www.distasio.com.au; 31 Fitzroy St; ☉ 11am-11pm; ☐ 3, 12. 16, 96) Within red Pompidou-style scaffolding – the work of artist Callum Morton – lies this buzzing, sophisticated spot, dominated by a grand marble bar and plaster-chipped walls behind lit glass. Waiters seemingly plucked from Venice's Caffè Florian mix perfect spritzes while dishing out bites, from lightly fried local seafood to elegant pastas (available till close). Book ahead; it's extremely popular.

★ Pontoon BAR
(☑ 03-9525 5445; www.pontoonstkildabeach.com. au; 30 Jacka Blvd, St Kilda; ☉ noon-late; ☐ 3, 16, 96) Beneath fine-diner Stokehouse (p233) is its casual, buzzing bar-bistro, a light-soaked space with floor-to-ceiling windows and a deck over the beach, looking out to the sunset. Shared-plates deliver some decent bites, including pizzas, grain salads and the namesake cheeseburger (mains $16 to $32). Slip on the shades and sip craft suds or a local prosecco.

☆ Entertainment

Cinemas

★ Moonlight Cinema CINEMA
(www.moonlight.com.au; Gate D, Royal Botanic Gardens, Birdwood Ave, South Yarra; adult/family $20/65; ☉ Nov-Mar; ☐ 3, 5, 6, 16, 64, 67, 72) Melbourne's original outdoor cinema hits the Royal Botanic Gardens (p218) from the end of November through March, screening current releases and retro classics. Bring a

WORTH A TRIP

ATTICA

Attica (☑ 03-9530 0111; www.attica.com. au; 74 Glen Eira Rd, Ripponlea; tasting menu $295; ☉ 6pm-late Tue-Sat; ☐ 67, ☑ Ripponlea) is Australia's only restaurant on San Pellegrino's World's Top 50 Restaurants list. Ben Shewry creates contemporary dishes with native ingredients, like saltwater crocodile rib glazed with spiced honey, and dessert served in emu eggs. It's even more popular since starring in Netflix's *Chef's Table;* reservations are taken on the first Wednesday of the month for the next three months.

picnic hamper and booze, or buy some from cashless operators at the venue.

Astor CINEMA
(☑ 03-9510 1414; www.astortheatre.net.au; cnr Chapel St & Dandenong Rd, St Kilda; tickets $15-18.50; ☐ 5, 64, 78, ☑ Windsor) This 1936 art deco darling has had more ups and downs than a fading Hollywood star. Saved from permanent closure, it's one of Melbourne's best-loved landmarks, with double features many nights and a mix of recent releases, art-house films and cult classics. Discount tickets ($15) are available Monday and Thursday. Look out for movie marathon events, some lasting 24 hours.

Live Music
Check daily papers and street magazines **Beat** (www.beat.com.au) and **The Music** (www.themusic.com.au) for gig info. Radio station **3RRR** (102.7FM; www.rrr.org.au) covers local music and features a gig guide on their website.

★ Esplanade Hotel LIVE MUSIC
(☑ 03-9534 0211; www.hotelesplanade.com.au; 11 The Esplanade, St Kilda; ☉ noon-late; ☐ 16, 96) You could spend all day going from room to room now that the beloved 'Espy' is back, after a $15 million renovation. Antiques complement its Victorian bones and there's live music on three stages – best is the famed **Gershwin Room** – plus a dozen bars, including the **Ghost of Alfred Felton**. For eats there's **Espy Kitchen** and modern Cantonese restaurant **Mya Tiger**.

★ The Tote LIVE MUSIC
(☑ 03-9419 5320; www.thetotehotel.com; cnr Johnston & Wellington Sts, Collingwood; ☉ 4pm-

MELBOURNE & COASTAL VICTORIA MELBOURNE

Carlton

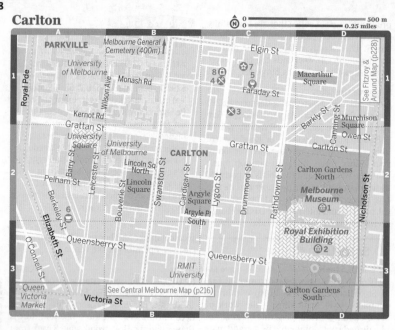

Carlton

⊙ Top Sights

⊗ Eating

⊙ Drinking & Nightlife

⊙ Entertainment

⊙ Shopping

1am Wed, 4pm-3am Thu-Sat, 4-11pm Sun; ☒86)
One of Melbourne's most iconic live-music
venues, this divey pub has been hosting a
roster of local and international punk, heavy
metal and hardcore bands since the '80s. It
has one of the best jukeboxes in the universe
and its temporary closure in 2010 saw people fiercely protest against the liquor-licens-
ing laws that were blamed for the closure.

Cherry LIVE MUSIC
(www.cherrybar.com.au; 68 Little Collins St, Melbourne; ⊙5pm-3am Wed & Sun, to 5am Thu, to 7am
Fri & Sat; ☒Parliament) In 2019 Melbourne's
most legendary live-rock bar had to vacate
its divey AC/DC Lane basement, ending
up a few blocks away in this heritage-listed
19th-century building, with a ground-floor
bar and dedicated band room upstairs.
Thursday is Soul Night, weekends see local

and international bands playing at 2am (the
party doesn't stop until breakfast-time) and
Sunday has free live blues acts.

Forum CONCERT VENUE
(☒1300 111 011; www.forummelbourne.com.au; 154
Flinders St, Melbourne; ☒Flinders St) One of the
city's most atmospheric live-music venues,
the Forum does double duty as a cinema
during the Melbourne International Film
Festival (p222). The striking Moorish exterior (an over-the-top fantasia with minarets,
domes and dragons) houses an equally interesting interior, with the southern night
sky rendered prettily on the domed ceiling.

Corner LIVE MUSIC
(☒03-9427 7300; www.cornerhotel.com; 57 Swan
St, Richmond; ⊙4pm-late Mon, noon-late Tue-Thu
& Sun, to 3am Fri & Sat; ☎; ☒70, ☒Richmond)

LGBTIQ+ MELBOURNE

Melbourne has a large LGBTIQ+ population – second in Australia only to Sydney – and it's generally a very accepting city. While there's still a handful of specifically gay venues scattered around the city, some of the best hang-outs are weekly takeovers of mainstream bars. The big event on the calendar is the annual **Midsumma Festival** (www.midsumma.org.au; ☺ Jan-Feb). It has a diverse program of cultural, community and sporting events, including the popular Midsumma Carnival at Alexandra Gardens, St Kilda's Pride March and much more. The **Melbourne Queer Film Festival** (www.mqff.com.au; ☺ Mar), Australia's largest, screens more than 100 films from around the world.

For more local info, pick up a copy of free magazine *Star Observer* (www.starobserver.com.au) from queer community bookshop Hares & Hyenas (p240), or music venues and some libraries (check online for distribution), or digitally subscribe to LOTL (formerly Lesbians on the Loose, www.lotl.com). LGBTIQ+ radio station JOY 94.9FM (www.joy.org.au) is another important resource for visitors and locals, as are the new Victorian Pride Centre (www.pridecentre.org.au), Gay & Lesbian Tourism Australia (www.visitgayaustralia.com.au), *DNA* magazine (www.dnamagazine.com.au) and Thorne Harbour Health (www.thorneharbour.org).

The band room here is one of Melbourne's most popular midsize venues. It's seen plenty of action over the years, from Dinosaur Jr to the Buzzcocks. If your ears need a break, there's a friendly front bar. The rooftop has city views but gets packed with a different crowd from the music fans below.

Theatre & Arts

Melbourne Theatre Company THEATRE
(MTC; ☎ 03-8688 0800; www.mtc.com.au; 140 Southbank Blvd, Southbank; ☺ box office 9am-5pm or start of evening performance Mon-Sat, 2hr prior to performance Sun; ⬚1) Founded in 1953, MTC is the oldest professional theatre company in Australia. It stages up to a dozen productions each year, ranging from contemporary (including many new Australian works) to Shakespeare and other classics. Performances take place in its award-winning Southbank Theatre, a striking black building enclosed within angular white tubing.

Classical Music

Melbourne Symphony Orchestra LIVE PERFORMANCE
(MSO; ☎ 03-9929 9600; www.mso.com.au; Hamer Hall, 100 St Kilda Rd, Southbank; ☺ box office 10am-6pm Mon-Fri; ⬚Flinders St) The MSO has a broad reach: while not afraid to be populist (it's done sell-out performances with Burt Bacharach and Kiss), it usually performs classical symphonic master works. It plays regularly at its Hamer Hall (☎1300 182 183; www.artscentremelbourne.com.au; 100 St Kilda Rd, Southbank; ☺ box office 10am-5.45pm; ⬚1, 3, 6, 16, 64, 67, 72, ⬚Flinders St) home, but also has a popular summer

series of free concerts at the **Sidney Myer Music Bowl** (☎13 61 00; www.artscentremelbourne.com.au; Kings Domain, 21 Linlithgow Ave, Southbank; ⬚3, 5, 6, 8, 16, 64, 67, 72) (BYO picnic).

Dance

Australian Ballet BALLET
(☎1300 369 741; www.australianballet.com.au; Level 6, 2 Kavanagh St, Southbank; ☺ box office 10am-4pm Mon-Fri; ⬚1) More than 50 years old, Melbourne-based Australian Ballet performs traditional and new works in the **Arts Centre** (☎03-9281 8000, tickets 1300 182 183; www.artscentremelbourne.com.au; 100 St Kilda Rd, Southbank; ☺ box office Theatres Building 9am-8.30pm Mon-Sat, 10am-5pm Sun, box office Hamer Hall 10am-5.45pm; ⬚Flinders St) and around the country. Take an hour-long Primrose Potter Australian Ballet Centre tour ($29) that includes a visit to the wardrobe department and dancer studios, or a two-hour production centre tour through a treasure trove of costumes, sets and props ($160). Bookings essential.

🔒 Shopping

◎ City Centre

★ **Craft Victoria** ARTS & CRAFTS
(☎03-9650 7775; www.craft.org.au; off Flinders Lane, Melbourne; ☺11am-6pm Mon-Wed, to 7pm Thu & Fri, 10am-5pm Sat; ⬚Flinders St) This retail arm of Craft Victoria showcases goods handmade exclusively by Victorian artists and artisans. Its range of jewellery, textiles, accessories, glass and ceramics bridges the art/craft divide and makes for some wonderful Melbourne mementos.

MELBOURNE & COASTAL VICTORIA MELBOURNE

TICKETS

Tickets for concerts, theatre, comedy, sports and other events are usually available from one of the following agencies:

Halftix (www.halftixmelbourne.com; 208 Little Collins St, Melbourne; ⊙10am-2pm Mon, 11am-6pm Tue-Thu, to 6.30pm Fri, 10am-4pm Sat; ⊠ Flinders St) Discounted theatre tickets are sold on the day of performance.

Moshtix (www.moshtix.com.au)

Ticketek (☑13 28 49; www.ticketek.com.au; 252 Exhibition St; ⊙9am-5pm Mon-Fri, 10am-2pm Sat)

Ticketmaster (☑13 61 00; www.ticketmaster.com.au; Forum, 150-152 Flinders St; ⊙9am-6pm Mon-Fri)

There are also a few galleries with changing exhibitions; admission is free. Pop in for a guide to the **Craft Cubed Festival** in August.

★**Melbournalia** GIFTS & SOUVENIRS
(☑03-9663 3751; www.melbournalia.com.au; Shop 5/50 Bourke St; ⊙10am-6pm Mon & Tue, to 7pm Wed-Fri, 11am-6pm Sat & Sun; ⊠Parliament) This bright corner shop is the place to stock up on singular souvenirs from more than a hundred local designers – prints featuring city icons, tram socks, native Aussie-inspired earrings and great books on Melbourne, as well as maps, guides, soaps, scents, gift cards, postcards and more. The friendly staff can help ship items home. Extended December hours.

Hill of Content BOOKS
(☑03-9662 9472; www.hillofcontentbookshop.com; 86 Bourke St, Melbourne; ⊙9am-6pm Mon-Thu, to 8pm Fri, 10am-6pm Sat, 11am-5pm Sun; ⊠Parliament) Melbourne's oldest bookshop (established 1922) has a large range of general titles and an extensive stock of books on art, classics and poetry.

Original & Authentic Aboriginal Art ART
(☑03-9663 5133; www.authaboriginalart.com.au; 90 Bourke St, Melbourne; ⊙10am-6pm Mon-Sat, 11am-5pm Sun; ⊠Parliament) For more than 20 years this centrally located gallery has sourced traditional and contemporary Indigenous art from the Central and Western Deserts, the Kimberley and Arnhem Land.

It subscribes to the City of Melbourne's code of practice for Indigenous art, ensuring authenticity and ethical dealings with artists.

City Hatters HATS
(☑03-9614 3294; www.cityhatters.com.au; 211 Flinders St; ⊙9am-6pm Mon-Fri, to 5pm Sat, 10am-4pm Sun; ⊠Flinders St) Located beside the main entrance to Flinders St Station, this evocatively old-fashioned men's hat shop is the most convenient place to purchase an iconic Akubra hat, a kangaroo-leather sun hat or something a little more unique.

◉ Fitzroy

★**Third Drawer Down** HOMEWARES
(☑03-9534 4088; www.thirddrawerdown.com; 93 George St, Fitzroy; ⊙10am-6pm; ☒86) This 'museum of art souvenirs' stocks both beautiful and absurdist pieces with a sense of humour, many of which are collaborations with well-known designers and artists. Giant burger-shaped stools sit next to ceramic plates, silk scarves and squeezy stress bananas.

Rose St Artists' Market MARKET
(☑03-9419 5529; www.rosestmarket.com.au; 60 Rose St, Fitzroy; ⊙10am-4pm Sat & Sun; ☒11) One of Melbourne's most popular art-and-craft markets showcases the best of local designers. Here you'll find up to 120 creatives selling jewellery, clothing, ceramics and iconic Melbourne screen prints. Nearby you can find local produce from **Fitzroy Mills Market** (9am to 2pm Saturday) or head to **Industry Beans** (☑03-9417 1034; www.industrybeans.com; 3/62 Rose St, Fitzroy; mains $12-25; ⊙7am-4pm Mon-Fri, from 8am Sat & Sun; ☎; ☒11, 96) around the corner for a coffee fix.

Hares & Hyenas BOOKS
(☑03-9495 6589; www.hares-hyenas.com.au; 63 Johnston St; ⊙9am-6.30pm Mon-Fri, 10am-6.30pm Sat, 11.30am-6.30pm Sun; ☒11, 96) Serving the LGBT+ community for three decades, this bookshop stocks a huge range of gay-friendly and gender-diverse books (fiction and non-fiction), along with magazines, DVDs and other items sourced from around the world. It also has its own live performance space, **The Hare Hole**, with regular gigs.

Crumpler FASHION & ACCESSORIES
(☑03-9417 5338; www.crumpler.com; 87 Smith St, Fitzroy; ⊙10am-6pm Mon-Sat, 10am-5pm

Sun; 🚲86) Crumpler's bike-courier bags – designed by two former couriers looking for a bag they could hold their beer in while cycling home – are what started it all. The brand's durable, practical designs now extend to bags for cameras, laptops and tablets, and can be found around the world. The original messenger bags start at around $150.

◉ Carlton & Brunswick

Readings   BOOKS
(📞03-9347 6633; www.readings.com.au; 309 Lygon St, Carlton; ⊘9am-11pm Mon-Sat, 10am-9pm Sun; 👶; 🚌200, 207, 🚊1, 6) A wander around this defiantly prosperous indie bookshop can occupy an entire afternoon, if you're so inclined. There's a dangerously loaded (and good-value) specials table and switched-on, helpful staff. Just next door is its specialty children's bookshop.

◉ Prahran & Windsor

Chapel Street Bazaar   VINTAGE
(📞03-9529 1727; www.facebook.com/Chapel StreetBazaar; 217 Chapel St, Prahran; ⊘10am-6pm; 🚊6, 78, 🚉Prahran) This old arcade is a sprawling, retro-obsessive riot and the closest thing you'll find to Aladdin's 'Cave of Wonders'. There are trinkets, jewellery and treasures, but you can also pick up everything from modernist furniture and classic Hollywood posters to Noddy eggcups, vintage clothing, cameras, vinyl and old toys. Prepare to lose track of time.

Design a Space   CLOTHING
(📞03-9510 0144; www.designaspace.com.au; 142 Chapel St, Windsor; ⊘noon-5pm Mon, 10am-6pm Tue-Sat, noon-4pm Sun; 🚊78, 🚉Windsor) You know the envy you feel when someone tells you they bought an incredible item of clothing overseas? Your payback is now at this colourful, quirky and unique fashion shop. Around 60 up-and-coming independent Australian designers have their own section selling clothing, jewellery and accessories.

Greville Records   MUSIC
(📞03-9510 3012; www.grevillerecords.com.au; 152 Greville St, Prahran; ⊘10am-6pm Mon-Thu & Sat, 10am-7pm Fri, 11am-5pm Sun; 🚊6, 72, 78, 🚉Prahran) One of the last bastions of the 'old' Greville St, this banging music shop from 1979 has such a loyal following that Neil Young invited the owners on stage during a

Melbourne concert. The forte here is vinyl, with no shortage of eclectic and limited-edition discs (a super-limited Bob Dylan *Live in Sydney 1966* double vinyl has been discovered here).

◉ St Kilda

St Kilda Esplanade Market   MARKET
(www.stkildaesplanademarket.com.au; Esplanade, St Kilda; ⊘10am-4pm Sun May-Sep, to 5pm Oct-Apr; 🚊3, 12, 16, 96) Fancy a shop by the seaside? Take a stroll along St Kilda's Esplanade, where a kilometre of local makers' trestle tables join end to end every Sunday. Pick up everything from ceramics, sculpture, glassware and woodwork to photographic prints, organic soaps, jewellery and tongue-in-cheek tea towels.

ⓘ Information

DANGERS & ANNOYANCES

Melbourne is a safe city, but as is the case anywhere, common sense goes a long way.
➡ There are occasional reports of alcohol-fuelled violence in the city centre late at night, particularly on King St. Steer clear of the heavily intoxicated and don't linger outside clubs.
➡ Screaming matches between those struggling to kick a drug habit are not uncommon in Collingwood's backstreets and on Fitzroy St, St Kilda. Ignore those involved and they'll most likely ignore you too.

INTERNET ACCESS

Free wi-fi is available at central city spots such as Federation Sq, Flinders St Station, Crown Casino and the State Library. It's also the norm in most midrange accommodation, although you sometimes have to pay for access in both budget and top-end stays. Many cafes also offer free wi-fi. There are plenty of libraries around Melbourne with computer terminals, though you'll need to bring ID to sign up and pre-booking is recommended.

MEDICAL SERVICES

Belgium, Finland, Ireland, Italy, Malta, the Netherlands, New Zealand, Norway, Slovenia, Sweden and the UK have reciprocal health-care agreements with Australia so their citizens can access some free or subsidised health services through Medicare; see www.humanservices.gov. au for more details.

  If you've been bitten by a snake or spider or have consumed something you think might be poisonous, contact the **Victorian Poisons Information Centre** (📞13 11 26; www.austin.org. au/poisons; ⊘24hr) for advice.

CAMBERWELL SUNDAY MARKET

Camberwell Sunday Market (www.
camberwellsundaymarket.org; Market Pl,
Camberwell; gold coin donation; ⊙6.30am-
12.30pm Sun; 🚃 Camberwell) Established
in 1976, the beloved secondhand market
is where Melburnians come to offload
unwanted items and antique hunters
dig for vintage gold. It's brilliant for
discovering preloved clothing cheaper
than you'll find in opportunity shops
and vintage stores, finding some holiday
reading and uncovering curiosities and
unusual souvenirs. Closed for the 10
days prior to Christmas.

HOSPITALS

Royal Children's Hospital (☑03-9345 5522;
www.rch.org.au; 50 Flemington Rd, Parkville;
⊙8am-noon & 2-8pm, emergency 24hr;
🚃58, 59)

Royal Melbourne Hospital (☑03-9342 7000;
www.thermh.org.au; 300 Grattan St, Parkville;
⊙10am-8pm, emergency 24hr; 🚃19, 58, 59)

MEDICAL CLINICS

La Trobe St Medical (TVMC; ☑03-9650 0023; www.
melbournecentralpharmacy.com.au; Melbourne Central, 211 La Trobe St, Melbourne;
⊙8.30am-5pm Mon-Thu, to 4pm Fri; 🚃Mel-
bourne Central)

Travel Doctor (TVMC; ☑03-9935 8100; www.
traveldoctor.com.au; L3, 393 Little Bourke St,
Melbourne; ⊙9am-5pm Mon-Wed & Fri, to
7.30pm Thu, to 1pm Sat)

**Royal Women's Hospital Sexual Assault
Unit** (☑03-9635 3610; www.thewomens.org.
au/patients-visitors/clinics-and-services/vio-
lence-sexual-assault/sexual-assault-re
sponse-service; 20 Flemington Rd, Parkville;
🚃58, 59)

PHARMACIES

Prahran Midnight Pharmacy (☑03-9510
3977; www.midnightpharmacy.com.au; 416
High St, Prahran; ⊙9am-midnight; 🚃6)

Pharmacy4Less (☑03-9663 4747; www.
pharmacy4less.com.au; Shop LG50, Melbourne Central, 300 Lonsdale St; ⊙8am-7pm
Mon-Wed, to 8pm Thu & Fri, 10am-6pm Sat
& Sun)

Tambassis Pharmacy (☑03-9387 8830; 32
Sydney Rd, Brunswick; ⊙8am-8pm Mon-Fri,
9am-5pm Sat & Sun; 🚃19, 🚃Jewell)

TOURIST INFORMATION

Melbourne Visitor Booth (https://whatson.
melbourne.vic.gov.au; Bourke St Mall, Melbourne; ⊙9am-5pm; 🚃86, 96) Official city
booth dispensing free tourist information.

Melbourne Visitor Hub (☑03-9658 9658;
https://whatson.melbourne.vic.gov.au; 90-130
Swanston St, Melbourne; ⊙9am-6pm; 🚃1, 3,
5, 6, 16, 64, 67, 72) Official tourism hub with
comprehensive information on things to do in
Melbourne and regional Victoria.

🛈 Getting There & Away

Most travellers arrive via Melbourne Airport,
which is well connected to the city by dedicated
shuttle bus and taxi (though not by public transport). There are also interstate trains and buses,
a direct boat from Tasmania and two minor
domestic airports nearby.

Flights, cars and tours can be booked online at
lonelyplanet.com/bookings.

AIR

Melbourne Airport

Melbourne Airport (☑03-9297 1600; www.
melbourneairport.com.au; Departure Dr,
Tullamarine; 🛜), 22km northwest of the city
centre in Tullamarine, is the city's only international and main domestic airport. It has
all of the facilities you'd expect from a major
airport, including **baggage storage** (☑03-
9338 3119; www.baggagestorage.com.au;
Terminal 2, International Arrivals, Melbourne
Airport; large bag per 4/8/24hr $12/14/17;
⊙5am-12.30am).

Dozens of airlines fly here from destinations
in the South Pacific, Asia, the Middle East and
the Americas. The main domestic airlines are
Qantas (☑13 13 13; www.qantas.com), **Jetstar**
(☑13 15 38; www.jetstar.com), **Virgin Australia** (☑13 67 89; www.virginaustralia.com) and
Regional Express (Rex; ☑13 17 13; www.rex.
com.au).

Avalon Airport

Jetstar flights to/from Sydney, Adelaide and
the Gold Coast, as well as AirAsia flights to/
from Kuala Lumpur and Citilink services to/
from Bali (Indonesia) use **Avalon Airport**
(☑03-5227 9100; www.avalonair
port.com.au; 80 Beach Rd, Lara), around 55km
southwest of Melbourne's city centre.

BOAT

The ferry **Spirit of Tasmania** (☑03-6419 9320,
1800 634 906; www.spiritoftasmania.com.au;
Station Pier, Port Melbourne; adult/car one-way
from $89/99; 🛜🚌) crosses Bass Strait from
Melbourne to Devonport, Tasmania, at least
nightly; there are also day sailings during peak

season. The crossing takes between nine and 11 hours.

BUS

The main terminus for long-distance buses is within the northern half of Southern Cross Station. Here you'll find counters for all the main bus companies, along with **luggage lockers** (☑ 03-9619 2588; www.southerncrossstation. net.au; Southern Cross Station, 99 Spencer St; per 3/24hr from $6/12; ☉ during train-service hours).

Firefly (☑ 1300 730 740, 03-8318 0318; www. fireflyexpress.com.au) Overnight coaches to and from Sydney ($70, 12 hours), Albury ($70, 3½ hours), Ballarat ($65, 1¾ hours) and Adelaide ($60, 9¾ hours).

Greyhound (☑ 1300 473 946; www.greyhound. com.au) Coaches to Albury (from $57, four hours), Sydney (from $99, 12 hours) and Canberra (from $69, eight hours).

V/Line (☑ 1800 800 007; www.vline.com.au; Southern Cross Station, Spencer St) Services destinations within Victoria, including Korumburra ($15.60, two hours), Mansfield ($30.40, three hours) and Echuca ($30.40, three hours).

CAR & MOTORCYCLE

The most direct (and boring) route between Melbourne and Sydney is the Hume Hwy (870km). The Princes Hwy hugs the coast and is much more scenic but also much longer (1040km) and slower. Likewise, the main route to and from Adelaide is the Western/Dukes Hwy (730km), but this bypasses the Great Ocean Road.

TRAIN

Southern Cross Station is the terminus for intercity and interstate trains.

Journey Beyond Rail Expeditions (☑ 1800 703 357; www.journeybeyondrail.com.au) Runs the *Overland* between Melbourne and Adelaide (from $114, 10 hours, twice weekly), though at the time of research this service was at risk of cancellation due to uncertainty over government subsidies.

NSW TrainLink (☑ bookings 13 22 32; www. nswtrainlink.info) Twice-daily services to and from Sydney ($117, 11½ hours) via Benalla ($30, 2¼ hours), Wangaratta ($43, 2½ hours), Albury ($60, 3¼ hours) and Wagga Wagga ($80, 4½ hours).

V/Line Operates the Victorian train and bus networks. Trains head to and from Warrnambool ($38.60, 3¾ hours) and Albury ($40.20, four hours), among others. Fares to Geelong ($13.40, one hour), Ballarat ($22.20, 1½ hours), Bendigo ($33.40, two hours), and Traralgon ($31.20, 2¼ hours) must be paid with a **myki**.

ⓘ Getting Around

TO/FROM THE AIRPORT

Melbourne Airport The **SkyBus** (☑ 1300 SKY-BUS, 03-9335 2811; www.skybus.com.au; adult/child one way $19.75/5, return $37.50/10; ⊠ Southern Cross) departs regularly and connects the airport to Southern Cross Station 24 hours a day. There are also services to other parts of Melbourne, including St Kilda.

Avalon Airport Near the neighbouring city of Geelong, but connected to Melbourne's Southern Cross Station by the Avalon City Express service of **SkyBus** (adult/child one way $24/5, return $46/10; 🕿).

Southern Cross Station Long-distance trains and buses arrive at this large station on the Docklands side of the city centre. From here it's easy to connect to metropolitan trains, buses and trams.

BICYCLE

➡ Cycling maps and information are available from the Melbourne Visitor Hub and **Bicycle Network** (☑ 03-8376 8888; www.bv.com.au).

➡ Helmets are compulsory.

➡ Conventional bikes can be taken on trains (but not the first carriage), but only folding bikes are allowed on trams or buses. Front bike racks are being trialled on some bus routes.

➡ For bike hire, try Rentabike (p221).

CAR & MOTORCYCLE

Driving in Melbourne presents its own set of challenges, due to the need to share the road with trams.

➡ Where trams run along the centre of the road, drivers cannot pass them once they indicate that they're stopping, as passengers board and alight from the street.

➡ In the city centre many intersections are marked 'right turn from left only'. This is the counter-intuitive 'hook turn', devised to stop vehicles from blocking trams and other cars. Right-turning drivers are required to move into the far left of the intersection (it's marked) and then turn right once the lights on that side of the intersection turn green (or in other words, just after the lights in front of you turn red). See www.vicroads.vic.gov.au for further details.

Car Hire

Most car and campervan hire places have offices at Melbourne Airport and in the city or central suburbs. There are some great comparison websites if you're looking for a bargain in advance.

Avis (☑ 13 63 33; www.avis.com.au)
Britz Australia (☑ 03-8398 8855; www.britz. com.au; Central West Business Park, 2/9

Ashley St, Braybrook; ⊗8am-4pm Sep-Apr, 8am-4pm Mon-Sat May-Aug)

Budget (📱1300 362 848; www.budget.com.au)

Hertz (📱13 30 39; www.hertz.com.au)

Rent a Bomb (📱03-9696 7555; www.rentabomb.com.au; 149 Clarendon St, South Melbourne; ⊗8am-6pm Mon-Fri, 9am-3pm Sat & Sun; 🚉12)

Thrifty (📱1300 367 227; www.thrifty.com.au)

Parking

Parking inspectors are particularly vigilant in the city centre and popular suburbs like St Kilda, Collingwood and Fitzroy. Most street parking is metered. Many areas now let you pay via credit card with smartphone app PayStay.

Keep an eye out for 'clearway' zones, which can result in sizeable fines and vehicles being towed. There are plenty of parking garages in the city, but rates can be exorbitant during the day from Monday to Friday.

Toll Roads

Both drivers and motorcyclists will need to purchase a Melbourne Pass ($5.50 start-up fee, plus tolls and a 55¢ or 30¢ vehicle-matching fee per trip, depending on the toll road) if planning on using one of the two toll roads: **CityLink** (📱13 33 31; www.citylink.com.au), which runs from Tullamarine Airport to the city and eastern suburbs, or **EastLink** (📱03-9955 1400; www.eastlink.com.au), from Ringwood to Frankston. Pay online or via phone – but pay within three days of using the toll road to avoid a fine.

Rental cars are sometimes set up for automatic toll payments with a toll tag installed; check when you hire.

PUBLIC TRANSPORT

Bus

Melbourne has an extensive bus network, with over 300 routes covering all the places that the trains and trams don't go. Most routes run from 6am to 9pm weekdays, 8am to 9pm Saturdays and 9am to 9pm Sundays. Night Bus services operate after midnight on many suburbs.

Train

Flinders St Station is the main city hub for Melbourne's 17 train lines. Trains start around 5am weekdays, run until midnight Sunday to Thursday, and all night on Friday and Saturday nights. Trains generally run every 10 to 20 minutes during the day and every 20 to 30 minutes in the evening – although during peak hour (7am to 9am into the city, and 4pm to 6pm out), trains run every three to five minutes.

Tram

Trams are intertwined with the Melbourne identity and an extensive network covers the city. They run roughly every 10 minutes during the day (more frequently in peak periods), and every 20 minutes in the evening. Services run until around 12.30am Sunday to Thursday and 1am Friday and Saturday on most lines; night service is available all night (every 30 minutes) on Friday and Saturday on lines 19, 67, 75, 86, 96 and 109.

The entire city centre is a free tram zone; listen for announcements telling you to 'touch on' your myki card as you approach the paid zone. Note that there's no need to 'touch off' your myki transport card on trams, as all zone 1 journeys are charged at the same rate – although it won't matter if you do.

Tickets & Passes

Melbourne's buses, trams and trains use **myki**, a 'touch on, touch off' travel-pass system. It's not particularly convenient for short-term visitors as it requires you to purchase a $6 plastic myki card and then add credit before you travel. Travellers should consider buying a **myki Explorer** ($16), which includes the card, one day's travel and discounts on various sights; it's available from SkyBus terminals, PTV hubs and some hotels. Otherwise, standard myki cards can be purchased (and topped up) at 7-Elevens, newsagents and major train stations. You can either top up with pay-as-you-go **myki Money** or purchase a seven-day unlimited **myki Pass** ($45); if you're staying more than 28 days, longer passes are available.

For travel within metropolitan Melbourne (zones 1 and 2), the pay-as-you-go fare is $4.50 for two hours, capped at $9 for the day ($6.50 on weekends and public holidays). There are large fines for travelling without having touched on a valid myki card; ticket inspectors are vigilant, unforgiving and sometimes undercover.

For timetables, maps and a journey planner, see the website of **PTV** (Public Transport Victoria; 📱1800 800 007; www.ptv.vic.gov.au). Handy smartphone apps like tramTRACKER or CityMapper will help organise your outings.

TAXI

➤ Melbourne's taxis are metered and require an estimated prepaid fare when hailed between 10pm and 5am (you may need to pay more or get a refund depending on the final fare). Two of the largest taxi companies are **Silver Top** (📱135 000; www.silvertop.com.au) and **13 Cabs** (📱13 22 27; www.13cabs.com.au).

➤ Ride-sharing services such as **Uber** (www.uber.com), **DiDi** (www.didiglobal.com) and **Shebah** (www.shebah.com.au), with female drivers offering rides for women and children, operate here.

GREAT OCEAN ROAD & BELLARINE PENINSULA

The Great Ocean Road (B100) is one of Australia's most famous touring routes. It takes travellers past world-class surfing breaks, through pockets of rainforest and calm seaside towns, and under koala-filled tree canopies. It shows off sheer limestone cliffs, dairy farms and heathland, and gets you up close and personal with the crashing waves of the Southern Ocean.

Hunt out the isolated beaches and lighthouses in between the towns and the thick eucalyptus forest of the Otway hinterlands to really escape the crowds. Rather than heading straight to the Great Ocean Road, a fork in the road at Geelong can take you the long, leisurely way there, through the Bellarine Peninsula, with visits to charming Queenscliff and wineries en route.

Geelong

POP 157,104

As Victoria's second-largest city, Geelong is a proud town with an interesting history and pockets of charm. While Melburnians love to deride their little cousin as a boring backwater, in reality few of the knockers have veered off its main thoroughfare enough to know what makes the town tick. Geelong's new bypass means travellers can skip the city and head straight to the Great Ocean Road; however, there are lots of reasons to stop here.

With the recent closure of major industry, Geelong is in the process of reinventing itself as a tourist town. It's centred on the sparkling Corio Bay waterfront and the city centre, where heritage buildings from the boom days of the gold-rush era and the thriving wool industry have undergone tasteful conversions into attractive restaurants and bars.

◉ Sights

Geelong Waterfront WATERFRONT
(Beach Rd) Geelong's sparkling revamped waterfront precinct is a great place to stroll, with plenty of restaurants set on scenic piers, plus historical landmarks, a 19th-century **carousel** (☑03-5224 1547; www.geelon-

gaustralia.com.au/carousel; $5; ⊙11am-4.30pm Mon-Fri, 10.30am-5pm Sat & Sun, longer hours summer), sculptures, grand homes, swimming areas, playgrounds and grassy sections ideal for picnics. In summer you can cool off at popular **Eastern Beach**, with a 1930s bathing pavilion complete with diving boards, sunbathing area and toddler pool. Jan Mitchell's 100-plus painted **Baywalk Bollards** are scattered the length of the waterfront.

Geelong Art Gallery GALLERY
(☑03-5229 3645; www.geelonggallery.org.au; 55 Little Malop St; ⊙10am-5pm) FREE With over 6000 works in its collection, this long-established gallery features celebrated Australian paintings such as Eugene von Guérard's *View of Geelong* and Frederick McCubbin's *A Bush Burial*. It also exhibits contemporary works and has free drop-in tours on weekends (from 11am to 1pm, plus 2pm to 4pm on Sunday).

Narana Aboriginal Cultural Centre CULTURAL CENTRE
(☑03-5241 5700; www.narana.com.au; 410 Torquay Rd, Charlemont; ⊙9am-5pm Mon-Fri, to 4pm Sat & Sun, cafe 9am-4pm, to 3pm Sat) FREE The Wathaurung people – the original inhabitants and traditional custodians of Geelong – called the area Jillong, and this precinct on its outskirts offers a fascinating insight into their culture. There's a range of things going on: a **gallery** featuring Victoria's largest collection of Aboriginal art; a fusion **cafe** that offers contemporary dishes using Indigenous ingredients; didgeridoo performances (or play one yourself); a boomerang-throwing gallery; and a native garden (admission by donation) that features emus, wallabies and kangaroos. Call ahead for daily tours.

National Wool Museum MUSEUM
(☑03-5272 4701; www.geelongaustralia.com.au/nwm; 26 Moorabool St; adult/child/family $10/6/30; ⊙9.30am-5pm Mon-Fri, 10am-5pm Sat & Sun) More interesting than it may sound, this museum showcases the importance of the wool industry in shaping Geelong economically, socially and architecturally – many of the grand buildings in the area are former wool-store buildings, including the museum's 1872 bluestone edifice. There's a sock-making machine and a massive 1910 Axminster carpet loom that gets chugging at regular intervals throughout the day.

Great Ocean Road & Southwest Coast

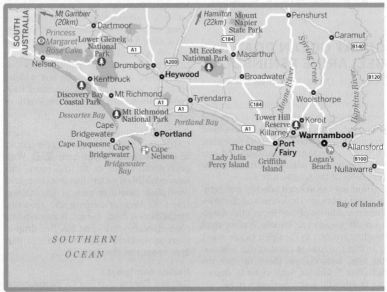

🛏 Sleeping

Gatehouse on Ryrie GUESTHOUSE **$$**
(📞 0417 545 196; www.gatehouseonryrie.com.au;
83 Yarra St; d incl breakfast $120-155; P @ 🛜)
In a prime location in the centre of town,
this guesthouse is one of Geelong's best
midrange choices. Built in 1897, it features
gorgeous timber floorboards throughout,
spacious rooms (most with shared facili-
ties), and a communal kitchen and lounge
area. Breakfast is in the glorious front room.

Devlin Apartments APARTMENT **$$**
(📞 03-5222 1560; www.devlinapartments.com.au;
312 Moorabool St; r $170-500; ❄ 🛜) Geelong's
most stylish offerings are these boutique
apartments, housed in a 1926 heritage-listed
building (the former Gordon Tech school).
Many of the apartments feature themed
designs, including 'New Yorker' loft-style
decor with arched windows; 'Modernist',
furnished with Danish designer chairs; and
'Industrial', featuring wrought iron, rustic
wood and tiled brick bathrooms.

🍴 Eating

Geelong Boat House FISH & CHIPS **$**
(📞 03-5222 3642, 0427 319 019; www.geelongboat
house.com.au; Geelong Waterfront, Western Beach;
fish & chips from $12; ⏰ 10am-8pm, bistro noon-3pm
& 5.30-8pm) Jutting out into the water, this

fish-and-chip joint is built atop a barge once
used to dredge the Yarra River. Grab a chair
on the deck or rooftop, or laze on one of its
picnic blankets on the grassy banks. There's
also a seafood restaurant in the boat shed.

Beach House Geelong CAFE **$$**
(📞 03-4214 2000; www.thebeachhousegeelong.com.
au; 95 Eastern Beach Rd, Geelong Waterfront; dishes
$16-26; ⏰ 7am-9pm) 🍃 It's been a few years in
between drinks for this historical waterfront
kiosk, but the much-loved Beach House is
back, and refitted with a modern coastal de-
cor to accompany the sparkling bay views.
The menu of contemporary cafe fare takes in
anything from açai bowls and cheeseburgers,
to filter coffees and Bloody Marys.

⭐ IGNI AUSTRALIAN **$$$**
(📞 03-5222 2266; www.restaurantigni.com; Ryan Pl;
8 courses $150, with wine pairing $245; ⏰ 6-10pm
Thu, noon-4pm & 6-10pm Fri & Sat, noon-4pm Sun)
Creating a buzz among food lovers is this latest venture by lauded chef (and local boy) Aar-
on Turner. The set tasting menus change on a
whim, incorporating a mix of Indigenous and
European flavours from saltbush to oyster
leaf, and marron to squab, using a wood-fired
grill fuelled by ironbark and red gum.

Staff are exemplary, bringing a fine-dining
experience without a hint of stuffiness, and
you're likely to hear the Ramones or Nick

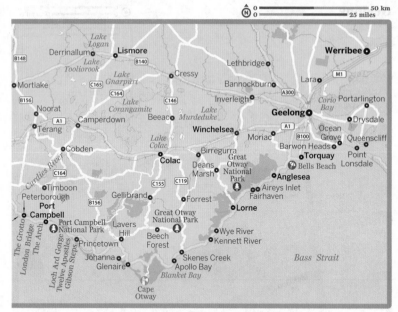

Cave on the sound system. Foodies with an interest in watching the action can grab a stool to dine at the bar overlooking the open kitchen. Stick around for a Geelong-roasted coffee and complimentary freshly baked cakes.

For something more casual, check out its Hot Chicken Project (p250).

🍷 Drinking & Entertainment

⭐ **Little Creatures &
White Rabbit** MICROBREWERY
(🎫 Little Creatures 03-5202 4009, White Rabbit 03-5202 4050; www.littlecreatures.com.au; cnr Fyans & Swanston Sts; ⊙10am-5pm Mon & Tue, to 10pm Wed-Fri, 8am-10pm Sat & Sun; 🛜🅿) Sharing space within the historic red-brick woollen-mill complex are these two separate, well-respected breweries that have come together to create a giant playground for beer-lovers. Little Creatures is the bigger operation, a vast, vibrant indoor-outdoor space, while White Rabbit, relocated from Healesville in 2015, is the more boutique offering, with a chic set-up among its brewing equipment.

Little Creatures, which began in Fremantle, Western Australia, has six core beers, including its Geelong-born Furphy – a hit with locals – which you can sample on a tasting paddle. Order a pizza and find a table inside, or nab an outdoor picnic table. In summer there's an outdoor cinema, craft markets and even a resident barber parked in a caravan. Tours of the brewery ($20) operate a few times a day and include free tastings. Kids will love the sand-pits and the room to run around.

White Rabbit offers more refined decor, but it's equally relaxed and you can enjoy its range of beers as the brewers work away on the next batch. It has five core beers, along with a seasonal on tap that's always worth checking out. There's a tempting charcuterie selection, and a few mains (the likes of roasted lamb shoulder; $26), plus an attached shop selling beer merchandise. There are info boards for self-guided tours of the brewery, or there's usually someone to show you around.

Barwon Club LIVE MUSIC
(🎫03-5221 4584; www.barwonclub.com.au; 509 Moorabool St; ⊙11am-late) The BC has long been Geelong's premier live-music venue, and has spawned the likes of Magic Dirt, Bored! and Warped, seminal bands in the 'Geetroit' rock scene. As well as a place to catch local and international bands, it's great for a beer and a pub meal.

ℹ️ Information

TOURIST INFORMATION
Geelong Visitor Information Centre (🎫03-5222 2900, 1800 755 611; www.visit

Geelong

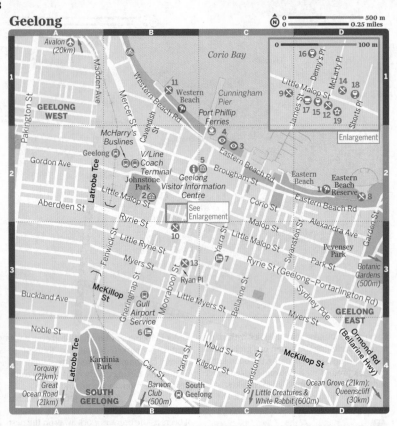

Geelong

⊙ Sights
1 Eastern Beach	D2
2 Geelong Art Gallery	B2
3 Geelong Waterfront	C2
4 Geelong Waterfront Carousel	C2
5 National Wool Museum	C2

🛏 Sleeping
6 Devlin Apartments	B4
7 Gatehouse on Ryrie	C3

⊗ Eating
8 Beach House Geelong	D2
9 Caruggi	C1
10 El Santo De Los Tacos	B3
11 Geelong Boat House	B1
12 Hot Chicken Project	D1
13 IGNI	B3
14 Pistol Pete's Food n Blues	D1

🍸 Drinking & Nightlife
15 18th Amendment Bar	D1
16 Blackman's Brewery	D1
17 Cartel Coffee Roaster	D1
18 Geelong Cellar Door	D1
The Continental	(see 15)

✪ Entertainment
19 Workers Club Geelong	D1

geelongbellarine.com.au; 26 Moorabool St; ⊙9am-5pm; 🛜) is the city's main tourist office, with brochures on Geelong, the Bellarine Peninsula and the Great Ocean Road, as well as free wi-fi.

ⓘ Getting There & Away

AIR

Avalon Airport (p242) 22km north of Geelong; count on around a 25-minute drive from town. Jetstar (p242) has services to and from Sydney, Adelaide and the Gold Coast; AirAsia (☐ 02-

8188 2133; www.airasia.com) has direct flights from Avalon to Kuala Lumpur (Malaysia) and **Citilink** (☑ 86-555 7081; www.citilink.co.id/en) flies to Denpasar, Bali (Indonesia). Plans were in place for a service to Vietnam's Ho Chi Minh City through VietJet Air.

Skybus (☑ 1300 759 287; www.skybus.com. au) Three to four buses a day from Avalon to/ from Geelong ($11, 35 minutes), making stops at the city and train stations. It also has buses to Melbourne's Southern Cross Station ($24, 1¼ hours).

BUS

Gull Airport Service (☑ 03-5222 4966; www. gull.com.au; 45 McKillop St; ⊙ office 9am-5pm Mon-Fri, 10am-noon Sat) Has regular services between Geelong and Melbourne Airport (adult/child $35/22, 1¼ hours), departing from the city centre and Geelong Station.

McHarry's Buslines (☑ 03-5223 2111; www. mcharrys.com.au; Geelong Station, Gordon Ave) Runs frequent buses from Geelong Station to Torquay ($3.40, 40 minutes) and the Bellarine Peninsula.

V/Line (☑ 1800 800 007; www.vline.com. au; Geelong Station, Gordon Ave) Buses run from Geelong Station to Apollo Bay ($20.60, 2½ hours, four daily) via Torquay ($3.60, 25 minutes), Anglesea ($7, one hour) and Lorne ($12.80, 1½ hours). On Monday, Wednesday and Friday a bus continues to Port Campbell ($36.20, 5¼ hours) and Warrnambool ($41, 6½ hours); both services involve a transfer at Apollo Bay. The train is a much quicker and cheaper option for those heading direct to Warrnambool, though you'll miss out on the Great Ocean Road experience. Heading inland, there's a bus to Ballarat ($11.20, 1½ hours).

CAR

Geelong is 75km south of Melbourne along the Geelong Rd (Princes Fwy; M1). The 25km Geelong Ring Rd runs from Corio to Waurn Ponds, bypassing Geelong entirely. To get to Geelong city, be careful not to miss the Princes Hwy exit from the left lanes.

FERRY

Port Phillip Ferries (☑ 03-9514 8959; www. portphillipferries.com.au; Geelong Waterfront) A new service linking Geelong with Melbourne's Docklands (one way adult/child $18/10, 1½ hours) was launched in late 2019, departing twice a day. Though it's slightly pricier and slower compared to the train, it's a more scenic way of getting between the two cities, plus there's a cafe, bar and free wi-fi onboard.

TRAIN

V/Line (☑ 1800 800 007; www.vline.com.au; Gordon Ave) trains run frequently from Geelong Station to Melbourne's Southern Cross Station ($9.50 to $13.60, one hour). Trains also head from Geelong to Warrnambool ($28.20, 2½ hours, four daily).

Bellarine Peninsula

For many a generation Melburnians have been making the drive down the Princes Hwy (Geelong Rd) to the seaside villages along the Bellarine Peninsula. The adjoining townships of Queenscliff, Ocean Grove, Point Lonsdale and Barwon Heads are all worth a look, known for family-friendly and surf beaches, lovely cafes and a relaxed coastal ambience. The area is also famous for its wonderful cool-climate wineries.

As well as linking up with the Great Ocean Road, it's just a short ferry trip from here over to the Mornington Peninsula.

❶ Getting There & Away

From Melbourne the Bellarine Peninsula is easily accessible via the Princes Fwy (M1) to Geelong. Be sure not to take the Geelong bypass; instead, take the Geelong exit and follow the signs to the Bellarine Hwy (B110).

BUS

McHarry's Buslines Connects Geelong with Barwon Heads (30 minutes), Ocean Grove (45 minutes), Portarlington (45 minutes), Point Lonsdale (55 minutes) and Queenscliff (one hour). A two-hour/daily ticket costs $3.40/6.80; myki card required.

FERRY

Port Phillip Ferries (☑ 03-9514 8959; www. portphillipferries.com.au; Portarlington Pier, Portarlington) A serious boon for the region is the introduction of a ferry service linking Portarlington with Melbourne's Docklands (one way adult/child $16/8, 1½ hours, twice daily).

Queenscliff–Sorrento Ferry (☑ 03-5257 4500; www.searoad.com.au; 1 Wharf St East, Queenscliff; one way foot passenger adult/ child $13/9, car incl driver $69, bicycle free; ⊙ hourly 6am-6pm, to 7pm peak season) Runs between Queenscliff and Sorrento (40 minutes).

BICYCLE

Bring along your bike from Melbourne on the train and get off at South Geelong Station to pedal the **Bellarine Rail Trail** (www.railtrails. org.au) for 35km to Queenscliff. The path

GEELONG CITY LANEWAY FINDS

When folk talk of Geelong's emergence as a cool, happening destination, inevitably they'll cite Little Malop precinct in the CBD as the place to go (not to be confused with the Market Square side, the domain of Geelong mallrats).

Hot Chicken Project (☑03-5221 8977; www.thehotchickenproject.com; 84a Little Malop St; mains from $19; ☺noon-10pm) Authentic Nashville hot chicken paired with natural wines and craft beers.

Blackman's Brewery (☑03-5221 5262; www.blackmansbrewery.com.au; Denny's Pl; tasting paddles $16; ☺4.30-10pm Tue-Thu, 3.30pm-midnight Fri & Sat, 3-8pm Sun) Popular taproom pouring beers brewed in Torquay.

Cartel Coffee Roaster (☑03-5221 4757; www.coffeecartel.com.au; 1-80 Little Malop St; ☺7am-5pm Mon-Fri, 8am-4pm Sat) A big player in Australia's third-wave coffee movement is this single-origin microroaster pouring coffees whichever way you like it.

18th Amendment Bar (www.the18thamendmentbar.com.au; 82a Little Malop St; ☺5pm-midnight Wed-Sat) Prohibition-style bar with a dark, low-lit space offering table service of original and classic cocktails.

Caruggi (☑03-5229 6426; www.caruggi.com.au; 66 Little Malop St; mains $16.50-38; ☺noon-2.30pm & 5.30-8.30pm Tue-Sat, noon-2.30pm Sun) Northern Italian dining with awesome pizzas.

El Santo De Los Tacos (☑03-5221 2880; www.elsanto.com.au; 115 Ryrie St; 2 tacos $15, mains $22-28; ☺11.30am-2.30pm & 5.30-9pm Mon-Fri, 5.30-11pm Sat, 5.30-9pm Sun; ☑) Vibrant Mexican cantina, just up from Little Malop.

Pistol Pete's Food n Blues (☑03-5221 0287; www.pistolpetesfoodnblues.com.au; 93a Little Malop St; mains $10-24; ☺11.30am-10pm Tue, Wed & Sun, to 11pm Thu, to 12.30am Fri & Sat) Louisiana-style cuisine paired with rye bourbon and swampy blues.

Geelong Cellar Door (☑03-5229 9568; www.geelongcellardoor.com.au; 97-99 Little Malop St; ☺noon-11pm Tue-Sun) Classy wine bar to sample the region's tipples by an open fire or in the red-brick courtyard.

Workers Club Geelong (☑03-5222 8331; www.theworkersclubgeelong.com.au; 90-92 Little Malop St; ☺5pm-late Wed-Sat) American-style barbecue accompanied by craft beers and live indie bands.

The Continental (☑03-5222 5677; www.facebook.com/thecontinentalgeelong; 82 Little Malop St; ☺4pm-1am) Retro Italian-style diner for wines, cocktails and stripped-back European bistro cuisine.

follows the historical train line, away from the road.

Queenscliff

POP 1315

Historic Queenscliff is a charming seaside town that mixes a salty maritime character with one of Victoria's most picturesque streetscapes. Many of its heritage-listed 19th-century buildings have been converted into hotels, restaurants and art galleries. It's a great base from which to explore the nearby wineries and beaches, along with the various historical sites and museums in town. The views across the Port Phillip Heads and Bass Strait are glorious.

☉ Sights & Activities

Fort Queenscliff HISTORIC SITE
(☑03-5258 1488; www.fortqueenscliff.com.au; cnr Gellibrand & King Sts; 90min tours adult/child/family $17/7.50/38; ☺11am Mon-Fri, 11am & 1.45pm Sat & Sun, school holidays 11am, 1.45pm & 3pm daily) Queencliff's fort was first used as a coastal defence in 1882 to protect Melbourne from a feared Russian invasion. It remained a base until 1946, and was then used as the Army Staff College until late 2012; today it functions as the Defence Department's archive. Tours take in the military museum (not always accessible), the magazine, cells and the twin lighthouses (including the iconic black lighthouse). It's a defence area, so bring ID for entry and arrive 10 minutes early.

A separate operator, Geraldine (a sixth-generation local with plenty of tales; 0410 512 472), leads tours (adult/child/family $15/7/35) midweek at 11am during the non-holiday period.

Queenscliffe Maritime Museum MUSEUM
(☑ 03-5258 3440; www.maritimequeenscliffe.org.au; 2 Wharf St; adult/child $10/5; ⊙ 11am-4pm) Home to the last lifeboat to serve the Rip (the treacherous stretch of water linking Port Phillip Bay to Bass Strait), this museum has displays on the intriguing current-day pilot-boat process, shipwrecks, lighthouses and steamships. Head out the back to see the heritage-listed 1895 boat shed, with paintings that served as a record of passing ships in the bay.

Scubabo Dive Victoria DIVING
(☑ 0447 008 809, 03-5258 1188; www.dive.scubabo.com/melbourne; 37 Learmonth St; per dive with/without gear $155/65) Scubabo offers SSI diving courses and trips for all levels, from intro to technical. There are some 200 sites in the area, taking in rich marine life and shipwrecks from the past three centuries, including WWI submarines and ex-HMAS *Canberra*, scuttled in 2009. Snorkel trips are also possible. Visit the website for upcoming trips and training courses.

🛌 Sleeping

Cobb & Co Lodge HOSTEL $
(☑ 03-5258 1188; www.cobbandcolodge.com.au; 37 Learmonth St; dm/d with shared bathroom $50/140; ⸙ 🖳) Run by Scubabo Dive Victoria, this is Bellarine's only backpacker-style accommodation and makes a great option for budget travellers and divers alike. The modern shared kitchen and lounge facilities are bright and airy, while the simple rooms are out the back. It was built in 1864, when it was used as a Cobb & Co horse coach stables.

★ Vue Grand HOTEL $$$
(☑ 03-5258 1544; www.vuegrand.com.au; 46-48 Hesse St; r incl breakfast $205-445; ⸙ 🖳) One of Queenscliff's most elegant historic buildings, the Vue has everything from standard pub rooms to a modern turret suite (boasting 360-degree views) and bay-view rooms with freestanding baths in their lounges.

Its front **bistro** (46 Hesse St; mains $17-32; ⊙ noon-10pm Wed-Sun, daily in summer) is a relaxed spot for a drink and a meal, while its stately dining room does dinners on Friday and Saturday.

🍴 Eating & Drinking

Circa 1902 INTERNATIONAL $$
(☑ 0499 771 674; www.circa1902.com.au; 59 Hesse St; tapas $10-18, mains $18.50-40; ⊙ 11.30am-2pm & 5.30-8pm Wed-Fri, noon-3pm & 6-8.30pm Sat & Sun, extended hours in summer; 🛈) On the main street, this historic hotel (c 1902, surprise surprise...) is a popular place to soak up Queenscliff's heritage atmosphere. It does multinational cuisine ranging from Goan chicken curry to seafood pies, but it's best known for its tapas-style shared plates. It's a good spot to sample regional wines and beers.

Upstairs there's no-frills but well-priced accommodation ($125 to $145) with shared bathrooms.

Queenscliff Brewhouse PUB
(☑ 03-5258 1717; www.queenscliffbrewhouse.com.au; 2 Gellibrand St; ⊙ 11am-late) Branching out from its Otways base (p260), Prickly Moses has set up a second brewhouse here in Queenscliff. The full range is showcased on tap, plus there are a few of its own local beers, as well as a selection of guest brewers, best enjoyed in the beer garden. It's also started distilling gin, and there's an upstairs whisky bar.

ℹ️ Information

Queenscliff Visitor Centre (☑ 03-5258 4843; www.queenscliff.com.au; 55 Hesse St; ⊙ 9am-5pm; 🛈) Has plenty of brochures on the area.

Torquay

POP 16,948

In the 1960s and '70s Torquay was just another sleepy seaside town. Back then, surfing in Australia was a decidedly countercultural pursuit, its devotees hippie dropouts living in clapped-out vans, smoking pot and making off with your daughters. These days it's become unabashedly mainstream, and the town's proximity to world-famous Bells Beach and its status as the home of two iconic surf brands – Rip Curl and Quiksilver, both initially wetsuit makers – ensure Torquay's place as the undisputed capital of the country's surf industry. It's one of Australia's fastest-growing towns, experiencing a population increase of 67% between 2001 and 2013 that these days makes it feel almost like an outer suburb of Geelong.

It has some lovely beaches, plus a growing number of contemporary cafes and restaurants, and one of Victoria's more innovative breweries.

⦿ Sights & Activities

★ Australian National Surfing Museum
MUSEUM

(☑ 03-5261 4606; www.australiannationalsurf ingmuseum.com.au; Surf City Plaza, 77 Beach Rd; adult/child/family $12/8/25; ⊙ 9am-5pm) The perfect starting point for those embarking on a surfing safari is this superbly curated museum that pays homage to Australian surfing. Here you'll see Simon Anderson's ground-breaking 1981 thruster, Mark Richard's retro airbrushed board-art collection and, most notably, Australia's Surfing Hall of Fame. It's full of great memorabilia (including Duke Kahanamoku's wooden longboard), videos and displays on surf culture from the 1960s to the '80s. Its themed shows throughout the year are always quality too.

Go Ride a Wave
SURFING

(☑ 1300 132 441; www.gorideawave.com.au; 1/15 Bell St; 2hr lessons adult/child from $72/62) This outfit offers surfing, stand-up paddleboarding (SUP) and kayaking, and hires boards, too. It runs several camps along the Great Ocean Road and Bellarine Peninsula; check the website for locations.

🛏 Sleeping

Bells Beach Backpackers
HOSTEL $

(☑ 03-5261 4029; www.bellsbeachbackpackers. com.au; 51-53 Surfcoast Hwy; van sites per double $24-32, dm $28-38, d with shared bathroom $80-110; @ 🛜) On the main highway in Torquay (not Bells Beach), this laid-back backpackers does a great job of fitting into the fabric of this surf town. Run by friendly owner Sean, along with his black lab, Bella, it has a super-chilled beach-house vibe, with basic rooms that are clean and in good nick, and a large kitchen that 'van packers' can also use.

Torquay Foreshore Caravan Park
CAMPGROUND $

(☑ 1300 736 533, 03-5261 2496; www.torquaycara vanpark.com.au; 35 Bell St; powered sites $50-105, glamping $113-190, cabins $134-400; ❋ 🛜) Just behind the back beach is the largest on the Surf Coast. It has good facilities and premium-priced cabins with sea views. Wi-fi is limited.

✗ Eating & Drinking

Ginger Monkey
CAFE $$

(☑ 03-5291 9734; www.gingermonkeycafe.com; 4 Baines Cres; meals from $17; ⊙ 8am-4pm; 🛜 🖉) This rustic-chic cafe has the best vegetarian food in town, offering nasi goreng or mushroom ragout with poached egg for brekkie, and chunky homemade vegetarian sausage rolls for lunch. If you're around on Friday, head out to the car park for its famous paella cook-up (vegetarian/seafood $15/17.50). It does fantastic coffee, too, using Proud Mary beans from Melbourne.

★ Blackman's Brewery
MICROBREWERY

(☑ 03-5261 5310; www.blackmansbrewery.com. au; 26 Bell St; ⊙ noon-10pm Wed-Sun, daily summer) One of Victoria's best microbreweries is this brewpub, where you can taste all eight Blackman's beers, which are produced on-site. Go the tasting paddle ($16) to sample the range of IPAs, unfiltered lager, pale ale and inventive seasonals – enjoy by a roaring fire or in the AstroTurf beer garden, along with a menu of pizzas, tacos and burgers.

★ Bomboras
BAR

(www.bomboras.com.au; 48 The Esplanade, Fisherman's Beach; ⊙ noon-9.30pm 1 Oct–Easter) The place to be in summer, this pop-up rooftop beach bar has prime ocean views. Enjoy local brews on tap, cocktails, pizza, and live music or DJs.

It also has a **pizzeria** (☑ 03-5264 7881; www.bomboras.com.au; 37 The Esplanade; pizzas from $24; ⊙ 6am-10pm) up the road that's open throughout the year for quality breakfasts and mains.

🛍 Shopping

Rip Curl Surf Factory Outlet
FASHION & ACCESSORIES

(Baines Surf Seconds; ☑ 03-5261 0057; 16 Baines Cres; ⊙ 9am-5.30pm) Rip Curl's shiny main outlet is in Surf City Plaza, but head round the back to the industrial estate for the factory outlet, where you'll get 30% off the price of last season's clothing and wetsuits. A big-name global brand these days, Rip Curl was founded in Torquay in 1969.

ℹ Information

Torquay Visitor Information Centre (☑ 03-5261 4219; www.torquaylife.com.au; Surf City Plaza, Beach Rd; ⊙ 9am-5pm; 🛜) Sharing space with the Australian National Surfing Museum,

BELLARINE WINERIES & PRODUCE

Well known for its cool-climate pinot noir, chardonnay and shiraz, the Bellarine/Geelong region has more than 50 wineries. It's also famous for its produce, from goat's-milk cheese and olives to mussels and blueberries. Combine a winery hop with the **Bellarine Taste Trail** (www.thebellarinetastetrail.com.au) for a fantastic day out. See a full list of wineries at www.winegeelong.com.au.

Scotchmans Hill (03-5251 3176; www.scotchmans.com.au; 190 Scotchmans Rd, Drysdale; mains $18-26; 10.30am-4.30pm) One of the Bellarine's first wineries remains one of its best, producing quality sauvignon blanc, pinot noir, chardonnay and cool-climate shiraz.

Jack Rabbit (03-5251 2223; www.jackrabbitvineyard.com.au; 85 McAdams Lane, Bellarine; dishes from $18; tastings from 10am, restaurant noon-3pm Sun-Thu, noon-3pm & 6-11pm Fri & Sat) Come to this boutique winery for stunning bay views while enjoying pinot and a bowl of mussels. Its fine-dining restaurant serves creative dishes made using local ingredients.

Terindah Estate (03-5251 5536; www.terindahestate.com; 90 McAdams Lane, Bellarine; mains $28-40; tastings 10am-4pm daily, restaurant noon-4pm Thu, Fri & Mon, 8-10am, noon-4pm & 6-10pm Sat, 8-10am & noon-4pm Sun) This winery has incredible water views, quality pinots and fine dining in its glasshouse shed.

Bennetts on Bellarine (03-8751 8194; www.bennettsonbellarine.com; 2171 Portarlington Rd, Bellarine; 11am-5.30pm Thu-Mon, daily Jan) Enjoy wood-fired pizzas and pinot on the back patio of this stylised tin shed looking out to vines.

Merne at Lighthouse (03-5251 5541; www.merne.com.au; 650 Andersons Rd, Drysdale; 2/4 courses $65/89; noon-3pm & 6-10pm Thu-Mon) Overlooking olive groves is this fine-dining restaurant with a grazing menu of creative modern Australian cuisine using seasonal Bellarine produce.

Flying Brick Cider Co. (03-5250 6577; www.flyingbrickciderco.com.au; 1251-1269 Bellarine Hwy, Wallington; bar 10am-5pm Sun-Thu, to late Fri & Sat, restaurant 11.30am-3pm Mon-Thu, 11.30am-3pm & 6-9pm Fri & Sat, noon-4pm Sun) A popular stop along the highway, this cider house produces quality apple and pear ciders, to be enjoyed in its grassy outdoor area.

Basils Farm (03-5258 4280; www.basilsfarm.com.au; 43-53 Nye Rd, Swan Bay; 10am-4pm Mon, Thu & Fri, to 5pm Sat & Sun, daily Jan) Enjoy their prosecco, a produce platter and fabulous Swan Bay views at this boutique winery.

Banks Road (0431 896 331; www.banksroad.com.au; 600 Banks Rd, Marcus Hill; 11am-4pm Thu-Sun, or by appointment) Have a glass of pinot gris while looking out at open-air sculptures in a pastoral setting, shared with a smart bistro.

Whiskery (Bellarine Distillery; 0468 926 282; www.bellarinedistillery.com.au; 1 Scotchmans Rd, Drysdale; tastings from $10; 11am-5pm Thu-Sun) As well as producing a single-malt, this distillery is renowned for gins; pop in for a tasting accompanied by pizzas and local-produce platters.

Oakdene (03-5256 3886; www.oakdene.com.au; 255 Grubb Rd, Wallington; mains $25-35; cellar door 10am-4pm, cafe 11am-2.30pm & 5.30-7.30pm daily, restaurant 6.30pm-late Wed-Fri, from noon Sat & Sun) Set in a quirky upside-down barn and surrounded by arty objects, this is a vineyard with a difference.

McGlashan's Wallington Estate (03-5250 5760; www.mcglashans.com.au; 225 Swan Bay Rd, Wallington; platters for 2-4 people $19-48; 11am-5pm Thu-Sun, daily Jan) Unpretentious winery with tastings in a motor-memorabilia-decorated barn.

Tuckerberry Hill (03-5251 3468; www.tuckerberry.com.au; 35 Becks Rd, Drysdale; 9am-5pm Sat & Sun mid-Oct–Dec & Feb-May, 9am-8pm daily Jan) Pick your own berries, or sample blueberry beer, muffins, milkshakes or berry ice cream.

Little Mussel Cafe (03-5259 1377; www.facebook.com/littlemusselcafe; 40-42 Newcombe St, Portarlington; mains $16-29; 9am-10pm Mon-Fri, from 8am Sat & Sun) Sample local mussels and oysters, served as chowder, in bowls of tomato and chilli or on tasting plates.

this well-resourced visitor centre makes a good starting point along the Great Ocean Road to fine-tune your itinerary. There's free wi-fi and internet access at the library next door.

ℹ Getting There & Away

Torquay is 15 minutes' drive from Geelong on the B100, around 103km south of Melbourne.

McHarry's Buslines (p249) Bus 51 runs hourly from 9am to 8pm (around 5pm weekends) between Geelong and Torquay ($3.40, 40 minutes).

V/Line (p249) Buses run four times daily from Geelong to Torquay ($3.60, 36 minutes).

Torquay to Anglesea

The Great Ocean Road officially begins on the stretch between Torquay and Anglesea. A slight detour takes you to famous **Bells Beach**, the powerful beach break that's part of international surfing folklore; it has hosted Australia's premier surfing event, the Bells Classic, since 1973. When the right hander is working, it's one of the longest rides in the country, but it's a wave for experienced surfers only. (It was here too, in name only, that Keanu Reeves and Patrick Swayze had their ultimate showdown in the film *Point Break*.)

★ Koorie Cultural Walk   WALKING

A highly recommended detour signposted off the Great Ocean Road is the fantastic Koorie Cultural Walk, a 2km trail (one-hour return) that details how the Indigenous Wathaurung people lived here for millennia. It's a lovely bushwalk through the Great Otway National Park, with echidnas and wallabies, and spectacular coastal outlooks of dramatic cliffs and pristine beaches, including lovely **Addiscott Beach**.

It's part of the **Surf Coast Walk** (www.surfcoastwalk.com.au), and the sands here stretch all the way to the clothing-optional beach at **Point Addis**.

In 1836 a community of some 700 Wathaurung people resided in the immediate area; tragically, by 1853 this number had been reduced to a mere 35 as a direct result of European settlement. In the car park at the top of the hill there's a plaque about William Buckley, an escaped convict who spent 32 years living with the Wathaurung from 1803.

Anglesea
POP 2545

Mix sheer orange cliffs falling into the ocean with hilly, tree-filled 'burbs and a population that booms in summer and you've got Anglesea, where sharing fish and chips with seagulls by the Anglesea River is a decades-long family tradition for many.

It's another coastal town that's emerged as an epicurean destination, with a new generation of youthful owners opening beach-chic cafes and casual fine-dining bistros.

Anglesea Golf
Club Kangaroo Tours   WILDLIFE WATCHING
(🕿 03-5263 1582; www.angleseagolfclub.com.au; Anglesea Golf Club, Golf Links Rd; 20min kangaroo tours adult/child/family $12.50/5/30; ⊙10am-3pm, later hours mid-Jan–mid-Feb) Get up close to eastern grey kangaroos on a tour of Anglesea's golf course, famous for its mob of 300-odd resident roos that have lived here for many a year. Tours in open-air electric buggies are informative and offer good photo ops.

If you don't want to do a tour, you can chance your luck spotting kangaroos from the road or, even better, pair your sightings with a round of golf (nine/18 holes from $30/55, club hire nine/18 holes $25/35). There's a bar and bistro here, too.

Anglesea Backpackers   HOSTEL $
(🕿 03-5263 2664; www.angleseabackpackers.com; 40 Noble St; dm $30-35, d/f from $115/150; @ 🛜) While most hostels like to cram 'em in, this simple, homey backpackers has just two dorm rooms and one double/triple, and is clean, bright and welcoming. In winter the fire glows warmly in the cosy living room. There are free bikes for guests and the owner can pick you up from town or as far away as Torquay.

Anglesea Family
Caravan Park   CAMPGROUND $
(🕿 1300 475 505, 03-5295 1990; www.angleseafamilycaravanpark.com.au; 35 Cameron Rd; powered sites $45-108, cabins $149-395; @ 🛜 ⛱) Beach- and riverfront caravan park with powered sites and comfortable cabins, along with a pool, wi-fi, two camp kitchens, a jumping pillow, an indoor spa and a games room.

★ Captain Moonlite   AUSTRALIAN $
(🕿 03-5263 2454; www.captainmoonlite.com.au; from $12; ⊙noon-6pm) At the time of research

MELBOURNE & COASTAL VICTORIA TORQUAY TO ANGLESEA

Anglesea's finest restaurant was in the process of relocating to a new address, but in the meantime they've just launched **Fish by Moonlite** (Shop 4, 87–89 Great Ocean Road), offering gourmet fish and chips, and fresh seafood to cook up back home.

Last One Inn CAFE $
(0425 749 645; www.lastoneinn.com.au; 113 Great Ocean Rd; dishes $10-23; 7.30am-3pm Mon-Wed, to 10pm Thu-Sun) Overlooking the Anglesea River is this spruced-up weatherboard that exudes a nostalgic endless-summer beach vibe. It's best known for smoky flame-grilled beef burgers, but it's also a top spot for tasty cooked brekkies and old-school thick shakes. Drop by sunset for spritz cocktails, craft beers, regional wines and tasty bar snacks.

ℹ Information

Anglesea Visitor Information Centre (www.visitgreatoceanroad.org.au/towns-and-villages/anglesea; Anglesea River, Great Ocean Rd; 9am-5pm;) Located at the estuary, this tiny volunteer-run information centre has a heap of brochures, including on local walks in the Great Otway National Park.

ℹ Getting There & Away

The Geelong bypass has reduced the time it takes to drive from Melbourne to Anglesea to around 1½ hours.

There are four to six daily V/Line buses between Geelong and Anglesea ($7, one hour).

Aireys Inlet & Around
POP 802

Midway between Anglesea and Lorne, Aireys Inlet is an attractive coastal hamlet that makes for an essential stop along the Great Ocean Road. It's home to a historic lighthouse that forms the backdrop to glorious stretches of beach, including **Fairhaven** and **Moggs Creek**. Its microbrewery, gin distillery and acclaimed restaurant are other reasons to stop.

⭐ **Split Point Lighthouse** LIGHTHOUSE
(1800 174 045, 03-5263 1133; www.splitpointlighthouse.com.au; Federal St; self-guided tours $10; 10am-2pm, longer hours in summer) Scale the 136 steps to the top of the beautiful 'White Queen' lighthouse for sensational 360-degree views. Built in 1891, the 34m-high lighthouse is still operational,

though it's now fully automated. You can visit on self-guided tours, where a staff member awaits up top to field questions about the area's history. The lighthouse was used as a setting for the popular TV show *Round the Twist*.

Blazing Saddles HORSE RIDING
(0418 528 647, 03-5289 7322; www.blazingsaddlestrailrides.com; Lot 1, Bimbadeen Dr; 1hr bush rides from $65, 2½hr beach & bush rides $140) People come from around the world to hop on a Blazing Saddles horse and head along stunning Fairhaven Beach or into the bush.

Aireys Inlet Holiday Park CABIN $
(03-5289 6230; www.aicp.com.au; 19-25 Great Ocean Rd; unpowered sites $32-70, powered sites $35-90, cabins $119-450;) The only budget option in Aireys itself is this well-maintained caravan park that's more cabin town than tent city. Facilities are all spick and span, and it's conveniently located for the pub, top shops and beach.

WORTH A TRIP

GREAT OCEAN ROAD CHOCOLATERIE & ICE CREAMERY

Great Ocean Road Chocolaterie & Ice Creamery (03-5263 1588; www.gorci.com.au; 1200 Great Ocean Rd, Bellbrae; ice cream from $4.80, mains $8.50-23; 9am-5pm) A sure way to placate those backseat cries of 'are we there yet?' is this chocolaterie located 4km outside Anglesea. It's a massive site that makes all its own chocolates and truffles on-site (including a bush-tucker range), a process you can observe through the gallery window. There are plenty of free samples, as well as 20 flavours of ice cream and a cafe.

On most Saturdays they host chocolate-making courses (from $20); book online.

Pole House RENTAL HOUSE **$$$**
(03-5220 0200; www.greatoceanroadholidays.com.au; 60 Banool Rd, Fairhaven; per night from $680) One of the most iconic houses along the Great Ocean Road, the Pole House is a unique architectural creation that, as the name suggests, sits atop a pole, with extraordinary ocean views. Access to the house is via an external pedestrian bridge. It's not suitable for children.

Willows Tea House CAFE **$**
(03-5289 6830; 7 Federal St; scones $4.50, breakfast & lunch $7-16; 9am-4pm;) Soak up Aireys' seafaring atmosphere at this teahouse set within a historic weatherboard cottage a few steps from the lighthouse. Stop by for morning or afternoon tea to indulge in homemade scones with jam and cream, enjoyed in the cosy interior or at outdoor tables. The new owners have introduced a quality brunch menu, including lip-smacking bacon-and-egg rolls with smoky relish.

★ **a la grecque** GREEK **$$**
(03-5289 6922; www.alagrecque.com.au; 60 Great Ocean Rd; small plates $10-28, large plates $29-34; noon-2.30pm & 6-9.30pm Wed-Sun, closed winter, open daily Jan) This outstanding modern Greek taverna is a Great Ocean Road institution that balances fine dining with a relaxed coastal approach. Meze such as seared scallops or chargrilled local octopus and mains of grilled

rack of lamb with *melitzanosalata* (eggplant dip) are sensational. So is the wine list.

★ **Aireys Pub** PUB, BREWERY
(03-5289 6804; www.aireyspub.com.au; 45 Great Ocean Rd; 11.30am-late;) Established in 1904, this pub is a survivor, twice burning down before closing in 2011, only to be revived by locals chipping in to save it. Now it's better than ever, with an on-site brewery, **Salt Brewing Co** (www.saltbrewing.co). The food is gourmet pub fare (mains $24 to $42), enjoyed by a roaring fire or out in its sprawling beer garden.

ⓘ Getting There & Away

From Melbourne, count on a 1¾-hour drive for the 123km trip to Aireys Inlet, or a bit longer if you're heading via Torquay (27km, 25 minutes).

Departing from Geelong Station, V/Line has four to six daily buses to Aireys Inlet ($9.60, 70 minutes), which continue on to nearby Fairhaven, Moggs Creek and Eastern View for the same fare.

Lorne
POP 1114

One of the Great Ocean Road's original resort towns, Lorne may be a tad overdeveloped these days, but it retains all the charms that have lured visitors here since the 19th century. Beyond its main strip it has an incredible natural beauty: tall old gum trees line its hilly streets, and Loutit Bay gleams irresistibly. It backs onto the lovely eucalyptus forest, fern gullies and waterfalls that inspired Rudyard Kipling to pen his poem 'Flowers' in 1891.

⊙ Sights & Activities

Lorne's picturesque beach is as nice as you'll find along the Great Ocean Road, with a long stretch of sand and gentle waves rolling in. At the back of Lorne there's lush rainforest, with 10 waterfalls to visit within a 10km radius – the most famous being **Erskine Falls** (Erskine Falls Access Rd).

★ **Qdos Art Gallery** GALLERY
(03-5289 1989; www.qdosarts.com; 35 Allenvale Rd; 9am-5pm) **FREE** Set amid the lush forest behind Lorne, Qdos always has something interesting showing at its contemporary gallery, to go with its open-air sculpture garden. There's also a lovely little

cafe doing wood-fired pizzas and superb *ryokan*-style accommodation.

Great Ocean Road Story · MUSEUM
(15 Mountjoy Pde; ⊙9am-5pm) FREE Inside Lorne Visitor Centre, this permanent exhibition of multimedia displays, videos and books offers informative background to the Great Ocean Road's remarkable construction that took place from 1919–32.

Live Wire Park · CLIMBING
(☑1300 548 394; www.livewirepark.com.au; 180 Erskine Falls Rd; entry adult/child $16/12, zip coaster $48/42, rope circuit from $66/60; ⊙9am-5pm, to 6pm summer) This adventure park with a state-of-the-art zip line and high-ropes tree courses is in the rainforest 900m from town. Its most thrilling feature is the Shockwave Zip Coaster, a zip line that flies through a twisting eucalyptus-canopy circuit, covering 525m in 1½ minutes. The two rope circuits (lasting from one to two hours) encompass swings, zip lines, tree climbs, obstacles and suspension bridges.

🛏 Sleeping

Great Ocean Road Cottages · HOSTEL $
(☑03-5289 1070; www.greatoceanroadcottages.com; 10 Erskine Ave; dm $35-50, d $100-180; ❈🐾🛜) On a lovely garden property replete with trees and birdlife, this friendly backpackers has dorm and private double options, both with cooking facilities. It's a five-minute walk from town, up a steep road running past the IGA supermarket. Cash bookings bring discounted rates.

Lorne Foreshore Caravan Park · CAMPGROUND $
(☑03-5289 1382, 1300 364 797; www.lornecaravanpark.com.au; 2 Great Ocean Rd; unpowered sites $41-82, powered sites $46-103, glamping $139-190, cabins $113-285; ❈🛜) Book at the Foreshore for all of Lorne's five caravan parks. Of these, Erskine River Caravan Park is the prettiest, though note that there's no swimming in the river. It's on the left-hand side as you enter Lorne, just before the bridge. Book well ahead for peak-season stays. Wi-fi is limited.

★Qdos · RYOKAN $$$
(☑03-5289 1989; www.qdosarts.com; 35 Allenvale Rd; r incl breakfast $325-420; 🛜) The perfect choice for those seeking a romantic getaway or forest retreat, Qdos' luxury Zen tree houses are fitted with tatami mats, rice-paper screens and no TV. Two-night minimum at weekends; no kids.

🍴 Eating & Drinking

★Lorne Beach Pavilion · AUSTRALIAN $$
(☑03-5289 2882; www.lornebeachpavilion.com.au; 81 Mountjoy Pde; breakfast $6-25, mains $14-34; ⊙9am-6pm Mon-Thu, to 9pm Fri, 8am-9pm Sat, 9am-4pm Sun) With its unbeatable foreshore location, life here is literally a beach, especially with a cold drink in hand. Cafe-style breakfasts and lunches hit the spot, while a more upmarket modern Australian menu of seafood and rib-eye steaks is on for dinner. Come at happy hour (3pm to 6pm) for $8 pints and $12 cocktails, or swing by sunset for a bottle of prosecco.

MELBOURNE & COASTAL VICTORIA LORNE

FREE CAMPING ON THE GREAT OCEAN ROAD

The following free campgrounds operate on a first-come, first-served basis, so you'll need to chance your luck. All sites have basic set-ups, with fire pits and non-flushing toilets.

Hammond Road Campground (☑13 19 63; www.parkweb.vic.gov.au; Hammond Rd, Wensleydale; free) Located 13km from Aireys Inlet.

Allenvale Mill Site Campground (☑13 19 63; www.parkweb.vic.gov.au; free) In the bush just behind Lorne.

Big Hill Track (☑13 19 63; www.parkweb.vic.gov.au; 1265 Deans Marsh-Lorne Rd, Benwerrin; free) Hidden away 15km north of Lorne.

Stevensons Falls Campground (Roadknight Creek Rd, Barramunga; free) Just outside Forrest, a 45-minute drive to Apollo Bay.

Sawpit Campground (Mount Clay State Forest; free) A short drive east of Portland.

WORTH A TRIP

FORREST

Tucked away in the hinterland of the Otways, a 30-minute drive north from Apollo Bay, the former logging town of Forrest has emerged as a tourist hotspot.

Since the closure of the logging industry the town has reinvented itself as one of the best mountain-biking destinations in the state; download a trail map at www.rideforrest.com.au/trails. In addition to renting out mountain bikes, **Forrest Hire Bikes** (☑ 0448 843 236; www.forresthirebikes.com.au; 33 Grant St, Forrest; bike hire half-/full day $50/80; ⊙ 8am-5pm Sat & Sun or by appointment) has a wealth of info.

Located 7km from Forrest is scenic Lake Elizabeth, famous for its population of platypuses and surreal scenery of dead trees jutting from the glassy water. **Otway Eco Tours** (☑ 0419 670 985; www.platypustours.net.au; adult/child/family $85/50/300) runs canoe trips at dusk and dawn to spot platypuses.

The town is also very well known for its microbrewery, the **Forrest Brewing Company** (☑ 03-5236 6170; www.forrestbrewing.com.au; 26 Grant St, Forrest; ⊙ 9am-5pm Sun-Wed, to 9pm Thu-Sat; ☜), where you can sample eight beers brewed on-site and dig into quality pub meals. The **Forrest General Store** (☑ 03-5236 6496; www.forrestgeneralstore.com.au; 33 Grant St; dishes from $8; ⊙ 7.30am-5pm) is also worth popping into to taste the artisanal gin they've started producing.

Chocolate is another reason to come by, with **Platypi Chocolate** (☑ 0433 362 639; www.platypichocolate.com.au; 73 Grant St; dishes $6.50-17; ⊙ 10am-5pm) offering a range of delectable homemade Belgian chocolates.

★ **Ipsos**   GREEK **$$**
(☑ 03-5289 1883; www.ipsosrestaurant.com.au; 48 Mountjoy Pde; sharing plates $7-26, larger plates $28-66; ⊙ noon-3pm & 6-10pm Thu-Mon, longer hours summer, closed winter) From the same family that ran Kosta – a much-loved Lorne restaurant – comes this smart taverna that occupies the same location where it all started in 1974. Run by sociable, young owner Dom, it has a menu comprising mainly Greek-influenced sharing plates, or go for the signature slow-roasted lamb shoulder ($66 for two people).

It received back-to-back *Good Food Guide* hats in 2019–20.

★ **MoVida Lorne**   SPANISH **$$**
(☑ 03-5289 1042; www.movida.com.au; 176 Mountjoy Pde; tapas $4.50-10, raciones $12-75; ⊙ noon-3pm & 5.30-10pm) One of Melbourne's hottest restaurants has gone for a sea change: setting up on the ground floor of the Lorne pub, MoVida has brought its authentic Spanish cuisine to the Great Ocean Road. The menu features a mix of classic dishes made with flair using regional produce.

Lorne Hotel   PUB
(☑ 03-5289 1409; www.lornehotel.com.au; 176 Mountjoy Pde; ⊙ noon-late) Since opening its doors in 1876, this pub has been Lorne's best spot for a beer. Its AstroTurf rooftop deck, overlooking the main street and ocean, is the place to be come summer, with regular bands and DJs. There's a whisky and gin bar downstairs, and its bistro also has views and is popular for its seafood platters.

The pub's **accommodation** (r $160-300; ❄ ☜) recently underwent a full refurb.

❶ Information

Lorne Visitor Centre (☑ 03-5289 1152, 1300 891 152; www.lovelorne.com.au; 15 Mountjoy Pde; ⊙ 9am-5pm; ☜) Has stacks of information (including heaps of ideas for walks in the area), helpful staff, fishing licences, bus tickets and accommodation referrals. Also has a gift shop, internet access, free wi-fi and a charger out the front for electric cars.

❶ Getting There & Away

If you're driving from Melbourne allow just under two hours for the 143km journey. Birregurra and Forrest, inland, are both around a 45-minute drive away.

V/Line buses pass through daily from Geelong ($12.80, 1½ hours) en route to Apollo Bay ($5.60, 50 minutes).

Wye River

POP 63

The Great Ocean Road snakes spectacularly around the cliff from Cumberland

River before reaching the tiny township of Wye River. Nestled discreetly in the pretty (steep) hillsides, just across from the ocean, it's a ripper of a community, and despite its small size it boasts one of the best pubs and one of the best cafes on the entire coast.

On Christmas Day 2015 major bushfires destroyed 116 homes in the area, and the entire town was evacuated; fortunately, no deaths were recorded.

Big4 Wye River Holiday Park CAMPGROUND $
(☑ 03-5289 0241; www.big4wyeriver.com.au; 25 Great Ocean Rd; unpowered sites $30-51, powered sites $38-78, cabins $135-185, houses $310-395; ✴ 🛜) Just back from the beach, this popular caravan park sprawls over 10 hectares. Featuring an Otways forest backdrop, it has grassy sites that are great for camping, and there's a range of comfortable units for couples and groups. There's a minimum two-night stay in summer.

★**Wye General** CAFE $$
(☑ 03-5289 0247; www.thewyegeneral.com; 35 Great Ocean Rd; mains $15-30; ⊙ 7.30am-4.30pm Mon-Sat, to 4pm Sun) This well-loved general store has provisions and groceries, but it's most noteworthy for its contemporary indoor-outdoor cafe-bar. With polished-concrete floors, timber accents and a sophisticated retro ambience, it does old-fashioned cocktails, beers on tap and a menu of breakfasts and all-day brunch items such as burgers and sourdough toasties.

★**Wye Beach Hotel** PUB
(www.wyebeachhotel.com.au; 19 Great Ocean Rd; ⊙ noon-11pm; 🛜) This is undoubtedly one of the finest coastal pubs in Victoria, if not Australia – the ocean views don't get much better. It has an unpretentious, local vibe and an all-regional craft-beer selection on tap, with brews from Forrest, Torquay and Aireys Inlet as well as one of its own.

🛈 Getting There & Away

Wye River is 159km from Melbourne, around a 2½-hour drive. It's positioned approximately halfway between Lorne and Apollo Bay on the Great Ocean Road.

There are several buses a day from Geelong ($15.80, two hours).

Kennett River

Located 25km east of Apollo Bay is Kennett River, a tiny, relaxed coastal community comprising not much other than a caravan park, a kiosk and holiday homes. As well as its fantastic beach, it's known for its great koala spotting by day, and glow-worms come evening.

Unfortunately, the town has suffered from the many tour buses that descend to see the koalas and feed the birds and has become a bit of a circus. Heed the signs, and *do not feed the birds,* especially as it will likely make them sick.

The friendly **Kennett River Holiday Park** (☑ 1300 664 417, 03-5289 0272; www.kennettriver.com; 1-13 Great Ocean Rd; unpowered sites $35-62, powered sites $41-72, cabins $120-244; ✴ 🛜) is one of the best sites along the coast, equally popular with surfers, families, travellers and young couples. The beach-view cabins have amazing vistas. There's free electric barbecues and a camp kitchen for cooking.

Kennett River is located directly on the Great Ocean Road, 165km from Melbourne. It's a 30-minute drive to Lorne. From Geelong there are three buses a day ($17.40, 2¼ hours).

Apollo Bay

POP 1598

One of the larger towns along the Great Ocean Road, Apollo Bay has a tight-knit community of fisherfolk, artists, musicians and seachangers. Rolling hills provide a postcard backdrop to the town, while broad, white-sand beaches dominate the foreground. It's an ideal base for exploring magical Cape Otway and the adjoining national park. There are some decent restaurants and lively pubs, and it's one of the best towns on the Great Ocean Road for budget travellers, with numerous hostels and ready transport access. It's also a popular stop for international package-bus tourists.

The Gadubanud people are the traditional custodians of Apollo Bay and the Otways region.

🏃 Activities

★**Mark's Walking Tours** WALKING
(☑ 0417 983 985; tours $25) Take a walk around the area with local Mark Brack, son of the Cape Otway lighthouse keeper. He

knows this stretch of coast, its history and its ghosts better than anyone around. Daily options include shipwreck tours, historical tours, glow-worm tours and the Great Ocean Walk (p262). Minimum two people.

★ **Apollo Bay Surf & Kayak** ADVENTURE
(☑03-5237 1189, 0405 495 909; www.apollobay surfkayak.com.au; 157-159 Great Ocean Rd; 2hr kayak tours $85, 1½hr surfing lesson $70) For a memorable wildlife encounter, grab a paddle and head out by kayak to visit an Australian fur-seal colony on these well-run tours. Weather-pending, they depart from Marengo Beach (south of the town centre); No children under 12 years. Also offers surfing and SUP lessons, plus board and mountain-bike hire ($40 per half-day).

🛏 Sleeping

Surfside Backpacker HOSTEL $
(☑03-5237 7263, 0419 322 595; www.surfsideback packer.com; cnr Great Ocean Rd & Gambier St; dm from $35, tw/d with shared bathroom $85/105; 🛜) Right across from the sand, this fantastic, sprawling 1940s beach house will appeal to those looking for a more quirky-style backpacker with true Apollo Bay character. Run by delightful owner Robyn, it has a homey lounge with couches, board games and huge windows looking out onto the ocean. Koalas are often spotted in the trees.

Pisces Big4 Apollo Bay CAMPGROUND $
(☑03-5237 6749; www.piscespark.com.au; 311 Great Ocean Rd; unpowered sites $36-58, powered sites $44-118, cabins $118-428; 🛜🏊) It's the unbeatable views from the oceanfront villas (from $180) that set this family-oriented park apart from the others. It's a sprawling site, with a suburbia-like layout, complete with street signs.

★ **Beacon Point Ocean View Villas** VILLA $$
(☑03-5237 6218; www.beaconpoint.com.au; 270 Skenes Creek Rd, Skenes Creek; r incl breakfast $170-370; 🅿🛜) With a commanding hill location among the trees, this wonderful collection of comfortable one- and two-bedroom villas is a luxurious yet affordable bush retreat. Most villas have sensational coast views, balcony and wood-fired heater. It's in Skenes Creek, 6km east of Apollo Bay. There's also a popular **restaurant** (☑03-5237 6411; www.chriss. com.au; 280 Skenes Creek Rd; breakfast $13-21, mains from $42-55; ⊙8.30-10am & 6pm-late daily, plus noon-2pm Sat & Sun; 🛜).

🍴 Eating & Drinking

Apollo Bay

Fishermen's Co-op FISH & CHIPS $
(☑03-5237 1067; www.facebook.com/apollobay fishcoop; Breakwater Rd; flake $8; ⊙11am-7pm) The best fish and chips in town is at the local fisherman's co-op, directly on the wharf. Most of its fish and crayfish is caught locally; check the Facebook page for the latest catch.

★ **Great Ocean Road Brewhouse** PUB
(☑03-5237 6240; www.greatoceanroadbrewhouse. com.au; 29 Great Ocean Rd; ⊙pub 11am-11pm Mon-Thu, to 1am Fri & Sat, Tastes of the Region noon-7pm Mon-Fri, from 11am Sat & Sun) Set up by renowned Otways brewery Prickly Moses, this taphouse pours an impressive range of its own and guest ales. The front bar is a classic pub and bistro, but through the back is the 'Taste of the Region' room, with a dozen of its own beers on tap to enjoy with tasting platters.

Grab a tasting paddle ($10) to sample five of its brews, which range from pale and golden ales to Pilsner, lagers and seasonals such as chardonnay IPA. You can also choose from a heap of other Aussie craft beers and an extensive regional wine selection. It has good-value pub rooms (from $75) too.

If that's not enough, its new **Apollo Bay Distillery** opened across the road in early 2020, producing gin and single-malt whisky, along with a pizzeria and local micro-roaster specialising in single-origin coffee.

ℹ Information

Great Ocean Road Visitor Centre (☑1300 689 297; www.visitapollobay.com; 100 Great Ocean Rd; ⊙9am-5pm; 🛜) Modern and professional tourist office with a heap of info on the area. Has free wi-fi and can book bus tickets too.

ℹ Getting There & Away

From Melbourne the fastest route is inland via the Geelong bypass that leads to Birregurra and Forrest, a 200km drive. If you're taking the scenic route along the Great Ocean Road (highly recommended), count on a 4½-hour trip.

Apollo Bay is easily reached by public transport from Melbourne ($30.80, four hours) via train to Geelong and then transfer to a connecting bus. There are three daily buses to/from Apollo Bay; stops include Torquay ($17.40, two hours), Anglesea ($12.80, 1½ hours) and Lorne ($5.60, 50 minutes). Heading west, there are three buses a week to Port Campbell ($12.80, two hours and 10 minutes) and Warrnambool

($23.80, 3½ hours), both departing on Monday, Wednesday and Friday.

Cape Otway

If you thought the Great Ocean Road was one long coastal drive, then this leg through the Otways may surprise you. Here the road heads inland, through shady rainforest with towering trees and fern gullies; it's home to a plethora of wildlife, most notably koalas. Cape Otway is the second-most-southerly point in mainland Australia (after Wilsons Promontory), and features a lighthouse that overlooks a beautiful, rugged coastline that's notoriously treacherous for shipping.

The Otway region is home to the Gadubanud people; you can learn about their culture at the Cape Otway Lightstation.

★**Cape Otway Lightstation**   LIGHTHOUSE
(☑03-5237 9240; www.lightstation.com; Lighthouse Rd; adult/child/family $19.50/7.50/49.50; ⊙9am-5pm, last entry 4.30pm) The oldest surviving lighthouse in mainland Australia, Cape Otway Lightstation was built in 1848 without mortar by more than 40 stonemasons. There are sublime coastal views from its observation deck, while the **Telegraph Station** has fascinating displays on the 250km undersea telegraph-cable link with Tasmania, laid in 1859. It's a sprawling complex with plenty to see, from Aboriginal cultural sites to a WWII radar bunker built to detect potential Japanese threats.

★**Bimbi Park**   CARAVAN PARK $
(☑03-5237 9246; www.bimbipark.com.au; 90 Manna Gum Dr; unpowered sites $25-40, powered sites $30-45, cabins $60-245; 🛜) 🏊 Down a dirt road 3km from the lighthouse is this character-filled caravan park with bush sites, cabins, bunkhouses, pods and old-school caravans. It's fantastic for families, backpackers and hikers on the Great Ocean Walk (p262). There's plenty of wildlife about, including koalas, and there's a rock-climbing wall ($15) and outdoor cinema. It has eco-cred too, with its use of solar power and water-saving initiatives.

Great Ocean Ecolodge   LODGE $$$
(☑03-5237 9297; www.greatoceanecolodge.com; 635 Lighthouse Rd; r incl activities from $395) 🏊 Reminiscent of a luxury African safari lodge, this mud-brick homestead stands in pastoral surrounds with plenty of wildlife. It's all solar powered and rates go towards the on-site **Centre for Conservation Ecology** (www.conservationecologycentre.org). Prices include a dusk wildlife walk with an ecologist, where you'll visit a tiger-quoll and potoroo enclosure. Bookings are mostly only available for weekdays.

Cape Otway Lightstation   B&B $$$
(☑03-5237 9240; www.lightstation.com; Lighthouse Rd; r incl breakfast & entry to lighthouse $255-395) There's a range of options at this romantic, windswept historic lighthouse. You can book out the whole Head Lightkeeper's House (sleeps 16) or the smaller Lighthouse Lodge (sleeps two), as well as other two-bedroom options for larger groups.

WORTH A TRIP

BRAE

Brae (☑03-5236 2226; www.braerestaurant.com; 4285 Cape Otway Rd, Birregurra; 8-course tasting plates per person $290, matched wines additional $180; ⊙noon-3pm Fri-Mon, from 6pm Thu & Sat) Regarded as one of Australia's best restaurants, Brae was established in 2012 by acclaimed chef Dan Hunter, who made his name at Dunkeld's Royal Mail Hotel. The restaurant mostly uses whatever's growing in its 12 hectares of organic gardens to create delightful gastronomic concoctions, all masterfully presented and with plenty of surprises.

Set within an attractive farmhouse cottage, Brae serves an eight-course tasting menu that changes daily, with flavours reflecting what traditionally grows in the area, including many Indigenous ingredients, which are arguably the highlight. Food is matched with regional wines, as well as offerings from local breweries and distilleries. For good reason the restaurant is a regular on the list of the World's Best 100 Restaurants; it reached number 44 in 2017. Reservations are essential, and need to be made well in advance. Their on-site boutique **accommodation** (☑03-5236 2226; www.braerestaurant.com; 4285 Cape Otway Rd; r incl breakfast from $615; ❄🛜) is also wonderful for a splurge.

WALKING THE GREAT OCEAN ROAD

The superb multiday **Great Ocean Walk** (www.greatoceanwalk.com.au) starts at Apollo Bay and runs all the way to the Twelve Apostles. It takes you through ever-changing land-scapes – along spectacular clifftops, past deserted beaches and into the dense eucalypt forests of the Great Otway National Park.

It's possible to start at one point and arrange a pick-up at another (public-transport options are few and far between). You can do shorter walks or the whole 104km trek over eight days. Designated campgrounds are spread along the walk, catering for registered walkers only; bring cooking equipment and tents (no fires allowed). Otherwise, there are plenty of comfortable accommodation options, from luxury lodges to caravan parks. Check out the helpful FAQ page on the website for all the info.

Walk 91 (☑ 03-5237 1189; www.walk91.com.au; 157-159 Great Ocean Rd, Apollo Bay; 3-day & 4-night self-guided walks incl accomodation from $663) and **Hike2Camp** (☑ 0497 132 047; www.hike2camp.com.au; per person 4-/6-day walks $690/890) can arrange your itinerary, transport and equipment hire, and can shuttle your backpack to your destination.

Port Campbell National Park

West of the Otways, the Great Ocean Road levels out and enters narrow, flat, scrubby escarpment lands that fall away to sheer, 70m-high cliffs along the coast between Princetown and Peterborough – a distinct change of scene. This is Port Campbell National Park, home to the **Twelve Apostles**, the most famous and most photographed stretch of the Great Ocean Road.

However, don't for a moment think that the Twelve Apostles constitute the road's end point. There's a string of iconic rock stacks west of Port Campbell, some arguably more scenic than the Apostles themselves, among them the **Bay of Islands** and **London Bridge**.

Other than the bay at Port Campbell, none of the beaches along this stretch are suitable for swimming because of strong currents and undertows.

The Kirrae Whurrong are the traditional custodians of this coastline.

◎ Sights

★**Twelve Apostles**   LANDMARK
(Great Ocean Rd; ⊘ 24hr) FREE The most iconic sight and enduring image for most visitors to the Great Ocean Road, the Twelve Apostles provide a fitting climax to the journey. Jutting out from the ocean in spectacular fashion, these rocky stacks stand as if they've been abandoned to the waves by the retreating headland. Today only seven Apostles (p265) can be seen from a network of viewing platforms connected by timber boardwalks around the clifftops.

Gibson Steps   BEACH
Follow 86 steps, hacked by hand into the cliffs by 19th-century landowner Hugh Gibson (and more recently replaced by concrete ones), down to wild Gibson Beach. You can walk along the beach, but be careful not to get stranded by high tides. It's a 50m walk from the car park, or a 2.2km return walk along a trail that sets out from the **Twelve Apostles Visitor Centre** (⊘ 10am-5pm Sun-Fri, to 5.30pm Sat).

Loch Ard Gorge   BEACH
Close to the Twelve Apostles, Loch Ard Gorge is where the Shipwreck Coast's most famous and haunting tale unfolded when two young survivors of the wrecked iron clipper *Loch Ard* made it to shore. There are several walks in the area, the most popular being the path down to the picturesque beach and cave where the pair took shelter. Further trails from here lead to scenic viewpoints, a cemetery, a blowhole and another rugged beach.

The Arch   LANDMARK
Offshore from Point Hesse, and well worth stopping for, the Arch is an intact bridge-like rock formation. It's believed that it will, one day – imminently – break into two separate rock stacks. There are some good photo ops from the various viewing points looking down on it.

London Bridge   LANDMARK
Around 7.5km west of Port Campbell, en route to Peterborough, London Bridge has indeed fallen down. It was once a double-arched rock platform linked to the mainland, but in January 1990 the bridge collapsed, leaving two terrified tourists ma-

rooned on the world's newest island – they were eventually rescued by helicopter. It remains a spectacular sight nevertheless. At dusk keep an eye out for penguins, which are often spotted on the beach, generally about 40m away.

The Grotto VIEWPOINT
A scenic stopover heading west from Port Campbell is the Grotto, where steep stairs lead down to a hollowed-out cavelike formation where waves crash through. It's approximately halfway between Port Campbell and Peterborough, a short drive from London Bridge.

★ **Bay of Islands Coastal Park** VIEWPOINT
Past Peterborough (12km west of Port Campbell), the lesser-visited Bay of Martyrs and Bay of Islands have spectacular lookout points from which to see rock stacks and sweeping views. Both bays have fantastic coastal walks, and there's a great beach at Crofts Bay.

🛈 **Getting There & Away**

V/Line runs a coach service from Apollo Bay to Princetown ($11.20, one hour and 10 minutes) three times a week on Monday, Wednesday and Friday, en route to Port Campbell and Warrnambool. However, having your own car is pretty much the only way to go in terms of exploring this area. The Apostles are 15km east of Port Campbell, with Loch Ard Gorge a little closer to town (around 12km). Other rock formations stretch 18km west of Port Campbell.

You can also arrange a **helicopter flight** (☑ 03-5598 8283; www.12apostleshelicopters.com.au; per person 15min flights $145) to take you over this dramatic stretch of coast. **Go West Tours** (☑ 03-9485 5290; www.gowest.com.au; from $125) and **Ride Tours** (☑ 0432 586 183; www.ridetours.com.au; tours $235) make the trip here from Melbourne.

Port Campbell
POP 478
This small, laid-back coastal town was named after Scottish captain Alexander Campbell, a whaler who took refuge here on trading voyages between Tasmania and Port Fairy. It's a friendly town with some nice little eating and drinking spots, which makes it an ideal place to debrief after visiting the Twelve Apostles. Its pretty bay has a lovely sandy beach, and is one of the few safe places for swimming along this tempestuous stretch of coast.

◉ **Sights**

Port Campbell Visitor Centre VISITOR CENTRE
(☑ 1300 137 255; www.visit12apostles.com.au; 26 Morris St; ◎9am-5pm) As well as invaluable tourist info and a fascinating display of items salvaged from historic shipwrecks (including the *Loch Ard* and the *Fiji*), this visitor centre offers a heap of activities. They very generously hire out free binoculars (for those visiting the penguins at the Twelve Apostles or doing some whale watching), a massive Newtonian reflector telescope for stargazing, as well as cameras, GPS gadgets and even an anemometer to measure wind speeds.

🛏 **Sleeping**

Port Campbell Guesthouse Flashpackers GUESTHOUSE $
(☑ 0407 696 559, 03-5598 6126; www.portcampbellguesthouseandflashpackers.com.au; 54 Lord St; r with shared/private bathroom from $100/140; ❋ 🛜) A place for independent-minded budget travellers who aren't into the hostel scene, this guesthouse feels more like going around to a mate's place. Set up within a historic cottage are four cosy rooms, a comfy lounge and a country kitchen with filter coffee. Its ultrarelaxed owner, Mark, is knowledgeable about the area.

If you're after added privacy there's a separate motel-style section up the front with en-suite rooms.

Port Campbell Hostel HOSTEL $
(☑ 03-5598 6305; www.portcampbellhostel.com.au; 18 Tregea St; dm/s/d/tr/q/f from $30/70/120/130/260/460; @🛜) This modern, sprawling double-storey backpackers has a range of clean mixed dorms and private rooms, along with a huge shared kitchen and an even bigger lounge area. It's a short stroll to the beach, and there's a bar with **Sow & Piglets** (☑ 03-5598 6305; ◎4-10pm) ales on tap and pizzas in the evenings ($10). Wi-fi in the lobby only.

Port Campbell Recreation Reserve CAMPGROUND $
(☑ 0431 128 790, 0407 666 610; www.facebook.com/PortCampbellRecReserve; 90 Hennessy St; unpowered/powered sites from $10/20; 🛜) For those with tents or campervans, this is the cheapest option in town. Head up just past the footy oval, where you'll find the

tin-shed reception to check in; if no one's around there's an honour system. There's a kitchen, laundry facilities, a toilet and shower block, and wi-fi. Rates increase peak season.

Sea Foam Villas   APARTMENT $$
(☑03-5598 6413; www.seafoamvillas.com.au; 14 Lord St; r $185-570; ❋🅿️) Located directly across from the water, Sea Foam undoubtedly has the best views in town. It's only really worth it, however, if you can snag one of the bay-view apartments, which are large, comfortable and luxurious.

🍴 Eating

★Forage on the Foreshore   CAFE $$
(☑03-5598 6202; www.forageontheforeshore.com.au; 32 Cairns St; dishes $13-36; ⊙9am-4pm Thu-Tue, longer hours in summer; 🅿️) In the old post office is this seafront cottage cafe with wooden floorboards, art on the walls, an open fireplace and a vintage record player spinning vinyl. There's an all-day breakfast menu, gourmet sandwiches and burgers, along with a seasonal menu of mains using fresh seafood and regional produce.

It serves local wines and top-notch single-origin coffee roasted by Cartel in Geelong.

12 Rocks Cafe Bar   CAFE $$
(☑03-5598 6123; www.12rocksbeachbar.com.au; 19 Lord St; breakfast $7-24, mains $16.50-38; ⊙9.30am-11pm) Your classic coastal beachside bistro, 12 Rocks is just about perfect for those who want a feed and a drink with waterfront views. Try an Otways beer with modern Australian pub fare such as beer-battered fish and chips, paprika-spiced calamari or their Rocks beef burger. They also serve up hearty breakfasts and decent coffee, along with ice cream from nearby Timboon.

ℹ Getting There & Away

V/Line buses leave Geelong on Monday, Wednesday and Friday and travel through to Port Campbell ($36.20, 5¼ hours), but you'll need to transfer to a different bus in Apollo Bay (2¼ hours), which generally leaves 30 minutes later. There's also a bus from Port Campbell to Warrnambool ($8.60, 1¼ hours) that leaves on the same days.

Warrnambool

POP 30,709

Once a whaling and sealing station, Warrnambool these days is the big smoke of the southwest, booming as a regional commercial and tourism centre. It has an attractive city centre, grand old buildings, numerous beaches, gardens and tree-lined residential streets, but the major housing and commercial development at the city fringes has rendered these areas much like city suburbs anywhere in Australia.

It's the whales that Warrnambool is most famous for, but it also has some great art galleries and historical sights. The sizeable population of uni students gives the town some spark, and you'll find cool bars and cafes.

The Gunditjmara people are the traditional owners of the land.

◎ Sights & Activities

★Flagstaff Hill
Maritime Village   HISTORIC SITE
(☑03-5559 4600; www.flagstaffhill.com; 89 Merri St; adult/child/family $19/9/49.50; ⊙9am-5pm, last entry 4pm) The world-class Flagstaff Hill precinct is of equal interest for its shipwreck museum, heritage-listed lighthouses and garrison as for its reproduction of an 1870s port town. It also has the nightly Tales of the Shipwreck Coast (adult/child/family $31/17/79), an engaging 70-minute sound-and-light show telling the story of the Loch Ard's plunge. The village has ye olde shoppes such as blacksmiths, candle makers and shipbuilders. If you're lucky the Maremma dogs will be around for you to meet.

★Warrnambool Art Gallery   GALLERY
(WAG; ☑03-5559 4949; www.thewag.com.au; 165 Timor St; ⊙10am-5pm Mon-Fri, to 3pm Sat & Sun) FREE One of Australia's oldest art galleries (established 1886), WAG has a stellar collection of works by prominent Australian painters. Its most famous piece is Eugene von Guérard's landscape Tower Hill, which is so detailed that it was used by botanists as a historical record when regenerating the Tower Hill area. There are contemporary pieces too, and several exhibitions run concurrently.

Logan's Beach
Whale-Watching Platform   VIEWPOINT
(Warrnambool Foreshore Promenade) Southern right whales come to mate and nurse their young in the waters near Logan's Beach from July to September, breaching and fluking off the platform. It's a major tour-

---

HOW MANY APOSTLES?

The Twelve Apostles are not 12 in number and, from all records, never have been. From the viewing platform you can clearly count seven, but maybe some obscure others. We consulted widely with Parks Victoria officers, tourist-office staff and even the cleaner at the lookout, but it's still not clear. Locals tend to say, 'It depends where you look from', which really is true.

The Apostles are known as 'stacks' in geological parlance, and they were originally called the 'Sow and Piglets'. In the 1960s someone (nobody can recall who) thought they might attract some tourists with a more venerable name, so the formations were renamed 'the Apostles'. Since apostles come in a dozen, the number 12 was added sometime later. The two stacks on the eastern (Otway) side of the viewing platform are not technically among the Apostles – they're Gog and Magog.

The soft limestone cliffs are dynamic and changeable, with constant erosion from the unceasing waves – one 70m-high stack collapsed into the sea in July 2005 and the Island Archway lost its archway in June 2009.

---

ist drawcard, but sightings are not guaranteed. Check the Warrnambool Whale Watch Facebook page or www.visitwarrnambool.com.au to see if the cetaceans are about.

★ **Deep Blue Hot Springs**　　SPA
(☑ 03-5559 2050; www.thedeepblue.com.au; 16 Pertobe Rd; hot springs weekday/weekend $55/66; ☺ 9am-7pm) After years in the making, Deep Blue's hot-spring sanctuary was unveiled in late 2019 to rave reviews. Featuring naturally geothermal waters sourced from 850m below, its 15 open-air pools (ranging from 36C° to 42C°) are arranged among beautifully landscaped grounds. Its bathing options offers an intriguing mix of experiences – from soaking in aromatherapy pools, to spas in rock-pools fitted with sensory sound-and-light features. Others include hydrotherapy spas, those with rainforest showers, foot spas and cold plunge pools. The sanctuary's stunning entrance features a futuristic contemporary design and a sci-fi salt cleansing room, while the surrounding lawn offers space to relax. Grab a detox beverage and a healthy bite from the grazing menu in the 'nourish dome' to round out the experience.

While the hot springs are for bathers 18 years and over, the adjoining day spa with indoor bathhouse is family-friendly, and offers an alluring range of spa treatments.

It's all part of a colossal resort complex with turret towers, located close to Warrnambool's main beach.

🛏 Sleeping

Warrnambool Beach Backpackers　　HOSTEL $
(☑ 03-5562 4874; www.beachbackpackers.com.au; 17 Stanley St; camping per person $15, dm $33-37, d from $90; @ 🛜) A short stroll from the beach, this hostel meets all backpackers' needs, with a huge living area, a kitschy Aussie-themed bar, free wi-fi, a kitchen and free pick-up from the train station. Rooms are basic but clean. 'Vanpackers' can stay here for $15 per person. There's bike, surfboard, stand-up paddleboard, wetsuit, kayak and fishing-equipment hire, and free use of boogie boards.

It's a 25-minute walk into the city, or there's a bus from here. It can also assist foreign backpackers looking for work in the area.

Hotel Warrnambool　　PUB $$
(☑ 03-5562 2377; www.hotelwarrnambool.com.au; cnr Koroit & Kepler Sts; d with shared/private bathroom from $110/120; ❄ 🛜) Renovations to this 1894 hotel have seen rooms upgraded to the more boutique end of the scale while keeping a classic pub-accommodation feel. The downside is that things can get noisy from the bar downstairs.

🍴 Eating & Drinking

Simon's Waterfront　　CAFE $$
(☑ 03-5562 1234; www.simonswaterfront.com.au; Level 1, 80 Pertobe Rd; breakfast $8-26, mains $18-31; ☺ 8.30am-10pm Tue-Sun, to 3pm Mon; 🛜) Feeling more Bondi than Warrnambool, this uber-trendy cafe has killer seafront views. Along with the usual cooked-egg options it does buttermilk pancakes with bacon and maple syrup, while for lunch there's a pleasing choice of seafood chowder, burgers and

nourish bowls. It's also a great place for a beer, or coffee from Melbourne roaster Seven Seeds.

★**Dart & Marlin** BAR
(☑03-5562 8659; www.facebook.com/thedartandmarlin; 216-218 Timor St; ☺5-10pm Tue-Fri, 2-10pm Sat, 4-10pm Sun) The city's coolest drinking den, this old-fashioned-style bar has plenty of character – from church-pew booth seating, art deco features and distressed walls to a battered piano that beckons to be played. Pull up a stool at the wooden bar to order from the quality selection.

It does artisan cocktails, local beers on tap and co-op cider. You can order pizza from the attached **Standard Dave** (www.standarddavepizza.com; pizza $16-24; ☺5-10pm Tue-Fri, 2-10pm Sat, 4-10pm Sun), run by the same folk. There's a beer garden out back for when the weather's nice.

Hotel Warrnambool PUB
(☑03-5562 2377; www.hotelwarrnambool.com.au; cnr Koroit & Kepler Sts; ☺noon-late; ☎) One of Victoria's best coastal boozers, the Hotel Warrnambool mixes pub charm with bohemian character and serves a range of beers and wines, along with wood-fired pizzas and other gastropub fare (mains $14 to $41). Its front dining room offers a more refined atmosphere and menu.

Rough Diamond CAFE
(☑03-5560 5707; www.roughdiamondcoffee.com.au; 203 Koroit St; ☺7am-2pm Mon-Fri, 8am-2pm Sat) So cool that it rocks an ugly brick 1970s motel-style facade – decked out with Astro-Turf and hipster signage – Rough Diamond does awesome single-origin coffee. Choose between African and Latin American beans for pour over coffees, and order from a menu featuring brekkie brioche buns, *croque monsieurs* and superfood salads.

ⓘ Information

Warrnambool Visitor Centre (☑1800 637 725; www.visitwarrnambool.com.au; 89 Merri St; ☺9am-5pm, extended hours in summer) For the latest on whale sightings, local tour and accommodation bookings, and walking-trail maps.

ⓘ Getting There & Away

Warrnambool is an hour's drive west of Port Campbell on the Great Ocean Road, and about 3½ hours' drive from Melbourne on the Princes Hwy (A1).

V/Line (☑1800 800 007, 03-5562 9432; www.vline.com.au) trains run to Melbourne ($39.20, 3½ hours, three or four daily).

There are two V/Line buses a week along the Great Ocean Road to Apollo Bay ($23.80, 3½ hours) on Wednesday and Friday, as well as four daily buses to both Port Fairy ($5.20, 30 minutes) and Portland ($13.80, 1½ hours). There's also a bus to Halls Gap ($30.80, three hours) three days a week on Sunday, Tuesday and Friday, via Dunkeld ($20.60, two hours), en route to Ararat ($36.20, three hours and 40 minutes). A coach to Ballarat ($20.60, two hours and 50 minutes) departs Warrnambool at 6.40am Monday to Friday.

ⓘ Getting Around

Cycling is a good way of getting to Port Fairy or Tower Hill (via Koroit) on the rail trail.

Otherwise there's Uber and local **taxis** (☑13 10 08) for getting around.

Tower Hill Reserve

Tower Hill, 15km west of Warrnambool, is a vast caldera born from a volcanic eruption 35,000 years ago. Aboriginal artefacts unearthed in the volcanic ash show that Indigenous people lived in the area at the time and, today, the Worn Gundidj Aboriginal Cooperative operates the **Tower Hill Natural History Centre** (☑0448 509 522, 03-5565 9202; www.towerhill.org.au; 1½hr walks adult/child $25.50/11.50; ☺10am-4pm, guided walks 11am & 1pm) **FREE**.

The centre is housed within a UFO-like building designed by renowned Australian architect Robin Boyd in 1962. Bushwalks led by Indigenous guides depart daily at 11am and 1pm and include boomerang-throwing and bush-tucker demonstrations. **Spotlighting night walks** (8pm; adult/child/family $28.95/14/65) are available with 24 hours' advance notice. The centre also sells handicrafts, artwork and accessories designed by the local Worn Gundidj community.

There are also excellent self-guided walks, including the steep 30-minute **Peak Climb**, with spectacular 360-degree views.

After a century of deforestation and environmental degradation, a detailed 1855 painting of Tower Hill by Eugene von Guérard (now exhibited in the Warrnambool Art Gallery) was used to identify species for a replanting program; over 300,000 trees have been replanted since 1961.

Parks Victoria manages the park and it's one of the few places where you'll spot wild emus, kangaroos and koalas hanging out together. It's also home to over 200 avian species, with its wetland habitat attracting both resident and migratory birds.

A short trip along the **Port Fairy–Warrnambool rail trail** (www.railtrails.org.au) is the historical township of **Koroit**, with a proud Irish heritage. It's noteworthy for its famed art noveau **pub** (☑03-5565 8201; www.mickeybourkes.com.au; 101 Commercial Rd; ⊗meals noon-2pm & 6-8pm, pub till late) as well as its new microbrewery, **Noodledoof Brewing Co** (☑03-5545 3178; www.noodledoof.com; 128 Commercial Rd, Koroit; tasting paddle from $16; ⊗7am-11pm Thu-Sat, to 5pm Sun).

Port Fairy

POP 3029

Established as a whaling and sealing station in 1833, Port Fairy has retained its historic 19th-century maritime charm. Here it's all about wide, tree-lined streets, heritage bluestone and sandstone buildings, whitewashed cottages and fishing boats. Add a dose of bohemian flair, and music festivals throughout the year, and you'll get a further idea of what makes the town tick.

With several nice beaches, surfing, fishing and plenty of wildlife to see, it was no wonder it was voted the world's most liveable small community in 2012.

⊙ Sights

Wharf PORT

Back in the 1850s the town's port was one of the busiest in Australia, serving as the main departure point for ships heading to England laden with wool, gold and wheat. Today there's still plenty going on at this charming marina, from luxury yachts to the weather-worn fishing boats moored here, along with a fancy new fish-and-chip restaurant.

Battery Hill HISTORIC SITE

Located across the bridge from Port Fairy's picturesque harbour, Battery Hill is worthy of exploration, with cannons and fortifications positioned here in 1887 to protect the town from the then perceived threat of Russian warships. Keep an eye out for the black wallabies that reside here. It was originally used as a flagstaff, so the commanding views don't disappoint.

WORTH A TRIP

12 APOSTLES GOURMET TRAIL

Head through the Corangamite hinterland on the **12 Apostles Gourmet Trail** (www.12apostlesfoodartisans.com) to indulge in a day of tasting cheese, chocolate, ice cream and single-malt whisky, among other fine regional produce. It's a 20-minute drive from Port Campbell.

Griffiths Island ISLAND

Where the Moyne River meets the ocean, Griffiths Island is home to a protected short-tailed shearwater (mutton-bird) colony; they descend on the town each October and stay until April (dusk is the best time to visit) before commencing their extraordinary 15,000km northern migration to Alaska. The 3km circuit makes for a lovely one-hour walk, passing the lighthouse (c 1859) and some swimming spots along the way.

✵ Festivals & Events

★ **Port Fairy Folk Festival** MUSIC

(www.portfairyfolkfestival.com; tickets $195-295, free events in town; ⊗Mar) Australia's premier folk-music festival is held on the Labour Day long weekend in March. It includes an excellent mix of Australian and international acts, and the streets are abuzz with buskers. Accommodation can book out a year in advance.

🛏 Sleeping

Port Fairy YHA HOSTEL $

(☑03-5568 2468; www.yha.com.au/hostels/vic/great-ocean-road/port-fairy; 8 Cox St; dm/s/d/f from $27/47/79/125; @🛜) Easily the best budget option in town, in the rambling 1844 home of merchant William Rutledge, this friendly, well-run hostel has a large kitchen, a pool table, free cable TV, a homely lounge and peaceful backyard. The owners Alison and Kadir are excellent sources of local info.

Merrijig Inn INN $$

(☑03-5568 2324; www.merrijiginn.com; 1 Campbell St; d from $130; 🛜) At the heritage-listed Merrijig, one of Victoria's oldest inns, you can choose between the quaint doll's-house 'attic' rooms upstairs and roomier, more comfortable rooms downstairs. There's a wonderful back lawn with veggie garden and silkie bantam chickens, plus comfy lounges with fireplaces throughout. Its restaurant (p268) is another reason to stay; add $30 for a delicious breakfast.

★ Drift House
BOUTIQUE HOTEL $$$

(📞 0417 782 495, 03-5568 3309; www.drifthouse.com.au; 98 Gipps St; d from $425; ❄️ 🐾) An intriguing mix of 19th-century grandeur and 21st-century design, Drift House is a must for architecture-lovers. Its grand frontage is that of the original 1860 double Victorian terrace, yet rooms feature ultra-slick open-plan designs and are decked out with boutique fittings. It's won a bunch of awards and is undoubtedly *the* spot to treat yourself in town.

Its next-door Edwardian weatherboard has also recently undergone a modern conversion and offers a tasteful balance between original and contemporary.

✕ Eating

Randy's Burgers
BURGERS $

(📞 03-4508 4202; www.facebook.com/eatrandys burgers; 24 Bank St; burgers $11-18; ⊙ 11.30am-2.30pm & 5.30-8.30pm) While Port Fairy may still miss its acclaimed fine-dining restaurant, Fen, the good news is that the owners Kirstyn and Ryan are back, and this time they're flipping burgers. The opportunity to dig into a burger cooked by a chef with two Good Food Guide hats is too good to pass up, and the likes of a 200g Wagyu cheeseburger won't disappoint.

★ Coffin Sally
PIZZA $$

(📞 03-5568 2618; www.coffinsally.com.au; 33 Sackville St; pizzas $14-22; ⊙ 4.30-8.30pm Mon-Sat, from 12.30pm Sun) This historic building, once used by a coffin maker, is now well regarded for traditional thin-crust pizzas, cooked in an open kitchen and wolfed down on street-side stools or in dimly lit dining nooks out the back next to an open fire. Its bar is one of Port Fairy's best spots for those into craft beers and well-made cocktails.

Merrijig Kitchen
AUSTRALIAN $$$

(📞 03-5568 2324; www.merrijiginn.com; 1 Campbell St; mains from $32; ⊙ 6-9pm Thu-Mon; 🐾 🍷) Here at Port Fairy's most atmospheric restaurant you can warm yourself by the open fire and enjoy superb dining with a menu that owner-chef Tanya Connellan changes daily, according to what's seasonal and what's local. It has a kitchen garden, house-cured meats and home-smoked fish, and features an award-winning wine list. Delectable food with great service.

ℹ️ Information

Port Fairy Visitor Centre (📞 03-5568 2682; www.portfairyaustralia.com.au; Railway Pl, Bank St; ⊙ 9am-5pm; 🐾) Provides spot-on tourist information, walking-tour brochures, free wi-fi, V/Line tickets, tourism brochures and publications. There's also bike hire (half-/full day $20/30), as well as free beach wheelchairs for travellers with disabilities.

ℹ️ Getting There & Away

Port Fairy is 20 minutes' drive west of Warrnambool on the A1 and just under an hour's drive to Portland further west. If you're coming from Melbourne it's a 288km journey, with the most direct route along the B140 highway from Geelong.

Taking public transport from Melbourne, it's a 4½-hour journey ($40.40) involving a train to Warrnambool, from where **V/Line** (📞 1800 800 007; www.vline.com.au) runs four to five connecting buses a day to Port Fairy (35 minutes). The bus here also heads to Tower Hill ($4.80) and Koroit ($4.80). There's also a bus from Port Fairy to Portland ($9.60, 55 minutes).

Portland
POP 10,061

Portland's claim to fame is as Victoria's first European settlement, founded as a whaling and sealing base in the early 1800s. Despite its colonial history, appealing architecture and beaches, blue-collared Portland feels much more like a regional hub than a tourist town.

That being said said, there's a lot on offer. The Great South West Walk (p270) is a big attraction, as are seafood and fishing, whale watching in winter, plus other unique wildlife encounters, and some good surf breaks outside town.

◉ Sights

Portland Maritime Discovery Centre
MUSEUM

(📞 1800 035 567; Lee Breakwater Rd; adult/student/child under 15yr $7.60/6.60/free; ⊙ 9am-5pm) Visit for excellent displays on shipwrecks and Portland's whaling history. Other highlights include a sperm-whale skeleton that washed ashore, a giant squid caught in 1997 and the original 1858 wooden lifeboat used to save 19 passengers after the disastrous wreck of the SS *Admella*. The **cafe** (📞 03-5521 7341; www.facebook.com/thecaptainsgalleyportland; mains $18-22; ⊙ 9.30am-3.30pm) has one of the best views in town.

Cape Nelson Lighthouse
LIGHTHOUSE

(☑ 0438 012 352; www.capenelsonlighthouse.com. au; Cape Nelson Rd; adult/child/family $15/10/40; ☺ tours 11.30am & 2pm) Head to the top of the still-operational Cape Nelson lighthouse (c 1884) for fantastic views overlooking the edge of the world. You'll be shown around the premises while hearing tales of shipwrecks and the history of area. The Australian film *South Solitary*, starring Miranda Otto, was shot here. It's 13km southwest from town, a 15-minute drive.

There's also **accommodation** (☑ 0428 131 253; www.capenelsonlighthouse.com.au; Cape Nelson Lighthouse; 1-/2-bedroom cottages incl breakfast from $200/270; ❄ ☎) in the historic lighthouse keeper's cottage.

Point Danger Gannet Colony
BIRD SANCTUARY

(Point Danger Coastal Reserve; ☺ Jul-Mar) Bird-lovers won't want to miss the opportunity to visit Australia's only mainland gannet colony, which can be viewed from a platform at Point Danger Coastal Reserve. However, for a truly unique Galapagos-style encounter, get in touch with the Portland Visitor Centre, which, with enough notice, can arrange the keys to open the fox-proof gate so that you can stand mere metres from these beautiful seabirds, who go about their business unfussed.

🛏 Sleeping & Eating

Hotel Bentinck
HISTORIC HOTEL $

(☑ 03-5523 2188; cnr Bentinck & Gawler Sts; motel s/d from $80/95, hotel r from $170; ❄ ☎) A rather grand **pub** (c 1856) on the main street, the Bentinck offers plush heritage rooms that strike the right balance between period touches and modern comforts. Room 27 is the pick, with water views, a spa bath and chesterfield couches. There are also motel rooms around the back; they're generic but get the job done.

Bahloo Portland
CAFE $$

(☑ 03-5548 4749; www.facebook.com/bahlooportland; 85 Cliff St; mains $15-26; ☺ 7.30am-4pm Mon-Fri, from 8am Sat & Sun; ☎) Housed in the original bluestone watchkeeper's house, across from the harbour, is one of Portland's best spots for hearty cooked breakfasts, loaded salad bowls, bagels and burgers. Its terrace is perfect for a coffee or glass of wine.

ℹ Getting There & Away

Portland is an hour's drive west of Port Fairy on the Princes Hwy (A1).

CAPE BRIDGEWATER

Home to one of Australia's finest stretches of white-sand surf beach, Cape Bridgewater makes for an essential 21km detour off the Portland–Nelson Rd. Its powdery white sands and turquoise waters resemble Queensland more than a remote Victorian beach. Though the beach is the main drawcard, there are also a number of walks featuring some dramatic scenery. It's a 1½-hour (return) walk to a viewing deck, from where you can observe the only place where Australian and New Zealand fur seals coexist; it's best to bring binoculars.

V/Line buses connect Portland with Port Fairy (from $9.60, 55 minutes) and Warrnambool (from $13.80, 1½ hour) four times daily on weekdays and twice a day on weekends. Buses depart from Henty St.

ℹ Information

Portland Visitor Centre (☑ 1800 035 567; www.iamportland.com.au; Lee Breakwater Rd; ☺ 9am-5pm) In a modern building on the waterfront, this excellent information centre has knowledgeable, helpful staff, with a stack of suggestions for things to do and see.

Nelson

POP 190

Tiny Nelson is the last outpost before the South Australian border – just a general store, a pub, a petrol station and a handful of places to stay. It's a popular holiday and fishing spot at the mouth of the Glenelg River, which flows through Lower Glenelg National Park. It's pretty much the halfway mark between Melbourne and Adelaide, and likes to think of itself as the beginning of the Great Ocean Road. Note that Nelson uses South Australia's 08 telephone area code.

◉ Sights & Acitivies

★ **Princess Margaret Rose Cave** CAVE
(☑ 08-8738 4171; www.princessmargaretrose-cave.com; Princess Margaret Rose Caves Rd, Mumbannar, Lower Glenelg National Park; adult/child/family $22/15/48; ☺ tours 10am, 11am, noon, 1.30pm, 2.30pm, 3.30pm & 4.30pm, reduced hours winter) Opened to the public in 1940, this limestone cave with surreal,

GREAT SOUTH WEST WALK

The 250km signposted loop that is the Great South West Walk begins and ends at Portland's visitor centre. It takes in some of the southwest's most stunning natural scenery: from the remote, blustery coast, through the river system of Lower Glenelg National Park, and back through the hinterland to Portland. The whole loop takes at least 10 days, but it can be tackled in sections, and parts can be done as day walks or even a two-hour loop. Maps are available from visitor centres in Portland (p269) and Nelson.

Visit www.greatsouthwestwalk.com for information and registration details.

gleaming calcite formations remains one of Australia's finest show caves. It can only be visited as part of a guided tour, which takes 45 minutes along the cave's illuminated walkways. The interpretative centre has good info on the cave's history. It's within Lower Glenelg National Park, 17km north of Nelson, and crosses the border before looping back over.

★ **Nelson Canoe Hire** CANOEING
(☑0409 104 798; www.nelsoncanoehire.com. au; hire per half-/full day kayak $40/65, canoe $45/70) Exploring the 65km stretch of scenic river along Lower Glenelg National Park on a multiday canoe trip is one of Victoria's best secret adventures. This outfit can kit you out for leisurely paddles or serious river-camping expeditions (three days including waterproof barrels; $150). There's no office, but it'll deliver all the gear; BYO tent and supplies.

Nelson Boat Hire BOATING
(☑08-8738 4048; www.nelsonboathire.com. au; dinghy per 1/4hr $55/130, motorboat per hr $65, houseboat per 2 nights $450-490; ☺Sep-Jul) Whether you head out for a few hours' fishing or hire a self-contained houseboat, cruising along the scenic waters of Lower Glenelg National Park will likely be the most relaxing part of your trip. The best bit is you don't need a boat licence. Houseboats sleep six and have a bathroom, fridge and kitchen; there's a two-night minimum hire period.

🛏 Sleeping & Eating

★ **Nelson Hotel** PUB
(☑08-8738 4011; www.facebook.com/Nelson Pub3292; 37 Kellett St; ☺11am-late; ☜) As real as outback pubs come, the Nelson Hotel (established 1848) is an essential stop for a beer and a friendly yarn with locals. It's got a character-filled front bar, featuring a dusty stuffed pelican, and a bistro serving quality meals (mains from $15). Owner-publican Neil is at the helm, and has the place back to its former glory.

Its budget accommodation is another selling point, with its basic rooms (singles/doubles with shared bathroom $45/75) recently refurbed and featuring character aplenty.

ℹ Information

Nelson Visitor Centre (☑08-8738 4051; www. nelsonvictoria.com.au; Leake St; ☺10am-12.30pm & 1.30-5pm; ☜) Good info on both sides of the border; particularly helpful for the parks and the Great South West Walk.

ℹ Getting There & Away

Nelson is 65km from Portland, and 4km from the South Australian border. Mt Gambier is the closest big town for provisions.

There's no public transport, so you'll need your own wheels. You could also walk here on the Great South West Walk.

MORNINGTON PENINSULA

This boot-shaped area of land between Port Phillip Bay and Western Port Bay has been Melbourne's summer playground since the 1870s, when paddle steamers ran down to Portsea. Today, much of the interior farming land has been replaced by vineyards and orchards – foodies love the peninsula, where a winery lunch is a real highlight – but it still retains lovely stands of native bushland.

The calm 'front beaches' are on the Port Phillip Bay side, where families holiday at bayside towns stretching from Mornington to Sorrento. The rugged ocean 'back beaches' face Bass Strait and are easily reached from Portsea, Sorrento and Rye; there are stunning walks along this coastal strip, part of the Mornington Peninsula National Park.

The bay heads are so close that it's just a short hop by ferry across from Sorrento to Queenscliff on the Bellarine Peninsula.

ℹ Information

Peninsula Visitor Information Centre (📞 1800 804 009, 03-5950 1579; www. visitmorningtonpeninsula.org; 359b Nepean Hwy, Dromana; ⊙ 10am-4pm; 🛜) The visitor information centre along the peninsula can book accommodation and tours, and stocks an abundance of brochures.

Love the Pen (www.lovethepen.com.au) Has a website offering food reviews, along with local tips and experiences.

ℹ Getting There & Away

The fastest way to Mornington Peninsula is via the tollway Eastlink (M3), exiting at the Mornington Peninsula Fwy (M11) via Peninsula Link. Point Nepean Rd (B110) also feeds into the Mornington Peninsula Fwy (M11), the main peninsula access. Alternatively, exit Moorooduc Hwy to Mornington and take the coast road around Port Phillip Bay.

Frequent Metro trains run from Melbourne to Frankston, Hastings and Stony Point.

BOAT

Westernport Ferries (📞 03-5257 4565; www. westernportferries.com.au; one way adult/ child/bicycle $13/6/4) Runs between Stony Point and Phillips Island via French Island.

Queenscliff–Sorrento Ferry (📞 03-5257 4500; www.searoad.com.au; foot or car passenger one way adult/child $13/9, driver & car one way/return $69/128; ⊙ hourly 7am-6pm, to 7pm Jan & long weekends) Sails between Sorrento and Queenscliff, enabling you to cross Port Phillip Bay by car or bicycle.

BUS

Public Transport Victoria (PTV; 📞 1800 800 007; www.ptv.vic.gov.au) Offers public buses across the peninsula.

Sorrento & Portsea

Historic Sorrento is the standout town on the Mornington Peninsula for its beautiful limestone buildings, ocean and bay beaches, and lively seaside summer atmosphere. This was the site of Victoria's first official European settlement, established by an expedition of convicts, marines, civil officers and free settlers who arrived from England in 1803.

The last village on the peninsula, posh Portsea is a bit like Victoria's equivalent of

---

WORTH A TRIP

MORNINGTON PENINSULA REGIONAL GALLERY

Mornington Peninsula Regional Gallery (MPRG; 📞 03-5950 1580; www. mprg.mornpen.vic.gov.au; Civic Reserve, Dunns Rd; adult/student $4/2; ⊙ 10am-5pm Tue-Sun; 🚌 785 from Frankston) One of Victoria's most impressive regional galleries, the MPRG has a permanent collection focusing on the cultural heritage of Mornington Peninsula as well as a notable collection of modern and contemporary Australian works on paper. Its exhibitions often explore the distinctive coastal environment and feature works by artists with a local connection. There are free guided tours at 3pm on Saturday and Sunday.

---

the Hamptons, where many of Melbourne's wealthiest have built seaside mansions. Other than the pub, of most interest for tourists are the dive shops here offering a number of tours – from wreck dives and snorkelling to sea-kayak trips to visit seals and dolphins – as well as nearby Point Nepean National Park.

🏃 Activities

⭐ **Bayplay** DIVING, WATER SPORTS
(📞 03-5984 0888; www.bayplay.com.au; 3755 Point Nepean Rd, Portsea; diving/snorkelling from $130/99; 🚌 788 from Frankston) This dive operator offers PADI courses as well as guided diving and snorkelling trips to see a heap of marine life, including sea dragons. It's also popular for its **sea-kayaking tours** (adult/child $99/88), where you can regularly spot dolphins and seals. Also available are SUP tours (two hours $75), sailing trips (from $99) and kayak hire (single/double from $55/70).

For landlubbers Bayplay organises camping and hires out bikes (per day $35) to explore the nearby Point Nepean National Park.

🛏 Sleeping

Sorrento Foreshore Camping Ground CAMPGROUND $
(📞 03-5950 1011; www.mornpen.vic.gov.au/activities/camping; Nepean Hwy, Sorrento; sites unpowered $26-55, powered $40-70; ⊙ late Oct-Apr; 🚌 788 from Frankston) Hilly, bush-clad sites between the bay beach and the main road into Sorrento.

Hotel Sorrento
HERITAGE HOTEL **$$**

(☑03-5984 8000; www.hotelsorrento.com.au; 5-15 Hotham Rd, Sorrento; weekdays/weekends d from $195/255, apt from $310/355; **P✿❀🐾**; 🚌788 from Frankston) The legendary 1871 Hotel Sorrento has well-equipped rooms in the main historical limestone building and 'On the Hill' double and family apartments in an adjoining modern block. The latter have airy living spaces, spacious bathrooms and private balconies with water views. Both its pub and rooftop bar have great views – a good spot for a drink.

🍴 Eating & Drinking

Sorrento Brewhouse
PUB FOOD **$$**

(☑03-5972 2483; www.sorrentobrewhouse.com.au; 154-164 Ocean Beach Rd, Sorrento; burger with chips $24; ⊙noon-3pm & 5.30-9.30pm) What food goes well with beer? Burgers and pizza of course. That's what's on offer at this popular brewhouse in an old house on Sorrento's main strip. They have nine of their beers on tap, and also serves boutique wine from the region. Sit inside or in the beer garden.

Morgan's Sorrento
SEAFOOD **$$**

(☑03-5984 3121; www.morganssorrento.com.au; 1 Esplanade, Sorrento; mains $25-65; ⊙11.30am-9pm; ❀) 🍴 This breezy beach bistro along Sorrento's foreshore has undergone a smart revamp, as well as a shift in culinary focus to create a menu driven by sustainable, local seafood. All of its produce is sourced from accredited sustainable suppliers, which features in well-prepared dishes such as seafood linguine, ceviche and shellfish mains, along with your classic fish and chips, and fish burgers.

★ Bistro Elba
AUSTRALIAN **$$$**

(☑03-5984 4995; www.bistroelba.com.au; 100-102 Ocean Beach Rd, Sorrento; mains $32-46; ⊙noon-10pm; 🐾; 🚌788 from Frankston) Its name references the sun-kissed Tuscan island, and Bistro Elba's menu reflects this Mediterranean inspiration. Stylishly casual, it's one of Sorrento's best restaurants and is sure to offer something to suit most palates. There's a fixed-price two-course lunch with a glass of wine ($40) and a popular happy hour (5pm to 6pm) when oysters are half-price.

Portsea Hotel
PUB

(☑03-5984 2213; www.portseahotel.com.au; 3746 Point Nepean Rd; ⊙11.30am-late; 🐾; 🚌788 from Frankston) Come to the historic, Tudor-clad Portsea Pub to take the local pulse. It's where the rich and powerful Melburnians who summer here flock to see and be seen, especially come polo season. Renovated in 2018, it offers three bars, a spectacular beer garden with bay views, wood-fire pizzas, and a mix of upmarket and classic pub fare.

WORTH A TRIP

BUDJ BIM CULTURAL LANDSCAPE

The traditional homeland of the Gunditjmara people, the Unesco World Heritage–listed **Budj Bim region** offers a fascinating insight into the ancient settlements of the Aboriginal people who've resided here for tens of thousands of years.

Of most interest to visitors is the **Tyrendarra Indigenous Protected Area**, the site of some of the oldest constructed aquaculture systems in the world, built by the Gunditjmara some 6600 years ago. A nature trail loops around the lava flow and wetlands, where you'll see a system of eel and fish traps and channels, as well as reproductions of the traditional round stone-and-thatch dwellings found in the region. While the area was badly hit by bushfires in late 2019, remarkably the damage revealed expansive new ancient aquaculture that previously was concealed beneath vegetation.

The best way to visit is through **Budj Bim Tours** (☑0458 999 315; www.budjbimtours.net; 12 Lindsay St, Heywood; 2½/4hr tours $70/100; ⊙from 10am Tue-Thu), an organisation run by the Gunditjmara that will guide you through the area, explaining the culture, traditions and land. However, the outfit is often difficult to get hold of, so aim to book two weeks in advance via email at leighboyer@windamara.com. Otherwise, it's possible to visit independently, with useful information boards along the way offering details of the trail.

It's on Taylors Rd, off Tyrendarra–Ettrick Rd, 2.5km north of the Princes Hwy (A1) and 32km northeast of Portland.

CAPE SCHANCK LIGHTHOUSE

Built in 1859, this working lighthouse (☎ 0407 348 478; www.facebook.com/theladyof history; 420 Cape Schanck Lighthouse Rd; tours incl museum & lighthouse adult/child/family $13/7/38; ☺ select weekends) sits in majesty on the peninsula's remote southwest tip. It's part of a historic precinct that you can explore anytime but to go inside the lighthouse itself you'll need to visit as part of a 30-minute tour, held on select weekends throughout the year and more regularly during high summer. Check the Facebook page for upcoming times.

From here you can explore the Mornington Peninsula National Park (www.park web.vic.gov.au/explore/parks/mornington-peninsula-national-park) along the 26km signed Coastal Walk to London Bridge near Portsea; other walks are detailed on the park's website

Accommodation (r with shared/private bathroom from $160/260; ✻ ☎) is available, too.

ℹ Information

Sorrento Beach Visitor Centre (☎ 03-5984 0065; www.sorrentobeachsidetourism. com.au; cnr Ocean Beach Rd & George St; ☺ 10am-4pm; ☎; ☐ 788 from Frankston) The visitor centre on the main drag has friendly staff who can offer advice about things to do and places to stay in the area.

ℹ Getting There & Away

Sorrento and Portsea are accessed from Melbourne, just under a two-hour drive, along Eastlink (M3) and the Mornington Peninsula Freeway (M11). By public transport, from Melbourne take the train to Frankston Station from where you can transfer to bus 788 to Sorrento and Portsea. Otherwise, the ferry (p271) is a great way to get across to Queenscliff, from where you can explore the Bellarine Peninsula and the Great Ocean Road.

Point Nepean National Park

Boasting expansive ocean views, this windswept national park (www.parkweb.vic.gov.au/ explore/parks/point-nepean-national-park; Point Nepean Rd; ☺ 8am-5pm, to 6pm late Dec-Mar; ℗; ☐ 788 from Frankston) on the peninsula's western tip was a seasonal base of its traditional owners, the Boon Wurrung people. After colonisation, a Quarantine Station was established here in 1852. Fort Nepean (www. parkweb.vic.gov.au/explore/parks/point-nepean-national-park; ☺ 8am-5pm, to 6pm late Dec-Mar), which played an important role in defending Australia from military threat, was built in stages from the late 1870s. Original gun emplacements remain there, as do the 50-odd

heritage buildings that made up the Quarantine Station.

There are a number of scenic walking and cycling trails in the park; gnarled Moonah trees *(Melaleuca lanceolata)* bent by the strong winds dot most of the landscape and local fauna including echidnas and wallabies can be spotted. Coles Track links the Quarantine Station with Gunners Cottage and Fort Nepean. En route keep an eye out for the Harold Holt memorial, the site where Australia's former prime minister remarkably disappeared after a swim here in December 1967.

The visitor centre (☎ 03-8427 2099; www.parkweb.vic.gov.au/explore/parks/point-ne pean-national-park; Quarantine Station; ☺ 10am-1pm & 1.30-5pm) offers walking maps or hire a bike (per three hours standard/electric bike $19.40/43.70); they often book out, so arrive early to avoid disappointment. Audio tours of Fort Nepean, the Quarantine Station and the park can be downloaded from the Parks Victoria website or the iTunes Store.

From Gunners Cottage car park, it's 2.6km. Alternatively a hop-on/hop-off wheelchair-accessible shuttle bus (adult/child return $12/8) travels between the Quarantine Station and the fort operating every 30 minutes between 10.30am and 4pm. This connects with the Portsea public bus stop (bus 788 to/from Frankston) three times daily; check the Parks Victoria website for details.

PHILLIP ISLAND

POP 10,387

Synonymous with penguins and petrolheads, Phillip Island attracts a curious mix of holidaymakers. At its heart, the island is still a farming community, but nature has conspired to turn it into one of Victoria's most popular tourist destinations. Apart from the major draws of the Penguin Parade and the annual Motorcycle Grand Prix, there's rich Indigenous history here (the Boon Wurrung people are the traditional custodians), as well as abundant birdlife and fauna. And there are also wonderful beaches, which are a major attraction in summer.

⊙ Sights

★**Penguin Parade**   WILDLIFE RESERVE
(⏹ 03-5951 2800; www.penguins.org.au; 1019 Ventnor Rd, Summerland Beach; general viewing adult/child/family $26.60/13.20/66.40; ⊙ parade times vary, access doors open 1hr before; 🅿) One of Victoria's major tourist draws, this evening parade of little penguins *(Eudyptula minor)* showcases the world's smallest, and probably cutest, penguins. The newly built multi-million-dollar complex includes interactive displays and amphitheatres that hold up to 3800 spectators who come to see the little fellas just after sunset as they waddle from the sea to their land-based nests. An underground viewing section, premium seats and VIP platforms are available for those wanting prime views; book well in advance.

★**Antarctic Journey**   OBSERVATORY, THEATRE
(⏹ 03-5951 2800; www.penguins.org.au/attractions/recreational-areas/the-nobbies; 1320 Ventnor Rd, Nobbies Centre, Summerlands; adult/child/family $18/9/45; ⊙ 10am–2hrs before sunset) Developed with the World Wide Fund for Nature (WWF), this cutting-edge multimedia exhibition has a spectacular location on the southwest tip overlooking the Nobbies. Its interactive displays focusing on the shared waters between this coast and Antarctica are highly informative, with clever augmented-reality features. There are 20-minute guided tours (included in the ticket price) at 11am, 1pm and 3pm daily. It's only a five-minute drive from the Penguin Parade, so aim to visit in mid-afternoon if you're seeing the penguins.

The Nobbies Boardwalk   VIEWPOINT
(⏹ 03-5951 2800; Summerlands; ⊙ 10am–1hr before sunset) **FREE** On the island's southwestern tip you'll pass by memorable landscapes of windswept grassy plateaus and rugged coastal scenery, leading to the Nobbies Centre that houses the multimedia Antarctic Journey. From here a boardwalk winds down to vantage points to view the offshore rock formations and the Seal Rocks, which are inhabited by one of Australia's largest colonies of fur seals; the boardwalk's one-in-14 gradient makes it reasonably accessible for people with a disability. Coin-operated binoculars ($2) allow you to view the seals.

🏃 Activities & Tours

Outdoor pursuits include hiking, cycling and – most notably – surfing. Beginners and families can go to **Smiths Beach**, where **Island Surfboards** (⏹ 03-5952 3443; www.islandsurfboards.com.au; 225 Smiths Beach Rd; lessons from $70, surfboard hire per hr/day $12.50/40; ⊙ 9am-5pm) offers surfing lessons and hires out gear.

In summer, the beaches at Cape Woolamai, Smiths Beach and Cowes are patrolled.

Phillip Island Circuit   ADVENTURE SPORTS
(⏹ 03-5952 9400; www.phillipislandcircuit.com.au; Back Beach Rd, Cowes) Petrolheads love the Island's motor-racing circuit, home to the annual Australian Motorcycle Grand Prix and a host of other motor racing events, on two wheels and four. The visitor centre runs **guided circuit tours** (adult/child/family $27.50/17.50/70; ⊙ tours 2pm), or check out the **History of Motorsport Museum** (adult/child/family $17.50/8.50/42; ⊙ 9am-5pm).

Wild Ocean Eco Boat   WILDLIFE WATCHING
(⏹ 1300 763 739, 03-5952 3501; www.wildlifecoastcruises.com.au/cruises/express-eco-boat-tour; 11-13 Jetty Triangle, Cowes; adult/child/family $85/65/235; ⊙ office 8.30am-4.30pm Jun-Aug, 9am-5pm Sep-May) 🛥 These high-speed boat tours visit the Australian fur seal colony at Seal Rocks and pass by the blowhole and 'pirate's cave' at Nobbies. A variety of other cruises and experiences are offered, so check the website for what's on.

🎉 Festivals & Events

Australian Motorcycle Grand Prix   SPORTS
(⏹ 1800 100 030; www.motogp.com.au; ⊙ Oct) The island's biggest event, this motorcycle race is held at the Phillip Island Circuit, which is generally acknowledged to be one of the most scenic circuits on the MotoGP international calendar. Its three days of petrolhead action are usually held in October, at which time the island's population jumps from 8000 people to over 150,000.

MICROBREWERIES & DISTILLERIES

Mornington may be famous as a wine-producing region, but a bunch of microbreweries and distilleries that have opened up, adding to the region's reputation as an epicurean destination. Check out the **Beer, Cider & Spirits Trail** (www.visitmp.org/BCSTrail).

St Andrews Beach Brewery (☑03-5988 6854; www.standrewsbeachbrewery.com.au; 160 Sandy Rd, Fingal; ☺11am-8pm; 🐾) Enjoy quality crafted beers at this upmarket microbrewery set within the former stables of Australia's finest racehorses.

Red Hill Brewery (☑03-5989 2959; www.redhillbrewery.com.au; 88 Shoreham Rd, Red Hill South; ☺11am-6pm Thu-Sun, extended hours summer; 🅿) Stop in for a pint at this bush brewery, who were producing interesting, non-mainstream beers well before the craft-beer explosion.

Mornington Peninsula Brewery (☑03-5977 0596; www.mpbrew.com.au; 72 Watt Rd; ☺3-9pm Wed, to 11pm Thu & Fri, noon-11pm Sat, to 7pm Sun; ☐781 from Frankston) This well-regarded, Mornington-based microbrewery does quality beers and wood-fired pizzas.

Jetty Road Brewery (☑03-5987 2754; www.jettyroad.com.au; 12-14 Brasser Ave, Dromana; ☺4-9pm Wed & Thu, noon-11pm Fri & Sat, noon-9pm Sun) A part of Dromana's backstreet boozy 'Bermuda Triangle', this popular taphouse brews top-notch beers and does tasty food.

Two Bays Brewing Co. (☑03-5910 0880; www.twobays.beer; 1/2 Trewhitt Ct, Dromana; ☺3-8pm Fri, noon-6pm Sat, noon-5pm Sun) Also in the gritty backstreets of Dromana is this gluten-free beer maker that also cooks up gluten-free pizzas.

Bass & Flinders (☑03-5989 3154; www.bassandflindersdistillery.com; 40 Collins Rd, Dromana; ☺11am-5pm Fri-Sun) The first distillery on the Mornington Peninsula was this artisanal gin producer, who were one of the first to use local Indigenous Australian botanicals.

JimmyRum Distillery (☑03-5987 3338; www.jimmyrum.com.au; 6 Brasser Ave, Dromana; ☺11am-10pm Thu-Sun) Artisanal rum made by aficionados who know their stuff.

Little Rebel (☑0421 875 772; www.littlerebel.com.au; 22 Collins Rd, Dromana; ☺8am-2pm Mon-Fri) 🐾 Third-wave micro-roaster who brews the best coffee on the peninsula.

🛏 Sleeping

Island Accommodation HOSTEL $
(☑03-5956 6123; www.theislandaccommodation.com.au; 10-12 Phillip Island Rd, Newhaven; dm/d from $29/135; 🅿🖾@🐾) 🐾 This YHA-affiliated backpackers hostel has two living areas complete with air-con in summer and fireplaces for winter. There are also two communal kitchens and a rooftop deck with terrific views. The cheapest dorms sleep 12 and doubles are motel-standard. The location isn't the best – you'll need your own transport to do any exploring. In summer, book ahead.

Cowes Foreshore Tourist Park CAMPGROUND $
(☑03-5952 2211; www.cowesforeshoretouristpark.com.au; 164 Church St, Cowes; sites/cabins from $41/95; 🖾🐾) Located right next to the beach, this park offers a range of powered and unpowered campsites as well as ensuite cabins sleeping up to six guests – the better ones have air-con and water views. Facilities include a children's playground and a camp kitchen. It's an easy walk into the centre of Cowes.

⭐**Clifftop** BOUTIQUE HOTEL $$$
(☑03-5952 1033; www.clifftop.com.au; 1 Marlin St, Smiths Beach; d $235-290; 🅿🖾🐾) It's hard to imagine a better location for your island escape than this classy place perched above Smiths Beach. Of the eight luxurious suites, the top four have ocean views and private balconies, while the downstairs rooms open onto gardens. All have comfortable beds and an attractive 'boho-luxe' decor. The communal lounge has a bar, wood fire and pool table.

🍴 Eating & Drinking

Bani's Kitchen MEDITERRANEAN $$
(☑0433 074 281, 03-5952 3106; www.baniskitchen.com.au; 10 Thompson Ave, Cowes; mains $18-52; ☺noon-3pm & 6-10pm Wed-Fri, 10am-9pm Sat & Sun; 🖾🐾🖾) Chef Manpreet Singh Tung seems an

unlikely candidate to be operating this place, as his cooking pedigree includes stints with acclaimed chefs Guy Grossi and Pam Talimanidis. But here on Phillip Island he is, and Bani's is a delight. Meat eaters should opt for the slow-cooked lamb or a souvlaki; vegetarians for the herb-laden vegan bowl.

Cape Kitchen MODERN AUSTRALIAN $$$
(☑03-5956 7200; www.thecapekitchen.com.au; 1215 Phillip Island Rd, Newhaven; mains $19-44; ⊘8.30am-4.30pm Fri-Mon; 🐾) Book a window table so that you can admire the ocean vistas while enjoying the contemporary bistro food served at the island's most fashionable dining option. The service is far better than most places in town, as is the wine list. It's a great breakfast.

Ocean Reach Brewing BREWERY
(☑03-5952 5274; www.oceanreach.beer; 47 Thompson Ave, Cowes; ⊘4-9pm Wed & Thu, noon-10pm Fri & Sat, to 7pm Sun, extended hours in summer) Close to the main beach in Cowes, this popular family-owned taphouse serves regular and seasonal beers brewed in Cowes – try the fruity and hoppy Island Pale Ale, or hedge your bets and opt for a tasting paddle (from $16). The on-site food truck serves American-style burgers ($17 to $21), buffalo wings ($14) and the like.

🛈 Information

Phillip Island Visitor Information Centre
(☑1300 366 422; www.visitbasscoast.com. au; 895 Phillip Island Tourist Rd, Newhaven; ⊘9am-5pm, to 6pm summer school holidays; 🐾) The main visitor centre on the island has a wall of brochures and maps. It sells tickets to

---

DON'T MISS

PENINSULA HOT SPRINGS

There are lots of spas and massage centres popping up along the peninsula but none can hold an aromatherapy candle to the large and luxurious **Peninsula Hot Springs** (☑03-5950 8777; www.peninsulahotsprings.com; Springs Lane, Fingal; bathhouse adult/child under 15 Mon-Fri $45/25, Sat & Sun $55/35, sanctuary $110, private bathing 45min $175; ⊘bathhouse 7am-10pm). It's proving to be a game changer for the region, with tourists coming far and wide to utilise the hot, mineral-rich waters pumped from deep underground.

---

the Penguin Parade, as well as discounted sights packages. It also offers a helpful accommodation booking service.

Cowes Visitor Information Centre (☑1300 366 422; www.visitphillipisland.com; cnr Thompson Ave & Church St, Cowes; ⊘9am-5pm) This smaller visitor centre offers a more convenient alternative for those staying in Cowes.

🛈 Getting There & Away

Located about 140km from Melbourne by car, Phillip Island can only be accessed by crossing the bridge between San Remo and Newhaven. From Melbourne take Monash Fwy (M1) and exit at Pakenham, joining South Gippsland Hwy at Koo Wee Rup.

If you're on foot or bicycle, you can get here by ferry from Stony Point to Cowes.

By public transport you'll need to take two V/Line coaches and one South Coast Bus coach to travel from Southern Cross Station to Cowes, a 2¾ hour trip via Koo Wee Rup ($15.80).

Westernport Ferries (☑03-5257 4565; www. westernportferries.com.au; Cowes Jetty; one way adult/child/bicycle $13/6/4; ⊘departures 8.35am-6pm Mon-Fri, to 5.30pm Sat & Sun) Runs between Stony Point on the Mornington Peninsula and Cowes via French Island. Check the website for the schedule.

WILSONS PROMONTORY & GIPPSLAND

The Great Ocean Road gets the crowds, but Gippsland hides all the secrets. Gippsland is one region where it pays to avoid the cities – the towns along the Princes Hwy are barely worth a glance. But beyond the highway are some of the state's most unspoilt and beautiful wilderness areas and beaches.

Along the coast there's Wilsons Promontory National Park, a fabulous destination for hikers and sightseers alike. This is only the start when it comes to stirring beaches. Epic Ninety Mile Beach yields to Cape Conran Coastal Park and Croajingolong National Park. Put them together and it's one of the wildest, most beautiful coastlines on Earth.

Unfortunately the area was badly affected by the 2019-20 bush fires which tore through the eastern part of the state.

Fish Creek

POP 827
Travellers in the know have been stopping for a bite to eat at Fish Creek on their way to

MORNINGTON PENINSULA WINERY RESTAURANTS

In addition to hitting the coast, taking an inland detour for a day of wine tasting and dining is a highly recommend part of any visit to the Mornington Peninsula. For an overview, check out **Mornington Peninsula Wineries & Region** (www.mpva.com.au).

Pt. Leo Estate (☑ 03-5989 9011; www.ptleoestate.com.au; 3649 Frankston-Flinders Rd, Merricks; tastings $10, sculpture park adult/concession/family $10/5/25; ☉ 11am-5pm daily, 6-10pm Thu-Sat; P 🍴) Overlooking Western Port Bay, this swanky multi-million dollar winery has two acclaimed restaurants and a huge sculpture garden.

Jackalope (☑ 03-5931 2500; www.jackalopehotels.com; 166 Balnarring Rd, Merricks North; r incl breakfast from $540; P ❋ 🛜 ☒) One of the peninsula's most fashionable wineries is this upmarket estate comprising cellar door, fine dining and luxury accomodation.

Lindenderry at Red Hill (☑ 03-5989 2933; www.lancemore.com.au/lindenderry; 142 Arthurs Seat Rd, Red Hill; pizza $22-24; ☉ cellar door noon-3pm Sat & Sun, restaurant noon-3pm Fri-Sun & 6-10pm Mon-Sat) Choose between fine-dining, cellar-door pizzeria or a picnic in its gorgeous gardens. Its luxurious hotel is one of peninsula's best.

Main Ridge Estate (☑ 03-5989 2686; www.mre.com.au; 80 William Rd, Red Hill; ☉ noon-5pm Fri-Sun) One of Mornington's oldest wineries, here you can taste its estate-grown pinot and chardonnay, enjoyed with shared plates.

Montalto (☑ 03-5989 8412; www.montalto.com.au; 33 Shoreham Rd, Red Hill South; mains $26-36, restaurant set menu $160; ☉ cafe 11am-5pm, restaurant noon-2.30pm daily & from 6pm Fri & Sat; P 🍴) A long-time crowd pleaser, this winery offers fine dining, a garden cafe and whimsical sculpture garden.

Port Phillip Estate (☑ 03-5989 4444; www.portphillipestate.com.au; 263 Red Hill Rd, Red Hill South; bistro 2-course meal $38, restaurant 2-/3-course meal $68/85; ☉ cellar door 11am-5pm, bistro noon-3pm Sat-Tue, restaurant noon-3pm Wed-Sun & 6.30-8.30pm Fri & Sat; P ❋) Inside an architecturally resplendent winery building that resembles a Bond villain's lair is a restaurant, bistro, magnificent cellar door and boutique accommodation.

Red Hill Estate (☑ 03-5989 2838; www.redhillestate.com.au; 53 Shoreham Rd, Red Hill South; ☉ cellar door 11am-5pm) This well-respected winery makes quality food and wine, enjoyed with magnificent views over the vines down to Western Port Bay.

Ten Minutes By Tractor (☑ 03-5989 6080; www.tenminutesbytractor.com.au; 1333 Mornington-Flinders Rd, Main Ridge; ☉ cellar door 11am-5pm, restaurant noon-3pm Wed-Sun & 6.30-10pm Thu-Sat) A perennial favourite, this elegant fine diner and wine cellar is looking better than ever after its reopening in late 2019.

the coast or Wilsons Promontory for years. These days it has developed into a little bohemian community, with craft shops, galleries, studios, bookshops and some great cafes. The **Great Southern Rail Trail** (www.gsrt.com.au) passes through too.

Fish Creek Hotel PUB $
(☑ 03-5683 2404; 1 Old Waratah Rd; d with shared bathroom $85-100, with private bathroom $110-130; ☉ noon-2pm & 6-9pm; ❋ 🛜) The colossal art deco Fish Creek Hotel, universally known as the Fishy Pub, is an essential stop for a beer or **bistro meal** (mains $18-34; ☉ kitchen 11.45am-2.30pm & 5.30-8.30pm) and serves as a handy base for trips into Wilsons Prom. There's a choice of comfortable pub rooms upstairs (no TV or kettle) with shared bathrooms, and motel accommodation at the back.

Paddock CAFE $
(☑ 03-5605 9413; www.facebook.com/thepaddockcoffeehouse; 2 Old Waratah Rd; mains $10-19; ☉ 8am-2.30pm Wed-Sun) One of the best spots for coffee in South Gippsland is this rustic cafe-provedore with a countrified inner-Melbourne vibe. Its menu is big on local produce, as well as pies and cakes.

★**Gurneys Cider** CIDERY
(☑ 0423 039 863; www.gurneyscider.com.au; 343 Fish Creek-Foster Rd; ☉ 11am-5pm Wed-Sun, daily summer, Fri-Sun winter) Run by a family of ex-pat Brits, Gurneys is an impressive, hands-on team of cider-makers who are passionate about producing real dry English ciders. Everything is made on-site using 30 types of apples that grow in its orchards. Tasting paddles are available ($10 to $14), or you can

buy cider by the bottle to enjoy the pastoral views with a produce platter (from $22).

❶ Getting There & Away

For Fish Creek, follow the signs off the South Gippsland Hwy at Foster (13km) or Meeniyan (28km). It's 24km (20 minutes) from the Wilsons Promontory entrance gate. There are four direct daily buses from Melbourne's Southern Cross Station ($22.20, three hours).

Wilsons Promontory National Park

If you like wilderness bushwalking, stunning coastal scenery and secluded white-sand beaches, you'll absolutely love the Prom. Given its accessibility from Melbourne, its network of more than 80km of walking tracks, its swimming and surf beaches, and its abundant wildlife, it's hardly surprising that Wilsons Promontory is one of the most popular national parks in Australia.

The southernmost part of mainland Australia, the Prom once formed part of a land bridge that allowed people to walk to Tasmania. The Brataualung clan from the Gunai and Kurnai nation are the traditional custodians of this land.

Tidal River, 30km from the park entrance, is the hub, home to the Parks Victoria office, a general store, a cafe and accommodation. The wildlife around Tidal River is incredibly tame, but to prevent disease, don't feed the animals or birds.

◉ Sights & Activities

Norman Beach   BEACH

(Tidal River) The Prom's most popular beach is this beautiful stretch of golden sand, conveniently located at Tidal River Campground. It's patrolled by surf life-savers in January; at other times, don't swim beyond waist depth as there are rips.

Wilsons Promontory Cruises   CRUISE

(☑0428 400 155; www.promcruises.com.au; Tidal River; 2½hr cruise adult/child/family $135/85/430; ⊙departures 11am daily & 2pm mid-Dec–late Mar) Launching directly off the beach in custom-made, yellow amphibious boats, these new eco-boat tours offer memorable up close views of the Prom's spectacular coastline and natural landmarks. Trips include passing by the mysterious

Skull Rock, and you'll often encounter seals, dolphins and whales.

🛏 Sleeping & Eating

The main accommodation base is Tidal River, comprising campsites and cabins. There are bush sites in the southern and northern sections of the park. Book online or through the visitor centre (p280) at Tidal River.

Otherwise, surrounding towns have B&Bs and motels that you can use as a base for visiting the park on a day trip.

Park Campsites   CAMPGROUND $

(☑03-8427 2122, 13 19 63; www.parkweb.vic.gov.au; unpowered/powered sites from $31.40/35) Campsites are sprawled across the Tidal River precinct and along the foreshore close to the beach. A maximum of six campers are allowed at each site. There's access to hot showers, flush toilets, a dishwashing area, rubbish-disposal points and gas barbecues. No campfires permitted.

Park Huts   HUT $

(☑13 19 63, 03-8427 2122; www.parkstay.vic.gov.au; Tidal River; 4-/6-bed huts from $118/181) If you're travelling tent free, these cosy wooden huts are a decent option, with bunks, small fridge, kitchenette and cooking utensils. Bathrooms are shared. Bring your own linen, pillows and towels.

★ Wilsons Promontory Lightstation   COTTAGE $$$

(☑13 19 63, 03-5680 9555; www.parkweb.vic.gov.au; d cottages $383-415, 12-bed cottages per person $138-150) These isolated, heritage-listed 1850s cottages, attached to a working lightstation on a small dot of land that juts into the ocean, are a real getaway. Kick back after the 19km hike (around six hours) from Tidal River and watch ships or whales passing by. Banks Cottage is ideal for couples, while the other cottage has bunks ideal for groups.

All have a fully equipped kitchen, so bring food for cooking. At the bunk cottage you'll need to bring your own linen and towels.

Wilderness Retreat   TENTED CAMP $$$

(☑03-8427 2122, 13 19 63; www.parkweb.vic.gov.au; d $338.40, extra person $26) Nestled in bushland, these large safari tents each have their own deck, bathroom, queen-size bed, fridge and heating, and there's a communal tent kitchen. Tents sleep up to four.

Wilsons Promontory National Park

Snake Island

Entrance Point

Shelter Cove

Freshwater Cove

Mt Singapore (147m)

Fish Creek (16km); Foster (25km)

C444 Yanakie

Dalgleish Rd

Limosa Rise

Duck Point

Yanakie Beach

Tin Mine Cove

Mt Hunter (347m)

Hunter Point

Foley Rd

Black Cockatoo Cottages

Corner Inlet

Corner Inlet Marine National Park

Chinaman Long Beach

Lighthouse Point

Millar Rd

Foster-Promontory Rd

Top of the Prom at Promview Farm

Long Island

Mt Margaret (218m)

Tin Mine Track

Three Mile Beach

Park Entrance Booth

Bennison Island

Three Mile Point

Stockyard Camp

Big Drift Walk

Chinamans Knob

Johnnie Souey Cove

Wilsons Promontory Rd

Millers Landing

Mt Roundback (316m)

Burry Creek

Chinaman Creek

Johnny Souey Track

Five Mile Rd

St Kilda Junction

Monkey Point

Cotters Beach

Vereker Lookout

Vereker Range

Five Mile Beach

Shellback Island

Emergencies Only

Mt Vereker (586m)

Darby Bay

Darby Beach

Lookout Rocks

Darby Creek

Mt Leonard (556m)

Latrobe Range

Mt Latrobe (754m)

The Cathedral

Tongue Point

Sparkes Lookout

Mt Bishop (319m)

Tidal River

Sealers Creek

Sealers Cove

Horn Point

Whisky Bay

Picnic Bay

Telegraph Saddle Car Park

Mt Ramsay

Sealers Cove Walk

Hobbs Head

Norman Island

Leonard Point

Squeaky Beach

Tidal River

Telegraph Saddle

Wilsons Range

Refuge Cove

Brown Head

Norman Bay

Mt Oberon (558m)

Kersops Peak

Norman Point

Little Oberon Bay

Mt Wilson (705m)

Little Waterloo Bay

Cape Wellington

Great Glennie Island

Oberon Bay

Oberon Point

Growler Creek

Mt Boulder (501m)

Waterloo Bay

Dannevig Island

Mt Norgate (419m)

Telegraph Track

Fraser Creek

Waterloo Point

Citadel Island

McHugh Island

Wilsons Promontory Marine National Park

Boulder Range

Lighthouse

Wilsons Promontory Lightstation

South West Point

Roaring Meg Creek

Anser Island

Wattle Island

South Point

South-East Point

Skull Rock

BASS STRAIT

TOP PROM WALKS

There's an extensive choice of marked walking trails, taking you through forests, marshes, valleys of tree ferns, low granite mountains and beaches lined with sand dunes. The Parks Victoria office at Tidal River has brochures with details of walks, from 15-minute strolls to multiday hikes.

Day Hikes

Mt Oberon Summit Starting from the Telegraph Saddle car park, this moderate-to-hard 7km-return walk is an ideal introduction to the Prom, with stunning panoramic views from the summit.

Lilly Pilly Gully Nature Walk An easy 5km (1½-hour) return walk through heathland and eucalypt forest, with lots of wildlife.

Squeaky Beach Nature Walk An easy 5km (two-hour) return stroll from Tidal River through coastal tea trees and banksias leads to a sensational white (and squeaky) sand beach.

Prom Wildlife Walk In the north of the park, this short 2.3km (45-minute) loop trail yields good potential kangaroo, wallaby and emu sightings. It's off the main road about 14km south of the park entrance.

Sealers Cove This popular 19km hike (six hours' return) takes you through pristine forest and along boardwalks that lead to a gorgeous sandy cove. There's a campsite here if you want to spend the night.

Vereker Outlook In the north of the park, this walk leads from the Five Mile Rd car park (6km, two hours' return) through varied bush landscapes and past granite boulders, with fantastic coastal views along the way.

Big Drift Walk A short walk from Stockyard Campground at the park's entrance are these spectacular sand dunes best viewed at sunrise or sunset.

Overnight Hikes

For all overnight walks you'll need to arrange a campsite ($7 per person per night) before setting off. You can do this online at www.parks.vic.gov.au, but you'll need to check in at the Tidal River information centre before heading off.

The best overnight hike, the **Southern Prom Hike (Southern Circuit)**, is a two-day walk that starts at Telegraph Saddle and heads down Telegraph Track to overnight at beautiful **Little Waterloo Bay** (12km, 4½ hours). The next day, walk on to **Sealers Cove** via the lovely beach at **Refuge Cove** and return to Telegraph Saddle (20km, 7½ hours).

The most popular long-distance hike, the **Lighthouse Walk (Southern Circuit)**, is a moderate 51km circuit across to Sealers Cove from Tidal River, down to Refuge Cove, Waterloo Bay and the **lighthouse**, and then back to Tidal River via Oberon Bay. Allow three days and coordinate your walk with tide times, as creek crossings can be hazardous. It's possible to visit or stay at the lightstatioby prior arrangement through the website or the park office.

Overnight walks in the **Northern Circuit** are through remote wilderness with no set trails. They're suitable only for seasoned trekkers with honed navigational skills.

You'll feel as though you're on an African safari with a kookaburra soundtrack.

Tidal River General Store & Cafe CAFE $
(☑ 03-5680 8520; dishes from $6; ⊘ 9am-5pm Mon-Fri, to 6pm Sat, to 4pm Sun, longer hours Jan) Tidal River's general store has grocery items, ice, some camping equipment and gas bottles, but if you're hiking or staying a while it's cheaper to stock up in Foster. The cafe

serves takeaway food such as pies, burgers, fish and chips and sandwiches, as well as all-day breakfasts, and meats and bread for a barbecue. No alcohol is sold here.

Information

Tidal River Visitor Centre (☑ 03-5680 9555, 03-8427 2122, 13 19 63; www.parkweb.vic.gov. au; ⊘ 8.30am-4.30pm, to 4pm winter) Handles all park accommodation (including permits for camping away from Tidal River) and offers info on the area's hiking options. It also has lockers for campers to charge devices, and a range of equipment, including all-terrain and beach wheelchairs, for travellers with limited mobility.

ⓘ Getting There & Away

Tidal River is approximately 224km southeast of Melbourne. There's no fuel here; the closest petrol station is at Yanakie, 7km north from the park's entrance gate.

There's no direct public transport between Melbourne and the Prom. The closest towns accessible by direct V/Line bus are Fish Creek ($22.20, three hours) and Foster ($25, 3¼ hours, three daily). From there you'll need to find a lift by other means.

Lakes District

The Gippsland Lakes form the largest inland waterway system in Australia, with the three main interconnecting lakes – Wellington, King and Victoria – stretching from Sale to beyond Lakes Entrance. The lakes are actually saltwater lagoons, separated from the ocean by the Gippsland Lakes Coastal Park and the coastal strip of sand dunes known as Ninety Mile Beach. Apart from the beach and taking to the water, the highlights here involve hanging out at the relaxed seaside communities.

Ninety Mile Beach

To paraphrase the immortal words of Crocodile Dundee...that's not a beach, *that's* a beach. Isolated Ninety Mile Beach is a narrow strip of dune-backed sand punctuated by lagoons and stretching unbroken for more or less 90 miles (150km) from near McLoughlins Beach to the channel at Lakes Entrance. The area is great for surf fishing, camping and *long* beach walks, though the crashing surf can be dangerous for swimming, except where patrolled at Seaspray, Woodside Beach and Lakes Entrance.

Lakes Entrance

POP 6071

With the shallow Cunninghame Arm waterway separating the town from ocean beaches, Lakes Entrance basks in an undeniably pretty location. In holiday season it's a packed-out, tacky tourist town with a graceless strip of motels, caravan parks, mini-golf courses and souvenir shops lining

KROWATHUNKOOLOONG KEEPING PLACE

A stirring and well-curated cultural exhibition space, **Krowathunkooloong Keeping Place** (☑ 03-5150 0737, 03-5152 1891; www.batalukculturaltrail.com. au; 37-53 Dalmahoy St; adult/child/family $6/4/15; ⊙ 10am-4pm Mon-Fri) offers a fascinating insight into the history and traditions of the Gunai and Kurnai nation and its five clans, who've lived in the East Gippsland region for well over 30,000 years. The exhibition traces the Gunai and Kurnai from their Dreaming ancestors, Borun the pelican and his wife, Tuk the musk duck, and features an impressive display of original artefacts and traditional cultural items, including canoes, boomerangs and contemporary Aboriginal art.

It's one several stops along the **Bataluk Cultural Trail** (www.batalu kculturaltrail.com.au), a must for those seeking further engagement with the traditions and culture of the Gunai and Kurnai.

the Esplanade. Still, the bobbing fishing boats, fresh seafood, endless beaches, and cruises out to Metung and Wyanga Park Winery should win you over.

The Tatungalung and Krauatungalung clans from the Gunai and Kurnai nation are the traditional custodians of this land. The Aboriginal community that lives both here and at nearby Lake Tyers is the second-largest in the state behind that of Shepparton.

🏃 Activities

★ **Venture Out**   ADVENTURE SPORTS

(☑ 0427 731 441; www.ventureout.com.au; 347b The Esplanade; mountain-bike, SUP & kayak hire per 2hr/day from $29/59, tours from $49; ⊙ 9am-5pm Tue-Sat Feb-Apr & Sep-Nov, daily Dec & Jan, 10am-4pm Tue-Sat May-Aug) Owner-guide Sarah offers excellent mountain-bike tours and sunset SUP and kayak trips, including one that paddles to a local winery ($69 with lunch). Mountain bikes and e-bikes are available for rent, perfect for tackling the **Gippsland Lakes Discovery Trail** (www.railtrails.org.au).

RAYMOND ISLAND

Home to a colony of around 250 koalas, **Raymond Island** offers pretty much guaranteed sightings of the cute marsupials in the wild. Directly across from Paynesville, the island (population 548) is easily accessed by a five-minute ferry ride, from where there's a signed 1.2km Koala Trail (20 minutes) leading you through the residential streets and a tract of forest; look up in the trees to spot koalas snoozing or munching eucalyptus leaves. Echidnas are also regularly seen.

Lonsdale Eco Cruises CRUISE
(☑ 0413 666 638; www.lonsdalecruises.com.au; Cunningham Quay; 3hr cruises adult/child/family $50/25/120; ⊘1pm Thu-Tue) ∅ These scenic cruises head out to the Entrance, Metung and Lake King on a former Queenscliff–Sorrento passenger ferry. Dolphin sightings are common. Prices include a Devonshire tea.

🛏 Sleeping

Lakes Entrance has stacks of accommodation, much of it typical motels, holiday apartments and caravan parks squeezed cheek by jowl along the Esplanade. Prices more than double during holiday periods (book ahead), but there are good discounts out of season.

Goat & Goose B&B $
(☑ 03-5155 3079, 0478 697 269; www.goatandgoose.com; 27b McRae St; d $90-150; 🐾) Bass Strait views are maximised at this wonderfully unique, multistorey, timber-pole-framed house, with quaint rooms featuring spa baths.

Kalimna Woods COTTAGE $$
(☑ 03-5155 1957; www.kalimnawoods.com.au; Kalimna Jetty Rd; d $144-245; ❄🐾) Retreat 2km from town to Kalimna Woods, set on a large bush-garden property complete with friendly resident sugar gliders and parrots. The country-style cottages (some with baths) are spacious, private and cosy, and come with barbecues and wood-burning fireplaces.

Bellevue on the Lakes HOTEL $$
(☑ 03-5155 3055; www.bellevuelakes.com; 201 The Esplanade; d from $179, 2-bedroom apt from $249; ❄🐾🏊) Right in the heart of the Esplanade, Bellevue is the plushest option along the main drag, with neatly furnished earth-toned rooms, most with water views. For extra luxury, go for the spacious spa suites or two-bedroom self-contained apartments. The foyer bar is another reason to stay here.

🍴 Eating & Drinking

Miriam's Restaurant STEAK, SEAFOOD $$
(☑ 03-5155 3999; cnr The Esplanade & Bulmer St; small plates $8.50-18, large plates $25-39; ⊘noon-late) The upstairs dining room at Miriam's overlooks the waterfront, and the Gippsland steaks, local-seafood dishes and casual cocktail-bar atmosphere are excellent. Try the epic 'Greek fisherman's plate': 1kg of local seafood for $79. There's a good choice of local wines and craft beers too. Happy-hour oysters ($2.50 each) are available from 4pm to 5pm.

Albert & Co BISTRO $$
(☑ 03-5155 1209; www.albertandco.com.au; Bellevue on the Lakes, 201 The Esplanade; dishes $12-34; ⊘7am-3pm daily & 6-10pm Wed-Sat) Bringing some urban style to the Esplanade is this diner doing a menu of modern breakfasts, local seafood and Gippsland steaks. The front bar is perfect for a pre-dinner tipple, offering cocktails, Gippsland wines and Lakes Entrance craft beers; happy hour runs from 4pm to 6pm ($12 cocktails).

★ Waterwheel Beach Tavern PUB
(☑ 03-5156 5855; www.thewaterwheel.com.au; 577 Lake Tyers Beach Rd, Lake Tyers Beach; ⊘10am-late; 🐾) Head to the adjoining township of Lake Tyers, 9km east of Lakes Entrance, for this relaxed coastal pub looking out to Ninety Mile Beach. There are Lakes Entrance craft beers on tap and local fish and chips to wolf down on its waterfront terrace, constructed from recycled materials (including the local jetty, and glass from the Sydney Opera House!).

Call ahead for the courtesy bus from Lakes. There's backpacker **accommodation** (dm from $20; 🐾) here too, including free first night camping.

Red Bluff Brewery MICROBREWERY
(☑ 0409 944 921; www.redbluffbrewers.com; 11 Old Bunga Rd; ⊘10am-5pm Mon-Fri, to 2pm Sat) Red Bluff has been brewing here for years now, but only in 2019 did it open the doors for folk to taste its beers – a pale and tropical ale, Kolsch, lager, pilsner and seasonal brews.

ℹ Information

Lakes Entrance Visitor Centre (☏ 03-5155 1966, 1800 637 060; www.discovereast gippsland.com.au; cnr Princes Hwy & Marine Pde; ☺ 9am-5pm, 10am-4pm winter; ☎) Free accommodation- and tour-booking services.

Also check out www.lakesentrance.com.

ℹ Getting There & Away

Lakes Entrance is 314km from Melbourne along the Princes Hwy.

V/Line (☏ 1800 800 007; www.vline.com.au) runs a train-bus service from Melbourne to Lakes Entrance ($43.40, around four hours, three to four daily) via Bairnsdale.

Metung

POP 1213

Curling around Bancroft Bay, little Metung is one of the prettiest towns in the Lakes District. Locals call it the Gippsland Riviera, and with its waterfront location and unhurried village charm, it's hard to argue.

It's a popular destination for yachties, and **Riviera Nautic** (☏ 03-5156 2243; www.rivieranautic.com.au; 185 Metung Rd; boat hire per 2hr/day from $90/200, yachts & cruisers per 3 days from $1164) can arrange liveaboard boats and motorised yachts – the perfect

way to visit if you have a group. No boat licence is required.

Moorings at Metung   APARTMENT $$
(☏ 03-5156 2750; www.themoorings.com.au; 44 Metung Rd; apt $170-445; ✷ ☎ ⊠) At the end of the road in Metung, and with water views to Lake King or Bancroft Bay, this contemporary complex has a range of apartments, from spacious studios to two-bedroom, split-level townhouses. The grounds have a tennis court, indoor and outdoor pools, a spa and a marina. Outside peak season it's good value.

★ **Metung Hotel**   PUB FOOD $$
(☏ 03-5156 2206; www.metunghotel.com.au; 1 Kurnai Ave; mains $19.50-35; ☺ kitchen noon-2pm & 6-8pm, pub 11am-late; ☎) In an unbeatable location overlooking Metung Wharf, this iconic pub has big windows and a deck, making the most of the water views. The bistro serves top-notch pub food with a focus on fresh local seafood. Items on the bar menu (from $19.50) are well priced, as are the **pub rooms** (r with shared bathroom $85).

ℹ Getting There & Away

Metung lies south of the Princes Hwy along the C606; the turn-off is signposted at Swan Reach, from where it's a 15km drive. The nearest major

---

EPICUREAN EAST GIPPSLAND

Bairnsdale has emerged as something of a culinary destination, with some superb new restaurants, wineries and gastropubs within a 20km radius of the town.

Sardine (☏ 03-5156 7135; www.sardineeaterybar.com; 3/69a The Esplanade; small plates $6-22, larger dishes $24-34; ☺ noon-3pm & 6-9pm Tue-Sun) In nearby Paynesville, don't miss the opportunity to treat yourself at Gippsland's only restaurant to be awarded a coveted *Good Food Guide* chef's hat. Opened by the former head chef at the celebrated Vue de Monde, Sardine offers casual fine dining, with a tasty menu of regional, sustainable produce that's big on local fish and seafood.

Long Paddock (☏ 03-5157 1638; www.longpaddock.com.au; 95 Main Rd, Lindenow; breakfast $9-18, mains $18-26; ☺ 7.30am-3.30pm Thu & Fri, 8am-10pm Sat, 8am-4pm Sun) 🍃 This esteemed restaurant in the tiny town of Lindenow, 18km west of Bairnsdale, adds to regional Victoria's culinary cachet. Run by a husband-and-wife team – who together boast an impressive résumé (Cumulus Inc, Vue de Monde and Michelin-starred restaurants) – it occupies a charming old bakery with original wood-fired scotch oven and serves divine dishes made from scratch using local ingredients.

Lightfoot & Sons (☏ 03-5156 9205; www.lightfootwines.com; 717 Wy Yung-Calulu Rd, Calulu; ☺ 11am-5pm Fri-Sun) Sample some of Gippsland's finest wines at this stylised rustic tin-shed cellar door, 11km northwest of Bairnsdale.

Northern Ground (☏ 03-5152 1544; www.northernground.com.au; 144 Main St; mains $12-25; ☺ 8am-5pm Mon-Thu, to 9pm Fri & Sat) Opened in late 2018, this bistro by expat British chef Rob Turner is symbolic of Bairnsdale's great gastronomic leap forward. Here the star is Gippsland produce, sourced from the immediate area to create a menu of fresh, seasonal and inventive takes on breakfast and lunch staples.

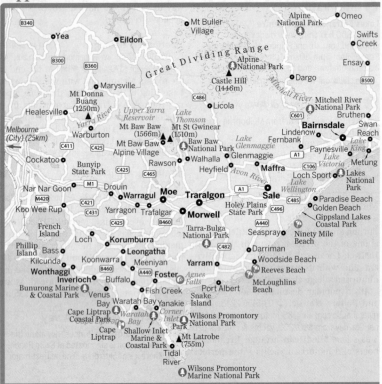

towns are Bairnsdale (28km away) and Lakes Entrance (24km). There's no public transport to Metung; the closest you'll get is Swan Reach, where the bus stops en route to Lakes Entrance or Bairnsdale.

East Gippsland & the Wilderness Coast

Beyond Lakes Entrance stretches a wilderness area of spectacular coastal national parks and old-growth forest.

In early 2020 severe bushfires ravaged the region, destroying some 900,000 hectares of East Gippsland's pristine forests and resulting in a monumental loss of wildlife. While it'll take time to recover, tourism in the area has reopened for business, and the local communities need you back here more than ever.

Cape Conran Coastal Park

This blissfully undeveloped part of the coast is one of Gippsland's most beautiful corners,

with long stretches of remote white-sand beach. The 19km coastal route from Marlo to Cape Conran is particularly pretty, bordered by banksia trees, grass plains, sand dunes and the ocean. Sadly the region suffered significant damage during the 2019-20 bushfires..

The region offers fantastic fishing, good surf and lovely walks – it's one for those seeking long, lazy days spent between the campsite and the beach. There's no internet or mobile coverage, so bring a good book!

For qualified divers, Marlo-based **Cross Diving Services** (☑ 03-5154 8554, 0407 362 960; www.crossdiving.com.au; 20 Ricardo Dr; ⊙ shore dives with equipment hire $50, boat dives with/without equipment $100/50, 4-day open-water course $660) offers dives most weekends.

The Aboriginal Gunai and Kurnai people are the traditional custodians of Cape Conran. The Krauatungalung clan lived here for tens of thousands of years, as evidenced by midden sites you can visit at **Salmon Rocks**, a stop along the Bataluk Cultural Trail (p281).

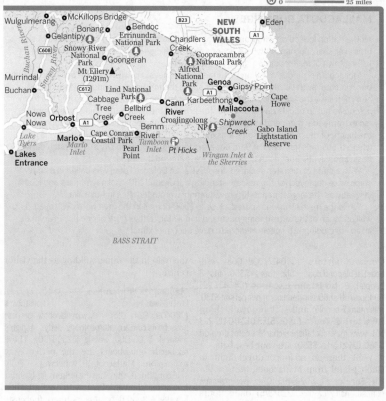

Parks Victoria runs two accommodation options in Cape Conran Coastal Park – **camping** (☏03-5154 8438; www.parkweb.vic. gov.au; Marlo-Conran Rd; unpowered sites $20.10) and **cabins** (☏03-5154 8438; www.parkweb. vic.gov.au; cabins from $180). At the time of research both remained closed due to the bush fires, so call ahead to confirm they've reopened.

Cape Conran Coastal Park lies south of the Princes Hwy, 405km from Melbourne. The well-signposted turn-off from the highway lies just east of the small settlement of Cabbage Tree. There's no public transport.

Mallacoota

POP 1063

One of Gippsland's, and indeed Victoria's, little gems, Mallacoota is the state's most easterly town, snuggled in the vast Mallacoota Inlet and surrounded by the tumbling hills and beachside dunes of beautiful Croajingolong National Park. Those who come this far are treated to long, empty ocean-surf beaches,

tidal estuaries, and swimming, fishing and boating on the inlet.

It's good for wildlife too, with kangaroos, as well as koalas, echidnas and lyrebirds inhabiting the area.

◎ Sights & Activities

★ **Gabo Island**   ISLAND

Located 14km offshore from Mallacoota, the windswept 154-hectare **Gabo Island Lightstation Reserve** is home to seabirds and one of the world's largest colonies of little penguins (you'll only see them if you stay overnight). There's also a fur-seal colony, and whales and dolphins are regularly sighted. The snorkellin is outstanding and there is an operating red-granite **lighthouse** (1862) that's one of the tallest in the southern hemisphere – you can stay in the **old keepers' cottages** (☏03-5158 0255, Parks Victoria 13 19 63; www.parkweb.vic.gov.au; Gabo Island; cottages $361-402).

Boat access to the island is often restricted due to bad weather; **Wilderness**

MALLACOOTA BUSHFIRES

As the nation looked on with horror as it endured some of the most catastrophic bush fires ever seen, perhaps nowhere epitomised the struggle more than in the laid-back fishing town of Mallacoota on New Years Eve, 2019.

Mallacoota is hidden away on Victoria's far southeast tip, with only the one road in and one road out; swift southwesterly wind changes meant the town suddenly found itself hemmed in by the fires and completely cut off from the outside world. Leaving the town no choice but to buckle down and bear the brunt of the fast approaching maelstrom (so extreme that it generated its own lighting), the entire population – at full capacity at the height of the holiday season – was evacuated to Mallacoota's foreshore. It was here where thousands gathered at 9am under a menacing blood-red sky in near pitch darkness; apocalyptic images that were broadcast around the world.

With a state of disaster declared, the Australian Defence Force was called in as navy ships were deployed for the rescue; shipping out around 1500 holidaymakers and locals in what was the largest peace-time evacuation ever undertaken in Australia.

While the main strip was spared, close to 1000 homes in the area were destroyed, as well as much of the surrounding bushland and a staggering figure of one billion animals killed – including 126 species feared to have become extinct.

Coast Charters (0417 398 068; wildcoast1@bigpond.com; 5hr tours $360, fits 8 people), **Gabo Island Escapes** (0437 221 694; parrotfish65@hotmail.com; per person $130, minimum 7 people) and **Mallacoota Fishing Charters & Tours** (03-5158 0124, 0419 223 101; www.mallacootafishingcharters.com; drop-off $360, day charter $550) are your best bets.

While there are no longer direct flights to Gabo Island from Mallacoota, **Merimbula Air Services** (02-6495 1074; www.mairserv. com.au; half-/full day $325/375) offers tours and can arrange a drop-off and pick-up service (a four-seater costs $775 one way).

Mallacoota Hire Boats BOATING
(0438 447 558; www.mallacootahireboats.com; 10 Buckland Dr; motorboats per 2/8hr $90/180, kayaks 1/2 people per 2hr $30/40; 7.30am-6pm) Hires out kayaks, motorboats, pedal boats and fishing equipment. No boat licence required; cash only. Houseboats can also be arranged. It's based at Mallacoota Foreshore Holiday Park.

🛏 Sleeping

Mallacoota Foreshore Holiday Park CARAVAN PARK $
(03-5158 0300; cnr Allan Dr & Maurice Ave; unpowered sites $18.50-50, powered sites $26-60; 📶) Curling around the waterfront, the grassy sites here constitute one of Victoria's largest, most sociable and scenic caravan parks, with sublime views of the inlet and its population of black swans and pelicans. There are no cabins, but this is the best of Mallacoota's many parks for campers. Reception is across the road in the same building as the visitor centre.

Mallacoota Wilderness Houseboats HOUSEBOAT $
(0409 924 016; www.mallacootawilderness houseboats.com.au; Karbeethong Jetty; 4 nights midweek $800-1100, weekly $1250-1700) These six-berth houseboats are the perfect way to explore Mallacoota's waterways. Fully self-contained, they have kitchen, fridge and hot-water shower, along with two attached kayaks. A $500 deposit is required; fuel costs are deducted from this upon return. No boat licence necessary.

⭐ **Karbeethong Lodge** GUESTHOUSE $$
(03-5158 0411; www.karbeethonglodge.com. au; 16 Schnapper Point Dr; r incl breakfast $150-220; 📶) Sit on the broad verandah of this early-1900s timber guesthouse and take in uninterrupted views over Mallacoota Inlet and the expansive gardens. The large guest lounge and dining room have an open fire and period furnishings, there's a mammoth kitchen, and the pastel-toned bedrooms are small but tastefully decorated.

🍴 Eating & Drinking

⭐ **Lucy's** CHINESE $
(03-5158 0666; 64 Maurice Ave; mains $9-30; 9am-3pm & 5.30-9pm) Lucy's is popular for delicious and great-value homemade rice noodles with chicken, prawn or abalone, as well as dumplings stuffed with ingredients from the garden. There's a cheap and cheerful wine list too. Cash only, and order at the counter.

★ Origami Coffee COFFEE
(www.facebook.com/origamicoffeemallacoota; 19
Dorron Ave; ⊙6.30am-12.30pm Thu-Sun, daily summer) A one-man operation run by Japanese expat Takeshi, this quirky outdoor cafe is set up in a tiny cabin on a vacant lot. Takeshi does some of the best coffee ($3.50) in Gippsland, using Dukes beans from Melbourne in a hand-lever espresso machine; the whisked *matcha* (powdered green tea) is also superb. All drinks are topped with anime latte art.

There are seats on the lawn, and it's BYO food. Also check out his origami and DIY kits.

ℹ Information

Mallacoota Visitor Centre (📞03-5158 0800; www.visitmallacoota.com.au; cnr Allan Dr & Maurice Ave; ⊙9am-5pm; 📶) On the main strip across from the water, this extremely helpful tourist centre has a ton of info.

ℹ Getting There & Away

Mallacoota is 23km southeast of Genoa (on the Princes Hwy), which is 492km from Melbourne.

Taking public transport from Melbourne to Mallacoota entails a long journey ($56.40, 8½ hours): from Southern Cross Station, take the train to Bairnsdale, then the V/Line bus to Genoa (3½ hours); the Mallacoota–Genoa bus meets the V/Line bus on Monday, Thursday and Friday, plus Sunday during school holidays, and runs to Mallacoota (30 minutes).

Croajingolong National Park

Croajingolong is one of Australia's finest coastal-wilderness parks, recognised by its listing as a Unesco World Biosphere Reserve. The park covers 875 sq km, stretching for about 100km from the town of Bemm River to the NSW border. Unspoilt beaches, inlets, estuaries and forests make it ideal for camping, walking, swimming and surfing. The five inlets, **Sydenham**, **Tamboon**, **Mueller**, **Wingan** and **Mallacoota** (the largest and most accessible), are popular canoeing and fishing spots.

FREE CAMPING

Pick up a copy of the *Free Camping Gippsland* brochure from visitor centres along the way. Sites can't be pre-booked, so you have to chance your luck.

Ninety Mile Beach (p281) A string of free foreshore camping grounds between Seaspray and Golden Beach.

Franklin River Reserve (4929 South Gippsland Hwy, Toora; free) An hour's drive from the Prom.

Lake Tyers State Park (📞13 19 63; www.parkweb.vic.gov.au; Pettman Rd; free) Has four free sites, of which Pettmans Beach is the best.

Regrettably, this was another region badly damaged during the devastating 2019–20 bush fires.

Point Hicks was the first part of Australia to be spotted by Captain Cook and the *Endeavour* crew in 1770, and was named after Lieutenant Zachary Hicks. A monument stands on the rocks on the oceanfront at remote **Point Hicks Lighthouse** (📞13 19 63; www.parkweb.vic. gov.au; Lighthouse Track, Tamboon; ⊙tours 1pm Fri-Mon) FREE, where you can arrange to spend the **night** (📞13 19 63; www.park stay.vic.gov.au/point-hicks-lighthouse; bungalows $126-146, cottages $332-388).

The area is the country of the Bidwell, and Gunai and Kurnai Indigenous people, along with the Monero-Ngarigo people from across the NSW border.

It lies 492km east of Melbourne. Access roads of varying quality lead south off the Princes Hwy and into the park from various points between Cann River and the NSW border. Among these are tracks leading to camping grounds at Wingan Inlet, Mueller Inlet, Thurra River and Shipwreck Creek.

Brisbane & Around

Best Places to Eat

➡ Joy (p310)

➡ Same Same (p309)

➡ Maeve Wine (p307)

➡ Carl's (p311)

➡ Eat Street Northshore (p308)

Best Places to Sleep

➡ Calile Hotel (p305)

➡ Ovolo the Valley (p305)

➡ Fantauzzo – Art Series Hotel (p303)

➡ Emporium Hotel (p303)

➡ Next (p300)

Why Go?

From urban sophistication to spectacular island beaches, the greater Brisbane region delivers on all fronts. The star of the show is Brisbane itself: the traditional home of the Jagera and Turrbal people, it's a lush, ever-evolving metropolis, with booming culinary and cultural scenes that attest to its coming of age. The city is home to one of Australia's most vibrant live-music scenes and some of its hottest dining destinations, not to mention one of the world's top galleries of contemporary Asian-Pacific art. Add to this a vibrant riverfront and effortlessly cool inner-city neighbourhoods and any preconceptions of a big provincial town seem positively quaint.

Lapping at Brisbane's eastern fringe is Moreton Bay and its low-lying islands: Moreton and North Stradbroke. Here, urbane pleasures are substituted for natural highs, from adrenaline-pumping sand dunes and tea-tree-tinted lakes, to endless miles of turquoise surf, the latter famed for its passing parades of whales, turtles and dolphins.

When to Go
Brisbane

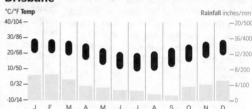

Feb School is back, making it an ideal time to hit the North Stradbroke Island surf.

May–Aug Cooler temperatures and blue skies make sightseeing a breeze.

Sep Warmer temperatures and hot-ticket arts events in Queensland's capital city.

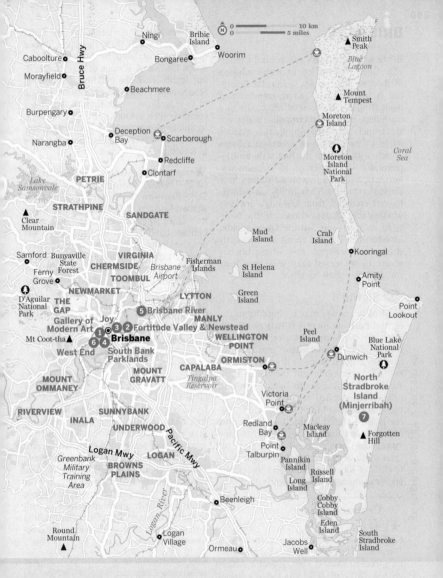

Brisbane & Around Highlights

1 Gallery of Modern Art (p291) Plugging into top-tier art at Brisbane's cultural heavyweight.

2 Fortitude Valley & Newstead (p315) Roaming on-point boutiques, cafes and music venues in the inner north.

3 Joy (p310) Scoring a reservation at one of Australia's hottest dining destinations.

4 South Bank Parklands (p291) Chilling and swimming at Brisbane's best-loved riverside hang-out.

5 Cycling the Brisbane River (p295) Cruising the

city's impressive riverside bikeways.

6 West End (p291) Exploring Brisbane's most bohemian neighbourhood.

7 North Stradbroke Island (p324) Enjoying flawless beaches, fresh seafood and Indigenous culture on an easily accessible island.

BRISBANE

POP 2.5 MILLION

Brisbane is Australia's subtropical Cinderella. Once mocked by brawnier siblings Melbourne and Sydney, Queensland's capital is in makeover mode, transforming itself from a provincial afterthought to a confident, polished metropolis. Statement skyscrapers are redefining the skyline, while in its patchwork of urban villages – each with its own distinct style and topography – an explosion of on-point restaurants, bars and live-music venues have the nation talking. Thankfully, some things haven't changed, from the city's enviable weather and affable attitude, to the beauty of its river and historic Queenslander architecture. The end result is a distinctly Brisbane experience, one where big-city pleasures are served against an easy, lush, frangipani-scented backdrop.

◉ Sights

Most of Brisbane's major sights lie in the central business district (CBD) and South Bank directly across the river. While the former offers colonial history and architecture, the latter is home to Brisbane's major cultural institutions and the South Bank Parklands. Behind South Bank, West End offers indie-spirited street life, while directly northeast of the CBD, Fortitude Valley is Brisbane's nightlife epicentre. East of it lies New Farm, home to the Brisbane Powerhouse arts centre. East of the CBD (and south of the Valley) lie the panoramic cliffs of Kangaroo Point and the Gabba sports stadium of Woolloongabba.

◎ Central Brisbane

★ **City Hall**   LANDMARK
(☑ 07-3339 0845; www.brisbane.qld.gov.au; King George Sq; ⊙ 8am-5pm, from 9am Sat & Sun, heritage tours 10.30am, 11.30am, 1.30pm & 2.30pm daily; 🏍; 🚉 Central) FREE Fronted by a row of sequoia-sized Corinthian columns, Australia's largest city hall was built between 1920 and 1930. Although they are free, fascinating heritage tours (45 minutes) of the sandstone behemoth should be booked in advance (online or by phone); tours are also available on the day from the excellent on-site Museum of Brisbane. Alternatively, free tours of the building's 85m-high clock tower run every 15 minutes from 10am to 5pm; grab tickets from the museum.

Interestingly, the marble in City Hall's foyer was sourced from the same Tuscan quarry as that used by Michelangelo to sculpt his *David*. It's one of many fascinating details about the building. The Rolling Stones played their first-ever Australian gig in its magnificent auditorium in 1965, itself complete with a 4300-pipe organ, mahogany and blue-gum floors, and offers free concerts at noon every Tuesday from February to November.

★ **Old Government House**   HISTORIC BUILDING
(☑ 07-3138 8005; www.ogh.qut.edu.au; 2 George St; ⊙ 10am-4pm Sun-Fri, tours by appointment 10.30am Tue & Thu; 🚉 QUT Gardens Point, 🚉 Central) FREE Queensland's most important heritage building, this 1862 showpiece was designed by estimable government architect Charles Tiffin as a residence for Sir George Bowen, Queensland's first governor. The lavish interior was restored in 2009 and the property offers free podcast tours and one-hour guided tours; the latter must be booked in advance. The 1st floor houses the worthy **William Robinson Gallery**, dedicated to the Australian artist and home to an impressive collection of his paintings, prints, drawings, sculpture and ceramics.

★ **Museum of Brisbane**   MUSEUM
(☑ 07-3339 0800; www.museumofbrisbane.com.au; Level 3, Brisbane City Hall, King George Sq; ⊙ 10am-5pm, to 7pm Fri; 🏍; 🚉 Central) FREE On the 3rd floor of City Hall, this forward-thinking museum explores historic and modern aspects of Brisbane, offering fresh, progressive insights into Queensland's capital. Exhibitions to date have explored themes as varied as contemporary Brisbane fashion, the city's robust music scene and the relationship between architecture, art, people and place. The result is a snapshot of a metropolis much more complex than many give it credit for.

City Botanic Gardens   PARK
(www.brisbane.qld.gov.au; Alice St; ⊙ 24hr; 🏍; 🚉 QUT Gardens Point, 🚉 Central) FREE Originally a collection of food crops planted by convicts in 1825, this is Brisbane's favourite green space. Descending gently from the Queensland University of Technology campus to the river, its manicured lawns, tangled Moreton Bay figs, bunya pines, rainforest and mangroves are a soothing elixir for frazzled urbanites. Grab a complimentary printed guide at the rotunda, from where free one-hour guided tours leave at 11am

and 1pm Monday to Saturday. On Sundays, the gardens host the popular **Brisbane Riverside Markets** (☑07-3870 2807; www.theriversidemarkets.com.au).

Parliament House HISTORIC BUILDING
(☑07-3553 6470; www.parliament.qld.gov.au; cnr Alice & George Sts; ⊙tours non-sitting days 1pm, 2pm, 3pm & 4pm Mon-Fri; ⬛QUT Gardens Point, ⎗Central) FREE With a roof clad in Mt Isa copper, this lovely blanched-white stone, French Renaissance–style building dates from 1868 and overlooks the City Botanic Gardens. The only way to peek inside is on one of the free 30-minute tours, which leave at the listed times (2pm only when parliament is sitting). Arrive five minutes before tours begin and don't forget to bring photo ID; no need to book.

Roma Street Parkland PARK
(www.visitbrisbane.com.au/Roma-Street-Parkland-and-Spring-Hill; 1 Parkland Blvd; ⊙24hr; ⬛; ⎗Roma St) FREE This beautifully maintained, 16-hectare downtown park is one of the world's largest subtropical urban gardens. Formerly a market and a railway yard, the park opened in 2001 and is a showcase for native Queensland vegetation, complete with a rainforest and fern gully, waterfalls, skyline lookouts, playgrounds, free-to-use BBQs and no shortage of frangipani. It's something of a maze: easy to get into, hard to get out of.

Commissariat Store Museum MUSEUM
(☑07-3221 4198; www.commissariatstore.org.au; 115 William St; adult/child $7/4; ⊙10am-4pm Tue-Fri; ⬛North Quay, ⎗Central) Built by convicts in 1829, this former government storehouse is the oldest occupied building in Brisbane. Inside is an immaculate little museum whose main focus is the region's convict and colonial history. Don't miss the wince-inducing convict 'fingers'.

St John's Cathedral CHURCH
(☑07-3835 2222; www.stjohnscathedral.com.au; 373 Ann St; ⊙9.30am-4.30pm; ⎗Central) FREE A magnificent symphony of stone, carved timber and stained glass just west of Fortitude Valley, St John's Cathedral is a beautiful example of Gothic Revival architecture. The building is a true labour of love: construction began in 1906 and wasn't finished until 2009, making it one of the world's last cathedrals of this architectural style to be completed.

◎ South Bank & West End

★**Gallery of Modern Art** GALLERY
(GOMA; ☑07-3840 7303; www.qagoma.qld.gov.au; Stanley Pl; ⊙10am-5pm; ⬛; ⬛South Bank Terminals 1 & 2, ⎗South Brisbane) FREE All angular glass, concrete and black metal, must-see GOMA celebrates modern and contemporary art, with a particular emphasis on Australian, Asian and Pacific artists. Regularly changing exhibitions spotlight everything from painting, sculpture and photography to video and installation art, while GOMA's Australian Cinémathèque screens unique, often rare films and video several times weekly. The gallery also includes a Children's Art Centre, well-stocked book-and-design shop, and both a casual **cafe** (☑07-3842 9906; www.qagoma.qld.gov.au; sandwiches & salads $15-16; ⊙10am-3pm, from 9am Sat & Sun; 🛜⬛) and smarter Modern-Australian **restaurant** (☑07-3842 9916; www.qagoma.qld.gov.au; mains $39-48, 5-course tasting menu $110; ⊙noon-3pm Thu-Sun, plus 5.30pm-late Fri & Sat; 🛜).

★**Queensland Art Gallery** GALLERY
(QAG; ☑07-3840 7303; www.qagoma.qld.gov.au; Melbourne St; ⊙10am-5pm; ⬛; ⬛South Bank Terminals 1 & 2, ⎗South Brisbane) FREE While Brisbane's main art museum includes numerous international works, its forte is its Australian collection. This includes works by heavyweights like Sidney Nolan, Russell Drysdale, Arthur Boyd, Charles Blackman, William Dobell, Margaret Olley and Howard Arkley. A robust collection of Indigenous Australian works features paintings and pottery by artists from the Hermannsburg School movement, among them the great Albert Namatjira, the first Indigenous person to be granted conditional Australian citizenship in 1957.

★**South Bank Parklands** PARK
(www.visitbrisbane.com.au; Grey St; ⊙24hr; ⬛; ⬛South Bank 1 & 2, 3, ⎗South Brisbane, South Bank) FREE Should you sunbake on a sandy beach, saunter through a rainforest, or eye-up a Nepalese peace pagoda? You can do all three in this 17.5-hectare park overlooking the city centre. Its canopied walkways lead to performance spaces, lush lawns, eateries and bars, and regular free events ranging from fitness classes to film screenings. The star attractions are **Streets Beach** (☑07-3156 6366; ⊙6am-midnight; ⬛; ⬛South Bank Terminals 1 & 2, 3, ⎗South Bank) FREE, an

Greater Brisbane

Enoggera Barracks
(Gallipoli Barracks)
Military Area

Enoggera Creek

ASHGROVE

Wardell St

KELVIN GROVE

Waterworks Rd

Coopers Camp Rd

Jubilee Tce

Boundary St

BARDON

14 28

Latrobe Tce

16 30

PADDINGTON

See West End &
Petrie Terrace
Map (p302)

Mt Coot-tha
Reserve

Frederick St

AUCHENFLOWER

Milton

MT COOT-THA

Sir Samuel Griffith Dr

Milton Rd

Auchenflower

Coronation Dr

5
1

M5

Western Fwy

TOOWONG

Regatta

2

Toowong

West End

TARINGA

Moggill Rd

Coronation Dr

Taringa

ST LUCIA

CHAPEL HILL

M5

Moggill Rd

Indooroopilly

Coonan St

INDOOROOPILLY

St Lucia
Golf Links

Chelmer

Brisbane River

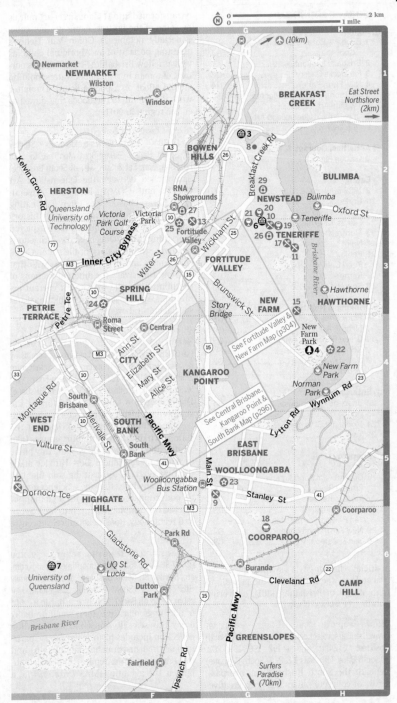

0 2 km
0 1 mile

BRISBANE & AROUND BRISBANE

Newmarket

NEWMARKET

Wilston

Windsor

BREAKFAST
CREEK

Eat Street
Northshore
(2km)

(10km)

A3

BOWEN
HILLS

26

3
8

BULIMBA

Kelvin Grove Rd

HERSTON

Queensland
University of
Technology

Victoria
Park Golf
Course

Victoria
Park

RNA
Showgrounds

27

10

25 Fortitude
Valley

13

Breakfast Creek Rd

29

NEWSTEAD

21 20
6 10

Bulimba

Oxford St

Teneriffe

19

26 TENERIFFE

Wickham St

31

77

Inner City Bypass

M3

Water St

26

Fortitude
Valley

15

17

11

Brisbane River

Hawthorne

PETRIE
TERRACE

10

24

Petrie Tce

Roma
Street

Spring
Hill

Central

FORTITUDE
VALLEY

Brunswick St

Story
Bridge

NEW
FARM

15

HAWTHORNE

33

10

M3

Ann St

CITY

Elizabeth St

Mary St

Alice St

15

KANGAROO
POINT

See Fortitude Valley &
New Farm Map (p304)

New
Farm
Park

4

New Farm
Park

22

23

Montague Rd

WEST
END

South
Brisbane

10

Merivale St

SOUTH
BANK

Pacific Mwy

See Central Brisbane,
Kangaroo Point &
South Bank Map (p296)

Norman
Park

Wynnum Rd

Vulture St

South
Bank

41

EAST
BRISBANE

Lytton Rd

12

Dornoch Tce

HIGHGATE
HILL

Woolloongabba
Bus Station

Main St

WOOLLOONGABBA

9

23

Stanley St

41

Coorparoo

Gladstone Rd

Park Rd

M3

18

COORPAROO

7

University of
Queensland

UQ St
Lucia

Buranda

22

CAMP
HILL

Dutton
Park

15

Cleveland Rd

Brisbane River

GREENSLOPES

Fairfield

Ipswich Rd

Pacific Mwy

Surfers
Paradise
(70km)

Greater Brisbane

artificial, lagoon-style swimming beach (packed on weekends); and the near-60m-high Wheel of Brisbane (p301), delivering 360-degree views of town.

Pillars Project   PUBLIC ART
(www.thepillarsproject.com; Merrivale St, South Brisbane; ⊙24hr; 💧; 🚌192, 196, 199, 202, 🚤South Bank Terminals 1 & 2, 🚈South Brisbane) Beneath the South Brisbane rail overpass, a row of concrete pillars has been creative-

ly transformed into 11 giant street-art murals by some of the hottest names on the scene. Especially notable is Guido Van Helten's arresting portrait of an Aboriginal child, as well as fellow Brisbanite Fintan Magee's portrait of a man in rising floodwaters, holding a child afloat on a boogie board. The latter work is a tribute to the floods that devastated the region in 2011.

State Library of Queensland   LIBRARY
(☎07-3840 7666; www.slq.qld.gov.au; Stanley Pl, South Bank; ⊙9am-8pm Mon-Thu, to 5pm Fri, 10am-5pm Sat & Sun; 💧; 🚈South Brisbane) Sandwiched between the Queensland Art Gallery and GOMA, Brisbane's pre-eminent library hosts free, often fascinating exhibitions exploring the region's history and culture. Past exhibitions have explored everything from Queensland's Indigenous languages to the history of the state's Greek community and its coffee shops. Note that opening times vary for different sections of the library; see the website for current exhibitions, specific gallery opening times and special cultural events.

Queensland Museum &
Sciencentre   MUSEUM
(☎07-3840 7555; www.qm.qld.gov.au; cnr Grey & Melbourne Sts; museum free, Sciencentre adult/child $15.50/12.50; ⊙9.30am-5pm; 💧; 🚤South Bank Terminals 1 & 2, 🚈South Brisbane) Dig deeper into Queensland history at the state's main historical repository, where intriguing exhibits include a skeleton of the state's own dinosaur Muttaburrasaurus (aka 'Mutt'), and the *Avian Cirrus*, the tiny plane in which Queenslander Bert Hinkler made the first England-to-Australia solo flight in 1928. Meanwhile, the site's Sciencentre is an educational funhouse with a plethora of interactive exhibits delving into life science and technology. Book tickets for Sciencentre online.

Queensland Maritime Museum   MUSEUM
(☎07-3844 5361; www.maritimemuseum.com.au; Stanley St, South Brisbane; adult/child/family $16/7/38; ⊙9.30am-4.30pm; 🚤Maritime Museum, 🚈South Bank) If you're a hardcore fan of all things maritime, then you'll probably enjoy this sea-salty museum. Its sprawling collection includes historic lighthouse parts, navigational instruments, model ships and the odd ship-cabin replica. The real highlight is the gigantic HMAS *Diamantina*, a

restored WWII frigate that you can clamber aboard and explore.

Fortitude Valley & New Farm

Brisbane Riverwalk BRIDGE
(; 195, 196, 199, Sydney St) Jutting out over the city's big, brown waterway, the Brisbane Riverwalk offers a novel way of surveying the Brisbane skyline. The 870m-long path – divided into separate walking and cycling lanes – runs between Howard Smith Wharves and the salubrious suburb of New Farm. The Riverwalk replaces the original floating walkway, which washed away in the floods of 2011.

New Farm Park PARK
(https://newfarmpark.com.au; Brunswick St; 24hr; ; 195, 196, New Farm Park) On the tail end of Brunswick St by the river, herit-

age-listed New Farm Park provides urban respite with its jacaranda trees, rose gardens and picnic areas. It's a perfect spot to spend a lazy afternoon, with electric BBQs and free wi-fi. Younger kids will especially love the playground – a Crusoe-esque series of platforms among vast Moreton Bay fig trees. The park also hosts the popular **Jan Powers Farmers Market** (www.janpowers farmersmarkets.com.au; Brisbane Powerhouse, 119 Lamington St; 6am-noon Sat) on Saturday mornings.

Activities

Brisbane's subtropical climate encourages physical activity, with a slew of activities ranging from cycling and rock-climbing, to swimming, kayaking and more. In many cases, these activities offer the best views of the city itself, making them sightseeing experiences in themselves. You'll find a plethora of excellent art and heritage walking trails around

BRISBANE'S GALLERY SCENE

Beyond Brisbane's heavyweight Gallery of Modern Art (p291), aka GOMA, and Queensland Art Gallery (p291) is a healthy crop of smaller and lesser-known galleries where you can mull over both the mainstream and the cutting-edge.

University of Queensland Art Museum (UQ Art Museum; 07-3365 3046; https://art-museum.uq.edu.au; Bldg 11, University of Queensland, University Dr, St Lucia; 10am-4pm Mon, Tue & Thu-Sat, to 8pm Wed; 412, UQ St Lucia) FREE Best reached by river on the CityCat, this progressive venue claims one of Queensland's most important public art collections, including a nationally significant cachet of self-portraits. Exhibitions change throughout the year, with a general focus on contemporary Australian art.

Institute of Modern Art (IMA; 07-3252 5750; www.ima.org.au; 420 Brunswick St, Fortitude Valley; 11am-6pm Tue-Sat; Fortitude Valley) FREE An excellent noncommercial gallery with an industrial vibe and regular showings by both local and international names working in media as diverse as installation art, photography and painting. Located inside the Judith Wright Centre of Contemporary Arts in Fortitude Valley.

TW Fine Art (0437 348 755; www.twfineart.com; 22 Masters St, Newstead; 10am-5pm Wed-Sat, to 3pm Sun; 470) FREE A crisp Newstead gallery eschewing the 'keep it local' mantra for intellectually robust, critically acclaimed contemporary art from around the world. It also runs an innovative online gallery of limited-edition prints, which you can browse at the gallery and have couriered straight to your home.

Fireworks Gallery (07-3216 1250; www.fireworksgallery.com.au; 9/31 Thompson St, Bowen Hills; 10am-6pm Tue-Fri, to 5pm Sat; 306, 322, 393) FREE Hidden away in an industrial corner of Bowen Hills, Fireworks is one of Brisbane's best-loved commercial galleries. With an emphasis on group exhibitions, the space showcases mainly painting and sculpture from emerging and established Australian artists, both Indigenous and non-Indigenous.

Milani (07-3846 6046; www.milanigallery.com.au; 270 Montague Rd, West End; 11am-6pm Tue-Fri, to 5pm Sat; 60, 192) FREE A well-regarded commercial gallery in West End with rotating exhibitions of edgy, sometimes confronting, contemporary Australian artwork. Numerous artists represented are Brisbane based, making it a good spot to savour the local scene.

Central Brisbane, Kangaroo Point & South Bank

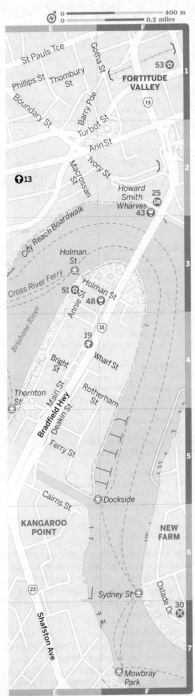

town at www.brisbane.qld.gov.au/things-to-see-and-do/experiences-and-culture/public-art/public-art-trails.

Riverlife
ADVENTURE SPORTS

(07-3891 5766; www.riverlife.com.au; Naval Stores, Kangaroo Point Cliffs Dv, Kangaroo Point; bike/rollerblade hire per 4hr $39/45, kayaks per 2hr $39; 9am-5pm Mon-Thu, to 10pm Fri, 8.30am-10pm Sat, 8.30am-5pm Sun; ; Thornton St) Based at the bottom of the Kangaroo Point Cliffs, Riverlife offers numerous active tours and experiences. Rock climb (from $59), abseil ($55) or opt for a kayak river tour (from $39). The last includes a booze-and-food 'Paddle and Prawns' option (from $105) on Friday nights and a 'Paddle and BBQ' on Saturday nights.

Student, child and family discounts are available on many tours, as well as bike, kayak, rollerblade and scooter (manual and electric) rental.

Story Bridge
Adventure Climb
ADVENTURE SPORTS

(07-3188 9070; https://storybridgeadventure climb.com.au; 170 Main St, Kangaroo Point; climb from $129; ; 234, Thornton St, Holman St) Conquering Brisbane's most famous bridge is thrilling, with unbeatable views of the city – morning, twilight (our favourite) or night. The climb scales the southern half of the structure, taking you 80m above the Brisbane River. Dawn climbs and climb-and-abseil combos ($159) run on Saturdays. Most climbs last two hours, with the climb-and-abseil experience lasting three hours. Minimum age six years.

Pinnacle Sports
CLIMBING

(07-3368 3335; www.pinnaclesports.com. au; River Tce, Kangaroo Point; abseiling/climbing $89/99;) Climb the Kangaroo Point Cliffs or abseil down them: either way it's a lot of fun! Options include three-hour day and evening rock-climbing sessions, as well as a two-hour sunset abseil. Kids aged eight and over welcome.

Tours

★ CityCat
BOATING

(13 12 30; www.translink.com.au; $4.90; 5am-midnight;) Ditch the bus or Uber and catch a CityCat catamaran along the Brisbane River for a calmer, often breathtaking perspective. Ferries run every 15 to 30 minutes between the Northshore Hamilton terminal northeast of the city to the

BRISBANE & AROUND BRISBANE

Central Brisbane, Kangaroo Point & South Bank

University of Queensland in the southwest, stopping at 16 terminals en route.

Useful stops include Teneriffe (handy for Newstead), New Farm Park, Riverside and North Quay (both in the CBD) and South Bank 2 (also handy for West End).

BlackCard Cultural Tours WALKING
(📞 07-3899 8153; www.theblackcard.com.au; walking tours from $55; 🚶) This Aboriginal-owned operator offers enlightening Indigenous walking tours in central Brisbane. Options include a 1½-hour art-and-culture-themed

tour and two three-hour walks: one also focused on art and culture, the other on traditional bush foods. Each tour generally runs thrice weekly, and a minimum of two people per tour is required; see the website for details and booking.

Brisbane Greeters WALKING
(📞 07-3156 6364; www.brisbanegreeters.com. au; Brisbane City Hall, King George Sq; ⊘10am; 🚃 Central) Free, small-group, multilingual introductory tours of Brisbane with affable volunteers. Book online at least three hours

in advance; walk-ups not accepted. You can also opt for a 'Your Choice' tour (these must be booked seven days in advance), based on your personal interests and schedule. While not compulsory, an online donation is appreciated to help support the programme.

Brisbane Ghost Tours   TOURS
(☑0401 666 441; http://brisbaneghosttours.com.au; walking tour adult/child $26/15, bus tours adult/child $50/40; ⊕) 'Get creeped' on these 1½-hour guided walking tours or 2½-hour bus tours of Brisbane's haunted heritage: murder scenes, cemeteries, eerie arcades and the infamous Boggo Road Gaol. There are several tours a week; bookings essential.

🏫 Courses

Golden Pig   COOKING
(☑07-3666 0884; www.goldenpig.com.au; 38 Ross St, Newstead; 4hr class $180; ⊒300, 302, 305) In a converted warehouse on the edge of Newstead, chef Katrina Ryan – who's worked at several prolific restaurants – runs this popular cooking school and pan-Asian restaurant. Four-hour cooking courses span numerous themes, from sourdough baking and charcuterie making, to European, Middle Eastern, Asian and South American cuisines. See the website for class times and types, which usually run Mondays, Saturdays and Sundays.

🎆 Festivals & Events

Bigsound Festival   MUSIC
(www.bigsound.org.au; ⊕Sep) Held over four huge nights in September, Australia's premier new-music festival draws buyers, industry experts and fans of fresh Aussie music. The fest features around 150 up-and-coming artists playing at 18 venues in Fortitude Valley.

Brisbane Festival   PERFORMING ARTS
(www.brisbanefestival.com.au; ⊕Sep) One of Australia's largest and most diverse arts festivals, running for three weeks in September and featuring an impressive schedule of concerts, plays, dance and fringe events. The festival ends with the spectacular 'Riverfire', an elaborate fireworks show over the Brisbane River.

Brisbane Street Art Festival   ART
(www.bsafest.com.au; ⊕May) The hiss of spray cans underscores this booming two-week celebration, which sees local and international street artists transform city walls into arresting artworks. Live mural art aside, the programme includes exhibitions, music, performance and street-art workshops.

Brisbane International   SPORTS
(www.brisbaneinternational.com.au; Queensland Tennis Centre, Tennyson; ⊕Jan; ☒Yeerongpilly) Featuring the world's top players, and running over a week in early January, this pro tennis tournament is a prologue to Melbourne's Grand Slam Australian Open.

BrisAsia Festival   CULTURAL
(www.brisbane.qld.gov.au; ⊕Feb-Mar) Running through much of February (and sometimes early March), the BrisAsia Festival celebrates both traditional and modern Asian cultures with over 100 events across the city. The festival programme includes dance, music and theatre performances, film screenings, interactive community events and no shortage of Asian bites.

Brisbane Comedy Festival   COMEDY
(www.briscomfest.com; ⊕Feb-Mar) Feeling blue? Check yourself into this month-long laughfest, usually running from late February to late March. Showcasing around 80 comedy acts from Australia and beyond (including high-profile names), festival gigs take place at the riverside Brisbane Powerhouse arts hub as well as at a number of other venues, including Fortitude Music Hall and Brisbane City Hall.

CMC Rocks Queensland   MUSIC
(www.cmcrocks.com; ⊕Mar) The biggest country and roots festival in the southern hemisphere takes place over three days in March at Willowbank Raceway in the southwest outskirts of Brisbane. Expect a mix of prolific American acts as well as home-grown country A-listers. Note that tickets usually sell out months in advance.

Anywhere Festival   PERFORMING ARTS
(https://anywhere.is; ⊕May) For over two weeks in May, all of Brisbane, Noosa and the Sunshine Coast becomes a stage as hundreds of performances pop up across the region in the most unconventional of places. Expect anything from theatre in laneways to cabaret in antique shops and bellowing sopranos in underground reservoirs.

Queensland Cabaret Festival   PERFORMING ARTS
(http://queenslandcabaretfestival.com.au; ⊕Jun) Come June, the state's southeast cranks up

BRISBANE & AROUND BRISBANE

the sass and subversion with the Queensland Cabaret Festival. Held over two weeks, its modestly sized programme includes both Australian and international acts.

Queensland Music Festival MUSIC
(QMF; www.qmf.org.au; ☉ Jul) Renowned singer-songwriter Katie Noonan is the current artistic director of this biennial statewide festival, which serves up an eclectic program of music ranging from the classical and operatic, to the contemporary. Held over three weeks, only in odd-numbered years, many of its events are free.

'Ekka' Royal Queensland Show CULTURAL
(www.ekka.com.au; Brisbane Showgrounds, 600 Gregory Tce, Bowen Hills; ☉ Aug; ⛟; ☐ 370, 375, ◪ Exhibition) Country and city collide at this epic 10-day event in August. Head in for fireworks, showbags, theme-park rides, concerts, shearing demonstrations and prize-winning livestock by the truckload. There's also a cooking stage, with demonstrations and the odd celebrity chef.

Brisbane Writers Festival LITERATURE
(BWF; https://bwf.org.au; ☉ Sep; ◪ South Brisbane) Queensland's premier literary event has been running for over five decades. With events held at the State Library of Queensland (p294), Queensland Art Gallery (p291) and Gallery of Modern Art (p291), the four-day programme includes readings, discussions and other thought-provoking events featuring both Australian and international writers and thinkers.

Oktoberfest CULTURAL
(www.oktoberfestbrisbane.com.au; Brisbane Showgrounds; ☉ Oct; ☐ 370, 375, ◪ Fortitude Valley) Australia's biggest German shindig. Held over two weekends, it's a sud-soaked blast, with traditional German grub, yodellers, oompah bands and a dedicated 'Kinder Zone' with rides, puppet shows, face painting and more for little aspiring Germans.

🛌 Sleeping

Brisbane's slumber options are varied, ranging from plush suites in heritage buildings to self-contained apartments and party-prone hostels. In general, prices do not abide by any high- or low-season rules; they are often higher midweek, as well as during major events and holiday periods.

🗺 Central Brisbane

Brisbane Quarters HOSTEL $
(☑ 07-3832 1663; https://brisbanequarters.com. au; 413 Upper Edward St; dm from $25, d with/without bathroom from $90/70; ✳ 🛜 ⛟; ◪ Central) Emerald-green tiles, macaw-pimped wallpaper and hot-pink splashes make for a lush introduction at this brand-new boutique hostel, complete with outdoor pool and fitness area. While the eight-bed dorms are tight on space, bunks and pods are comfy, with handy bedside USB ports. Bathrooms are suitably stylish, with en-suite facilities in some private single and double rooms. High-speed internet and breakfast are included.

An on-site restaurant, club and rooftop bar are also in the works.

Brisbane City YHA HOSTEL $
(☑ 07-3236 1004; www.yha.com.au; 392 Upper Roma St; dm from $22, d with/without bathroom $95/82, f from $115; P ✳ @ 🛜 ⛟; ◪ Roma St) A clean, well-run hostel with good-quality facilities, including a rooftop pool. The maximum dorm size is six beds; most have bathrooms. Big on security and kitchen space (there are lots of fridges), the property is within walking distance of the city centre and major South Bank art galleries. Parking costs $12 per night and is best booked ahead as spots are limited.

Base Brisbane Uptown HOSTEL $
(☑ 07-3238 5888; www.stayatbase.com; 466 George St; dm/d/tw from $20/100/100; ✳ @ 🛜; ◪ Roma St) This purpose-built hostel near Roma St station flaunts its youth with mod interiors, decent facilities and overall cleanliness. Dorms range from four to 14 beds (women only dorms are available), and all rooms feature air-con and en-suite bathroom. The property is also wheelchair accessible. The downstairs bar is a party palace, and daily hostel activities range from pub crawls to drag-queen bingo.

★ Next HOTEL $$
(☑ 07-3222 3222; www.snhotels.com/next/brisbane; 72 Queen St; r from $178; ✳ 🛜 ⛟; ◪ Central) Above the Queen St Mall, Next delivers stylish, affordable accommodation. Rooms are generic though svelte and contemporary, with high-tech touchscreen and app technology and decent beds. The outdoor lap pool flanks a buzzing bar, itself adjacent to a handy traveller lounge (with massage chairs and showers) for guests who check in early or want a place to relax before a late flight.

BRISBANE & AROUND BRISBANE

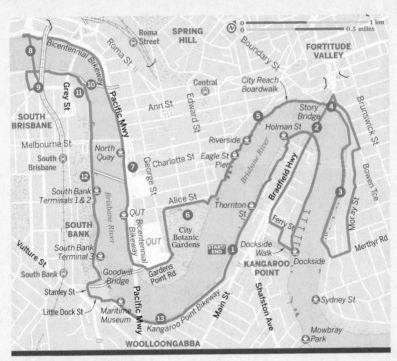

Cycling Tour
Riverside Brisbane

START RIVERLIFE
END RIVERLIFE
LENGTH 16KM; 1½ HOURS

Hire a bike from **1** **Riverlife** (p297) and follow the riverside path north, riding under Story Bridge and heading south along Kangaroo Point's eastern riverbank. Veer right into Dockside Walk, which leads to Ferry St. Cross Deakin St and turn right onto the path leading onto **2** **Story Bridge**. Once crossed, swing right into Bowen Tce, eventually veering right into Moray St. Turn right into Merthyr Rd, which leads to the **3** **Brisbane Riverwalk** (p295). Follow it north to the **4** **Howard Smith Wharves**, cycling through the redevelopment to reach the riverside City Reach Boardwalk. Note the domed, heritage-listed **5** **Customs House** and then cycle along the waterfront to the **6** **City Botanic Gardens** (p290).

The park path parallel to Alice St veers left, leading to Gardens Point Rd. Follow the road down to the Bicentennial Bikeway and head north on it, passing the convict-built **7** **Commissariat Store** (p291). Further along, cross the **8** **Go Between Bridge** and immediately turn right into Bouquet St, then right again onto the riverside pathway. The depiction of an Aboriginal child beneath the South Brisbane rail overpass – by renowned artist Matt Adnate – is one of numerous large street-art murals constituting the **9** **Pillars Project** (p294). Further along the river are the iconic **10** **Kurilpa Bridge**, **11** **Gallery of Modern Art** (p291) and **12** **Wheel of Brisbane** (☎07-3844 3464; www.thewheelofbrisbane.com.au; Grey St; adult/child/family $22/14.50/64; ☉10am-10pm, to 11pm Fri & Sat; ☻; ☒South Bank Terminals 1 & 2, ☒South Brisbane).

The riverfront pathway leads up to Stanley St (which becomes Little Dock St). Turn left into it and follow it to the Kangaroo Point Bikeway, passing numerous contemporary sculptures and the heritage-listed **13** **Kangaroo Point Cliffs**. The cliffs are a former quarry, whose stone was used to construct numerous historical buildings, including the Commissariat Store. The bikeway leads right back to Riverlife and the end of your two-wheeled adventure.

West End & Petrie Terrace

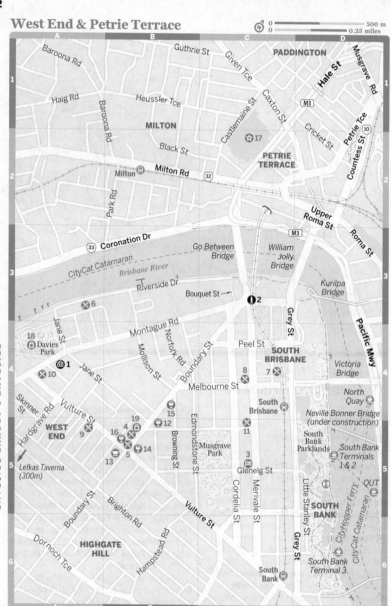

There's also an on-site gym and limited valet parking ($55 per night).

Ibis Styles HOTEL **$$**
(☎07-3337 9000; www.ibisstylesbrisbaneeliza beth.com.au; 40 Elizabeth St; d from $119; ❄@☎; ☒Central) Smart, contemporary digs at the world's largest Ibis hotel. Multicoloured carpets and striking geometric shapes set a playful tone in the lobby, and while the standard rooms are smallish, all are comfortable, with fantastic mattresses, smart TVs and impressive river and South Bank views. Property perks include a small

West End & Petrie Terrace

gym with quality equipment and guest laundry facilities.

★Ovolo Inchcolm BOUTIQUE HOTEL **$$$**
(☐ 07-3226 8888; https://ovolohotels.com.au/ovoloinchcolm; 73 Wickham Tce; d from $240; ☐❄🛜; 🚏Central) Built in the 1920s as doctors' suites, the Inchcolm excels in contrasting heritage features with bold, modern touches, from colour-saturated wallpaper and pop-art rock-star portraits to a cabinet of curiosities in the lobby-cum-bar. Ranging from compact to spacious, rooms are plush, seductively textured and kitted out with iPad Mini, Apple TV, Alexa speaker, complimentary treats, Nespresso machine and super-sleek bathrooms.

Fantauzzo –
Art Series Hotel BOUTIQUE HOTEL **$$$**
(☐ 07-3515 0700; www.artserieshotels.com.au/fantauzzo; 5 Boundary St; r from $223; ❄🛜🏊; 🚣Riverside, 🚏Central) Acclaimed Melbourne-based artist Vincent Fantauzzo is the muse at this on-point boutique hotel, part of the Howard Smith Wharves waterfront redevelopment. His works, which include portraits of famous Australians, create visual intrigue throughout the 166-room property. Smart, modernist-inspired rooms feature emerald-green velvet sofas, heavenly beds and art tomes; opt for a river-view room to avoid looking straight at a cliff face.

🛏 South Bank & West End

★Emporium Hotel BOUTIQUE HOTEL **$$$**
(☐ 07-3556 3333; www.emporiumhotels.com.au; 267 Grey St, South Brisbane; d from $450; ☐❄🛜🏊; 🚏South Bank Terminal 3, 🚏South Bank) From the lipstick-red glass-shard panels to the Japanese-inspired spa and spectacular rooftop infinity pool, Brisbane's most decadent boutique hotel roars 'wow factor'. All 143 rooms room are fabulously spacious, with sublime king-sized beds, 55in flatscreen TVs, coffee-pod machines and marble bathrooms with dual basins and Molton Brown amenities. Higher-priced rooms face the river, while cheaper rooms look over leafy suburbia.

Rydges South Bank HOTEL **$$$**
(☐ 07-3364 0800; www.rydges.com; 9 Glenelg St, South Brisbane; r from $200; ☐❄🛜🏊; 🚏South Brisbane) This refurbished, 12-floor winner is within walking distance of South Bank Parklands (p291) and major galleries. In rich hues of silver, grey and purple, standard rooms are large and inviting (try to get one facing the city), with sublimely comfortable beds, smart TVs, free wi-fi, motion-sensor air-con and small but modern bathrooms.

Check the hotel website for good-value, last-minute deals. Valet parking costs $45 per night ($38 for stays booked directly through the hotel).

🛏 Fortitude Valley & New Farm

Bowen Terrace GUESTHOUSE **$**
(☐ 07-3254 0458; www.bowenterrace.com.au; 365 Bowen Tce, New Farm; dm from $21, s/d without bathroom from $59/89, d/f with bathroom from $89/107; 🛜🏊; ☐195, 196, 199) In a restored, century-old Queenslander, Bowen Terrace offers modestly priced lodging in a real-estate hotspot. Simple rooms include TV, bar fridge, quality linen and lofty ceilings with fans (no air-con). There's a communal kitchen, laundry facilities and

BRISBANE & AROUND BRISBANE

Fortitude Valley & New Farm

0 — 200 m
0 — 0.1 miles

St Pauls Tce
9
Barry Pde
Alfred St
Brunswick St
Fortitude Valley
Alden St
29
Constance St
Wickham St
Brookes St
25
5
Barry Pde
Ann St
East St
12
Wickham St
Brunswick St
Warner St
30
7
FORTITUDE VALLEY
CHINATOWN
14
Ballow St
Ann St
21
Chester St
16
27
2
Bakery La
15
23
Winn La
19
18
McLachlan St
25
Wandoo St
17
28
10
33
4
Doggett St
Ann St
24
Winn St
Berwick St
James St
Duncan St
(Chinatown Mall)
34
Ivory St
31
Robertson St
Boundary St
15
Martin St
20
Arthur St
Bowen Tce
Harcourt St
Howard
Smith
Wharves
Kent St
Story
Bridge
Kent St
NEW
FARM
Terrace St
James St
8
CT White
Park
6
13
Heal St
CityHopper Ferry
Annie St
Pablo (350m);
Brisbane
Powerhouse (1km);
Jan Powers Farmers
Market (1km)
26
11
32
Barker St
3
22
Browne St
1
Bowen Tce
Brunswick St
Villiers St
Brisbane River
Moray St
Moreton St
Moreton St
Merthyr Rd
Moreton St
New Farm Park
(200m)

New Farm
Confectionery
(650m)

BRISBANE & AROUND BRISBANE

Fortitude Valley & New Farm

a pool. Soundproofing between the rooms isn't great, but it's good value for money, with more class than your average hostel.

Spicers Balfour Hotel BOUTIQUE HOTEL $$
(1300 597 540; www.spicersretreats.com/spicers-balfour-hotel; 37 Balfour St, New Farm; r from $189, ste from $269; P ❄ 📶; 🚌195, 196, 199) Sophisticated Spicers occupies two renovated heritage buildings on the same street. Slumber in one of the small, plush rooms in the old Queenslander or upgrade to a spacious, deco-inspired suite in the 1920s villa, four of which come with free-standing bath. All rooms and suites feature gorgeous beds, Bose sound systems and Nespresso machines. There's also a reputable restaurant and cocktail bar.

Tryp BOUTIQUE HOTEL $$
(07-3319 7888; www.trypbrisbane.com; 14-20 Constance St, Fortitude Valley; r from $149; ❄ 📶; 🚆Fortitude Valley) Fans of street art will appreciate this hip 65-room place, complete with a small gym, rooftop bar and glass-panelled lift affording views of the graffiti-strewn shaft. Each of the hotel's four floors features work by a different Brisbane street artist, and while standard rooms are small, all are comfy and feature coffee machines, interactive TVs and fabulous marshmallow beds.

★ **Calile Hotel** BOUTIQUE HOTEL $$$
(07-3607 5888; www.thecalilehotel.com; 48 James St, Fortitude Valley; r from $270; P ❄ 📶 🏊; 🚌470, 🚆Fortitude Valley) Worldly and sophisticated, the Calile turns many local rivals a shade of green. The statement-making, cabana-flanked pool is the stuff of fashion shoots, while its 175 uncluttered rooms come in on-trend shades of pastel blue, green and pink (the latter with poolside balconies). In-room perks include gorgeous king-size beds, Nespresso machines, Bluetooth soundbars and coveted amenities from Grown Alchemist.

Ovolo the Valley BOUTIQUE HOTEL $$$
(07-3253 6999; https://ovolohotels.com.au/ovolothevalley; 1000 Ann St, Fortitude Valley; d from $206; P ❄ 📶 🏊; 🚌60, 300, 302, 305, 306, 322, 🚆Fortitude Valley) With striking pink mesh in the lobby and inflatable flamingos in the rooftop pool, it's clear that Ovolo values quirkiness. Its 103 rooms spark wide grins with their luxe, playful takes on '70s and '80s chic, including retro bangers on the sound system. Entry-level 'Medium Rooms' are small but comfortable, while 'Valley Suites' impress with huge, hot-tub-fitted bathrooms.

✕ Eating

Brisbane's food scene is flourishing – a fact not lost on the nation's food critics and switched-on gluttons. From Mod Oz degustations to curbside food trucks, the city offers an increasingly competent, confident array of culinary highs. Particularly notable is the growing number of eateries fusing high-end culinary sophistication with an easy, casual vibe that is indelibly Brisbane.

Central Brisbane

Strauss CAFE $
(☎07-3236 5232; www.straussfd.com; 189 Elizabeth St; dishes $7.50-17; ⊙6.30am-3pm Mon-Fri; 🛜📶♿; 🚢Riverside, Eagle St Pier, 🚉Central) Strauss shrugs off its corporate surrounds with low-key, Brooklyn-esque cool and a neighbourly vibe. Head in for quick-fix banana bread, or settle in for simple locavore dishes that include omelettes, vibrant salads and sandwiches with combos like red-bean-and-beetroot falafel, pumpkin hummus and avocado. The place takes its coffee seriously, with espresso, filtered and bottled cold brew, mainly from local roaster Sundays.

Bahn Mi Now SANDWICHES $
(168 Adelaide St; sandwiches $7-9; ⊙8am-3pm Mon-Fri, from 11am Sat; 📶♿; 🚉Central) Vietnamese-born Ashleigh Ng heads this hole-in-the-wall takeaway, pumping out affordable, mouth-watering Vietnamese-style sandwiches under a neon-pink sign. Choose your protein (crackling pork is the crowd favourite) and watch the team stuff it into your fresh, crusty baguette, along with cardamom-infused pâté, mayo, pickled carrots and daikon, cucumber and (for those who like it hot) chilli. A vegetarian option is available.

Govinda's VEGETARIAN $
(☎07-3210 0255; www.brisbanegovindas.com.au; 358 George St; all-you-can-eat $12.90; ⊙7am-8pm Mon-Fri, from 11am Sat; 📶; 🚌470, 475, 476, 🚉Roma St) Grab a plate and pile it high with the likes of vegetarian curry, salads, poppadoms, chutneys and semolina fruit pudding at this no-frills budget eatery, run by the Hare Krishnas. For light eaters (or those on an especially tight budget), you can also opt for one dish with rice for $7.

You'll find another branch in **West End** (☎0404 173 027; www.brisbanegovindas.com.au; 82 Vulture St, West End; all-you-can-eat $12.90; ⊙11am-3pm & 5-8pm Mon-Sat; 🚌199).

Felix for Goodness CAFE $$
(☎07-3161 7966; https://felixforgoodness.com; 50 Burnett Lane; dishes $12-24; ⊙7am-3pm Mon-Fri, 8am-2pm Sat; 🛜📶♿; 🚢North Quay, 🚉Central) 🌿 Spruced-up Felix channels Melbourne with its laneway locale, industrial fit-out and effortlessly cool vibe. Produce-driven, all-day-brunch dishes might include poppy-seed pikelets with whipped ricotta, roasted stone fruit and saffron-cardamon syrup, or a bowl of golden falafel served with cauliflower, currants, tabbouleh, sauerkraut and *muhammara* (hot pepper dip). Wash it down with speciality coffee, craft beer, a natural wine or feel-good smoothie.

Greenglass FRENCH $$
(☎0403 966 671; www.greenglasswine.com; 336 George St; mains $23-40; ⊙11.30am-2pm Mon-Fri, 5.30-9pm Tue-Fri; 🚉Roma St) Up a flight of stairs wedged between a discount chemist and a topless bar is this pared-back, loft-style favourite. Here, produce is king, translating into a French-inspired, Italian-accented menu that might offer crumbed, fried olives stuffed with cream cheese and capsicum or a classic Wagyu steak frites good enough for fastidious French palates. The enlightened wine list champions smaller producers.

Arc Dining AUSTRALIAN $$$
(☎07-3505 3980; www.arcdining.com.au; Howard Smith Wharves, 5 Boundary St; mains $36-42, degustation menus $68-98; ⊙noon-3pm & 6-10pm Wed-Sun; 🚢Riverside, 🚉Central) Reminiscent of a designer beach shack, Arc is the top dining option at Howard Smith Wharves. Floor-to-ceiling windows deliver smashing bridge-and-city views, which are a perfect match for Arc's beautifully executed menus. Local farmers, smaller producers and ingredients from an on-site kitchen garden are celebrated in dishes like albacore crudo with bush tomato and celeriac, or goose prosciutto with asparagus, peach and macadamia.

Wines lean towards organic, sustainable and minimal-intervention drops. Book ahead.

South Bank & West End

Messina GELATO $
(☎07-3844 0416; https://gelatomessina.com/stores/south-brisbane; 1/109 Melbourne St, South Brisbane; gelato from $5.30; ⊙noon-10.30pm, to 11.30pm Fri & Sat, to 10pm Sun; 📶♿; 🚌192, 196,

199, 202, ⌂ South Brisbane) Sydney's cult-status artisanal gelateria keeps Brisbanites cool with its extensive, rotating repertoire of freshly churned flavours. The emphasis is on natural ingredients, shining through in options like apple pie, panna cotta with fig jam and amaretti (almond biscuits), macadamia crunch, and salted coconut with mango salsa (made using Queensland mangoes, naturally). Gluten-free and vegan gelato are available.

★ **Maeve Wine** AUSTRALIAN **$$**
(https://maeve.wine; Level 1, 39 Melbourne St, South Brisbane; dishes $10-30; ☺ 4-11pm Mon-Wed, to midnight Thu-Sat; ☑; ⌂ South Brisbane) This narrow, timber-panelled nirvana for food and wine lovers (book ahead) is split into separate bar and bistro areas. Its sharing-style menu showcases superb Australian produce in nuanced, modern dishes like Spencer Gulf kingfish carpaccio with goat's yoghurt, black garlic and green tomato. Thoughtfully chosen wines focus on European drops and New World vino produced in an old-world style.

★ **Gauge** AUSTRALIAN **$$**
(☑ 07-3638 0431; www.gaugebrisbane.com.au; 77 Grey St, South Brisbane; breakfast & lunch dishes $14-32, dinner mains $28-38; ☺ 5-11pm Wed-Sat, 8am-2.30pm Sat & Sun; ☒ South Bank Terminals 1 & 2, ⌂ South Brisbane) In a crisp, sparse space punctuated by black-spun aluminium lamps and a smashing wine list, clean, contemporary dishes burst with Australian confidence. Signatures include a provocative 'blood taco' packed with roasted bone marrow, mushroom and native thyme, and a brilliant black garlic bread with burnt vanilla and brown butter.

★ **Morning After** CAFE **$$**
(☑ 07-3844 0500; www.morningafter.com.au; cnr Vulture & Cambridge Sts, West End; breakfast $10-24, lunch mains $19-25; ☺ 7am-4pm; ☜☑☗; ☐ 199) Decked out in blonde-wood furniture, terrazzo flooring and bold green accents, airy, contemporary Morning After turns out exceptional, produce-driven fare. Expect mod-Oz twists on Mediterranean and Asian flavours, whether it's crunchy granola with smooth kaffir lime and lemongrass panna cotta, a blue-swimmer-crab omelette topped

WORTH A TRIP

ATMOSPHERIC PADDINGTON

Speckled with hilly side streets, 19th-century workers' cottages and rickety tin-and-timber Queenslanders, inner-city Paddington couldn't feel further apart from the high-rises and hustle of other inner-city neighbourhoods. It's an evocative neighbourhood and one worth a morning or afternoon wander.

The suburb's nerve centre is Given Tce (which becomes Latrobe Tce) and the 1.3km stretch between Guthrie and Collingwood Sts is the most interesting to explore. Worthy pitstops include tiny **Sun & Company** (☑ 0432 170 675; www.facebook.com/sunandcompanystore; 28 Latrobe Tce; ☺ 10am-5pm Tue-Fri, to 4pm Sat & Sun; ☐ 375, 377), an ethically minded shop selling small-batch, locally made gifts. Further west, **Remy's** (☑ 07-3073 3986; http://remys.com.au; 106 Latrobe Tce, Paddington; breakfast dishes $6-21, burgers $11-18; ☺ 7am-9pm Mon-Sat, 8am-8pm Sun; ☜☑☗; ☐ 61, 375, 385) is famed for its great-value burger deals: two-for-one burgers on Sundays from 3.30pm to 6.30pm and half-price burgers on Mondays from 5pm to 7pm. The cafe's weekly events include live blues, jazz and DJs, all listed on its Facebook page.

Further west still, **Green Tangerine** (☑ 07-3367 3511; www.greentangerine.com.au; 157 Latrobe Tce; ☺ 10am-4pm Tue, to 5pm Wed-Fri, 9.30am-5pm Sat, 10am-3.30pm Sun; ☐ 375) stocks Australian design objects and gifts, while a few doors away, antiques emporium **Empire Revival** (☑ 07-3369 8088; www.empirerevival.com.au; 167 Latrobe Tce; ☺ 10am-5pm, to 4pm Sun; ☐ 375) occupies a heritage-listed theatre dating from 1929. If you manage to find your way out, cross Collingwood St and settle in at **Naïm** (☑ 07-3172 1655; www.naimrestaurant.com.au; 14 Collingwood St; brunch dishes $15-27, dinner mains $21-35; ☺ 8am-2pm Tue-Sun, also 5-8.30pm Thu-Sat; ☜☑☗; ☐ 375), a relaxed cafe-style eatery with verdant views of Paddington and fresh, gorgeous dishes inspired by the Middle East.

To reach Paddington, catch bus 385 from the Cultural Centre bus station on Melbourne St in South Bank or from King George Sq in central Brisbane.

EAT STREET NORTHSHORE

A relaxing CityCat catamaran ride away, family-friendly **Eat Street Northshore** (🖉 0428 485 242; www.eatstreetmarkets.com; 221d MacArthur Ave, Hamilton; admission adult/child $3/free, meals from $10; ⊙ 4-10pm Fri & Sat, noon-8pm Sun; 🖉 🏕; 🚻 Northshore Hamilton) is Brisbane's hugely popular take on the night food market. Divided into themed sections reminiscent of an amusement park, its veritable village of shipping-containers-turned-kitchens peddle everything from freshly shucked oysters to Japanese yakisoba, South American grilled meats, American mac-and-cheese and Sicilian cannoli. Add craft brews, two live-music stages and a handful of quirky retailers and you have one of the city's most atmospheric nights out. The venue is an easy 200m walk west of the Northshore Hamilton CityCat stop.

with tangy papaya salad and fried shallots, or lunchtime Peking-duck tacos with chilli and pickled ginger.

Hello Please   VIETNAMESE **$$**
(http://helloplease.co; cnr Fish Ln & Hope St, South Brisbane; dishes $13-26; ⊙ 5pm-late Tue-Thu, from noon Fri-Sun; 🚉 South Brisbane) Hawker-inspired bar-cum-eatery Hello Please is all about punchy, knockout flavours in a South Brisbane laneway. Vietnamese inspired and East-Asian accented, options include spectacular rice-paper spring rolls jammed with pork, salads with combos like Hainanese chicken, pickled vegetables and aromatic herbs, plus East-West mash-ups that might see shiitake-mushroom congee tweaked with sharp Grana Padano cheese. Well-crafted cocktails crank up the good vibes.

Plenty West End   CAFE **$$**
(🖉 07-3255 3330; www.facebook.com/plenty westend; 284 Montague Rd, West End; dishes $6-21; ⊙ 6.30am-2.30pm, 7am-1.30pm Sat, 7.30am-1.30pm Sun; 🛜 🖉 🏕; 🚌 60, 192, 198) 🖉 In the far west of West End lies this graphics-factory-turned-cafe, a rustic, industrial backdrop for farm-to-table edibles. Scan the counter for freshly made cakes, or the blackboard for headliners that might include buttermilk pancakes with peanut-butter mousse and

smoked honey, or house-made hash browns with creamed corn, salsa verde and poached eggs. Libations include fresh juices, kombucha and fantastic coffee.

Grown   VEGETARIAN **$$**
(🖉 07-3036 7213; https://grownbne.com; G03/21 Buchanan St, West End; brunch dishes $13-18, dinner dishes $14-27; ⊙ 7.30am-2.30pm & 5.30-9pm Tue-Sat, 7.30am-2.30pm Sun; 🛜 🖉; 🚌 60, 192) 🖉 At West End's western edge, this airy, sustainable cafe-restaurant champions local produce and meat-free dining. Almost everything is made in-house, including a very Aussie 'Vegemite' made using black sesame and tamari. The result is vibrant, feel-good dishes such as pearl couscous with chickpeas, heirloom tomatoes, fermented pumpkin and citrus salad. Drinks include excellent, locally roasted coffee and vegan wine and beer.

Julius   ITALIAN **$$**
(🖉 07-3844 2655; www.juliuspizzeria.com.au; 77 Grey St, South Brisbane; pizzas $22-26, pasta $25-27; ⊙ noon-9.30pm Tue, Wed & Sun, to 10pm Thu, to 10.30pm Fri & Sat; 🚉 South Bank Terminals 1 & 2, 🚉 South Brisbane) This svelte Italian fires up proper pizzas, divided into *pizze rosse* (with tomato sauce) or *pizze bianche* (without). The former includes a simple, beautiful marinara, cooked the proper Neapolitan way (sans seafood). The pasta dishes are also solid, with *fritelle di ricotta* (fried ricotta dumplings filled with cherry jam) making a satisfying epilogue.

The place takes no reservations after 12.30pm at lunch and 5.45pm at dinner, so consider heading in early to avoid the wait (Friday and Saturday nights are super busy).

Chop Chop Chang's   ASIAN **$$**
(🖉 07-3846 7746; www.chopchopchangs.com.au; 185 Boundary St, West End; dishes $9-33; ⊙ 11.30am-3pm & 5.30-9pm Mon-Thu, to 10pm Fri, 11.30am-10pm Sat, 11.30am-9pm Sun; 🖉 🏕; 🚌 199) 'Happiness never decreases by being shared.' So said the Buddha. The hordes at this casual, cavernous stalwart concur, sharing bowls of flavour-packed, pan-Asian street food like *larb moo* (ground-pork with sawtooth, chilli, lime and sugarloaf), crispy Szechuan eggplant with pickled daikon, and cooling watermelon and pomelo salad. A dedicated vegan banquet ($35) is offered on Tuesdays, with optional matching vegan wines.

BRISBANE & AROUND BRISBANE

Lefkas Taverna   GREEK **$$**
(☑07-3844 1163; www.facebook.com/lefkastav
ernabrisbane; 170 Hardgrave Rd, West End; mains
$16-28; ⊙11am-9.30pm Tue-Thu, to 10pm Fri &
Sat; 🖍🖼) Sage Brisbanites snub Brisbane's
hipper, pricier Greek hotspots for this sub-
urban stalwart. Light-filled and refresh-
ingly unpretentious, its classic repertoire
includes succulent *dolmathakia* (rice-filled
vine leaves), juicy grilled meats and impec-
cably grilled baby octopus that will leave
you salivating for days. Much of what is
served is made from scratch, from the dips
to the naughty *galaktoboureko* (Greek cus-
tard pie).

Ramen Danbo   RAMEN **$$**
(☑07-3844 5365; https://ramendanbo.com.au;
52 Merivale St, South Brisbane; ramen from $14;
⊙11am-10pm; 🖍🖼; ☒South Brisbane) Japanese pop and a chorus of *'Irasshaimase!'*
greet punters at this casual, upbeat Japanese
import. The cult-status pork-bone tonkotsu
is lifted by a house-made special sauce and
run through a Japanese filter to ensure that
Brisbane's version is true to the original.
Diners can tweak their dishes, from spice
level and toppings to noodle firmness. Vegetarian and vegan options available.

★**Signature**   AUSTRALIAN **$$$**
(☑07-3556 3333; www.emporiumhotels.com.au;
Emporium Hotel, 267 Grey St, South Brisbane;
mains $36-55, 5-/7-course tasting menu $75/95; ⊙5.30-
9.30pm Tue-Sat; 🛜🖍; ☒South Bank Terminal 3,
☒South Bank) Elegant dining thrives in this
award-winning, deco-inspired dining room,
complete with flawlessly attentive staff, a
1000-glass-bauble ceiling installation and
floor-to-ceiling showpiece wine cabinet. The
latter is home to around 6500 wines, per-
fectly complementing technically brilliant,
locavore-focused dishes like Brisbane Valley
quail with pancetta, hazelnut and wattle-seed
granola or refreshing Queensland spanner
crab with pomelo, ruby grapefruit, jamon,
rockmelon and mandarin sorbet.

A handful of à-la-carte vegan dishes (mains
$26) are available. Book ahead.

★**Stokehouse Q**   MODERN AUSTRALIAN **$$$**
(☑07-3020 0600; https://stokehouseq.com.au;
River Quay, Sidon St; mains $38-56; ⊙noon-late,
from 11am Fri-Sun; 🛜; ☒South Bank Terminal 3,
☒South Bank) Sophisticated bistro fare and
relaxing river views make this one of Brisbane's destination restaurants. At crisp,
linen-clad tables, urbanites toast to locally

sourced produce, shining in polished dishes
like cornbread topped with fresh Fraser-Isle
spanner crab and lemon myrtle, or the signature soda-batter fish with triple-cooked
chips and seaweed salt. Tip: come here for
lunch to fully appreciate the view.

✗ Fortitude Valley, New Farm & Bowen Hills

Ben's Burgers   BURGERS **$**
(☑07-3195 3094; www.bensburgers.com.au; 5b
Winn Lane; burgers $12; ⊙11am-9pm, to 11pm Fri
& Sat; 🖍; ☒Fortitude Valley) Top-notch ingredients drive Ben's, a tiny bolthole in a laneway
off Ann St. The menu is an uncomplicated
affair: three brioche-bun burgers, among
them a meat-free mushroom-and-Parmesan
option. Sides are equally straightforward
– fries or chilli-cheese fries – with brown-
ies and pecan pie making for a fitting end.
Drinks include house-made cherry cola and
ginger ale, shakes and beer.

★**Same Same**   THAI **$$**
(☑07-3188 1418; www.samesamerestaurant.com.
au; Shop AM3, Ada Lane, 46 James St, Fortitude
Valley; larger dishes $23-48; ⊙restaurant 5.30-
10.30pm Tue-Thu, noon-3pm & 5.30-11pm Fri &
Sat, noon-3pm & 5.30-10.30pm Sun, upstairs bar
5.30pm-midnight Thu, from 3pm Fri-Sun; 🗐470,
☒Fortitude Valley) Book an early feed to
avoid a wait at one of Brisbane's hottest
dining spots. Here, Thai-inspired recipes,
top-tier ingredients and contemporary
Australian flair underscore sharing-style
plates that are big on flavour. From silky
Hervey Bay scallops with chilli, garlic, pep-
percorns and basil, to Bundaberg Bay bug
in a coconut-and-turmeric curry, bites are
punchy, balanced and worthy of the hype.

Upstairs, Same Same leaps across the
Pacific with its green-tiled bar, Los, home
to an impressive selection of tequilas.

★**Happy Boy**   CHINESE **$$**
(☑0413 246 890; http://happyboy.com.au; East
St; dishes $6-30, banquets $35-45; ⊙11.30am-
2pm & 5.30-8.30pm Tue, Wed & Sun, to 9.30pm
Thu-Sat; 🖍; ☒Fortitude Valley) Fun, loud and
always pumping, this ever-hip place draws
all types with its toothsome Chinese, good
enough to make your uncle weep. Dive into
smashing dishes like twice-cooked dry and
sticky beef rib in sweet sauce, Chongqing
chilli chicken, and smoky, burnt broccolini
with black-bean butter.

WORTH A TRIP

MT COOT-THA FOREST

Commanding city views and hiker-friendly bushland are the order of the day at **Mt Coot-tha Forest**, an easy 5km west of central Brisbane. Spanning over 1600 hectares of open eucalypt forest and rainforest gullies, the reserve is topped by 287m Mt Coot-tha, the city's highest point. The **summit lookout** (☑07-3369 9922; www.brisbanelookout. com; 1012 Sir Samuel Griffith Dr; ♠; ◻471), which includes a cafe and restaurant, offers a prime-time panorama of the Brisbane skyline and greater metro area. On a clear day you'll even spot the Moreton Bay islands. The hillsides are traced by walking trails, with downloadable walking maps available at www.brisbane.qld.gov.au (click on 'Things to see and do').

At its base, the 52-hectare **Brisbane Botanic Gardens** (☑07-3403 2535; www. brisbane.qld.gov.au/botanicgardens; Mt Coot-tha Rd; ☉8am-6pm, to 5pm Apr-Aug; ♠; ◻471) FREE harbours a plethora of mini-ecologies, from cactus, bonsai and herb gardens, to rainforests and arid zones. Free guided walks run at 11am and 1pm (public holidays excepted). Self-guided tours, which include an Aboriginal plant trail, can be downloaded from the website.

At the entrance to the gardens is the **Sir Thomas Brisbane Planetarium** (☑07-3403 2578; www.brisbane.qld.gov.au/planetarium; Mt Coot-tha Rd; shows adult/child $16.40/10; ☉10am-4pm Tue-Thu, to 7.30pm Fri, 10.45am-7.30pm Sat, 10.45am-4pm Sun; ◻471), its Cosmic Skydome screening numerous outer-space shows; bookings are strongly recommended. The planetarium's free exhibition gallery includes a fascinating section on traditional Aboriginal and Torres Strait Islander astronomy.

It takes around 30 minutes to reach Mt Coot-tha by bus (route 471) from Adelaide St in the city, opposite King George Sq. The bus drops you off at the lookout, stopping outside the botanic gardens and planetarium en route.

Weekday lunch includes some good-value specials, with most dishes around $14. Next door is Happy Boy's moody, on-point wine bar, Snack Man.

★ **Joy** AUSTRALIAN $$$
(☑0412 425 626; www.joyrestaurant.com.au; Shop 7 Bakery Lane, 694 Ann St, Fortitude Valley; chef's menu $110; ☉6-10.30pm Thu-Sun; ☑; ◻Fortitude Valley) Advance planning is the only way to secure a place at this 10-seat, omakase-inspired 'it kid', one of Australia's hottest eateries. Behind its compressed-stone counter, powerhouse chefs Tim and Sarah Scott serve up knock-out Mod-Oz creations like venison-tartare spring rolls or mont blanc with roasted artichoke caramel, Italian meringue and salted Chantilly cream.

Reservations usually open a couple of months in advance and book out immediately; see the website. Vegetarian options must be requested when booking.

★ **Little Valley** CHINESE $$$
(☑0431 619 884; https://little-valley.com.au; 6 Warner St; set dinner menus $65-85; ☉noon-3pm & 5.30-10.30pm Wed-Sun; ☑; ◻Fortitude Valley) Award-winning Little Valley has established

quite a reputation for its contemporary, regional Chinese cuisine. Order an on-point cocktail and snap your chopsticks at sophisticated, creative bites such as lobster-and-chive *har gow* (dumplings), roasted pork belly with sweet-and-sour peaches, or East-meets-West Chinese bolognese with nduja XO sauce and prawn floss. Book ahead.

If you're on a tighter budget, opt for the weekday lunch dim sum ($39).

Montrachet FRENCH $$$
(☑07-3367 0030; https://montrachet.com. au; 1/30 King St, Bowen Hills; mains $44-60, 4-/7-course degustation $90/120, Sat 5-course set menu $110; ☉noon-3pm & 6-10pm Tue-Fri, 5.30-10pm Sat; ◻301, 320, ◻Fortitude Valley) Seductive accents, French posters and classic Gallic fare: is this Bowen Hills or Burgundy? You'll feel much closer to France at this *comptoir*-bistro hybrid, hands down Brisbane's top French restaurant. Prime regional ingredients power polished dishes like double-baked crab-and-Gruyère soufflé and brined, slow-roasted Aylesbury duck with cherry-pickled lion's mane mushroom and salt-baked celeriac. Wine offerings are impressive and the service near-flawless. Book ahead.

Baja MEXICAN **$$$**
(☑07-3625 0069; www.bajamodernmexican.com;
211 Brunswick St, Fortitude Valley; dishes $12-23;
⏱5.30-10pm Tue-Sat, noon-3pm Thu & Fri; ▨;
🚇Fortitude Valley) Piñatas are ditched for
Tasmanian oak, natural clay and Queens-
land marble at dimly lit, next-gen Baja,
where smart, Mexican-inspired dishes
flaunt top local ingredients. If available,
don't miss the Baja fish taco or the twice-
cooked octopus tentacles, the latter paired
with chilli oil and a squid-ink-burnt jala-
peño soy sauce. Drinks include well-crafted
cocktails and an ever-expanding list of mes-
cals and tequilas.

✖ Newstead & Teneriffe

★Sourced CAFE **$**
(☑07-3852 6734; www.sourcedgrocer.com.au;
11 Florence St, Teneriffe; dishes $9-24; ⏱7am-
3pm Mon-Sat, from 8am Sun; 🖶; 🚌 60, 199, 393,
🚊Teneriffe) Decked out with a vine-laced
front deck and open kitchen, chilled, ware-
house-turned-cafe Sourced serves beautiful,
seasonal cafe fare. Check the blackboard
for creative salad specials that might pair
bitter radicchio with roasted beetroot and
caramelised purple carrots, or opt for the
smashing, long-running cabbage pancake
with crispy fried broccoli, soft egg and
goat's-milk cheese.

La Macelleria GELATO **$**
(☑0423 286 542; www.lamacelleriagelateria.
com; 10-29 Florence St, Teneriffe; gelato from $5;
⏱11am-10pm, to 11pm Fri & Sat; 🚌60, 199, 🚊Ten-
eriffe) After opening their first gelateria in
an old butcher's shop in Bologna (La Macel-
leria means 'The Butchery'), Italians Matteo
Zini and Matteo Casone turned their atten-
tion to Brisbane. Made from scratch using
quality ingredients, their gelato flavours
range from classic roasted pistachio to a
heavenly buffalo-milk ricotta with caramel-
ised figs. Sorbets are seasonal. Bargain $2
espresso coffee noon to 3pm weekdays.
 You'll find another two inner-city branch-
es in Bowen Hills and West End.

★Carl's AUSTRALIAN **$$**
(☑07-3054 7144; www.carlsnewstead.com.
au; 22 Wyandra St, Newstead; 1-/2-/3 courses
$30/50/60; ⏱3-9pm Wed-Sat, to 7pm Sun, bar to
10.30pm; 🚌60/199, 🚊Teneriffe) Carl's is the intimate, continental-spirited bistro-wine bar
you wish you had on your street. A handful
of tables share space with the open kitchen,
where rotating guest chefs prepare clever,
nuanced dishes such as kingfish crudo with
apple sorbet, buttermilk and horseradish.
Skilled sommelier Mark Whitaker steers the
wine offerings, which might include a Can-
berra-region Marsanne or perhaps a Geor-
gian Saperavi.
 Charcuterie offerings are house-cured,
smoked and aged at sibling venue City Winery (p315). Book ahead Friday and Saturday
evenings.

★Nodo CAFE **$$**
(☑07-3852 2230; https://nododonuts.com; 1 Ella
St, Newstead; dishes $13-23; ⏱7am-3pm; 🛜▨;
🚌300, 302, 305, 306, 322, 470) Light-washed
Nodo serves up Brisbane's poshest dough-
nuts, with combos like Valrhona choco-
late with beetroot. They're gluten-free,
baked (not fried) and sell out quickly. The
rest of the cafe menu is equally inspired,
from porcini waffles with black garlic but-
ter, mushrooms, kale, soft-fried duck egg,
toasted hazelnut ricotta and wattleseed,
to crushed avocado with camel-milk feta,
Vegemite togarashi and black lime.
 Great coffee too.

✖ New Farm

Chouquette BAKERY **$**
(☑07-3358 6336; www.chouquette.com.au; 19
Barker St; pastries from $2.90, baguettes $8.50-10;
⏱6.30am-4pm Wed-Sat, to 2.30pm Sun; ▨▨;
🚌195, 199) The best patisserie this side of
Toulouse? Something to think about as you
grab a coffee and a bag of the namesake
chouquettes (small choux pastries topped
with granulated sugar), a shiny slice of *tarte
au citron* (lemon tart), or a lunchtime ba-
guette stuffed with the likes of slow-cooked
pork rillettes and cornichons. Charming
French-speaking staff.

Pablo CAFE **$$**
(☑07-3113 3660; www.facebook.com/pablonew
farm; 4/220 James St, New Farm; dishes $14-19;
⏱6am-2pm Tue-Sat, 7am-1pm Sun; 🛜▨🖶;
🚌199) An idiosyncratic mix of midcentury
design, antiques and Australian-themed
street art, affable, Pablo is a brunch favourite among New Farmers. Local produce and
tweaks on cafe staples underscore the menu,
which might see smashed avocado served
with mango-and-pomegranate salsa and co-
conut-tahini yoghurt, or French toast paired
with spiced poached pears and saffron fairy
floss. Great coffee too.

Double Shot
CAFE **$$**

(📞 07-3358 6556; www.facebook.com/doubleshot
newfarm; 125 Oxlade Dr; mains $13-21; ⏰7am-
3pm Wed, Thu & Sat, to 9pm Fri, 8am-3pm Sun;
🅿🛈; 🚌196, 🚢Sydney St) With its button-cute
porch and manicured hedge, laid-back Dou-
ble Shot is a hit with the locals. Join the New
Farm crew for good coffee, homemade co-
conut bread with whipped ricotta, Spanish
sardines on sourdough or refreshing green
papaya, coconut and chicken salad. A short
evening menu of small plates, deli boards,
burgers and themed dishes is served from
3pm on Friday.

Himalayan Cafe
NEPALI **$$**

(📞 07-3358 4015; 640 Brunswick St; mains $17-
29; ⏰5.30-9.30pm Tue-Thu & Sun, to 10.30pm Fri
& Sat; 🅿; 🚌195, 196, 199) Awash with prayer
flags, this highly atmospheric neighbourhood stalwart pulls in the punters with its
authentic Tibetan and Nepalese dishes,
from *phali* (oven-baked savoury pastries) to
tender *fhaiya deakau* (diced lamb with vegetables, coconut milk, sour cream and spic-
es). Some dishes impress more than others;
the goat curry is a hit. Vegetarian, vegan and
gluten-free options are available.

Kangaroo Point & Woolloongabba

Pearl Cafe
CAFE **$$**

(📞 07-3392 3300; www.facebook.com/pearl.cafe.
brisbane; 28 Logan Rd, Woolloongabba; breakfast
$9-23, lunch mains $22-28; ⏰7am-2pm Mon, to
3pm Tue-Sun; 🚌174, 175, 204) Euro-spirited
Pearl is one of Brisbane's best-loved week-
end brunch spots, with freshly baked cakes
on the counter and beautiful cafe fare on
the menu. Kickstart the day with the likes
of buttermilk pancakes with charred pine-
apple, fresh berries, toasted coconut and
mascarpone or scan a lunch menu that
spans light, nourishing salads to impressive
pasta mains. Grazing boards also available.

⭐1889 Enoteca
ITALIAN **$$$**

(📞 07-3392 4315; www.1889enoteca.com.au; 10-12
Logan Rd, Woolloongabba; pasta $24-45, dinner mains
$32-55; ⏰noon-2.30pm & 6-10pm Tue-Fri, 6-10pm
Sat, noon-2.30pm Sun; 🚌174, 175, 204) Italian
purists rightfully adore this moody, sophisticated bistro and wine shop, where pasta is
not served with a spoon and a Roman-centric
menu delivers seductive dishes such as fried
zucchini flowers stuffed with mozzarella and
anchovies, or *cacio e pepe* (spaghetti with

24-month-aged pecorino Romano and black
pepper). The superlative wine list champions
natural drops from lauded, smaller Italian
producers.

🍷 Drinking & Nightlife

From a booming microbrewery scene new
wine bars focused on artisanal winemak-
ers and interesting varietals, Brisbane's
drinking scene has grown up significantly
in recent years. The city's live-music scene
is also booming, with cult-status venues
like Newstead's Triffid and the Valley's Fortitude Music Hall serving up impressive
independent talent, both homegrown and
touring. Tip: always carry photo ID.

🍸 Central Brisbane

⭐Felons Brewing Co
MICROBREWERY

(📞 07-3188 9090; https://felonsbrewingco.com.au;
Howard Smith Wharves, 5 Boundary St; ⏰11am-
late; 🛈; 🚢Riverside, 🚉Central) The long timber
deck at this sprawling, polished microbrewery – part of the Howard Smith Wharves
redevelopment – offers a knockout panorama of the river and Brisbane skyline. Drink
in the view while knocking back Felons'
easy-drinking ales, citrusy lager, IPA, or the
cider made using local apples. Bites include
charcuterie boards, tasty wood-fired pizzas,
burgers and virtuous salad bowls.

Brooklyn Standard
BAR

(📞 07-3221 1604; www.facebook.com/brooklyn
standardbar; Eagle Lane; ⏰4pm-late Mon-Fri, from
6pm Sat; 🚢Riverside, 🚉Central) The red neon
sign sets the tone: 'If the music is too loud,
you are too old'. Booming, live funk, soul or
rockabilly is what you get at this rocking
cellar bar, decked out in NYC paraphernalia,
a 1940s shoe-polish dispenser and murals
by local artist Dan Farmer. The Americana
theme extends to the menu, which includes
Brooklyn lager and tater tots.

Mr Percival's
BAR

(📞 07-3188 9090; www.mrpercivals.com.au; Howard Smith Wharves, 5 Boundary St; ⏰11am-late;
🛈; 🚢Riverside, 🚉Central) While the pool-
boy-cute barkeeps and caviar service might
scream Hamptons, the spectacular skyline
view from the outdoor deck confirms otherwise. Jutting out over the Brisbane River,
this breezy, pastel-hued bar is the poshest
place to drink at Howard Smith Wharves,
pouring cocktails, spritzes, boutique wines
and craft beers.

John Mills Himself

CAFE, BAR

(☑ bar 0422 294 146, cafe 0434 064 349; www.
johnmillshimself.com.au; 40 Charlotte St; ☺ cafe
6.30am-3.30pm Mon-Fri, bar 4-9pm Mon, to 10pm
Tue-Thu & Sat, to midnight Fri; ☒ Central) Tiny
John Mills transforms from daytime coffee
shop to evening cocktail den. While the former brews excellent coffee, the latter pours
outstanding Australian artisanal spirits
that might see your martini made with
Tasmanian sheep's-whey gin. Local craft
beers flow from six taps while the wine list
champions Queensland's Granite Belt. Accessible from both Charlotte St and an alley
off Elizabeth St.

Gresham Bar

BAR

(☑ 0437 360 158; www.thegresham.com.au; 308
Queen St; ☺ 7am-late, from noon Sat, from 4pm
Sun; ☎; ☒ Central) Tucked into one corner of
a noble, heritage-listed bank building, the
Gresham evokes the old-school bars of New
York; we're talking pressed-metal ceiling,
Chesterfields and a glowing cascade of spirit
bottles behind a handsome timber bar (complete with library-style ladder). It's a dark,
buzzing, convivial spot, with an especially
robust selection of whiskies and a snug side
room.

Alba Bar & Delicatessen

BAR

(www.albabar.com.au; 34 Burnett Lane;
☺ noon-midnight Mon-Fri, from 3pm Sat; ☎;
☒ Central) *Pintxos* and hip-hop beats make
for interesting bedfellows at Alba, a new-
school laneway bar from former *Masterchef
Australia* contestant Jamie Fleming. Drinks
include cocktails and lesser-known wine
varietals, paired perfectly with rotating
lunchtime *bocadillos* (Spanish sandwiches;
served until 3pm weekdays only) and all-day
tapas-style bites, served Monday to Saturday. The latter include a knockout *morcil-
la* (blood sausage) with polenta, truffle and
radish.

Coffee Anthology

CAFE

(☑ 07-3210 1881; www.facebook.com/coffeean
thology; 126 Margaret St; ☺ 7am-3.30pm Mon-
Fri, 7.30am-noon Sat; ☎ ⓦ; ☒ Central) Coffee
Anthology brews a rotating selection of
blends from A-list Aussie roasters like
Sydney's Sample Coffee and Melbourne's
Small Batch Roasting Co (take-home bags
available). It's a contemporary, semi-al-
fresco space, also serving high-quality,
creative breakfasts and lunches that might
include leatherwood-honey panna cotta
with tarragon chiffon and granola or an

BEER YOGA

You can slurp *and* stretch simultaneously at Brisbane's weekly beer yoga
sessions, hosted by **Felons Brewing Co**
(felonsbrewingco.com.au) at its spectacular riverside location. The 45-min-
ute Vinyasa Slow Flow sessions run
every Monday at 5.30pm, drawing a mix
of punters happily sipping a local craft
ale or cider in between slow, relaxed
moves suitable for rookies. Sessions
are free; simply bring your own yoga
mat and purchase any drinks at the bar
before the session begins. Check the
Felons Brewing Co website for updates.

Asian-inspired pulled-pork burger with
house-made BBQ sauce, wombok and shal-
lot mayo.

Pablo & Rusty's Coffee Roasters

CAFE

(☑ 07-3236 4525; https://pabloandrustys.com.au;
200 Mary St; ☺ 6.30am-3.30pm Mon-Fri; ☒ Eagle St Pier, ☒ Central) In Brisbane's financial
heartland, glass-and-timber Pablo & Rusty's
pours beautiful brews for coffee connoisseurs. Options include espresso, batch brew,
chilled filter and Nitro, with coffee flights
available for those wanting to sample the
day's best brews. Speciality hot chocolate,
cold-pressed juices and kombucha are also
on offer, along with pastries and simple,
fresh (if generally unremarkable) breakfast
and lunch bites.

🍽 South Bank & West End

Terrace

ROOFTOP BAR

(☑ 07-3556 3333; www.emporiumhotels.com.
au; Emporium Hotel, 267 Grey St, South Brisbane;
☺ 6.30am-11pm; ☎; ☒ South Bank Terminal 3,
☒ South Bank) Brisbane's most spectacular
(and luxe) rooftop bar rolls out a blockbuster view of the Brisbane River and the
city's imposing skyline. The bar itself is
impressive, with floor-to-ceiling windows,
a dramatic onyx bar, lush greenery and a
sweeping al-fresco balcony with coveted
bar tables. Sip a *shuzo* and soda, slurp some
oysters and gaze out at your new favourite
Australian city.

Maker

COCKTAIL BAR

(☑ 0437 338 072; 9 Fish Lane, South Brisbane;
☺ 4pm-midnight Tue-Sun; ☒ South Bank Terminals 1 & 2, ☒ South Brisbane) Intimate, black-
clad and spliced by a sexy brass bar, Maker

LGBTIQ+ BRISBANE

While Brisbane's LGBTIQ+ scene is significantly smaller than its Sydney and Melbourne counterparts, the city has an out-and-proud presence. Newstead and Teneriffe have become residential epicentres for gay men. Other LGBTIQ+-friendly neighbourhoods include the arty, more alternative West End across the river, as well as Fortitude Valley, Bowen Hills, and Paddington.

Fortitude Valley's **Wickham Hotel** (☑07-3051 7621; www.thewickham.com.au; 308 Wickham St; ⊘10am-late; ⛴Fortitude Valley) remains the epicentre of Brisbane's low-key LGBTIQ+ scene, with regular drag shows and special weekly events. The Valley is also home to **Beat MegaClub** (☑07-3852 2661; www.thebeatmegaclub.com.au; 677 Ann St; ⊘8pm-late Mon-Sat, from 5pm Sun; ⛴Fortitude Valley). Closer to the city centre, Spring Hill's **Sportsman Hotel** (☑07-3831 2892; www.sportsmanhotel.com.au; 130 Leichhardt St; ⊘1pm-1am, to 2.30am Fri & Sat; ☒372, 373, ⛴Central) is a blue-collar pub with pool tables, drag shows, good pub meals and a rather eclectic crowd.

Major events on the city's rainbow-hued calendar include the **Brisbane Queer Film Festival** (www.bqff.com.au; ⊘Mar), arts festival **Melt** (https://brisbanepowerhouse.org; Brisbane Powerhouse, 119 Lamington St, New Farm; ⊘Jun/Jul; ☒196, ⛴New Farm Park) and the **Brisbane Pride Festival** (https://brisbanepride.org.au; ⊘Sep).

crafts seasonal cocktails using house liqueurs, out-of-the-box ingredients and a splash of whimsy. Here, classic Negronis are made with house-infused vermouth, while gin and tonics might get native with quandong and finger lime. You'll also find a selection of boutique wines by the glass and beautiful bar bites.

Cobbler BAR
(☑0455 686 968; www.cobblerbar.com; 7 Browning St, West End; ⊘5pm-1am Mon, 4pm-1am Tue-Thu & Sun, 4pm-2am Fri & Sat; ☒60, 192, 198, 199, ⛴South Brisbane) Whisky fans will weep tears of joy at the sight of Cobbler's imposing bar, graced with over 450 whiskies from around the globe. Channelling a speakeasy vibe, this dimly lit West End wonder also pours a cognoscenti selection of rums, tequilas and *amari* (Italian digestifs), not to mention a crafty selection of cocktails that add modern twists to the classics.

Catchment Brewing Co BREWERY
(☑07-3846 1701; www.catchmentbrewingco.com.au; 150 Boundary St, West End; ⊘11am-10pm Tue-Thu & Sun, to 1am & Sat; ☎; ☒199) An understatedly hip, two-level microbrewery with notable, seasonal nosh and live music (mainly jazz) in the front room Saturday evenings and Sunday afternoons. House brews include Pale Select, a nod to the signature beer of the defunct West End Brewery, with other libations including Australian organic wines, craft gins and coffee.

Jungle BAR
(☑0448 925 912; www.facebook.com/junglewestend; 76 Vulture St, West End; ⊘4pm-late Thu-Sun; ☒199) Aloha and welcome to paradise... Well, at least to Brisbane's only proper tiki bar. An intimate, hand-built bamboo hideaway pimped with wood-carved stools, a green-glowing bar and DJ-spun Hawaiian tunes, it's an apt place to cool down with a tropical beverage. Keep it classic with piña colada (served in a pineapple, naturally), or neck a Red Stripe lager from Jamaica.

Blackstar Coffee Roasters CAFE
(☑07-3217 2323; www.blackstarcoffee.com.au; 44 Thomas St, West End; dishes $12-23; ⊘7am-5pm; ☎⭐; ☒199) One of Brisbane's top coffee roasters, laid-back Blackstar pulls in West End bookworms, hipsters and hippies. Kick back and slurp a single-origin espresso or cool down with a bottle of cold-pressed coffee. Food options include a French toast sandwich with fresh ricotta and banana, and a range of roti dishes (including a meat-free mushroom version with chilli jam and smoked hummus).

Archive Beer Boutique BAR
(☑07-3846 6680; www.archivebeerboutique.com.au; 100 Boundary St, West End; ⊘11am-late; ☒198, 199) Whether you're hankering for a Brisbane chilli-choc porter, a Melbourne American IPA or a Sydney guava gose, chances are you'll find it pouring at this foaming juggernaut. There are more than 20 rotating beers on tap, as well as a bounty of Aussie and imported bottled brews. Decent grub (available

until 9pm) includes grilled meats, burgers and pizzas.

Fortitude Valley & New Farm

⭐ Savile Row
COCKTAIL BAR

(📞0455 686 968; https://savilerowbar.com.au; 677 Ann St; ⏰5pm-3am; 🚇Fortitude Valley) Snug, wood-panelled Savile Row hides its assets behind an unmarked orange door. This is one of the city's best-stocked cocktail boltholes, with some 750 spirits, including around 500 whiskies from Scotland to India and Taiwan. Cocktails are superb, inspired by creative flavour combinations and made using cold-pressed juices.

⭐ Gerard's Bar
WINE BAR

(📞07-3252 2606; www.gerardsbar.com.au; 13a/23 James St; ⏰4pm-late Mon-Fri, from noon Sat & Sun; 🚌470, 🚇Fortitude Valley) Gerard's is a stylish, grown-up bar that's one of Brisbane's best. Perch yourself at the polished-concrete bar, choose from the sharply curated wine list, and pair your selection with standout bar snacks, including prized Spanish charcuterie and beautiful cheeses. If you're craving a cocktail, expect meticulous creations like the Tipsy Gerardine, a climate-appropriate medley of vodka, pomegranate molasses, grenadine, rose water, pineapple and passion fruit.

City Winery
WINE BAR

(📞07-3054 7144; www.citywinery.com.au; 11 Wandoo St; ⏰11am-10pm Tue-Thu & Sun, to 11pm Fri & Sat; 🚇Fortitude Valley) The first microwinery to open in Brisbane since 1860, City Winery makes vino from varietals grown in different corners of Australia. Good-value lunch specials are offered daily (noon to 2pm) in the front cellar-bar, while the impressive backroom restaurant runs at lunch Friday to Sunday and dinner Wednesday to Sunday.

Heading the kitchen is talented chef Travis Crane, cooking gorgeous, locally sourced produce using a 4m fire pit.

Head in for all-day tastings or twice-daily winery tours (11.30am and 3pm), the latter requiring pre-booking online.

Eleven
ROOFTOP BAR

(📞07-3067 7447; www.elevenrooftopbar.com.au; 757 Ann St; ⏰8.30am-midnight Tue-Thu, to 3am Fri, noon-3am Sat, noon-midnight Sun; 🛜; 🚇Fortitude Valley) Slip into your slinkiest threads for the Valley's finest rooftop retreat, with a competent list of drinks, including pickled-onion-pimped martinis and high-flying French champagnes.

Drink in the multi-million-dollar view, which takes in the city skyline and Mt Coot-tha beyond, and schmooze to DJ-spun tunes later in the week. The dress code is especially strict on Friday and Saturday evenings; see the website.

Family
CLUB

(📞07-3852 5000; www.thefamily.com.au; 8 McLachlan St; ⏰Fri & Sat; 🚇Fortitude Valley) Queue up for one of Brisbane's biggest and mightiest clubs. The music here is phenomenal, with multiple dance floors, a rooftop bar and elite DJs from Oz and abroad. See Family's Facebook page for upcoming events and guest acts.

Bloodhound Corner Bar & Kitchen
BAR

(📞07-3162 6402; www.bloodhoundcornerbar.com.au; 454 Brunswick St; ⏰noon-10pm, to midnight Fri & Sat; 🚇Fortitude Valley) Starting life as a grocery store, this 19th-century pile is now a new-school Valley bar with a solid selection of rotating craft beers. Vintage brick walls, mottled floorboards and open fireplaces share the space with street art and plenty of hipster beards. Check its Facebook page for upcoming gigs featuring local and touring music acts. Decent bar grub includes softshell tacos.

Bear Bones Coffee
CAFE

(📞0466 271 740; www.bearbones.com.au; 2/66 McLachlan St; ⏰7am-2pm Mon-Fri; 🚌196, 🚇Fortitude Valley) Occupying a warehouse washed with geometric street art, this Valley micro-roaster pulls everyone from thirsty local tradies to Brisbane's coffee intelligentsia. Single-origin coffees change daily, with three house blends rotating throughout the week. Brewing options include nitro, batch and cold brew, complemented by a short list of simple bites, from toast to eggs with avocado, goat's cheese and grapefruit balsamic.

Gertie's Bar & Lounge
WINE BAR

(📞07-3358 5961; https://gertiesbar.com.au; 699 Brunswick St; ⏰4pm-midnight Tue-Thu, from 3pm Fri & Sat, 3-11pm Sun; 🚌195, 196, 199) With its rotating fans, potted palms and its Latin-American staff, moody Gertie's wouldn't look out of place in Havana or Buenos Aires. It's a justifiable hit with locals, who sip vino, beer and (well-priced) martinis while people watching to Latin beats. Food options are tasty, with live music served up Friday and Saturday evenings.

Death Before Decaf COFFEE
(www.facebook.com/deathbeforedecaf247;
3/760 Brunswick St; ⊙24hr; ☐195, 196, 199)
Kick-ass speciality coffee, brewed all day
and all through the night: this ink-loving,
head-banging legend is a godsend for people
craving a decent cup after 4pm. Death Before
Decaf, we salute you.

Newstead & Teneriffe

★**Industry Beans** CAFE
(☑07-3180 1190; https://industrybeans.com; 18
Proe St, Newstead; dishes $12-29; ⊙7am-4pm;
☑☑; ☐60, 393) Melbourne siblings Trevor and Steven Simmons are behind this
luminous, statement-making cafe-roastery,
complete with coffee-plant greenhouse. Beyond its meticulously brewed single origins
and blends are some out-of-the-box offerings, including a spritz made using yuzu
syrup and cascara (the dried fruit of coffee
cherries). Bites include pastries from New
Farm's Chouquette (p311) and sophisticated, seasonal dishes that raise the bar for
cafe grub.

★**Triffid** BAR
(☑07-3171 3001; www.thetriffid.com.au; 7-9 Stratton
St, Newstead; ⊙noon-late Wed-Sun; ☐60, 393) Not
only does the Triffid have an awesome beer
garden (complete with shipping-container
bars and a cassette-themed mural honour-
ing Brisbane bands), but it's also one of the
city's top live-music venues. Acts span local,
Aussie and international talent, playing in
a barrel-vaulted WWII hangar with killer
acoustics. It's hardly surprising given that the
place is owned by former Powderfinger bassist John Collins.

Green Beacon Brewing Co MICROBREWERY
(☑07-3257 3565; www.greenbeacon.com.au;
26 Helen St, Teneriffe; ⊙noon-late; ☎; ☐393,
470, ☑Teneriffe) In a cavernous warehouse,
Green Beacon brews some of Brisbane's
best beers. The liquid beauties ferment
in vats behind the long bar before flow-
ing through the taps and onto your grateful palate. Choose from nine core beers,
a house cider, or seasonal specials like a
blood-orange IPA. Decent bites include
fresh local seafood, and there's typically a
guest food truck out front.

Newstead Brewing Co MICROBREWERY
(☑07-3367 0490; https://newsteadbrewing.com.
au; 85 Doggett St, Newstead; ⊙10am-late; ☎;

☐60, 393, ☑Teneriffe) What was once a bus
depot is now a pumping microbrewery, its
12 taps pouring six standard house brews,
one cider and five seasonal beers. For an en-
lightening overview, order the paddle board
of different brews. If beer doesn't rock your
boat, knock back cocktails, craft spirits or
wine from a small, engaging list of smaller
producers.

Kangaroo Point & Woolloongabba

★**Black Sheep Coffee** CAFE
(☑0477 552 292; https://blacksheepcoffee.com.
au; 109 Norman St, Woolloongabba; ⊙6am-2pm
Mon-Fri, 7am-1pm Sat & Sun; ☎☑; ☐200) What
began life as Brisbane's first speciality-coffee
cart is now this welcoming industrial space,
roasting and brewing the city's best joe on
a Woolloongabba backstreet. Monthly rotating single origins are ethically sourced,
with house blends including Black Sheep's
five-bean, milk-friendly Feeling Woolly.
Hand-picked, hand-rolled single-origin teas
are also available, along with fresh pastries
from Sprout Artisan Bakery.

Electric Avenue BAR
(☑07-3891 2316; www.electricavenuejr.com.au; 23
Logan Rd, Woolloongabba; ⊙5pm-midnight Tue,
noon-midnight Wed-Sat, noon-5pm Sun; ☐174, 175,
204) Take a moody, antiques-decorated bar,
add a worthy bistro, throw in a speakeasy
and you have Electric Avenue. Downstairs,
serious cocktails – both classic and creative – are accompanied by craft beers and
gins, well-chosen wines and seasonal dishes. Lurking upstairs is Prohibition-inspired
Mrs Jack Rabbits, an intimate, old-world
spot perfect for savouring a niche whisky...
or perhaps another gin martini.

Grinders COFFEE
(☑07-3514 5904; www.grinderscoffee.com.
au; 7/11 Logan Rd, Woolloongabba; ⊙7am-4pm;
☐174, 175, 204) The Brisbane outpost of
Melbourne speciality-coffee roaster Grinders is an impressive sight: sleek pink-
ish-marble counters, sculptural neon and
lush greenery. Sip top-notch coffee brewed
using numerous methods, from old-school
espresso to V60, cold drip and Aeropress.
Local artisan Brasserie Bakery supplies the
pastries, and the cafe also runs brewing
and coffee-appreciation classes ($15; first
Sunday of the month).

Bar Spritz CAFE

(☑ 07-3391 7771; www.barspritz.com.au; 29 River Tce, Kangaroo Point; ⊙ 7am-midnight; ⚲; ⌨ 234) Looking out at the river, skyline and City Botanic Gardens, lofty Bar Spritz arguably has the best view of Brisbane. It's a casual, shaded, alfresco pavilion, with a drinks list that includes coffee and a number of variations on the ubiquitous Aperol spritz. Food options are heavily Italian, though the place is best for a casual drink.

Sea Legs Brewing Co MICROBREWERY

(☑ 0480 178 695; www.sealegsbrewing.com.au; 89 Main St, Kangaroo Point; ⊙ noon-10pm, to midnight Fri & Sat; ⚲; ⌨ 234, ⛴ Holman St) What was an old boxing gym in the shadow of Story Bridge is now Kangaroo Point's first microbrewery, the passion project of five engineering mates. Spacious and child-friendly, the brewery's house range includes ales, IPAs, a tropical lager, milk stout and dry-hopped gose. Experimental and seasonal brews, along with guest beers from other local microbreweries, also flow from the taps.

☆ Entertainment

Most big-ticket international bands have Brisbane on their radar, and the city regularly hosts top-tier DJ talent. World-class cultural venues – among them the Queensland Performing Arts Centre (QPAC) and the Brisbane Powerhouse – offer a year-round program of theatre, dance, music, comedy and more. Film offerings range from mainstream to art-house, screened everywhere from multiplex cinemas to inner-city parks.

Fortitude Music Hall LIVE MUSIC

(https://thefortitude.com.au; 312-318 Brunswick St, Fortitude Valley; ⊙ hours vary; ⛲ Fortitude Valley) A steroids shot for Brisbane's already muscly live-music scene, ballroom-inspired Fortitude Music Hall has some serious backers, including ex-Powderfinger bassist John 'JC' Collins. From Boy & Bear to Pixies and the National, the venue hosts high-cred indie music acts (both home-grown and international), as well as the odd high-profile comedian.

Zoo LIVE MUSIC

(☑ 07-3854 1381; www.thezoo.com.au; 711 Ann St, Fortitude Valley; ⊙ 6pm-late Thu-Sat; ⛲ Fortitude Valley) Going strong since 1992, the Zoo remains a grungy spot for indie rock, folk, acoustic, hip-hop, reggae and electronic acts, with no shortage of raw talent.

BARGAIN MASSAGE

Hidden away on a Newstead side street, **Q Academy** (☑ 1300 204 080; www. qacademy.com.au; 20 Chester St, Newstead; 1hr massage $35; ⌨ 393) offers one-hour myotherapy, relaxation or remedial massage for a bargain $35. Although the practitioners are massage students at the accredited academy, all have extensive theoretical training and enough experience to leave you feeling lighter. It's a very popular spot, so book online (or by using the Q Academy app) at least a week in advance. Cards only; no cash payments.

Acts that have hit the stage include Welsh post-hardcore band Mclusky, Ned Flanders–themed US metal rockers Okilly Dokilly and Sunshine Coast indie-folk duo the Dreggs. Book tickets directly on the website.

Queensland Performing Arts Centre PERFORMING ARTS

(QPAC; ☑ guided tours 07-3840 7444, tickets 13 62 46; www.qpac.com.au; Queensland Cultural Centre, cnr Grey & Melbourne Sts, South Brisbane; ⊙ box office 9am-8.30pm Mon-Sat, Tony Gould Gallery 10am-4pm Tue-Sat during exhibitions; ⛴ South Bank Terminals 1 & 2, ⛲ South Brisbane) Known locally as QPAC, Brisbane's main performing arts centre comprises four venues and the Tony Gould Gallery, the latter a small exhibition space focused on the performing arts. The centre's busy calendar includes world-class ballet, concerts, theatre, musicals and comedy, from both Australian and international acts.

Brisbane Powerhouse PERFORMING ARTS

(☑ box office 07-3358 8600; https://brisbanepow erhouse.org; 119 Lamington St, New Farm; ⌨ 196, ⛴ New Farm Park) Originally a 1920s power station, Brisbane Powerhouse is now a hub of nationally and internationally acclaimed theatre, music, comedy, dance and more. The complex also hosts a number of special series, festivals and exhibitions throughout the year, some of which are free. See the website for what's on.

Tivoli ARTS CENTRE

(☑ 07-3852 1711; www.thetivoli.net.au; 52 Costin St, Fortitude Valley; ⌨ 379, ⛲ Fortitude Valley) From music to comedy, you can expect interna-

OUTDOOR CINEMA

One of the best ways to spend a warm summer night in Brisbane is with a picnic basket and some friends at an outdoor cinema. **Moonlight Cinema** (www.moonlight.com.au; Amphitheatre, Roma Street Parkland, 1 Parkland Blvd; adult $15, family $50; ⊙ Tue-Sun mid-Dec–Mar; ⊕; ℝ Roma St) runs from mid-December to the end of March at Roma Street Parkland, on the edge of the CBD. Films, which include current mainstream releases and modern cult classics, usually screen from Tuesday to Sunday, flickering into life around 7.15pm; gates open at 5.30pm and it's a good idea to arrive early to get a good spot. Food and drink (including alcohol) are available for purchase (card payments only).

Another option is **American Express Openair Cinemas** (www.openaircinemas.com. au; City Botanic Gardens, 147 Alice St; adult/child $20/17; ⊙ mid-Jul–mid-Aug; ⊕; ☀ South Bank Terminals 1 & 2, ℝ South Brisbane), where from mid-July to mid-August you can watch recent-release films and retro favourites under the stars (or clouds). Most sessions sell out online prior to the night of the screening, so book ahead. See the website for location and screening details.

tional notables and local success stories treading the boards at this elegant art-deco stager, built in 1917 and known for its great acoustics. Acts to date have included Canadian electronic musician Peaches, British superstar Mika and Grammy Award–winning singer-songwriter Patty Griffin. Check the website for upcoming gigs.

Foundry BAR
(www.thefoundry.net.au; 228 Wickham St; ⊙ 8pm-late Thu & Fri, from 5pm Sat; ℝ Fortitude Valley) The Foundry serves up good times in the form of pool tables and a solid line-up of top-notch, up-and-coming Aussie bands. The joint is a proper music and arts incubator, with both rehearsal spaces and accommodation for music acts upstairs, as well as a number of in-house creative studios. Expect anything from indie acoustic pop to punk.

Riverstage LIVE MUSIC
(☑ 07-3403 7921; www.brisbane.qld.gov.au/facilities-recreation/arts-and-culture/riverstage; 59 Gardens Point Rd; ☀ QUT Gardens Point, ℝ South Bank) Evocatively set in the City Botanic Gardens, this outdoor arena hosts plenty of prolific national and international music acts, with past acts including Billy Idol, Fatboy Slim, UK rapper Stormzy and Aussie music legend Paul Kelly. See the website for upcoming acts.

Underground Opera Company OPERA
(☑ 07-3143 5384; www.undergroundopera. au; Spring Hill Reservoir, Wickham Tce, Spring Hill; ⊙ hours vary; ☐ 30, ℝ Central) A professional, Brisbane-based performing-arts company running annual seasons of opera and Broadway musical recitals in the subterranean Spring Hill Reservoir, built between 1871

and 1882. See the website for season dates and prices.

Brisbane Jazz Club JAZZ
(☑ 07-3391 2006; www.brisbanejazzclub.com.au; 1 Annie St, Kangaroo Point; admission varies; ⊙ Thu-Sun; ☀ Holman St) Straight out of the bayou, this tiny riverside jazz shack has been Brisbane's jazz beacon since 1972. Anyone who's anyone in the scene plays here when they're in town, and the venue offers a pub-style dining menu for those wanting a bite with the tunes. Check the website for upcoming music acts, times and ticket prices.

Cineplex South Bank CINEMA
(☑ 07-3112 9003; www.cineplex.com.au; cnr Grey & Ernest Sts; adult/child from $8.50/5; ⊕; ☀ South Bank Terminals 1, 2 & 3, ℝ South Bank) A short walk from South Bank Parklands, this is the cheapest complex for mainstream releases, screened in either 2D or 3D. Screenings are cheapest before 6pm on weekdays (and all day Tuesday), with adult tickets an especially low $6.50. See the website for other special deals.

New Farm Six Cinemas CINEMA
(☑ 07-3358 4444; https://fivestarcinemas.com.au/new-farm; 701 Brunswick St, New Farm; adult/child $17/12; ⊙ 9.30am-late; ⊕; ☐ 195, 196, 199) When those subtropical heavens open up, take refuge at New Farm's historic movie palace. Remodelled and restored, its state-of-the-art screening rooms show mostly mainstream new releases. Tuesday is popular with penny-pinching film buffs, with all tickets $12. If you're a student (with official student ID), head in on Thursday nights for even cheaper $7.50 tickets.

Judith Wright Centre of Contemporary Arts
PERFORMING ARTS

(☑ 07-3872 9000; www.judithwrightcentre.com; 420 Brunswick St, Fortitude Valley; 🛜; 🚇 Fortitude Valley) The Valley's free-thinking arts incubator hosts an eclectic array of cultural treats, including contemporary dance, circus and visual arts. It's also the hub for the hugely popular Bigsound Festival (p299), a four-night music fest held each September. Scan the website for upcoming performances and exhibitions.

Gabba
STADIUM

(Brisbane Cricket Ground; ☑ 1300 843 422; www.thegabba.com.au; 411 Vulture St, Woolloongabba; 🚴; 🚌 113, 117, 124, 125, 172, 198, 203, 234) You can cheer both AFL football and interstate and international cricket at the Gabba in Woolloongabba, south of Kangaroo Point. If you're new to cricket, try to get along to a Twenty20 (T20) match, which sees the game in its most explosive form. The cricket season runs from late September to March; the football from late March to September.

Suncorp Stadium
STADIUM

(☑ 07-3331 5000; www.suncorpstadium.com.au; 40 Castlemaine St, Milton; 🚌 61, 375, 377, 470, 475, 🚇 Milton) In winter, rugby league is the big spectator sport here and local team the Brisbane Broncos call this stadium home. The stadium also hosts the odd major rock concert.

🔒 Shopping

Brisbane's retail landscape is eclectic, spanning the indie records, vintage fashion and well-stocked bookshelves of West End to the high-end, on-point Australian fashion and accessories of Fortitude Valley's James St. In between you'll find everything from boutiques championing local ceramics and jewellery, to city-centre department stores and weekly markets peddling everything from organic produce to art and sustainable skincare.

🏠 Central Brisbane

Noosa Chocolate Factory
FOOD

(☑ 1300 720 668; www.noosachocolatefactory.com.au; 144 Adelaide St; ⊘ 8am-7pm Mon-Thu, to 9pm Fri, 9am-6pm Sat, 10am-5pm Sun; 🚴; 🚇 Central) 🍫 Don't delude yourself: the small-batch, artisanal chocolates from this Sunshine Coast Willy Wonka will override any self-control. Best sellers include gen-

erous, marshmallowy Rocky Road and a very Queensland concoction of unroasted macadamias covered in Bowen-mango-flavoured chocolate. Varieties rotate frequently and, best of all, none contain palm oil. A second branch at No 156 serves speciality coffee and hot chocolate.

Maiocchi
FASHION & ACCESSORIES

(☑ 07-3012 9640; www.maiocchi.com.au; Brisbane Arcade, 117 Adelaide St; ⊘ 9am-5.30pm Mon-Thu, to 8pm Fri, to 4pm Sat, 11am-4pm Sun; 🚇 Central) Home-grown Maiocchi is well known for its fun, vintage-inspired frocks. Brighten your wardrobe with custom prints, '50s silhouettes and the odd Japanese influence. Your next summer cocktail dress aside, the boutique also stocks tops and pants, plus fresh, quirky Australian jewellery, bags and colourful sandals. You'll find it to the left of the Adelaide St entrance to the heritage-listed Brisbane Arcade.

Double Double
FASHION & ACCESSORIES

(☑ 07-3210 2003; https://doubledouble.store; Level 1, 115 Queen St; ⊘ 10am-6pm Mon-Thu, to 8pm Fri, to 5pm Sat, noon-5pm Sun; 🚇 Central) An inconspicuous lift takes the style council up to Double Double, quite possibly Brisbane's edgiest unisex fashion boutique. Its edits of youthful, street-smart clothing and accessories aren't cheap, but they are unique and progressive, with labels including Japan's Comme des Garçons, Wacko Maria and N Hoolywood, Denmark's Norse Projects, and independent LA eyewear company Akila.

Folio Books
BOOKS

(☑ 07-3210 0500; https://foliobooks.com.au; 133 Mary St; ⊘ 8.30am-6pm Mon-Thu, to 7pm Fri, to 5pm Sat, 10am-4pm Sun; 🚢 Eagle St Pier, 🚇 Central) Bibliophiles flock to Folio for an eclectic, sophisticated collection of titles covering everything from Canberra politics and Queensland modernism, to international art, gastronomy, design, travel and fiction. Staff are well read, friendly and helpful, and the place is utterly dangerous for those skilled at losing track of time.

Brisbane City Markets
MARKET

(www.brisbanecitymarkets.com.au; Reddacliff Pl, George St; ⊘ 8am-6pm Wed; 🚢 North Quay, 🚇 Central) Central Brisbane lives out its bucolic village fantasies when local growers and artisans descend on Reddacliff Pl to sell their prized goods. Fill your shopping bags with fruit and vegetables, meat, seafood, artisan breads, pastries, raw honey and more. Stock up for a picnic in the City Botanic Gardens, or simply grab a coffee and a ready-to-eat, multiculti bite.

A smaller edition takes place every Thursday from 8am to 2.30pm in Cathedral Sq, located on the corner of Ann and Wharf Sts.

South Bank & West End

Jet Black Cat Music MUSIC
(☑0419 571 299; www.facebook.com/jetblackcat music; 72 Vulture St, West End; ☺10.30am-5pm Tue, Wed & Fri, to 3pm Thu, 10am-4pm Sat, 10am-2pm Sun; ☑199) Serious music fans know all about Shannon Logan and her little West End record shop. She's usually behind the piano-cum-counter, chatting with a loyal fan base who drop in for an in-the-know, hard-to-find booty of indie vinyl. Logan only sells what she's passionate about, and the place also hosts occasional in-store gigs showcasing well-known local and international indie talent.

Where the Wild Things Are BOOKS
(☑07-3255 3987; https://wherethewildthingsare. com.au; 191 Boundary St, West End; ☺8.30am-6pm, to 5pm Sun; ☑; ☑199) Little sister to Avid Reader next door, Where the Wild Things Are stocks a whimsical collection of books for toddlers, older kids and teens. The bookshop also runs regular activities, from weekly story-time sessions to book launches, signings and crafty workshops covering topics such as book illustration. Scan the bookshop's website and Facebook page for upcoming events.

Davies Park Market MARKET
(www.daviesparkmarket.com.au; Davies Park, West End; ☺6am-2pm Sat; ☑60, 192) Shaded by huge Moreton Bay fig trees, this popular, atmospheric market heaves with fresh produce, not to mention a gut-rumbling booty of multicultural food stalls. Grab an organic coffee from **Gyspy Vardo**, sip it on a milk crate, then scour the place for organic fruit and veg, herbs, flowers, handmade jewellery, natural skincare and even the odd bonsai.

Swop Clothing Exchange FASHION & ACCESSORIES
(https://swop.net.au; 161 Boundary St, West End; ☺10am-6pm Mon-Fri, to 5pm Sat, to 4pm Sun; ☑198, 199) Sustainably minded Swop sells (and buys) high-quality threads, accessories and footwear from the '60s to today. Flick through colour-coded racks for fun frocks, skirts, jumpsuits and shirts, some

from coveted Australian and international designers like Scanlan Theodore and DKNY. Mix-and-match with rockstar cowboy boots, or shop a smaller selection of men's shirts, tees, denim and trousers.

Fortitude Valley & Bowen Hills

Artisan DESIGN
(☑07-3215 0808; https://artisan.org.au; 45 King St, Bowen Hills; ☺10am-5pm Tue-Fri, to 4pm Sat; ☑301, 320, ☒Fortitude Valley) True to its name, this contemporary Bowen Hills gallery-shop celebrates the work of independent, mostly local creatives. Prices are reasonable, with objects ranging from handmade bowls, cups and vases, to idiosyncratic jewellery, striking textiles and accessories that might include twine and raffia bags from the Torres Strait Islands. A worthy stop for those seeking unique Queensland (and Australian) gifts and design.

James Street FASHION & ACCESSORIES
(www.jamesst.com.au; James St; ☑470, ☒Fortitude Valley) Channelling West LA with its low-slung architecture, lush streetscape and sports cars, this is the Valley's most glamorous strip. The addition of the Calile Hotel (p305) complex has boosted the street's upmarket offerings, which include numerous high-end Australian fashion labels. Standouts include colourful Camilla, Sass & Bide, indie-chic Gorman and multi-brand Wolfe & Ordnance, known for stocking harder-to-find homegrown designers.

Libertine PERFUME
(☑07-3216 0122; www.libertineparfumerie.com.au; 181 Robertson St; ☺10am-5pm Mon-Fri, 9.30am-5pm Sat, 10am-4pm Sun; ☑470, ☒Fortitude Valley) While you won't stumble across any celeb-endorsed eau de toilettes at Libertine, you will discover some of the world's most coveted and hard-to-find perfume and skincare brands for women and men. Among them is Amouage (established for the Sultan of Oman), Carthusia and Creed, the latter's in-store offerings including the very fragrance created for Princess Grace on her wedding day.

Newstead & Teneriffe

New Farm Confectionery FOOD
(☑07-3139 0964; www.newfarmconfectionery. com.au; 16 Waterloo St, Newstead; sweets from $3; ☺7am-5.30pm Mon-Fri, 9am-4pm Sat; ☑; ☑60,

TO MARKET, TO MARKET

Beyond the weekly farmers markets that feed the masses in central Brisbane, New Farm (p295) and West End is a string of other fantastic local markets, peddling anything from handmade local fashion and bling to art, skincare and out-of-the-box giftware. Hit the stalls at the following options.

Young Designers Market (☑ 07-3844 2440; www.youngdesignersmarket.com.au; Little Stanley St; ☺ 10am-4pm 1st Sun of the month; ☢ South Bank Terminal 3, ☒ South Bank) Explore the work of up to 80 of the city's best emerging designers and artists, selling mostly women's fashion, accessories and jewellery, as well as art, homewares and the occasional furniture piece. Held beside South Bank Parklands, the market generally runs on the first Sunday of the month.

Finders Keepers (www.thefinderskeepers.com/brisbane-markets; Brisbane Showgrounds, 600 Gregory Tce, Bowen Hills; adult/child $5/free; ☺ Jun & Nov; ☐ 370, 375, ☒ Fortitude Valley) A cool, biannual market with live music, street food and over 200 stalls showcasing the wares of independent Australian designers, artists and craftspeople. It's a great spot to score high-quality, one-off fashion pieces, jewellery, bags and more from local and interstate creatives. The three-day event takes place at the Marquee, located inside the Brisbane Showgrounds in Bowen Hills.

Collective Markets South Bank (www.collectivemarkets.com.au; Stanley St Plaza; ☺ 5-9pm Fri, 10am-9pm Sat, 9am-4pm Sun; ⛟ ; ☢ South Bank Terminal 3, ☒ South Bank) South Bank's Collective Markets may draw the tourist hordes, but its modest sweep of stalls do sell some great items, most notably breezy summer frocks and kidswear. Other offerings include contemporary handmade jewellery, candles, skincare, photography and (sometimes kitschy) art.

☢ Teneriffe) For a locavore sugar rush, hit this lauded confectioner. From the macadamia brittle and raspberry marshmallow to the ruby chocolate bars, all of the products are made using natural, top-tier ingredients. Dairy- and gluten-free treats are available, and the store also runs occasional chocolate and confectionary workshops for DIY gluttons; see the website for upcoming offerings.

Commercial Road Antiques ANTIQUES (☑ 07-3852 2352; http://commercialroadantiques.com.au; 85 Commercial Rd, Teneriffe; ☺ 10am-5pm; ☐ 393, 470, ☢ Teneriffe) Whether you're on the prowl for a Victorian dresser, a mid-century armchair or a '60s beatnik frock, chances are you'll find it in this warren of eclectic antiques and retro. There's a solid selection of vintage threads and jewellery, no shortage of porcelain (including Chinese antiques), plus kookier items ranging from retro toys and film-themed postcards to the odd Burmese marionette.

ⓘ Information

INTERNET ACCESS

Brisbane City Council offers free wi-fi access in much of central Brisbane (the CBD), and you will also find free wi-fi hotspots at South Bank Parklands, Roma Street Parkland, the State Library of Queensland, James St in Fortitude Valley and New Farm Park.

Brisbane Square Library (☑ 07-3403 4166; www.brisbane.qld.gov.au; 266 George St; ☺ 9am-6pm Mon, Tue & Thu, to midnight Wed & Fri, to 4pm Sat, 10am-3pm Sun; 🔊 ⛟ ; ☢ North Quay, ☒ Central) Contemporary public library with free wi-fi access.

MEDICAL SERVICES

CBD Medical Centre (☑ 07-3211 3611; www.cbdmedical.com.au; Level 1, 245 Albert St; ☺ 7am-7pm Mon-Fri, 8.30am-5pm Sat, 9am-5pm Sun; ☒ Central) General medical services and vaccinations.

Royal Brisbane & Women's Hospital (☑ 07-3646 8111; https://metronorth.health.qld.gov.au/rbwh; cnr Butterfield St & Bowen Bridge Rd, Herston; ☐ 310, 321, 330, 333, 340, 370, 375) Located three kilometres north of the city centre, it has as a 24-hour casualty ward. In case of emergency, call 000 for an ambulance.

Travel Doctor – TMVC (Travellers' Medical & Vaccination Centre; ☑ 07-3815 6900; www.traveldoctor.com.au; Level 5, West Tower, 410 Ann St; ☺ 8.30am-4.30pm Mon-Fri; ☒ Central) Travellers' medical services.

MONEY

Travelex (☑ 07-3174 1018; www.travelex.com.au; 300 Queen St; ☺ 9.30am-4pm Mon-Thu, to

5pm Fri; 🚢 Riverside, Eagle St Pier, 🚉 Central) Money exchange. Currency can be ordered online, commission free, and picked up at the branch.

POST

Main Post Office (GPO; 📞 13 13 18; www. auspost.com.au; 261 Queen St; ⊙7am-6pm Mon-Fri, 9am-12.30pm Sat; 🚢 Riverside, Eagle St Pier, 🚉 Central) Brisbane's main post office offers foreign-currency exchange.

TOURIST INFORMATION

Brisbane Visitor Information Centre (📞 07-3006 6290; www.visitbrisbane.com.au; The Regent, 167 Queen St; ⊙ 9am-5.30pm Mon-Thu, to 7pm Fri, to 5pm Sat, 10am-5pm Sun; 🚉 Central) Terrific one-stop info counter for all things Brisbane, with brochures, maps and information on city attractions and events. Staff can also book a range of tours.

South Bank Visitor Information Centre (📞 07-3029 1797; www.visitbrisbane.com.au; Stanley St Plaza; ⊙9am-5pm; 🛜; 🚢 South Bank Terminal 3, 🚉 South Bank) One of Brisbane's official tourist information hubs, with brochures, maps and festival guides, plus tour and accommodation bookings, and tickets to entertainment events. Free wi-fi is available, though you'll get a more reliable signal at the State Library of Queensland, further north on South Bank.

❶ Getting There & Away

AIR

Brisbane Airport (www.bne.com.au; Airport Dr), around 14km northeast of the city centre, is the third-busiest airport in Australia. It's the main international airport serving Brisbane and southeastern Queensland, with nonstop international flights to New Zealand, the Pacific islands, North America and Asia (with onward connections to Europe and Africa).

The airport has separate international and domestic terminals about 2km apart, connected via a free airport shuttle bus (4am to 11pm). Both terminals are also connected by the Airtrain (terminal transfer adult/child $5/free).

BUS

Brisbane Coach Terminal (Parklands Cres; 🛜) serves long-distance regional and interstate buses. The terminal is located beside Roma St train station, directly opposite platform 10.

Booking desks for Greyhound Australia (p526) and **Murrays** (📞13 22 51; www.murrays.com. au) can be found at the coach terminal.

Long-haul routes include Cairns, Darwin and Sydney, though it's usually just as affordable to fly, not to mention a lot quicker.

CAR & MOTORCYCLE

The M1 runs through Brisbane's eastern suburbs, shooting north towards the Sunshine Coast and northern Queensland and south towards the Gold Coast and Sydney. See Transurban's **Linkt** (📞13 33 31; http://brisbane-network.linkt.com.au) website for toll details and fees.

Major car hire companies have offices at Brisbane Airport and in the city. Smaller hire companies with branches near the airport (and shuttles to get you to/from there) include **Ace Rental Cars** (📞1800 620 408; www. acerentalcars.com.au; 330 Nudgee Rd, Hendra; ⊙7am-6:30pm, to 9:30pm Thu & Fri), **Apex Car Rentals** (📞07-3868 3355, 1800 2739 2277; www.apexrentacar.com.au; 400 Nudgee Rd, Hendra; ⊙7am-6pm) and **East Coast Car Rentals** (📞1800 327 826; www.eastcoast-carrentals.com.au; 504 Nudgee Rd, Hendra; ⊙7am-10pm).

TRAIN

Brisbane's main station for long-distance trains is Roma St. For reservations and information contact **Queensland Rail** (📞13 16 17; www. queenslandrail.com.au). For services between Brisbane and Sydney see https://transportnsw. info/regional.

❶ Getting Around

Brisbane's excellent public transport network – bus, train and ferry – is run by TransLink. Information on public transport is available at the tourist offices in the city centre and at South Bank. Complementing the network is a nifty network of bike paths.

TO/FROM THE AIRPORT

Train

Airtrain (📞1800 119 091; www.airtrain.com. au; adult one way/return $19.50/37) services connect Brisbane airport's two terminals to central Brisbane before continuing south to the Gold Coast. Children 14 years and under travel free when accompanied by an adult. Tickets purchased online in advance are cheaper (especially if purchased a week or more in advance). Translink *go cards* are also valid.

Trains run every 15 to 30 minutes from 5am (6am on weekends), with the last train departing the airport at 10pm.

Bus

Con-X-ion (📞07-5556 9888, 1300 910 943; www.con-x-ion.com) runs regular shuttle buses between the airport and hotels in the Brisbane city centre (one way/return $20/38). It also connects Brisbane Airport to Gold Coast hotels and private residences (one way/return $54/99), as well as to Sunshine Coast hotels and private residences (one way/return from around $59/99). Book tickets online.

Taxi

A taxi to central Brisbane costs around $45 to $55.

BICYCLE

Brisbane has an extensive network of bikeways and shared pathways across the city and suburbs.

Brisbane's bike-share programme is called **CityCycle** (☑1300 229 253; www.citycycle. com.au; access per day/month $2/5; ☉24hr). To use it, purchase a 24-hour casual pass ($2 per day) on the website or at any of the 150 bike-share stations with credit-card facilities. It can be pricey to hire for more than an hour, so make use of the free first 30 minutes per bike and ride from station to station, swapping bikes as you go. Inconveniently, only about half of the bikes include a helmet (compulsory to wear). For real-time information on bike availability at each station, download the official CityCycle app 'AllBikesNow'.

CAR & MOTORCYCLE

Brisbane's comprehensive public transport system will make driving altogether unnecessary for most visitors. If you do decide to get behind the wheel, however, consider investing in a GPS; the city's convoluted and one-way streets can quickly cause frustration.

➡ Ticketed, time-limited parking is available on many streets in the CBD and the inner suburbs. Heed the signs: Brisbane's parking inspectors can be ruthless. Download the free CellOPark Australia app, which allows you to pay for parking using your smartphone.

➡ For more detailed information on parking, see www.visitbrisbane.com.au/parking.

PUBLIC TRANSPORT

Buses, trains and ferries operate on an eight-zone system: all of the inner-city suburbs are in Zone 1, which translates into a single fare per adult/child of $4.90/2.40. If travelling into Zone 2, tickets are $6/3.

If you plan to use public transport for more than a few trips, you'll save money by purchasing an electronic **Go Card** (www.translink. com.au/tickets-and-fares/go-card; starting balance adult/child $10/5). Purchase the card, add credit and then use it on city buses, trains and ferries, and you'll save more than 30% off individual fares. go cards are sold (and can be recharged) at transit stations, 7-Eleven convenience stores, newsagents, by phone or online. You can also top-up on CityCat catamaran services (cash only). go cards can also be used on local transport on the Gold Coast and Sunshine Coast, as well as to hire CityCycle bikes.

Boat

CityCat (p297) catamarans serve 18 ferry terminals between the University of Queensland in St Lucia and Northshore Hamilton. Handy stops include South Bank (Terminals 1 and 2), three CBD terminals (North Quay, QUT Gardens Point and Riverside), New Farm Park (for Brisbane Powerhouse), Teneriffe (handy for Newstead) and Northshore Hamilton (for Eat Street Northshore). Services run every 15 to 30 minutes from around 5am to around 11pm (midnight on Fridays and Saturdays). Tickets can be bought on board or, if you have one, use your electronic go card.

CityHopper Ferries are free but slower, zigzagging back and forth across the water between North Quay, South Bank (Terminal 3), Maritime Museum, the CBD (Eagle St Pier), Kangaroo Point and New Farm. These additional services run roughly every 40 minutes from about 6am to around midnight.

Cross River Ferries connect Kangaroo Point (Thornton St and Holman St) with the CBD (Eagle St Pier) and Teneriffe with Bulimba. These ferries run from around 6am to around 11pm, roughly every 12 to 35 minutes to/from the CBD, every 15 minutes to/from New Farm Park, and every 15 minutes to/from Teneriffe. Standard TransLink fares/zones apply as per all other Brisbane transport.

For more information, including timetables, see www.transdevbrisbane.com.au.

Bus

Brisbane's bus network is extensive and especially handy for reaching West End, Paddington, Kangaroo Point, Woolloongabba, Fortitude Valley and Newstead.

In the city centre, the main stops for local buses are the underground **Queen St Bus Station** and **King George Square Bus Station**. You can also pick up many buses from the stops along Adelaide St, between George and Edward Sts.

➡ Buses generally run every 10 to 30 minutes, from around 5am (around 6am or later Saturday and Sunday) till about 11pm. Special NightLink buses run all night on some routes on Friday and Saturday.

➡ CityGlider and Buz services are high-frequency services along busy routes. Tickets cannot be purchased on board CityGlider services; use a go card. CityGlider services run all night on Friday and Saturday.

➡ Free hop-on, hop-off City Loop and Spring Hill Loop bus services circle the CBD and Spring Hill, stopping at key spots like QUT, Queen St Mall, City Botanic Gardens, Central Station and Roma Street Parkland. Buses run roughly every 10 to 20 minutes on weekdays from around 7am to around 6pm (about 7pm on the Spring Hill Loop).

Train

TransLink's (☑ 13 12 30; www.translink. com.au) Citytrain network has six main, colour-coded lines, which run as far north as Gympie on the Sunshine Coast and as far south as Varsity Lakes on the Gold Coast. All trains go through Roma Street, Central and Fortitude Valley stations; three of the lines (Ferny Grove and Beenleigh, Shorncliffe and Cleveland, Airport and Gold Coast) also run through South Brisbane and South Bank stations.

The Airtrain (p322) service integrates with the Citytrain network in the city centre and along the Gold Coast line.

Trains run from around 4am, with the last train on each line leaving Central Station between 11pm and 1am (later on Friday and Saturday). On Sunday, the last train can depart as early as 9.30pm or 10.30pm on some lines.

Single train tickets can be bought at train stations, or use your *go card* (p323).

See www.translink.com.au for timetables and a network map.

TAXI

The main taxi companies are **Black & White** (☑ 13 32 22; www.blackandwhitecabs.com.au) and **Yellow Cabs** (☑ 13 19 24; www.yellowcab. com.au).

NightLink flat-fare taxis run on Friday and Saturday nights (11pm to 5am) and can be hailed from dedicated ranks. These ranks are located at George St (near Queen St) and Eagle St (between Wharf and Creek Sts) in the city centre, and on Warner St (near Wickham St) in Fortitude Valley. Pay your fare at the beginning of the journey (cash only).

Numerous ride-sharing services are available in Brisbane, including Uber (www.uber.com), DiDi (www.didiglobal.com) and Ola (https://ola. com.au). Shebah (www.shebah.com.au) operates an all-female fleet of drivers offering rides for women and children.

AROUND BRISBANE

North Stradbroke Island

POP 2100

An easy 30-minute ferry chug from the Brisbane suburb of Cleveland, unpretentious North Stradbroke Island (Minjerribah) serves up glorious powdery white beaches, great surf, sleepy beach towns and Indigenous art and culture. It's also a hotspot for spying dolphins, turtles, manta rays and, between June and November, humpback

whales. 'Straddie' also offers freshwater lakes and 4WD tracks.

There are only a few small settlements on the island, with a handful of accommodation and eating options – mostly near **Point Lookout** in the northeast. On the west coast, **Dunwich** (Goompi) is where the ferries dock. **Amity** is a small village on the northwestern corner. Much of the island's southern section is closed to visitors due to sand mining.

Interestingly, North and South Stradbroke Islands used to be one single island, but a savage storm blew through the sand spit between the two in 1896.

◎ Sights

★**Cylinder Beach**   BEACH
(♿) Bordered by Cylinder and Home Beach Headlands, this broad, beautiful beach is patrolled by lifesavers, offers easy access from the car park, and generally has smaller waves than neighbouring beaches like the ominously named Deadman's Beach. As you'd expect, it's popular with families. Remember to swim between the flags.

**North Stradbroke
Island Historical Museum**   MUSEUM
(☑ 07-3409 9699; www.stradbrokemuseum.com. au; 15-17 Welsby St, Dunwich; adult/child $5/1; ⊙10am-2pm Tue-Sat, 11am-3pm Sun) Once the 'Dunwich Benevolent Asylum' – a home for the destitute – this small but engaging museum describes shipwrecks and harrowing voyages, and gives an introduction to the island's rich Aboriginal history (the Quandamooka are the traditional owners of the island). Island artefacts include handmade bricks made by 19th-century convicts and the impressive shell of a green turtle found on a local beach.

**Salt Water Murris Quandamooka
Aboriginal Art Gallery**   GALLERY
(☑ 07-3415 2373; www.facebook.com/SWMQuan damooka; 3 Ballow Rd, Dunwich; ⊙9am-2pm Tue-Sun) On Dunwich's main street, this Aboriginal-owned gallery space exhibits crafts and contemporary art by the island's traditional owners, the Quandamooka.

🏃 Activities

At Point Lookout, the breathtaking **North Gorge Walk** (Mooloomba Rd; ♿) is an absolute highlight. It's an easy 20-minute loop around the headland along boardwalks, with the thrum of cicadas as your

Point Lookout

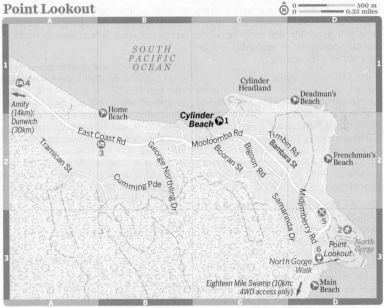

soundtrack. Keep an eye out for turtles, dolphins and manta rays offshore. The view from the headland down Main Beach is epic in scale.

About 8km east of Dunwich on Alfred Martin Way is the car park for **Naree Budjong Djara National Park** (www.nprsr.qld.gov. au/parks/naree-budjong-djara; Alfred Martin Way). From here, take the 2.6km walking track to Straddie's glittering centrepiece, **Blue Lake (Kaboora)**: keep an eye out for forest birds, skittish lizards and swamp wallabies along the way. There's a wooden viewing platform at the lake, which is encircled by a forest of paperbarks, eucalypts and banksias. You can cool off in the water, if you don't mind the spooky unseen depths.

★ **Straddie Adventures**   KAYAKING
(☑ 0433 171 477; www.straddieadventures.com. au; adult/child sea-kayaking trips from $75/40, sandboarding $35/30; 🚸) Operated by the area's traditional Aboriginal owners, this outfit runs highly recommended sea-kayaking trips with an Indigenous cultural bent, meaning fascinating insight into the island's ancient cultural history and its rich wildlife. Sandboarding sessions are also run, as well as combo trips (adult/ child from $100/65) that include both activities.

Manta Lodge & Scuba Centre   DIVING
(☑ 07-3409 8888; www.mantalodge.com.au; 132 Dickson Way, Point Lookout; wetsuit/surfboard/ bike hire per day $15/50/33, one-day beginner scuba-diving course $349) Based at the YHA, Manta Scuba Centre offers a broad range of options. You can hire wetsuits, snorkelling equipment, GoPro gear, surfboards

and bikes, or take the plunge with a diving course. To explore Moreton Bay Marine Park's rich marine life, sign up for one of the popular snorkelling or scuba-diving trips ($99 and $155 respectively).

North Stradbroke Island Surf School
SURFING

(📞 0407 642 616, 0400 443 591; www.northstrad brokeislandsurfschool.com.au; Cylinder Beach, Mooloomba Rd, Point Lookout; group lesson from $50, private lesson $100) Small-group, 1½-hour surf lessons for rookies, intermediate and advanced wave riders. One-hour solo lessons are also available if you're feeling bashful. Book ahead.

Straddie Super Sports
ADVENTURE SPORTS

(📞 07-3409 9252; www.facebook.com/StraddieSu perSports; 18 Bingle Rd, Dunwich; bodyboard/bike hire per day $10/50, 4hr kayak hire $30; ⊙ 8am-4.30pm, to 3pm Sat, to noon Sun) A friendly shop hiring out mountain bikes, kayaks and SUPs, surfboards and bodyboards. The place also sells fishing gear and camping accessories.

🛏 Sleeping

Manta Lodge YHA
HOSTEL $

(📞 07-3409 8888; www.mantalodge.com.au; 132 Dickson Way, Point Lookout; dm/d from $30/99; ❄ @ 🛜) This affable, beachside hostel has clean (if unremarkable) rooms, with four, six and eight-bed dorms, as well as private rooms. There's a communal firepit out the back, a spacious kitchen, cosy communal spaces, plus a dive school downstairs. Rental options include surfboards, bodyboards, SUPs, bikes and snorkelling gear. Wi-fi is free in communal areas and $5 for 24 hours in the rooms.

★ Sea Shanties
CABIN $$

(📞 07-3409 7161; www.seashanties.com.au; 9a Cook St, Amity Point; cabins $160-200; 🛜 🐾) Dotted with upcycled sculptures and tropical plants, this waterfront oasis offers seven gorgeous, self-contained cabins. Lime-washed timber floors and stylish furnishings deliver a chic, nautical look, and each comes with fridge, hotplates, microwave and coffee machine (BYO grinds). Facilities include a well-equipped outdoor kitchen and BBQ area, lounge, private jetty (complimentary snorkelling gear available) and laundry.

Wi-fi is limited to the communal lounge, though you'll hopefully be too busy gazin out at crystalline waters from your deckchair.

Allure
APARTMENT $$

(📞 07-3415 0000; www.allurestradbroke.com.au; 43-57 East Coast Rd, Point Lookout; bungalows/ villas from $166/220; ❄ 🛜 🐾) Set in a leafy compound with a pool and gym for guests, Allure offers large, contemporary bungalows and villas. Bungalows are studio-style affairs with kitchenettes and mezzanine bedrooms, while villas offer full kitchens and separate bedrooms. All have private laundry facilities and outdoor deck with BBQs. While there isn't much space between the shacks, they're cleverly designed with privacy in mind.

Check for minimum stays.

🍴 Eating & Drinking

Island Fruit Barn
CAFE $

(📞 07-3409 9125; www.islandfruitbarn.com; 16 Bingle Rd, Dunwich; meals $10-18; ⊙ 7am-2pm; 🛜 🚗 ♿) On Dunwich's main strip, free-spirited Island Fruit Barn is a casual, with tasty breakfasts, salads, sandwiches, spinach pies, cakes and pastries. There's a good choice of gluten-free, vegetarian and vegan bites, as well as great coffee. The cafe exhibits (and sells) locally made ceramics and woven items, and usually hosts monthly gigs featuring local musicians or artists.

Blue Room Cafe
CAFE $

(📞 0438 281 666; 27 Mooloomba Rd, Point Lookout; sandwiches & burritos $10-12; ⊙ cafe 7.30am-2pm, provedore 7.30am-5.30pm Mon-Sat, to 2pm Sun; 🚗 ♿) Looking straight off the set of Aussie surf-side soap *Home & Away*, this youthful, beach-shack-chic cafe has a small alfresco terrace and a counter of fresh, ready-to-eat options like burritos, wraps, salads and fruit cups. Sweet treats range from brownies and bitter-chocolate tarts to a vegan, gluten-free Snickers slice. The adjoining provedore is aptly named the Green Room.

Point Lookout Surf Life Saving Club
BAR

(📞 07-3409 8158; www.pointlookoutslsc.com.au; 24 Kennedy Dr, Point Lookout; ⊙ 2pm-twilight Sat & Sun; ♿) On weekend afternoons, locals and in-the-know out-of-towners head here to kick back on the outdoor deck, sipping cheap beers and soaking up the spectacular ocean view. Indeed, this is one of the greatest vantage points for whale watching (June to November).

ⓘ Getting There & Away

The hub for ferries to North Stradbroke Island is the Brisbane bayside suburb of Cleveland.

Stradbroke Ferries (☑ 07-3488 5300; www.stradbrokeferries.com.au; Toondah Harbour, 12 Emmett Dr, Cleveland; one way per vehicle incl passengers from $60, walk-on adult/child $8/5) runs passenger/vehicle services between Cleveland and Dunwich on North Stradbroke Island (45 to 50 minutes, 11 to 13 times daily). If travelling with a vehicle, always book online to secure a place; there is no need to print tickets.

Stradbroke Flyer Gold Cats (☑ 07-3286 1964; www.flyer.com.au; Middle St, Cleveland; return adult/child $20/10) operates passenger-only trips between Cleveland and Dunwich (25 minutes, 14 to 15 times daily). A free Stradbroke Flyer courtesy bus picks up water-taxi passengers from the Cleveland train station 10 minutes prior to most water taxi departures (see the website for exclusions). Tickets can be purchased on the water taxi; advance bookings not required.

Citytrain (p324) services run regularly from Brisbane's Central and Roma St Stations (as well as the inner-city stations of South Bank, South Brisbane, Fortitude Valley and Bowen Hills) to Cleveland station ($9.10, one hour). Buses to the ferry terminal (seven minutes) meet the trains at Cleveland station.

ⓘ Getting Around

Straddie is big: it's best to have your own wheels to explore it properly. If you plan to go off-road, you can get information and buy a 4WD permit ($52.75) from **Minjerribah Camping** (☑ 07-3409 9668; www.minjerribahcamping.com.au; 1 Junner St, Dunwich; ☺ 8am-4pm Mon-Fri, to 1pm Sat).

Stradbroke Island Buses (☑ 07-3415 2417; www.stradbrokeislandbuses.com.au) meet the ferries at Dunwich and run to Amity Point and Point Lookout (one-way/return $5/10). Services run roughly every hour and the last bus to Dunwich leaves Point Lookout at 6.20pm. Cash only.

Scooters on Straddie (☑ 0497 777 933; https://scootersonstraddie.com.au; 9 Sturt St, Dunwich; scooter hire per day $75; ☺ 8.30am-5pm Wed-Mon) hires 50cc scooters from Dunwich, with surfboard rack an optional $5 per day. Drop-off and pick-up in Amity Point and Point Lookout is available for an extra $10 (return).

Straddie Super Sports in Dunwich rents out mountain bikes.

Stradbroke Cab Service (☑ 0408 193 685) charges around $60 from Dunwich to Point Lookout.

Moreton Island

POP 245

If you're not going further north in Queensland than Brisbane but fancy an island getaway, sail over to Moreton Island (Moorgumpin). The third-largest sand island in the world, its unspoilt beaches, dunes, bushland and lagoons are protected, with 98% of the isle comprising the **Moreton Island National Park & Recreation Area** (https://parks.des.qld.gov.au/parks/moreton-island). Off the west coast are the rusty, hulking **Tangalooma Wrecks**, which provide excellent snorkelling and diving.

Moreton Island has a rich history. Shell middens and bone scatters speak of the island's original inhabitants, the Ngugi people, a clan belonging to the Quandamooka group. The island is also the site of Queensland's first and only whaling station at Tangalooma, which operated between 1952 and 1962.

There are four small settlements, all on the west coast: **Tangalooma** (home to the island's only resort), **Bulwer** near the northwestern tip, **Cowan Cowan** between Bulwer and Tangalooma, and **Kooringal** near the southern tip.

◎ Sights & Activities

Around half a dozen bottlenose dolphins swim in from the ocean and take fish from the hands of volunteer feeders each evening. Be aware that only visitors who have booked official day trips or select overnight stays with Tangalooma Island Resort have access to the dolphin-feeding sessions. Note also that feeding dolphins can teach them to be dependent on humans, and animal welfare activists advise against it.

The resort also houses the **Tangalooma Eco Centre** (☑ 1300 652 250; www.tangalooma.com; Tangalooma Island Resort; ☺ 10am-noon & 1-4pm; ♿), which has a display on the diverse marine and bird life of Moreton Bay.

Island bushwalks include a desert trail (two hours) leaving from Tangalooma Island Resort, as well as the strenuous trek up Mt Tempest, 3km inland from Eagers Creek – worthwhile, but you'll need transport to reach the start.

Cape Moreton Lighthouse offers great views when the whales are passing by. Built in 1857, it's also Queensland's oldest operating lighthouse.

Australian Sunset Safaris (☑ 1300 553 606, 07-3287 1644; www.sunsetsafaris.com.au;

tours from Brisbane adult/child from $199/164; 🚐)
runs 4WD trips with an eco or adventure
focus, and convenient pick up from central
Brisbane. The one-day 'Get Wrecked Tour'
(adult/child $199/164) includes a guided
snorkelling tour (weather permitting), kayaking in see-through kayaks, sand tobogganing
and time for swimming. The highly recommended two-day tour (adult/child $359/324)
includes an evocative, optional kayaking tour
of the island's shipwrecks at night ($45) and
accommodation in dorms, twin-share units
or luxe glamping tents.

Adventure Moreton Island (☑1300
022 878; www.adventuremoretonisland.com; 220
Holt St, Pinkenba; day tours from $99) runs a
handful of day tours, among them an Island
Adrenaline package (from $199), which
includes bike, kayak (or SUP) and snorkel
hire, and the choice of either a jet-boat ride
or parasailing session. Tours depart from
Holt Street Wharf in Brisbane. Overnight
resort accommodation packages also available (per person an extra $120).

🛌 Sleeping

Tangalooma hosts the island's sole **resort**
(☑1300 652 250; www.tangalooma.com; Tangalooma; d/apt from $209/399; ❄@🅿🛜🏊).
There are also five national park camping
areas on Moreton Island: North Point, Blue
Lagoon, Ben-Ewa, the Wrecks and Com-
boyuro Point. All have toilets, cold showers
and running water (treat before using).
Book online before you get to the island,

well in advance during peak Australian
summer and school-holiday periods.

❶ Getting There & Away

Several ferries operate from the mainland. To explore once you get to the island, bring a 4WD or
take a tour. Most tours are out of Brisbane, and
include ferry transfers. Timetables are available
on each ferry company's website.

Amity Trader (☑0475 740 097, 07-3820 6557;
www.amitytrader.com; Victoria Point Jetty,
Masters Ave, Victoria Point; 4WD/walk-on passengers return $280/50) Runs vehicle barges
for 4WD vehicles and walk-on passengers from
the Brisbane suburb of Victoria Point to Kooringal on Moreton Island several times monthly.
Sailing time is roughly two hours one-way; see
the website for the current timetable.

Micat (☑07-3909 3333; www.moretonislan
dadventures.com.au; 14 Howard Smith Dr, Port
of Brisbane; one way 4WD $65-140, adult/child
$28.50/18.50) Vehicle ferry service from the
Port of Brisbane to Tangalooma. Bookings are
essential and service frequency is based on
demand, with one to two sailings daily in quiet
periods and between one and five sailings daily
in busy periods, such as local school holidays.
Journey time is around 1½ hours one way; see
the website for current sailing times.

Tangalooma Flyer (☑07-3637 2000; www.
tangalooma.com; 220 Holt St, Pinkenba; return
adult/child $84/46) Fast passenger catama-
ran operated by Tangalooma Island Resort. It
makes the 1¼-hour trip to the resort four times
daily from Holt St Wharf in the Brisbane suburb
of Pinkenba (see the website for directions).

The Gold Coast

Best Places to Eat

➡ Songbirds (p344)

➡ Fishhouse (p340)

➡ Commune (p340)

➡ Elk Espresso (p337)

➡ BSKT Cafe (p338)

Best Places to Sleep

➡ La Costa Motel (p343)

➡ Burleigh Break (p340)

➡ Mouses House (p345)

➡ One The Esplanade (p333)

➡ Xanadu (p336)

Why Go?

Built for pleasure and remaining a place dedicated to sun, surf and the body beautiful, this strip of coast is the Australia visitors from cooler climes fantasise about. Its multitude of shimmering high-rises seems incongruous against the beach, and its reputation for tackiness is occasionally deserved. But this is far outstripped by the area's youthful spirit and startling beachy beauty: some 52km of pristine sand with countless epic surf breaks, blissful water temperatures and 300 sunny days a year.

While Surfers Paradise's malls and bars entertain the party kids, the other neighbourhoods have distinct charms of their own, from booming culinary scenes and coastal chic to retro beach holiday nostalgia and laid-back local flavour. Not to be overlooked is the lush, misty subtropical rainforest of the hinterland – a good place to get in touch with the spirit of the traditional owners of this land, the Yugambeh people.

When to Go
Surfers Paradise

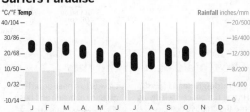

Dec–Feb The best time for sunshine, higher temperatures and busy beaches.

Jun–Aug Winter brings sun-chasers from cooler climes, and still-swimmable water.

Oct & Nov Perfect weather, lower prices; time your visit to miss 'Schoolies week.

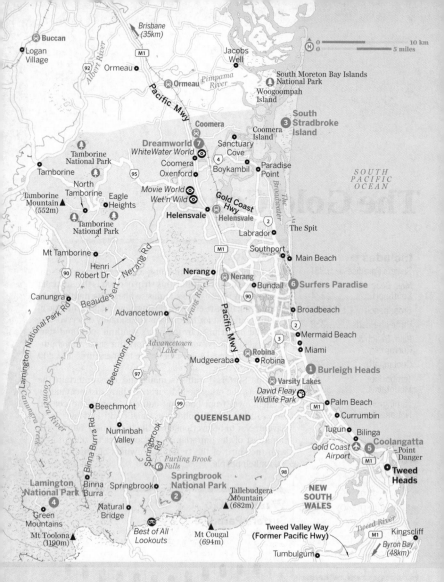

The Gold Coast Highlights

1 Burleigh Heads (p338) Hitting the beach then diving into the creative culinary scene.

2 Springbrook National Park (p345) Taking in the vista at the aptly named Best of All Lookout.

3 South Stradbroke Island (p336) Retreating from the

crowds to a near-deserted expanse of beach and bush.

4 Lamington National Park (p345) Bushwalking through craggy gorges and densely canopied rainforest.

5 Coolangatta (p342) Braving a dawn surf at the Superbank break, or a picnic with a view on Point Danger.

6 Surfers Paradise (p331) Drinking, dancing and watching the sun come up on the beach.

7 Theme Parks (p346) Testing your nerve (and your stomach) on the Gold Coast's rides, such as those at Dreamworld.

ℹ️ Getting There & Away

AIR

Gold Coast Airport (p524) is 21km south of Surfers Paradise, near Coolangatta. Domestic routes are handled by Qantas, Jetstar and Virgin Australia, while AirAsia X, Air New Zealand and Scoot join them on international routes. Brisbane Airport (p524) is 84km northwest of Surfers Paradise and accessible by train. It is a useful arrival point for the Gold Coast, especially for international visitors.

BUS

Greyhound (📞 07-3155 1550; www.greyhound. com.au) has services to/from Brisbane ($14 to $24, 1¼ hours, five daily), Byron Bay ($25 to $37, 3½ hours, three daily), Coffs Harbour ($83, seven hours, three daily), Newcastle ($161, 12¾ to 14¼ hours, two daily) and Sydney ($100 to $200, 14 to 16¾ hours, three daily).

TRAIN

TransLink (📞 07-3851 8700; www.translink. com.au) services connect Brisbane's Airport and Central Station with the Gold Coast every hour, but the stations are all slightly inland. For holidaymakers, the most useful stops are Coomera (where buses run to the theme parks) and Helensvale (where the G:Link tram connects to Surfers). For Helensvale, a single paper ticket costs $16 from Central Station (68 minutes) and $35 from the Airport (1½ hours).

ℹ️ Getting Around

TO/FROM GOLD COAST AIRPORT

Skybus (📞 1300 759 287; www.skybus.com. au; adult/child $15/2) Departs every half hour from the domestic-arrivals end of the airport and heads to over 400 Gold Coast hotels and apartments. A separate bus runs to Byron Bay.

Con-X-ion Airport Transfers (📞 07-5556 9888; www.con-x-ion.com) Door-to-door transfers to/from Gold Coast Airport and your hotel (from $15 to Surfers), as well as from Brisbane Airport (from $35); prebooking essential. Private pickups also available.

Surfside Buslines (📞 13 12 30; www.surfside. com.au) From Gold Coast Airport, route 777 is a limited-stop service running every 15 minutes from 5.16am to 11.36pm via Palm Beach, Burleigh Heads, Miami and Mermaid Beach to Broadbeach South tram station ($6, 27 minutes), where you can transfer to the G:link tram.

BOAT

Hopo (📞 07-5655 3528; www.hopo.com.au; 1 zone $5, day pass $25) has 14 services a day between Surfers Paradise (Appel Park wharf on the Nerang River) and Broadwater Parklands via HOTA and Marina Mirage.

Boats for South Stradbroke Island (p336) depart from Mariner's Cove.

PUBLIC TRANSPORT

Southeast Queensland has an integrated public transport smart card known as the *Go* card (available from convenience stores, news agencies and stations for a $10 refundable deposit) covering TransLink trains, Surfside buses and G:link trams. Paper tickets are also available, but the *Go* card fares are at least 30% cheaper.

Note, there are no public transport services to the national parks of the hinterland.

Bus

Surfside Buslines, a subsidiary of Brisbane's main TransLink operation, runs regular buses up and down the Gold Coast.

Tram

G:link (www.translink.com.au) is a light rail service connecting Helensvale train station and Broadbeach via Southport and Surfers Paradise. If you're likely to do more than one trip, it's worth buying a 'go explore' day pass (adult/child $10/5; available online, at tram stops and from convenience stores and the information centre). It gives you unlimited travel on TransLink buses and the tram. Otherwise, you can buy single-trip tickets from a machine on the tram platform.

Surfers Paradise

POP 23,700

Some may mumble that paradise has been lost amid the skyscrapers and shopping centres, but Surfers' gloriously long stretch of golden sand still attracts a phenomenal number of visitors – 20,000 per day at its peak. For all the high-rises, the main commercial centre only occupies a few frenetic blocks. Party-hard teens and early-20-somethings come here for a heady dose of clubs and bars, perhaps fitting in a bit of beach time as a hangover remedy before it all starts again. Families are attracted by the ready availability of spacious apartments, loads of kid-friendly eating options and, yes, that beautiful beach. If crashing waves aren't your thing, cut across to sheltered Budds Beach on the Nerang River.

🔾 Sights & Activities

SkyPoint   VIEWPOINT
(www.skypoint.com.au; Level 77, 3003 Surfers Paradise Blvd; adult/child $27/17; ⏱️7.30am-10pm) For an eagle-eye view of the coast and hinterland, zip up to this 230m-high observation deck near the top of Q1; at 322m, it's the world's tallest residential building. Save money on Friday and Saturday nights when it turns into

Surfers Paradise

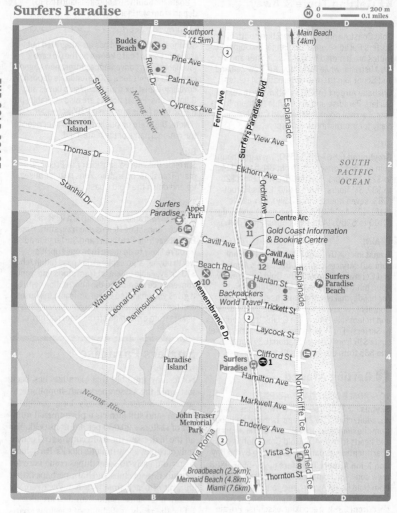

Surfers Paradise

◉ Sights
1 SkyPoint C4

✪ Activities, Courses & Tours
2 Australian Kayaking Adventures B1
3 Cheyne Horan School of Surf C3
4 Whales in Paradise B3

🛏 Sleeping
5 Bunk C3
6 Moorings on Cavill B3

7 One The Esplanade D4
8 Surfers Beachside D5
The Island .... (see 5)

✗ Eating
9 Bumbles B1
10 Paradox Coffee Roasters C3
11 Stairwell Coffee C3

🍷 Drinking & Nightlife
12 Surfers Paradise Beer Garden C3

a cocktail bar from 8pm to 11pm (admission $10). You can also tackle the SkyPoint Climb (sunrise/day/twilight/night $107/77/97/87) up the spire to a height of 270m.

Cheyne Horan School of Surf   SURFING
(📞1800 227 873; www.cheynehoran.com.au; shop 5, Surfers International Bldg, Hanlan St; 2hr lesson $59; ⏰lessons 10am & 2pm) Learn to carve up the waves at this school, run by former pro surfer Cheyne Horan. Multilesson packages reduce the cost per class.

Australian Kayaking Adventures   KAYAKING
(📞0412 940 135; www.australiankayakingadventures. com.au; 13 River Dr; half-day tours adult/child $85/75, sunset tours $55/45) Paddle out to underrated South Stradbroke Island on a morning tour, or take a dusk paddle around Chevron Island in the calm canals behind Surfers.

Balloon Down Under   BALLOONING
(📞07-5500 4797; www.balloondownunder.com.au; 30min/1hr flight $250/299) Head up, up and away on sunrise flights over the Gold Coast. Choose to end with a 'champagne' breakfast for an extra $25. Passengers are transported from the Mercure Resort Gold Coast (64 Palm Meadows Dr, Carrara) to the launch site.

Whales in Paradise   WHALE WATCHING
(📞07-5538 2111; www.whalesinparadise.com.au; 58 Cavill Ave; adult/child/family $99/69/267; ⏰Jun-Oct) Leaves central Surfers up to five times a day for three hours of whale watching.

✱✱ Festivals & Events

Gold Coast Film Festival   FILM
(www.gcfilmfestival.com; ⏰Apr) Mainstream and art-house flicks from all over the world feature over 12 days in mid-April on outdoor screens, including SIPFest, two nights of short films screened right on the beach.

Bleach   CULTURAL
(www.bleachfestival.com.au; ⏰Apr) Art shows, contemporary dance, music of all genres, theatre and performances all feature, held over 12 days in a variety of indoor and outdoor spaces. There's a late-summer party vibe, with the occasional superstar performer heading the bill, as well as some edgy and provocative work.

Gold Coast 600   SPORTS
(www.supercars.com; ⏰Oct) For three days in late October, the streets of Surfers are transformed into a temporary race circuit for high-speed cars.

🛏 Sleeping

Bunk   HOSTEL $
(📞07-5676 6418; www.bunksurfersparadise.com.au; 6 Beach Rd; dm $37-42; ✱@🛜🏊) Retro motel turned boutique hostel, Bunk features private pod-style bunks equipped with reading lights and chargers, and all dorms come with en-suite bathroom, in-room safe, balcony and much-needed air-con. Cool off in the pool, soak it up in the spa or hang out in the bar.

Rhapsody Resort   APARTMENT $$
(📞07-5618 8300; www.rhapsodyresort.com. au; 3440 Surfers Paradise Blvd; apt from $169; P✱🛜🏊) You might find yourself rhapsodising about the views from this 41-floor tower block, especially if you're barbecuing on the rooftop terrace. The ground-floor pool is small, but the beach is only a block away. Apartments range from studios to two-bedroom units, all with kitchen and laundry.

The Island   HOTEL $$
(📞07-5538 8000; www.theislandgoldcoast. com.au; 3128 Surfers Paradise Blvd; r/ste from $159/189; P✱🛜🏊) The Islander Hotel has been reborn as the Island and it's indeed an island of contemporary style – more of an LA/Palm Springs vibe than Gold Coast. Spacious rooms have natural timber, matte-black tapware and king-sized beds, and there are plenty of spaces to be seen, from the street-side Goldie's restaurant to the umbrella-lined pool and the rooftop bar.

Moorings on Cavill   APARTMENT $$
(📞07-5538 6711; www.mooringsoncavill.com.au; 63 Cavill Ave; apt from $182; P✱🛜🏊) Managed with a smile, this roomy apartment tower at the river end of Cavill Ave is great for families: the vibe is quiet and respectful. The location is hard to beat too: close to the beach, shops and restaurants. Minimum two-night stay, with maximum discounts for week-long stays.

★One The Esplanade   APARTMENT $$$
(📞07-5538 3154; www.oneontheesplanade.com.au; 1 The Esplanade; apt from $235; P✱🛜🏊) One of the few apartment blocks directly on the beach, this complex has friendly management, a saltwater pool, barbecues and secure underground parking. All the stylish apartments have north-facing balconies.

Surfers Beachside   APARTMENT $$$
(📞07-5570 3000; www.surfersbeachside.com.au; 10 Vista St; apt $199-315; P✱🛜🏊) The delightful management is a huge plus at this unpretentious, family-friendly spot, which

is surprisingly quiet given it's only a block back from the beach. Each apartment is individually owned and decorated, but all interiors are clean, comfortable and unfussy, and all have balconies. There's a minimum three-night stay in high season, but that's sometimes open to negotiation.

✕ Eating

Stairwell Coffee
CAFE $

(📞 0449 976 707; www.stairwellcoffee.com. au; Centre Arcade, 3131 Surfers Paradise Blvd; mains $5-13; ⊙ 7am-4pm Mon-Sat) Escape to this hole-in-the-wall cafe, hidden down a shabby shopping arcade, for well-made coffee using locally roasted beans and a short menu of jaffles (Aussie for toasted sandwiches), croissants and bagels. We're particularly fond of 'the Mortgage', a bagel slathered in smashed avocado, feta and smoked paprika.

★ Paradox Coffee Roasters
CAFE $$

(📞 07-5538 3235; www.paradoxroasters.com; 7/10 Beach Rd; mains $16-22; ⊙ 7am-2pm) Sustainably sourced beans are roasted on-site to produce some seriously good brews at this impressive cafe, where red-brick walls support a high ceiling looking a little like an inverted ice tray. The menu is concise but delicious, featuring the likes of barramundi (Australian sea bass) burgers and slow-braised lamb shanks served with baba ganoush (smoky eggplant paste).

Bumbles
CAFE $$

(📞 07-5538 6668; www.bumblescafe.com; 19 River Dr; mains $14-24; ⊙ 7am-4pm Fri-Wed, to 10pm Thu; 🐾) This gorgeous converted house (actually, at one stage, a brothel) is the place for cooked breakfasts and non-run-of-the-mill lunches, such as miso salmon with soba noodles. Otherwise, just cosy up in one of the eclectically furnished rooms for coffee and cake.

ℹ SCHOOLIES ON THE LOOSE

Every year in November, thousands of teenagers flock to Surfers Paradise to celebrate the end of their high-school education in a three-week party known as Schoolies Week. Although local authorities have stepped in to regulate excesses, boozed-up and drug-addled teens are still the norm. It's not pretty.

🍷 Drinking & Entertainment

Surfers Paradise Beer Garden
BAR

(📞 07-5570 1322; www.surfersbeergarden.com.au; Cavill Ave; ⊙ 10am-late) Not so much a garden – more a terrace bar with a retractable roof and a long balcony above a tired shopping mall overlooking leafy Cavill Ave. Steel yourself with a few cold ones on the balcony before you hit the clubs, or catch the regular bevy of live bands and live-screened UFC (mixed martial arts) and boxing matches. Good times.

HOTA
ARTS CENTRE

(Home of the Arts; 📞 07-5588 4000; www.hota. com.au; 135 Bundall Rd; ⊙ box office 9am-9pm Mon-Sat, 10am-8pm Sun, gallery 10am-5pm) A bastion of culture and civility beside the Nerang River, this arts centre has two cinemas, a cafe, a bar, an outdoor stage and a 1200-seat theatre, which regularly hosts impressive productions (theatre, comedy, jazz, opera, kids' concerts etc). If you're travelling after 2021, the colourful six-level HOTA art gallery should be completed.

ℹ Information

Backpackers World Travel (📞 07-5538 7417; www.backpackersworld.com; 3063 Surfers Paradise Blvd; ⊙ 10am-6pm Mon-Sat; 🐾) Accommodation, tour and transport bookings.

Gold Coast Information & Booking Centre (📞 07-5570 3259; www.destinationgoldcoast. com; 2 Cavill Ave; ⊙ 8.30am-5pm) The main Gold Coast tourist information booth; also sells theme-park tickets and has public transport info.

My Doctors Clinic (📞 07-5592 2299; www. mydoctorsclinicsurfers.com.au; 16/3221 Surfers Paradise Blvd; ⊙ 24hr) General medical centre and pharmacy. Book an appointment online.

Main Beach & Southport

POP 35,800

North of Surfers Paradise, the pace eases up but the apartment towers are only slightly less lofty. Main Beach makes for a serene base if you're here for views, beach time and generally taking it easy. Tedder Ave may no longer possess place-to-be cache, but it still has a pleasantly village-like atmosphere.

Further north, the Spit separates the Southport Broadwater from the Pacific Ocean, stretching 5km to almost meet South Stradbroke Island. Its southern end is home to Marina Mirage, an upmarket shopping centre with a few waterfront dining options, along with Mariner's Cove, a base for aquatic activities. The beach up here, backed as it is

Main Beach & Southport

Marine Parade, Southport; adult/child $6.20/4.60; ⊙5am-8pm Mon-Fri, 6am-4pm Sat, 8am-3pm Sun).

Main Beach Pavilion ARCHITECTURE
(Macarthur Pde; ⊙6.30am-late) **FREE** The lovely but somewhat shabby Spanish Mission–style Pavilion (1934) is a remnant from pre-boom days. Inside there's a cafe, toilets and changing rooms, and some fabulous old photos of the Gold Coast before the skyscrapers.

Federation Walk WALKING
(www.federationwalk.org) This pretty 3.7km (each way) trail takes you through patches of fragrant littoral rainforest, flush with beautiful birdlife, and runs parallel to one of the world's most beautiful strips of surf beach. Along the way, it connects to the Gold Coast Oceanway, which heads 36km to Coolangatta. The walk begins in the Phillip Park car park, on Sea World Dr.

⌂ Sleeping

Surfers Paradise
YHA at Main Beach HOSTEL $
(☑07-5571 1776; www.yha.com.au; 70 Sea World Dr, Main Beach; dm $34-36, r without bathroom $84, f with bathroom $104; [P][@][⚡]) Despite being called Surfers Paradise YHA, this is actually a great 1st-floor spot overlooking the Mariner's Cove marina in Main Beach, with sky-blue dorms kitted out with basic metal bunks. There's a free shuttle bus, pub crawls

with dunes and native parkland, is surprisingly quiet. It also has some very uncrowded surf breaks that deliver when nothing else does.

Across the Broadwater is Southport, a densely populated suburb with a large, very popular shopping centre.

◎ Sights & Activities

Broadwater Parklands PARK
(Marine Pde, Southport) Hugging the water's edge on the Southport side of the Broadwater estuary, this large park features free barbecues, beach volleyball, a swimming pontoon, restaurants and the Great Lawn, where big public events like the Mayor's Christmas Carols are held. Best of all is **Rockpools**, a free water park for toddlers, where colourfully painted marine critters squirt water into a series of paddling pools. It's also home to the large outdoor pools of the **Gold Coast Aquatic Centre** (☑07-5582 8282; www.cityofgoldcoast.com.au/aquaticcentre;

SOUTH STRADBROKE ISLAND

A narrow, 21km-long sand island, 'South Straddie' is largely undeveloped and car-free – the perfect antidote to the Gold Coast's busyness. At its northern end, the narrow channel separating it from North Stradbroke Island is a top fishing spot; at its southern end, where the Spit is only 200m away, you'll find breaks so good they have Gold Coast surfers braving the swim over.

South Stradbroke was once attached to North Stradbroke, until a huge storm in 1896 blasted through the isthmus that joined them. The ensuing isolation has been a boon for South Stradbroke's natural habitat, with wallabies aplenty and pristine bush, sand and sea to explore.

There's very little on the island apart from a few rustic campgrounds and a family-friendly resort. The easiest way to visit on a day trip is to take the **Couran Cove ferry** (☑ 07-5597 9999; www.courancove.com.au; Mariner's Cove, 60-70 Seaworld Dr; return adult/child $38/18) to the island resort of the same name. Boats depart four or five times a day for the 30-minute journey. From the resort, it's roughly a 2km walk along shady bush tracks to the surf beach. If you get peckish, the resort has a bistro overlooking the marina and a burger bar by its pool.

on Thursday and Saturdays, and the hostel is within wobbling distance of a tavern. It can also arrange tours and activities.

Meriton Suites Southport APARTMENT $$
(☑ 07-9277 1111; www.meritonsuites.com.au; 2 Como Cres, Southport; apt from $125; P✳🅰🛜🏊) This vast tower has 228 one-, two- or three-bedroom fully equipped apartments, and a pricing structure which means there's often a bargain to be had if you book far enough ahead – and there's almost always a room if you leave it to the last moment. The complex also has indoor and outdoor pools, a gym, a sauna and a supermarket.

Ashmore Palms
Holiday Village RESORT $$
(☑ 07-5539 3222; www.ashmorepalmsgoldcoast. com.au; 71 Hinde St, Ashmore; cottage from $153; P✳🛜🏊) There's a big range of family-friendly cottages – ranging from humble two-bedroom Hibiscus Chalets to two-storey Macaw Mansions – tucked between the palms in this nearly six-hectare, tightly packed, resort village. Kids will love the parrot-filled aviaries, two swimming pools and very cool playgrounds, plus there are tennis courts and barbecue areas. It's 4km inland from the Broadwater, so best with a car.

Main Beach Tourist Park CARAVAN PARK $$
(☑ 07-5667 2720; www.goldcoasttouristparks.com. au; 3600 Main Beach Pde, Main Beach; sites/cabins from $48/122; P✳🛜🏊) Just across the road from the beach and surrounded by a phalanx of high-rise apartments, this caravan park is a family favourite. There are good facilities, including an inviting pool, and it's all very well maintained.

★ **Xanadu** RESORT $$$
(☑ 07-5557 0400; www.xanadumainbeach.com. au; 59 Pacific St, Main Beach; apt from $420; P✳🛜🏊) Spacious two-bedroom, two-bathroom apartments (150 in total) with full kitchen and laundry facilities are the norm in this pair of massive 1990s-built towers. It's just across the road from Main Beach but there are also indoor and outdoor pools, two tennis courts, a gym, spa pools, a sauna and guest barbecues. All it lacks is Olivia Newton-John in roller skates.

Sheraton Grand Mirage Resort RESORT $$$
(☑ 07-5577 0000; www.sheratongrandmirage goldcoast.com; 71 Sea World Dr, Main Beach; r/ste from $256/555; P✳🛜🏊) This 295-room absolute-beachfront hotel has a relaxed glamour, and rooms are nicely low-slung and set among 6 hectares of tropical gardens. The large oasis pool has a swim-up bar, and a delightful strip of Spit beach is accessible down a little path. Discounted rates can often be found online.

Pacific Views APARTMENT $$$
(☑ 07-5527 0300; www.pacificviews.com.au; 5-11 Woodroffe Ave, Main Beach; apt from $219; P✳🛜🏊) If you can cope with decor surprises, these individually owned and furnished apartments have amazing floor-to-ceiling views, spacious balconies and helpful staff. They're just one block back from the beach and there's a cafe downstairs.

✖ Eating & Drinking

Peter's Fish Market
SEAFOOD **$**

(🖉07-5591 7747; www.petersfish.com.au; 120 Sea World Dr, Main Beach; meals $9-18; ⊙9am-7.30pm) A no-nonsense fish market and fish-and-chip shop selling fresh and cooked seafood, which can be eaten on a few tables out the front by the river. The kitchen opens at midday.

Southport Surf Lifesaving Club
BAR

(🖉07-5665 3900; www.sslsc.com.au; Macarthur Pde, Main Beach; ⊙8am-midnight) This beautiful, airy pavilion-style club has spectacular views. The deck is open from 8am for coffee, or head here for lazy, beery afternoons.

🔒 Shopping

Gourmet Farmers Market
MARKET

(🖉07-5555 6400; www.facebook.com/marinamiragefarmersmarket; Marina Mirage, 74 Sea World Dr, Main Beach; ⊙7am-noon Sat) On Saturday mornings, the open spaces of the Marina Mirage mall fill with stalls selling seasonal fruit and veg, baked goods, pickles, oils, vinegars, seafood, pasta and more, all from small-scale producers and makers.

Broadbeach

POP 5510

Directly south of Surfers Paradise, Broadbeach still has apartment towers and malls, but it's decidedly more upmarket than its northern neighbour, with carefully landscaped streets and smart places to eat, drink and shop. If you're after a big but somewhat classy night out, it's the best option on the GC. Of course, the stretch of golden beach is gorgeous.

🛏 Sleeping & Eating

Meriton Suites Broadbeach
APARTMENT **$$**

(🖉07-5579 6200; www.meritonsuites.com.au; 2669 Gold Coast Hwy; apt from $150; P❄🎦🏊) The golden pegasus on the lawn between the indoor and outdoor pools is the only concession to quirkiness at this tastefully but demurely furnished complex. Apartments have laundry facilities and proper kitchens with coffee makers and dishwashers. If you get peckish, there's a yum-cha restaurant and convenience store downstairs.

Peppers Broadbeach
APARTMENT **$$$**

(🖉07-5635 1000; www.peppers.com.au/broadbeach; 21 Elizabeth Ave; 1-/2-/3-bedroom apt from $239/295/719; ❄🎦🏊) When you want flawless if somewhat predictable comfort, these two large, curvy apartment towers are for you. Think marble dining tables, European kitchen appliances, wrap-around balcony and high-thread-count linen. The three-bedroom 'sky homes' really take the luxury to town. There are two pools, a gym, teppanyaki barbecues, a zen garden and a tai chi lawn.

Cardamom Pod
VEGETARIAN **$**

(🖉0452 218 108; www.cardamompodbroadbeach.com; 1/2685 Gold Coast Hwy; 1/2/3 dishes with rice $10/18/25; ⊙11am-9pm Mon-Thu, from 8am Fri-Sun; 🖉) 🌱 Vegetarians and vegans rejoice! This meat-free place has a counter full of salads and warmer-tray curries, vegan lasagne and cheesy bakes. Finish off with a cake, many of which are raw, gluten- and sugar-free. Everything is made from scratch on the premises.

★Elk Espresso
CAFE **$$**

(www.elkespresso.net; Oasis bldg, Old Burleigh Rd; mains $16-20; ⊙6am-4pm; 🚼) Stroll across the road from the beach and brush off your sandy feet for some seriously good breakfasts at this breezy corner cafe, generously garlanded with hanging plants. A beloved local institution, Elk serves sophisticated, beautifully presented meals and great coffee.

🍷 Drinking & Nightlife

Roosevelt Lounge
COCKTAIL BAR

(🖉07-5613 2335; www.therooseveltlounge.com.au; 75 Surf Pde; ⊙6-10pm Tue, to 1am Thu-Sat) It's Professor Green in the library with a cocktail in this darkened, semisecret speakeasy at the rear of the Loose Moose. Dress up and be prepared for some hefty prices for the signature cocktails ($22 to $28). The gin, tonic and whisky lists are particularly impressive. Tuesday is comedy night and Thursday a live soul session.

Broadbeach Bulls
SPORTS BAR

(🖉07-5531 5913; www.broadbeachbowlsclub.com; 169 Surf Pde; ⊙11.30am-8pm) The Broadbeach Bowling Club is home to the best greens in Australia – it hosted the bowling competition for the 2018 Commonwealth Games. Its bright and breezy bar serves pub-style food and hosts regular live gigs. Come for a sunset beer on the terrace, and perhaps a round of barefoot bowls.

Mermaid Beach & Miami

POP 13,400

The high-rises disappear and you get a glimpse of the Gold Coast of old as you hit these neighbourhoods of low-rise blocks and rambling beach cottages. However, nestled within these suburban streets and low-key shopping strips you'll find some of the region's most innovative eating and drinking options. The stretch of beach here is lovely with a laid-back, local feel.

◉ Sights

Miami Marketta   MARKET

(☑0488 590 599; www.miamimarketta.com; 23 Hillcrest Pde; ⊙5-10pm Wed, Fri & Sat) A street market in a previously abandoned warehouse strewn with fairy lights, this lively space has food, fashion, art and live music. Work your way through food stalls hawking Japanese tempura, tacos, homemade pasta and home-baked cakes. Grab a drink at the cocktail bar and browse the latest art exhibition.

✖ Eating & Drinking

★ BSKT Cafe   CAFE $$

(☑07-5526 6565; www.bskt.com.au; 4 Lavarack Ave, Nobby Beach; mains $17-23; ⊙6am-4pm Sun-Thu, 7am-10pm Fri & Sat; 🕸🚲🖨) This satisfyingly industrial-styled cafe is only metres from the beach, but that's far from its only charm. It's the brainchild of four buddies whose focus is organic produce, and the dishes and service punch well above cafe level (we love the crusty banh mi). Vegans and paleos will be equally at home here, as will children (there's a play area).

Glenelg Public House   STEAK $$$

(☑07-5575 2284; www.theglenelgpublichouse.com. au; 2460 Gold Coast Hwy, Mermaid Beach; mains $26-54; ⊙5pm-midnight Mon-Thu, from noon Fri-Sun) A passionate place, this atmospheric eating and drinking den uses premium produce; the epic steak list takes in quality cuts from Queensland, NSW and Tasmania. If you're not here for slabs of meat, dishes such as Wagyu meatballs, pan-roasted barramundi or free-range roast chicken fill out the menu. Early diners can take advantage of the good-value 'sunset menu'.

Cambus Wallace   COCKTAIL BAR

(☑07-5575 3420; www.thecambuswallace.com. au; 4/2237 Gold Coast Hwy, Nobby Beach; ⊙5pm-midnight Tue-Sun) This moody, maritime-themed bar attracts a good-looking but relaxed local crew. Settle in with something from its massive rum and whisky list, or try a Gold Coast take on cocktail classics (there's no Dark 'n' Stormy, but a coconut, pineapple, lime and rum Maiden Voyage could not be better suited to the climate). The sliders are great too.

Burleigh Heads

POP 10,100

The superchilled surfie enclave of Burleigh (drop the 'Heads' if you don't want to out yourself as a tourist) has long been a family favourite, but is definitely enjoying its moment in the sun on a broader scale. Its gently retro vibe and palpable youthful energy epitomise both the Gold Coast's timeless appeal and its new, increasingly interesting spirit. You'll find some of the region's best cafes and restaurants dotted around its little grid and, yes, that famous right-hand point break still pumps, while the beautiful pine-backed beach continues to charm everyone who lays eyes on it.

◉ Sights

Burleigh Head National Park   NATIONAL PARK

(www.npsr.qld.gov.au/parks/burleigh-head; Goodwin Tce) FREE Burleigh Head is known as Jellurgal to the local Kombumerri clan of the Yugambeh people, who trace its formation to a creation spirit called Jabreen. As you walk the 1.2km (each way) Oceanview Track that edges this 27-hectare rainforest reserve, look out for the six-sided basalt columns Jabreen is said to have left in his wake. You might also spot sea eagles and, from May to November, whales. Side tracks lead up to a pair of lookouts.

The broad mouth of the Tallebudgera Creek, on its southeastern edge, is a popular swimming spot.

Jellurgal   CULTURAL CENTRE

(☑07-5525 5955; www.jellurgal.com.au; 1711 Gold Coast Hwy; tours adult/child from $30/15; ⊙8am-3.30pm Mon-Fri) 🌿 FREE This Aboriginal cultural centre at the base of Burleigh Head (Jellurgal) showcases a collection of artefacts and artwork, and offers a variety of cultural tours taking in sites important to the local Yugambeh people, who have lived here for tens of thousands of years. Tours range from the 2½-hour *Jellurgal*

Burleigh Heads

0   500 m
0   0.25 miles

Map labels:

Black Hops Brewing (380m);
Paddock Bakery (580m)
Solnamara (280m)
Gold Coast Hwy
Second Ave
First Ave
The Esplanade
Acanthus Ave
Burleigh St
Burleigh St
W Burleigh Rd
Acanthus Ave
West St
Park Ave
Connor St
Ocean St
James St
Goodwin Tce
Tweed St
Hayle St
George St W
George St E
Burleigh Ridge Park
Tabilban St
David Fleay Wildlife Park (1.5km);
Burleigh Brewing Company (3.5km)
Burleigh Beach
Burleigh Head
SOUTH PACIFIC OCEAN
Tallebudgera Creek
The Collective (3km); Currumbin (5km);
Currumbin Wildlife Sanctuary (5.5km);
Balter (6.3km); Coolangatta (11km)

Burleigh Heads

◉ Sights
1 Burleigh Head National Park D4
2 Village Markets B2

🛌 Sleeping
3 Burleigh Beach Tourist Park C3
4 Burleigh Break B1

🍴 Eating
5 Borough Barista B2
6 Commune A1
7 Fishhouse C3
8 Harry's Steak Bistro & Bar B2
9 Justin Lane B2
10 Rick Shores C3

Walkabout (adult/child $30/15), venturing onto their Dreaming mountain, to longer tours involving traditional dance and an ochre ceremony; book in advance.

David Fleay Wildlife Park   WILDLIFE RESERVE
(☎07-5669 2051; www.qld.gov.au/davidfleay; Loman Lane, West Burleigh; adult/child/family $25/12/64; ◷9am-5pm) Opened by the naturalist who first succeeded in breeding platypuses and wedge-tailed eagles, this wildlife park has enclosures housing koalas, cassowaries, emus, crocs, wallabies, kangaroos, snakes and a very cute platypus. There are plenty of informative native wildlife shows throughout the day. Just outside the park, boardwalks traverse the mangroves fringing Tallebudgera Creek.

Village Markets   MARKET
(www.thevillagemarkets.co; Burleigh Heads State School, 1750 Gold Coast Hwy; ◷8.30am-1pm 1st & 3rd Sun of month) This long-running market highlights local designers, makers and collectors, with fashion and lifestyle stalls, lots of live music and a strong local following.

🛏 Sleeping

⭐ Burleigh Break   MOTEL $$
(📱 0418 113 411; www.burleighbreak.com.au; 8 Fourth
Ave; s/d from $95/100; [P][❄][📶]) A progressive
renovation has seen one of the Gold Coast's
beloved midcentury motels transformed into
a friendly and great-value place to stay. Classic
motel design means highway views, but you're
still just a minute's amble from the beach.
Rooms have retained vintage features where
possible, but otherwise are fresh and simple.
There's a guest lounge and barbecue.

Burleigh Beach Tourist Park   CARAVAN PARK $$
(📱 07-5667 2750; www.goldcoasttouristparks.com.
au; 36 Goodwin Tce; sites/cabins from $48/148;
[P][❄][@][📶]) This park is snug, but it's well run
and in a good spot near the beach. All the
cabins have two bedrooms and sleep four to
eight people.

Solnamara   APARTMENT $$$
(📱 07-5535 1022; www.solnamara.com.au; 202 The
Esplanade; apt from $279; [P][❄][📶][🏊]) Separated
from the beach by just a road and a strip
of tropical plants, this modern block offers
slick apartments angled for ocean views. Relax into the Burleigh lifestyle on your own
private balcony or beside the kidney-shaped
pool. On rainy days, raid the book and DVD
library at reception.

🍴 Eating

Borough Barista   CAFE $
(www.boroughbarista.com.au; 14 The Esplanade;
mains $13-16; ⊘ 5am-2pm) It's all cool tunes
and friendly vibes at this little open-walled
espresso shack across from the beach.
Join local surfers for their dawn espresso
or cold brew, and postsurf head here for a
smoked-salmon bagel, wrap or açai bowl on
a footpath bench.

Paddock Bakery   BAKERY $
(📱 07-5508 2573; www.paddockbakery.com; 20 Hi-
biscus Haven; dishes $10-19; ⊘ 6am-3pm; 🖉) An
antique wood-fired oven sits in the heart of
this beautiful old weatherboard cottage and
turns out wonderful bread, croissants and
pastries. The semi-sourdough doughnuts
have a devoted fan base. There's a full breakfast and lunch menu, too, as well as top coffee,
smoothies, milkshakes and cold-pressed juices. Grab a seat in the garden and tuck in.

⭐ Commune   CAFE $$
(📱 07-5520 3377; 1844 Gold Coast Hwy; mains
$14-22; ⊘ 6am-3.30pm; 🖉) The hippest kid
in Burleigh, this excellent cafe serves all
the açai, chia seed and paleo muesli power bowls you could ever hope for, but we'll
be ordering the coriander corn fritters. Or
possibly the cacao pancakes, chilli-crab
scrambled eggs or fish tacos... Band posters gaze down on the big communal table
inside, and there are others on the street.

Justin Lane   PIZZA $$
(📱 07-5576 8517; www.justinlane.com.au; 1708
Gold Coast Hwy; mains $20-26; ⊘ 5pm-late Mon
& Tue, from noon Wed-Sun) One of the key
players in Burleigh's eating and drinking
scene, Justin Lane has colonised most of
an old shopping arcade with a downstairs
pizzeria and rooftop bar offering lovely
foreshore views. Great pizzas, simple but
flavour-packed pasta dishes and a fantastic
wine list make it a must, even if you're not
here for the party vibe.

⭐ Fishhouse   SEAFOOD $$$
(📱 07-5535 7725; www.thefishhouse.com.au;
50 Goodwin Tce; mains $42-50; ⊘ noon-3pm &
5.30-10pm) This stylish whitewashed brick
building across from the beach is well
known for its seaside specialities, with the
best sustainably caught fish sourced both
locally and from around Australia. Choose
individual mains (such as coral trout in a
smoky mussel broth) or order a whole fish
for the table. Complimentary side dishes
are delicious.

Harry's Steak Bistro & Bar   STEAK $$$
(📱 07-5535 2699; www.harryssteakbistro.com.au;
1744 Gold Coast Hwy; mains $25-52; ⊘ 5pm-late
Mon-Thu, from noon Fri-Sun) Harry's is a stylish paean to 'beef, booze and banter' which
is superserious about its steaks, with each
accredited with the name of its producer
and region. Sweet staff will go out of their
way to make sure you get a cut you'll enjoy.
They also do a tasty Wagyu cheeseburger,
and a token fish dish and mushroom pasta.

Rick Shores   ASIAN $$$
(📱 07-5630 6611; www.rickshores.com.au; 43
Goodwin Tce; mains $34-54; ⊘ noon-midnight)
This acclaimed modern Asian restaurant offers beachfront dining at its most
beachy, with windows that open out to let
in the breeze and the sound of the crashing
waves. Portions are large and designed for
sharing, but be sure to start with the sensational fried Moreton Bay bug roll all to
yourself. Excellent service, too.

LOCAL KNOWLEDGE

GOLDIE'S BEST SURF BREAKS

The Gold Coast possesses some of the longest, hollowest and best waves in the world, and is lauded for its epic consistency. The creation of the 2km Superbank sand bar has made for a decade of even better waves, even more often.

Snapper Rocks A highly advanced point break at Coolangatta's far south; home to the Pro World Surfing League, and home break to Australian pro surfers Stephanie Gilmore and Nick Fanning.

Duranbah Universally known as D-bah, this beach break has world-class A-frames and is good for those who like their waves technical and punchy.

Greenmount Classic beach break that benefits from a southerly swell.

Kirra Beautiful beach break that doesn't work that often, but, oh when it does.

Burleigh Heads Strong currents and boulders to watch out for, but a perfect break that's more often on than not.

Miami to Surfers Paradise This immense stretch of beach offers plenty of relatively empty breaks.

The Spit One of north Goldie's stalwarts, this peaky beach break can work even when the surf is small.

Drinking & Nightlife

Black Hops Brewing BREWERY
(📞0435 830 466〖〗; www.blackhops.com.au; 15 Gardenia Grove; ⏱noon-7pm Wed-Sun) The Black Hops crew run a friendly and fun taproom, where you can enjoy a tasting paddle or sample whatever craft delight they've currently got on their 14 taps. You can also pick up bottles of beer to take home, plus there's usually a food truck pulled up outside on weekends.

Burleigh Brewing Company BREWERY
(📞07-5593 6000; www.burleighbrewing.com.au; 2 Ern Harley Dr; ⏱3-8.30pm Fri & Sat, 2-6pm Sun) Hang out in this cavernous space with fellow beer lovers, or grab a seat in the courtyard to listen to live music and fuel up from the food trucks. There's a 24-tap line-up of Burleigh brews; tasting paddles are available.

Palm Beach & Currumbin

POP 17,600

Around the point from Burleigh, Palm Beach has a particularly lovely stretch of sand, backed with a few old-style beach shacks. Its numbered streets are also home to some great coffee stops and dining options. Further south again, Currumbin is a sleepy, family-focused town, with a beautiful surf beach, safe swimming in Currumbin Creek and some interesting midcentury architecture. It's also home to a well-known wildlife sanctuary.

Sights & Activities

Currumbin Wildlife Sanctuary WILDLIFE RESERVE
(📞07-5534 1266; www.currumbinsanctuary.com.au; 28 Tomewin St, Currumbin; adult/child/family $50/40/150; ⏱8am-5pm) This nicely restrained, old-style operation includes Australia's biggest rainforest aviary, where you can hand-feed a technicolour blur of rainbow lorikeets. There's also kangaroo and crocodile feeding, photo ops with koalas, reptile shows, a treetop ropes course and Aboriginal dance displays (some activities have fees). There's often an adults-at-kids-prices special online. Note, the parking is $10 extra – or you can park for two hours around the corner for free.

Currumbin Rock Pools SWIMMING
(Currumbin Creek Rd, Currumbin Valley) **FREE**
These natural swimming holes are a cool spot during the hot summer months, and feature grassy banks for kids to run around and rocky ledges from which brave teenagers like to plummet. It's 14km up Currumbin Creek Rd from the coast.

Eating & Drinking

The Collective INTERNATIONAL **$$**
(📞07-5534 6707; www.thecollectivepalmbeach.com.au; 1128 Gold Coast Hwy, Palm Beach; mains $15-32; ⏱noon-late) Five kitchens here serve one rambling indoor-outdoor communal dining space, strung with fairy lights, flush with pot plants and packed with happy eaters. There are two bars, one of them a

Coolangatta

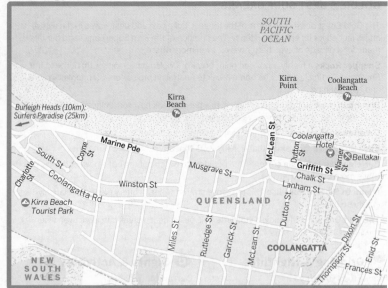

balmy rooftop affair. Choose from burgers, pizza, pan-Asian, Mexican and Mod Oz share plates; there are also gluten-free and vegan options.

Balter   BREWERY
(☑ 07-5525 6916; www.balter.com.au; 14 Traders Way, Currumbin; ⊙ 3-8pm Wed-Fri, from noon Sat & Sun) Surf star Mick Fanning (the guy who punched a shark, right?) and his fellow circuit legends Joel Parkinson, Bede Durbidge and Josh Kerr are all partners in this wonderful brewery, hidden away at the back of an industrial estate. Come and sample the sought-after Balter XPA or a seasonal special. Tours are also available, including a four-beer tasting paddle ($35).

Coolangatta

POP 5950

The conjoined towns of Coolangatta (Queensland) and Tweed Heads (NSW) sit on either side of the state border, separated only by broad Boundary St. You can walk along the median strip with a foot in each state.

'Coolie' has quality surf beaches (including the legendary Superbank) and a tight-knit, very real community that makes it feel less touristy. The **Coolangatta Gold** (www.sls.com.au/coolangattagold; ⊙ Oct) surf-lifesaving comp happens here every October and the **Corona Open Gold Coast** (www.world surfleague.com; Point Danger; ⊙ Mar-Apr) kicks off surfing's most prestigious world tour at Snapper Rocks each March. Follow the boardwalk north around Kirra Point for another beautiful long stretch of beach, sometimes challenging surf and locally loved cafes and bars with an indie atmosphere.

◉ Sights & Activities

Captain Cook Memorial   LIGHTHOUSE
The headland of Point Danger marks the border between Queensland and New South Wales. There are amazing views from here both ways along the coast, and you can use it as a starting point or picnic end to several coastal walks. As well as being a memorial to James Cook, the 1970-built brutalist concrete tower that marks the spot (and the cardinal directions) is a working lighthouse. Once a laser, it's now a tried-and-true electric beacon.

Gold Coast Surfing Centre   SURFING
(☑ 0417 191 629; www.goldcoastsurfingcentre.com; Marine Pde; group lessons $45) Former professional surfer and Australian surfing-team coach Dave Davidson promises to get you up and surfing in your first lesson. Look for the branded vans at Rainbow Bay and Greenmount Beach.

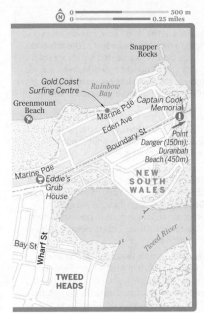

0 ———— 500 m
0 ———— 0.25 miles

Snapper Rocks

Gold Coast Surfing Centre — Rainbow Bay

Greenmount Beach

Marine Pde — Captain Cook Memorial

Eden Ave

Boundary St — Point Danger (150m); Duranbah Beach (450m)

Marine Pde — Eddie's Grub House

NEW SOUTH WALES

Tweed River

Bay St — Wharf St

TWEED HEADS

🛏 Sleeping

Kirra Beach Tourist Park   CARAVAN PARK $
(📞 07-5667 2740; www.goldcoasttouristparks.com.au; 10 Charlotte St; sites from $37, r without bathroom $69, cabin $131; ✳@🛜🛜✳) This large council-run park has plenty of trees, wandering ibises and a camp kitchen, playground and heated swimming pool. There are good-value self-contained two-bedroom cabins, as well as twin and double 'lodging rooms'.

⭐ La Costa Motel   MOTEL $$
(📞 07-5599 2149; www.lacostamotel.com.au; 127 Golden Four Dr, Bilinga; r/apt from $145/205; ✳🛜) One of the few motels of 1950s 'highway heritage', this mint-green weatherboard has stayed true to its roots on the outside, while the interiors are stylish, comfortable and include kitchenettes. A lovely apartment with private deck suits longer stays. It's super handy for the airport and only a short stroll from North Kirra Beach.

🍴 Eating & Drinking

Bellakai   CAFE $$
(📞 07-5599 5116; www.bellakai.cafeleader.com; 82 Marine Pde; mains $14-21; ⊘5am-2pm) Open extra early for presurf coffee and sustenance, Bellakai is popular with locals as a meeting and chatting spot. Substantial cooked breakfasts shift into sharing plates as the day progresses.

Eddie's Grub House   BAR
(📞 07-5599 2177; www.eddiesgrubhouse.com; 171 Griffith St; ⊘noon-late Tue-Sun) The walls are covered in photos of rock legends, from Bowie to Motörhead, at this totally old-school hard rock and metal bar. Yes, there's grub to be had, and Eddie's 'dive bar comfort food' is exactly that, but this is predominantly a place for drinking, dancing and catching local bands.

Coolangatta Hotel   PUB
(📞 07-5589 6888; www.thecoolyhotel.com.au; cnr Marine Pde & Warner St; ⊘9am-late) The hub of Coolangatta's sometimes boisterous nocturnal scene, this huge pub, right across from the beach, pumps with live bands, pool comps, trivia nights, pub meals – basically, the works. Big Sunday sessions.

GOLD COAST HINTERLAND

Inland from the surf, sand and half-nakedness of the Gold Coast, the densely forested mountains of the McPherson Range feel a million miles away. There are some wonderful national parks here, packed with subtropical jungle, waterfalls, lookouts and rampant wildlife.

Tamborine Mountain

POP 7030

The mountaintop rainforest community of Tamborine Mountain – comprising Eagle Heights, North Tamborine and Mt Tamborine – is 45km inland from the Gold Coast beaches. It has cornered the arts-and-craft, package-tour, chocolate-fudge-liqueur market in a big way – if this is your bag, Gallery Walk in Eagle Heights is the place to stock up.

👁 Sights & Activities

Tamborine National Park   NATIONAL PARK
(www.nprsr.qld.gov.au/parks/tamborine; ⊘sunrise-8pm Oct-Mar, to 6pm Apr-Sep) Queensland's oldest national park comprises 13 sections stretching across an 8km plateau. Pick up a map at the information centre in North Tamborine for easy-to-moderate walking trails to features such as the Witches Falls and Cameron Falls. In the Joalah section of the park, a 1.1km return walk through pretty rainforest leads to the Curtis Falls, tucked

GOLD COAST THEME PARKS

The gravity-defying roller coasters and water slides at the Gold Coast's theme parks offer some seriously dizzying action and, despite a tragic fatal accident at Dreamworld in 2016 (killing four people), they still attract huge crowds. Discounted tickets are sold in most of the tourist offices on the Gold Coast or can be bought online. Multiday passes (seven/14 days $159/189) grant unlimited entry to the four parks owned by **Village Roadshow** (☑ 13 33 86; www.themeparks.com.au), including Warner Bros Movie World, Wet'n'Wild and Paradise Country.

Some tips: the parks can get insanely crowded, so arrive early or face a long walk from the far side of the car park; booking online will usually save you money; the parks don't let you bring in your own food or drinks. Note, Lonely Planet chooses not to publicise parks that keep captive cetaceans such as performing dolphins.

Dreamworld (☑ 07-5588 1111; www.dreamworld.com.au; Dreamworld Pkwy, Coomera; adult/child $99/89; ⊙ 10am-5pm; ⛟) Australia's biggest theme park has stomach-churning thrill rides (with names like The Giant Drop and The Claw), whiz-bang multisensory rides (such as the Sky Voyager) and an excellent Corroboree section, featuring Aboriginal cultural displays and lots of native critters. Other attractions include the resident tigers of Tiger Island, Wiggles World and the DreamWorks Experience. Tickets give you entry to both Dreamworld and neighbouring WhiteWater World.

Paradise Country (☑ 13 33 86; www.paradisecountry.com.au; Production Dr, Oxenford; adult/child $39/29; ⊙ 9.30am-4.30pm; ⛟) Younger kids love this 'Aussie Farm Experience', which features native animals (koalas, kangaroos, Tasmanian devils, wombats, dingoes) alongside farm animals and other furry cuties (marmosets, tiger cubs). Shows include the obligatory sheep-shearing demonstration.

Warner Bros Movie World (☑ 13 33 86; www.movieworld.com.au; Pacific Hwy, Oxenford; adult/child $99/89; ⊙ 9.30am-5.30pm) Movie-themed shows, rides and attractions, including the DC Rivals Hypercoaster, Batwing Spaceshot, Justice League 3D Ride and Scooby-Doo Spooky Coaster. Actors dressed as Batman, Austin Powers, Porky Pig et al roam through the crowds.

Wet'n'Wild (☑ 13 33 86; www.wetnwild.com.au; Pacific Hwy, Oxenford; adult/child $79/74; ⊙ 10am-5pm) The ultimate water slide here is the Kamikaze, where you plunge down an 11m drop in a two-person tube at 50km/h. This vast water park also has pitch-black slides, white-water rapids and wave pools.

WhiteWater World (☑ 07-5588 1111; www.dreamworld.com.au; Dreamworld Pkwy, Coomera; adult/child $59/49; ⊙ 10am-5pm) This water park, next door to Dreamworld, features the Cave of Waves, Pipeline Plunge and numerous other water activities and slides. Bring coins for the extortionately priced lockers.

The Surfside Buslines (p331) TX7 bus (from Coomera Station) stops at the main theme parks, as does Con-X-ion Airport Transfers (p331).

just below a busy road; look out for lyrebirds and platypuses.

From the Cedar Creek car park it's a short walk past a picnic area to the **Cedar Creek Falls** lookout. The track continues down through a rock-walled gorge to natural pools at their base. You can swim here, but follow the instructions on the signs.

Note that the waterfalls are at their most impressive after heavy rains; they reduce to little more than a trickle in drought conditions.

Skywalk   WALKING
(☑ 07-5545 2222; www.rainforestskywalk.com.au; 333 Geissmann Dr, North Tamborine; adult/child/

family $20/10/49; ⊙ 9.30am-4pm) Take a 1.5km walk along forest-floor trails to pretty Cedar Creek, with spectacular elevated steel viewpoints and bridges cutting through the upper canopy along the way. Look out for rare Richmond birdwing butterflies en route. It's a hefty charge for a 30-minute stroll, though.

🛏 Sleeping

★ **Songbirds**   BOUTIQUE HOTEL $$$
(☑ 07-5545 2563; www.songbirds.com.au; Lot 10, Tamborine Mountain Rd; villa from $288, 2-/3-course meal $65/85; ⊙ restaurant noon-3pm & 6-9pm Thu-Sat, noon-3pm Sun; 🅿 ❄ 🛜) Set within 20

hectares of lush rainforest, Songbirds offers six Southeast Asian–inspired villas, each with a double spa bath. It's also home to one of the Gold Coast's most innovative restaurants, producing highly technical dishes making good use of produce grown on-site. Rates drop for stays of two nights or more, and dining-inclusive deals are available.

ℹ Information

Tamborine Mountain Visitor Information Centre (☑ 07-5545 3200; www.tamborine mtncc.org.au; Doughty Park, Main Western Rd, North Tamborine; ⏱ 9.30am-3.30pm; 🛜)

Lamington National Park

Dense rainforest cloaks the valleys and steep cliffs of the McPherson Range, reaching elevations of 1100m on the Lamington Plateau. The 206-sq-km Lamington National Park is part of the vast Gondwana Rainforests of Australia World Heritage Area, the most extensive expanse of subtropical rainforest in the world.

It's known as Woonoongoora to the local Yugambeh people, meaning 'quiet and timeless', and you could spend days exploring this impressive part of the hinterland on its more than 160km of walking trails. However, it also offers short walks, waterfalls, birdwatching and picnic areas for day trippers. The two most accessible sections of the park are Binna Burra on the eastern side and Green Mountains (O'Reilly's) on the western side.

The park was affected by the major bush fires that swept through Australia in 2019/2020. At the time of writing, rangers were confident that tracks, roads and accommodation would eventually be repaired and re-established.

ℹ Information

There are Queensland Parks & Wildlife Services (QPWS) information centres at **Green Mountains** (☑ 07-5544 0600; www.parks.des. qld.gov.au; 3579 Lamington National Park Rd; ⏱ 8am-4pm Sat & Sun) and at **Binna Burra** (☑ 07-5533 3584; www.parks.des.qld.gov.au; 890 Binna Burra Rd; ⏱ 8am-4pm Sat & Sun).

Springbrook National Park

Springbrook National Park (☑ 13 74 68; www.nprsr.qld.gov.au/parks/springbrook) is a steep remnant of the huge Tweed Shield volcano that centred on nearby Wollumbin/Mt Warn-

ing in NSW more than 20 million years ago. It's a wonderland for hikers, with excellent trails through cool-temperate, subtropical and eucalypt forests offering a mosaic of gorges, cliffs and waterfalls. Like Lamington National Park, it's part of the Gondwana Rainforests of Australia World Heritage Area.

The park is divided into four sections. The 900m-high **Springbrook Plateau** is home to the township of Springbrook, which fans out along Springbrook Rd. Laced with waterfalls, trails and eye-catching lookouts, this section receives the most visitors. **Mt Cougal**, accessed via Currumbin Creek Rd, has several waterfalls and swimming holes (watch for submerged logs and slippery rocks). The **Natural Bridge** section has a walking circuit leading to a scenic waterfall-cave formation, while **Numinbah Valley** to the north is the most heavily forested section of the park.

◎ Sights & Activities

Excellent viewpoints in the park include the appropriately named **Best of All Lookout** (Repeater Station Rd), the **Canyon Lookout** (Canyon Pde), also the start of a 4km circuit walk to Twin Falls, and the superb lookout beside the 60m **Goomoolahra Falls** (Springbrook Rd), giving views across the plateau and all the way back to the coast.

The **Purling Brook Falls** (Forestry Rd) tumble 106m over the edge of a broad canyon, its sheer rock walls painted in orange and black. A 4km (two-hour) circuit starts here; you're best to tackle it in a clockwise direction to avoid ending with a punishing set of stairs.

🛏 Sleeping

Settlement Campground   CAMPGROUND $
(☑ 13 74 68; www.nprsr.qld.gov.au/parks/spring brook; 52 Carricks Rd, Springbrook; sites per person/family $7/27) There are 11 grassy sites at this pretty, trim camping ground (the only one at Springbrook) with toilets and gas BBQs. Book your permit online.

★ **Mouses House**   CHALET $$$
(☑ 07-5533 5192; www.mouseshouse.com.au; 2807 Springbrook Rd, Springbrook; chalet from $270; 🅿❄🛜) Linked by softly lit boardwalks, these 14 cedar chalets hidden in the magical misty woods are intimate mountain hideaways. Each has a spa bath and a wood fire, and some have outdoor hot tubs. Breakfast, lunch and dinner hampers are available.

THE GOLD COAST LAMINGTON NATIONAL PARK

Noosa & the Sunshine Coast

Why Go?

A place of flawless beaches, coveted surf breaks and laid-back, sun-kissed resort towns, the Sunshine Coast stretches a golden 100km from the tip of Bribie Island to the Cooloola Coast. 'Sunny's' towns and cities flaunt their own particular appeal and vibe, from breezy, informal Caloundra to chic, polished Noosa Heads, as they vie for the attention of holidaymakers from cooler climes.

The Sunshine Coast hinterland is a lush, green and peaceful backdrop to the coast. Here you'll find the ethereal Glass House Mountains, dramatic volcanic plugs shrouded in ancient mythology. Further north, the Blackall Range features bird-filled rainforest, lush pastures and quaint rural villages alive with colourful markets, artisanal food and crafty boutiques.

For tens of thousands of years, these coastal plains have belonged to the Kabi Kabi (Gubbi Gubbi) people, known as the mwoirnewar (the saltwater people) to the Jinibara people of the hinterland.

Best Places to Eat

➡ Spirit House (p368)

➡ Sum Yung Guys (p364)

➡ Il Vento (p361)

➡ Noosa Beach House (p353)

➡ Little Humid (p353)

Best Places to Sleep

➡ YHA Halse Lodge (p351)

➡ Rumba Resort (p358)

➡ Oceans (p361)

➡ Monaco (p358)

➡ Glass House Mountains Ecolodge (p357)

When to Go
Noosa

May Gourmets and gluttons nosh and slosh at the four-day culinary festival Noosa Eat & Drink.

Aug Smaller crowds, milder weather and the region-wide food festival the Curated Plate.

Sep/Oct Caloundra draws music fans with its rocking surfside Caloundra Music Festival.

Noosa & the Sunshine Coast Highlights

1 Noosa (p348) Switching between nature hikes, surfing and bar-hopping in the coast's A-list beach town.

2 Glass House Mountains (p356) Soaking up magnificent vistas of the hinterland's surreal volcanic landmarks.

3 Great Sandy National Park (p365) Cruising up one of Australia's most spectacular natural highways, the Great Beach Drive.

4 Regional feasting (p352) Savouring local produce, culinary ingenuity and craft brews at Noosa's burgeoning food scene.

5 Noosa Everglades (p367) Encountering a dugong in a rare, precious ecosystem.

6 Eumundi Markets (p367) Shopping yourself silly in a wonderland of crafts, artists and street food at Australia's top artisan market.

7 Mary Cairncross Scenic Reserve (p369) Cooing over pademelons in an ancient rainforest.

8 Caloundra (p357) Riding waves, sipping speciality coffee and snapping street art in Sunny's understated hub of cool.

ℹ Getting There & Around

AIR

Sunshine Coast Airport (p363) is at Marcoola, 10km north of Maroochydore and 26km south of Noosa. Jetstar (www.jetstar.com) and Virgin Australia (www.virginaustralia.com) have daily direct flights from Sydney and Melbourne; Jetstar also runs direct flights from Adelaide one to three times weekly. Qantas (www.qantas.com.au) flies direct from Sydney.

The airport also hosts seasonal direct flights to Auckland, New Zealand. Once expansion works are completed in late 2020, it's expected to introduce other international flights.

BUS

Greyhound Australia (p526) has several direct daily connections between Brisbane and Mooloolaba/Maroochydore (from $24/25, 1¼ to 2¾ hours) and Noosa (from $28, 2¼ to three hours). It runs morning and afternoon services from Brisbane to Australia Zoo ($21, 1¼ hours).

Premier Motor Service (☑13 34 10; www.premierms.com.au) runs one daily service each way between Brisbane and Noosa ($24, 2½ hours) via Mooloolaba and Maroochydore ($24, 1½ hours).

Several companies offer transfers from Sunshine Coast Airport and Brisbane to points along the coast. Fares from Brisbane cost from $45 to $65 and from Sunshine Coast Airport from $18 to $35.

Con-X-ion (p322) Does airport transfers from the Sunshine Coast and Brisbane Airports.

Henry's Airporter (☑1300 954 199, 07-5474 0199; www.henrys.com.au) Runs a door-to-door service from Sunshine Coast Airport to points north as far as Noosa Heads and Tewantin.

Sunbus (☑Marcoola Depot 07-5450 7888; www.sunbus.com.au) Local routes include Caloundra to Maroochydore ($6, 55 minutes) and Maroochydore to Noosa ($9.10, 1¼ hours). Services also run between Nambour train station and Noosa ($9.10, 1¼ hour) via Eumundi. TransLink Go Cards are accepted.

Noosa

POP 52,125

One of Australia's most fashionable resort towns, Noosa's restrained, low-rise centre nestles between pristine subtropical rainforest and calm, crystalline waters. The result is intimate, relaxed and exclusive. The town itself is within the Noosa Biosphere Reserve, a Unesco-recognised area famous for its highly diverse ecosystem.

While the designer boutiques, stylish restaurants and canal-side villas draw urban elites, the beach and bush are free and welcoming to all, leading to a healthy intermingling of fashionistas, laid-back surfers and family groups. Noosa encompasses three main zones: upmarket **Noosa Heads** (around Laguna Bay and Hastings St), the more relaxed **Noosaville** (along the Noosa River) and the administrative hub of **Noosa Junction**. All three occupy the traditional land of the Kabi Kabi (or Gubbi Gubbi) people, whose territory stretches from Fraser Island south to the Pumicestone Passage and west towards the Conondale and Blackall Ranges.

◉ Sights

★**Noosa National Park**   NATIONAL PARK
(www.noosanationalpark.com; Noosa Heads; 🔁) Noosa's unmissable national park delivers spectacular coastal views (expect to see dolphins) and ambrosial beaches like **Tea Tree Bay**. The most scenic way to reach it is on the accoya-tree boardwalk along the coast from town. At the entrance, the Noosa National Park Information Centre (p354) has free walking maps and information on the day's koala sightings; the adjoining kiosk brews great coffee. The most popular trail is the **Coastal Walk**; allow at least 1½ hours for the return trip.

Noosa Main Beach   BEACH
(Laguna Bay; Noosa Heads; 🔁) Only steps away from the restaurants, bars and boutiques of Hastings St, Noosa's most popular beach is patrolled year-round. It's one of the east coast's few north-facing beaches, offering gentle to moderate waves ideal for families and rookie surfers.

🏃 Activities

Merrick's Learn to Surf   SURFING
(☑0418 787 577; www.learntosurf.com.au; Beach Access 14, Noosa Main Beach, Noosa Heads; group lesson $70; ⊙ group lessons 8.45am & 1.15pm, private lessons 11.15am; 🔁) Merrick's is one of the most popular surf schools on the Sunshine Coast, offering super-fun, two-hour group lessons twice daily, as well as the option of private tutorials (from $180). Kids aged seven and over are welcome, and the outfit runs special five-day kids' lessons during the school holidays. Lessons can be conducted in French, too – *très bien!*

Foam & Resin   SURFING, WATER SPORTS
(☑0424 985 687; 53 Hastings St, Noosa Heads; surfboard/SUP rental from $25/30; ⊙9am-5pm)

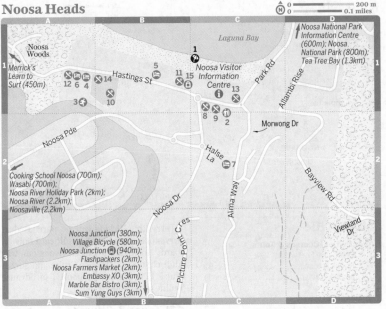

Noosa Heads

Noosa Heads

◎ Sights
1 Noosa Main Beach...................................C1

✪ Activities, Courses & Tours
2 Foam & Resin...C2
3 Noosa Ferry..A1

🛏 Sleeping
4 10 Hastings...A1
5 Accom Noosa...B1
  Fairshore...(see 5)
6 Hotel Laguna...A1
7 YHA Halse Lodge....................................C2

✗ Eating
8 Betty's Burgers & Concrete Co.............C1
9 Cafe Le Monde.......................................C1
  El Capitano..(see 8)
10 Hard Coffee..B1
11 Hastings Street Bakery........................B1
12 Kaali...A1
13 Massimo's...C1
14 Noosa Beach House..............................B1

🍷 Drinking & Nightlife
  Miss Moneypenny's..........................(see 6)

🛍 Shopping
15 Noosa Longboards................................B1

Owned and run by an affable Kiwi expat, this open-air surf rental kiosk sits opposite the visitor centre in Noosa Heads. It's generally cheaper than its competitor on the beach and offers good-quality equipment, including longboards, shortboards and SUPs. Opening times can vary.

Adventure Sports Noosa WATER SPORTS
(☎07-5455 6677; www.kitesurfaustralia.com.au; 136 Eumundi Noosa Rd, Noosaville; SUP/kitesurfing lessons $125/299; ◉9am-5pm Mon-Fri, to 2pm Sat Aug-Apr, reduced hours rest of year) As well as running popular kitesurfing and

SUP lessons, Adventure Sports offers hire of kayaks and SUPs (either from $35 per half day). Kayaks include those with or without a rudder.

Noosa Wave BOATING
(☎0458 997 188; www.noosawave.com.au; the jetty, 186 Gympie Tce, Noosaville; adult/child $75/60, family $250, snorkelling $99) With 850HP pushing you over the waves, this has to be Noosa's most exhilarating boat ride. The 1½-hour Epic Adventure ride takes you out around Noosa Heads National Park, where you may

Noosaville

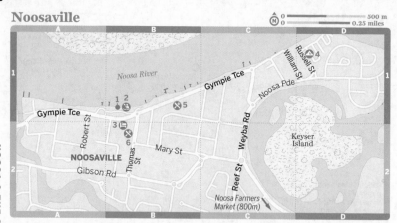

Noosaville

🏃 Activities, Courses & Tours
1 Discovery Fraser B1
2 Kayak Noosa B1
  Noosa Wave .... (see 1)

🛏 Sleeping
3 Islander Noosa Resort B2
4 Noosa River Holiday Park D1

🍴 Eating
5 Little Humid B1
6 Mexican Joint B2
  Noosa Boathouse .... (see 2)

spot turtles, whales, dolphins or manta rays. Guided snorkelling trips are also available.

Kayak Noosa　　　　　　　　　　KAYAKING
(☎0448 567 321, 07-5455 5651; www.kayaknoosa. com; 194 Gympie Tce, Noosaville; tours adult/child $60/45; 👫) Runs commendable kayaking tours exploring the mangrove corridors and sand flats of the Noosa River estuary. Also offers SUP tours along the river, as well as rental of kayaks (one hour/day $15/60) and SUPs ($15/70).

Noosa Ferry　　　　　　　　　　　CRUISE
(☎07-5449 8442; www.noosaferry.com; Ferry Tour all-day pass adult/child $25/10; 👫) This excellent ferry service runs a hop-on, hop-off Ferry Tour between Tewantin and the Sofitel Noosa Pacific Resort jetty in Noosa Heads. It's an informative and scenic way to get around greater Noosa. It also offers an Eco Cruise (adult/child $59/29) on Tuesdays and Thursdays, and a one-hour Sunset Cruise (BYO alcoholic drinks; per adult/child $25/12.50) from Tuesday to Saturday.

Ferry Tour tickets can be purchased at ferry stops or on board (credit card only on board; Noosaville to Noosa Heads one way adult/child $15/7.50). Eco Cruise and Sunset Cruise tickets must be booked in advance (online or by phone).

👉 Tours & Courses

⭐**Discovery Fraser**　　　　　　　DRIVING
(☎07-5449 0393; www.discoveryfraser.com; 186 Gympie Tce, Noosaville; tours adult/child $165/130; 👫) This place runs a great one-day, 4WD tour of Fraser Island, with pick-up available on the Sunshine Coast between Sunshine Beach and Noosa. Tours also depart daily from Rainbow Beach.

Bike On Australia　　　　MOUNTAIN BIKING
(☎07-5474 3322; www.bikeon.com.au; 12/20 Venture Dr, Noosaville; guided tours from $60, bike hire per day from $30) This operation offers a variety of tours, including self-guided and adventurous eco-jaunts. The fun, half-day Off the Top Tour – downhill on a mountain bike – costs $80, with a minimum of four people required. See the website for numerous hire locations in Noosa Heads and Noosaville. Delivery also available.

Cooking School Noosa　　　　　COOKING
(☎07-5449 2443; www.thecookingschoolnoosa. com; 2 Quamby Pl, Noosa Heads; ⏱half-/full-day class from $140/250) Lauded restaurant Wasabi (p353) also runs hands-on cooking courses at its purpose-built cooking school. Helmed by in-house chefs, as well as special guest chefs from around the country, regular options include Japanese, Southeast Asian, Italian and French courses, all of which use

seasonal local produce and conclude with lunch or dinner and sommelier-picked accompanying wines or beer.

⭐ Festivals & Events

Noosa Festival of Surfing SURFING
(www.noosafestivalofsurfing.com; ⊘ Feb/Mar) A week of wave-riding action in Februrary or March. There's a huge range of competition divisions, from invite-only pros to amateur competitions spanning all age brackets. Water action aside, events include surf talks and workshops as well as live music. Hang around for the dog surfing championships after the humans have finished. See the website for dates.

Noosa Eat & Drink FOOD & DRINK
(www.noosaeatdrink.com.au; ⊘ May) A four-day tribute to all manner of gastronomic delights, featuring a wife array of chefs, masterclasses and special lunches and dinners, as well as themed food and wine tours.

Noosa Alive CULTURAL
(www.noosaalive.com.au; ⊘ Jul) A 10-day festival of world-class music, dance, theatre, visual arts, literature and more. The programme includes both local and world premieres, as well as high-profile festival guests.

🛏️ Sleeping

For an extensive list of short-term holiday rentals, try Noosa Visitor Information Centre (p354) or **Accom Noosa** (☑ 07-5447 5374, 1800 072 078; www.accomnoosa.com.au; Shop 5/41 Hastings St, Noosa Heads; ⊘ 8.30am-6pm).

⭐ **YHA Halse Lodge** HOSTEL $
(☑ 07-5447 3377; https://halselodge.com.au; 2 Halse Lane, Noosa Heads; dm/r from $38/99; P @ 🛜) This splendid, colonial-era Queenslander is a legendary backpacker stopover and well worth the clamber up its steep drive. There are four-, six- and 16-bed dorms, twins, doubles and a lovely wide verandah. Popular with locals, the bar is a mix-and-meet bonanza, offering great meals (mains $18 to $27) and cheap happy-hour drinks from 5pm to 6.30pm. Close to the Main Beach action.

Flashpackers HOSTEL $
(☑ 07-5455 4088; www.flashpackersnoosa.com; 102 Pacific Ave, Sunshine Beach; dm from $38, d with/without bathroom from $125/100; ❄️ 🛜 🏊) Flashpackers challenges the notion of hostels as flea-bitten dives. Thoughtful touches

to its neat four- and six-bed dorms include full-length mirrors, personal reading lights, ample wall sockets and the free use of surfboards and bodyboards. Other freebies include cheese and wine on Mondays, a sausage BBQ on Fridays and a courtesy bus to/from the main bus station and around Noosa.

Noosa River Holiday Park CARAVAN PARK $
(☑ 07-5449 7050; www.noosaholidayparks.com.au; 4 Russell St, Noosaville; unpowered/powered sites $61/63; 🛜) 🏄 This park is especially appealing for its location on the banks of the Noosa River, right between Noosa Heads and Noosaville. The latter's cafes and bars are within walking distance and the site itself has lovely spots to take a dip in the river. Recent upgrades include brand new amenities, among them clean, spacious showers. It's a justifiably popular place: book well ahead.

Hotel Laguna APARTMENT $$
(☑ 07-5447 3077; www.hotellaguna.com.au; 6 Hastings St, Noosa Heads; studio/apt from $195/270; P ❄️ 🛜 🏊) Neatly wedged between the river and Hastings St, Hotel Laguna consists of self-contained apartments and smaller studios. While all are privately owned and individually decorated, you can expect smart, pleasant digs. There's a communal guest laundry and courtyard-style pool area. The location means you are only a roll-out-of-bed to the beach and Hastings St cafes, bars, restaurants and shopping.

⭐ **10 Hastings** MOTEL $$$
(☑ 07-5455 3340; www.10hastingsstreet.com. au; 10 Hastings St, Noosa Heads; studio/apt from $200/350; ❄️ 🛜) A rarity along Noosa's Hastings St, this renovated boutique motel is a refreshing alternative to the resorts. Clean, fresh, beach-chic rooms come as compact two-person studios and a larger studio suite (sleeping two adults and two children). Larger still is the two-bedroom apartment (sleeping up to six). Beach towels are complimentary. Check for minimum stays.

Islander Noosa Resort RESORT $$$
(☑ 07-5440 9200; www.islandernoosa.com.au; 187 Gympie Tce, Noosaville; 2-/3-bedroom apt from $270/335; P ❄️ 🛜 🏊) Set on 1.6 hectares of tropical gardens, with a central lagoon-style pool area and wooden boardwalks meandering through the trees, this is a good family option in the heart of Noosaville. Check the website for specials. Facilities include a gym and two tennis courts. Apartments are a little

dated, but are comfy and pleasant with full kitchen and laundry facilities.

Fairshore
APARTMENT $$$

(☑07-5449 4500; www.fairshorenoosa.com. au; 41 Hastings St, Noosa Heads; apt from $550; P❋🐾🐱) A smart, family-friendly apartment resort with direct access to Noosa Main Beach and buzzing Hastings St, Fairshore comes with a magazine-worthy, palm-fringed pool area. Two-bedroom apartments offer one or two bathrooms; though each apartment varies in style, all have laundry facilities and most are airy and contemporary. There's also a small gym. Parking is free (vehicle height restriction 1.85m).

✖ Eating

Noosa is a culinary hub, with no shortage of renowned restaurants boasting international flair and local flavours. That said, dining in Noosa is rarely cheap, with mains commonly north of $30. If you're watching your budget, picnic by the river, lunch at casual cafes, or grab a bite at bakeries such as **Tanglewood Organic Sourdough Bakery** (☑07-5473 0215; www.facebook.com/tanglewoodorganicsourdough; Belmondos Organic Market, 59 Rene St, Noosaville; pastries from $5; ⊙7am-4pm Mon-Sat; 🐾🖐) and **Hastings Street Bakery** (☑0429 183 391; 3/49 Hastings St, Noosa Heads; items from $4; ⊙6am-4pm; 🖐). There are several major supermarkets around town, as well as the fantastic Noosa Farmers Market (p354) on Sundays.

Betty's Burgers & Concrete Co
BURGERS $

(☑07-5455 4378; www.bettysburgers.com.au; 2/50 Hastings St, Noosa Heads; burgers $10-17; ⊙10am-8.30pm Sun-Thu, to 9pm Fri & Sat; 🖐) Betty's has achieved cult status all the way down Australia's east coast, which explains the queues at its lush, semi-al-fresco Noosa outlet. The burgers are worth the wait for pillowy soft buns and flawlessly grilled, premium-meat patties (veggie option available), the perfect fries are wonderfully crispy and the moreish concretes (frozen custard; $5) come in seasonally changing flavours like lemon-raspberry cheesecake.

Hard Coffee
CAFE $

(☑0410 673 377; 18 Hastings St, Noosa Heads; meals $10-22; ⊙7am-5pm, kitchen closes 3pm) One of the cheaper options on Hastings St, super-casual Hard Coffee lurks inside a nondescript food court. The food is simple but tasty, with options like sun-dried tomato focaccia, steak sandwich and a basic but satisfying avocado smash. Good coffee and no shortage of regulars reading the paper or discussing the morning surf.

Massimo's
GELATO $

(☑07-5474 8033; 75 Hastings St, Noosa Heads; gelato from $5.50; ⊙9.30am-9.30pm, to 10pm Fri & Sat; 🖐) While the 'no tastings' policy seems a little mean-spirited, rest assured that Massimo's icy treats are creamy and natural in flavour. You'll find both milk-based and sorbet options, from cinnamon and macadamia to climate-appropriate options like mango and passion fruit.

★ Mexican Joint
MEXICAN $$

(☑0423 768 064; www.facebook.com/themexicanjoint; Thomas St, Noosaville; tacos $8, mains $18-36; ⊙noon-late) Away from the hustle, this relaxed, casual restaurant serves up seriously good tacos (mushroom, prawn, pulled beef, achiote chicken and more), plus generous nachos and superb sizzling fajitas. The compact, well-executed menu covers all the bases (including vegetarian), plus cocktails and Mexican beer. See the specials board for seasonal additions like burritos (bowl-style if you wish) or spicy chicken wings.

Cafe Le Monde
INTERNATIONAL $$

(www.cafelemonde.com.au; 52 Hastings St, Noosa Heads; lunch $14-38, dinner mains $25-39; ⊙6am-10pm, to late Fri-Sun; 🐾🖐) There's not a fussy palate or dietary need that isn't catered for on Cafe Le Monde's expansive menu. Its large, blue-and-white patio buzzes with surfers, hipsters and everyone in between digging into options as varied as paleo breakfast waffles, burgers, local seafood and pasta. Baked goods are from organic sibling Tanglewood Bakery, while the wines are mainly certified organic or biodynamic.

El Capitano
PIZZA $$

(☑07-5474 9990; www.elcapitano.com.au; 52 Hastings St, Noosa Heads; pizzas $22-25; ⊙5-10pm, to 11pm Fri & Sat) Down an easy-to-miss path and up some stairs is one of Noosa's best pizzerias, a hip spot with bar seating, louvred windows and marine-themed street art. The light, fluffy pizzas are gorgeous, made with sourdough bases, topped with artisanal ingredients. Get started with the handcrafted meats, pickled vegetables and buffalo mozzarella available from the *salumi e mozzarella* bar. Booking advised.

Noosa Boathouse
MODERN AUSTRALIAN **$$**

(📞07-5440 5070; www.noosaboathouse.com.au; 194 Gympie Tce, Noosaville; mains $24-38; ⊘cafe 6am-6pm, restaurant 11.30am-3pm & 5-8pm Tue-Sun; 🖪) This floating eatery offers numerous sections: cafe, fish-and-chip kiosk, rooftop bar (open for sunset drinks Tuesday to Sunday) and a Cape Cod–style restaurant. The restaurant's modern, bistro-style menu features Italian and Asian accents, though the best value is found at the fish-and-chip kiosk, which offers the same great battered fish from $17. Picnic tables are not too far away.

Kaali
INDIAN **$$**

(📞07-5474 8989; www.kaaligourmetindian.com; 2/2 Hastings St, Noosaville; mains $19-33; ⊘4.30-9.30pm Mon, 12.30-2.30pm & 4.30-9.30pm Tue-Sun; 🖉) After all the Mod Oz cuisine on offer in Noosa Heads, this touch of India offers some spicy relief. At the western end of Hastings St, it's a casual spot, cooking up excellent curries, including the signature lamb shank *nilgiri*, and great tandoori breads.

★ Noosa Beach House
MODERN AUSTRALIAN **$$$**

(📞07-5449 4754; www.noosabeachhousepk.com. au; 16 Hastings St, Noosa Heads; dinner mains $39-48, 3-/6-course menu $85/115, bar tapas 3 for $33; ⊘6.30-10.30am & 5.30-9.30pm, plus noon-2.30pm Sat & Sun; 🖉) White walls, glass and timber set an uncluttered scene at this effortlessly chic restaurant, the stamping ground of celebrity chef Peter Kuruvita. Seasonal ingredients and fresh local seafood underscore a contemporary menu whose deeply seductive Sri Lankan snapper curry with tamarind and *aloo chop* (potato croquette) nods to Kuruvita's heritage. Herbivorous foodies can opt for a seven-course degustation ($100).

The stylish (if boisterous) front bar is a popular spot for all-day dining, an evening aperitif, fantastic cocktails, people watching and live music on Friday and Saturday evenings and Sunday afternoon.

★ Wasabi
JAPANESE **$$$**

(📞07-5449 2443; www.wasabisb.com; 2 Quamby Pl, Noosa Heads; 7/11 courses from $95/165; ⊘5-9.30pm Wed, Thu & Sat, noon-9.30pm Fri & Sun) An award-winning, waterside destination restaurant, Wasabi is well known to visiting gourmets. Premium produce from the region and Wasabi's own farm stars in delicate, technically brilliant dishes such as local line-caught fish, *ponzu* (citrus) butter, pickled young bamboo, cucamelon and greens followed by nasturtium ice cream, rosella granita, *biwa* (loquat) blossom and sake syrup. Book ahead.

★ Little Humid
MODERN AUSTRALIAN **$$$**

(📞07-5449 9755; www.littlehumid.com.au; 2/235 Gympie Tce, Noosaville; dinner mains $35-44; ⊘noon-2pm Thu-Sun & 6pm-midnight daily; 🖉) This deservedly popular place serves up beautiful, seasonal bistro fare with subtle twists: flash-fried cuttlefish with green papaya, avocado salsa, palm sugar and chilli; or crispy-skin duck confit with sweet-potato puree, baby beets, broccolini, orange, anise and vanilla glaze. Vegetarian options available. Book for dinner.

🍷 Drinking & Nightlife

★ Land & Sea Brewery
MICROBREWERY

(Fortune Distillery; 📞07-5455 6128; www.landandseabrewery.com; 19 Venture Dr, Noosaville; ⊘11am-late Mon-Fri, 10am-late Sat & Sun; 🖪) Noosa's first microbrewery fills an impressive warehouse space in Noosaville's industrial area (ring about its courtesy bus). The brews are balanced, easy-drinking and mostly vegan. There are eight to 10 beers on rotation, with regularly rotating IPAs, occasional collaborations and more unusual creations such as Japanese rice lager.

The warehouse is also home to a new venture: **Fortune Distillery**. The stainless-steel brewery alongside beautiful copper stills make a dramatic backdrop to the innovative, varied and good-value lunch and dinner menu, which includes, among other dishes, Milanese arancini, Wagyu beef tataki, vegan poke and a simple fish of the day.

★ Village Bicycle
BAR

(📞07-5474 5343; https://villagebicyclenoosa.com; 16 Sunshine Beach Rd, Noosa Junction; ⊘4pm-midnight, from 3pm Fri-Sun) Splashed with street art, Village Bicycle is a convivial, indie-spirited space, packed nightly with loyal regulars here to knock back beers (mainstream as well as local craft brews), cocktails and vino, and tuck into quality tacos, burgers and hot dogs. Best of all, the kitchen is open until 11pm.

Clandestino Roasters
COFFEE

(📞1300 656 022; www.clandestino.com.au; Belmondos Organic Market, 59 Rene St, Noosaville; ⊘7am-4pm Mon-Fri, to 3pm Sat; 🖪🖪) It might be off the tourist radar, but this cavernous warehouse and micro-roaster on the outskirts of Noosa packs in hipsters, surfers and suits, all here for Noosa's top coffee. Choose from three blends and six single origins served many ways, including espresso-style, cold-drip, pour-over and batch brew. Also serves nitro cold brew and health-promoting elixirs created by an on-site naturopath.

Miss Moneypenny's COCKTAIL BAR
(☑ 07-5474 9999; www.missmoneypennys.com; 6 Hastings St, Noosa Heads; cocktails from $19; ☺ 11.30am-midnight; ☎) Award-winning Miss Moneypenny's sets a sophisticated scene for languid toasts. Well-crafted cocktails fall into numerous categories, from Seasonals and Sours to tongue-in-cheek '80s Cruise Ship Drinks. Not that irony gets in the way of quality: even the piña colada is shaken with original Coco Lopez coconut cream. Nosh includes posh bar bites and pizzas ($19 to $31), served till late.

🔒 Shopping

Noosa Farmers Market MARKET
(www.noosafarmersmarket.com.au; Noosa Australian Football Club Grounds, 155 Weyba Rd, Noosaville; ☺ 6am-noon Sun) Whet your appetite at this wonderful weekly ode to all things fresh and artisanal. Bag organic veggies, aromatic herbs, local seafood, meats and olives, condiments, crusty bread, aromatic skincare and more. Look out for **Cedar Street Cheeserie**; its buffalo mozzarella is coveted by several leading restaurants. You'll also find international street food, good coffee and live music to bop to.

Thomas Surfboards FASHION & ACCESSORIES
(http://thomassurfboards.com; 4 Project Ave, Noosaville; ☺ 7am-5pm Mon-Wed & Fri, to 9pm Thu, to 3pm Sat; ☎) Behind glass panels, Thomas makes Noosa's finest surfboards, both ready-to-ride and custom made. It also stocks its own fashion label, alongside niche street- and surf-wear brands like McTavish and The Snake Hole. There's an in-house cafe-bar here, along with a hipster barber called **Captain Sip Sop's**, plus a gallery space with rotating exhibitions of surf-oriented art, both local and international.

Noosa Longboards SPORTS & OUTDOORS
(☑ 07-5447 4776; www.noosalongboards.com; 2/55 Hastings St, Noosa Heads; ☺ 9am-5pm) Established in 1994, this iconic brand was one of the first to sell traditional-style longboards at the beginning of the longboard renaissance in Oz. Two decades on, it's fa-

mous for handcrafting them with a contemporary twist. Boards aside, the shop stocks its own quality beachwear label, threads from veteran Aussie label Okanui, as well as authentic, vintage Hawaiian shirts.

ℹ Information

POST

Post Office (☑ 13 13 18; www.auspost.com.au; 91 Noosa Dr, Noosa Junction; ☺ 9am-5pm Mon-Fri, to 12.30pm Sat) In Noosa Junction.

TOURIST INFORMATION

Noosa Visitor Information Centre (☑ 07-5430 5000; www.visitnoosa.com.au; 61 Hastings St, Noosa Heads; ☺ 9am-5pm; ☎) Helpful tourist office covering Noosa and surrounds. Free wi-fi too.

Noosa National Park Information Centre (☑ 07-5447 3522; ☺ 9.15am-4.45pm) At the entrance to Noosa National Park, this information centre offers trail maps and information on the park's flora and fauna, as well as a black-board listing the morning's koala sightings. Also sells provisions, including water, snacks and sunscreen.

ℹ Getting There & Away

Long-distance bus services stop at the **Noosa Junction Bus Station** on Sunshine Beach Rd. Greyhound Australia (p526) has several daily bus connections from Brisbane to Noosa (from $28, 2¼ to three hours), while Premier Motor Service (p348) has one ($24, 2½ hours).

Most hostels have courtesy pick-ups.

Sunbus (p348) operates frequent services from Noosa to Maroochydore ($9.10, 1¼ hours) and Nambour train station ($9.10, 1¼ hours). Journeys to Nambour may require a transfer in Maroochydore. TransLink Go Cards are valid on these services.

ℹ Getting Around

BICYCLE

Bike On Australia (p350) rents out bicycles from several locations in Noosa, including the Noosa River Holiday Park (p351) in Noosaville and Flashpackers (p351) in Sunshine Beach. Alternatively, bikes can be delivered to and from your door for $35 (or free if the booking is over $100).

BOAT

Noosa Ferry (p350) operates ferries between Noosa Heads and Tewantin several times a day (all-day pass adult/child $25/10). **Noosa Water Taxi** (☑ 0411 136 810; www.noosawatertaxi. com; 15min hire up to 6 guests $60; ☺ 9am-late) operates a water-taxi service around

Noosa Sound from 9am to late; call or text to book. The service is also available for private charters.

BUS
Sunbus (p348) has local services that link Noosa Heads, Noosaville, Noosa Junction and Tewantin. TransLink Go Cards can be used on these services.

CAR & MOTORCYCLE
Most of the major car-rental brands can be found in Noosa; rentals start at around $70 per day.
Noosa Car Rentals (☐ 0429 053 728; www. noosacarrentals.com.au)
Scooter Mania (☐ 0404 086 462; www.scootermania.com.au; 6/24hr from $45/70)

Bribie Island
POP 18,190

Known as Yarun ('hunting ground') to the island's original inhabitants, the Joondoobarrie people, Bribie Island lies at the northern end of Moreton Bay. The only island in the bay linked to the mainland by bridge, Bribie today is a sedate place, popular with young families and retirees looking for a waterfront holiday or home. While it's far more developed than Stradbroke and Moreton Islands, the island does harbour some beautiful, sweeping sandy beaches.

🛏 Sleeping & Eating

Bribie Island National Park Camping   CAMPGROUND $
(☐13 74 68; www.npsr.qld.gov.au/parks/bribie-island; campsites per person $6.65) On the island's west coast, **Poverty Creek** is a large, grassy campground; facilities include toilets, a waste disposal facility and cold showers. Just south, **Ocean Beach** offers similar facilities. On the east coast, the **Gallagher Point** camping area has a few bush campsites, with no toilets or other facilities. All three sites are accessible by 4WD.

On the Beach Resort   APARTMENT $$$
(☐07-3400 1400; www.onthebeachresort.com. au; 9 North St, Woorim; apt from $220; ❄❄) This place out-luxes anything else on the island, with reliable service and great facilities, including a saltwater pool. Apartments are modern, bright and breezy, with fully equipped kitchens and laundry facilities. There's usually a two-night minimum stay that increases to a four-night minimum stay during the Christmas and Easter holiday periods.

Sandstone Point Hotel   PUB FOOD $$
(☐07-3475 3001; https://sandstonepointhotel. com.au; 1800 Bribie Island Rd, Sandstone Point; mains $24-39; ☺8am-9pm, to 9.30pm Sat; ⚹⛾) The best place to eat round here is on the mainland side of the bridge. This sprawling, modern waterfront pub is divided into numerous bars and dining areas, including a spacious outdoor deck. Good-quality, globally inspired bites range from breakfast egg-based classics to graze-friendly oysters, charcuterie boards and pizzas, and more substantial grilled steaks and seasonal Australian seafood dishes.

ℹ Information

Bribie Island Visitor Information Centre
(☐07-3408 9026; http://visitbribieisland.com. au; Benabrow Ave, Bellara; ☺9am-4pm) Pick up maps featuring 4WD tracks, camping sites and more.

ℹ Getting There & Away
There is no 4WD hire on Bribie, and you'll need a vehicle access permit ($53.50 per week) for the island's more off-track spots. Pick up one at **Surfside Newsagency** (☐07-3408 1796; 1/10 North St, Woorim; ☺6.30am-5pm Mon-Fri, to 2.30pm Sat & Sun), **Gateway Bait & Tackle** (☐07-5497 5253; www.gatewaybaitand-tackle.com.au; 1383 Bribie Island Rd, Ningi; ☺5.30am-5pm, to 2pm Wed, 4.30am-5pm Sat, 4.30am-3pm Sun) or online (https://parks.des. qld.gov.au).

Frequent Citytrain services run from Brisbane to Caboolture, from where **Bribie Island Coach-**

CABOOLTURE TREASURES

Caboolture lies about 64km or one hour's drive north of Brisbane on the Bruce Hwy (M1). Though it is gradually being engulfed by suburbia, the once-rural town has a couple of interesting museums worth seeking out.

The impressive and surprising **Abbey Museum** (✆07-5495 1652; www.abbeymuseum.com.au; 63 The Abbey Pl, off Old Toorbul Point Rd, Caboolture; adult/child $12/7; ⊙10am-4pm Mon-Sat) houses an eclectic collection of art and archaeology that spans some 500,000 years. Once the private collection of Englishman 'Reverend' John Ward, the pieces include neolithic tools, ancient earthenware, sculpture and burial artefacts from across the Mediterranean, medieval manuscripts, and even an ancient Greek foot-guard (one of only four worldwide).

The neighbouring **church** has more original stained glass from Winchester Cathedral than is actually left in England. Free guided tours of the church run at 11am on Tuesday and Thursday (staff and availability permitting). In July, Australia's largest **medieval festival** (✆07-5495 1652; www.abbeymedievalfestival.com; Abbey Museum, 63 The Abbey Pl, Caboolture; ⊙Jul; ♿) is held on the grounds.

The Abbey Museum is on the road to Bribie Island, 6km from the Bruce Hwy turn-off. At the turn-off is the Caboolture Airfield and the **Caboolture Warplane Museum** (✆07-5499 1144; www.caboolturewarplanemuseum.com; Hangar 104, Caboolture Airfield, McNaught Rd, Caboolture; adult/child $10/5; ⊙9am-3pm). The museum, a must-see for aircraft enthusiasts and those interested in Australia's aviation history, houses a booty of restored WWII warplanes, including a P51D Mustang, CAC Wirraway and Cessna Bird Dog. All in flying order, they are accompanied by a collection of aircraft engines and wartime memorabilia.

es (✆07-3408 2562; www.bribiecoaches.com.au) route 640 runs to Bribie Island via Ningi and Sandstone Point. Buses run roughly every hour, stopping in Bongaree and continuing through to Woorim. Regular Brisbane TransLink bus fares apply (one way from central Brisbane $12).

Glass House Mountains

The Glass House Mountains rise abruptly from the plains 30km southwest of Caboolture. Australia's finest example of an eroded central volcano complex, they are listed on the National Heritage Register.

The traditional owners, the Jinibara people and Kabi Kabi (Gubbi Gubbi) people, have inhabited the area for millennia. According to Dreaming legend, these looming volcanic plugs – formed some 24 to 27 million years ago – are a family of mountain spirits. To British explorer James Cook, their shapes recalled the conical glass-making furnaces of his native Yorkshire. Not surprisingly, they have inspired countless artists and writers.

The Glass House Mountains National Park is broken into several sections (all close to Beerwah), with picnic grounds and lookouts but no campgrounds. The peaks themselves are reached by a series of roads, some unsealed, that head inland from Steve Irwin Way, itself home to Australia Zoo, founded by the world-famous Crocodile Hunter.

The easiest and most stunning panoramic viewing point of the Glass House Mountains is the **Glass House Mountains Lookout** (Glasshouse-Woodford Rd; ♿), 9km from the visitor information centre. The lookout includes BBQ facilities and toilets. On clear days, you can even (just) see the Brisbane skyline.

Hikers are spoilt for choice in the Glass House Mountains National Park, which offers a series of graded, signposted walking tracks. Detailed information on the various trails can be obtained at the helpful **Glass House Mountains Visitor & Interpretive Centre** (✆07-5458 8848; www.visitsunshinecoast.com.au; cnr Bruce Pde & Reed St; ⊙9am-4pm; 🛜).

Accommodation in the immediate area is relatively limited, with worthy options including luxe **Glass on Glasshouse** (✆07-5496 9608, 0431 101 208; www.glassonglasshouse.com.au; 182 Glasshouse-Woodford Rd; cottages incl breakfast $325-425; ❄🛜) and quirky **Glass House Mountains Ecolodge** (✆07-5493 0008; www.glasshouseecolodge.com; 198 Barrs Rd; r from $128; ❄🛜) 🖊.

Campers can pitch their tent (or park their caravan) at the basic **Coochin Creek Camping Area** (https://qpws.usedirect.com/qpws; off Roys Rd, Beerwah State Forest; per person $6.65) in nearby Beerwah State Forest. The Glass House Mountains are an easy day trip from Brisbane and the Sunshine Coast, where you'll find a plethora of accommodation options.

The tiny town of Glasshouse Mountains is home to a small supermarket and a handful of eateries, including the **Glasshouse Mountains Tavern** (07-5493 0933; 10 Reed St; mains $13-28; 10am-8.30pm, to midnight Fri, to 9.30pm Sat, kitchen closes 2-5.30pm), where you can get a decent meal. It also has a train station on the North Coast line with regular connections to Brisbane (see https://translink.com.au).

Caloundra

POP 51,095

Straddling a headland at the southern end of the Sunshine Coast, once sleepy Caloundra has reinvented itself as a centre of cool. Beyond its golden beaches, water sports and beautiful **Coastal Pathway** is a low-key creative scene, spanning top-notch coffee shops and bars to impressive street art and a microbrewery, not to mention the coast's most sharply curated regional art galleries. The cherry on top of the proverbial cake is the Caloundra Music Festival one of Queensland's biggest, best-loved annual music events.

Sights & Activities

Caloundra's main draw are its beaches – they curve around the headland so you'll always find a sheltered beach no matter how windy it gets. **Bulcock Beach** captures a good wind tunnel, making it popular with kitesurfers. There's an appealing foreshore promenade that extends around to family-friendly **Kings Beach**, home to a free saltwater swimming pool on the rocks. The Coastal Pathway continues around the headland to **Point Cartwright**. Depending on the conditions, **Moffat Beach** ('Moffs' to the locals) and **Dicky Beach** have the best surf breaks; Moffat Beach is the choice hang-out for local surfies and hipsters, and especially popular for Sunday brunch or afternoon drinks.

The town's small but excellent **regional art gallery** (07-5420 8299; http://gal-lery.sunshinecoast.qld.gov.au; 22 Omrah Ave; 10am-4pm Tue-Fri, to 2pm Sat & Sun) FREE is located a short walk north of Bulcock St, Caloundra's main shopping strip.

Queensland Air Museum MUSEUM
(07-5492 5930; www.qam.com.au; 7 Pathfinder Dr; adult/child $20/10; 10am-4pm) Occupying two hangars beside Caloundra airport, the volunteer-run QAM houses about 100 civilian and military aircraft, including a mid-century Douglas DC-3 (the world's first mass-produced all-metal airliner) and a supersonic F-111 fighter jet belonging to the Royal Australian Air Force.

Caloundra Surf School SURFING
(0413 381 010; www.caloundrasurfschool.com.au; 1½hr lessons from $50) The pick of the local surf schools, with board hire also available. Depending on conditions, lessons may take place at Happy Valley, Currimundi Beach or Dicky Beach.

Caloundra Jet Ski BOATING
(0434 330 660; www.caloundrajetski.com.au; The Esplanade; rides $150-280) Affable, joke-cracking local Ken Jeffrey owns and operates these thrilling jet-ski tours of the Pumicestone Passage, the narrow waterway separating Caloundra and the northern tip of Bribie Island. Ken and his jet skis can be found on the boardwalk opposite the corner of the Esplanade and Otranto Ave.

Sunshine Coast Skydivers SKYDIVING
(07-3067 0715, 1300 759 348; www.sunshinecoastskydivers.com.au; Caloundra Aerodrome, 1 Pathfinder Dr; tandem jumps from $230) Send your adrenaline into overdrive as you plummet towards Caloundra and the Pacific Ocean from 4300m.

Festivals & Events

Caloundra Music Festival MUSIC
(www.caloundramusicfestival.com; Sep-Oct) A four-day, family-friendly music festival held at Kings Beach, with 40,000-strong crowds and a diverse line-up of entertainment, featuring prolific current and veteran Australian rock, indie pop, blues and soul acts, as well as international guests.

Sleeping & Eating

Dicky Beach Family Holiday Park CARAVAN PARK $
(07-5491 3342; www.sunshinecoastholidayparks.com.au; 4 Beerburrum St; camp sites from $43, cabins from $161;) You can't get any

NOOSA & THE SUNSHINE COAST CALOUNDRA

Caloundra

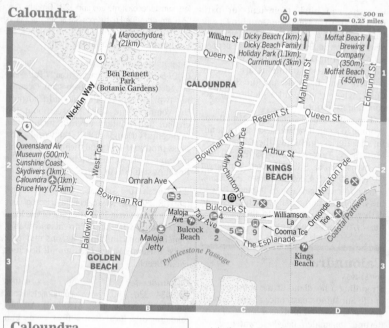

Caloundra

closer to Dicky, one of Caloundra's most popular beaches. The brick cabins are as ordered and as tidy as the grounds and there's a tennis court, as well as a small swimming pool for the kids.

Caloundra Backpackers HOSTEL $
(☎07-5499 7655; www.caloundrabackpackers.
com.au; 84 Omrah Ave; dm from $28, d with/with-

out bathroom from $80/70; ☎) Caloundra's only hostel is a no-nonsense budget option with a sociable courtyard and free weekly BBQ. The place is looking a little tired, however, the six- and three-bed dorms are clean, there's a decent kitchen and free use of SUPs, surfboards and bicycles.

Monaco APARTMENT $$
(☎07-5490 5490; www.monacocaloundra.com.au; 12 Otranto Ave; apt from $180; P❋☎❀) Modern, good-sized apartments one block from Bulcock Beach. They're individually owned, so styles vary; the more expensive apartments offer full water vistas. Wi-fi is free but capped, and apartments are serviced every eight days. Property perks include a stylish, heated lap pool, separate kids' pool, spa, sauna, gym and games rooms. Minimum two-night stay, with cheaper rates for longer stays.

★Rumba Resort RESORT $$$
(☎07-5492 0555; www.rumbaresort.com.au; 10 Leeding Tce; r from $235; P❋☎❀) This sparkling white playground is one of the slickest slumber pads in town. Studio rooms are light, spacious and modern, each with high-quality mattresses, two-person Jacuzzi, home-theatre system and fully equipped kitchen. The pool area is worthy of a photo

shoot, with two heated pools and a flanking bar. Easy walking access to the beachfront to boot.

Green House Cafe VEGETARIAN $

(☑ 07-5438 1647; www.greenhousecafe.com.au; 5/8 Orumuz Ave; mains $10-18; ⊙8am-3pm, to 2pm Sat & Sun; ✍⚫) A showcase for local ingredients, this chilled laneway spot serves up fresh, organic and filling vegetarian grub such as avocado on sourdough with either cashew cheese or herbed feta. Or there's crunchy waffles with seasonal fresh fruit and coconut nutmeg ice cream. Lighter bites and baked treats are also available, alongside virtuous smoothies, cold-pressed juices, kombucha and Hinterland-roasted organic coffee.

Dom's at Kings ITALIAN $$

(☑ 07-5492 8889; www.domsatkings.com; 4/79 Edmund St, Kings Beach; mains $15-29; ⊙kitchen 7.30-10.30am, 11.45am-1.45pm & 5.30-7.30pm) Sometimes you just want a traditional thin-crust pizza or well-balanced pasta in a noisy, bustling Italian joint with few pretensions, a decent wine list and espresso *perfetto*. Dom's fits the bill. Hearty breakfasts are also available. Enter from Ormonde Tce.

Kings Beach Bar AUSTRALIAN $$

(☑ 07-5341 8475; www.kingsbeachbar.com.au; 1/8 Levuka Ave, Kings Beach; meals $17-24; ⊙6am-5pm, to 9pm Wed-Sat, to 8pm Sun, kitchen closes earlier; 🛜⚫) This chilled, Kings Beach-front cafe serves tasty cafe fare and good coffee. Morning options might include poached peaches with berry labneh or gluten-free granola and caramelised fennel, while the lunch and dinner repertoire includes fish tacos, poke bowls, an excellent seafood linguine, and various burgers, among them a roast-pumpkin and halloumi burger with spinach, pickled slaw and house-made tomato chutney. Live music Thursday and Sunday.

🍷 Drinking & Nightlife

Moffat Beach Brewing Company MICROBREWERY

(☑ 07-5491 4023; www.moffatbeachbrewingco.beer; 12 Seaview Tce, Moffat Beach; ⊙7am-4pm Mon, to 8pm Tue, to late Wed-Sun) This award-winning microbrewery offers a rotating cast of house brews on tap, from a cult-status double IPA Iggy Hop to a vanilla latte stout. There's a four-brew paddle ($20) for the curious, as well as low-alco-

hol and gluten-free bottled beers. Breakfast, lunch and dinner are served. Live tunes add atmosphere on Thursday and Friday from 5pm, Saturday and Sunday from 4pm.

Lamkin Lane Espresso Bar CAFE

(www.facebook.com/lamkinlane; 31 Lamkin Lane; ⊙6am-4pm, 7am-noon Sat & Sun) The hearts of coffee snobs sing at minimalist Lamkin Lane, where affable baristas like nothing more than chatting about their two speciality blends and rotating trio of single origins (try their nuanced cold brew). The team here has a strong relationship with its coffee farmers, which means your brew is as ethical as it is smooth and aromatic.

ℹ️ Getting There & Away

The **Caloundra Transit Centre** (Caloundra Bus Interchange; 23 Cooma Tce) is the main bus station for both long-distance and local buses, a short walk south of Bulcock St.

Sunbus (p348) has frequent services between Caloundra and Maroochydore ($6, one hour). Transfer in Maroochydore for buses to Noosa ($6). TransLink Go Cards can be used on Sunbus services.

Mooloolaba & Maroochydore

Mooloolaba seduces many with its sublime climate, family-friendly beaches and resort lifestyle. Once a humble fishing village, it's now one of the Sunshine Coast's main holiday hubs – its lively esplanade and riverfront is lined with high-rises, cafes, bars, boutiques and restaurants. The town is also a launching pad for numerous activities and tours, including diving and snorkelling.

Further north, booming Maroochydore takes care of the business end, with a sprawling shopping centre, buzzing eateries and bars. It too claims a stretch of sandy beachfront.

◉ Sights & Activities

Sea Life Sunshine Coast AQUARIUM

(www.underwaterworld.com.au; Wharf Marina, Parkyn Pde, Mooloolaba; adult/child $40/28; ⊙9am-3pm; ⚫) Kids will love this tropical oceanarium, complete with an 80m-long transparent underwater tunnel for close-up views of rays, reef fish and several species of shark. There's interactive exhibits, live

Maroochydore

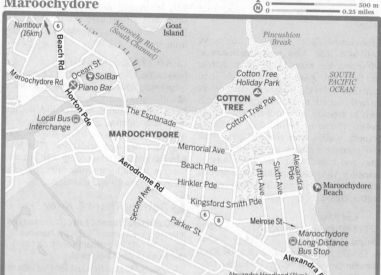

Nambour (16km)
Goat Island
Maroochy River (South Channel)
Pincushion Break
Beach Rd
Ocean St
SolBar
Piano Bar
Maroochydore Rd
Horton Pde
Cotton Tree Holiday Park
SOUTH PACIFIC OCEAN
COTTON TREE
Cotton Tree Pde
The Esplanade
Local Bus Interchange
MAROOCHYDORE
Memorial Ave
Beach Pde
Aerodrome Rd
Hinkler Pde
Fifth Ave
Sixth Ave
Alexandra Pde
Maroochydore Beach
Kingsford Smith Pde
Second Ave
Parker St
Melrose St
Maroochydore Long-Distance Bus Stop
Alexandra Pde
Alexandra Headland (1km); Oceans (2km); Spice Bar (2km); Mooloolaba (3km)

0 — 500 m
0 — 0.25 miles

shows, presentations and – during school holidays – the option of sleeping at the aquarium overnight ($99 per person). Book online for discounted admission.

While visitors can also swim with seals, it's worth considering that animal-welfare groups believe captivity is debilitating and stressful for marine animals and exacerbated by human interaction.

Sunreef DIVING
(☎07-5444 5656; www.sunreef.com.au; Shop 11-12, The Wharf, Parkyn Pde, Mooloolaba; dives from $99; ⊙8am-5pm, to 4pm Sun) This outfit offers numerous dives at the wreck of sunken warship HMAS *Brisbane,* including daytime double dives (from $165) and single night dives (from $99). It also runs a snorkelling day trip to Flinders Reef (from $199), which claims the highest number of coral species of any subtropical reef system along Australia's east coast. The trip includes equipment and lunch.

PADI Open Water Diver courses start at $649.

Sunreef Hire WATER SPORTS
(☎07-5444 5656; www.hirehut.com.au; Shop 11-12, The Wharf, Parkyn Pde, Mooloolaba; kayak/jet ski hire from $30/180) This operation hires out kayaks (first hour/additional hours $30/15),

SUPs ($30/15), jet skis (one hour $180) and boats (first hour/additional hours $60/30). It also hires out numerous types of bicycles (one hour/day $10/50), including mountain bikes, hybrids and kids' bikes.

Robbie Sherwell's XL Surfing Academy SURFING
(☎0423 039 505; www.xlsurfingacademy.com; Mooloolabah Beach; 1hr private/group lessons $100/50) Dip a toe into Aussie surf culture at this long-established school, headed by former surfing champion Robbie Sherwell, once ranked fifth in the world. The outfit caters to all levels, from rookie to advanced. Also uses neighbouring Alexandra Headland Beach.

⛵ Tours

Coastal Cruises Mooloolaba CRUISE
(☎0419 704 797; www.cruisemooloolaba.com.au; Wharf Marina, 123 Parkyn Pde, Mooloolaba; cruises from $35) Two-hour sunset and 1½-hour seafood lunch cruises through Mooloolaba Harbour, the river and canals.

Whale One WILDLIFE
(☎1300 942 531; www.whaleone.com.au; Shop 11-12, The Wharf, Parkyn Pde, Mooloolaba; whale-watching tours adult/child $75/55; 👶) Between June and early November, Whale One runs cruises that get you close to the

spectacular acrobatic displays of humpback whales, which migrate north from Antarctica to mate and give birth.

🎊 Festivals & Events

Big Pineapple
Music Festival   MUSIC
(www.bigpineapplemusicfestival.com; ☺May) The one-day 'Piney Festival' is one of the region's top music events, with four stages showcasing titans of the current Aussie music scene. Campsites and pre-pitched tents are available and sell out quickly.

🛏 Sleeping & Eating

Cotton Tree Holiday Park   CAMPGROUND $
(☑07-5459 9070; www.sunshinecoastholiday parks.com.au; Cotton Tree Pde, Cotton Tree, Maroochydore; campsites/villas from $58/223; 🛜) In this popular area of Maroochydore, Cotton Tree Holiday Park enjoys direct access to the beach and Maroochy River.

Facilities include BBQs and laundry. The one- and two-bedroom villas are air-conditioned; each has private kitchen, bathroom and linen supplied. Weekly rates are cheaper; see the website for details.

Mooloolaba Beach
Holiday Park   CARAVAN PARK $
(☑07-5444 1201; www.sunshinecoastholidayparks. com.au; Parkyn Pde, Mooloolaba; powered sites $55) A well-maintained property fronting beautiful Mooloolaba Beach, with powered caravan sites with concrete slabs as well as powered tent sites backing on to the sand dunes. Mooloolaba cafes, bars and eateries are a short walk away.

Kyamba Court Motel   MOTEL $$
(☑07-5444 0202; www.kyambacourtmotel.com. au; 94 Brisbane Rd, Mooloolaba; s/d from $99/110; P ❄ 🛜 ≋) Although this motel is on a busy road, the side fronts the canal and the clientele is not of the party-hardy kind. The motel's owners take pride in the property and the rooms, which are clean and nicely sized (except for smallish bathrooms). It's a short walk into town and to the beach. Free breakfast provisions, too. Great value.

Ring for a discount on multinight stays.

⭐ Oceans   RESORT $$$
(☑07-5444 5777; www.oceansmooloolaba.com. au; 101-105 Mooloolaba Esplanade, Mooloolaba; 2-/3-bedroom apt from $625/725; P ❄ 🛜 ≋) Cascading water greets guests at this superlative five-star apartment resort, directly across from the beach and in the heart of Mooloolaba. Ocean views are de rigueur in the apartments, which are sleek, sparklingly clean and contemporary, with spas and quality appliances. Apartments are serviced daily, with property perks including adults' and children's pools and a gym. Free parking and wi-fi.

Dockside Apartments   APARTMENT $$$
(☑07-5478 2044; www.docksidemooloolaba. com.au; 50 Burnett St, Mooloolaba; 2-/3-bedroom apt from $260/280; P ❄ 🛜 ≋) The fully equipped apartments here are all privately owned, meaning that decor and appeal can vary significantly. That said, you can expect neat, clean, comfortable digs and friendly management. It sits in a quiet spot away from the hubbub, but is an easy walk from Mooloolaba's main strip, surf club, beach and wharf precinct. Minimum two- to three-night stay.

⭐ Il Vento   ITALIAN $$
(☑07-5444 7849; www.facebook.com/ilventomool oolaba; The Wharf, 123 Parkyn Pde, Mooloolaba; pizzas $18-27, pasta & mains $25-37; ☺noon-2pm & 5-9pm, to 8.30pm Sun) Part of Mooloolaba's revamped Wharf, boisterous, bistro-style 'The Wind' has blown in proper, thin-crust pizzas made in a wood-fired oven, and homemade pasta (including gluten-free), such as *spaghetti con gamberetti* (with prawns, chilli and garlic). Wrap things up with the cannoli, filled fresh to order with sweetened ricotta and crumbed pistachio.

⭐ Velo Project   CAFE $$
(☑07-5444 8693; www.theveloproject.com. au; 19 Careela St, Mooloolaba; dishes $10-23; ☺7am-3pm; 🛜 🚲) A wonderful mishmash of recycled furniture and vintage ephemera, side-street Velo is an easy-going, breezy affair. Here, locals play board games while munching on date-and-macadamia compote with fresh banana, salted butterscotch and ice cream, or toasted ciabatta topped with Fraser Isle spanner crab, tomato salsa, asparagus, avocado and wasabi-and-turmeric mayo. Great, locally roasted coffee too.

Good Bar   AMERICAN $$
(☑07-5477 6781; www.thegoodbar.com.au; 5/19-23 First Ave, Mooloolaba; burgers $16-22; ☺11am-late) Tiles-and-concrete Good Bar serves quality American comfort food with craft beers, spirits and cocktails. Succulent and indulgent burgers dominate the menu, how-

Mooloolaba

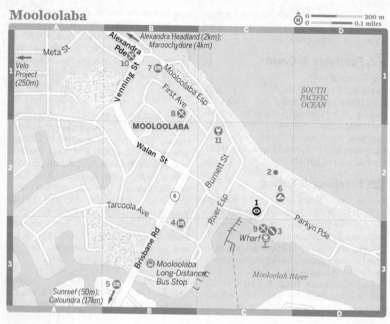

Mooloolaba

ever, there's also fried chicken, smokehouse ribs and a 20-hour smoked Cape Grim brisket. Weekly events include trivia on Tuesday nights, $12 burgers on Thursdays, and live tunes on Saturdays and Sundays.

Piano Bar MEDITERRANEAN $$
(0422 291 249; www.thepianobar.com.au; 22-24 Ocean St, Maroochydore; tapas $8-24; 5pm-late, from noon Fri & Sat) Bohemian down to its tasselled lampshades and Liberace tomes, Piano Bar peddles generously sized, pan-Mediterranean tapas (order one or two at a time). Try the pan-seared gnocchi with mushrooms and crispy pancetta, or the very tender charred marinated octopus. Selected

wine varietals plus live blues, funk or jazz Wednesday to Monday seal the deal.

★ **Spice Bar** FUSION $$$
(07-5444 2022; www.spicebar.com.au; 1st fl, 123 Mooloolaba Esplanade, Mooloolaba; small plates $16-18, large plates $28-36; noon-3pm & 6pm-late Wed-Sun) Slick, contemporary Spice Bar dishes up superb Asian-fusion fare. The menu is a share-plates affair, with highlights including Hervey Bay scallops, and an aromatic duck prepared using a six-year-old master stock. For a satisfying overview, opt for one of the degustation menus (five/seven/10 courses $59/79/95). A bar menu operates between 3pm and 6pm.

Drinking & Nightlife

Taps@Mooloolaba   BAR
(☏07-5477 7222; www.tapsaustralia.com.au; cnr Esplanade & Brisbane Rd, Mooloolaba; ☺noon-late) A beer fiend's nirvana, loud, buzzing Taps lets you pull your own beers. It may sound gimmicky, but it's serious business: there are almost 30 taps located throughout the venue, pouring craft and other brews to quench the most serious of post-surf thirsts. Sud-soaking bites include cream-cheese-stuffed jalapeños, burgers, loaded fries, wings and a taco salad.

SolBar   CLUB
(☏07-5443 9550; www.solbar.com.au; 10/12-20 Ocean St, Maroochydore; ☺10am-midnight Mon-Thu, to 3am Fri, 11am-3am Sat, to midnight Sun) SolBar is a godsend for city-starved indie fans, with a constantly surprising line-up taking to the stage (Friday, Saturday and Sunday), plus budding singer-songwriters testing their tunes on Wednesday's open-mic night. Thursday is trivia night. The venue doubles as a popular cafe-bar-restaurant, with discounted tap beers, house wine and cider from 5pm to 7pm. Food options include salads, risottos, burgers and pizzas.

ℹ Information

In Marcoola the Sunshine Coast Airport houses a **tourist information centre** (☏07-5448 9088; www.visitsunshinecoast.com.au; Sunshine Coast Airport, Friendship Dr, Marcoola; ☺9am-3pm; 🛜).

ℹ Getting There & Away

AIR

Sunshine Coast Airport (Maroochydore Airport; ☏07-5453 1500; www.sunshinecoastairport.com; Friendship Ave, Marcoola) Gateway airport for the Sunshine Coast, with direct daily flights to Sydney and Melbourne and thrice-weekly non-stop flights to Adelaide. Also hosts seasonal direct flights to Auckland, New Zealand. Once current expansion works are completed in late 2020, the airport is expected to introduce new international routes to Asia, the west Pacific and possibly Hawaii.

BUS

In Mooloolaba, the **bus stop** for long-distance buses is in front of the Mooloolaba Bowls Club on Brisbane Rd. In Maroochydore, the **bus stop** (Sixth Ave) is on Sixth Ave, a block back from the beach. Maroochydore is also the main interchange hub for local buses heading either north or south along the Sunshine Coast or further inland. The **interchange station** (Horton Pde, Maroochydore) is outside Sunshine Plaza shopping centre.

Greyhound Australia (p526) buses run several times daily to Brisbane (departing Mooloolaba/Maroochydore from $24/25, 1¼ to 2¾ hours).

Premier Motor Service (p348) runs once daily to and from Brisbane (one way $24, 1½ hours).

Sunbus (p348) has frequent services between Mooloolaba and Maroochydore ($4.90, 20 minutes) and on to Noosa ($9.10, 55 to 80 minutes). TransLink Go Cards are valid on these services.

Coolum
POP 8500

Rocky headlands shelter a number of secluded coves before the coastline opens out onto the fabulously long stretch of golden sand and rolling surf of Coolum Beach. Like much of the coast along here, the backdrop is spreading suburbia, but Coolum remains a quieter option to the more popular and overcrowded holiday scenes at Mooloolaba and Maroochydore.

◉ Sights & Activities

Mt Coolum   MOUNTAIN
(https://parks.des.qld.gov.au/parks/mount-coolum; Tanah St West, Mt Coolum) Looming 4km south of Coolum Beach is Mt Coolum (208m), an ancient volcanic dome whose peak offers spectacular views of the Sunshine Coast and its hinterland. Mt Coolum is a favourite early-morning hiking spot for locals and visitors alike and responsible for many a toned calf muscle. From the car park, the walking trail (1.6km return) leads through open eucalypt forest, shrub and montane heath. There's a drinking fountain in the car park.

Coolum Surf School   SURFING
(☏0438 731 503; www.coolumsurfschool.com.au; Tickle Park, David Low Way, Coolum Beach; 2hr lesson $60) Coolum Surf School will have you riding the waves in no time. Instructors are friendly, enthusiastic and patient, so even the most awkward of rookies won't feel embarrassed. The outfit also hires out surfboards/bodyboards (from $30/15 for a day).

🛏 Sleeping & Eating

Coolum Beach

Holiday Park   CARAVAN PARK $
(✆07-5446 1474; www.sunshinecoastholiday
parks.com.au; 1827 David Low Way, Coolum
Beach; powered sites from $48, cabins from
$163; ❄🐾) Location, location, location:
this dog-friendly park (excluding cabins)
not only fronts a patrolled beach, but is
also across the road from Coolum's main
restaurant and cafe strip. Communal facilities include showers, a camp kitchen with
TV, fridge, hotplates and BBQs, as well as
laundries.

Coolum Seaside   RESORT $$$
(✆07-5455 7200; www.coolumseaside.com; 6-8
Perry St, Coolum Beach; studio/apt from $200/210;
P🅿❄@❄🏊) Two blocks from the surf, this
immaculately maintained, spacious resort
has three pools, a tennis court, BBQs and a
small gym. The studios and one-, two- and
three-bedroom apartments are wonderful-
ly spacious; the apartments feature fully
equipped kitchen and laundry facilities.

Element on Coolum Beach   APARTMENT $$$
(✆07-5455 1777; www.elementoncoolumbeach.
com.au; 1808 David Low Way, Coolum Beach; apt
from $220; P🅿❄❄🏊) Coolum Beach's smart-
est digs features a heated pool, central location and 49 huge, stylish apartments. Each
apartment is individually owned, so interiors will vary. Expect them to be spotless and
fully equipped with contemporary design
in soothing neutral tones, and floor-to-ceiling windows leading out to a wide balcony.
Rates come down for week-long stays; minimum two-night stay.

The Caf   CAFE $$
(✆07-5446 3564; www.thecafcoolum.com;
21 Birtwill St, Coolum Beach; mains $15-20;
⏱6.30am-4pm; ❄🐾) Off the main drag, this
relaxed cafe has pleasant, shaded seating
and whips up creative, feel-good fare. The
menu is always changing, but expect veg
and vegan bowls, salads with seared tuna,
great all-day breakfasts, and a share plate of
delicious nibbles. Drinks include smoothies,
juices, wine, bottled beers and cocktails.

Castro's Bar & Restaurant   MEDITERRANEAN $$
(✆07-5471 7555; cnr Frank St & Beach Rd,
Coolum Beach; pizzas $22-26, mains $25-36;
⏱5-8.30pm, to 9pm Fri & Sat, to 8pm Sun) Although not even vaguely Cuban, this popular, casual spot does enjoy a Fidel-like
longevity thanks to its mouth-watering

repertoire of mainly Mediterranean dishes. Tuck into satisfying wood-fired pizzas,
gorgeous risottos, or surrender to Castro's
slow-cooked confit duck, wood-fired and
served with roast potatoes and poached
pear stuffed with date chutney.

Peregian Beach & Sunshine Beach

The low-rise, low-key beach suburbs of Peregian Beach and Sunshine Beach punctuate
a 15km stretch of uncrowded, unobstructed
beach that shoots north from Coolum to the
rocky headland of Noosa National Park.

At the southern end, Peregian Beach is
all about long, solitary beach walks, excellent surf breaks and the not-so-uncommon
spotting of whales offshore. It's also popular with locals catching up at breezy cafes
with yoga mats in tow. Further north, the
laid-back-latte ethos and burgeoning foodie scene of Sunshine Beach attracts Noosa
locals and surfies escaping the migrating
summer hordes. On the beach itself, sandy
walks morph into bush trails over the headland, leading to the wild sweep of Alexan-
dria Bay and, further on, Noosa's Laguna
Bay. Road access to Noosa National Park is
from McAnally Dr or Parkedge Rd in Sunshine Beach.

✕ Eating & Drinking

★Le Bon Delice   CAFE $
(✆07-5471 2200; www.facebook.com/lebondeli
cepatisserie; cnr Heron St & David Low Way, Peregian Beach; pastries from $4, ice cream from $5,
lunch $12-22; ⏱7am-4.30pm Mon & Wed-Sat, to
2.30pm Sun; 🐾) From the tarts and eclairs
to the *dacquoises* (made with almond and
hazelnut meringue), the calorific concoctions from French-born owner and *pâtis-
sier* Jean Jacques are as beautiful as they
are delicious. Jean's cult-status millefeuille
(French vanilla slice) is only available on
Thursdays and usually sells out by noon.
Excellent homemade ice cream and sorbets
too. Lunch bites include quiches.

Also opens on Tuesdays during the school
holidays.

★Sum Yung Guys   ASIAN $$
(✆07-5324 1391; www.sumyungguys.com.au;
8/46 Duke St, Sunshine Beach; dishes $22-39;
⏱noon-2.30pm & 5-11.30pm) Flavours explode
and thrill at this fun and popular place,
co-owned by 2016 *Masterchef Australia*

runner-up Matt Sinclair. He's usually in the kitchen, whipping up knockout dishes inspired by the tang, heat and intrigue of Southeast Asia. The result: anything from cuttlefish with green mango, lemongrass and betel leaf, to chargrilled chicken with green chilli and a sesame-and-ginger cream.

The naan bread and cocktails are equally impressive. Booking well ahead is advised. The last sitting for dinner is at 8.30pm.

Embassy XO　　　　　　　CHINESE $$$
(☑07-5455 4460; www.embassyxo.com.au; 56 Duke St, Sunshine Beach; mains $38-48; ⊙3-9.30pm Wed & Thu, from noon Fri-Sun) Embassy XO is not your average suburban Chinese joint, with a smashing wine list and quality produce driving dishes such as 12-hour poached pork belly, and steamed Coral Coast barramundi. Other options include gorgeous five-course banquets ($72, vegetarian available), yum cha banquet lunches ($38) Friday to Sunday, and bar snacks from 3pm.

Pitchfork　　　　　MODERN AUSTRALIAN $$$
(☑07-5471 3697; www.pitchforkrestaurant.com. au; 5/4 Kingfisher Dr, Peregian Beach; mains $28-36; ⊙noon-2pm & 5pm-late Tue-Sun; ☑) The award-winning chefs at this bright, casually chic restaurant – flanking Peregian Beach's lush green square – pump out a concise, seasonal, contemporary menu. You might find grilled peach with prosciutto, goat's curd, basil and candied walnut, or the day's fresh fish served in a coconut-and-lemongrass broth accompanied by a green papaya salad. Vegetarian menu available.

Marble Bar Bistro　　　　　　　　BAR
(☑07-5455 3200; www.marblebarbistro.com; 40 Duke St, Sunshine Beach; ⊙noon-9pm, to midnight Fri & Sat; ☑) Kick back in a cushioned lounge or perch at one of the concrete bar tables at this sheltered, al-fresco bar. Bites include tapas ($10 to $20) and pizzas ($18 to $20), though the place is probably best for a drink rather than a memorable feed.

Cooloola Coast

Stretching for 50km between Noosa and Rainbow Beach, the Cooloola Coast is a remote strip of long sandy beach backed by the Cooloola Section of the Great Sandy National Park. Although it's undeveloped, the 4WD and tin-boat set flock here in droves, so it's not always as peaceful as you might imagine. If you head off on foot or by canoe

along one of the many inlets or waterways, however, you'll soon escape the crowds. The coast is famous for the **Teewah coloured sand cliffs**, estimated to be about 40,000 years old.

Great Sandy National Park: Cooloola Section

Extending from Lake Cootharaba north to Rainbow Beach, this 54,000 hectare section of **national park** (www.australiasna turecoast.com) offers wide ocean beaches, soaring cliffs of richly coloured sands, pristine bushland, heathland, mangroves and rainforest, all of which are rich in bird life, including rarities such as the red goshawk and the grass owl. One of the most extraordinary experiences here is driving along the beach from Noosa North Shore to Double Island Point, around 50km to the north.

The route is only accessible to 4WDs with a vehicle permit (available from www.npsr. qld.gov.au) and forms part of the **Great Beach Drive**, a spectacular coastal touring route linking Noosa and Hervey Bay. At Double Island Point, a 1.1km-long **walking trail** leads up to spectacular ocean views and a lighthouse dating back to 1884. From June to October, it's also a prime place for spotting majestic **humpback whales**.

From the Double Island Point section of the beach, a 4WD track cuts across the point to the edge of a large tidal lake (perfect for kids and less confident swimmers) and then along Rainbow Beach to the town of Rainbow Beach, passing along the way spectacular coloured cliffs made of ancient, richly oxidised sands in over 70 earthy shades. According to local Indigenous legend, the sands obtained their hues when Yininigie (a spirit represented by a rainbow) plunged into the cliffs after fighting an evil tribesman. The black sand is rutile, once locally mined to make titanium for American space technology.

Great Beach Drive aside, another memorable way to explore the national park is by boat or canoe along the numerous tributaries of the Noosa River. Boats can be hired from Tewantin and Noosa (along Gympie Tce), Boreen Point and Elanda Point on Lake Cootharaba.

There are also some fantastic walking trails starting from Elanda Point on the shore of Lake Cootharaba, including the

WOODSTOCK DOWN UNDER

The **Woodford Folk Festival** (www.woodfordfolkfestival.com; ⊙Dec-Jan;) draws around 135,000 people each year with its bumper program of music and culture. It includes over 2000 national and international performers, playing everything from folk and world music, to Indigenous music, indie rock and electro, as well as buskers, cabaret performers, belly dancers, arts and craft workshops, visual-arts performances, environmental talks and more.

The festival is held at Woodfordia, a property near the town of Woodford, from 27 December to 1 January each year. Camping grounds are set up on site with toilets, showers and a range of foodie marquees, but prepare for a mud bath if it rains. The festival is licensed, so leave your booze at home. Tickets purchased online cost $130 ($150 at the gate) per day, or $537 ($600 at the gate) for the season, with camping an additional $35 per night or $120 for the season. Discounted rates apply for attendees aged 17 and under. Check online for programmes and the latest prices.

Woodford is 35km northwest of Caboolture. Shuttle buses run regularly from the Caboolture train station to and from the festival grounds.

46km **Cooloola Wilderness Trail** to Rainbow Beach and a 7km trail to Kinaba.

Great Beach Drive 4WD Tours (☑07-5486 3131; www.greatbeachdrive4wdtours.com; tours adult/child $195/120;) offers intimate, eco-centric 4WD tours of the spectacular Great Beach Drive from Noosa to Rainbow Beach. Epic Ocean Adventures (p383) runs adventure tours departing both Rainbow Beach and Noosa, and including dolphin- and turtle-spotting kayaking trips.

Hoof it along the beach with **Rainbow Beach Horse Rides** (☑0412 174 337; www.rainbowbeachhorserides.com.au; Clarkson Dr; rides from $185), options include an evocative, two-hour Full Moon Ride ($250).

The most popular (and best-equipped) camping grounds are **Fig Tree Point** (☑13 74 68; https://parks.des.qld.gov.au/parks/cooloola/camping; sites per person $6.65), at the northern end of Lake Cootharaba; **Harry's** (sites per person $6.65), about 4km upstream; and **Freshwater** (sites per person $6.65), about 8km south of Double Island Point. You can also camp at designated zones on the beach if you're driving up to Rainbow Beach.

Rainbow Beach Ultimate Camping (☑0419 464 254; www.rainbow-beach-hire-a-camp.com.au; per minimum 2-night stay incl permit from $731) takes all the hard work out of camping by providing most of the equipment and setting it up for you, from the tent, mattresses, stretchers and crockery, to the dining table, BBQ, private toilet and shower.

The **QPWS Great Sandy Information Centre** (☑07-5449 7792; 240 Moorindil St, Tewantin; ⊙7.30am-3.30pm) provides information on park access, tide times and fire bans within the park. The centre also issues car and camping permits for both Fraser Island and the Great Sandy National Park, but these are cheaper if booked online via https://parks.des.qld.gov.au.

Lake Cooroibah

A couple of kilometres north of Tewantin, the Noosa River widens into Lake Cooroibah. Surrounded by bushland, the glassy, relatively shallow lake is an idyllic spot to push out a canoe or kayak and relish the silence.

Noosa North Shore Retreat (☑07-5447 1225; www.noosanorthshoreretreat.com.au; Beach Rd, Noosa North Shore; camp sites from $32, tent/r/cottage from $130/140/170;) has everything from camp sites and permanent 'village tents' to motel rooms and cottages, along with the Great Sandy Bar & Restaurant (mains $20 to $28).

ⓘ Getting There & Away

From the end of Moorindil St in Tewantin, cash-only **Noosa North Shore Ferries** (☑07-5447 1321; www.noosanorthshoreferries.com.au; one way pedestrian/car $1/7; ⊙5.30am-10.20pm, to 12.20am Fri & Sat) shuttle across the river to Noosa North Shore, from where the eastern shore of the lake is accessible. To reach the lake's western shore from Noosa, follow the signs to Tewantin and head west out of town on McKinnon Dr. Turn right into Lake Cooroibah Rd, which winds its way north towards the lake.

Lake Cootharaba & Boreen Point

Relatively shallow and warm, Cootharaba is the largest lake in the Cooloola Section of Great Sandy National Park, measuring about 5km in width and 10km in length.

Perched on its western shore is the sleepy hamlet of Boreen Point, home to one of Queensland's most atmospheric pubs, and remote Elanda Point. Lake Cootharaba is also the gateway to the glassy, ethereal Noosa Everglades (Great Sandy National Park: Cooloola Section). One of only two everglades systems in the world, the pristine wetlands make for an exceptional escape, with canoeing, bushwalking and tranquil bush camping all possibilities.

🏃 Activities

⭐ **Everglades Eco Safaris** CRUISE
(☑ 07-5485 3165; www.evergladesecosafaris.com.au; 204 Lake Flat Rd, Elanda Point; adult/child $130/90; ▣) This outfit runs fantastic boating tours of the Noosa Everglades. The Eco Safari cruise includes a boat trip with morning tea and lunch (meat-free options available on request) back at base, Habitatnoosa. Free shuttle-bus pick-up and drop-off from Noosa Heads and Noosaville.

Kanu Kapers KAYAKING
(☑ 07-5485 3328; www.kanukapersaustralia.com; 11 Toolara St, Boreen Point; guided tours adult/child from $189/105, self-guided tours from $99) Offers guided and self-guided day tours of the Noosa Everglades, as well two- and three-day kayaking and camping adventures (from $495) to Cooloola National Park. See the website for details of the tour meeting location (north of Boreen Point).

🛏 Sleeping & Eating

Boreen Point
Camping Ground CAMPGROUND $
(☑ 07-5485 3244; www.noosaholidayparks.com.au; Esplanade, Boreen Point; powered/unpowered camp sites from $36/30) On shallow Lake Cootharaba, this bucolic little camping ground dominated by large gum trees is usually crowd-free and provides your own secluded patch of lakefront, native bush. The closest major supermarket is in Tewantin, 20km away, so stock up on provisions before heading in; you will also need to bring your own water supply. Canoe rental available.

Habitatnoosa TENTED CAMP $
(☑ 07-5485 3165; www.habitatnoosa.com.au; 204 Lake Flat Rd, Elanda Point; camp sites from $33, permanent tent $150, en-suite tent $250) Flanked by the warm, shallow waters of Lake Cootharaba, this spacious camping ground includes powered and unpowered sites, plus roomy, basic tents that sleep four. Top billing goes to the glamping tents, equipped with stylish timber furniture, fridge, wine glasses and spacious en-suite bathrooms. Facilities include two kitchens, laundry, showers, kayak hire and a high-quality bistro-cum-microbrewery, **Cootharabar** (☑ 07-5447 1333; www.habitatnoosa.com.au/bistro-bar; Lake Flat Rd, Elanda Point; mains $24-42; ⊙ bar from 11am daily, kitchen noon-2pm Mon-Wed, noon-2pm & 6-8pm Thu-Sun; ▣).

Apollonian Hotel PUB FOOD $$
(☑ 07-5485 3100; www.apollonianhotel.com.au; 19 Laguna St, Boreen Point; mains $20-29; ⊙ 10am-9pm, to 10pm Fri, to 9.30pm Sat, to 6pm Sun; ▣) Framed by palms, jacarandas and quandong trees, this atmospheric pub – complete with shady verandahs and a beautifully preserved interior – dates back to the late 19th century. Moved here from its original Gympie location in 1985, the place is famous for its Sunday spit-roast lunch (bookings essential; adult/child $25/15), accompanied by live blues, bluegrass or jazz.

Eumundi

POP 2220

While the weatherboard pubs, broad verandahs and tin-roof cottages evoke classic rural Queensland, historic Eumundi has a quirky New Age vibe. The hilly hamlet is most famous for its Eumundi Markets, a twice-weekly, hippy-hearted sprawl of crafts, clothing, produce and artisanal bites, shaded under heritage-listed fig trees.

◉ Sights & Activities

⭐ **Eumundi Markets** MARKET
(☑ 07-5442 7106; www.eumundimarkets.com.au; 80 Memorial Dr; ⊙ 8am-1.30pm Wed, 7am-2pm Sat; ▣) This is one of Australia's most atmospheric artisan markets, attracting over 1.6-million visitors a year to its 600-plus stalls. Dive into a leafy, bohemian wonderland of hand-crafted furniture, jewellery, clothing and accessories, art, fresh local produce, gourmet provisions and more. Get

NOOSA & THE SUNSHINE COAST EUMUNDI

your muscles pummelled, your tarot cards read or simply tuck into a world's worth of street food, from *gözleme* (Turkish stuffed flatbread), empanadas and gyoza to local artisan pastries.

Majestic Theatre CINEMA
(☑ 07-5485 2330; www.themajestictheatre.com.au; 5 Factory St, Pomona; tickets adult/child $15/10; ⊙ screenings noon 2nd & 4th Sat of month; ⛶) The charming Majestic is the longest-running commercial theatre in Australia. The venue screens films from the silent era – complete with live accompaniment – twice a month. It also hosts other events, from screenings of modern film classics to live music; see the website. You'll find the theatre in the town of Pomona, roughly 10km northwest of Eumundi.

Tom Wegener Surfboards SURFING
(www.tomwegenersurfboards.com; Cooroy) Internationally renowned surfboard shaper Tom Wegener offers homestays where you can spend a day or two learning the craft of 'corky' surfboard shaping. (You can also have him make a fibreglass-free board for you.) The homestay in Cooroy, about 8km northwest of Eumundi, costs $350 per day (excluding materials) and includes eight hours in the studio, plus meals and surfing sessions. Book online two months in advance.

🛏 Sleeping & Eating

Harmony Hill B&B $
(☑ 0418 750 643, 07-5442 8685; www.airbnb. com.au/rooms/9636472; 81 Seib Rd; train carriage/homestead $95/100; 🕏🐨) This 12-acre, hilltop property includes a restored, self-contained 1912 railway carriage that sleeps up to four people, as well as a tastefully appointed, three-bedroom homestead with full kitchen. Communal perks include an outdoor pool, grazing kangaroos and gorgeous sunsets.

Eumundi Dairy GUESTHOUSE $$$
(https://eumundidairy.com.au; 33 Grasstree Rd; homestead/dairy per night $350/550; 🕏🕏) Expect to leave yearning for your own escape from the city at this 60-acre property, complete with grazing cows, Monet-style lily ponds and two self-contained holiday homes. The three-bedroom Queenslander homestead offers snug, carpeted rooms, a large wraparound verandah and winter fireplace. The four-bedroom converted dairy has a lighter, more contemporary feel. Minimum two-night stay; midweek deals available.

Imperial Hotel PUB FOOD $$
(☑ 07-5442 8811; www.imperialhoteleumundi. com.au; 1 Etheridge St; lunch $16-23, dinner mains $20-38; ⊙ 10am-10pm, to midnight Fri & Sat) An atmospheric, colonial-style pub with kooky bohemian touches, the Imperial is much-loved for its beer garden and live music acts. The tasty menu covers all bases, from chickpea-and-ricotta corn fritters to salt-and-pepper calamari, burgers, steaks, interesting salads and a graze-friendly cheese board. The place is also home to the **Eumundi Brewery** (☑ 07-5442 8811; www.imperialhotele umundi.com.au/eumundi-brewery; Imperial Hotel, 1 Etheridge St; ⊙ tours 11am, noon, 1pm & 2pm Wed & Sat), which runs behind-the-scenes tours (book these in advance).

⭐ Spirit House THAI $$$
(☑ 07-5446 8994; www.spirithouse.com.au; 20 Nindery Rd, Yandina; mains $38-52, banquet $80-115; ⊙ noon-3pm daily, 6-9pm Wed-Sat; ⛶) One of Queensland's top dining destinations (book well ahead for weekends), Spirit House evokes the deep jungles of Southeast Asia with its moody tropical setting and sophisticated Thai-inspired menu. Savour honey and clove-spiced chicken with cashew puree and papaya salad, or whole crispy fish with chilli tamarind sauce.

Its casual **Hong Sa Bar** serves impressive cocktails and sharing platters, and the restaurant also runs a **cooking school** (four-hour classes from $150). Yandina is 11km south of Eumundi.

❶ Information

Discover Eumundi Heritage & Visitor Centre
(☑ 07-5442 8762; www.discovereumundi. com; 73 Memorial Dr; ⊙ 10am-3pm Mon-Fri, to 2pm Sat) Also houses the town's compact and interesting local history museum.

SUNSHINE COAST HINTERLAND

Inland from Nambour, the **Blackall Range** forms a stunning backdrop to the Sunshine Coast's beaches a short 50km away. A relaxed half- or full-day circuit drive from the coast follows a winding road along the razorback line of the escarpment, passing through quaint mountain villages and offering spectacular views of the coastal lowlands.

Maleny

POP 3735

Perched high in the rolling green hills of the Blackall Range, Maleny offers an intriguing melange of artists, musicians and other creative souls, ageing hippies, 'tree-changers' and co-op ventures. Its bohemian edge underscores a thriving commercial township that has moved on from its timber and dairy past without yielding to the kitschy 'ye olde' tourist-trap developments of nearby mountain villages. It's also home to one of the region's most respected microbreweries. The town itself sits on the traditional land of the Jinibara people.

◎ Sights

★**Mary Cairncross**
Scenic Reserve   NATURE RESERVE
(☑ 07-5429 6122; www.mary-cairncross.com.au; 148 Mountain View Rd; by donation; ⊙ rainforest walking tracks 7am-6pm, Discovery Centre 9am-4.30pm; ⊕) The ethereal, 55-hectare Mary Cairncross Scenic Reserve wraps visitors in a remnant of the subtropical rainforests that once blanketed the Blackall Range. Its state-of-the-art Rainforest Discovery Centre leads visitors through interactive exhibitions and out onto easy walking tracks that snake through the rainforest. Boasting over 120 species of birds the forest is rarely silent. The cool, shaded forest floor is also home to a healthy number of unbearably cute red-legged pademelons.

Beside the Rainforest Discovery Centre is a cafe serving light snacks and more substantial meals plus magnificent views overlooking the spectacular Glass House Mountains.

Maleny Botanic Gardens   GARDENS
(☑ 0400 091 731; www.malenybotanicgardens.com.au; 233 Maleny-Stanley River Rd; adult/child $16/free, incl aviary $35/14; ⊙ 9am-4.30pm; ⊕ 🐾) This privately owned oasis comprises 18 acres of steep escarpment that has been manicured into a tapestry of paths, hedges, lawns and ponds with sweeping views of the Glasshouse Mountains. Botanical highlights include rare cycads, orchids, roses, azaleas and annuals. The gardens are also home to a trio of aviaries, with 600-plus birds.

🛏 Sleeping & Eating

Maleny Views Motel   MOTEL $$
(☑ 0428 772 212, 07-5494 2944; www.malenyviewsmotel.com.au; 2 Panorama Pl; r $110-150; 🅿 ❄ 🤶) All the rooms at this welcoming place, which was previously known as the Morning Star Motel, have outstanding. previously have outstanding elevated views to the coast. Standard rooms are typically 'cosy motel' in size, but notably spotless and sporting modern bathrooms. Deluxe suites (one is wheelchair accessible) boast a corner spa. Located near the turn-off to the Mary Cairncross reserve; there are three restaurants close by.

★**Marketplace Maleny**   CAFE $
(☑ 07-5435 2493; 55 Maple St; mains $13-20; ⊙ 6.30am-5pm; 🍴) Head uphill to the top of the main drag to this rejuvenated garage for great organic coffee, muffins, big breakfasts, healthy salads and more. Using seasonal produce from its own garden, it offers daily specials and plenty of vegetarian options. The atmospheric old workshop and its breezy front verandah are comfortable and relaxing places to recharge.

🍷 Drinking & Nightlife

Brouhaha Brewery   MICROBREWERY
(☑ 07-5435 2018; www.brouhahabrewery.com.au; 6/39 Coral St; ⊙ 11am-late Wed-Sun; 🤶) This hip microbrewery has established itself as one of the region's best. Its rotating brews include IPAs, stouts, saisons and sours, some made with local produce. Can't choose? Order the well-priced tasting paddles (four/10 beers for $14/32). A clipboard menu of quality eats (meals $22 to $35) includes grazing plates, burgers and seafood and meaty mains (booking recommended).

There's a great selection of Australian craft spirits, to boot. Live music on Fridays from 4pm.

Fraser Island & the Fraser Coast

Best Places to Eat

➡ Maddigan's Seafood (p376)

➡ Paolo's Pizza Bar (p376)

➡ Brents Burgers (p384)

➡ Coast (p376)

➡ Mammino Gourmet Ice Cream (p387)

Best Places to Sleep

➡ Kingfisher Bay Resort (p381)

➡ Hervey Bay YHA (p374)

➡ Debbie's Place (p384)

➡ Scarness Beachfront Tourist Park (p375)

➡ Mango Tourist Hostel (p373)

Why Go?

North of Noosa, this near-tropical pocket of quintessential coastal Queensland boasts the World Heritage–listed Fraser Island, easy-going coastal communities such as Hervey Bay and Rainbow Beach, the sugar-cane and rum capital Bundaberg, and numerous old-fashioned country towns never too far from the ocean.

Fraser Island is the world's largest sand island, home to ancient rainforests and luminous perched lakes, moody ocean swells, a beach highway and photogenic shipwrecks – few leave unimpressed. Across the waters of the Great Sandy Strait, Hervey Bay appeals to retirees and young travellers alike, and from July to October welcomes migrating humpback whales, especially nursing mothers and calves, into its protected waters. Further south, tiny Rainbow Beach is a backpacker hotspot with great surfing.

When to Go
Bundaberg

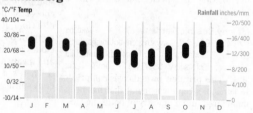

Aug Shake a leg at the Gympie Music Muster; celebrate whales at the Hervey Bay Ocean Festival.

Jul–Nov Watch humpback whales – optimal sighting time is August to October.

Nov–Mar Spy on turtles laying eggs or hatching at Mon Repos.

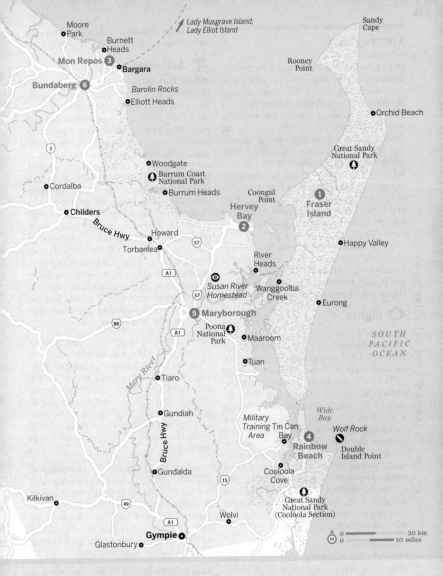

Fraser Island & the Fraser Coast Highlights

1 Fraser Island (p377)
Cruising up the beach 'highway', swimming in crystal freshwater lakes and camping under the stars.

2 Hervey Bay (p372)
Watching the whales at play in the bay, then wining and dining at one of several excellent restaurants.

3 Mon Repos (p390)
Witnessing female loggerhead turtles lay their eggs, or cute hatchlings take their first flipper-stumble down the beach.

4 Rainbow Beach (p383)
Surfing the long break at Double Island Point and gazing over the rainbow cliffs from atop the Carlo Sandblow.

5 Maryborough (p385)
Stepping back into pre-Federation times and paying homage to the creator of Mary Poppins at this historic river port.

6 Bundaberg Rum Distillery (p388) Sampling Queensland's much-loved 'liquid gold' at its sugary source in Bundaberg.

Hervey Bay

POP 53,035

One of the Fraser Coast's more alluring destinations, Hervey Bay, a conglomeration of seaside suburbs, unfurls itself lazily along a bayside shorefront. Pialba, Torquay, Scarness and Urangan pack in plenty of restaurants, pubs and tour operators. Young travellers rub shoulders with grey nomads passing languidly through camping grounds and serious fisherfolk recharging in pursuit of the one that got away. Throw in the chance to see majestic humpback whales frolicking here from July to November, and the town's convenient access to the Unesco–listed Fraser Island, and it's easy to understand the broad appeal of Hervey Bay.

Fraser Island shelters Hervey Bay from the ocean surf and the sea here is shallow and usually calm – perfect for kiddies and summer holiday snapshots. The Butchulla people are the traditional owners here.

⦿ Sights

★ **Fraser Coast Cultural Centre**   MUSEUM, GALLERY
(☑ 07-4197 4206; www.ourfrasercoast.com.au; 166 Old Maryborough Rd, Pialba; ☺ 10am-4pm; 🅿 👪)
FREE Home to both the **Fraser Coast Discovery Sphere** and **Hervey Bay Regional Gallery**, this boldly designed cultural centre is landmarked by 'Nala', the 20-tonne humpback-whale sculpture that 'breaches' 12m into the air from its forecourt. Especially enjoyable for kids, the Discovery Sphere educates visitors about the Unesco-listed Great Sandy Biosphere through captivating and interactive exhibits, all with a background soundtrack of eerie whale song. The gallery gives space to local artists, alongside thoughtfully curated temporary shows.

Urangan Pier   PIER
(Urangan) This historic pier (c 1913–17), jutting nearly 1km into the Great Sandy Strait, makes for a fine stroll, on which you may spot a pod of dolphins or snap a serene sunset. It's also a top place to drop a line.

Wetside Water Park   AMUSEMENT PARK
(☑ 1300 79 49 29; www.frasercoast.qld.gov.au/wetside; cnr Main St & the Esplanade, Pialba; ☺ 10am-5pm; 👪) **FREE** On hot days, this watery playground on the foreshore can't be beaten. There's plenty of shade, gorgeous old trees, a cafe, fountains, tipping buckets and a boardwalk with water infotainment. Paid

attractions include a waterslide ($6 for 10 slides) and a wave pool ($7 per person).

🏃 Activities

Whale Watching

Whale-watching tours operate out of Hervey Bay every day (weather permitting) during the annual migrations between late July and early November. Around 7000 humpbacks pass through here each year, allowing operators to 'guarantee' sightings from August to the end of October (a subsequent trip is free if the whales don't show). Outside of the peak season, many boats offer dolphin-spotting tours. Boats cruise from **Whale Bay Marina** (Buccaneer Dr, Urangan) or the adjacent **Great Sandy Straits Marina** (☑ 07-4125 3822; http://greatsandystraitsmarina.com.au; 17 Buccaneer Dr, Urangan) out to Platypus Bay in the lee of Fraser Island, then zip around from pod to pod to find the most active whales. Most vessels offer half-day tours, and most include lunch and/or morning or afternoon tea. Tour bookings can often be made through your accommodation, or through the information centres.

Spirit of Hervey Bay   WHALE WATCHING
(☑ 1800 642 544; www.spiritofherveybay.com; Whale Bay Marina, Buccaneer Dr, Urangan; adult/child from $100/95; ☺ 8.30am & 1.30pm) The three-level *Spirit* is Hervey's largest whale-watching vessel, and the only one offering a money-back guarantee in the event of a cetacean no-show (between 18 July and 26 October). Afternoon tours are $10 cheaper for adults.

Freedom Whale Watch   WHALE WATCHING
(☑ 1300 879 960; www.freedomwhalewatch.com.au; Great Sandy Straits Marina, Buccaneer Dr, Urangan; adult/child incl lunch $140/100; 👪) Watch the whales from three levels on the 58ft catamaran *Freedom III*. This large, well-regarded operation can also arrange private charters and dive trips.

Blue Dolphin Marine Tours   WHALE WATCHING
(☑ 07-4124 9600; www.bluedolphintours.com.au; Berth B7, Great Sandy Straits Marina, Buccaneer Dr, Urangan; adult/child $160/130; 👪) 🎐 This well-regarded, experienced outfit scouts for whales, dolphins and other marine visitors to Hervey Bay. Smaller groups (24 maximum) aboard the 11.6m sailing catamaran *Blue Dolphin* ensure an intimacy that is difficult to replicate on larger vessels. Dolphin tours (when the whales aren't around) cost $85/55 per adult/child.

Tasman Venture WHALE WATCHING
(☑1800 620 322; www.tasmanventure.
com.au; Great Sandy Straits Marina, Buccaneer Dr, Urangan; whale-watching adult/child
$125/65; ◷8.30am & 1.30pm Jul-early Nov;
🖝) One of the best of Hervey's numerous
whale-watching outfits, Tasman Venture
runs a catamaran with underwater micro-
phones and viewing windows. Sightings
are guaranteed during the season – you get
a free subsequent trip if the whales don't
show. Throw in a Fraser Island day trip
(adult/child $205/195) to explore the less-
er-known western coast of Fraser.

Other Activities

Hervey Bay Ecomarine Tours CRUISE
(☑07-4128 9800; www.herveybayecomarinetours.
com.au; Great Sandy Straits Marina, Buccaneer
Dr, Urangan; 4hr tours adult/child from $115/70)
Cruise on the 12m, glass-bottomed boat
Milbi ('sea turtle' in the local Butchulla language) for snorkelling and coral viewing in
the clear waters of the Great Sandy Strait,
followed by an island BBQ. *Milbi* also takes
whale-watching cruises in season, and transfers to nearby Weenandin ('Round Island').
Tours are designed for minimal ecological
impact, and some involve education from
Butchulla guides.

Air Fraser Island SCENIC FLIGHTS
(☑1300 172 706; www.airfraserisland.com.au; Hervey Bay Airport; scenic flights 30/60min $135/220)
Air Fraser offers scenic flights over Fraser
Island and chances to land and explore.
Leaving from either Hervey Bay or Sunshine
Coast Airport, it sells packages including
accommodation and 4WD (from $575 per
person for two nights).

Aquavue WATER SPORTS
(☑07-4125 5528; www.aquavue.com.au; 415a
The Esplanade, Torquay; 🖝) Operating from a
prime spot on the Torquay foreshore, Aquavue hires out paddleboards and kayaks ($20
per hour) and jet skis ($50/150 per 15/60
minutes). A more involved option is a jet-ski
tour across the Great Sandy Strait to explore
Fraser Island's less-visited west cost, with
lunch served at the delightful Aquavue Cafe
on return ($450, 3½ hours).

Susan River Homestead HORSE RIDING
(☑07-4121 6846; www.susanriver.com; Lot 56,
Noble Rd, off Maryborough–Hervey Bay Rd, Susan River; 🖝) This 1600-acre homestead
offers horse-riding packages (adult/child
$250/160) including accommodation, all

meals and use of the on-site swimming pool
and tennis courts. Day trippers can canter
off on two-hour horse rides (adult/child
$85/75) while night rides ($130/105) are
held around each full moon, with a bonfire
and BBQ dinner included.

🔰 Tours

Fraser Experience TOURS
(☑07-4124 4244; https://fraserexperiencetours.
com.au; 28 Southern Cross Circuit, Urangan; adult/
child from $213/150; ◷7am-5pm) This outfit
runs small-group tours of Fraser Island;
it offers some freedom with the itinerary,
though only one departure per day (meals
included). Also available is a somewhat
conspicuous Hummer tour (adult/child
$295/238). The company has an office near
the airport, but will collect guests from their
Hervey Bay digs.

Fraser Explorer Tours TOURS
(☑07-4194 9222; www.fraserexplorertours.com.
au; 1-/2-day tours $239/399; 🖝) Very expe-
rienced drivers take daily trips to Fraser
Island, leaving from Hervey Bay or Rainbow Beach. Premium tours include lunch
at Eurong Beach Resort (p379) and sunset
drinks, while two-day visitors overnight at
the resort. Vehicles take 40 passengers (or
18 for the premium tour).

🎉 Festivals & Events

Hervey Bay Ocean Festival CULTURAL
(www.herveybayoceanfestival.com.au; ◷Jul/
Aug) Held to coincide with a pit stop tak-
en every year in Hervey Bay by humpback
whales migrating north, this festival offers
music, talks, food, parties and the chance to
get out on the water to marvel at the giant
mammals. Conservation and education are
key focuses.

🛏 Sleeping

Mango Tourist Hostel HOSTEL $
(☑07-4124 2832; www.mangohostel.com; 110
Torquay Rd, Scarness; dm/d $26/56; 🅿🌀🖥)
🖉 A small hostel run by knowledgeable
local Phil, who can arrange tailored Hervey Bay and Fraser Island itineraries, and
put guests in contact with yachts seeking
crew. Intimate and loaded with character,
the old Queenslander, set on a quiet street
away from the beach, sleeps guests in a
four-bed dorm room and two very homey
doubles.

Hervey Bay

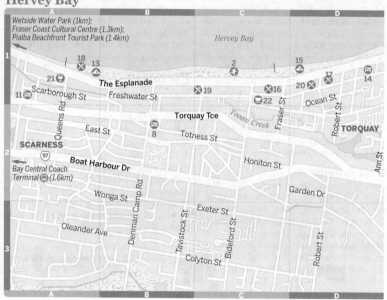

FRASER ISLAND & THE FRASER COAST HERVEY BAY

Hervey Bay

◎ Sights
1 Urangan Pier...G1

✚ Activities, Courses & Tours
2 Aquavue..C1
3 Blue Dolphin Marine Tours....................H2
   Freedom Whale Watch.......................(see 3)
4 Hervey Bay Ecomarine Tours.............H3
5 Spirit of Hervey Bay..............................H3
   Tasman Venture....................................(see 3)

🛏 Sleeping
6 Arlia Sands Apartments..........................E1
7 Colonial Lodge...E1
8 Flashpackers..B2
9 Grange Resort..F1
10 Hervey Bay YHA.....................................G3

11 Mango Tourist Hostel.............................A1
12 Pier One..G1
13 Scarness Beachfront Tourist Park........A1
14 Shelly Bay Resort...................................D1
15 Torquay Beachfront Tourist Park.........D1

🍴 Eating
16 Bayaroma Cafe..C1
   Coast...(see 14)
17 Eat at Dan & Steph's..............................D1
18 Enzo's on the Beach...............................A1
19 Maddigan's Seafood...............................C1
20 Paolo's Pizza Bar....................................D1

🍷 Drinking & Nightlife
21 Beach House Hotel..................................A1
22 Minimalist Coffee Roasters...................C1

Flashpackers HOSTEL $
(☑ 07-4124 1366; www.flashpackersherveybay.com; 195 Torquay Tce, Torquay; dm from $22, d $80; ⌗ ⬆ 🛜 🗷) It's impossible to be bored at Flashpackers: with beach volleyball, a pool, pool table, games room, 'cinema' with free movies and BBQ area, you may find yourself ready for some alone time even before evening events such as the Friday-night sausage sizzle swing round. The four-to-seven-bed dorms are functional and clean,

queen doubles are available, and continental breakfast is included.

★ Hervey Bay YHA HOSTEL $
(☑ 07-4125 1844; www.yha.com.au; 820 Boat Harbour Dr, Urangan; dm/d/cabins from $25/48/149; ⌗ @ 🛜 🗷) This excellent YHA is set on 8 hectares of tranquil bushland close to the Great Sandy Straits Marina and the beach. It's a lovely spot, thick with ambience, possums and parrots. Facilities include a pool, tennis and basketball courts, and a sociable

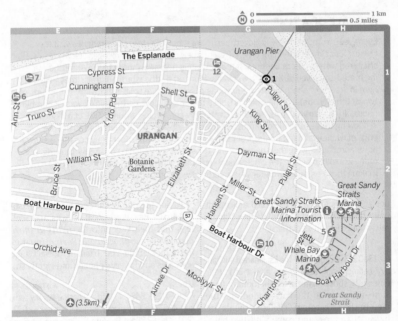

bar-restaurant. All dorm rooms come with their own dining tables and desks, and stand-alone single beds.

Scarness Beachfront
Tourist Park
CARAVAN PARK $

(☑ 07-4128 1274; www.beachfronttouristparks.com.au; The Esplanade, Scarness; powered/unpowered sites from $43.50/35.50; 🛜) This is one of three caravan parks fronting Hervey Bay's exquisitely long sandy beach. It's equipped with a camp kitchen, BBQs and picnic areas, and is just over the road from shops and restaurants.

Other branches are at **Pialba** (☑ 07-4128 1399; www.beachfronttouristparks.com.au; 267 The Esplanade, Pialba; powered/unpowered sites from $43.50/35.50; 🛜) and **Torquay** (☑ 07-4125 1578; www.beachfronttouristparks.com.au; 367a The Esplanade, Torquay; powered/unpowered sites from $43.50/35.50; 🛜).

Colonial Lodge
APARTMENT $$

(☑ 07-4125 1073; www.herveybaycoloniallodge.com.au; 94 Cypress St, Torquay; 1-/2-bedroom apt $121/171; 🅿✳🛜🌊) With just self-contained apartments at this hacienda-style lodge across from the water, guests sometimes get to know each other hanging out by the pool or communal BBQ area. Staff are friendly and the apartments are bigger than average, with a lovely place to sit out the front.

Shelly Bay Resort
APARTMENT $$

(☑ 1800 240 797, 07-4125 4533; www.shellybayresort.com.au; 466 The Esplanade, Torquay; 1-/2-bedroom units $155/195; ✳🛜🌊) The bright, breezy beach-facing apartments at Shelly Bay Resort are some of the best value in town, especially the two-bedroom ones, which have prime corner locations overlooking the lagoon-style pool. There's a half-sized tennis court and BBQ area, and customer service is first class.

Arlia Sands Apartments
APARTMENT $$

(☑ 07-4125 4360; www.arliasands.com.au; 13-15 Ann St, Torquay; 1-/2-bedroom apt from $130/170; 🅿✳🛜🌊) Packing plenty of interior space into smallish footprints, these one- and two-bedroom apartments a few streets back from the beach are good value for money. There's a communal BBQ area, saltwater pool and well-informed help arranging tours and activities at reception.

Grange Resort
RESORT $$$

(☑ 07-4125 2002; www.thegrange-herveybay.com.au; 33 Elizabeth St, Urangan; 1-/2-/3-bedroom villas from $175/235/305; 🅿✳🛜🌊) Reminiscent of a stylish desert resort with fancy split-level condos and filled with life's little luxuries, this biscuit-coloured, palm-shaded complex is close to the beach and town. Pets are very welcome in most apartments – a rarity in these parts – but

A WHALE OF A TIME

Every year, from July to early November, more than 7000 humpback whales visit the Fraser Coast, most spending time fattening their calves and frolicking in Hervey Bay's sheltered waters before continuing their arduous migration south to the Antarctic. Having mated and given birth in the warmer waters off northeastern Australia, they arrive here in groups of about a dozen (known as pulses), before splitting into smaller groups of two or three (pods). The new calves utilise the time to develop the thick layers of blubber necessary for survival in icy southern waters by consuming around 600L of milk daily.

Viewing these majestic creatures, many of which are now accustomed to the presence of whale-watching boats, is simply awe-inspiring. You'll most likely see these showy aqua-acrobats waving their pectoral fins, tail slapping, breaching or simply 'blowing', and many will roll up beside the whale-watching boats with one eye clear of the water... making those on board wonder who's actually watching whom.

not at the fabulous pool bar. Each apartment has a full kitchen, laundry and garage. Nightly rates reduce for longer stays.

Pier One
RESORT $$$
(☑ 1300 213 792; 558-559 The Esplanade, Urangan; 1-/2-bedroom apt $210/260; P✳🛜🏊) Pier One suits short-term travellers looking for a view of the sea in the background and the pool in the foreground. The apartments are bigger than most and come with two bathrooms, shiny surfaces, modern furniture and a very reasonable price tag.

🍴 Eating

⭐ **Maddigan's Seafood** FISH & CHIPS $
(☑ 07-4128 4202; 1/401 The Esplanade, Torquay; fish & chips $9.90-14.90; ⊙ 8am-8pm) Deservedly popular with the locals, Maddigan's is an old-school Australian seaside fish and chippery that fries fresh. Grab coral trout and chips, or perhaps a burstingly full family pack ($30.90) and eat your spoils across the road on Torquay Beach. The catch is displayed on ice at the front of the shop if you'd prefer to purchase it fresh.

Bayaroma Cafe
CAFE $
(☑ 07-4125 1515; https://bayaroma.com.au; 428 The Esplanade, Torquay; meals $11-22; ⊙ 6am-3.30pm; ☑) Famous for its coffee, all-day breakfasts and people-watching position across from the beach in Torquay, Bayaroma has a jam-packed menu that truly has something for everyone – including vegetarians. Attentive, chirpy service is an added bonus.

⭐ **Paolo's Pizza Bar** ITALIAN $$
(☑ 07-4125 3100; www.paolospizzabar.com.au; 2/446 The Esplanade, Torquay; mains $16-28; ⊙ 5-9pm Thu-Mon) A wood-fired oven and a proper feeling for Italian food in the kitchen combine

at Paolo's to produce the best pizza and pasta in Hervey Bay. Fresh local prawns and scallops find their way onto the *frutti di mare* pizza, while the *gnocchi alla Sorrentina* uses fresh mozzarella and basil. It doesn't take bookings and is very popular (and rightly so).

Coast
AUSTRALIAN $$
(☑ 07-4125 5454; https://coasttherveybay.com.au; 469 The Esplanade, Torquay; mains $21-32; ⊙ 11.30am-2.30pm Thu-Sun, 5.30pm-late Tue-Sun) One of the finest restaurants in Hervey Bay, Coast brings big-city sophistication to its cuisine, which is designed to share and to turn great produce into even greater dishes. Smaller plates such as Hervey Bay scallops with garlic butter and pancetta are followed by larger ones like pan-seared market fish with miso mayo, edamame, fennel and carrot-and-ginger dressing.

Enzo's on the Beach
CAFE $$
(☑ 07-4124 6375; www.enzosonthebeach.com.au; 351a The Esplanade, Scarness; mains $10-24; ⊙ 6.30am-5pm Mon-Wed, to 7pm Thu & Sun, to late Fri & Sat) With a deck opening onto the beach, this sleek and inviting cafe-restaurant offers different pleasures throughout the day: breakfast might be eggs Benedict; lunch might be a burger, nachos or crispy Southern-fried barramundi. Dinner dishes, including share 'feasts' designed for two ($40 to $60), such as the chart-topping Seafood Fiesta, are offered Thursday to Sunday.

Also lovely for coffee, cocktails, a cleansing ale or wine. Happy hour is 3pm to 5pm.

Eat at Dan & Steph's
AUSTRALIAN $$
(☑ 0475 850 173; https://danandsteph.com.au; 1b/449 The Esplanade, Torquay; mains $20-25; ⊙ 6am-3pm Mon, Wed & Thu, 6am-3pm & 5.30-10.30pm Fri, 7am-3pm & 5.30-10.30pm Sat, 7am-3pm Sun) Dan and Steph, winners of a TV

cooking show, do a lip-smacking all-day menu covering breakfast (perhaps house-made sausage with spinach croquette, poached eggs and Hollandaise) and lunch (maybe tacos filled with delicious butter-milk-marinated and panko-crumbed ca-lamari with kimchi and fresh avocado). Dinner, on Friday and Saturday, might include a house-made gnocchi with a creamy mushroom ragout, among other dishes.

🍷 Drinking & Nightlife

⭐ Minimalist Coffee Roasters   CAFE
(Shop 8,16 Bideford St; espresso from $4; ⊙6am-3.30pm Mon-Fri, 7-11.30am Sat) Roasting their own ethically sourced beans, the folks at Minimalist know their way around coffee. The cafe sits at the back of a cooperative including crafty Cargo Alehouse, a craft-beer outlet, and Echo Alpha Tango, an eatery. The latter provides Minimalist with a breakfast menu on Saturday mornings. The secretive entrance is on Truro St.

Beach House Hotel   PUB
(📞07-4196 9366; www.beachhousehotel.com.au; 344 The Esplanade, Scarness; ⊙10am-10pm Mon-Wed, to 11pm Thu, to 2am Fri, 9-2am Sat, 9am-10pm Sun; 🍴🐕) The Beach House is perhaps Hervey's most popular pub, thanks to an expensive fit-out, a prime viewpoint on Scarness Beach and a willingness to give the people what they want: numerous beer taps, gambling, big-screen sport, picture windows that open to let in the offshore breeze, a huge courtyard, decent food and accessible live music most nights of the week.

ℹ️ Information

Aside from the main **Hervey Bay Visitor Information Centre** (📞1800 811 728; www.visitfrasercoast.com; 227 Maryborough-Hervey Bay Rd, Urraween; ⊙9am-5pm), on the southern approach to town from Maryborough, there's a **kiosk** (📞07-4128 9800; www.gssm.net.au; Great Sandy Straits Marina, Buccaneer Dr, Urangan; ⊙7am-5.30pm) at the Great Sandy Straits Marina.

ℹ️ Getting There & Away

AIR
Hervey Bay Airport (📞07-4194 8100; www.frasercoastairport.com.au; Don Adams Dr, Urangan; ⊙6am-½hr after last scheduled flight) is just off Booral Rd. **Qantas** (📞13 13 13; www.qantas.com) and **Virgin** (📞13 67 89; www.virginaustralia.com) have regular flights to/from Sydney and Brisbane.

BOAT
Ferries to Fraser Island leave from River Heads, about 10km south of town, and various whale-watching and tour boats leave from Whale Bay Marina (p372) and Great Sandy Straits Marina (p372).

BUS
Buses depart from **Bay Central Coach Terminal** (Hervey Bay Coach Terminal; Stockland Shopping Centre, 6 Central Ave, Pialba). **Greyhound** (📞1300 473 946; www.greyhound.com.au) and **Premier Motor Service** (📞13 34 10; www.premierms.com.au) have several services daily to/from Brisbane ($41 to $98, 5¼ to 7½ hours), Maroochydore ($27 to $75, five to 5½ hours), Bundaberg ($18 to $29, 1¼ to 2½ hours) and Rockhampton ($53 to $97, 5¼ to 7¼ hours).

Tory's Tours (📞07-4128 6611; www.torystours.com.au) has a daily service to Brisbane city or airport (adult/child $60/49). **Wide Bay Transit** (📞07-4121 3719; www.widebaytransit.com.au) runs buses from the Stockland Shopping Centre (6 Central Ave, Pialba) to meet the Rockhampton and Bundaberg Tilt Trains in Maryborough ($13, one hour).

ℹ️ Getting Around

Hervey Bay is the best place to hire a 4WD for Fraser Island.

Aussie Trax (📞07-4124 4433; www.fraserisland4wd.com.au; 56 Boat Harbour Dr, Pialba)

Fraser Magic 4WD Hire (📞07-4125 6612; www.fraser4wdhire.com.au; 5 Kruger Ct, Urangan; ⊙6.30am-6.15pm)

Hervey Bay Rent A Car (📞07-4194 6626, 0417 340 574; www.herveybayrentacar.com.au; 6 Pier St, Urangan; ⊙8am-4.30pm Mon-Sat)

Safari 4WD Hire (📞07-4124 4244; www.safari4wdhire.com.au; 28 Southern Cross Circuit, Urangan; ⊙7am-5.30pm Mon-Fri, 8am-4pm Sat & Sun)

Fraser Island

The local Butchulla people call it K'gari – 'paradise' – and for good reason. Sculpted by wind, sand and surf, the striking blue freshwater lakes, crystalline creeks, giant dunes and lush rainforests of this gigantic sandbar form an enigmatic island paradise unlike any other. Fraser Island is the largest sand island in the world (measuring 120km by 15km) and the only known place where rainforest grows on sand.

Inland, the vegetation varies from dense tropical rainforest and wild heath to wetlands and wallum scrub, with sand blows, mineral streams and perched freshwater

Fraser Island

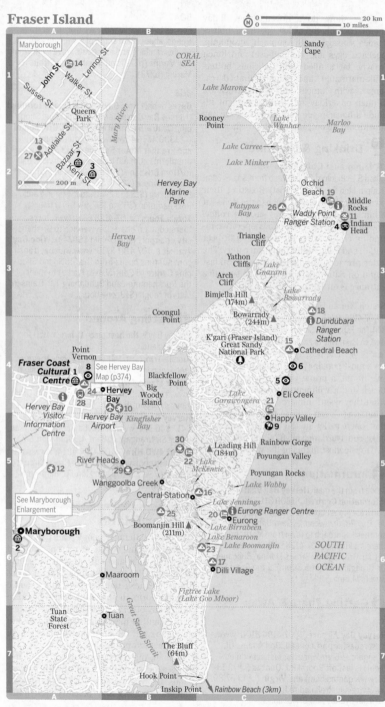

0   20 km
0   10 miles

Maryborough

John St
Walker St
Lennox St
14
Sussex St
Queens Park
Adelaide St
13
27
Bazaar St
Kent St
7
3
0   200 m

Mary River

CORAL SEA

Sandy Cape

Lake Marong

Rooney Point

Lake Wanhar

Lake Carree

Lake Minker

Marloo Bay

Hervey Bay Marine Park

Orchid Beach 19
Middle Rocks
26
Waddy Point Ranger Station
11 Indian Head
4

Platypus Bay

Hervey Bay

Triangle Cliff

Yathon Cliffs

Arch Cliff

Bimjella Hill (174m)

Lake Gnarann

Lake Bowarrady

Bowarrady (244m)

18
Dundubara Ranger Station

Coongul Point

K'gari (Fraser Island) Great Sandy National Park

15
Cathedral Beach

Point Vernon

Fraser Coast Cultural Centre 1
8
See Hervey Bay Map (p374)

Blackfellow Point

6

Hervey Bay Visitor Information Centre
24
Hervey Bay
28
10

Big Woody Island

Lake Garawongera

5
Eli Creek

21

Happy Valley
9

Hervey Bay Airport

Kingfisher Bay

Hervey Bay

River Heads
12
29
Wanggoolba Creek

30
22
Lake McKenzie

Leading Hill (184m)

Rainbow Gorge

Poyungan Valley

Poyungan Rocks

Lake Wabby

Central Station
16
Lake Jennings

Lake Garawongera

25

Boomanjin Hill (211m)

20
Eurong Ranger Centre
Eurong

Lake Birrabeen

Lake Benaroon

23
Lake Boomanjin

SOUTH PACIFIC OCEAN

17
Dilli Village

Maryborough
2

Maaroom

Figtree Lake (Lake Goo Mboor)

See Maryborough Enlargement

Tuan State Forest

Tuan

Great Sandy Strait

The Bluff (64m)

Hook Point
Inskip Point
Rainbow Beach (3km)

Fraser Island

FRASER ISLAND & THE FRASER COAST FRASER ISLAND

lakes flanked by long sandy beaches. The island, most of which is protected as part of the Great Sandy National Park, is home to a profusion of bird life and wildlife, including the famous dingo, while offshore waters teem with dugong, dolphins, manta rays, sharks and migrating humpback whales.

◉ Sights & Activities

Starting at Fraser's southern tip, where the ferry leaves for Inskip Point on the mainland, a high-tide access track cuts inland, avoiding sometimes-dangerous Hook Point, and leads to the eastern beach, which serves as the main thoroughfare for an island with no paved roads. Heading north, the first settlement is Dilli Village, a former sand-mining centre now home to a campground and research centre, while Eurong, with shops, fuel, an inexpensive resort (☑1800 678 623, 07-4120 1600; www.eurong.com.au; Eurong; r from $129, 2-bedroom apt $219; ❇@☎❇) and places to eat, is another 9km north. From here, an inland track crosses to Wanggoolba Creek (for the ferry to River Heads).

Right in the middle of the island is the ranger centre and forest campground at Central Station (☑13 74 68; http://parks.des.qld.gov.au; per person/family $6.65/26.60), the starting point for numerous walking trails. From here

you can drive (or walk, if you have abundant time) to the beautiful McKenzie, Jennings, Birrabeen and Boomanjin Lakes. Lake McKenzie is spectacularly clear and ringed by white-sand beaches, making it a great place to swim. Lake Birrabeen sees fewer tour and backpacker groups, but is no less inviting.

About 4km along the beach north of Eurong, a signposted walking trail leads across to the beautiful Lake Wabby, the most accessible of Fraser's lakes. An easier route is from the Lake Wabby Lookout, off Cornwell's Break Rd from the inland side. Lake Wabby is surrounded on three sides by eucalyptus forest, while the fourth side is a massive sand blow that encroaches on the lake at a rate of about 3m a year. Wabby is deceptively shallow, so be warned that diving is very dangerous.

As you drive further north along the eastern beach, consider times of high tide as you approach Poyungan and Yidney Rocks, which may require a deviation inland. North of here is Happy Valley, with places to stay, a shop and a bistro; about 10km further north again is Eli Creek, a fast-moving, crystal-clear waterway that also requires care due to the many streams that bisect Fraser's eastern shore. About 2km after Eli Creek is the salt-rotted hulk of the Maheno, a condemned passenger liner blown ashore by a cyclone in

1935; its oxidised ribs now provide Fraser's classic photo opportunity.

Roughly 5km north of the *Maheno* you'll find the **Pinnacles**, an eroded section of coloured sand cliffs, and about 10km beyond those, Dundubara, with a ranger station and an excellent **camping ground** (☑13 74 68; http://parks.des.qld.gov.au; per person/family $6.65/26.60). There is then a 20km stretch of beach before you come to the rocky prominence of **Indian Head**, named by Captain Cook for the 'Indians' who gathered here to watch him sail past in 1770. Sharks, manta rays, dolphins and (during the migration season) whales can often be seen from the top of this headland.

Between Indian Head and Waddy Point, the trail branches inland, passing **Champagne Pools**, a natural swimming site that offers the only wholly safe saltwater dip on the island. There's good beach camping at **Waddy Point** (☑13 74 68; http://parks.des.qld.gov.au; per person/family $6.65/26.60) near Orchid Beach, the island's most northerly settlement. Many tracks north of here are closed for environmental protection, and to 4WDs hired from companies that don't want to see their vehicles stranded in impossible terrain.

Air Fraser Island (p381) has a terrific-value 'Day Away' tour ($150) for those looking to land on the island and explore a little on foot. Depart from Hervey Bay or Sunshine Coast.

FRASER ISLAND GREAT WALK

Meandering 90km through the island's interior from Dilli Village to Happy Valley, the Fraser Island Great Walk is a stunning way to experience this unique environment. Broken up into seven sections of around 6km to 16km each, plus some side trails, the walk follows the pathways of Fraser Island's original inhabitants, the Butchulla people. En route it passes underneath rainforest canopies, circles around some of the island's vibrantly blue perched lakes, and courses through shifting dunes.

It's imperative that you visit the **Queensland Parks & Wildlife** (☑13 74 68; www.des.qld.gov.au) website for maps, dingo safety advice, updates on the track (which can close when conditions are bad) and camping permits.

🛏 Sleeping

Camping permits, which need to be displayed, are required to camp at the 45 Queensland Parks & Wildlife (p383) camping grounds across Fraser. The most developed sites, with coin-operated hot showers, toilets and BBQs, are at Waddy Point, Dundubara and Central Station. Campers with vehicles can also use the smaller camping grounds at **Lake Boomanjin** (☑13 74 68; http://parks.des.qld.gov.au; per person/family $6.55/26.60), and at **Ungowa** (☑13 74 68; http://parks.des.qld.gov.au; per person/family $6.65/26.60) and **Wathumba Spit** (☑13 74 68; http://parks.des.qld.gov.au; per person/family $6.65/26.60) on the west coast.

Walkers' camps are set away from the main camping grounds, along the Fraser Island Great Walk (p383) trail. The trail map, available from Queensland Parks, lists the camp sites and their facilities. Camping is permitted on designated stretches of the eastern beach, but there are no facilities. Fires are prohibited except in communal fire rings at Waddy Point and Dundubara – bring your own firewood in the form of untreated, milled timber, and ensure no fire ban is in place.

Supplies on the island are limited and costly. Stock up well before arriving, and be prepared for mosquitoes and March flies.

Dilli Village   CAMPGROUND $
(☑07-4127 9130; www.usc.edu.au; site per person from $10, r/cabin $70/160) Managed by the University of the Sunshine Coast, which uses this precinct as a base for environmental education and research purposes, Dilli Village offers good sites on a softly sloping, dingo-fenced campground. Rooms in the bunkhouses sleep two. The self-contained cabins, which can sleep five, are particularly good value.

Cathedrals on Fraser   CARAVAN PARK $$
(☑07-4127 9177; www.cathedralsonfraser.com.au; Cathedral Beach; powered/unpowered sites for 2 $65/49, tent from $99, 2-bed cabins with/without bathroom $270/250; @) This spacious dingo-fenced park offers abundant, flat, grassy sites and a range of cabins. There's a shop selling fuel, alcohol, food and groceries on site, two camp kitchens, a laundry, communal firepits and plenty of picnic areas.

Fraser Island Retreat   CABIN $$
(☑07-4127 9144; www.fraserislandretreatqld.com.au; Happy Valley Dr, Happy Valley; d/apt from $150/215; @ 🡒 🡒) Located in the relatively remote Happy Valley, halfway along the east coast of the island, this retreat's nine timber

ⓘ DEALING WITH DINGOES

Despite its many natural attractions and opportunities for adventure, there's nothing on Fraser Island that gives a thrill comparable to your first glimpse of a dingo. Believed to be among the most genetically pure in the world, the dingoes of Fraser are sleek, spry and utterly beautiful. They're also wild beasts that can become aggressive at the drop of a hat (or a strong-smelling food sack). While attacks are rare, there are precautions that must be taken by every visitor to the island.

➡ However skinny they appear, or whatever woebegone look they give you, never feed dingoes. Dingoes that are human-fed quickly lose their shyness and can become combative and competitive. Feeding dingoes is illegal and carries heavy fines.

➡ Don't leave any food scraps lying around, and don't take food to the lakes: eating on the shore puts your food at 'dingo level', an easy target for scrounging scavengers.

➡ Stay in groups, and keep any children within arm's reach at all times.

➡ Teasing dingoes is not only cruel, but dangerous. Leave them alone, and they'll do the same to you.

➡ Dingoes are best observed at a distance. Pack a zoom lens and practise some silence, and you'll come away with some brilliant photographs...and all your limbs intact.

cabins (each sleeping up to four people) are great for a comfortable nature experience. The cabins are airy, nestled in native foliage and close to the beach. On site there's a camp kitchen, a licensed restaurant and a shop that sells fuel.

★**Kingfisher Bay Resort**   RESORT **$$$**
(☑ 07-4194 9300, 1800 072 555; www.kingfisher bay.com; Kingfisher Bay; d from $199, 2-bedroom villa from $289; ❄@☀) 🄿 Set in delightful native gardens, this elegant eco-resort has hotel rooms with private balconies, and sophisticated two- and three-bedroom timber villas designed to minimise environmental impact (three-night minimum stay in high season). The **Seabelle Restaurant** is terrific (mains $28 to $40), while the three bars are great fun in summer at sunset, especially the backpacker-friendly **Dingo**.

There are boutique shops, pools, a day spa and daily ranger-guided, eco-accredited tours of the island, taking in everything from its history, plants and animals to bush foods and medicines.

Eliza Fraser Lodge   LODGE **$$$**
(☑ 0418 981 610; www.elizafraserlodge.com.au; 8 Eliza Ave, Orchid Beach; per person $410) Occupying a stunning purpose-built house, Eliza Fraser is the island's finest lodging. Serviced directly by **Air Fraser Island** (☑ 1300 172 706; www.airfraserisland.com.au) and Brisbane Helicopters, the two-level house is perfect for families or small groups. The hosts are expert guides and will organise fishing trips,

nature hikes and 4WD adventures, or just let you enjoy the spectacular surrounds. Minimum four people, three nights.

ⓘ Information

You must purchase permits from Queensland Parks & Wildlife Service (p383) for vehicles (up to one month $52.75) and to camp in QPWS camping grounds (adult/family per night $6.65/26.50) before you arrive. Permits aren't required for private camping grounds or resorts. Buy permits online or check with visitor centres for up-to-date lists of where to buy them.

Ranger stations at **Eurong** (☑ 07-4127 9128), **Dundubara** (☑ 07-4127 9138) and **Waddy Point** (☑ 07-4127 9190) are not public-facing offices, open in scheduled hours – they're often unattended, as the rangers are out on patrol.

ⓘ Getting There & Away

Before crossing via ferry from either Rainbow Beach or Hervey Bay, ensure that your vehicle has suitably high clearance (if you're one of the few not visiting on a tour, that is) and, if camping, that you have adequate food, water and fuel.

AIR

Air Fraser Island (p381) charges from $150 for a one-way flight to the island's eastern beach, departing Hervey Bay airport.

BOAT

Vehicle ferries connect Fraser Island with **River Heads**, about 10km south of Hervey Bay, or further south at **Inskip Point**, near Rainbow Beach.
Fraser Venture Barge (☑ 1800 227 437, 07-4194 9300; www.fraserislandferry.com.au)

SAND SAFARIS

The only way to explore Fraser Island (besides walking) is with a 4WD. For most travellers there are three options: tours (tag-along or fully guided); hiring a 4WD; or taking a day tour from a resort on Fraser. Bear in mind the greater the number of vehicles, the greater the environmental damage. With an average of more than 1000 people visiting the island each day, Fraser can sometimes feel like a giant sandpit with its own peak hour and congested beach highway.

Tag-Along Tours

Popular with backpackers, tag-along tours see travellers pile into 4WD convoys, following a lead vehicle with an experienced guide and driver. Travellers take turns driving the other vehicles, which can be great fun, but has also led to accidents. Rates hover around $500 for three days – be sure to check if your tour includes everything you'd expect.

Advantages Highly social; driving the beaches is exhilarating.

Disadvantages If food isn't included, you'll have to cook; groups can be even bigger than on bus tours.

Dropbear Adventures (📞 0487 333 606, 1800 061 156; www.dropbearadventures.com.au; 2-/3-day tour $399/549) Lots of departures from Rainbow Beach and Noosa to Fraser Island; easy to get a spot.

Dingos Fraser Island 4X4 Tag Along Tour Departs from Rainbow Beach; maintains the friendly backpacker vibe established before departure.

Nomads (📞 07-5447 3355; www.nomadsfraserisland.com; 3-day tour $529) Departs from Noosa.

Pippies Beach House (p384) Departs Rainbow Beach; well organised and has small convoys with high safety standards.

Organised Tours

Most organised tours cover Fraser's hotspots: rainforests, Eli Creek, Lake McKenzie, the Pinnacles and the *Maheno* shipwreck.

Advantages Removes the worry of driving in sand; expert commentary; decent food and comfortable accommodation; often the most economical choice.

Disadvantages Day-tour buses often arrive en masse at the same place at the same time.

Cool Dingo Tours (📞 07-4120 3333; www.cooldingotour.com; 2-/3-day tours twin share per person from $459/595) The party option, Cool Dingo leaves from Hervey Bay or Rainbow Beach.

Fraser Experience (p373) Small group tours offer greater freedom with the itinerary; departing from Hervey Bay.

Fraser Explorer Tours (p373) Multiple departures from Hervey Bay or Rainbow Beach; includes accommodation on the island.

Remote Fraser Island Tours (📞 1800 620 322; www.tasmanventure.com.au; tours adult/child $185/110) Day tours from Hervey Bay to the less-visited west coast.

4WD Hire

You can hire a 4WD from Hervey Bay, Rainbow Beach or on Fraser Island itself. All companies require a hefty bond.

When planning your trip, reckon on covering 20km an hour on the inland tracks and 40km an hour on the eastern beach. Most companies will help arrange ferries, permits and camping gear. Rates range from $270 to $600 for one day, falling for multiday hires.

Advantages Freedom to roam the island and escape the crowds.

Disadvantages You may encounter beach and track conditions that even experienced drivers find challenging; expensive.

There are rental companies in Hervey Bay (p377) and Rainbow Beach (p385). On the island, Aussie Trax hires out 4WDs from Kingfisher Bay Resort.

Makes the 30-minute crossing from River Heads to Wanggoolba Creek on the west coast of Fraser Island (return fares: pedestrian adult/child $60/30, vehicle and four passengers $225). It departs daily from River Heads at 8.30am, 10.15am and 4pm, and returns from the island at 9am, 3pm and 5pm.

Kingfisher Bay Ferry (☑1800 227 437, 07-4194 9300; www.fraserislandferry.com) Operates a daily 50-minute vehicle and passenger service (pedestrian adult/child return $60/30, vehicle and four passengers return $225) from River Heads to **Kingfisher Bay**, departing at 6.45am, 9am, 12.30pm, 3.30pm and 6.45pm (plus 9.30pm in peak periods) and returning at 7.50am, 10.30am, 2pm, 5pm and 9pm (plus 11pm in peak periods).

Manta Ray (☑07-5486 3935, 0418 872 599; www.mantarayfraserislandbarge.com.au; vehicle incl passengers return $130; ⊙6am-5.15pm) Leaving from Inskip Point, Manta Ray has two ferries continuously running the 15-minute crossing to a beach just west of Hook Point on Fraser Island, from 6am to 5.15pm daily (vehicle including passengers return $130).

❶ Getting Around

A 4WD is necessary if you're driving on Fraser Island and you must have a vehicle permit from Queensland Parks & Wildlife Service (p383), which costs $52.75 for up to one month. Expensive fuel is available from shops at Cathedral Beach, Eurong, Kingfisher Bay, Happy Valley and Orchid Beach. If your vehicle breaks down, call the tow-truck service in Eurong: **Fraser Island Towing** (0428 353 164, 07-4127 9449).

The 4WD **Fraser Island Taxi Service** (☑07-4127 9188, 0429 379 188; www.fraserservice.com.au) operates all over the island. Bookings are essential, as there's only one cab for the island.

If you want to hire a 4WD while on Fraser, **Aussie Trax** (☑07-4124 4433; www.fraserisland4wd.com.au; full-day hire from $554) has a medium-sized fleet of Suzuki Jimnys and Toyota Land-Cruisers, available at the Kingfisher Bay Resort.

Rainbow Beach

POP 1249

Named for cliffs of colourful, mineral-rich sand, Rainbow Beach is an idyllic, low-key Australian beach town at the base of the Inskip Peninsula. Though understated, it is beloved of European backpackers as a base for excursions to Fraser Island. It's a great place to try your hand at different outdoor activities, tap into the backpacker party scene, or just chill out with family and friends. Ideally reached via the Cooloola Section of the Great Sandy National Park, a dramatic

approach possible only for 4WDs, it's more easily and conventionally accessed by excellent roads from Gympie, 73km southwest.

◎ Sights & Activities

Carlo Sand Blow   NATURAL FEATURE

(🏛) This great bowl of wind-blown sand above Rainbow Beach is arrestingly beautiful. Named for a crew-member on Cook's first voyage to these parts, it's reached by a short climb through subtropical forest, after which the foliage parts to reveal a vast scoop of golden sand, with views to Fraser Island and Inskip Point to the north, and Rainbow Beach and Double Island Point to the south. Don't slide down the flanks of the environmentally fragile Sand Blow, as this damages them.

Take Cooloola Dr to its highest point to reach the car park and short walking track, and try to time your visit for sunrise or sunset: either will take your breath away.

Rainbow Paragliding   PARAGLIDING

(☑0418 754 157; www.paraglidingrainbow.com; glides $200) Rainbow Beach is recognised as one of the best coastal places in the world for paragliding, with its safe launch and landing, smooth air flows and spectacular sights. Experienced operator Jean Luc has been taking tandem flights with exhilarated customers here since 1995.

Epic Ocean Adventures   WATER SPORTS

(☑0408 738 192; www.epicoceanadventures.com.au; 1/6 Rainbow Beach Rd; 3hr surf lessons $69, 3½hr kayak tours $89; ⊙8am-6pm) With a shopfront on the main drag in Rainbow Beach, this surf school has experienced instructors to guide beginners through nearby Double Island Point's sometimes-challenging breaks. Its fantastic dolphin-spotting sea-kayak tours also leave from this 4WD-accessible beach.

Wolf Rock Dive Centre   DIVING

(☑07-5486 8004, 0498 743 795; www.wolfrockdive.com.au; 2 Goondi St; double-dive charters $210) Wolf Rock, a quartet of volcanic pinnacles off Double Island Point, is one of Queensland's best scuba-diving sites. This shop takes divers here to see endangered grey-nurse sharks year-round, and you may also see turtles, rays, giant gropers and even whales.

**Dingos Fraser Island
4X4 Tag Along Tour**   ADVENTURE SPORTS

(☑08-8131 5750; www.dingofraser.com; 18 Spectrum St, Rainbow Beach; 3-day tours $519) A number of Rainbow Beach operators organise 'tag-along' tours to Fraser Island, where participants drive 4WDs in convoy. Dingos tours take in principal sights and activities such as Lakes McKenzie and Wabby, the *Maheno* shipwreck and Indian Point, and are seriously fun. Meals, camping, permits and barge fees are all included.

Surf & Sand Safaris ADVENTURE SPORTS
(☑07-5486 3131; www.surfandsandsafaris.com.au; half-day tours adult/child $85/50) This outfit offers half-day 4WD tours through the Great Sandy National Park and along the beach to the coloured sands and lighthouse at Double Island Point. Full-day beach-drive tours to Noosa can also be arranged through a partner operator (adult/child $195/120).

Pippies Beach House DRIVING
(☑07-5486 8503; www.pippiesbeachhouse.com.au; 3-day 2-night tag-along tours $469) Departing Rainbow Beach, these well-organised, small convoys to Fraser Island with reportedly high safety standards take a maximum 34 guests. They rate well with returning backpackers.

🛌 Sleeping

Rainbow Beach
Holiday Village CARAVAN PARK $
(☑07-5486 3222, within Australia 1300 366 596; www.rainbowbeachholidayvillage.com; 13 Rainbow Beach Rd; powered/unpowered sites $45/38, villas from $165; ⓟ❄🐕🏊) This popular, central caravan park offers generous, grassy sites (some with ocean outlooks) and a range of villas and chalets. There's also a camp kitchen, laundry, swimming pool, gas BBQs and a store for essentials, petrol and permits.

Freedom Rainbow Beach HOSTEL $
(☑1800 180 288, 07-5401 5500; www.freedomhostels.com; 20 Spectrum St; dm/tw/d from $28/89/99; ⓟ❄🐕🏊) A classically gregarious and youthful hostel, Freedom Rainbow Beach accommodation is decent and clean, with dorms, twins and doubles. There's a pool, bar, laundry, BBQs, pool- and table-tennis tables, and a front desk organising tours to Fraser Island and surfboard hire. Nightly entertainment includes music, games and karaoke.

Pippies Beach House HOSTEL $
(☑07-5486 8503; www.pippiesbeachhouse.com.au; 22 Spectrum St; dm/d/apt from $25/75/140; ⓟ❄🏊) Catering mainly to young backpackers, this hostel offers decent kitchen and laundry facilities, free toast-and-jam breakfasts, a pool and organised group activities including tag-along Fraser Island tours. Extra

touches such as thumb drives loaded with current films, loaned to guests on check-in, demonstrate an above-and-beyond attitude. Two-bedroom, self-contained family units, located away from the hostel, sleep five.

★**Debbie's Place** B&B $$
(☑0423815980,07-54863506; www.rainbowbeachaccommodation.com.au; 30 Kurana St; d/ste from $160/180, 3-bedroom apt from $350; ⓟ❄🐕🏊) Debbie's meticulously kept Queenslander is the standard bearer for Rainbow Beach holiday accommodation. The motel- and apartment-style rooms are fully self-contained, with private entrances and verandahs, the effervescent Debbie is a mine of information, and the gardens are verdant with hanging baskets and tropical blooms. There's one wheelchair-friendly room, and several with excellent outdoor cooking facilities.

Plantation Resort at Rainbow RESORT $$$
(☑07-5486 9600, within Australia 1800 556 423; www.plantationresortatrainbow.com.au; 1 Rainbow Beach Rd; d from $329; ⓟ❄🐕🏊) Rainbow Beach's swankiest digs span several floors in the heart of town, with lovely ocean views from most apartments. All are self-contained, with spa baths, BBQs and clean-lined modern fittings across lounge rooms and bedrooms. There's a communal pool, underground parking and rooftop penthouses for absolute luxury. Two-night minimums may apply.

🍴 Eating

Rainbow Fruit CAFE $
(☑07-5486 3126; 13b/1 Rainbow Beach Rd; breakfast from $12.50, dishes $4.50-16; ⏰7.30am-5pm Mon-Fri, to 4pm Sat, to 3pm Sun; 🍴) Fresh fruit and vegetables are sliced, diced and pureed for a range of juices, wraps and salads at this humble cafe and greengrocer just off the main strip. Spicy Thai curries are worth a try too.

★**Brents Burgers** BURGERS $$
(☑07-5486 8877; 8 Rainbow Beach Rd; burgers & mains $14-18; ⏰10am-late) Cool burger bar that serves up a great range of burgers, including vegan and veg options, with sidewinder chips. Very good fish and chips, too. Clandestino coffee from Noosa and irresistible gelato from Maleny. Fully licensed.

Cafe Jilarty at Rainbow CAFE $$
(☑07-5486 3277; 12 Rainbow Beach Rd; pizzas & mains $13-21; ⏰6am-8.30pm) Breezy, casual cafe with indoor and outdoor seating where you can grab a coffee or smoothie, burrito or

wrap, fish and chips, and decent thin-crust pizzas. BYO only and no corkage (there's a bottle shop close by).

Deck at Sea Salt
BISTRO $$

(☑ 0499 008 624; 2 Rainbow Beach Rd; mains $17-20; ⊙ 8am-6pm Sun & Mon, to 7pm Tue, to 9pm Wed & Thu, to 11pm Fri & Sat) The prime corner location – a deck open to the ocean breeze in the heart of town – is the obvious draw here, but the food's not bad either. Check to see what's on special. If you don't fancy a full meal such as ribs or a burger, there are always drinks, and tapas options such as spicy Spanish potatoes and grilled paprika octopus.

🛈 Getting There & Away

Greyhound (☑ 1300 473 946; www.greyhound. com.au) and **Premier Motor Service** (☑ 13 34 10; www.premierms.com.au) are the two principal bus companies offering daily services to/from Brisbane ($31 to $54, five to 5½ hours), Noosa ($20 to $38, 2½-2¾ hours) and Hervey Bay ($16 to $32, two hours); all stop on Spectrum St near Freedom Rainbow Beach hostel.
Active Tours & Transfers (☑ 07-5313 6631; www.activetransfers.com.au) runs a shuttle bus to Rainbow Beach from Brisbane Airport ($135, three hours) and Sunshine Coast Airport ($95, two hours).

Most 4WD-hire companies will also arrange permits and barge costs to Fraser Island ($130 per vehicle return), and hire out camping gear. Try **Rainbow Beach 4x4 Hire** (☑ 07-5486 8300; www.rainbowbeach4x4hire.com.au; 66 Rainbow Beach Rd; 2-3 days per day $200; ⊙ 8.30am-4.30pm) or **Rainbow Beach Adventure Centre 4WD Hire** (☑ 07-5486 3288, 0419 663 271; www.adventurecentre.com.au; 13 Spectrum St; per day $270; ⊙ 7am-5pm).

Gympie
POP 18,267

Gympie is a pleasant former gold-rush town featuring some fine heritage architecture and interesting relics of the days when gold and timber lured pioneers to this fertile land, traditionally owned by the Kabi Kabi (Gubbi Gubbi) people. Come in August for one of the best country music festivals in Australia.

Gympie Gold Mining & Historical Museum
MUSEUM

(☑ 07-5482 3995; www.gympiegoldmuseum.com. au; 215 Brisbane Rd; adult/child/family $10/5/25; ⊙ 9am-4pm; [P][♿]) Spread over 15 historical buildings, Gympie's gold-mining museum holds a diverse collection of mining equip-

ment and steam engines. There's a decent cafe, open 9am to 4pm, and activities such as gold panning.

Gympie Music Muster
MUSIC

(www.muster.com.au; ⊙ Aug) Held in the Amamoor Creek Forest near Gympie over four days every August, the Muster is one of Queensland's largest country-music festivals. All proceeds go to charity.

Gympie Muster Inn
MOTEL $$

(☑ 07-5482 8666; www.gympiemusterinn.com. au; 21 Wickham St; d from $140; [P][✳][🛜][🏊]) If you can't muster up the energy to drive any further, then this friendly motel with wheelchair accessible and family rooms will suffice. Decorated grey, black and red, rooms are like small units. Wickham St is aka Bruce Hwy.

Maryborough
POP 22,206

Founded in 1847 to take advantage of the broad Mary River, Maryborough is one of Queensland's oldest towns. Traditionally land of the Butchulla people, this major 19th-century river port welcomed thousands of free settlers looking for a better life. This legacy is visible in the many heritage-listed buildings, Victorian parks and handsome Queenslanders that line Maryborough's broad streets.

History is celebrated in a clutch of intriguing local museums and sites around Wharf St. Maryborough is also Adding to the birthplace of Pamela Lyndon (PL) Travers, creator of the umbrella-wielding Mary Poppins. You can take part in Poppins-themed walks, and there's a life-sized statue of the world's most famous nanny on the corner of Richmond and Wharf Sts, outside the bank building where Travers was born. The Mary Poppins Festival (p386) is in June/July.

◉ Sights

Portside Heritage Precinct
HISTORIC SITE

(☑ 07-4190 5722; www.ourfrasercoast.com.au/ Portside; Wharf St; Portside pass adult/child $20/ free; ⊙ 9.30am-3.30pm Mon-Fri, to 12.30pm Sat & Sun) In the historic area beside the Mary River, Portside has 13 heritage-listed buildings, parkland and museums. The Portside Centre, located in the former Customs House, has interactive displays on Maryborough's history. Part of the centre, but a few doors down, the Bond Store Museum also highlights key periods in Maryborough's history.

Downstairs is the original packed-earth floor and even some liquor barrels from 1864.

Story Bank
MUSEUM

(☑1300 794 929; www.storybankmaryborough. com.au; cnr Kent & Richmond Sts; adult/child $10/5; ⊙9.30am-2.30pm) Upstairs, in a bedroom of the former Australian Joint Stock Bank (c 1882), Helen Goff (aka PL Travers), the author of the Mary Poppins stories, was born. The building has been lovingly restored into a creative and interactive 'story-trading' bank. Outside the building is a life-size statue of the Mary Poppins character.

Brennan & Geraghty's Store
MUSEUM

(☑07-4121 2250; www.nationaltrust.org.au; 64 Lennox St; adult/family $5.50/13.50; ⊙10am-3pm; 🚻) This National Trust–classified store traded for 100 years (1871 to 1972) before closing its doors. Two generations of owners had kept a lot of old stock, and the museum is crammed with tins, bottles and packets, including early Vegemite jars, Victorian-era curry powder and stock- and credit-ledgers. It's a nostalgic wonderland for anyone interested in consumer and advertising ephemera.

Maryborough Military & Colonial Museum
MUSEUM

(☑07-4123 5900; www.maryboroughmuseum. org; 106 Wharf St; adult/couple/family $12/20/26; ⊙9am-3.30pm Mon-Fri, to 12.30 Sat & Sun; 🚻) Occupying a brick warehouse built for JE Brown in 1879, this museum houses over 7000 military and colonial artefacts. Check out the only surviving three-wheeler Girling car, originally built in London in 1911. There's also a replica Cobb & Co coach and one of the largest military libraries in Australia. If you're also visiting the Bond Store and Customs House, buy a Portside Pass, which covers all three museums for just $20.

Gatakers Artspace
GALLERY

(www.ourfrasercoast.com.au/Gatakers-Artspace; 311 Kent St; ⊙10am-4pm Mon-Fri, to 1pm Sat & Sun) FREE Inside the restored Gatakers Buildings (behind the Military & Colonial Museum) are four galleries exhibiting contemporary art from the region and beyond. All art pieces are original and many are for sale. See the website for the latest workshops and events.

👉 Tours

Maryborough Guided Walks
WALKING

(⊙9am Mon-Sat) FREE Free guided walks depart from the City Hall and take in the town's many sites.

Tea with Mary
TOURS

(☑07-4190 5722; $20; ⊙9.30am Thu & Fri) Tour of the historic precinct with a 'Mary Poppins inspired' guide, finishing with morning tea. Tours run on request – book through the visitor centre (p387).

🎉 Festivals & Events

Mary Poppins Festival
CULTURAL

(☑07-4196 9630; www.marypoppinsfestival.com. au; ⊙Jun-Jul; 🚻) A supercalifragilisticexpialidocious festival celebrating Maryborough local PL Travers and the famous Miss Poppins. Held over nine days during the June/July school holidays, it involves storytelling, music and pop-up events around town.

🛏 Sleeping & Eating

Le Piaf on Treasure
B&B $$

(☑0438 195 443; www.piaftreasure.com.au; 13 Treasure St; d incl breakfast $130; 🛜) One ensuite bedroom in a lovingly-restored 1940s Queenslander, 'Le Piaf' is run by Cecile, the French-Australian language teacher who also owns Eco Queenslander, the adjacent B&B built and restored at the same time. The immaculate, light-filled room has its own entrance, opening onto a shaded verandah, and a fridge for perishables.

Eco Queenslander
BUNGALOW $$

(☑0438 195 443; www.ecoqueenslander.com; 15 Treasure St; per couple from $140; 🛜) 🌿 Lovely Cecile, the French adventurer who fell in love with Maryborough, is an enthusiastic host in the old Queenslander she tastefully restored. As well as a comfy lounge, full kitchen, laundry and cast-iron bathtub, there are sustainable features such as solar power, rainwater tanks, energy-efficient lighting and bikes for guest use. Minimum two-night stay.

Best Western Kimba Lodge
MOTEL $$

(☑07-4123 3999; www.kimbalodge.com.au; 177 John St; d from $145; ❄️🛜🏊) This handy central motel is on the road out to, or in from, Hervey Bay and feature spotless rooms, modern bathrooms and comfortable beds. Also available are fully-self-contained two-bedroom apartments.

Alowishus Delicious
CAFE $

(☑07-4302 8631; www.alowishus.com.au; 232-244 Adelaide St; mains $7-18; ⊙7am-5pm Mon-Thu, 7pm Fri, 8am-9pm Sat, 8am-4pm Sun; 🛜) 🌿 The Maryborough outpost of a Bundaberg favourite, Alowishus is the slickest, shiniest cafe in central Maryborough. The breakfast menu is like a 'greatest hits' of the Australian cafe genre – smashed avocado on sourdough with feta, eggs Benedict, zucchini and sweetcorn fritters – while there's something for everybody at lunch – wraps, burgers, salads, quiche, lasagna and a handful of veggie choices.

ℹ Information

Maryborough Fraser Island Visitor Information Centre (🖊 1800 214 789; www.visitfraser coast.com; City Hall, 388 Kent St; ⊙ 9am-5pm Mon-Fri, to 1pm Sat & Sun) Free walks leave from this well-stocked and helpful tourist office at 9am, Monday to Saturday. Also books Fraser Island tours and sells Queensland Parks & Wildlife permits and licences.

ℹ Getting There & Away

Queensland Rail (🖊 1300 131 722; www. queenslandrailtravel.com.au) has two services: the *Spirit of Queensland* ($99, 4½ hours) and the Tilt Train ($75, four hours) connecting Brisbane with Maryborough West station. The station is 7km west of the centre, and is connected via a shuttle bus.

Greyhound (🖊 1300 473 946; www.greyhound. com.au) and **Premier Motor Service** (🖊 13 34 10; www.premierms.com.au) have buses to Gympie ($11 to $38, one to 2¼ hours), Bundaberg ($20 to $46, three to 3½ hours) and Brisbane ($39 to $79, 4½ to six hours). Buses leave from the old railway station on Lennox St.

Wide Bay Transit (🖊 07-4121 4070; www. widebaytransit.com.au) runs shuttles between Maryborough and Hervey Bay, timed to meet the Rockhampton and Bundaberg Tilt Trains ($16.50, one hour).

Childers

POP 1584

Surrounded by fertile fields and the rich red soil of an area traditionally owned by the Dunaburra of the Kabi Kabi (Gubbi Gubbi) people, Childers is a charming little town. Easily imagined in its formative Victorian years, its main street is lined with tall, shady trees and lace-trimmed historical buildings. Most notable are the early-20th-century Federal Hotel, and the rebuilt Palace Hotel, burnt down by an arsonist in 2000 and now home to a memorial to the 15 backpackers who perished in the blaze. Backpackers still flock to Childers for fruit-picking and farm work.

Childers Palace Memorial & Art Gallery GALLERY
(Childers Art Space; 🖊 07-4130 4876; www.bun dabergregionalgalleries.com.au; 72 Churchill St; ⊙ 9am-4pm Mon-Fri, to 3pm Sat & Sun) FREE Fifteen backpackers tragically died when the hostel that once operated here was consumed by a deliberately-lit fire in 2000. The two-storey balconied Palace Hotel was erected in 1903, when the 1890 original was destroyed in an earlier fire. Drop in to see a moving memorial wall commemorating the 15 victims, plus rotating exhibitions of art.

Mango Hill B&B B&B $$
(🖊 1800 816 020, 0408 875 305; www.mangohill cottages.com; 8 Mango Hill Dr; d incl breakfast from $150; 🕸) Attached to the **Hill of Promise Winery**, just east of Childers, Mango Hill comprises two restful timber cottages with rural outlooks. Nothing is too much trouble for the effusive hosts, who channel their Sicilian-Australian heritage into heartfelt hospitality and biodynamic semillon, Grenache and blended wines and liqueurs. Self-serve breakfasts include the owners' preserves, and can be vegan and/or gluten free.

★**Mammino Gourmet Ice Cream** ICE CREAM $
(🖊 07-4126 2880; www.mammino.com.au; 115 Lucketts Rd; ice-cream cups $6; ⊙ 9am-5pm) Locally famous, Mammino's ice cream is made in a factory on this rural property just outside Childers. It's made with all-natural ingredients, and you can sample one of its macadamia or fruit flavours from the small retail outlet here, or from the Paragon Theatre Espresso Bar in town.

Paragon Theatre Espresso Bar CAFE $
(🖊 0478 066 724; www.paragontheatre.com.au; 75 Churchill St; ⊙ 7.30am-4.30pm) In the restored, heritage-listed Paragon Theatre (c 1927) is a charming cafe serving toasted sandwiches, Buddha bowls, cakes, Mammino gourmet ice cream and espresso coffee. Customers can take a peek at the historical theatre (still in use) with its deck-chair seating and improvised interior decoration. La Scala it ain't, but the pride and resourcefulness of early Childers is evident.

Federal Hotel PUB FOOD $$
(🖊 07-4126 1438; 71 Churchill St; mains $15-34; ⊙ 10am-midnight) A classic, wrought-iron-wrapped, two-storey Federation-era hotel, the Feddy is a quintessential Australian pub, though the swinging saloon doors may have you briefly imagining you are in an American western. There's a decent menu of favourites such as rump steak, chicken Kiev and bangers and mash.

FRASER ISLAND & THE FRASER COAST CHILDERS

ⓘ Information

Childers Visitor Information Centre (☑07-4126 3886, 1300 722 099; 72 Churchill St; ⊙9am-4pm Mon-Fri, to 1pm Sat & Sun) is on the ground floor of the Palace Hotel, below the Palace Memorial & Art Gallery.

ⓘ Getting There & Away

Childers is 50km south of Bundaberg. **Greyhound Australia** (☑1300 473 946; www.greyhound.com.au) and **Premier Motor Service** (☑13 34 10; www.premierms.com.au) both stop on Crescent St, behind the post office, and have at least one daily service to/from Brisbane ($47 to $101, 5½-8½ hours), Hervey Bay ($11 to $20, one to 1¾ hours) and Bundaberg ($11 to $29, 50 minutes to 1½ hours).

Burrum Coast National Park

Shifting between a lowland vegetation of stringybark trees, dense mangroves and flat coastal dunes, **Burrum Coast National Park** (https://parks.des.qld.gov.au/parks/burrum-coast) is a popular spot for knowledgeable campers, birdwatchers, fishers, canoeists and hikers. It's divided into two sections: the Woodgate section begins at the southern end of the Esplanade in Woodgate, 42km east of Childers, and has attractive beaches and abundant fishing. The more isolated, thickly wooded Kinkuna section boasts a fine, secluded beach.

There are several places to overnight: the **NRMA Woodgate Beach Holiday Park** (☑07-4126 8802, within Australia 1300 414 448; www.woodgatebeachtouristpark.com; 88 The Esplanade, Woodgate; powered site $38, cabin $93, beachfront villa $140; P❄) in Woodgate; the Queensland Parks–run camping ground at **Burrum Point** (https://parks.des.qld.gov.au; Walkers Point Rd; per person/family $6.65/26.60), accessible only by 4WD; and more isolated bush-camping areas in the Kinkuna section of the park. Camping permits should be acquired in advance, online..

Burrum Coast National Park is 55km south of Bundaberg, and you'll need your own vehicle to get there.

Bundaberg

POP 69,061

Bundaberg is the largest centre on the Fraser Coast. It's known throughout Australia for its sugar-cane fields, eponymous dark rum, tongue-tingling ginger beer and fruit-farming backpackers. The town is an agricultural centre with some pubs and a decent art gallery. However, in many people's eyes, the beach hamlets around 'Bundy' are more attractive than the town. Some 25km to the north are the wide, flat beaches of **Moore Park**; to the east, nesting loggerhead turtles seek the sands of **Mon Repos**; while holidaymakers head to **Bargara** and, to the south, **Elliott Heads**.

◉ Sights & Activities

★**Bundaberg Rum Distillery**   DISTILLERY
(☑07-4131 2999; www.bundabergrum.com.au; Hills St; adult/child museum $19/9.50, guided tour $28.50/14.25; ⊙10am-5pm Mon-Fri, to 4pm Sat & Sun) Bundaberg's biggest claim to fame is the iconic Bundaberg Rum: you'll see the brand's polar bear on billboards and bumper stickers.. Choose from either a self-guided tour through the museum or a guided tour of the distillery, which commenced production in 1889. Tours depart on the hour, and both include a tasting for the over-18-year-olds. Wear closed shoes.

Lady Elliot Day Trip   TOURS
(☑07-5536 3644, 1800 072 200; www.ladyelliot.com.au; adult/child $445/299; 🚤) Fly to Lady Elliot Island, spend five hours on the Great Barrier Reef, use the resort's facilities, take free guided reef walks and snorkel in the lagoon. Lunch and a glass-bottomed boat tour are also included. Flights leave Bundaberg at 8.40am and return at 4.30pm; flight time is 30 minutes.

Bundaberg Barrel   BREWERY
(☑07-4154 5480; www.bundaberg.com; 147 Bargara Rd; adult/child $12/free; ⊙9am-4.30pm Mon-Sat, 10am-3pm Sun) Bundaberg's nonalcoholic ginger beer and other soft drinks aren't as famous as Bundy Rum, but they run a deserved close second. Visit the Barrel to take an audio tour of the small museum, taste 14 flavours and take a six-pack home with you (included in the tour price).

Burnett River Cruises   CRUISE
(☑0427 099 009; www.burnettrivercruises.com.au; 11e Petersen St; 2½-hr tours adult/child $27.50/10; ⊙office 9am-2pm Tue-Sun) The *Bundy Belle,* a restored river ferry, chugs at a pleasant pace to the mouth of the Burnett River. Cruises depart from the south bank of the river, near Daphne Geddess Park – see the website or call for tour times.

Bundaberg Aqua Scuba   DIVING
(☑07-4153 5761; www.aquascuba.com.au; 239 Bourbong St; diving courses from $349; ⊙shop

Bundaberg

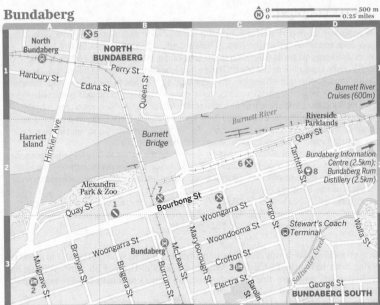

9am-5pm Mon-Sat) This experienced operator leads dives to nearby sites around Coral Cove, plus longer cruises to Lady Musgrave Island (one/two dives $296/346) and interesting wrecks in the area. It also offers basic accommodation for $20/115 per night/week.

🛏 Sleeping & Eating

Bunk Inn HOSTEL $
(www.bunkinnhostel.com.au; 25 Barolin St; dm from $32.50; ❄🛜) This hostel is the best choice of budget digs in town with four- or five-bed mixed dorms supplied with fresh linen and towels. Shared kitchen and bathrooms are clean and there's a supermarket very close by. Air-conditioned from 8pm to 8am.

Bundaberg Spanish Motor Inn MOTEL $$
(☑07-4152 5444; www.bundabergspanish motorinn.com; 134 Woongarra St; r from $115; 🅿❄🛜🏊) A Spanish hacienda-style motel does not feel out of place in the hot Bundaberg climate, and this old-fashioned motor inn in a quiet side street off the main drag is *muy bueno*. Spotless units are self-contained and all overlook the central pool, and there's a BBQ and laundry for guest use.

Alowishus Delicious CAFE $
(☑07-4154 2233; www.alowishus.com.au; Earl's Court, 4/176 Bourbong St; mains $13-16; ⊗7am-

Bundaberg

⊕ Activities, Courses & Tours
1 Bundaberg Aqua Scuba.....................B2

⊜ Sleeping
2 Bundaberg Spanish Motor Inn...........A3
3 Bunk Inn...C3

⊗ Eating
4 Alowishus Delicious............................C2
5 Oodies Cafe...A1
6 Spicy Tonight.......................................C2
7 Spotted Dog Tavern...........................B2

⊕ Drinking & Nightlife
8 Bargara Brewing Company...............D2

6pm Mon-Wed, to 9pm Thu, to 11pm Fri, 8am-11pm Sat, 8am-5pm Sun) This upbeat cafe down an arcade off Bourbong St is the place to go for well-made coffee in Bundaberg. The food's great too: breakfasts like corn-and-zucchini fritters with poached egg, guacamole and salsa, and lunches like a crispy sweet-chilli chicken burger always hit the mark. Note: the kitchen closes at 3pm.

Spicy Tonight THAI $$
(☑07-4154 3320; www.spicytonight.com.au; 1 Targo St; dishes $18-23; ⊗11am-2.30pm Mon-Sat, 5-9pm daily; ❄🍴) Step behind the grand, columned facade of this former bank to

TURTLE ENCOUNTERS

Mon Repos, 15km northeast of Bundaberg, is one of Australia's most accessible turtle rookeries and home to the **Mon Repos Turtle Centre** (☑ 1300 722 099, 07-4159 1652; https://parks.des.qld.gov.au/parks/mon-repos/turtle-centre; 141 Mon Repos Rd; ⊗ 9am-4pm; 🚻) **FREE**. From November to late March, female loggerheads lumber up the beach to lay eggs in the sand. About eight weeks later, the hatchlings dig their way to the surface, and, under cover of darkness, emerge en masse to scurry down to the water as quickly as possible.

The Bundaberg Information Centre has information on turtle conservation and reports on turtle numbers, and takes bookings (until 4pm) for nightly Turtle Encounter tours (adult/child $27/14, from 7pm during the season). Bookings are mandatory and need to be made through the visitor centre or online at www.bundabergregion.org.

Warning: upwards of 300 people nightly descend on the turtles as they try to go about their business. Groups of 60 take turns for 30 minutes on the beach, which means you may be delayed for quite some time until your group gets in (good thing you can pick up fish and chips in nearby Bargara).

Bundaberg Coaches (☑ 07-4153 1037; www.bundaberg-coaches.com.au) runs the Turtle Express (adult/child/family $62/49/185), which will pick you up from your Bundaberg accommodation between 5.30pm and 5.50pm.

discover a delightful family-run restaurant serving both Indian and Thai food. While the Indian offerings are fine, you should stick to the superb Thai dishes, which betray the origins of the chef. *Tom yum* soup with succulent prawns, or *pad cha* (spicy seafood stir-fry) will delight pescatarians.

Oodies Cafe
CAFE **$$**
(☑ 07-4153 5340; www.oodies.com.au; 103 Gavin St; mains $15-22; ⊗ 6.30am-3.30pm Mon-Fri, to 2pm Sat & Sun; 🚸🐾) A double garage on the edge of Bundaberg's city centre is the unlikely venue for Bundaberg's most cosmopolitan cafe. Lounge on leather armchairs under art-spangled walls, surveying the bric-a-brac as you sip an expertly made coffee and wait for your super salad or breakfast bruschetta.

Spotted Dog Tavern
PUB FOOD **$$**
(☑ 07-4198 1044; www.spotteddogtavern.com.au; 217 Bourbong St; lunch mains $13-19, dinner mains $21-37; ⊗ 8am-midnight) Bundaberg's most popular hotel-restaurant is busy all day. The pub food is a step above the competition with tapas, share plates, pizzas, steaks and seafood. It doesn't look much from the outside, or from the inside for that matter, but the restaurant, cafe, bar, beer garden and live music keep the locals streaming through the door.

🍺 Drinking & Nightlife

Bargara Brewing Company
MICROBREWERY
(☑ 07-4152 1675; www.bargarabrewingco.com.au; 10 Tantitha St; ⊗ 11am-9pm Wed & Thu, to 10pm Fri & Sat, to 3pm Sun) This buzzing craft brewery and taproom serves pizzas, sliders, jerky and

other drinking food ($14 to $17) to accompany pints of Drunk Fish, Thirsty Turtle and Hip Hop. Occasionally has live music too.

ℹ️ Information

Bundaberg Information Centre (☑ 1300 722 099, 07-4153 8888; www.bundabergregion.org; 36 Avenue St; ⊗ 9am-5pm) This reliable tourist office has helpful staff and reams of brochures.

ℹ️ Getting There & Away

AIR

Daily **Virgin** (☑ 13 67 89; https://virginaustralia. com) and **Qantas** (☑ 13 13 13; www.qantas.com. au) flights connect Bundaberg to Brisbane.

BUS

The **coach terminal** (☑ 07-4153 2646; 66 Targo St) is on Targo St. Both **Greyhound** (☑ 1300 473 946; www.greyhound.com.au) and **Premier Motor Service** (☑ 13 34 10; www.premierms.com. au) have daily services connecting Bundaberg with Brisbane ($53 to $111, eight to nine hours), Hervey Bay ($18 to $29, 2½-2¾ hours) and Rockhampton ($41 to $56, 3½ to five hours).

Duffy's City Buses (☑ 1300 383 397; www. duffysbuses.com.au) has nine services every weekday (and four on Saturday) to Bargara ($4, 20 minutes), leaving from behind Target on Woongarra St.

TRAIN

The Queensland Rail (p387) Tilt Train runs from Brisbane to Bundaberg (from $89, 4½ hours). The *Spirit of Queensland* (from $81, 5½ hours, five weekly) also stops here between Brisbane and Cairns.

Capricorn Coast & the Southern Reef Islands

Best Places to Eat

➜ Headrick's Lane (p399)

➜ Getaway Garden Café (p395)

➜ Lightbox (p396)

➜ TruFusion Indian Bar & Grill (p399)

Best Places to Sleep

➜ Svendsen's Beach (p403)

➜ Takarakka Bush Resort (p405)

➜ Backpackers @ 1770 (p394)

➜ Lady Elliot Island Eco Resort (p397)

Why Go?

This sometimes overlooked stretch of Queensland's coast straddles the Tropic of Capricorn, and comprises the southernmost islands of the Great Barrier Reef. Here, local families seek escape from the inland heat of centres such as beef capital Rockhampton among dreamy beaches, mangroves and reef-fringed islands, while the less-accessible coast and hinterland hold some of the state's most arrestingly beautiful national parks.

Beachside towns of Agnes Water, Town of 1770, Gladstone and Yeppoon are jumping-off points for the reef and the southern reef islands, replete with bushwalking, great beaches, remote resorts and places to camp under the stars; kayaking, snorkelling and surfing also beckon. Inland, travellers can try their luck fossicking in the Gemfields or hike in search of ancient Aboriginal rock art amid the epic gorges of Carnarvon National Park.

When to Go
Rockhampton

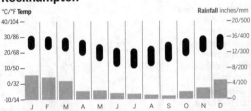

Feb The Agnes Blues and Roots Festival rocks in the Discovery Coast.

May–Sep Warm winter temperatures are ideal for swimming and sun-seeking.

Dec Nature puts on a light show during the summer solstice at Capricorn Caves.

Capricorn Coast & the Southern Reef Islands Highlights

1 Heron Island
(p397) Marvelling at the coral gardens of one of Australia's great diving and snorkelling sites.

2 Lady Elliot Island (p397) Diving with mantas and exploring shipwrecks off this tiny cay.

3 Carnarvon National Park
(p404) Hiking through ancient river-carved gorges to find Aboriginal rock art.

4 Great Keppel Island (p401) Clambering over rocky headlands to claim your own perfect, coral-fringed beach.

5 Agnes Water
(p393) Surfing or chilling in this friendly beach town, site of Queensland's most northerly surf beach.

6 Rockhampton
(p398) Tucking into a huge steak and delving into the culture and history of the Darumbal people.

7 Capricorn Caves
(p399) Wandering open-mouthed through water-carved limestone caverns, spotting ancient coral and tiny bats.

8 Gemfields
(p403) Fossicking for fortune-changing sapphires in these sun-baked inland diggings.

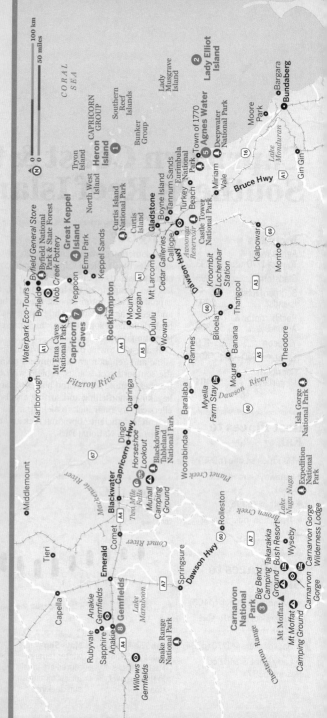

Agnes Water & Town of 1770

POP 2286

Tucked away on gorgeous coastal lands owned traditionally by the Gureng Gureng people, Agnes Water is a former milling town turned holiday destination, named after a schooner that was lost at sea en route from Mackay to Brisbane. Bordered by national parks, coves, paperbark wetlands and the rolling Pacific, Agnes Water has the east coast's most northerly surf beach and some excellent hostels.

Just 8km up the road, at the end of a narrow promontory, is the site of Captain Cook's first landing in Queensland. The tiny settlement of 1770 is a perfect for kayaking, paddleboarding and fishing excursions around the inlets of the 'Discovery Coast' and the jumping-off point for boat trips to the Great Barrier Reef and Eurimbula National Park.

The Bustard Bay Lookout is a great short walk; you can also hike along the beach between the two settlements.

◉ Sights & Activities

Agnes Water Museum   MUSEUM

(☑07-4974 9511; www.agneswatermuseum.com. au; Springs Rd, near cnr Captain Cook Dr, Agnes Water; adult/child $3/free; ☉10am-2pm Wed-Mon) This fine little museum is a labour of love that delves deeply into local history, such as Captain Cook's 1770 landing and voyage of exploration, displaying extracts from Cook's journal and detailed botanical drawings of the plants collected. Then there's the story of the 1868 Bustard Head lighthouse and the strange lives of its denizens, plus Aboriginal bark paintings from Arnhem Land and a wealth of Aboriginal weaponry and tools.

1770 SUP   WATER SPORTS

(☑0421 026 255; www.1770sup.com.au; 1½/2hr tours $45/50) Explore the calm waters and sandy banks of 1770 with a top-notch stand-up paddleboarding (SUP) instructor. Tours include an intro lesson, or just rent your own board (one hour/day $25/70). The roving SUP trailer can often be found on the 1770 waterfront across from the Tree bar, facing 580 Captain Cook Dr.

Pedal-powered (you'll see) SUPs also available ($30/45 for half/one hour).

1770 Liquid Adventures   KAYAKING

(☑0428 956 630; www.1770liquidadventures.com. au; Captain Cook Dr) This experienced outfit makes the most of 1770's delightful surrounds on its sunset tours ($60). You'll be guided around the usually placid waters off Eurimbula National Park, before retiring to Bustard Bay beach for drinks and snacks in the gloaming – keep an eye out for dolphins. You can also rent kayaks for self-directed fun (single/double kayaks per hour $20/25).

Family tours ($45/35 per adult/child) focus on bird and marine life and will appeal to any child who is comfortable paddling alone.

1770 LARC Tours   TOURS

(☑07-4974 9422; www.1770larctours.com.au; 1770 Marina, 535 Captain Cook Dr, Town of 1770; day trips adult/child $160/99) ✔ The hot-pink, ex–Vietnam War Lighter Amphibious Resupply Cargo (LARC) vehicle makes a comfortable ride for exploring the natural joys of Bustard Headland and Eurimbula National Park. Aside from the signature seven-hour day trip (lunch and sandboarding included), this outfit also runs hour-long afternoon tours (adult/child $40/18) and the Goolimbil Walkabout ($85/45).

On the latter, guests accompany a guide from the local Gureng Gureng people through mangroves and coastal forest, learning traditional hunting-and-gathering knowledge.

1770 Reef   BOATING

(☑07-4972 7222; www.1770reef.com.au; 1770 Marina, 535 Captain Cook Dr, Town of 1770; day trip adult/4-14yr/family $208/108/558; ⓓ) This ship-shape outfit runs day trips to the 14-hectare coral cay Lady Musgrave Island in the Capricorn Bunker Group. Following the 90-minute cruise through the waters of the Great Barrier Reef, you can snorkel a coral-skirted lagoon, kick back in a glass-bottomed boat, or spot nesting birdlife on guided land tours. Trip departs at 8.30am and returns at 5pm.

Book Lady Musgrave trips well ahead during school holidays.

Moondoggie Beach & Bush Tours   OUTDOORS

(☑07-4974 7916, 0407 118 390; www.moondog gietours.wordpress.com; day tour per person from $95) The bushland beauty of Eurimbula and Deepwater National Parks needs a 4WD and some local knowledge to fully enjoy: local guide Arty provides both. Depending on the season, and your inclinations, you may spot turtles or whales, wander through deep green rainforest, swim in peaceful rock pools, learn to surf or try your hand at stand-up paddleboarding.

Pickup can be arranged from the Caltex service station in Agnes, or your accommodation.

Paperbark Forest Boardwalk   WALKING
(Springs Rd; ◷24hr) One of Agnes Town's non-watery attractions, this 400m boardwalk meanders its way through a coastal floodplain ecosystem some 3km south of town. Hop along the stumpy steps as you gaze up at the paperbark-tea trees, clad in skirts of climbing maidenhair ferns. If you're lucky, you may spot flying foxes that feed on the flowers.

Nighttime sees the emergence of the giant burrowing cockroaches that feed on dead vegetative matter and act as forest caretakers.

Lazy Lizard Surf School   SURFING
(☑0488 177 000; www.lazylizardsurfschool.com.au; 7 Agnes St; 2hr lesson $40; ▣) Offering lessons for smaller groups (six students per coach, minimum age 14), Lazy Lizard will be sure to get you up in the gentle surf in front of the clubhouse. Private lessons for groups ($150 for four) and individuals ($60 per hour) can also be arranged.

✷ Festivals & Events

Agnes Blues & Roots Festival   MUSIC
(☑07-4974 7570; www.agnesbluesandroots.com.au; SES Grounds, Agnes Water; 3-day pass $154; ◷Feb) This weekend-long, single-stage festival in idyllic surrounds consistently attracts Australian and international musicians.

🛏 Sleeping

Cool Bananas   HOSTEL $
(☑07-4974 7660; www.coolbananasbackpackers.com; 2 Springs Rd, Agnes Water; dm $27-29; ☜) This breezy backpacker hang-out is sociable without being a party place. Roomy eight-bed dorms (including women only) are perfectly comfortable, and management encourages mingling during 'family time' each evening from 6pm to 8pm, with communal meals going for $6. Further fraternisation occurs during nightly events such as Aloha Mondays (leis and cocktails) and during surfing lessons.

Cool Bananas hires surfboards (half-full day $20/30) and is just five minutes from the beach. Vans can park here for $13 per person per night.

★Backpackers @ 1770   HOSTEL $
(☑0408 533 851; www.backpackers1770.com.au; 20-22 Grahame Colyer Dr, main entry from Captain Cook Dr, Agnes Water; dm/d $27/70; ▣☜) Actually in Agnes Water, this gregarious, great-value

hostel is a model of the genre. Run by divemaster Oscar, it offers spotless dorms, three smart doubles and a lush communal garden where meals are taken, guitars strummed and stories shared. There are nightly events such as trivia, beer pong and movies, and you can play billiards beneath a canopy of surfboards.

Dinner and breakfast are available ($5 per meal), as are bikes (half-full day $10/15) and surfboards ($15/20).

1770 Camping Ground   CAMPGROUND $
(☑07-4974 9286; www.1770campingground.com.au; 641 Captain Cook Dr, Town of 1770; powered/unpowered sites from $43/38, beachfront sites $52; ☜) This campground, with its beach frontage, is superpopular with vacationing families. The site is well shaded with palm and fig trees, and there's a laundry, cafe and camp kitchen available. Campfires are allowed on the beachfront, and sunsets are stunning. During holidays, caravans and tents sit cheek by jowl, so don't expect glorious solitude.

1770 Southern Cross Backpackers   HOSTEL $
(☑07-4974 7225; www.1770southerncross.com; 2694 Round Hill Rd, Agnes Water; dm/d incl breakfast $30/90; ☜▣) Spread over a large gum-treed property some 2km out of Agnes Water, this chilled-out backpackers' abode abounds with extras, such as giant trampoline, pool and movie room, BBQs for guest use, plus the fun Scooter Roo tours. Free shuttles whisk you into town and the on-site buzzy nightspot (Karma Bar) acts as a reveller magnet.

For greater rusticity, there's also a camp site (unpowered/powered sites $15/18).

The Lovely Cottages   COTTAGE $$
(☑07-4974 9554; www.thelovelycottages.com.au; 61 Bicentennial Dr, Agnes Water; cottages $155; ▣❄☜▣) This aptly named eco-retreat and outdoor gallery epitomises casual Queensland bush chic. Four colourful two-bedroom cottages (one equipped for disabled access) each sleep up to three people, sharing a BBQ and enticing lagoon-style pool. Two-night minimums apply, while discounted rates for longer stays can be found on the website.

★1770 Getaway   VILLA $$
(☑07-4974 9323; www.1770getaway.com.au; 303 Bicentennial Dve, Agnes Water; villas $195; ❄☜▣) These five delightful one-bedroom villas are set among 1.5 hectares of riotous tropical vegetation just out of the centre of Agnes. Decorated in soothing creams,

each has an airy, open feel, well-appointed kitchens and shady private verandahs with BBQs. Breakfast by the pond at the lovely Getaway Garden Cafe can be included ($35 for two).

✖ Eating

Holidays Cafe CAFE $
(☑ 07-4974 9619; www.holidayscafe.com.au; 55 Jeffery Crt; mains $11-22; ☺ 7am-4pm; 🅿🚼) Appealingly situated beneath the casuarina trees, this beachfront cafe inside a caravan park draws you in with a killer mixture of sea views, pick-me-up juices, organic coffee, ample breakfasts (eggs every which way, full Aussie fry-ups, moreish burritos) and crowd-pleaser lunches (burgers, salads, fish tacos).

★ Getaway Garden Café CAFE $$
(☑ 07-4974 9323; www.1770getaway.com.au; 303 Bicentennial Dr, Agnes Water; breakfast & lunch mains $16-22, dinner per person $28; ☺ 8am-2.30pm Sun-Fri, with booking 5.30-7:30pm Wed & Sun; 🐾) This open-sided, teak-doored pavilion, set in restful tropical gardens, is where travellers invariably find themselves chasing Agnes' best meal. Tuck into eggs Benedict with brisket on brioche, smashed avocado on sourdough or paleo muesli in the morning, then come back for sandwiches, salads and burgers at lunchtime.

Bookings are essential for Wednesday and Sunday dinners of wood-fired pizza and spit-roasted lamb.

Codie's Place AUSTRALIAN $$
(☑ 07-4974 7004; www.codiesplace.com.au; 7 Agnes St; mains $11-29; ☺ 8am-9pm; 🅿🚼) 🍃 This down-to-earth, family-run restaurant doesn't bang on about 'taking you on a journey'; instead, they serve up generous platefuls of slow-cooked lamb, homemade gnocchi with pesto, grilled catch of the day with seasonal veg and other deceptively simple, beautifully executed dishes. Egg dishes, wraps and burgers fill your belly earlier in the day and these guys have strong eco credentials.

ⓘ Information

Agnes Water Visitor Information Centre
(☑ 07-4902 1533; www.visitagnes1770.com.au; 71 Springs Rd, Agnes Water; ☺ 8.30am-4.30pm Mon-Fri, 9am-4pm Sat, to 1pm Sun) Staffed by above-and-beyond volunteers who even leave out information and brochures when it's closed, just in case a lost soul blows into town.

ⓘ Getting There & Away

Greyhound (☑ 1300 473 946; www.greyhound.com.au; Round Hill Rd) buses detour off the Bruce Hwy to Agnes Water; daily services include Brisbane ($143, 8½ hours, two daily), Bundaberg ($30, 1½ hours, two daily) and Cairns ($214, 23 hours, nightly).

The road linking Agnes Water to the main highway is prone to flooding during the rainy season.

Eurimbula & Deepwater National Parks

South of Agnes Water is **Deepwater National Park** (www.parks.des.qld.gov.au/parks/deepwater), an unspoiled coastal landscape with long sandy beaches, freshwater creeks, good fishing spots and two camping grounds. It's also a major breeding ground for loggerhead turtles, which dig nests and lay eggs on the beaches between November and February.

The 78-sq-km **Eurimbula National Park** (www.parks.des.qld.gov.au/parks/eurimbula), on the northern side of Round Hill Creek, is a landscape of dunes, mangroves and eucalyptus forest, as well as pristine creeks full of marine life, ideal for snorkelling and boating. Both offer delightful beaches, hikes in the Australia bush, while Eurimbula has the added bonus of a historic lighthouse, with its share of unexplained deaths and tragic mysteries.

Moondoggie Beach & Bush Tours (p393) does tours of both national parks, but only 1770 LARC Tours (p393) will let you access the Bustard Head lighthouse.

From the northern park entrance at Deepwater, drive 5km to the basic camping ground at Middle Rock (no facilities) and a further 2km to the Wreck Rock camping ground.

There are two basic camping grounds in Eurimbula, one at Middle Creek with toilets only and the other at Eurimbula Creek with toilets and limited rainwater.

Gladstone

POP 34,215
Surrounded by mangrove-fringed waterways on land owned traditionally by the Gureng Gureng people, Gladstone is a major centre for the mining and energy industries, with the best connections to the southern Great Barrier Reef. Its marina (on Bryan Jordan Dr) is the main departure point for

boats to the southern coral cay islands of Heron, Masthead and Wilson. In town itself, the best concentration of food, drink and accommodation can be found at the port end of Gondoon St.

🛏 Sleeping

Gladstone Backpackers
HOSTEL $

(📞 07-4972 5744; www.gladstonebackpackers.com.au; 12 Rollo St; dm/tw $25/60; @🛜🏊) Set inside a big blue Queenslander down by the marina, Gladstone Backpackers offers a large communal kitchen and shared bathrooms, plus well-maintained dorms and twins. Grey-haired nomads, itinerant miners and European wanderers find common ground on the airy verandah. There's free use of bicycles and free pickups from all principal transport points.

Harbourview Motel
MOTEL $

(📞 07-4972 4222; 23 Coon St; r $80; P🌀🛜) This friendly place looks down upon Gladstone from its lofty hill vantage point. The decor of its spacious rooms with kitchenette and fan probably won't make your social media posts for good nor ill, but it's a nice overnighter.

WORTH A TRIP

CURTIS ISLAND

Curtis Island, just across the water from Gladstone, can't be confused with a resort island. Apart from swimming, fishing and lolling about on the dunes, its main drawcard is the annual appearance of rare flatback sea turtles on its eastern shores between October and January. Permits for camping at the Turtle Street, Joey Lees and Yellow Patch sites (per person/family $6.55/26) can be booked online via **Queensland Parks & Wildlife** (📞 13 74 68; https://qpws.usedirect.com/qpws) or you can stay at the friendly **Capricorn Lodge** (📞 07-4972 0222; www.facebook.com/capricornlodge; Seaview Esplanade lodgings from $70).

Curtis Ferry Services (📞 07-4972 6990; www.curtisferryservices.com.au; 215 Alf O'Rouke Dr, Gladstone Marina) connects the island with Gladstone every day bar Tuesday and Thursday (return adult/child $30/18, family from $84).

🍴 Eating & Drinking

Dock @ East Shores
AUSTRALIAN $$

(📞 07-4976 9596; www.thedockgroup.com.au; 17 Flinders Pde; mains $19-29; ⊘ 8am-9pm Mon-Thu, to 11pm Fri & Sat, to 8pm Sun; 🛜) A favourite on the Gladstone waterfront, this breezy cafe-restaurant is ideal for breakfast on the verandah (perhaps sweetcorn fritters with pesto mayonnaise, tomato salsa and poached eggs), afternoon beer and 'tapas', or a proper feed at dinnertime (maybe pan-fried red emperor with greens, followed by macadamia-coconut crumble). Gelato and freshly made doughnuts are ideal for drop-in treats.

★ Lightbox
WINE BAR

(📞 07-4972 2698; www.lightboxgladstone.co; 56 Goondoon St; ⊘ 7am-2pm Mon & Sun, to 10pm Tue-Thu, to midnight Fri & Sat) With its clean lines and open facade, this slick espresso-and-wine bar is Gladstone's most 'urban' haunt. The wine list offers some Italian vintages alongside those from across Australia and New Zealand, the coffee's skilfully prepared, and breakfasts such as rösti with haloumi, soft egg and beef-brisket stock are delicious. Charcuterie, pizza and small plates take over later in the day.

ℹ Information

Gladstone Visitor Information Centre (📞 07-4972 9000; www.gladstoneregion.info; 72 Bryan Jordan Dr; ⊘ 8.30am-4.30pm Mon-Fri, 9am-4pm Sat, 9.30am-2pm Sun) Located at the marina, the departure point for boats to Heron Island, this well-staffed tourist office has all the information you need. It can arrange tours of the local power station (Queensland's largest), the port facilities, or the LNG plants on Curtis Island.

ℹ Getting There & Away

AIR

Qantas (www.qantas.com) and Alliance Airlines (www.allianceairlines.com.au) operate several flights daily between Brisbane and **Gladstone Airport** (📞 07-4977 8800; www.gladstoneairport.com.au; 31 Aerodrome Rd), around 7km from the city centre.

BOAT

Curtis Ferry Services has regular services to Curtis Island via Facing Island (same price) on Monday, Wednesday, Friday, Saturday and Sunday, leaving from the Gladstone marina. Transport to other nearby islands can be arranged on request.

You can also access the islands with various charter operators.

If you've booked a stay on Heron Island, the resort operates a launch (one-way per person $64, two hours).

BUS

Greyhound Australia (☑ 1300 473 946; www.greyhound.com.au) has several coach services from Brisbane ($164, 10 to 13 hours, two daily) via Bundaberg ($50, three to 3½ hours), and Rockhampton ($22, 1¼ hours, 20 daily). The terminal is at the Puma service station, about 200m southwest of the centre.

TRAIN

Queensland Rail (www.queenslandrail.com.au) has frequent north- and southbound services passing through Gladstone's **train station** (☑ 07-3606 6630, 1300 131 722; www.queenslandrailtravel.com.au). The Tilt Train and Spirit of Queensland call in at Gladstone from Brisbane (from $119, 7½ hours) and Rockhampton ($39, 1½ hours) daily.

Southern Reef Islands

While much hype surrounds the Great Barrier Reef's northern splendour, the Southern Reef Islands are the place of 'castaway' dreams: tiny coral atolls fringed with sugary white sand and turquoise seas, and hardly anyone within flipper-flapping reach. From beautiful Lady Elliot Island, 85km northeast of Bundaberg, secluded and uninhabited coral reefs and atolls dot the ocean for about 140km up to Tryon Island. Lady Musgrave is a blue lagoon in the middle of the ocean, while Heron Island is a natural escape for adventurous families and world-class scuba diving.

Several cays in this part of the reef are excellent for snorkelling, diving and just getting back to nature – though reaching them is generally more expensive than reaching islands nearer the coast. Some of the islands are important breeding grounds for turtles and seabirds, protected within the Capricornia Cays Important Bird Area.

Lady Elliot Island

The Great Barrier Reef's southernmost coral cay, Lady Elliot is a 45-hectare vegetated shingle cay populated with nesting sea turtles and an impressive number of seabirds. It's considered to offer the best snorkelling in the southern Great Barrier Reef and the diving is good too: explore a seabed of shipwrecks, coral gardens, bommies (coral pinnacles or outcroppings) and blowholes, and abundant marine life, including barracuda, giant manta rays and harmless leopard sharks. Sitting in one of the Barrier Reef's 'Green Zones', it enjoys the highest level of environmental protection – which is also enjoyed by the migrating humpback whales between June and October.

Lady Elliot Island is not a national park; your only accommodation option is the low-key **Eco Resort** (☑ 1800 072 200; www.ladyelliot.com.au; r with half board & activities from $315/130 per adult/child). Accommodation here comprises safari tents, simple motel-style units or more expensive two-bedroom, self-contained suites. Rates include breakfast and dinner, snorkelling gear and some tours.

Heron Island

Part of the Capricornia Cays, Heron Island is among the world's finest scuba-diving regions, with a majority of the Reef's fish and coral species found here. Visitors generally come to spend time beneath the waves around the 34-sq-km Heron Reef, but the island's rugged beauty is reason enough to stay above the surface. A true coral cay, with excellent beaches, superb snorkelling and wall dives, plus turtle-watching, it's densely vegetated with pisonia and casuarina trees. There's a resort and research station on the northeastern third of the island; the remainder is national park.

Heron Island Resort (☑ 1800 875 343; www.heronisland.com; d//f/ste from $308/364/404; ✳) is your only accommodation choice, with tiled and spacious rooms and floor-to-ceiling windows; the incredible natural surrounds are more of an attraction.

The **Heron Islander** (☑ 1800 875 343; www.heronisland.com; one-way adult/child $69/35) ferry departs Gladstone at 9.30am every day except Tuesday and Thursday and takes two hours.

For a more glamorous approach, take a **seaplane** (☑ 1800 875 343; www.heronisland.com; one-way $349) from Gladstone. Departures are daily, subject to demand, and times can vary.

North West Island

North West is a spectacular 106-hectare coral cay, the second-biggest on the reef. Like much of the Capricornia Cays National Park, it's a remote tropical haven, growing steadily more popular. It is also an important site for nesting green turtles and birds; every October, hundreds of thousands of wedge-tailed shearwaters (70% of the east-coast Australian breeding population) descend on the island to nest, squabble and scare the wits out of campers with their creepy night-time howls. There's a basic camping ground here, nestled in pisonia forest and with access to the beach; sites (per person/family $6.55/26) can be booked online via Queensland Parks & Wildlife.

Rockhampton & Around

POP 80,665

Welcome to Rockhampton ('Rocky' to its residents), where the hats, boots and pickup trucks are big, and the bulls are even bigger. With more than 2.5 million cattle within a 250km radius, Rocky justifiably calls itself Australia's Beef Capital. Originally a gold-rush town founded in 1858 on land owned by the Darumbal people, and built on 'Sin, Sweat and Sorrow', it's now the administrative and commercial centre of Central Queensland, with fine Victorian buildings reflecting the region's 19th-century mining heyday.

Straddling the tropic of Capricorn 40km inland, Rocky can be scorching hot and unbearably humid in summer. Its walkable centre has a smattering of museums and cultural centres, a pleasant riverfront promenade and some great dining, but appeals most to travellers as a gateway to the coastal gems of Yeppoon and Great Keppel Island, and the Byfield National Park to the north.

◉ Sights

★ Dreamtime Cultural Centre
CULTURAL CENTRE

(☑07-4936 1655; www.dreamtimecentre.com.au; 703-751 Yaamba Rd, Parkhurst; adult/child $16/7.50; ⊙9am-3pm Mon-Fri, tours 10.30am & 1pm; ℗⊞) The stories of the local Darumbal people and Torres Straits islanders are well-conveyed here. Self-guide through exhibits such as 'The Vanishing Culture of the Sandstone Belt' or join an excellent, 90-minute, hands-on tour with knowledgeable guides. You will learn about the significance of rock paintings found in Carnarvon National Park, watch a didgeridoo demonstration and try your hand at throwing a boomerang. The Centre is on the Bruce Hwy, 7km north of town.

Check out the exhibition dedicated to Aboriginal sporting achievements and don't miss the paintings by the late artist Brian Fisher, the fluid lines depicting kangaroos, goannas, platypuses and other wildlife.

Rockhampton Art Gallery
GALLERY

(☑07-4936 8248; www.rockhamptonartgallery.com.au; 62 Victoria Pde; ⊙9am-4pm Mon-Fri, from 10am Sat & Sun; ℗) FREE Founded in 1967, this great regional gallery owns an impressive collection of modernist Australian paintings, including works by Russell Drysdale, Arthur Boyd, John Brack and Sidney Nolan. You'll also see a rotating collection of pieces by Aboriginal artists, significant British and Japanese works, and photography by the Queensland Evolve collective.

Archer Park Rail Museum
MUSEUM

(☑07-4936 8191; www.archerparkrailmuseum.com; 51-87 Denison St; adult/child/family $9.50/5.80/28; ⊙10am-3pm Mon-Thu, to 1pm Sun; ℗) Housed in a handsome heritage-listed railway station dating to 1899, this museum tells the station's story through photographs, artefacts, 'speaking' mannequins, and the enthusiasm of the curator, happy to relay the history of the regional railways. Climb aboard the locomotive or ride the museum's rare French-built Purrey steam tram (10am to 1pm Sunday) – the last operational example left anywhere and the last remaining of Rockhampton's nine trams that plied its streets between 1909 and 1939.

🛏 Sleeping

Heritage Hotel Rockhampton
HISTORIC HOTEL $

(☑07-4927 6996; www.facebook.com/heritagehotelrock; 228 Quay St; r $60; ℗⊜❋) Revamped and reopened after years of shuttered decay, this 19th-century hotel has a Wild West vibe, plenty of wrought-iron detail and river views from the front-facing rooms. Yes, the air-con sounds a bit like a plane taking off, and bathroom facilities are strictly shared and reminiscent of school changing rooms, but it's central and excellent value for money.

Criterion
HISTORIC HOTEL $

(☑07-4922 1225; www.thecriterion.com.au; 150 Quay St; hotel s/d/ste $70/80/90, motel r from $115; ⊙pub 6.30am-midnight Sun-Thu, to 3am Fri & Sat; ℗❋🛜) Dating from 1889, with one of the finest facades on historic Quay St, the Criterion is Rockhampton's grandest old pub. Replacing a pub built in 1867, it retains its elegant foyer and characterful period rooms, while out front is a friendly bar (and a steakhouse to avoid).

All the old hotel rooms have showers, although the toilets are down the hall. If you prefer more comfort, there are a number of modern motel rooms next door.

CAPRICORN CAVES

Capricorn Caves (☑07-4934 2883; www.capricorncaves.com.au; 30 Olsens Caves Rd; adult/child/family $35/17/87; ⊙tours 9am-4pm; P⚲) Riddling the Berserker Range some 24km north of Rockhampton, this vast cave complex is one of the Capricorn Coast's foremost attractions. Technically not subterranean (the caves were formed by water working on the limestone of an ancient reef, thrust upward by tectonic pressure) they contain cave coral, stalactites, dangling fig-tree roots and little insectivorous bats. The most popular (one-hour) tour showcases their remarkable acoustics with a classical-music recording in Cathedral Cave, and is suitable for all ages and most fitness levels.

The cathedral has become a popular wedding spot, and hosts several concerts throughout the year. In December, around the summer solstice (1 December to 14 January), sunlight beams through a 14m vertical shaft into Belfry Cave, creating an electrifying light show. If you stand directly below the beam, reflected sunlight colours the whole cavern with whatever colour you're wearing.

There are other tours that focus on palaeontology and fossils. Also, daring spelunkers over 16 years old and of decent fitness can book a two-hour 'adventure tour' ($90), which has you crawling through tight spots with names such as 'Fat Man's Misery'. A less strenuous family version of this tour is also offered (adult/child $50/40; also two hours long).

The Capricorn Caves complex has barbecue areas, a pool, a kiosk and accommodation (powered sites $35, cabins from $150).

★Denison
Boutique Hotel   BOUTIQUE HOTEL $$
(☑07-4923 7378; www.denisonhotel.com.au; 233 Denison St; d incl breakfast $135; P❄🌐) Occupying a handsome, wrought-iron-wrapped, two-storey Victorian building, built in 1886 for the railway administration and now on the National Heritage register, the Denison is Rockhampton's most characterful hotel. Period splendour meets 21st-century creature comforts: king-size four-poster beds with pillow-top mattresses, heavy velvet drapes, high ceilings and spa baths in each en suite.

Coffee House   MOTEL $$
(☑07-4927 5722; www.coffeehouse.com.au; 51 William St; d/tw/ste/apt from $150/175/185/185; ❄🌐⛆) The Coffee House features compact, tiled motel rooms, self-contained apartments and spa suites, all decorated with botanical-themed art and dark-wood writing desks. There's a scafe-restaurant–wine bar on-site.

✗ Eating & Drinking

You'd think that in the 'beef capital of Australia' finding a good steak would be easy, right? But no: while most places will throw a slab of meat on the grill, few will do it justice.

Two Professors   CAFE $
(☑07-4927 2301; www.thetwoprofessors.cafeleader.com; 49 William St; mains $10-18; ⊙5.30am-4.30pm Mon-Fri, 6am-2pm Sat & Sun; ❄🌐) Approaching coffee with a reverence given to alchemy, Rocky's best coffee shop turns speciality beans from a Brisbane roastery into highly satisfying brew using Chemex, V60 and other processes. Coffee aside, this is a haven for those wanting to read their paper or clack on a laptop over a leisurely brunch.

★TruFusion Indian Bar & Grill   INDIAN $$
(☑07-4291 2990; www.facebook.com/trufusionrocky; 137 East St; mains $19-28; ⊙5-9pm Mon-Wed, 11.30am-2pm & 5-9pm Thu-Sat; 🖉) This restaurant is a contender for 'Best Indian/Sri Lankan Food in Queensland'. Biryanis come studded with tender pieces of smoked goat, 'devil' dishes hit you with twin punches of sweet heat and sourness, and your palate will appreciate the tandoori lamb cutlets, fringed with crisp ribbons of fat. Bindi masala and chargrilled eggplant are nonmeaty pleasers.

Bartlett's Tavern   STEAK $$
(☑07-4927 2699; www.bartlettstavern.com.au; 166 Kent St; mains $18-29; ⊙11.30am-2.30pm & 5-9pm; 🖉) Ask locals where to find superlative steaks in Rocky and most will direct you to this unassuming, family-run bistro. What it lacks in character it makes up for in spades with its rump and porterhouse steaks, thrown on the grill just long enough to sear in all the right places. Daily specials are terrific value, too.

★Headrick's Lane   AUSTRALIAN $$$
(☑07-4922 1985; www.headrickslane.co; 189 East St; mains $16-45; ⊙kitchen 7am-9pm Tue-Sat, to 2pm Sun; 🌐) All clean lines and industrial decor,

this high-ceilinged restaurant and microbrewery makes intelligent use of a heritage-protected merchant's store in central Rockhampton, and is still the most urbane place to eat in town. It morphs to meet needs throughout the day, serving inventive breakfasts, calorific bar food and more refined dinners.

Great Western Hotel
PUB

(☑ 07-4922 3888; www.greatwesternhotel.com.au; 39 Stanley St; ⊘ 11am-midnight Wed & Thu, to 3am Fri & Sat) Dating from 1862, the GWH is part country pub, part concert venue and part of Rockhampton's social fabric. Out the back is a bullring – try to time your visit for a Wednesday or Friday night, when cattlefolk get tossed in the air by bucking bulls and broncos.

ⓘ Information

Tropic of Capricorn Spire Visitor Centre
(☑ 07-4936 8000; www.advancerockhampton. com.au; 176 Gladstone Rd; ⊘ 9am-5pm Mon-Sat, to 3pm Sun) This helpful centre sits on the highway right beside the tropic of Capricorn marker, 3km south of central Rockhampton. Brochures include guides to fishing on the Fitzroy River.

ⓘ Getting There & Away

AIR

QantasLink (www.qantas.com) and Virgin (www. virginaustralia.com) connect Rockhampton with Brisbane and Mackay. The airport (☑ 1300 225 577; www.rockhamptonregion.qld.gov.au/coun cilservices/rockhampton-airport; 81 Canoona Rd) is about 4km west of the centre of town. Young's Bus Service (☑ 07-4922 3813; www.youngsbus-service.com.au; 171 Bolsover St) runs bus 20 to and from the airport a dozen or so times daily.

BUS

Greyhound (www.greyhound.com.au) buses run from Rockhampton to Brisbane ($179, 11¼ to 14½ hours, three daily), Mackay ($70, four hours, three daily) and Cairns ($222, 17 hours, daily), among other destinations. Premier Motor Service (www.premierms.com.au) offers cheaper but less frequent services. Buses stop at the Puma (93/101 George St) petrol station.

TRAIN

From the train station (Depot Hill), 450m southwest of the city centre, Queensland Rail (www.queenslandrailtravel.com.au) runs at least one daily service to Brisbane ($135, 7¾ to 10½ hours) via Gladstone ($39, 1½ hours), plus Cairns (seat/sleeper $289/404, 16¼ hours, four weekly) via Mackay and Townsville.

Yeppoon
POP 19,003

The natural point of embarkation for the Keppel Bay Islands, Yeppoon is a breezy, laid-back town with good sleeping, eating and shopping options and a long, beautiful beach backed by apartments and restaurants. If you're here on the first Sunday of the month, drop in on the **Figtree Creek Markets**, a craft-and-produce market held in the grounds outside the Capricorn Coast Visitor Information Centre. Nearby, **Byfield National Park** makes for an entertaining diversion, particularly if you have a 4WD.

◉ Sights

★ Cooberrie Park
WILDLIFE RESERVE

(☑ 07-4939 7590; www.cooberriepark.com.au; 9 Stones Rd; adult/child/family $30/15/70; ⊘ 10am-3pm, animal show 1pm; 🚗) At this small wildlife sanctuary, your contribution goes towards the rehabilitation of injured and orphaned animals following the wildfires of 2019-20. You can stroll the 10 hectares of bushland, feed grass pellets to kangaroos, peacocks and emu wandering freely through the grounds. It's 15km north of Yeppoon.

🛏 Sleeping

While Away B&B
B&B $$

(☑ 07-4939 5719; www.whileawaybandb.com.au; 44 Todd Ave; s/d incl breakfast $115/140; ❄🔊) This perennially popular B&B has good-sized, immaculately clean rooms (one with wheelchair access) and a quiet location 100m back from the beach. It offers complimentary nibbles, tea, coffee, port and sherry, as well as generous breakfasts. All four rooms on the ground floor can be group-booked for $400.

★ Coral Inn Yeppoon
INN $$

(☑ 07-4939 2925; www.coralinn.com.au; 14 Maple St; r from $135; ❄🔊🏊) Beautifully landscaped grounds and contemporary rooms make this a great find in Yeppoon's quiet backstreets. Families in particular benefit from the quad room, communal kitchen, BBQ, pizza oven, and mini 'beach' area with hammocks and pool. Buffet breakfast is $12 extra, and there's an open bar (5pm to 6pm).

Coral Inn isn't appropriate for backpackers.

🍴 Eating

Whisk
CAFE $$

(☑ 0413 053 398; www.whiskyeppoon.com.au; 15 James St; mains $13-27; ⊘ 7am-2pm; 🔊) Aussies do brunch in a big way; nothing new there. But Whisk deserves credit for adding fun twists to the classics to make them particularly hipster-pleasing (behold: sweet-potato eggs Benny, red-velvet waffles and Buddha bowls brimming over with red quinoa).

ℹ️ Information

Capricorn Coast Visitor Information Centre
(📞07-4939 4888; www.capricorncoast.com.au; 1 Scenic Hwy; ⏰9am-5pm) Has plenty of information on the Capricorn Coast and Great Keppel Island, and can book accommodation and tours.

Out the back you'll find the genuinely interesting **Shell World**, a collection of more than 2000 seashells, some elaborate and beautiful beyond imagination, that has been growing since 1962.

ℹ️ Getting There & Away

Yeppoon is 43km northeast of Rockhampton, and 7km north of Keppel Bay Marina at Rosslyn Bay. Young's Bus Service runs frequent buses throughout the week from Rockhampton to Yeppoon ($6.30, 40 minutes) and down to Keppel Bay Marina ($6.30, one hour).

If you're driving, there's a free daytime car park at Keppel Bay Marina. For longer, secure undercover parking, the **Great Keppel Island Security Car Park** (📞07-4933 6670; 422 Scenic Hwy; per day from $15) is by the turn-off to the marina, south of Yeppoon.

Keppel Konnections (p404) and **Funtastic Cruises** (📞0438 909 502; www.funtastic cruises.com; Red Pier, Rosslyn Bay; day cruise adult/child $110/90; ♿) both leave from Keppel Bay Marina daily to Great Keppel Island and the Keppel Bay Islands National Park.

Great Keppel Island

Known as Wop-pa to its Woppaburra traditional owners, Great Keppel is the largest of the group of 18 islands that bears its name. The 4-sq-km island was a party destination in the '80s ('Get Wrecked on Keppel'), but is currently a laid-back, blissed-out destination for hardy bushwalkers keen to tackle its rocky, headlands and ridge trails, and sun seekers who are drawn by Keppel's 17 pristine beaches and the reef denizens found in its cerulean coastal waters. An old resort, which closed in 2012, had been acquired at research time by Asian developers, and a $400 million megaresort, complete with golf course, marina and airport may yet come to pass.

👁️ Sights

Beaches

The beaches of Great Keppel rate among Queensland's best. Fisherman's Beach and adjoining Putney Beach both have sheltered waters, good for swimming. Leeke's Beach, accessible either from the north end of Putney Beach or via the 1st Lookout (one hour) is a long but exposed stretch of sand. A steep 25-minute walk via the the rocky headland brings you to Monkey Beach, ideal for both swimming and snorkelling. Accessible either via a 4WD track or short hop across the headland from Monkey Beach, Long Beach is the best on the island: white sand, cerulean waters and a naturist section at its north end.

WORTH A TRIP

BYFIELD

Byfield is a village in Byfield National Park, 40km north of Yepoon, a well-concealed landscape of rare diversity: empty sand dunes running up to rocky pinnacles, wetlands and semitropical rainforests. A 4WD will get you to remote hiking paths and isolated beaches beautiful enough to warrant a much longer stay.

Nob Creek Pottery (📞07-4935 1161, 0428 192 601; www.nobcreekpottery.com.au; 216 Arnolds Rd; ⏰10am-4pm Thu-Mon) FREE is a working pottery and gallery nestled in leafy rainforest. The gallery showcases hand-blown glass, woodwork and jewellery; the handmade ceramics are outstanding. Take a boat trip through the rainforest with **Waterpark Eco-Tours** (📞0488 351 171; www.waterparkfarm.com.au; 201 Waterpark Rd; 2½hr tour $28; ♿), keeping an eye out for bright blue kingfishers, baby turtles and big daddy eels.

There are five **camping grounds** (📞13 74 68; www.parks.des.qld.gov.au; per person/family $6.55/26) to choose from (prebook). Nine Mile Beach and Five Rocks are on the beach and you'll need a 4WD to access them.

Set on 26 hectares of richly scented, cacophonous rainforest splendour, **Byfield Mountain Retreat** (📞0428 192 601, 07-4935 1161; www.byfieldmountainretreat.org; 140 Flanders Rd; house per night from $260) is only a short drive from Byfield village and will suit anyone looking for a deep nature experience.

Great Keppel Island

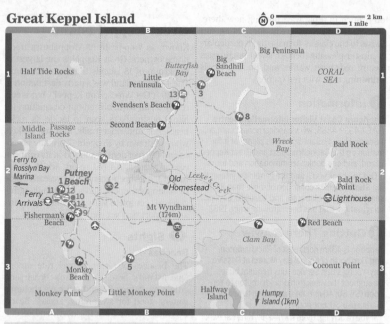

Great Keppel Island

🏃 Activities

Water Sports

Great Keppel is a haven for all manner of watery pursuits, from kayaking, paddleboarding and wakeboarding to some of Queensland's best snorkelling. Swimming is good also, though swimmers must beware the rip tides around the island's many points.

Keppel Watersports   WATER SPORTS
(📞0439 797 733; Fisherman's Beach; ⊙8am-4pm; 🚻) Operating from a hut on the main beach, this friendly operation hires out snorkelling equipment (per day $15), kayaks (one hour $25) and stand-up paddleboards (one hour $20), and also runs jet-ski tours ($185 per person). Snorkelling tours and beach dives are available; contact them in advance to request a boat drop on one of the island's far beaches.

Bushwalking

There is excellent bushwalking on the island; make sure to take plenty of water and a hat. Times below are from Fisherman's Beach.

Take the dirt track and partially paved road to the **1st Lookout** (40 minutes). Just beyond, you can hike up to the summit of **Mt Wyndham** (178m) for terrific views of the island (1½ hours). It's best to retrace your steps, since the trail on the other side of the viewpoint is overgrown. Alternatively, descend to the wetlands from the 1st Lookout, skirt them, and carry on straight along the dirt track all the way to **Butterfish Bay** (2¼ hours), past **Svendsen's Beach** (two hours). A trail to **Clam Bay** (two hours) branches off from the wetlands track, just past the **Old Homestead**. Also from the wetlands track, a relatively demanding trail climbs up a ridge and continues all the way to the 'lighthouse' (7.7km, three hours).

From Butterfish Bay, a sandy trail leads past the large sand dune to the terrific snorkelling spot of Wreck Beach (30 minutes).

From Fisherman's Beach, you can also do the Leeke's Beach Circuit (3.8km, two hours) by descending to Leeke's Beach from the 1st Lookout and then making your way back via Putney Beach after scrambling up a short, steep trail at the west end of Leeke's Beach. Also from Fisherman's Beach, you can do another loop (two hours), taking in Long Beach, Monkey Beach and Shelving Beach.

Sailing

Sail Capricornia CRUISE
(☑0421 709 238; www.sailcapricornia.com.au; Keppel Bay Marina; full-day cruises incl lunch adult/child $130/85) Sail Capricornia offers full-day snorkelling jaunts in the waters around Great Keppel Island on board the catamaran *Grace*. Sunset ($55) and private cruises ($1600 to $1900) are also available.

Freedom Fast Cats CRUISE
(☑07-4933 6888; www.freedomfastcats.com; Pier 1, John Howes Dr) Operates tours (adult/child from $78/50) of the surrounding reef and islands from its base at Keppel Bay Marina in Rosslyn Bay (7km south of Yeppoon). Glass-bottomed boats leave at either 9.15am or 10.30am, while seven-hour adventure tours (adult/child $138/93) with snorkelling and

'boomnetting' (trawling behind the boat in a net) are booked in advance.

🛏 Sleeping

Great Keppel Island
Holiday Village HOLIDAY PARK $
(☑07-4939 8655, 1800 537 735; www.gkiholiday village.com.au; 80 The Esplanade; unpowered sites $25, r $100, glamping tents $120, cabins $160) 🖋 This beachside holiday park offers good budget accommodation to suit all (dorms, basic twin rooms, cabins, safari tents), with access to a large communal kitchen, barbecue area, shared bathrooms and hammocks under a tree. Snorkelling gear can be rented for $5, and Geoff picks guests up from the boat.

⭐ **Svendsen's Beach** CABIN $$
(☑07-4938 3717; www.svendsensbeach.com; 2-person tent/studio/house $120/160/240) 🖋 Three-night minimum stays are barely enough at this secluded eco-retreat on the 'other' side of Great Keppel. It runs on solar and wind power, and has a bush-bucket shower. The perfect place for snorkelling and bushwalking, it's BYO food. Owner Lyndie will pick you up in her boat from the ferry.

Great Keppel Island Hideaway RESORT $$
(☑07-4939 2050; www.greatkeppelislandhidea way.com.au; f with shared bathroom $155, tr $180, cabins $240-335) Its sublime bend of Fisherman's Beach propped up by giant sandbags, this hideaway is set on leafy grounds, with

---

OFF THE BEATEN TRACK

THE GEMFIELDS

Comprising the townships of **Sapphire**, **Rubyvale** and **Anakie**, the Gemfields of Central Queensland are a tough and often sun-scorched landscape, drawing seasonal prospectors who eke out a living until a jackpot (or sunstroke) arrives. There are over 3000 mines within a 900-sq-km radius, and fossickers descend in winter – in the baking summers the towns are nearly deserted – to seek sapphires, zircons and, very rarely, rubies. The town of Emerald, 61km east of the Gemfields, is the gateway to the Gemfields (misleadingly, emeralds are not actually found here).

Some 1.2km beyond Rubyvale is **Miners' Heritage Walk-in Mine Tour** (☑07-4985 4444; www.minersheritage.com.au; 97 Heritage Rd, Rubyvale; adult/child $20/10; ⊗9am-5pm), a former sapphire mine. Informative 40-minute underground tours, in which you descend into a maze of tunnels, begun in 1906 and reaching 17m beneath the surface, are available throughout the day. Tours usually start at 15 minutes past the hour, and under-12s are charged just $5. You can also buy a bag of 'mine wash' and have a go at fossicking; the on-site jewellers will then tell you whether your finds are of gem quality. You can pick up reasonably priced gems and jewellery in the shop attached to the mine, and also at the **Rubyvale Gem Gallery** (☑07-4985 4388; www.rubyvalegemgallery.com; 3 Main St; ⊗9am-5pm) in the heart of Rubyvale; the owners have several spacious apartments for rent out back ($125) if you want to extend your Gemfields adventure.

the distance between the various cabins and houses lending an air of peaceful isolation to a family holiday. The cheapest family rooms share facilities, or else you can splurge on airy A-frame houses by the seafront.

Fresh air fiends and water babies will welcome the wakeboarding, kayak tours and jet-ski circumnavigation of the island.

ⓘ Getting There & Away

Regular ferries make the 30-minute trip from Keppel Bay Marina in Rosslyn Bay, 7km south of Yeppoon, to **Fisherman's Beach** on Great Keppel. **Keppel Konnections** (☑ 0484 241 505; www.keppelkonnections.com.au; Red Pier; adult/child one way from $25/15) has twice-daily services to the island, departing Rosslyn Bay at 9am and 3pm and returning at 10am and 4pm, with an extra service from Friday to Sunday. Freedom Fast Cats (p403) leaves Rosslyn Bay between 7.30am and 10.30am and returns between 8am and 3.45pm, depending on the day and the season (adult/child/family return $45/30/135). For day trippers, there are sometimes daily specials ($30 return).

ⓘ Getting Around

With the exception of taking boat cruises around the island, pretty much the only way to get any-

GREAT KEPPEL'S BEST DIVING & SNORKELLING SITES

Great Keppel's underwater topography is a terrific playground for snorkellers and divers. The following sites are reachable on foot.

Shelving Beach & Monkey Beach Numerous coral varieties, often attract turtles.

Wreck Beach An abundance of coral varieties, including huge brain coral, plus clownfish, spider conchs.

Second Beach Small coral patch, lots of small reef fish, occasional turtles.

The following spots are accessed by boat.

Half Tide Rocks Olive sea snakes, clownfish, soft and hard corals.

Passage Rocks Deep north–south channel, numerous hard coral species.

Middle Island Several snorkelling spots, including the former Underwater Observatory that attracts numerous reed fish.

where on Great Keppel is on your own two feet, meaning that fit bushwalkers have most of the beaches all to themselves. Take plenty of water. **Theo** (☑ 0431 622 281) runs 4x4 drop-offs to Long Beach and Monkey Beach. Keppel Watersports (p402) can drop you off by boat at a beach of your choice; ask in advance for prices.

CAPRICORN HINTERLAND

The central highlands, west of Rockhampton and the traditional lands of the Ghungalu people, are home to the tremendous Carnarvon National Park. Particularly popular during the cooler months, it offers spectacular gorges, unique flora, millennia-old Aboriginal rock art and one of Australia's Great Walks.

In the Gemfield beyond Emerald, 270km inland, try fossicking for sapphires in the heat and rubble – you'll be surrounded by the good people and vibe of the outback.

Carnarvon National Park

Significant to the Bidjara, Karingbal and Kara Kara people for around 4000 years, Carnarvon Gorge is a primeval landscape of sandstone cliffs, pinnacles, river and verdant vegetation. This 30km-long, 200m-high fissure was carved out over millions of years by Carnarvon Creek and its tributaries. Left behind is a lush oasis along the bottom of the gorge, where life flourishes. You'll find giant cycads, king ferns, river oaks, flooded gums, cabbage palms, deep pools, and platypuses in the creek. Escaped convicts once took refuge here, among caves that still bear ancient rock paintings. Wildlife is plentiful.

For most, Carnarvon Gorge *is* the Carnarvon National Park, as the other sections – including Mt Moffatt, Ka Ka Mundi and Salvator Rosa – are difficult to access.

🏃 Activities

★ **Australian Nature Guides**   WALKING
(☑ 07-4984 4652; www.carnarvongorge.info; tours per person $25-75) The only locally based guide service, Australian Nature Guides takes small groups through this fascinating landscape on a range of day hiking tours, as well as night wildlife safaris. Guides are your best bet for coming away from Carnarvon suitably edified. Regular tours run April to October; tailor-made tours run anytime.

HIKING IN CARNARVON NATIONAL PARK

Carnarvon National Park has some terrific hikes to suit all abilities, ranging from gentle, 20-minute nature trails and day hikes to the multiday Great Walk.

There are gentle walks not far from the entrance to the gorge. The 1.5km **Nature Trail** loop is particularly good at dawn or dusk, when you may spot night gliders, plus platypus in the creek. The 600m-return **Rock Pool** trail takes you to a deep swimming hole, which makes for a refreshing dip.

In the gorge itself, the **Boolimba Bluff Walk** (6.4km return) makes for a strenuous workout; it's a stiff climb up to the rim of the gorge and the 'roof of Queensland', particularly magical at dawn or sunset.

A wonderful day hike is the 19km-return **Big Bend Walk** (allow seven to eight hours) that takes you as far as the Big Bend camping ground. For the most part, it's a level and partially shaded walk along the bottom of the gorge, with numerous creek crossings. It also allows you to check out some of the gorge's top highlights along the side gorges branching off from the main trail: the millennia-old Aboriginal cave art at **Art Gallery** and **Cathedral Cave**, the hidden garden of the **Amphitheatre**, and the natural phenomena of the **Moss Garden** and **Wards Canyon**. It's best to hike to the furthest point of your walk first, and then visit the side gorges on the way back.

Carnarvon National Park's tour de force is the 87km-long, six-day **Carnarvon Great Walk**, a loop that links Carnarvon Gorge with Mount Moffat. It's hiked clockwise from the Big Bend camping ground, traversing the gorge and ascending ridgelines to lofty woodland plateaus. It's a serious undertaking, best done between April and October; the trail tends to be closed for maintenance from December to March.

🛏 Sleeping

There are nine basic national-park camp sites along the Great Walk within the gorge itself. Only **Big Bend** (https://qpws.usedirect.com/qpws; sites per person/family $6.55/26) is open year-round. The **Carnarvon Gorge Campground** (sites per person/family $6.55/26), right next to the entrance to the gorge, is open only during Easter and the June to July and September to October school holidays.

⭐ **Takarakka Bush Resort** RESORT $$
(☏07-4984 4535; www.takarakka.com.au; Obriens Rd; unpowered/powered sites from $30/36, cabins $165-215) 🦘 Popular with families and bushwhackers due to its variety of accommodation – tent and caravan sites, safari tents ($125 to $165), cabins ($195) and cottages ($248) – in a stunning location at the head of some fine walking trails. You'll see plenty of wildlife, from wallabies to platypus. Takarakka is 5km from the gorge.

Carnarvon Gorge Wilderness Lodge LODGE $$$
(☏07-4984 4503, 1800 644 150; www.carnarvon-gorge.com; Obriens Rd; cabins from $220; ⊙mid-Feb–Nov; @🛜🏊) This is outback chic set deep in the bush, with abundant wildlife in stunning surrounds. Excellent guided tours are available, plus a full-board package (from $155 to $300 per person). The Carnarvon Gorge Discovery Centre is on-site.

The centre hosts the informative Afternoon Park Presentation at 4.30pm each day between March and October (gold-coin donation).

ℹ Information

Carnarvon Gorge Visitor Centre (☏07-4984 4505; www.parks.des.qld.gov.au; ⊙8am-4pm; 🛜) Right near the entrance to the gorge, this sometimes unstaffed information centre has detailed info on the park's history and wildlife.

ℹ Getting There & Away

There are no bus services to Carnarvon – you'll need your own wheels.

The 40km access road to the park branches off from the Carnarvon Hwy (Rte A7), 62km south of Rolleston at the intersection of Rte A7 and Rte 60, and 112km north of Injune, also on the A7. The road is sealed all the way to the park entrance, barring a couple of kilometres. Following heavy rain, sections of the road are prone to flooding.

Petrol is not available anywhere in the gorge – fill up at Rolleston or Injune.

Wildlife Spotter's Guide

An encounter with any of Australia's charismatic creatures is among the highlights of a journey here. Here are 10 iconic species to watch out for.

1. Eastern Grey Kangaroo
At home across Australia's eastern third, the eastern grey can stand 2m tall and weigh more than 65kg.

2. Koala
The koala is found from Chillagoe in Far North Queensland to close to the Victoria–South Australia border. It spends much of its life sleeping, and has very poor eyesight.

3. Platypus
Platypus are common but shy, inhabiting freshwater streams and river margins from Far North Queensland to coastal Victoria.

4. Wombat
The common wombat is nocturnal and lives in dry forests and coastal scrub in eastern NSW, eastern Victoria and Tasmania.

5. Echidna
One of only two egg-laying mammals (monotremes) on earth (the platypus is the other), echidnas are one of the oldest species of mammal. They can live everywhere from forests to farmlands.

6. Dingo
One of Australia's largest carnivores, the dingo arrived in Australia around 4000 years ago. Pure-breeds, such as those on Fraser Island, have sandy, ginger or black fur.

7. Saltwater Crocodile
The estuarine (saltwater) crocodile can grow up to 6m long, can live in both fresh and saltwater, and can live over 70 years. They eat fish, birds and mammals.

8. Humpback Whale
Reaching up to 16m long, humpback whales migrate along Australia's east coast between June and November. Males produce a song that can last 20 minutes.

9. Eastern Brown Snake
The world's second-most venomous land snake, the eastern brown is common throughout eastern Australia, except in densely forested areas.

10. Cassowary
This beautiful, flightless bird is the world's second-heaviest bird species, and is the third-tallest bird species (after ostrich and emu)..

Whitsunday Coast

Best Places to Eat

➡ Bommie (p429)

➡ Fish D'Vine (p421)

➡ Dispensary (p414)

➡ 9th Lane Grind (p414)

➡ Paddock &
Brew Company (p414)

➡ Shuckz Oyster &
Champagne Bar (p419)

Best Places to Sleep

➡ Elysian Retreat (p426)

➡ Qualia (p427)

➡ Stoney Creek Farmstay
(p416)

➡ Coral Sea Resort (p419)

➡ Platypus Bushcamp (p416)

➡ Eungella Mountain Edge
Escape (p416)

Why Go?

Many travellers to Australia, especially those with a sailing pedigree or penchant for camping under the stars, head straight for the Whitsundays – an archipelago of mostly uninhabited islands in the Coral Sea – and struggle to leave. Photogenic teal waters and white-sand beaches fringe the forested isles, while around them tropical fish swarm through the world's largest coral garden – the Great Barrier Reef Marine Park. The gateway to the islands, Airlie Beach, is a compact backpacker hub with a parade of tanned faces zinging between boats, beaches and bars.

South of Airlie, art deco meets street art and great food in the coastal Queensland town of Mackay. It's the jumping-off point for trips to Eungella National Park – a lush hinterland oasis where platypuses cavort in the wild – as well as wallaby-spotting in Cape Hillsborough National Park. Sugar-cane- and mango-growing dominate the coast, for those interested in harvest work.

When to Go
Mackay

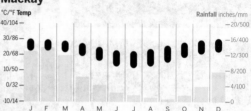

Jun–Oct The perfect time to enjoy sunny skies, calm days, mild weather and stinger-free seas.

Aug Sailing boats skim across the water and parties are held during Airlie Beach Race Week.

Sep–Oct Optimal conditions for kayaking around the islands.

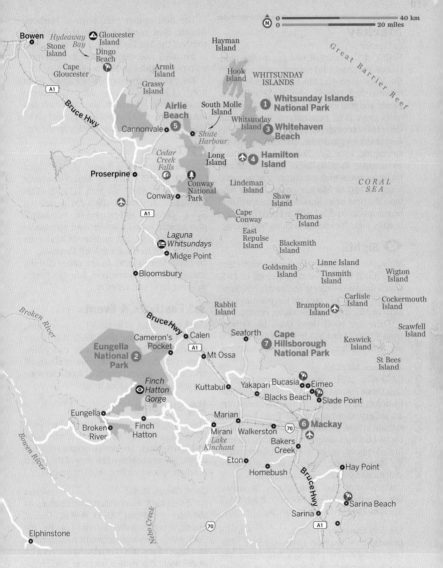

Whitsunday Coast Highlights

1 **Whitsunday Islands National Park** (p423) Sailing through magnificent aquamarine waters and camping under the stars.

2 **Eungella National Park** (p415) Waiting patiently for a glimpse of a shy platypus and walking in the misty rainforest.

3 **Whitehaven Beach** (p430) Being dazzled by the bright-white silica sand at this impossibly photogenic beach.

4 **Hamilton Island** (p427) Hiking the steep forest trails away from the resort buzz.

5 **Airlie Beach** (p417) Swilling beer and partying hard in fun-lovin' Airlie Beach.

6 **Mackay** (p410) Enjoying the diverse dining scene and checking out street art in this appealing town.

7 **Cape Hillsborough National Park** (p417) Spotting wallabies at dawn where the bush meets the beach.

Mackay

POP 125,000

Sitting at the heart of vast sugar-cane plantations covering land owned traditionally by the Yuibera people, Mackay is a prosperous regional hub named after the Scottish explorer and mariner John Mackay. The town's main draw is its proximity to Eungella and Cape Hillsborough National Parks, though its easy-going tropical vibe, artificial lagoon for swimming, appealing botanical gardens and picturesque location twixt the marina and the mangroves may encourage you to spend a day or two in Mackay proper. Those who have the time or inclination to linger will find broad streets studded with art deco facades, a healthy nightlife and the region's best dining.

◉ Sights

Mackay's impressive art-deco architecture owes much to a devastating cyclone in 1918, which flattened many of the town's buildings. Enthusiasts should pick up the pamphlet *Art Deco in Mackay* from the visitor centre.

There are good views over the harbour from **Rotary Lookout** in North Mackay and over the beach at **Lampert's Lookout**.

Artspace Mackay   GALLERY
(☑07-4961 9722; www.artspacemackay.com.au; Civic Centre Precinct, Gordon St; ☺10am-5pm Tue-Fri, to 3pm Sat & Sun) FREE This contemporary art gallery showcases works from local and visiting artists, including pieces by the Indigenous Lockhart River Art Gang. Exhibits may include photos of South Pacific Islanders and the stories behind their tattoos as well as installations by renowned Japanese artists.

Chew over the masterpieces at on-site cafe **Foodspace** (☑07-4961 9719; mains $14-15; ☺7.30am-2pm Mon-Fri, 8.30am-1pm Sat).

Mackay Laneway Project   PUBLIC ART
(www.facebook.com/mackaylanewayproject; Fifth Lane; ☺24hr) For Mackay's tag artists, the city is their canvas. Download the Zappar app and aim your phone at the barcodes in this alleyway to make the psychedelic mandala and rainforest animals come to life.

This is part of the city's *Art Walk*; pick up a brochure from the tourist information centre to locate all the sculptures and murals that dot the city centre.

Beaches

Mackay has plenty of beaches, although not all are ideal for swimming.

The best option near town is **Harbour Beach**, 6km north of the centre and just south of the Mackay Marina. The beach here is patrolled and there's a foreshore reserve with picnic tables and barbecues.

Even better are the beaches about 16km north of Mackay. At long, flat, residence-encroached **Blacks Beach**, the sand stretches out for 6km, while **Bucasia** is the most undeveloped and arguably the prettiest of the lot.

☞ Tours

Reeforest Adventure Tours   TOURS
(☑1800 500 353, 07-4959 8360; www.reeforest.com; tours adult/child from $135/99) This well-established outfit offers day tours such as a platypus-and-rainforest 'eco-safari', plus longer expeditions around the Mackay region's reefs and rainforests, and even a 12-day trip to the Cape York Peninsula in far-north Queensland. In the cane-crushing season (June to December), you can tour a working farm and refinery.

✯ Festivals & Events

Mackay Festival of Arts   CULTURAL
(☺Jul) Going strong since 1985, this 10-day extravaganza in July features everything from comedy, music and cabaret to visual arts, workshops and plenty of food and wine in various venues across town.

⨶ Sleeping

There are plenty of motels strung along busy Nebo Rd, southwest of the centre, while several apart-hotels are dotted around the city centre. There are also a few digs of the beach hotel and motel variety near the marina.

Coral Sands Motel   MOTEL $
(☑07-4951 1244; www.coralsandsmotel.com.au; 44 Macalister St; s/d from $90/99; ✴☞☒) One of Mackay's better wallet-friendly options, the Coral Sands boasts ultrafriendly management and large rooms in a central location. It's a bit tropi-kitsch, but with a saltwater pool, high-speed internet, plus the river, shops, pubs and cafes on your doorstep, you will overlook the cheesy decor.

Riviera Mackay   APARTMENT $$
(☑07-4914 2460; www.rivieramackay.com.au; 5-7 Nelson St; 1-/2-bedroom apt from $169/274; 🅿✴☞) This light, stylish property, architecturally inspired by Palm Springs, presents you with well-appointed apartments in a monochrome palette cut by slashes of gold and yellow. Enjoy basic kitchens,

Mackay

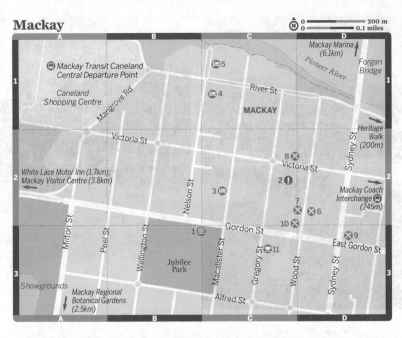

Mackay

◉ Sights
1 Artspace Mackay B3
2 Mackay Laneway
   Project C2

🛏 Sleeping
3 Coral Sands Motel C2
4 Oaks Rivermarque
   Mackay C1
5 Riviera Mackay C1

🍴 Eating
6 9th Lane Grind D2
7 Dispensary D2
   Foodspace .... (see 1)
8 Fusion 128 .... C2
9 Oscar's on Sydney D3
10 Paddock & Brew Company C2

🍺 Drinking & Nightlife
11 Woodsman's Axe Coffee C3

walk-in showers, air-conditioning and other mod-cons, plus access to a rooftop terrace equipped with a BBQ and all-encompassing river views.

Oaks Rivermarque Mackay   APARTMENT $$
(📞1300 550 409; 55-65 River St; r/apt from $144/169; P⊖❄🌐🏊) This apart-hotel is part of a local chain, but it has a lot going for it. The location is very central, the decor minimalist and you can opt for a cheaper double instead of a fully-equipped apartment if you're keen on dining out. Great amenities, too: pool, gym, spa...

White Lace Motor Inn   MOTEL $$
(📞07-4951 4466; www.whitelace.com.au; 73 Nebo Rd; r from $115, studio $170; P⊖❄🌐🏊) Who

said that a motel can't be characterful? From its Victorian-style exterior with shady verandah and white wrought-iron 'lacework' to the bright splashes of contemporary art in its rooms, it's the most appealing option along busy Nebo Rd. Light sleepers ought to ask for a room facing the back.

🍴 Eating

Oscar's on Sydney   FUSION $
(📞07-4944 0173; www.oscarscafe.com.au; cnr Sydney & Gordon Sts; mains $12-21; ⏰7am-4pm Mon-Fri, to 3pm Sat, from 7.30am Sun; ❄🌐) *Poffertjies* (little sugar-dusted Dutch pancakes) are a standout breakfast item at this popular cafe, where the menu encompasses such crowd-pleasers as huevos rancheros, macadamia muesli,

412

1. Strand jetty, Townsville (p433) 2. Airlie Beach Lagoon (p417)
3. Port Douglas (p479)
4. Great Barrier Reef (p502)

JEN WATSON / SHUTTERSTOCK ©

Gateways to the Reef

There are many wonderful ways to approach Australia's massive undersea kingdom. You can head to a popular gateway town and join an organised tour, sign up for a multiday sailing or diving trip exploring less-travelled outer fringes of the reef, or fly out to a remote island, where you'll have the reef largely to yourself.

The Whitsundays

Bathed in turquoise waters, and blessed with coral gardens and palm-fringed beaches, the Whitsundays have many options for reef exploring: base yourself on an island, go sailing or stay at Airlie Beach and island-hop on day trips.

Cairns

Among the most popular gateways to the reef, Cairns has dozens of boat operators offering snorkeling day trips, as well as multiday reef explorations on liveaboard vessels. For the uninitiated, Cairns is also a good place to learn to dive.

Port Douglas

An hour's drive north of Cairns, Port Douglas is an affluent, laid-back beach town with excellent water-sport options, including diving and snorkelling tours heading out to more than a dozen sites, including pristine outer reefs such as Agincourt.

Townsville

Australia's largest tropical city is far from the outer reef (2½ hours by boat), but has some exceptional draws, including access to Australia's best wreck dive, an excellent aquarium and marine-themed museums. Townsville is a departure point for liveaboard dive boats and for Magnetic Island.

Southern Reef Islands

For an idyllic getaway off the beaten path, book a trip to one of several remote reef-fringed islands on the southern edge of the Great Barrier Reef. You'll find fantastic snorkelling and diving just offshore.

smashed avocado and all manner of egg-tastic dishes. At lunchtime, the focus shifts onto salads, and steak sandwiches.

★ **9th Lane Grind**   CAFE **$$**
(☑0428 897 861; www.facebook.com/9thlanegrind; 43 Wood St; mains $15-28; ☺6.30am-3.30pm Mon-Fri, to 2.30pm Sat; ▣) Locally known for its short, eclectic menu that changes frequently according to the chef's whim, this popular 'bruncherie' excels when it comes to beautifully presented, calorific concoctions such as pork-belly croque-monsieur eggs Benny and Eton Mess French toast. Great coffee, too, and a sweet lunch menu that spans the globe.

Paddock & Brew Company   BARBECUE **$$**
(☑0487 222 880; www.facebook.com/thepad dockandbrewcompany; 94 Wood St; mains $15-34; ☺5pm-midnight Mon-Wed, from noon Thu & Fri, from 7am Sat & Sun) Grab some carnivorously inclined friends, head for this US-style 'meatery' and craft-beer bar and go straight for the Pit Master's Plate – a platter heaped with slow-cooked, tender brisket, pulled pork, smoked sausages and so much more. Less peckish? The burgers really hit the spot, as do the breads made with one of 140 beers on offer.

★ **Dispensary**   MODERN AUSTRALIAN **$$$**
(☑07-4951 3546; http://thedispensary.nefood.com. au; 84 Wood St; mains $18-46; ☺6am-2.30pm Mon, to midnight Tue-Sat) The dark, cavern-like interior with dark-wood banquettes is a boon for those who've come here to romance their sweetie over share plates of scallops with apple and hazelnut butter and tempura zucchini flowers. But most days, you'll find a lively crowd filling the tables outside, pairing their smart Mod Oz mains with carefully chosen wines. Dress up come evening.

In the mornings, it's a popular brunch and coffee spot.

Fusion 128   MODERN AUSTRALIAN **$$$**
(☑07-4999 9329; www.fusion128.com.au; 128 Victoria St; mains $30-43; ☺11.30am-2pm Tue-Sat, 5.30-9pm Tue-Thu, to 10pm Fri & Sat) One of the highlights of Mackay's food scene, Fusion 128 blends low-lit industrial design and a casual atmosphere. On the menu, Asian flavours meet classical European techniques with mixed results: the barramundi and twice-cooked pork belly are triumphs, while the seafood laksa is overburdened with a random explosion of celery. Cocktails like the lychee martini provide apt accompaniments.

 Drinking & Nightlife

Woodsman's Axe Coffee   COFFEE
(☑0437 773 776; www.woodmansaxe.com; 47 Gordon St; ☺6am-3pm Mon-Fri, to 2pm Sat) The best coffee in town (from $4.50) – either espresso or filter, made from ever-changing single-origin beans – is bulked out with light eats at this thimble-sized, self-styled 'eclectic hipster' coffee bar.

 Information

Mackay Visitor Centre (☑1300 130 001, 07-4837 1228; www.mackayregion.com; 320 Nebo Rd; ☺9am-5pm Mon-Fri; ☏) About 3km south of the centre, this visitor centre offers plenty of information on the region and beyond.

The Mackay region's main visitor information centre is in **Sarina** (☑07-4837 1228; www. mackayregion.com; Field of Dreams, Bruce Hwy, Sarina; ☺9am-5pm May-Oct, 9am-5pm Mon-Fri, to 3pm Sat, to 1pm Sun Nov-Apr).

ℹ Getting There & Away

AIR

Mackay Airport (☑07-4957 0201; www.mack ayairport.com.au; Boundary Rd E) is about 3km south of the centre of Mackay. TransLink bus 303 runs to the airport from the Caneland shopping mall at the western end of River St, along River St and then south down Gregory St (11 daily Monday to Friday, four daily Saturday).

Jetstar, Qantas and Virgin have daily flights to/from Brisbane, Rockhampton and Townsville.

BUS

Buses stop at the **Mackay Coach Interchange** (Caltex, cnr Victoria & Tennyson Sts), where tickets can also be booked. **Greyhound** (☑1300 473 946; www.greyhound.com.au) travels up and down the coast, connecting Mackay to Airlie Beach ($36, two hours, three daily), Townsville ($78, seven hours, two daily), Cairns ($129, 12½ hours, daily) and Brisbane ($242, 17 to 18½ hours, two daily).

Premier Motor Service (☑13 34 10; www.pre mierms.com.au) runs to the same destinations for less money, but has fewer services.

TRAIN

The *Spirit of Queensland*, operated by **Queensland Rail** (☑1300 131 722; www.queensland railtravel.com.au), runs five times weekly from Mackay to Brisbane ($161, 13½ hours), Cairns ($129, 11½ hours) and cities between. The train station is in Paget, 5km south of the city centre.

ℹ Getting Around

Major car-rental firms have desks at Mackay Airport – see www.mackayairport.com.au for listings. **NQ Car & Truck Rental** (☑ 07-4953 2353, 1800 736 828; www.nqcartruckrentals. com.au; 6 Malcomson St, North Mackay; ⊙ 8.30am-5pm Mon-Fri) is a reliable local operator.

Mackay Transit Coaches (☑ 07-4957 3330; www.mackaytransit.com.au) has several services around the city, many leaving from **Caneland shopping centre** (Mangrove Rd) and connecting the city with the harbour, airport and northern beaches; pick up a time-table at the visitor centre or look online.

For a taxi, call **Mackay Taxis** (☑ 13 10 08; www.mackaytaxi.com.au).

Eungella National Park

You have an excellent chance of spotting the elusive platypus in the rivers and creeks of the mystical, mountainous Eungella National Park, located on the traditional land of the Birra Gubba people. The park covers nearly 500 sq km of the lofty Clarke Range, but is largely inaccessible except for the established hiking trails around Broken River and Finch Hatton Gorge. The park's isolation from other rainforest areas for thousands of years has resulted in unique species, including the orange-sided skink and the Eungella honey-eater. There are also ongoing attempts by the Lazarus Project to resurrect the now-extinct Eungella gastric-brooding frog, which incubated its eggs in its stomach and gave birth to live young by spitting them out.

The park is divided into two sections: Broken River's subtropical rainforest and the tropical rainforest, waterfalls and swimming holes of Hatton Gorge, a 30km drive away.

◉ Sights

Finch Hatton Gorge

Finch Hatton Gorge is a remarkable, prehistoric slice of rugged subtropical rainforest, dotted with enormous granite boulders. The 12km road branches off the main Eungella–Mackay road and cuts its way through sugar-cane fields to the gorge turn-off, terminating in a parking and picnic area from which you can access two hiking trails.

Broken River

Broken River centres on the small bridge across the eponymous river, and comprises the picnic and camping grounds as well as tracts of ancient forest that border the river. The main attraction is platypus-spotting; other river life you're sure to see are large northern snapping turtles and brilliant azure kingfishers. Connecting Eungella hamlet, Broken River and Crediton Hall further south, hiking trails of varying strenuousness wind their way through the forest – a remarkable tangle of ferns and vines, beneath a canopy of Mackay cedars with their mighty buttressed roots, tulip oaks and cabbage palms.

Maps are available from the **information centre** (☑ 07-4958 4745; ⊙ 10am-3pm) near the platypus-viewing platforms in Broken River. It's sporadically staffed, but luckily there are information boards with maps at the trailheads.

Eungella

The hamlet of Eungella (*young*-gulluh; meaning 'land of clouds') sits perched 600m above sea level on the edge of a plateau overlooking the Pioneer Valley, with wonderful vistas over the Mackay hinterland towards the ocean. Some 6km north of Broken River, and 15km west of Finch Hatton (the town), Eungella is a convenient jumping-off point for Eungella National Park – in fact, one of the longer hiking trails starts in the hamlet – but staying here is less atmospheric than near the platypus habitat just down the road.

Lively markets are held in Eungella on the first Saturday of each month (April to December) from 9am at the town hall on North St.

🔅 Activities

Rainforest Scuba   DIVING
(☑ 0434 455 040; www.rainforestscuba.com; 55 Anzac Pde, Finch Hatton; per diver certified/non-certified $120/170) Claiming to be the world's first rainforest dive operator, these guys offer a fun experience. Expect to submerge in crystal-clear creeks where you're likely to see turtles and fish, but considerably less likely to see a shy platypus. Dives are generally held at 2pm, with no time limit, and certified divers can opt for a night dive.

Hiking

In Finch Hatton Gorge, there are two excellent hiking trails. A gorgeous 1.6km trail with mild inclines leads through the rainforest to Araluen Falls, with its tumbling waterfall and deep swimming hole; you'll see daredevils diving off the surrounding rocks. A further 1km hike takes you to the Wheel of Fire Falls, a series of cascades ending in another deep swimming hole.

Between Eungella and Broken River, there are six interconnected hiking trails, with another two following Broken River southeast

STONY CREEK RETREAT

Stoney Creek Farmstay (☑07-4954 1177; www.stoneycreekfarmstay.com; 180 Stoney Creek Rd, Eton, off Peak Downs Hwy; dm/stables/cottages $25/150/195; ℗), 32km south of McKay, offers accommodations such as an endearingly ramshackle cottage, a rustic livery stable or the charismatic **Dead Horse Hostel**, and forget all about wi-fi and flushin' loos: this is dead-set bush livin'. Two-hour horse rides cost $125 per person, there's plenty of wildlife to spot and hostel accommodation is free if you ride for two consecutive days.

'Family rides' of just an hour (under/over 10 years old $65/85) are more suitable for small children.

towards **Crediton Hall**, with longer hikes possible in the Denham Range to the south.

Starting in Eungella, the gentle **Pine Grove Circuit** (1.6km) loops through subtropical forest. It joins the more strenuous **Cedar Grove Track** (2.8km) that dwarfs you with its red cedars and tulip oaks and crosses several creeks. It ends at the **Sky Window Circuit** (250m), a level, easy loop that offers great views of the Pioneer Valley below. From here, you can continue to Broken River via the moderately demanding **Clark Range Track** (8.2km), with some short uphill sections and stairs.

At Broken River, there are two easy, pleasant, interlinked loops that meander through the rainforest and along the river: the **Rainforest Discovery Circuit** (780m) and the **Granite Bend Circuit** (1.6km). The challenging **Crediton Creek Track** (8km) branches off from the latter and follows the course of the river to the **Wishing Pool Circuit** (1.7km). On the last two trails there are greater chances of seeing large monitor lizards and some of the forest's serpentine denizens that like to hide in the piles of rotting leaves.

🛏 Sleeping & Eating

🛏 Finch Hatton Gorge

⭐**Platypus Bushcamp** CAMPGROUND $
(☑07-4958 3204; www.bushcamp.net; 672 Gorge Rd, Finch Hatton; sites/huts $10/100; ❈❅) 🌿 Situated in gorgeous rainforest next to a platypus swimming hole, this bush retreat was handbuilt 30 years ago by Wazza, the eccentric

owner. Canvas-clad, open-sided tree houses come equipped with mosquito nets, and you and your sweetie can watch platypuses from your bed in the secluded 'Honeymoon Suite'. The rustic kitchen/lounge engenders camaraderie among guests, and stays get extended indefinitely. Bring your own food and linen. Wazza's place is due to be taken over by new management in 2020 or 2021.

River Rock Cafe CAFE $
(☑07-4958 3281; mango smoothie $10; ⊙10am-5pm Wed-Sun) An essential stop for mango smoothies on your way to or from a sweaty hike to the Finch Hatton Gorge swimming holes, this shady space also offers light meals and other smoothie flavours.

🛏 Broken River

Fern Flat CAMPGROUND $
(www.parks.des.qld.gov.au; sites per person/family $6.55/26) With eight shady sites adjacent to the river and a basic outdoor privy, the campground is 500m down a gravel road, past the information centre (where you'll also find a kiosk, picnic tables, BBQs, proper loos and hot showers for $2). Register online.

Broken River Mountain Resort RESORT $$
(☑07-4958 4000; www.brokenrivermr.com.au; Eungella Dam Rd; d $140-200; ❈❅❈) Goannas and brush-tailed possums share space with humans at this lovely retreat, which has cosy cedar cabins, ranging from small, motel-style units to a large self-contained lodge sleeping up to six. There's a guest lounge with an open fire and the **Possums Table Restaurant & Bar** (mains $35-36; ⊙breakfast & dinner), serving meat-heavy Aussie classics.

The resort organises several (mostly free) activities for its guests, including spotlighting (nocturnal animal-spotting), birdwatching and guided walks, and can arrange shuttle transfers for longer walks.

Platypus Lodge Restaurant CAFE $
(☑07-4958 4785; mains $8-17; ⊙10am-3pm Wed-Sun) Next to the information centre, this appealing cafe serves good coffee, cakes and a few Aussie standards, like shepherd's pie.

🛏 Eungella

⭐**Eungella Mountain Edge Escape** CABIN $
(☑07-4958 4590; www.mountainedgeescape.com.au; North St; 1-/2-bedroom cabin $120/140; ❈) The three neat, self-contained wooden cabins with balcony on the edge of the escarp-

ment form a wonderful vantage point for appreciating Eungella. The grounds are perfectly manicured and each cabin is warmly decorated and fully equipped with barbecue and DVD player. Minimum stays apply during holidays and the owners can arrange meals.

ℹ Getting There & Away

From Mackay, it's a 70km drive west along the Eungella–Mackay road to Finch Hatton Gorge, 88km to Broken River and 82km to Eungella. There are no buses to Eungella or Finch Hatton, but Reeforest Adventure Tours (p410) runs day trips from Mackay and will drop off and pick up those who want to linger.

The turn-off for Finch Hatton Gorge is just before the town of Finch Hatton. The last 2km of the 10km drive from the main road is on unsealed roads, with several creek crossings that can become impassable after heavy rain. A dramatically winding mountain road climbs up to Eungella and Broken River.

Cape Hillsborough National Park

Comprising broad beaches, rocky headlands, sand dunes, mangroves, hoop pines and rainforest, this 10.2-sq-km national park lies some 50km northwest of Mackay. Along the four short, easy-to-moderate walking trails through the headlands, you may spot kangaroos, wallabies and sugar gliders. Turtles are common close to shore, and roos might be seen on the beach in the evening and early morning. To get here, follow Bruce Hwy north from Mackay for 20km, then follow the signs along partly paved roads.

On the approach to the foreshore area, a 1.2km (40-minute) boardwalk circuit leads through a tidal mangrove forest, past a vast Aboriginal midden testifying to historic shellfish feasts. From the picnic area, the Beachcomber Cove Track (2.2km return, 1½ hours) passes through eucalyptus groves and rainforest before ending at the eponymous cove. Just south of the picnic area, the Yuibeira Plant Trail (1.2km return, 30 minutes) educates you about the traditional use of plants. You may also spot the remnants of stone fish traps, left by the Yuibeira people. Finally, Andrews Point Track (2.8km return, two hours), a steep and rocky walk from the south end of the beach, is worth it for the numerous scenic viewpoints.

Accommodation options consist of the little Smalleys Beach Campground (☑13

74 68; www.parks.des.qld.gov.au; sites per person/family $6.55/26) and the Cape Hillsborough Nature Resort (☑07-4959 0152; www.capehillsboroughresort.com.au; 51 Risley Pde; unpowered/powered sites $33/38, cabins $110-260; ✳ ✳).

Airlie Beach

POP 1208

Situated along a coastline traditionally owned by the Ngaro and Gia peoples, and squeezed in between Pioneer Bay and a hillside dotted with apartment buildings, compact Airlie is the gateway to the unparalleled Whitsunday Islands and an essential stop on most east-coast road trips. Its multiple hostels, beer gardens and tour operators are strung along the short stretch of Shute Harbour Rd, separated from the yachts bobbing on the waters by a lovely lawn-fringed swimming lagoon (📷) FREE.

Between the bustling cafes, thronged with backpackers, and the forests of masts of the Coral Sea and Port of Airlie marinas, you'll find all you need in this beachside holiday hub: bars, restaurants, supermarkets and accommodation to suit all budgets. Those looking to avoid the party scene – families especially – will have no trouble finding quieter lodgings close enough to the centre of town.

🏃 Activities

Mostly water-based, and understandably focused on the Whitsundays, Airlie offers a dazzling array of outdoor diversions: sailing

ℹ PLATYPUS VIEWING

Most days of the year, you can be pretty sure of seeing a platypus or two in Broken River at the rightfully renowned platypus-viewing platforms (there are two, both a couple of minutes' walk along paved footpaths on either side of the bridge) and under the bridge itself. Broken River is reputedly one of the most reliable spots on earth to catch these meek monotremes at play and we can vouch for it – few people leave disappointed. The best times are around sunrise and in the afternoons, from around 3pm till dusk. You must remain patient, silent and still. Platypus activity peaks from May to August, when the females are fattening themselves up in preparation for gestating their young.

(p428), kayaking, skydiving, helicopter tours – you name it. You can hire sea kayaks and paddleboards near Airlie Lagoon for a paddle around Airlie Bay.

Whitsunday Dive Adventures   DIVING
(☑07-4948 1239; www.whitsundaydivecentre.com; Shute Harbour Rd, Coral Sea Marina; ⊙9am-6pm; ➍) This experienced shop runs day trips to Tongue Bay on Whitsunday Island, leaving from Abell Point Marina at 7.45am each day, including meals and snorkelling equipment ($209/107 per adult/four-to-12-year-old child). Certified divers can take one or two dives for $90 and $150 respectively. The outfit also offers four-day PADI open-water certification for $485, plus diving options for kids.

Airlie Beach Skydivers   SKYDIVING
(☑1300 759 348; www.airliebeachskydivers.com.au; 2/273 Shute Harbour Rd; 3048m/4267m jump $244/295; ⊙8am-5.30pm) This friendly team with a shopfront on Shute Harbour Rd can take you as high as 4267m for tandem jumps; they're the only outfit to offer a landing on Airlie Beach.

Skydive Airlie Beach   SKYDIVING
(☑1300 585 224; www.skydive.com.au/airlie-beach; 1/265 Shute Harbour Rd; skydives from $199; ⊙7am-9pm) With operations in four Australian states, this organised-but-relaxed outfit offers tandem jumps from 2134m and 4572m at Airlie Beach, and 4572m at Whitehaven Beach, with free return shuttles from its office in central Airlie.

👉 Tours

Salty Dog Sea Kayaking   KAYAKING
(☑07-4946 1388; www.saltydog.com.au; Shute Harbour Rd, Shute Harbour; half-full day trips $90/145) Based in Shute Harbour, Salty Dog offers guided day tours to South Molle Island, kayak rental (half-full day $60/90) and longer kayak-and-camping missions, including a wonderful six-day expedition ($1850) to Whitsunday and Hook Islands. It's a very hands-on intro to the Whitsundays, with the chance to spot sea turtles, dolphins, reef fish and (between July and September) humpback whales.

The company also offers half-day tours manageable by children (adult/child $90/80) and rents kayaks to experienced kayakers only.

Air Whitsunday Seaplanes   TOURS
(☑07-4946 9111; www.airwhitsunday.com.au; Shute Harbour Rd, Terminal 1, Whitsunday Airport; tours from $310) Air Whitsunday offers a range of tours aboard Cessna and de Havilland seaplanes. These include flyovers of the Outer Reef, where you don't leave the aircraft (which nonetheless performs a 'touch-n-go' water landing en route, just for thrills) and excursions landing at Whitehaven Beach and Heart Reef, where passengers disembark to snorkel, sightsee and bliss out.

✨ Festivals & Events

Airlie Beach Race Week   SAILING
(www.abrw.com.au; ⊙Aug) Held during the mild, calm subtropical winter, this week-long regatta sees more than 100 sports boats from around the world descend on Airlie to compete in the surrounding azure waters. Diversions include live music, food and drink and a fun run.

Festivities centre on the Whitsunday Sailing Club (☑07-4946 6138; www.whitsundaysailingclub.com.au; Airlie Point, 11 Ocean Rd; ⊙10am-10pm).

Airlie Beach Festival of Music   MUSIC
(www.airliebeachfestivalofmusic.com.au; 1-/3-day pass $150/250; ⊙Nov) First held in 2012, this sunny music festival spans 18 venues and three days in November. With the principal marquee beautifully located waterside at the Whitsunday Sailing Club, the mainly Australian line-up blends new acts with established legends such as The Church.

🛏 Sleeping

Airlie Beach is a backpacker haven, with hostels ranging from party central to basic beds for the night. There's also a remarkable variety of midrange accommodation suitable for families, ranging from boutique hotels to apartments, although little at the top end.

Backpackers by the Bay   HOSTEL $
(☑07-4946 7267; www.backpackersbythebay.com; 12 Hermitage Dr; dm $24-27, d & tw $72; ❇🛜🌊) This hostel will suit those who like to be sociable without engaging in crush-your-beer-can-against-your-forehead party action. Run by folks who genuinely cater to backpacker needs, this place sees guests congregating in the garden, saltwater pool and games room; there's also a laundry, BBQ area and kitchen, and good ratio of guests per bathroom.

Magnums Backpackers HOSTEL $

(☑1800 624 634; www.magnums.com.au; 366 Shute Harbour Rd; powered/unpowered sites $35/30, dm/d from $28/60; ❄@🛜) Expect to be kept up late by revellers from the attached Magnums Bar, which is either a boon or a bane, depending on your morning routine or reason for staying in Airlie. Either way, this place, with average dorms and basic doubles in a tropical garden, is the place to meet other travellers and cut loose for a few days.

Airlie Beach YHA HOSTEL $

(☑07-4946 6312; www.yha.com.au; 394 Shute Harbour Rd; dm $33, d with/without bathroom $85/75, f $160; ❄@🛜≋) Trust YHA to provide a genuine alternative to sordid hostels and bush dumps for young travellers. Central and reasonably quiet, with a pool and ample kitchen facilities, this is arguably the best hostel in central Airlie, with six- and eight-bed en-suite dorms, plain but serviceable doubles and a family room, sleeping up to five.

★**Sunlit Waters** APARTMENT $$

(☑07-4946 6352; www.sunlitwaters.com; 20 Airlie Cres; studios from $135, 1-bedroom apt $155; P❄🛜≋) Representing some of the best value in Airlie, these tiled studios and apartments have a lot going for them: the lofty hillside location overlooking the Abell Point Marina, well-equipped kitchenettes, ceiling fans and splashes of bold colour in the decor.

Waterview APARTMENT $$

(☑07-4948 1748; www.waterviewairliebeach. com.au; 42 Airlie Cres; studios from $155, 1-bedroom units from $170; P❄🛜) Waterview's compact units are an excellent choice for self-caterers aiming for a central yet quiet location, coupled with creature comforts. There are gorgeous views of the bay from the balconies, eye-catching splashes of contemporary art, spacious and comfy sitting areas and kitted-out kitchenettes – all a stone's throw from the main street but without the bustle.

Airlie Beach Hotel HOTEL $$

(☑07-4964 1999; www.airliebeachhotel.com.au; cnr Airlie Esplanade & Coconut Grove; motel/hotel r from $149/229; P❄🛜≋) Given the ideal central location, the sea-facing hotel rooms here are some of the best in town at this price. With smartly furnished rooms and a pool, popular pub and immense liquor store on-site, this place attracts bargain-savvy travellers.

Heart Hotel & Gallery BOUTIQUE HOTEL $$

(☑1300 847 244; www.hearthotelwhitsundays.com. au; 277 Shute Harbour Rd; r $149-270, ste $449; ❄🛜) This smart hotel in the heart of Airlie couldn't be more central. Architecturally inspired by early Queensland homes, the white-washed, fan-cooled rooms are smallish but elegant, with top-quality bedding, up-to-date tech fittings (Bose sound systems, Nespresso machines, massive flat-screen TVs) and luxurious bathrooms. The gallery, on the top floor, shows the work of local artists.

★**Coral Sea Resort** RESORT $$$

(☑1800 075 061, 07-4964 1300; www.coralsearesort. com; 25 Ocean View Ave; d from $225; P❄@🛜≋) An excellent option for sedate travellers, this is a place where you can watch the waves from your spa bath or by dangling in your hammock on your private verandah (if you book a suite, that is). Sea-view rooms have stunning vistas, but you'll save plenty by going for a garden view.

Peninsula Airlie Beach APARTMENT $$$

(☑07-4964 1600; www.peninsulaairliebeach.com; apt $349-599; P❄🛜≋) All chrome and floor-to-ceiling glass, this set of luxury apartments perches on a rock peninsula just south of the Abell Point Marina. The light-filled, thoroughly contemporary apartments are decked out in neutral shades and all come with sea views, and guests can watch the yachts set sail from the marina while floating in the infinity pool.

✗ Eating

Central Airlie offers everything from cheap takeaway kebab shops to fancier restaurants. Self-caterers will find a massive **Woolworths** (cnr Shute Harbour Rd & Waterson Way; ⊙8am-9pm Mon-Fri, to 6pm Sat, from 9am Sun) supermarket behind the main strip in the centre of town.

Wisdom Cafe CAFE $

(☑07-4946 5199; 1b/273 Shute Harbour Rd; mains $7-17; ⊙7.30am-4pm; ✐) The smell of strong coffee beckons you inside this deservedly busy corner cafe. Perch at the limited indoor and outdoor tables and dig into the fresh juice combos and smoothies, breakfast classic like eggs Benny and sourdough topped with smashed avocado and cairns of crumbled feta. Later in the day, the focus shifts to handmade sandwiches and flatbread pizza.

★**Shuckz Oyster & Champagne Bar** SEAFOOD $$

(☑07-4948 0599; 263 Shute Harbour Rd; dozen oysters from $22; ⊙12.30-8.30pm Wed-Sun)

Airlie Beach

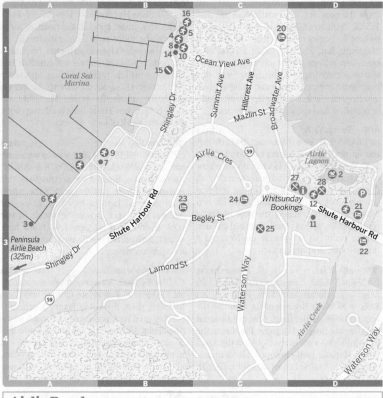

Some food combinations are so perfect that they require little embellishment. Oysters and champagne are one such combo. Have your succulent Coffin Bay molluscs 10 different ways, gulp them down in oyster shooters, sip your flute of Brut, and perhaps peel some

chutney, homemade muesli or cauliflower omelette with pesto), organic coffee and the homey, cluttered interior where you can peruse some children's books or acquire some organic body scrub.

Cool Lala Asian Cuisine ASIAN $$
(☑0484 220 777; www.facebook.com/coolla laairlie; 7/265 Shute Harbour Rd; mains $18-28; ⊙noon-2.30pm & 5.30-8.30pm Wed-Sun) This place keeps somewhat erratic hours, but catch it open and feast on punchy kimchi, delicate steamed dumplings, Korean drumsticks that pummel your taste buds with twin hits of heat and sweetness, and bites of crispy Taiwanese chicken. It is excellent drinking food, aching to be paired with a Chang or Asahi beer. More substantial dishes are on the menu come evening.

★Fish D'vine SEAFOOD $$$
(☑07-4948 0088; www.fishdvine.com.au; 303 Shute Harbour Rd; mains $30-33; ⊙5-11pm) Picture yourself in a vast dining area, where bartenders are shaking dark and stormy cocktails at the centrepiece bar. Meanwhile, waiters flit by, bearing platters of oysters, bowls of fish curry, platters of oven-baked barramundi and Seafood Extravaganza while diners tuck into chilli crab, covering themselves with sauce and shell fragments.

Sport eaters can take on the 'Seafood Indulgence', a two-tiered cascade of shells, claws and fins for two to share ($149).

🍷 Drinking & Nightlife

It's said that Airlie Beach is a drinking town with a sailing problem. The bar at Magnums (p418), a huge hostel in the centre of town, is always crowded, and a popular place to kick off a raucous evening.

Northerlies Beach Bar & Grill BAR
(☑1800 682 277; www.northerlies.com.au; 116 Pringle Rd, Woodwark; ⊙10am-8.30pm Sun-Thu, to 9pm Fri & Sat) Tucked away on a tranquil shore-front in Woodwark, facing Airlie across Pioneer Bay, Northerlies is just the place for a sundowner. The timber-floored bar and restaurant, open-sided to get the most of the views and the bay breezes, is set up to linger over craft beers, cocktails and well-chosen wines from Australia, New Zealand and Europe.

ℹ️ Information

Whitsunday Bookings (☑07-4948 2201; www. whitsundaybookings.com.au; 5/263 Shute Harbour Rd; ⊙8am-6pm) This office has been

local prawns and tear into the sweet white flesh of some Moreton Bay bugs.

Little Vegas Burger & Bar BURGERS $$
(☑07-4948 2853; www.facebook.com/littleve gasbb; 3/259 Shute Harbour Rd; burgers $16-24; ⊙noon-3pm & 5-9pm Wed-Mon) You're surrounded by trippy, Pop art-style faces of Elvis, Marilyn Monroe and other Vegas luminaries as you bite into a beef patty piled high with blue cheese, bacon, mushroom and caramelised onions, or panko-crusted trout with smashed avocado, or a pulled-pork sandwich overflowing with slaw and barbecue sauce. It's a sticky finger kind of place.

Cafe One 3 VEGETARIAN $$
(☑0419 783 313; 13 Waterson Way; mains $14-17; ⊙6.30am-2.30pm Mon-Fri; 🍴) Everything about this family-run cafe says 'wholesome': the menu, full of vegetarian and vegan dishes such as vegan muffin with avocado and

helping travellers book the right tour for years. Call for out-of-hours service.

ℹ Getting There & Away

AIR

The closest major airports, **Whitsunday Coast** (Proserpine Airport; www.whitsundaycoastairport.com.au; Lascelles Ave, Gunyarra) at Proserpine and **Hamilton Island** (Great Barrier Reef Airport; ☑ 07-4946 8620; www.hamiltonisland.com.au/getting-here/airport; Airport Dr) aka Great Barrier Reef Airport, have regular connections with Sydney, Melbourne and Brisbane.

Whitsunday Airport (p425), a small airfield 6km east of Airlie Beach (midway between Airlie Beach and Shute Harbour), doesn't have regular scheduled flights, but helicopter flights operate from here.

BOAT

For the general public, the only regular, daily boats from Airlie Beach to Whitsunday Islands are operated by Cruise Whitsundays (p425) and run between the **Port of Airlie** (☑ 1800 676 526; www.portofairlie.com.au; 13 The Cove Rd) and Hamilton Island ($62, one hour, 10 daily), plus Daydream Island ($37, 30 minutes, nine daily), as well as between the two islands ($40, 30 minutes, eight daily).

Campers heading to Hook, Whitsunday or the South Molle Island group need to make advance arrangements with **Scamper** (☑ 07-4946 6285, 0487 226 737; www.whitsundaycamping.com.au; Shute Harbour Rd) at Shute Harbour, some 8km southeast of Airlie Beach. **Island Transfers** (☑ 0488 022 868; www.islandtransfers.com; Shute Harbour Rd, Shute Harbour; ⊙ 6am-6pm) also drop campers off at Whitsunday and South Molle, and run several daily services to Palm Bay on Long Island.

BUS

Greyhound (☑ 1300 473 946; www.greyhound.com.au) buses detour off the Bruce Hwy,

connecting Airlie Beach to all the major centres along the coast, including Brisbane ($264, 18¼ to 21 hours, three daily), Mackay ($36, two hours, three daily), Townsville ($50, 3¼ to five hours, three daily) and Cairns ($108, nine to 10¼ hours, two daily). Premier Motor Service (www.premierms.com.au) offers lower fares to the same destinations.

Long-distance buses stop at the **Heart of the Reef Transit Terminal** (The Cove Rd, Port of Airlie).

ℹ Getting Around

Whitsunday Transit connects Proserpine (for Whitsunday Coast Airport), Cannonvale, Abell Point Marina, Airlie Beach and Shute Harbour (one to two hourly, from 6am to around 6.30pm). There are several stops in the centre along Shute Harbour Rd, at the junction with Broadwater Ave, plus the Port of Airlie.

Conway National Park

This serene national park encompasses the Conway Peninsula, once the hunting grounds of the Giru Dala and still home to large swaths of lowland tropical rainforest, remote mangroves, rocky uplands, and pandanus and paperbark woodlands. The day-use area, plus two car parks, 7km, 8km and 11km east of Airlie Beach, respectively, are the starting points for two easy-to-moderate walking trails apiece. The Whitsunday Transit bus from Airlie Beach to Shute Harbour (one to two hourly) takes just 20 minutes and can drop you at the trailheads.

From the day-use area, the Coastal Fringe Circuit (1.2km) traverses coastal rainforest, with Hayward Gully (1.6km) branching off into a rocky gully.

Mt Rooper car park is the starting point for the Swamp Bay traverse (2.1km), ending

---

ℹ CYCLONE WARNING

In Queensland's far north, between November and April each year, cyclones – known in the northern hemisphere as hurricanes – are a part of life, with an average of four or five forming each season. It's rare for these cyclones to escalate into full-blown destructive storms; however, in March 2017 Severe Tropical Cyclone Debbie made landfall near Airlie Beach, causing significant damage and flooding in South East Queensland and the Northern Rivers area of New South Wales. Airlie Beach and Bowen were affected as well. Bringing torrential rain, strong winds and ferocious seas, the storm killed at least 12 people in Australia, primarily as a result of extreme flooding.

During the season, keep a sharp ear out for cyclone predictions and alerts. If a cyclone watch or warning is issued, stay tuned to local radio and monitor the Bureau of Meteorology website (www.bom.gov.au) for updates and advice. Locals tend to be complacent about cyclones, but will still buy out the off-license when a threat is imminent!

TOP BEACHES

If the Whitsundays have some of Australia's finest beaches, and Australian beaches are some of the best in the world, then beach connoisseurs have hit the jackpot. Although there are plenty of secluded, postcard-perfect, sandy bays in this tropical archipelago, the following are reasonably accessible for nonyachting folk.

Whitehaven Beach (p430) With azure-blue waters lapping the pure-white silica sand, Whitehaven on Whitsunday Island is absolutely stunning.

Chalkies Beach Opposite Whitehaven Beach, on Haslewood Island, this is another idyllic, white-sanded beach. It's not on the usual tourist circuit, though some operators do stop there. Otherwise, charter a boat yourself.

Langford Island At high tide, Langford is a thin strip of sand on the rim of a ludicrously picturesque, coral-filled turquoise lagoon. More a sandbank than a beach, but surreally beautiful nonetheless.

Butterfly Bay On the northern side of Hook Island is this protected bay, which flutters with butterfly song each winter. Popular with discerning bareboat-charter-goers, who snorkel in the shallows and lob on the sand like happy beached whales.

Escape Beach This sheltered, sandy cove, lapped by cerulean waters, is Hamilton Island's loveliest beach – all the more because you're likely to have it all to yourself. To get here, it's a scenic 1¾-hour hike from the trailhead behind Whitsunday Apartments.

at the beach overlooking the Molle island group, as well as the ascent of Mt Rooper (2.3km, 221m). Combine the two trails via the 5.4km Mt Rooper Circuit, with good views of the Whitsunday Islands.

Just above Shute Habour, the Coral Beach trail (1.1km) takes you to the eponymous beach from the Coral Bay car park, with an additional 600m leading to The Beak lookout overlooking the Whitsunday Passage.

17km west of Airlie Beach, the Forestry Rd car park (off Shute Harbour Rd) is the jumping-off point for the demanding 27km Conway Circuit that brings you back to Airlie Beach, with bush camping en route.

Finally, beautiful **Cedar Creek Falls** (Cedar Creek Falls Rd), a popular swimming spot when there's sufficient water, can be reached by turning east from the Proserpine–Airlie Beach road at Conway Rd (18km southwest of Airlie) then following the signs. Expect to see butterflies, orchids, white cedars, Alexander Palms and perhaps turtles and monitor lizards.

THE WHITSUNDAYS

Rising out of the aquamarine sea, the 74 thickly forested, white-sand-fringed Whitsunday Islands are one of Australia's loveliest destinations, an unmatched playground for yachties, divers, campers, fishers and resort-loungers. Sheltered by the Great Barrier

Reef, these warm waters are particularly good for sailing, as exploited by the 100-plus yachts that gather here each August for Airlie Beach Race Week (p418). When Captain Cook sailed these waters in 1770, naming the islands after his sponsors, it was the seasonal home of the Ngaro people – and these islands also shelter some of the oldest archaeological sites on Australia's east coast. Four of them have resorts, some are private, but most are uninhabited (or offer camping), so that you can play out your *Shipwrecked* fantasy. Whitehaven Beach on Whitsunday Island is acknowledged as one of the finest beaches in Australia, while mainland hub Airlie Beach (p417) is a great base for exploring this archipelago.

🏃 Activities

Day Trips

Day trips usually involve going to Whitehaven Beach on Whitsunday Island, with other activities thrown in – including snorkelling and bushwalking. Other than the superfast *Camira*, operated by Cruise Whitsundays or the yacht Lady Enid, sailing boats aren't able to make it all the way to Whitehaven Beach on a day trip from Airlie Beach. Instead, they usually go to the lovely Langford Reef and Hayman Island (p431), stopping for lunch and snorkelling. If going to Whitehaven is a dealbreaker, you're better off signing on for a day trip on a catamaran or speedboat.

Whitsunday Islands

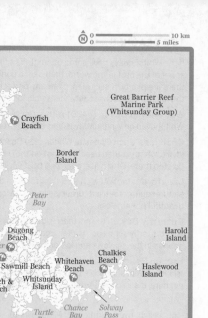

0   10 km
0   5 miles

Arkhurst Island

Hayman Island

Black Island

Langford Island

Great Barrier Reef Marine Park (Whitsunday Group)

Bird Island

Crayfish Beach

Hook Island

Border Island

Nara Inlet

Peter Bay

North Molle Island

Daydream Island

South Molle Island

Cid Island

Dugong Beach

Cid Harbour

Harold Island

Airlie Beach

Swamp Bay

Mt Rooper Lookout

Planton Island

Sawmill Beach

Whitehaven Beach

Chalkies Beach

Haslewood Island

Beak Lookout

Shute Harbour

Nari's Beach & Joe's Beach

Whitsunday Island

Denman Island

Shute Harbour

Henning Island

Turtle Bay

Chance Bay

Solway Pass

Long Island

Dent Island

Hamilton Island

Whitsunday Passage

CORAL SEA

Conway National Park

The Narrows

Dent Passage

Pentecost Island

Maher Island

Cedar Creek Falls

Lindeman Island

Conway Beach

Repulse Bay

Great Barrier Reef Marine Park (Whitsunday Group)

Shaw Island

Mansell Island

Thomas Island

★ **Ocean Rafting**
BOATING

(☎07-4946 6848; www.oceanrafting.com.au; Shingley Dr, Coral Sea Marina; adult/child/family $159/102/476; ⊕) A great way to see the Whitsundays' top attractions in a single day is on an adrenaline-packed Northern Exposure or Southern Lights trips (the former is better for snorkelling; the latter gives more time on the beach). The iconic yellow semirigid boats zoom to Whitehaven Beach, with lunch on a sandbar, and take in two snorkelling stops off Hook Island.

Red Cat Adventures
BOATING

(☎07-4946 4444; www.redcatadventures.com.au; 350 Shute Harbour Rd; tours from $179; ⊙7am-6pm) This excellent family-owned operation offers three distinct tours. Its popular day trip involves dashing to Whitehaven Beach in a speedboat, stopping for snorkelling on Whitsunday and Hook islands en route. Longer trips include the Ride to Paradise (one/two nights $309/599), which takes in several Whitsunday highlights before overnighting in Paradise Cove, a resort north of Airlie. Departures leave from Abell Point Marina.

Lady Enid   BOATING
(☑07-4948 3000; www.ladyenid.com.au; Coral Sea Marina, Port of Airlie; cruise $245) This gorgeous yacht, built in 1961 and the victor in the first Sydney-Brisbane yacht race, now leads a more sedate life cruising to Whitehaven Beach with a maximum of 24 passengers. Lunch, snacks, optional snorkelling and a stroll up to the Hill Inlet viewpoint are included. There is a strict 18-plus policy. The nine-hour cruise departs from Port of Airlie marina at 7.30am.

Whitehaven Xpress   BOATING
(☑07-4946 1585; www.whitehavenxpress.com.au; Shute Harbour Rd, Abell Point Marina; day trips adult/4-14yr $190/130) This operator offers various boat excursions, the most popular being its daily speedboat jaunt to Whitehaven Beach, which includes snorkelling, a glass-bottomed boat and beach BBQ. It departs from Airlie Beach's Abell Point Marina at 8.45am, returning around 4.45pm, with courtesy bus connection to your accommodation in Airlie.

Cruise Whitsundays   CRUISE
(☑07-4846 7000; www.cruisewhitsundays.com; 24 The Cove Rd, Port of Airlie; day cruise adult/4-14yr from $209/145) Cruise Whitsundays offers trips to various Whitsunday Islands and reefs, including Whitsunday Island and Hardy Reef. A delightful option is overnighting on the company's pontoon at spectacular Hardy Reef, 39 nautical miles offshore (from $525 per person). Also memorable are day trips around Whitsunday Island on the catamaran *Camira* (adult/child $209/145).

Diving
You'll notice a lack of dedicated dive shops in Airlie Beach and the Whitsundays. While the Great Barrier Reef may beckon, most dives in this area visit the fringing reefs around the Whitsundays (especially on their northern tips) because they are much easier to reach and often hold more abundant soft corals. PADI open-water courses start at around $450, while one/two dives for those already certified cost around $80/140.

Based in Airlie, Whitsunday Dive Adventures (p418) is your best bet.

A number of sailing cruises include diving as an optional extra. Prices start from $100 for introductory or certified dives. Cruise Whitsundays offers dives (from $119) on day trips to its reef pontoon.

Most of the island resorts also have dive schools and free snorkelling gear.

🛏 Sleeping

On the Whitsundays, accommodation tends to be split between resorts and remote beach camping.

Resorts
Resorts are located on Daydream, Long, Hamilton and Hayman islands, with Hamilton having the greatest choice and the more affordable accommodation options, as well as a number of independent cafes and restaurants. Some of the resorts are open to day trippers, making it possible to enjoy their ample facilities on a wallet-friendly budget, while others are completely exclusive, guests-only affairs. For resort guests, most travel agents will put together a range of discounted package deals combining airfares, transfers, accommodation and meals.

Camping
Queensland Parks & Wildlife (☑13 74 68; https://qpws.usedirect.com/qpws) manages Whitsunday Islands National Park camping grounds on Whitsunday, Hook, Henning, Molle, Lindeman, Shaw, Repulse and Smith islands for independent campers as well as groups on commercial trips. Camping permits (per person/family $6.55/26) are available online or at Queensland Parks' Airlie Beach office (☑13 74 68, 07-4946 1480; cnr Shute Harbour & Mandalay Rds; ⊘9am-4.30pm Mon-Fri).

Camping grounds are *basic* and most tend to have pit toilets, rainwater tanks and picnic tables, so you must be self-sufficient and bring insect repellent, food and 5L of water per person per day, plus three days' extra supply in case you get stuck. You should also have a fuel stove, as wood fires are banned.

❶ Getting There & Away

AIR
The two main airports for the Whitsundays are Hamilton Island (p422) and Whitsunday Coast (p422) at Proserpine. In Flametree, about 6km east of Airlie Beach, is the small **Whitsunday Airport** (☑07-4946 9180; www.whitsundayairport.com.au; Shute Harbour Rd, Flametree), used by charter services.

From Proserpine, Jetstar (www.jetstar.com) flies to Sydney, Melbourne and Brisbane, Virgin (www.virginaustralia.com) flies to Brisbane. From Hamilton Island, Qantas (www.qantas.com) and its partners fly to Sydney, Melbourne, Brisbane and Cairns, Virgin flies to Sydney, Melbourne and Brisbane, and Jetstar flies to Sydney.

BUS

Greyhound (☑1300 473 946; www.greyhound.com.au) and Premier Motor Service (www.premierms.com.au) detour off the Bruce Hwy to Airlie Beach. **Whitsunday Transit** (☑07-4946 1800; www.whitsundaytransit.com.au) connects Proserpine, Cannonvale, Airlie Beach, Flametree and Shute Harbour.

Whitsundays 2 Everywhere (☑0447 997 111; www.whitsundaytransfers.com) operates transfers from Whitsunday Coast Airport (Proserpine) to Airlie Beach for around $22 per adult one way.

BOAT

Cruise Whitsundays (p425) runs multiple daily ferries to Daydream and Hamilton island, plus services between the two; ideal for day trippers.

If you want to camp, contact Scamper (p422) in advance. Its boat leaves from Shute Harbour and can drop you at South Molle Island ($65 return) and its tiny satellites, Whitsunday Island ($105 to $155) and Hook Island ($160). Camping transfers include complimentary 5L water containers. You can also hire camp kits ($50 first night, $25 subsequent nights), which include a tent, gas stove, cooler and more. The website is full of more helpful information. Alternatively, contact Island Transfers (p422); it offers drop-offs at South Molle and Whitsunday islands for comparable prices and also does several trips daily to Palm Bay on Long Island on demand (four-person minimum).

The rest of the islands are accessible only to those with their own boats.

Long Island

Mostly classified as national park, thickly forested Long Island has secluded, pretty white beaches, lots of adorable wild rock wallabies and 17km of walking tracks. Ten kilometres long, it narrows to a neck just 400m wide – hence the name. There are two resorts here (one open to day trippers), plus a **basic campsite** (☑13 74 68; www.parks.des.qld.gov.au; sites per person/family $6.55/26) overlooking a sheltered beach. Long Island is reachable via private transfer from Shute Harbour with Island Transfers (p422); arrange in advance.

★ **Elysian Retreat**   RESORT $$$
(☑1800 765 687; www.elysianretreat.com.au; all-inclusive villas from $650 per person; 🔊) 🌿
Ten light-filled, thatch-roofed villas at this intimate, solar-powered boutique resort, accommodating a maximum of 20 guests, overlook a private stretch of reef near the south end of Long Island. Spend your tranquil days kayaking, paddleboarding or snorkelling, dining on gourmet organic meals from a daily changing menu and getting

pampered in the spa. Get here by boat or helicopter.

Palm Bay Resort   RESORT $$$
(☑1300 655 126; www.palmbayresort.com.au; villas/bungalows/suites from $299/370/420; 🐟) Occupying Long Island's narrow 'neck', this luxury self-catering resort offers a range of villas, *bures* ('Balinese-inspired' cottages), bungalows and houses, each with designer trimmings and either ocean views or easy beach access. There's a huge pool, day spa, tennis court, bar and shop, with snorkelling, kayaking and bushwalking the prime attractions for guests. Get here with Island Transfers (p422).

Hook Island

The 53-sq-km Hook Island, the second-largest island in the Whitsunday group, is predominantly national-park territory, its highest point being Hook Peak (450m). There are good beaches dotted around the island, and decent diving and snorkelling locations, such as Manta Ray Bay and Butterfly Bay. There are three basic camping grounds at Maureen's Cove, Steen's Beach, Curlew Beach and Crayfish Beach; Curlew Beach is the prettiest location, but the other three are shadier.

Buy camping permits (adult/family per night $6.55/26) online from Queensland Parks & Wildlife (p425). Scamper (p422) carries passengers from Shute Harbour to the camping grounds (return per person $160).

South Molle Island

The largest of the Molle Islands group, South Molle is virtually joined to its reef-fringed siblings, Mid and North Molle Islands. The island is mostly national park and is crisscrossed by 15km of walking tracks, with some superb lookout points. There are two partially shaded camping grounds for overnighting, as well as a basic camping ground apiece on the tiny Planton and Denman satellite islets (for that *Shipwrecked* experience). Day trippers and campers can get to the Molle islands with Scamper (p422) for $65 return.

Buy camping permits (adult/family per night $6.55/26) online from Queensland Parks & Wildlife (p425) before visiting.

Daydream Island

The rainforest-cloaked, reef-fringed Daydream Island (day trip resort fee per adult/

child $38/19) is only 1km long and 200m wide, and very popular with day visitors due to its accessibility. Much of it is taken up by the vast Daydream Island Resort & Spa, and day trippers may use the restaurants, pools and bars, wander the coral-strewn main beach, sunbathe at Lovers' Cove and walk the 1km Rainforest Trail. Cruise Whitsundays ferries connect the island with Port of Airlie ($37, nine daily) and Hamilton Island ($40, eight daily).

**Daydream Island
Resort & Spa** RESORT $$$
(07-3259 2350; www.daydreamisland.com; Daydream Island; r/ste from $350/1052; ❄️ ☎️ 🛜 ☰) The only lodgings on Daydream Island are white and airy, with a vertical garden in the main atrium and facilities galore. The Daydream team know their clientele – families with kids, international travellers and time-poor holidaymakers – and understand how to capitalise on the buzz generated by the location. Air-conditioned rooms are luxuriously kitted-out, and many face the glorious Coral Sea.

Hamilton Island
POP 1208

If you arrive by water, Hamilton greets you with the sight of a marina lined with yachts, villas and apartment towers peeping out of the hillside greenery, jet skis whizzing across the bay, golf buggies meandering along the winding roads, planes coming in to land and waterfront restaurants buzzing with punters.

The most developed of the Whitsundays, Hamilton has much to offer, whether you're a bushwalker looking to tackle a host of rocky walking trails, a fresh-air fiend into water sports (above and below the waves), a family of day trippers from Airlie Beach, or a lounge lizard wishing to combine sunbathing on

white-sand beaches with wandering in and out of air-conditioned boutiques and sipping a cold beer on the waterfront. One thing you're less likely to find here is solitude and tranquility...unless you stay in the most exclusive resorts or hit the remotest trails.

⊙ Sights

Hamilton Island Wildlife WILDLIFE RESERVE
(07-4946 8635; www.hamiltonisland.com.au/nature-and-wildlife/wildlife-hamilton-island; 1 Resort Dr; adult/child $27/16; ⊙8am-5pm; 🚼) This wildlife centre is a good place to introduce your kids to various marsupials, including wallabies and koalas, as well as a dingo, parrots and an assortment of reptiles. There are several options for meeting koalas, the best one being the pricey but worthwhile 'VIP Experience'.

🏃 Activities

You can hire stand-up paddleboards, kayaks, windsurfers, catamarans, jet skis and other equipment from centrally located Catseye Beach, or go parasailing or waterskiing. Nonmotorised equipment costs around $15 for half-hour rental, $30 for an hour. Jet-ski tours and diving and snorkelling excursions are offered by operators along the marina.

🛏 Sleeping & Eating

⭐**Qualia** RESORT $$$
(1300 780 959; www.qualia.com.au; 20 Whitsunday Blvd; villas from $1300; ❄️ @ 🛜 ☰) Hamilton's premier resort is serenity personified. Its 60 'pavilions' (timber-rich, luxuriously furnished villas) are divided into 'Leeward' (better for sunsets) and 'Windward' (glorious sea views), and are scattered among tropical foliage on the island's secluded northern peninsula. Qualia's boons include a private beach, two excellent, guests-only restaurants, a luxe spa,

WHITSUNDAY COAST HAMILTON ISLAND

HIKING HAMILTON

Hamilton Island has around 20km of decent bushwalking trail, the access point being the resort trail entrance (near the Whitsunday Apts shuttle stop). From there, you can hike up to **Resort Junction** in order to reach **Resort Lookout** (1.7km), or proceed onwards to **Saddle Junction** (1.8km), the gateway to the rest of the trails. If you only have time for one walk, clamber up scenic **Passage Peak** (239m), a 1¼-hour hike that rewards you with 360-degree views of the Whitsundays. However, if you really want to challenge yourself, do a loop from Saddle Junction to Passage Peak, then descend to **South East Head**, the remotest point on the island, before making your way to Escape Beach and hiking back up to Saddle Junction (allow six to seven hours for this). **Coral Cove Beach** and Resort Lookout can also be accessed via dirt road from near the Golf Driving Range shuttle stop (Blue line), but you're likely to be sharing it with dust-rousing ATV tours.

SAILING THE WHITSUNDAYS

The Whitsundays are the place to skim across fantasy-blue waters on a tropical breeze. If you're flexible with dates, last-minute standby rates can considerably reduce the price and you'll also have a better idea of weather conditions. Many travellers hang out in Airlie Beach for a few days for this exact purpose, although you may end up spending your savings in the pub!

Most vessels offer snorkelling on the fringing reefs, where the colourful soft corals are often more abundant than on the outer reef. Equipment and meals are always included; diving and other activities nearly always cost extra.

Some of the better-known boats berthing in Airlie Beach are as follows:

ISail Whitsundays (☑ 1800 550 751; www.isailwhitsundays.com; Shingley Dr, Coral Sea Marina; s/d $539/699 per person) Two-day, two-night adventures, stopping at Hayman, Hook and Whitsunday islands, either on a 14m catamaran or a 15m yacht. Paddleboards and sea scooters included.

TallShip Adventures (☑ 1800 334 773; www.tallshipadventures.com.au/overnight-sail ing-alexander-stewart; Shingley Dr, Coral Sea Marina; s/d $395/495 per person) 🍃 Overnight trips to Whitehaven Beach on a classic timbered 70ft yacht. Includes snorkelling and learning the traditional art of sailing.

Atlantic Clipper (☑ 07-4946 5755; www.atlanticclipper.com.au; Shingley Dr, Abell Point Marina, Airlie Beach; 2-day, 2-night trips from $489) A 53-berth party boat offering two-day cruises to Whitehaven Beach, Langford Island and other highlights. Diving offered.

Prima Sailing (☑ 1800 550 751; www.primasailing.com.au; Shingley Dr, Port of Airlie; 2-day, 2-night tours s/d $399/890) This 14m sloop, custom-built to cruise these waters, takes parties of up to 12 on two-night trips to sites only smaller boats can reach.

Once you've decided, book at one of the many agencies in Airlie Beach.

Bareboat Sailing

Rent a yacht or catamaran without skipper, crew or provisions. You don't need formal qualifications, but you (or one of your party) have to prove that you can competently operate a vessel.

Expect to pay between $700 and $1000 a day in high season (roughly June to August, when the weather is mild and calm) for a yacht sleeping four to six people, plus a book-ing deposit and a security bond (refunded when the boat is returned undamaged). Most companies have a minimum hire period of three to five days.

There are a number of bareboat charter companies around Airlie Beach, including the following.

Charter Yachts Australia (☑ 1800 639 520; www.charteryachtsaustralia.com.au; Shingley Dr, Coral Sea Marina; per night from $650)

Cumberland Charter Yachts (☑ 1800 075 101; www.ccy.com.au; Shingley Dr, Coral Sea Marina; yachts/catamarans per night from $495/695)

Queensland Yacht Charters (☑ 1800 075 013; www.yachtcharters.com.au; Shingley Dr, Coral Sea Marina; yachts/catamarans per night from $690/850)

Whitsunday Escape (☑ 1800 075 145; www.whitsundayescape.com; Shingley Dr, Coral Sea Marina; yachts/catamarans per night from $750/1000)

Crewing

In return for a free bunk, meals and a sailing adventure, crewing will see you hoisting the mainsail and cleaning the head. Look for 'Crew Wanted' signs around the marina, and at restaurants and hotels. Your experience will depend on the vessel, skipper, other crew members (if any) and your own attitude. Be sure to let someone know where you're going, with whom and for how long.

swimming pools and a plethora of water sports. Minimum stays apply.

Those keen to emerge from Qualia's cocoon of luxury can arrange sailing, diving, snorkelling and plenty of other pleasant diversions.

Reef View Hotel   HOTEL $$$
(✆ 02-9007 0009; www.hamiltonisland.com.au; 12 Resort Dr; d from $390, f $600; ❄🛜⊠) Aptly named, this hilltop resort has spectacular views of Hamilton's forested hills on one side, and the beach and fringing reef on the other (if you opt for the pricier ocean-view doubles). Centrally located and popular with families and groups, its rooms are spacious and decked out in soothing neutrals, with easy access to Catseye Beach.

Manta Ray Cafe   INTERNATIONAL $$
(✆ 07-4946 9999; Marina Village; mains $24-49; ⊙noon-10pm; 🧒) Set right on the water, this bright and airy restaurant distinguishes itself with a succinct menu, prompt service and smart composition of ingredients. There are international classics (prawn linguine, tuna tataki), some meat-free pleasers (vegetarian Buddha bowl) and an interesting take on the rib-eye (encrusted with paprika and coffee). It's a popular lunch and dinner spot.

★Bommie   AUSTRALIAN $$$
(✆ 07-4946 9999; Hamilton Island Yacht Club, Front St; 4-course/tasting menus $125/150; ⊙6pm-late Tue-Sat) Bommie is Hamilton's swankiest, most atmospheric restaurant, with excellent cocktails to boot. Take your loved one and choose from the compact menu of ingredient-driven, elaborately constructed dishes (like octopus with sherry caramel and lemon thyme, venison with tarragon emulsion), or else splurge on the tasting menu.

❶ Getting There & Away

AIR

Hamilton Island Airport (p422), the main arrival centre for the Whitsundays, is serviced by Qantas (www.qantas.com) to/from Sydney, Melbourne, Brisbane and Cairns, Virgin (www.virginaustralia.com) to/from Sydney, Melbourne and Brisbane, and Jetstar (www.jetstar.com.au) to/from Sydney.

BOAT

Cruise Whitsundays (p425) connects Hamilton Island Airport and the marina with the Port of Airlie in Airlie Beach (adult/child one-way $62/40, one hour, 10 daily) and also with Daydream Island ($37/18, 30 minutes, eight daily).

❶ Getting Around

Free shuttle buses (Green and Blue) follow two routes: Green runs along the marina and to the hotels by Catseye Beach every 15 minutes, while Blue connects the hotels to the north and south ends of the island every 20 minutes from 7am to 11pm. You can also hire a golf buggy (one/two/three hours $49/65/69, overnight $87) on which to whizz around the island. The buggies are available at the airport or marina.

Hayman Island

The most northerly of the Whitsunday group, little Hayman is just 4 sq km in area and rises to 250m above sea level. It has forested hills, valleys and beaches, and a luxury five-star resort – one of Australia's most celebrated, and long a stage for the lifestyles of the rich and famous. Access to the island is only possible if you're a guest at the resort.

InterContinental Hayman Island Resort   RESORT $$$
(✆ 07-4940 1838; www.hayman.com.au; r/ste incl breakfast from $405/708; ❄@🛜⊠) An avenue of stately date palms leads to one of the most gilded playgrounds on the Great Barrier Reef, with its hectare of swimming pools (open around the clock), landscaped gardens, state-of-the-art spa, five restaurants and pristine beaches. The rooms vary from well-appointed poolside cabins to deluxe three-bedroom suites and stand-alone villas.

Resort guests must first fly to Hamilton Island Airport, before being escorted to Hayman's fleet of luxury cruisers at the Port of Airlie for a pampered transfer to the resort.

Lindeman Island

The best known of the 13 coral-fringed specks in the Lindeman Islands National Park, this island is traditionally owned by the Ngaro, an Aboriginal seafaring people. The Club Med resort that opened here in 1992 closed 20 years later, and awaits redevelopment by its new owners. Now nature photographers and hikers are the main visitors, exploring a sea-claimed volcano mostly covered by national park, with splendid empty bays, reefs for snorkelling, and over 16km of walking trails.

Basic camping is available at Boat Port (adult/family per night $6.55/26) – an open site on a quiet beach backed by rainforest, with numerous walking trails nearby. Book online with Queensland Parks & Wildlife (p425) before arrival.

Whitsunday Island

The largest of the paradisaical group to which it gives its name, Whitsunday Island is ruggedly forested, and surrounded by clear teal waters and coral gardens. Its most visited site is the dazzling 7km-long **Whitehaven Beach** (Whitsunday Island) – one of Australia's finest – visited by pretty much every sailing/snorkelling tour from Airlie Beach but still managing to seem uncrowded. The more intrepid will also enjoy the Hill Inlet lookout at the north end of Whitehaven Beach.

There are six basic camp sites on the island, some with more shade than others. It's hard to beat the Whitehaven Beach camp site for its five-star location. Book camp sites online with Queensland Parks & Wildlife (p425), and see Scamper (p422) for camping transfers ($105 to $155 return per person).

Bowen

POP 10,377

A small coastal town built on the traditional lands of the Ngaro and Gia people and set on a hill north of Airlie Beach, Bowen is famous around Australia for its mangoes and tomatoes – it gets busy during fruit-picking season (April to January) – and is known locally for its secret bays and inlets. Its wide, quiet streets, clapboard Queenslander houses, landscaped esplanade and laid-back vibe make it an appealing place for an overnighter (or a lengthy stay, if you're inclined towards fruit picking). There are also some truly stunning – and little-visited – beaches and bays northeast of the town centre, including the stinger-free Queen's Beach and petite Horseshoe Bay, a favourite with snorkellers.

Baz Luhrmann's epic movie *Australia* was shot here in 2007, but there is nothing left of the 1940s Darwin film set; even the 'Bowenwood' sign on the town's water tower has been painted over with tropical fish. The locals feel it's time to move on.

🛏 Sleeping & Eating

Queens Beach Tourist Village   CABIN $$
(☑ 07-4785 1313; www.qbtvbowen.com.au; 160 Mount Nutt Rd; camping per site $36, cabin $105-125; ⊠) The holy trinity of location, cleanliness and top-notch facilities align at this beautifully kept, palm-studded holiday park, just a few minutes' walk from Bowen's lovely main beach. Pool, well-equipped kitchen and laundry are at the disposal of campers (take your pick of shady, grassy spots) and cabin-dwellers alike and the wafting scent of meat on the barbie fills the air.

Port Denison Motor Inn   MOTEL $$
(☑ 07-4786 6822; www.portdenisonmotorinn.com.au; 11 Dalrymple St; r $130-135; P ❋ 🛜) In a it's-hard-to-get-more-central location in the town proper, half a block from the beach, this exemplary motel is looked after by kind and welcoming staff and is a short shuffle from Bowen's clutch of diners and services. Expect spotless, if not terribly exciting, rooms with kitchenette and barbecue access.

★ Bird's Fish Bar   FISH & CHIPS $
(☑ 07-4786 4631; www.facebook.com/bowenfishermans.seafood.9; Henry Darwen Dr; fish & chips $11-15; ⊗ 8.30am-8pm Mon-Sat, from 11am Sun) This melange of nautical cliches (rum barrels, dangling buoys, octopuses adorning walls) and fish plucked fresh from Poseidon's realm is a wonderful spot to tuck into fish and chips, wrapped in butcher's paper and enjoyed against a backdrop of sea views. Devour some red emperor, crumbed scallops or some local bug tails (the meatiest part of this toothsome Australian crustacean).

Jochheims Pies   BAKERY $
(☑ 07-4786 1227; www.facebook.com/jochheimspies; 49 George St; pies $6.50; ⊗ 5am-3.30pm Mon-Fri, to 1pm Sat) Jochheims has been keeping Bowen bellies full of homemade pies and other baked treats since 1963. Pies, including innovative varieties such as prawn in garlic-and-white-wine sauce (sold on Thursdays), are the main stock in trade, but quiches, robust breakfasts and scones are also top-notch.

The 'hunky beef' pie is so named because it was Hugh Jackman's favourite while filming *Australia*.

ℹ Information

There's a **visitor centre** (☑ 07-4786 4222; www.tourismbowen.com.au; Bruce Hwy; ⊗ 8.30am-5pm Mon-Fri, 9am-3pm Sat & Sun) 7km south of Bowen on the Bruce Hwy.

ℹ Getting There & Away

Greyhound (www.greyhound.com.au) and Premier Motor Service (www.premierms.com.au) have frequent bus services running to/from Brisbane ($263, 20 hours, two daily) via Airlie Beach ($26, one hour), and Cairns ($78 to $97, 8½ hours to 9¼ hours, two daily). Buses leave from outside **Bowen Travel** (☑ 07-4786 1611; www.bowentravel.com.au; 40 Williams St; ⊗ 9am-5pm Mon-Sat).

Townsville to Mission Beach

Best Places to Eat

➜ Enrico's @ Tyto (p444)

➜ JK's Delicatessen (p444)

➜ PepperVine (p450)

➜ Oliveri's Continental Deli (p452)

➜ Longboard Bar & Grill (p436)

➜ Tusker's Tuckerbox (p450)

Best Places to Sleep

➜ Orpheus Island Lodge (p443)

➜ Licuala Lodge (p449)

➜ Sejala (p449)

➜ Paluma Rainforest Inn (p441)

➜ Rambutan (p435)

➜ Base Backpackers (p440)

Why Go?

Between Cairns and the Whitsunday Islands, this lesser-known, rainforested stretch of coast lacks both the glamour and the crowds of the Far North Queensland coast, and is all the better for it. Giant endangered cassowaries graze within sight of beautiful beaches, and koalas nap in gum trees on islands encircled by turquoise seas. Oft-overlooked Townsville is a real slice of urban North Queensland life, while Magnetic Island, offshore, is one of Australia's most underrated wildlife-watching destinations. North of Townsville is beautiful Mission Beach, a laid-back village that ironically attracts thrill seekers by the busload, all eager to skydive over the reef and on to white-sand beaches, or go on an adrenaline-pumping white-water rafting trip along the Tully River. Up in the hills, Paluma is like a high-altitude oasis of rainforest trails and quiet villages.

When to Go
Townsville

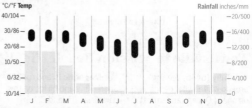

May–Sep Stinger-free seas make this the best time for water activities.

Aug Townsville shows off its cultural side during the Australian Festival of Chamber Music.

Oct Warm and humid but lower crowds and fine beach weather, unless the rains arrive early.

Map labels:

Wooroonooran National Park
Millaa Millaa
Ravenshoe
Innisfail
Mamu Tropical Sky Walk
Mourilyan
Eubenangee Swamp National Park
Flying Fish Point
Silkwood
El Arish
Kurrimine
Bingil Bay
Tully Gorge National Park
3 Mission Beach
Wongaling Beach
Dunk Island
South Mission Beach
Tully
Murray Falls
Tully River
Herbert River
Girringun National Park (Edmund Kennedy Section)
Goold Island
Cardwell
Hinchinbrook Island
Girringun National Park
Burdekin River
Lucinda
Halifax
Pelorus Is (North Palm Island; Yanooa Island)
Orpheus Island (Goolboddi)
Curacoa Island (Noogoo)
Great Palm Island
6 Wallaman Falls
Ingham
Forest Beach
Fantome Island (Eumilli)
Jourama Falls
Mt Spec (1000m)
Havannah Island
Mt Fox (811m)
Lake Paluma
Mutarnee
Herald Island
2 Paluma Range National Park
Paluma
Rattlesnake Island
Magnetic Island
4 Horseshoe Bay
Nelly Bay
Cape Cleveland
Australian Institute of Marine Science
7 Townsville
Thuringowa
Nome
Bowling Green Bay National Park
Yongala
Alva Beach **5**
Giru
Mt Elliot National Park
Woodstock
Ayr
Home Hill
Clare
Burdekin River
Mingela
Charters Towers 8
Ravenswood
Millaroo

CORAL SEA
Great Barrier Reef
Burdekin River

0 — 50 km
0 — 25 miles

Townsville to Mission Beach Highlights

1 Tully (p445) Veering around white-water bends on one of Queensland's most exciting rivers.

2 Paluma Range National Park (p441) Exploring rainforest on winding trails.

3 Mission Beach (p447) Spotting cassowaries in this laid-back, tropical town.

4 Magnetic Island (p439) Snorkelling and hiking on this paradisiacal island.

5 Yongala (p440) Scuba diving at one of Australia's greatest wreck dives.

6 Wallaman Falls (p444) Enjoying the view then schlepping down Australia's highest single-drop waterfall.

7 Townsville (p433) Catching the urban, tropical charm of Far North Queensland's premier town.

8 Charters Towers (p438) Watching an outdoor ghost film in this outback gold-rush town.

9 Innisfail (p452) Discovering art-deco treasures in this untouristed town.

Townsville

POP 229,031

Northern Queensland's often-overlooked major city is easy on the eye: at Townsville's heart is its handsome, endless esplanade, an ideal viewing platform to fabulous Magnetic Island, a short ferry ride offshore. A better museum and aquarium you'll struggle to find in Queensland, and this pedestrian-friendly city has grand, refurbished 19th-century buildings offering loads of landmarks. For the best views, climb bright-red Castle Hill.

The Wulgurukaba Indigenous people claim to be the traditional owners of the Townsville city area, but these are also the traditional lands of the Bindal, Girrugubba, Warakamai and Nawagi. Indigenous Australians make up almost 10% of the population here, and they're part of a diverse modern population, with university students, armed forces members and old-school locals joined by fly-in, fly-out mine workers, and summer-seekers lapping up the average 320 days of sunshine per year.

☉ Sights

★ Reef HQ Aquarium   AQUARIUM

(☑ 07-4750 0800; www.reefhq.com.au; Flinders St E; adult/child/family $28/14/70; ⊙ 9.30am-5pm) A staggering 2.5 million litres of water flow through the coral-reef tank here at what they claim is the world's largest living coral-reef aquarium. It's home to 130 coral and 120 fish species. Kids will enjoy feeding and interacting turtles at the turtle hospital. Talks and tours (included with admission) occur throughout the day – check the website for times.

★ Museum of Tropical Queensland   MUSEUM

(☑ 07-4726 0600; www.mtq.qm.qld.gov.au; 70-102 Flinders St E; adult/child/family $15/8.80/38; ⊙ 9.30am-5pm) The award-winning Museum of Tropical Queensland provides a snapshot of this diverse region, from World Heritage–listed rainforest and reefs to the story of the shipwrecked HMS *Pandora,* the ship sent to capture the *Bounty* mutineers. The museum's family-friendly exhibitions explore life in the tropics from prehistoric times to the modern day. School-holiday programs offer something for kids of all ages.

Billabong Sanctuary   WILDLIFE RESERVE

(☑ 07-4778 8344; www.billabongsanctuary.com.au; Bruce Hwy; adult/child/family $38/25/110; ⊙ 9am-5pm) 🍴 Just 17km south of Townsville, this eco-certified wildlife park offers up-close-and-personal encounters with Australian wildlife – from dingoes to cassowaries – in their natural habitat. You could easily spend all day at the 11-hectare park, with feedings, shows and talks every half-hour or so. Although a memorable photo opportunity, remember that programs that allow you to have your picture taken holding a koala or a wombat can actually cause significant stress to the animal.

Castle Hill   VIEWPOINT

(Castle Hill Rd) FREE This striking 286m-high pink granite monolith dominates Townsville's skyline and offers stunning views of the city and across Cleveland Bay to Magnetic Island. Walk up via the rough 'goat track' (2km one-way) from Hillside Cres. Otherwise, drive via Gregory St up the narrow, winding 2.6km Castle Hill Rd. A signboard up top details short trails leading to various lookout points.

⚡ Activities

Diving is the main activity here, but you can also swim, skydive, hike and go horse riding. White-water rafting operators plying the Tully River can arrange Townsville pickups.

Strand   SWIMMING

Stretching 2.2km, Townsville's waterfront is interspersed with parks, pools, cafes and playgrounds – with hundreds of palm trees providing shade. Its golden-sand beach is patrolled and protected by two stinger enclosures (the only places you can swim from November to March).

At the northern tip is the **rock pool** (The Strand; ⊙ 24hr) FREE, an enormous artificial swimming pool surrounded by lawns and sandy beaches. Alternatively, head to the chlorinated safety of the heritage-listed, Olympic-size swimming pool, **Tobruk Memorial Baths** (☑ 07-4772 6550). There's also a fantastic **water playground** (⊙ 10am-8pm Dec-Mar, to 6pm Sep-Nov, Apr & May, to 5pm Jun-Aug) FREE for the kids.

☞ Tours

★ Australian Institute of Marine Science   TOURS

(AIMS; ☑ 07-4753 4444; www.aims.gov.au; 1526 Cape Cleveland Rd, Cape Ferguson; ⊙ 10am Fri Apr-Nov) 🍴 FREE Fascinating two-hour tours run weekly from April to November at this marine-research facility conducting research into issues such as coral bleaching

Townsville

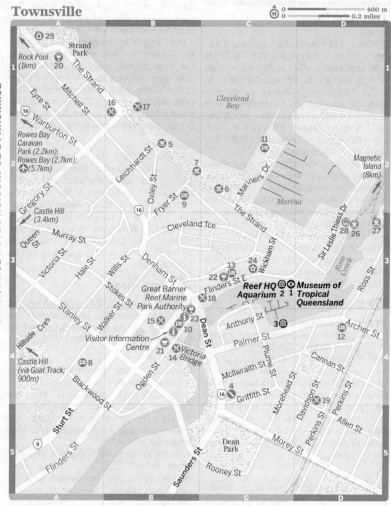

and management of the Great Barrier Reef; advance bookings are essential. The turn-off from the Bruce Hwy is 37km southeast of Townsville; the institute is 13km from the turn-off.

Townsville History Walking Tour WALKING
(📞 0400 560 471; www.townsvillehistorywalking
tours.com.au; tours from $20) These historical walking tours of Townsville are proving popular with locals and curious visitors. There are traditional history-focused tours as well as a cemetery tour and one that delves into the city's shadowy past.

🎊 Festivals & Events

**Australian Festival
of Chamber Music** MUSIC
(📞 07-4771 4144; www.afcm.com.au; ⊙ Jul-Aug) Townsville hosts this internationally renowned festival at various venues across the city. It's usually held in August, but can begin in late July.

Townsville 400 SPORTS
(www.supercars.com/townsville; adult/child 3-day pass from $292/182; ⊙ Jul) Racing cars roar through a purpose-built street circuit during the Supercar Championship.

Townsville

🛌 Sleeping

★ Civic Guest House   HOSTEL $
(📞07-4771 5381; www.civicguesthousetownsville.
com.au; 262 Walker St; dm $21-26, d with shared/
private bathroom from $60/75; @🖥) This old-
fashioned hostel respects the independent
traveller's needs for cleanliness, comfort,
security and easy company – it's a slightly
old-fashioned but welcome change from the
boisterous backpacker trend. Free transport
to/from the ferry or bus station.

★ Rambutan   HOSTEL $
(📞07-4771 6915; www.rambutantownsville.com.au;
113-119 Flinders St; dm/d from $15/84) One of the
coolest places to stay in Far North Queensland, central Rambutan has swish accommodation: choose from spick-and-span dorms
to tastefully decorated rooms (groups might
want to consider the villas). There's a terrific **rooftop bar** (📞07-4771 6915; www.rambutan
townsville.com.au/rooftop-bar; ⊙noon-late) that
also serves food and a street-side cafe, which
means some may struggle to find a reason to
leave the premises.

Rowes Bay Caravan Park   CARAVAN PARK $
(📞07-4444 4090, 1800 751 845; www.rowesbay
holidaypark.com.au; 46 Heatley Pde; powered/
unpowered sites from $44/34, cabins with/without
bathroom from $110/90, villas $135-160; ☀@🖥🏊)

This leafy park sits directly opposite Rowes
Bay's beachfront – there's plenty of shade and
you couldn't be closer to the beach. The villas
are smaller than the cabins, but spiffier.

Oaks Metropole Hotel   HOTEL $$
(📞07-4753 2900; www.oakshotels.com/en/
oaks-metropole-hotel; 81 Palmer St; d from $95;
P🚗☀🖥🏊) Perfect for an after-party or
predinner in-room drinks, the Oaks Metro-
pole is right at the end of the Palmer St shuf-
fle. The rooms are small, stylish and popular
with single professionals. Parking is free,
service is discreet and there's a small gym.

Hotel Grand Chancellor Townsville HOTEL $$
(📞07-4729 2000; www.grandchancellorhotels.com/
hotel-grand-chancellor-townsville; 334 Flinders St;
r/apt from $115/135; ☀🖥🏊) Large, spacious
rooms and apartments, many with water
and/or city views, in a fine central location attract numerous repeat visitors. A perfect mix
whether you're here for business or pleasure,
and with eminently reasonable prices, what's
not to like? The look is contemporary and
there's a rooftop swimming pool.

Mariners North   APARTMENT $$$
(📞07-4722 0777; www.marinersnorth.com.au; 7
Mariners Dr; 2-/3-bedroom apt from $235/375;
P🚗☀🖥🏊) The pick for families in
Townsville is Mariners North, in the newer

GREAT BARRIER REEF TRIPS FROM TOWNSVILLE

The Great Barrier Reef lies further offshore from Townsville than it does from Cairns and Port Douglas. On the upside, it's less crowded (and the reef suffers less from the effects of crowds). Trips from Townsville are generally dive-oriented; if you only want to snorkel, take a day trip that just goes to the reef – the *Yongala* wreck (p440) is diving only.

The visitor information centre (p438) has a list of Townsville-based operators offering PADI-certified learn-to-dive courses with two days' training in the pool, plus at least two days and one night living aboard the boat. Prices for three-day open-water courses start at $750, and you'll need to obtain a dive medical (around $60).

Recommended operators that run both diving and snorkelling trips include the following.

Adrenalin Dive (p440) Arranges day snorkelling trips to the reef, and dive excursions to Yongala (from $289), including two dives. Liveaboard trips and dive-certification courses are also available.

Remote Area Dive (p440) Runs day dive or snorkel trips (from $235) to the reef, and to Orpheus and Pelorus Islands. Also liveaboard trips and dive courses.

section of the marina, with a sandy stretch out the front and a delightful pool. The apartments are very good, particularly the ground-floor ones with direct pool and garden access; others may prefer views over Cleveland Bay.

✗ Eating

Perpendicular to the Strand, Gregory St has a clutch of cafes and takeaway joints. The Palmer St dining strip offers a diverse range of cuisines: wander along and take your pick. Many of Townsville's bars and pubs also serve food. The **City Lane Precinct**, accessed off the north side of Flinders and Stanley Sts, is a hugely popular laneway with six different restaurants serving international cuisine.

Harold's Seafood SEAFOOD $$
(☎07-4724 1322; www.haroldseafood.com.au; cnr the Strand & Gregory St; mains $12-31; ☉8am-9pm Mon-Thu, 9am-9.30pm Fri-Sun) The big fish-and-chip joint on the corner whips up fish burgers and large servings of barramundi and salad.

★**Longboard Bar & Grill** AUSTRALIAN $$
(☎07-4724 1234; www.longboardbarandgrill.com; The Strand, opposite Gregory St; mains $17-37; ☉11am-3pm & 5.30pm-late Mon-Sat, 11am-3pm Sun) The coolest place in Townsville for a light meal and a party overlooking the water is this surf-themed pub-restaurant, which does terrific nightly specials including tacos and buffalo wings. The regular steak, seafood and pasta menu is very reliable if unimaginative. Orders are taken at the bar, the vibe is right most nights and staff are fast and efficient.

Cowboys Leagues Club AUSTRALIAN $$
(☎07-4724 8000; www.cowboysleagues.com.au; 313-335 Flinders St; mains $19-27; ☉10am-1am Mon, to 2am Tue & Thu-Sat, from 8.45am Wed, 9am-1am Sun) Right in the heart of town, this sprawling complex connected to the North Queensland Cowboys Rugby League Club has two restaurants. The Match Restaurant & Grill serves up tasty bistro-size meals, while the Star Graze is about share plates and build-your-own burgers. The atmosphere is casual, loud and parochial, a real slice of north Queensland life.

Buy a temporary membership ($2) for meal and drink discounts.

Wayne & Adele's Garden of Eating AUSTRALIAN $$
(☎07-4772 2984; 11 Allen St; mains $18.50-42; ☉6.30-10.30pm Mon & Thu-Sat, noon-3pm Sun) There's irreverence at every turn in this husband-and-wife-run gourmet restaurant situated in an Aussie backyard (well, courtyard at least). Those who like a side serving of quirky with their grub shouldn't miss mains such as 'Hopping Mad' (kangaroo fillet with juniper, Madagascan vanilla and bacon mash). And on no account bypass the cashew cheesecake if it's on the menu.

A Touch of Salt AUSTRALIAN $$$
(☎07-4724 4441; www.atouchofsalt.com.au; 86 Ogden St; mains lunch $24, dinner $34-43; ☉noon-3pm & 5.30-11pm Fri, 5.30-11pm Tue-Thu & Sat; ☑) Although the favoured high-end dining experience for Townsville's posh set doesn't look very stylish upon entry, the bar is slick, the service is fussy and the sophisticated fusion cuisine, which changes with the seasons, is ambitious (though can overreach at times). Vegetarians get their own menu.

Drinking & Nightlife

Most nightlife is concentrated around Flinders St East, while Palmer St and the Strand offer lower-key spots. Check listings in Thursday's edition of the *Townsville Bulletin*. Nightclubs generally stay open until 5am.

★ **Townsville Brewery** BREWERY
(☑ 07-4724 2999; www.townsvillebrewery.com.au; 252 Flinders St; ☉ 11.30am-11pm Mon-Thu, to late Fri & Sat) Craft brews are made on-site at this hopping, stunningly restored 1880s former post office. Soak up a Townsville Bitter or Bandito Loco, and take a brewery tour ($15 per person including tasting) at 3.30pm on Friday.

Beach Bar BAR
(☑ 07-4724 4281; www.watermarktownsville.com.au/bar; Watermark Hotel, 72-74 The Strand; ☉ 11am-late) The place to be seen in Townsville. Well, if it's good enough for Missy Higgins and Silverchair, then it's good enough for the rest of us. Some serious Sunday sessions take place in the tavern bar with prime ocean views down the flash end of the Strand.

Coffee Dominion CAFE
(☑ 07-4724 0767; www.coffeedominion.com.au; cnr Stokes & Ogden Sts; ☉ 6am-3pm Mon-Fri, to noon Sat & Sun) 🍃 An eco-conscious establishment roasting beans sourced from the Atherton Tablelands to Mombasa. If you don't find a blend you like, invent your own and they'll grind it fresh.

Heritage Exchange BAR
(☑ 07-4724 1374; www.theheritagetownsville.com; 137 Flinders St E; ☉ 5pm-late Tue-Thu, 4pm-3am Fri, 5pm-3am Sat) At this surprisingly chic craft bar, suave 'mixologists' deliver creative cocktails ($18) to a cool crowd looking for something more than a beer-barn swill-fest. It also has a sophisticated bar menu for meals (think BBQ-bourbon pork, and scallop and chorizo gnocchi), as well as tipsy nibbles such as coconut prawns. Live music Friday and Saturday from 8pm.

☆ Entertainment

Flynns LIVE MUSIC
(☑ 07-4721 1655; www.flynnsbar.com; 101 Flinders St E; ☉ 5pm-late Tue-Sun) A jolly Irish pub that doesn't try too hard to be Irish. Wildly popular for its live music every night. Nothing too challenging – just good, honest live music.

🛍 Shopping

Cotters Market MARKET
(www.facebook.com/sundayonflinders.cotters market; 320 Flinders St; ☉ 8.30am-1pm Sun) With around 200 craft and food stalls, as well as live entertainment, it's one of the best weekly markets in north Queensland.

Strand Night Market MARKET
(☑ 0477 477 040; www.townsvillerotarymarkets.com.au; The Strand; ☉ 5-9pm 1st Fri of month Feb-Dec) Once a month on the first Friday of the month from February to December, head to the Strand for curios, crafts and knick-knacks in the balmy evening air.

ℹ Information

Great Barrier Reef Marine Park Authority
(☑ 07-4750 0700; www.gbrmpa.gov.au; 280 Flinders St) National body overseeing the Great Barrier Reef.

Visitor Information Centre (☑ 07-4721 3660; www.townsvilleholidays.info; 280 Flinders St; ☉ 9am-5pm Mon-Sat, to 1pm Sun) Extensive

NORTH QUEENSLAND COWBOYS

They love their rugby up here in Townsville, and they're passionate about home-town team, the North Queensland Cowboys (www.cowboys.com.au), which joined the elite national competition, now known as National Rugby League (NRL), in 1995. Locals still talk about the Cowboys dramatic last-gasp victory over the better-fancied Brisbane Broncos in the 2015 NRL Grand Final. It remains the Cowboys' only premiership to date.

From 2020, all home games will be played at the dazzling 25,000-seat state-of-the-art North Queensland Stadium (also known as the Queensland Country Bank Stadium; www.northqueenslandstadium.com.au). If you're in the area during the NRL season (which runs from mid-March to early October), you can buy tickets online or at the stadium on the day of the match. Stop by also for a meal year-round at the Cowboys Leagues Club, the home base for many a Cowboys fan.

The **Cowboys Team Shop** (☑ 07-4724 8002; https://cowboys.shopdesq.com; 335 Flinders St; ☉ 10am-7pm Mon, to 8pm Tue-Sat, 9am-7pm Sun) sells merchandise – great for a gift back home.

CHARTERS TOWERS

The 19th-century gold-rush settlement of Charters Tower sits 137km southwest of Townsville. With a long main street lined with verandahs and covered walkways, it's a fine example of a rural Aussie town which owes its current form to gold; prior to the discovery of gold, these were the traditional lands of the Gudjal Indigenous people. With almost 100 mines, some 90 pubs and a stock exchange, the town became known simply as 'the World'. Today, a highlight of a visit to the Towers is strolling past its glorious facades recalling the grandeur of those heady days.

The **Stock Exchange Arcade** (☑ 07-3223 6666; www.nationaltrust.org.au/qld; 76 Mosman St; ⊗ 9am-5pm), with its barrel-vaulted portico, was the commercial hub in the late 19th century. Today it features a breezy, sun-filtered **cafe** (☑ 07-4787 7954; breakfast $4-22, mains $7-19, lunch specials $13; ⊗ 8am-2.30pm) and a fine art gallery.

Come nightfall, panoramic **Towers Hill**, the site where gold was first discovered, is the atmospheric setting for an open-air cinema showing the 20-minute film *Ghosts After Dark* – check seasonal screening times and buy tickets ($10) at the visitor centre. **Tors Drive-In** (☑ 07-4787 1086; www.torsdrive-in.com; 130 New Queen Rd, Queenton; adult/child $9.50/7.50; ⊗ gates open 6.30pm, films start 7pm) is another possibility.

Staying at the atmospheric and friendly old **Royal Private Hotel** (☑ 07-4787 8688; www.royalprivate-hotel.com.au; 100 Mosman St; s/d from $75/125; ❋ ☎) feels like something between time travel and visiting a museum. The creaky wooden beds and black-and-white-checked bathroom tiles are charming (or cheesy, depending how you look at it).

The excellent **Charters Towers Visitor Centre** (☑ 07-4761 5533; www.visitcharterstowers.com.au; 74 Mosman St; ⊗ 9.30am-5pm) books all tours in town.

visitor information on Townsville, Magnetic Island and nearby national parks.

ⓘ Getting There & Away

AIR

Airlines flying to/from **Townsville Airport** (☑ 07-4727 3211; www.townsvilleairport.com.au) include the following:

Airnorth (☑ 1800 627 474; www.airnorth.com.au) Darwin and the Gold Coast.

Jetstar (☑ 13 15 38; www.jetstar.com.au) Melbourne, Sydney and Brisbane.

Qantas (☑ 13 13 13; www.qantas.com.au) Melbourne, Sydney, Brisbane, Cairns, Mackay, Mt Isa and Cloncurry; dozens of onward connections.

Virgin (☑ 13 67 89; www.virginaustralia.com) Sydney and Brisbane.

BOAT

SeaLink (☑ 07-4726 0800; www.sealinkqld.com.au) runs Magnetic Island ferries almost hourly from **Breakwater** (2/14 Sir Leslie Thiess Dr; lockers per day $4-6) in Townsville (return adult/child including all-day bus pass $30/17, 25 minutes) between 5.30am and 11.30pm. Car parking is available in Townsville.

Magnetic Island Ferries (☑ 07-4796 9300; www.magneticislandferry.com.au; Ross St, South Townsville) operates a car ferry from **Fantasea Car Ferry Terminal** (Ross St, South Townsville), from the south side of Ross Creek (eight times daily, seven on weekends, 35 minutes). It costs $210 (return) for a car and up to three passengers, and $30/15 (adult/child return) for foot passengers only. Bookings are essential and bicycles go free.

BUS

Greyhound (☑ 1300 473 946; www.greyhound.com.au; The Breakwater, Sealink Travel Centre, Sir Leslie Thiess Dr) has three daily services to Brisbane (from $279, 24 hours), Rockhampton ($142, 11½ hours), Airlie Beach ($42, 4¾ hours), Mission Beach ($46, 3½ hours) and Cairns ($58, six hours). Buses pick up and drop off at the Breakwater Ferry Terminal.

Premier (☑ 13 34 10; www.premierms.com.au) has one service a day to/from Brisbane ($190, 23½ hours) and Cairns ($57, 5½ hours), stopping in Townsville at the Fantasea Car Ferry Terminal.

TRAIN

Townsville's **train station** (Charters Towers Rd) is 1km south of the centre.

The Brisbane–Cairns *Spirit of Queensland* travels through Townsville five times a week. Journey time between Brisbane and Townsville is 18½ hours (one-way $189 to $442), and Townsville to Cairns is 6½ hours ($50 to $109). Contact **Queensland Rail** (☑ 1300 131 722; www.queenslandrailtravel.com.au).

Getting Around

TO/FROM THE AIRPORT

Townsville Airport is 5km northwest of the city centre in Garbutt. A taxi to the centre costs about $25, while **Townsville Shuttle Services** (☑ 0478 160 036; www.shuttletsv.com.au; per person $5-10) runs between the airport, Townsville hotels and the Magnetic Island Ferry Terminal. The more people in your group, the cheaper the per-person fare. Bookings can be made online.

TAXI

Taxis congregate at ranks across town, or you can call **Townsville Taxis** (☑ 13 10 08; www.tsvtaxi.com.au).

Magnetic Island

POP 2650

Almost within swimming distance offshore from Townsville, Magnetic Island (Maggie to her friends) is one of Queensland's most laid-back addresses. The local population, who mostly commute to Townsville or cater for the tourist trade, must pinch themselves as they come home to the stunning coastal walking trails, gum trees full of dozing koalas and surrounding bright turquoise seas.

Over half of this mountainous, triangular-shaped island's 52 sq km is national park, with cycling, scenic walks and abundant wildlife, including a large allied rock wallaby population. Inviting beaches and waters close to shore offer water sports, or simply the chance to bask in the sunshine. The granite boulders, hoop pines and eucalyptus are a fresh change from the tropical-island paradise.

Prior to white settlement, Magnetic Island was known as Yunbenun and was home to the island's traditional owners, the Wulgarukaba people.

Sights

Horseshoe Bay
BAY

Horseshoe Bay, on the north coast, is the best of Maggie's accessible beaches and attracts its share of young, hippy-ish nature lovers and older day trippers. You'll find water-sports gear for hire, a stinger net, a row of cafes and a fantastic pub. Bungalow Bay Koala Village has a **wildlife park** (☑ 07-4778 5577; www.bungalowbay.com.au; 40 Horseshoe Bay Rd; adult/child/family $30/13/80; ☺ 2hr tours 10am, noon & 2.30pm), where you can interact with koalas. Pick up local arts and crafts at Horseshoe Bay's **market** (☑ 0457 023 095; Pacific Dr Foreshore; ☺ 9am-

2pm 2nd & last Sun of month), which sets up along the beachfront.

Picnic Bay
BAY

Picnic Bay is one of the most low-key spots on the island, dominated more by a community of friendly locals than anything else. There's a stinger net during the season (November to May) and the swimming is superb. There's also a fine jetty if you'd like to throw in a line or simply contemplate the sea.

Nelly Bay
BAY

Magnetic Harbour in Nelly Bay will be your first taste of life on the island. There's a wide range of busy but relaxing eating and sleeping options and a decent beach. There's also a children's playground towards the northern end of the beach, and good snorkelling on the fringing coral reef.

Arcadia
VILLAGE

Arcadia village is a conglomerate of shops, cafes and accommodation. Its main beach, **Geoffrey Bay**, has a reef at its southern end (reef walking at low tide is discouraged). By far its prettiest beach is the cove at **Alma Bay**, with huge boulders tumbling into the sea. There's plenty of shade here, along with picnic tables and a children's playground.

If you head to the end of the road at **Bremner Point**, between Geoffrey Bay and Alma Bay, you can see wild allied rock wallabies. Although some people feed the wallabies

---

BEST WILDLIFE EXPERIENCES – TOWNSVILLE TO MISSION BEACH

Magnetic Island Tracking down dozing koalas and hand-feeding rock wallabies.

Paluma Range National Park Following bird trails and looking for shy platypus amid rainforested hills.

Mission Beach (p451) Watching for cassowaries in the forest fringe.

Innisfail (p452) Going on croc and wildlife boat tours.

Yongala Wreck (p440) Viewing turtles, rays, barracuda and all manner of marine life on an epic scale.

Tyto Wetlands (p444) Marvelling at agile wallabies and hundreds of birds at Ingham.

this can cause them to become dependent on humans and it's not recommended.

🏃 Activities

⭐ Forts Walk WALKING
Townsville was a supply base for the Pacific during WWII, and the forts were designed to protect the town from naval attack. If you're going to do just one walk, then the Forts Walk (2.8km, 1½ hours return) is a must. It starts near the Radical Bay turn-off, passing lots of ex-military sites, gun emplacements and false 'rocks'.

At the top of the walk is the observation tower and command post, which have spectacular coastal views, and you'll almost certainly spot koalas lazing about in the treetops. Return the same way or continue along the connecting paths, which deposit you at Horseshoe Bay (you can catch the bus back).

Nearby Balding Bay is Magnetic Island's unofficial nude beach.

Big Mama Sailing BOATING
(☑ 0437 206 360; www.bigmamasailing.com; Pacific Dr; full-day cruises adult/child $195/110) Hit the water with passionate boaties Stu, Lisa and Fletcher, who made their name with the *Big Mama* before moving here from Mission Beach. You can even sail aboard *Ragamuffin 111*, a former Sydney to Hobart Yacht Race (p80) hero.

Horseshoe Bay Ranch HORSE RIDING
(☑ 07-4778 5109; www.horseshoebayranch.com.au; 38 Gifford St, Horseshoe Bay; 2hr rides $130; ⊙8.30am & 2.30pm) Ride into the not-so-crashing surf on this popular bushland-to-beach two-hour tour.

Magnetic Island Sea Kayaks KAYAKING
(☑ 07-4778 5424; www.seakayak.com.au; 93 Horseshoe Bay Rd, Horseshoe Bay; morning tours adult/child $95/75, evening $65/50; ⊙8am, 3.45pm & 4.30pm) 🐟 Magnetic Island is a perfect destination for sea kayaking, with plenty of launching points, secret beaches, marine life, and laid-back cafes to recharge in after your paddle. Join an eco-certified morning or sunset tour, or go it alone on a rented kayak.

🛏 Sleeping

Magnetic Island has an excellent range of accommodation for all budgets. Nelly Bay and Arcadia have the most options, while Picnic Bay and Horseshoe Bay are quieter.

Holiday cottages and apartments can offer better value and an 'I'm a local!' feel: check out www.bestofmagnetic.com or www.townsvillenorthqueensland.com.au/destinations/magnetic-island.

⭐ Base Backpackers HOSTEL $
(☑1800 242 273; www.stayatbase.com; 1 Nelly Bay Rd, Nelly Bay; camping per person from $13, dm $32-39, d from $125; @🔊🏊) Base must be one of the best-located hostels in Australia, situated between Nelly and Picnic Bays. It's famous

---

DIVING THE YONGALA WRECK

Widely considered one of Australia's top wreck dives, the SS Yongala Wreck is a steamship that sank in a cyclone while passing through the Great Barrier Reef in 1911 (one year before the *Titanic* met a similar fate); 122 passengers lost their lives. Diving here involves prolific marine life, more so than almost anywhere else on the reef.

Almost guaranteed are giant groupers, giant marble rays, eagle rays, trevally, barracuda, eagle rays, turtles, sea snakes, bull sharks and more against a backdrop of a coral-crusted wreck. Yongala Dive (☑07-4783 1519; www.yongaladive.com.au; 56 Narrah St, Alva Beach) does dive trips (one day, two dives from $264 including gear) out to the *Yongala* wreck from Alva Beach, 17km northeast of Ayr. It takes only 30 minutes to get out to the wreck from here, instead of a 2½-hour boat trip from Townsville. Book ahead for backpacker-style accommodation at its onshore dive lodge (☑07-4783 1519; www.yongaladive.com.au; 56 Narrah St, Alva Beach; powered/unpowered sites $36/28, dm $40, d $94-130; @), with free pickups from Ayr. There are also a number of Townsville-based operators, such as Adrenalin Dive (☑07-4724 0600; www.adrenalinedive.com.au; 252 Walker St; 9hr snorkel trip per person from $249) and Remote Area Dive (RAD; ☑07-4721 4425; www.remoteareadive.com.au; 16 Dean St). From Magnetic Island, try Pleasure Divers (☑07-4778 5788; www.pleasuredivers.com.au; 10 Marine Pde, Arcadia; introductory dives from $150; ⊙8.30am-5pm) and Pro Dive Magnetic (☑0424 822 450; www.prodivemagnetic.com; 43 Sooning St, Nelly Bay).

PALUMA RANGE NATIONAL PARK

It's worth venturing off the Bruce Hwy via the Paluma Range National Park, southern gateway to the Wet Tropics World Heritage Area. The park is divided into two parts: the Mt Spec section and the northern Jourama Falls section. Both offer a variety of water-holes, inland beaches, hiking and mountain-biking trails, and prolific birdlife. The traditional owners of the park are the Nywaigi people.

For more information on the park, visit www.parks.des.qld.gov.au/parks/paluma-range.

Mt Spec

The Mt Spec part of the park (61km north of Townsville, 40km south of Ingham) is a misty Eden of rainforest and eucalyptus trees criss-crossed by walking tracks. This range of habitats houses an incredibly diverse population of birds, from golden bowerbirds to black cockatoos.

From the northern access route of the Bruce Hwy, take the 4km-long partially sealed Spiegelhauer Rd to **Big Crystal Creek**; from there, it's an easy 100m walk from the car park to **Paradise Waterhole**, a popular spot with a sandy beach and lofty mountain views; we couldn't take our eyes off the transparent water when the sun came out. The **Big Crystal Creek Camping Ground** (☑13 74 68; www.parks.des.qld.gov.au/parks; sites per person/family $6.65/26.60) has gas BBQs, toilets, cold showers and picnic tables; get here early to secure a site.

The southern access route (Mt Spec Rd) is a sealed, albeit twisty, road that writhes up the mountains to **Paluma Village**. In Paluma village the cool **Rainforest Inn** (☑07-4770 8688; www.rainforestinnpaluma.com; 1 Mt Spec Rd; d $130; ✳) has well-designed rooms and a nearby restaurant-bar. En route to Paluma, be sure to stop off at **Little Crystal Creek**, a picturesque swimming hole with a cute stone bridge, picnic area and waterfalls.

Jourama Falls

Waterview Creek tumbles down Jourama Falls and other cascades past palms and umbrella trees, making this northern section of the park a fine place for a picnic. It's a steep climb to the lookout; keep your eyes peeled for kingfishers, freshwater turtles and endangered mahogany gliders on the way up. There's bush camping with no facilities in the area.

This part of the park is reached via a 6km sealed road (though the creek at the entrance can be impassable in the wet season), 91km north of Townsville and 24km south of Ingham. Be sure to fuel up before veering off the highway.

Platypus in Paluma

Paluma Range National Park is one of the best places in Queensland to see a platypus. All the park's creeks and rivers are possible sites, but platypuses are shy and rarely appear in areas with lots of visitors. The pick of the spots is **Running River**, close to **Hidden Valley Cabins** (☑07-4770 8088; www.hiddenvalleycabins.com.au; CMB 46; r/cabin from $90/160) 🌿, west of Paluma. Hidden Valley Cabins runs two-hour platypus-spotting safaris, as well as night tours on which you might see bettongs and other nocturnal native mammals and birds. Advance bookings are essential.

for wild full-moon parties, and things can get raucous at any time at the infamous on-site **Island Bar**. Sleep, food and transport package deals are available. Dorms and double rooms are serviceable and clean, but it's all about the action at Base.

Arcadia Beach Guest House GUESTHOUSE $
(☑07-4778 5668; www.arcadiabeachguesthouse.com.au; 27 Marine Pde, Arcadia; dm from $35, r with private/shared bathroom from $135/75; ✳🛜🏊) Well priced and staffed by effusive profes-

sionals, Arcadia Beach Guest House does a lot right, including providing an enormous variety of sleeping quarters. Will you stay in a bright, beachy room (named after one of Magnetic Island's bays) or a dorm? Go turtle-spotting from the balcony, rent a canoe, a Moke, a 4WD...or all of the above?

Magnetic Island B&B B&B $$
(☑07-4758 1203; www.magneticislandbedand breakfast.com; 11 Dolphin Ct, Horseshoe Bay; d $170; 🛜🏊) The double rooms here book out

quickly, but the Bush Retreat ($220) sleeps four and is a great deal for natural seclusion. Rooms are bright and breezy, and the hosts are astutely professional. There's a neat saltwater pool, and the included breakfasts are wholesome and delicious. Minimum two-night stay applies.

Shambhala Retreat BUNGALOW $$
(☏0448160580;www.shambhala-retreat-magnetic-island.com.au; 11 Barton St, Nelly Bay; d $115-135; ❄❄) 🐾 With some of the best-value, self-contained, tropical units on the island, Shambhala is a green-powered property with Buddhist influences evident in the wall hangings and water features. Two units have outdoor courtyard showers; all have fully equipped kitchen, large bathroom and laundry facilities. Local wildlife is often drawn to the patios. Minimum stay is two nights.

Island Leisure Resort RESORT $$
(☏07-4778 5000; www.islandleisure.com.au; 4 Kelly St, Nelly Bay; burés d/f from $129/189; ❄🛜❄) Self-contained, Polynesian-style cabins (burés) give this by-the-beach spot an extra-tropical feel. Private patios allow guests to enjoy their own piece of paradise: a lagoon pool and BBQ area beckon social souls.

★ Peppers Blue on Blue Resort RESORT $$$
(☏07-4758 2400; www.peppers.com.au/blue-on-blue; 123 Sooning St, Nelly Bay; d/apt from $214/252; ❄🛜❄) Overlooking the Nelly Bay marina, Peppers Blue on Blue is one of the island's premier addresses. Rooms are stylishly turned out, with fresh, muted colours and island photographs on the walls (if you can tear yourself away from the ocean views). The swimming pool seems to go on forever.

The penthouse and some three-bedroom apartments have private plunge pools.

✖ Eating

★ Cafe Nourish CAFE $
(☏07-4758 1885; www.facebook.com/cafenourish hsb; 3/6 Pacific Dr, Horseshoe Bay; mains $12-19; ⊙7am-2pm Mon-Fri, to 3pm Sat & Sun) Horseshoe Bay has become quite the hip cafe strip and this favourite cafe does the small things well: fresh healthy wraps, breakfasts, smoothies and energy balls. Try the Vietnamese chicken salad or the salmon bruschetta. Great coffee too. Service is energetic and heartfelt.

Early Bird CAFE $$
(☏07-4758 1195; www.facebook.com/theearlyb; 2/11 Pacific Dr, Horseshoe Bay; breakfasts $10-18, mains from $16.50; ⊙7am-2pm) With a devoted local following, the Early Bird deserves its place along the popular Horseshoe Bay cafe strip. There is a certain echo of paradise in having breakfast under a frangipani tree while gazing out upon a turquoise tropical sea. The Hawaiian French toast is almost as intriguing as the pear and ricotta bruschetta, and the halloumi and mango salad is pretty special too.

Marlin Bar PUB FOOD $$
(☏07-4758 1588; www.themarlinbar.com.au; 3 Pacific Dr, Horseshoe Bay; mains $19-27; ⊙11am-2am, kitchen closes 9.30pm) Marlin Bar is popular with sailing crews dropping anchor in Horseshoe Bay and locals looking for some live music in the evenings. Meals are on the large side and (surprise!) revolve around seafood, except on Wednesday, which is steak night (from $15). Dogs are welcome.

Picnic Bay Hotel PUB FOOD $$
(☏07-4778 5166; www.picnicbayhotel.com.au; 1 The Esplanade, Picnic Bay; mains $14-34; ⊙9.30am-10pm) There are worse places to settle in for a drink than the quiet Picnic Bay, with Townsville's city lights sparkling across the bay. There's an all-day grazing menu and huge salads. Wednesday is $14 schnitzel night.

ⓘ Getting There & Away

SeaLink (☏07-4726 0800; www.sealinkqld.com.au) runs an excellent ferry service to Magnetic Island from Townsville (return adult/child including all-day bus pass $30/17, 25 minutes). There's roughly one trip per hour between 5.30am and 11.30pm. All ferries arrive and depart Magnetic Island from the terminal at Nelly Bay.

Magnetic Island Ferries (☏07-4796 9300; www.magneticislandferry.com.au) operates a car ferry crossing eight times daily (seven on weekends) from the south side of Townsville's Ross Creek to Magnetic Island (35 minutes). It costs $210 (return) for a car and up to three passengers, and $30/15 (adult/child return) for foot passengers only. Bookings are essential and bicycles are transported free.

ⓘ Getting Around

There's one main road across the island, which goes from Picnic Bay, past Nelly and Geoffrey Bays, to Horseshoe Bay. Local buses ply the route regularly. Walking trails through the bush also link the main towns. Maps are available at the ferry-terminal ticket desk.

BUS

Sunbus (www.sunbus.com.au/magnetic-island) ploughs between Picnic and Horseshoe Bays, meeting all ferries and stopping at major accom-

ORPHEUS ISLAND

Orpheus, the traditional homeland of the Manbarra people, is a heavenly 13-sq-km island 80km north of Townsville, with a national park that's part of the Great Barrier Reef Marine Park. Its dry sclerophyll forest is a geographical anomaly this far north, one where bandicoots, green tree frogs, echidnas, ospreys and pesky feral goats roam free (the last as part of a madcap 19th-century scheme to provide food for potential shipwreck survivors). Visitors gravitate towards the eucalyptus-scented hiking trails and crystal-clear snorkelling.

Part of the Palm Islands group, Orpheus is surrounded by magnificent fringing reef that's home to a mind-blowing collection of fish (1100 species) and a rich variety of both hard and soft corals. While the island is great for snorkellers and divers year-round (pack a stinger suit in summer), seasonal treats such as manta-ray migration (August to November) and coral spawning (mid-November) make the trip out here even more worthwhile.

Tours

SeaLink Queensland (📞 07-4726 0800; www.sealinkqld.com.au; half-day tours per adult/child/family from $119/89/359) Full-day tours to Orpheus from Townsville, usually with time for snorkelling and lunch. It may leave you wanting more (you'll only get a taste of Orpheus' charms), but it's still a gorgeous day out.

Sleeping & Eating

Choose between two distinct worlds: stay at one of the flashiest resorts in all of Queensland or go bare-bones camping at **Yank's Jetty** (📞 13 74 68; adult/family $6.65/26.60), **Pioneer Bay** (📞 13 74 68; adult/family $6.65/26.60) or **South Beach** (📞 13 74 68; adult/family $6.65/26.60). The three camping grounds can be reached only by private boat; the first two have toilets and picnic tables. Book online (https://qpws.usedirect.com/qpws; 13 74 68).

Orpheus Island Lodge (📞 07-4839 7937; www.orpheus.com.au; d incl full board from $1600) Orpheus Island Lodge is arguably the finest five-star resort in Queensland, rivalling the more famous Hayman Island for sheer tropical splendour. While not particularly large or opulent, the rooms are magazine-chic with wood floors and a white-linen look, and complement the beachfront surrounds. The real draws though are the food, service and prestige. You also have a rarely visited corner of the Great Barrier Reef to yourself.

Getting There & Away

There are no scheduled ferry services to Orpheus Island, which leaves two options. The first is to ask around the town of Lucinda to arrange a boat ride or water taxi over. **Absolute North Charters** (📞 0419 712 577; return transfers $90-175) is a good place to start – it has an office in Lucinda but leaves from the Cardwell jetty. You'll need to arrange a pickup time. **Nautilus Aviation** (📞 07-4034 9000; www.nautilusaviation.com.au; return to/from Townsville $590) runs helicopters from Townsville at 2pm daily. The spectacular trip takes 30 minutes.

---

modation places. A day pass covering all zones is $7.60, or you can include it in your ferry ticket price. Be sure to talk to the bus drivers, who love chatting about everything to do with the island.

MOKE & SCOOTER

Moke and scooter-hire places abound. You'll need to be over 21 years old, have a current driving licence and leave a credit-card deposit. Scooter hire starts at around $40 per day and Mokes at about $75. Try **Tropical Topless Car Rentals** (📞 07-4758 1111; www.tropicaltopless.com; 138 Sooning St, Nelly Bay; ⊗ 8am-5pm) for a classic Moke, or **Roadrunner Scooter Hire** (📞 07-4778 5222; 56a Kelly St, Nelly Bay; ⊗ 8.30am-5pm) for scooters and trail bikes.

Ingham & Around

POP 4357

Ingham is a cane-cutting centre with a proud Italian heritage – in August they celebrate the **Australian Italian Festival** (📞 07-4776 5288; www.australianitalianfestival.com.au; ⊗ Aug). With origins that go back much further, the Nywaigi are the traditional owners of the land around Ingham. **Mungalla Station** (📞 07-4777 8718, 0428 710 907; www.mungallaaboriginaltours.com.au; 2hr tours adult/child $75/40) 🚗, 15km east of Ingham, runs insightful Aboriginal-led tours, including boomerang throwing

THE PUB WITH NO BEER

The poem that inspired the iconic Slim Dusty hit 'Pub With No Beer' (1957) was written in the **Lees Hotel** (☑07-4776 1577; www.facebook.com/leeshotelmotel; 58 Lannercost St, Ingham; s/d from $95/110; ❉⑤) by Ingham cane-cutter Dan Sheahan in 1943, after American soldiers drank the place dry.

and stories from the local Nywaigi culture, plus a traditional Kupmurri lunch. A minimum of 10 needed, so call ahead to check.

Ingham is also the guardian of the 120-hectare **Tyto Wetlands** (☑07-4776 4792; www.tyto.com.au; Cooper St), which has 4km of walking trails and attracts around 240 bird species. The locals – hundreds of agile wallabies – love it too, converging at dawn and dusk. The town is the jumping-off point for the majestic **Wallaman Falls** (www.parks. des.qld.gov.au/parks/girringun-wallaman); at 305m, it's the longest single-drop waterfall in Australia.

🛏 Sleeping & Eating

Wallaman Falls Campground　CAMPGROUND $
(☑13 74 68; www.parks.des.qld.gov.au/parks/girrin gun-wallaman; sites per person/family $6.65/26.60) At this excellent camping ground 51km west of Ingham, close to Wallaman Falls, facilities include BBQs, picnic tables and cold showers, plus there are regular wildlife visits, including platypus in the swimming hole.

Hinchinbrook Marine Cove Resort RESORT $$
(☑07-4777 8395; www.hinchinbrook-marine-cove-resort.com.au; 54 Dungeness Rd, Lucinda; d/bungalows from $115/135, 3-bedroom apt $350; ❉❈) The award-winning Marine Cove Resort is terrific value given the bright, spacious bungalows sleep up to five, management is hands-on and there's easy access to Hinchinbrook Island. The resort is in Lucinda, 27km northeast of Ingham.

★ **JK's Delicatessen**　DELI $
(☑07-4776 2828; 78 Lannercost St; mains $5-17; ☺8am-5pm Mon-Fri, 8.30am-2.30pm Sat; 🖉) An enticing mix of deli items, many of the gourmet Italian variety, light meals (lasagne, sandwiches, pies, wraps, pastries, all-day breakfasts, Turkish breads) and great coffee, tea and milkshakes add up to a favourite Ingham lunch spot; it's just as good if you're stocking up for a picnic. The staff can put together some spectacular antipasto platters if you give them time.

There are plenty of vegetarian and gluten-free options, too.

★ **Enrico's @ Tyto**　ITALIAN $$$
(☑07-4776 1109; www.enricosrestaurant.com. au; 73 Mcilwraith St, Tyto Precinct; mains $29-38; ☺6-9pm Tue-Sat) Part of the Tyto Wetlands precinct, Enrico's is Ingham's best Italian restaurant. The dishes here have a refreshing modern twist. Start with the hickory-smoked pork belly or kangaroo and pancetta cigars, and follow up with the homemade gnocchi with Moreton Bay bugs and lemon myrtle. There's a kids menu, too.

ℹ Information

Hinchinbrook Visitor Information Lounge
(☑07-4776 4792; www.tropicalcoasttourism. com.au; cnr Cooper St & Bruce Hwy; ☺9am-5pm Mon-Fri, to 4pm Sat & Sun) Information on the town and region.

ℹ Getting There & Away

Greyhound (☑1300 473 946; www.greyhound. com.au) Buses to Cairns ($59, 3¾ hours), Townsville ($38, 1½ hours) and Brisbane (from $315, 26 hours).

Premier (☑13 34 10; www.premierms.com. au) Runs services to Cairns ($35, 4¼ hours), Townsville ($27, 1½ hours) and Brisbane ($196, 25 hours).

CASSOWARY COAST

The Cassowary Coast, situated between Innisfail in the north and Cardwell and Hinchinbrook Island in the south, is one of the least-touristed stretches of coast fronting the Great Barrier Reef in Far North Queensland. Part of the region's secret is that, for the most part, the Bruce Hwy between Cairns and Townsville rarely draws near to the coast, thereby sheltering immaculate beaches and buzzing seaside towns, such as Mission Beach, from the crowds. The Cassowary Coast also has a fascinating hinterland with waterfalls, national parks and small villages never far from the water. And yes, this is the best place in the world to see the charismatic cassowary, one of the world's largest and more curious-looking birds.

Cardwell

POP 1309

Cardwell is an appealing place with plenty of sand, a walkable foreshore and a jetty with uninterrupted views of Hinchinbrook Island. The Girramay are the land's traditional owners. Plenty of travellers linger here for seasonal fruit picking – if you're looking for this kind of work, there are far worse places in the world to do it (check at the backpackers hostel for information). For everyone else, sit back and enjoy one of the town's famous crab sandwiches while gazing out at the view.

◉ Sights

★ **Girringun Aboriginal Art Centre** GALLERY
(☑ 07-4066 8300; www.art.girringun.com.au; 235 Victoria St, Bruce Hwy; ⊙8.30am-5pm Mon-Thu, 9am-2pm Fri) ⊘ Traditional woven baskets, paintings and colourful wooden sculptures are among the works for sale at this cooperative of Aboriginal artists from nine different Indigenous groups that cover 25,000 sq km. The centre is one of the best in this part of Queensland, and you'll often find the artists at work here. It also serves as a Keeping Place, with 150 years of cultural history on display.

🛏 Sleeping & Eating

Cardwell Beachcomber Motel & Tourist Park CARAVAN PARK $
(☑ 07-4066 8550; www.cardwellbeachcomber.com.au; 43a Marine Pde; powered/unpowered sites $40/32, d cabins & studios $105-170; ❉@🛜🏊) With a very sweet location across from the sea, the Beachcomber has a good variety of options, though the camp sites are a little tight. Cute studios and modern ocean-view villas by the pool will take the heat off your east-coast adventure. There's a small on-site restaurant.

Cardwell Central Backpackers HOSTEL $
(☑ 07-4066 8404; 6 Brasenose St; dm $26-32; @🛜🏊) Good feedback from the banana-farm workers suggests Cardwell Central is a reliable place to stay and source work. It also accepts overnighters. Accommodation is simple, and the pool table's a hit.

Vivia Cafe CAFE $$
(☑ 07-4066 8030; 135 Victoria St; mains $12-22; ⊙7.30am-3.30pm Sat-Wed, to 7pm Thu & Fri) A candidate for Cardwell's best cafe, hugely popular Vivia serves everything from lasagne and calamari to steak sandwiches and fish burgers. Order a crab sandwich ($13.20) and walk across the road to the jetty to eat it.

Seaview Cafe FAST FOOD $$
(☑ 07-4066 8690; 87 Victoria St; mains $12-26; ⊙24hr) Known as the place with the giant crab on the roof, the cavernous Seaview is a famous stopover for hungry drivers. Trucker chefs dish up local flavours in the form of seafood sandwiches and a mammoth all-day breakfast ($20). It ain't fancy, and gets pretty mixed reviews, but if you're driving past at 3am, you'll be glad it's there.

ℹ Information

Rainforest & Reef Centre (☑ 07-4066 8601; www.greatgreenwaytourism.com; 142 Victoria St; ⊙8.30am-5pm Mon-Fri, 9am-1pm Sat & Sun) The Rainforest & Reef Centre, next to Cardwell's jetty, has an ageing interactive rainforest display and detailed info on Hinchinbrook Island and other nearby national parks.

ℹ Getting There & Away

Buses on the Brisbane–Cairns route stop at Cardwell's Seaview Cafe.
Greyhound (☑1300 473 946; www.greyhound.com.au) Runs services to Cairns (from $57, three hours) and Townsville (from $43, 2½ hours, three daily).
Premier (☑13 34 10; www.premierms.com.au) Buses to Cairns ($31, three hours), Mission Beach ($24, one hour) and Townsville ($27, two hours).

WORTH A TRIP

CARDWELL FOREST DRIVE

From the town centre, Cardwell Forest Drive, a scenic 26km round-trip through nearby forests, is chock-a-block with lookouts, walking tracks and picnic areas signposted along the way. There are super swimming opportunities at **Attie Creek Falls**, as well as at the aptly named **Spa Pool**, where you can sit in a rock hollow as water gushes over you.

Other highlights include the picnic area at **Dead Horse Creek** (4WD only) and **Cardwell Lookout**.

Cardwell's visitor centre has brochures detailing other walking trails and swimming holes in the park.

HINCHINBROOK ISLAND

Australia's largest island national park (399 sq km) is a holy grail for walkers, but getting here requires advance planning. Granite mountains rise dramatically from the sea and wildlife creeps through the foliage. The mainland side is dense with lush tropical vegetation, while long sandy beaches and tangles of mangrove curve around the eastern shore. Hinchinbrook forms part of the traditional lands of the Biyaygiri people, who called the island Pouandai.

Hinchinbrook Island Cruises (☑ 0499 335 383; www.hinchinbrookislandcruises.com.au) Runs a service from Cardwell's Port Hinchinbrook Marina to Hinchinbrook's Ramsay Bay boardwalk (one-way/return per person from $99/140, 1½ hours) It also operates a four-hour, two-island tour (adult/child $110/99) that includes a cruise between Goold and Garden Islands spotting dolphins, dugongs and turtles, before docking at Ramsay Bay boardwalk for a walk on the 9km-long beach and a picnic lunch.

Thorsborne Trail (www.npsr.qld.gov.au) Hinchinbrook's highlight is the Thorsborne Trail (also known as the East Coast Trail), a very challenging 32km coastal track. It's recommended that you take three nights to complete the trail; return walks of individual sections are also possible. Be prepared for hungry native beasts (including crocs), saber-toothed mosquitoes and very rough patches. You'll have to draw (or carry) your own water.

As only 40 walkers are allowed to traverse the trail at any one time, the parks service recommends booking a year ahead for a place during the high season and six months ahead for other dates. Cancellations are not unheard of, so if you've arrived without a booking it's worth asking, but don't count on being lucky.

Tully

POP 2390

Tully calls itself the 'wettest town in Australia'. A gigantic golden gumboot at Tully's entrance is as high as the waters rose (7.9m) in 1950; climb the spiral staircase to the viewing platform up top to get a sense of just how much that is! And while boggy Babinda challenges Tully's claim, the fact remains that all that rain ensures plenty of raftable rapids on the nearby Tully River, and shimmering fruit farms in need of travelling labour.

☞ Tours

Banana Farm Tours TOURS
(☑ 07-4065 4823; www.bananafarmtours.com. au; 132 Cowley Creek Rd, Silkwood; adult/child/ family $25/10/60; ☺ 9am Tue & Wed) Bananas are a mainstay of local life in these parts and the two-hour banana-farm tours at Banana Farm Tours offer a fantastic behind-the-scenes look at growing, harvesting and packing, with a light lunch to finish things off.

The farm is at Silkwood, 26km northwest of Mission Beach.

🛏 Sleeping & Eating

Banana Barracks HOSTEL $
(☑ 07-4068 0455; www.bananabarracks.com; 50 Butler St; 8-/4-bed dm weekly $135/165; @ 🕸 🖭) Banana Barracks is the go-to backpackers for wannabe fruit pickers in the Tully region. The hostel is also the hub of Tully's nightlife, with an on-site nightclub, Rafters Bar.

Mount Tyson Hotel PUB $
(☑ 07-4068 1088; www.mttysonhotel.com.au; 23 Butler St; s/d $60/105; 🕸 🕿) This pub was renovated after Cyclone Yasi hit in 2011 and is a bit bland in terms of ambience, but the motel rooms are fresh and clean and provide good value for a short stay. You're also right in the heart of town.

Ripe Harvest Cafe CAFE $
(☑ 07-4068 0606; www.ripeharvestcafe.com.au; Shop 1, 18 Butler St; mains $10-18; ☺ 5.30am-3pm Mon-Fri, 7am-noon Sat; ☞) Fresh tastes and friendly service go nicely with the all-day breakfasts and premade lunches. It's all about healthy eating with plenty of vegetarian and gluten-free options, and an emphasis on organic, fresh produce straight from the farmer.

ⓘ Information

Tully Visitor & Heritage Centre (☑ 07-4068 2288; Bruce Hwy; ☺ 9am-4.30pm Mon-Fri, to

1pm Sat, from 10am Sun) has a brochure outlining a self-guided heritage walk around town, with 17 interpretative panels (including one dedicated to Tully's higher-than-average tally of UFO sightings), and walking-trail maps for the nearby national parks. The centre also has free wi-fi and a book exchange.

ℹ Getting There & Away

BUS

Buses stop alongside Tully's Banyan Park on the Brisbane–Cairns route.

Greyhound (📞 1300 473 946; www.greyhound.com.au) Goes to Cairns ($29, 2½ hours) and Townsville ($45, 3¼ hours).

Premier (📞 13 34 10; www.premierms.com.au) Runs services to Cairns ($27, 2½ hours) and Townsville ($31, 3¼ hours).

TRAIN

Tully is on the **Queensland Rail** (📞 1800 872 467; www.traveltrain.com.au) Brisbane–Cairns train line, with the *Spirit of Queensland* passing through five times a week. Destinations include Cairns ($33 to $55, 2½ hours) and Townsville ($50 to $85, 3¼ hours).

Mission Beach

The rainforest meets the Coral Sea at Mission Beach, a tropical enclave of beach hamlets that has long threatened to take the Australian getaway circuit by storm, but never quite gets overrun. With the new owners of Dunk Island having also brought up a number of properties across Mission Beach in 2019, that could finally change.

Until it does, this Coral Sea bolthole has maintained a beautiful balance between yoga living, backpacker bravado and eco-escape, plus it has Australia's highest density of cassowaries – this is your best chance to see this extraordinary bird. Hidden among World Heritage listed rainforest, a short 30km detour from the Bruce Hwy, Mission Beach is also one of the closest access points to the Great Barrier Reef, and is the gateway to Dunk Island.

These are the traditional lands of the Djiru people.

🏃 Activities

There's white-water rafting on the Tully River or, if you've your own board, Bingil Bay is one of the few spots inside the reef where it's possible to surf, with small, consistent 1m swells. Stinger enclosures at Mission Beach

ℹ **WARNING**

While Mission's coastline seems to scream 'toe dip!', don't just fling yourself into the water any old where: stick to the **swimming enclosures**, lest you have a nasty encounter with a marine stinger...or a croc.

and South Mission Beach provide safe year-round swimming.

Local walking and cycling trails abound – pick up the *Rotary Mission Beach Walk & Ride Map* from the visitor centre (p451).

⭐ **Charley's Chocolate Tour** TOURS
(Charley's Chocolate Factory; 📞 07-4068 5011; www.charleys.com.au; 388 Cassowary Dr, Mt Edna; adult/child/family $34/22/98; ⊙ 10.30am Thu & Sun) Follow the trail from cocoa tree to chocolate at this terrific chocolate factory, where you'll learn the history of chocolate, how it is made and get to taste the final product. An Aussie Farm Lunch (barbecued burger) is included in the tour, and there's a shop where you can buy chocolate. Advance bookings are essential.

Skydive Mission Beach SKYDIVING
(📞 1300 800 840; www.skydive.com.au/mission-beach; 1830/4270m tandem dives from $199/329) Mission Beach is rightfully one of the most popular spots in Australia for skydiving, with views over gorgeous islands and blue water, and a soft landing on a white-sand beach. Skydive Australia, known locally as Skydive Mission Beach, runs several flights per day.

Coral Sea Kayaking KAYAKING
(📞 0484 791 829; www.coralseakayaking.com; Jackey Jackey St, South Mission Beach; single/double kayak per day $90/120, 3-day expedition per person $990) This outfit offers kayak rental and

---

TULLY RIVER RAFTING

The Tully River provides thrilling white water year-round thanks to Tully's trademark downpours and the river's hydro-electric floodgates. Rafting trips are timed to coincide with the daily release of the gates, resulting in Grade IV rapids foaming against a backdrop of stunning rainforest scenery.

Wildside Adventures (📞 07-4088 6212; www.wildsideadventures.com.au; half-/full-day rafting from $129/189) is an option out of Mission Beach.

Mission Beach

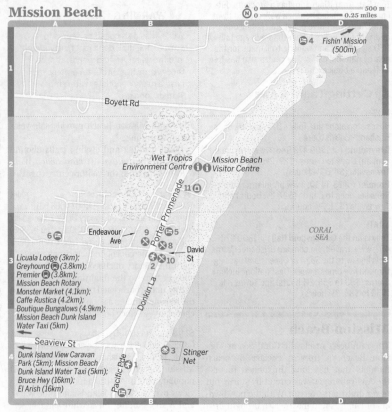

Mission Beach

Activities, Courses & Tours
1 Drift Spa..B4
2 Skydive Mission Beach.......................B3
3 Stinger Enclosure...............................B4

Sleeping
  Castaways Resort & Spa..............(see 1)
4 Mission Beach Ecovillage....................D1
5 Mission Beach Retreat.........................B3
6 Nautilus B&B..A3
7 Sejala...B4

Eating
8 Chippy No 1..B3
9 Early Birds Cafe...................................B3
10 Garage...B3
   PepperVine.....................................(see 8)
   Pippi's on the Beach.....................(see 10)

Shopping
11 Mission Beach Markets........................B2

a range of tours with knowledgable guides, from three-day trips to the Family or Barnard Islands, to seven-day yoga or Hinchinbrook Island expeditions.

Sleeping

★ Jackaroo Treehouse Hostel   HOSTEL $
(☏ 07-4210 6008; www.jackarootreehouse.com; 13 Frizelle Rd; camping sites from $15, dm from $25, d with shared bathroom incl breakfast from $68; P @ 🛜 🛋) Drive inland past Clump Mountain and while away the days in this timber pole-frame retreat deep in the rainforest by a huge jungle pool overlooking the Coral Sea. Find a quiet double room and pull up next to young backpackers bronzing in the tropical sun.

**Dunk Island View
Caravan Park**   CARAVAN PARK $
(☏ 07-4068 8248; www.dunkislandviewcaravan park.com; 21-35 Webb Rd, Wongaling Beach; sites

$36, 1-/2-bedroom units $117/149; 🌸 🛜 🏊 🛏) One of the best caravan parks in northern Queensland; its views of Dunk Island are stupendous and the grounds are impeccably kept. The small pool is welcome in stinger season, and there's also an on-site cafe serving fish and chips. Cabins are simple but clean.

Mission Beach Retreat HOSTEL $
(✆07-4088 6229; www.missionbeachretreat. com.au; 49 Porter Promenade; dm $26-30, d $63; 🌸 @ 🛜 🏊) Bang in the centre of town, with the bonus of being beachfront, this is an easy, breezy backpacker spot that's hard not to like. YHA-accredited, it fills up quickly. Extras include a shuttle service to the supermarket and free wi-fi. Staff insist on friendly interaction with guests.

★**Licuala Lodge** B&B $$
(✆07-4068 8194; www.licualalodge.com.au; 11 Mission Circle; s/d/tr incl breakfast from $120/140/190; 🛜 🏊) You'll need your own car at this peaceful B&B 1.5km from the beach and pretty much everything else. Guests alternate between the wonderful verandah, where terrific breakfast can be had overlooking landscaped gardens, and the swimming pool surrounded by a rock garden. Cassowaries pop by regularly to check out the scene. Sue and Mick are welcoming hosts.

Mission Beach Ecovillage CABIN $$
(✆07-4068 7534; www.ecovillage.com.au; Clump Point Rd; d $129-169, 2-bedroom bungalows from $245; 🌸 🛜 🏊) With its own banana and lime trees scattered around the tropical gardens, and a direct path through the rainforest to the beach, this 'ecovillage' makes the most of its environment. Clustered around a rocky pool, the bungalows are a little worn, but there's a licensed restaurant and bubbly enough service to compensate.

Boutique Bungalows B&B $$
(✆07-4068 9996; 3 Spurwood Cl, Wongaling Beach; bungalows $110-130; P 🐾 🌸 🛜 🏊) This welcoming B&B has large and stylish accommodation not far from Wongaling Beach. Steve and Sharon are welcoming hosts and travellers consistently give it the thumbs-up.

Nautilus B&B B&B $$
(✆0419 100 011; 1 Nautilus St; 2-bedroom apt from $195) Two pristine white-tiled apartments sit side-by-side atop a hill overlooking town, offering an enjoyable stay. The lounge and open-plan kitchen are great for enjoying your breakfast ($18 per person)

WORTH A TRIP

PARONELLA PARK

Set beside a series of creeks and waterfalls 50km northwest of Mission Beach (and with at least one resident croc), this unusual, tropical **Paronella Park** (✆07-4065 0000; www.paronellapark. com.au; 1671 Japoonvale Rd, Mena Creek; adult/child $47/26; ⊙9am-7.30pm) is a romantic, Dalí-esque escape from reality. Day trippers wander dreamily among its moss-covered steps, lush tropical foliage and huge palatial structures straight from some Victorian-Mayan movie set. Tours run every hour, starting at 9.30am and the last leaving at 4.30pm.

Self-made Spanish immigrant José Paronella built Paronella Park as a gift to his wife Margarita. He opened the incongruously sited property and pleasure gardens to a grateful public shortly after their construction. He died in 1948, and the park is now privately owned and National Trust–listed. The whole place is filled with magic and mystery.

and planning the day ahead. Look out for wallabies grazing nearby at sunset.

While bookings are technically only available online through internet booking services, it's worth popping past Nautilus B&B and asking Dena if she can help you out.

★**Sejala** CABIN $$$
(✆07-4088 6699; www.sejala.com.au; 26 Pacific Pde; d from $290; 🌸 🏊) Choose from 'Waves', 'Coral' and 'Beaches': three self-contained beach 'huts' within snoring distance of the coconut palms. Each one comes with rainforest shower, deck with private BBQ and loads of character. Ideal for hiding away with a partner.

Castaways Resort & Spa RESORT $$
(✆07-4068 7444; www.castaways.com.au; Pacific Pde; d $100-279, 1-/2-bedroom apt $299/329; 🌸 @ 🛜 🏊) Stare longingly out to sea from your apartment in this mainstay of the Mission Beach family-holiday scene. Travellers on a budget can play it smart in a simple rainforest room and take advantage of the two elongated pools, a luxurious **spa** (✆07-4068 7444; www.castaways.com.au/mission-beach-day-spa) and stunning beach views from its tropical-style bar-restaurant. Come on Tuesday for tropical high tea.

MAMU TROPICAL SKYWALK

Part of **Wooroonooran National Park** (www.parks.des.qld.gov.au/parks/wooroonooran), 27km from Innisfail, the **Mamu Tropical Skywalk** (☑ 07-4064 5294; www.mamutropicalskywalk.com.au; Palmerston Hwy; adult/child/family $26/15/76; ⊘ 9.30am-5.30pm, last entry 4.30pm) and other trails passing through the rainforest for more than 1km (350m elevated, 2.5km return in total) are wonderful excursions. Climb up 100 steps to Far North Queensland's highest rainforest observation tower (37m); the views are fabulous. Allow at least an hour to complete the 2.5km, wheelchair-accessible circuit.

This passes through the traditional lands of the Ma:Mu and panels along the way introduce you to their traditional culture.

The Palmerston Hwy continues west of here to Millaa Millaa, passing the entrance to the Waterfalls Circuit.

✖ Eating

Chippy No 1 FISH & CHIPS $
(☑ 07-4088 6765; www.facebook.com/thechippyno1; Porter Promenade; mains from $8.50; ⊘ 10am-7pm Mon-Thu, to 8pm Fri & Sat, 11am-7pm Sun) Mission Beach's best fish and chips? Plenty of locals think so. The barra, a seafood basket or the tropical burger (with pineapple)? Take your pick – as Gwyneth would say, it's all good.

Early Birds Cafe CAFE $$
(☑ 07-4088 6000; www.facebook.com/earlybirdsonthebeach; 47 Porter Promenade; mains $9-26; ⊘ 6am-3pm Thu-Mon; ☑) One of few places open first thing in the morning, Early Birds wins return customers with its honest, cheap, cafe-style breakfasts and bigger-than-average fresh juices. Specials range from steak to fish and chips or Thai chicken curry.

★ Bingil Bay Cafe CAFE $$
(☑ 07-4068 7146; www.bingilbaycafe.com.au; 29 Bingil Bay Rd; mains $19-32, pizzas $25; ⊘ 7am-10pm; ☑) Sunshine, rainbows, coffee and gourmet grub make up the experience at this lavender landmark with a great porch for watching the world drift by. Breakfast is a highlight, but it's open all day. The tiger-prawn and Spanish-mackerel linguini is excellent, and the sirloin is well-priced and

deservedly popular. Regular art displays and live music ensure a creative clientele.

★ Tusker's Tuckerbox AUSTRALIAN $$
(☑ 0414 395 164; www.tuskers.com.au; 154 Kennedy Esplanade, South Mission Beach; mains lunch from $16, dinner $18-48; ⊘ noon-9pm Fri-Sun) Something of a South Mission Beach institution as the week winds down, Tusker's gets many people's vote for the best fish and chips in Far North Queensland. It also does a beef-rump enchilada, goat casserole and a range of steaks and burgers, sometimes with everything on one epic platter. Lunch options are much lighter.

Caffe Rustica ITALIAN $$
(☑ 07-4068 9111; www.caffe-rustica.com.au; 24 Wongaling Beach Rd; mains $20-23, pizzas $12-25; ⊘ 5pm-late Wed-Sat, 10am-9pm Sun; ☑) Traditional pizza and pasta are the staples at this evening haunt set inside a corrugated-iron beach shack; it also makes its own gelato and sorbet. Bookings are encouraged as it's popular with locals year-round.

Garage AUSTRALIAN $$
(☑ 07-4088 6280; www.thegaragemissionbeach.com; 41 Donkin Lane; share plates $9-26, pizzas $18-25; ⊘ 4-10pm Wed-Sun; ❋ ☑) A hotspot in Mission with the 20-something set, the Garage is famous for its delicious sliders (miniburgers) and free-pour cocktails ($14). The hard-working chef mixes up the menu regularly and management ensures there's a festive vibe in the beer garden, with an eclectic playlist and tapas specials.

Pippi's on the Beach SEAFOOD $$
(☑ 07-4088 6150; 42 Donkin Lane; mains $25-39; ⊘ noon-2.30pm & 5-9.30pm Fri-Tue) This beachfront venue has the best beach views in Mission Beach (get here early for a front-row table). It serves up a small range of mains from tiger-prawn risotto to twice-cooked pork belly.

★ PepperVine AUSTRALIAN $$$
(☑ 07-4088 6538; www.peppervine.com.au; Shop 2, 4 David St; tapas from $8.50, mains $27-44; ⊘ 4.30pm-late Mon, Thu & Fri, from 10am Sat & Sun) On the Village Green, PepperVine is an contemporary restaurant borrowing from Italian, Spanish and Mod Oz culinary influences, and nailing atmosphere and service. Wood-fired pizza and a glass of Australian wine is the early-evening staple; the fine dining (including premium steaks) announces itself after sunset as the crowd descends.

🛍 Shopping

Mission Beach Markets　　MARKET
(Porter Promenade; ⊙8am-1pm 1st & 3rd Sun of month) Local arts, crafts, jewellery, tropical fruit, homemade gourmet goods and more overflow from stalls at the Mission Beach Markets.

**Mission Beach Rotary
Monster Market**　　MARKET
(☑07-4068 7220; Marcs Park, Cassowary Dr, Wongaling Beach; ⊙7.30am-12.30pm last Sun of month Easter-Nov) Wonderful stuff, including handmade log furniture.

ℹ Information

Mission Beach Visitor Centre (☑07-4068 7099; www.missionbeachtourism.com; 55 Porter Promenade; ⊙9am-5pm Mon-Sat, 10am-2pm Sun) The main visitor centre in town has reams of information in multiple languages.

Wet Tropics Environment Centre (☑07-4068 7197; www.wettropics.gov.au; Porter Promenade; ⊙10am-5pm Mon-Sat, to 2pm Sun) Located next door to the Mission Beach Visitor Centre you'll find displays and movies about the local environment, including, of course, the cassowary.

ℹ Getting There & Away

Greyhound (☑1300 473 946; www.greyhound.com.au) and **Premier** (☑13 34 10; www.premierms.com.au) buses stop in Wongaling Beach next to the 'big cassowary'. Fares with Greyhound/Premier are $26/20 to Cairns (2¼ hours) and $48/46 to Townsville (3½ to four hours).

Dunk Island

Dunk is known to the Djiru people, the traditional owners of this land, as Coonanglebah (the island of peace and plenty). They're not wrong: this is pretty much your ideal tropical island, with lush jungle, white-sand beaches and impossibly blue water.

Walking trails criss-cross (and almost circumnavigate) Dunk: the **circuit track** (9.2km) is the best way to explore the island's interior and encounter wildlife. There's snorkelling over bommies (coral pinnacles or outcroppings) at **Muggy Muggy** and swimming at beautiful **Coconut Beach**. On weekends in high season there are often special events such as bongo lessons or a ukulele band – check with the Mission Beach Visitor Centre.

THE CASSOWARY: ENDANGERED NATIVE BIRD

This flightless prehistoric bird struts through the rainforest like something out of Jurassic Park. It's as tall as a fully grown adult, has three razor-sharp, dagger-style clawed toes, a bright-blue head, red wattles (the lobes hanging from its neck), a helmetlike horn and shaggy black feathers similar to an emu's. Meet the cassowary, an important link in the rainforest ecosystem. It's the only animal capable of dispersing the seeds of more than 70 species of trees whose fruit is too large for other rainforest animals to digest and pass (the end product also acts as fertiliser).

It is estimated that there are anywhere between 1500 and 6000 cassowaries left in the wilds of northern Queensland. An endangered species, the cassowary's biggest threat is loss of habitat, and most recently the cause has been natural. Tropical Cyclone Yasi stripped much of the rainforest around Mission Beach bare, threatening the struggling population with starvation. The cyclone also left the birds exposed to the elements, and more vulnerable to dog attacks and cars as they venture out in search of food.

The Mission Beach area has the highest density of cassowaries in Australia, and you're most likely to see cassowaries in the wild around **South Mission Beach** (watch for them around the caravan park and along South Mission Beach Rd in particular), **Etty Bay** (where you might see them on the beach) and the Cape Tribulation section of the Daintree National Park (p486). Cassowaries, sometimes with young, frequently wander through the garden at Licuala Lodge (p449) in Mission Beach. Cassowaries can be aggressive, particularly if they have chicks, although attacks on human beings are extremely rare. Do not approach them; if one threatens you, don't run – give the bird right-of-way and try to keep something solid between you and it, preferably a tree.

Next to the Mission Beach Visitor Centre, there are cassowary conservation displays at the Wet Tropics Environment Centre, staffed by volunteers from the Community for Coastal & Cassowary Conservation (www.cassowaryconservation.asn.au). Proceeds from gift-shop purchases go towards buying cassowary habitat. The website www.savethecassowary.org.au is also a good source of info.

ⓘ Getting There & Away

Mission Beach Dunk Island Water Taxi (☑ 07-4068 8310; www.missionbeachwatertaxi.com; Banfield Pde, Wongaling Beach; adult/child return $40/20, 3hr tours $50/25) makes the 20-minute trip from Mission Beach's Wongaling Beach at 9am, 10am and 11am. Return trips are at noon, 3.30pm or by arrangement.

Innisfail

POP 7775

Innisfail is a handsome, unhurried north Queensland town known for river fishing, farming and a remarkable collection of art-deco edifices. Only 80km south of Cairns, there's not a tourist in sight; you can join the locals on the wide Johnstone River and dodge tractors along the pretty main street.

Relaxing, beachside **Flying Fish Point** is 8km northeast of Innisfail's town centre, while turn-offs south of town lead to exquisite **Etty Bay**, with its wandering cassowaries, rocky headlands, rainforest, large stinger enclosure and a simple but superbly sited caravan park.

These are the traditional lands of the Ma:Mu people, who still make up nearly 20% of the population.

✵ Festivals & Events

Feast of the Senses FOOD & DRINK
(☑ 0447 037 476; www.feastofthesenses.com.au; ⊙ Mar) This tropical-food showcase is a highlight of the northern Queensland culinary calendar. The final-day market extravaganza takes place along the Bruce Hwy in the centre of town.

⚡ Activities

Snapping Tours WILDLIFE
(☑ 0448 814 655; www.snappingtours.com.au; Fitzgerald Esplanade, Innisfail Jetty; adult/child/family from $40/20/110; ⊙ 8.30am, 10.30am, 3.30pm & 5.30pm) These two-hour boat trips up the Johnstone River are primarily in search of saltwater crocs, but there are plenty of other creatures to grab your attention, too, such as rich birdlife and mud crabs, as well as Unesco World Heritage–listed rainforest. Another highlight is the Indigenous cultural tour.

🛏 Sleeping & Eating

Backpackers Shack HOSTEL $
(☑ 0499 042 446, 07-4061 7760; www.backpackersshack.com; 7 Ernest St; dm per week $195; P ❉ @) Modest, dormitory-style accommodation awaits guests at the Shack, a locally operated, unofficial employment agency for seasonal fruit workers.

Barrier Reef Motel MOTEL $$
(☑ 07-4061 4988; www.barrierreefmotel.com.au; Bruce Hwy; r $135-200; ❉ @ 🛜 ≋) More than a road-trip stopover, the Barrier Reef Motel is almost reason enough to hang out an extra day or so in Innisfail. The Barrier Reef has above-average motel-style rooms, with soothing tiled floors and large bathrooms. It's just south of the centre, and the saltwater pool and bar is an added bonus.

★**Oliveri's Continental Deli** DELI $
(☑ 07-4061 3354; www.oliverisdeli.com.au; 41 Edith St; sandwiches $8-12; ⊙ 8.30am-5pm Mon-Fri, to noon Sat; ☑) An Innisfail institution, this culinary superstar offers goodies including 60-plus varieties of European cheese, ham and salami, and scrumptious sandwiches.

Innisfail Seafood SEAFOOD $
(☑ 07-4061 1579; www.facebook.com/innisfailseafood; 51 Fitzgerald Esplanade; mains from $11; ⊙ 9am-5.30pm Mon, to 7.30pm Tue-Sat, to 2pm Sun) This fish shop sells fresh-as-it-gets fish to throw on the BBQ and organic cooked prawns by the bagful ($18 to $20 per kg). Chippy Tuesday (fish and chips for $7 on Tuesdays) is a terrific deal.

ⓘ Information

The visitor information centre (☑ 0428 228 962; www.tropicalcoasttourism.com.au/innisfail; Anzac Park, Bruce Hwy; ⊙ 9am-3pm Mon-Fri, to 1pm Sat) has local info and a full list of accommodation options that can help with finding work.

ⓘ Getting There & Away

➡ Bus services operate once daily with **Premier** (☑ 13 34 10; www.premierms.com.au) and several times daily with **Greyhound** (☑ 1300 473 946; www.greyhound.com.au) between Innisfail and Townsville ($51, 4¼ hours) and Cairns ($23, 1½ hours).

➡ Innisfail is on the Cairns–Brisbane train line; contact Queensland Rail (p529) for information.

Cairns & the Daintree Rainforest

Best Places to Eat

➡ Coco Mojo (p473)
➡ Ganbaranba (p464)
➡ Prawn Star (p465)
➡ Flames of the Forest (p485)
➡ Little Larder (p484)
➡ Yachty (p485)

Best Places to Sleep

➡ Peppers Beach Club (p484)
➡ Bailey (p464)
➡ Travellers Oasis (p462)
➡ Cape Trib Beach House (p491)
➡ Lizard Island Resort (p492)
➡ On the Wallaby (p467)

Why Go?

Tropical, touristy Cairns is an unmissable stop on any east-coast traveller's itinerary. Experienced divers and first-time toe-dippers swarm to the steamy city for its easy access to the Great Barrier Reef. Those more interested in submerging themselves in boozy good times are well served by a barrage of bars and clubs. The Atherton Tablelands – home to cooler climes, volcanic crater lakes, jungly waterfalls and gourmet food producers – are a short, scenic drive inland.

The winding road north of Cairns hugs stunning sections of shoreline en route to ritzy Port Douglas; keep going and you'll meet the mighty Daintree River's vehicular ferry. From here, profuse rainforest stretches to Cape Tribulation and beyond, tumbling onto long swaths of white-sand beaches; don't forget to watch for crocs!

This region is the traditional home of numerous Aboriginal groups, including the Yirrganydji, Yidinji, Djabugay, Kuku Yalanji, Guugu Yimithirr and Djirrbal.

When to Go
Cairns

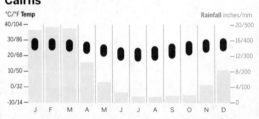

May Port Douglas pizzazz at Carnivale. Stinger season comes to an end.

Aug Milder temps and the Cairns Festival make this an ideal time to visit.

Nov Divers delight in the reef's annual coral spawning.

Cairns & the Daintree Rainforest Highlights

1 Great Barrier Reef (p483) Diving, snorkelling and swimming among fish, turtles and multicoloured corals.

2 Kuku-Yalanji Dreamtime Gorge Walk (p487) Walking alongside Mossman Gorge's clear waters with traditional owners.

3 Kuranda (p475) Riding the Skyrail above the rainforest to the markets, then returning to Cairns by rail.

4 Palm Cove (p472) Indulging in the romantic restaurants and resorts of this picture-postcard town.

5 Atherton

Lizard Island (60km)

CORAL SEA

Cape Bedford

Endeavour River National Park

Cooktown

Mt Cook National Park

Archer Point

Trevathen Falls

Endeavour Falls

Endeavour River

Amman River

Annan River Gorge

Helenvale

Black Mountain National Park

Rossville

Endeavour River

Lakeland

Peninsula Developmental Rd

Quinkan Reserve

Palmer River Roadhouse

Cedar Bay (Mangkal-Mangkalba) National Park

Bloomfield Lodge

Wujal Wujal

Ayton

Bloomfield Falls

Emmagen Beach

Bloomfield Track

8 Cape Tribulation

Myall Beach

Thornton Beach

Cow Bay

Daintree National Park (Cape Tribulation Section)

Wonga Beach

Daintree Village

9 Daintree River

Newell

Daintree National Park

Mossman

2 Kuku-Yalanji Dreamtime Gorge Walk

Port Douglas **7**

Snapper Island National Park **6**

Four Mile Beach

Craigilie

Mulligan Hwy

Mt Carbine

Mulligan Hwy

1 Great Barrier Reef

50 km
25 miles

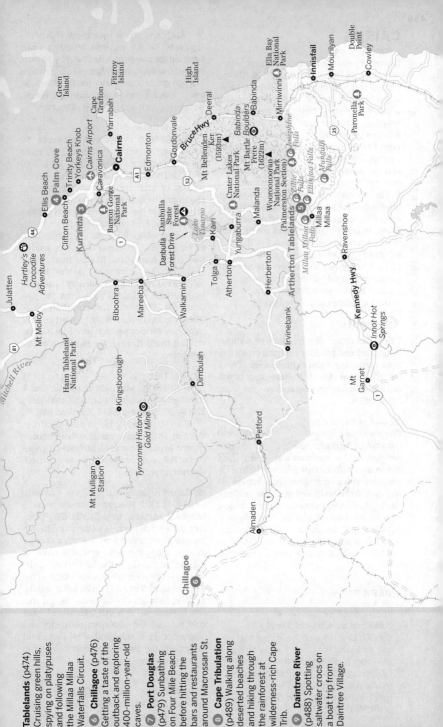

Tablelands (p474)
Cruising green hills, spying on platypuses and following the Millaa Millaa Waterfalls Circuit.

6 Chillagoe (p476)
Getting a taste of the outback and exploring 400-million-year-old caves.

7 Port Douglas (p479) Sunbathing on Four Mile Beach before hitting the bars and restaurants around Macrossan St.

8 Cape Tribulation (p489) Walking along deserted beaches and hiking through the rainforest at wilderness-rich Cape Trib.

9 Daintree River (p488) Spotting saltwater crocs on a boat trip from Daintree Village.

CAIRNS

POP 152,729

Cairns (pronounced 'cans') has come a long way since its humble beginnings as a boggy swamp and rollicking goldfields port. Heaving under the weight of an ever-growing number of resorts, tour agencies, souvenir shops, backpacker bars and a million reminders of its proximity to the Great Barrier Reef, Cairns is unabashedly geared towards tourism. Recent luxury-hotel developments and an increasingly busy cruise-ship port confirm its status as a holiday hotspot.

The city centre is more board shorts than briefcases, and you'll find yourself throwing away all notions of speed and schedules here, thanks to heady humidity and a hearty hospitality. There's no beach in town, but the magnificent Esplanade lagoon more than makes up for it; otherwise, the northern beaches are but a local bus ride or short drive away.

The Cairns region is the traditional land of the Yirrganydji and Yidinji peoples.

☉ Sights

Cairns has plenty of attractions in addition to the reef and outdoor adventures, including a thriving arts and cultural scene. Check out the Cairns Arts & Culture Map (www.cairnsartsandculturemap.com.au) for more information.

★ **Cairns Esplanade, Boardwalk & Lagoon** WATERFRONT
(www.cairns.qld.gov.au/esplanade; ☉lagoon 6am-9pm Thu-Tue, from noon Wed; P ♿) FREE
Sunseekers and fun-lovers flock to Cairns Esplanade's spectacular swimming lagoon on the city's reclaimed foreshore. The artificial, sandy-edged, 4800-sq-metre saltwater pool with its *Woven Fish* sculptures, is lifeguard patrolled and illuminated nightly. The adjacent 3km foreshore boardwalk has picnic areas, birdwatching vantage points, sculptures,

PARK PASS

The Capta 4 Park Pass (www.capta.com.au, adult/child/family $95/47.50/237.50) covers entry into four parks that are easily reached on day trips from Cairns: the Australian Butterfly Sanctuary (p475) and Rainforestation (p475) in Kuranda; Wildlife Habitat (p481) in Port Douglas and Cairns Zoom & Wildlife Dome (p459).

free BBQs and fitness equipment. Follow the signposts for the excellent **Muddy's** (www.cairns.qld.gov.au/esplanade/facilities/playgrounds/muddys; Esplanade; ☉9am-7pm; ♿) FREE, which has playgrounds and water fun for little kids, and a skate ramp, beach volleyball courts, bouldering park and Fun Ship playground.

★ **Cairns Botanic Gardens** GARDENS
(☎07-4032 6650; www.cairns.qld.gov.au/cbg; 64 Collins Ave; ☉grounds 7.30am-5.30pm, visitor centre 8.30am-4pm Mon-Fri, to 1pm Sat & Sun) ✔ FREE These gorgeous gardens are an explosion of greenery and rainforest plants. Highlights include a section devoted to Aboriginal plant use, the **Gondwana Heritage Garden**, the **Flecker Garden** and an excellent conservatory filled with butterflies and exotic flowers. Tag along on a free guided walk (daily from 10am) to learn more.

Follow the **Rainforest Boardwalk** to Saltwater Creek and Centenary Lakes, a birdwatcher's delight. Uphill from the gardens, **Mt Whitfield Conservation Park** (www.cairns.qld.gov.au/facilities-sport-leisure/parks/mt-whitfield-conservation-park; Edge Hill) has walking tracks through the rainforest to city viewpoints.

★ **Reef Teach** CULTURAL CENTRE
(☎07-4031 7794; www.reefteach.com.au; 2nd fl, Mainstreet Arcade, 85 Lake St; adult/child/family $23/14/60; ☉lectures 6.30-8.30pm Mon, Wed, Fri) ✔ Take your knowledge to new depths at this fun, informative centre, where marine experts explain how to identify specific species of fish and coral, and how to approach the reef respectfully.

★ **Cairns Aquarium** AQUARIUM
(☎07-4044 7300; www.cairnsaquarium.com.au; 5 Florence St; adult/child/family $42/28/126; ☉9am-5pm, last admission 4pm; ♿) Cairns' multi-million-dollar aquarium is well worth a visit for its vast and gorgeously presented range of marine life, the Great Barrier Reef in miniature and offbeat experiences such as 'sleeping with the sharks' and a 5D submarine simulator ride. Fittingly, displays focus on the marine habitats of Far North Queensland – not only the reef, but also rivers, estuaries and billabongs. Free talks and shows are held throughout the day, covering everything from sea turtles to reef conservation.

Cairns Art Gallery GALLERY
(☎07-4046 4800; www.cairnsartgallery.com.au; cnr Abbott & Shields Sts; ☉9am-5pm Mon-Fri, from 10am Sat, to 2pm Sun) FREE The permanent

DIVE COURSES & TRIPS

Cairns, the scuba-dive capital of the Great Barrier Reef, is a popular place to attain Professional Association of Diving Instructors (PADI) open-water certification. A staggering number of courses (many multilingual) are available; check inclusions thoroughly. All operators require you to have a dive medical certificate, which they can arrange (around $80).

Keen certified divers should seek out specialised dive opportunities such as night diving, the annual coral spawning and trips to Cod Hole, near Lizard Island, one of Australia's premier diving locations. Recommended dive schools and operators include the following.

Mike Ball Dive Expeditions (07-4053 0500; www.mikeball.com; 3 Abbott St; 3-night Cod Hole $1987, 7-night liveaboard safari from $3910, PADI courses from $245)

Tusa Dive (07-4047 9100; www.tusadive.com; cnr Shields St & Esplanade; adult/child day trips from $220/145, introductory dive $290/215)

Cairns Dive Centre (CDC; 07-4051 0294; www.cairnsdive.com.au; 121 Abbott St; day trips from $140, dive courses from $545)

Divers Den (07-4046 7333; www.diversden.com.au; 319 Draper St; day trips from $160)

Pro-Dive (07-4031 5255; www.prodivecairns.com.au; 116 Spence St; day trips from $233, PADI courses from $955)

collection of this acclaimed gallery has an emphasis on local and Indigenous work. It also hosts prominent visiting exhibitions and workshops; attached is an excellent gift shop and Perrotta's (p465) cafe.

Reef Eye FERRIS WHEEL
(www.thereefeye.com.au; Esplanade; adult/child $10/8; ⊙10am-10pm Jun-Jan) Soak up stunning views of the Coral Sea and Cairns city aboard this 35m-high Ferris wheel. The fully enclosed gondolas rotate 360 degrees (passengers control the spinning themselves); rides last about 10 minutes. Located beside the lagoon.

Cairns Museum MUSEUM
(07-4051 5582; www.cairnsmuseum.org.au; cnr Lake & Shields St; adult/child/family $15/6/30; ⊙10am-4pm Mon-Sat) This contemporary museum features four well-curated galleries covering the history of Cairns and Far North Queensland in pictures, exhibits and local stories. It offers a refreshing glimpse into the region's soul beyond the touristy glitz.

Crystal Cascades WATERFALL
(via Redlynch) FREE About 14km from Cairns, 'Crystals' is a series of beautiful waterfalls and idyllic, croc-free swimming holes that locals would rather keep to themselves. The area is accessed by a 1.2km (30-minute) pathway. Crystal Cascades is linked to Lake Morris (the city's reservoir) by a steep rainforest walking trail (allow three hours return); it starts near the picnic area.

There is no public transport to the pools. Drive to the suburb of Redlynch, then follow the signs.

Captain Cook Statue LANDMARK
(225 Sheridan St) You won't be able to miss this mammoth statue, one of Australia's most controversial 'Big Things'. Looming over the city's main road since 1972, the 10m-high concrete likeness of Captain James Cook – depicted with his right arm extended and outstretched hand palm-down – evokes a whirlwind of sentiment from both visitors and locals. Some feel it's disrespectful to local Indigenous people, while others claim it's a city icon. Pretty much everyone wonders why he's doing *that* salute.

The statue was built nearly 50 years ago as a roadside gimmick promoting the now-demolished Captain Cook Motel. Local lore has it that permission to build the hulking Cook was accidentally given – apparently the Council mistook the planned statue's dimensions (given in metres) for Imperial measurements.

In January 2017, the statue was hung (by folks unknown) with a giant sign reading 'SORRY', in apparent reference to Australia Day, which is referred to by many as Invasion Day. That same year, Aboriginal artist Munganbana Norman Miller suggested a giant boomerang be given to Cook to hold. Debate rages on as to the statue's future.

🏃 Activities & Tours

A staggering 800-plus tours drive, chug, sail and fly out of Cairns daily, making the selection process almost overwhelming. Many offer transfers to/from your accommodation. We recommend operators with years of experience, who cover the bases of what visitors

Cairns

500 m
0.25 miles

200 m
0.1 miles

Esplanade

Abbott St

Spence St

CAIRNS

Reef Teach

Lake St

Mainstreet Arcade
City Arcade
Grafton St
Shields St

Sheridan St

Enlargement

Cairns Harbour

Pier Marina

Cairns Esplanade, Boardwalk & Lagoon

Esplanade

Aplin St

Cairns Aquarium

Abbott St

Florence St

Cairns Private Hospital

Minnie St

Munro Martin Park

Grafton St

Upward St

Sheridan St

McLeod St

Water St

Lake St

Grove St

Charles St

Digger St

Esplanade

NORTH CAIRNS

Sheridan St

McKenzie St

Thomas St

Smith St

Trinity Bay

Martyn St

James St

Grove St

Gatton St

Little St

Cairns Cemetery

MANUNDA

Wilkinson St

The Lakes (640m);
Tanks Arts Centre (1.4km);
Cairns Botanic Gardens (1.6km);
Mt Whitfield Conservation Park
Walking Tracks (2km); NOA (2.1km);
Edge Hill (2.2km); (4.2km);
Smithfield (13km)

are generally looking for. Shop around for special deals.

★ Cairns Canyoning OUTDOORS

(☏07-4243 3242; www.cairnscanyoning.com; tours from $184) Give the salty stuff a break and join this fantastic freshwater expedition to beautiful Behana Gorge, a rainforest oasis of pools, waterfalls and canyons 45 minutes south of Cairns. The all-day tours include abseiling, cliff jumping, snorkelling and swimming; you'll be shown the ropes (literally) on the day. Transfers and lunch included.

Cairns Zoom & Wildlife Dome ADVENTURE SPORTS

(☏07-4031 7250; www.cairnszoom.com.au; Reef Hotel Casino; wildlife entry adult/child $25/12.50, wildlife & zoom from $45/28.50; ☉9am-6.15pm; 👪) Cards, croupiers and...crocodiles? Sitting on top of the Reef Hotel Casino (p469), this unusual park brings the best of Far North Queensland's outdoors inside, with a native-creatures zoo, aviary and recreated rainforest. The complex is criss-crossed with zip lines, swings, obstacle courses and more; the truly adventurous can venture outside for a nerve-testing dome climb.

Aussie Drifterz OUTDOORS

(☏07-4031 3460; www.aussiedrifterz.com.au; 19-21 Barry St; tubing adult/child/family $90/70/310) Scenic and serene, a relaxing bob down Behana Gorge on an inner tube is tough to beat. The crystal-clear river runs through natural tree tunnels, and you'll almost certainly catch glimpses of curious wildlife. Tours include return transfers.

Cairns Boat Hire BOATING

(☏07-4051 4139; www.cairnsboathire.net.au; Berth A1, Marlin Marina; tinny per hour/half-/full-day $50/189/300; ☉8.30am-5pm) Explore the open waterways and mangrove mazes of Trinity Inlet in a four-person tinny or eight- or 10-person pontoon (from $65 per hour). Fishing gear also available for hire. No boat licence required; minimum two-hour hire.

★ NQ Watersports ADVENTURE

(☏0411 739 069; www.nqwatersports.com.au; B-Finger, Marlin Marina; jet-ski croc tours solo/tandem $190/260; ☉9am-4pm) It's a world first: croc-spotting tours...on a jet ski! Zip down Trinity Inlet in search of supersized salties, while nesting eagles soar dramatically overhead. The company also offers jet-ski hire (from $90), parasailing (from $90) and

Cairns

bumper tubing (from $35). Combo packages available.

AJ Hackett Bungy & Minjin BUNGEE JUMPING
(☏07-4057 7188; www.ajhackett.com/cairns; McGregor Rd, Smithfield; bungee $179, swing $129, combos from $269; ⊙10am-5pm) Bungee jump from the 50m rainforest tower or drop 45m

and swing through the trees at 120km/h in the jungle harness swing. Price includes return transfers from Cairns.

**Smithfield Mountain
Bike Park** MOUNTAIN BIKING
(www.parks.des.qld.gov.au/parks/smithfield; McGregor Rd, Smithfield) FREE Smithfield

Mountain Bike Park, 17km north of Cairns, is a world-class championship course with more than 60km of linked cross-country trails that wind and bump through rainforest, over creeks and down treacherous descents. The trails are graded easy (green), intermediate (blue) and extreme (black). Rent a bike from the nearby **Cairns Mountain Bike Tours & Hire** (0452 294 035; www.cairnsmountainbiketours.com; Shop 13 5-21 Faculty Close, Smithfield; bike hire half-/full-day from $88/99, tours $99-145; 8.30am-5pm Mon-Fri, to 1pm Sat).

Scenic Flights

GBR Helicopters   SCENIC FLIGHTS
(07-4081 8888; www.gbrhelicopters.com.au; Helipad, Pierpoint Rd; flights per person from $189) This outfit offers a range of scenic helicopter flights, from a 10-minute soar above Cairns city to an hour-long hover over the reef and rainforest ($699).

GSL Aviation   SCENIC FLIGHTS
(1300 475 000; www.gslaviation.com.au; Cairns Airport, 83 Royal Flying Doctor St; 40min flight per person from $219) Those wanting to see the reef from above would do well to consider these scenic flights; they are cheaper than chopper tours, and offer more time in the air. Charter flights also available.

White-Water Rafting

Raging Thunder   ADVENTURE SPORTS
(07-4030 7990; www.ragingthunder.com.au; 59-63 Esplanade; rafting half/full day from $136/169) This experienced operator offers rafting trips down the Tully and Barron rivers, as well as canyoning, hot-air ballooning and Fitzroy Island tours.

Foaming Fury   RAFTING
(07-4031 3460; www.foamingfury.com.au; 19-21 Barry St; half-/full-day trips from $145/200) Full-day trips on the Russell River, and half-day trips down the Barron. Prices include transfers and pickup. Family rafting and multiday package options are also available.

Ballooning & Skydiving

Hot Air Cairns   BALLOONING
(07-4039 9900; www.hotair.com.au/cairns; Reef Fleet Terminal; 30min flights adult/child from $290/249) Balloons take off from Mareeba to float through dawn over the Atherton Tablelands. Prices include return transfers from Cairns. These trips are worth the 4am wake-up call.

Skydive Cairns   SKYDIVING
(1300 815 960; www.skydive.com.au/cairns; 52-54 Fearnley St; tandem jumps $199-309) Tandem jumps from 4600m (15,000ft) or 2300m (7500ft) with serene views of the reef and rainforest. Transfers available from accommodation in Cairns or Port Douglas.

City Tours

Cairns Discovery Tours   TOURS
(07-4028 3567; www.cairnsdiscoverytours.com; 36 Aplin St; adult/child/family $87/45/260) Eye-opening half-day tours that take in the sights of the city, Barron Gorge, the Botanic Gardens (includes a horticulturalist-guided tour; p456) and Palm Cove. Also books Great Barrier Reef and Cooktown tours.

Fishing

Fishing Cairns   FISHING
(0448 563 586; www.fishingcairns.com.au; half/full-day trips from $120/220, share charter reef trips from $280) Choose from a burley-bucket-load of half- to multiday fly-, sports- and game-fishing tours and charters, on calm rivers, estuaries or open-water reef. Prices vary accordingly.

Catcha Crab Tours   FISHING
(07-4051 7992; www.cairnscatchacrab.com.au; B-Finger, Marlin Marina; adult/child $95/75;) These long-running tours offer visitors the chance to catch tasty mud crabs, and are a relaxing way to take in the mangroves and mudflats of Trinity Inlet. The four-hour tours, which include morning or afternoon tea plus a fresh crab lunch, depart at 8.30am and 1pm. There are free pickups if you're staying in the city centre.

Festivals & Events

Cairns Festival   FAIR
(www.cairns.qld.gov.au/festival; end Aug–early Sep) The Cairns Festival takes over the city with a packed programme of performing arts, visual arts, music and family events.

Sleeping

Cairns is the most budget-friendly place in Far North Queensland, and its hostels range from The most converted houses to hangar-sized resorts. Holiday-apartment complexes dot the city; dozens of drive-in motels line Sheridan St.

Families and groups should check out **Cairns Holiday Homes** (0438 134 173; www.cairnsholidayhomes.com.au). If you plan to stick around for a while for work, **Cairns Share-**

house (☑07-4041 1875; www.cairns-sharehouse. com; per week from $120; ❈ 🤍 ⛱) has around 200 long-stay rooms strewn across the city.

★ Travellers Oasis   HOSTEL $

(☑07-4052 1377; www.travellersoasis.com.au; 8 Scott St; dm/s/d from $29/60/70; P ❈ @ 🤍 ⛱) Folks adore this little hippy hostel, hidden away in a side street behind Cairns Central Shopping Centre. It's intimate, inviting and less party-centric than many of Cairns' other offerings. A range of room types – from three-, four- and six-bed dorms to single, twin and deluxe double rooms – is available. Air-conditioning costs $1 per three hours.

★ Tropic Days   HOSTEL $

(☑07-4041 1521; www.tropicdays.com.au; 28 Bunting St, Bungalow; dm/d incl breakfast from $25/62; P ❈ @ 🤍 ⛱) Tucked behind the showgrounds (with a courtesy bus into town), this popular hostel has a tropical garden with hammocks, pool table, fresh linen and towels, free wi-fi and a relaxed vibe. Its Monday night croc, emu and roo BBQs are legendary. Air-conditioning is $1 for three hours. Free bikes for guests' use.

★ Bounce   HOSTEL $

(☑07-4047 7200; www.bouncehostels.com; 117 Grafton St; dm/apt incl breakfast from $21/140; P ❈ 🤍 ⛱) Bounce is a cut above many Cairns budget spots, with tidy dorms and neat studio-style apartments with kitchen and balcony, sleeping four. The central deck, pool and games room are great for socialising. Fantastic freebies – including wi-fi, hot breakfasts, guided hikes each Friday and a Saturday BBQ – seal the deal.

Mad Monkey   HOSTEL $

(☑07-4229 0888; www.madmonkey.com.au; cnr Esplanade & Aplin St; dm/d incl breakfast from $20/70; ❈ 🤍) This branch of the popular Mad Monkey chain has prime position on the Esplanade, with bars, restaurants and the lagoon (p456) a mere stagger away. That's assuming you make it out of the hostel itself, a tough call given it has its own bar, themed nightly events, free hot breakfasts and a gaming room. Dorms are sparkling if unexciting.

Cairns Coconut Holiday Resort   CARAVAN PARK $

(☑07-4054 6644; www.coconut.com.au; cnr Bruce Hwy & Anderson Rd, Woree; powered/unpowered

---

INDIGENOUS EXPERIENCES

Scratch beneath the surface of Cairns' touristy streets, shops and shindigs and you'll discover something timeless: Indigenous culture. Aboriginal and Torres Strait Islander people have been living in the Far North for more than 40 millennia, and their culture, stories and unique perspectives offer visitors a deeper connection with and understanding of Cairns' lands and waters. Especially recommended are the following.

Dreamtime Dive & Snorkel (☑07-4030 7920; www.dreamtimedive.com; Reef Fleet Terminal; adult/child/family $189/99/484) 🐾 Local Indigenous sea rangers take visitors on a reef journey that lasts five hours and spans tens of thousands of years, incorporating snorkelling and dives with stories from the Dreaming, traditional dance and cultural interaction.

Tjapukai Aboriginal Cultural Park (☑07-4042 9999; www.tjapukai.com.au; 4 Skyrail Drive, Smithfield; adult/child/family $62/45/166; ⏲9am-5pm & 7-9.30pm; P ♿) 🐾 Managed by the area's original custodians, this award-winning cultural extravaganza tells the story of creation using giant holograms and actors. There's a dance theatre, a gallery, boomerang- and spear-throwing demonstrations, bush-tucker walks and more.

Mandingalbay Ancient Indigenous Tours (☑07-4056 8283; www.mandingalbay.com. au; adult/child/family $97/48.50/250) 🐾 These 100%-Indigenous-owned and operated three-hour ecotours cross Trinity Inlet to reach the traditional lands of the Mandingalbay Yidinji people, where guides introduce visitors to the 'bush supermarket and pharmacy' of Grey Peaks National Park.

Cairns Indigenous Arts Fair (CIAF; www.ciaf.com.au; ⏲Jul) 🐾 Artists from far-flung Indigenous communities display and sell their work at this annual event. The dance, song, theatre, fashion and food of the world's oldest living culture are also showcased.

Yarrabah Arts Centre (☑07-4056 9249; www.facebook.com/pg/yarrabahartcentre; Museum Rd, Yarrabah; ⏲9am-4pm Mon-Thu) 🐾 FREE This small centre houses the works of artists from Yarrabah, a small, scenic Aboriginal coastal community about 50km from Cairns city. Ogle everything from local ceramics to traditional weaving; all pieces are for sale.

sites from $44/42, cabins/units/villas/condos from $125/135/175/250; P✶🕸☒) If you're travelling with kids and don't mind being a bit out of town (8km), this holiday park is a destination unto itself. It has a massive water park, two pools with slides, playgrounds, a humongous jumping pillow, tennis courts, minigolf, spas, an outdoor cinema and much more, all spread over 11 immaculate hectares.

Gilligan's Backpacker's Hotel & Resort   HOSTEL $

(☎07-4041 6566; www.gilligans.com.au; 57-89 Grafton St; dm/r incl breakfast from $20/140; ✶🕸☒) Huge and central, Gilligan's is a loud, proud, party-hardy flashpacker resort, where all four- to 10-bed dorms have a bathroom and most have a balcony. Higher-priced rooms come with fridge and TV. Good on-site restaurant and fab lagoon pool. Gilligan's mammoth bar/club (☎07-4040 2777; www.gilligans.com.au; 57-89 Grafton St; ◷11am-late) is synonymous with 'having a big one' in Cairns-speak. Pickup central.

Castaway's   HOSTEL $

(☎07-4051 1238; www.castawaysbackpackers.com. au; 207 Sheridan St; dm/s/d $24/45/55, d with ensuite $75; P✶🕸☒) Castaway's, operating here for more than 25 years, is an intimate and very friendly hostel with a sociable pool and BBQ area, no-bunk dorms and a free shuttle bus to the city centre. The on-site van park ($15) is a great deal for campervanners. There's a free weekly communal BBQ, a pool table, movies room and more.

Caravella Backpackers   HOSTEL $

(☎07-4051 2431; www.caravella.com.au; 149 Esplanade; dm $17-22, s/d $58/63, d with bathroom $73-83; ✶🕸☒) Caravella nicely blurs the lines between backpacker hostel and budget guesthouse – if you don't want a dorm bed there's a good range of clean, private rooms available and it's not a 20-something party joint. Add a nice pool and common area, cheerful staff and Esplanade location for a winning combination. There's another Caravella hostel at 72 Grafton St.

Lake Placid Tourist Park   CARAVAN PARK $

(☎07-4039 2509; www.lakeplacidtouristpark.com; Lake Placid Rd; powered sites from $44, bungalows/cottages from $75/125, en-suite cabins from $118; P✶🕸☒🐾) A mere 15-minute drive from the city centre, but far enough away to revel in rainforesty repose, this delightful spot overlooks the aptly named Lake Placid: it's an excellent alternative to staying centrally if you're

driving. Camping and a variety of well-priced, tasteful accommodation options are available. Within striking distance of a wide range of attractions and the northern beaches.

Cairns Plaza Hotel   HOTEL $$

(☎07-4051 4688; www.cairnsplaza.com.au; 145 Esplanade; d/studios/ste from $180/210/280; P✶@🕸☒) One of Cairns' original high-rise hotels, the Plaza is – thanks to recent renovations and professional staff – a good choice in this price range. Rooms have crisp, clean decor and functional kitchenettes; many enjoy stunning views over Trinity Bay. A guest laundry and friendly around-the-clock reception staff make it an excellent choice. Directly across from Muddy's (p456).

Cascade Gardens   APARTMENT $$

(☎07-4047 6300; www.cascadegardens.com. au; 175 Lake St; studio from $175, 1-/2-bedroom apt from $200/280; P✶🕸☒) These tasteful tropical apartments are sparkling and bright, something that could equally be said about the cheery staff here. All apartments have good kitchen and balcony. It's a two-minute walk to the Esplanade.

Pacific Hotel   HOTEL $$

(☎07-4051 7888; www.pacifichotelcairns.com; cnr Esplanade & Spence St; d $191-256; P✶🕸☒) In a prime location at the southern-end start of the Esplanade, this iconic hotel has been lovingly maintained and refurbished with fresh, modern amenities. All rooms have a balcony. Friendly, helpful staff help to make this an excellent midrange choice. The fun Bushfire Flame Grill (☎07-4044 1879; www.bushfirecairns.com; mains $29-41, churrasco per person $55; ◷breakfast 6.30-9.30am, dinner 5.30pm-late) restaurant is attached.

Reef Palms   APARTMENT $$

(☎07-4051 2599; www.reefpalms.com.au; 41-47 Digger St; apt $125-185; P✶🕸☒) Couples and families appreciate the excellent value and friendly service at this quiet complex. The squeaky-clean apartments have cooking facilities and either balcony or courtyard; larger apartments include a lounge area and spa.

Harbour Lights   APARTMENT $$

(☎07-4057 0800; www.cairnsharbourlightshotel. com.au; 1 Marlin Pde; apt from $169-319; P✶🕸☒) This collection of slick, self-contained apartments overlooks the marina from its prime position above the Reef Fleet Terminal (p470). Take in the splendid views from your balcony (request one facing the water) or the glorious saltwater pool. There's a collection of excellent restaurants just down the stairs (on the boardwalk).

★ Bailey
BOUTIQUE HOTEL $$$

(☑ 07-4253 4000; www.crystalbrookcollection.com/bailey; 163 Abbott St; d/ste from $245/655; P❄🛜≋) Billed as the 'arty one' of Cairns' three Crystalbrook Collection five-star hotels, Bailey's green, eye-catching facade is already a cityscape icon, despite having only opened in 2019. It's just as snazzy inside, with thoroughly modern rooms, ever-changing art exhibitions, supercool on-site restaurants and bars, and a fabulous rooftop pool. Worth the splurge.

201 Lake Street
HOTEL $$$

(☑ 07-4053 0100; www.201lakestreet.com.au; 201 Lake St; r/apt from $260/330; P❄🛜≋) Looking as though it's been lifted from the pages of a trendy magazine, this gorgeous apartment complex has a stellar pool and a whiff of exclusivity. Grecian white predominates and guests can choose between swish hotel rooms or contemporary apartments with an entertainment area, a large-screen TV and a balcony.

The Lakes
RESORT $$$

(☑ 07-4053 9400; www.thelakescairns.com.au; 2 Greenslopes St; apt from $250; P❄🛜≋) These gigantic resort apartments are a winning choice for families, groups, or anyone who wants to be away from the hustle and bustle of the CBD. All apartments are amply equipped for self-caterers; some have huge fan-cooled lanais (Hawaiian-style verandahs). The resort's four pools are a blessing on hot days (so, almost every day). Sandflies can be an issue: bring mozzie repellent.

Shangri-La
HOTEL $$$

(☑ 07-4031 1411; www.shangri-la.com/cairns; 1 Pierpoint Rd, The Pier; d/ste from $250/360; P❄🛜≋) Towering over the marina, this is one of Cairns' swishest hotels. All stylishly appointed rooms and suites have private balcony; if you have cash to splash, consider a Horizon Club suite, with wraparound views of the water and 74 sq metres of designer space. Service is as attentive as you'd expect from this luxury chain.

✖ Eating

There's something to tickle every taste bud up here; you'll find top-notch grub in the pubs, an overwhelming variety of chow-houses along the Esplanade – including the busy, cheap **Night Markets** (www.facebook.com/cairnsnightmarkets; Esplanade; dishes $8-17; ☉10am-11pm) – refined restaurants along the marina and an eclectic sprinkling of city cafes, particularly along Grafton St. There's plenty for vegetarians and vegans too.

For fresh fruit, veg and other local treats, hit Rusty's Markets (p469) on the weekend; for groceries, try **Cairns Central Shopping Centre** (☑ 07-4041 4111; www.cairnscentral.com.au; cnr McLeod & Spence Sts; ☉9am-5.30pm Mon-Wed, Fri & Sat, to 9pm Thu, 10.30am-4pm Sun).

★ Ganbaranba
JAPANESE $

(☑ 07-4031 2522; 14 Spence St; mains $11-17; ☉11.30am-2.30pm & 5-8.30pm; ❄) You'll recognise this tiny place by the queues outside: Ganbaranba is a local cult joint, and without a doubt the best place for ramen and gyoza in Cairns. Slurpers can watch the chefs making noodles; if the view proves too tempting, you can ask for a refill for a mere $1.50. Absolutely worth the wait.

Snoogies
VEGETARIAN $

(☑ 0409 340 024; www.facebook.com/snoogieshealthbar; 82 Grafton St, Mainstreet Arcade; snacks from $2, mains $5-12; ☉9am-2pm Mon-Fri) This superfresh vegan cafe has been a stalwart on Cairns' healthy-eating scene for more than a decade. Tucked down a quirky little arcade running between Lake and Grafton Sts, Snoogies serves up tropical smoothies and juices and inventive salads, wraps, curries, soups and more. Try its sweet treats (the lime-pistachio slice is outstanding) for a guilt-free indulgence.

Corea Corea
KOREAN $

(☑ 07-4031 6655; Orchid Plaza, 58 Lake St; mains $10-16; ☉lunch 11am-4pm Mon-Fri, from noon Sat & Sun, dinner 6-9pm daily) Disregard the empty-mall atmosphere at Orchid Plaza and head upstairs to dig into authentic sizzling, spicy Korean fare at this very popular hangout.

Bagus
INDONESIAN $

(☑ 07-4000 2051; www.baguscafe.info; 149 Esplanade; mains $11-29; ☉6.45am-2.30pm Mon-Sat, from noon Sun, plus 5.30-8.30pm Mon, Tue, Thu, Sat & Sun) The heady aromas of traditional Indonesian street food waft from this friendly little hole-in-the-wall cafe; the nasi goreng and chicken satay could be straight from a beach cafe in Bali. Breakfasts ($4.50 to $11.50) are good value. Opposite Muddy's (p456) playground.

SOLE FOOD: CAIRNS' TOP SEAFOOD SPOTS

While Cairns has more fish-and-chips shops than you can shake a seagull at, those looking for a seafood splurge are well catered for with some top-notch restaurants on the waterfront and beyond. Delish fish and other local undersea delicacies to look for on menus include mud crabs, crayfish, barramundi, coral trout and prawns. Grab a bib, your stretchiest shorts and prepare to pig out, pescatarian-style.

Prawn Star (☑0497 007 225; www.facebook.com/prawnstarcairns; E-Finger, Marlin Marina; seafood $30-110; ⊙11am-9pm) This trawler restaurant is tropical-dining perfection: clamber aboard and fill yourself with prawns, mud crabs, oysters and whatever else was caught that day, while taking in equally delicious harbour views.

Dundee's (☑07-4051 0399; www.dundees.com.au; Marlin Pde, beneath Harbour Lights; mains $20-46; ⊙11.30am-late) Waterfront fave offering appealing appetisers (chunky seafood chowder, tempura soft-shell crab) and mains including barbecued lobster, garlic yabbies and enormous seafood platters.

Tha Fish (☑07-4041 5350; www.thafish.com.au; 1 Pierpoint Rd, The Pier; mains $30-47; ⊙lunch 11am-3pm, dinner 5.30pm-late; ℗✳🛜) The ultimate in DIY-seafood scoffing without *actually* having to do it yourself, Tha Fish lets diners choose between five types of fish (barra, salmon, coral trout et al) then match it with an ever-changing roster of five to six cooking styles (lime-battered, chargrilled, curry-spiced), each with scrumptious sides.

Meldrum's Pies in Paradise　　BAKERY $
(☑07-4051 8333; www.facebook.com/meldrumspiesinparadise; 97 Grafton St; pies $6.20-7.70; ⊙7am-3pm Mon-Fri, 6.30am-2.30pm Sat; ☑) Multi-award-winning Meldrum's deserves the accolades bestowed upon its seemingly innumerable renditions of the humble Aussie pie; it's been at it since 1972, an achievement that speaks volumes in a transient tourist town such as Cairns. For something different, try the chicken and macadamia satay or tuna mornay with spinach pies; the vegetarian options are delicious.

⭐**NOA**　　TAPAS $$
(☑07-4032 3117; www.noaeat.com.au; cnr Collins Ave & Pyne St, Edge Hill; tapas $9-38, mains $24-38; ⊙7am-10pm; 🛜☑) Edge Hill, Cairns' hippest suburb, has plenty going for it: the botanic gardens, Centenary Lakes, a sprinkling of boutiques and coffee joints, and this place. Known locally as *the* place to sip, savour, see and be seen, the exceedingly atmospheric NOA tempts with tapas (reef fish ceviche, Wagyu tataki), mains (tandoori spatchcock, local-seafood spaghetti) and cocktails to set you swooning.

⭐**Pacifico**　　INTERNATIONAL $$
(☑0415 467 126; www.facebook.com/pacifico cairns; 183 Bunda St; mains $20-33; ⊙10am-10pm Tue-Sat; ✳🛜) Formerly Green Ant Cantina, Pacifico – opened in late 2019 – carries on the traditions of its predecessor: huge portions of Tex-Mex and gourmet pub grub, strong cocktails and a rollicking after-dinner party scene. Though the menu spans everything from kangaroo burgers to veggie bowls, it's spicy food that's the star of the show here: try the Wings of Satan... if you dare!

Iyara by Sakare　　THAI $$
(☑07-4041 4748; www.iyarabysakare.com; 91 Esplanade, upstairs; mains $24-38; ⊙6-10.30pm; ✳☑) The exceptional, authentic Thai food here has induced more than a few swoons from delighted diners. Beautifully presented dishes such as hot-and-sour barramundi and red-curry duck with grapes seem custom-made for #foodporn snaps...if your camera hand can beat your chopsticks hand to it, that is (unlikely). Bonus points for dreamy sea views, artfully presented cocktails and attentive staff.

Bayleaf Balinese Restaurant　　BALINESE $$
(☑07-4047 7955; www.bayleafrestaurant.com.au; cnr Lake & Gatton Sts; mains $20-35; ⊙lunch noon-2pm Tue-Fri, dinner 6pm-late nightly; ℗✳) One of Cairns' best restaurants isn't along the waterfront or in the lobby of a flash hotel, but attached to a midrange apartment complex. The Balinese food created here by specialist chefs is wholly authentic. Order a ton of starters, go for the banquet or share mains such as gado gado or *bebek kalas* (duck curry with green papaya).

DAY TRIPS FROM CAIRNS

Great Barrier Reef

Reef trips generally include transport, lunch, stinger-suits and snorkelling gear. When choosing a tour, consider the vessel type, its capacity, inclusions and destination: outer reefs are more pristine but further afield; inner reefs can be patchy and show signs of decay and bleaching.

Reef Magic (07-4031 1588; www.reefmagiccruises.com; Reef Fleet Terminal; adult/child/family day trips from $239/119/597;) Reef Magic's high-speed catamaran sails to its all-weather Marine World pontoon moored on the edge of the outer reef. If you don't want to get your feet wet, try a glass-bottomed boat ride, hop in the semisubmersible or chat with the marine biologist on the sundeck.

Reef Encounter (07-4037 2700; www.reefencounter.com.au; 100 Abbott St; 2-night liveaboards from $705) If a day on the reef isn't enough, try an overnight 'reef sleep' with Reef Encounter. Twenty-seven air-conditioned en-suite cabins accommodate a maximum of 42 guests; you don't even have to snorkel or dive to appreciate this floating hotel. A wide range of programmes, plus meals and daily departures from Cairns, make this excellent value.

Cape Tribulation & the Daintree

Active Tropics Explorer (07-4031 3460; www.capetribulationadventures.com.au; 19-21 Barry St; day tours adult/child/family from $185/165/640) These fun all-day trips take in the sights and cultural highlights of Mossman Gorge, the Daintree and Cape Trib; overnight tours and add-ons including horse riding, sea kayaking and 'jungle surfing' are also available. Tours include pickup.

Billy Tea Safaris (07-4032 0077; www.billytea.com.au; day trips $149-205) This reliable, eco-certified bunch offers comprehensive 4WD small-group day trips to Daintree and Cape Trib, the Tablelands and Chillagoe, as well as multiday safaris.

Atherton Tablelands

Skyrail Rainforest Cableway (07-4038 5555; www.skyrail.com.au; 6 Skyrail Dr, Smithfield; adult/child/family one-way from $55/27.50/137.50, return $82/41/205; 9am-5.15pm) At 7.5km

---

Perrotta's at the Gallery INTERNATIONAL **$$**
(07-4031 5899; 38 Abbott St; mains $13-29; 6.30am-10pm;) This unmissable cafe, attached to the Cairns Art Gallery (p456), tempts you onto its covered deck with splendid gourmet breakfasts (6.30am to 3pm), fresh juices, barista coffees and inventive lunch and dinner menus (hello, octopus-watermelon-radish-avocado-'nduja-sausage salad!). It's a chic spot with an interesting crowd and ideal people-watching perches.

Lillipad CAFE **$$**
(07-4051 9565; www.lillipadcafe.com; 72 Grafton St; mains $15-26; 7am-3pm & 5-9.30pm;) With humongous feasts, from crêpes to wraps and a truckload of vegetarian options, this is one of the best-value options in town. It's a little bit hippie, and a whole lot busy. Don't miss the fresh juices. The menu has an international flavour: all-day breakfast options include shakshuka and huevos rancheros while lunch/dinner choices run from burritos to vegan lasagne.

Marinades INDIAN **$$**
(07-4041 1422; www.marinadescairns.com.au; 43 Spence St; mains $18.50-25; 5-9.30pm Mon-Thu & Sun, to 10pm Fri & Sat;) This has long been one of Cairns' most popular Indian restaurants, and for good reason. Its comprehensive menu of aromatic dishes includes Goan prawn curry, the best vindaloo in town and some memorable veggie options.

Rocco MEDITERRANEAN **$$**
(07-4252 7711; www.crystalbrookcollection.com/riley/food-and-drink/rocco; Riley, 131-141 Esplanade; mezze $15-22, mains $22-36; noon-late;) Perched on the top of the 12-storey glass tower that is Riley (one of Cairns' three Crystalbrook Collection hotels), this smart, eco-conscious restaurant boasts 270-degree vistas of the city and the sea: it's the highest restaurant in Cairns. The contemporary Mediterranean mezze, share plates and mains – heavy on local and artisanal produce – are as delectable as the views.

long, spectacular Skyrail is one of the world's longest gondola cableways, offering a bird's-eye view over the ancient rainforest between Cairns and Kuranda. Allow about 90 minutes for the one-way trip, including two stops en route, featuring jungly boardwalks with interpretive panels and lookouts – including new glass-floor perch the Edge – over the mighty **Barron Falls**.

Upgrade to a glass-floored 'diamond view' gondola (one-way is an extra $20/10), or – for full-on adventure seekers – book the amazing, open-air **Canopy Glider** (an extra $110 per person; age restrictions apply).

The last departures from Cairns and Kuranda are at 2.45pm for a return journey and 3.30pm for one-way; transfers to and from the terminals are available.

Skyrail and Kuranda Scenic Railway offer combination tickets (adult/child from $114.50/57.25).

Kuranda Scenic Railway (☑ 07-4036 9333; www.ksr.com.au; adult/child/family one-way from $50/25/125, return from $76/38/190) Winding 34km from Cairns to Kuranda through picturesque mountains, the track used by the Kuranda Scenic Railway was completed in 1891: workers dug tunnels by hand, battling sickness, steep terrain and venomous creatures. The two-hour pleasure trip includes seating in heritage-style carriages, audio commentary, a souvenir trip guide and a stop at the Barron Falls viewing platform.

Trains depart Cairns Central train station (p470) at 8.30am and 9.30am daily, returning from the delightful, flower-strewn Kuranda station at 2pm and 3.30pm.

Uncle Brian's Tours (☑ 07-4033 6575; www.unclebrians.com.au; $129) High-energy, small-group day trips taking in the Babinda Boulders, Josephine Falls, Millaa Millaa, Yungaburra, Lake Eacham and more. Bring your togs! Pickup from Cairns accommodation.

On the Wallaby (☑ 07-4033 6575; www.onthewallaby.com; day tours $119-169) Excellent activity-based tours of the Tablelands' rainforests and waterfalls including swimming, cycling, hiking and canoeing. Based in Yungaburra but has daily morning pickups from Cairns.

Savannahlander (☑ 07-4053 6848; www.savannahlander.com.au; tours adult/child from $430/300; ☉ Mar-Dec) This classic 1960s train chugs out of Cairns on a variety of overnight and multiday outback tours to destinations including Chillagoe, Mt Surprise and Forsayth. The popular three-day Savannah Rail Runner goes from Cairns to Forsayth.

★ **Ochre** AUSTRALIAN $$$
(☑ 07-4051 0100; www.ochrerestaurant.com.au; Marlin Pde; mains $20-44; ☉ lunch 11.30am-3pm, snacks 3-5.30pm, dinner 5.30-9.30pm; ✳) The menu at this award-winning waterfront restaurant makes innovative use of native Aussie fauna (such as salt-and-native-pepper-leaf crocodile and prawns, or wallaby fillet) and flora (wattle-seed, lemon myrtle, Davidson plum glaze). Tablelands steaks are cooked to perfection. Can't decide? Order a tasting plate (from $108) or a platter ($30 to $76).

🍷 **Drinking & Nightlife**

Cairns is the undisputed party capital of the north. Dip your toe into the mayhem with **Cairns Ultimate Party** (☑ 07-4041 0332; www.ultimatepartycairns.com; cnr Lake & Shields Sts; per person $40; ☉ Wed & Sat nights), a wild-n-crazy pub/club crawl that takes in five suitably frenetic venues over six hours.

You'll find some of Cairns' best coffee in the cafes lining Grafton St and in the arcades running off it.

★ **Three Wolves** BAR
(☑ 07-4031 8040; www.threewolves.com.au; Red Brick Laneway, 32 Abbott St; ☉ 4pm-midnight; 🖵) Intimate, understated and bang on trend (think Edison bulbs, copper mugs and mixologists in old-timey barkeep aprons), this laneway bar delivers a welcome dash of Melbourne to the tropics. It has an excellent selection of speciality spirits, cocktails and beers, plus a hip bar menu: $10 Tapas Tuesdays never fail to pull the crowds.

★ **Salt House** BAR
(☑ 07-4041 7733; www.salthouse.com.au; 6/2 Pierpoint Rd; ☉ noon-2am Mon-Fri, from 7am Sat & Sun; 🖵) On the waterfront by the yacht club, Cairns' coolest, classiest bar caters to a hip and happy crowd. With killer cocktails, tremendous views, live music and DJs, and a superb mod-Oz nibbles-and-mains menu, the Salt House is absolutely not to be missed. The pizzeria here is justifiably popular.

The Jack PUB

(☎07-4051 2490; www.thejack.com.au; cnr Spence & Sheridan Sts; ☺11am-2am) The Jack is a kick-arse pub by any standards, housed in an unmissable heritage Queenslander with an enormous shaded beer garden. There are nightly events, including live bands and DJs, great pub grub and an adjacent hostel (dorm/room from $21/50) for those who just can't tear themselves away.

Hemingway's Cairns BREWERY

(☎07-4099 6663; www.hemingwaysbrewery.com/cairns-wharf; 4 Wharf St; ☺11am-late) Housed in a revamped shed on the Cairns Wharf, the ginormous Hemingway's sports a 19m bar and 20 beer taps. Many of the brews are named after bawdy characters from the region's past. Check out the shiny vats and brewing pipes while enjoying a tasting paddle ($15). Meals are also available.

Pier Bar BAR

(☎07-4031 4677; www.thepierbar.com.au; Pier Shopping Centre, 1 Pierpoint Rd; ☺11.30am-3am) This local institution is much loved for its killer waterfront location and daily happy hour (5pm to 7pm). Its Sunday sessions are legendary, with live music, food and drink specials and an always-happening crowd.

Conservatory Bar WINE BAR

(☎0431 858 137; www.theconservatorybar.com.au; 12-14 Lake St; ☺4pm-late Wed-Sat) Tucked away in a little room in a little laneway, this is Cairns' best wine bar, and one of the city's top places for a low-key tipple, whatever your flavour. It also makes fabulous cocktails and has loads of craft beers. It's relaxed, friendly and oozes a tropical sophistication all its own. It regularly hosts exhibitions and live (mellow) music.

Grand Hotel PUB

(☎07-4051 1007; www.grandhotelcairns.com.au; 34 McLeod St; ☺10am-midnight; 🐾) Established in 1926, this laid-back haunt is worth visiting just to rest your beer on the bar – an 11m-long carved crocodile! There's usually live music on the weekend. It's a decent place to loiter with the locals rather than the backpacker crowd.

Woolshed BAR

(☎07-4031 6304; www.thewoolshed.com.au; 24 Shields St; ☺9pm-late) This enduring backpacker magnet and meat market is where young travellers, dive instructors, pickup artists and living-it-up locals get happily hammered en masse. To a groan of dismay heard around the globe, the Woolshed's infamous dancing tables were removed (insurance issues) in late 2019.

PJ O'Briens IRISH PUB

(www.pjobriens.com.au/cairns; cnr Lake & Shields Sts; ☺11.30am-late) It has sticky carpets and reeks of stale Guinness, but Irish-themed PJ's still packs the backpackers in with party nights and dirt-cheap meals. Tuesday is trivia night, Wednesday is karaoke.

Bang & Grind COFFEE

(☎07-4051 7770; www.facebook.com/bangandgrind; 8/14 Spence St; ☺6am-2.30pm Mon-Fri, from 6.30am Sat; 🐾) Pull up a seat in the retro space for a Ransom caffeine fix; locals rate this as some of the best coffee in Cairns. It serves breakfast and lunch.

☆ Entertainment

Elixir Music Bar LIVE MUSIC

(☎0407 403 681; www.facebook.com/elixirbarcairns; 92 Abbott St; ☺5pm-midnight Wed-Sat, from 4pm Sun; 🐾) This offbeat little bar rocks to the beat of some of Cairns' best – and oft-unheralded – live-music groups and performers. Blues is a speciality, but acts can be a genre-spanning mixed bag. It also hosts open-mike nights, slam-poetry gigs, comedy and more.

A PUB CRAWL ON THE FLY

We've all heard of the Flying Circus, but how about a flying pub crawl? The five-hour **Heli Pub Tour** (☎07-4035 9935; www.helitoursnq.com.au; pub tour from $799) choppers thirsty revellers between four scenic watering holes spread between southern Cairns, Lake Tinaroo and the Tablelands.

Once your feet are back on the ground, continue your quest for quirky quenchers at **Macalister Brewing Company** (☎0408 086 814; www.facebook.com/macalisterbrewingcompany; 3/6 Danbulan St, Smithfield; ☺noon-7pm Wed, Thu & Sun, to 10pm Fri & Sat; 🐾), a cruisy brewpub set amid a sea of sugar cane, or **Flamingos** (www.flamingostikibar.com.au; 43 Esplanade, under Pacific Hotel; ☺4pm-midnight Tue-Sun; 🐾), a superkitsch Tiki basement bar with fishbowl cocktails and literally hundreds of rums on offer.

SEX ON THE REEF

If you're a keen diver or just a romantic at heart, try to time your visit with the annual coral spawning, an all-in orgy in which reef corals simultaneously release millions of eggs and sperm into the water. The ejaculatory event has been described as looking like a psychedelic snowstorm, with trails of reproductive matter streaking the sea in rainbow colours visible from miles away.

The spawning occurs sometime in November or December; the exact date depends on factors including water temperature (it must be 26°C or above), the date of the full moon, the stillness of the water and the perfect balance between light and dark (who doesn't appreciate a bit of mood lighting?). Most Cairns-based diving outfits offer special spawning night dives for those looking to get in on the action. Even if you're on land, you may notice an, um, 'amorous' aroma on the night of the mass love-in.

Tanks Arts Centre   LIVE PERFORMANCE
(☑ 07-4032 6600; www.tanksartscentre.com; 46 Collins Ave) Next to the Botanic Gardens (p456), Tanks is one of Cairns' premier live-music and performance venues, hosting a regular lineup of touring bands, theatre and comedy acts. See the website for what's on.

Reef Hotel Casino   CASINO
(☑ 07-4030 8888; www.reefcasino.com.au; 35-41 Wharf St; ⊗ 9am-5am) In addition to table games and pokies, Cairns' casino has five dining spots and three bars, including the enormous Casino Sports Arena bar. Catch dinner and a show at the adults-only Paramour Cabaret Theatre.

🛍 Shopping

★ **Rusty's Markets**   MARKET
(☑ 07-4040 2705; www.rustysmarkets.com.au; 57-89 Grafton St; ⊗ 5am-6pm Fri & Sat, to 3pm Sun) No weekend in Cairns is complete without a visit to this busy, vibrant multicultural market. Weave (and taste) your way through piles of seasonal tropical fruits, veggies and herbs, plus farm-fresh honey, locally grown flowers, excellent coffees, curries and other hot meals, cold drinks, antiques and more.

Doongal Aboriginal Art   ART
(☑ 07-4041 4249; www.doongal.com.au; 49 Esplanade; ⊗ 9am-9pm) This place stocks authentic artworks, boomerangs, didgeridoos and other traditional artefacts by local and Central Australian Indigenous artists. Worldwide shipping is available.

Crackerbox Palace   VINTAGE
(☑ 07-4031 1216; 228 Sheridan St; ⊗ 10am-5pm Mon-Fri, to 3pm Sat) This treasure trove of all things vintage has been luring in the locals for more than 20 years. It's crammed full of one-off clothes, furniture, records, knick-knacks and awesome oddities.

Night Markets   MARKET
(☑ 07-4051 7666; www.facebook.com/cairns nightmarkets; 71-75 Esplanade; ⊗ shops 5-11.30pm, food court 10am-11pm) Head here if your supply of shark-bite T-shirts is running low, or you need your name engraved on a grain of rice. It's souvenir city, but worth a stroll around; the vibe is fun and frantic. There are many massage operators here: be sure to agree on the price before your rubdown begins. Enter via the Esplanade or Abbott St.

ℹ Information

MEDICAL SERVICES

Cairns 24 Hour Medical Centre (☑ 07-4052 1119; www.cairns24hourmedical.com.au; cnr Grafton & Florence Sts; ⊗ 24hr) Centrally located medical centre; also does dive medicals.

Cairns Hospital (☑ 07-4226 0000; 165 Esplanade) Largest hospital in Far North Queensland.

POST

Post Office (☑ 13 13 18; www.auspost.com. au; 38 Sheridan St; ⊗ 8.30am-5.30pm Mon-Fri, 9am-12.30pm Sat)

TOURIST INFORMATION

The Cairns Regional Council's website (www. cairns.qld.gov.au/region/tourist-information) has tons of details on events, activities and transport in the region.

You'll find privately run tourist information centres and booking offices around town; they all book the same trips at similar prices but you can usually get better deals booking through your accommodation, especially at backpacker hostels.

ℹ Getting There & Away

AIR

Qantas (☑ 13 13 13; www.qantas.com.au), **Virgin Australia** (☑ 13 67 89; www.virginaustralia.com) and **Jetstar** (☑ 13 15 38; www.jetstar.com.au), plus a handful of international carriers, arrive in and depart from **Cairns Airport** (📞07-4080 6703; www.cairnsairport.com; Airport Ave), with direct services to all Australian capital cities except Canberra and Hobart, and to regional centres including Townsville, Weipa and Horn Island. Direct international connections include Bali, Singapore, Shenzhen, Tokyo and Port Moresby.

Hinterland Aviation (📞07-4040 1333; www.hinterlandaviation.com.au; Cairns Airport) has at least two flights daily from Cairns to Cooktown.

Skytrans (📞1300 759 872; www.skytrans.com.au; Cairns Airport) services Cape York communities and the Torres Strait Islands.

BOAT

Almost all reef trips from Cairns depart the Marlin Wharf (sometimes called the Marlin Jetty or Marlin Marina), with booking and check-in facilities inside the **Reef Fleet Terminal** (Pierpoint Rd). A handful of smaller operators may have their check-in facilities boat-side, on the wharf itself. Be sure to ask for the correct berth number.

International cruise ships and **SeaSwift** (📞1800 424 422, 07-4035 1234; www.seaswift.com.au; office 41-45 Tingira St, Portsmith; one-way/return from $670/1065) cargo ships to the Torres Strait and Seisia on Cape York dock and depart from the **Cairns Seaport** (📞07-4052 3888; www.portsnorth.com.au/cairns; cnr Wharf & Lake Sts).

BUS

Long-distance buses arrive at and depart from the **Interstate Coach Terminal** (Reef Fleet Terminal) and Cairns Central Railway Station. Operators include the following.

Cairns Cooktown Express (📞07-4059 1423; www.cairnscooktownexpress.com.au)

Greyhound Australia (📞1300 473 946; www.greyhound.com.au)

Premier Motor Service (📞13 34 10; www.premierms.com.au)

Tablelands Tours & Transfers (📞07-4045 1882; www.tablelandstoursandtransfers.com.au)

Trans North (📞07-4095 8644; www.transnorthbus.com; Cairns Central Railway Station)

CAR & MOTORCYCLE

Major car-rental companies have airport and city (usually on Sheridan St) branches. Daily rates start at around $30 for a compact auto and $80 for a 4WD. **Cruising Car Rental** (📞07-4041 4666; www.cruisingcarrental.com.au; 196 Sheridan St; per day from $35) and **Rent-a-Bomb** (📞07-4031 4477; www.rentabomb.com.au; 144 Sheridan St; per day from $30) have cheap rates on older model vehicles. If you're looking for a cheap campervan, **Jucy** (📞1800 150 850; www.jucy.com.au; 55 Dutton St, Portsmith; per day $35-75), **Spaceships** (📞1300 132 469; www.spaceshipsrentals.com.au; 397 Sheridan St;

per day from $35), **Lucky Campervan Rentals** (📞1800 808 881; www.lucky-rentals.com.au; 107 Bunda St; ☉from $37 per day) and **Hippie Camper Hire** (📞1800 777 779; www.hippie-camper.com; 432 Sheridan St; per day from $22) have quality wheels at budget prices.

If you're in for the long haul, check hostels and www.gumtree.com.au for used campervans and ex-backpackers' cars.

If you prefer two wheels to four, try **Choppers Motorcycle Tours & Hire** (📞07-4051 6288; www.choppersmotorcycles.com.au; 150 Sheridan St; 90min ride $130, motorcycle hire per day from $150) or **Cairns Scooter & Bicycle Hire** (📞07-4031 3444; www.cairnsbicyclehire.com.au; 47 Shields St; scooters/bikes per day from $50/15; ☉8am-5pm Mon-Fri, 9am-4.30pm Sat).

Royal Automobile Club of Queensland (RACQ; 📞07-4042 3100, road conditions info 13 19 05; www.racq.com.au; Stockland Shopping Centre, 537 Mulgrave Rd, Earlville; ☉8.30am-5pm Mon-Fri) has maps and information on road conditions state-wide, including Cape York.

TRAIN

The Kuranda Scenic Railway (p467) runs daily; the Savannahlander (p467) offers a miscellany of rail journeys into the outback from **Cairns Central train station** (Bunda St).

Queensland Rail (📞1300 131 722; www.queenslandrailtravel.com.au) operates services between Brisbane and Cairns.

ⓘ Getting Around

TO/FROM THE AIRPORT

The airport is about 6km north of central Cairns; many hotels and hostels offer courtesy pickups.

Airport Connections Cairns (📞07-4049 2244; www.cairnsbuscharters.com) meets incoming flights and runs a shuttle (adult/child $19/9.50) directly to your Cairns accommodation; it also runs to/from the airport and Port Douglas (adult/child $46/23) and the Northern Beaches.

Cairns Airport Shuttle (📞0432 488 783; www.cairnsairportshuttle.com.au) is a good option for groups; the more passengers, the cheaper the fare.

Taxis to the city centre cost around $25 (plus $4 airport surcharge).

BICYCLE

Cairns is criss-crossed with cycling paths and circuits; some of the most popular routes take in the Esplanade, Botanic Gardens and Centenary Lakes. There's a detailed list of routes and maps at www.cairns.qld.gov.au/region/tourist-information/things-to-do/cycle. Some backpacker hostels rent out bikes. Otherwise try Cairns Scooter & Bicycle Hire.

BUS

Cairns has a fairly efficient and comprehensive city-bus system run by **Translink** (Sunbus; www.translink.com.au/cairns). All buses stop at the **Cairns Transit Mall** (Lake St).

TAXI

Cairns Taxis (☑ 07-4048 8333, 13 10 08; www.cairnstaxis.com.au)

AROUND CAIRNS

Islands off Cairns

Green Island

Showing some of the scars that come with fame and popularity, this pretty coral cay (45 minutes from Cairns) nevertheless retains much of its beauty. The island has a rainforest interior with interpretive walks, a fringe of white-sand beach, and superb snorkelling just offshore; it's great for kids. You can walk around the island (which, along with its surrounding waters, is protected by national- and marine-park status) in about 30 minutes.

The star attraction at family-owned aquarium **Marineland Crocodile Park** (☑ 07-4051 4032; www.greenislandcrocs.com.au; adult/child $20/9.50; ☺ 9.30am-4pm; ⊞) is Cassius, the world's largest croc in captivity at 5.5m. Believed to be more than 110 years old, he's fed daily at 10.30am and 1.30pm.

If you don't want to get your hair wet, **Seawalker** (☑ 07-4044 9944; www.seawalker.com.au; per person $180) allows you to don a helmet and go for a (guided) stroll on the sea floor, 5m below the surface.

Luxurious **Green Island Resort** (☑ 07-4031 3300; www.greenislandresort.com.au; r from $250, ste $745-845; ⊞@☜⊠) maintains a sense of privacy and exclusivity despite having sections opened to the general public, including restaurants, bars, an ice-cream parlour and water-sports facilities. Spacious split-level suites feature tropical themes, timber furnishings and inviting balconies.

Big Cat (☑ 07-4051 0444; www.greenisland.com.au; Reef Fleet Terminal; adult/child/family $98/49/245) and **Great Adventures** (☑ 07-4044 9944; www.greatadventures.com.au; Reef Fleet Terminal; Green Island transfer adult/child/family $85/43/213; ⊞) run transfers and day-return tours to Green Island.

Fitzroy Island

A steep mountaintop rising from the sea, fabulous Fitzroy Island has clinking coral beaches, giant boulders and rainforest walking tracks, one of which ends at a now-inactive lighthouse. It's a top spot for swimming and snorkelling; one of the best places to lay your towel is Nudey Beach, which, despite its name, is not officially clothing-optional.

The **Cairns Turtle Rehabilitation Centre** (www.cairnsturtlerehab.org.au; adult/child $11.50/7; ☺ tours from 1pm; ⊞) looks after sick and injured sea turtles before releasing them back into the wild. Daily educational tours (45 minutes, maximum 15 guests) take visitors through the turtle hospital to meet recovering residents. Bookings through the Fitzroy Island Resort are essential.

Fitzroy Island Resort (☑ 07-4044 6700; www.fitzroyisland.com; studios/bungalow/cabins/ste/apt from $170/175/293/270/315; ⊞☜⊠) has tropi-cool accommodation ranging from sleek studios, suites and beachfront cabins through to luxurious apartments. The restaurant, bar and kiosk are open to day trippers. Budgeteers can book here for a site at the **Fitzroy Island Camping Ground** (☑ 07-4044 6700; www.fitzroyisland.com; sites $37).

The **Fitzroy Island Flyer** (www.fitzroyisland.com; return adult/child/family $80/40/211) departs Cairns' Marlin Wharf (berth 20) at 8am, 11am and 1.30pm (bookings essential) and whisks you to Fitzroy Island in just 45 minutes. It returns to Cairns at 9.30am, 12.15pm and 5pm.

Frankland Islands

If the idea of hanging out on one of five uninhabited, coral-fringed islands with excellent snorkelling and stunning white-sand beaches appeals, cruise out to the Frankland Group National Park. These continental islands are made up of High Island to the north, and Normanby, Mabel, Round and Russell Islands to the south.

Frankland Islands Reef Cruises (☑ 07-4033 0081; www.franklandislands.com.au; adult/child from $204/119) runs excellent day trips that include a cruise down the Mulgrave River, snorkelling gear, tuition and lunch.

Cairns' Northern Beaches

Despite what some brochures may infer, Cairns city doesn't have a genuine swimmable beach. But a 15-minute drive (or a local bus ticket) will get you out to a string of lovely beach communities, each with their own character: Yorkeys Knob is popular with sailors, Trinity is big with families and Palm Cove is a swanky honeymoon haven with plenty of upmarket accommodation and restaurants. The last beach, Ellis, makes for a relaxing break en route to Port Douglas.

The narrow coastal strip between Cairns and Port Douglas is the traditional home of the Yirrganydji people, surrounded by the broader Djabugay (Tjapukai) country that stretches inland.

Yorkeys Knob

POP 2760

Yorkeys Knob is a laid-back beach community best known for its marina and **golf course** ([] 07-4055 7933; www.halfmoonbaygolf.com.au; 66 Wattle St; 9/18 holes $29/49, club hire $25), and the cheeky crocs that frequent it. The 'Knob' part of the name elicits sniggers from easily amused locals; others wonder where the apostrophe went. Yorkeys has a stinger net in summer.

Blazing Saddles ([] 07-4055 7400; www. blazingsaddles.com.au; 96 Yorkeys Knob Rd; horse rides from $135, quad bikes from $145; []) has half-day horse-riding tours that meander through rainforest, mangroves and sugar-cane fields.

For fresh seafood and delightful views of the marina's expensive floating toys from the expansive dining deck, **Yorkeys Knob Boating Club** ([] 07-4055 7711; www.ykbc.com. au; 29 Buckley St; mains $16-40; [] noon-3pm & 6-9pm) is worth the trip from Cairns.

Trinity Beach

Trinity Beach, with its gorgeous stretch of sheltered sand, pretty esplanade and sensibly priced dining and accommodation, has managed to stave off the tourism vibe, despite being a holiday hotspot and popular dining destination for locals in the know. There's not much to do here except eat, sleep and relax, but Trinity Beach's central position makes it easy to get out and about if you're feeling active.

One of the most handsome blocks on the beachfront, **Sea Point on Trinity Beach** ([] 07-4057 9544; www.seapointontrinitybeach.com; 63 Vasey Esplanade; apt $130-360; [] [] [] []) offers indoor-outdoor balconies, tiled floors and breezy outlooks.

Don't let the easy-breezy beach-shack vibe fool you into thinking the food at **Fratelli on Trinity** ([] 07-4057 5775; www.fratelli.net.au; 47 Vasey Esplanade; mains $20-35; [] 7am-10pm Wed-Sun, from 4.30pm Tue) is anything less than top class. Pastas are superb; their delectable crab-and-zucchini fritters might even distract you from the million-dollar views.

Blue Moon Grill ([] 07-4057 8957; www. bluemoongrill.com.au; Shop 6, 22-24 Trinity Beach Rd; mains $22-36; [] 5-9pm Mon-Fri, 7.30-11.30am & 5-9pm Sat & Sun) wows with a creative, original menu presented with passion. Where else can you try crocodile popcorn?

Palm Cove

POP 2059

Stunning, sophisticated Palm Cove is a destination in its own right. More intimate than Port Douglas and more upmarket than Cairns' other beaches, Palm Cove is a cloistered coastal community with a beautiful promenade along the melaleuca-lined Williams Esplanade. Its gorgeous stretch of white-sand beach and its sprinkling of fancy restaurants do their best to lure young lovers from their luxury resorts; invariably, they succeed.

If you can drag yourself away from the beach or the pool, Palm Cove has some excellent water-sports operators, including **Palm Cove Watersports** ([] 0402 861 011; www.palmcovewatersports.com; 149 Williams Esplanade; kayak hire per hour single/double $25/35, SUP hire $25) and **Pacific Watersports** ([] 0413 721 999; www.pacificwatersports.com. au; 41 Williams Esplanade), which offers three-hour kayak tours to see turtles ($80).

✦ Festivals & Events

Palm Cove Reef Feast   FOOD & DRINK
(www.reeffeast.com.au; [] early Oct) Get a taste of the tropics over three gut-busting days of food stalls, markets and al-fresco dining events.

🛏 Sleeping & Eating

★ **Cairns Beaches Flashpackers**   HOSTEL $
([] 07-4055 3797; www.cairnsbeachesflashpackers.com; 19 Veivers Rd; dm/d $39/89; [] [] [] [])
Palm Cove's first and only hostel is a splendid, spotless place just 100m from the beach. It's more a restful retreat than party palace. The bunk-free dorms are tidy and comfortable; the private rooms have bathrooms and sliding-door access to the pool. Cook in the immaculate communal kitchen. Scooter and bike hire is available.

Palm Cove Holiday Park
CAMPGROUND **$**

(☑1800 736 741; www.nrmaparksandresorts.com.au/palm-cove; 149 Williams Esplanade; powered/unpowered sites from $40/32; P 🛜) Stake out a spot at this modern, well-run beachfront camping ground near the jetty. It packs out in the high season when there's a seven-night minimum but rates reduce from October to April. It has a good camp kitchen, a BBQ area and a laundry.

Sarayi
BOUTIQUE HOTEL **$$**

(☑07-4059 5600; www.sarayi.com.au; 95 Williams Esplanade; d from $170, apt $250-319; P ❄ 🛜 ≋) White, bright and perfectly located among a grove of melaleucas across from the beach, Sarayi is a wonderful, affordable choice for couples, families and the growing number of visitors choosing to get married on its rooftop terrace.

★Reef House
Resort & Spa
BOUTIQUE HOTEL **$$$**

(☑07-4080 2600; www.reefhouse.com.au; 99 Williams Esplanade; r/apt from $305/445; P ❄ 🛜 ≋) Once the private residence of an army brigadier, Reef House is more intimate and understated than most of Palm Cove's resorts. The whitewashed walls, wicker furniture, big beds romantically draped in muslin and luxurious day spa add to the air of refinement. The **Brigadier's Bar** works on an honesty system; complimentary punch is served by candlelight at twilight.

27 Degrees
CAFE **$**

(☑0419 661 946; www.27degreesqld.com; cnr French St & Williams Esplanade; bowls $15-18, baguettes $13; ⊙8am-2pm Wed-Sun; ✐) Though it's but a hole-in-the-wall, you won't be able to miss 27 Degrees, thanks to its bright *Miami Vice* decor and gaggle of satisfied customers chowing down on veggie poké bowls and dairy-free smoothies in blue slouch chairs outside. Excellent banh mi and other baguettes, too. Even visitors from Melbourne rave about 27's superb coffees (hot and cold-press).

★Coco Mojo
INTERNATIONAL **$$**

(☑07-4059 1272; www.cocomojoclifton.com; 14 Clifton Rd, Clifton Beach; mains $23-40; ⊙11.30am-9pm Mon-Wed & Fri, 10.30am-8pm Thu, 9am-9pm Sat & Sun; ❄ 🛜) A five-minute drive from Palm Cove, Coco Mojo at Clifton Beach is worth a special trip. The menu focuses on the wildly varying street foods of the world, covering cuisines from Nigerian to Texan, Indonesian to Lebanese; somehow, the experienced international chefs

make it work. The tasting plates and heaving share platters (from $75) are the stars of the show.

★Chill Cafe
CAFE **$$**

(☑0439 361 122; www.chillcafepalmcove.com; 41 Williams Esplanade; mains $25-38; ⊙6am-late; ❄ 🛜) The prime position on the corner of the waterfront esplanade, combined with fun, friendly and attentive service, sexy tunes and a huge airy deck, are all great reasons to try the oversized, tasty treats (think fish tacos and chunky club sandwiches) offered by this hip cafe. Opens early for breakfast, though the Bloody Marys start at 10am.

Nu Nu
AUSTRALIAN **$$$**

(☑07-4059 1880; www.nunu.com.au; 1 Veivers Rd; mains $26-125, tasting menu per person from $89; ⊙7am-late; ❄ 🛜) Trendy Nu Nu uses fresh local produce to create Mod Oz masterpieces including wok-fried mud crab and smoked Wagyu rump cap. It's destination dining – come for lunch or breakfast if you want to get a taste for the place without the huge bill.

🍷 Drinking & Nightlife

Apres Beach Bar & Grill
BAR

(☑07-4059 2000; www.apresbeachbar.com.au; 119 Williams Esplanade; ⊙11.30am-midnight Mon-Thu, to 1am Fri-Sun) The most happening place in Palm Cove, with a fun crowd, regular live music and a fab cocktail list. Good eats, too.

🛍 Shopping

Palm Cove Markets
MARKET

(Williams Esplanade; ⊙8am-2pm 1st Sun Oct-Aug) Browse more than 130 stalls for local

---

THE CAIRNS OF CAIRNS

As if the natural scenery on the road to Port Douglas wasn't distracting enough, the comely Captain Cook Hwy has another eye-catcher: hundreds upon hundreds of mysterious, precariously piled rocks. The stone stackers' identity and mission has puzzled and delighted both locals and #instatravellers looking for a hot shot: is it a play on 'cairns'? Conceptual art? Whatever's going on, pull over for a peek and a ponder as many passers-by do. You'll find the cryptic collection just north of Ellis Beach.

handicrafts, offbeat souvenirs and regional produce. Live entertainment, food stalls and kids' activities to boot.

Ellis Beach

Little Ellis Beach is the last – and possibly best of Cairns' northern beaches and the closest to the highway, which runs right past it. The long, sheltered bay is a stunner, with a palm-fringed, lifeguard-patrolled swimming beach, and a stinger net in summer. Cairns' only (unofficial) clothing-optional beach, **Buchans Point**, is at the southern end of Ellis; there's no stinger net here, so consider your valuable assets before diving in in your birthday suit.

North of Ellis Beach towards Port Douglas, **Hartley's Crocodile Adventures** (☑ 07-4055 3576; www.crocodileadventures.com; Captain Cook Hwy, Wangetti Beach; adult/child/family $41/20.50/102.50; ⊘ 8.30am-5pm; 🐾) offers a daily range of squeal-inducing events including croc-farm tours, feedings, 'crocodile attack' and snake shows, and croc-infested lagoon cruises.

Ellis Beach Oceanfront Bungalows (☑ 1800 637 036, 07-4055 3538; www.ellisbeach.com; Captain Cook Hwy; powered/unpowered sites from $43/36, cabins with shared bathroom from $115, bungalow d $170-210; 🅿 ❄ 🛜 🛝) has camping, cabins and contemporary bungalows, the best of which have direct ocean views. Just *try* to drive past the happening **Ellis Beach Bar 'n' Grill** (☑ 07-4055 3534; www.ellisbeachbarandgrill.com.au; Captain Cook Hwy; mains $14-28; ⊘ 8am-8pm; 🐾) and not stop for a burger.

South of Cairns

Babinda

Babinda is a small working-class village on the highway about 60km south of Cairns. The main attraction is the **Babinda Boulders** FREE, 7km inland, where a photogenic but potentially dangerous – heed all warning signs – creek rushes between 4m-high granite rocks. **Kayaking** (☑ 07-4067 2678; www.babindakayaking.com.au; 330 Stager Rd, Mirriwinni; kayak & SUP hire half/full day $45/70) on the Babinda Creek is also popular.

Babinda is part of the traditional tribal lands of the Yidinji people.

There's free camping at **Babinda Boulders Camping Area** and the **Rotary Park Campground** (Howard Kennedy Dr).

Wooroonooran National Park

Part of the Wet Tropics World Heritage Area, steamy, dreamy Wooroonooran National Park brims with stunning natural spectacles, including Queensland's highest peak (Mt Bartle Frere; 1622m), dramatic falls, tangled rainforest, unusual flora and fauna and blissfully cool swimming holes. It's heaven for serious hikers, or anyone looking to escape the (relative) rat race of bustling Cairns.

This part of the park was part of the traditional tribal lands of the Yidinji and Ngadjonjii rainforest people.

Head here with your own wheels or on a day trip with **Wooroonooran Safaris** (☑ 07-4033 1886; www.wooroonooran.com; day tour adult/child $219/99.50). Contact **NPRSR** (DES; ☑ 13 74 68; www.parks.des.qld.gov.au/parks/wooroonooran) about camping permits.

ATHERTON TABLELANDS

Climbing back from the coast between Innisfail and Cairns is the fertile food bowl of the far north, the Atherton Tablelands. Quaint country towns, eco-wilderness lodges and luxurious B&Bs dot greener-than-green hills between patchwork fields, pockets of rainforest, spectacular lakes, waterfalls and Queensland's highest mountains, Bartle Frere (1622m) and Bellenden Ker (1593m).

This region makes for a great getaway from the swelter of the coast: it's almost always a few degrees cooler than Cairns, and on winter nights things get downright chilly.

The Tablelands are the traditional home of the Djirrbal and Ngadjonji tribes of the Djirrbalngan language group, while the area around Kuranda and Yungaburra is the land of the Djabugay (Tjapukai) and Yidinji peoples.

🛈 Getting There & Away

Four main roads lead in from the coast: the Palmerston Hwy from Innisfail, Gillies Hwy (turn-off just before Gordonvale), Kennedy Hwy (known locally as the Kuranda Range) from Smithfield, and Rex Range Rd between Mossman and Port Douglas. Though there are frequent buses from Cairns to the main towns on the Tablelands, it's worth hiring your own wheels to fully explore the area.

Trans North (p470) has regular bus services connecting Cairns with various towns on the Tablelands, including Kuranda ($6.90, 30 minutes), Mareeba ($20.10, one hour), Atherton ($26.60, 1¾ hours) and Herberton/Ravenshoe

($33.50/39.20, two/2½ hours, Monday, Wednesday, Friday).

Kuranda

POP 3008

Tucked away in thick rainforest, arty, alternative Kuranda is one of Cairns' most popular day trips. During the day, this hippy haven swarms with tourists soaking up the vibe, visiting animal sanctuaries and poking around its famous markets and souvenir shops; after the markets close at 3pm, you can almost hear the village sigh as the streets and pubs are reclaimed by mellow locals (and the occasional street-hopping wallaby).

Kuranda and the Barron Gorge region are the traditional home of the Djabugay (Tjapukai) people, many of whom are involved in the local arts and cultural scene.

⊙ Sights & Activities

★ Kuranda Original
Rainforest Markets MARKET
(☑07-4093 9440; www.kurandaoriginalrainforest-market.com.au; 7-11 Therwine St; ☺9.30am-3pm) Follow the clouds of incense down to these atmospheric village markets. Operating since 1978, they're still the best place to see artists at work and hippies at play. Pick up everything from avocado ice cream to organic lingerie and sample local produce such as honey and fruit wines.

Rainforestation PARK
(☑07-4085 5008; www.rainforest.com.au; Kennedy Hwy; adult/child/family $51/25.50/127.50; ☺9am-4pm; ☒) You'll need a full day to properly explore this enormous complex, divided into three sections: a koala & wildlife park, the interactive Pamagirri Aboriginal Experience, and a river & rainforest tour aboard the amphibious Army Duck boat-truck.

The park is 3km east of Kuranda. Shuttles (return adult/child $12.50/6.25) run every half-hour between the park and Kuranda village.

Heritage Markets MARKET
(☑07-4093 8060; www.kurandamarkets.com.au; Rob Veivers Dr; ☺9.30am-3.30pm) At this touristy market you'll find Australiana souvenirs – think emu oil, kangaroo-skin bow ties and Akubra hats – by the busload. It's also home to Frogs (☑07-4093 8952; www.frogsrestaurant.com.au; mains $10-38; ☺9am-3.30pm; ☒☒) cafe and a handful of wildlife sanctuaries, including Kuranda Koala Gardens (☑07-

TABLELANDS MARKETS

As is seemingly obligatory for any quaint country region, the tiny towns of the Tablelands host a miscellany of monthly markets. Kuranda's blockbuster bazaars are legendary, but for something a bit more down-home, check out the following.

Atherton Undercover Markets (Merriland Hall, Robert St; ☺7am-noon 2nd Sun of month)

Malanda Markets (www.facebook.com/malandamarkets; Malanda Showgrounds; ☺7.30am-12.30pm 3rd Sat of month)

Mareeba Markets (www.mareebamarkets.org.au; Centenary Park, Byrnes St; ☺7.30am-12.30pm 2nd & 5th Sat of month)

Tumoulin Country Markets (Tumoulin Rd, Ravenshoe; ☺8am-noon 4th Sun of month)

Yungaburra Markets (www.yungaburramarkets.com; Gillies Hwy; ☺7.30am-12.30pm 4th Sat of month)

4093 9953; www.koalagardens.com; adult/child $19/9.50; ☺9am-4pm), Australian Butterfly Sanctuary (☑07-4093 7575; www.australian-butterflies.com; adult/child/family $20/10/50; ☺9.45am-4pm) and Birdworld (☑07-4093 9188; www.birdworldkuranda.com; adult/child $19/9.50; ☺9am-4pm); grab a Kuranda Wildlife Experience Pass (adult/child $51/25/50) on-site for discounted entry to all three attractions.

Kuranda Riverboat CRUISE
(☑0412 159 212; www.kurandariverboat.com.au; adult/child/family $20/10/50; ☺hourly 10.45am-2.30pm) Hop aboard for a 45-minute calm-water cruise along the Barron River in search of freshwater crocodiles, or opt for an hour-long interpretive rainforest walk (adult/child from $35/17.50) in a secluded spot accessible only by boat.

Located on the jetty behind the train station; buy tickets for the cruise on board, or book online for the walk.

🛏 Sleeping & Eating

Between 9am and 3pm there are numerous local cafes catering to the tourist dollar, including some fabulous places at the Original Markets (p475): must-tries include the to-die-for falafels at Falafellicious (www.

WORTH A TRIP

CHILLAGOE

This charismatic former gold-rush town will fulfil your wildest, most romantic outback dreams. With a raw, unhurried quality, it's at the centre of an area that has impressive limestone caves, Indigenous rock-art sites and the creepy-cool ruins of an early-20th-century **smelting plant** (www.parks.des.qld.gov.au/parks/chillagoe-caves/chillagoe-smelters.html) FREE. **Chillagoe Observatory** (☑ 07-4094 7155; www.coel.com.au; Hospital Ave; adult/child from 6 years $25/15; ⊙ 7.30pm Easter-Oct) offers the chance to scan the clear savannah skies through two huge telescopes.

Stop in at the **Hub** (☑ 07-4094 7111; www.qwe.com.au/chillagoe/the_hub.html; Queen St; ⊙ 8am-3.30pm) for help with finding some of Chillagoe's more hidden highlights. The **Chillagoe–Mungana Caves National Park** (☑ 07-4094 7111; www.parks.des.qld.gov.au/parks/chillagoe-caves; 1-/2-/3-cave tours $28.75/45.80/57.60; ⊙ tours 9am, 11am & 1.30pm) website has information on walking tracks and tours in the area.

Chillagoe's big annual events are the **rodeo** (⊙ May) and **Great Wheelbarrow Race** (www.greatwheelbarrowrace.com; ⊙ May).

facebook.com/falafelkuranda; Original Kuranda Rainforest Markets; falafel $10; ⊙ 10am-3pm Sun-Fri; 🍴) and creamy crêpes at **Petit Cafe** (☑ 0421 799 131; Original Kuranda Rainforest Markets; crêpes $6.50-24; ⊙ 8am-3pm). Only a few places, including the Barron Falls Hotel (aka the 'top pub'), are open in the evening.

Kuranda Rainforest Park　CARAVAN PARK $
(☑ 07-4093 7316; www.kurandarainforestpark.com.au; 88 Kuranda Heights Rd; powered/unpowered sites $37/30, s/d without bathroom from $35/55, units & cabins from $105; 🅿🌸🛜🐕) This well-tended park lives up to its name, with grassy campsites enveloped in rainforest. Basic but cosy budget rooms open onto a tin-roofed timber deck, units come with poolside or garden views, and cabins are snuggled up by the forest. There's an excellent on-site **restaurant** (mains $16-29; ⊙ 5.30-8.30pm Wed-Sun; 🍴) serving local produce. It's a 10-minute walk from town via a forest trail.

⭐ **Cedar Park Rainforest Resort** RESORT $$$
(☑ 07-4093 7892; www.cedarparkresort.com.au; 250 Cedar Park Rd, Koah; r incl breakfast $229-300; 🅿🌸🛜) 🍃 Set deep in the bush (a 20-minute drive from Kuranda towards Mareeba), this unusual property is part Euro-castle, part Aussie-bush-retreat. In lieu of TV, guests look out for wallabies, peacocks and dozens of native birds. There are hammocks aplenty, creek access, a fireplace, and a gourmet restaurant with well-priced meals and free port.

German Tucker　GERMAN $
(www.germantucker.com; Therwine St; sausages $6.50-11; ⊙ 10am-3pm) Fill up on classic *würste* or try the tasty emu and crocodile sausages at this amusing place, where they blast oompah music and splash out steins of top-notch German beer.

Kuranda Hotel　PUB FOOD $$
(☑ 07-4093 7206; www.kurandahotel.com; cnr Arara & Coondoo Sts; mains $15-26.50; ⊙ 10am-4pm; 🅿🌸🛜🐕) Locally known as the 'bottom pub', the Kuranda Hotel has generous, good-value pub-grub meals, with some higher-end options as well. The broad deck overlooking the train station is usually busy at lunchtime, when hungry tourists tuck into local barramundi, kangaroo pot-pies, enormous burgers and chicken parmas.

ⓘ Information

Kuranda Visitor Information Centre (☑ 07-4093 9311; www.kuranda.org; Centenary Park; ⊙ 10am-4pm)

ⓘ Getting There & Away

Kuranda is as much about the journey (from Cairns) as the destination: choose between the Skyrail Rainforest Cableway (p466) and the Kuranda Scenic Railway (p467), or do both with a combination return ticket.

Fares to Kuranda from Cairns are $6.90 with Trans North (p470), $16 on the Cairns Cooktown Express (p470).

Kuranda is a 25km drive up the Kuranda Range from Cairns.

Mareeba

POP 11,079

Whether it's lassos or lattes that whet your whistle, you'll have a right knees-up in Mareeba. The dusty town – gateway to Cape York to the north and Chillagoe to the west – plays host to one of Australia's biggest rodeos (www.mareebarodeo.com.au; tickets $20-50; ☉ Jul), featuring two days of buckin' broncos, bull riding and crazy clowns. Mareeba is also one of the country's prime coffee-growing regions; an estimated 70% of Australia's coffee crop is grown here. Learn all about it over a cup o' joe at **Coffee Works** (☏ 07-4092 4101; www.coffeeworks.com.au; 136 Mason St; museum adult/child $19/10; ☉ cafe 9am-4pm, museum to 2pm).

This region was once the heart of the country's main tobacco-growing region, but Mareeba now has turned its soil to more wholesome produce, with fruit orchards and distilleries in addition to the coffee farms: try local spirits and liqueurs at **Mt Uncle Distillery** (☏ 07-4086 8008; www.mtuncle.com; 1819 Chewko Rd, Walkamin; ☉ 10am-4pm). Mareeba's drier landscape differs dramatically from the higher-altitude central Tablelands.

Mareeba ('Meeting of the Waters') is the traditional home of the Muluridji people. **Granite Gorge Nature Park** (☏ 07-4093 2259; www.granitegorge.com.au; 332 Paglietta Rd, Chewko; entry adult/child $13/6; ☉ 9am-6pm; ♿), 12km from Mareeba, occupies an alien landscape of humongous granite boulders, caves, turtle-inhabited swimming holes and wildlife galore.

Campers can use the **rodeo campgrounds** (☏ 0448 472 548; www.mareebarodeo.com.au; Kerribee Park; unpowered/powered sites per 2 people $16/20) year-round.

Atherton

POP 7331

The largest settlement and unofficial capital of the same-name Tablelands, Atherton is a spirited country town that makes a decent base for exploring the region's highlights. It's the best place up here to shop for supplies.

Many backpackers head up to the Tablelands for year-round fruit-picking work; the **Atherton Visitor Information Centre** (☏ 1300 366 361; athinfocentre@trc.qld.gov.au; cnr Main & Silo Sts; ☉ 9am-5pm) can help with up-to-date work info.

Thousands of Chinese migrants came to the region in search of gold in the late 1800s. All that's left of Atherton's Chinatown is the tin-and-timber **Hou Wang Miau Temple** (☏ 07-4091 6945; www.houwang.org.au; 86 Herberton Rd; adult/child/family $10/5/20; ☉ 9am-4pm Wed-Fri, to 1pm Sat). Admission includes a guided tour.

Crystal Caves (☏ 07-4091 2365; www.crystalcaves.com.au; 69 Main St; adult/child/family $25/12.50/65; ☉ 9am-5pm; ♿) is a gaudy mineralogical museum that houses one of the world's biggest amethyst geodes (more than 3m high and weighing 2.7 tonnes).

For a caffeine fix or sugar rush, hit **Petals & Pinecones** (P&P; ☏ 0436 412 559; www.petalsandpinecones.com; 6-8 Herberton Rd; coffee/shakes from $4.50/9; ☉ 9am-4.30pm Tue-Fri, to 4pm Sat & Sun; ♿), a quirky cafe-gallery offering excellent coffee and teetering freakshakes. It's behind the Supercheap Auto shop.

Lake Tinaroo

Lake Tinaroo, also known as Tinaroo Dam, was allegedly named when a prospector stumbled across a deposit of alluvial tin and, in a fit of excitement, shouted 'Tin! Hurroo!'. Today, Cairnsites flee the swelter of the coast for boating, waterskiing and shoreline lolling. **Barramundi fishing** (☏ 0438 012 775; www.tinaroobarra.com; half-/full-day fishing $350/600) is permitted year-round, though if you're not joining a charter, you'll need to pick up a permit from local businesses.

The 28km **Danbulla Forest Drive** winds its way through rainforest and softwood plantations along the north side of the lake. The unsealed but well-maintained road passes the pretty **Lake Euramoo** and the boardwalk-encircled **Cathedral Fig**, a gigantic 500-year-old strangler fig similar to the Curtain Fig in nearby Yungaburra; it's also accessible via a signposted road off the Gillies Hwy.

There are five Queensland Parks **camping grounds** (☏ 13 74 68; www.parks.des.qld.gov.au/parks/danbulla/camping.html; camping permits per person/family $6.55/26.60) in the Danbulla State Forest. All have water, BBQs and toilets; advance bookings are essential.

Lake Tinaroo Holiday Park (☏ 07-4095 8232; www.laketinarooholidaypark.com.au; Tinaroo Falls Dam Rd; powered/unpowered sites $39/29, cabins $135-150; P ❄ 🛜 ♿ 🐾) is a modern, well-equipped and shady camping ground with tinnies, canoes and kayaks for rent.

Yungaburra

Wee, winsome Yungaburra ticks every box on the country-cute checklist: within one lap of its tree-lined streets, you'll find 19 heritage-listed sites, a welcoming 1910 corner pub, boho-boutiques and cafes, and a dedicated platypus-watching platform. Its proximity to Lake Tinaroo and some of the region's top natural attractions makes Yungaburra a contender for best base on the Tablelands.

The town's lyrical name is thought to mean 'place of questioning' in the local Yidinyji language.

The sacred, 500-year-old **Curtain Fig tree** (Fig Tree Rd, East Barron) FREE, signposted 3km out of town, is a must-see for its gigantic, other-worldly aerial roots that hang down to create an enormous 'curtain'. If you're very quiet, you might catch a glimpse of a timid monotreme at the **platypus-viewing platform** (Gillies Hwy) FREE on Peterson Creek.

Explore the wilds around Yungaburra with **Alan's Wildlife Tours** (☑ 07-4095 3784; www.alanswildlifetours.com.au; tours $110-550), led by a passionate local naturalist.

Tablelands Folk Festival (www.tablelandsfolkfestival.org.au; ☉ Oct) is a fabulous community event featuring music, workshops, performances and a market.

🛏 Sleeping & Eating

★ **On the Wallaby** HOSTEL $
(☑ 07-4095 2031; www.onthewallaby.com; 34 Eacham Rd; van sites per person $15, dm/d with shared bathroom from $28/50; P 🛜) 🍴 This cosy ecofriendly hostel features handmade timber furniture, lots of green-energy touches (solar, rainwater tanks), spotless rooms and no TV. Nature-based tours ($40) include night canoeing and

mountain-biking; popular tour packages and transfers are available from Cairns. Cook for yourself in the communal kitchen, or join the nightly BBQ.

Yungaburra Hotel PUB FOOD $$
(Lake Eacham Hotel; ☑ 07-4095 3515; www.yungaburrahotel.com.au; 6 Kehoe Pl; mains $14-37; ☉ restaurant noon-2pm & 6-8.30pm; 🍴) This wonderful, welcoming, original-timber country pub is one of the most evocative in the state, let alone on the Tablelands. It often hosts live jams and bands; otherwise, just order a schooner, meet the locals and soak up the old-school atmosphere. The restaurant does huge, wholesome meals, including a Saturday-night buffet ($25).

ℹ Information

Yungaburra Information Centre (☑ 07-4095 2416; www.yungaburra.com; Maud Kehoe Park; ☉ 9am-5pm Mon-Sat, 10am-4pm Sun) The delightful volunteers at this immaculate centre can help recommend accommodation, provide info on walks and tours and generally chat about all things Yungaburra.

Crater Lakes National Park

Part of the Wet Tropics World Heritage Area, the two mirror-like, rainforest-fringed volcanic crater lakes of **Lake Eacham** and **Lake Barrine** are popular for swimming: no salties!

DON'T MISS

TABLELANDS FOR FOODIES

The Tablelands are the perfect place to savour the flavour of some of the country's top artisanal food and drink offerings. Great epicurean experiences include the following.

Rainforest Bounty (☑ 07-4076 6544; www.rainforestbounty.com.au; 66 Lindsay Rd, Malanda; courses from $190) Riverside slow-cooking school using local ingredients in its one-day courses.

Cheesemaking & More (☑ 07-4095 2097; www.cheesemakingandmore.com.au; Quinlan Rd, Lake Eacham) Two-day cheesemaking classes, and one-day courses on making bread and butter and hard cheese.

Gallo Dairyland (☑ 07-4095 2388; www.gallodairyland.com.au; Atherton-Malanda Rd; ☉ 9.30am-4.30pm; 🍴) FREE Working farm with cheese factory and handmade chocolates.

Honey House (☑ 07-4093 7261; www.honeyhousekuranda.com; 7 Therwine St; ☉ 9am-3.30pm; 🍴) Kuranda institution with high-quality raw local honeys, hives and a resident beekeeper.

Honesty stalls: Pick up fresher-than-fresh batches of fruit, veggies, jams and more from any of the unmanned stalls lining Tablelands roads and tracks. Just drop your coins in the honesty box!

Find local info at the **Rainforest Display Centre** (McLeish Rd, Lake Eacham; 9am-1pm Mon, Wed & Fri).

Spot water dragons and tortoises or simply relax and soak up the views on a 45-minute **cruise** (07-4095 3847; www.lakebarrine.com.au/cruises; adult/child/family $18/8/40; 9.30am & 11.30am) around Lake Barrine; book and board at the excellent **Lake Barrine Teahouse** (07-4095 3847; www.lakebarrine.com.au; Gillies Hwy; Devonshire teas from $12; 9am-4pm).

Chambers Wildlife Rainforest Lodges (07-4095 3754; www.chamberslodges.com.au; Eacham Close; lodge $140-210) is the bee's knees for nature lovers, with 10 self-contained rainforest lodges, a wildlife-viewing platform, walking paths and all manner of critters scarpering about the grounds.

Malanda & Around

Malanda has been a byword for 'milk' in north Queensland ever since 560 cattle made the 16-month overland journey from NSW in 1908. Check out the **Malanda Dairy Centre** (07-4095 1234; 8 James St; 9am-3pm Wed-Sun) FREE, which has a great cafe and kid-friendly exhibits on the region's bovine history.

Rainforest-shrouded Malanda and its surrounds – including the other-worldly **Mt Hypipamee** (www.parks.des.qld.gov.au/parks/mount-hypipamee; Crater Rd) FREE crater – are also home to shy, rare Lumholtz's tree-kangaroos; bring a low-wattage torch for an evening of spotlighting.

Spot a platypus at the **Australian Platypus Park & Tarzali Lakes Aquaculture Centre** (07-4097 2713; www.australianplatypuspark.com; 912 Millaa Millaa-Malanda Rd, Tarzali; guided tour adult/child $8.50/6; 9am-4pm, tours every half-hour), or take in a flick at the heritage-listed **Majestic** (07-4096 5726; www.majestictheatre.com.au; 1 Eacham Pl, Malanda; tickets single/family $10/30; Fri-Sun), which claims to be the country's longest-operating commercial movie theatre. **Malanda Falls Visitor Centre** (07-4089 2583; www.trc.qld.gov.au/locations/malanda-falls-visitor-information-centre; 132 Malanda-Atherton Rd; 9am-4.30pm) has thoughtful displays and guided rainforest walks.

Millaa Millaa

Evocatively nicknamed the 'Village in the Mist', charming Millaa Millaa is a small and gloriously green dairy community famous for its wonderful waterfalls. Surrounded by rolling farmland dotted with black-and-white cows, it's a picturesque spot to stop for lunch or to spend a few quaint and quiet nights.

There's accommodation at **Millaa Millaa Tourist Park** (07-4097 2290; www.millaacaravanpark.com.au; cnr Malanda Rd & Lodge Ave; powered/unpowered sites $32/27, cabins $65-110) and the **Millaa Millaa Hotel** (07-4097 2212; 15 Main St; s/d from $88/98). Stop in at the **Falls Teahouse** (07-4097 2237; www.thefallsteahouse.com.au; 6 Theresa Creek Rd; mains $9.50-17.50; 10am-4pm Mon-Wed & Fri, from 9.30am Sat & Sun, plus 6-9pm Fri) for a Devonshire tea, or a cheese platter at **Mungalli Creek Dairy** (07-4097 2232; www.mungallicreekdairy.com.au; 254 Brooks Rd; meals $9.50-19.50; 10am-4pm).

WORTH A TRIP

WATERFALLS CIRCUIT

Take in four of the Tableland's most picturesque waterfalls on the leisurely 15km Waterfalls Circuit (www.millaamillaa.com). Start by swinging on to Theresa Creek Rd, 1km east of Millaa Millaa on the Palmerston Hwy. Surrounded by tree ferns and flowers, the **Millaa Millaa Falls**, 1.5km along, are easily the best for swimming and have a grassy picnic area. The beautiful 12m falls tumble into a large, shallow pool. **Zillie Falls**, 8km further on, are reached by a short walking trail that leads to a lookout peering down (with some vertigo) on the falls from above. Pretty **Ellinjaa Falls** are reached via a steep 200m trail down to a rocky swimming hole at the base of the falls. Although not part of the circuit, **Mungalli Falls** is another set of rapids a further 5.5km off the Palmerston Hwy (past Mungalli Creek Dairy).

PORT DOUGLAS

POP 3504

Port Douglas (Port or PD) is Far North Queensland's most glamorous resort town, and a fab gateway to the Great Barrier Reef – the Outer Reef is just an hour offshore. Apart from the million-dollar marina, dreamy Four Mile Beach and five-star

Port Douglas

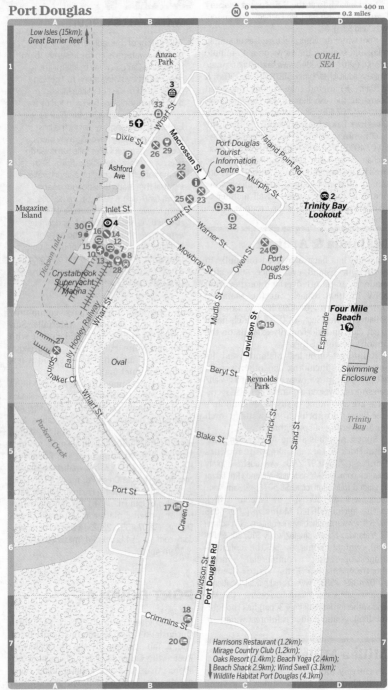

Low Isles (15km);
Great Barrier Reef

Anzac
Park

CORAL
SEA

Wharf St

Macrossan St

Dixie St

Island Point Rd

Ashford
Ave

Port Douglas
Tourist
Information
Centre

Murphy St

Magazine
Island

Inlet St

Trinity Bay
Lookout

Grant St

Warner St

Dickson Inlet

Crystalbrook
Superyacht
Marina

Mowbray St

Owen St

Port
Douglas
Bus

Mudlo St

Four Mile
Beach

Esplanade

Davidson St

Oval

Beryl St

Reynolds
Park

Swimming
Enclosure

Trinity
Bay

Bally Hooley Railway

Wharf St

Spinnaker Cl

Garrick St

Sand St

Packers Creek

Blake St

Port St

Craven Cl

Davidson St

Port Douglas Rd

Crimmins St

Harrisons Restaurant (1.2km);
Mirage Country Club (1.2km);
Oaks Resort (1.4km); Beach Yoga (2.4km);
Beach Shack 2.9km); Wind Swell (3.1km);
Wildlife Habitat Port Douglas (4.1km)

Port Douglas

resorts big enough to warrant their own postcode, the town itself is filled with excellent if pricey restaurants, stylish boutiques and earthy pubs. It's flash, fun and a fine place for discovering all that's good about the north, plus it's also an excellent base for visiting Cape Tribulation, the Daintree and Mossman Gorge.

The peninsula that PD occupies is the traditional home of the Yirrganydji people.

◉ Sights

★ **Four Mile Beach**   BEACH
(⟨♿⟩) This broad stretch of squeaky sand wraps around the eastern side of the peninsula in a near-perfect arc of sand and swaying palms – access is off the eastern end of Macrossan St, the town's main thoroughfare, and various points south. There's a patrolled swimming area in front of the surf life-saving club (with a stinger net in summer) and sunloungers available for hire.

★ **Wildlife Habitat Port Douglas**   ZOO
(⟨📞⟩07-4099 3235; www.wildlifehabitat.com.au; Port Douglas Rd; adult/child/family $37/18.50/92.50; ⟨🕐⟩8am-5pm; ⟨♿⟩) 🐾 This sanctuary endeavours to keep and showcase native animals in enclosures that mimic their natural environment, while allowing you to get up close to koalas, kangaroos, crocs, cassowaries and more. Tickets are valid for five days. For an extra special experience book for Breakfast with the Birds (adult/child/family incl admission $60/30/150; ⟨🕐⟩9-10.30am; ⟨♿⟩) or Lunch with the Lorikeets (adult/child/family incl admission $62/31/155; ⟨🕐⟩noon-1.30pm; ⟨♿⟩). The Predator Plank is a walkway across the saltwater-croc enclosure, while nocturnal visits (adult/child/family $43/32/118) are also possible.

★ **Trinity Bay Lookout**   VIEWPOINT
(Island Point Rd) **FREE** Head up to Flagstaff Hill for sensational views over Four Mile Beach and the Coral Sea. Drive or walk up via Wharf St, or there's a walking path leading up from the north end of Four Mile Beach.

St Mary's by the Sea   CHURCH
(⟨📞⟩0418 456 880; 6 Dixie St) **FREE** Worth a peek inside (when it's not overflowing with wedding parties), this quaint, nondenominational, white timber church was built in 1880, rebuilt after a cyclone in 1911 and restored in 1989. Services take place at 11am on Sundays.

Court House Museum   MUSEUM
(⟨📞⟩07-4098 1284; www.douglashistory.org.au; Wharf St; adult/child $2/free; ⟨🕐⟩10am-1pm Tue, Thu, Sat & Sun) The quaint and quiet 1879 Court House contains historical exhibits, including the story of Ellen Thompson, who was tried for murdering her husband in 1887 and the only woman ever hanged in Queensland.

🏃 Activities

Beach Yoga   YOGA
(www.beachyogaportdouglas.com; Four Mile Beach; per person $15-20; ⟨🕐⟩8am Mon-Sat) Morning

beach yoga near the southern end of Four Mile Beach is a gorgeous way to start the day. It's beginner-friendly, kids under 12 are free, and it's cheaper if you prepay online; otherwise, bring cash ($20). Look for the big, yellow hibiscus flower.

Golf

Port Douglas has a number of excellent golf courses, including the championship links-style **Palmer Sea Reef** (☑ 07-4087 2222; www.palmergolf.com.au; 9/18 holes with cart from $80/105), and the Peter Thomson–designed **Mirage Country Club** (☑ 07-4099 5537; www.miragecountryclub.com.au; 9/18 holes with cart $75/95, driving range from $11).

Diving

An introductory, controlled scuba dive, with no certification or experience necessary, costs around $300, and a three-day PADI Open Water course starts at $850; certified divers will pay around $350 for a full-day trip with three dives with all gear included.

Blue Dive DIVING
(☑ 0427 983 907; www.bluedive.com.au; 3-day dive courses $875) Port Douglas' most acclaimed dive operator offers a range of programmes including liveaboard trips and PADI certification. Private, guided scuba dives of the reef aboard Poseidon or *Calypso* are available.

Tech Dive Academy DIVING
(☑ 07-4015 2915; www.tech-dive-academy.com; Crystalbrook Marina; 2-/4-day open-water courses from $1280/2000) 🥾 Highly regarded dive school offering individual (one-to-one or two-to-one for couples) instruction in a range of courses from PADI Open Water to technical and Nitrox diving. The two-day course certifies divers to only 12 metres. Dive boats depart from Crystalbrook Marina.

Sailing & Water Sports

Crystalbrook Superyacht Marina (☑ 07-4099 5775; www.crystalbrookmarina.com; 44 Wharf St) FREE is the hub of water-based activities in Port Douglas.

★**Wind Swell** WATER SPORTS
(☑ 0427 498 042; www.windswell.com.au; cnr Barrier & Reef Sts; lessons from $50) Kitesurf the Coral Sea, or go stand-up paddleboarding down a rainforest creek – there's something for everyone from beginners to high-flyers. Kitesurfing lessons and paddleboarding

tours from the beach start at $50, but there are also plenty of advanced options.

Port Douglas Boat Hire BOATING
(☑ 07-4099 6277; www.pdboathire.com.au; Berth C1, Crystalbrook Marina; rentals per 1/4hr from $47/159; ☺ 8.30am-5.30pm; ⛵) Rents canopied, family-friendly pontoon boats that can carry up to six people. An excellent way to explore the calm inland estuaries or go fishing.

Port Douglas Yacht Club BOATING
(☑ 07-4099 4386; www.portdouglasyachtclub.com.au; 1 Spinnaker Close; ☺ from 4pm Wed) Free sailing with club members every Wednesday afternoon: sign on from 4pm. Those chosen to go sailing are expected to stay for dinner and drinks in the club afterwards.

🧭 Tours

Port Douglas is a hub for Far North Queensland tours. Many tours based out of Cairns offer pickups from Port Douglas, and vice versa.

★**Tony's Tropical Tours** TOURS
(☑ 07-4099 3230; www.tropicaltours.com.au; day tours adult/child from $198/170) 🥾 This luxury, small-group (eight to 10 passengers) ecotour operator specialises in day trips to out-of-the-way sections of the Mossman Gorge and Daintree Rainforest (adult/child $198/170), and Bloomfield Falls and Cape Tribulation (adults only $235 – good mobility required). A third tour heads south to the Tablelands.

Port on a Plate FOOD & DRINK
(☑ 0421 906 465; www.portonaplate.com.au; per person $160) An excellent addition to Port's portfolio of tours, Port on a Plate takes you on a chef-guided tour of the area, visiting local farms, a chocolate producer and other food-orientated stops. A three-course lunch is included.

Blue Adventures WILDLIFE
(☑ 0427 983 907; www.blueadventures.com.au; adult/child $265/250) Small-group, wildlife-focused tours take you to a range of habitats, including Daintree Rainforest, Atherton Tablelands and the Outback fringe. The full-day tours offer what is probably your best chance of seeing platypuses and tree kangaroos in the wild. Private tours are also possible.

Bike N Hike CYCLING
(☑ 07-4099 5799; www.bikenhiketours.com.au; 3 Warner St; per person from $219; ☺ 9am-5pm) Mountain bike down the aptly named Bump

VISITING THE GREAT BARRIER REEF FROM PORT DOUGLAS

The outer reef (known here as Agincourt), is closer to Port Douglas than it is to Cairns. Several operators visit the Low Isles, a small group of islands surrounded by beautiful coral reef just 15km offshore; there's a good chance of spotting turtles, reef sharks and giant clams here.

Most day tours depart from Crystalbrook Marina. Tour prices usually include reef tax, snorkelling, transfers from your accommodation, lunch and refreshments. Make bookings directly through the operators or (for the same price) at the Port Douglas Tourist Centre (p485).

Full-Day

One of the most popular day trips is **Quicksilver** (☑ 07-4087 2100; www.quicksilver-cruises.com; Crystalbrook Marina; adult/child/family $257.50/129.50/645), which offer fast cruises to its private pontoon on Agincourt Outer Reef. It's an especially good option for families, as you're not restricted to a boat for the whole day, which includes around 3½ hours of snorkelling and time for a guided trip in a minisubmarine. Additional activities are possible for extra cost.

Most other full-day excursions to the Outer Reef spend up to five hours snorkelling, and take you to three different snorkelling spots (off the back of the boat). Recommended operators offering these types of trips include **Poseidon** (☑ 07-4087 2100; www.poseidon-cruises.com.au; Crystalbrook Marina; adult/child $254/182), **Tropical Journeys** (☑ 07-4099 6999; www.tropicaljourneys.com; Shop 44, Crystalbrook Marina; adult/child day tours $255.50/185.50; ⊕), **Silversonic** (☑ 07-4087 2100; www.silverseries.com.au; adult/child $247.50/172.50) and **Wavelength** (☑ 07-4099 5031; www.wavelength.com.au; Shop 12, Crystalbrook Marina; day tour adult/child/family $239.50/189.50/824); most have on-board marine biologists.

Half-Day

A cheaper and quicker alternative to the Outer Reef snorkelling trips is a half-day excursion to the Low Isles. **Reef Sprinter** (☑ 07-4099 6127; www.reefsprinter.com.au; Shop 3, Crystalbrook Marina; adult/child from $140/120; ⊕) offers a range of options, including 2¼-hour or 3½-hour trips, which usually include about 1½ hours snorkelling. **Calypso** (☑ 07-4099 6999; www.calypsoreefcruises.com; adult/child half day $199/159, full day $255.50/185.50) is another option. Both companies also offer half-day trips to the Outer Reef.

Track on a cross-country bike tour, or take on an action-packed night tour. Also does half-day cycling and hiking trips.

Bush & Boat KAYAKING
(☑ 0447 546 926; www.bushandboat.com.au; 2913 Mossman-Daintree Rd; tours adult/child from $85/55) Guided sea kayaking, and river tours in the Daintree rainforest. Pick-ups from Port Douglas, Mossman and Daintree Village. Most tours operate out of Thala Beach Nature Reserve (p484).

Back Country Bliss Adventures ADVENTURE
(☑ 07-4099 3677; www.backcountrybliss.com.au; tours from $105) Go with the flow as you drift-snorkel down the Mossman River. Also small-group bushwalking and Daintree adventure trips.

Boat Tours
Numerous operators run sunset boat tours around Port Douglas. Contact the Port Douglas Tourist Information Centre (p485) for options.

Lady Douglas BOATING
(☑ 0408 986 127; www.ladydouglas.com.au; Crystalbrook Marina, Wharf St; 1½hr cruises adult/child/family $40/25/110; ⊗ cruises 10.30am, 12.30pm, 2.30pm & 4.30pm; ⊕) A lovely paddle steamer running four daily croc-spotting river tours (plus an evening cruise on Fridays) along the Dickson Inlet.

✯ Festivals & Events

For 10 days in May, Port Douglas comes alive to the tune of its own **Carnivale** (www.carnivale.com.au): there's a parade, live music, performances galore and lashings of good food and wine.

In October there's more merriment with **Portoberfest** (Crystalbrook Marina).

🛌 Sleeping

⭐ Coral Beach Lodge HOSTEL $
(☑ 07-4099 5422; www.coralbeachlodge.com; 1 Craven Close; dm $23-39, d $120; ⚙ @ 🛜 🏊) 🐟 A cut above most backpacker places, this chilled-out hostel has well-equipped en-suite dorms (with four or five beds) and double or triple rooms that put some motels in the shade – flat-screen TVs, modern bathrooms and comfy beds. Each room has an outdoor area with hammocks, and there's a lovely pool, a games room, a kitchen and helpful owners.

Dougies HOSTEL $
(☑ 1800 996 200, 07-4099 6200; www.dougies.com.au; 111 Davidson St; tent/bungalow per person $28/30, dm/d $20/75; ⚙ @ 🛜 🏊) It's easy to hang about Dougies' sprawling grounds in a hammock or pool by day and move to the bar at night. If you can summon the energy, bikes and fishing gear are available for rent and the beach is a 300m walk east. Free pickup from Cairns on Monday, Wednesday and Saturday.

Pink Flamingo BOUTIQUE HOTEL $$
(☑ 07-4099 6622; www.pinkflamingo.com.au; 115 Davidson St; d studio/villa $150/210; ⚙ @ 🛜 🏊) Flamboyantly painted rooms, private walled courtyards and a groovy al-fresco bar make the Pink Flamingo Port Douglas' hippest gay-friendly digs. With just two studios and 10 villas, it's an intimate stay in a sea of megaresorts. A heated pool, a gym and bike rental are also on offer.

⭐ Peppers Beach Club RESORT $$$
(☑ 1300 737 444; www.peppers.com.au/beach-club; 20-22 Davidson St; spa ste from $295, 1-/2-bedroom ste from $475/530; ⚙ 🛜 🏊) A killer location and an exceptional, enormous, sandy lagoon pool, combined with luxurious, airy apartments with high-end furnishings and amenities, put Peppers right up there with Port Douglas' best in its price range. Some rooms have balcony spas, others swim-up decks or full kitchens. Family friendly, but still recommended for young romantics too.

> ### ⓘ PORT DOUGLAS ACCOMMODATION
> For booking local accommodation, try Port Douglas Getaways (www.portdouglasgetaways.com.au), Sanctuary Stays (www.sanctuarystays.com.au), or Executive Retreats (www.executiveretreats.com.au).

Thala Beach Nature Reserve RESORT $$$
(☑ 07-4098 5700; www.thalabeach.com.au; Captain Cook Hwy; d $375-800; ⚙ 🛜 🏊) On a private coastal headland 15km south of Port Douglas, Thala Beach is a sublime upmarket eco-retreat so relaxing that even locals come here to splash out and chill for the weekend. Luxurious tree-house-style bungalows are scattered throughout the jungle with easy access to a private stretch of beach, two pools, walking trails and a treetop restaurant.

Oaks Resort RESORT $$$
(☑ 07-4099 8900; www.oakshotels.com; 87-109 Port Douglas Rd; d from $210; ⚙ @ 🛜 🏊) Formerly QT, Oaks has had a makeover but is still fun and aimed at a trendy, 20- to 30-something crowd, though families will find a lot to like. There's a lagoon pool and swim-up bar, a gym, a spa and tidy minimalist rooms. The breakfast buffet is highly rated.

🍴 Eating

Self-caterers can stock up on supplies at the large Coles Supermarket (☑ 07-4099 5366; www.coles.com.au; 11 Macrossan St; ⊙ 6am-9pm) in the Port Village shopping centre. For ice cream and gelato, Capannina (☑ 0419 605 814; www.facebook.com/portdouglasdessertbar; 3/32 Macrossan St; ice cream from $5; ⊙ noon-9.30pm) is easily Port Douglas' best.

Mocka's Pies BAKERY $
(☑ 07-4099 5295; 9 Grant St; pies $5.50-7; ⊙ 8am-4pm) Local institution serving Aussie pies with exotic fillings such as crocodile laksa and bush kangaroo.

Grant Street Kitchen BAKERY $
(☑ 0478-769 987; www.grantstreetkitchen.com.au; Shop 4/5 Grant St; mains $7-16; ⊙ 6am-3pm; 🐟) Delicious egg-and-bacon rolls, ham-and-cheese croissants or fruit salads are breakfast treats at this awesome little artisanal bakery. For lunch try the homemade pies (such as prawn and coral trout) or the sushi bowl.

⭐ Little Larder CAFE $$
(☑ 07-4099 6450; www.facebook.com/thelittlelarderportdouglas; 53-61 Macrossan St; mains $12-30; ⊙ 7.30am-3pm; 🛜 🐟) Breakfast on turmeric crab omelette until 11.30am, then it's gourmet sandwiches, fab dishes like Szechuan salt-and-pepper squid or Balinese-style duck and killer cocktails from noon. Good coffee, or try freshly brewed and super smoothies. Little Larder is effortlessly cool and outrageously good.

Yachty MODERN AUSTRALIAN $$
(07-4099 4386; www.portdouglasyachtclub.com.
au; 1 Spinnaker Close; mains $22-30; 5.30-8pm
Wed-Fri, noon-2.30pm & 5.30-8pm Sat & Sun) One
of the best-value nights out is the local yacht
club, where well-crafted meals, from kanga-
roo spring rolls or cauliflower arancini to
dukkah-spiced crocodile, are served nightly
with sunset views over Dickson Inlet. The
lunch menu is similar but a little cheaper.

On the Inlet SEAFOOD $$
(07-4099 5255; www.ontheinlet.com.au; 18-20
Wharf St; mains $24-36; noon-3pm & 5.30-
10pm) This local institution was moved out
of its overwater location on Dickson Inlet
in 2018, but it has been reborn across the
road on Wharf St. No water views or visits
from George the grouper anymore, but it
still has the $18 bucket of prawns and drink
deal (noon to 3pm) and all-round good-value seafood.

Beach Shack MODERN AUSTRALIAN $$
(07-4099 1100; www.the-beach-shack.com.
au; 29 Barrier St; mains $26-31, pizza $15.50-26;
5.30-10pm) It's quite a hike down to the
southern end of Four Mile Beach, but this
locals' favourite is worth the trip for sublime
pizzas, tapas and tasty dishes like crispy-
skin barramundi or macadamia-crusted
eggplant. The lantern-lit garden completes
the beach theme with its sandy floor. Satur-
day is $10 pizza night.

★**Harrisons
Restaurant** MODERN AUSTRALIAN $$$
(0455 594 011; www.harrisonsrestaurant.com.au;
Sheraton Grand Mirage, Port Douglas Rd; mains $34-
52; noon-3pm & 5-9pm Tue-Sat) Marco Pierre
White–trained chef-owner Spencer Patrick
whips up culinary gems that stand toe to toe
with Australia's best. Fresh, locally sourced
produce is turned into dishes such as smoked
duck breast with burnt honey and lavender.
Harrisons is ensconsed in the flash Sheraton
Grand Mirage, but is open to nonguests.

★**Flames of
the Forest** MODERN AUSTRALIAN $$$
(07-4099 3144; www.flamesoftheforest.com.au;
dinner with show, drinks & transfers per person from
$195; Tue, Thu & Sat) This unique experience
goes way beyond the traditional concept of
'dinner and a show', with diners escorted
deep into the rainforest for a truly immersive
night of theatre, culture and gourmet cuisine.
Transport is provided from Port Douglas or
Cairns (no self-drive). Bookings essential.

Drinking & Entertainment

Check out www.whatsoninport.com.au for
entertainment, dining and events listings.

★**Hemingway's** MICROBREWERY
(07-4099 6663; www.hemingwaysbrewery.com;
Crystalbrook Marina, 44 Wharf St) Hemingway's
makes the most of a fabulous location at the
marina with a broad deck, a long bar and
Dickson Inlet views. There are usually six
brews on tap, including Hard Yards dark la-
ger and Pitchfork Betty's pale ale. Naturally,
food is available, but this is one for the beer
connoisseurs. A tasting paddle is $15. Ask
about their brewery tours or craft gin.

Iron Bar PUB
(07-4099 4776; www.ironbarportdouglas.com.
au; 5 Macrossan St; 11am-3am) This place
has wacky outback-meets-Wild–West decor
featuring corrugated iron and old timber,
setting the scene for a wild night out. Don't
miss the nightly cane-toad races ($5) for a
bit of comic relief.

Shopping

Macrossan St is crammed with boutiques
and souvenir shops, and there are local
markets on Wednesday (Crystalbrook Marina,
Wharf St; 11am-5pm Wed) and Sunday (Anzac
Park, Macrossan St; 8am-2pm Sun).

Ngarru Gallery ARTS & CRAFTS
(0402 861 029; www.ngarrugallery.com.au; 1/31
Macrossan St; 10am-6pm) Indigenous art from
across Australia, including from Arnhem
Land and the Western Desert, lightly fills this
beautiful space. Some is for collectors, other
pieces are more accessible, and there's some
jewellery and other crafts as well.

Perrin Clarke Photography PHOTOGRAPHY
(07-4099 4532; www.perrinclarkephotography.
com.au; 1/38 Macrossan St; 10am-6pm Mon-Fri, to
4pm Sat & Sun) Stunning photography from Far
North Queensland, available for printing in a
conveniently wide range of sizes and formats.

Information

The *Port Douglas & Mossman Gazette* comes out
every Thursday, and has local info, gig guides
and more.

There's no official government-accredited
visitor information centre in Port Douglas, but
private bookings agents abound, such as **Port
Douglas Tourist Information Centre** (07-
4099 5599; www.infoportdouglas.com.au; 23
Macrossan St; 8am-6.30pm).

ⓘ Getting There & Away

About half of the 65km drive between Cairns and Port Douglas hugs the coast, affording magical vistas. Several shuttle companies make this trip daily, via the airport and Cairns' northern beaches.

Cairns (p470) is the nearest airport to Port Douglas.

BUS

Port Douglas Bus (☏ 07-4099 5665; www.portdouglasbus.com.au; 53-61 Macrossan St) operates daily between Port Douglas, Cairns and Cairns Airport.

Trans North (☏ 07-4095 8644; www.transnorthbus.com.au) picks up in Port Douglas on the coastal drive between Cairns and Cooktown.

ⓘ Getting Around

Hire bikes at **Bike Shop & Hire** (☏ 07-4099 5799; www.portdouglasbikehire.com.au; 3 Warner St; 4/24hr from $20/24; ⊙9am-5pm Mon-Sat); backpackers hostels also have bikes for hire.

Minibuses, such as those run by **SR Coaches** (☏ 0469 723 071; www.srcoaches.com.au/local_shuttle), shuttle between town and the highway for around $5.

Major car-rental chains have branches here, or try **Comet Car Hire** (☏ 07-4099 6407; www.cometcarhire.com.au; 3/54 Macrossan St) and keep it local.

DON'T MISS

BEST DAINTREE INDIGENOUS ENCOUNTERS

The Kuku Yalanji people are the traditional custodians of the Daintree region, including Daintree Village, Mossman, Cow Bay and Cape Tribulation. Genuine encounters with local indigenous people are possible.

Janbal Gallery Spend an hour or two watching local artists work and learning about their world.

Walkabout Cultural Adventures Indigenous-led cultural tours.

Kuku Yalanji Cultural Habitat Tours Coastal indigenous culture through the eyes of a traditional guide.

Kuku-Yalanji Dreamtime Gorge Walk Explore Mossman Gorge with an indigenous guide.

THE DAINTREE

The oldest rainforest on the planet, the Unesco World Heritage–listed Daintree Rainforest is one of Australia's most beautiful corners. Sheltered within this vast and extraordinary forest is all manner of wildlife, especially along the Daintree River, but also deep within the forest, from cassowaries to tree kangaroos. Here, the rainforest tumbles right down to the coast, to remote and deserted beaches that seem to go on forever, while offshore lies the peerless Great Barrier Reef. Put it all together, and we challenge you to find another place where so many world-class natural attractions come together.

Mossman

POP 1937

Surrounded by sugar-cane fields, the workaday town of Mossman, 20km north of Port Douglas, is best known for beautiful Mossman Gorge, part of the Daintree National Park. The town itself is worth a stop to get a feel for a Far North Queensland working community and to stock up if you're heading further north.

Nearly one-fifth of the town's population are Aboriginal people and three of Far North Queensland's best Indigenous tours are based here and at nearby Cooya Beach.

⊙ Sights

★ **Janbal Gallery**   GALLERY
(☏07-4098 3917; www.janbalgallery.com.au; 5 Johnston Rd; ⊙9am-5pm Mon-Fri; ⊕) 🏻FREE Browse and buy the art at this Aboriginal-run gallery, or create your own masterpiece (canvas or boomerang) under the guidance of artist-in-residence, Binna. One-hour workshops (adult/child $50/25) are held at 9am and 3pm Monday to Friday.

ⓒ Tours

Walkabout Cultural Adventures   CULTURAL
(☏0429 478 206; www.walkaboutadventures.com.au; half/full-day tours $165/209) 🏻 Local Indigenous guide Juan Walker heads these authentic, small-group cultural tours around Mossman, Cooyee Beach and further into the Daintree rainforest of the Kuku Yalanji people. Tours include learning about seasonal bush tucker, culture and traditions of the local inhabitants and their relationship with the land, and even some boomerang throwing.

MOSSMAN GORGE

In the southeast corner of Daintree National Park, 5km west of Mossman town, **Mossman Gorge** (www.mossmangorge.com.au; ⊙8am-6pm; 🚻) forms part of the traditional lands of the Kuku Yalanji people. The gorge is a boulder-strewn valley where sparkling water washes over ancient rocks and passes through dense rainforest. Taking a Dreamtime Gorge Walk with an indigenous guide is the best way to explore. Otherwise, it's 4km by road from the visitor centre to a viewpoint and swimming hole; depending on conditions, swimming may not be permitted.

You can walk the 4km, but visitors are encouraged to take the shuttle (adult/child/family return $11.80/5.90/29.50, every 15 minutes). There are several kilometres of walking trails on boardwalks and a picnic area at the gorge, but no camping.

Kuku-Yalanji Dreamtime Gorge Walk (adult/child/family $78/38.50/194.50; ⊙10am, 11am, noon, 1pm & 3pm) These unforgettable 1½-hour Indigenous-guided walks of Mossman Gorge include a smoking ceremony, bush tea and damper, and a guided walk through the forest, with a focus on medicinal plants. Book through the Mossman Gorge Centre.

Mossman Gorge Centre (📞07-4099 7000; www.mossmangorge.com.au; ⊙8am-6pm) The flashy gateway to the Mossman Gorge has an Indigenous art gallery, retail section and bush-tucker cafe. It's here you can book in for one of the organised walks or take the shuttle bus to the gorge.

Kuku Yalanji Cultural Habitat Tours CULTURAL
(📞07-4098 3437; www.kycht.com.au; Cooya Beach; half-day tour adult/child $90/75, night walk per person $150) Based at Cooya Beach, 6km east of Mossman, these unique Indigenous tours focus on the coastal environment and traditional hunting techniques such as spearfishing and mudcrabbing. The night tour includes an after-dark beach walk and spearfishing by boat.

🛏 Sleeping & Eating

Mossman Motel Holiday Villas VILLA $$
(📞07-4098 1299; www.mossmanmotel.com.au; 1-9 Alchera Dr; r $112-215; 🅿❄🛜🏊) These great-value, spacious villas occupy lovely landscaped grounds complete with rock waterfall and natural pool on the southern entrance to town.

⭐**Silky Oaks Lodge** RESORT $$$
(📞07-4098 1666; www.silkyoakslodge.com.au; Finlayvale Rd; tree houses $455-998, ste $898-1250; ❄🛜🏊) This eco-resort on the Mossman River woos honeymooners and stressed-out execs with amazing architecturally designed tree houses, riverside lodge suites, luxury hammocks, rejuvenation treatments, polished-timber interiors and private spa baths. Activities include tennis, gym, yoga classes and canoeing. Its stunning **Treehouse Restaurant & Bar** (mains $31-47; ⊙7-10am, noon-2.30pm & 6-8.30pm) is open to interlopers with advance reservation.

ⓘ Getting There & Away

Port Douglas Bus has return shuttles from Port Douglas to Mossman Gorge (adult/child/family return $29/17/85, 9am and noon). Numerous tour companies run buses from Cairns and Port Douglas to the gorge. Self-driving is the easiest way to explore the region north of Mossman.

Daintree Village

Daintree Village feels like the end of the road, a tiny green settlement set on a plateau of farmland alongside the Daintree River and surrounded by stands of rainforest. Wildlife- and croc-spotting tours (p488) leave on small-boat cruises from the village jetty.

🛏 Sleeping & Eating

Red Mill House B&B $$
(📞07-4098 6233; www.redmillhouse.com.au; 11 Stewart St; s/d from $185/235; ❄🛜) Photographers and birdwatchers will love the Red Mill with its emphasis on information and observation. There are four lovely en-suite rooms in the 'Tremaine' and a family room in the main house, along with a communal lounge, library and rainforest garden.

⭐**Daintree Eco Lodge & Spa** RESORT $$$
(📞07-4777 7377; www.daintree-ecolodge.com.au; 3189 Mossman-Daintree Rd; tree houses $380-480; ❄@🛜🏊) The sublime boutique 'banyans' (pole cabins; 10 with private spa) here sit in seclusion high in the rainforest canopy a

WILDLIFE & CROC-WATCHING TOURS

Half a dozen local operators run croc-spotting and birdwatching boat tours of the Upper Daintree from the jetty in the village and the Lower Daintree from near the cable ferry.

Daintree River Wild Watch (📞 0447 546 926; www.daintreeriverwildwatch.com.au; 3hr cruises adult/child $60/35; ♿) runs informative sunrise birdwatching cruises, and sunset photography nature cruises with avid birdwatcher and expert guide Ian 'Sauce' Worcester. The focus is on birds, but also takes in crocs and plant life. A two-hour land-based option, run by coowner Alex Pawlow, sets off straight after the morning cruise and is an excellent way to see some rainforest birds, as well as swamp wallabies.

Remarkably, **Solar Whisper** (📞 07-4098 7131; www.solarwhisper.com; adult/child/family $30/15/70; ⊘ 9.30am, 10.45am, 11.45am, 12.45pm, 2.15pm & 3.30pm; ♿) 🏊 is still the only solar-powered tour boat on the Daintree. Departing from the lower Daintree just before the ferry crossing on the south bank, Solar Whisper's one-hour croc-spotting cruises are quiet and ecofriendly with a good chance of seeing wildlife. The up-close 'croc cam' is another selling point. Two-hour cruises can also be arranged.

The experienced **Bruce Belcher's & Son Daintree River Cruises** (📞 07-4098 7717; www.daintreerivercruises.com.au; 1hr cruises adult/child/family $30/14/75; ⊘ 8.15am, 9.30am, 11am, noon, 1.30pm, 2.30pm & 4pm; ♿) is also recommended, with one-hour cruises on a covered boat from close to Daintree Village.

Crocodile Express (📞 07-4098 6120; www.crocodileexpress.com; 1hr cruises adult/child/family $30/15/70; ⊘ 8.30am, 9.45am, 11am, 12.30pm, 2pm & 3.30pm; ♿) has six daily cruises from two separate locations, one on the Upper Daintree from Daintree Village and the other on the Lower Daintree from the ferry crossing. The village booking office also has tourist info and souvenirs. Online bookings get a 10% discount.

Daintree River Cruise Centre (📞 07-4098 6115; www.daintreerivercruisecentre.com.au; 2914 Mossman-Daintree Rd; adult/child/family $30/15/80; ⊘ 9.30am-3.30pm; ♿) Runs up to eight one- to 1½-hour cruises daily from a private jetty south of the village. There are usually places available, but it's worth booking ahead for the 9.30am or 9.50am departures. Morning or afternoon tea included.

few kilometres south of Daintree Village. Even the day spa is eco-minded, with its own range of organic, Indigenous-inspired products and treatments. Nonguests are welcome at its superb **Julaymba Restaurant** (📞 07-4098 6100; www.daintree-ecolodge.com.au; 3189 Mossman-Daintree Rd; mains $30-40; ⊘ dinner from 6pm), which uses local produce, including native berries, nuts, leaves and flowers.

Big Barramundi Garden   CAFE $
(📞 07-4098 6186; www.bigbarra.daintree.info; 12 Stewart St; mains $18-20, burgers $7-10; ⊘ 10am-4pm) You can't miss the giant barramundi next to this open-sided cafe. It serves exotic burgers (barra, crocodile and kangaroo), pies and smoothies or fruit juices (black sapote, paw paw) as well as Devonshire teas.

ℹ Getting There & Away

Daintree Village is around 35km north of Mossman, or a 20km-each-way detour from the Mossman-Daintree Rd. There's no public transport and no fuel is available in Daintree Village.

Cow Bay & Around

Tiny Cow Bay is the first community you reach after the Daintree ferry crossing. On the steep, winding road between Cape Kimberley and Cow Bay, the **Walu Wugirriga Lookout** (Alexandra Range Lookout) offers sweeping views beyond the Daintree River inlet; it's especially breathtaking at sunset.

The white-sand and mostly deserted **Cow Bay Beach**, 5km east of the main road at the end of Buchanan Creek Rd, rivals any coastal paradise.

◉ Sights & Activities

⭐ **Daintree Discovery Centre** NATURE RESERVE
(📞 07-4098 9171; www.discoverthedaintree.com; Tulip Oak Rd; adult/child/family $35/16/85; ⊘ 8.30am-5pm; ♿) 🏊 This award-winning attraction's **aerial walkway**, which includes a 23m tower used to study carbon levels, takes you high into the forest canopy. A theatre screens films on cassowaries, crocodiles, conservation and climate change. An excellent audio-guide tour

and interpretive booklet is included in the admission fee; tickets are valid for reentry for seven days. Dinosaur models in the surrounding forest make the point that this is one ancient rainforest, although it does cheapen the experience a little.

Tickets are valid for seven days.

🛏 Sleeping

⭐**Epiphyte B&B** B&B $
(☑07-4098 9039; www.rainforestbb.com; 22 Silkwood Rd; s/d/cabins from $80/130/170) This lovingly built, laid-back place is set on a lush 3.5-hectare property. Individually styled rooms are of varying sizes, but all have their own verandah. A spacious, private cabin features a patio, kitchenette and sunken bathroom. Minimum two-night stay.

⭐**Daintree Wilderness Lodge** LODGE $$$
(☑07-4098 9105; www.daintreewildernesslodge. com.au; 1780 Cape Tribulation Rd; cabin from $310; ❄🛜🏊) Beautiful wood-floored cabins with balcony deep in the rainforest make this a top place for immersion in the Daintree. Service is impeccable, there's a good restaurant and there's a real sense of having found your own rainforest hideaway.

🍴 Eating

⭐**Daintree Ice Cream Company** ICE CREAM $
(☑07-4098 9114; www.daintreeicecream.com. au; Lot 100, Cape Tribulation Rd; ice-cream tasting cup $7.50; ⏰11am-5pm) We dare you to drive past this all-natural ice-cream producer with a range of flavours that changes daily. The tasting cup includes four flavours – you might get macadamia, black sapote, wattleseed or soursop, but they're all delicious.

Cow Bay Hotel PUB FOOD $$
(☑07-4098 9011; 1480 Cape Tribulation Rd; mains $12-26; ⏰noon-2.30pm & 6-8.30pm, bar 10am-10pm) If you're craving a decent counter meal, a coldie and that Aussie country pub atmosphere, the Cow Bay is the only real pub this side of the Daintree River. Also has motel-style rooms.

ℹ Getting There & Away

It's around 15km from the **Daintree River Ferry** (www.douglas.qld.gov.au/community/daintree-ferry; one-way/return car $17/30, motorcycle $7/12, pedestrian & bicycle $1/2; ⏰6am-midnight) via a steep and winding road to Cow Bay, then another 30km to Cape Trib. It's sealed all the way but still slow going; watch out for wildlife, especially cassowaries.

Trans North (p470) stops here on its Cairns to Cooktown run.

Cape Tribulation

POP 118

Cape Trib is at the end of the winding sealed road from the Daintree River and, with its two magnificent beaches, laid-back vibe and rainforest walks, it's a little slice of tropical paradise, the classic rainforest-meets-the-sea destination with a true sense of wilderness thrown in. Despite the backpacker bars and tour operators, Cape Trib retains a frontier quality, with road signs alerting drivers to cassowary crossings, and croc warnings giving evening beach strolls added excitement. It's a glorious place, worth more than the day most travellers dedicate to visiting here.

You can only get here by a slow car ferry or 4WD track, which adds to the sense of this being a special place.

MT SORROW RIDGE WALK

The beach at Cape Tribulation can get busy with day-trippers, especially in high season. To really escape the crowds, consider taking the demanding sea-to-summit day hike up to **Mt Sorrow**. The trail starts in a lowland rainforest valley, full of trees with large buttress roots and a canopy woven with large woody vines. As the ridge ascends, feather-leafed palms become more common. On the ridge, the vegetation is dominated by acacias (wattles). From the lookout, you can watch spangled drongos and small flocks of topknot pigeons in the air, while a variety of butterflies drift around on the wind. On a clear day, the beautiful Daintree coastline can be seen stretching southwards to Snapper Island and beyond.

In the humid tropical air, it's a steep climb from sea level to 680m in just 3.5km, so pacing yourself is essential. The first 2km is a gentle climb but the last gruelling 1.5km heads for the clouds. Along the way, watch for cassowaries and Bennett's tree kangaroos.

Cape Tribulation Area

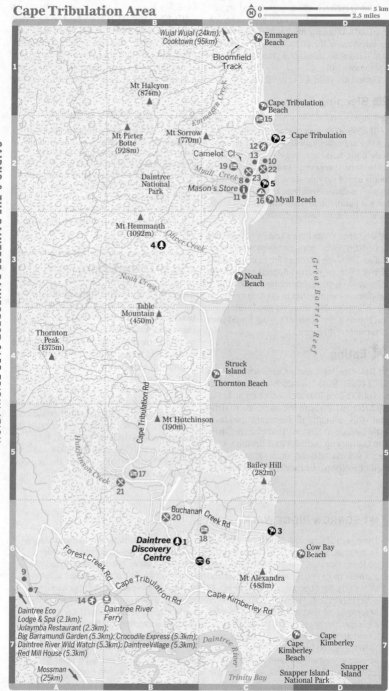

0 ___ 5 km
0 ___ 2.5 miles

Wujal Wujal (24km);
Cooktown (95km)

Emmagen
Beach

Bloomfield
Track

Emmagen Creek

Mt Halcyon
(874m)

Cape Tribulation
Beach

15

Mt Pieter
Botte
(928m)

Mt Sorrow
(770m)

2 Cape Tribulation

12

Camelot Cl

13

Myall Creek

19

10

Daintree
National Park

8

23

22

5

Mason's Store

11

16 Myall Beach

Mt Hemmanth
(1092m)

Oliver Creek

4

Great Barrier Reef

Noah Creek

Noah
Beach

Table
Mountain
(450m)

Thornton
Peak
(1375m)

Struck
Island

Thornton Beach

Cape Tribulation Rd

Mt Hutchinson
(190m)

Hutchinson Creek

Bailey Hill
(282m)

17

21

Buchanan Creek Rd

20

3

Daintree
Discovery
Centre

1

18

Cow Bay
Beach

6

Mt Alexandra
(483m)

9

7

Forest Creek Rd

Cape Tribulation Rd

Cape Kimberley Rd

14

Daintree
River
Ferry

Daintree Eco
Lodge & Spa (2.1km);
Julaymba Restaurant (2.3km);
Big Barramundi Garden (5.3km); Crocodile Express (5.3km);
Daintree River Wild Watch (5.3km); Daintree Village (5.3km);
Red Mill House (5.3km)

Daintree River

Cape
Kimberley

Cape
Kimberley
Beach

Snapper Island
National Park

Snapper
Island

Mossman
(25km)

Trinity Bay

Cape Tribulation Area

◉ Sights & Activities

Enjoy long walks on the stunning swaths of **Cape Tribulation** and **Myall** beaches where you can usually swim (or at least paddle) safely outside stinger season. Do heed warnings and local advice about croc sightings. There are boardwalk trails at **Dubuji** (Myall Beach), **Kulki** (Cape Trib Beach) and, further south towards Noah Creek, the rainforest **Marrdja Boardwalk**.

⛵ Tours

★ **Ocean Safari** SNORKELLING
(☑ 07-4098 0006; www.oceansafari.com.au; Cape Tribulation Rd; adult/child/family from $154/99/459; ☺ 8am & noon) This operation leads small groups (25 people maximum) on morning and afternoon snorkelling cruises to the Great Barrier Reef, just half an hour offshore by fast inflatable. The sea

turtles in this stretch of reef are a highlight. Wetsuit hire ($8) is available.

Mason's Tours WALKING, DRIVING
(☑ 07-4098 0070; www.masonstours.com.au; Mason's Store, Cape Tribulation Rd; walks up to 4 people 2hr/half day $350/550) Long-time local Lawrence Mason conducts enlightening rainforest walks, including a night walk; 4WD tours up the Bloomfield Track to Cooktown are also available (groups of up to five people half/full day $880/1375). Find out more at the popular Mason's Cafe (p492).

Jungle Surfing Canopy Tours OUTDOORS
(☑ 07-4098 0043; www.junglesurfing.com.au; Cape Tribulation Rd; zip lines $109, night walks $49; ☺ 8am-5.30pm, night walks 7.30pm) Get right up into the rainforest on an exhilarating two-hour flying-fox (zip line) surf through the canopy. Guided night walks follow biologist-guides who shed light on the rainforest after dark – the chance to see tree kangaroos is a real highlight. Rates include pickup from Cape Trib accommodation (self-drive not permitted).

Cape Trib Horse Rides HORSE RIDING
(☑ 1800 111 124; www.capetribhorserides.com.au; rides adult/child from $110/70; ☺ 8am & 2.30pm) Leisurely morning and afternoon rides along the beach and into the forest.

🛏 Sleeping

★ **Cape Trib Beach House** HOSTEL, RESORT $
(☑ 07-4098 0030; www.capetribbeach.com.au; 152 Rykers Rd; dm $35-49, cabins $180-255; ✳@☒) The Beach House has everything that's great about Cape Trib – a secluded patch of rainforest facing a pristine beach and a friendly vibe that welcomes backpackers, couples and families. Clean dorms and rustic almost-beachfront cabins make the most of the location. The open-deck licensed **restaurant** (mains lunch $16-26, dinner $18-34; ☺ 7-9.30am, noon-2.30pm & 6-8pm; 🖼) and bar is well regarded enough that locals often eat and drink here.

Cape Tribulation Camping CAMPGROUND $
(☑ 07-4098 0077; www.capetribcamping.com.au; Lot 11, Cape Tribulation Rd; powered/unpowered sites per adult $22/17) Myall Beach is just steps away from this lovely laid-back campground. Grassy sites are fairly well spaced, facilities are good (unless you want a pool) and the **Sand Bar** (pizzas $15-20; ☺ 5-8pm Mon-Sat Apr-Nov) is a sociable verandah restaurant serving Cape Trib's best wood-fired pizzas.

LIZARD ISLAND

The five islands of the Lizard Island Group lie 33km off the coast about 100km north of Cooktown. Lizard, the main island, has rocky, mountainous terrain, glistening white beaches and spectacular fringing reefs for snorkelling and diving. Most of the island is national park and teeming with wildlife, but most people visit for the sumptuous accommodation and dining epitomised by the five-star luxury at the ultra-exclusive **Lizard Island Resort** (☑1300 863 248; www.lizardisland.com.au; Anchor Bay; d from $1969; ✳ @ 🛜 🖵).

Lizard Island has historically been a sacred place used by the Dingaal (Walmbaria) people for initiation ceremonies and for hunting turtles and dugong.

Guided Tours

Lizard Island Day Tour (Daintree Air Services; ☑07-4034 9300; www.daintreeair.com. au; per person $790) This full-day tour flies you up from Cairns to Lizard Island and back again, with time for hiking, snorkelling and simply lazing on the island's beaches.

Getting There & Away

At the time of writing there were no scheduled flights to Lizard Island. For guests at Lizard Island Resort, charter flights are organised as part of the booking for $770 return per person.

Rainforest Hideaway   B&B **$$$**
(☑07-4098 0108; www.rainforesthideaway.com; 19 Camelot Close; d $149) 🍃 This colourful B&B, consisting of one room in the main house and a separate cabin, was single-handedly built by its owner, artist and sculptor 'Dutch Rob' – even the furniture and beds are handmade. A sculpture trail winds through the property and traditional Thai massage is available (one hour $75). Minimum two nights. It's a 20-minute walk through the rainforest to the beach.

🍴 Eating

There's a **supermarket** (☑07-4098 0015; Cape Tribulation Rd; ⊙8am-6pm) stocking very basic supplies for self-caterers – fussy shoppers should stock up in Cairns or Port Douglas.

Mason's Store & Cafe   CAFE **$**
(☑07-4098 0016; www.facebook.com/masonscaf ecapetrib; 3781 Cape Tribulation Rd; mains $9-20, tasting plates from $28; ⊙10am-4pm) Everyone calls into Mason's for tourist info, for the liquor store (open until 5.30pm), or to dine out on exotic meats. Pride of place on the menu at this laid-back al-fresco cafe goes to the croc burger, but you can also try camel, emu and kangaroo in burgers or tasting plates. A short walk away is a crystal-clear, croc-free swimming hole ($1).

★**Whet**   AUSTRALIAN **$$**
(☑07-4098 0007; www.whet.net.au; 1 Cape Tribulation Rd; mains lunch $17-22, dinner $17-36; ⊙11am-3pm & 6-8pm) 🍃 Whet is regarded as Cape Trib's most sophisticated place to eat, with a loungey cocktail-bar feel and romantic, candlelit, al-fresco dining. Tempura wild barramundi and house chicken curry grace the menu. You'll often find locals at the bar and the owners pride themselves on fresh produce and ecofriendly processes.

🛈 Information

Mason's Store (☑07-4098 0070; www. facebook.com/masonscafecapetrib; Cape Tribulation Rd; ⊙11am-7pm Mon-Sat, to 4pm Sun) The best place for regional info including Bloomfield Track conditions.

🛈 Getting There & Away

The road to Cape Trib is sealed so it's suitable for any hire vehicle, but north of here the Bloomfield Track is 4WD-only for the 32km or so to Wujal Wujal. From there, the road is sealed all the way to Cooktown. The Daintree River Ferry carries wanderers and their wheels across the river every 15 minutes or so, thereby connecting Cape Tribulation with the rest of the region.

Trans North (p470) runs from Cairns to Cape Tribulation three times a week year-round, continuing on to Cooktown, depending on road conditions.

Understand East Coast Australia

History

Australia is an ancient continent. Rocks here have been dated back beyond the Archaean eon 3.8 billion years ago, and its Indigenous peoples have been here more than 50,000 years. Given this backdrop, 'history' as we describe it can seem somewhat fleeting...but it sure makes an interesting read!

First Australians

Many academics believe Indigenous Australians came here from somewhere else, with scientific evidence placing them on the continent at least 40,000 to 60,000 years ago. Aboriginal peoples, however, believe they have always inhabited the land.

Before the coming of Europeans, culture was the common link for Indigenous peoples across Australia – through the many aspects common to all the Aboriginal nations they were able to interact with each other. In postcolonial Australia it is also the shared history that binds Aboriginal peoples.

At the time of European contact the Aboriginal population was grouped into 300 or more different nations, with distinct languages and land boundaries. Most Aboriginal peoples did not have permanent shelters but moved within their territory and followed seasonal patterns of animal migration and plant availability. The diversity of landscapes in Australia meant that each nation varied in their lifestyles, and although they were distinct cultural groups, there were also many common elements: each nation had several clans or family groups who were responsible for looking after specific areas, for example. For thousands of years Aboriginal people lived within a complex kinship system that tied them to the natural environment. From the desert to the sea, Aboriginal peoples shaped their lives according to their environments and developed different skills and a wide body of knowledge on their territory.

Intruders Arrive

By sunrise, the storm had passed. Zachary Hicks was keeping sleepy watch on the British ship *Endeavour* when suddenly he was wide awake. He summoned his captain, James Cook, who climbed into the brisk

TIMELINE	50,000 years ago	43,000 BCE	3000 BCE
	The earliest record of Indigenous Australians inhabiting the land. The country is home to lush forests, teeming lakes and giant marsupials – including a wombat the size of a rhinoceros.	A group of Indigenous Australians sits down in the Nepean Valley near current-day Sydney and makes some stone tools. Archaeological sites like this have been found across Australia.	The last known large immigration to the continent from Asia occurs. Over 300 languages are spoken among the myriad groups living in Australia.

morning air to a miraculous sight. Ahead of them lay an uncharted land of wooded hills and gentle valleys. It was 19 April 1770, and they had found what would later be called Point Hicks, in eastern Victoria. In the coming days Cook began to methodically draw the first European map of Australia's east coast.

Two weeks later Cook led a party of men onto a narrow beach. As they waded ashore, two Aboriginal men stepped onto the sand and challenged the intruders with spears. Cook drove the men off with musket fire. For the rest of that week, the Aboriginal people and the intruders watched each other warily. The local Aboriginal people called the place Kurnell; Cook called it 'Botany Bay'. The fertile eastern coastline of Australia is now teeming with Cook's place names – including Hervey Bay (after an English admiral), Endeavour River and Point Solander (after one of the scientists on the *Endeavour*).

One night, in the seas off the great rainforests of the Kuku Yalanji Aboriginal people, in what is now known as Far North Queensland, the *Endeavour* was inching gingerly through the Great Barrier Reef when the crew heard the sickening sound of ripping timbers. They had run aground near a cape that is a tourist paradise today. Cook was in a glowering mood: he named it Cape Tribulation 'because here began all our troubles'. Seven days later Cook managed to beach the wounded ship in an Aboriginal harbour named Charco (Cook renamed it Endeavour), where his carpenters patched the hull.

When the *Endeavour* reached the northern tip of Cape York, blue ocean opened up to the west. Cook and his men could smell the sea route home. And on a small, hilly island ('Possession Island'), Cook raised the Union Jack. Amid volleys of gunfire, he claimed the eastern half of the continent for King George III.

Convict Beginnings

Eighteen years later, in 1788, the British were back to stay. They numbered 751 ragtag convicts and children, and around 250 soldiers, officials and their wives. This motley 'First Fleet' was under the command of a humane and diligent naval captain, Arthur Phillip. As his orders dictated, Phillip dropped anchor at Botany Bay, but the paradise that had so delighted Joseph Banks – a botanist on the First Fleet whose descriptions of Australia's plants captured the imagination of the British public, and who became a leading advocate of British settlement in Australia – filled Phillip with dismay. The land was marshy, there was little fresh water, and the anchorage was exposed to wind and storm. So Phillip left his floating prison and embarked in a small boat to search for a better location. Just a short way up the coast his heart leapt as he sailed into the finest harbour in the world. There, in a small cove, in the idyllic lands of the Eora people, he

Before Europeans arrived, Australia contained an estimated 750,000 Indigenous people, scattered among 300 or more Aboriginal nations. Among them, they spoke at least 300 Indigenous languages and dialects.

1606	1770	1776	1788
Dutch seaman Willem Janszoon 'discovers' Cape York on a foray from the Dutch East Indies, although he mistakes it for part of New Guinea.	English captain James Cook maps Australia's east coast in the scientific ship *Endeavour*. He then runs aground on the Great Barrier Reef near a place he names Cape Tribulation.	The 13 British colonies in the US declare independence, leaving King George III's government without a place to ship convicts. Authorities turn their attention to the vast Australian continent.	The Eora people of Bunnabi discover they have new neighbours; 11 ships arrive bearing soldiers and convicts, dropping anchor in what the new arrivals call Botany Bay.

established a British penal settlement on 26 January 1788. He renamed the place after the British Home Secretary, Lord Sydney.

Robert Hughes' outstanding book *The Fatal Shore* (1987) depicts convict Australia as a terrifying gulag where Britain tormented rebels, vagrants and criminals. Women (who were outnumbered five to one) lived under constant threat of sexual exploitation. Female convicts who offended their gaolers languished in the depressing 'female factories'. Male reoffenders were cruelly flogged, and could even be hanged for minor crimes, such as stealing. Re-offenders were sent to newly established colonies at Port Arthur in Van Diemen's Land (later called Tasmania) or Norfolk Island in the remote Pacific.

Even so, many convicts soon earned their 'ticket of leave', a kind of parole that gave them the freedom of the colony and the right to seek work on their own behalf. At first Sydney and these smaller colonies depended on supplies brought in by ship. Anxious to develop productive farms, the government granted land to soldiers, officers and emancipated convicts. After 30 years of trial and error, their farms began to flourish.

On the Land

Each year settlers pushed deeper into the Aboriginal territories in search of pasture and water for their stock. These people became known as squatters (because they 'squatted' on Aboriginal lands) and many held this territory with a gun. Aboriginal Australians still recount how their waterholes were poisoned and their people massacred. Some of the most bitter struggles occurred in the remote mining districts of central Queensland. In Tasmania the impact of settlement was so devastating that today all of the island's Indigenous Australians are of mixed heritage.

On the mainland many of the squatters reached a truce with the defeated Indigenous peoples. In remote regions it became common for Aboriginal Australians to take low-paid jobs on farms, working on sheep and cattle stations as drovers, rouseabouts, shearers and domestics. This arrangement continued in outback pastoral regions until after WWII.

THE MAKING OF MELBOURNE

In 1835 a young squatter named John Batman sailed from Van Diemen's Land to Port Phillip Bay on the mainland. On the banks of the Yarra River, he chose the location for Melbourne, famously announcing that 'This is the place for a village'. Batman then worked a staggering swindle: he persuaded the local Aboriginal people to 'sell' him their traditional lands (a whopping 2500 sq km) for a crate of blankets, flour, knives and knick-knacks. Back in Sydney, Governor Burke declared the contract void, not because it was unfair, but because the land officially belonged to the British Crown.

1824	1835	1844–45	1871
The government establishes the brutal penal colony of Moreton Bay, a place of blood, sweat and tears. A second penal colony, Brisbane, follows two years later.	John Batman arranges the 'purchase' of 2500 sq km from Aboriginal Australians of the Dutigalla tribe for flour and trinkets. Melbourne is established on the north bank of the Yarra River..	The first guidebook to Australia is written in the form of a journal by Ludwig Leichhardt. It chronicles his party's exploration from Brisbane almost to Darwin. In 1848 he vanishes without a trace.	Aboriginal stockman Jupiter discovers gold in Queensland and the rush is on. Within 10 years Brisbane has made its fortune from both gold and wool.

Gold & Rebellion

Transportation of convicts to eastern Australia ceased in the 1840s. This was just as well: in 1851 prospectors discovered gold in New South Wales (NSW) and central Victoria. The news hit the colonies with the force of a cyclone. From every social class, young men and some adventurous women headed for the diggings. Soon they were caught up in a great rush of prospectors, entertainers, publicans, sly-groggers, prostitutes and quacks from overseas. In Victoria the British governor was alarmed – both by the way the Victorian class system had been thrown into disarray, and by the need to finance law and order on the goldfields. His solution was to compel all miners to buy an expensive monthly licence, in the hope that the lower orders would return to their duties in town.

But the lure of gold was too great and, after three years, the easy gold at Ballarat was gone and miners were toiling in deep, water-sodden shafts. Infuriated by a corrupt and brutal system that held them in contempt and united under the leadership of a charismatic Irishman named Peter Lalor, they raised the flag of the Southern Cross and swore to defend their rights and liberties. They armed themselves and gathered inside a rough stockade at Eureka, where they waited for the government to make its move.

In the predawn of Sunday 3 December 1854, a force of troopers attacked the stockade. In 15 terrifying minutes, they slaughtered 30 miners and lost five soldiers. The story of the Eureka stockade is often told as a battle for nationhood and democracy – as if a true nation must be born out of blood – but these killings were tragically unnecessary. The eastern colonies were already in the process of establishing democratic parliaments, with the full support of the British authorities. In the 1880s Lalor himself became Speaker of the Victorian parliament.

The gold rush also attracted boatloads of prospectors from China. The Chinese prospectors endured constant hostility and were the victims of ugly race riots on the goldfields at Lambing Flat (now called Young) in NSW in 1860–61. Chinese precincts developed in the backstreets of Sydney and Melbourne and many Chinese people went on to establish themselves as important members of the business community.

Gold and wool brought immense investment and gusto to Melbourne in particular. By the 1880s there were gaslights in the streets, railways and that great new invention: the telegraph. The southern capital became known as 'Marvellous Melbourne', so opulent were its theatres, hotels, galleries and fashions.

Meanwhile, the huge expanses of Queensland were remote from the southern centres of political and business power. It was a tough, raw frontier colony, in which money was made by hard labour – in mines, in the forests and on cattle stations. In the coastal sugar industry, southern

The handsome blue-and-white Southern Cross flag flown at the Eureka stockade in 1854 has since become a symbol of union movements in Australia.

1891	1901	1915	1918
A shearers' strike around Barcaldine, Queensland, establishes a labour legend; the confrontation leads to the birth of the Australian Labor Party.	The Australian colonies federate; a new national parliament meets in Melbourne. The White Australia policy is passed, which bans non-Europeans from immigrating.	In line with Australia's close ties to Britain, Australian and New Zealand Army Corps (the Anzacs) join the Allied invasion of Turkey at Gallipoli. The Anzac legend is born.	The Great War ends. From a country of 4.9 million, 320,000 were sent to war in Europe and almost 20% were killed. Cracks appear in Australian–British relations.

investors grew rich on a plantation economy that exploited tough Pacific Island labourers (known as 'Kanakas'), many of whom had been kidnapped from their islands.

Nationhood

On 1 January 1901 Australia became a federation. When the members of the new national parliament met in Melbourne, their first aim was to protect the identity and values of a European Australia from an influx of Asians and Pacific Islanders. Their solution was what became known as the White Australia policy. It became a racial tenet of faith in Australia for the next 70 years. For those who were welcome to live in Australia (ie whites), this was to be a model society, nestled in the skirts of the British Empire.

Just one year later, white women won the right to vote in federal elections. In a series of radical innovations, the government introduced a broad social-welfare scheme and protected Australian wage levels with import tariffs. Its mixture of capitalist dynamism and socialist compassion became known as 'the Australian settlement'. It was an impressive start, although its benefits were closed to both non-white immigrants and Indigenous Australians.

War & the Great Depression

Living on the edge of this forbidding land, and isolated from the rest of the world, most Australians took comfort from the idea that they were still a part of the British Empire. When war broke out in Europe in 1914, thousands of Australian men rallied to the Empire's call. They had their first taste of death on 25 April 1915, when the Australian and New Zealand Army Corps (or the Anzacs) joined British and French troops in an assault on the Gallipoli peninsula in Turkey. It was eight months before the British commanders acknowledged that the tactic had failed, but by then 8141 young Australians were dead. Soon the Australian Imperial Force was fighting in the killing fields of Europe. By the time the war ended, 60,000 Australian men had been slaughtered. Ever since, on 25 April, Australians have gathered at war memorials around the country and at Gallipoli for the sad and solemn services of Anzac Day.

Australia careened wildly through the 1920s, investing in immigration and growth, until the economy collapsed into the abyss of the Great Depression in 1929. Unemployment brought its shame and misery to one in three houses. For those who were wealthy – or who had jobs – the Depression was hardly noticed. In fact, the fall in prices actually meant that the purchasing power of their income was enhanced. For everyone else, it was a dire and difficult time.

Revered by many critics as the great Australian novel, Patrick White's *Voss* (1957) was inspired by the story of the Prussian explorer Leichhardt. It's a psychological tale, a love story and an epic journey over the Australian desert.

Written in 1895 by AB 'Banjo' Paterson, 'Waltzing Matilda' is widely regarded as Australia's unofficial national anthem. Some say the song paid homage to striking sheep shearers during the 1890s labour uprisings.

1929	1937	1941	1956
The Great Depression: thousands go hungry as the economy crashes. Unemployment peaks at 28% in 1932 – one of the highest rates in the industrialised world (second only to Germany).	Cane toads are released into the wild to control pests damaging Queensland's sugar-cane fields. The action proves disastrous, creating a plague that spreads to other states.	The Japanese bomb Townsville. The war in the Pacific is on. Hundreds of thousands of Australian troops pour out to battlefields worldwide; thousands of American troops pour in and drink a lot of beer.	The summer Olympics are held in Melbourne – the first time the games are held in the southern hemisphere. Australia places third in the medal tally behind the USSR and the USA.

WWII

As the economy began to recover, the whirl of daily life was hardly dampened when, in 1939, Australian servicemen sailed off to Europe for a new war. Though Japan was menacing, Australians took it for granted that the British navy would keep them safe. In December 1941 Japan bombed the US fleet at Pearl Harbor. Weeks later the 'impregnable' British naval base in Singapore crumbled, and soon thousands of Australians and other Allied troops were enduring the savagery of Japan's prisoner-of-war camps.

As the Japanese swept through Southeast Asia and into Papua New Guinea, the British announced that they could not spare any resources to defend Australia. But the legendary US commander General Douglas MacArthur saw that Australia was the perfect base for American operations in the Pacific. In a series of savage battles on sea and land, Allied forces gradually turned back the Japanese advance. Importantly, it was the USA, not the British Empire, that came to Australia's aid. The days of the British alliance were numbered.

Peace, Prosperity & Multiculturalism

When WWII ended, a new slogan rang through the land: 'Populate or Perish!' The Australian government embarked on an ambitious scheme to attract thousands of immigrants. With government assistance, people flocked from Britain as well as from non-English-speaking countries, including Greece, Italy, Czechoslovakia, Serbia, Croatia, the Netherlands and Poland, and, later, from Turkey, Lebanon and many other countries. These 'new Australians' were expected to assimilate into a suburban stereotype known as the 'Australian way of life'.

Many migrants found jobs in the growing manufacturing sector, in which companies such as General Motors and Ford operated with generous tariff support. In addition, the government embarked on audacious public works schemes, notably the mighty Snowy Mountains Hydro-Electric Scheme in the mountains near Canberra. Today environmentalists point out the devastation caused by this huge network of tunnels, dams and power stations, but the Snowy scheme was an expression of a new-found postwar optimism and a testimony to the cooperation among the labourers of many nations who completed the project.

This era of growth and prosperity was dominated by Robert Menzies, the founder of the modern Liberal Party and Australia's longest-serving prime minister, with over 18 years in office. Menzies was steeped in British history and tradition, and liked to play the part of a sentimental monarchist; he was also a vigilant opponent of communism. As Asia succumbed to the chill of the Cold War, Australia and New Zealand entered a formal military alliance with the USA – the 1951

The most accessible version of the Anzac legend is Peter Weir's epic film *Gallipoli* (1981), with a cast that includes a fresh-faced Mel Gibson.

1962	1969	1970s	1972
Indigenous Australians gain the right to vote in federal elections – but they have to wait until 1967 to receive full citizenship, which happens overwhelmingly in a nationwide referendum.	Setting the political scene in Queensland for the next 21 years, Joh Bjelke-Petersen becomes premier. His political agenda was widely described as 'development at any price'.	Inflation, soaring interest rates and rising unemployment bring the golden postwar days to an end. As house prices skyrocket, home ownership moves out of reach for many.	The Aboriginal Tent Embassy is erected on the lawns of Parliament House in Canberra. Over the next decades it serves as a reminder that Indigenous peoples have been denied sovereignty of their land.

TERRA NULLIUS & MABO

In May 1982 Eddie Mabo led a group of Torres Strait Islanders in a court action to have the traditional title to their land on Mer (Murray Island) recognised. Their argument challenged the legal principle of terra nullius (literally, 'land belonging to no one') and demonstrated their unbroken relationship with the land over a period of thousands of years. In June 1992 the High Court found in favour of Eddie Mabo and the Torres Strait Islanders, rejecting the principle of terra nullius – this became known as the Mabo decision. The result has had far-reaching implications in Australia ever since, including the introduction of the *Native Title Act* in 1993.

Anzus security pact. When the USA hurled its righteous fury into a civil war in Vietnam, Menzies committed Australian forces to the battle, introducing conscription for military service overseas. The following year Menzies retired, leaving his successors a bitter legacy – the antiwar movement would split Australia.

There was a feeling, too, among many artists, intellectuals and the younger generation that Menzies' Australia had become a rather dull, complacent country, more in love with US and British culture than with its own talents and stories. In an atmosphere of youthful rebellion and emerging nationalism, the Labor Party was elected to power in 1972 under the leadership of an idealistic lawyer named Gough Whitlam. In just four years his government transformed the country: he ended conscription and abolished all university fees, and he introduced a free universal health-care scheme, no-fault divorce, the principle of Aboriginal Australian land rights, and equal pay for women. The White Australia policy had been gradually falling into disuse, and under Whitlam it was finally abandoned altogether. By now, around one million migrants had arrived from non-English-speaking countries, and they had filled Australia with new languages, cultures, foods and ideas. Under Whitlam this achievement was embraced as 'multiculturalism'.

By 1975 the Whitlam government was rocked by a tempest of economic inflation and scandal. At the end of 1975 his government was controversially dismissed from office by the governor general, the Queen's representative within Australia. But the general thrust of Whitlam's social reforms was continued by his successors.

Best History Encounters

The Rocks Discovery Museum (Sydney)

Museum of Sydney (Sydney)

Melbourne Museum (Melbourne)

Queensland Museum (Brisbane)

National Museum of Australia (Canberra)

Modern Challenges

Today Australia faces new challenges. In the 1970s the country began dismantling its protectionist scaffolding. New efficiency brought new prosperity. At the same time, wages and working conditions, which were once protected by an independent tribunal, became more vulnerable as

1975	2000	2008	2011
The Great Barrier Reef Marine Park is created. It later becomes a World Heritage Site, which angers Bjelke-Petersen, who intended to explore for oil on the reef.	Sydney hosts the summer Olympics, which are a triumph of spectacle and goodwill. Aboriginal runner Cathy Freeman lights the flame at the opening ceremony and wins gold in the 400m event.	On behalf of parliament, Prime Minister Kevin Rudd delivers a moving apology to Aboriginal Australians for laws and policies that 'inflicted profound grief, suffering and loss'.	Powerful floods inundate vast areas of Queensland, including Brisbane, killing 35 people and causing billions of dollars of damage. Cyclone Yasi follows weeks later, devastating parts of north Queensland.

egalitarianism gave way to competition. And after two centuries of development, the strains on the environment were starting to show – on water supplies, forests, soils, air quality and the oceans.

Under John Howard, Australia's second-longest-serving prime minister (1996–2007), the country grew closer than ever to the USA, joining the Americans in the war in Iraq. Some Australians were dismayed by the conservative Howard government's harsh treatment of asylum seekers, its refusal to acknowledge the reality of climate change, its anti-union reforms and the prime minister's lack of empathy for Aboriginal Australians. But Howard presided over a period of economic growth that emphasised the values of self-reliance and won him continuing support.

In 2007 Howard was defeated by the Labor Party's Kevin Rudd, an ex-diplomat who issued a formal apology to Indigenous Australians for the injustices they had suffered over the past two centuries. Though it promised sweeping reforms in environment and education, the Rudd government found itself faced with a crisis when the world economy crashed in 2008. In 2010 Rudd lost his position in a leadership spill.

Incoming Prime Minister Julia Gillard, along with other world leaders, now faced three related challenges: climate change, a diminishing fuel supply and a shrinking economy. Since 2013 the prime minister's chair has changed hands several times with a run of leaders after Gillard: Rudd (again); then three Liberal Party leaders in quick succession, Tony Abbott, Malcolm Turnbull and Scott Morrison. A May 2019 election saw the Morrison-led Liberal Party retain control.

Governing the nation, almost 120 years after it was created, has proven to be quite a challenge in the 21st century.

Reading Australian History

History of Australia (Manning Clark; 1962)

The Fatal Shore (Robert Hughes; 1986)

Birth of Melbourne (Tim Flannery; 2004)

First Footprints (Scott Cane; 2013)

HISTORY MODERN CHALLENGES

2016 & 2017	2019	2019	2020
Two catastrophic 'bleaching' events, caused by warmer-than-usual water temperatures, have a severe impact on the Great Barrier Reef.	The incumbent conservative Liberal/National Party coalition, led by Prime Minister Scott Morrison, wins a surprise re-election in the national elections; the coalition first won power in 2013.	Devastating bushfires ravage communities across Australia's eastern seaboard, especially in eastern Victoria and New South Wales, sparking a national debate on the impact of climate change.	Australia records its first case of the COVID-19 on January 25 and by mid-March the country is in full lockdown. As restrictions ease in May, Australians mostly embrace the 'new normal' of spatial distancing.

Environment

Australia's environment is unlike anywhere else on the planet. It's an astonishingly rich place, home to the world's largest coral reef, the earth's oldest rainforests, and animals that simply don't exist elsewhere. Making this glorious, endemic diversity of Australia's natural world a priority of your trip will repay you with highlights many times over. And yet, Australia's fragile ecosystems face unprecedented challenges, from climate change to feral species driving Australia's native creatures towards extinction. It's a fascinating story of our time.

The Land & Coast

There is an epic quality and scale to Australia's landscapes: rugged in places yet extremely fragile elsewhere, sometimes unmistakably Australian, just as often altered by ill-considered human intervention. Much of the natural environment here – especially around the cities – has been damaged or replaced by trees and creatures from Europe. In other places, extraordinary fragments of the original environment have been preserved and many are relatively easy to access.

Great Barrier Reef

Unlike mainland Australia, today's Great Barrier Reef (GBR) is relatively young, geologically speaking. Its foundations formed around 500,000 years ago, with northern Australia surrounded by tropical waters as it drifted gradually northward from the massive South Pole land mass that was Gondwana. The GBR grew and receded several times in response to changing sea levels. Coastal plains that are now the sea floor were occupied by Indigenous Australians only 20,000 years ago, when the ice-age sea level was 130m lower than it is today. As the ice caps contracted, seas flooded continental shelves and stabilised near their current levels about 6000 to 8000 years ago. Corals settled atop high parts of the Queensland shelf, initiating the unique combination of biological and geological processes that have built the reef ecosystem we see today.

The ecosystem of the Great Barrier Reef includes the sea-floor habitats between the reefs, hundreds of continental islands and coral cays, and coastal beaches, headlands and estuaries. The 2900 reefs (ranging from less than 1km to 26km long) that make up the GBR system truly astounding biological diversity, with over 1500 species of fish, over 400 species of reef-building coral, and hundreds of species of molluscs (clams, snails, octopuses), echinoderms (sea stars, bêches-de-mer, sea urchins), sponges, worms, crustaceans and seaweed. The GBR is also home to marine mammals (such as dolphins, whales and dugongs) and six of the planet's seven species of sea turtles. The GBR's 900-or-so islands range from unvegetated or sparsely vegetated sand cays to densely forested continental islands.

Established in 1975, the 360,000-sq-km Great Barrier Reef Marine Park is about the same size as Italy. About 30% of the park is closed, and the remainder is open to commercial and recreational fishing. There are a handful of coastal cities along the reef's southern half (notably Cairns, Townsville, Mackay and Gladstone), some with ports to service cattle and

After separating from the prehistoric Gondwana landmass 120 million years ago, Australia broke free from Antarctica and headed north. The Unesco-listed rainforests in New South Wales, southeastern Queensland and Far North Queensland have been around since then: they're the oldest on earth. Only 1% of Australia's original rainforests survive.

sugar export, and mineral export and import. Shipping lanes traverse its length and breadth, and ore carriers, cargo ships and cruise liners must use local marine pilots to reduce the risk of groundings and collisions.

Great Dividing Range

Separating East Coast Australia's coastal littoral from the country's interior, the Great Dividing Range is more than a mountain range. These may not be the highest mountains on the planet – Mt Kosciuszko, Australia's highest mountain in southern New South Wales (NSW), rises just 2228m. But this is the fifth-longest continuous range on earth (around 3500km long), and the range has a profound impact upon the Australian landscape; the fertile coastal strip is in stark contrast to the lands west of the range, which are drier and get progressively more so on their way to the outback. Historically, the Great Dividing Range also served as a barrier to exploration and settlement – it took decades longer for European settlers to expand their reach beyond the hills.

The Great Dividing Range begins (or ends, depending on your perspective) at Dauan Island off the tip of Far North Queensland, and doesn't stop until it reaches the Grampians in western Victoria, around 3500km later.

Wildlife

The first naturalists to investigate Australia were astonished by what they found. Here the swans were black – to Europeans this was a metaphor for the impossible – and mammals such as the otherworldly platypus and echidna lay eggs. It really was an upside-down world, where the larger animals hopped and where each year the trees shed their bark rather than their leaves. That's because Australia has been isolated from the other continents for a very long time (around 80 million years). Unlike those on other habitable continents that have been linked by land bridges, Australia's birds, mammals, reptiles and plants have taken their own separate and very different evolutionary journeys. The result is one of the world's most distinct natural realms.

Birds

Australia has 898 recorded bird species, although an estimated 165 of these are considered to be vagrants, with only a handful of sightings (or even only one) recorded. Nearly half of all Australian birds are not found anywhere else on earth. A 2014 study by the Commonwealth Scientific and Industrial Research Organisation (CSIRO) warned that 10% of Australia's birds could become extinct by the end of the century. Relatively few of Australia's birds are seasonal breeders, and few migrate – instead, they breed when the rain comes.

Mammals

Australia is home to a remarkable 379 different mammal species; more than 94% of these are native to Australia. The majority of these mammals are marsupials (159) and bats (76).

For advice on the best places to see many iconic Australian mammals, see the East Coast Australia Outdoors (p46) chapter.

Kangaroos & Wallabies

Australia is, of course, famous as the home of the kangaroo (aka 'roo'). There are three main species of kangaroo: red kangaroo, eastern grey kangaroo and western grey kangaroo. Of these, only the eastern grey kangaroo is found along East Coast Australia.

The lifestyles of these hopping marsupials are exquisitely attuned to Australia's harsh conditions. Have you ever wondered why kangaroos,

---

ENVIRONMENT WILDLIFE

The Coastal Studies Unit at the University of Sydney has deemed there to be an astonishing 10,685 beaches in Australia. (It defines a beach as a stretch of sand that's more than 20m long and remains dry at high tide.)

Birdlife Australia (www.birdlife.org.au) is the nation's peak birding body; it organises birding excursions and publishes a regular newsletter. Watch its website for updates on unusual sightings.

alone among the world's larger mammals, hop? It turns out that hopping is the most efficient way of getting about at medium speeds. This is because the energy of the bounce is stored in the tendons of the legs – much like in a pogo stick – while the intestines bounce up and down like a piston, emptying and filling the lungs without needing to activate the chest muscles. When you travel long distances to find meagre feed, such efficiency is a must.

There are also at least 15 different types of wallaby (a smaller version of the kangaroo), including rock-wallabies and nail-tail wallabies, as well as wallaroos, potoroos and pademelons. The most commonly seen species along the coast and its hinterland are agile wallabies and swamp wallabies.

Koalas

Marsupials are so energy-efficient that they need to eat one-fifth less food than equivalent-sized placental mammals (everything from bats to rats, whales and ourselves). But some marsupials have taken energy efficiency much further. If you visit a wildlife park or a zoo, you might notice that faraway look in a koala's eyes. It seems as if nobody is home – and this, in fact, is near the truth.

Several years ago biologists announced that koalas are the only living creatures that have brains that don't fit their skulls. Instead they have a shrivelled walnut of a brain that rattles around in a fluid-filled cranium. Other researchers have pointed out that the brains of the koalas examined for the study may have shrunk because these organs are so soft. Whether soft-brained or empty-headed, there is no doubt that the koala is not the Einstein of the animal world, and we now believe that it has sacrificed its brain to energy efficiency – brains cost a lot to run. Koalas eat gum leaves, which are so toxic they use 20% of their energy just detoxifying this food. This leaves little energy for the brain, but fortunately living in the treetops – where there are so few predators – means they can get by with few wits at all.

Koalas live in highly fragmented populations, and suffered massive losses in the 2019–20 bushfires that swept through southeastern and eastern Australia. The greatest threat to koalas is habitat loss – of nearly 900 species of eucalyptus trees in Australia, koalas eat the leaves of fewer than 50, and prefer just 10.

Platypuses & Echidnas

Two unique monotremes (egg-laying mammals) live in Australia: the bumbling echidna, something akin to a hedgehog; and the platypus, a bit like an otter, with webbed feet and a ducklike bill. Echidnas are common along bushland trails, but platypuses are elusive, and only seen at dawn and dusk in quiet rivers and streams.

Mostly nocturnal, the platypus stores food in cheek pouches until it is ready to chew. Males have a poisonous spur on each hind ankle, and the webbing on their feet, which enables them to swim so rapidly underwater, can be folded out of the way when they need to walk on land.

Echidnas have an exceptionally long and sticky tongue, which is ideal for cleaning out ant nests and termite mounds. They are found throughout Australia and can survive in all kinds of habitats.

Wombats

The koala's nearest relative, the wombat (of which there are three species), has a large brain for a marsupial. These creatures live in complex burrows and can weigh up to 35kg, making them the largest herbivorous burrowers on earth. Because their burrows are effectively air-conditioned, they have the neat trick of turning down their metabolic activity when they are

Bats live in large treetop colonies where they roost during the day, leaving en masse every night to forage for food. One of the largest such nightly spectacles is around the Port Douglas suburb of Craiglie in Far North Queensland. The nightly exodus includes spectacled flying foxes.

in residence. One physiologist, who studied wombats' thyroid hormones, found that biological activity ceased to such an extent in sleeping wombats that, from a hormonal point of view, they appeared to be dead!

Wombats can remain underground for a week at a time, and can get by on just one-third of the food needed by a sheep of equivalent size. One day, perhaps, efficiency-minded farmers will keep wombats instead of sheep; at the moment, however, that isn't possible.

The largest of the wombat species, the northern hairy-nose, is one of the world's rarest creatures, with only around 196 surviving in a remote nature reserve in central Queensland. The last census was taken in 2013. Other wombat species aren't so rare and can be seen in various places (p46) along, or just inland from, the east coast.

Whales

Whaling, a driving economic force across much of southern Australia from the time of colonisation, was finally banned in Australia in 1979. The main species on the end of the harpoon were humpback, blue, southern right and sperm whales, which were culled in huge numbers in traditional breeding grounds such as Sydney Harbour, the Western Australia coast around Albany and Hobart's Derwent River estuary. The industry remained profitable until the mid-1800s, before drastically depleted whale numbers, the lure of inland gold rushes and the emergence of petrol as an alternative fuel started to have an impact.

Humpback whales, around 16m in length, are commonly seen in Australian waters. They spend the Australian summer (roughly from December to March) feeding on krill around Antarctica. They begin to head north in April and reach the waters off Victoria around June. From June to August, they migrate north along Australia's eastern coast to mate and to calve in the warm, tropical waters off the north Queensland coast. In September they begin the return journey, and are seen until November when they again approach Antartica, completing a more-than-10,000km return migration.

Over recent years (and much to locals' delight), whales have made cautious returns to both Sydney Harbour and the Derwent River. Whale watching has emerged as a lucrative tourist activity in migratory hotspots such as Warrnambool in Victoria, Eden and beyond Sydney Harbour in NSW, and Hervey Bay in Queensland.

Reptiles

One thing you will see lots of in Australia are reptiles. Snakes are abundant, and they include five of the 10 most venomous species known in nature. Where the opportunities to feed are few and far between, it's best not to give your prey a second chance, hence the potent venom. Snakes will usually leave you alone if you don't fool with them. Observe, back quietly away and don't panic, and you should be OK.

Feeling right at home in rivers, estuaries and ocean shallows north of Airlie Beach, the saltwater crocodile is the world's largest living reptile – old males can reach an intimidating 6m long.

Environmental Issues

The European colonisation of Australia, commencing in 1788, heralded a period of catastrophic environmental upheaval. The result today is that Australians are struggling with some of the most severe environmental problems to be found anywhere in the world. It may seem strange that a population of just 24 million, living on a continent the size of the USA (minus Alaska), could inflict such damage on its environment, but Australia's long isolation, its fragile soils and difficult climate have made it particularly vulnerable to human-induced change.

With only half of the 2019–20 summer gone, fires had destroyed near-ly 19 million hectares (190,000 sq km, or 73,360 sq miles) across most Australian states. Worst hit were communities along the length of the NSW coast, and in eastern Victoria, southeastern Queensland around Noosa, and Kangaroo Island in South Australia. Thirty people died and more than 2000 homes were destroyed.

One university study at the height of the crisis estimated that the fires had killed one billion animals (800 million in NSW alone). Everyone agreed that the figures likely underestimated the true impact, and that numerous species were pushed closer to extinction. And while Australia's plants, and the habitat they provide for native species, long ago adapted to cycles of flood, drought and fire, scientists fear that the frequency with which fire events have occurred in recent years means that some may never recover.

The slow response of Australia's national government, led by Prime Minister Scott Morrison, to the growing crisis caused widespread anger in Australia. The government's consistent refusal to accept and address the human causes for global warming over the years, and its initial un-willingness to accept that climate change may have played a role in the fires, also didn't help.

Barely seven months earlier, the government had won re-election, and part of its platform included fast-tracking approval for Adani, a contro-versial coal mine, which, environmentalists claim, could pose a significant threat to the Great Barrier Reef near Townsville in Far North Queensland, quite apart from the impacts of perpetuating Australia's dependence on coal exports. Although the government changed tack in their public state-ments and suggested a new approach was on the horizon, many remained sceptical, and with good reason. At the height of the fires, in December 2019, the Climate Change Performance Index (www.climate-change-performance-index.org) ranked Australia as the world's worst performer in terms of climate policy. If nothing else, the debate has shifted.

Feral Animals & the Extinction Crisis

Of all the continents, Australia has the worst record on the extinction of mammals, with around 30 mammal species having become extinct since European settlement in 1788. There are many causes, including deforest-ation, land clearing and habitat loss. The introduction to Australia of non-native predators is another.

Beginning with the escape of domestic cats into the Australian bush shortly after 1788, a plethora of vermin – from foxes and wild camels to cane toads – have run wild in Australia, causing extinctions in the native fauna. One out of every 10 native mammals living in Australia prior to European colonisation is now extinct, and many more are high-ly endangered. Extinctions have also affected native plants, birds and amphibians.

Non-native species (the full list includes foxes, rabbits, cats, pigs, goats, donkeys, horses, camels, starlings, sparrows, cane toads, mosquito fish and carp) contribute significantly to the fragmentation of ecosys-tems and the extinction of native animals in Australia. Each brings a unique suite of problems – some as predators of native animals, others as competitors for the limited resources of food, water and shelter.

According to one recent scientific study, there are 2.3 million feral cats in Australia and they may be killing millions of native animals every night. In addition to government programmes to restore and pro-tect habitats and species in national parks, private organisations such as Australian Wildlife Conservancy (AWC; www.australianwildlife.org) and Bush Heritage (www.bushheritage.org.au) are buying up vast areas across the country, fencing them and eradicating pests and feral animals, allowing the land and its wildlife to recover.

Food & Drink

Australians once proudly survived on a diet of 'meat and three veg'. Fine fare was a Sunday roast; lasagne or croissants were exotic. Fortunately the country's cuisine has evolved, and these days Australian gastronomy is keen to break rules, backed up by top chefs, world-renowned wines, excellent coffee and a burgeoning craft-beer scene. All along the east coast you'll find incredible seafood, from humble fish-and-chippers to fine-dining restaurants overlooking the ocean, while fantastic food markets and hip cafe culture make for top-notch culinary exploring.

Modern Australian (Mod Oz)

Australia has never really had its own cuisine, and its culinary offering was essentially the sum total of all the cuisines brought to the Australian kitchen by immigrants and influences from around the world. Over time though, something quintessentially Australian has emerged. The phrase Modern Australian (Mod Oz) has been coined to classify contemporary Australian cuisine: a melange of East and West; a swirl of Atlantic and Pacific Rim; a flourish of authentic French and Italian.

Immigration has been the key to this culinary blend. An influx of immigrants since WWII, arriving from Europe, Asia, the Middle East and Africa, introduced new ingredients and new ways to use staples. Vietnam, Japan, Fiji – no matter where the food is from, there are expat communities and interested locals keen to cook and eat it.

As the Australian appetite for diversity and invention grows, so does the food culture surrounding it. Cookbooks and foodie magazines are bestsellers, and Australian celebrity chefs – highly sought overseas – reflect Australia's multiculturalism in their backgrounds and dishes.

If all this sounds overwhelming, never fear. The range of food in Australia is a true asset. You'll find that dishes are characterised by bold and interesting flavours and fresh ingredients. All palates are catered for along the east coast: the chilli meter spans gentle to extreme, seafood is plentiful, meats are full-flavoured and vegetarian needs are considered (especially in the cities).

The total at the bottom of a restaurant bill is all you really need to pay in Australia. Tipping isn't mandatory, but is appreciated when service has been provided with a smile. Around 10% is the norm (perhaps more if your kids have trashed the dining room).

BEER & BREWERIES

Balter (07-5525 6916; www.balter.com.au; 14 Traders Way, Currumbin; 3-8pm Wed-Fri, from noon Sat & Sun) Surfside beers from Currumbin, Queensland.

BentSpoke Brewing Co (02-6257 5220; www.bentspokebrewing.com.au; 38 Mort St, Braddon; 11am-midnight) Canberra-based brewer consistently among Australia's best.

Burleigh Brewing Company (07-5593 6000; www.burleighbrewing.com.au; 2 Ern Harley Dr; 3-8.30pm Fri & Sat, 2-6pm Sun) Stalwart craft brewer at Burleigh Heads on the Gold Coast.

Stone & Wood (02-6685 5173; www.stoneandwood.com.au; 100 Centennial Circuit; 10am-5pm Mon-Fri, noon-6pm Sat & Sun, meals noon-3pm) Creates a Byron Bay brew that's so popular country-wide it's almost mainstream.

Young Henry's (02-9519 0048; www.younghenrys.com; 76 Wilford St, Newtown; noon-7pm; Newtown) Bold brews from Newtown in Sydney's inner west. And a distillery!

Local Delicacies

Australia's size and diverse climate – from the tropical north to the temperate south – mean that there's an enormous variety of produce on offer.

Seafood connoisseurs prize Sydney rock oysters and scallops from Queensland. Rock lobsters (aka crayfish) are fantastic and fantastically expensive; mud crabs, despite the name, are a sweet treat. Another odd-sounding delicacy is 'bugs' – like shovel-nosed lobsters without a lobster's price tag; try the Balmain and Moreton Bay varieties. Aussie prawns are also superb, particularly the school prawns or the eastern king (Yamba) prawns found along the northern New South Wales coast.

Aussies love their seafood, but they've not lost their love of a hefty chunk of steak. Rockhampton is the beef capital of Australia, although the vast cattle stations of western Queensland produce some of the world's highest-quality cuts. Lamb from Victoria's lush Gippsland is also highly prized.

Queensland's fertile fields are dappled with banana and mango plantations, orchards and vast seas of sugar cane. In summer mangoes are so plentiful that Queenslanders actually get sick of them. The macadamia, a buttery native nut, grows throughout southeastern Queensland – you'll find them tossed in salads, crushed in ice cream and petrified in sticky cakes.

There's a small but brilliant farmhouse-cheese movement in Australia, hampered by the fact that all the milk must be pasteurised. Despite this, the results can be spectacular. Cheese obsessives can go a step further and make their own on a course at Yungaburra's farm-based **Cheesemaking & More** (☑07-4095 2097; www.cheesemakingand-more.com.au; Quinlan Rd, Lake Eacham).

Vegemite: you'll either love it or hate it. For reference, Barack Obama diplomatically called it 'horrible'. It's certainly an acquired taste, but Australians consume more than 22 million jars of the stuff each year.

Coffee Culture

Coffee has become an Australian addiction. There are Italian-style espresso machines in every cafe, boutique roasters are all the rage and, in urban areas, the qualified barista is ever-present (there are even barista-staffed cafes attached to petrol stations). Sydney and Melbourne have given rise to a whole generation of coffee snobs, with the two cities slugging it out for bragging rights as Australia's coffee capital (Melbourne currently has the edge). The cafe scene in Melbourne is particularly artsy, and the best way to immerse yourself in it is by wandering the city centre's cafe-lined laneways. Beyond the big cities, you'll be able to find a decent coffee in most towns, but you might still struggle in rural areas.

Foodie Touring Hot Spots

The vine-covered Hunter Valley (a few hours north of Sydney) produces far more than just wine. Among the rolling hillsides, you'll find farmhouse cheeses, smoked fish and meats, seasonal produce (ike figs,

THE AUSSIE BBQ

The iconic Australian barbecue (BBQ, or barbie) is a near-mandatory cultural experience. In summer locals invite their mates around in the late afternoon and fire up the barbie, grilling burgers, sausages (snags), steaks, seafood, and veggie, meat or seafood skewers – if you're invited, bring some meat and cold beer. The BBQ is wheeled out year-round at weekends for quick-fire lunches. There are also coin-operated and free BBQs in parks around the country – a terrific, traveller-friendly option.

> **BRING YOUR OWN**
>
> If a restaurant is 'BYO', it means you can bring your own alcohol. If the eatery also sells alcohol, you can usually only bring your own bottled wine (no beer, no cask wine) and a 'corkage' charge is added to your bill. The cost is either per person or per bottle, and can be up to $20 per bottle in fine-dining places.

citrus, peaches and avocados), Belgian-style chocolate, boutique beer, olives and much more. For a memorable assemble-your-own picnic, it doesn't get much better than this.

In the Atherton Tableland in north Queensland, you can get a first-hand look at the nation's best coffee-growing plantations. Even better, you'll get to sample the good stuff, plus coffee liqueur and dark-chocolate-coated coffee beans.

Farmers Markets

Local farmers markets are terrific places to sample the culinary riches of the region, support local growers and enjoy the affable airs (including live music, friendly banter and free food sampling). You'll find fruit, veggies, seafood, nuts, meat, bread and pastries, liqueurs, beer, wine, coffee and much more in markets all along the east coast. For locations, check the website of the Australian Farmers' Markets Association (www.farmersmarkets.org.au).

Wine Country

South Australia may be the nation's wine-production behemoth, but the Hunter Valley is Australia's oldest wine region (dating from the 1820s). The Hunter is home to more than 120 wineries, with a mix of boutique, family-run outfits and large-scale commercial vintners. The Lower Hunter is known for shiraz and unwooded semillon. Upper Hunter wineries specialise in cabernet sauvignon and shiraz, with forays into verdelho and chardonnay.

To the south, Victoria has more than 500 wineries. Just northeast of Melbourne, the celebrated Yarra Valley is a patchwork of vines producing fine pinot noir, peachy chardonnay and crisp sparkling wine. Further south, the hills and valleys of the Mornington Peninsula and Bellarine Peninsula produce beautiful cool-climate reds and whites – most famously pinot noir, chardonnay, pinot gris and pinot grigio.

There's even a wine region in Queensland – the Granite Belt, two hours southwest of Brisbane – which has been carving out a name for itself in recent years. The neighbouring towns of Stanthorpe and Ballandean are gateways to this understated region.

Most wineries are open to visitors, with free tastings, though some keep limited hours (opening only on weekends).

Top Foodie Sites

www.broadsheet.com.au (Melbourne, Sydney & Brisbane)

https://grabyourfork.blogspot.com (Sydney)

www.melbournegastronome.com (Melbourne)

www.gourmettraveller.com.au

Sport

Whether they're filling stadiums, glued to the big screen at the pub, or on the couch in front of the TV, Australians invest heavily in sport – both fiscally and emotionally. The federal government kicks in more than $300 million every year – enough cash for the nation to hold its own against formidable international sporting opponents. Despite slipping to 10th place at the 2016 Rio Olympics (down from 58 medals and fourth place in Sydney in 2000), expectations are always high.

Sporting Obsessions

All three east-coast states can stake legitimate claims to the title of Australia's sporting mecca (even Canberra has pro teams and more than its fair share of sports-mad residents). The object of passion, however, varies from state to state. In New South Wales (NSW) and Queensland it's the gladiatorial arena of rugby league, while down south, Victoria is a smouldering cauldron of Australian Football League (AFL). Cricket unifies everyone and is a nationwide obsession in summer.

But these sports are hardly the only games in town. Australians love all sport, from basketball and Formula One to tennis, soccer, horse racing, netball, surfing and even bull riding. When competition is afoot, the roaring crowds will appear (case in point: Brisbane's Australia Day Cockroach Races attract upwards of 7000 cheering fans each year).

Australian Rules Football

Australia's most attended sport is Australian Rules football (Aussie Rules). The Australian Football League (www.afl.com.au) has expanded its popularity across the country, including rugby-dominated NSW and Queensland. Long kicks, high marks and brutal collisions whip crowds into frenzies, and the roar of 50,000-plus fans yelling 'Baaall!!!' upsets dogs in suburban backyards for kilometres around.

During the season (March to September) Australians go footy mad, entering tipping competitions, discussing groin and hamstring strains and savouring the latest in loutish behaviour (on and off the field). It all culminates on the last Saturday in September, when Melbourne hosts the AFL grand final – the whole city goes berserk. Around 100,000 fans pack into the Melbourne Cricket Ground and millions more watch on TV.

Some teams – notably Essendon, Richmond and Port Adelaide – run Indigenous programmes designed to promote the sport in Aboriginal communities across the country, and all teams recruit Indigenous players.

Starting in 2017, the AFL Women's (AFLW) was an instant success. It began with eight teams (all connected with their male counterparts) and expanded to 14 in 2020. Adelaide won in 2017 and 2019, and the Western Bulldogs took the 2018 premiership. The eight-round season begins in February, with the finals in April.

Rugby

The National Rugby League (NRL; www.nrl.com) is the most popular sporting competition north of the Murray River. The competition, which parallels the AFL season from March to September, features 16 teams – 10 from NSW, three from Queensland, and one each from the Australian Capital Territory (ACT), New Zealand and Victoria. To witness an NRL game is to appreciate all of Newton's laws of motion – bone-crunching!

One of the most anticipated events in the league calendar (apart from the grand final in October) is the State of Origin series held in June or July, when all-star players from Queensland take on their counterparts from NSW in explosive state-against-state combat. Queensland's Maroons won eight in a row from 2006 to 2013, although NSW restored some pride with victories in 2014, 2018 and 2019.

The women's national rugby league team is known as the Australian Jillaroos; it won the last two World Cups, in 2013 and as hosts in 2017.

Rugby Union (www.rugby.com.au) is almost as popular as rugby league, at least when it comes to the national team. Historically, union was an amateur sport played by upper-class gents from prestigious British public-school systems, while league was associated with working-class communities of northern England. The ideological divide carried over to Australia, where it has remained to a large degree over the past century.

The national union team, the Wallabies, won the Rugby World Cup in 1991 and 1999, and were runners-up in 2003 and 2015. In between world cups, annual Bledisloe Cup matches between Australia and arch-rival New Zealand (the world-beating All Blacks) draw huge crowds. Bledisloe matches form part of the annual southern-hemisphere Rugby Championship (https://super.rugby/therugbychampionship) played between Australia, New Zealand, South Africa and Argentina.

NRL Premiers

2015 North Queensland Cowboys

2016 Cronulla Sharks

2017 Melbourne Storm

2018 Sydney Roosters

2019 Sydney Roosters

Cricket

The Aussies dominated both test and one-day cricket for much of the noughties, holding the number-one world ranking for most of the decade. But the subsequent retirement of once-in-a-lifetime players such as Shane Warne and Ricky Ponting has sent the team into an extended 'rebuilding' phase. Losses in the biennial Ashes series against arch-enemy England came in 2009, 2011, 2013 and 2015, despite momentary redemption in an unusual 2014 series (the competition is usually only held in odd-numbered years) when Australia demoralised England 5-0. The Ashes trophy is a tiny terracotta urn containing the ashen remnants of an 1882 cricket bail (the perfect Australian BBQ conversation opener: ask a local what a 'bail' is).

In 2018, Australian cricket was throw into chaos by the revelation that members of the team were involved in ball-tampering, a form of cheating in this 'gentleman's game', while on tour in South Africa. Three leading players were banned for up to a year. Improbably, the team retained the Ashes in 2019.

The Women's National Cricket League (WNCL) began in 1996 and involves all states and the ACT playing each other in 50-over one-day games. Since 2008, there has also been the Australian Women's Twenty20 Cup (replaced by the Women's Big Bash League in 2015). The Australian national team has won the Women's World Cup five times (most recently in 2013) and the T20 World Cup five times, including in 2018 and 2020. For current cricketing info, see www.espncricinfo.com or www.cricket.com.au.

The first Australian cricket team to tour England was 100% Victorian Aboriginal – in 1868. The subsequent 'whiteness' of the sport in Australia meant that this achievement was unheralded until quite recently.

Soccer

Australia's national men's soccer team, the Socceroos (www.socceroos.com.au), qualified for the 2006, 2010, 2014 and 2018 World Cups after a long history of almost-but-not-quite getting there. Results have been mixed, from advancing to the second knockout stage of the comp in 2006 to a straight-sets elimination in 2014 and 2018.

The national women's team, the Matildas (www.matildas.com.au), has been much more successful, reaching the quarter-finals of the World Cup in

SURF'S UP!

Australia has been synonymous with surfing ever since the Beach Boys enthused about 'Australia's Narrabeen', one of Sydney's northern beaches, in *Surfin' USA*. Other east-coast surfing hot spots, such as Bells Beach, the Pass at Byron Bay, and Burleigh Heads on the Gold Coast, resonate similarly with international wave addicts. Ironman and surf-life-saving competitions are also held on beaches around the country, attracting dedicated fans.

Quite a few Australian surfers have attained world-champion status. Legendary names in the men's competition include Mark Richards, Tom Carroll, Joel Parkinson and three-time champ Mick Fanning; and in the women's competition there's Wendy Botha, seven-time champion Layne Beachley, six-time winner Stephanie Gilmore and Tyler Wright.

2007, 2011 and 2015. In early 2020, the team was ranked sixth in the world, and Sam Kerr, the team captain, is considered one of the global superstars of the game.

The national men's A-League (www.a-league.com.au) has enjoyed increased popularity in recent years, successfully luring a few big-name international players to bolster the home-grown talent pool.

Tennis

Rod Laver is Australia's most successful men's tennis player, having won 11 Grand Slam titles between 1960 and 1969. Margaret Court won a remarkable 24 Grand Slam singles titles, although her controversial views against same-sex marriage have since made her a divisive figure in Australian public life.

Every January in Melbourne, the Australian Open (www.australianopen. com) attracts more people to Australia than any other sporting event. The men's competition was last won by an Australian, Mark Edmondson, back in 1976 – and after former world number-ones Pat Rafter and Lleyton Hewitt retired in 2003 and 2016 respectively, it appears likely that the wait will continue for a while longer.

An Australian last won the women's competition in 1978, when Chris O'Neil took home the cup. Queenslander Ashleigh (Ash) Barty is Australia's great hope, having won the US Open in 2019 and topping the world women's rankings at the end of 2019.

Swimming

Australia is girt by sea and pockmarked with pools; unsurprisingly, Australians know how to swim. Australia's greatest female swimmer, Dawn Fraser, won the 100m freestyle gold at three successive Olympics (1956–64), plus the 4 x 100m freestyle relay in 1956. Australia's greatest male swimmer, Ian Thorpe (aka Thorpie or the Thorpedo), retired in 2006 aged 24, with five Olympic golds swinging from his neck. In early 2011 Thorpe announced his comeback, with his eye fixed on the 2012 London Olympics, but he failed to make the team in the selection trials. Australia's swim team won 20 medals (including six golds) at the 2008 Olympics, but more recent results at the 2012 and 2016 Games (10 medals at each, one and three golds respectively) have prompted much soul-searching.

Horse Racing

Michelle Payne became the first female jockey to win the Melbourne Cup, when she rode Prince of Penzance to victory in 2015.

Australia's biggest race – the 'race that stops a nation' – is the Melbourne Cup (www.flemington.com.au/melbourne-cup-carnival), which occurs on the first Tuesday in November. The most famous Melbourne Cup winner was the New Zealand–born horse Phar Lap, who won in 1930 before dying of a mysterious illness (suspected arsenic poisoning) in America. Phar Lap is now a prize exhibit in the **Melbourne Museum** (⏍13 11 02; www.museum victoria.com.au; 11 Nicholson St, Carlton; adult/child $15/free; ⊙10am-5pm; 🚻; 🚊City Circle, 86, 96, 🚆Parliament). The British-bred Makybe Diva is a more recent star, winning three cups in a row before retiring in 2005.

The Melbourne Cup, and the Australian horse-racing industry in general, has lost some of its lustre (and popular support) in recent years, with damning media reports on the mistreatment of current and former racehorses.

Survival Guide

Directory A–Z

Accessible Travel

Disability awareness in Australia is reasonably high. Legislation requires that new accommodation must meet accessibility standards and tourist operators must not discriminate. Facilities for wheelchairs are improving in accommodation, but there are still many older establishments where the necessary upgrades haven't been made: call ahead to confirm.

Download Lonely Planet's free Accessible Travel guides from http://lptravel.to/AccessibleTravel.

Resources

Australian Tourist Commission (www.australia.com) Publishes detailed, downloadable information for people with disabilities, including travel and transport tips and contact addresses of organisations in each state.

Deaf Australia (https://deaf australia.org.au)

National Disability Services (☑02-6283 3200; www.nds.org.au) The national industry association for disability services.

National Information Communication & Awareness Network (NICAN; https://catalogue.nla.gov.au) Australia-wide directory providing information on access, accommodation, sports and recreational activities, transport and specialist tour operators.

Travellers' Aid (www.travellers aid.org.au) Help for visitors with special needs, including equipment hire and care-taking services.

Vision Australia (www.vision australia.org) Australia's largest provider of services for the blind and partially sighted.

Bargaining

Gentle haggling can be observed at weekend markets and vintage shops, but it's generally not the done thing in Australia, where prices are fixed. It's acceptable to ask for a discount on expensive items when paying cash or buying more than one item. In most instances you're expected to pay the stated price.

Customs Regulations

Entering Australia you can bring in most articles free of duty, provided customs officers are satisfied they're for personal use and that you'll be taking them with you when you leave. See www.border.gov.au for more information.

➡ There's a duty-free quota per person of 2.25L of alcohol (if you're over 18 years of age), 25 cigarettes (yes, you read that right) plus an open packet and dutiable goods up to the value of $900 ($450 if you're under 18).

➡ Amounts of more than A$10,000 cash (or its equivalent) must be declared.

➡ Authorities take biosecurity very seriously, and are vigilant in their efforts to prevent introduced pests getting into the

---

PRACTICALITIES

Newspapers Leaf through the daily *Sydney Morning Herald*, Melbourne's *Age*, Brisbane's *Courier-Mail* or the national *Australian* newspapers.

Radio Tune in to ABC radio (www.abc.net.au/radio).

TV The main free-to-air TV channels are the government-sponsored ABC, multicultural SBS and the three commercial networks – Seven, Nine and Ten – plus numerous additional channels from these main players.

Smoking Illegal in pubs, bars, restaurants, offices, shops, theatres etc, and within certain signposted distances of public-facility doorways (airports, bus depots, cinemas etc).

Weights & Measures Australia uses the metric system.

country. Be sure to declare all goods of animal or vegetable origin. Dispose of any fresh food and flowers. If you've recently visited farmland or rural areas, it's best to scrub your shoes before you get to the airport; you'll also need to declare them to Customs.

Discount Cards

Senior Cards Travellers over 60 with some form of identification (eg a Seniors Card: www.australia.gov.au/information-and-services/benefits-and-payments/older-australians/seniors-card) are often eligible for concession prices. Most Australian states and territories issue their own versions of these, which can be used Australia-wide.

Student, Youth & Teacher Cards The internationally recognised International Student Identity Card (www.isic.org) is available to full-time students aged 12 and over. The card gives the bearer discounts on accommodation, transport and admission to various attractions. The same organisation also produces the International Youth Travel Card (IYTC), issued to people under 26 to 30 years of age (depending on country of provider) and not full-time students. It has benefits equivalent to the ISIC. Also similar is the International Teacher Identity Card (ITIC), available to teaching professionals. All three cards are available online or from student travel companies ($30).

Etiquette

There are very few rules of etiquette to take into account in Australia.

Greetings Usually a simple 'G'day', smile or nod suffices when passing people. Shake hands with men or women when meeting for the first time. Australians expect a firm handshake with eye contact.

Aboriginal Communities Direct eye contact can be considered

overbearing. Be respectful, wait to be acknowledged and respond in a like manner.

Dry Communities Check whether alcohol restrictions apply when visiting remote communities. You may be breaking the law if you have booze in your vehicle.

BBQs Bring your own drinks, and some sausages (aka 'snags') if invited to a BBQ.

Photography Ask before taking pictures of people. Particularly bear in mind that for Aboriginal Australians, photography can be highly intrusive, and photographing cultural places, practices and images, sites of significance and ceremonies may not be welcomed. Respect is essential.

Electricity

Type I
230V/50Hz

Embassies & Consulates

Canberra has a full suite of foreign embassies, while many countries also maintain consulates in Sydney and/or Melbourne. There are also some in Brisbane and a couple in Cairns. See http://protocol.dfat.gov.au.

EATING PRICE RANGES

The following price ranges refer to a main course.

$ less than $15

$$ $15–32

$$$ more than $32

Health

Although there are plenty of hazards in Australia, few travellers should experience anything worse than sunburn or a hangover. If you do fall ill, health-care standards are high.

Health Insurance

Health insurance is essential for all travellers. You may prefer a policy that pays doctors or hospitals directly rather than requiring you to pay on the spot and claim later. If you have to claim later make sure you keep all documentation. Check that the policy covers ambulances and emergency medical evacuations by air.

Availability & Cost of Health Care

The Medicare system covers Australian residents for some health-care costs. Visitors from countries with which Australia has a reciprocal health-care agreement are eligible for benefits specified under the Medicare program. Agreements are currently in place with Belgium, Finland, Italy, Malta, the Netherlands, New Zealand, Ireland, Norway, Slovenia, Sweden and the UK; check the details before departing these countries. For further details, visit www.humanservices.gov.au/customer/subjects/medicare-services. But even if you're not covered by Medicare, a short consultation with a local GP will usually only set you back $60 or $70.

PHARMACEUTICALS

Painkillers, antihistamines for allergies, and skincare products are widely available at chemists (pharmacies) throughout Australia. You may find that medications readily available over the counter in some countries are only available in Australia by prescription. These include the oral contraceptive pill, some medications for asthma and all antibiotics.

Tap Water

Tap water in Australia is generally safe to drink. Water taken from streams, rivers and lakes should be treated before drinking.

Insurance

A good travel-insurance policy covering theft, loss and medical problems is essential. Some policies specifically exclude designated 'dangerous activities' such as scuba diving, white-water rafting and even bushwalking. Make sure the policy you choose fully covers you for your activity of choice, and covers ambulances and emergency medical evacuations by air.

Worldwide travel insurance is available at www.lonelyplanet.com/travel-insurance. You can buy, extend and claim online anytime – even if you're already on the road.

Internet Access

➡ By far the easiest way to access the internet is to buy a local prepaid SIM card, pop it in your (unlocked) phone and sign up for a data package. Expect to pay around $2 for the SIM, then $30 to $50 for a month of calls, texts and data.

➡ Nearly all hotels and hostels provide wi-fi connections, although some, especially top-end places, charge for the service, or make the free service so slow that you are virtually forced to pay for 'premium' access.

➡ Many cafes and bars offer free wi-fi. Most public libraries and shopping centres also offer it.

➡ Pay-as-you-go wi-fi hotspots are common in busy areas such as airports.

Legal Matters

➡ Australia is very strict when it comes to driving under the influence of alcohol or illegal drugs. There is a significant police presence on the roads, and they have the power to stop your car and see your licence (you're required to carry it), check your vehicle for roadworthiness and insist that you take a breath test for alcohol or a drug test. The legal limit is 0.05 blood alcohol concentration (measured as grams per 100mL, equivalent to what many other countries would call 0.5). If you're over, you face a hefty fine and other sanctions.

➡ First offenders caught with small amounts of illegal drugs are likely to receive a fine rather than go to jail, but a conviction may affect your visa status.

➡ If you remain in Australia after your visa expires, you will officially be an 'overstayer' and could face detention and expulsion, and then be prevented from returning to Australia for up to three years.

LGBTIQ+ Travellers

Australia's east coast – Sydney especially – is a popular destination for LGBTIQ+ travellers. The legendary annual **Sydney Gay & Lesbian Mardi Gras** (www.mardigras.org.au; ⊙Feb-Mar) draws huge numbers of visitors, as does Melbourne's **Midsumma Festival** (www.midsumma.org.au; ⊙Jan-Feb).

In general, Australians are open-minded about same-sex relationships, but the further out of the cities you get, the more likely you are to run into homophobia. Same-sex acts are legal in all states.

Gay and lesbian magazines include *DNA*, *Lesbians on the Loose (LOTL)* and the Sydney-based *SX* (resurrected under a new owner in 2019). In Queensland look for *Queensland Pride*. The country-wide *Star Observer* is Australia's longest-running publication for the LGBTIQ+ community.

In Melbourne, tune into JOY 94.9FM for Australia's only LGBTIQ+ radio station.

Resources

Gay & Lesbian Tourism Australia (https://visitgayaustralia.com.au)

Gay News Network (www.facebook.com/gaynewsnetwork)

QNews (https://qnews.com.au)

Same Same (www.facebook.com/samesame)

Maps

You'll find plenty of maps available when you arrive in Australia. Visitor centres usually have free maps of the region and towns, although quality varies. Automobile associations are a good source of reliable road maps. Hema Maps (www.hemamaps.com) produces excellent, inexpensive road maps of Australia's various regions. Maps.ME is a useful app that works even if you're offline; download the relevant part of the country in advance.

Unfortunately, Geoscience Australia (www.ga.gov.au) has stopped printing its excellent topographic sheet maps, which are useful for bushwalking and other activities that require large-scale maps. However, they are still available digitally and are free to download.

Money

There are ATMs everywhere and major credit cards are widely accepted, though there's often a surcharge. Cryptocurrency (particularly Bitcoin) is accepted at some major tourist destinations.

ATMs, Eftpos & payWave

ATMs ATMs proliferate in east-coast cities, but don't expect to find them everywhere, certainly not off the beaten track or in small towns. Most ATMs accept cards issued by other banks (for a fee) and are linked to international networks.

Eftpos & payWave Many service stations, supermarkets, restaurants, cafes and shops have Electronic Funds Transfer at Point of Sale (Eftpos) facilities, allowing you to make purchases (with your credit or debit card) and even withdraw cash (with your debit card), though this has mostly been superseded by payWave, which is hugely common.

Fees Remember that withdrawing cash through ATMs or Eftpos may incur significant fees – check the costs with your bank first.

Credit & Debit Cards

Credit cards such as Master Card and Visa are widely accepted for most accommodation and services, and a credit card is essential to hire a car. They can also be used to get cash advances over the counter at banks and from many ATMs, depending on the card – but these withdrawals incur immediate interest. Diners Club and American Express cards are not as widely accepted.

Businesses often pass on their bank fees to customers, so a 1% to 2% surcharge is common if you pay by card. An increasing number of places don't take cash, but there are also places that don't take cards.

Currency

The Australian dollar comprises 100 cents. There are 5c, 10c, 20c, 50c, $1 and $2 coins, and $5, $10, $20, $50 and $100 notes.

Money Changers

Changing foreign currency is usually no problem at banks throughout Australia, or at licensed money changers such as Travelex or AmEx in airports and cities. Expect substantial fees.

Taxes & Refunds

There's a 10% goods and services tax (GST) automatically added to almost everything you buy, Australia-wide. If you purchase goods with a total minimum value of $300 from any one shop within 60 days of departure from Australia, the Tourist Refund Scheme entitles you to a refund of any GST paid (see www.abf.gov.au/entering-and-leaving-australia/tourist-refund-scheme for more information).

Tipping

Tipping isn't traditionally part of Australian etiquette, but it's increasingly the norm to tip around 10% for good service in restaurants, and a few dollars for porters (bell-hops) and taxi drivers.

Opening Hours

Business hours vary from state to state, but use the following as a guide:

Banks 9.30am–4pm Monday to Thursday, to 5pm Friday

Bars 4pm–late

Cafes 7am–5pm

Nightclubs 10pm–4am Thursday to Saturday

Post offices 9am–5pm Monday to Friday; some also 9am–noon Saturday

Pubs 11am–midnight

Restaurants noon–2.30pm and 6–9pm

Shops 9am–4pm

Supermarkets 7am–9pm

Post

Australia Post (www.auspost.com.au) is the nationwide provider. Most substantial towns have a post office, or an Australia Post desk within a bank. Services are reliable, but slower than they used to be (recent cost-saving cutbacks are to blame). Express Post delivers a parcel or envelope interstate within Australia by the next business day; otherwise, allow four days for urban deliveries, and longer for country areas.

Public Holidays

Public holidays vary from state to state (and sometimes year to year). The following is a list of the main national and state public holidays; check locally for precise dates.

National

New Year's Day 1 January

Australia Day 26 January

Easter (Good Friday to Easter Monday inclusive) Late March or early April

Anzac Day 25 April

Queen's Birthday Second Monday in June

Christmas Day 25 December

Boxing Day 26 December

Australian Capital Territory

Canberra Day Second Monday in March

Bank Holiday First Monday in August

Labour Day First Monday in October

New South Wales

Bank Holiday First Monday in August

Labour Day First Monday in October

Queensland

Labour Day First Monday in May

Royal Queensland Show Day (Brisbane) Second or third Wednesday in August

EMERGENCY APP

There's a new app put out by Emergency services to help locate people in an emergency – recommended for download by bushwalkers etc. It's called Emergency+ (https://emergencyapp.triplezero.gov.au).

Victoria

Labour Day Second Monday in March

Melbourne Cup Day First Tuesday in November

School Holidays

Below are key times when prices are highest and much accommodation is booked out in advance:

➡ Christmas holiday season (mid-December to late January)

➡ Easter (March–April)

➡ Shorter (two-week) school-holiday periods generally fall in mid-April, late June to mid-July, and late September to mid-October.

Safe Travel

Australia is a relatively safe and friendly place to travel, but natural disasters regularly wreak havoc. Bush fires, floods and cyclones can devastate local areas as weather events become more extreme and unpredictable.

➡ Check weather warnings and don't venture into affected areas without an emergency plan.

➡ Crime is low but don't let your guard *too* far down.

➡ Beware of online house rental scams in Australia. Follow best practice when transferring money overseas.

➡ Wild swimming can be dangerous here thanks to rips, sharks, jellyfish and

crocodiles – always seek reliable information.

➡ Watch for wandering wildlife on roads, especially at night. Kangaroos are very unpredictable.

Surviving Bush Fires

Bush fires in Australia tend to last longer and cause more devastation every summer and may well affect your travel plans if you're travelling during fire season.

Check weather forecasts in advance. If it looks like an existing bush fire is likely to affect your destination, consider changing your plans.

One of the best apps for monitoring wildfires is **Australian Fires**, divided into five regional apps, it provide up-to-date information about the location and severity of fires.

Each district in Australia is given a Fire Danger Rating on any given day, ranging from Low-Moderate to Code Red (catastrophic). The rating is your prompt to take action to stay safe.

If the destination you're in is threatened by bush fires, pay attention to the news and heed official warnings. Follow orders to evacuate if such orders are given.

During a bush fire emergency in your area, you may receive an emergency warning on your mobile phone if you have an Australian SIM card. Find out more about the Emergency Alert system at www.emergencyalert.gov.au.

If it's likely that you may have to drive through an area affected by wildfires, it's worth buying a particulate respirator mask in advance. It needs to have P95 or P100 filters to give you some protection from smoke particles.

Should you be in a destination where evacuation routes are cut off by fire, do the following:

➡ Stock up on water and make sure you have a torch as power is likely to be shut off.

➡ If you're an asthmatic, make sure you have your medication to hand.

➡ Take shelter inside your hotel or guesthouse and close all doors, windows, blinds, vents and curtains to prevent flames, embers and smoke from entering.

➡ Fill your bath, sinks and any buckets with water so you can put out any fires that start inside.

➡ Place wet towels around your door and window edges to stop embers and smoke from entering.

Telephone

Mobile Phones

Use global roaming (check with your service provider to see whether it has a free roaming agreement with Australia) or pick up a local SIM card with a prepaid account from one of the four main providers (Telstra, Optus, Vodafone or Virgin). ID is usually required. The east coast generally gets good mobile-phone reception, but service can be haphazard or non-existent in the interior and far north (eg the Daintree Rainforest). Local numbers with the prefix 04xx belong to mobile phones.

Local Calls

➡ Local calls from private phones cost 30c and are untimed.

➡ Local calls from public phones cost 50c and are untimed.

➡ Calls to mobile phones attract higher rates and are timed.

International Calls

➡ When calling overseas you need to dial the international access code from Australia (0011), the country code then the area code (without the initial 0).

➡ If calling Australia from overseas, the country code is 61 and you need to drop the 0 in the state/territory area codes.

Long Distance Calls & Area Codes

➡ STD (long-distance) calls can be made from private phones, mobile phones and virtually any public phone and are cheaper during off-peak hours (7pm to 7am).

➡ When calling from one area to another area within the same area code, there's no need to dial the area code before the local number. If these calls are long-distance (more than 50km away), they're charged at long-distance rates, even though they have the same area code.

➡ Area codes on the east coast:

State/Territory	Area Code
ACT	✎02
NSW	✎02
Queensland	✎07
Victoria	✎03

Information & Toll-Free Calls

➡ Toll-free numbers (prefix 1800) can be called free of charge, though they may not be accessible from certain areas or from mobile phones.

➡ Calls to numbers beginning with 13 or 1300 are charged at the rate of a local call.

➡ To make a reverse-charge (collect) call within Australia, dial 1800-REVERSE (1800 738 3773) from any public or private phone.

➡ Telephone numbers beginning with either 1800, 13 or 1300 cannot be dialled from outside Australia.

Phonecards

A variety of phonecards can be bought at newsagents, hostels and post offices for a fixed dollar value (usually $10, $20 etc) and can be used with any public or private phone. Shop around.

Most public phones use phonecards; some also accept credit cards. Old-fashioned coin-operated public phones are rare.

VoIP

The cheapest way to call abroad from Australia is using Skype, WhatsApp, FaceTime or other inexpensive/free Voice over Internet Protocol services.

Time

Australia is divided into three time zones:

Eastern Standard Time (GMT plus 10 hours) Queensland, New South Wales (NSW), Australian Capital Territory (ACT), Victoria and Tasmania.

Central Standard Time (half-hour behind Eastern Standard Time) Northern Territory, South Australia.

Western Standard Time (two hours behind Eastern Standard Time) Western Australia.

Note that Queensland remains on Eastern Standard Time all year, while most of the rest of Australia switches to daylight saving time over the summer (October to early April), when clocks are wound forward one hour.

Toilets

➡ Toilets in Australia are sit-down Western style and plentiful at roadside rest areas and gas stations.

➡ Most public toilets are free of charge and reasonably well looked-after.

➡ See www.toiletmap.gov.au for public toilet locations, including disabled-access toilets.

Tourist Information

Tourist information is provided in Australia by various regional and local offices – often info centres staffed by volunteers in key tourist spots. Each state also has a government-run tourist organisation ready to inundate you with information:

New South Wales (www.visitnsw.com)

Queensland (www.queensland.com)

Victoria (www.visitvictoria.com)

The Australian Tourist Commission (www.australia.com) is the countrywide government body charged with luring foreign visitors.

Visas

All visitors to Australia need visas; only New Zealanders are granted a visa on arrival. Apply online through the **Department of Immigration & Border Protection** (✎02-6275 6666, 1300 363 263; www.homeaffairs.gov.au).

eVisitor (651)

➡ Many European passport holders are eligible for a free eVisitor visa, allowing stays in Australia for up to three months within a 12-month period.

➡ eVisitor visas must be applied for online. They are electronically stored and linked to individual passport numbers, so no stamp in your passport is required.

➡ It's advisable to apply at least 14 days prior to the proposed date of travel to Australia.

Electronic Travel Authority (ETA; 601)

➡ Passport holders from the European countries eligible for eVisitor visas, plus passport holders from Brunei, Canada, Hong Kong, Japan, Malaysia, Singapore, South Korea and the USA, must apply for either a visitor ETA or business ETA.

➡ ETAs are valid for 12 months, with stays of up to three months on each visit.

➡ ETA visas cost $20.

Visitor (600)

➡ Short-term Visitor visas have largely been replaced by the eVisitor and ETA. However, if you're from a country not covered by either, or you want to stay longer than three months, you'll need to apply for a Visitor visa.

➡ Standard Visitor visas allow one entry for a stay of up to three, six or 12 months, and are valid for use within 12 months of issue.

➡ Visitor visas cost from $145 to $1065.

Work & Holiday (462)

➡ Nationals from Argentina, Austria, Chile, China, Czech Republic, Ecuador, Greece, Hungary, Indonesia, Israel, Luxembourg, Malaysia, Peru, Poland, Portugal, San Marino, Singapore, Slovak Republic, Slovenia, Spain, Thailand, Turkey, Uruguay, USA and Vietnam aged between 18 and 30 can apply for a Work and Holiday visa prior to entry to Australia.

➡ Applicants from Indonesia, Singapore, Thailand, Turkey and Vietnam must apply online through ImmiAccount (https://immi.homeaffairs.gov.au/help-support).

➡ Once granted, this visa allows the holder to enter Australia within three months of issue, stay for up to 12 months, leave and re-enter Australia any number of times within those 12 months, undertake temporary employment to supplement a trip, and study for up to four months.

➡ The application fee is $485.

Working Holiday (417)

➡ Young (aged 18 to 30) visitors from Belgium, Canada, Cyprus, Denmark, Estonia, Finland, France, Germany, Hong Kong, Ireland, Italy, Japan, the Republic of Korea, Malta, the Netherlands, Norway, Sweden, Taiwan and the UK are eligible for a Working Holiday visa, which allows you to visit for up to 12 months and gain casual employment.

➡ Holders can leave and re-enter Australia any number of times within those 12 months.

➡ Holders can only work for any one employer for a maximum of six months.

➡ Apply prior to entry to Australia (up to a year in advance); you can't change from another tourist visa to a Working Holiday visa once you're in Australia.

➡ Conditions include having a return air ticket or sufficient funds ($5000) for a return or onward fare.

➡ Application fee $485.

➡ Second Working Holiday visas can be applied for once you're in Australia, subject to certain conditions.

➡ Second Working Holiday visa holders may apply for a third Working Holiday visa once they are in Australia, subject to certain conditions.

Visa Extensions

If you want to stay in Australia for longer than your visa allows, you'll need to apply for a new visa (usually a Visitor visa 600). Apply online (https://immi.homeaffairs.gov.au/visas) at least two or three weeks before your visa expires.

Volunteering

Lonely Planet's *Volunteer: A Traveller's Guide to Making a Difference Around the World* provides useful information about volunteering.

Resources

Conservation Volunteers Australia (www.conservation volunteers.com.au) Nonprofit organisation involved in tree planting, walking-track construction, and flora and fauna surveys.

Go Volunteer (www.govolunteer.com.au) National website listing volunteer opportunities.

Greening Australia (www.greeningaustralia.org.au) Helps volunteers get involved with environmental projects in the bush or in plant nurseries.

Reef Check (www.reefcheck australia.org) Trains volunteers to monitor the health of the Great Barrier Reef (not so healthy of late...).

Sea Turtle Foundation (www.seaturtlefoundation.org) Volunteer opportunities in sea-turtle conservation.

Volunteering Australia (www.volunteeringaustralia.org) Support, advice and volunteer training.

Volunteering Queensland (www.volunteeringqld.org.au) Volunteering info and advice across Queensland.

Willing Workers on Organic Farms (www.wwoof.com.au) A website with information about WWOOFing, where you do a few hours' work each day on a farm in return for bed and board.

Women Travellers

The east coast is generally a safe place for women travellers, although the usual sensible precautions apply. Sexual harassment is rare, though it still occurs – especially in rural areas when macho Aussie males have been drinking. Hitchhiking isn't such a great idea anywhere in Australia these days, even when travelling in pairs.

Work

If you come to Australia on a tourist visa then you're not allowed to work for pay. You'll need either a Work & Holiday (462) or Working Holiday (417) visa; see www.home affairs.gov.au for details.

Finding Work

Casual hospitality work can often be found during peak season in tourist hubs, such as Cairns, the Gold Coast and resort towns along the Queensland coast.

Seasonal fruit picking (harvesting) relies on casual labour, and there is something to be picked, pruned or farmed somewhere in Australia year-round (just don't expect to make a fortune).

People with computer, secretarial, nursing and teaching skills can find work temping in the major cities (via employment agencies).

Resources

Backpacker noticeboards and local newspapers are good resources for local work opportunities.

Australian JobSearch (www. jobsearch.gov.au) Myriad jobs across the country.

Career One (www.careerone. com.au) General employment site; good for metropolitan areas.

Harvest Trail (www.harvesttrail. gov.au) Harvest job specialists.

National Harvest Telephone Information Service (☎1800 062 332) Advice on when and where you're likely to pick up harvest work.

Seek (www.seek.com.au) General employment site; good for metropolitan areas.

Travellers at Work (www.taw. com.au) Excellent site for working travellers in Australia.

Workabout Australia (www. workaboutaustralia.com.au) Gives a state-by-state breakdown of seasonal work opportunities.

Income Tax

If you're earning money in Australia, you'll be paying tax in Australia and will have to lodge a tax return. See the website of the Australian Taxation Office (www.ato. gov.au) for info on how to do this, including getting a payment summary from your employer, timing and dates for lodging returns, and receiving your notice of assessment.

As part of this process you'll need to apply for a Tax File Number (TFN) to give your employer. Without it, tax will be deducted at the maximum rate from your wages. Apply online via the Australian Taxation Office; it takes up to four weeks to be issued.

Transport

GETTING THERE & AWAY

Australia's east coast is a long way from just about everywhere (including Australia's west coast) – getting here usually means a long-haul flight. Flights, tours and rail tickets can be booked online at lonelyplanet.com/bookings.

Entering the Country

If you're arriving on the east coast on an international flight, the process is usually straightforward and efficient, with the usual passport checks and customs declarations.

Air

High season (with the highest prices) for flights into Australia is roughly over the country's summer (December to February); low season generally tallies with the winter months (June to August), though this is actually peak season in the tropical north.

Airports & Airlines

On the east coast, most international flights head to Sydney, Melbourne or Brisbane, though Cairns and the Gold Coast, Canberra and Geelong also receive the occasional international flight.

Brisbane Airport (www.bne.com.au; Airport Dr)

Cairns Airport (✈07-4080 6703; www.cairnsairport.com; Airport Ave)

Canberra Airport (✈02-6275 2222; www.canberraairport.com.au; Terminal Ave, Pialligo)

Gold Coast Airport (OOL; ✈07-5589 1100; www.goldcoastairport.com.au; Eastern Ave, Bilinga)

Melbourne Airport (✈03-9297 1600; www.melbourneairport.com.au; Departure Dr, Tullamarine; ☎)

Sydney Airport (Kingsford Smith Airport, Mascot Airport; ✈02-9667 9111; www.sydneyairport.com.au; Airport Dr, Mascot; ☒Domestic Airport, ☒International Airport)

Australia's international carrier is Qantas (www.qantas.com), which has an outstanding safety record. Qantas offers a discount-fare Walkabout Pass for passengers flying into Australia from overseas with Qantas or American Airlines. The pass allows you to link around 29 domestic Australian destinations for less than you'd pay booking flights individually. See www.qantas.com for more information.

Land

If you're exploring the whole of Australia, travelling overland to the east coast from elsewhere in this wide red land may well be how you arrive.

CLIMATE CHANGE & TRAVEL

Every form of transport that relies on carbon-based fuel generates CO_2, the main cause of human-induced climate change. Modern travel is dependent on aeroplanes, which might use less fuel per kilometre per person than most cars but travel much greater distances. The altitude at which aircraft emit gases (including CO_2) and particles also contributes to their climate change impact. Many websites offer 'carbon calculators' that allow people to estimate the carbon emissions generated by their journey and, for those who wish to do so, to offset the impact of the greenhouse gases emitted with contributions to portfolios of climate-friendly initiatives throughout the world. Lonely Planet offsets the carbon footprint of all staff and author travel.

Bus

Aside from bus routes linking the states along the east coast, long-distance buses truck into Queensland from the Northern Territory (NT), and into Victoria and New South Wales (NSW) from South Australia (SA). Greyhound (www.greyhound.com.au) is the main interstate player.

Car & Motorcycle

The highways rolling into Victoria, NSW and Queensland from SA and the NT are in good shape and well trafficked.

Train

Trains from Adelaide roll into Melbourne, and into Sydney from as far off as Perth; Journey Beyond Rail (https://journeybeyondrail.com.au) is the operator.

Sea

Cruise & Cargo Ship

P&O Cruises (www.pocruises.com.au) operates holiday cruises between Brisbane, Melbourne or Sydney and destinations in New Zealand and the Pacific.

Alternatively, some freighter ships allow passengers to travel on board as they ship cargo to/from Australia: see websites such as www.freighterexpeditions.com.au and www.freightercruises.com for options.

Yacht

It is possible (if not straightforward) to travel between Australia and Papua New Guinea, Indonesia, New Zealand and the Pacific islands by hitching rides or crewing on yachts – usually you have to at least contribute towards food. Ask around at marinas and sailing clubs in places such as Coffs Harbour, Great Keppel Island, Airlie Beach, the Whitsundays and Cairns. April is a good time to look for a berth in the Sydney area.

GETTING AROUND

Air

East coast Australia is well serviced by airlines big and small.

FlyPelican (www.flypelican.com.au) Connects Sydney with Newcastle, Byron Bay, Taree and other NSW destinations.

Hinterland Aviation (www.hinterlandaviation.com.au) Connects Cairns to Cooktown, Kowanyama, Palm Island and other north Queensland destinations.

Jetstar (www.jetstar.com) Budget offshoot of Qantas; has extensive services to destinations all over Australia, plus Tasmania.

Qantas (www.qantas.com) Australia's main player; extensive services.

REX (www.rex.com.au) Connects Melbourne, Adelaide, Sydney, Brisbane, Cairns, Townsville and Perth with small regional airports.

Skytrans (www.skytrans.com.au) Serves northern Queensland and the Torres Strait, flying from Cairns to Kowanyama, Saibai Island and other little-visited locations.

Virgin Australia (www.virginaustralia.com.au) Services major destinations throughout Australia.

Bicycle

Whether you're hiring a bike to ride around a city or wearing out your sprockets on a long-distance haul, the east coast is ideal for cycling. There are bike paths in most cities, and in the country you'll find thousands of kilometres of good (and not too hilly) roads. Many touring cyclists carry camping equipment, but it's feasible to travel from town to town staying in hostels, hotels or caravan parks.

> ### DEPARTURE TAX
> Departure tax is included in the price of a ticket.

Legalities Bicycle helmets are compulsory, as are white front lights and red rear lights for riding at night.

Weather and safety Always carry plenty of water. Wear high-vis clothing, a helmet with a peak (or a cap under your helmet), use sunscreen and avoid cycling in the middle of the day. Beware summer northerlies that can make a northbound cyclist's life hell. It can get very cold in Victoria and inland NSW, so pack appropriate clothing.

Bicycle Hire

Rates charged by most rental outfits for road or mountain bikes range from $10 to $15 per hour and $25 to $50 per day. Security deposits can range from $50 to $200, depending on the rental period.

Buying a Bike

For a new road or mountain bike in Australia, your bottom-level starting price will be around $600. With all the requisite on-the-road equipment (panniers, helmet, lights etc) you're looking at upwards of $1700.

To sell your bike (or buy a secondhand one), try hostel noticeboards or online at Trading Post (www.tradingpost.com.au), Gumtree (www.gumtree.com.au) or Bike Exchange (www.bikeexchange.com.au).

Resources

Each state and territory has a cycling organisation that can help with local information and put you in touch with touring clubs:

Bicycle Network Victoria (www.bicyclenetwork.com.au)

Bicycle NSW (www.bicyclensw.org.au)

Bicycle Queensland (www.bq.org.au)

Pedal Power ACT
(www.pedalpower.org.au)

TRANSPORT BOAT

Boat

There are no formal east-coast ferry services, but sailing up and down the coast in a yacht is a possibility. Ask around at marinas in Coffs Harbour, Great Keppel Island, Airlie Beach, the Whitsundays, Sydney and Cairns.

Bus

East coast Australia's bus network is reliable, but not the cheapest for long hauls. Most buses have air-con and toilets; all are smoke-free. There are no separate classes on buses. Book seats at least a day ahead (a week or two during summer). Small towns eschew formal bus terminals for an informal drop-off/pick-up point, usually outside a post office or shop.

Bus Companies

Long-distance bus route operators include the following:

Con-x-ion (www.con-x-ion.com) Connects Sydney, Melbourne, Brisbane, Gold Coast and Sunshine Coast airports with surrounding areas.

Firefly Express (www.firefly express.com.au) Runs between Sydney, Melbourne and Adelaide.

Greyhound Australia (www.greyhound.com.au) The main player, with an extensive nationwide network.

NSW TrainLink (https://transportnsw.info) Coach and train services in NSW.

Premier Motor Service (www.premierms.com.au) Greyhound's main competitor on the east coast. Runs hop-on, hop-off services between major destinations.

Trans North (www.transnorthbus.com.au) Cairns to Cooktown via the inland route (Kuranda, Mareeba) or the coast (Port Douglas, Daintree).

V/Line (www.vline.com.au) Bus connections from the likes of

Ballarat, Seymour and Gippsland, complementing Victorian regional train services.

Costs

Following are typical, non-discounted, one-way bus fares for some popular east-coast routes:

Route	Fare ($)	Duration (hr)
Brisbane–Airlie Beach	260	19
Brisbane–Cairns	347	29-32
Melbourne–Canberra	83	8
Melbourne–Sydney	107	12
Sydney–Brisbane	178	13-15½
Sydney–Byron Bay	158	10½-12½
Townsville–Cairns	63	5½

Reservations

During summer, school holidays and public holidays, you should book well ahead, especially on intercity services. At other times you should have few problems getting onto your preferred service.

Reserve at least a day in advance if you're using a travel pass.

Bus Passes

Bus passes are a good option if you plan on multiple stopovers. Book online or phone at least a day ahead to reserve a seat.

Greyhound offers myriad money-saving passes; check the website for comprehensive info. The main options:

Hop-On/Hop-Off Passes Up to 90 days of one-direction travel along eight popular long-haul routes – including Cairns to Melbourne ($579) and Brisbane to Cairns ($365) – stopping as often as you like.

Whimit Pass Gives you go-anywhere flexibility, plus the choice to backtrack within a certain time period.

Fifteen-/60-/365-day passes cost $329/449/1699.

Premier Motor Service offers several passes for one-way travel along the east coast, including a one- and six-month pass between Sydney and Cairns ($230/361), a three-month pass between Sydney and Brisbane ($103) and a six-month pass from Byron Bay to Cairns ($278).

Car & Motorcycle

The most flexible way to see the east coast is by car – it's certainly the only way to access interesting out-of-the-way places without taking a tour.

Motorcycles are popular, as the climate is ideal for bikes for much of the year. A fuel range of 350km will easily cover fuel stops along the coast. The long, open roads here are really made for large-capacity motorbikes (750cc and up).

Driving Licences

To drive in Australia you'll need to hold a current driving licence issued in English from your home country. If the licence isn't in English, you'll also need to carry an International Driving Permit, issued in your home country.

Fuel

Diesel and unleaded petrol are available from service stations. LPG (gas) is also available in populated areas, but not always at more remote service stations. On main east-coast highways there's usually a small town or petrol station every 50km or so.

Prices vary from place to place, but at the time of writing the average price of unleaded was hovering around $1.55 in the cities. Out in the country, prices can soar.

Automobile Associations

The national **Australian Automobile Association** (AAA; ☎02-6247 7311; www.

aaa.asn.au) is the umbrella organisation for the various state associations.

The state organisations have reciprocal arrangements with other states and with similar organisations overseas, including AAA in the USA and RAC or AA in the UK. Bring proof of membership with you.

NRMA (☑13 11 22; www.my nrma.com.au) Covers NSW and the Australian Capital Territory (ACT).

RACQ (☑13 19 05; www.racq. com.au) Covers Queensland.

RACV (☑13 72 28; www.racv. com.au) Covers Victoria.

Hire

There are plenty of car-rental companies, big and small, ready to put you behind the wheel. The main thing to remember is distance – if you want to travel far, you'll need unlimited kilometres.

Larger car hirecompanies have drop-offs in major cities and towns. Smaller local firms are sometimes cheaper but may have restrictions. The big firms sometimes offer one-way rentals, which may not cost any extra. Most companies require drivers to be over the age of 21, though in some cases it's 18 and in others it's 25. Typical rates are from $45/65/85 per day for a small/medium/ large car.

The usual big international companies (Avis, Budget, Europcar, Hertz, Thrifty) all operate in Australia. The following websites offer rate comparisons and last-minute discounts:

Carhire.com (www.carhire.com.au)

Drive Now (www.drivenow.com.au)

Webjet (www.webjet.com.au)

CAMPERVANS

Companies for campervan hire – with rates from around $100 (two berths) or $160 (four berths) per day, usually with minimum five-day hire

and unlimited kilometres – include the following:

Apollo (☑1800 777 779; www. apollocamper.com)

Britz (☑1300 738 087; www. britz.com.au)

Hippie Camper (☑1800 777 779; www.hippiecamper.com)

Jucy (☑1800 150 850; www. jucy.com.au)

Maui (☑1800 827 821; www. maui.com.au)

Mighty Campers (☑1800 821 824; www.mightycampers. com.au)

Spaceships (☑1300 132 469; www.spaceshipsrentals.com.au)

Travelwheels (☑0412 766 616; www.travelwheels.com.au)

FOUR-WHEEL DRIVES

Having a 4WD enables you to get right off the beaten track and revel in the natural splendour that many travellers miss. Something midsized like a Nissan X-Trail costs around $110 to $160 per day; for a Toyota LandCruiser you're looking at around $165 up to $220, which should include unlimited kilometres. Check insurance conditions carefully, especially the excess, as they can be onerous.

The major car-hire companies have 4WD rentals, or try Apollo or Britz.

ONE-WAY RELOCATIONS

Relocations are usually cheap deals, although they don't allow much time flexibility. Most of the large hire companies offer deals, or try the following operators:

Drive Now (www.drivenow.com.au)

imoova (www.imoova.com)

Transfercar (www.transfercar.com.au)

Insurance

Third-Party Insurance In Australia, third-party personal-injury insurance is included in the vehicle-registration cost, ensuring that every registered vehicle carries at least minimum insurance. We recommend

extending that minimum to at least third-party property insurance – minor collisions can be amazingly expensive.

Rental Vehicles When it comes to hire cars, understand your liability in the event of an accident. You can pay an additional daily amount to the rental company that will reduce your liability in the event of an accident from upwards of $3000 to a few hundred dollars.

Exclusions Be aware that if you're driving on dirt roads you may not be covered by insurance (even if you have a 4WD); if you have an accident you'll be liable for all costs. Also, many insurance policies don't cover damage to windscreens or tyres – always read the small print.

Purchase

If you plan to stay several months and do plenty of driving, buying a car will probably work out to be cheaper than renting one. You can buy from a car dealer or a private seller. In Sydney, consult www.sydneytravellerscar market.com.au for advice and vehicle listings, or check the used-car outlets lining Parramatta Rd.

Sydney and Cairns are particularly good places to buy cars from backpackers who have finished their trips: try hostel noticeboards. Travellers' Autobarn (www. travellers-autobarn.com.au) is a useful site for buyers and sellers alike.

REGISTRATION & LEGALITIES

When you buy a vehicle in Australia, you need to transfer the registration into your own name within 14 days. Each state has slightly different requirements and different organisations that do this. Similarly, when selling a vehicle you need to advise the state or territory road transport authority of the sale and change of name.

In NSW, Queensland and Victoria, the buyer and seller need to complete and sign a transfer-of-registration form.

In the ACT there's no form, but the buyer and seller need to co-sign the reverse of the registration certificate.

Note that it's much easier to sell a car in the same state in which it's registered, otherwise you (or the buyer) must re-register it in the new state, which can be a hassle.

It's the buyer's responsibility to ensure the car isn't stolen and that there's no money owing on it; check the car's details with the Personal Property Securities Register (www.ppsr.gov.au).

ROADWORTHY CERTIFICATE

Sellers are required to provide a roadworthy certificate when transferring registration in the following situations:

ACT – Once the vehicle is six years old; annual inspection record also required for vehicles running on gas.

NSW – Once the vehicle is five years old.

Queensland – Safety Certificate required for all vehicles; certificate also required for vehicles running on gas.

Victoria – Certificate of roadworthiness required for all vehicles.

If the vehicle you're considering doesn't have a roadworthy certificate, it's worth having a roadworthiness check done by a mechanic before you buy it. The state automobile associations have lists of licenced vehicle testers.

ROAD TRANSPORT AUTHORITIES

For more information about processes and costs:

Access Canberra (www.rego.act.gov.au) Covers ACT.

Roads & Maritime (www.rta.nsw.gov.au) Covers NSW.

Department of Transport & Main Roads (www.tmr.qld.gov.au) Covers Queensland.

VicRoads (www.vicroads.vic.gov.au) Covers Victoria.

Road Hazards

Fatigue Be wary of the weary; driving long distances (particularly in hot weather) can be utterly exhausting. Falling asleep at the wheel is not uncommon. On a long haul, stop and rest every two hours or so – do some exercise, change drivers or have a coffee.

Heat If travelling in the outback, particularly during the hotter months, be aware that outside temperatures can be 45°C or higher and that the reflective (ground) temperature can be around 65°C, which is why deaths are caused every year by heat exposure when motorists break down, even if they are carrying adequate amounts of water.

Roadkill A huge problem in Australia. Many Australians avoid travelling once the sun drops because of the risks posed by nocturnal animals on the roads.

Two-Lane Roads East coast Australia has few multilane highways, although there are stretches of divided road (four or six lanes) in busy areas such as the toll roads in Sydney, Melbourne and Brisbane. Two-lane roads, however, are the only option for many routes.

Unsealed Roads Conditions vary wildly and cars perform differently when braking and turning on dirt. Don't exceed 80km/h on dirt roads; if you go faster you won't have time to respond to a sharp turn, stock on the road or an unmarked gate or cattle grid. If you're in a rental car, check your contract to ensure you're covered for driving on unsealed roads.

Wildfires Bush fires have become a fact of life, particularly during the hot, dry summers. Roads may be closed due to hazardous conditions, so it's good to download a wildfire locator app (such as National Bushfires, BushFire or Australian Fires) to stay on top of changing conditions.

Road Rules

Australians drive on the left-hand side of the road; all cars are right-hand drive.

Drink-Driving Random breath tests are common. If you're caught with a blood alcohol concentration of more than 0.05 grams per 100mL, expect a court appearance, a fine and/or the loss of your licence. Police can randomly pull any driver over for a breathalyser or drug test.

Give Way If an intersection is unmarked (unusual) and at roundabouts, you must give way to vehicles entering the intersection from your right.

Mobile Phones Using a mobile phone while driving is illegal (excluding hands-free technology).

Seatbelts and car seats Seatbelt usage is compulsory. Children up to the age of seven must be belted into an approved safety seat.

Speed Limits The general speed limit in built-up and residential areas is 50km/h (sometimes 60km/h). Near schools the limit is usually 25km/h to 40km/h around school drop-off and pick-up times. On the highway it's 100km/h or 110km/h. Police have speed radar guns and cameras and are fond of using them in strategic locations.

TOLL ROADS

There are a handful of toll roads on the east coast – mostly on major freeways around Melbourne, Sydney and Brisbane. Ensure you pay tolls online or you'll face hefty fines – whether you're travelling in your own vehicle or in a rental. Unless you've organised a toll pass ahead of time, you usually have two or three days to pay after driving the toll road. Pay tolls in NSW, Queensland and Victoria by signing up for a pass online: www.linkt.com.au.

Parking

One of the big problems with driving around big cities like Sydney, Brisbane and Melbourne (or popular tourist towns like Byron Bay) is finding somewhere to park. Even if you do find a spot there's likely to be a time restriction, a meter (or ticket machine) or both. Parking fines range from about $50 to $120 and if you park in a clearway your car will be towed away or clamped – check the signs.

In the cities there are large car parks where you can park all day for $20 to $40.

Hitching & Ride-Sharing

Hitching is never entirely safe in any country in the world, and we don't recommend it. Travellers who decide to hitch should understand that they are taking a small but potentially serious risk. People who do choose to hitch will be safer if they travel in pairs and let someone know where they are planning to go.

People looking for travelling companions for car journeys around the east coast often leave notices on boards in hostels and backpacker accommodation.

In Sydney there's a women-and-children only carshare scheme called Shebah (www.shebah.com.au).

Local Transport

Brisbane, Melbourne and Sydney have public-transport systems utilising buses, trains, ferries and/or trams. Larger regional towns and cities have their own local bus systems. Sizeable towns also have taxis. There's almost no

service north of Cairns, so your only option is to join a tour or hire a car.

The relatively new Gold Coast Rapid Transit (https://ridetheg.com.au) links 16 stops over 22km between Helensvale and Broadbeach.

Train

Train travel is a comfortable option for short- or long-haul sectors along the east coast, but it's also a few dollars more than travelling by bus and it may take a few hours longer.

Rail services within each state (and sometimes extending interstate) are run by that state's rail body:

NSW TrainLink (☑13 22 32; www.nswtrainlink.info) Operates from Sydney south to Canberra and Melbourne, and along the coast north to Brisbane (but not Byron Bay).

Queensland Rail (☑1300 131 722; www.queenslandrailtravel.com.au) Connects Brisbane with the Gold Coast and Sunshine Coast, extending to Cairns with offshoots to Charleville, Mt Isa and Longreach.

Sydney Trains (☑13 15 00; www.transportnsw.info) Connects Sydney with the Blue Mountains, south coast and central coast.

V/Line (☑1800 800 007; www.vline.com.au; Southern Cross Station, Spencer St) Connects Victoria with NSW, SA and the ACT.

Costs

Children, students and backpackers can generally secure a discount on standard fares. If you can stretch your budget to a sleeper cabin, we highly recommend it (sleeping upright in a seat surrounded by snoring train

companions isn't always a great way to travel). Note that cheaper fares are generally nonrefundable with no changes permitted. Some typical fares:

Brisbane–Cairns Adult/child seated from $221/184; in a cabin from $389/311

Sydney–Brisbane Adult/child seated $117/65; cabin $271/180

Sydney–Canberra Adult/child seated $51/28

Sydney–Melbourne Adult/child seated $117/65; cabin $271/180

Reservations

During national holidays, school holidays and weekends, book your seat a week or two in advance if possible. Many discount fares require you to reserve well in advance.

Rail Passes

Coverage of the east coast by rail isn't bad, and several useful passeLGBTIQ+ s are sold.

Discovery Pass Allows travel with unlimited stops in any direction on the NSW TrainLink regional train and coach network, including extensions to Melbourne, Brisbane and Canberra; available for 14 days ($232), one month ($275), three months ($298) or six months ($420). Routes must be prebooked.

Queensland Coastal Pass Available only to international visitors; allows one month ($209) or two months ($289) of one-direction travel on the main Queensland Rail trains, between the Gold Coast and Cairns.

Queensland Explorer Pass Available only to international visitors; allows one month ($299) or two months ($389) of travel in any direction on the whole Queensland Rail network.

Behind the Scenes

SEND US YOUR FEEDBACK

We love to hear from travellers – your comments keep us on our toes and help make our books better. Our well-travelled team reads every word on what you loved or loathed about this book. Although we cannot reply individually to your submissions, we always guarantee that your feedback goes straight to the appropriate authors, in time for the next edition. Each person who sends us information is thanked in the next edition – the most useful submissions are rewarded with a selection of digital PDF chapters.

Visit **lonelyplanet.com/contact** to submit your updates and suggestions or to ask for help. Our award-winning website also features inspirational travel stories, news and discussions.

Note: We may edit, reproduce and incorporate your comments in Lonely Planet products such as guidebooks, websites and digital products, so let us know if you don't want your comments reproduced or your name acknowledged. For a copy of our privacy policy visit lonelyplanet.com/privacy.

WRITER THANKS

Cristian Bonetto

Many thanks to those who offered tips and support, among them Drew Westbrook, Jordy Goričanec, Warren Foster and Mark Whitaker. At Lonely Planet, a big thank you to Kathryn Rowan for the commission. Back home in Melbourne, grazie mille to my family for their constant support and understanding during those intense write-up periods.

Lindsay Brown

I am very grateful for the assistance provided by numerous friendly folks from Bribie Island to Bundaberg. The volunteers in the visitor information centres were all excellent ambassadors for their respective regions. Thanks to Kathryn Rowan for always being available for editorial and technical queries and thanks to Jenny for being the best travelling companion.

Jayne D'Arcy

Massive thanks to Kathryn Rowan for sending me to Byron! Thanks to Penny and Louise (and kids) and David who made the road trip up and back so friendly, and my children, Miles and Ruby, the most delightful travel companions ever. Thanks also to Dad for looking after the guinea pigs, and Mum, for travelling with us in spirit

Peter Dragicevich

Huge thanks are due to my big brother, Tony Dragicevich, and sister-in-law, Debbie Dragicevich, for their generous hospitality in Sanctuary Cove. Thanks too to my other big brother Robert Dragicevich for providing excellent company while researching South Stradbroke Island and Surfers Paradise. Special thanks too to Drew, Linda and Catherine.

Anthony Ham

Thanks to Kat Rowan for entrusting me with such a wonderful area. Thanks also to everyone at the Wet Tropics Information Centre in Mission Beach and to Dr. Bill Laurance for teaching me so much about cassowaries, rainforest ecosystems and the like. Thanks to Marina, Carlota, Valentina, Javi, Sandra, Sara and Ana for being such wonderful companions on the roads of Far North Queensland, and to Jan for always keeping the home fires burning.

Trent Holden

A massive thanks to Kathryn Rowan and Anne Mason for commissioning me to cover my home state of Victoria, a great honour indeed! Thanks also to the Lonely Planet production team – eds, cartos and designers ¬– for all your hard work inhouse. A big shout out to my fellow writers, too. I'd also like to acknowledge the fire affected communities that I visited in East Gippsland, and wish you a speedy recovery. Finally, lots of love to my family, friends and fiancée Kate.

Anna Kaminski

I would like to thank Kat and Anne for entrusting me with my stretch of the Queensland coast, my fellow scribes for all your helpful ideas and input and everyone who's helped me along the way, including Sammy and Macca (Town of 1770), Jill (Carnarvon National Park), Lisa and Pat (Gemfields), Wong (Mackay), Wayne and Francis (Rockhampton), Lyndie and Geoff (Great Keppel Island), plus various boat captains in the Whitsundays and Southern Reef Islands.

Ali Lemer

Many thanks to Joel Balsam, Stephanie Foden and MaSovaida Morgan for cat-sitting; to Cindy Frost and Suzanne Thomson for their wonderful hospitality; to Tarnay Sass at ACMI; and to LPers Kat Rowan, Tim Richards and Anna Kaminski for their help in putting it all together. Big thanks to all my old friends and workmates for hanging out while I was in town. And last but not least, thanks to marvellous Melbourne, my second hometown.

Monique Perrin

Thanks to my research buddies Bob Scott, Shalini Perera, Dan Farley and Zyra McAuliffe, and to all my Sydney mates who shared their favourite clubs, cafes and vegan kitchens. Enormous thanks also to Andy Symington and Kat Rowan at LP.

Tim Richards

Thanks to my co-writer Ali Lemer, who brought a fresh perspective from New York City to the hip streets of Melbourne. Also much gratitude to my wife Narrelle Harris, who had to listen to me babbling about places I'd walked to in the research (but did benefit when we tested out new restaurants together). Finally, thanks to all the great people of Melbourne who happily answered questions and gave useful tips about their fun city.

Tamara Sheward

Sweaty Cairns hugs and hearty thanks to my friends, family, local experts and random ring-ins who helped me delve ever deeper into the wonders of my erstwhile hometown and surrounds; it's always an eye-opener being a traveller/travel writer in one's own backyard. At LP, massive thanks to Kat Rowan for the gig and for helping me out with any write-up hiccups. As ever, the biggest clink of the coconuts goes to my gorgeous geckos Dušan and Masha.

Tom Spurling

Thanks to Kat Rowan for sending me to this beautiful part of the world. Thanks to Lucy, Oliver and Poppy for enduring my chaotic demands on the road. Thanks to Jess for minding the cat. Thanks to Bob and H and Anna and the Kemps for giving me permission to procrastinate. Thanks to tech support for, you know, everything. Baba Nam Kevalam!

Andy Symington

I owe many thanks to lots of helpful people along the way but particularly to excellent Sydney co-author Monique Perrin and to Rachel Boyd for her valuable opinions on the Sydney restaurant scene. Most of all, I owe deep gratitude to my father Neville who was always a bastion of encouragement and who will be sorely missed.

Benedict Walker

Huge thanks to Kat and Kirsten at LP for getting me back on the road again. To Sally and Roger Brock, the Walkers, aunty Meg and Collywols for backing me, still. To Andy, for kicking cancer to the curb; to Lozzie, Granto, Cole, Jack & the Kirkmans for helping me come home, and to my friends in Leipzig and Berlin, for remembering me, until I can return. I dedicate all my words and journeys to you, Mum - without your unfaltering love, kindness and belief in me, there would be silence.

ACKNOWLEDGEMENTS

Climate map data adapted from Peel MC, Finlayson BL & McMahon TA (2007) 'Updated World Map of the Köppen-Geiger Climate Classification', *Hydrology and Earth System Sciences*, 11, 1633–44.

Cover photograph: Kangaroo at Casuarine Beach, Cape Hillsborough National Park, Mark Fitzpatrick/Getty Images ©

Illustrations p62-63 by Javier Zarracina

THIS BOOK

This 7th edition of Lonely Planet's *East Coast of Australia* guidebook was researched and written by Cristian Bonetto, Lindsay Brown, Jayne D'Arcy, Peter Dragicevich, Anthony Ham, Trent Holden, Anna Kaminski, Ali Lemer, Monique Perrin, Tim Richards, Tamara Sheward, Tom Spurling, Andy Symington and Benedict Walker. The previous edition was also coordinated by Andy Symington. This guidebook was produced by the following:

Senior Product Editor Kathryn Rowan

Senior Cartographer Julie Sheridan

Product Editors Fergus O'Shea, Amy Lynch

Book Designer Wibowo Rusli

Assisting Editors Michelle Bennett, Nigel Chin, Kellie Langdon

Cartographers Diana Von Holdt, Valentina Kremenchutskaya

Assisting Book Designers Ann Brooks, Fergal Condon

Cover Researcher Brendan Dempsey-Spencer

Thanks to Joel Cotterell, Sandie Kestell, Anne Mason, Genna Patterson, Angela Tinson

532

Index

Map Legend

Sights

- Beach
- Bird Sanctuary
- Buddhist
- Castle/Palace
- Christian
- Confucian
- Hindu
- Islamic
- Jain
- Jewish
- Monument
- Museum/Gallery/Historic Building
- Ruin
- Shinto
- Sikh
- Taoist
- Winery/Vineyard
- Zoo/Wildlife Sanctuary
- Other Sight

Activities, Courses & Tours

- Bodysurfing
- Diving
- Canoeing/Kayaking
- Course/Tour
- Sento Hot Baths/Onsen
- Skiing
- Snorkelling
- Surfing
- Swimming/Pool
- Walking
- Windsurfing
- Other Activity

Sleeping

- Sleeping
- Camping
- Hut/Shelter

Eating

- Eating

Drinking & Nightlife

- Drinking & Nightlife
- Cafe

Entertainment

- Entertainment

Shopping

- Shopping

Information

- Bank
- Embassy/Consulate
- Hospital/Medical
- Internet
- Police
- Post Office
- Telephone
- Toilet
- Tourist Information
- Other Information

Geographic

- Beach
- Gate
- Hut/Shelter
- Lighthouse
- Lookout
- Mountain/Volcano
- Oasis
- Park
- Pass
- Picnic Area
- Waterfall

Population

- Capital (National)
- Capital (State/Province)
- City/Large Town
- Town/Village

Transport

- Airport
- Border crossing
- Bus
- Cable car/Funicular
- Cycling
- Ferry
- Metro station
- Monorail
- Parking
- Petrol station
- Subway station
- Taxi
- Train station/Railway
- Tram
- Underground station
- Other Transport

Routes

- Tollway
- Freeway
- Primary
- Secondary
- Tertiary
- Lane
- Unsealed road
- Road under construction
- Plaza/Mall
- Steps
- Tunnel
- Pedestrian overpass
- Walking Tour
- Walking Tour detour
- Path/Walking Trail

Boundaries

- International
- State/Province
- Disputed
- Regional/Suburb
- Marine Park
- Cliff
- Wall

Hydrography

- River, Creek
- Intermittent River
- Canal
- Water
- Dry/Salt/Intermittent Lake
- Reef

Areas

- Airport/Runway
- Beach/Desert
- Cemetery (Christian)
- Cemetery (Other)
- Glacier
- Mudflat
- Park/Forest
- Sight (Building)
- Sportsground
- Swamp/Mangrove

Note: Not all symbols displayed above appear on the maps in this book

Tamara Sheward

Cairns After years of freelance travel writing, rock'n'roll journalism and insalubrious authordom, Tamara leapt at the chance to join the Lonely Planet ranks in 2009. Since then, she's worked on guides to an incongruous jumble of countries including Montenegro, Australia, Serbia, Russia, the Samoas, Bulgaria and Fiji. She's written a miscellany of travel articles for the BBC, The Independent, Sydney Morning Herald et al; she's also fronted the camera as a documentary presenter for Lonely Planet TV, Nat Geo and Al-Jazeera. Tamara's based in far northern Australia, but you're more likely to find her roaming elsewhere, tattered notebook in one hand, the world's best-travelled preschooler in the other.

Tom Spurling

Canberra & South Coast New South Wales Tom is a freelancer writer and school teacher currently based in Perth, Western Australia. He has contributed to 17 LP titles, including Turkey, India, Central America on a Shoestring, Australia, Japan, China and South Africa, Lesotho & Swaziland. When not reviewing surf beaches, long blacks and pillow menus for the world's most famous guidebook company, he trudges through a doctorate on international students in the hope of one day becoming an expert on international students, or even an international student himself.

Andy Symington

Sydney Andy has written or worked on over a hundred books and other updates for Lonely Planet (especially in Europe and Latin America) and other publishing companies, and has published articles on numerous subjects for a variety of newspapers, magazines, and websites. He part-owns and operates a rock bar, has written a novel and is currently working on several fiction and non-fiction writing projects. Andy, from Australia, moved to Northern Spain many years ago. When he's not off with a backpack in some far-flung corner of the world, he can probably be found watching the tragically poor local football side or tasting local wines after a long walk in the nearby mountains.

Benedict Walker

North Coast New South Wales A beach baby from Newcastle (AU), Benedict turned 40 in 2017 and decided to start a new life in Leipzig (DE)! Writing for LP was a childhood dream. He insists it's a privilege, a huge responsibility and loads of fun! He is thrilled to have covered big chunks of Australia, Canada, Germany, Japan, USA (inc. Las Vegas!), Switzerland, Sweden and Japan, for you. Come along for the ride, on Insta! @wordsandjourneys.